HORROR
AND
SCIENCE FICTION
FILMS:
A Checklist

by
Donald C. Willis

The Scarecrow Press, Inc.
Metuchen, N.J. 1972

Willis, Donald C
  Horror and science fiction films.

  1. Moving-pictures--Plots, themes, etc.--Horror.
2. Moving-pictures--Plots, themes, etc.--Science
fiction. I. Title.
PN1995.9.H6W5   791.43'0909'16   72-3682
ISBN 0-8108-0508-1

To Forrest J Ackerman,
who started it all

INTRODUCTORY NOTES

My interest in horror-film research began around 1960 with the local "shock theatre"-type, television horror-movie packages ("The Late Show," "Mystery Mansion," "Friday Night Frights") and was further cultivated by the complementary stills and information in magazines like <u>Famous Monsters</u> and <u>Castle of Frankenstein.</u> (Before even seeing any of the films, I had been fascinated by the titles --SCARED TO DEATH, THE FROZEN GHOST--of these movies apparently so strange and terrifying that they could only be shown late at night so that the weak-hearted would not accidentally stumble upon them.) It was about the time the late shows went off the air (1963-4) that I began looking in earnest through old magazines and microfilmed newspapers for new titles and credit information.

The finished main listing, extensive as it may seem, is not of course complete. Countries like India and Malaya make many films, but documentation is haphazard, if available. And there are even reports of movies made for particular regions in the U.S. that are never shown elsewhere.

If I am nearly complete in any one area, it's the American old-house horror-mystery (or the "thunderstorm mystery" as Leslie Halliwell calls it) of the Twenties, Thirties, and Forties. It's this group of movies I most enjoyed "discovering": SECRET WITNESS, STRANGE PEOPLE, BEFORE MIDNIGHT, BEFORE DAWN, MURDER AT DAWN, TRICK FOR TRICK, DANGEROUS PEOPLE, PHANTOM OF CRESTWOOD, ONE FRIGHTENED NIGHT, TEMPLE TOWER, TOMORROW AT SEVEN, WHO KILLED AUNT MAGGIE?, THE THIEF IN THE DARK, MISS PINKERTON, MURDER BY INVITATION, etc.

To aid in deciding what movies qualified as horror or science fiction, I formulated a few general rules. These were helpful--sometimes. For instance, "deals with the devil" seemed a likely horror theme. But sometimes it's strictly for laughs, as in UP IN SMOKE, BEDAZZLED, or BEAUTY OF THE DEVIL. Also, death-semblance serum is a horror-movie staple, but in some movies it is a very insignificant element. Ghosts haunting houses, castles, operas, ranches, mines or hills are always horror. But in TOPPER TAKES A TRIP the ghosts haunt Roland Young in a purely light-comical manner. But in TOPPER RETURNS we are back to the "haunted" house.

The 1935 GREAT IMPERSONATION is horror, but the other two versions are not. Horror elements were added to a spy story to make the '35 version a horror movie and were removed in 1942 to make the story a straight spy story again. Hypnosis when used for "evil" purposes is horror, but not when used for comedy. Death and the threat of death are central to horror, so Death personified is always horror (except as a "bit" role). "Black" magic is horror; "trick" or stage magic is not.

The fantasy film poses special problems. Fantasies like THE WIZARD OF OZ and MARCH OF THE WOODEN SOLDIERS have horror scenes which are more horrifying than those of most horror movies. And fantasy is easy to confuse with science fiction. Either can yield the same results, as in the case of scientific invisibility (e.g., THE INVISIBLE MAN) vs. magical invisibility (e.g., THE INVISIBLE WRESTLER). Movies which include excerpts from horror or s-f movies and which have no horror/s-f elements of their own are in the "out" list, as are movies with insignificant, incidental horror/s-f elements.

Shorts before 1930 (admittedly an arbitrary date) are included on the main list because live-action shorts were of about equal importance with features for several years after features were first introduced (around 1913). The shorts and animated cartoon section at the end of this book is sketchier than the main one since I did not go out of my way to research post-1930 shorts. Animated films have always been of minor importance in the s-f/horror film field and deserve a checklist of their own.

I would like to be able to list my favorite horror and s-f movies in some kind of order, and have tried to, but I have seen some of them too many times, some of them too few, and it is difficult enough just deciding what to list. I think NOSFERATU may be the best, or METROPOLIS, and I have a particular affection for MARK OF THE VAMPIRE, THE THING, and INVADERS FROM MARS, but I think they are all very good:

v

ALPHAVILLE, BRIDE OF FRANKENSTEIN, CURSE OF THE DEMON, DEAD OF NIGHT, FIVE MILLION YEARS TO EARTH, FORBIDDEN PLANET, THE HAUNTING, HAXAN, HORROR OF DRACULA, THE INNOCENTS, INVADERS FROM MARS, THE INVISIBLE MAN, ISLE OF THE DEAD, KING KONG, THE LAST WARNING, LOKIS, MARK OF THE VAMPIRE, METROPOLIS, NOSFERATU, THE THING, 2001, and THE UNINVITED.

Some of my favorites on the main list aren't necessarily horror or s-f, but have a little of one, the other, or both. I think BEAUTY AND THE BEAST is easily the best of these, though ORPHEUS could stand another viewing: THE ADVENTURES OF BARON MUNCHAUSEN, AND THEN THERE WERE NONE, BEAUTY AND THE BEAST, THE MANCHURIAN CANDIDATE, MEET JOHN DOE, NIGHT OF THE HUNTER, ORPHEUS, THE TESTAMENT OF DR. MABUSE, THE THREE AGES, WEEKEND, and THE WIZARD OF OZ.

Some movies that I have wanted to see (I'm not quite out of lists yet) have eluded me for years. (I caught up with MURDERS IN THE RUE MORGUE just recently.) Among the horror and s-f movies on this list that I have not seen and that I would most like to see (and which are to the best of my knowledge extant) are THE BAT WHISPERS, LONDON AFTER MIDNIGHT, THE SPIDER (1931), MIRACLES FOR SALE, the French FALL OF THE HOUSE OF USHER, TRICK FOR TRICK, WAXWORKS, LA JETEE, THE UNKNOWN PURPLE, UGETSU, SVENGALI (1931), MURDER BY THE CLOCK, THE LODGER (1926), THESE ARE THE DAMNED, THE GORILLA (1939), HOUSE OF FEAR (1939), and last and probably least, DEVIL BAT.

There are about 4,400 titles in the main listing. The last title added was BLOOD FROM THE MUMMY'S TOMB, on October 20, 1971.

Acknowledgments

Of those who helped me I wish to thank particularly Walter W. Lee, Jr., and Ronald V. Borst, who are compiling similar lists and who gave me access to them. Walt Lee was of especial help on silent films, and Ron Borst on detailed information on American sound films.

I would also like to thank Forrest J Ackerman for the use of his files, notes, and stills; the library staff at the Academy of Motion Picture Arts and Sciences for its assistance; and Don Glut, Les Otis, and Bill Warren.

TABLE OF CONTENTS

EXPLANATORY NOTES

The general order of information in each entry of the main listing is as follows: title (parentheses in titles indicate spelling variations)/country of origin (if not the U.S.)/ studio, production company (on foreign films released in the U.S., U.S. distributor is generally listed first)/year (on films released more than a year after they were made, the date of completion, in parentheses, follows the date of release)/color and scope indication/running time/alternate titles/director/screenplay, story/photography/music/art direction and set design/special effects/makeup/editor/producer/narrator/reference and picture sources/cast/synopsis and comment.

"Sound" or "silent" is indicated for pictures made during the silent-sound transition (1928 to 1930). The color process (if indicated) generally refers to English-language prints. Sources vary in the amount of information they give on a title. Records of early silents usually only indicate the production company and the running time.

There are four addenda at the end of the book: "Titles Announced for Release in 1971-1972"; "Shorts (1930-1971), and Animated and Puppet Films"; "Out List" (films which for one reason or another I decided not to enter in the main sequence); and "References." The first three are self-explanatory, and use the same abbreviations as in the main list. The "References" is a listing of books and periodicals used in the preparation of this work; it contains fuller citations to secondary works mentioned in the main sequence.

ABBREVIATIONS

Production companies:

AA - Allied Artists
AI - American International Pictures
AM&B - American Mutoscope and Biograph
Biog - Biograph
BV - Buena Vista
CFF - Children's Film Foundation
Col - Columbia
C&M - Cricks and Martin
Cont - Continental
E-L - Eagle-Lion
Educ - Educational
Emb - Embassy
Ess - Essanay
F Nat - First National
Fox - Twentieth Century-Fox or Fox
Gaum - Gaumont
MGM - Metro-Goldwyn-Mayer
Mono - Monogram
Para - Paramount
Rep - Republic
S3 - Sigma III
7A - Seven Arts
TEC - Television Enterprises Corporation
T-L - Trans-Lux
UA - United Artists
Univ - Universal or Universal-International
Vita - Vitagraph
WB - Warner Brothers
WB&E - Williams, Brown and Earle

Credits:

B - British
F - French

I - Italian
J - Japanese
Arg - Argentine
Braz - Brazilian
G - German
Russ - Russian
Hung - Hungarian
Fili - Filipino
Yug - Yugoslav
D - director
SP - screenplay by
PH - photography by
Ref - references, sources
m - minutes
Mus sc - musical score by
Mus D - music direction by
Art D - art direction by
Ed - edited by
P - produced by
Assoc P - associate producer
Ass't D - assistant director
Add'l Dial - additional dialogue by
Adap - adapted by
Cost - costumes by
SpFX - special effects by
SpPH - special photography by
Prod Des - production designed by
Narr - narration by
Pic - pictures, photos
Exec P - executive producer
Sup - supervised by
pbk - pressbook
mm - millimeter
c - circa
sfa - same film as?
aka - also known as

References:

Annuario - Annuario del Cinema Italiano 1966-1967
Bios - The Bioscope
Boxo - Boxoffice
Brit Cinema - British Cinema
CNW - Continued Next Week
COF - Castle of Frankenstein
DDC - Dictionnaire du Cinema
EncicDS - Enciclopedia della Spettacolo

FanMo - Fantastic Monsters
F&F - Films and Filming
FD - Film Daily
FDY - Film Daily Yearbook
FEFN - Far East Film News
FFacts - Film Facts
F Index - The Film Index (magazine)
FIR - Films in Review
FM - Famous Monsters
FMO - For Monsters Only
HM - Horror Monsters
Ital P - Italian Production
LC - Library of Congress
M&H - Monsters and Heroes
M Bee - The Modesto Bee
MFB - The Monthly Film Bulletin
MM - Mad Monsters
MMF - Midi-Minuit Fantastique
ModM - Modern Monsters
MPH - Motion Picture Herald
MPN - Motion Picture News
MPW - Moving Picture World
M/TVM - Movie/TV Marketing
NYT - The New York Times
PM - Parents' Magazine
La Prod Cin Fr - La Production Cinématographique
   Française
Rep Gen - Repertoire Generale
RVB - Ronald V. Borst
S&S - Sight and Sound
S Bee - The Sacramento Bee
SF Film - Science Fiction Film
SF in the Cinema - Science Fiction in the Cinema
SM - Spaceman
SpCinema - The Spanish Cinema
S Union - The Sacramento Union
TBG - The Bad Guys
TVG - TV Guide
TVFFSB - Television Feature Film Source Book
TVK - TV Key Movie Guide
UFQ - Unijapan Film Quarterly
V - Variety (weekly)
V(d) - Variety (daily)
V&FI - Views and Film Index
VV - The Village Voice

A CHECKLIST OF HORROR AND SCIENCE-FICTION FILMS

A III-ES see IN ROOM THREE (1919/1937)

A.D.3 OPERATION WHITE WHALEFISH (I) Madison Film 1966 (A.D.3 OPERAZIONE SQUALO BIANCO. OPERATION WHITE SHARK--TV) D: Stanley Lewis. SP: Luigi Angelo. Story: I. Fasan, F. Ratti, L. Angelo. PH: V. Natalucci. Ref: Annuario. TVFFSB. with Rodd Dana, Francesco Mulè, Franca Polesello, Janine Reinaud. Atomic bombs manufactured cheaply with "new formula."

A-HAUNTING WE WILL GO Fox 1942 67m. D: Alfred Werker. SP: Lou Breslow. Story: L. Breslow, Stanley Rauh. PH: Glen MacWilliams. Mus D: Emil Newman. Art D: Richard Day, Lewis Creber. P: Sol M. Wurtzel. Ref: COF 6:4. with Stan Laurel, Oliver Hardy, Elisha Cook, Jr., Dante the Magician, Sheila Ryan, John Shelton, Don Costello, Edward Gargan, Addison Richards, Robert Emmet Keane, Willie Best, George Lynn, Walter Sande, Mantan Moreland, Frank Faylen, Judy Ford (Terry Moore), Wade Boteler. Three gangsters search for a coffin they think belongs to an illusionist.

A LA CONQUETE DE L'AIR see CONQUEST OF THE AIR, The

A NOUS LA LIBERTE (F) Films Sonores Tobis 1931 97m. SP,D; René Clair. PH: Georges Perinal. Mus: Georges Auric. Art D: L. Meerson. Ed: René Le Henatt. Ass't D: Albert Valentin. Ref: The London Times. Imagen. with Henri Marchand, Raymond Cordy, Rolla France, Paul Olivier, Jacques Shelly, André Michaud, Germaine Aussey, Léon Lorin, Alex d'Arcy. A vision of a future world dominated by cybernetics.

A PIED, A CHEVAL ET EN SPOUTNIK see DOG, A MOUSE AND A SPUTNIK, A

A QUATORZE MILLIONS DE LIEUES DE LA TERRE see SKY SHIP, The

A TOUT COUER A TOKYO POUR O.S.S. 117 see TERROR IN TOKYO

AADHI RAAT KE BAAD (India) 1965 Ref: Shankar's 8/1/65. with Ashok Kumar (Mister X) An invisible man battles crooks.

AADMI see MAN, The

AARAVALLI (India) Modern Theatres Ltd. 1957 210m. D: S. V. Krishnan. Ref: FEFN 12/20/57. with M. Mynavathi. "Witch magic" restores poisoned man to life.

ABANDONED ROOM, The (novel by C. Wadsworth Camp) see LOVE WITHOUT QUESTION

ABBOTT AND COSTELLO GO TO MARS Univ 1953 77m. (ON TO MARS. ROCKET AND ROLL) D: Charles Lamont. SP: John

Grant, D. D. Beauchamp. Story: D. D. Beauchamp, Howard
Christie. PH: Clifford Stine. Mus D: Joseph Gershenson.
Art D: Alexander Golitzen, Robert Boyle. SpFX: David S.
Horsley. Makeup: Bud Westmore. Ref: RVB. with Bud Ab-
bott, Lou Costello, Robert Paige, Martha Hyer, Mari Blanchard,
Horace McMahon, Joe Kirk, Hal Forrest, Harold Goodwin, James
Flavin, Jack Kruschen, Jean Willes, Anita Ekberg, Russ Conway,
Sid Saylor, Rex Lease, Dale Van Sickel, Jackie Loughery, Gloria
Paul. If you don't follow the action closely, you may wonder how
they ended up on Venus instead of Mars. (Who gets the Venus-
flight rap?)

ABBOTT AND COSTELLO IN AFRICA see AFRICA SCREAMS

ABBOTT AND COSTELLO MEET DR. JEKYLL AND MR. HYDE
Univ 1953 77m. D: Charles Lamont. SP: John Grant, Lee
Loeb. Based on stories by Sidney Field and Grant Garrett and
"The Strange Case of Dr. Jekyll and Mr. Hyde" by Robert Louis
Stevenson. PH: George Robinson. Mus D: Joseph Gershenson.
Art D: Bernard Herzbrun, Eric Orbom. Makeup: Bud West-
more. Pix: FM 2:24.11:37,38. Ref: RVB. with Bud Abbott,
Lou Costello, Craig Stevens, Boris Karloff, Helen Westcott, John
Dierkes, Reginald Denny, Clyde Cook, Donald Kerr. Jekyll
Hyde, and wax models of Dracula and Frankenstein's monster.

ABBOTT AND COSTELLO MEET FRANKENSTEIN Univ 1948 90m.
(MEET THE GHOSTS or ABBOTT AND COSTELLO MEET THE
GHOSTS--England. THE BRAIN OF FRANKENSTEIN) D: Charles
T. Barton. SP: Robert Lees, Frederic Rinaldo, John Grant. PH:
Charles Van Enger. Mus sc & D: Frank Skinner. Art D:
Bernard Herzbrun, Hilyard Brown. Sets: Russell A. Gausman,
Oliver Emert. SpFX: David S. Horsley, Jerome H. Ash. Make-
up: Bud Westmore. Ref: RVB. FM 13:7.17:23.35:12. HM 7:19
COF 7:42. Based on characters in "Dracula" by Bram Stoker, "Frank-
enstein" by Mary Shelley, and "The Invisible Man" by H. G. Wells.
with Bud Abbott, Lou Costello, Bela Lugosi (Count Dracula), Lon
Chaney, Jr. (The Wolf Man), Glenn Strange (the monster), Lenore
Aubert, Jane Randolph, Frank Ferguson, Vincent Price (the voice
of the Invisible Man), Joe Kirk, Bobby Barber, Harry Brown.

ABBOTT AND COSTELLO MEET THE GHOSTS see ABBOTT AND
COSTELLO MEET FRANKENSTEIN

ABBOTT AND COSTELLO MEET THE INVISIBLE MAN Univ 1951
82m. D: Charles Lamont. SP: Robert Lees, Frederic Rinaldo,
John Grant. Based on ideas in "The Invisible Man" by H. G.
Wells. PH: George Robinson. Mus D: Joseph Gershenson.
Art D: Bernard Herzbrun, Richard H. Riedel. Makeup: Bud
Westmore. Ed: Virgil Vogel. Ref: RVB. Mod M 1:34. with
Bud Abbott, Lou Costello, Arthur Franz, Nancy Guild, Gavin
Muir, Sheldon Leonard, Adele Jergens, William Frawley, George
J. Lewis, Bobby Barber, Ed Gargan, Harold Goodwin, Donald
Kerr. A doctor's formula makes a boxer invisible. Weak.

ABBOTT AND COSTELLO MEET THE KILLER, BORIS KARLOFF
Univ 1949 82m. D: Charles T. Barton. SP: John Grant,
Howard Snyder, Hugh Wedlock, Jr. PH: Charles Van Enger.
Mus: Milton Schwartzwald. Art D: Bernard Herzbrun, Richard
H. Riedel. SpFX: David S. Horsley. Makeup: Bud Westmore.

Ref: RVB. with Bud Abbott, Lou Costello, Boris Karloff,
Lenore Aubert, Gar Moore, Donna Martell, Alan Mowbray, James
Flavin, Roland Winters, Mikel Conrad, Percy Helton, Murray
Alper, Billy Gray. Series of murders in hotel. Very weak.
ABBOTT AND COSTELLO MEET THE MUMMY Univ 1955 79m.
  (IL MISTERO DELLA PIRAMIDE--Italy) D: Charles Lamont.
SP: John Grant. Story: Lee Loeb. PH: George Robinson.
Mus D: Joseph Gershenson. Art D: Bernard Herzbrun. Make-
up: Bud Westmore. Ref: RVB. Mod M 1:34. with Bud Abbott,
Lou Costello, Marie Windsor, Richard Deacon, Mel Welles, Eddie
Parker (Klaris, the mummy), Dan Seymour, Michael Ansara, Kurt
Katch, Jan Arvan, Donald Kerr. A few funny routines. Last of
their Universal horror series. And no ABBOTT AND COSTELLO
MEET THE CREATURE FROM THE BLACK LAGOON?
THE ABOMINABLE DR. PHIBES (U. S. -B) AI 1971 color by Movie-
lab 94m. (DR. PHIBES. THE CURSE OF DR. PHIBES) D:
Robert Fuest. SP: James Whiton, William Goldstein. PH:
Norman Warwick. Mus sc: Basil Kirchen. Ref: V 5/26/71.
M/TVM 10/70:23. with Vincent Price, Joseph Cotten, Hugh
Griffith, Terry-Thomas, Virginia North. Doctor employs the
"10 Curses" in getting revenge on the doctors responsible for his
wife's death. Static direction, mediocre script except for the
curses, which are interesting if sometimes improbable. The
director's idea of a scene is to have the actors meet at one spot
before the camera and get the dialogue out of the way quickly.
ABOMINABLE COUNT YORGA, The see RETURN OF COUNT
  YORGA, The
THE ABOMINABLE SNOWMAN (OF THE HIMALAYAS) (B) Fox/
Regal/Hammer 1957 85m. (THE SNOW CREATURE) D: Val
Guest. SP: Nigel Kneale, from his story "The Creature." PH:
Arthur Grant. Prod Des: Bernard Robinson. Makeup: Phil
Leakey. Ref: RVB. Pic: FM 80:55. with Forrest Tucker,
Peter Cushing, Maureen Connell, Richard Wattis, Robert Brown.
Expedition to the Himalayas discovers that the missing link is a
superior being and not a beast. Placid but atmospheric.
ABOVE ALL LAW see INDIAN TOMB, The
THE ABSENT-MINDED PROFESSOR BV 1961 97m. D: Robert
Stevenson. SP: Bill Walsh, from the story "A Situation of
Gravity" by Samuel Taylor. P: B. Walsh, Walt Disney. Ref:
FFacts. Sequel: SON OF FLUBBER. with Fred MacMurray,
Keenan Wynn, Nancy Olson, Tommy Kirk, Ed Wynn, Leon Ames,
Elliott Reid, Edward Andrews, Jack Mullaney, Wally Brown, Alan
Carney, James Westerfield. Professor invents anti-gravity sub-
stance.
THE ACCURSED CAVERN (F) 1898 Melies (LA CAVERNE
MAUDITE) Ref: DDC III:350. Ghosts.
ACE DRUMMOND Univ 1936 serial 13 episodes 6. Evil Spirits.
D: Cliff Smith, Ford Beebe. SP: Wyndham Gittens, Ray Trampe,
Norman Hall. PH: Richard Fryer. From the newspaper feature
created by Eddie Rickenbacker. Ref: SF Film. Lee. STI 2:35.
FanMo 2:35. with John King, Jean Rogers, Noah Beery, Jr., Lon
Chaney, Jr., Russell Wade, House Peters, Jr. Atomic ray guns.
ACE OF PIC, OPERATION COUNTER ESPIONAGE see OPERATION

COUNTERSPY
ACE OF SCOTLAND YARD   Univ   1929   silent and sound versions
    serial 10 episodes   5. Menace of the Mummy. D: Ray Taylor.
    Sequel to BLAKE OF SCOTLAND YARD with Crauford Kent,
    Florence Allen, Grace Cunard. "Spooky.... Much creeping about
    in the night"--CNW.
"ACE OF SPADES"--COUNTER-ESPIONAGE OPERATION   see
    OPERATION COUNTERSPY
ADAM'S RIB   Para   1923   110m.   D: Cecil B. DeMille.   SP:
    Jeanie Macpherson. Ref: Lee. MPN 27:381. with Milton
    Sills, Theodore Kosloff, Anna Q. Nilsson.   Vision of the life of
    the cave man.
THE ADAPTIVE ULTIMATE (by John Jessel)   see   SHE DEVIL
ADVENTURE AT THE CENTER OF THE EARTH (Mex) Sotomayor /
    Col   1964 (AVENTURA EN EL CENTRO DE LA TIERRA)   D:
    Alfredo B. Cravenna.   SP: J. M. F. Unsain.   PH: Raul M.
    Solares.   Mus: S. Guerrero.   Ref: Indice.   Imagen.   Pix:
    FM 44:45. 45:62.   with Kitty de Hoyos, Javier Solis, Jose Elias
    Moreno, Ramon Bugarini, David Reynoso.   Dinosaurs, including
    a cyclopean monster, a duck-bill dinosaur, and a winged reptile.
An ADVENTURE IN THE NIGHT (Mex)   Anda /Azteca   1947 90m.
    (UNE AVENTURA EN LA NOCHE)   SP, D: Rolando Aguilar.
    Story: Chano Urueta.   PH: Raul M. Solares.   Mus: R.
    Ramirez.   Art D: J. G. Granada.   Ref: Aventura.   Lee.   with
    Luis Aguilar, Miroslava, Jorge Reyes, Carlos Villarias.   Ghosts,
    medium, murder.
ADVENTURE OF GARGANTUAS   see WAR OF THE GARGANTUAS
ADVENTURE OF THE CARDBOARD BOX, The (by Arthur Conan
    Doyle) see CARDBOARD BOX, The
ADVENTURE OF THE DANCING MEN, The (by Arthur Conan Doyle)
    see SHERLOCK HOLMES AND THE SECRET WEAPON
ADVENTURE OF THE DEVIL'S FOOT, The (by Arthur Conan Doyle)
    see DEVIL'S FOOT, The
ADVENTURE OF THE SIX NAPOLEONS, The (by Arthur Conan
    Doyle) see PEARL OF DEATH /SIX NAPOLEONS, The
ADVENTURE OF THE SPECKLED BAND, The (by Arthur Conan
    Doyle) see SPECKLED BAND, The (1912 /1923 /1931)
ADVENTURE UNLIMITED see WHITE PONGO
THE ADVENTURES OF BARON MUNCHAUSEN (G)   UFA   1943
    color (MUNCHAUSEN.   BARON MUNCHAUSEN)   D: Joseph Von
    Baki.   SP: B. Burger.   Mus: G. Haentzschel.   Art D: Werner
    Klein.   Sets: Emil Hasler, Otto Gulstorff.   SpFX: Konstantin
    Jrmenin-Jschet.   Ref: RVB.   Pix: DDC I: 50. II:307.   with Hans
    Albers, Werner Scharf, Leo Slezak, Käthe Haack, Brigitte Horney.
    An invisible Munchausen, a disembodied head on the moon, and
    many other special effects marvels.
ADVENTURES OF BARON MUNCHAUSEN, The see FABULOUS
    BARON MUNCHAUSEN, The
The ADVENTURES OF CAPTAIN MARVEL   Rep 1941   serial 12
    episodes (THE RETURN OF CAPTAIN MARVEL--'45 reissue)
    D. William Witney, John English.   SP: Ronald Davidson,
    Norman Hall, Archie Heath, Joseph Poland, Sol Shor.   Based on
    the Fawcett Publications comic strip characters.   PH: William

Nobles. Mus sc: Cy Feuer. Ref: RVB. Barbour. with Tom
Tyler, Frank Coghlan, Jr., William Benedict, Louise Currie,
Robert Strange, John Davidson, George Pembroke, Reed Hadley,
Jack Mulhall, Kenne Duncan, Nigel de Brulier, John Bagni,
Carleton Young, Tetsu Komai. Pix: FanMo 2:36. Mod M 3:58.
A superhero who smiles as bullets bounce off him, a villain
called the Scorpion ("The Scorpion wants your lens"), and of
course Shazam ("I am Shazam"; "I'm Billy").
The ADVENTURES OF CUCURUCHITO AND PINOCHO   (Mex)
Cimesa 1942 serial 10 episodes (LAS AVENTURAS DE
CUCURUCHITO Y PINOCHO) SP,D: Carlos Vejar, Jr. Story:
S. Bartolozzi, M. Donato. PH: Ross Fisher. Ref: El Cine Grafico
11/22/42. 1/1/43. Indice. with Francisco Jambrina, Alicia
Rodriguez, Marta Ofelia Galindo, Maruja Grifell (the witch
Piruli), Carlos Guerrero. Dragon.
ADVENTURES OF QUIQUE AND ARTHUR THE ROBOT, The see
DISINTEGRATING RAY, The
THE ADVENTURES OF SHERLOCK HOLMES Fox 1939 85m.
D: Alfred Werker. SP: Edwin Blum, William Drake, from the
play "Sherlock Holmes" by William Gillette. PH: Leon Shamroy.
Mus D: Cyril J. Mockridge. Art D, Richard Day, Hans Peters.
Sets: Thomas Little. P: Darryl F. Zanuck. Ref: COF 16:22.
RVB. Pix: TBG:39. with Basil Rathbone, Nigel Bruce, Ida
Lupino, George Zucco, Alan Marshal, Terry Kilburn, Henry
Stephenson, E. E. Clive, Mary Gordon, Arthur Hohl, Holmes
Herbert. Family curse; club-footed "monster" in fog; Zucco as
Moriarty.
The ADVENTURES OF SIR GALAHAD Col 1949 serial 15 epi-
sodes D: Spencer G. Bennet. SP: George H. Plympton, Lewis
Clay, David Mathews. PH: Ira H. Morgan. P: Sam Katzman.
Ref: The Serial. with George Reeves, Charles King, William
Fawcett, Hugh Prosser, Lois Hall, Nelson Leigh, Don Harvey,
John Merton, Rick Vallin, Ray Corrigan. Sorcerer's spell;
ambulatory tree; magic ring of fire; Black Knight that multiplies
into three knights.
The ADVENTURES OF SUN WU KUNG (J) Toho 1959 color/scope
98m. (SONGOKU) D: Kajiro Yamamoto. SP: Takeo Murata,
K. Yamamoto. PH: Hajime Koizumi. Ref: UFQ 5. with
F. Ichikawa, Norihei Miki, N. Chiba, Reiko Dan. Sun Wu Kung
combat "Devils" who believe they will live 10,000 years if they
eat the flesh of a holy man.
ADVENTURES OF SUPERMAN, The see SUPERMAN FLIES
AGAIN/SUPERMAN AND THE MOLE MEN
ADVENTURES OF TAKLA MAKAN (J) Toho 1965 Eastmancolor/
scope 100m. (KIGANJO NO BOKEN) SP,D: Senkichi Tani-
guchi. PH: K. Yamada. Mus: Akira Ifukube. Ref: Toho
Films 1965. with Toshiro Mifune, Mie Hama, Tadao Nakamura,
Tatsuya Mihashi. Giant birds; wizards.
THE ADVENTURES OF THREE NIGHTS Eiko 1913 48m. Ref:
Bios 8/28/13. "Weird story of a warning by a ghostly countess"
in an old castle.
ADVENTUROUS VOYAGE OF THE ARCTIC, The see VOYAGE OF
THE "ARCTIC," The

AELITA (Russ) Amkino/Vufku/Mezrabpom-Russ 1924 (1929--
U. S.) 77m. (REVOLT OF THE ROBOTS) D: Iakov Protazanov.
SP: F. Otzep, A. Faiko, from the novel by Tolstoi. PH:
Iuri Zheliabuzhski, E. Schöneman. Art D & Sets: V. Simov,
I. Rabinovich, A. Exter, Sergei Kozlovski. Ref: Imagen. FM
15:22. SM 1:3. Pix: DDC II:308. Le Surrealisme au Cinema:
128C. Pict. Hist. Cinema:44. with Igor Ilinski, Iulia Sointseva,
Nikolai Tseretelli, Konstantin Eggert. Civilization of robots
found on Mars.
The AERIAL ANARCHISTS (B) Kineto 1911 Ref: Bios 10/19/11.
SF in the Cinema:17. Anarchists construct "gigantic aeroplane. "
AEROCAB AND VACUUM PROVIDER, The see PROF. PUDDEN-
HEAD'S PATENTS
AERIAL SUBMARINE (B) Kineto 1910 12m. Ref: Bios 11/24/
10. Silent FF. Combination submarine-plane of the future.
AERIAL TORPEDO see AIRSHIP DESTROYER, The
AERIAL WARFARE see AIRSHIP DESTROYER, The
The AFFAIR LAFARGE 1938 90m. Ref: Repertoire General
'47:14. with Erich von Stroheim, P. Renoir, M. Chantal.
Woman "devoted to witchcraft" suspect in murder mystery.
AFFAIRE DES POISONS, L' see POISON AFFAIR, The
AFFAIRS OF A VAMPIRE see CURSE OF THE UNDEAD
AFRICA SCREAMS UA 1949 79m. (ABBOTT AND COSTELLO
IN AFRICA) D: Charles T. Barton. SP: Earl Baldwin. PH:
Charles Van Enger. Mus: Walter Schumann. Art D: Lewis
Creber. SpFX: Carl Lee. P: Edward Nassour. Ref:
V 4/29/49. with Bud Abbott, Lou Costello, Frank Buck, Clyde
Beatty, Hillary Brooke, Max Baer, Buddy Baer, Shemp Howard,
Joe Besser. Gigantic ape in brief sequence.
AFRITET ISMAIL YASSINE see ISMAIL YASSINE AND THE GHOST
AFTER DEATH (I) Kleine/Cines 1913 36m. (DOPO LA MORTE)
Ref: Bios 10/30/13. DDC III. with Hesperia. Death-sem-
blance serum.
AFTER THE WELSH RAREBIT Edison 1913 20m. (AFTER THE
WELSH RABBIT) Ref: Bios 4/17/13:xix. The Edison Kine-
togram 2/15/13. with William Wadsworth. Man dreams he's
tortured in hell.
AFTER WORLDS COLLIDE (novel by Edwin Balmer and Philip
Wylie) see WHEN WORLDS COLLIDE
AGAIN (SP-I) Trebol/Empire 1966 color/scope 93m. (I CALDI
AMORI DI UNA MINORENNE) SP, D: Julio Buchs. SP: also
De Urrutia, S. Continenza. PH: Manuel Rojas. Mus: G.
Ferrio. Art D: G. Postiglione. SpFX: Paul Perez. Ref:
MFB'71:45. with Brett Halsey, Marilù Tolo, Romina Power,
Gérard Tichy. Drug combined with music induces loss of self-
control.
AGAINST ALL ODDS see BLOOD OF FU MANCHU
AGENT FOR H. A. R. M. Univ 1966 color 84m. (THE HARM
MACHINE--England) D: Gerd Oswald. SP: Blair Robertson.
PH: James Crab. Mus: Gene Kauer, Douglas Lackey. SpFX:
Harry S. Wollman. P: Joseph Robertson. Ref: RVB.
FFacts. with Mark Richman, Wendell Corey, Barbara Bouchet,
Martin Kosleck, Rafael Campos, Carl Esmond, Donna Michelle,

Alizia Gur, Robert Quarry. Spore from meteorite turns humans
to fungus. Campos' showy performance is the sole interest.
AGENT JOE WALKER: OPERATION FAR EAST (I) Cinesecolo
1966 (AGENTE JOE WALKER OPERAZIONE ESTREMO ORI-
ENTE) D: Frank Kramer (aka Gianfranco Parolini). SP:
Kramer, S. Commermann, W. Kauff. Story: S. Commermann.
PH: F. Izzarelli. Ref: Annuario. with Tony Kendall, Brad
Harris, Barbara Frey, John F. Little Words, Charles Tamblin.
Scientist invents a super-laser.
AGENT 077, FROM THE EAST WITH FURY (I-SP-F) Fida/Epoca/
Jacques Roitfeld 1965 color/scope 102m. (AGENTE 077,
DALL'ORIENTE CON FURORE. FROM THE ORIENT WITH
FURY) D: Terence Hathaway (aka Sergio Grieco). SP: De
Riso, Scolaro, S. Continenza, Martin, Coscia. PH: Juan
Julio Baena. Mus: Piero Piccioni. Ref: MFB'67:43. Ital P.
with Ken Clark, Philippe Hersent, Margaret Lee, Evi Marandi.
Inventor of the "beta ray weapon" uses it against the villains.
AGENT SO3, OPERATION ATLANTIS see OPERATION ATLANTIS
AGENT SIGMA 3--MISSION GOLDWATHER (SP-I) Estela/Imexcine
1968 color/scope 82m. (AGENTE SIGMA 3--MISION GOLD-
WATHER. SIGMA III) D: Gian Paolo Callegari. SP: Tiziano
Longo. PH: Romolo Garroni. Mus: M. Carra. Art D: J. L.
Galicia. Ref: Sp Cinema. TVFFSB. with Jack Taylor, Silvia
Solar, Diana Martin, Armando Calvo. Gang of criminals "hiber-
nates" the inventor of the "Wall Ray."
AGENTE LEMMY CAUTION MISSIONE ALPHAVILLE see ALPHA-
VILLE
AGENTE JOE WALKER OPERAZIONE ESTREMO ORIENTE see
AGENT JOE WALKER: OPERATION FAR EAST
AGENTE 003, OPERACION ALTANTIDA see OPERATION AT-
LANTIS
AGENTE 007, DALL'ORIENTE CON FURORE see AGENT 007,
FROM THE EAST WITH FURY
AGENTE SEGRETO 777 OPERAZIONE MISTERO see SECRET
AGENT 777 OPERATION MYSTERY
AGENTE SIGMA 3--MISION GOLDWATHER see AGENT SIGMA
3--MISSION GOLDWATHER
AGENTE SPAZIALE K 1 see HUMAN DUPLICATORS, The
The AGONY OF FEAR Selig 1915 40m. D: Giles R. Warren.
SP: William E. Wing. Ref: MPN 10/9/15. LC. Man dies of
fright.
AHKEA KKOTS see BAD FLOWER, The
AIDO--SLAVE OF LOVE (J) Hani Productions/Shochiku 1969
color/scope D: Susumu Hani. Ref: M/TVM 6/69. with
Yuri Suemasa, Kenzo Kawarazaki. "Aido, girl incarnated from
a married woman's sex desires, seduces all the men she meets."
AIMEZ-VOUS LES FEMMES? see DO YOU LIKE WOMEN?
AIR ADVENTURES OF JIMMIE ALLEN see SKY PARADE, The
AIR FURY (story by Ben Pivar) see AIR HAWKS
AIR HAWKS Col 1935 66m. D: Albert Rogell. SP: Griffin
Jay, Grace Neville, from the story "Air Fury" by Ben Pivar.
PH: Henry Freulich. Ref: RVB. FD. Pix: SM 4:1.
with Ralph Bellamy, Tala Birell, Douglass Dumbrille, Edward

Van Sloan, Wiley Post, Victor Kilian, Robert Allen, Robert
Middlemass. Owner of an airline uses a scientist's death ray
against another airline.
The AIR TORPEDO (F) 1912 (LA TORPILLE AERIENNE) Ref:
DDC III: 331. with Edouard Mathé.
The AIR TORPEDO (G) Warner's Features /Deutsche Kinema-
tographen G. 1913 (DAS LUFT-TORPEDO) 40m. Ref: MPW
20:1272. Lee. Remote-control bomb.
The AIRMAN'S ENEMY (F) Film de Paris 1913 48m. Ref:
Bios 10/30/13. "A drama of hypnotism."
The AIRSHIP Vita 1908 (100 YEARS HENCE) D: J. Stuart
Blackton. Ref: MPW'08:377. SF Film. Futuristic aircraft.
The AIRSHIP DESTROYER (B) Urban 1909 22m. (AERIAL
TORPEDO. AERIAL WARFARE. BATTLE IN THE CLOUDS)
Ref: MPW'09:973. Silent FF. Torpedo directed at airship "by
wireless."
AKUMA GA YONDEIRU see TERROR IN THE STREETS
AKUMA NO KESHIIN see EVIL BRAIN FROM OUTER SPACE, The?
ALADDIN AND HIS LAMP Mono 1952 Cinecolor 67m. D: Lew
Landers. SP: Howard Dimsdale, Millard Kaufman. PH:
Gilbert Warrenton. Mus: Marlin Skiles. Art D: David Milton.
P: Walter Wanger. Ref: HR 2/4/52. with Patricia Medina,
John Sands, John Dehner, Billy House, Ned Young, Noreen Nash,
Rick Vallin. Genie "capable of assuming other forms" threatens
to kill Aladdin.
ALADDIN AND HIS WONDERFUL LAMP see ALIF LAILA
ALADDIN AND THE WONDERFUL LAMP Pathe 1906 15m. Ref:
V&FI 12/29/06. Vases become "grotesque human faces";
magician; gnome; giant.
ALADDIN AND THE WONDERFUL LAMP Fox 1917 90m. D:
C. M. & S.A. Franklin. SP: Bernard McConville. Ref: MPN
16:2580. with Violet Radcliffe, Virginia Corbin, Buddy Mes-
singer, Elmo Lincoln. Evil magician; evil spirit.
ALAS, I AM INVISIBLE! see HELP, I'M INVISIBLE
The ALCHEMIST Kinematograph 1913 color 30m. Ref: Bios
4/3/13. MPW 15:681. "Stars tell" of girl's peril.
The ALCHEMIST'S HALLUCINATION (F) 1897 Melies
(L'HALLUCINATION DE L'ALCHIMISTE) color Ref: DDC III:
350. Star with five female heads; giant face which spews people
out through its mouth. Fairly amusing tinted Melies.
ALERT TO THE SOUTH (F-I) Neptune-Sirius 1953 color 110m.
(ALERTE AU SUD. ALLARME AU SUD) D: Jean Devejure.
PH: Lucien Joulin. Mus: Joseph Kosma. Art D: Robert
Hubert. Ref: Laclos. La Prod.Cin.Fr. DDC III:60,422.
Repertoire General'54:242. with Jean Murat, Gianna-Maria
Canale, J.C.-Pascal, Jean Tissier. A ray "which paralyzes
or kills" is detected in the heart of the Sahara.
ALFRED HITCHCOCK HOUR, The see DARK INTRUDER
ALGOL (G) Deutsche Licht. 1920 D: Hans Werckmeister.
SP: Hans Brenert. PH: Axel Graatkjar, H. Kricheldorff.
Art D: Walter Reimann. Ref: Fantastique. SF in the
Cinema:22. with Emil Jannings, John Gottowt, Käthe Haack,
Hanna Ralph. An evil spirit from the star Algol leaves a man

a machine which can make him ruler of the world.
ALGY TRIES PHYSICAL CULTURE (B) Gaum 1910 (The Adventures
of the Hon. Algy Slacker series) Ref: Bios 5/5/10. Dr.
Knuttz' preparation makes Algy strong.
ALIAS FUMANCHU (Fili) 1964 Ref: M/TVM 5/64:51 (ALYAS
FUMANCHU)
ALIAS NICK BEAL Para 1949 93m. D: John Farrow. SP:
Jonathan Latimer, from a story by Mindret Lord. PH: Lionel
Lindon. Mus sc: Franz Waxman. Art D: Hans Dreier, Franz
Bachelin. with Ray Milland, Audrey Totter, Thomas Mitchell,
George Macready, Fred Clark, Darryl Hickman, Nestor Paiva. A
politician makes a deal with the devil. A cross between Lew-
ton (horror) and Capra (political drama). Many good touches.
ALIF LAILA (India) 1953 P,D: K. Amarnath. Story: M.R.
Nawab. Adapted from "Aladdin and His Wonderful Lamp." PH:
M. Billimoria. Mus: S. Sunder. Ref: Filmfare 5/15/53.
with Nimmi, Pran, Vijay Kumar. An evil magician strikes
Aladdin blind; genie; magic sword.
ALL THAT MONEY CAN BUY see DEVIL AND DANIEL WEBSTER,
The
ALL WERE ENEMIES see MAKING THE HEADLINES
ALLARME AU SUD see ALERT TO THE SOUTH
ALLEY OF NIGHTMARES see SHE FREAK
The ALLIGATOR PEOPLE Fox/Associate Producers 1959 74m.
D: Roy Del Ruth. SP: Orville Hampton. Story: Hampton,
Charles O'Neal. PH: Brydon Baker. Art D: Lyle Wheeler,
John Mansbridge. Ref: RVB. COF 6:4. with Richard Crane,
Beverly Garland, Lon Chaney, Jr., Bruce Bennett, George
Macready, Douglas Kennedy, Frieda Inescort. Man cured of
injuries by hormone extracted from alligators.
ALONE WITH THE DEVIL. (Dan?) Nordisk 1914 53m. Ref:
Bios 3/5/14. "Diabolical plot"; hypnotism.
ALONG WITH GHOSTS see JOURNEY WITH GHOST ALONG
TOKAIDO ROAD
ALPHAVILLE (F-I) Pathe-Contemporary/Chaumiane-Filmstudio
1965 98m. (ALPHAVILLE, UNE ETRANGE AVENTURE DE
LEMMY CAUTION or UNE NOUVELLE AVENTURE DE LEMMY
CAUTION--France. UNA NUOVA AVVENTURA DI LEMMY
CAUTION or AGENTE LEMMY CAUTION MISSIONE ALPHA-
VILLE--Italy. TARZAN VS. IBM) SP,D: Jean-Luc Godard.
PH: Raoul Coutard. Mus: Paul Misraki. Ed: Agnès Guille-
mot. Ass't D: Charles Bitsch, J.-P. Savignac, H.
Kalouguine. P: André Michelin. Ref: M/TVM 8/65. An-
nuario. COF 8:46. 9:6. with Eddie Constantine, Anna Karina,
Howard Vernon, Akim Tamiroff, Laszlo Szabo, Michel Dela-
haye, Jean-Andre Fieschi, Jean-Louis Comolli (Professor
Jeckell). Private eye Lemmy Caution battles the giant com-
puter which runs Alphaville. Very amusing, with a great
vending-machine gag.
ALRAUNE (G) Luna 1918 Ref: Lee.
ALRAUNE (G) UFA/Ama-Film 1928 (MANDRAKE. UNHOLY
LOVE) D,SP: Henrik Galeen, from a novel by Hanns Heinz
Ewers. PH: Franz Planer. Art D: Walter Reimann, Max

Heilbronner. silent Ref: The Haunted Screen. FM 10:26.
Imagen. Pix: DDC II:413. with Brigitte Helm, Paul Wegener,
Ivan Petrovich, John Loder, Alexander Sascha. A scientist
creates an "artificial woman of great beauty."
ALRAUNE (G) UFA 1930 sound (MANDRAKE. DAUGHTER OF
EVIL) D: Richard Oswald. SP: C. Roellinghoff, R. Weisbach,
from a novel by Hanns Heinz Ewers. PH: Günther Krampf.
Mus: Bronislaw Kaper. Art D: Otto Erdmann, Hans Sohnle.
Ref: The Haunted Screen. FD. with Brigitte Helm, Albert
Bassermann, Agnes Straub, Käthe Haack, Martin Kosleck. "A
scientist's experiments in creating life."
ALRAUNE (G) Styria-Carlton 1952 (MANDRAKE. UNNATURAL
--'56 U.S.) D: Arthur-Maria Rabenalt. Other credits: Robert
Herlth, Kurt Heuser, Werner Heymann. From a novel by
Hanns Heinz Ewers. Ref: DDC III:35, 38, 39, 40. I:250. with
Hildegarde Neff, Erich von Stroheim, Karl Boehm, Trude Hes-
terberg. Pix: "La Belle et La Bete."
ALRAUNE AND THE GOLEM see GOLEM, The (1915)
ALTAR OF BLOOD see SCREAM OF THE DEMON LOVER
ALTER EGO (radio play by Arch Oboler) see BEWITCHED
ALYAS FUMANCHU see ALIAS FUMANCHU
AM ENDE DER WELT see AT EDGE OF WORLD
AM RANDE DER WELT see AT EDGE OF WORLD
AMA NO BAKEMONO YASHIKI see HAUNTED CAVE, The
AMANT DE LA LUNE see LOVER OF THE MOON
AMANTE DEL VAMPIRO, L' see VAMPIRE AND THE BALLERINA,
  The
AMANTI D'OLTRETOMBA see NIGHTMARE CASTLE
The AMAZING COLOSSAL MAN AI/Malibu 1957 80m. SpFX, P, D:
Bert I. Gordon. SP: Mark Hanna, Gordon. PH: Joseph
Biroc. Mus sc & D: Albert Glasser. Props: Paul Blaisdell.
Ref: RVB. FM 14:19. Pic: FM2:15. 18:26. Sequel: WAR OF
THE COLOSSAL BEAST. with Glenn Langan, Cathy Downs,
William Hudson, James Seay, Russ Bender, Judd Holdren,
Scott Peters, Frank Jenks. An army officer is caught in a
plutonium explosion. Pretty silly s-f.
The AMAZING DR. G (I-Sp) AI-TV/FIDA--Epoca 1966 color
85m. (DUE MAFIOSI CONTRO GOLDFINGER. TWO MAFIOSI
AGAINST GOLDGINGER) D: G. Simonelli. Ref: TVFFSB.
M/TVM 8/68. Fernsehen. with Franco Franchi, Ciccio In-
grassia, Gloria Paul, Fernando Rey, Elisa Montes. Dr. Gold-
finger plots to robotize government personnel.
AMAZING MR. H, The see MADMEN OF MANDORAS
THE AMAZING MR. X Eagle-Lion 1948 79m. (THE SPIRITUAL-
IST) D: Bernard Vorhaus. SP: Muriel Roy Bolton, Ian
Hunter. Story: Crane Wilbur. PH: John Alton. Mus sc:
Alexander Laszlo. Sp Art FX: Jack Rabin. Makeup: Ern and
Frank Westmore. Ref: RVB. COF 6:4. with Turhan Bey,
Richard Carlson, Lynn Bari, Cathy O'Donnell, Donald Curtis.
Woman in the clutches of a fake spiritualist. Some eerie
scenes.
THE AMAZING TRANSPARENT MAN AI 1960 60m. D: Edgar
Ulmer. SP: Jack Lewis. PH: Meredith Nicholson. Mus sc & D:

23 Amazing

Darrell Calker. Prod Des: Ernest Fegte. SpFX: Howard
Anderson Co. Ref: RVB. with Marguerite Chapman, Douglas
Kennedy, James Griffith, Ivan Triesault. Man uses invisibility
serum for criminal purposes. Not one of Edgar Ulmer's best.
The AMAZING TRANSPLANT 1971 Ref: LA Times/FJA "His
was the most unique [sic] of all."--advertisement.
The AMBUSHERS Col 1967 Technicolor 102m. D: Henry Levin.
SP: Herbert Baker, from the book by Donald Hamilton. PH:
Burnett Guffey, Edward Coleman. Mus: Hugo Montenegro.
See also The SILENCERS. Third in The Matt Helm series. Ref:
FFacts. RVB. with Dean Martin, Senta Berger, Janice Rule,
James Gregory, Kurt Kasznar, Albert Salmi, Beverly Adams.
Fanatical group takes U.S. spaceship out of orbit; "flying sau-
cer"; metal vaporizers.
The AMERICAN SUICIDE CLUB Lux 1910 10m. Ref: Bios 212:25.
AMMIE, COME HOME (book by Barbara Michaels) see HOUSE
THAT WOULD NOT DIE, The
AMMUTINAMENTO NELLO SPAZIO see MUTINY IN OUTER
SPACE
AMONG THE LIVING Para 1941 68m. D: Stuart Heisler. SP:
Lester Cole, Garrett Fort. Story: Cole, Brian Marlow. PH:
Theodor Sparkuhl. Art D: Hans Dreier, Haldane Douglas. P:
Sol C. Siegel. Ref: RVB. V 9/3/41. FM 52:13. Pic:
MadM 9:8. TBG. with Albert Dekker, Susan Hayward, Harry
Carey, Frances Farmer. Psychological horror film: Insane boy
hidden in mansion. Offbeat, but in uninteresting ways. Dekker
does good things with his voice in dual role.
AMORE ALL'ITALIANA see SUPER DIABOLICAL
AMORE ATTRAVERSO I SECOLI, L' see OLDEST PROFESSION
IN THE WORLD, The
AMOROUS GHOST, The see MAN ALIVE
AMOUR DE POCHE, Un see GIRL IN HIS POCKET
The AMPHIBIAN MAN (Russ) AI-TV/Lenfilm 1962 color 99m.
(CELOVEK ANFIBJA. THE AMPHIBIOUS MAN) D: Gennadi
Kazansky, Vladimir Chebotaryov. SP: A. Xenofontov, A.
Kapler, A. Golburt, from a story by A. Belyayev. PH: Eduard
Razovsky. Ref: RVB. DDC III:153. EncicDS'55:330. with
Vladimir Korenev, Anastasia Vertinskaya, Mikhail Kozakov,
Anatoly Smiranin. Scientist's son has shark gills instead of
lungs. Dull and melodramatic.
AMPHIBIANS, The see UNDERWATER CITY, The
AMPHIBIOUS MAN, The see AMPHIBIAN MAN, The
ANABEL LEE (by Edgar Allan Poe) see AVENGING CONSCIENCE,
The
ANAK NG KIDLAT see DAUGHTER OF LIGHTNING
ANAK PONTIANAK see SON OF THE VAMPIRE, The
ANARBALA (India) 1940 Advance Pictures P,D: A. M. Khan.
Story: M. Nayab. Mus: Mahomed. Ref: Dipali 5/10/40:10, 24.
with Shanta Kashmiri, Benjamin, Jani Babu, S. Alam. A king's
"adventures against Black Magic."
THE ANATOMIST (B) Dola Films/Richard Gordon 1961 73m.
D: Leonard William. Based on a play by James Bridie. Ref:
Boxo 10/30/61. with Alastair Sim, George Cole, Adrienne

Corri, Jill Bennett, Michael Ripper. The Burke and Hare story.

An ANCESTOR'S LEGACY Ambrosio 1914 18m. Ref: Bios 6/25/14. "Gruesome details in old castle cause weird dream in which the various horrors attack their victim with ultra-modern accessories."

ANCHIN TO KIYOHIME see PRIEST AND THE BEAUTY, The

The ANCIENT ROMAN (I) Cines 1909 11m. Ref: Bios 7/29/09. Three professors discover a living Roman gladiator in his tomb.

The ANCINES WOODS (Sp) Amboto 1969 color (EL BOSQUE DE ANCINES. EL BOSQUE DEL LOBO. THE WOLFMAN OF GALICIA. THE WOLF'S FOREST) D: Pedro Olea. SP: Juan Antonio Porto, from a novel by Carlos M. Barbeito. PH: Aurelio G. Larraya. Ref: V 5/6/70. 9/9/70:24. SpCinema'71. Epileptic murderer believed to be werewolf.

AND SOON THE DARKNESS (B) Levitt-Pickman/EMI/Associated British 1970 Technicolor 100m. D: Robert Fuest. SP: Brian Clemens, Terry Nation. PH: Ian Wilson. Mus: Laurie Johnson. Ref: V 7/22/70. Motion Picture Exhibitor 7/22/70. with Pamela Franklin, Michele Dotrice, Sandor Eles, Clare Kelly, John Nettleton. Two English girls on a bicycle tour through France separated. "Horror film"--PM.

AND THE DOG CAME BACK 1907 Ref: MPW'07:252. Dog put through sausage machine returns.

AND THEN THERE WERE NONE Fox 1945 90m. P, D: René Clair. SP: Dudley Nichols, from the novel "Ten Little Indians" or "The Nursery Rhyme Murders" and the play "Ten Little Niggers" by Agatha Christie. PH: Lucien Andriot. Mus D: Charles Previn. Art D: Ernest Fegte. Ref: RVB. with Barry Fitzgerald, Walter Huston, Louis Hayward, June Duprez, Roland Young, Sir C. Aubrey Smith, Judith Anderson, Mischa Auer, Richard Haydn, Queenie Leonard, Harry Thurston. Mysterious "host" of mansion on lonely island commits multiple murder. Does very well as a comedy and a mystery, with Haydn and Young the most amusing of several amusing characters.

ANDALUSIAN SUPERSTITION (F) Pathe 1912 13m. Ref: Silent FF. Bios 6/27/12. "Hideous little living creatures bottled in spirits" in cavern; "ghostly hand."

ANDERE, Der see OTHER, The (1913/1930)

ANDERE ICH, Das see OTHER SELF, The

ANDROMEDA GALAXY, The see CLOUD OF ANDROMEDA, The

ANDROMEDA NEBULA, The see CLOUD OF ANDROMEDA, The

The ANDROMEDA STRAIN Univ 1971 Technicolor/scope 127m. D: Robert Wise. SP: Nelson Gidding, from the novel by J. Michael Crichton. PH: Richard H. Kline. Mus: Gil Melle. Art D: William Tuntke. Prod. Des: Boris Leven. Ref: V 3/10/71. with Arthur Hill, David Wayne, James Olson, Kate Reid, Paula Kelly. Biological invasion from outer space.

ANDROMEDA, THE MYSTERIOUS see CLOUD OF ANDROMEDA, The

An ANGEL FOR SATAN (I) Discobolo 1966 color (UN ANGELO PER SATANA) D: Camillo Mastrocinque SP: Mastrocinque,

Mangione. PH: Giuseppe Acquari. Mus: F. De Masi. Ref:
Ital P. with Barbara Steele, Anthony Steffen, Ursula Davis,
Aldo Berti, Mario Brega, Claudio Gora. The statue of a
woman rises from a lake.
ANGEL ISLAND (Play by Bernie Angus) see FOG ISLAND
ANGELI BIANCHI...ANGELI NERI see WITCHCRAFT '70
ANGELO PER SATANA, Un see ANGEL FOR SATAN, An
ANGER OF THE GOLEM see IT!
ANGOISE L' (play by P. Mills and C. Vylars) see LATIN
   QUARTER, The
The ANGRY RED PLANET AI 1960 Eastmancolor/Cinemagic
   83m. (INVASION OF MARS. JOURNEY TO PLANET FOUR)
   D: IB Melchior. SP: Melchior, Sid Pink. PH: Stanley
   Cortez. SpFX: Herman Townsley. Ref: RVB. Pic: FM
   7:11. 19:13. SM 6:25. with Gerald Mohr, Les Tremayne,
   Jack Kruschen, Nora Hayden. Visitors to Mars find a bat-rat-
   spider-crab monster, carnivorous plants, etc. Some adequate-
   ly imaginative effects, but not nearly enough for a whole movie.
The ANIMAL WORLD WB/Windsor 1956 82m. SP, D, P: Irwin
   Allen. PH: Harold Wellman. Mus D: Paul Sawtell. Art D:
   Bill Tuttle. Supervising Animator: Willis O'Brien. Animation:
   Ray Harryhausen. Narr: Theodore Von Eltz, John Storm.
   Ref: RVB. Pic: FM 21:17. 43:22. dinosaurs and other, less
   interesting, animals.
An ANIMATED ARMCHAIR (F) Pathe 1910 9m. Ref: Bios
   5/18/11: "Haunted room."
An ANIMATED DOLL Essanay 1908 Ref: MPW'08:463. In-
   ventor's automaton.
ANITA (Austrian) Wiener Kunstfilm 1920 (TRANCE) D: Luise
   Kolm, Jakob Fleck. SP: Fritz Lohner-Beda. Ref: Osterr. with
   Lola Urban-Kneidinger, Wilhelm Klitsch, Julius Strobl, Nora
   Herbert. "Existence under hypnosis."
ANITA (India) 1967 Ref: Shankar's 4/30/67. with Sadhana,
   Manoj, Sajjan, I. S. Johar, Bela Bose, Madhumati. Hero
   trails "dead" girl to old, decaying mansion, meets "life-sized
   ghosts."
ANOTHER'S GHOST Pathe 1910 Ref: MPW 7:1006. "Spectre"
   haunts innkeeper who "killed" variety artist.
ANSIKTET see MAGICIAN, The (1958)
ANTI-HAIR POWDER 9m. 1908 Ref: MPW'08:480 Dr. Quack's
   powder removes hair instantly.
ANTIGONE see YEAR OF THE CANNIBALS
ANTINEA, L'AMANTE DELLA CITTA SEPOLTA see JOURNEY
   BENEATH THE DESERT
AOOM (Sp) Hersua Interfilms 1969 Eastmancolor 93m. D:
   Gonzale Suarez. SP: Suarez, Gustave Hernandez. PH: Fran-
   cisco Marin. Mus: Alfonso Sainz. Ref: V 7/22/70. with
   Lex Barker, Teresa Gimpera, Julian Ugarte. Man's soul
   enters doll, then corpse.
The APE Mono 1940 62m. (GORILLA--France, Germany) D:
   William Nigh. SP: Curt Siodmak, Richard Carroll, from
   "The Ape" by Adam Hull Shirk. PH: Harry Neumann. Mus D:
   Edward Kay. Art D: E. R. Hickson. Ref: RVB. COF 6:4.

Pic: FM 46:11. 56:15. with Boris Karloff, Maris Wrixon, Henry Hall, George Cleveland, Gertrude Hoffman, Selmer Jackson. A doctor needs spinal fluid to experiment on a cure for paralysis.

The APE MAN Mono 1943 70m (LOCK YOUR DOORS--England) D: William Beaudine. SP: Barney Sarecky, from the story "They Creep in the Dark" by Karl Brown. PH: Mack Stengler. Mus D: Edward Kay. Art D: David Milton. P: Sam Katzman, Jack Dietz. Ref: RVB. COF 6:5. 8:23. Pic: FM 33:74. MW 4:38. with Bela Lugosi, Wallace Ford, Louise Currie, Minerva Urecal, Henry Hall, Emil Van Horn (the ape), J. Farrel MacDonald, Wheeler Oakman, Jack Mulhall. A man turns into an ape. A mysterious man hovering around in the background provides the only surprise and makes a joke of the whole movie, if that isn't redundant. Lugosi, in an embarrassing role, has one good Lugosi line: "Tell him he's wanted in surgery. "

The APE WOMAN (I) 1964 Emb/Interfilm--Champion 97m. (LA DONNA SCIMMIA. A MOST UNUSUAL WOMAN) D: Marco Ferreri. SP, Ferreri, Rafael Azcona. PH: Aldo Usuelli. P: Carlo Ponti. Ref: RVB. DDC II:329. COF 6:56. with Annie Girardot, Ugo Tognazzi, Achille Majeroni, Filippo Marcelli. Pic: FM28:9. A promoter discovers a young woman covered with hair.

An APISH TRICK Pathe 1909 9m. Ref: Bios 11/25/09. A wife inoculates her husband with monkey serum which makes him act like an ape.

APOKAL (G) 1970 Anczy/Unset Eastmancolor 86m. SP,D: Paul Anczykowski. From a story by Edgar Allan Poe. PH: L. Loosen. Mus: Peter Janssens. Ref: V 5/26/71: "Grotesque. " with Christopher Nel, R. de Neve, Dorit Amann.

The APPARITION (F) Melies/Star 1903 (LE REVENANT) Ref: DDC III:352. Man at hotel bothered by moving candles, etc.

APPEARANCE OF SUPER GIANT, The see INVADERS FROM SPACE?

APRADHI KAUN? See WHO IS GUILTY?

APRIL 1, 2000 (Austrian) Martin S. Lewis/Wien Films 1952 D: Wolfgang Liebeneiner. SP: R. Brunngraber, E. Marboe. Ref: FM 26:4. DDC III:2,55. RVB. with Curt Jurgens, Paul Hörbiger, Waltraut Haas, Hilde Krahl, Karl Ehmann. Pic: SM 1:13. 3:30.

AQUA SEX see MERMAIDS OF TIBURON, The

The AQUARIANS Univ-TV 1970 96m. D: Don McDougall. SP: Leslie Stevens, Winston Miller. Story: Ivan Tors, Alan Caillou. PH: Clifford Poland. Mus: Lalo Schifrin. Art D: Gene Harris. D (Underwater Sequences): Ricou Browning. with Ricardo Montalban, Jose Ferrer, Kate Woodville, Leslie Nielsen, Chris Robinson, Curt Lowens. Underwater nuclear-powered laboratory; nerve gas.

ARANAS INFERNALES see SPIDERS FROM HELL

ARAIGNEE VAMPIRE, L' see SPIDER, The (1958)

The ARC (G) 1919 D: Richard Oswald. Ref: Lee. FIR'63: 95. The future of civilization.

ARE YOU DYING, YOUNG MAN? see BEAST IN THE CELLAR, The
ARGOMAN SUPERDIABOLICO see HOW TO STEAL THE CROWN OF ENGLAND
ARGONAUTS, The see GIANTS OF THESSALY
ARMS OF THE AVENGER see WEAPONS OF VENGEANCE
AROUND A STAR see TRIP TO A STAR (F)
AROUND THE WORLD UNDER THE SEA MGM/Tors 1966 Metrocolor/scope 117m. P,D: Andrew Marton. SP: Arthur Weiss, Art Arthur. PH: Clifford Poland. SpFX: Projects Unlimited. Ref: TVG. with Lloyd Bridges, Shirley Eaton, Brian Kelly, David McCallum, Keenan Wynn, Marshall Thompson, Gary Merrill, Celeste Yarnall. Sea monster; "special submarine."
ARREST BULLDOG DRUMMOND Para 1938-9 57m. D: James Hogan. SP: Stuart Palmer, from the book "The Final Count" by H. C. McNeil. PH: Ted Tetzlaff. Art D: Hans Dreier, Franz Bachelin. Ref: FD 1/17/39. Pic: FM 26:68. with John Howard, George Zucco, Heather Angel, H. B. Warner, Reginald Denny, E. E. Clive, Zeffie Tilbury, Leonard Mudie, Clyde Cook, George Regas, Claude Allister, John Sutton, John Davidson. A ray ("atomic disintegrator") "that will detonate explosives at a distance of half a mile" is stolen.
ARRIVANO I TITANI see MY SON, THE HERO
The ARROW MAIDEN Mutual (Reliance) 1915 15m. Ref: MPW 25:726. MPN 7/17/15. Medicine woman revives Indian from spell; latter frightens other brave who thought he was dead.
ARSENIC AND OLD LACE WB 1944 118m. D: Frank Capra. SP: Julius J. Epstein, Philip G. Epstein. From the play by Joseph Kesselring. PH: Sol Polito. Mus sc: Max Steiner. SpFX: Byron Haskin, Robert Burks. Ref: RVB. Pic: TBG. FMO 5:35. with Cary Grant, Raymond Massey, Peter Lorre, Priscilla Lane, Josephine Hull, Jean Adair, Jack Carson, John Alexander, Edward Everett Horton, James Gleason, Grant Mitchell, John Ridgely. Mortimer Brewster runs into his long-lost brother Jonathan, who acts like someone out of a horror movie. Great lines ("Gentlemen, be seated") and a controversial, energetic performance by Grant.
ARTISTS AND MODELS Para 1955 Technicolor/scope 109m. D: Frank Tashlin. SP: Tashlin, Hal Kanter, Herbert Baker. Adap: Don McGuire. From "Rock-a-Bye, Baby!" by Norman Lessing and Michael Davidson. Mus D: Walter Scharf. Art D: Hal Pereira, Tambi Larsen. PH: Daniel L. Fapp. P: Hal B. Wallis. Ref: FDY. with Dean Martin, Jerry Lewis, Dorothy Malone, Shirley MacLaine, Eva Gabor, Eddie Mayehoff, Anita Ekberg, George "Foghorn" Winslow, Jack Elam, Herbert Rudley, Richard Webb, Kathleen Freeman, Art Baker, Steven Geray, Emory Parnell, Carleton Young, Frank Jenks, Eve Meyer, Nick Castle. Lewis "dreams up" lurid space adventures which sell to comic books.
The ARTIST'S DREAM AM&B 1903 Ref: Niver. Woman becomes skeleton.
AS DE PIC, OPERACION CONTRAESPIONAJE see OPERATION COUNTERSPY

ASESINO INVISIBLE, El See INVISIBLE MURDERER, The
ASESINO LOCO Y EL SEXO, El see WRESTLING WOMEN VS.
THE MURDERING ROBOT, The
ASESINOS DE OTROS MUNDOS see MURDERERS FROM
ANOTHER WORLD
ASHRIDGE CASTLE (B) 1926 short (HAUNTED CASTLES
series) D: C. C. Calvert. Ref: Brit. Cinema. V 2/24/26.
ASSASSINO HA LE ORE CONTATE, L' see COPLAN SAVES HIS
SKIN
ASSEDIO DI SIRACUSA, L' see SIEGE OF SYRACUSE, The
ASSIGNMENT: ISTANBUL see CASTLE OF FU MANCHU, The
ASSIGNMENT--OUTER SPACE (I) 1960 AI/Ultra--Titanus/Fred
Gebhardt/4 Crown color (SPACE MEN) D: Anthony Dawson
(Antonio Margheriti). SP: Vassiliz Petrov. PH: Marcello
Masciocchi. Mus: Gordon Zahler. SpFX: Caesar Peace.
Exec P: Hugo Grimaldi. Ref: RVB. Imagen. Pic: SM 4:11.
with Rik Von Nutter, Archie Savage, Alain Dejon, Gaby Farinon,
Franco Fantasia, Aldo Pini. A malfunctioning computer sends
a spaceship out of control. Confusing, poorly dubbed, but not
altogether uninteresting.
ASSIZE OF THE DYING (book by Edith Pargeter) see SPANIARD'S
CURSE, The
"ASSO DI PICCHE," OPERAZIONE CONTROSPIONAGGIO see
OPERATION COUNTERSPY
The ASTOUNDING SHE MONSTER AI/Hollywood Int'l. 1957
60m. (THE MYSTERIOUS INVADER--Eng. THE ASTOUNDING
SHE CREATURE) P, D: Ronnie Ashcroft. SP: Frank Hall.
PH: William C. Thompson. Mus: G. Kauer. Ref: MFB'58:
144. RVB. Pic: FM 2:41. with Robert Clarke, Kenne
Duncan, Marilyn Harvey, Jeanne Tatum, Shirley Kilpatrick (the
alien). One of those that have to be seen to be believed,
they're so bad.
ASTRO-ZOMBIES Ram Ltd./Seymour Borde/Genini 1968
Eastmancolor 94m. P,D: Ted V. Mikels. SP: Mikels, Wayne
Rogers. PH: Robert Maxwell. Mus: Nico Karaski. Art D:
Wally Moon. Ref: V 5/1/68:20. Boxo 11/11/68. S Union.
with Wendell Corey, John Carradine, Rafael Campos, Tom
Pace, Joan Patrick, Tura Satana, William Bagdad. Dr. De
Marco has several people murdered in order to get vital or-
gans for his "astro-man."
The ASTRONAUTS (Mex) Azteca/Zacarias 1960 (LOS ASTRO-
NAUTAS) SP, D: Miguel Zacarias. PH: M. G. Urquiza. Mus:
G. C. Carrion. Art D: R. R. Granada. Story: R. G.
Bolaños. with Viruta, Capulina, Gina Romand, Norma Mora,
Erna Martha Bauman. Ref: Indice.
ASTRONAUTS (novel by S. Lem) see FIRST SPACESHIP ON
VENUS
The ASTRONOMER'S DREAM (F) Melies 1898 3m. (LE REVE
D'UN ASTRONOME or LA LUNE A UN METRE or L'HOMME
DANS LA LUNE--France. A TRIP TO THE MOON--Lubin
pirated version) Ref: Silent FF. SF Film. Imagen.
Astronomer dreams he travels on rope ladder to moon. A
lesser Melies.

ASYLUM OF HORROR   see   HISTOIRES EXTRAORDINAIRES (1931)
AT EDGE OF WORLD   (G)   UFA.   1926   (AM ENDE DER WELT
   or AM RANDE DER WELT)   D: Karl Grune.   SP: Karl Mayer.
   Art D: A. D. Weppach.   Ref: Lee.   RVB.   COF   13:47.   V
   12/21/27. 6/20/28.   with Brigitte Helm, Wilhelm (William)
   Dieterle, Max Schreck.   War of the future.
AT THE SIGN OF THE JACK O'LANTERN   Hodkinson/Renco   1922
   65m.   SP, D: Lloyd Ingraham.   SP: also David Kirkland.   Ref:
   AFI.   with Betty Ross Clark, Earl Schenck, Wade Boteler,
   Victor Potel, Mrs. Raymond Hatton, Monte Collins.   "Ghostly
   events" in a country house.
AT THE SIGNAL OF THE THREE SOCKS   1915   Ref: MPW'15:555
   (Episode Five of "The Mysterious Lady Baffles and Detective
   Duck" series) Maid dresses as ghost to scare couple; "rubber-
   scope" acts like TV.
AT THE VILLA ROSE   (B)   Stoll   1920   ("Eminent British Authors"
   series) 56m.   D: Maurice Elvey.   SP: Sinclair Hill.   Sets:
   Walter W. Murton.   Ref: SilentFF.   with Teddy Arundell,
   Norman Page.   From the novel by A.E.W. Mason.   Remade as
   HOUSE OF MYSTERY (1941), MYSTERY AT THE VILLA ROSE
   (1930/1932).
ATACAN LAS BRUJAS   see SANTO ATTACKS THE WITCHES
ATAUD DEL VAMPIRO, El   see   VAMPIRE'S COFFIN, The
ATLANTIDE, L' (novel by Pierre Benoit)   see   ATLANTIS/
   JOURNEY BENEATH THE DESERT/LOST ATLANTIS/SIREN OF
   ATLANTIS
ATLANTIS   (Dan-G) Nordisk   1913   D: Ole Olsen.   SP: Gerhardt
   Hauptmann, from his novel.   Ref: DDC II:367. III:511.   Imagen.
   RVB.   with Olaf Fönss.
ATLANTIS   (F) Gaumont   (L'ATLANTIDE)   103m.   D: Jacques
   Feyder.   Based on a novel by Pierre Benoit.   Ref: SilentFF.
   Pic: DDC I:58.   III:455.   with Stacia Napie(r)kowska, Jean Angelo,
   Georges Melchior.
ATLANTIS   see   SIREN OF ATLANTIS
ATLANTIS, THE LOST CONTINENT (US-B)   MGM/Galaxy   1961
   Metrocolor 90m.   P, D: George Pal.   SP: Daniel Mainwaring,
   from a play by Sir Gerald Hargreaves.   PH: Harold Wellman.
   Mus sc: Russell Garcia.   Art D: George W. Davis, William
   Ferrari.   SpFX: A. Arnold Gillespie, Lee LeBlanc, Robert R.
   Hoag.   Animation: Projects Unlimited (Jim Danforth & Associates),
   Makeup: William Tuttle.   Narr: Paul Frees.   Rev: RVB.   FM
   11:8.   Pic: FM 18:42.   PM.   with Ed Platt, Joyce Taylor,
   Anthony Hall, John Dall, Bill Smith, Frank DeKova, Jay Novello,
   Edgar Stehli, Wolfe Barzell, Berry Kroeger.   Atlantans plan to
   conquer the world with "atomic energy."   The effects almost
   save the rest, which is quite a feat.
ATLAS AGAINST THE CZAR   (I) Regal Int'l. /John Alexander   1964
   color   89m.   (MACISTE ALLA CORTE DELLO CZAR.   GIANT
   OF THE LOST TOMB.   SAMSON VS. THE GIANT KING)   D:
   Amerigo Anton.   SP: Anton, Mario Moroni, Alberto De Rossi.
   PH: Aldo Giordani.   Ref: MFB.   Boxo 8/23/65.   TVG.   with
   Kirk Morris, Massimo Serato, Gloria Milland, Ombretta Colli.
   Soldiers of the tyrannical Czar Nicolaiev find the body of

Maciste in a tomb and bring him back to life.
ATLAS IN THE LAND OF THE CYCLOPS (I) Medallion-TV 1960
color 100m. (MACISTE NELLA TERRA DEI CICLOPI. ATLAS
VS. THE CYCLOPS. MACISTE IN THE LAND OF THE CY-
CLOPS) D: Leonviola. (MONSTER FROM THE UNKNOWN
WORLD--England) Ref: Orpheus 3:31. Pic: MW 10:50. with
Gordon Mitchell, Chelo Alonso, Aldo Padinotti (the cyclops).
ATOM AGE VAMPIRE (I-F) AI 1960 ('63-U.S.) 87m. (SED-
DOK, L'EREDE DI SATAN. LE MONSTRE AU MASQUE)
D: Richard McNamara (Anton Majano). SP: Majano, Piero
Monviso Gino de Sanctis, Alberto Bevilacqua. P: Mario
Bava. Ref: RVB. FM 10:10. with Alberto Lupo, Susanne
Loret, Ivo Garrani, Sergio Fantoni. Scientist's serum restores
scarred girl's beauty. A lot of mirrors get broken.
ATOM MAN VS. SUPERMAN Col 1950 serial 15 episodes D:
Spencer G. Bennet. SP: George H. Plympton, Joseph F.
Poland, David Mathews. PH: Ira H. Morgan. P: Sam Katz-
man. Ref: Barbour. pic: MW 10:22. FanMo 1:14. 4:54.
From "Superman" and "Action" comics and the "Superman"
radio show. with Kirk Alyn, Noel Neill, Lyle Talbot, Tommy
Bond, Pierre Watkin, Jack Ingram, Don Harvey, Terry Frost.
"Heat ray," "phantom zone," "flying saucer."
ATOMIC BRAIN, The see MONSTROSITY
ATOMIC DUCK, The see MR. DRAKE'S DUCK
The ATOMIC KID Rep 1954 87m. D: Leslie Martinson. SP:
John Fenton Murray, Benedict Freeman. Story: Blake Edwards.
PH: John L. Russell, Jr. Ref: RVB. with Mickey Rooney,
Robert Strauss, Whit Bissell, Elaine Davis, Bill Goodwin, Joey
Forman, Robert Emmet Keane, Peter Leeds. Rooney, caught in
an atomic blast, becomes radioactive. A staple at kiddie
matinees in the Fifties.
The ATOMIC MAN (B) AA/Todon 1955 78m. D: Ken Hughes.
SP: Charles Eric Maine, from his story, "The Isotope Man."
(TIMESLIP) PH: A. T. Dinsdale. Mus D: Richard Taylor.
Art D: George Haslam. Ref: FDY. Lee. with Gene Nelson,
Faith Domergue, Peter Arne, Vic Perry. Nuclear scientist is
dead on the operating table for seven seconds. No story to go
with the intriguing central gimmick.
ATOMIC MONSTER, The see MAN MADE MONSTER
ATOMIC RULERS OF THE WORLD (J) 1957 Manley-TV/Shintoho
83m. (INVINCIBLE SPACEMAN. ATOMIC RULERS. SUPER
GIANT. SUPAH JAIYANTO #3 & #4: INVADERS FROM THE
PLANETS or KOTETSU NO KYOGIN-KAISEIJI NO MAJYO and
THE EARTH IN DANGER or KOTETSU NO KYOGIN-CHIKYO
METSUBO SUNZEN) D: Teruo Ishii, also A. Mitsuwa and ?.
SP: I. Miyagawa. Ref: FEFN 6/28/57. Imagen. Cahiers.
Bianco. COF 11:57. Rep Gen'61. Super Giant pamphlet.
with Ken Utsui, Junko Ikeuchi, Minoru Takada. The creatures
of the Emerald Planet send Starman to save earth.
The ATOMIC SUBMARINE AA/Gorham 1960 73m. D: Spencer
G. Bennet. SP: Orville Hampton. Produced in association
with Jack Rabin and Irving Block. PH: Gilbert Warrenton.
Electronic mus sc & d: Alexander Laszlo. Art D: Don Ament,

Daniel Haller. SpFX: Rabin, Block, Louis DeWitt. P: Alex
Gordon. Ref: RVB. Pic: FM 7:16. with Arthur Franz, Dick
Foran, Brett Halsey, Tom Conway, Bob Steele, Joi Lansing,
Selmer Jackson, Victor Varconi, Paul Dubov, Jack Mulhall,
Sid Melton. Sub finds flying saucer in Arctic waters. Trite.
ATOMIC WAR BRIDE 1966 United Screen Arts/Medallion-TV
   77m. Ref: TVFFSB. with Anton Vodak, Eva Krewskan. In
   the "final war" the President authorizes an atomic attack.
ATRAGON (J) 1965 AI/Toho Pathecolor 88m. (ATORAGON--
   FLYING SUPERSUB. KAITEI GUNKAN) D: Inoshiro Honda.
   SP: Shinichi Sekizawa. PH: Hajime Koizumi. Mus sc & D.
   Akira Ifukube. SpFX: Eiji Tsuburaya. Ref: RVB. PM. with
   Tadao Takashima, Kenji Sahara, Hiroshi Koizumi, Jun Tazaki.
   Underwater Mu Empire and monster-machine Atragon threaten
   the world. The dubbing hurts ("Don't move 'cause I'll blow you
   all up").
ATTACK FROM SPACE (J) 1958-7 Manley-TV/Shintoho 79m.
   (SUPER GIANT. SUPER GIANT AGAINST THE SATELLITES.
   SUPAH JAIYANTO #5 & #6: THE SINISTER SPACESHIP or
   JINKO EISEI TO JINRUI NO HAMETSU and THE DESTRUCTION
   OF THE SPACE FLEET or UCHUTEI TO JINKO EISEI NO
   GEKITOTSU) partly in color D: Teruo Ishii. SP: Ichiro
   Miyagawa. Story: Shinsuke Negishi. PH: Hiroshi Juzuki.
   Ref: COF 11:57. FEFN 4/4/58. Super Giant pamphlet.
   Cahiers. Bianco. UFQ-1. with Ken Utsui, Utako Mitsuya, Kan
   Hayashi, Teruhisa Ikeda, Hiroshi Asami, Junko Ikeuchi, Minoru
   Takada. Invaders from the Sapphire galaxy employ a Japanese
   scientist in their plot to take over the earth.
ATTACK OF THE BLOOD LEECHES see GIANT LEECHES, The
ATTACK OF THE CRAB MONSTERS AA/Los Altos 1957 64m.
   P,D: Roger Corman. SP: Charles Griffith. PH: Floyd
   Crosby. Mus sc & D: Ronald Stein. with Richard Garland,
   Pamela Duncan, Russell Johnson, Mel Welles, Ed Nelson, Beech
   Dickerson. H-bomb fallout creates giant land crabs which ab-
   sorb the mental power of their victims. Basically silly ideas
   nonetheless make for some eerie scenes. One of Corman's (and
   Griffith's) more interesting early works.
ATTACK OF THE FIFTY-FOOT WOMAN AA/Woolner 1958 65m.
   D: Nathan Hertz. SP: Mark Hanna. PH: Jacques Marquette.
   Mus sc & D: Ronald Stein. P: Bernard Woolner. Ref: RVB.
   FDY. with Allison Hayes, William Hudson, Yvette Vickers,
   Roy Gordon, Ken Terrell. Woman sees a spaceship land.
   Really rotten.
ATTACK OF THE GIANT LEECHES see GIANT LEECHES, The
ATTACK OF THE LIVER EATERS see SPIDER BABY
ATTACK OF THE MAYAN MUMMY (Mex-U.S.) 1963 85m. D:
   (U.S. footage): Jerry Warren. with Richard Webb, Nina Knight,
   John Burton. A girl is regressed through hypnosis into a past
   life. A primer on how to avoid dubbing and how not to make a
   movie. The camera will remain stationary for minutes on end
   while the characters in the added U.S. footage talk out the plot.
   Then there'll be a chunk of original footage with very little
   dialogue; and even then dubbing is usually got around somehow.

Incredible nihilistic ending.   Almost fascinating in its primitive techniques.

ATTACK OF THE MONSTERS see GAMERA VS. GUIRON

ATTACK OF THE MUSHROOM PEOPLE AI-TV/Toho (J) 1963 Eastmancolor/scope 89m. (MATANGO. MATANGO--FUNGUS OF TERROR--Eng.) D: Inoshiro Honda. SP: Takeshi Kimura. PH: Hajime Koizumi. SpFX: Eiji Tsuburaya. Ref: MFB'69. FM 30:10. with Hiroshi Koizumi, Akira Kubo, Kenji Sahara. Offbeat tale of a strange substance found on an island. Some bizarre sequences, but the dubbing ruins most of it.

ATTACK OF THE PUPPET PEOPLE AI/Alta Vista 1958 78m. (SIX INCHES TALL. THE FANTASTIC PUPPET PEOPLE) Fx, P, D: Bert I. Gordon. SP: George W. Yates. PH: Ernest Laszlo. Mus sc & d: Albert Glasser. Ref: FM 2:20. 14:19. 28:14. Pic: FM 16:40. 17:14. with John Hoyt, John Agar, June Kenny, Scott Peters, Susan Gordon, Marlene Willis, Laurie Mitchell. A toymaker shrinks people. Film fails to exploit the limitless potential of its premise.

ATTACK OF THE ROBOTS (F-Sp) 1962 Speva/Cine-Alliance/ Hesperia 93m. (CARTES SUR TABLE-F. CARTAS BOCA ARRIBA-Sp. CARDS ON THE TABLE) D: Jesus Franco. SP: Jean-Claude Carriere. PH: A. Macasoli. Mus: Paul Misraki. Art D: J. A. D'Eaubonne. Ref: La Prod. Cin. Fr. FIR'68. with Eddie Constantine, Francoise Brion, Sophie Hardy, Fernando Rey, "Lemmy Constantine." An international organization uses killer-robots in an attempt to conquer the world.

AU SECOURS! see HELP!

AU SECOURS, JE SUIS INVISIBLE! see HELP, I'M INVISIBLE!

AUBERGE ENSORCELEE, L' see BEWITCHED INN, The

AUF WIEDERSEHEN (by G. Morris and M. Barteaux) see SIX HOURS TO LIVE

AUGEN DER MUMIE MA, Die see EYES OF THE MUMMY

AUGEN DES DR. MABUSE, Die see ONE THOUSAND EYES OF DR. MABUSE, The

AUNT ELIZA RECOVERS HER PET (F) Pathe Freres? c1908 7m. Ref: SilentFF. A thief steals a bird and cooks and eats it. A detective hypnotizes him, then saws him in half to free the bird.

AURA (novel by Carlos Fuentes) see WITCH IN LOVE, The

AUTOMAT NA PRANI see WISHING MACHINE, The

AUTOMATAS DE LA MUERTE, Los see NEUTRON VS. THE DEATH ROBOTS

AUTOMATIC MOTORIST, The (B) Urban 1911 D: Walter Booth. Ref: SF Film. Brit. Cinema. Robot chauffeur.

AUTOMOBILE CHASE, The (F) Melies 1905 (LE VOYAGE AUTO-MOBILE PARIS--MONTE CARLO EN DEUX HEURES) Ref: s-f Film.

AUTOMOBILE MOTORIST, The (B) Kineto 1911 11m. Ref: Bios 3/16/11. A trip to the stars.

AUTOPSY OF A GHOST (Mex) Rodriguez 1967 (AUTOPSIA DE UN FANTASMA) D: Ismael Rodriguez. Ref: M/TVM 9/66.

MMF 18-19:15. with Basil Rathbone, John Carradine, Cameron Mitchell, Amedee Chabot.

AVARICE Imp 1917 SP, D: E. Magnus Ingleton. Ref: MPW 31:904. "death Reviews the horrors" of a miserly woman's life. She thrusts gold into his face--"which gradually changes into a skull" --and falls dead. with Claire McDowell, T. D. Crittenden (Death), Leo Pearson, Betty Schade.

AVATAR (by T. Gautier) see HE WHO DIES OF LOVE

AVENGER, The (G) 1960 Roberts & Barry /Kurt Ulrich (DER RAECHER) D: Karl Anton. From the novel by Edgar Wallace. Ref: FIR'63:378. '67. RVB. Pic: FM 18:8.19:19.49:51. with Heinz Drache, Ingrid van Bergen, Klaus Kinski, Rainer Brandt. Ape-like murderer decapitates his victims.

AVENGING CONSCIENCE, The: Thou Shalt Not Kill 1914 Ess P, D: D. W. Griffith. PH: Billy Bitzer. Ref: FM 11:40. 47: 60. RVB. FIR'65. Based on "The Black Cat," "The Conquering Worm," "The Tell-Tale Heart," "The Pit and the Pendulum," and "Annabel Lee" by Edgar Allan Poe. with Henry B. Walthall, Dorothy Gish, Donald Crisp, Blanche Sweet, Spottiswoode Aitken, Mae Marsh. Psychological horror.

AVENGING HAND, The (B) Crick 1915 P: Charles Calvert. Ref: Hist. Brit. Film. A murder is committed by the stolen hand of an Egyptian mummy.

AVENGING SPECTER, The (I) Roma 1914 Ref: Lee (SPETTRO VENDICATORE)

AVENTURA EN EL CENTRO DE LA TIERRA see ADVENTURE AT THE CENTER OF THE EARTH

AVENTURA EN LA NOCHE, Une see ADVENTURE IN THE NIGHT, An

AVENTURAS DE CUCURUCHITO Y PINOCHO, Las see ADVENTURES OF CUCURUCHITO AND PINOCHO, The

AVENTURAS DE QUIQUE Y ARTURO EL ROBOT, El see DISINTEGRATING RAY, The

AVIATION HAS ITS SURPRISES (F) Pathe Freres 1909 9m. Ref: SilentFF. Mixture inflates man like a balloon, & he rises into the air.

AWFUL DR. ORLOF, The (F-I-Sp) Sigma III /Newman--Leo Lax-- Hispamer 1962 ('65--U. S.) 90m. (L'HORRIBLE DOCTEUR ORLOF--F. IL DIABOLICO DOTTOR SATANA--I. GRITOS EN LA NOCHE--Sp. THE DEMON DOCTOR. CRIES IN THE NIGHT) D, SP: Jesus Franco. From a story by David Kuhne. PH: Godofredo Pacheco. Ref: FM 28:7. with Howard Vernon, Perla Cristal, Diana Lorys, Conrado San Martin, Faustino Cornejo. A mad doctor kidnaps women for his skin-grafting experiments.

AYESHA, THE RETURN OF SHE see VENGEANCE OF SHE

AZ ELET KIRAYLA see PICTURE OF DORIAN GRAY, The (Hung) ('17)

AZIMAT see SEAL OF SOLOMON, The

AZTEC MUMMY, The (Mex) Calderón 1957 (LA MOMIA. LA MOMIA AZTECA. THE MUMMY. THE MUMMY STRIKES) D: Rafael Portillo. PH: Enrique Wallace. Mus: Antonio Díaz Conde. Ref: Aventura. Bianco. COF-A:46. Lee. Pic:

Babes

34

FM 28:49. MadM 4:29. with Ramon Gay, Rosita Arenas, Crox Alvarado, Luis Aceves Castañeda, Arturo Martinez, Jorge Mondragón.

BABES IN THE WOODS Miles Bros. 1907 Ref: MPW'07:491. Mrs. Bear invites two children into her home and prepares to "roast them for dinner."
BABES IN THE WOODS (F) Pathe Freres 1913 15m. Ref: SilentFF. Based on the fairy tale.
BABES IN THE WOODS Fox 1917 70m. D: C. M. & S. A. Franklin. SP: Bernard McConville, from "Hansel and Gretel." Ref: Lee.
BABES IN TOYLAND BV 1961 Technicolor 105m. D: Jack Donohue. SP: Joe Rinaldi, Ward Kimball, Lowell S. Hawley. From the operetta by Victor Herbert and Glenn McDonough. PH: Edward Coleman. Art D: Carroll Clark, Marvin Davis. Mus: George Bruns. SpFX: Robert Mattey. Makeup: Pat McNalley. Ref: FFacts. with Ray Bolger, Annette Funicello, Tommy Sands, Tommy Kirk, Ed Wynn, Kevin Corcoran, Henry Calvin, Gene Sheldon, Ann Jilliann, Brian Corcoran. Toymaker's invention that shrinks people; Bogeyland.
BABES IN TOYLAND see MARCH OF THE WOODEN SOLDIERS
The BABY INCUBATOR Gaum 1910 8m. Ref: Bios 3/24/10. Doctor's incubator warms, animates baby until he steps out of it and begins talking.
BABY'S GHOST Lux 1911 7m. Ref: Bios 2/8/12. "Great white ghost" frightens burglars.
BACHELOR BRIDES PDC 1926 83m. D: William K. Howard. SP: Garrett Fort, C. Gardner Sullivan, from a play by C. H. Malcolm. PH: Lucien Andriot. P: Cecil B. DeMille. Art D: Max Parker. Ass't D: Henry Hathaway. Ref: MPW 80:346. Lee. AFI. with Rod LaRocque, Eulalie Jensen, Sally Rand, Elinor Fair, George Nichols, Lucien Littlefield, Eddie Gribbon. Castle; secret passages; hairy clutching hand.
BACK FROM THE DEAD Fox/Regal 1957 79m. D: Charles Marquis Warren. SP: Catherine Turney, from her novel, "The Other One," or "The Possessed." PH: Ernest Haller. Mus sc & d: Raoul Kraushaar. Art D: James Sullivan. with Arthur Franz, Peggie Castle, Marsha Hunt, Jeanne Bates, James Bell. Girl possessed by spirit of husband's first wife.
BACK TO EARTH Univ 1923 25m. SP,D: Al Herman. Ref: Lee. MPN 28:1363. Flying house with magnetic gadgets.
BACK TO LIFE AFTER 2000 YEARS (F) Pathe 1910 13m. (THE ROMAN'S AWAKENING--Eng.) Ref: Bios 3/31/10. MPW 7:423,463. Ancient Roman emerges from sepulchre to tour modern Rome.
BACK TO THE STARS (by E. von Daeniken) see MEMORIES OF THE FUTURE
The BAD AND THE BEAUTIFUL MGM 1952 118m. D: Vincente Minnelli. SP: Charles Schnee. Story: George Bradshaw. PH:

Robert Surtees. Mus: David Raksin. Art D: Cedric Gibbons, Edward Carfagno. P: John Houseman. Ref: V(d) 11/19/52. Newsweek 1/26/53. with Lana Turner, Kirk Douglas, Dick Powell, Walter Pidgeon, Barry Sullivan, Gloria Grahame, Gilbert Roland, Leo G. Carroll, Paul Stewart, Ivan Triesault, Elaine Stewart, Kathleen Freeman, Robert Burton, Francis X. Bushman, Sandy Descher, Barbara Billingsley, Dabbs Greer, Pat O'Malley, Frank Gerstle. Horror-movie maker ("The Catmen") modeled on Val Lewton.

The BAD FLOWER (Korean) Sunglim Film 1961 (AHKEA KKOTS) D: Yongmin Lee. Based on "Dracula" by Bram Stoker and the film HORROR OF DRACULA. Ref: FEFN 1/61, 5/61. with Chimi Kim, Yechoon Lee.

The BAD SEED WB 1956 127m. P, D: Mervyn LeRoy. SP: John Lee Mahin, from the play by Maxwell Anderson and the novel by William March. PH: Hal Rosson. Mus: Alex North. with Nancy Kelly, Patty McCormack, Henry Jones, William Hopper, Eileen Heckart, Jesse White, Evelyn Varden, Paul Fix, Gage Clarke, Frank Cady, Dayton Lummis, Shelley Fabare(s), Pat Morrow, Don C. Harvey. Mother fears her daughter is a victim of "inherited" evil.

The BAD SEED (Turkish) Pesen/And Film 1964 D: Nevzat Pesen. From the play by Maxwell Anderson and the novel by William March. Ref: M/TVM 2/64. with Lale, Alev Oraloglu.

BADDESLEY MANOR (B) 1926 short (HAUNTED CASTLES series) D: Maurice Elvey. Ref: Brit.Cinema. V 2/24/26. Man loses wager with Death.

The BADGER PALACE (J) Toho 1958 color/scope 98m. (OHATARI TANUKI GOTEN) D: Kozo Saeki. SP: Tatsuo Nakada. Story: K. Kimura. Ref: FEFN 3/7/58. with Shinji Yamada, I. Arishima, Y. Nanto. "Badger princess" lured into the web of the "spider queen."

BADGES (play by M. Marcin & E. Hammond) see GHOST TALKS, The

BADSHAH see HUNCHBACK OF NOTRE DAME, The (1954)

BAG OF MONKEY NUTS, A see MAN MONKEY, The

BAGHDAD THIRUDAN see THIEF OF BAGHDAD ('60/Indian)

BALAOO (F) Union/Univ (Eclair) 1913 45m. (BALAOO OU DES PAS AU PLAFOND. BALAOO, THE DEMON BABOON) D: Victorin Jasset. Based on the novel by Gaston Leroux. Ref: MPW 16:507. Mitry II. with M. Bataille (the baboon), H. Gouget. Apeman murderer: "Weirdest animal ever created." See also WIZARD, The. DR. RENAULT'S SECRET.

BALLAD OF A WITCH, The (I) Ambrosio/Warwick 1909 10m. (LA BALLETA DI UNA STREGA. THE WITCH'S BALLAD) PH: Giovanni Vitrotti. Ref: Lee. Bios 4/21/10. Witch causes fisherman to drown himself.

BAMANAVATAR (India--Bengali) Radha Film 1939 D: Hari Bhanja. Ref: Dipali 1/5/40. with Ahindra Chowdhury (Bali, king of the demons), R. Roy, Nibhanani. "Conflict between the gods and the demons."

The BAMBOO SAUCER World Entertainment 1968 100m. DeLuxeColor SP, D: Frank Telford, from a story by Rip Von

Ronkel and John Fulton. PH: Hal Mohr. Mus: Edward Paul.
Art D: Theodore Holsopple. SpFX: Fulton, Glen Robinson.
Ref: V 11/6/68. with Dan Duryea, John Ericson, Lois Nettleton, Bernard Fox, Vincent Beck. A flying saucer is reported hidden in a Red Chinese village. A U.S. team attempts to track
it down.

BANCHO SARAYASHIKI see GHOST STORY (1957)

BANCO A BANGKOK POUR O.S.S. 117 see SHADOW OF EVIL

BANDE DES SCHRECKENS, Die see TERRIBLE PEOPLE, The

The BANDIT (India) Bharati 1960 153m. (JAGGA DAKU) D:
Chandrakant. Ref: FEFN 2/60. with Jabeen, Jairaj. The
king's daughter enlists the aid of a man with supernatural powers against an army commander and a witch.

BANG BANG (U.S.-Sp-I) Sidney Pink--Westside Int'l. /L.M.
Film/Domino 1968 color/scope 87m. (THE BANG BANG
KID) D: Stanley Praeger (Luciano Lelly). SP: José L.
Bayonas. PH: A. Macasoli. Mus: Nino Fidenco. Ref:
M/TVM 8/68. Sp. Cinema'69. with Guy Madison, Tom Bosley,
Sandra Milo, Dianik Zurakowska. Lawman uses robot against
ranch owner who lives in imported castle.

The BANSHEE K.B. 1913 35m. Ref: Bios 10/16/13. Dream:
A Man murders his best friend.

BARAN see VARAN

BARBARELLA (I-F) Para 1968 color 98m. D: Roger Vadim.
SP: Vadim, Terry Southern, Jean Claude Forest, Brian Degas,
Claude Brule, Clement Wood, Tudor Gates, Vittorio Bonicelli.
PH: Claude Renoir. From the book by Forest. Art D: Enrico Fea. Sets: Giorgio Hermann. Costumes: Jacques Fon-
teray. with Jane Fonda, John Philip Law, David Hemmings,
Milo O'Shea, Marcel Marceau, Anita Pallenberg, Claude Dauphin, Ugo Tognazzi, Veronique Vendell. The adventures of a
female astronaut in the year 40,000. Moderately amusing but
hardly ever more.

The BARBER'S QUEER CUSTOMER AM&B 1902 Ref: Niver.
Man turns into owl, monkey, etc.

BARCA SIN PESCADOR, LA see BOAT WITHOUT THE FISHER-
MAN, The

The BAREFOOT BOY Mono 1938 63m. D: Karl Brown. SP:
John T. Neville. PH: Gilbert Warrenton. Ed: Finn Ulback.
P: Harold Lewis. Ref: FDY. MFB'38:257. with Jackie
Moran, Marcia Mae Jones, Ralph Morgan, Claire Windsor,
Charles D. Brown. Children locate missing bonds in a haunted
house.

BARGAIN WITH SATAN, A see STUDENT OF PRAGUE, The
(1913)

BARNUM see FREAKS

BARON DEL TERROR, El see BRAINIAC, The

BARON FANTOME, Le see PHANTOM BARON, The

BARON MUNCHAUSEN see ADVENTURES OF BARON MUNC-
HAUSEN, The /CAPTURING THE NORTH POLE /FABULOUS
BARON MUNCHAUSEN, The

BARON MUNCHAUSEN'S DREAM (F) Pathe 1911 12m. (BARON
MUNCHAUSEN. LES HALLUCINATIONS DU BARON DE

MUNCHAUSEN?) /Melies? From stories by Rudolph E. Raspe.
Ref: Bios 9/21/11. Dream: dragon, "fierce men."
BARON PRASIL see FABULOUS BARON MUNCHAUSEN, The
The BARTON MYSTERY (B) Stoll 1920 72m. PH: E. Harvey
Harrison. Ref: SilentFF. with Lyn Harding, Edward O'Neil,
Arthur Pusey, Little Enid Bell. Psychic solves murder.
The BASILISK (B) Hepworth 1914 42m. SP, PH: C. M. Hep-
worth. Ref: Hist. Brit. Film. with William Felton, Alma
Taylor, Tom Powers. Girl in clutches of man with occult
powers.
The BAT UA 1926 103m. D, SP: Roland West. PH: Arthur
Edeson. From the play by Mary Roberts Rinehart and Avery
Hopwood and the novel by M. R. Rinehart. Story: Julien
Josephson. Titles: George Marion, Jr. Art D: William
Cameron Menzies. Ref: Clarens. AFI. with Louise Fazenda,
Jack Pickford, Emily Fitzroy, Eddie Gribbon, Robert McKim,
Sojin, Lee Shumway, Andre de Beranger. "Haunted" house.
The BAT AA/Liberty 1959 80m. SP, D: Crane Wilbur, from
the play by Mary Roberts Rinehart and Avery Hopwood and the
novel by M. R. Rinehart. PH: Joseph Biroc. Art D: David
Milton. Sets: Rudy Butler. with Vincent Price, Agnes
Moorehead, Gavin Gordon, John Sutton, Lenita Lane, Elaine
Edwards, Darla Hood, Robert B. Williams. Killer lurks near
supposedly haunted house, "The Oaks." Film breaks S. S. Van
Dine's 4th rule for detective stories and Ronald A. Knox's 7th,
but doesn't do much else.
The BAT WHISPERS UA 1930 82m. SP, D: Roland West. From
the play by Mary Roberts Rinehart and Avery Hopwood and the
novel by M. R. Rinehart, "The Bat." PH: Ray June, Robert
H. Planck. Ed: James Smith. Art D: Paul Crawley. Ref:
FDY, AFI. with Chester Morris, Una Merkel, Chance Ward,
Richard Tucker, DeWitt Jennings, Grayce Hampton, Maude
Eburne, Spencer Charters, William Bakewell, Gustav Von Seyf-
fertitz.
BATMAN Col 1943 serial 15 episodes D: Lambert Hillyer.
SP: Victor McLeod, Leslie Swabacker, Harry Fraser. Based
on the comic created by Bob Kane. PH: James S. Brown, Jr.
Mus: Lee Zahler. with Lewis Wilson, Douglas Croft, J. Carrol
Naish, William Austin, Robert Fiske, Charles Middleton.
1. The Electrical Brain. 2. The Bat's Cave. 3. The Mark of
the Zombies. 4. The Living Corpse.
BATMAN Fox/Greenway 1966 DeLuxeColor 105m. D: Leslie
H. Martinson. SP: Lorenzo Semple, Jr., from the comic
characters created by Bob Kane. PH: Howard Schwartz. Mus:
Nelson Riddle. Art D: Jack Martin Smith, Serge Krizman.
SpFX: L. B. Abbott. with Adam West, Burt Ward, Lee Meri-
wether, Cesar Romero, Burgess Meredith, Frank Gorshin,
Alan Napier, Neil Hamilton, Stafford Repp, Madge Blake,
Reginald Denny, Milton Frome, George Sawaya. The Joker,
the Penguin, Catwoman, and the Riddler join forces and hijack
the yacht of the inventor of a "dehydrater" that turns people into
dust.
BATMAN AND ROBIN Col 1949 serial 15 episodes (THE NEW

ADVENTURES OF BATMAN AND ROBIN)   D: Spencer G. Bennet.
SP: George Plympton, Joseph F. Poland, Royal K. Cole. PH:
Ira H. Morgan. Mus: Mischa Bakaleinikoff. P: Sam Katzman.
Based on the comic created by Bob Kane. Ref: MFB'50:170.
Lee. with Robert Lowery, Johnny Duncan, Jane Adams, Lyle
Talbot, Don C. Harvey, William Fawcett, Rick Vallin, Michael
Whalen, House Peters, Jr. The Wizard's machine paralyzes
traffic and industry.

BATMAN FIGHTS DRACULA (Fili) 1967 Ref: M/TVM 9/67.

BATMEN OF AFRICA see DARKEST AFRICA

BATTLE BENEATH THE EARTH (B) MGM/DDD/Cherokee
1968 Technicolor 92m. D: Montgomery Tully. SP: L. Z.
Hargreaves. PH: Kenneth Talbot. Mus: Ken Jones. Art D:
Jim Morahan. SpFX: Tom Howard. with Kerwin Mathews,
Viviane Ventura, Robert Ayres, Peter Arne, Bill Nagy, Bessie
Love. Red Chinese dig tunnels under the U.S.; laser-borer.

BATTLE BEYOND THE STARS (U.S.-J) MGM/Toei/Southern
Cross 1969 color 90m. (THE GREEN SLIME, DEATH AND THE
GREEN SLIME. GAMMO SANGO UCHU DAISAKUSEN) D:
Kinji Fukasaku. SP: Charles Sinclair, William Finger, Tom
Rowe. PH: Y. Yamasawa. Art D: S. Eno. SpFX: Akira
Watanabe. P: Walter Manley, Ivan Reiner. Ref: M/TVM 6/69:
33. with Robert Horton, Richard Jaeckel, Luciana Paluzzi,
Ted Gunther. Swamp on asteroid is alive with a jelly-like green
substance.

BATTLE BEYOND THE SUN (Russ) Dovzhenko 1959 (THE HEA-
VENS CALL) color 90m. D: Alexandr Kosir. SP: A Sasonov,
E. Romeschikov, M. Kariukov. PH: Nikolai Kulchitski. Ref:
Imagen. with Ivan Pereverzev, A. Shvorin, T. Litvinenko.
Spaceship intended for Mars lands on a star.

The BATTLE CRY OF PEACE Vita 1915 100m. SP,D: J. Stuart
Blackton. From the book "Defenseless America" by Hudson
Maxim. Ref: NYT 6/7/16. MPW 25:1291. MPN 8/21/15.
with Charles Richman, Norma Talmadge. Invading force
reaches American shores, takes New York City.

BATTLE IN OUTER SPACE (J) Col/Toho 1960 EastmanColor
90m. (UCHU DAISENSO. THE WORLD OF SPACE) D: Inoshiro
Honda. SP: Shinichi Sekizawa. Story: Jotaro Okami. PH:
Hajime Koizumi. SpFX: Eiji Tsuburaya. with Ryo Ikebe, Kyoko
Anzai, Minoru Takada, Harold Conway. A series of catastro-
phes sweeps the globe. Cloddish.

BATTLE IN THE CLOUDS see AIRSHIP DESTROYER, The

BATTLE IN THE DARK Kalem 1916 (#8 in THE GIRL FROM
'FRISCO series) Ref: MPN 14:2056. Hindu mystic pretends to
communicate with the spirit world.

BATTLE OF THE ASTROS see INVASION OF ASTRO-MONSTER

BATTLE OF THE GIANTS see ONE MILLION B.C.

BATTLE OF THE WILLS Imp 1911 10m. Ref: Bios 11/16/11.
MPW'11:479. Girl under influence of hypnotist.

The BATTLE OF THE WORLDS (I-U.S.) AI/Topaz/Ultra 1960
('63-U.S.) color 84m. (IL PIANETA DEGLI UOMINI SPENTI.
THE PLANET OF EARTH. THE OUTSIDER. THE PLANET OF
EXTINGUISHED MEN) D: Anthony Dawson (Antonio Margheriti).

PH: Cesare Allion.   Ref: FFacts. Musee du Cinema.   with
Claude Rains, Bill Carter, Maya Brent, Umberto Orsini. Lost
plante; electronic brain.
BATU BELAH BATU BERTANGKUP see DEVOURING ROCK, The
BAUL MACABRO, EL see MACABRE TRUNK, The
BAWANG PUTEH, BAWANG MERAH (Malayan) Keris Films
1960 101m. D: S. Roomai Noor. Ref: FEFN 3/60. with
Latiffa Omar, Umi Kalthum, M. Maarof. Woman casts "evil
spells."
BEACH GIRLS AND THE MONSTER, The see MONSTER FROM
THE SURF
BEACH PARTY IN A HAUNTED HOUSE see GHOST IN THE IN-
VISIBLE BIKINI
BEAR, The see LOKIS
BEAST, The see WOLF MAN, The (1924)
BEAST, The see BEAST WITH FIVE FINGERS/SWORD AND THE
DRAGON, The
BEAST FROM GREEN HELL see MONSTER FROM GREEN HELL
BEAST FROM HAUNTED CAVE AA/Filmgroup 1960 64m.
(CREATURE FROM THE CAVE) D: Monte Hellman. SP:
Charles Griffith. PH: Andy Costikyan. P: Gene Corman.
Sound: Beech Dickerson. Ref FFacts. with Michael Forest,
Sheila Carol, Frank Wolff, Wally Campo, Christopher Robin-
son (the beast). Spider-like monster inhabits cave. Sheila
Carol's classy, self-confident performance acts very agreeably
against the generally dismal tone of the proceedings. The movie
is mainly a showcase for her talent and style, but there are a
few shudders.
BEAST FROM OUTER SPACE, The (by A. Zimbalist and B.
Gordon) see KING DINOSAUR
EBAST FROM SPACE, The see 20 MILLION MILES TO EARTH
The BEAST FROM 20,000 FATHOMS WB 1953 80m. D: Eugene
Lourie. SP: Lou Morheim, Fred Freiberger, from "The Fog-
horn" by Ray Bradbury. PH: Jack Russell. Mus: David But-
tolph. Art D: Lourie. SpFX: Willis Cook. TechnicalFX: Ray
Harryhausen. Ref: FDY. with Paula Raymond, Paul Christian,
Cecil Kellaway, Kenneth Tobey, Donald Woods, Jack Pennick,
Lee Van Cleef, Ross Elliott, King Donovan, Frank Ferguson,
Mary Hill, Michael Fox. Monster revived by atomic testing.
Fair.
The BEAST IN THE CELLAR (B) Cannon/Tigon--Leander 1971 color
101m. (ARE YOU DYING, YOUNG MAN? YOUNG MAN, I THINK
YOU'RE DYING!) D,SP: James Kelly, PH: Harry Waxman.
Mus: Tony Macauley. Ref: NYT4/15/71. Boxo 5/3/71. with
Beryl Reid, Flora Robson, John Hamill, Tessa Wyatt. "Killer-
thing" hidden in cellar.
BEAST OF BLOOD (U.S.-Fili) Hemisphere 1970 Eastmancolor
90m. (BLOOD DEVILS--Eng. HORRORS OF BLOOD ISLAND.
RETURN TO THE HORRORS OF BLOOD ISLAND) SP,D,D:
Eddie Romero. Story: Beverly Miller. PH: Justo Paulino. Art
D: Ben Otico. Mus: Tito Arevalo. SpFX: Teofilo Hilario. Ref:
MFG'71:236. Boxo 2/9 & 8/17/70. COF 15:46. with John Ashley,
Celeste Yarnall, Eddie Garcia. Nice color photography and

nothing else. One of the worst.

The BEAST OF HOLLOW MOUNTAIN UA /Peliculas Rodriguez
(U.S.-Mex) 1956-4 80m. DeLuxeColor /scope (EL MONSTRUO
DE LA MONTAÑA HUECA. VALLEY OF THE MISTS. Second
Script RING AROUND SATURN filmed as THE BRAVE ONE)
D: Edward Nassour, Ismael Rodriguez. SP: Robert Hill, from
a story by Willis O'Brien. PH: Jorge Stahl, Jr. Mus: Raul
Lavista. Art D: Jack De Witt. SpFX: Jack Rabin, Louis De Witt.
with Guy Madison, Patricia Medina, Eduardo Noriega, Carlos
Rivas, Pascual Garcia Pena. Ref: Indice, Bill Warren. Clarens.
An exciting few minutes of animated monster tacked on to the end
of a really dull western.

BEAST OF MOROCCO (B) Schoenfeld /Assoc.Brit.-Pathe 1966
Technicolor 73m. (THE HAND OF NIGHT) D: Frederic Goode.
SP: Bruce Stewart. PH: William Jordan. Mus: John Shakespeare.
Makeup: Cliff Sharpe. Ref: MFG'68:180. Boxo 11 /11 /68.   MMF
18-19:2, 16. with William Sylvester, Edward Underdown, Terence
De Marney, Diane Clare, Alizia Gur. Vampirism and a beautiful
female ghost.

BEAST OF PARADISE ISLAND see PORT SINISTER

BEAST OF THE YELLOW NIGHT (U.S.-Fili) New World 1971
DeLuxeColor SP,D, P: Eddie Romero. Ref: Boxo 5 /31 /71:K-3.
with John Ashley, Mary Wilcox.

BEAST OF YUCCA FLATS Cardoza-Francis /Crown-Int'l.-TV 1960
60m. SP, D: Coleman Francis. Mus: I. Nafshun, Al Remington.
Ref: TVFFSB. RVB. with Tor Johnson, Douglas Mellor, Barbara Francis, Tony Cardoza. Man caught in middle of bomb
test becomes monster.

The BEAST THAT KILLED WOMEN Mahon 1965 color 60m.
(THE BEAST THAT RUINED WOMEN. THE BEAST THAT
MOLESTED WOMEN) Ref: COF 8:6. Gorilla loose in nudist
camp.

BEAST WITH A MILLION EYES American Releasing Corp. /San
Mateo Prods. /Pacemaker 1955 78m. D: David Kramarsky.
SP: Tom Filer. PH: Everett Baker. Mus: John Bickford.
Ref: V 12 /14 /55. with Paul Birch, Lorna Thayer, Dona Cole,
Richard Sargeant, Chester Conklin. Creature from another
planet. Projects its mind into all living things nearby. Unpleasant.

BEAST WITH FIVE FINGERS WB 1946 88m. D: Robert Florey.
SP: Curt Siodmak, from the story, "The Beast," by W. F.
Harvey. PH: Wesley Anderson. Mus: Max Steiner. Ref: FDY
S&S'68:213. with Robert Alda, Andrea King, Peter Lorre,Victor
Francen, J. Carrol Naish, Charles Dingle, Pedro de Cordoba.
Pianist's severed hand alive and out for revenge. Moments--
Lorre has some, the hand a few. But mainly it's a feeble comedy.
The film has a following, surprisingly enough.

BEATRICE FAIRFAX series see WAGES OF SIN, The (1916)

The BEAUTIFUL DREAMER (Mex) Mier & Brooks 1952 (EL
BELLO DURMIENTE) D: Gilberto M. Solares. SP: Solares,
Juan Garcia. PH: Raul M. Solares. Mus: Manuel Esperon. Ref:
Indice. Lee. LA Times 9 /30 /53. with Tin Tan, Wolf
Rubinski, Lilia Del Valle, Gloria Mestre, "Marcelo." Caveman
under witch doctor's spell 10,000 years; prehistoric animals.

BEAUTY AND THE BEAST (F) Pathe 1899 Ref: DDC? From the fairy tale by Gabrielle Suzanne.
BEAUTY AND THE BEAST (F) Pathe 1908 11m. (LA BELLE ET LA BETE) Based on the fairy tale by Madame Leprince de Beaumont. Ref: F Index 11/14/08. Ugly beast.
BEAUTY AND THE BEAST Rex (Univ) 1913 40m. P,D: H. C. Mathews. From the fairy tales by Gabrielle Suzanne and the Bros. Grimm. Ref: Bios 12/4/13. MPW 16:1340. with Elsie Albert.
BEAUTY AND THE BEAST Int'l. Film Service 1916 SP,D: H. E. Hancock. Ref: MPW 29:967. with Mineta Timayo (Sleeping Beauty).
BEAUTY AND THE BEAST (F) Discina--Lopert 1946 90m. (LA BELLE ET LA BETE) SP,D: Jean Cocteau. PH: Henri Alekan. Mus: Georges Auric. Sets: Christian Bérard, executed by René Moulaert. Ed: Claude Ibéria. Costumes: Bérard. P: André Paulvé. Technical adviser: René Clement. Production D: E. Darbon. Cameraman: Tiquet. Ref: Rep. Gen. '47:67. with Josette Day, Jean Marais, Mila Parely, Nane Germon, Marcel André, Michel Auclair. One of the few great fantasy films, with spirit, imagination, humor, warmth, and even a touch of horror. Everything seems (literally) to be alive.
BEAUTY AND THE BEAST UA 1963 Technicolor 77m. D: Edward L. Cahn. SP: George Bruce, Orville H. Hampton. PH: Gilbert Warrenton. Art D: Franz Bachelin. P: Robert E. Kent. Ref: FFacts. Pic: FM 67:57. with Joyce Taylor, Eduard Franz, Mark Damon, Michael Pate, Merry Anders, Walter Burke. Medieval duke victim of ancient curse which turns him into a beast every night.
BEAUTY AND THE BEAST 1966 color Choreographic D: Lew Christensen. Art D: Dik Rose. Costumes: Tony Duquette. The San Francisco Ballet Company's production of Tchaikovsky's "Beauty and the Beast." with Lynda Meyer, Robert Gladstein, David Anderson. Ref: TVG 12/24/68. Beauty is captured by an ugly beast.
BEAUTY AND THE DRAGON (J) 1955 Toei 100m. (BIJO TO KAIRYU. THE LADY AND THE DRAGON) D: Kimisaburo Yoshimura. SP: Kaneto Shindo, from the Kabuki play "Narukami." Ref: Toho Films. with Chiyonosuke Azuma, Nobuko Otowa. A high priest forces a dragon into a water pit.
BEAUTY AND THE ROBOT AA 1960 93m. (SEX KITTENS GO TO COLLEGE. TEACHER WAS A SEXPOT) Story, D, P: Albert Zugsmith. SP: Robert Hill. PH: Ellis Carter. SpFX: Augie Lohman. Ref: FFacts. with Mamie Van Doren, Tuesday Weld, Mijanou Bardot, Mickey Shaughnessy, Louis Nye, Pamela Mason, Martin Milner, Conway Twitty, Jackie Coogan, John Carradine, Vampira, Jody Fair, Charles Chaplin, Jr., Harold Lloyd, Jr. Electronic brain supplies professor with racing tips. Not half as funny as INVASION OF THE STAR CREATURES.
THE BEAUTY OF THE SLEEPING WOODS (F) Pathe Freres 1908 15m. (LA BELLE AU BOIS DORMANT. SLEEPING BEAUTY) PH: Segundo de Chomon. Based on "Sleeping Beauty" by Charles Perrault. Ref: MPW'08:299 SilentFF.

BEBE AND SPIRITUALISM (F) 1912 D: Louis Feuillade. Ref: DDC II:338. (BEBE FAIT DU SPIRITISME)

The BED SITTING ROOM (B) Lewenstein 1969 DeLuxeColor 91m. D: Richard Lester. SP: John Antrobus, from the play by Spike Milligan and Antrobus. Adap. Charles Wood. PH: David Watkin. Mus: Ken Thorne. SpFX: Phil Stokes. Ref: MFB'70:67. with Ralph Richardson, Rita Tushingham, Michael Hordern, Mona Washbourne, Peter Cook, Dudley Moore, Arthur Lowe, Milligan, Roy Kinnear, Dandy Nichols, Harry Secombe, Ronald Fraser. England left devastated by nuclear war. Too wild and disorienting to make much comic sense as a whole, but gag-for-gag a fairly good minor comedy.

BEDLAM RKO 1946 79m. (CHAMBER OF HORRORS) D: Mark Robson. P: Val Lewton. SP: Robson, Carlos Keith, from "Bedlam," plate 8 of "The Rake's Progress" by William Hogarth. PH: Nicholas Musuraca. Mus: Roy Webb. Art D: Albert S. D'Agostino, Walter E. Keller. Ref: FM 57:63. FDY. with Boris Karloff, Anna Lee, Billy House, Richard Fraser, Glenn Vernon, Ian Wolfe, Jason Robards, Robert Clarke, Elizabeth Russell, Leyland Hodgson, Joan Newton. Dark horse candidate for best of the Lewtons. Karloff in top form as the cruel master of the asylum. Elaborately-thought-out script.

The BEE AND THE ROSE Pathe 1908 Ref: F Index 12/19/08. Spider captures the "Queen of the bees" in his web.

BEE GIRL, The see WASP WOMAN

The BEECHWOOD GHOST Powers 1910 Ref: MPW 7:772. Fake ghost.

The BEETLE (B) Barker 1919 D: Alexander Butler. Ref: Brit. Cinema. Movie Monsters. with L. Douglas, Maudie Dunham. Soul of Egyptian princess in beetle seeks vengeance.

BEFORE DAWN RKO 1933 60m. D: Irving Pichel. SP: Garrett Fort, Marion Dix, Ralph Block. Mus: Max Steiner. From a short story, "Death Watch," by Edgar Wallace. Ref: NYT. FDY. with Stuart Erwin, Dorothy Wilson, Warner Oland, Dudley Digges, Frank Reicher, Jane Darwell, Gertrude W. Hoffman, Oscar Apfel. Clairvoyant girl in trance solves mystery; "supposedly haunted house, phosphorescent death mask floating along dark corridor," sliding doors.

BEFORE I DIE see TARGETS

BEFORE I HANG Col 1941 62m. D: Nick Grinde. SP: Robert D. Andrews. PH: Benjamin Kline. Art D: Lionel Banks. Ref: FDY. TVG. with Boris Karloff, Evelyn Keyes, Bruce Bennett, Pedro de Ccrdoba, Edward Van Sloan, Don Beddoe, Robert Fiske. A doctor "develops a compulsion to kill" after taking a serum.

BEFORE MIDNIGHT Col 1933 63m. D: Lambert Hillyer. SP: Robert Quigley. PH: John Stumar. Ref: V 1/16/34. NYT 1/10/ 34. with Ralph Bellamy, June Collyer, Claude Gillingwater, Betty Blythe, Arthur Pierson, Joseph Crehan, Bradley Page. Man who had premonition he would be murdered is, in a spooky old house.

The BEGGAR KING Lubin 1916 25m. SP, D: Wilbert Melvillw. Ref: MPN 13:3271. with Robert Gray, Jay Morely. "Automatic

typewriter which transmits messages to another machine any
distance away. "
BEGINNING OF THE END Rep 1957 73m. P, D: Bert I. Gordon.
SP: Fred Freiberger, Lester Gorn. Ref: FDY. with Peggie
Castle, Peter Graves, Morris Ankrum, Richard Benedict, James
Seay, Don C. Harvey. Giant grasshoppers run amok. Army
risks charges of insecticide in killing them. Very tacky.
BEGINNING OF THE GAME OF DIABOLO (F) Pathe 1908 6m.
Ref: V&FI 9/19/08. Skeletons play the devil's new game.
BEHEMOTH, SEA MONSTER see GIANT BEHEMOTH, The
BEHIND RED CURTAINS (novel by M. Scott) see ONE HOUR
BEFORE DAWN
BEHIND THE CURTAIN Univ 1924 55m. D: Chester M. Frank-
lin. SP: Emil Forest, Harvey Gates. Story: William J. Flynn.
PH: Jackson Rose. Ref: AFI. with Lucille Ricksen, Johnny Har-
ron, George Cooper, Winifred Bryson, Charles Clary. Fake
spiritualist commits murder.
BEHIND THE DOOR see MAN WITH 9 LIVES, THE
BEHIND THE MASK Col 1932 70m. D: John Francis Dillon.
SP: Jo Swerling, from his story, "In the Secret Service." PH:
Teddy Tetzlaff. Continuity: Dorothy Howell. Ed: Otis Garrett.
Ref: FDY. with Edward Van Sloan, Jack Holt, Boris Karloff,
Claude King, Constance Cummings, Willard Robertson. Mad
doctor/criminal mastermind threatens to torture hero. Enjoy-
ably ludicrous, especially in Van Sloan's delivery of his riper
lines ("The pain when I am going through the layers of your
skin will not be unendurable. It is only when I begin to cut on
the inside that you will realize that you are having an experi-
ence").
BEI VOLLMUND MORD see WEREWOLF IN A GIRLS' DORMI-
TORY
BEISS MICH, LIEBLING see BITE ME, DARLING
BELA LUGOSI MEETS A BROOKLYN GORILLA Jack Broder Prods.
1953 75m. (THE BOYS FROM BROOKLYN. THE MONSTER
MEETS THE GORILLA. LUGOSI MEETS A BROOKLYN GORIL-
LA) D: William Beaudine. SP: Tim Ryan. PH: Charles Van
Enger. Mus: Richard Hazards. Assoc P: Herman Cohen. Ref:
TVFFSB. with Duke Mitchell, Sammy Petrillo, Bela Lugosi,
Muriel Landers. Mad doctor turns man into a gorilla. Petrillo,
imitating Jerry Lewis's early style, is similarly irritating, which
is better than nothing.
BELLE ET LA BETE, La see BEAUTY AND THE BEAST (1908/
1946)
BELLE AU BOIS DORMANT, La see BEAUTY OF THE SLEEP-
ING WOODS, The/SLEEPING BEAUTY (1902)
BELLO DURMIENTE, El see BEAUTIFUL DREAMER, The
The BELLS Reliance 1913 30m. D: Oscar C. Apfel. Ref:
MPW 15: 792. Bios 9/25/13. Mathias, murderer, haunted by
vision of victim.
The BELLS Gaum 1914 (B) Ref: Lee. with H. B. Irving
(Mathias).
The BELLS Pathe 1918 SP: Gilson Willets, Jack Cunningham.
Ref: NYT 9/16/18. D: Ernest C. Warde. with Lois Wilson,

Frank Keenan, Joseph Dowling, Ed Coxen, Ida Lewis. Man haunted by murder goes insane.

The BELLS Chadwick 1926 80m. SP, D: James Young. From the play "Le Juif Polonais" by Erckmann-Chatrian. PH: L. William O'Connell. Ref: AFI. Clarens. with Lionel Barrymore, Edward Phillips, Boris Karloff, Gustav von Seyffertitz, Otto Lederer, Lola Todd. Man haunted by vision of murder victim. Mesmerist.

BENEATH THE PLANET OF THE APES Fox 1970 DeLuxeColor/ scope 95m. D: Ted Post. SP: Paul Dehn. Story: Dehn, Mort Abrahams, from characters created by Pierre Boulle. PH: Milton Krasner. Mus: Leonard Rosenman. Art D: Jack Martin Smith, William Creber. SpPHFX: L. B. Abbott, Art Cruickshank. Makeup design: John Chambers. with James Franciscus, Kim Hunter, Maurice Evans, Linda Harrison, Paul Richards, Victor Buono, James Gregory, Jeff Corey, Thomas Gomez, Tod Andrews, Charlton Heston. Sequel to THE PLANET OF THE APES.

BENEATH THE SEA Lubin 1915 35m. SP: Wilbert Melville, S. Roland White. Ref: MPN 2/27/15. with Charles Fowler, Velma Whitman, George Routh. Submarine boat invention.

BENEATH THE TOWER RUINS (B) Urban/Eclipse 1911 14m. Ref: MPW 8:904. Ghost.

BENIGHTED (novel by J. B. Priestley) see OLD DARK HOUSE, The (1932/1963)

BERENICE (by E. A. Poe) see HORROR/PREMATURE BURIAL, The

The BERLINER (G) 1948 ('53--U.S.) Narr: Henry Morgan. Ref: The Society of Cinema Arts bulletin. In the year 2050 a 100-year-old movie on TV tells the story of Otto Averageman confronted by a 6-1 ratio of women to men.

BERLINO, APPUNTAMENTO PER LE SPIE see SPY IN YOUR EYE

BERSERK (B) Col/Herman Cohen 1968 Technicolor 96m. (CIRCUS OF BLOOD. CIRCUS OF TERROR) D: Jim O'Connolly. SP: Cohen, Aben Kandel. PH: Desmond Dickinson. Mus sc & d: Patrick John Scott. Art D: Maurice Pelling. Ref: LA Times 2/16/68. with Joan Crawford, Ty Hardin, Diana Dors, Michael Gough, Judy Geeson, Sydney Tafler, Milton Reid. Maniac causes circus "accidents."

BERTIE'S BOOK OF MAGIC (B) Hepworth 1912 6m. Ref: Bios 10/24/12. Bertie learns how to turn a woman into a black cat. To change her back a butcher cuts the cat's throat.

BESO DE ULTRATUMBA, El see KISS FROM BEYOND THE GRAVE, The

The BEST HOUSE IN LONDON (B) MGM/Ponti 1969 Metrocolor 97m. D: Philip Saville. SP: Denis Norden. PH: Alex Thomson. Mus: Mischa Spoliansky. Prod Des: Wilfrid Shingleton. Ref: COF 16:53. V 7/30/69. Int'l. Mot. Pic. Exhibitor 7/30/69. with David Hemmings, Joanna Pettet, George Sanders, Dany Robin, Maurice Denham, Martita Hunt. 300-foot balloon-craft; Sherlock Holmes-Dr. Watson bit.

BETTY'S ELECTRIC BATTERY Pathe 1910 7m. Ref: Bios

9/15/10 Battery makes people spin.
BETWEEN THE NETS (SP-F-I) Balcazar /CFDF /Fida 1967 color /
scope 93m. (ENTRE LAS REDES-Sp) D: Riccardo Freda. SP:
J. A. de la Loma. Story: R. P. Kenny. PH: J. Gelpi.
Mus: J. Lacome. Art D: J. A. Soler. Ref: Sp. Cinema'68.
with Lang Jeffries, Sabine Sun, Silvia Solar, Frank Oliveras,
Ida Galli. Coplan film; subterranean center for making atomic
weapons.
BETWEEN TWO WORLDS see DYBBUK, The (1968)
BETWEEN WORLDS see DESTINY
BEWARE, SPOOKS! Col 1939 68m. D: Edward Sedgwick. SP:
Richard Flournoy, from "Spook House" by Flournoy. SP: also
Albert Duffy, Brian Marlow. PH: Allen G. Siegler. Ref:
FDY. with Joe E. Brown, Mary Carlisle, Clarence Kolb, Marc
Lawrence, Don Beddoe, George J. Lewis. Fake ghosts; Coney
Island spook house.
BEWILDERING CABINET, The 1907 Ref: MPW'07:426 Two girls
in cabinet turned into "ugly ogres."
BEWITCHED MGM 1945 65m. SP, D: Arch Oboler, from his
radio play "Alter Ego." PH: Charles Salerno. Mus: Bronislau
Kaper. Art D: Cedric Gibbons, Malcolm Brown. P: Jerry
Bresler. Ref: FDY. FM 67:16. with Edmund Gwenn, Phyllis
Thaxter, Henry M. Daniels, Jr., Addison Richards, Will
Wright, Oscar O'Shea, Minor Watson, Virginia Brissac. Girl
with split personality; hypnosis separates the two.
BEWITCHED see WITCHCRAFT (1961)
The BEWITCHED INN (F) Melies /Star 1897 3m. (L'AUBERGE
ENSORCELEE) Ref: DDC III:350. SilentFF. Candle explodes,
chair moves, etc.
BEWITCHED LOVE OF MADAME PAI, The see MADAME WHITE
SNAKE
The BEWITCHED MANOR HOUSE (F) Pathe 1909 7m. Ref:
MPW 5:101. Haunted castle; "spook faces"; "ferocious beasts";
satan.
The BEWITCHED MESSENGER Bat /Brockliss 1910 12m. Ref:
Bios 10/13/10. Witch curses "tri-car."
The BEWITCHED MATCHES (F) Eclair 1913 8m. Ref: MPW
16:597. Witch turns man into skeleton.
The BEWITCHED TRAVELLER AM&B (B) 1904 P: Cecil Hep-
worth. Ref: Niver. Appearing and disappearing objects.
The BEWITCHED WINDOW Pathe 1911 12m. Ref: Bios 11/30/11.
Spirit and devil torment painter.
BEYOND LOVE AND EVIL (F) AA /Comptoir Français 1970 90m.
D: Jacques Sandelari. SP: Sandelari, Jean Stuart, Jean-Pierre
Deloux. (LA PHILOSOPHIE DANS LE BOUDOIR) PH: Jean-
Marc Ripert. Mus: Jean-Claude Pelletier. Ref: V 3/17/71. HR
3/4/71: "Horror film." with Souchka, Lucas de Chabanieux,
Fred Saint-James. Castle of torture.
BEYOND THE FLAME BARRIER see FLAME BARRIER, The
BEYOND THE HORIZON (India) 1937 Prabhat Cinetone (VAHA)
SP, D: Narayan Kalay (K. Kale). PH: V. Avadoot. Ref: Dipali.
Filmindia 8/37:19. with Shanta Apte. Prehistory.
BEYOND THE MOON 1954 From the "Rocky Jones, Space Ranger"

TV show.

BEYOND THE TIME BARRIER AI 1960 75m. (THE WAR OF 1995) D: Edgar G. Ulmer. PH: Meredith Nicholson. Mus: Darryl Calker. SP: Arthur G. Pierce. Ref: FFacts. with Robert Clarke, Darlene Tompkins, Arianne Arden, Vladimir Sokoloff, John van Dre(e)len. Air Force pilot crashes through the time barrier into the earth of the future. Not one of Edgar Ulmer's best.

BEYOND THE WALL see DESTINY

BHAKTA-PRALHAD (India) Saraswati Cinetone 1934 D: K. P. Bhave. Ref: Dipali 5/11 & 6/8/34. with K. Kant, Salvi. Lion-like monster. "Trick scenes."

BHARTRUHARI (India--Hindustani) 1945 D: Doshi. SP: Wali. Ref: Lee: Filmindia 12/45. with Surendra. Skeleton steps out of body.

BHOOLOKA RAMBHAI (India--Tamil) 1958 Ref: FEFN 12/13/57 & 2/21/58. with Anjali. Girl rescued by the god Siva from the devil.

BHOOT BUNGLA (India) 1965 Ref: Shankar's 5/16/65. with Mahmood, Asit Sen. Haunted house, ghosts.

BHUTIO MAHAL see HAUNTED HOUSE (1931)

The BIBULOUS CLOTHIER Edison 1899 2m. Ref: Niver. Clothier's customer takes a drink, grows larger, etc.

The BIG BAD WOLF 1966 color 53m. Ref: TVG. Ideal Catalogue '67-'70. From the fairy tale by the Bros. Grimm. Hungry wolf after 7 baby goats.

The BIG BROADCAST OF 1936 Para 1935 97m. D: Norman Taurog. SP: Walter De Leon, Francis Martin, Ralph Spence. PH: Leo Tover. Ref: FDY. with Jack Oakie, George Burns, Gracie Allen, Lyda Roberti, Wendy Barrie, C. Henry Gordon, Akim Tamiroff, Bing Crosby, Amos n' Andy, Ethel Merman, Mary Boland, Charlie Ruggles, Bill Robinson, Gail Patrick, Sir Guy Standing, Virginia Weidler, Henry Wadsworth. "Radio-eye" television.

The BIG BROADCAST OF 1938 Para 1938 90m. D: Mitchell Leisen. SP: Walter De Leon, Francis Martin, Ken Englund. PH: Harry Fishbeck. Story: F. H. Brennan. SpFX: Gordon Jennings. Ref: MFB'38. FDY. with W. C. Fields, Bob Hope, Tito Guizar, Martha Raye, Shirley Ross, Lynne Overman, Ben Blue, Leif Erickson, Russell Hicks, Kirsten Flagstad, Dorothy Lamour, Grace Bradley. Flying golf cart; radio invention that makes boat go 65 knots. Fields steals the show ("Had a hard time killing a flying wombat... gets in your shoes"), but it's petty Larsen E. The plot gets in his way, and the musical numbers get in the way of the plot. What little is left is all Fields'.

BIG COMET, The see JOHNNY VENGMAN AND THE BIG COMET

BIG DUEL IN THE NORTH SEA see GODZILLA VS. THE SEA MONSTER

A BIG GREY-BLUE BIRD Filmverlag Der Autoren/T.S. (W.G.) 1970 color 98m. (EIN GROSSER GRAUBLAUER VOGAL) P,D: Thomas Schamoni. SP: Schamoni, Uwe Brandner, Hans Noever, Max Zielmann. PH: Dieter Lohmann, Bert Fiedler. Ref: V 7/14/71. with Olivera Vuco, Sylvia Winter, Klaus

Lemke, Umberto Orsini.   Five scientists succeed in "disinte-
grating" time.
The BIG MESS (G) Kairos Film 1971 color 90m.   (Der
    GROSSE VERHAU) SP, D: Alexander Kluge, from "The Mono-
    pole Capitalism" by Baran and Sweezy.   PH: Thomas Mauch,
    Alfred Tichawsky. SpFX: Bernd Hoeltz. Ref: V 9/22/71. with
    Vinzenz and Maria Sterr, Sigi Graue, Silvia Forsthofer. In the
    year 2034 two astronauts wreck spaceships and sell them to in-
    surance companies.
The BIG NOISE Fox 1944 74m.   D: Mal St. Clair. PH: Joe
    MacDonald. Ref: TVG. FDY. with Stan Laurel, Oliver Hardy,
    Doris Merrick, Arthur Space, Veda Ann Borg, Bobby Blake,
    Frank Fenton, Philip Van Zandt, Selmer Jackson, Francis Ford,
    Jack Norton, Edgar Dearing, Charles Wilson. "New-type
    bomb"; remote-control airplane.
The BIG WORLD OF LITTLE CHILDREN (Polish) Film Polski
    1962 103m. (WIELKA, WIELKA I NAJWIEKSZA. THE BIG,
    THE BIGGER AND THE BIGGEST. THE MAGIC CAR) D: Anna
    Sokolowska. SP: Sokolowska, Jerzy Broszkiewicz. PH:
    J. Korcelli, A. Markowski. Ref: M/TVM 7/63. Film Polski
    '63. MMF 9:24. with Kinga Sienko, Wojciech Puzynski. Third
    of three episodes: Grozek and Ika enter a silver sphere and
    find a planet called Véga which has undergone atomic devastation.
BIGFOOT Universal Entertainments/Ellman 1971 94m. SP:
    Slatzer, James Gordon White. PH: Wilson S. Hong. Mus:
    Richard Podolar. Art D: Norman Houle. Ed: Hugo Grimaldi.
    P: Anthony Cardoza.
BIGGEST FIGHT ON EARTH, The see GHIDRAH
BIJO TO KAIRYU see BEAUTY AND THE DRAGON
BIJOTO EKITAI-NINGEN see H-MAN, The
BIKINI BEACH AI 1964 Pathecolor/scope 100m. D: William
    Asher. SP: Asher, Robert Dillon, Leo Townsend. Art D:
    Daniel Haller. Mus sc: Les Baxter. Ref: COF 6:50. FM
    30:64. 34:74. ModM 1:73. Variety, with Boris Karloff, Val
    Warren (Teenage Werewolf Monster), Frankie Avalon, Annette
    Funicello, Martha Hyer, Harvey Lembeck, Don Rickles, John Ash-
    ley, Jody McCrea, Candie Johnson, Meredith MacRae, James
    Westerfield, Donna Loren, Stevie Wonder, Keenan Wynn,
    Timothy Carey.
BIKINI PARTY IN A HAUNTED HOUSE see GHOST IN THE IN-
    VISIBLE BIKINI
BILDNIS DES DORIAN GRAY, Das see PICTURE OF DORIAN
    GRAY, The (G. -1917)
BILL BECOMES MENTALLY DERANGED Lux 1912 9m. Ref:
    Bios 3/7/12. Operation cures man of "water on the brain."
BILL BUMPER'S BARGAIN Ess 1911 18m. Ref: Lee. Bur-
    lesque on the opera "Faust" by Gounod. with Francis Bushman
    (the devil).
BILL TAKEN FOR A GHOST Lux 1911 8m. Ref: Bios 11/19/11.
    MPW 10:500. Tourists take Bill for a ghost in the Chateau of
    Spookeybrook.
BILLION DOLLAR BRAIN (B) UA/Lowndes 1967 color/scope
    111m. D: Ken Russell. SP: John McGrath. Based on the novel

by Len Deighton. PH: Billy Williams. Mus sc & d: R. R. Bennett. Art D: Bert Davey. Prod Des: Syd Cain. Ref: MFB'68:2. with Michael Caine, Karl Malden, Françoise Dorléac, Oscar Homolka, Ed Begley. "Giant computer"; oil millionaire who plans a private attack on Russia.

BILLY GETS MARRIED see HAUNTED HONEYMOON

BILLY THE KID VS. DRACULA Emb/Circle 1966 Pathecolor 72m. D: William Beaudine. SP: Karl Hittleman. Mus: Raoul Kraushaar. Based on the character in "Dracula" by Bram Stoker. with John Carradine, Bing Russell, Roy Barcroft, Melinda Plowman, Charlita, Harry Carey, Jr., Chuck Courtney, Marjorie Bennett. Odd-lines-for-Dracula dept.: (to his niece) "Marrying a notorious gunman? I won't hear of it!" Odd-lines-for-anyone dept.: "Oh, God--the vampire test!" Strenuously ridiculous.

BILLY'S SEANCE Imp 1912 13m. Ref: Bios 2/29/12. Billy employs an electric generator in his seance.

BIMI see KING OF THE WILD

The BIRDS Univ 1963 120m. Technicolor D: Alfred Hitchcock. SP: Evan Hunter, from the story by Daphne Du Maurier. PH: Robert Burks. Art D: Robert Boyle. SpFX: Lawrence A. Hampton. Sound: Bernard Hermann. Ref: FFacts. with Rod Taylor, Tippi Hedren, Jessica Tandy, Suzanne Pleshette, Veronica Cartwright, Ethel Griffies, Charles McGraw, Doodles Weaver, Karl Swenson, Elizabeth Wilson. Birds start attacking people for no apparent reason. The birds are okay; it's the people who are unbelievable. Auteurs had a tough time with this one.

BIRDS DO IT Col 1966 PatheColor 95m. D: Andrew Marton. SP: Arnie Kogen, Art Arthur. PH: Howard Winner. Story: Leonard Kaufman. Mus: Samuel Matlovsky. Exec P: Ivan Tors. Ref: FFacts. with Soupy Sales, Tab Hunter, Arthur O'Connell, Edward Andrews, Beverly Adams. A man becomes negatively ionized and finds he can fly.

BIRD'S NEST, The (by Shirley Jackson) see LIZZIE

BIRTH OF A FLIVVER 1915 Ref: FM 63:28. Two cavemen invent the wheel and make a wagon, which they hitch to a dinosaur.

BIRTH OF EMOTION, The Alhambra-Kriterion 1914 30m. Ref: MPN 1/16/15:45. The Stone Age.

BIRTH OF FRANKENSTEIN see CURSE OF FRANKENSTEIN

The BISHOP OF THE OZARKS FBO/Cosmopolitan 1923 70m. SP,D: Finis Fox. Story: Milford W. Howard. PH: Sol Polito. Ref: AFI. with Howard, Derelys Perdue, Cecil Holland, Fred Kelsey, William Kenton. Doctor's "evil influence" over girl, "occult powers of evil," seance, telepathy.

BITE ME, DARLING (G) Cinerama 1970 color 102m. (BEISS MICH, LIEBLING) P,D: Helmut Foernbacher. SP: Foernbacher, M. R. Becker, W. H. Riedl. PH: Igor Luther. Ref: V 10/14/70. with Eva Renzi, Patrick Jordan, Amadeus August. Psychiatrist returns from the grave as a vampire.

BIZARRE (B) 1970 color 91m. (EROS EXPLODING. SECRETS OF SEX) Noteworthy Films D: Antony Balch. SP: Martin Locke, John Eliot, Balch, Maureen Owen, Elliott Stein. Story: A. Mazure. PH: David McDonald. Mus: De Wolfe. Exec P:

49   Black

Richard Gordon. Ref: MFB'70:52. with Stein, Maria Frost,
Cathy Howard, Anthony Rowlands. Narr: Valentine Dyall. Five
stories: Mummified, damned soul travels through the ages ob-
serving the battle of the sexes.
The BLACK ABBOT (W. G.) 1961 CCC/Copri Int'l. 95m. (DER
SCHWARZE ABT) D: Franz J. Gottlieb. SP: Johannes Kai,
from a novel by Edgar Wallace. PH: Richard Angst. Mus:
Martin Mottcher. Mysterious hooded character attacks those
who come near hidden treasure on estate. with Joachim Fuchs-
berger, Dieter Borsche, Charles Regnier, W. Peters, Eddie
Arent, Klaus Kinski. One scene with some bats; otherwise the
usual muddled Wallace.
BLACK ALIBI (novel by C. Woolrich) see LEOPARD MAN
The BLACK BOX Univ 1915 serial 15 episodes D: Otis Turner.
Ref: CNW. MPN 3/27, 4/17, 6/12 & 6/26/15. with Herbert
Rawlinson, Anna Little, Frank Lloyd, William Worthington.
"Prehistoric ape man"; "electro-thought transference"; pocket
wireless telephone; televiewer; electrical device for hypnotism;
cloak of invisibility.
BLACK BUTTERFLIES (Mex) 1953 (MARIPOSAS NEGRAS. DARK
BUTTERFLIES) D: Carlos Hugo Christensen. SP: G. Meneses,
A. Naeza, Christensen. Ref: Indice. Lee. LA Times 12/8/53.
FM 67:14. Voodoo love potion. with Arturo de Cordova,
Virginia Luque, A. Barrion.
The BLACK CAMEL Fox 1931 D: Hamilton MacFadden. SP:
Barry Connors, Philip Klein. Adap: Hugh Stange. From a
story by Earl Derr Biggers. PH: Dan Clark. Ref: V 7/7/31.
FD 7/5/31. MPH 5/16/31. NYT. with Warner Oland, Bela
Lugosi, Sally Eilers, Dorothy Revier, Victor Varconi, J. M.
Kerrigan, Robert Young, Mary Gordon, Violet Dunn, Murray
Kinnell. Lugosi as psychic in Chan mystery.
The BLACK CASTLE Univ 1952 81m. D: Nathan Juran. S P:
Jerry Sackheim. PH: Irving Glassberg. Mus D: Joseph
Gershenson. P: William Alland. Art D: Bernard Herzbrun,
Alfred Sweeney. Ref: FDY. with Stephen McNally, Richard
Greene, Paula Corday, Boris Karloff, Lon Chaney, Jr., Michael
Pate, Tudor Owen, John Hoyt. Torture chamber; death-sem-
blance serum. Mediocre.
The BLACK CAT Univ 1934 65m. (HOUSE OF DOOM--Eng. THE
VANISHING BODY--'51 Realart reissue) D: Edgar G. Ulmer.
SP: Peter Ruric, from a story by Edgar Allan Poe. PH:
John Mescall. Art D: Charles D. Hall. P: Carl Laemmle, Jr.,
E. M. Asher. Ref: Orpheus 2: 4-17. ModM 3:7, 32: cut
scene. Pic: FM 10:13. 11:44. 13:33. 14:46. with Boris
Karloff, Bela Lugosi, David Manners, Herman Bing, Jacqueline
Wells (Julie Bishop), Lucille Lund, Egon Brecher, Henry
Armetta. None of the seven Karloff-Lugosi horror films was
really good. This merely had the distinction of being the first,
and, as such, is popular with some horror fans. Ulmer's
imaginative, fluid camera-work never quite saved movies with
poor material (like this and CLUB HAVANA), and poor material
was mostly what he got.
The BLACK CAT Univ 1941 70m. D: Albert S. Rogell. SP:

Robert Lees, Fred Rinaldo, Eric Taylor, Robert Neville. PH:
Stanley Cortez. Art D: Jack Otterson. Mus D: H. J. Salter.
SpFX: John P. Fulton. Ref: FDY. with Basil Rathbone, Hugh
Herbert, Broderick Crawford, Bela Lugosi, Gale Sondergaard,
Anne Gwynne, Gladys Cooper, Claire Dodd, John Eldredge,
Alan Ladd. The reading of the will in the eerie old mansion.
The novelty cast, though largely wasted, isn't as dull as the
usual mystery-comedy cast (although the plot is as dull).
Cortez comes up with a few striking camera angles. The
mansion has more secret passages than rooms.
BLACK CAT (India-Hindi) Sippy Films 1959 154m. D: N. A.
Ansari. Ref: FEFN XII:10-11. 5/16/58. with Minu Kumtaz,
Shammi. "A crime thriller of the Dr. Jekyll and Mr. Hyde
variety."
The BLACK CAT Hemisphere/Falcon Int'l. 1966 72m. P,D:
Harold P. Hoffman. with Robert Frost, Robyn Baker. Man
thinks cat is evil reincarnation of his father.
BLACK CAT (J) Toho 1968 scope 99m. (KURONEKO. YABU
NO NAKA NO KURONEKO) SP,D: Kaneto Shindo. PH:
Kiyomi Kuroda. Mus: Hikaru Hayashi. with Nobuko Otowa,
Kichiemon Nakamura Mother and daughter turn into monsters,
seek revenge on barbarian soldiers who raped and killed them.
BLACK CAT, The (by E. A. Poe) see AVENGING CONSCIENCE,
The/BLACK CAT, The (1934)/FIVE TALES OF HORROR/
HISTOIRES EXTRAORDINAIRES (1931)/MANIAC (1934)/
RAVEN, The (1912)/TALES OF TERROR
BLACK CAT MANSION (J) ShinToho 1958 partly in color
69m. (BOREI KAIBYO YASHIKI. GHOST CAT MANSION)
D, Nobuo Nakagawa. SP: Y. Ishikawa, J. Fujishima. PH:
Tadashi Nishimoto. Ref: UFQ-2. with Toshio Hosokawa,
Midori Chikuma, Fujie Satsuki, Shin Shibata. Woman bitten to
death by haunted cat which assumes her form.
BLACK CHRISTMAS see BLACK SABBATH
BLACK CLOAK see DARK INTRUDER
The BLACK CROOK Kalem 1915 60m. SP: Phil Lang. Based
on the play by Charles M. Barras. Ref: MPN 13:253. MPW
26:1986. with E. P. Sullivan. Pack with the devil to deliver
one soul a year.
The BLACK CROWN (F-Sp) Suevia Films 1952 (LA COURONNE
NOIRE. LA CORONA NEGRA) D: Luis Saslavsky. PH:
Bellesteros & Valentin Javier. SP: Miguel Mihura. Story:
Jean Cocteau. Ref: MMF 9:14. Lee. with Maria Felix,
Rossano Brazzi, Vittorio Gassman, Julia C. Alba. Nightmares
and witches, clutching hands from graves.
BLACK DRAGON OF MANZANAR see G-MEN VS. THE BLACK
DRAGON
BLACK DRAGONS Mono 1942 64m. D: William Nigh. SP:
Harvey Gates. PH: Art Reed. Mus: Lange & Porter. Art
D: Dave Milton. P: Sam Katzman, Jack Dietz. Ref: FDY.
with Bela Lugosi, Clayton Moore, J. Barclay, George Pem-
broke, Bob Frazer, Bob Fiske, Kenneth Harlan, I. Stanford
Jolley. Plastic surgery & drugs turn a man into a monster.
The BLACK FOREST Princess-TV 1954 63m. P,D: Gene

Martel. SP: Joe Liss, Irve Tunick. PH: Erich Claunick. Ref: MFB'55:37. with Peggy Ann Garner, Akim Tamiroff, Gordon Howard. Sadistic baron hunts men down (a la "The Most Dangerous Game" by Richard Connell).

BLACK FRIDAY Univ 1940 70m. D: Arthur Lubin. SP: Curt Siodmak, Eric Taylor. PH: Elwood Bredell. Mus D: H. J. Salter. Art D: Jack Otterson. Ref: Academy. FDY. with Boris Karloff, Bela Lugosi, Stanley Ridges, Anne Nagel, Anne Gwynne, Virginia Brissac, Paul Fix, Jack Mulhall, Joe King, Murray Alper, James Craig, Edward McWade, Eddie Dunn, Emmett Vogan, Edward Earle, Edwin Stanley, Harry Hayden, Frank Jaquet, Dave Willock, William Ruhl, Jessie Arnold, Wallace Reid, Jr. The brain of a dying gangster is transplanted into a professor's head. Worst of the Karloff-Lugosi horror films-- and with competition like The RAVEN that's saying plenty. Ridiculous plot twists. Ineptly-staged action. All the actors come off looking pretty bad.

BLACK LIMELIGHT (B) Alliance/Assoc. Brit. 1938 69m. D: Paul Stein. SP: Dudley Leslie. PH: Claude Friese-Greene. Ref: FD 7/6/39: "Killer working under moon-madness." CCF 7:10. Brit. Cinema. MFB'38: 180. with Raymond Massey, Joan Marion, Walter Hudd, Henry Oscar.

BLACK MAGIC Kalem 1916 25m. D: James W. Horne. SP: George B. Howard. (episode in THE SOCIAL PIRATES series) Ref: MPN 14:282. MPW 29:474. with Marin Sais, Ollie Kirkby. Hindu fakir keeps rich woman in his hypnotic power.

BLACK MAGIC Mono 1944 65m. (MEETING AT MIDNIGHT. CHARLIE CHAN AND BLACK MAGIC) D: Phil Rosen. SP: George Callahan. Based on the character Charlie Chan created by Earl Derr Biggers. PH: Arthur Martinelli. Mus sc: Alexander Laszlo. with Sidney Toler, Mantan Moreland, Frances Chan, Joseph Crehan, Jacqueline de Wit, Frank Jaquet, Edward Earle, Claudia Dell, Harry Depp, Richard Gordon. A murder is committed during a seance. Routine Chan film.

BLACK MAGIC (U.S.-I) UA 1949 102m. (CAGLIOSTRO-I.) P,D: Gregory Ratoff. SP: Charles Bennett. Add'l Dial: Richard Schayer. From "Memoirs of a Physician" and "Cagliostro" by Dumas. PH: Ubaldo Arata, Anchiso Brizzi. Art D: Jean D'Eaubonno, Ottavio Scotti. Ref: DDC III:322. with Orson Welles, Akim Tamiroff, Nancy Guild, Raymond Burr, Frank Latimore, Valentina Cortesa, Margot Grahame, Barry Kroeger, Gregory Gay, Lee Kresel. 18th-century hypnotist Cagliostro keeps a girl under his hypnotic spell.

BLACK MAGIC see WAJAN

BLACK MOON Col 1934 68m. D: Roy William Neill. SP: Wells Root, from the magazine story, "Haiti Moon," by Clements Ripley. PH: Joseph August. Ref: FDY. with Jack Holt, Fay Wray, Dorothy Burgess, Cora Sue Collins, Arnold Korff, Clarence Muse, Lumsden Hare, Madame Sul-te-wan, Lawrence Criner, Henry Kolker, Robert Fraz(i)er, Edna Tichenor. A white woman becomes fascinated by voodoo rituals.

The BLACK OPAL Ramo 1913 18m. Ref: Bios 12/4/13. "Tragic happenings" dog possessors of opal ring.

Black

52

BLACK ORPHEUS (Braz.-F.) Lopert 1959 Eastmancolor 95m.
D: Marcel Camus. SP: Jacques Viot, from "Orfeu da Conceicao"
by Vinicius de Moraes. PH: Jean Bourgoin. Mus: Antonio
Carlos Jobim, Luis Bonfa. Adap: Viot, Camus. with Breno
Mello, Marpessa Dawn, Lourdes de Oliveira. Ref: FFacts.
Woman pursued by Death. Moderately good.
BLACK OXEN 1923-24 90m. PH: Norbert Brodin. D: Frank
Lloyd. From a novel by Gertrude Atherton. Ref: NYT 1/7/24.
AFI. SF in the Cinema: 42. with Corinne Griffith, Conway
Tearle, Alan Hale, Clara Bow, Kate Lester. 58-year old
woman rejuvenated by doctor's x-ray operation.
BLACK PANTHER OF RATANA (G-I-Thai) Rapid/Cineproduzione/
Constantin 1963 100m. (DER SCHWARZE PANTHER VON
RATANA-G) D: Jurgen Roland. SP: Johannes Kai. PH: Klaus
von Rautenfeld. Mus: Gerd Wilden. Ref: German Pictures.
M/TVM 6/63. with Marianne Koch, Heinz Drache, Horst
Frank, Brad Harris. "Mysterious murderer" responsible for
series of "terrifying panther crimes."
BLACK PIT OF DR. M (Mex) Alameda Films 1958 (MISTERIOS
DE ULTRATUMBA. MYSTERIES FROM BEYOND THE GRAVE)
D: F. Mendez. PH: Victor Herrera. Ref: Aventura. TVG.
with Gaston Santos, Mapita Cortes, Rafael Bertrand. The spirit
of a scientist returns to seek revenge.
THE BLACK RAVEN PRC 1943 61m. D: Sam Newfield. SP:
Fred Myton . PH: Robert Cline. Mus D: David Chudnow. P:
Sigmund Neufeld. Ref: FDY. MFB'43. with George Zucco,
Wanda McKay, Noel Madison, Bob Randall, Byron Foulger,
Charles Middleton, Glenn Strange, I. Stanford Jolley. 3
murders in a gloomy roadside inn on a stormy night.
The BLACK RIDER (B) Balblair/Butchers 1955 66m. D: Wolf
Rilla. SP,P: A. R. Rawlinson. PH: Geoffrey Faithfull.
Mus: Wilfred Burns. Ref: MFB'55:23. with Jimmy Hanley,
Rona Anderson, Leslie Dwyer, Beatrice Varley, Lionel Jeffries.
Hooded figure thought to be the local ghost is actually a smug-
gler.
The BLACK ROOM Col 1935 67m. D: Roy William Neill. SP:
Henry Myers, from writings by Arthur Strawn. PH: Al Siegler.
Ref: FD 8/17/35. Pic: FD 7/26/35. FM 56:23. with Boris
Karloff, Marian Marsh, Katherine De Mille, Robert Allen, John
Buckler, Thurston Hall, Frederick Vogeding, Egon Brecher,
Edward Van Sloan, Henry Kolker. Some suspense in one of the
better minor thrillers of the mid-Thirties, with Karloff in a dual
role.
BLACK SABBATH (I-F-U.S.) Emmepi--Galatea/Lyre/AI 1963
Eastmancolor 99m. (I TRE VOLTI DELLA PAURA. THE
THREE FACES OF FEAR. BLACK CHRISTMAS. THE THREE
FACES OF TERROR) D: Mario Bava. SP: Bava, Marcello
Fondato, Alberto Bevilacqua. From "A Drop of Water" by Chek-
hov, "The Telephone" by F. G. Snyder, and "The Wurdalak" by
Alexei Tolstoy. PH: Ubaldo Terzano. Mus: (Ital.) Roberto
Nicolos(i); (dubbed) Les Baxter. Art D: Giorgio Giovannini. Ref:
Clarens. with Boris Karloff, Michèle Mercier, Mark Damon,
Suzy Anderson, Milly Monti. First story makes one of the best

horror shorts; 2nd isn't much; 3rd has fine moments but goes on
and on.
The BLACK SCORPION WB 1957 88m.   D: Edward Ludwig. SP:
David Duncan, Robert Blees, from a story by Paul Yawitz. PH:
Lionel Linden. Mus: Paul Sawtell. Art D: Edward Fitzgerald.
SpFX: Willis O'Brien. Ref: Clarens. with Richard Denning,
Mara Corday, Carlos Rivas, Mario Navarro, Pascual Pena.
Giant scorpions rampant in Mexico. Okay.
BLACK SHADOWS Fox 1920 60m. D: Howard M. Mitchell. SP:
J. Anthony Roach. Ref: MPW 44:42. with Estella Evans, Peggy
Hyland, Albert Roscoe. Victim of hypnotic spell steals.
The BLACK SKULL (Mex) c1960 (LA CALAVERA NEGRA) Ref:
FM 12.8 (Still)
The BLACK SLEEP UA 1956 81m. (DR. CADMAN'S SECRET)
D: Reginald Le Borg. SP: Le Borg, John C. Higgins. PH:
Gordon Avil. Mus D: Les Baxter. P: Howard W. Koch. Ref:
FDY. Les Otis. COF 3:35. Pic: FM 11:13, 23. 20:18. with
Basil Rathbone, Bela Lugosi, Lon Chaney, Jr., Akim Tamiroff,
John Carradine, Tor Johnson, Herbert Rudley, George Sawaya,
Sally Yarnell, John Sheffield, Patricia Blake, Phyllis Stanley,
Claire Carleton. Doctor seeks cure for wife's brain condition,
succeeds mainly in creating monsters. Not too hot, though
Tamiroff is amusing.
BLACK SUNDAY (I) AI/Galatea--Jolly Films 1960 84m. (LA
MASCHERA DEL DEMONIO. REVENGE OF THE VAMPIRE--
Eng. HOUSE OF FRIGHT. MASK OF THE DEMON. DIE
STUNDE WENN DRACULA KOMMT--Ger.) D: Mario Bava. SP:
Ennio DeConcini, Mario Serandre (Bava). From "The Vij" by
Gogol. PH: Ubaldo Terzano. Mus: (Ital) Roberto Nicolosi;
(dubbed) Les Baxter. Art D: Giorgio Giovannini. Ref: FM
11:13. Clarens. with Barbara Steele, John Richardson, Ivo
Garrani, Andrea Checchi, Arturo Dominici. Witch comes to life
when the cross guarding her tomb is removed.
BLACK TORMENT (B) Governor/Compton 1964 color 88m.
P, D: Robert Hartford-Davis. SP: Donald and Derek Ford. PH:
Peter Newbrook. Mus: Robert Richards. Art D: Alan Harris.
Ref: MMF. COF 6:56. with John Turner, Heather Sears, Ann
Lynn, Peter Arne, Raymond Huntley, Joseph Tomelty, Norman
Bird, Francis de Wolff, Edina Ronay. Witchcraft, murder, and
insanity in an old mansion.
BLACK WIDOW, The 1941 see BODY DISAPPEARS, The
The BLACK WIDOW Rep 1947 serial 13 episodes (SOMBRA,
THE SPIDER WOMAN--'66 feature) D: Spencer G. Bennet, Fred
Brannon. SP: Franklin Adreon, Basil Dickey, Jesse Duffy, Sol
Shor. PH: John MacBurnie. Assoc P: Mike Frankovich. Ref:
FIR'68:523. Barbour. with Bruce Edwards, (Brother) Theodore
Gottlieb (Hitomu), Virginia Lindley, Carol Forman, Anthony
Warde, Ramsay Ames, I. Stanford Jolley, Gene Stutenroth, Sam
Flint, Tom Steele, Dale Van Sickel, Forrest Taylor, Ernie Adams,
Robert Wilke. The dialogue tells the story: "And I don't think he'll
conquer the world--it's been tried"; "You're now gonna see the
next number one guy of the world"; Doctor (re: his sound disinte-
grator): "That too testifies to the soundness of my theory."

The BLACK ZOO AA 1962 Eastmancolor/scope 88m. D:
Robert Gordon. SP, P: Herman Cohen. PH: Floyd Crosby.
Mus: Paul Dunlap. Art D: William Glasgow. SpFX: Pat
Dinga. Ref: FFacts. with Michael Gough, Rod Lauren, Jerome
Cowan, Virginia Grey, Jeanne Cooper, Elisha Cook, Jr.,
Marianna Hill, Edward Platt. Mad zookeeper turns lions and
tigers loose on those who oppose him.
BLACKBEARD'S GHOST BV 1968 Technicolor 107m. D: Robert
Stevenson. SP: Bill Walsh, Don Da Gradi, from a novel by
Ben Stahl. PH: Edward Colman. Mus: Robert F. Brunner.
SpFX: Eustace Lycett, Robert A. Mattey. with Peter Ustinov,
Dean Jones, Suzanne Pleshette, Elsa Lanchester, Joby Baker,
Elliott Reid, Richard Deacon, Kelly Thordsen, Herbie Faye,
Gil Lamb, Alan Carney. Witch curses husband Blackbeard to
wander in limbo. He is conjured up in the present.
BLACKHAWK Col 1952 serial 1. Distress Call from Space.
7. Mystery Fuel. 10. Chase for Element X. D: Spencer G.
Bennet, Fred F. Sears. SP: George H. Plympton, Royal Cole,
Sherman Lowe. PH: William Whitley. Mus: Mischa Bakaleini-
koff. P: Sam Katzman. Based on the "Blackhawk" comic maga-
zine drawn by Reed Crandall. Ref: Barbour. Don Glut. with
Kirk Alyn, Carol Forman, John Crawford, Don C. Harvey, Rick
Vallin, William Fawcett. Disintegrator, etc.
BLADE IN THE BODY, The see MURDER CLINIC, The
BLAKE MURDER MYSTERY, The see HAUNTED HOUSE, The
(1940)
BLAKE OF SCOTLAND YARD Univ 1927 serial 12 episodes
1. The Castle of Fear. 10. The Lady in White. Sequel: ACE
OF SCOTLAND YARD. D: Robert F. Hill. Ref: LC. Lee/
Stringham: sf elements. with Hayden Stevenson, Gloria Gray,
Monty Montague, Grace Cunard.
BLAKE OF SCOTLAND YARD Victory/Bon Ami 1936 74m. D:
Robert F. Hill. SP: Hill, William Lord Wright. (Feature ver-
sion of 15-episode serial) P: Sam Katzman. Ref: COF 7:10.
STI 2:40. Pic: TBG. with Ralph Byrd, Joan Barclay, Herbert
Rawlinson, Lloyd Hughes, Dickie Jones, Bob Terry. Death ray;
villain with cloak and claw.
BLANCHEVILLE MONSTER, The see HORROR
BLAST OFF MCA-TV 1954 From the "Rocky Jones, Space
Ranger" TV series. Ref: TVG. with Richard Crane, Sally
Mansfield, Maurice Cass.
BLAST OFF see THOSE FANTASTIC FLYING FOOLS
BLAUE LICHT, Das see BLUE LIGHT, The
BLEARY OH! THE VILLAGE AVIATOR Gaum 1909 8m. Ref:
Bios 12/16/09. Combination motorcycle-and-wings flies over
roof or two before crashing.
A BLIND BARGAIN Goldwyn 1922 55m. PH: Norbert Brodin.
D: Wallace Worsley. SP: J. G. Hawks. From "The Octave
of Claudius" by Barry Pain. Ref: FM 2:6. 8:24. Pic: FM 15:
38. 16:40. 39:52. 63:54. AFI. with Lon Chaney (Dr. Lamb/
Ape Man), Raymond McKee, Virginia True Boardman, Jacqueline
Logan, Fontaine LaRue. Mad doctor's experiments result in
ape-man and other half-human creatures.

The BLIND BEAST (J) Daiei 1968 color/scope 84m. (MOJU)
D: Yasuzô Masumura. SP: Yoshio Shirasaka. Story: Rampo
Edogawa. PH: S. Kobayashi. Mus: H. Hayashi. Art D: S.
Mano. Ref: UFQ-44. MPH 3/26/69. with Eiji Funakoshi,
Mako Midori, N. Sengoku. Blind man traps girl in room of
horrors.
The BLIND GIRL OF CASTLE GUILLE Patheplay 1913 Ref:
MPW'13:988. Witch; vision of angel kills girl.
BLIND MAN'S BLUFF (B) Fox British 1936 70m. D: Albert
Parker. SP: Cecil Maiden, from the story "Smoked Glasses"
by William Foster. Ref: Lee. Focus on Films'70 #2. with
James Mason, Basil Sydney, Iris Ashley. "Sci-fi overtones":
invisible ray?
BLIND MAN'S BLUFF (Sp-U.S.) Hispamer/Weinbach 1967 97m.
(EL COLECCIONISTA DE CADAVERES. THE CORPSE COLLEC-
TORS. DEATH COMES FROM THE DARK. CAULDRON OF
BLOOD) Eastmancolor SP, D: Santos Alcocer (Edward Mann).
Story: Alcocer, J. Melson, J. L. Bayonas. PH: Francisco
Sempere. Mus: José Luis Navarro. Art D: Gil Parrando. Ref:
Sp. Cinema'68. with Jean-Pierre Aumont, Boris Karloff, Viveca
Lindfors, Rosenda Monteros, Ruben Rojo, Dianik Zurakowska.
Blind sculptor models on skeletons provided by his wife, who
murders for them.
BLIND WOMAN'S CURSE see HAUNTED LIFE OF A DRAGON-
TATTOOED LASS, The
BLITHE SPIRIT (B) UA/Two Cities 1945 color 94m. D: David
Lean. SP, P: Noel Coward, from his play. Mus: Richard
Addinsell. PH: Ronald Neame. with Rex Harrison, Margaret
Rutherford, Constance Cummings, Kay Hammond, Joyce Carey.
Ghosts & spiritualism. Sometimes witty, sometimes just
mechanically "clever" comedy. Rutherford has the shortest,
unheartiest (funniest) laugh on record. Harrison, as usual, is
just adequate.
The BLOB Para/Tonlyn 1958 DeluxeColor 85m. (THE MOLTEN
METEOR) D: Irvin S. Yeaworth, Jr. SP: Theodore Simonson,
Kate Phillips, from an idea by Irving H. Millgate. PH: Thomas
Spalding. Mus: Ralph Carmichael. Art D: William Jersey,
Karl Karlson. Ref: Lee. FM 26: 12. 35:75: DAUGHTER OF
HORROR poster in film. P: Jack Harris. with Steve McQueen,
Aneta Corseaut, Olin Howlin, Earl Rowe. McQueen gives maybe
his most interesting performance; the blob does some cute tricks;
but it's all very lackadaisical and flat.
The BLOCK SIGNAL Lumas/Gotham 1926 74m. D: Frank
O'Connor. SP: Edward J. Meagher. Story: F. Oakley
Crawford. PH: Ray June. Ref: MPW'26:371. AFI. with
Ralph Lewis, Jean Arthur, Sidney Franklin, George Chesebro.
Inventor's automatic braking device brings runaway train to dead
stop.
BLIND GORILLA see WHITE PONGO
BLONDE COMME CA! Une see MISS SHUMWAY CASTS A SPELL
BLONDIE HAS SERVANT TROUBLE Col 1940 70m. D: Frank
Strayer. SP: Richard Flournoy. Story: Albert Duffy. From
the comic by C. Young. PH: Henry Freulich. Ed: Gene

Havlick. Ref: FDY. with Penny Singleton, Arthur Lake, Larry Simms, Jonathan Hale, Arthur Hohl, Daisy, Danny Mummert, Esther Dale, Irving Bacon, Fay Helm. The Bumstead family moves into a "haunted" house.

BLONDINE (F) 1944 D: Henri Mahé. Ref: Rep.Gen'47. FM 28:18. with Georges Marchal, Nicole Maurey, Pieral. Fairy tale: giant.

BLOOD AND BLACK LACE (I-F.West G) AA/Woolner/Emmepi--de Beauregard--Monachia 1964 Eastmancolor 90m. (SEI DONNE PER L'ASSASSINO. SIX WOMEN FOR THE MURDERER) D: Mario Bava. SP: Bava, Marcello Fondato, Giuseppe Barilla. PH: Ubaldo Terzano. Mus: Carlo Rustichelli. Art D: A. Breschi. Ref: Clarens. COF 8:6. 6:52. "Horrific overtones." with Eva Bartok, Cameron Mitchell, Thomas Reiner, Harriet White, Claude Dantes. Masked murderer.

BLOOD AND LACE AI/Contemporary Filmakers--Carlin Co. 1971 87m. Movielab color D: Philip Gilbert. SP: Gil Lasky. PH: Paul Hipp. Mus ed: John Rons. Art D: Lee Fischer. Ref: V 3/17/71: "Cadavers, severed hand, spooky shadows." with Gloria Grahame, Melody Patterson, Milton Selzer.

BLOOD AND ROSES (F-I) Para/EGE--Documento 1960 Eastmancolor/scope 74m. (ET MOURIR DE PLAISIR. TO DIE WITH PLEASURE) D: Roger Vadim. SP: Vadim, Roger Vailland, Claude Brulé, Claude Martin. From "Carmilla" by Sheridan Le Fanu. PH: Claude Renoir. Mus: Jean Prodomidès. Art D: Jean André. Ref: Clarens. Orpheus 3:28. PM. FM 8:16. with Elsa Martinelli, Mel Ferrer, Annette Stroyberg, Gaby Farinon, Camilla Stroyberg, Marc Allegret. Woman comes under spell of vampire ancestor she resembles.

BLOOD BATH (U.S.-Yugos) AI 70m. (TRACK OF THE VAM-PIRE--TV) 1966 SP,D: Jack Hill, Stephanie Rothman. PH: Alfred Taylor. Mus: Mark Lowery. Ref: Les Otis. PM. Pic: FM 45:56. with William Campbell, Marrisa Mathes, Linda Saunders, Sandra Knight. An artist is possessed by the spirit of a vampire ancestor.

BLOOD BEAST FROM HELL see DEATHSHEAD VAMPIRE, The

BLOOD BEAST FROM OUTER SPACE (B) World Entertainment/Harris/New Art 1967 84m. (NIGHT CALLER. NIGHT CALLER FROM OUTER SPACE) D: John Gilling. SP: Jim O'Connaly, from the novel "Night Callers" by Frank Crisp. PH: Stephen Dade. Ref: V. COF 9:45. with John Saxon, Maurice Denham, Patricia Haines, John Carson, Jack Watson, Alfred Burke. A visitor from one of Jupiter's moons kidnaps girls to take back with him.

BLOOD BEAST TERROR, The see VAMPIRE BEAST CRAVES BLOOD, The

BLOOD BROTHERHOOD Rex 1914 Ref: Bios 2/12/14. 18m. "Hypnotic power."

BLOOD CREATURE see TERROR IS A MAN

BLOOD DEMON see SNAKE PIT, The

BLOOD DEVILS see BEAST OF BLOOD

The BLOOD DRINKERS (Fili) Hemisphere/Falcon 1966 88m. (VAMPIRE PEOPLE--TV) D: Gerardo deLeon. P: Cirio H.

Santiago.   Ref: Boxo 9/5/66.   COF 11:6.   with Amelia Fuentes,
Ronald Remy.   A band of vampires terrorizes a small village.
BLOOD DRINKERS, The   see   DR. TERROR'S GALLERY OF
HORRORS
BLOOD FEAST   Box Office Spectaculars   1963   Eastmancolor   61m.
D: Herschell G. Lewis.   SP: A. Louise Downe.   P: David
Friedman.   Ref: COF 6:56.   FM 39:66.   MMF.   with Connie
Mason, Thomas Wood, Scott Arnold.   Madman trying to bring
Egyptian love goddess to life removes members and organs of
various girls, without, as critic Michael Caen observed, the
least local anaesthetic.   Connie Mason gives one of the best
unintentional comic performances ever--luckily; all the explicit
gore would be too much to take straight.   Villain is crushed to
death in a garbage truck, and a witness notes: "He died a fit-
ting death for the garbage he was."   Totally inept technically.
BLOOD FROM THE MUMMY'S TOMB   (B)   EMI/Hammer   1971
Technicolor   94m.   D: Seth Holt.   SP: Christopher Wicking,
based on Bram Stoker's novel, "The Jewel of Seven Stars."   PH:
Arthur Grant.   Mus: Tristram Cary.   Art D: Scott Mac-
Gregor.   SpFX: Michael Collins.   Ref: V 10/27/71.   with
Andrew Keir, Valerie Leon, James Villiers, George Coulouris,
David Markham, Tamara Ustinov, Rosalie Crutchley.
BLOOD FIEND   see   THEATRE OF DEATH
BLOOD IS MY HERITAGE   see   BLOOD OF DRACULA
BLOOD MONSTER   see   HORROR OF THE BLOOD MONSTERS
BLOOD OF DRACULA   AI/carmel   1957   70m.   (BLOOD OF THE
DEMON.   BLOOD IS MY HERITAGE)   D: Herbert L. Strock.
SP: Ralph Thornton.   PH: Monroe Askins.   Mus: Paul Dunlap.
Art D: Leslie Thomas. Title inspired by "Dracula" by Bram
Stoker.   Asst D: Austen Jewell.   P: Herman Cohen.   Ref:
FM 2:16.   Pic: FM 1:39.   with Sandra Harrison, Louise Lewis,
Gail Ganley, Jerry Blaine, Malcolm Atterbury, Don Devlin,
Richard Devon.   The power to turn people into vampires by
remote-control hypnosis is supposed to someday end all wars.
Who said horror movies never have a social conscience?
BLOOD OF DRACULA'S CASTLE   A&E Film Corp.   1969
Pathecolor 84m.   D: Al Adamson.   SP: Rex Carlton.   PH:
Leslie Kovacs.   Mus: Lincoln Mayorage.   Based on the charac-
ter created by Bram Stoker in "Dracula."   Planned sequel:
DRACULA'S COFFIN.   Ref: Boxo 8/25/69.   with John Carra-
dine, Paula Raymond, Alex D'Arcy, Robert Dix.   Photographer
inherits old castle from his late uncle.
BLOOD OF FRANKENSTEIN   Independent Int'.   1971   (DRACULA
VS. FRANKENSTEIN)   Based on characters in "Frankenstein" by
Mary Shelley and "Dracula" by Bram Stoker.   Technical adviser:
Forrest J. Ackerman.   Ref: V 5/12/71:203.   FM 69: 24.   with
Lon Chaney, Jr., J. Carrol Naish, Angelo Rossitto, Zandor
Vorkov (Dracula), John Bloom (Frankenstein's monstor), Anthony
Eisley, Jim Davis.
BLOOD OF FU MANCHU   (Sp-G-US-B)   Commonwealth United/Ada--
Terra--Udastex--Towers of London   1968   Eastmancolor   92m.
(FU MANCHU Y EL BESO DE LA MUERTE-Sp. DIE RACHE DES
DR. FU MANCHU-G. DER TODESKUSS DES DR. FU MAN CHU-

G. DER TODESKUSS DES DR. FU MAN CHU-G. AGAINST ALL
ODDS-TV. KISS AND KILL. FU MANCHU'S KISS OF DEATH)
D: Jess Franco. SP: Peter Welbeck. Based on the character
created by Sax Rohmer. PH: Manuel Merino. Ref: Sp Cinema
'69. MFB'69:56. COF 13:27. F Bltn 10/27/69. M/TVM 3 &
5/69. with Christopher Lee, Richard Greene, Shirley Eaton,
Tsai Chin, Maria Rohm. Snake venom injection causes blindness
& death.
BLOOD OF GHASTLY HORROR Independent Int'l 1971 Ref: Boxo
9/6/71: W-5. with Kent Taylor, Tommy Kirk, John Carradine.
BLOOD OF NOSTRADAMUS (Mex) AI-TV c1960 98m. (LA
SANGRE DE NOSTRADAMUS) D: F. curiel. SP: C. Taboada,
Alfredo Ruanova. with Jermon Robles, Julio Aleman. Vampire
marks inspector for death. Some atmospheric shots; the usual
dubbed muddle.
BLOOD OF THE DEMON see BLOOD OF DRACULA
BLOOD OF THE VAMPIRE (B) Univ/Eros 1958 Eastmancolor
84m. D: Henry Cass. SP: Jimmy Sangster. PH: Geoffrey
Seaholme. Mus: Stanley Black. Art D: John Elphick. Makeup:
Jimmy Evans. P: Baker & Berman. Ref: MFB'58:126. Pic:
FM 19:70. with Donald Wolfit, Vincent Ball, Barbara Shelley,
Victor Maddern, John Le Mesurier, Milton Reid. A resuscitated
scientist conducts experiments at an asylum.
BLOOD OF THE VIRGINS (Mex) Azteca c1968 color (SANGRE DE
VIRGENES) D: Emilio Vieyra. P: Orestes Trucco. Ref:
poster. with Gloria Prat, Ricardo Bauleo, Susana Beltran,
Rolo Puente. Vampires.
BLOOD ON HER SHOE (book by Medora Field) see GIRL WHO
DARED, The
BLOOD ON HIS LIPS see HIDEOUS SUN DEMON, The
BLOOD ON SATAN'S CLAW, The see SATAN'S SKIN
BLOOD ROSE, The see RAVAGED
The BLOOD SEEDLING Selig 1915 30m. Ref: MPW 27: 2051,
2230. with Thomas Santschi, Leo Pierson, Thomas Bates.
Swedenborg's "spirit notions" influence man to hold seance to
expose murderer.
BLOOD SUCKERS, The see ISLAND OF THE DOOMED/DR.
TERROR'S GALLERY OF HORRORS
BLOOD TERROR, The see VAMPIRE BEAST CRAVES BLOOD,
The
BLOOD THIRST (U.S.-Fili) Chevron-Paragon/Journey 1971
(1965) (The HORROR FROM BEYOND. BLOOD SEEKERS)
D,P: Newton Arnold. SP: N. I. P. Dennis. PH: H. Santos.
Ref: MMF 13:60. FM 46:21. Film Bltn 6/71:32. COF 8:50.
Photon 21:5. with Robert Winston, Yvonne Nielson, Judy Dennis,
Vic Diaz. Mixture of blood and electric energy gives woman pro-
longed life. Boring and talky. The hero keeps making a fool of
himself with totally unfunny quips.
BLOOD VENGEANCE Ambrosio 1911 From a play by D'Annuncio.
Ref: MPW'12:126: "Eerie, literary atmosphere." Ghost orders
her daughter to kill her murderess with a "bag of asps."
The BLOODLESS VAMPIRE (U.S.-Fili?) Journey D: Michael du
Pont Ref: COF 8:48. MMF 13:60. with Charles Macauley,

Helen Thompson.
BLOODLUST   Crown Int'l.   1963-1   68m.   SP,D,P: Ralph Brooke.
From Richard Connell's "The Most Dangerous Game."   Ref:
HM 3:43.   with Robert Reed, Lylyan Chauvin, Wilton Graff, June
Kenny, Joan Lora.   Mad hunter uses humans as game.
The BLOODSTONE   Lubin   1908   Ref: F Index 10/24/08.   Ring
brings violence and death.
BLOODSUCKERS   (B)   Chevron-Paragon/Lucinda-Titan   1971
Movielab color   D: Robert Hartford-Davis.   SP: Julian More,
from "Doctors Wear Scarlet" by Simon Raven.   PH: Desmond
Dickinson.   Mus sc & d: Bobby Richards.   Ref: Photon 21:40.
Film Bltn 6/71:32.   with Peter Cushing, Patrick Macnee,
Patrick Mower, Alex Davion.   Vampire cult.   Dull, fragmented
story, poorly edited.
BLOODTHIRSTY BUTCHERS   Mishkin/Constitution   1970 color
79m.   PH,D,   Andy Milligan.   SP: Milligan, John Borske.
Sets: James Fox.   Ref: Boxo 2/12/70.   with John Miranda,
Annabella Wood, Berwick Kaller (Sweeney Todd).   Mysterious
alliance between murderer and proprietress of shop which
sells "meat pies."   The film was evidently edited by one of the
butchers.   A scene ends, another begins, and that's that.
Interminably talky.
BLOOD-THIRSTY EYES   see   DRACULA'S LUST FOR BLOOD
The BLOODY INN   (Mex)   Calderon   1941   (LA POSADA
SANGRIENTA)   D: Fernando A. Rivero.   SP: Mario de Lara.
Story: Ernesto Cortazar.   PH: Ross Fisher.   Ref: El Cine
Grafico'41:219. /Indice.   with David Silva, Gloria Marin,
Miguel Inclán, Alfredo Varela.   "Terror film.... Is the criminal
a man or a monster?"
BLOODY JUDGE, The   see   WITCH-KILLER OF BLACKMOOR, The
The BLOODY PIT OF HORROR   (I)   Pacemaker/Int'l.   Enter-
tainment Corp. -Ralph Zucker--MBS Cinematografica   1965
('67-U.S.)   Eastmancolor 80m.   (IL BOIA SCARLATTO.   THE
SCARLET EXECUTIONER.   THE RED HANGMAN.   VIRGINS
FOR THE HANGMAN.   THE SCARLET HANGMAN)   D:
Massimo Pupillo (aka Max Hunter).   SP: Roberto Natale,
Romano Migliorini.   PH: Luciano Trasatti.   Mus: Gino
Peguri.   Ref: Ital P.   RVB.   with Mickey Hargitay, Walter
Brandi, Moa Thai, Rita Klein, Mario Pupillo (aka Ralph Zuck-
er), Alfredo Rizzo (aka Alfred Rice).   Crazed actor tortures
intruders in his castle.
BLOODY PLEASURE   (Mex)   c1969   (PLACER SANGRIENTO)   D:
Emilio Vieyra.   SP: Antonio Rosso.   PH: Aribal Paz.   P:
Orestes Trucco.   with Justin Martin, Jose Orange, Greta
Williams.   Man in horror-mask casts spells to lure women to
his villa.   Crummy, with lame attempts at atmosphere to com-
pensate for lack of anything else.
BLOODY SCREAM OF DRACULA, The   see   DRACULA, PRINCE
OF DARKNESS
The BLOODY VAMPIRE   (Mex)   AI-TV/Tele-Talia   1962   110m.
(El VAMPIRO SANGRIENTO.   CONDE FRANKENSTEIN?
COUNT FRANK(EN)HAUSEN)   SP,D: Miguel Morayta.   PH:
Raul M. Solares.   Mus: L. H. Breton.   Art D: Manuel Fontanals.

Ref: Indice.   MMF-13:58. 9:22. FM 63:24.   M/TVM 5/63.
Pic: FM 57:14,16. with Carlos Agosti, Begoña Palacios, Antonio Raxell, Erna Martha Bauman. The vampire gets away at the end. So what.
BLOOMER AS A GHOST (I) Cines 8m. Ref: Bios 10/23/13. Spiritualists.
BLOW YOUR OWN HORN FBO 1923 70m. D: James W. Horne. SP: Rex Taylor, from the play by Owen Davis.   PH: Joseph Dubray.   Ref: AFI. with Warner Baxter, Ralph Lewis, Derelys Perdue, Ernest C. Warde, Eugene Acker. "Wireless power transmitting device" demonstrated.
BLOWN UPON Kriterion (Punch) 1915 Ref: MPN 1/30/15. Doctor's liquid "rigidizes anyone who is blown upon by the person who has taken a sip of the fluid."
BLUE DEMON (Mex) c1963 (EL DEMONIO AZUL) Ref: FM 46:15.   FJA pbk. Grafica 6/66:2 with Jaime Fernandez, Rosa Maria Vasquez, Mario Orea. Werewolf.
BLUE DEMON AGAINST THE SATANIC POWER (Mex) Col c1964 (BLUE DEMON CONTRA EL PODER SATANICON) Ref: FJA pic. with Martha Elena Cervantes, Jaime Fernandez.
The BLUE LIGHT (G) Sokal/Mayfair 90m.   (DAS BLAUE LICHT) 1932 ('34-U.S.) D: Leni Riefenstahl. SP: Riefenstahl, Bela Balazs. PH: Hans Schneeberger. Ref: FD 5/8/34. DDC I:201. with Leni Riefenstahl. A strange light on a mountain peak lures young men from a village to their death. A gypsy who has been to the light and lived is branded a witch. Simple, weak story; interesting use of the moon and light as almost supernatural powers.
The BLUE SEXTET 1971 color Ref: RVB. Murder victim's amateur vampire film shown for a group of people.
BLUEBEARD PRC 1944 73m. D: Edgar G. Ulmer. SP: Pierre Gendron. Story: Arnold Phillips, Werner Furst. PH: J. Feindel. Mus d: Leo Erdody. Art D: Paul Palmentola. Ref: FDY. with John Carradine, Nils Asther, Ludwig Stossel, Jean Parker, Henry Kolker, George Pembroke, Iris Adrian. Pic: TBG. Artist driven by compulsion to strangle his models. Overrated "sleeper," but decent enough.
The BOARDING SCHOOL (Sp) AI/Arturo Gonzalez-Anabel 1969 color/scope 105m. (LA RESIDENCIA. THE HOUSE THAT SCREAMED) D: Narciso Ibanez Serrador. SP: Luis Penafiel, from a story by Juan Tebar. PH: Manuel Berenguer. Mus: Waldo de Los Rios. Ref: V 3/11/70. with Lilli Palmer, Cristina Galbo, John Moulder Brown, Tomas Blanco. Headmistress' son decides to "find the right girl" by killing his favorites and assembling one from their members. The atmosphere is supposed to be menacing, but the production is just competent enough to be boring.
The BOAT WITHOUT THE FISHERMAN (Sp) Teide 1964 scope 83m. (LA BARCA SIN PESCADOR) D: José Maria Forn. SP: Alcofar. Story: A. Casona. PH: R. Albiñana. Mus: E. S. de la Maza. Art D: M. Infiesta. Ref: Sp Cinema'65. with Gerard Landry, Julian Ugarte, Mabel Karr, A. S. Leal. Deal with the devil.

BOBBY AT THE CHEMIST'S Gaum 10m. c1912 Ref: Bios.
Draught makes woman spin around and around; man takes nitro-
glycerin and explodes.
BOBBY "SOME" SPIRITUALIST Melies/Gaum 1912 9m. Ref:
MPW 20:104. Bios 11/14/12. (BOBBY TAKES UP SPIRITUAL-
ISM) Boy frightens members of seance with "manifestations."
BOB'S ELECTRIC THEATRE (F) Pathe 1909 7m. Ref: MPW
5:581, 588. Miniature "electric" theater.
BOB'S NIGHTMARE Mono Film 1912 9m. Ref: Bios 2/22/12.
Dream: Mysterious man and woman in white; giant knife cuts
head off.
BODIAM CASTLE (B) 1926 short (HAUNTED CASTLES series)
D: A. V. Bramble. Ref: Brit. Cinema. V 2/24/26.
The BODY BENEATH Nova Int'l 1970 85m. SP, D, PH: Andy
Milligan. color Ref: Boxo 3/1/71. with Gavin Reed, Jackie
Skarvellis, Susan Clark, Colin Gordon. Vampire arrives in
London to seek out the last members of the Ford family, ends
up in Carfax Abbey, à la Dracula.
The BODY DISAPPEARS WB 1941 71m. (The BLACK WIDOW)
D: D. Ross Lederman. SP: Scott Darling. Ref: V 12/3/41.
Pic: MadM 9:37. with Edward Everett Horton, Jane Wyman,
Jeffrey Lynn, Willie Best, Marguerite Chapman, Craig Stevens,
David Bruce, Ivan Simpson, DeWolf Hopper, Michael Ames,
Charles Halton, Natalie Schafer, Wade Boteler. A college pro-
fessor is perfecting a formula for making bodies invisible and
bringing the dead back to life.
BODY IS MISSING, The see WHO STOLE THE BODY
The BODY SNATCHER RKO 1945 77m. D: Robert Wise. P:
Val Lewton. SP: Carlos Keith, Philip MacDonald, from a story
by Robert Louis Stevenson. PH: Robert de Grasse. Mus: Roy
Webb. Art D: Albert D'Agostino, Walter F. Keller. Ref:
FIR'64. FM 10:26. COF 7:30. Pic: FM 11:12. with Boris
Karloff, Bela Lugosi, Henry Daniell, Rita Corday, Edith Atwater,
Robert Clarke, Russell Wade, Sharyn Moffett, Donna Lee. It's
ironic that the more well-known Lewtons (this one, CAT PEO-
PLE) are among his lesser ones. This has an interesting motif:
Death is indicated by sound suddenly choked off; but it's marred
by a weak co-plot and lines like "He taught me the mathematics
of surgery, but he couldn't teach me the poetry of medicine."
Karloff has another of his best villainous roles in a Lewton film.
The BODY SNATCHER (Mex) Internacional Cinematográfica 1956
(EL LADRON DE CADAVERES) D: Fernando Méndez. SP:
Méndez, Alejandro Verbitzky. PH: Victor Herrera. Mus:
Federico Ruiz. Art D: Gunther Gerszo. Ref: Indice. HM 3:17.
Pic: FM 9:18. 38:37. 57:16. with Columba Domínguez, Crox
Alvarado, Wolf Rubinski, Carlos Riquelme.
BODY SNATCHERS, The (book by Jack Finney) see INVASION OF
THE BODY SNATCHERS
BODY STEALERS, The see INVASION OF THE BODY STEALERS
The BOGEY WOMAN (F) Pathe 1909 7m. Ref: F Index 7/3/09.
The Bogey Woman turns kids into vegetables.
The BOGUS GHOST Kalem 1916 Ref: MPN 13:3433. Woman be-
lieved drowned becomes "mystic's spirit."

BOIA SCARLATTO, Il see BLOODY PIT OF HORROR, The
BOITE A MALICE, La see TRICK BOX, The
A BOLT FROM THE SKY Kalem 1913 18m. Ref: Bios 9/11/13.
  Scientist struck dead by fragment of meteorite.
The BOMB Lubin 1914 Ref: Lee. Super-bomb.
A BOMB WAS STOLEN (Rumanian) 1962 Studios Bucaresti 65m.
  (FURAT O BOMBA. S-A FURAT O BOMBA) SP,D: Ion Popescu-
  Gopo. Ref: M/TVM'62. Film Review 64/5. with Iurie Darie.
  Pieces of bomb have magical properties. Horror film (with
  Jekyll-Hyde theme) told in stills outside theatre playing "Mons
  Sex." Mainly uninspired, silly farce, with several inventive comic
  touches.
BOMBS FOR PEACE (Sp) 1959 Hispamex (BOMBAS PARA LA
  PAZ) D: Antonio Román. PH: Manuel Merino. SP: J. María
  Iglesias. Ref: Cine Espanol'59. with Fernando Fernán Gomez,
  Jalita Martinez, Jose Isbert, Susana Campos. A young chemist
  inherits the formula for making peace bombs and uses them at a
  political conference.
The BOOGIEMAN WILL GET YOU Col 1942 66m. D: Lew
  Landers. SP: Edwin Blum. Story: Paul Gangelin, Hal Fimberg,
  Robert Hunt. PH: Henry Freulich. Art D: Robert Peterson.
  Ref: FDY. Pic: COF-A:46. FM 7:22. FanMO 2:52. 6:15. FMO
  5:34. with Boris Karloff, Peter Lorre, Jeff Donnell, Larry
  Parks, Maude Eburne, Maxie Rosenbloom, Don Beddoe, Frank
  Puglia, George McKay. Mad doctor tries to create a superman.
  Some clever ribbing of standard horror-movie talk.
BOREI KAIBYO YASHIKI see BLACK CAT MANSION
BORMAN (I-F) Spettacolo-Saba/Radius 1966 Story,D: John Hus-
  ley. SP: Jack Savyam. PH: Bob Presley. Ref: Annuario. with
  Robert Kent, Liana Orfei, Dominique Boschero, Moa Thai, Paul
  Muller, Kitty Swan. Martin Borman lives and heads an organiza-
  tion "whose aim is to destroy most of manking leaving only a
  type of superman."
BORROWED FACE, The see LOST FACE, The
BOSQUE DE ANCINES, El see ANCINES WOODS, The
BOSQUE DEL LOBO, El see ANCINES WOODS, The
BOTAN-DORO see PEONIES AND STONE LANTERNS/TALE OF
  PEONIES AND STONE LANTERNS, A
The BOTTLE IMP Para 1917 60m. From "The Imp in the Bot-
  tle" by Robert Louis Stevenson. Ref: MPN 15:2194. with
  Sessue Hayakawa, Kehua Waipahu. Person damned who dies
  with bottle still in his possession.
BOTTLED UP (F) Pathe 1909 7m. Ref: F Index 5/29/09.
  Chemist uses fluid to liquify people.
BOWERY AT MIDNIGHT Mono 1942 63m. (BURIAL AT MID-
  NIGHT?) D: Wallace Fox. SP: Gerald Schnitzer. Story: Sam
  Robins. PH: Mack Stengler. Mus: Edward Kay. Art D: Dave
  Milton. P: Sam Katzman, Jack Dietz. Ref: DDC III:262. FDY.
  with Bela Lugosi, John Archer, Tom Neal, Wanda McKay, Dave
  O'Brien, Vince Barnett, Anna Hope, Wheeler Oakman, J. Farrell
  MacDonald. A chemical formula saves the people a gang's trigger
  man shoots.
The BOWERY BOYS MEET THE MONSTERS AA 1955 66m. D:

Edward Bernds. SP: Elwood Ulmann, Bernds. PH: Harry Neumann. Mus D: Marlin Skiles. SpFX: Augie Lohman. Makeup: Edward Polo. Ref: FanMo 4: 58. Pic: FM 19:73. with Huntz Hall, Leo Gorcey, Bernard Gorcey, Ellen Corby, Lloyd Corrigan, John Dehner, Paul Wexler ("vampire" man). Robot, haunted house, carnivorous plant, mad doctor, etc. Leo Gorcey's malapropisms are the sole attraction.

The BOY DETECTIVES (J) Toei 1959 color/scope 61m. (SHONEN TANTEIDAN) D: Eijiro Wakabayashi. Ref: FEFN 7/59. Group of highschool boys accidentally launched on "interplanetary rocket."

BOYS FROM BROOKLYN, The see BELA LUGOSI MEETS A BROOKLYN GORILLA

BOYS OF THE CITY see GHOST CREEPS, The

The BRAHMA DIAMOND AM&B 1909 19m. Ref: F Index 2/6/09. Mystic mirror, hypnosis used to recover diamond stolen from idol.

The BRAHMIN'S MIRACLE Pathe 1908 Ref: F Index 9/26/08. High priest turns mummy into maiden.

The BRAIN (B-W.G.) Governor/CCC 1962 83m. (VENGEANCE-Eng. EIN TOTER SUCHT SEINEN MORDER-G. OVER MY DEAD BODY) D: Freddie Francis. SP: Robert Stewart, Philip Mackie. From "Donovan's Brain" by Curt Siodmak. PH: Robert Huke. Mus: Ken Jones. Ref: COF-A:43. with Peter Van Eyck, Miles Malleson, Bernard Lee, Anne Heywood, Cecil Parker, Frank Forsyth, Allan Cuthbertson, Victor Brooks, Jack MacGowran, Siegfried Lowitz, Jeremy Spenser, Hans Neilsen. Scientist keeps dead tycoon's brain alive. Two or three very-well-staged, well-directed scenes highlight average shocker.

The BRAIN EATERS AI/Corinthian 1958 57m. (THE KEEPERS. THE BRAIN SNATCHERS. KEEPERS OF THE EARTH) D: Bruno VeSota. SP: Gordon Urquhart. PH: Larry Raimond. Mus: Tom Jonson. Art D: Bert Shomberg. P: Edwin Nelson. Ref: Orpheus 3:26. FM 2:23 FM-A'69: 35. with Nelson, Jody Fair, Leonard Nimoy, Alan Frost, Jack Hill, Joanna Lee. Parasites from inside the earth threaten mankind. Among the more interesting late-Fifties minor s-f films. Lines like "We have learned patience in 200 million years" and "brain eaters" that look like cupcakes with coconut-flake antennae.

The BRAIN FROM PLANET AROUS Howco Int'l 1957 70m. D: Nathan Hertz. SP: Ray Buffum. PH, P: Jacques Marquette. Mus: Walter Greene. Ref: HR 12/26/57. with John Agar, Joyce Meadows, Robert Fuller, Ken Terrell, Thomas B. Henry. Alien force takes over mind and body of scientist. The usual.

BRAIN OF BLOOD Hemisphere 1971 color 88m. D: Al Adamson. SP: Joe Van Rodgers, Kane W. Lynn. Ref: Boxo 8/9/71. with Kent Taylor, Grant Williams, Reed Hadley, John Bloom, Regina Carroll, Vicki Volante. "The vampires return to life!" Mad doctor transplants brain of ruler of Middle-Eastern nation.

BRAIN OF FRANKENSTEIN, The see ABBOTT AND COSTELLO MEET FRANKENSTEIN

BRAIN-SERUM Lubin 1909 Ref: LC. Lee.

BRAIN SNATCHERS, The see BRAIN EATERS, The

The BRAIN THAT WOULDN'T DIE AI 1963-60 71m. (THE
HEAD THAT WOULDN'T DIE) SP, D: Joseph Green. PH:
Stephen Hajnal. SpFX: Byron Baer. Makeup: George Fiala.
P: Rex Carlton. Ref: MMF 9:39. COF 7:49. with Jason
Evers, Virginia Leith, Adele Lamont. Pic: FM 19:21. A doc-
tor leaves the scene of an accident--with his fiancee's living
head. What follows is less plausible. Remarkably bad.
BRAIN TRANSPLANT see SECRET OF DR. CHALMERS, The
THE BRAINIAC (Mex) AI-TV /Cinematografica, A. B. S. A. 1961
85m. (EL BARON DEL TERROR) D: Chano Urueta. SP:
Adolpho Portillo. PH: Jose O. Ramos. Mus: G. C. Carrion.
Ref: Indice. Pic: FM 40:23. with Abel Salazar, Carmen
Montejo, Ariadne Welter, Rene Cardona, Ruben Rojo, Mauricio
Garces, Federico Curiel, German Robles. Sorcerer-turned-
monster responsible for literal brain drain. Execrable.
BRAINSNATCHER, The see MAN WHO LIVED AGAIN, The
BRAINSTORM WB 1965 114m. P, D: William Conrad. SP:
Mann Rubin. Story: Larry Marcus. PH: Sam Leavitt. Mus:
George Duning. Ref Boxo 5 /17/65: "Horror." FD 5/14/65:
"Chiller... Posing as a psychotic brings on a psychosis." with
Jeff Hunter, Anne Francis, Dana Andrews, Viveca Lindfors,
Michael Pate, Strother Martin, Pat Cardi.
BRAND OF EVIL Ess 1913 30m. Ref: MPW 18:835. Lee.
SP: Edward T. Lowe. D: H. Webster. with Thomas Commer-
ford. Hand that stole idol's eye withers.
BRAND OF SATAN Peerless-World 1917 55m. D: George
Archainbaud. SP: J. F. Looney. Ref: MPN 16:280. Lee.
with Montagu(e) Love. Strangler with split personality.
THE BRANDED FOUR Select 1920 serial 15 episodes D: Duke
Worne. Ref: CNW. Imagen. Pic: TBG. with Ben Wilson,
Neva Gerber, Joseph Girard, William Dyer. Children branded
at birth with mysterious marks that will only appear at
maturity; "ray of destruction. "
BRASIL ANO 2000 see BRAZIL YEAR 2000
BRANDNER KASPAR SCHAUT INS PARADIES see STRANGE
STORY OF BRANDNER KASPAR, The
The BRASS BOTTLE F Nat 1923 65m. D: Maurice Tourneur.
SP: Fred Myton, from the book by F. Anstey. PH:
Arthur Todd. Art D: Milton Menasco. Ref: AFI. FM
24: 77. with Ernest Torrence, Barbara La Marr, Roy
Collins (The Evil Eye, Cyclopean creature), Harry
Myers, Tully Marshall, Ford Sterling, Otis Harlan.
The BRASS BULLET Univ 1918 serial 18 episodes 8. The Mag
netic Rug. Remake: THE HAUNTED ISLAND (1928). D: Ben
Wilson. From "Pleasure Island" by Frank R. Adams. Ref:
CNW: "Chiller. " with Juanita Hansen, Jack Mulhall, Joseph W.
Girard.
The BRAVE LITTLE TAILOR Childhood /Cinecom Movielab color
Ad: ogre. Ref: S Union.
BRAVE ONE, The see BEAST OF HOLLOW MOUNTAIN, The
BRAZIL YEAR 2000 (Braz) Mapa Film 1969 color 95m.
(BRASIL ANO 2000) SP, D, P: Walter Lima, Jr. PH: Guido

Cosulich.   Ref: V 6/3/70.   M/TVM 8/69.   with Ancey Rocha,
Enio Goncalves, Helio Fernando.   Aftermath of World War III.
BREAKDOWN OF THE AEROMOBILES, The   (I) 1915 Ref: DDC
II:48. (LA PANNA DEGLI AEROMOBILI) with André Deed.
BRENN; HEXE, BRENN see MARK OF THE DEVIL
BRENNENDE GERICHT, Das see BURNING COURT, The
The BRIBE Victor (Univ) 1915 Ref: MPN 2/6/15. with Charles
Ogle, Mary Fuller. Girl made to steal under influence of hyp-
notism.
BRICK BRADFORD Col 1947 serial 15 episodes 2. Flight to
the Moon. 7. Into another Century. D: Spencer G. Bennet.
SP: George H. Plympton, Arthur Hoerl, Lewis Clay. PH: Ira H.
Morgan. Mus: Mischa Bakaleinikoff. P: Sam Katzman. Ref:
Barbour. SF Film. Showmen's 1/17/48. with Kane Richmond,
Rick Vallin, Linda Johnson, Pierre Watkin, Jack Ingram, John
Merton, Leonard Penn, Wheeler Oakman, Carol Forman, John
Hart, Helene Stanley, Nelson Leigh. "Time top," "Interceptor
Ray," anti-missile weapon; etc.
The BRIDE AND THE BEAST AA 1958 78m. Story, D, P: Adrian
Weiss. SP: Edward D. Wood, Jr. PH: Roland Price. Mus:
Les Baxter. Pic: FMO 1:35. with Lance Fuller, Charlotte
Austin, Johnny Roth, Slick Slavin, Jeanne Gerson, Steve Calvert.
Hunter finds out his bride was a gorilla in a former life. Stock
shots from "Man Eater of Kumaon."
BRIDE FROM HADES, The see TALE OF PEONIES AND STONE
LANTERNS, A
BRIDE OF FRANKENSTEIN Univ 1935 80m. (The RETURN OF
FRANKENSTEIN. FRANKENSTEIN LIVES AGAIN!) D: James
Whale. SP: William Hurlbut, John Balderston. PH: John Mes-
call. Mus: Franz Waxman. Mus D: Mischa Bakaleinikoff.
Based on characters in Mary Shelley's "Frankenstein." Art D:
Charles D. Hall. SpFX: John P. Fulton. Makeup: Jack Pierce.
Ed: Ted Kent, Maurice Pivar. P: Carl Laemmle, Jr. Sound:
Gilbert Kurland. Props: Kenneth Strickfaden. Ref: MMF. FM 1:33.
12:22. 46:76. Pic: FM 21:34. with Colin Clive, Boris Karloff,
Valerie Hobson, Elsa Lanchester, Ernest Thesiger, O. P.
Heggie, Dwight Frye, E. E. Clive, Una O'Connor, Douglas
Walton, Gavin Gordon, Mary Gordon, Tempe Piggott, Lucien
Prival, Grace Cunard, Rollo Lloyd, Walter Brennan, John Car-
radine, Neil Fitzgerald, Reginald Barlow, Ted Billings, Billy
Barty, Joan Woodbury, Monty Montague, Edward Piel, Sr.,
Josephine McKim. Though not a great movie, this is one of
the true originals of film history. Some scenes are badly mis-
calculated (e.g., the hermit) or routine (the forest), but unlike
Whale's FRANKENSTEIN, BRIDE doesn't date badly, if at all.
There is much bizarre comedy, and it's written and directed
with such mock-ghoulish gusto that it's almost exhilarating at
times.
The BRIDE OF MYSTERY Gold Seal 1914 40m. Ref: Bios 4/30/14.
MPW 19:678. Doctor brings apparently-dead, hypnotized girl to
life.
BRIDE OF THE ATOM see BRIDE OF THE MONSTER
BRIDE OF THE GORILLA Realart/Jack Broder 1951 76m. SP,D:

Curt Siodmak. PH: Charles Van Enger. Mus: Raoul Kraushaar. Art D: Frank Sylos(?). SpFX: Lee Zavitz. Ed: Francis D. Lyon. Ref: FDY. COF 7:11, 42. with Lon Chaney, Jr., Tom Conway, Barbara Payton, Raymond Burr, Paul Cavanagh, Giselle Werbisek, Woody Strode. Dumb horror movie. While you're waiting for Lon Chaney to turn into a wolf, Raymond Burr turns into a gorilla. Or does he? Who cares? Only for diehard ambiguity fans.

The BRIDE OF THE HAUNTED CASTLE Artistic/Pathe 1910 15m. Ref: Bios 6/23/10. 5/7/14. Bride trapped in castle encounters living skeleton which gives her a warning.

BRIDE OF THE MONSTER Banner/DCA 1956 67m. (BRIDE OF THE ATOM) P, D: Edward D. Wood, Jr. SP: Wood, Alex Gordon. Ref: FM 2:52 9:26. with Bela Lugosi, Tor Johnson, Ed Parker, William Benedict, Conrad Brooks, Loretta King. A mad scientist attempts to create a race of supermen. A veritable catalogue of cliche lines.

BRIDEGROOMS WANTED (India) 1935 Bhavnani SP, D: M. Bhavnani. Ref: Mov. Pic. Mo. 7/35. with Nargis, Fatty Prasad, S. Nayampally. Dream: "Dance of the ghosts"; "Dance of the witches, " who curse woman.

BRIDES OF BLOOD (Fili-U. S.) Hemisphere/Premier 1968 color 90m. (BRIDES OF DEATH. ORGY OF BLOOD. TERROR ON BLOOD ISLAND. BRIDES OF BLOOD ISLAND) D: Gerardo de Leon, Eddie Romero. Ref: COF 10:48. M/TVM 8/66. with John Ashley, Kent Taylor, Beverly Hills. Atomic testing responsible for mutant flora and fauna on South Pacific island.

BRIDES OF DR. JEKYLL, The see DR. ORLOFF'S MONSTER

BRIDES OF DRACULA (B) Univ/Hammer/Hotspur 1960 Technicolor 85m. D: Terence Fisher. SP: Jimmy Sangster, Peter Bryan, Edward Percy. Based on the character in "Dracula" by Bram Stoker. PH: Jack Asher. Mus: Malcolm Williamson. Art D: Bernard Robinson, Thomas Goswell. SpFX: Sydney Pearson. Makeup: Roy Ashton. Ref: FM 8:10. FFacts. Pic: FM 8:15. 9:11, 14. with Peter Cushing, Martita Hunt, Yvonne Monlaur, Freda Jackson, David Peel, Miles Malleson, Mona Washbourne, Andrée Melly, Michael Ripper. French teacher accidentally unleashes vampire on Transylvanian countryside. Some sharp bits but rather anemic overall.

The BRIDES OF FU MANCHU (B) 7A/Towers 1966 color 94m. D: Don Sharp. SP: Peter Welbeck. Based on characters created by Sax Rohmer. PH: Ernest Steward. Mus: Johnny Douglas. Art D: Frank White. Makeup: George Partleton. Ref: MMF. MMania 3:54. with Christopher Lee, Douglas Wilmer, Marie Versini, Heinz Drache, Howard Marion Crawford, Tsai Chin, Carole Gray, Harald Leipnitz, Roger Hanin, Rupert Davies. Fu Manchu attempts to rule the world with a sound wave.

The BRIDGE OF TIME Selig 1915 35m. Ref: MPN 10/16/15. MPW 26:323. Soul returns to body of wicked ancestor.

The BRIGHTON STRANGLER RKO 1945 67m. D: Max Nosseck. SP: Nosseck, Arnold Phillips. PH: J. Roy Hunt. Mus D: C. Bakaleinikoff. Art D: Albert D'Agostino. SpFX: Vernon L. Walker. Mus: Leigh Harline. Ref: FDY. with John Loder, June

Duprez, Rose Hobart, Miles Mander, Ian Wolfe, Gilbert Emery,
Matthew Boulton. Leading actor in a horror play assumes his
character's homicidal traits. Finale finds an unusual way to stop
a murder.

BRING ME THE VAMPIRE (Mex) AI-TV/Clasa 1965 (ECHENME
AL VAMPIRO. LA CASA DE LOS ESPANTOS?) D: Alfredo B.
Cravenna. SP: Alfredo Ruanova. PH: F. Colin. Ref: RVB.
Lee. M Bee. FM 31:18. with Carlos Riquelme, Maria
Eugenia San Martin, Hector Godoy, Mantequilla, Pascual Garcia
Pena, Ramon Bugarini. Heirs to fortune must spend time in
haunted castle. One, maybe two laughs.

The BROTHERHOOD OF SATAN Col 1971 Technicolor 92m. D:
Bernard McEveety. SP: William Welch. Story: Sean Mac-
Gregor. PH: J. A. Morril. Mus: J. Mendoza-Nava. Ref:
V 4/28/71. with Strother Martin, L. Q. Jones, Charles Bate-
man, Anna Capri, Alvy Moore. Witchcraft; "prince of dark-
ness"; supernatural force that takes over small town in New
Mexico.

BROTHERS GRIMM, The (by H. Gerstner) see WONDERFUL
WORLD OF THE BROTHERS GRIMM, The

BRUCE GENTRY Col 1949 serial 15 episodes D: Spencer G.
Bennet, Thomas Carr. SP: George H. Plympton, Joseph F.
Poland, Lewis Clay. PH: Ira H. Morgan. Mus: Mischa
Bakaleinikoff. P: Sam Katzman. Ref: Barbour. with Tom Neal,
Tristram Coffin, Eddie Parker, Judy Clark, Forrest Taylor,
Hugh Prosser, Ralph Hodges, Jack Ingram, Terry Frost, Dale
Van Sickel, Charles King, Stephen Carr. Mysterious discs
menace the world.

BRUDERGRIMM, Die see WONDERFUL WORLD OF THE
BROTHERS GRIMM, The

BRUJA, La see WITCH, The (1956)

BRUJA SIN ESCOBA, Una see WITCH WITHOUT A BROOM, A

The BRUTE Champion 1912 Ref: MPW'12:132. "The Grim
Reaper" "absorbs" a drunkard's soul.

BRUTE FORCE Biog 1912 30m. Ref: MPN 10/9/15 (reissue).
Dream: Cave-man days.

The BRUTE MAN PRC--Univ 1946 60m. D: Jean Yarbrough.
SP: M. Coates Webster, Dwight V. Babcock, George Bricker.
with Rondo Hatton, Tom Neal, Jane Adams, Jan Wiley. Pic:
TBG. Hideously scarred by acid, a football player becomes a
psychopathic killer; Hatton as "The Creeper."

The BUBBLE Oboler 1967 112m. SP, D, P: Arch Oboler. In
4-D. Ref: Boxo 1/23/67. with Michael Cole, Deborah Walley,
Johnny Desmond, Virginia Gregg, Victor Perrin, Olan Soule.
Citizens of small town trapped inside huge dome.

BUCK ROGERS Univ 1939 serial 12 episodes (DESTINATION
SATURN--'65 feature version. PLANET OUTLAWS--'53 feature)
D: Ford Beebe, Saul Goodkind. SP: Norman Hall, Ray Trampe.
PH: Jerry Ash. Ref: SM 5:38. FanMo 1:64. 5:37. with Buster
Crabbe, Tom Steele, Roy Barcroft, Constance Ford, C. Mon-
tague Shaw, Jackie Moran, Anthony Warde, Jack Mulhall,
Carleton Young, Dave Sharpe, Eddie Parker, Kenne Duncan,
Guy Usher, Henry Brandon, Wheeler Oakman, Reed Howes,

68

Philip Ahn. Ray guns; "Nirvano" gas that causes suspended
animation; invisible rays; "Filament Ray" helmets that change
humans to robots; Zuggs, sub-human zombies; etc.
A BUCKET OF BLOOD AI/Alta Vista 1959 65m. P, D: Roger
Corman. SP: Charles Griffith. PH: Jacques Marquette. Mus:
Fred Katz. Art D: Daniel Haller. Ref: Clarens. Pic: FM 7:15.
with Dick Miller, Julian Burton, Barboura Morris, Anthony Car-
bone, Ed Nelson, Judy Bamber, Burt Convy. Fairly delightful
black comedy until the plot becomes predictable, the characters
unsympathetic. Sculptor covers dead cat with clay, becomes
more ambitious.
BUCKET OF BLOOD, A see TELL TALE HEART, The (1934)
BUCKLIGE UND DIE TANZERIN, Der see HUNCHBACK AND THE
DANCER, The
The BUDDA'S CURSE Lux 1910 Ref: Bios 1/12/11. Indian priest
appears magically, curses household.
BUDDHAS LEBENDE see LIVING BUDDHAS
BUESCHSE DER PANDORA, Die see PANDORA'S BOX
BUHNE FREI FUR MARIKA see STAGE IS CLEARED FOR
MARIKA, The
BULLDOG DRUMMOND (by Sapper) see SOME GIRLS DO
BULLDOG DRUMMOND AT BAY (B) Rep 1937 63m. D: Norman
Lee. SP: Patrick Kirwan, James Parrish, from a story by
H. C. McNeil. PH: Walter Harvey. Ref: NYT. FDY. with
Victor Jory, John Lodge, Dorothy Mackaill, Claud(e) Allister,
Richard Bird. Robot plane's inventor kidnapped.
BULLDOG DRUMMOND COMES BACK Para 1937 59m. D: Louis
King. SP: Edward T. Lowe, from H. C. (Sapper) McNeil's
"The Female of the Species." PH: William C. Mellor. Mus:
Boris Morros. Art D: Hans Dreier, Franz Bachelin. Ref: FDY.
MFB'37. with John Howard, John Barrymore, Louise Campbell,
Reginald Denny, E. E. Clive, J. Carrol Naish, Helen Freeman,
Zeffie Tilbury, John Sutton, Rita Page. "Haunted house" with a
gas-filled chamber.
BULLDOG DRUMMOND ESCAPES Para 1937 67m. D: James
Hogan. SP: Edward T. Lowe. Story: Gerard Fairlie. Based
on the character created by H. C. McNeil. PH: Victor Milner.
Ref: FD. with Ray Milland, Sir Guy Standing, Heather Angel,
Porter Hall, Reginald Denny, E. E. Clive, Fay Holden, Walter
Kingsford, Clyde Cook. "Eerie manor house....atmosphere is
purposely fog-filled....chills and thrills."
BULLDOG DRUMMOND'S PERIL Para 1938 66m. D: James
Hogan. SP: Stuart Palmer, from "The Third Round" by H. C.
McNeil. PH: Harry Fischbeck. Art D: Hans Dreier, Robert
Odell. Mus D: Boris Morros. Assoc P: Stuart Walker. Ref:
FD. HM 9:20. with John Barrymore, John Howard, Louise Camp-
bell, Reginald Denny, E. E. Clive, Porter Hall, Elizabeth Pat-
terson, Nydia Westman, Halliwell Hobbes, Matthew Boulton,
Zeffie Tilbury, Clyde Cook. Synthetic diamond stolen.
BULLDOG DRUMMOND'S SECRET POLICE Para 1939 56m.
D: James Hogan. SP: Garnett Weston, from "Temple Tower" by
H. C. (Sapper) McNeil. PH: Merritt Gerstad. Ref: FD 4/12/39.
MFB'39:113. with John Howard, Heather Angel, Reginald Denny,

H. B. Warner, E. E. Clive, Elizabeth Patterson, Leo G. Car-
roll, Forrester Harvey, Clyde Cook. Castle with chamber of
horrors, subterranean caverns, secret passages.
BULLDOG DRUMMOND'S THIRD ROUND see THIRD ROUND, The
BUMBLES' DIMINISHER Univ 1913 9m. Ref: Bios 9/11/13.
 Powder from novelty shop "reduces everything."
BUMKE DISCOVERS THE TURNING MICROBE Elite 1913 11m.
 Ref: Bios 6/12/13. Bumke concocts a formula with the microbe
 that makes tops spin and wheels revolve.
BUMPKIN'S PATENT SPYOPTICON (B) Cricks & Martin 1910
 8m. Ref: Biox 11/17/10. Invention in a "Fun City" enables
 you "to see your friend as others see him."
BUNCO SQUAD RKO 1950 67m. D: Herbert I. Leeds. SP:
 George Callahan. PH: Henry Freulich. Mus: Paul Sawtell.
 Art D: Albert D'Agostino, Walter Keller. From a story by
 Reginald Taviner. with Robert Sterling, Joan Dixon, Ricardo
 Cortez, Douglas Fowley, Elisabeth Risdon, Marguerite
 Churchill, John Kellogg, Robert Bice, Dante. Woman makes
 "contact" with dead son at seance.
BUNTER'S PATENT BELLOWS (B) Cricks & Martin 1910 7m.
 Ref: Bios 9/8/10. Bellows cause miniature cyclones.
BURGLARY BY AIRSHIP Gaum 1910 7m. Ref: Bios 3/3/10.
 Burglar's airship has magnet attached to bottom; lifts safes,
 etc.
BURIAL AT MIDNIGHT see BOWERY AT MIDNIGHT
BURIED ALIVE (by E. A. Poe) see RAVEN, The (1912)
BURN, WITCH, BURN (B) AI/Independent Artists 1962 90m.
 (NIGHT OF THE EAGLE-Eng) D: Sidney Hayers. SP: George
 Baxt, Richard Matheson, Charles Beaumont, from "Conjure
 Wife" by Fritz Leiber. PH: Reginald Wyer. Mus: William
 Alwyn, Muir Mathieson. Art D: Jack Shampan. Ref: Clarens.
 with Janet Blair, Peter Wyngarde, Margaret Johnston, Anthony
 Nicholls, Colin Gordon, Kathleen Byron, Reginald Beckwith.
 Nice adaptation of the first half of the novel. Interesting black
 magic alternates with unfortunate melodramatic tendencies.
BURN, WITCH, BURN (by A. A. Merritt) see DEVIL DOLL (1936)
The BURNING COURT (F-I-W.G.) 1961 Int'l Prods/Comacico/
 Taurus/UFA 108m. (LA CHAMBRE ARDENTE-F. I PECCA-
 TORI DELLA FORESTA NERA-I. DAS BRENNENDE GERICHT-
 G. THE CURSE AND THE COFFIN--Eng) P,D: Julien Duvivier.
 SP: Duvivier, Charles Spaak. ('63-Trans-Lux-U.S.) From the
 novel by John Dickson Carr. PH: Roger Fellous. Art D: Schatz.
 Ref: MFB'65:38. FM 26:10. COF 4:4. with Nadja Tiller, Jean-
 Claude Brialy, Edith Scob, Antoine Balpetre, Claude Rich. Witch
 curses descendants of family of castle.
BURNT ROSE, The see RAVAGED
BUS CONDUCTOR, The (story by E. F. Benson) see DEAD OF
 NIGHT
BUSTER'S SPOOKS Univ 1929 25m. D: S. Newfield. Ref: Lee.
 FD. Deserted house, etc.
BUT YOU WERE DEAD see VERONIQUE'S LONG NIGHT
The BUTCHER'S DREAM Lux 1909 9m. Ref: Bios 9/30/09.
 Butcher dreams animals butcher him.

BY FOOT, HORSE AND SPUTNIK see DOG, A MOUSE AND A SPUTNIK, A

BY RADIUM'S RAYS Gold Seal (Univ) 1914 36m. Ref: Bios 6/18/14. Operation restores woman's reason.

BY ROCKET TO THE MOON see GIRL IN THE MOON

BY THE HOUSE THAT JACK BUILT Imp/Independent 1911 Ref: MPW'11: 730. Hag's sleeping potion causes girl's soul to leave her body; wicked queen of the gnomes has the heart of a prince stolen.

BY WHOSE HAND Col 1927 68m. D: Walter Lang. SP: Marion Orth. PH: J. O. Taylor. Ref: FD 11/27/27. MPH 1/7/28. with Ricardo Cortez, Eugenia Gilbert, Tom Dugan, Edgar Washington Blue, Lillian(ne) Leighton. Comedy-mystery; house suspected of being haunted.

BYAKU FUJIN NO YOREN see MADAME WHITE SNAKE

BYAKUYA NO YOJO see TEMPTRESS, The

CABEZA DE PANCHO VILLA, La see HEAD OF PANCHO VILLA, The

CABEZA VIVIENTE, LA see LIVING HEAD, The

CABIN IN THE SKY MGM 1943 100m. D: Vincente Minnelli. SP: Joseph Schrank. Based on the play by Lynn Root; lyrics by John Latouche, music by Vernon Duke. Added music and lyrics by E. Y. Harburg and Harold Arlen. PH: Sidney Wagner. Art D: Cedric Gibbons. P: Arthur Freed. Ref: V 2/10/43. with Ethel Waters, Eddie Anderson, Lena Horne, Louis Armstrong, Rex Ingram, Duke Ellington, Mantan Moreland, Willie Best, Butterfly McQueen. Lucifer, Jr., after man's soul.

The CABINET OF CALIGARI Fox 1962 104m. (THE CABINET OF DR. CALIGARI) P,D: Roger Kay. SP: Robert Bloch. CinemaScope PH: John Russell. Mus: Gerald Fried. Sets: Howard Bristol. Exec P: Robert Lippert. Ref: Orpheus 3:26. COF 2:15. Pic. FM 19:10. 21:12. with Dan O'Herlihy, Glynis Johns, Dick Davalos, Vicki Trickett, J. Pat O'Malley, Estelle Winwood, Lawrence Dobkin. Woman finds she is a prisoner in an old mansion.

The CABINET OF DR. CALIGARI (G) Decla-Bioscop/Goldwyn 1919 81m. (DES KABINETT EDS DR. CALIGARI) D: Robert Wiene. SP: Carl Mayer, Hans Janowitz (Fritz Lang). PH: Willy Hameister. Art D: Hermann Warm, Walter Reimann, Walter Röhrig. Name from "Unknown Letters" by Stendhal. P: Erich Pommer. Ref: SilentFF. FD 2/13/37: Planned remake by Feher. FM 13:6. COF 7:29. 8:36. Pic: FM 7:18.16:28.21:12. with Werner Krauss, Conrad Veidt, Lil Dagover, Rudolf Klein-Rogge, Friedrich Feher, Hans Heinz von Twardowski, Rudolf Lettinger. Somnambulist commits murders at hypnotist's bidding. The sets are all, and that's not enough.

The CACTUS CURE Arrow 1925 60m. D: Ward Hayes. Ref: AFI. with Dick Hatton, Yakima Canutt, Wilbur McGaugh, Marilyn Mills. Western. "Haunted" house.

The CAGE (F) Edic 1962 85m. (LA CAGE. MAMY WATTA)
D: Robert Darène. SP: P. Tristan, P. Maury, C. Garnier.
Adap: Claude Desailly. Dial: P. Andreota. PH: Jacques Lang.
Ref: M/TVM 5/63. Lee. La Prod. Cin. Fr. 11/62. with Jean
Servais, Marina Vlady, Alain Bouvette. African hex causes doc-
tor to see apparition of dead wife.
CAGE OF DOOM see TERROR FROM THE YEAR 5000
CAGLIOSTRO (F) Pathe Freres 1910 20m. From Dumas père.
Ref: SilentFF. DDC III:502. Bios 4/21/10. with Hélène du
Montel. Girl under Cagliostro's hypnotic spell.
CAGLIOSTRO (Austrian-G?) Micco-Film 1920 (DER GRAF VON
CAGLIOSTRO) D: Reinhold Schünzel. SP: Schünzel, Robert
Liebmann. PH: Karl Hoffman. Art D: O. F. Werndorff. Ref:
Osterr. EncicDS III:1509. with Conrad Veidt, Schünzel, Anita
Berber, Karl Götz.
CAGLIOSTRO (F-I?) 1928 Ref: DDC II:57. III:34. with Renée
Héribel, Rina De Liguoro.
CAGLIOSTRO (G) 1929 D: Richard Oswald. Ref: DDC III:529.
Encic DS VII:1421: "Fantasmagorico." Pic: DDC I:1. with
Alfred Abel.
CAGLIOSTRO see BLACK MAGIC (1948)
CAIN ADOLESCENTE (Sp?) D: Roman Chalbaud. A widow is
under the evil spell of a black magician in a poor quarter of
Venezuela. Ref: MMF 9:18.
CAKE IN THE SKY (I) Luce 1970 D: Lino Del Fra. Ref:
M/TVM 10/70:25. with Paolo Villaggio, Francesco Mule.
Scientist develops cake-shaped aircraft.
CALAVERA NEGRA, La see BLACK SKULL, The
CALDI AMORI DI UNA MINORENNE, I see AGAIN
CALEB POWERS see WITCHING HOUR, The (1916)
CALINO'S NEW INVENTION (F) 1912 Gaum 5m. D: Jean
Durand. Ref: SilentFF. with M. Migé. Invention electrifies
people in house.
CALL FROM THE DEAD Than 1915 15m. Ref: MPW 25:1910.
Corpse revenges murder.
CALLING DR. DEATH Univ 1943 63m. (Inner Sanctum series)
D: Reginald LeBorg. SP: Edward Dein. PH: Virgil Miller.
Mus: Paul Sawtell. SpPH: John P. Fulton. Art D: John B.
Goodman, Ralph M. DeLacy. Ref: Clarens. FDY. ModM
2:71. Pic: COF 6:25. with Lon Chaney, Jr., Ramsay Ames,
J. Carrol Naish, Holmes Herbert, David Bruce, Fay Helm, Lisa
Golm, George Eldredge. Man thinks he may have killed his wife
during bout of amnesia.
CALLING PAUL TEMPLE (B) Nettlefold Studios 1948 D:
Maclean Rogers. SP: A. R. Rawlinson, Kathleen Butler,
Francis Durbridge, from the radio serial by F. Durbridge.
D of PH: Geoffrey Faithfull. Cameraman: Arthur Grant. Mus
sc & d: Percival Mackey. Art D: C. H. Gilbert. Ass't D:
John Moxey. Ref: Brit. Fm. Ybk. '49:237. with John Bentley,
Dinah Sheridan, Alan Wheatley, Merle Tottenham, Celia Lipton.
Oriental doctor hypnotizes woman not to reveal secret; mystery.
CALTIKI--THE IMMORTAL MONSTER (I-U.S.) AA/Galatea-Bruno
Vailati 1959('61-U.S.) 75m. D: Robert Hampton (Riccardo

Freda); (Eng. version) Lee Kresel. (CALTIKI, THE UNDYING MONSTER) SP: Filippo Sanjust. PH: John Foam (Mario Bava). Mus: Roman Vlad. Ref: Orpheus 3:29. FM 9:15. 10:42. with Daniela Rocca, John Merivale, Didi Sullivan (aka Didi Perego), Giacomo Rossi-Stuart, Arturo Dominici. Monster emerges from subterranean pool in ancient Mayan city. Rather tame after an eerie beginning.

CANADIAN MOUNTIES VS. ATOMIC INVADERS Rep 1953 serial (MISSILE BASE AT TANIAK--'66 feature) D: Franklin Adreon. SP: Ronald Davidson. PH: John MacBurnie. SpFX:Howard and Theodore Lydecker. Ref: Barbour. Don Glut. with Bill Henry, Susan Morrow, Dale Van Sickel, Arthur Space, Harry Lauter, Tom Steele, Pierre Watkin, Gayle Kellogg. Foreign agents plan to launch missiles at U.S. from rocket centers in Canada.

CANDLES AT NINE (B) Brit. Nat'l-Anglo-American 1944 86m. D: John Harlow. Ref: COF 8:36. MPH. with Jessie Matthews, John Stuart, Beatrix Lehmann, Hugh Dempster, Winifred Shotter, John Salew. Murdered uncle's niece must spend month in his eerie mansion to inherit it; "spooky hands...ghostly shadows."

CANNIBAL ORGY see SPIDER BABY

The CANTERVILLE GHOST MGM 1944 95m. D: Jules Dassin. SP: Edwin Blum. From Oscar Wilde's story. PH: Robert Planck. Art D: Cedric Gibbons, Edward Carfagno. Ref: FDY. with Charles Laughton, Robert Young, Margaret O'Brien, Peter Lawford, Frank Faylen, Rags Ragland, William Gargan, Reginald Owen, Una O'Connor, Donald Stuart, Elisabeth Risdon, Lumsden Hare, Mike Mazurki, Marc Cramer. Ghost haunts old English castle.

CANTO DE LA SIRENA, El see SONG OF THE SIREN, The

The CAPE CANAVERAL MONSTERS CCM 1960 69m. SP, D: Phil Tucker. PH: W. Merle Connell. Mus sc: Guenther Kauer. Prod Des: Ken Letvin. Ref: RVB. with Katherine Victor, Jason Johnson, Scott Peters, Linda Connell. The scriptwriter was desperate: Common scientific terminology is passed off as clever dialogue. Candidate for worst musical score (along with BLOODTHIRSTY BUTCHERS, TORTURE DUNGEON, and I CON-FESS).

CAPTAIN AMERICA Rep 1944 serial 15 episodes (RETURN OF CAPTAIN AMERICA) D: John English, Elmer Clifton. SP: Royal Cole, Ronald Davidson, Basil Dickey, Jesse Duffy, Harry Fraser, Grant Nelson, Joseph Poland, PH: John MacBurnie. Mus: Mort Glickman. SpFX: Howard and Theodore Lydecker. Ref: Barbour. Pic: M&H 2:19. with Dick Purcell, Lorna Gray, Lionel Atwill, Charles Trowbridge, Russell Hicks, George J. Lewis, John Davidson, Frank Reicher, Hugh Sothern, Jay Novello, John Bagni, John Hamilton, Robert Frazer. One of the more interesting characteristics of Republic serials is the remarkable mucilaginous property of the actors' hats, which remain on in brawls, chases, cataclysms, and the presence of ladies.

CAPTAIN CLEGG see NIGHT CREATURES

CAPTAIN FROM TOLEDO (SP-I) Petruka-General Peron/Italcine

1966 color 102m. (LA MUERTE SE LLAMA MYRIAM. L'UOMO
DI TOLEDO. THE MAN FROM TOLEDO. DEATH IS CALLED
MYRIAM) D: Eugenio Martin. SP: Martin, H. Moretti. PH:
F. Vila. Mus: F. Lavagnino. Art D: E. Constantini. Ref: MFB
'68:160. SpCinema'67. Annuario. with Stephen Forsyth, Ann
Smyrner, Karl Mohner, Norma Bengell, José Calvo, Ivan Desny.
Secret weapon, "Greek Fire."
CAPTAIN MEPHISTO AND THE TRANSFORMATION MACHINE see
MANHUNT OF MYSTERY ISLAND
CAPTAIN MIDNIGHT Col 1942 serial 15 episodes D: James W.
Horne. SP: Basil Dickey, George H. Plympton, Jack Stanley,
Wyndham Gittens. From the radio serial. PH: James S. Brown,
Jr. Ref: Barbour. Lee. with Dave O'Brien, Dorothy Short,
James Craven, Guy Wilkerson, Joseph Girard, Ray Teal, George
Pembroke, Bryant Washburn. Pic: M&H 1:21. COF 3:40. Bor-
derline s-f.
CAPTAIN NEMO AND THE UNDERWATER CITY (B) MGM/Omnia
1969 Metrocolor/scope 106m. D: James Hill. SP: Pip Baker,
Jane Baker, R. Wright Campbell. Based on the character cre-
ated by Jules Verne. PH: Alan Hume. Mus: Walter Stott. Ref:
MFB'70:11. with Robert Ryan, Chuck Connors, Nanette Newman,
Luciana Paluzzi, Bill Fraser, Kenneth Connor, Allan Cuthbertson.
City produces gold as a byproduct of apparatus that supplies
oxygen.
CAPTAIN SIN(D)BAD MGM 1963 color 81m. D: Byron Haskin.
SP: Samuel B. West, Harry Relis. PH: Gunter Senftleben, Eugen
Shuftan. Mus: Michel Michelet. Art D: Werner & Isabelle
Schlichting. SpFX: Lee Zavitz, Augie Lohman. SpPHFX: Tom
Howard. P: Frank & Herman King. Ref: FFacts. with Guy
Williams, Pedro Armendariz, Geoffrey Toone, Abraham Sofaer,
Heidi Bruehl, Rolf Wanka. Giant mailed fist, giant birds, Scylla
monster, etc.
CAPTAIN ULTRA (J) Toei 1967 color D: Koichi Takemoto.
Ref: M/TVM 7/67. with Yuki Shirono, H. Nakata. Spacemen
vs. earthmen.
CAPTAIN VIDEO Col 1951 serial 15 episodes D: Spencer G.
Bennet, Wallace A. Grissell. SP: Royal Cole, Sherman L. Lowe,
Joseph Poland, George H. Plympton. From the TV series,
"Captain Video and His Video Rangers." PH: Fayte Browne.
SpFX: Jack Erickson. P: Sam Katzman. Ref: FM 15:22. FanMo
5:37. 6:42,50. Pic: MMania 3:32. FM 12:20. FanMo 1:14. with
Judd Holdren, Larry Stewart, George Eldredge (Tobor), Gene
Roth, Don C. Harvey, William Fawcett, Jack Ingram, I. Stanford
Jolley, Skelton Knaggs. Robots (from PHANTOM EMPIRE); the
Ozonator; the Isotopic Radiation Curtain; the Mu-Ray Camera; the
Disintegrator Ray Cannon; the Opticon Scillometer; etc.
CAPTIVE WILD WOMAN Univ 1943 60m. D: Edward Dmytryk.
SP: Griffin Jay, Henry Sucher. Story: Ted Fithian, Neil P.
Varnick. PH: George Robinson. Mus: H. J. Salter. Art D:
John B. Goodman. Sequels: JUNGLE WOMAN, JUNGLE CAP-
TIVE. Ref: HM 5:42. FM 2:20. 81:6-11. STI 5:19: footage from
The BIG CAGE. Pic: FM 20:21. with John Carradine, Acqua-
netta, Milburn Stone, Evelyn Ankers, Lloyd Corrigan, Fay Helm,

Martha MacVicar (or Vickers), Paul Fix, Vince Barnett, Ed
Peil (or Piel), Sr., Fern Emmett, Grant Withers, Harry Hol-
man, Anthony Warde. Mad scientist turns orang-utang into
girl. Reputedly not as bad as the title might lead you to believe,
actually it is. Ridiculous ideas and dialogue, many plot incon-
sistencies. The were-ape makup is all that's original.
CAPTIVE WOMEN RKO 1953 65m. (3000 A.D. /1000 YEARS
FROM NOW--'57 reissue) D: Stuart Gilmore. SP, P: Aubrey
Wisberg, Jack Pollexfen. PH: Paul Ivano. Mus: Charles Koff.
Ref: MFB'53:76. with Robert Clarke, Margaret Field, William
Schallert, Gloria Saunders, Ron Randell, Stuart Randall, Paula
Dorety. Barbarians and mutants in New York City in the 29th
Century A.D. Terrible.
CAPTURING THE NORTH POLE (B) Urban-Eclipse 1909 7m.
Ref: MPW'09:853. Baron Munchausen; "Spirit of the North";
hypnotism, etc.
CAPURCITA Y PULGARCITO CONTRA LOS MONSTRUOS see
TOM THUMB AND RED RIDING HOOD VS. THE MONSTERS
CARA DEL TERROR, La see FACE OF TERROR, The
The CARDBOARD BOX (B) Stoll 1923 30m. (Last Adventures
of Sherlock Holmes series) From "The Adventure of the Card-
board Box" by Sir Arthur Conan Doyle. Art D: Walter W.
Murton. Ref: SilentFF. with Eille Norwood, Hubert Willis, Tom
Beaumont. Mystery of a pair of human ears sent to a woman.
CARDS ON THE TABLE see ATTACK OF THE ROBOTS
CAREER OF A COMET (by J. Verne) see VALLEY OF THE
DRAGONS
CARMILLA (by S. Le Fanu) see BLOOD AND ROSES/TERROR IN
THE CRYPT/VAMPYR/VAMPIRE LOVERS, The
CARNAGE see CORRUPTION
CARNIVAL OF SINNERS see DEVIL'S HAND, The (1942)
CARNIVAL OF SOULS Herts-Lion/Harcourt 1962 80m. P, D:
Herk Harvey. SP: John Clifford. PH: Maurice Prather. Mus:
Gene Moore. Ref: MFB'67:59. with Candace Hilligoss, Harvey,
Frances Feist, Sidney Berger. Girl haunted by shadowy presence
of a man. Atmospheric; builds a little too slowly.
CAROLINA CANNONBALL Rep 1955 73m. D: Charles Lamont.
SP: Barry Shipman. Story: Frank Gill, Jr. PH: Reggie Lanning.
Mus: R. Dale Butts. SpFX: Howard and Theodore Lydecker.
Ref: TVG. withJudy Canova, Andy Clyde, Ross Elliott, Sig
Ruman, Jack Kruschen, Emil Sitka. The first atomic-powered
guided missile lands near a ghost town.
The CARPATHIAN CASTLE (Rumanian) 1957 D: Alberto Cavalcanti.
From "The Castle of the Carpathians" by Jules Verne. Ref:
DDC I: 337. Lee. Weird manifestations around castle explained
scientifically.
CARRY ON SCREAMING (B) Sigma III/Anglo 1966 color 97m.
(SCREAMING. CARRY ON, VAMPIRE) D: Gerald Thomas. SP:
Talbot Rothwell. PH: Alan Hume. Makeup: Geoff Rodway. P:
Peter Rogers. Ref: FM 23. 42:62-71. COF 12:50. with Ken-
neth Williams, Harry H. Corbett, Dennis Blake (the mummy
Rubbatiti), Tom Clegg (Odbodd, Frankenstein-monster-like),
Fenella Fielding (vampire-like Valeria), Joan Sims, Bernard

Bresslaw, Charles Hawtrey, Jon Pertwee. A mad doctor experiments in petrifying things.

CARTAS BOCA ARRIBA see ATTACK OF THE ROBOTS

The CARTER CASE Olive 1919 serial 15 episodes (THE CRAIG KENNEDY SERIAL) D: Donald MacKenzie. From the "Craig Kennedy" stories by Arthur B. Reeve. Ref: Lee. CNW. TBG. with Marguerite Marsh, Ethel Terry, Louie R. Wolheim. 1. The Phosgene Bullett. 2. The Vacuum Room. 7. The Nervagraph. 12. The X-Ray Detective. Invisible plane.

CARTES SUR TABLE see ATTACK OF THE ROBOTS

CASA DE LOS ESPANTOS, La see BRING ME THE VAMPIRE?

CASA DEL TERROR, La see FACE OF THE SCREAMING WEREWOLF

CASA EMBRUJADA, La see CURSE OF THE CRYING WOMAN, The

The CASE OF BECKY 1915 D: Frank Reicher. Ref: MPW'15:2252. FIR'65. with Blanche Sweet, Carlyle Blackwell, James Neill. Hypnotist imposes dual personality on girl.

The CASE OF BECKY 1921 Para 65m. D: Chester M. Franklin. SP: J. Clarkson Miller, from the play by Edward Locke. PH: George Folsey. Ref: NYT 10/10/21. AFI. with Constance Binney, Glenn Hunter, Montagu Love, Frank McCormack. Dual personality.

CASE OF CHARLES DEXTER WARD, The (by H. P. Lovecraft) see HAUNTED PALACE, The

CASE OF POISONS, The see POISON AFFAIR, The

CASE OF THE FRIGHTENED LADY see CRIMINAL AT LARGE/ FRIGHTENED LADY, The

CASE OF THE MISSING BRIDES see CORPSE VANISHES, The

The CASE OF THE TWO BEAUTIES (Sp-G) Montana-Edificio/ Aguila 1968 color/scope 92m. (EL CASO DE LAS DOS BELLEZAS) SP,D: Jesus Franco. Story: K.-H. Manchen. PH: Jorge Herrero. Mus: F. G. Morcillo. Art D: C. Viudes. Ref: SpCinema'69. with Janine Reynaud, Rossana Yanni, Adrian Hoven, Michel(e) Lemoine. Painter's servant, Morpho is a "strange being, half man half gorilla."

CASEY'S JUMPING TOOTHACHE 1909 4m. Ref: MPW'09:97. Man dreams dentist's gas causes him to float in air.

CASINO ROYALE (B) Col 1967 Technicolor 131m. D: Val Guest, Ken Hughes, John Huston, Robert Parrish, Joe McGrath. SP: Wolf Mankowitz, John Law, Michael Sayers. Suggested by the novel by Ian Fleming, with a character from "Frankenstein" by Mary Shelley. PH: Jack Hildyard. Add'l PH: John Wilcox, Nicolas Roeg. Mus sc & D: Burt Bacharach. SpFX: Cliff Richardson, Roy Whybrow. SpMatteWork: Les Bowie. Ref: FFacts. COF 12:50. with Peter Sellers, Ursula Andress, David Niven, Woody Allen, Joanna Pettet, Orson Welles, Daliah Lavi, Deborah Kerr, William Holden, Charles Boyer, Jean-Paul Belmondo, George Raft, John Huston, Terence Cooper, Barbara Bouchet, Peter O'Toole, Kurt Kasznar, Gabriella Licudi, Alexandra Bastedo, Jackie Bisset, Anna Quayle, Stirling Moss, Tracy Crisp, Colin Gordon, Bernard Cribbins, Tracy Reed, Percy Herbert. Flying Saucer.

CASK OF AMONTILLADO, The (by E. A. Poe) see HISTOIRES
EXTRAORDINAIRES (1948)/MASTER OF HORROR/TALES OF
TERROR
CASO DE LAS DOS BELLEZAS, El see CASE OF THE TWO
BEAUTIES, The
CASTELLO DEI MORTI VIVI, Il see CASTLE OF THE LIVING
DEAD
CASTELLO DI FU MANCHU, Il see CASTLE OF FU MANCHU,
The
CASTILLO DE FU MANCHU, El see CASTLE OF FU MANCHU,
The
CASTILLO DE LAS BOFETADES, El see CASTLE OF SLAPS, The
CASTILLO DE LOS MONSTRUOS, El see CASTLE OF THE
MONSTERS, The
CASTING THE RUNES (story by M. R. James) see CURSE OF
THE DEMON
The CASTLE GHOST Pathe 1910 9m. Ref: Bios 1/5/11.
"Haunted" house: Suitor meets apparition, shoots it. It turns
out to be girl.
The CASTLE GHOSTS Aquila 1908 Ref: MPW 12:497. Man
impersonates ghost.
A CASTLE IN FLANDERS (G) Tobis Magna 1937 90m. D: Geza
von Bolvary. Ref: MFB'37. with Marta Eggerth, Paul Hartman,
Georg Alexander. "Ghostly workings" and "mysterious happen-
ings" in castle.
CASTLE IN THE AIR (B) Hallmark 1952 90m. D: Henry Cass.
SP: Alan Melville, Edward Dryhurst, from a play by Melville.
PH: Erwin Hillier. Mus: Francis Chagrin. Ref: MFB'52. Boxo
2/7/53. with Margaret Rutherford, David Tomlinson, Helen
Cherry, A. E. Matthews, Patricia Dainton, Brian Oulton, Ewan
Roberts. "Spookery"; "family ghost."
CASTLE IN THE DESERT Fox 1942 62m. D: Harry Lachman.
SP: John Larkin, based on the character Charlie Chan created
by Earl Derr Biggers. PH: Virgil Miller. Ref: FDY. RVB.
with Sidney Toler, Sen Yung, Arleen Whelan, Lucien Littlefield,
Richard Derr, Douglas Dumbrille, Henry Daniell, Lenita Lane,
Ethel Griffies, Milton Parsons, Steven Geray. Potion distilled
from weed suspends heart-beat for short periods of time. Under-
ground chamber of horrors; clutching hands, etc. Daniell is
startlingly good. Plot above, humor below, par for Chan movie.
CASTLE MINERVA (by V. Canning) see MASQUERADE
CASTLE OF BLOOD (I-F) 1964 Woolner 90m. (LA DANZA
MACABRA or TERRORE-I. CASTLE OF TERROR-TV.
DIMENSIONS IN DEATH) D: Anthony Dawson (Antonio Marg-
heriti). SP: Jean Grimaud, Gordon Wilson, Jr., Corbucci,
Grimaldi. From "Danse Macabre" by Edgar Allan Poe. PH:
Riccardo Pallothin. Ref: MW 1:10. Annuario. MFB'67:139.
Pic: COF 9:48. with Barbara Steele, Georges Riviere, Margarete
Robsahm. Supernatural beings need blood for yearly renewal.
Starts slow, but builds to a nice shock ending.
CASTLE OF DOOM see VAMPYR
CASTLE OF EVIL United/WEC 1966 color 81m. (THE HAUNT-
ING AT CASTLE MONTEGO) D: Francis D. Lyon. SP: Charles

A. Wallace. PH: Brick Marquard. Mus: Paul Dunlap. Art D:
Paul Sylos, Jr. SpFX: Roger George. Makeup: Bob Dawn.
P: Earle Lyon. Ref: FJA script. with Scott Brady, Virginia
Mayo, David Brian, Lisa Gaye, Hugh Marlowe. Pic: FMO 5:28.
FM 57:11. "Mechanical monster," "spirit," etc.
The CASTLE OF FU MANCHU (I-G-Sp-B) Italian Int'l/Terra/Bal-
cazar/Towers 1970 color/scope 92m. (EL CASTILLO DE FU
MANCHU. FU MANCHU'S CASTLE. IL CASTELLO DI FU-
MANCHU. ASSIGNMENT ISTANBUL) D: Jesus Franco. SP:
M. Barthel. Dial: J. Balcázar. PH: Manuel Merino. Mus: M.
Shelby. Art D: S. Ontañon. also with J. M. Martin, Rosalba
Neri. Ref: M/TVM 11/68. SpCinema'71. with Christopher Lee,
Tsai Chin, Maria Perschy, Richard Greene.
The CASTLE OF LUST (G) Aquila 1968 color (IM SCHLOSS
DER BLUTIGEN BEGIERDE) D: Percy G. Parker. SP: Parker,
E. M. Schnitzler. PH: J. H. Martin, F. Hofer. Mus: Jerry
van Royen. Ref: M/TVM 12/68. with Janine Reynaud, Howard
Vernon, Michel Lemoine, Pier A. Caminneci, Jan Hendriks.
Dead revived.
The CASTLE OF SLAPS (Sp) 1945 (EL CASTILLO DE LAS
BOFETADES) D: J. de Orazal. SP,P: Juan Arajol. Mus:
Juan Hernandez. Art D: E. Bronchalo. Ref: MMF 9:14. with
Dolores Paris, Elena de Castilla, Domingo Bronchalo, Antonio
Martinez. In the wood young Pepito meets three witches who
take him to "a haunted house, from which no living person has
returned."
CASTLE OF TERROR see CASTLE OF BLOOD/HORROR CASTLE/
TERROR, The (1963)
CASTLE OF THE CARPATHIANS, The (by J. Verne) see CAR-
PATHIAN CASTLE, The
CASTLE OF THE LIVING DEAD (I-F) AI-TV/Serena-Francinor
1964 85m. (LE CHATEAU DES MORTS VIVANTS. IL CAS-
TELLO DEI MORTI VIVI-I. CRYPT OF HORROR-Eng) D:
Luciano Ricci (aka Herbert Wise). SP: Warren Kiefer. PH:
Aldo Tonti. Mus: A. Lavagnino. Art D: Carlo Gentili. Ref:
MMF 12:37. COF 12:30. MFB'68:58. Pic: Shriek 3:9,11.
with Christopher Lee, Gaia Germani, Philippe Leroy, Mirko
Valentin, Donald Sutherland. A count has discovered a chemical
which petrifies living matter. Average Italian (-French) horror
movie.
The CASTLE OF THE MONSTERS (Mex) Sotomayor (Col) 1957
(EL CASTILLO DE LOS MONSTRUOS) D: Julian Soler. SP:
Carlos Orellana. Story: Fernando Galiana. PH: Victor Herrera.
Mus: G. C. Carrion. Ref: Indice. FanMo 7:26. FM 17:10.
20:25. 31:19. Pic: FanMo 4:22. FM 31:18. 33:47. MW 1:17.
with Clavillazo, Evangelina Elizondo, German Robles (vampire).
Gorilla, mummy, werewolf, "Frentestein," "Bestia de la
Laguna seca."
CASTLE SINISTER (B) Unicorn 1947 49m. D: Oscar Burn.
Ref: MFB'48:29. with Mara Russell-Tavernan, A. Hunter,
James Liggatt, Robert Essex. Shrouded monk's "ghost."
The CASTLE WITH THE FIERY GATES (I-Sp) Prodimex/Hispamer-
Eureka 1970 color/scope D: Luis Merino. (sfa SCREAM OF

THE DEMON LOVER?) Ref: M/TVM 10/70:25: "Horror drama." with Charles Quiney, Erna Schurer.

The CAT AND THE CANARY Univ 1927 90m. D: Paul Leni. SP: Alfred A. Cohn, Robert F. Hill. From the play by John Willard. PH: Gilbert Warrenton. Art D: Charles Hall. Titles: Walter Anthony. Ref: Clarens. TBG. COF 7: 32. FM 24:8. Pic: DDC II:309. AFI. with Laura La Plante, Arthur-Edmund Carewe, Lucien Littlefield, Creighton Hale, For(r)est Stanley, Tully Marshall, Flora Finch, Gertrude Astor. Mysterious killer "haunts" Clifton Castle. This famous horror-mystery is drawn out by repetition and wan attempts at humor, but it has half-a-dozen striking visual effects, and the film is worth seeing just for them.

The CAT AND THE CANARY Para 1939 74m. D: Elliott Nugent SP: Walter De Leon, Lynn Starling. From the play by John Willard. PH: Charles Lang. Mus: Ernst Toch. Art D: Hans Dreier, Robert Usher. Ref: Clarens. Orpheus 4:57. Pic: FM 31:59. COF 9:23. ModM 3:32. with Bob Hope, Paulette Goddard, John Beal, Gale Sondergaard, George Zucco, John Wray, Elizabeth Patterson, Douglass Montgomery, Nydia Westman, George Regas. Comedy version of the horror play.

The CAT CREEPS Univ 1930 71m. D: Rupert Julian. SP: William Hurlbut, Gladys Lehman. From the play "The Cat and the Canary" by John Willard. PH: Jerry Ash, Hal Mohr. P: Carl Laemmle, Jr. Ref: COF 16:28:lost film. Clarens. New Yorker 11/15/30: "The big lonely house at midnight, sliding panels, an escaped madman, groping, clawlike hands in the shadows." with Helen Twelvetrees, Jean Hersholt, Montagu Love, Elizabeth Patterson, Raymond Hackett, Lawrence Grant, Lilyan Tashman, Theodore von Eltz, Blanche Frederici.

The CAT CREEPS Univ (Spanish version of above film) 1930 D: George Melford. SP: William Hurlbut, Gladys Lehman. From the play "The Cat and the Canary" by John Willard. Ref: FIR '67. (EL GATO) Pic: FM 16:28. with Antonio Moreno, Lupita Tovar, Manuel Granado.

The CAT CREEPS Univ 1946 58m. D: Erle C. Kenton. SP: Edward Dein, Jerry Warner. From a story by Gerald Geraghty. PH: George Robinson. Mus D: Paul Sawtell. Art D: Jack Otterson, Abraham Grossman. Ref: HM 8:17. FDY. with Paul Kelly, Noah Beery, Jr., Lois Collier, Douglas Dumbrille, Rose Hobart, Jonathan Hale. Cat's body supposedly harbors the spirit of a corpse. Unoriginal but pleasant.

CAT GIRL (B) AI/Malibu/Insignia 1957 67m. (THE CAT-WOMAN) D: Alfred Shaughnessy. SP: Lou Rusoff. PH: Peter Hennessy. Ref: FM 11:14. with Barbara Shelley, Robert Ayres, Kay Callard, Paddy Webster, John Watson. A girl believes she's under a curse. Slight.

CAT PEOPLE RKO 1942 75m. D: Jacques Tourneur. SP: De-Witt Bodeen. P: Val Lewton. PH: Nicholas Musuraca. Mus: Roy Webb. Art D: Albert D'Agostino, Walter E. Keller. Ref: COF 7:30. FM 10:26. FDY. with Simone Simon, Kent Smith, Jane Randolph, Tom Conway, Jack Holt, Alan Napier, A. Craig, Elizabeth Russell. Young woman believes she can turn into a

cat. Uneven; lots of touches, some helpful, some not-so-helpful.
Influential, but lesser, Lewton.
The CAT THAT WAS CHANGED INTO A WOMAN (F) Pathe 1909
12m. (LA CHATTE METAMORPHOSEE EN FEMME) D: Louis
Feuillade. Ref: Bios 6/30/10. DDC III:338. The gods change
a cat into a woman.
CAT-WOMAN, The see CAT GIRL, The
CAT-WOMEN OF THE MOON Astor--3-Dimensional Picture/AI-
TV 1954-3 64m. (ROCKET TO THE MOON) Remade as MIS-
SILE TO THE MOON. D: Arthur Hilton. SP: Roy Hamilton.
Story, P: Al Zimbalist, Jack Rabin. PH: William Whitley. Mus:
Elmer Bernstein. Art D: William Glasgow. Ref: MFB. with
Sonny Tufts, Victor Jory, Marie Windsor, William Phipps,
Douglas Fowley, Carol Brewster. Classic title, classic lines:
"Welcome to the moon" "Do you have a special earth girl?" "I
have a high regard for you--you're smart, you have courage, and
you're all woman. "
CATACOMBS see WOMAN WHO WOULDN'T DIE, The
CATHARSIS see TERROR IN THE CRYPT
CATMAN OF PARIS Rep 1946 65m. D: Lesley Selander. SP:
Sherman Lowe. PH: Reggie Lanning. Mus D: Richard Cherwin.
Art D: Gano Chittenden. SpFX: Howard and Theodore Lydecker.
Ref: FDY. Pic: FM 28: 69. 33:38. with Carl Esmond, Robert
Wilke, Lenore Aubert, Adele Mara, Gerald Mohr, John Dehner,
Douglas Dumbrille, Anthony Caruso, Fritz Feld, Francis Pierlot,
George Renavent. The position of the stars turns a man into a
were-cat. Derivative, mainly from CAT PEOPLE, LEOPARD
MAN, and THE WOLF MAN.
The CAT'S REVENGE Lux 1908 4m. Ref: MPW'08:549. Spirit
of cat haunts cook.
CAUCASIAN GHOST (J) Okura 1963 (KAIDAN IJIN YUREI) D:
Satoru Kobayashi. Ref: Unij. Bltn. 31. with Miyako Ichijo,
Kyoko Ogimachi. Ghost story.
CAUCHEMAR D'UN PECHEUR, Le see 20,000 LEAGUES UNDER
THE SEA (1907)
CAUCHEMAR FRANCO-ANGLAIS, Le see TUNNELING THE
CHANNEL UNDER THE SEA
CAUGHT BY TELEVISION see TRAPPED BY TELEVISION
CAULDRON OF BLOOD see BLIND MAN'S BLUFF (1967)
CAVALIER DE RION CLAIR, Le (novel by C. Boncompain) see
SORCERER, The
The CAVALIER'S DREAM Edison 1898 1m. D: Edwin S. Porter.
Ref: Niver. Dream of Death, the devil, etc.
The CAVE DWELLERS' ROMANCE Bison 1913 33m. Ref: Bios
11/20/13. Mysticism; man transformed into pony.
The CAVE MAN Vita 1912 15m. Ref: Bios 7/4/12: The CAVE
MAN; OR, BEFORE A BOOK WAS WRITTEN. Cave men.
The CAVE MAN Vita 1915 Ref: MPW 26. LC. Lee. with
Robert Edeson, Fay Wallace. Cave man comedy.
CAVE MAN see ONE MILLION B.C.
The CAVE MEN'S WAR Kalem 1913 35m. Ref: Bios 2/15/14.
The Shell People vis. the Cave Dwellers.
CAVE OF THE LIVING DEAD (Yug-W.G.) Trans-Lux/Objectiv--

Triglav 1963('66-U.S.) 88m. (DER FLUCH DER GRUNEN AUGEN. LA NUIT DES VAMPIRES-F) D: Akos von Rathony. SP: C. V. Rock. Story: Rathony. PH: Saric Hrvoj. Art D: Ivan Pengov. Exec P: Richard Gordon. Ref: MMF 18-19:102. FFacts. with Adrian Hoven, Erika Remberg, Carl Mohner, Wolfgang Preiss, Karin Field. Murders are linked to a cave under a village's castle and to the "curse of the green eyes."

CAVERNE MAUDITE, La see ACCURSED CAVERN, The

CELEBRATED LODGER, The (by Marie-B. Lowndes) see LODGER, The (1926/1944)/PHANTOM FIEND

CELLE QUI N'ETAIT PLUS (by Boileau and Narcejac) see DIABOLIQUE

CEREBRO DEL MAL, El see SANTO AGAINST THE DIABOLICAL BRAIN

CESTA DO PRAVEKU see JOURNEY TO THE BEGINNING OF TIME

CHAIN LIGHTNING Arrow 1922 60m. P: Ben Wilson. SP: J. Grubb Alexander, Agnes Parsons. Ref: FJA still. FD 3/19/22. Ray gun.

The CHAIRMAN (Brit-U.S.) Fox 1969 DeLuxeColor/scope 104m. (THE MOST DANGEROUS MAN IN THE WORLD--Eng) D: J. Lee Thompson. SP: Ben Maddow, from the novel by Jay Richard Kennedy. PH: John Wilcox, Ted Moore. Mus: Jerry Goldsmith. Art D: Peter Mullins. Ref: MFB. with Gregory Peck, Anne Heywood, Arthur Hill, Keye Luke. A scientist enters Red China to learn the secret of an enzyme which would allow crops to grow in any climate. A transmitter implanted in his skull enables him to communicate with London by satellite. Oddball "A" picture plays more like a '40s "B" updated and is evidently sort of successful at whatever it is it's trying to do.

The CHALLENGE ABC-TV/Fox 1970 color 72m. D: Allen Smithe. SP: Mark Norman. PH: John Nickolaus. Mus: Harry Geller. SpFX: L. B. Abbott. Ref: RVB. TVG. with Darren McGavin, Mako, James Whitmore, Broderick Crawford, Skip Homeier, Paul Lukas. As an alternative to war the U.S. and an Asian power choose representatives for a fight to the death.

The CHALLENGE OF THE GIANT (I) Plaza-Schermi Riuniti 1965 80m. (LA SFIDA DEI GIGANTI. THE GIANT'S CHALLENGE) D: Maurice Bright. SP: Enzo Gicca. Remake of HERCULES AND THE CAPTIVE WOMEN? PH: A. Mancori. Ref: Annuario. La Saison Cinem. with Reg Park, G. Sandri, Audrey Amber, Luigi Barbini. Gea, goddess of the earth, sends her son, the giant Anteo, to fight Hercules.

The CHALLENGING GHOST (J) Toei 1959 (THE MAN IN THE MOONLIGHT MASK. GEKKO KAMEN. MOONLIGHT MASK-- THE CHALLENGING GHOST) D: Shoichi Shimazu. Ref: Unijapan '60:96. with Fumitake Omura.

CHAMAK CHANDNI (India--Hindi) Bharati 1959 140m. D: M. Vyas. Ref: FEFN XII:16-17. with Shakila, Roopmala, Mahipal. "A princess of the earth is lured away to the moon as a result of a conspiracy between the prime minister of the kingdom and a lunar official."

CHAMBER OF HORRORS (B) Mono 1940 79m. (THE DOOR

WITH SEVEN LOCKS--Eng) Remade as THE DOOR WITH
SEVEN LOCKS. D: Norman Lee. SP: Lee, John Argyle, Gil-
bert Gunn, from a story by Edgar Wallace. Ref: FIR'67:79.
S&S'68:213. DDC III:465. with Leslie Banks, Lilli Palmer,
Gina Malo, Richard Bird. Advertised as a horror movie, film
is actually on the light side, with Banks as a witty sadist.
CHAMBER OF HORRORS WB 1966 99m. P, D: Hy Averback.
SP: Stephen Kandel. Story: Kandel, Ray Russell. "House of
Wax" TV series planned. Ref: Boxo 9/5/66. FFacts. FM 41:
34. ModM 3:7. with Cesare Danova, Wilfrid Hyde-White, Laura
Devon, Patrice Wymore, Suzy Parker, Patrick O'Neal, Tun Tun,
Jeanette Nolan, Marie Windsor, Berry Kroeger, Tony Curtis.
Madman loose in Baltimore. Film notable mainly for introducing
the Fear Flasher and the Horror Horn.
CHAMBER OF HORRORS see BEDLAM
CHAMBRE ARDENTE, La see BURNING COURT, The
CHAMPAGNE ROSE IS DEAD (Dutch-Swedish) Chanowski/Aspekt/
Swedish-TV 1970 color D: Calvin Floyd. Ref: V5/12/71:106,
182. with Francis Matthews (Paul Temple). Feature film "set
in the near future."
CHAN MAHI (Pakistani) Kamal Pictures 1957 140m. P, D:
A. K. Pasha. PH: R. Lodhi. Mus: R. Attrey. Ref: FEFN
8/23/57 with Aslam Parwez. Peasant sells soul for money.
CHAND SADAGAR (India-Bengali) Lakshmi 1934 D: Profulla
Roy. PH: B. Das. Ref: Dipali 3/30/34. with A. Chaudhury,
Padmavati. Snake-goddess; love that "defeats death."
CHANDRA SENA (India) Prabhat 1931 silent D: V. Shantaram.
Ref: Dipali 8/16/35.
CHANDRA SENA (India) Prabhat 1935 D: V. Shantaram. Ref:
Dipali 8/16/35. with N. Tarkhad, Rajani, Mane. "Demon
king...serpent king."
CHANDRASENA (India) Wadia Bros. 1959 150m. D: B. J.
Mistry. Ref: FEFN 11/59. Rama learns the secret of the
vulnerability of two demon-brothers and destroys them. "Fan-
tastic special-effects."
CHANDU ON THE MAGIC ISLAND 1935 For credits see RETURN
OF CHANDU. Ref: FIR'64:580. FIR'61:636: "A sequel to
RETURN OF CHANDU, both of which were released as 7-reel
features that were followed, in succeeding weeks, by eight 2-reel
chapters." COF 8:38. Screen: "Sequel to RETURN OF
CHANDU." Almost perfectly awful. Disembodied voices all over
the place; other nice and cheap "special effects."
CHANDU, THE MAGICIAN Fox 1932 75m. D: William Cameron
Menzies, Marcel Varnel. From the radio drama by Harry
Earnshaw, Vera Oldham, and R. R. Morgan. SP: Barry Con-
nors, Philip Klein. PH: James Wong Howe. Ed: Harold
Shuster. Ref: FDY. FM 9:6. 80:30-3. Photoplay 11/32. See
also CHANDU ON THE MAGIC ISLAND, RETURN OF CHANDU,
and TRICK FOR TRICK. Pic: FM 54:33. FanMo 5:22. with
Edmund Lowe, Bela Lugosi, Irene Ware, Henry B. Walthall,
Herbert Mundin, Weldon Heyburn, Virginia Hammond, June
Vlasek, Nestor Aber. The evil Roxor steals a death ray.
Great fun for kids.

CHANDU'S RETURN see RETURN OF CHANDU
CHANGE OF MIND Sagittarius 1969 98m. Eastmancolor D:
Robert Stevens. SP: Seeleg Lester, Richard Wesson. PH:
Arthur J. Ornitz. Mus: Duke Ellington. with Raymond St.
Jacques, Susan Oliver, Janet MacLachlan, Leslie Nielsen.
District Attorney's brain transplanted into body of dead Negro.
CHARIOTS OF THE GODS see MEMORIES OF THE FUTURE
The CHARLATAN Univ 1929 60m. part-talking D: Harold
Watterson. SP: B. W. Burton, Robert Jahns, from a play.
Titles: Tom Reed. PH: George Robinson. Ref: V 4/17/29.
Pic: A Pictorial Hist. Talkies. with George Melford, Rad-
cliffe Fellow, Margaret Livingston, Gary Cooper. Old mansion,
storm, screams, sinister Orientals, etc.
CHARLESTON (F) Epinay 1927 29m. (CHARLESTON-PARADE.
SUR UN AIR DE CHARLESTON.) P, D: Jean Renoir. SP:
Pierre Lestringuez, from an idea by André Cerf. PH: Jean
Bachelet. Mus: Clément Doucet. Ref: SF Film. Bazin's
"Jean Renoir." with Johnny Huggins, Catherine Hessling,
Pierre Braunberger, Lestringuez. In the year 2028 Europe is in
the grip of a new Ice Age. A few amusing scenes, special effects;
but just a curiosity of a film with nothing in it to suggest the warmth
and beauty of DAY IN THE COUNTRY, THE CRIME OF MR.
LANGE, or the other extraordinary films which Renoir was soon
to make.
CHARLIE CHAN AND BLACK MAGIC see BLACK MAGIC (1944)
CHARLIE CHAN AT THE OLYMPICS Fox 1937 71m. D: H.
Bruce Humberstone. SP: Robert Ellis, Helen Logan. Based
on the character created by Earl Derr Biggers. PH: Daniel
B. Clark. Mus D: Samuel Kaylin. Ref: FD 3/29/37.
V 5/26/37. with Warner Oland, Katherine de Mille, Pauline
Moore, Allen Lane, Keye Luke, C. Henry Gordon, John
Eldredge, Layne Tom, Jr., Jonathan Hale, F. Vogeding, Sel-
mer Jackson, Emmett Vogan, George Chandler, Minerva Urecal,
Paul W. Panzer, Philip Morris, Lee Shumway, Stanley Blystone.
A device for a remote-control robot airplane is stolen.
CHARLIE CHAN AT THE OPERA Fox 1936 66m. D: H. Bruce
Humberstone. SP: Charles Belden, Scott Darling. Story: Bess
Meredyth. Based on the character created by Earl Derr Big-
gers. Opera "Carnival" by Oscar Levant. Mus D: Samuel Kay-
lin. Art D: Duncan Cramer, Lewis Creber. PH: Lucien An-
driot. Ref: FM 2:31. FDY. V 12/16/36: "Nooks and crannies
provide spook atmosphere." with Warner Oland, Boris Karloff,
Keye Luke, Nedda Harrigan, William Demarest, Charlotte Henry,
Gregory Gay(e), Guy Usher, Frank Conroy, Fred Kelsey, Lee
Shumway, Joan Woodbury, Stanley Blystone. Karloff as madman/
amnesia victim.
CHARLIE CHAN AT THE WAX MUSEUM Fox 1940 63m. D: Lynn
Shores. SP: John Larkin. Based on the character created by
Earl Derr Biggers. PH: Virgil Miller. Art D: Richard Day,
Lewis Creber. Ref: COF 8:38. FDY. with Sidney Toler, Vic-
tor Sen Yung, Marguerite Chapman, Harold Goodwin, Archie
Twitchell, C. Henry Gordon, Marc Lawrence, Ted Osborne,
Michael Visaroff. Stormy night, killer with bandaged face, wax

models of Bluebeard and Jack the Ripper, secret room, trap
door, lights going out, peering faces, creaking doors, etc. A
few bright spots. Too few really.
CHARLIE CHAN AT TREASURE ISLAND Fox 1939 59m. D: Norman Foster. SP: John Larkin. Based on the character created by Earl Derr Biggers. PH: Virgil Miller. Ref: FDY.
with Sidney Toler, Cesar Romero, Douglas Dumbrille, Sen
Yung, Sally Blane, Douglas Fowley, Charles Halton, Trevor
Bardette, Pauline Moore, June Gale, Louis Jean Heydt. Dr.
Zodiac, fake seances, and real mind-reading. Not as plodding
as most Chans. One good horror moment.
CHARLIE CHAN IN EGYPT Fox 1935 65m. D: Louis King.
SP: Robert Ellis, Helen Logan. Based on the character cre-
ated by Earl Derr Biggers. PH: Daniel B. Clark. P: Edward
T. Lowe. Ref: COF 8:38. FDY. Pic: TBG. with Warner Oland,
Nigel de Brulier, Stepin Fetchit, Jameson Thomas, Frank Con-
roy, Rita Hayworth (Rita Cansino), Paul Porcasi, Arthur Stone,
Pat Paterson, Thomas Beck. Fake "living mummy." Thorough-
ly routine, listless.
CHARLIE CHAN IN RENO Fox 1939 70m. D: Norman Foster.
SP: Frances Hyland, Albert Ray, Robert E. Kent, from the
story "Death Makes a Decree" by Philip Wylie and the Charlie
Chan stories by Earl Derr Biggers. PH: Virgil Miller. Mus
D: Samuel Kaylin. Art D: Richard Day, David Hall. Ref:
FD 6/5/39. with Sidney Toler, Ricardo Cortez, Phyllis
Brooks, Slim Summerville, Kane Richmond, Sen Yung, Robert
Lowery, Hamilton MacFadden, Fred Kelsey, Jim Aubrey. Clue
takes Chan to "ghost village near Reno, where some good creepy
stuff develops."
CHARLIE CHAN'S MURDER CRUISE Fox 1940 75m. (CHARLIE
CHAN'S ORIENTAL CRUISE) D: Eugene Forde. SP: Lester
Ziffren, Robertson White. Based on the character created by
Earl Derr Biggers. Ref: FDY. with Lionel Atwill, Sidney
Toler, Robert Lowery, Marjorie Weaver, Don Beddoe, Sen Yung,
Leo G. Carroll, Cora Witherspoon, Harlan Briggs, Charles
Middleton, Leonard Mudie, James Burke, Montague Shaw.
Strangler in horror-mask on board ship.
CHARLIE CHAN'S SECRET Fox 1936 71m. D: Gordon Wiles.
SP: Helen Logan, Robert Ellis, Joseph Hoffman. Based on the
character created by Earl Derr Biggers. PH: Rudolph Mate.
Ref: FDY. with Warner Oland, Rosina Lawrence, Arthur Ed-
mund Carewe, Charles Quigley, Henrietta Crosman, Astrid
Allwyn, Herbert Mundin, Jonathan Hale, Egon Brecher. Se-
ances, apparitions, secret panels, secret passages, etc. Slug-
gish, with all those annoying "sinister glances"; brightened only
by a few of Chan's wise little sayings.
CHARLY Cinerama/Selmur 1968 103m. P, D: Ralph Nelson.
SP: Stirling Silliphant, from the story "Flowers for Algernon"
by Daniel Keyes. PH: Arthur Ornitz. Mus: Ravi Shankar.
Art D: Charles Rosen. Ref: V 7/3/68. with Cliff Robertson,
Claire Bloom, Leon Janney, Lilia Skala, Frank Dolan. Mentally retarded adult turned into genius. Pretty grim example of
(attempted) audience manipulation. Some of the worst scenes on

film in recent years.
CHARMED SWORD Pathe 1908 Ref: MPW'08:83. Sword defeats the "Evil One."
CHARRETIER DE LA MORT, La (by S. Lagerlof) see PHANTOM CHARIOT, The (1939)
CHARRETTE FANTOME, La see PHANTOM CHARIOT, The (1939)
CHARRO DE LAS CALAVERAS, El see RIDER OF THE SKULLS, The
CHATEAU DES MORTS VIVANTS, Le see CASTLE OF THE LIVING DEAD
CHATEAU EN SUEDE see NUTTY, NAUGHTY CHATEAU
CHATEAU HANTE, LE see HAUNTED CASTLE, The (1897)
CHATTE METAMORPHOSEE EN FEMME, La CAT THAT WAS CHANGED INTO A WOMAN, The
CHE OVNI (Arg) Beccaglia 1968 D: Aníbal Uset. SP: Gius. PH: Ignacio Souto. Mus: S. Mihanovich, O. L. Ruiz. Art D: A. Sanchez. Ref: Cine Argentino. with Marcela Lopez Rey, Jorge Sobral, Perla Caron, Erika Wallner. A singer is kidnapped by an envoy from another planet where love has been forgotten.
CHECK AND DOUBLE CHECK RKO 1930 71m. D: Melville Brown. SP: J. Walter Ruben. Story: Bert Kalmar, Harry Ruby. Art D: Max Ree. PH: William Marshall. Ref: FDY. New Yorker 11/8/30. AFI. with Freeman Gosden, Charles Correll, Sue Carol, Charles Morton, Ralf Harolde, Irene Rich, Rita La Roy, Russell Powell, Duke Ellington and his band. Amos'n'Andy in a "haunted" house. Pic: Pict. Hist. Talkies.
CHEF WUNSCHT KEINE ZEUGEN, Der see NO SURVIVORS, PLEASE
The CHESS PLAYER (F) 1926 82m. (JOUEUR D'ECHECS) D: Raymond Bernard. From "The Mysterious Automaton of Dr. Kempelen" by Henry Dupuy-Mazuel. Ref: Lee. Cinema'68. Pic: DDC I:218. with Charles Dullin. Villain killed by automata.
The CHESS PLAYER (F) Unity/Société Vega Films 1938 85m. D: Jean Dréville. (JOUEUR D'ECHECS) Ref: S&S'68:213. MFB'39:52. with Conrad Veidt, Francoise Rosay. Baron builds "life-size mechanical dolls," "working models of people."
The CHEVAL MYSTERY Victor 1915 35m. Ref: LC. MPN 7/3/15. with Harry Myers, Rosemary Theby. Hypnotist can turn girl "from her ordinary self into a raving maniac at will."
CHEVALIER DE LA NUIT, Le see KNIGHT OF THE NIGHT, The
CHI O SUU NINGYO see VAMPIRE DOLL, The
CHIEN DES BASKERVILLE, Le see HOUND OF THE BASKERVILLES, The (1914-F)
CHIKYU BOEIGUN see MYSTERIANS, The
CHIKYU SAIDAINO KESSEN see GHIDRAH
CHILDREN OF LIGHT, The (novel by H. L. Lawrence) see THESE ARE THE DAMNED
CHILDREN OF THE DAMNED (B) MGM 1963 81m. (THE CHILDREN. THE CHILDREN RETURN) D: Anton M. Leader. SP: Jack Briley; follow-up to VILLAGE OF THE DAMNED.

PH: Davis Boulton.   Mus: Ron Goodwin.   SpFX: Tom Howard.
Ref: COF 2:46.   Orpheus 3:31.   with Ian Hendry, Alan Badel,
Barbara Ferris, Lee Yoke-Moon, Alfred Burke, Bessie Love.
UNESCO investigators attempt to communicate with six "super-
children" brought to London from different countries. Clumsily
developed story surprises with its sudden bursts of pretension
but can't follow up on them.   Script has some ideas but nothing
to connect them.
CHILD'S PLAY   (B)   Group 3 /British Lion   1954   68m.   Adap, D:
Margaret Thomson.   SP: Peter Blackmore.   Story: Don Sharp.
PH: Denny Densham.   Mus: Antony Hopkins.   Art D: Michael
Stringer.   Exec P: John Grierson.   Ref: MFB.   with Mona
Washbourne, Peter Martyn, Carl Jaffe, Dorothy Alison, Ingeborg
Wells. Children produce "miniature atomic explosion" from toy
atomic set, also "manufacture atomic sweetmeat, Bangcorn."
The CHIMES   (B)   Hepworth   1914   35m.   Ref: Lee. From a story
by Charles Dickens.   Spirit accompanies man through "weird
scenes."
The CHINATOWN MYSTERY   Syndicate Picture   1928   silent serial
10 episodes   2. The Clutching Claw.   D: J. P. McGowan.   Ref:
CNW.   STI 1:14.   with Joe Bonomo, Ruth Hiatt, Francis Ford,
Al Baffert.   Villain called "the evil Sphinx"; formula for arti-
ficial diamonds.
CHINESE AND MINI SKIRTS   (Sp-G-I)   PCC /Aquila /Ticino   1968
color /scope   98m.   (CHINOS Y MINIFALDAS)   D: Ramón Comas.
SP: K. Luger, C. Chatterley, J. L. Madrid, R. Comas.   PH:
Eloy Mella.   Mus: Piero Umiliani.   Ref: SpCinema'69.   with
Adrian Hoven, Barth Warren, George Wang, Gerard Landry.
Mind-controlling drug.
The CHINESE PARROT   Univ   1927   D: Paul Leni.   SP: J. Grubb
Alexander, from a story by Earl Derr Biggers.   Ref: Clarens:
"Some eerie moments."   V: "Creepy."   FD 1 /8 /28: "Weird
orgy of mystery."   MPN 1 /7 /28: "Lots of spooky atmosphere";
curse on necklace.   with Anna May Wong, Sojin, Slim Summer-
ville, Edgar Kennedy, Hobart Bosworth, Marian Nixon, Etta Lee,
Edmund Burns.
CHINOS Y MINIFALDAS   see   CHINESE AND MINI SKIRTS
CHIOSU ME   see   DRACULA'S LUST FOR BLOOD
A CHRISTMAS CAROL   Ess   1908   Ref: F Index 12 /12 /08.   From
Dickens' story.
A CHRISTMAS CAROL   Edison   1910   17m.   Ref: SilentFF.   From
Dickens' story.
A CHRISTMAS CAROL   (B)   London   1914   22m.   P: Harold Shaw.
From Dickens' story.   Ref: SilentFF.   with Charles Rock, George
Bellamy.
A CHRISTMAS CAROL   Loew's Inc.   1938.   69m.   D: Edwin L.
Marin.   SP: Hugo Butler, from Dickens' story.   PH: Sydney
Wagner.   Art D: Cedric Gibbons.   P: Joseph L. Mankiewicz.
Ref: FDY.   with Reginald Owen, Gene Lockhart, Terry Kilburn,
D'Arcy Corrigan, Leo G. Carroll, Ann Rutherford, Ronald
Sinclair.
A CHRISTMAS CAROL   (B)   UA /Renown   1951   86m.   D, P: Brian
Desmond Hurst.   SP: Noel Langley, from Dickens' story.   Mus

sc: Richard Addinsell. PH: C. Pennington-Richards. Art D: Ralph Brinton. Ed: Clive Donner. Ref: FDY. with Alastair Sim, Kathleen Harrison, Jack Warner, Michael Hordern, Mervyn Johns, Hermione Baddeley, George Cole, Rona Anderson, Hattie Jacques, Francis DeWolff, Ernest Thesiger. Since the point of the visions is in Scrooge's reaction to them, the movie very wisely is never away from him long. Not up to Sim's best films (The GREEN MAN, the great The HAPPIEST DAYS OF YOUR LIFE), but moderately good.

CHRISTMAS CAROL, A see DREAM OF OLD SCROOGE, The/ OLD SCROOGE/RIGHT TO BE HAPPY, The/SCROOGE (1901/ 1913/1935/1970)

The CHRISTMAS MARTIAN (Canadian) Faroun Films 1971 color 66m. (LE MARTIEN DE NOEL) D: Bernard Gosselin. SP: Roch Carrier. PH: Alain Dostie. Mus: Jacques Perron. Sp sound FX: Robert Laferriere. Ref: V 6/9/71. Friendly Martian lands in Quebec.

CHRONICLES OF BLOOM CENTER Selig 1915 25m. (SPOOKS) Ref: MPN 13:102. Lee. with Sidney Smith, William Hutchinson. Man frightens spiritualists at seance by dressing as ghost. Then "real spirits" appear.

A CHUMP AT OXFORD UA 1939 (released 1941) 63m. D: Alfred Goulding. SP: Charles Rogers, Felix Adler, Harry Langdon. PH: Arthur Lloyd. Mus: Marvin Hatley. Exec P: Hal Roach. Ref: COF 8:39. V: "Ghost-at-midnight" routine. with Stan Laurel, Oliver Hardy, Peter Cushing, Forrester Harvey, Forbes Murray, Rex Lease, Wilfred Lucas, Stanley Blystone. Blow on head gives Laurel different personality.

CHUTE FE LA MAISON USHER, La see FALL OF THE HOUSE OF USHER, The (French, 1928)

CIEL SUR LA TETE, Le see SKY ABOVE HEAVEN

CIELO SULLA TESTA, Il see SKY ABOVE HEAVEN

CIEN GRITOS DE TERROR see 100 CRIES OF TERROR

CINCO ADVERTENCIAS DE SATANAS, Las see SATAN'S FIVE WARNINGS (1938/1945/1969)

CINQ GENTLEMEN MAUDITS, Les see FIVE DOOMED GENTLE- MEN, The/UNDER THE MOON OF MOROCCO

CINQUE TOMBE PER UN MEDIUM see TERROR CREATURES FROM THE GRAVE

The CIRCULAR STAIRCASE Selig 1915 60m. D: Edward J. Le Saint. Based on the novel by Mary Roberts Rinehart. Ref: MPW 26:522. with Eugenie Besserer, Stella Razeto, Guy Oliver, Edith Johnson. "Apparition" frightens man to death; secret room; secret passage.

CIRCUS OF BLOOD see BERSERK

CIRCUS OF DR. LAO, The (by C. G. Finney) see SEVEN FACES OF DR. LAO, The

CIRCUS OF HORRORS (B) AI/Lynx 1960 color 91m. D: Sidney Hayers. SP: George Baxt. PH: Douglas Slocombe. Mus: Franz Reizenstein and Muir Mathieson. Art D: Jack Shampan. Song "Look for a Star" by Mark Anthony. Makeup: Trevor Crole- Rees. Pic: FM 8:10. 18:44. 54:42. with Anton Diffring, Erika Remberg, Yvonne Monlaur, Yvonne Romain, Jane Hylton,

Donald Pleasance, Kenneth Griffith, Vanda Hudson, John Meri-
vale, Jack Gwillim.   Mad circus manager eliminates perform-
ers with "accidents." Strong (too strong) on sadism, with an
engaging performance by Diffring.
CIRCUS OF TERROR   see   BERSERK
CISARUV PEKAR, PEKARUV CISAR   see   EMPEROR AND THE
   GOLEM, The
CISARUV PEKAR, RELEKARUV CISAR   see   EMPEROR AND THE
   GOLEM, The
CITY BENEATH THE SEA   NBC-TV/Motion Pictures Int'l 1971
   color 96m.   Story, D, P: Irwin Allen. SP: John M. Lucas. PH:
   Kenneth Peach. Mus: Richard LaSalle. SpFX: L. B. Abbott,
   Art Cruickshank. Ref: RVB. TVG. with Stuart Whitman,
   Robert Wagner, Rosemary Forsyth, Robert Colbert, Burr De-
   Benning, Paul Stewart, Whit Bissell, Larry Pennell, Tom Drake,
   Richard Basehart, Joseph Cotten, Sugar Ray Robinson, James
   Darren.   Underwater metropolis; "fissionable H-128."
A CITY DESTROYED (F) 1924 P, D: Luitz Morat. SP : Jean-
   Louis Bouquet. (LA CITE FOUDROYEE) Ref: Imagen. DDC
   I:333. II:308. III:252, 253. Pic: DDC I:334. with Daniel
   Mendaille, Jane Maguenat, Armand Morins. Paris is destroyed
   by a mysterious ray.
CITY IN THE SEA (by E. A. Poe) see WAR-GODS OF THE DEEP
CITY OF THE DEAD   see   HORROR HOTEL
CITY UNDER THE SEA   see   WAR-GODS OF THE DEEP
The CLAIRVOYANT (B) Gaum 1935 72m. (THE EVIL MIND)
   D: Maurice Elvey. SP: Charles Bennett, Bryan Edgar Wallace.
   From a novel by Ernst Lothar. Remade as THE NIGHT HAS A
   THOUSAND EYES. PH: Errol Hinds. Ref: FM 47:15. Lee.
   London Mercury 9/35. with Claude Rains, Fay Wray, Ben
   Field, Jane Baxter, Mary Clare. Pic: DDC II:189. A fake
   fortune teller discovers he has real clairvoyant powers.
The CLAIRVOYANT SWINDLERS Kalem 1915 25m. Ref: MPN
   5/8/15. with Marin Sais. "Spirit" talks at seance.
CLAW MONSTERS, The   see   PANTHER GIRL OF THE KONGO
CLAWS OF SATAN (J) Toei 1958 scope 62m. (MAJIN NO
   TSUME) D: Eijiro Wakabayashi. Ref: Unijapan'60:94. FEFN
   XII:10-11: "Ray guns." Pic: FM 26:2: hunchback. with Fumi-
   take Kumira.
The CLIMAX Univ 1944 Technicolor 86m. P, D: George Waggner.
   SP: Lynn Starling, Curt Siodmak, from a play by Edward Locke.
   PH: Hal Mohr. Mus: Edward Ward. Art D: John B. Goodman,
   Alexander Golitzen. Ref: FDY. Pic: FM 12:13. with Boris Kar-
   loff, Susanna Foster, Turhan Bey, Ludwig Stossel, Gale Sonder-
   gaard, June Vincent, Jane Farrar, Thomas Gomez, George
   Dolenz, Scotty Beckett. Opera's physician has body of prima
   donna he murdered embalmed in his home. Poor follow-up to
   THE PHANTOM OF THE OPERA; almost as funny as A NIGHT
   AT THE OPERA. Bey grins his way through.
CLOAK, The (by R. Bloch) see HOUSE THAT DRIPPED BLOOD,
   The
The CLOCK-MAKER'S SECRET Pathe 1907 15m. Ref: MPW
   '07:636. An old clock maker is in league with the devil. When

the devil comes for his soul, his daughter makes him flee by
drawing out a cross.

The CLOUD OF ANDROMEDA (Russ) Dovjenko Studios 1968
color 85m. (ANDROMEDA, THE MYSTERIOUS. THE
ANDROMEDA GALAXY. THE ANDROMEDA NEBULA.
TUMANNOCT' ANDROMED) D: Eugeny Sherstobytov. From
work by Russian scientist Ivan Efremov. Ref: FM 54:8.
V 5/1/68:17. 7/10/68:19. RVB. SF Times 9/68. "Com-
munication with other planets."

The CLOUD PUNCHER Fox 1917 22m. SP, D: Charles Parrot.
MPW 31:1081. with Hank Mann, Lynn Staley. Bullets that
bring rain.

CLOUDS OVER EUROPE (B) Col 1939 78m. (Q PLANES) D:
Tim Whelan, Arthur Woods. SP: Ian Dalrymple. Story: Brock
Williams, Arthur Wimperis, Jack Whittingham. PH: Harry
Stradling. Ref: Brit. Cinema. Bill Warren. NYT 6/16/39.
with Laurence Olivier, Ralph Richardson, Valerie Hobson,
George Curzon, Hay Petrie, John Longden. Four British bomb-
ers disappear in a year. A camouflaged death ray on a trawler
is responsible.

The CLOWN AND THE ALCHEMIST Edison 1900 Ref: Niver.
Grotesque apparitions.

CLOWN AND THE AUTOMATON (F) Melies 1897 Ref: SF Film.
(GUGUSSE ET L'AUTOMATE)

CLOWN FERDINAND AND THE ROCKET see ROCKET TO NO-
WHERE

The CLOWN HERO Imp 1913 13m. Ref: Bios 9/4/13. Boy
dreams of "weird animals" which give him "an awful fright."

The CLUB PEST Biog 1915 8m. Ref: MPN 2/6/15. LC.
Man bets he can spend a night in a "haunted" house.

The CLUTCHING HAND Stage & Screen/Weiss 1936 serial 15
episodes 13. The Mystic Menace. 14. The Silent Spectre. SP:
Leon D'Usseau, Dallas Fitzgerald, from the "Craig Kennedy"
stories by Arthur B. Reeve. Ref: COF 8:38. Imagen. with
Jack Mulhall, Rex Lease, Mae Busch, William Farnum, Robert
Frazer, Joseph W. Girard, Robert Walker, Dick Alexander,
Snub Pollard, William Desmond, Bull Montana, Tom London,
Bryant Washburn. Formula for synthetic gold; secret passages;
"clutching hand." Wonderfully awkward action, acting, dialogue:
"You'll know when I pull it what I've got up my sleeve" "I
haven't that paper" "Since you have been in this room have you
heard anything? By that I mean have you heard any noise?" etc.

The CLUTCHING HAND (Fili) Sampaguita 1962 (HIRAM NA
KAMAY) D: Tony Cayado. Ref: M/TVM 3/62, 5/62:29:
"Horror." with Eddie Gutierrez, Josephine Estrada.

CLUTCHING HAND, The see EXPLOITS OF ELAINE, The

The COBRA STRIKES Eagle-Lion 1948 62m. D: Charles F.
Riesner. SP: Eugene Conrad. Dial D: Stewart Stern. PH: Guy
Roe. Art D: Armor Marlowe. PH FX: George J. Teague.
Makeup: Ern Westmore, Del Armstrong. Ref: pbk. with Sheila
Ryan, Richard Fraser, Leslie Brooks, James Seay, Richard
Loo, Philip Ahn, Leslie Dennison. Doctor's invention, a hypo-
gun, causes no pain, leaves no mark on victims.

COBRA WOMAN Univ 1944 70m. D: Robert Siodmak. SP:
Richard Brooks, Gene Lewis. Story: W. Scott Darling. PH:
George Robinson, W. Howard Greene. Mus: Edward Ward. Art
D: John B. Goodman, Alexander Golitzen. SpFX: John P.
Fulton. P: George Waggner. Ref: FDY. Pic: FM 11:19. with
Jon Hall, Sabu, Lon Chaney, Jr., Edgar Barrier, Maria Montez,
Samuel S. Hinds, Mary Nash, Lois Collier, Moroni Olsen.
Cobra bites twin sisters: one is immune, the other almost dies.
Two-pronged stick with cobra venom. Not one of Siodmak's best.
CODE OF THE AIR Bischoff 1928 silent 71m. SP: Barry
Barringer. D: James P. Hagan. Ed, Titles: DeLeon Anthony.
PH: William Miller. Ref: FD 12/16/28. Lee. AFI. with
William V. Mong, Kenneth Harlan, June Marlowe, Arthur Rankin,
Paul Weigel. Death ray.
CODE 645 see G-MEN NEVER FORGET
COFFIN, The see SADIST, The (1966)
The COFFIN MAKER 1928 SP, P: Robert Florey. Ref: NYT.
Revived dead, Death.
COFFIN OF TERROR see TERROR CREATURES FROM THE
GRAVE
The COLD HEART (G) Hermes-Film 1923 (DAS KALTE HERZ.
DER PAKT MIT DEM SATAN) D: Fred Sauer. SP:Sauer, W.
Wassermann, from the story by N. W. Hauff. Ref: Deutsche I.
with Fritz Schulz, Grete Reinwald, Frieda Richard.
The COLD HEART (G) Orbis-Film 1923 (DAS KALTE HERZ.
DAS WIRTSHAUS IM SPESSART) D: Adolf Wenter. SP: M. M.
Langen, from the story by N. W. Hauff. Ref: Deutsche I. with
Fritz Berger, Ellen Kürti, Dary Holm, Hans Staufen.
The COLD HEART (G) Mercedes-Film 1929 (DAS KALTE HERZ)
From the story by N. W. Hauff. Ref: Deutsche II.
The COLD HEART (E.G.) DEFA 1950 Agfacolor (DAS KALTE
HERZ. HEART OF STONE) 103m. SP, D: Paul Verhoeven.
SP: also Wolf von Gordan, from the story by N. W. Hauff. PH:
Bruno Mondi. Mus: Herbert Trantow. Ref: MFB'58:14. FM
28:18. Positif: 70:41. with Lutz Molk, Hanna Rucker, Paul Bildt
(Glass Manikin), Erwin Gschonneck (Dutch Michael), Paul Esser.
A charcoal burner swaps his heart with the giant, Dutch Michael,
for one of stone, in order to become rich.
The COLD SUN MCA-TV 1954 78m. D: Hollingsworth Morse.
SP: Warren Wilson. From the "Rocky Jones, Space Ranger"
TV series. P: Roland Reed. Ref: TVG. COF 8:39. with Richard
Crane, Sally Mansfield. A strange disturbance on the sun causes
the earth to grow cooler.
COLECCIONISTA DE CADAVERES, El see BLINDMAN'S BLUFF
(1967)
COLONEL BOGEY (B) Rank/Highbury 1947 51m. D: Terence
Fisher. SP: John Baines, W. E. C. Fairchild. PH: Gordon
Lang. Mus: Norman Fulton. Art D: Don Russell. P: John
Croyden. Ref: MMF 1:26. MFB'48:124. Brit. Fm.Ybk'49/'50:
220. with Jack Train, Mary Jerrold, Jane Barrett, John Stone,
Ethel Coleridge, Sam Kydd. A colonel's ghost haunts his own
house.
COLONNE DE FEU, La see COLUMN OF FIRE, The

Color

COLOR ME BLOOD RED Box Office Spectaculars 1966-64 color 74m. SP, PH, D: Herschell G. Lewis. P: David Friedman. Ref: RVB. with Don Joseph, Candi Conder, Scott H. Hall. Artist who uses real blood for the red in his paintings means it when he tells a girl, "This painting will be you." Not as (unintentionally) funny as BLOOD FEAST, but just as repellent in its unrestrained use of gore.

COLOR MOMMY DEAD see PICTURE MOMMY DEAD

The **COLOSSUS OF NEW YORK** Para 1958 70m. D: Eugene Lourie. SP: Thelma Schnee. Story: Willis Goldbeck. PH: John F. Warren. Art D: Sets: Hal Pereira, John Goodman. SpFX: John P. Fulton. P: William Alland. Ref: FFacts. Pic: FM 15:20. with Ross Martin, Mala Powers, Otto Kruger, Robert Hutton, Ed Wolff, John Baragrey, Charles Herbert. The brain of a brilliant researcher is transplanted into a robot.

COLOSSUS OF THE STONE AGE see FIRE MONSTERS AGAINST THE SON OF HERCULES, The

COLOSSUS--THE FORBIN PROJECT Univ 1970-69 Technicolor / scope 100m. (COLOSSUS 1980. DAY THE WORLD CHANGED HANDS. THE FORBIN PROJECT) D: Joseph Sargent. SP: James Bridges, from the novel "Colossus" by D. F. Jones. PH: Gene Polito. Mus: Michel Colombier. Art D: Alexander Golitzen, John J Lloyd. with Eric Braeden, Susan Clark, Gordon Pinsent, William Schallert, Robert Cornthwaite. U.S. super-computer merges with Russian counterpart. Not very dramatic since half the film it seems is "telescreen" calls, between the President and the computer base, etc. Some humor and ingenuity.

COLOUR OUT OF SPACE, The (by H. P. Lovecraft) see DIE, MONSTER, DIE!

The **COLUMN OF FIRE** (F) Melies 1899 1m. (LA COLONNE DE FEU) From an episode in H. Rider Haggard's "She." Ref: Imagen.

COMANDO DE ASESINOS see MURDERER'S COMMAND

COME RUBAMMO LA BOMBA ATOMICA see HOW WE STOLE THE ATOMIC BOMB

COME RUBARE LA CORONA D'INGHILTERRA see HOW TO STEAL THE CROWN OF ENGLAND

COME SI UCCIDE UNA SIGNORA? see TARGET FOR KILLING

The **COMEDY OF TERRORS** AI 1964 86m. (THE GRAVESIDE STORY) D: Jacques Tourneur. SP: Richard Matheson. PH: FloydCrosby. Mus: Les Baxter. Art D: Daniel Haller. Ref: FM 35:74. COF 5:24. Orpheus 4:52. with Vincent Price, Peter Lorre, Boris Karloff, Basil Rathbone, Joyce Jameson, Joe E. Brown, Beverly Hills, Linda Rogers. Undertaker takes to murder to perk up business. Often embarrassingly crude; sometimes effective even in its crudeness; sometimes ingenious, thanks mainly to Lorre's comic talent.

The **COMET** Kalem 1910 Ref: SF Film. Comet explodes cars, melts gold, etc.

THE COMET'S COME-BACK Beauty(Mutual) 1916 Ref: SF Film. MPN 13: 3434. with Dick Rosson, John Steppling. Comet emits gas which retards action.

The COMING AVIATOR'S DREAM Lux 1910 8m. Ref:Bios 4/7/10. Dream: A boy of the future makes an airplane out of furniture.

COMMANDO CODY Rep-TV 1953 12-episode TV series released theatrically Ref: Lee. See also RADAR MEN FROM THE MOON. Pic: SM 4:8. 5:23. with Judd Holdren, Aline Towne, William Schallert, Lyle Talbot. "Heat-ray gun, " etc.

COMME MARS EN CAREME see DON'T PLAY WITH MARTIANS

COMO SE MATA A UNA SENORA? see TARGET FOR KILLING

The COMPUTER WORE TENNIS SHOES BV 1969 Technicolor 90m. D: Robert Butler. SP: Joseph L. McEveety. PH: Frank Phillips. Mus: Robert F. Brunner. with Kurt Russell, Cesar Romero, Joe Flynn, William Schallert, Jon Provost, Pat Harrington, Fritz Feld. Computer's store of information transferred to student's brain in freak electrical accident.

CONDE DRACULA see COUNT DRACULA

CONDE FRANKENSTEIN see BLOODY VAMPIRE, The?

CONDEMNED MEN Toddy c1940 Ref: FJA poster. with Mantan Moreland, Dorothy Dandridge, Niel Webster. Zombies.

CONDEMNED TO DEATH (B) First Anglo/First Division 1932 71m. (THE JACK O'LANTERN MURDERS) D: Walter Forde. SP: Bernard Merrivale, H. Fowler Meare. From the play "Jack O'Lantern" by George Goodchild. PH: Sydney Blythe, William Luff. Ref: COF 8:40. DDC II:309. with Arthur Wontner, Gillian Lind, Jane Welsh, Norah Howard, Edmund Gwenn, Gordon Harker. Condemned man hypnotizes judge to kill.

CONDEMNED TO LIVE Chesterfield/Invincible 1935 67m. D: Frank Strayer. SP: Karen de Wolf. PH: M. A. Anderson. Ed: Roland D. Reed. Ref: RVB. FM 47:49. with Ralph Morgan, Mischa Auer, Maxine Doyle, Russell Gleason, Pedro de Cordoba, Carl Stockdale. A man whose mother was killed by a large bat develops a dual personality.

CONGO PONGO see WHITE PONGO

CONJURE WIFE (novel by F. Lieber) see BURN, WITCH, BURN/ WEIRD WOMAN

CONJURING A LADY AT ROBERT HOUDIN'S (F) 1896 Melies 2m. (ESCAMOTAGE D'UNE DAME CHEZ ROBERT HOUDIN) Ref: Silent FF. A stage conjurer causes a lady to vanish and a skeleton to appear in her place.

CONQUERING WORM, The (by E. A. Poe) see AVENGING CONSCIENCE, The

CONQUEROR OF ATLANTIS (I-Egyptian) Copro Film/PCA Produzione 1965 color/scope (IL CONQUISTATORE DI ATLANTIDE-I. KINGDOM IN THE SAND-Eng) D: Alfonso Brescia. Story, SP: Brescia, Franco D'Este. PH: Fausto Rossi. Ref: Annuario. Bianco #78. with Kirk Morris, Luciana Gilli, Hélène Chanel, Piero Lulli, Andrea Scotti, Mahmud El Sabba. The mysterious Shadow People of Atlantis are kidnapping Bedouins.

The CONQUEROR OF THE MOON (Mex) Col/Sotomayor 1960 (EL CONQUISTADOR DE LA LUNA) D: Rogelio Gonzalez. SP: J. M. F. Unsain, A. Varela, Jr. PH: Raul M. Solares. Mus: Raul Lavista. Ref: Indice. MadM 8:36. Pic: COF 3:54.

FanMo 2:63. with "Clavillazo," Ana Luisa Peluffo, Andres Soler. Monster brain that rules the moon; "Cyclo Ray" which paralyzes; radiation-infected underground moon-dwellers.

The CONQUEROR WORM (B) AI/Tigon 1968 PerfectColor 86m. D: Michael Reeves. SP: Reeves, Tom Baker. Based on the poem by Edgar Allan Poe and the book "Witchfinder General" by Ronald Bassett. PH: Johnny Coquillon. Mus: Paul Ferris. Art D: Jim Morahan. Ref: V(d) 5/14/68. with Vincent Price, Ian Ogilvy, Rupert Davies, Hilary Dwyer, Nicky Henson, Patrick Wymark, Robert Russell. A 17th-century witch-hunter travels from village to village in England torturing "witches."

CONQUEST OF SPACE Para 1955 Technicolor 81m. (MARS PROJECT) D: Byron Haskin. SP: James O'Hanlon. Adap: Barre Lyndon, George W. Yates, Philip Yordan. PH: Lionel Linden. Mus: Van Cleave. Art D: Hal Pereira, J. McMillan Johnson. P: George Pal. From a book by Wernher von Braun; title from the book by Chesley Bonestell and Willy Ley. Ref: Clarens. Pic: SM 1:10. with Eric Fleming, Walter Brooke, Phil Foster, Mickey Shaughnessy, Benson Fong, Ross Martin, William Redfield, William Hopper, Vito Scotti, Joan Shawlee. A group of men on a space station undertake the first trip to Mars. Good-natured, but trying in its attempts at homey charm, comedy. Little to offer except color (orange asteroids, etc.).

The CONQUEST OF THE AIR (F) Pathe 1901 (A LA CONQUETE DE L'AIR. LA CONQUETE DE L'AIR. THE FLYING MACHINE) D: F. Zecca. Ref: SF Film. EncicDS'55:326. Bicycle-type plane.

CONQUEST OF THE NORTH POLE (F) Melies 1912 20m. (A LA CONQUETE DU POLE) Ref: SilentFF. Prof Maboul's airship flies through the stars to the North Pole; Snow Giant. Inventive.

CONQUETE DE L'AIR, La see CONQUEST OF THE AIR, The

CONQUISTADOR DE LA LUNA, El see CONQUEROR OF THE MOON, The

CONQUISTATORE DI ATLANTIDE, Il see CONQUEROR OF ATLANTIS, The

The CONSCIENCE (F) Pathe Freres/Hubsch. 1905 9m. (DAS GEWISSEN-Ger) Ref: SilentFF. Bios 9/30/09. Murderer haunted by apparition of his victim, Death in the form of a black-robed woman.

CONSCIENCE Vita 1912 15m. (or, THE CHAMBER OF HOR-RORS) Ref: SilentFF. Night in chamber of horrors; death by fright.

The CONVICT GURADIAN'S NIGHTMARE (F) Pathe 1906 8m. Ref: Bios 7/15/09. Lee. Dream: Convict turns into "hideous grinning skeleton."

CONVICTED BY HYPNOTISM (F) Eclair 1912 30m. (A DOUBLE LIFE) Ref: Film Index. with Cécile Guyon, Charles Krauss. Wife under husband's hypnotic power accidentally kills her father.

COPLAN SAVES HIS SKIN (I-F) Cinesecolo/CFFP 1966 color 105m. (L'ASSASSINO HA LE ORE CONTATE-I. LES JARDINS DU DIABLE or COPLAN SAUVE SA PEAU-F. THE MURDER-

ER'S TIME IS SHORT. THE DEVIL'S GARDEN)D: Yves Boisset.
SP: Claude Veillot. PH: Pierre Lhomme. Ref: Ital P'67. Film-
kritik 9/68. V3/6/68. with Claudio Brook, Margaret Lee,
Klaus Kinski, Jean Servais. Mad scientist bent on destroying the
world; hunter hunting men a la "The Most Dangerous Game."
COPLAN TENTE SA CHANCE (by P. Kenny) see FX 18 SECRET
AGENT
COPPELIA (F) Melies 1900 (COPPELIA OU LA POUPEE ANIMEE)
From the ballet by Delibes. Ref: Mitry II. SF Film. Android.
COPPELIA (Dan) 1912 (KOPPELIA) Ref: Mitry II:95. CORONA
NEGRA, La see BLACK CROWN, The
The CORONER'S MISTAKE Miles Bros. 1907 8m. Ref: MPW
1:160. Lee. Comic ghost story.
CORPSE COLLECTORS, The see BLIND MAN'S BLUFF (1967)
The CORPSE GRINDERS Geneni 1971 Eastmancolor 67m. D, P:
Ted V. Mikels. SP: Arch Hall, Joseph L. Cranston. PH:
Bill Anneman. SpFX: Gary Heacock. Ref: V(d) 12/30/71.
with Sean Kenney, Monika Kelly, Sanford Mitchell, J. Byron
Foster, Ray Dannis, Vince Barbi. Human cat food turns cats
into killers. Not the worst, but close enough that it doesn't
matter. Grisly but dull. Poorly-staged shock scenes. Classy
title.
CORPSE-MAKERS, The see TWICE TOLD TALES
CORPSE VANISHED, The see REVENGE OF THE ZOMBIES
The CORPSE VANISHES Mono 1942 64m. (CASE OF THE
MISSING BRIDES) D: Wallace Fox. SP: Harvey Gates. Story:
Sam Robins, Gerald Schnitzer. PH: Art Reed. Mus: Lange &
Porter. Art D: David Milton. P: Sam Katzman, Jack Dietz.
Ref: FM 24:6. DDC III:14. COF 8:46. Pic: FMO 2:11,14.
with Bela Lugosi, Minerva Urecal, Joan Barclay, Gwen Kenyon,
Frank Moran, Kenneth Harlan, Elizabeth Russell, Angelo Ros-
sitto, Vince Barnett, George Eldredge, Luana Walters, Tristram
Coffin. A scientist uses the blood of brides to keep his wife
young.
CORRIDORS OF BLOOD (B) MGM/Producers Associates Prod. /
Altura 1958 ('62-U.S.) 85m. (DOCTOR OF SEVEN DIALS) D:
Robert Day. SP: Jean Scott Rogers. PH: Geoffrey Faithfull.
Mus: Buxton Orr. Art D: Anthony Masters. Ref: FFacts.
P: John Croydon. with Boris Karloff, Christopher Lee, Betta
St. John, Francis Matthews, Francis DeWolff, Adrienne Corri,
Finlay Currie, Charles Lloyd Pack, Frank Pettingell, Basil
Dignam, Nigel Green. Doctor encounters criminal group that
provide hospitals with cadavers. Heavy handed and dull.
CORRUPTION (B) Titan-Oakshire/Col 1967 color 90m.
(CARNAGE-F) D: Robert Hartford-Davis. SP: Donald & Derek
Ford. PH, P: Peter Newbrook. Mus:Bill McGuffie. Ref: MMF
18-19:14. V(d) 12/5/68 with Peter Cushing, Sue Lloyd, Noel
Trevarthen, Kate O'Mara. Mad doctor's disfigured wife goads
him into killing girls for their skin tissue glands.
COSMIC FRAME, The (by P. Fairman) see INVASION OF THE
SAUCERMEN
The COSMIC MAN AA 1959 72m. D: Herbert Greene. SP:
Arthur Pierce. PH: John F. Warren. Mus: Paul Sawtell, Bert

Shefter. SpFX: Charles Duncan. with John Carradine, Bruce Bennett, Paul Langton, Angela Greene, Scotty Morrow. Sphere from outer space. Poor.

COSMIC MAN APPEARS IN TOKYO, The see WARNING FROM SPACE

The COSMIC MONSTER(S) (B) DCA/Eros 1958 75m. (THE CRAWLING TERROR. STRANGE WORLD OF PLANET X) D: Gilbert Gunn. SP: Paul Ryder. From a novel by Rene Ray. PH: Joe Amber. Mus: Robert Sharples. Ref: MFB'58:49. with Forrest Tucker, Gaby Andre, Martin Benson, Wyndham Goldie, Patricia Sinclair, Hugh Latimer. A scientist experimenting in metal magnetics ruptures the magnetic field of the earth. Poor.

COSMIC VESSEL (Russ) 1936 (KOSMITCHESKY REIS. COSMICAL PASSAGE) D: V. Jouravliav. SP: Filimonov. PH: Galperin. Ref: Soviet Cinema. Musee Du Cinema: "Rare s-f-film for children."

COSMONAUTS ON VENUS see STORM PLANET

The COUGHING HORROR (B) Stoll 1924 23m. (Further Mysteries of Dr. Fu-Manchu series) Adap, D: Fred Paul. PH: Frank Canham. Art D: Walter W. Murton. Based on characters created by Sax Rohmer. Ref: SilentFF. with Harry Agar Lyons, Paul, Humbertson Wright. Nayland Smith investigates a series of murders.

COUNT DRACULA (G-Sp-I) Korona/Fénix/Filmar 86m. color/scope (NACHTS, WENN DRACULA ERWACHT-G. EL CONDE DRACULA-Sp. DRACULA '71) D: Jesus Franco. SP: Franco and Augusto Finochi. PH: Manuel Merino. Art D: Karl Schneider. Mus: Bruno Nicolai. From "Dracula" by Bram Stoker. See also VAMPYR (1971). Ref: V 4/7/71. SpCinema '71. Fernsehen. with Christopher Lee, Herbert Lom, Klaus Kinski, Soledad Miranda, Maria Röhm, Fred Williams, Jack Taylor, Paul Muller [or Miller].

COUNT FRANK(EN)HAUSEN see BLOODY VAMPIRE, The

COUNT YORGA--VAMPIRE see LOVES OF COUNT IORGA, The

COUNTDOWN WB/7A 1968 color 73m. D: Robert Altman. SP: Loring Mandel, from the novel "The Pilgrim Project" by Hank Searls. PH: William W. Spencer. Mus: Leonard Rosenman. Art D: Jack Poplin. Exec P: William Conrad. Ref: V(d) 2/12/68. PM. with James Caan, Robert Duvall, John Rayner, Barbara Baxley, Joanna Moore, Steve Inhat, Charles Aidman. The political overtones of the race to the moon.

COUNTERATTACK OF THE MONSTER see GIGANTIS

COUNTERBLAST (B) Brit.Nat'l 1948 100m. D: Paul L. Stein. SP: Jack Whittingham. Story: Guy Morgan. PH: James Wilson. Ref: COF. MFB'48:91. with Mervyn Johns, Nova Pilbeam, Karel Stepanek, Robert Beatty, Margaretta Scott. Scientist discovers treatment effective against plague germs. Mus: Hans May.

COUNTESS ANKARSTROM (G) Deutsche Bioscop 1910 20m. Ref: Bios 12/1/10. Gypsy's prophecy that the hand the duke shakes first will cause his death comes true.

COUNTESS DRACULA (B) Hammer 1970 color 93m. D: Peter Sasdy. SP: Jeremy Paul. Story: Alexander Paal, Sasdy, from an idea by Gabriel Ronay. PH: Ken Talbot. Mus sc: Harry

Robinson.   Art D: Philip Harrison.   SpFX: Bert Luxford.
Makeup: Tom Smith.   Ref: MFB '71.   with Ingrid Pitt, Nigel
Green, Maurice Denham.   Widow discovers that bathing in blood
rejuvenates her.
COURONNE NOIRE, La   see   BLACK CROWN, The
COUSINES, Les   see   FROM EAR TO EAR
CRACK IN THE WORLD   (B)   Para/Security   1965   color   96m.
   D: Andrew Marton.   SP: Julian Halevy, Jon Manchip White.   PH:
   Manuel Berenguer.   Mus: John Douglas.   Art D, SpFX: Eugene
   Lourie.   Pic: FMO 2:27.   with Dana Andrews, Kieron Moore,
   Janette Scott, Alexander Knox.   Explosion opens fault which
   runs around world.
CRACKED NUTS   Univ   1941   62m.   D: Edward Cline.   SP: W.
   Scott Darling, Erna Lazarus.   PH: Charles Van Enger.   Art D:
   Jack Otterson.   Ref: COF 8:40.   Boxo 8/2/41.   with Stu Erwin,
   Mischa Auer, Una Merkel, William Frawley, Astrid Allwyn, Man-
   tan Moreland, Will Wright, Pierre Watkin, Emmett Vogan, Mil-
   ton Parsons, Pat O'Malley, Dave Willock, Shemp Howard
   (robot).   Mad Russian invents "robot."
CRAGMIRE TOWER   (B)   Stoll   1924   21m.   (Further Mysteries of
   Dr. Fu-Manchu series)   Adap, D: Fred Paul.   PH: Frank Can-
   ham.   From stories by Sax Rohmer.   Art D: Walter W. Murton.
   Ref: SilentFF.   with Harry Agar Lyons, Paul, Humbertson
   Wright.
CRAIG KENNEDY   (books by A. B. Reeve)   see   CARTER CASE,
   The/CLUTCHING HAND, The (1936)
CRASH OF MOONS   MCA-TV   1954   78m.   From the "rocky
   Jones, Space Ranger" TV series.   Ref: COF 8:40.   TVG.   with
   Richard Crane, Sally Mansfield, Scotty Beckett.   Planetoid vs.
   "gypsy moon."
CRASHING LAS VEGAS   AA   1956   62m.   D: Jean Yarbrough.   SP:
   Jack Townley, PH: Harry Neumann.   Art D: David Milton.   Ref:
   FDY.   with Leo Gorcey, Huntz Hall, Mary Castle, Don Haggerty,
   Mort Mills, Minerva Urecal.   One of the Bowery Boys develops
   mysterious mental super-powers after an electric shock.
The CRAWLING EYE   (B)   DCA/Eros   1958   85m.   (THE FLYING
   EYE.   THE TROLLENBERG TERROR.   CREATURES FROM
   ANOTHER WORLD.   THE CREEPING EYE)   D: Quentin Law-
   rence.   SP: Jimmy Sangster, from a TV series by Peter Key.
   PH: Monty Berman.   Mus: Stanley Black.   P: Robert S. Baker,
   Berman.   Ref: FD 7/10/58.   Orpheus 3:27.   with Forrest
   Tucker, Janet Munro, Laurence Payne, Jennifer Jayne, Warren
   Mitchell, Frederick Schiller.   A tentacled monster lies in wait
   in a radioactive cloud.   Another of Hammer's early, competent
   s-f films.
The CRAWLING HAND   AI/Herts-Lion?   1963   88m.   (DON'T
   CRY WOLF.   THE CREEPING HAND.   TOMORROW YOU DIE)
   D: Herbert L. Strock.   SP: Strock, William Edelson,   PH:
   Willard Van der Veer.   P: Joseph Robertson.   Ref: Orpheus
   3:26.   FanMo 5:33.   with Rod Lauren, Peter Breck, Kent Taylor,
   Alan Hale, Allison Hayes, Richard Arlen.   Another dismembered
   hand on the loose.   Unforgivable; incredibly labored attempts at
   suspense.   Memorable little stomach-turning ending.

CRAWLING MONSTER, The   see   CREEPING TERROR, The
CRAWLING TERROR, The   see   COSMIC MONSTER(S), The
CRAZY ADVENTURE   (J)   1966   109m.   (DAIBOKEN)   D: Kengo
   Furusawa.   SP: R. Kasahara, Yasuo Tanami.   Ref: UFQ.   with
   Hitoshi Ueki, Reiko Dan.   Adolf Hitler is still alive and command-
   ing a garrison in the South Pacific.
The CRAZY DOPE   (F)   Pathe   1911   12m.   Ref: MPW 10:130.
   Chemist's elixir causes increased efficiency.
CRAZY KNIGHTS   see   GHOST CRAZY
The CRAZY RAY   (F)   Les Films Diamant   1923   61m.   (PARIS
   QUI DORT.   LE RAYON INVISIBLE)   SP, Ed, D: René Clair.
   PH: Maurice Desfassiaux, Paul Guichard.   Art D: André Foy.
   Ass't D: Claude Autant-Lara, Georges Lacombe.   Ref: Imagen.
   COF 8:40.   SilentFF.   with Henri Rollan, Albert Préjean,
   Madeleine Rodrigue.   Inventor's ray makes time stand still.
CREATION   see   KING KONG
CREATION OF THE HUMANOIDS   Emerson/Genie   1962   color
   75m.   D: Wesley E. Barry.   SP: Jay Simms;   PH: Hal Mohr.
   Ref: COF 6:60.   FanMo 5:56.   with Don Megowan, Erica
   Elliott, Frances McCann, Don Doolittle.   Robots take over the
   earth after World War III.   Pretty silly.   Choice line: "How do
   you apologize to someone for killing them?"
CREATURE, The (by N. Kneale)   see ABOMINABLE SNOWMAN, The
CREATURE FROM BLOOD ISLAND   see   TERROR IS A MAN
CREATURE FROM GALAXY 27, The   see NIGHT OF THE BLOOD
   BEAST
CREATURE FROM GREEN HELL   see   MONSTER FROM GREEN
   HELL
CREATURE FROM HIGHGATE POND, The   see   MONSTER OF
   HIGHGATE PONDS, The
CREATURE FROM THE BLACK LAGOON   Univ   1954   (3-D)   79m.
   D: Jack Arnold.   SP: Arthur Ross, Harry Essex.   PH: William E.
   Snyder.   Art D, Sets: Bernard Herzbrun, Hilyard Brown.   P:
   William Alland.   Ref: FM 10:26.   Clarens.   with Richard Carlson,
   Julia Adams, Richard Denning, Antonio Moreno, Whit Bissell,
   Nestor Paiva, Ricou Browning, Ben Chapman, Rodd Redwing,
   Julio Lopez.   Scientific expedition in an Amazon lagoon comes
   across a "Gill-Man."   Fair.
CREATURE FROM THE CAVE   see   BEAST FROM HAUNTED CAVE
CREATURE FROM THE HAUNTED SEA   Filmgroup   1960   60m.
   P, D: Roger Corman.   SP: Charles Griffith.   PH: Jacques Mar-
   quette.   Mus: Fred Katz.   Ref: FFacts.   with Ant(h)ony Carbone,
   Betsy Jones-Moreland, Edward Wain, Edmundo R. Alvarez,
   Robert Bean, B. Dickerson.   Monster lurks in the waters off a
   small Caribbean Island.   Flat comedy with nondescript actors,
   dull plot, and dumb narration and gags.   Corman (as an actor)
   contributes one of the infrequent good bits.
CREATURE OF THE WALKING DEAD   (Mex?)   ADP/Jerry Warren
   c1964   D: Frederic Corte.   SP: Joseph Unsain.   PH: Richard
   Wallace.   SpFX: Nicolas Reye.   Ref: RVB.   COF-A:6.   Pic: FM
   46:73.   with Rock Madison, Ann Wells, Bruno VeSota, Katherine
   Victor.   A doctor experiments in immortality.
The CREATURE WALKS AMONG US   Univ   1956   78m.   D: John

Sherwood. SP: Arthur Ross. PH: Maury Gertsman. Art D,
Sets: Alexander Golitzen, Robert E. Smith. P: William Alland.
Ref: FDY. with Jeff Morrow, Rex Reason, Leigh Snowden, Don
Megowan, Gregg Palmer. Followup to CREATURE FROM THE
BLACK LAGOON.

CREATURE WITH THE ATOM BRAIN   Col/Clover   1955   70m.
D: Edward L. Cahn. SP: Curt Siodmak. PH: Fred Jackman,
Jr. Mus D: Mischa Bakaleinikoff. Art D: Paul Palmentola. P:
Sam Katzman. Ref: FDY. Pic: FM 15:3. with Richard Denning,
Harry Lauter, Tristram Coffin, Angela Stevens, S. John
Launer, Gregory Gay, Lane R. Chandler, Don C. Harvey.
Gangster uses scientifically-created zombies against his ene-
mies. Another Katzman dud.

CREATURE WITH THE BLUE HAND   (G)   New World   c1970   color
D: Alfred Vohrer. SP: Alex Berg. Ref: Boxo 5/31/71. with
Klaus Kinski, Diana Kerner. Mad killer in castle.

The CREATURES   (F-Swedish)   New Yorker/Parc-Madeleine--
Sandrew 1966 102m. (LES CREATURES) SP, D: Agnes Varda.
PH: Willy Kurant. Mus: Pierre Barbaud. Art D: Claude Pignot.
Ref: LATimes 10/29/67. with Catherine Deneuve, Jacques
Charrier, Michel Piccoli, Eva Dahlbeck, Nino Castelnuovo.
Machine allows author to make people act out their subcon-
scious.

CREATURES FROM ANOTHER WORLD see CRAWLING EYE, The

CREATURES OF DESTRUCTION AI-TV/Azalea 1967 color 80m.
D: Larry Buchanan. Remake of SHE CREATURE. Ref: M/TVM
10/68. TVG. with Les Tremayne, Pat Delaney, Aron Kincaid.
A hypnotist predicts the time a sea monster will strike.

CREATURES OF EVIL see CURSE OF THE VAMPIRES

CREATURES OF THE PREHISTORIC PLANET see HORROR OF
THE BLOOD MONSTERS

CREATURES THE WORLD FORGOT   (B)   Col/Hammer   1971
Technicolor 95m. D: Don Chaffey. SP, P: Michael Carreras.
PH: Vincent Cox. Prod Des: John Stoll. Mus: Mario Nascim-
bene. SpFX: Sid Pearson. Ref: V 4/7/71. with Julie Ege,
Brian O'Shaughnessy. Rock Men, Mud Men, Marauder Men, and
"prehistoric beasts."

The CREEPER Fox/Reliance 1948 64m. D: Jean Yarbrough.
SP: Maurice Tombragel. Story idea: Don Martin. P: Bernard
Small. with Eduardo Ciannelli, Onslow Stevens, June Vincent,
Ralph Morgan, Janis Wilson, John Baragrey. Mad doctor's serum
turns man into catlike creature.

CREEPERS, The see ISLAND OF TERROR (1966)

CREEPING EYE, The see CRAWLING EYE, The

CREEPING HAND, The see CRAWLING HAND, The

CREEPING SHADOWS see LIMPING MAN, The (1931)

The CREEPING TERROR Teledyn/Metropolitan Int'l/Crown-Int'l-
TV 1964 75m. P: A. J. Nelson. (The CRAWLING MONSTER)
Ref: TVFFSB. FM 31:33. MW 1:12. Orpheus 3:32. COF 8:40.
SP: Robert and Allan Silliphant. with Vic Savage, Shannon
O'Neil.

The CREEPING UNKNOWN   (B)   UA/Hammer 1955 78m. (SHOCK.
THE QUATERMASS EXPERIMENT) Sequels: ENEMY FROM

SPACE. FIVE MILLION YEARS TO EARTH. D: Val Guest.
SP: Richard Landau, Guest. From a TV play by Nigel Kneale.
PH: Jimmy Harvey. Art D: J. Elder Wills. SpFX: Les Bowie.
Ref: FM 14:46. Clarens. with Brian Donlevy, Jack Warner,
Lionel Jeffries, Margia Dean, Thora Hird. Spaceship returns
to earth with monster. First, and not the best, of the Quater-
mass series.

The CRESCENT MOON (J) Toei 1955 55m. (YUMIHARI-ZUKI)
Part II of three-part serial. Ref: FEFN 10/14/55. with C.
Azuma, Y. Hasegawa, K. Yashioji. Famous bowman under
spell of "wicked sorcerer."

CRIES IN THE NIGHT see AWFUL DR. ORLOF, The

CRIME DE L'INGENIEUR LEBEL, Le see DEATH KISS, The

CRIME DE LORD ARTHUR SAVILE, Le see LORD ARTHUR SA-
VILE'S CRIME

CRIME DOCTOR see SHADOWS IN THE NIGHT

CRIME DOCTOR'S COURAGE Col 1945 66m. D: George
Sherman. SP: Eric Taylor. From a radio show by Max Mar-
cin. PH: L. W. O'Connell. Art D: John Datu. Ref: FDY.
COF 8:40. PM: "Eerie atmosphere." with Warner Baxter,
Hillary Brooke, Lloyd Corrigan, Anthony Caruso, King Kong
Kashay, Jerome Cowan, Robert Scott, Emory Parnell, Charles
Arnt, Stephen Crane, Lupita Tovar. Dancing team suspected of
being vampires.

CRIME DOES NOT PAY see GENTLE ART OF MURDER, The

CRIME IN THE MIRROR see DEATH ON THE FOUR POSTER

CRIME NE PAIE PAS, Le see GENTLE ART OF MURDER, The

The CRIME OF DR. CRESPI Rep 1935 63m. P,D: John Auer.
SP: Edwin Olmstead, Lewis Graham. From "The Premature
Burial" by Edgar Allan Poe. PH: Larry Williams. Ed:
Leonard Wheeler. Ref: FD. COF 8:42. 12:43. Pic: FM 10:
20. with Erich von Stroheim, Dwight Frye, Paul Guilfoyle,
Harriett Russell, Jeanne Kelly, John Bohn. Man turned into
helpless zombie by drug, buried alive.

CRIMES AT THE DARK HOUSE (B) 1940 61m. Eros/Brit. Lion
P,D: George King. From "The Woman in White" by Wilkie
Collins. Ref: COF 8:42. Pic: TBG. with Tod Slaughter,
Hay Petrie, Sylvia Marriott. A "woman in white," an eerie
boat house, and Dr. Fosco's "Home for Nervous Diseases."
Slaughter conjures up some choice images: "Red lips and red
wine for the rest of the evening, eh, my pretty?" "So you want-
ed to be a bride, eh? Well, so you shall be...a bride of death!"
"A little hunting trick I learned in Australia--kill the mother
and the waifs will follow."

CRIMES OF DR. MABUSE see TESTAMENT OF DR. MABUSE,
The (1932)

The CRIMES OF STEPHEN HAWKE (B) Eros 1936 65m.
(STRANGLER'S MORGUE) P,D: George King. SP: Paul White,
Jack Celestin. Ref: COF 8:42. with Eric Portman, Tod
Slaughter. An old moneylender is also a murderer known as "The
Spine-Breaker." The quintessence of Slaughter ("Your hands!--
They have sinews of steel!"), with a funny framing-story device.

CRIMES OF THE BODY SNATCHERS see GREED OF WILLIAM

HART, The?
CRIMES OF THE WAX MUSEUM see HOUSE OF WAX
CRIMINAL AT LARGE (B) Gainsborough/Helber 1932 70m.
   (THE FRIGHTENED LADY-Eng) D: T. Hayes Hunter. SP:
   Edgar Wallace, basis for his play, "The Case of the Frightened
   Lady." Ref: FD. FIR'67. DDC III:14,464. with Finlay
   Currie, Gordon Harker, Cathleen Nesbitt, Emlyn Williams,
   Belle Chrystall, D. A. Clarke-Smith. Madman has spells dur-
   ing which he strangles people.
The CRIMINAL HYPNOTIST Biog 1909 10m. Ref: Niver. V&FI
   IV-4:6. D: D. W. Griffith. with Owen Moore, Florence Law-
   rence, Mack Sennett. Girl under hypnosis helps robbers.
CRIMINALI DELLA GALASSIA, I see WILD, WILD PLANET
CRIMINALS OF THE GALAXY see WILD, WILD PLANET
The CRIMSON ALTAR (B) AI/Tigon 1968 color 89m. (THE
   CRIMSON CULT. WITCH HOUSE. THE REINCARNATION.
   CURSE OF THE CRIMSON ALTAR. SPIRIT OF THE DEAD)
   D: Vernon Sewell. SP: Mervyn Haisman, Henry Lincoln,
   Gerry Levy. Suggested by "The Dreams in the Witch-House"
   by H. P. Lovecraft. PH: Johnny Coquillon. Mus: P. Knight.
   Art D: Derek Barrington. Ref: V 9/18/68. with Boris Kar-
   loff, Barbara Steele, Christopher Lee, Mark Eden, Michael
   Gough, Rupert Davies. Witchcraft and reincarnation.
The CRIMSON GHOST Rep 1946 serial 12 episodes (CYCLO-
   TRODE X--'66 feature version) D: William Witney, Fred Bran-
   non. SP: Albert DeMond, Sol Shor, Basil Dickey, Jesse Duffy.
   Ref: Barbour. Pic: FM 14:47. 15:67. with Charles Quigley, I.
   Stanford Jolley, Linda Stirling, Clayton Moore, Kenne Duncan,
   Forrest Taylor, Emmett Vogan, Stanley Price, Tom Steele,
   Dale Van Sickel, Rex Lease, Wheaton Chambers. An arch-
   criminal is after a machine designed to repel atomic attacks;
   death-ray radium detector band kills. Another Republic serial
   with people jumping out of cars, trucks, planes, and boats just
   before they run off the cliff, blow up, collide, or sink. Favorite
   lines dept.: "We've been tricked by cleverness."
The CRIMSON MOTH Biog 1914 30m. Ref: MPN 1/2/15. LC.
   with Jack Drumier, Louise Vale. Curse on the House of Huntington that when the "crimson moth" appears one of the family
   dies.
The CRIMSON PIRATE (U.S.-I) WB/Norma 1952 Technicolor
   104m. D: Robert Siodmak. SP: Roland Kibbee. Ref: RVB.
   with Burt Lancaster, Nick Cravat, Eva Bartok, Torin Thatcher,
   James Hayter, Margot Grahame, Noel Purcell, Christopher
   Lee. 19th-century inventor perfects submarine, bomb, machine-
   gun, etc.
The CRIMSON STAIN MYSTERY Metro 1916 serial 16 episodes
   D: T. Hayes Hunter. Ref: LC. CNW. MPN 14:1398,2867.
   with Maurice Costello, Ethel Grandin. Doctor's drug turns
   men into criminals.
CRIPTA E L'INCUBA, La see TERROR IN THE CRYPT
CROISIERES SIDERALES see SIDEREAL CRUISES
The CROOKED CIRCLE World Wide 1932 70m. D: H. Bruce
   Humberstone. SP: Ralph Spence, Tim Whelan. PH: Robert B.

Kurrle. Ref: Harrison's 10/15/32. Cinema Digest 12/12/32.
with James Gleason, Roscoe Karns, Ben Lyon, ZaSu Pitts,
Irene Purcell, C. Henry Gordon, Raymond Hatton, Berton
Churchill, Spencer Charters, Robert Frazer, Frank Reicher,
Christian Rub, Ethel Clayton. House haunted by a phantom
violinist; skeleton; secret doors, etc.

The CROSS-EYED SUBMARINE Univ 1917 35m. D: W. Beaudine.
Burlesque of 20,000 LEAGUES UNDER THE SEA. Ref: LC.
MPN 15:3932.

CROSS OF IRON see HUSH, HUSH, SWEET CHARLOTTE

CROSSED WIRES (novel by C. R. Cooper) see FAST EXPRESS,
The

CROW HOLLOW (B) Eros/Bruton 1952 69m. D: Michael Mc-
Carthy. SP: Vivian Milroy. PH: R. Lapresle. Ref: COF 8:42.
MFB. TVFFSB: "Eerie old country mansion." with Donald
Houston, Natasha Parry, Nora Nicholson, Patricia Owen, Melis-
sa Stribling, Meadows White. A woman suspects that someone
wants to kill her.

CROWHAVEN FARM ABC-TV 1970 color 72m. P, D: Walter
Grauman. Exec P: Aaron Spelling. Assoc P, SP: John Mc-
Greevey. PH: Fleet Southcott. Mus sc: Robert Drasnin. with
Hope Lange, Paul Burke, Lloyd Bochner, John Carradine,
Cyril Delevanti, Patricia Parry, Virginia Gregg, Ross Elliott,
William Smith. Witches, reincarnation, and dreams. Ref:
RVB. TVG.

CRUEL GHOST LEGEND (J) Shochiku 1968 (CURSE OF THE
BLOOD) D: Kazuo Hase. (KAIDAN ZANKOKU MONOGATARI)
Ref: UFQ 41. with M. Tamura, Saeda Kawaguchi, Yusuke
Kawazu. Family curse; ghost.

CRY OF THE BANSHEE (B) AI 1970 Movielab color 87m.
D: Gordon Hessler. SP: Tim Kelly, Christopher Wicking. PH:
Johnny Coquillon. Mus: Les Baxter. Art D: George Provis.
Ref: MFB'71:6. V 8/5/70: Avenging spirit. with Vincent
Price, Elisabeth Bergner, Essy Persson, Hugh Griffith, Sally
Geeson, Hilary Dwyer, Patrick Mower, Quinn O'Hara. Hardly
enough plot or dialogue for a feature; sloppy-looking and careless
with close-ups. A total waste.

CRY OF THE BEWITCHED (Mex) Yates/Domino 1956 color
90m. (YAMBAO) D: Alfredo B. Cravenna (Crevenna?). SP:
J. A. de Castro (and Julio Alejandro?). Story: Julio Albo. PH:
Raul M. Solares. Mus: Lan Adomian. Ref: COF 8:42.
Indice. with Ninon Sevilla, Ramon Gay, Ricardo Roman. A
native girl uses witchcraft to gain the love of a plantation owner.
Lots of secret rites, chants, little else.

The CRY OF THE NIGHT HAWK (B) Stoll 1923 20m. (Mystery
of Dr. Fu-Manchu series) SP: A. E. Coleby, Frank Wilson.
From the stories by Sax Rohmer. PH: D. P. Cooper. Ref:
SilentFF. with Harry Agar Lyons, Joan Clarkson, Fred Paul,
Humbertson Wright.

CRY OF THE WEREWOLF Col 1944 65m. D: Henry Levin. SP:
Griffin Jay, Charles O'Neal. PH: L. W. O'Connell. Mus D:
Mischa Bakaleinikoff. Ref: FDY. COF 8:42. with Stephen
Crane, Nina Foch, Osa Massen, Barton MacLane, Blanche

Yurka, Fritz Leiber, John Abbott, Milton Parsons. A woman
finds out that her mother was a werewolf. Imitation-Lewton
suspense scenes. Awkward dialogue ("My father was killed here
under strange and desperate circumstances").

The CRYING WOMAN (Mex) Eco Films 1933 (LA LLORONA)
    D: Ramon Peon. SP: C. N. Hope, Guz Aguila. Story: Aguila,
    from a legend. PH: G. Baqueriza. Mus: Max Urban. Ref:
    Indice. Cine Universal 2/10/68. with Ramon Pereda, Carlos
    Orellana, Maria Luisa Zea, Antonio R. Frausto, Paco Martinez,
    Virginia Zuri, E. del Real.

The CRYING WOMAN (Mex) Bueno 1959 (LA LLORONA)
    D: Rene Cardona. SP: Adolfo Portillo. Story: C. T. de M.
    Sanchez, based on a legend. PH: Jack Draper. Mus: Luis
    M. Lopez. Ref: Indice. Cine Universal 2/10/68. with Maria
    Elena Marques, Eduardo Fajardo, Carlos Lopez Moctezuma,
    Mauricio Garces, Erna Martha Bauman.

CRYPT OF HORROR see CASTLE OF THE LIVING DEAD/TERROR
    IN THE CRYPT

4 [CUATRO], 3, 2, 1, MUERTE see MISSION STARDUST

CUATROS NOCHES DE LA LUNA LLENA, Las see FOUR NIGHTS
    OF THE FULL MOON

CUISINE MAGNETIQUE see MAGNETIC KITCHEN

CULT OF THE COBRA Univ 1955 82m. D: Francis D. Lyon.
    SP: Jerry Davis, Cecil Maiden, Richard Collins, PH: Russell
    Metty. Mus D: Joseph Gershenson. Art D: Alexander Golitzen,
    John Meehan. Ref: FDY. with Faith Domergue, Richard Long,
    Marshall Thompson, David Janssen, Jack Kelly, Kathleen Hughes.
    Six American soldiers fall under the curse of the Snake Goddess.
    Slight; borrows the monster's-eye technique from IT CAME FROM
    OUTER SPACE.

A CURE FOR MICROBES Cines 1909 7m. Ref: Bios 9/2/09.
    Doctor extracts liquid from man by means of a wooden tap on
    his stomach.

The CURE OF COWARDICE Pathe 1909 9m. Ref: Bios 1/27/10.
    Doctor cures man of cowardice; latter refuses to pay his bill,
    pushes streetcars out of the way, etc.

CURIOSITY SHOP, The see HAUNTED CURIOSITY SHOP, The

The CURIOUS FEMALE Fanfare 1970 Eastmancolor 87m. P, D:
    Paul Rapp, SP: Winston R. Paul. Ref: Boxo 11/30/70. with
    Michael Greer, Elaine Edwards, Angelique Pettyjohn, Charlene
    Jones. In the year 2427 a master computer rules Los Angeles.

A CURIOUS INVITATION (F) Pathe 1910 Ref: MPW 6:1117.
    Lee. Scientist reverses time.

CURIOUS WAY TO LOVE, A see PLUCKED

CURSE AND THE COFFIN, The see BURNING COURT, The

The CURSE OF BELPHEGOR (F) 1968-7 Radius (LA MALEDIC-
    TION DE BELPHEGOR) D: Georges Combret. Ref: MMF 18-19:
    16. with N. Noblecourt.

CURSE OF COUNT YORGA see RETURN OF COUNT YORGA, The

CURSE OF DARK SHADOWS MGM 1971 97m. color (NIGHT OF
    DARK SHADOWS) D: Dan Curtis. SP: Sam Hall. Story: Hall,
    Curtis. PH: Richard Shore. Mus: Robert Cobert. Art D:
    Trevor Williams. Ref: FilmBltn 6/71:18. V 8/11/71. Based

on the "Dark Shadows" TV series. with David Selby, Grayson Hall, Lara Parker, Nancy Barrett.

CURSE OF DR. PHIBES, The. see ABOMINABLE DR. PHIBES, The

CURSE OF DRACULA see RETURN OF DRACULA

CURSE OF FRANKENSTEIN (B) WB/Hammer 1957 (BIRTH OF FRANKENSTEIN) Eastmancolor 83m. D: Terence Fisher. SP: Jimmy Sangster. Based on the novel "Frankenstein" by Mary Shelley. PH: Jack Asher. Mus: James Bernard. Art D: Ted Marshall. Makeup: Phil Leakey. Ref: FDY. with Christopher Lee, Peter Cushing, Hazel Court, Valerie Gaunt, Robert Urquhart, Noel Hood, Hugh Dempster. Hammer's big early success isn't much.

The CURSE OF NOSTRADAMUS (Mex) AI-TV c1960 (LA MALDICION DE NOSTRADAMUS) D: Federico Curiel. SP: C. Taboada. 77m. Ref: COF 8:42. FM 33:8. with Jermon Robles, Domingo Soler, Julio Aleman. Just about the worst of the Nostradamus series, if such distinctions are possible.

CURSE OF SIMBA see CURSE OF THE VOODOO

CURSE OF THE ALLENBYS, The see SHE WOLF OF LONDON

The CURSE OF THE AZTEC MUMMY (Mex) AI-TV/Calderon 1959 85m. (LA MALDICION DE LA MOMIA AZTECA) D: Rafael Portillo. SP: Alfredo Salazar. Story: Salazar, Guillermo Calderon. PH: Enrique Wallace. Mus: A. D. Conde. Ref: Indice. Pic: COF 8:43. with Ramon Gay, Rosita Arenas. New super-hero the Angel--masked, caped, and haloed; faster than a speeding bullet, more powerful than a locomotive, much more ludicrous than you can imagine. An Aztec mummy is no match for him.

CURSE OF THE BLOOD see CRUEL GHOST LEGEND

CURSE OF THE BLOOD GHOULS see SLAUGHTER OF THE VAMPIRES, The

THE CURSE OF THE CAT PEOPLE RKO 1944 70m. D: Robert Wise, Gunther Fritsch. SP: DeWitt Bodeen. P: Val Lewton. PH: Nicholas Musuraca. Mus: Roy Webb. Art D, Sets: Albert D'Agostino, Walter E. Keller. Ref: FM 10:26. COF 7:30. 8:42. Clarens. with Simone Simon, Kent Smith, Jane Randolph, Ann Carter, Elizabeth Russell, Eve March, Julia Dean, Erford Gage, Sir Lancelot. Follow-up film to CAT PEOPLE. Child's fantasy world and the "real" world. Different, but a little too sweet, "sincere." One memorable melody.

CURSE OF THE CRIMSON ALTAR see CRIMSON ALTAR, The

The CURSE OF THE CRIMSON IDOL Phoebus 1914 37m. Ref: Bios 4/3/14:109: "Weird." Hindu appears and disappears mysteriously, seeks Hindu idol bought at sale.

The CURSE OF THE CRYING WOMAN (Mex) AI-TV/Cinematografica, ABSA 1961 74m. (LA MALDICION DE LA LLORONA. LA CASA EMBRUJADA. THE WITCH HOUSE) D: Rafael Baledon. SP: Baledon, F. Galiana. PH: J. O. Ramos. Mus D: G. C. Carrion. Ref: Indice. RVB. COF 8:42. with Abel Salazar, Rosita Arenas, Rita Macedo, Carlos Lopez Moctezuma, Domingo Soler. Girl inherits a house of horror.

CURSE OF THE DEAD see KILL, BABY, KILL

CURSE OF THE DEMON (B) Col/Sabre 1957-8 83m. (NIGHT
OF THE DEMON-Eng. HAUNTED) D: Jacques Tourneur. SP:
Hal Chester, Charles Bennett, from the story "Casting the
Runes" by Montague R. James. PH: Ted Scaife. Mus sc:
Clifton Parker. Mus D: Muir Mathieson. Art D: Ken Adam.
SpFX: George Blackwell, Wally Veevers. Ed: Michael Gordon.
P: Chester. Ref: FM 2:12. 37:72. 38:23-27. COF 7: 32. 8:20,
42. Pic: FM 17:42. 18:48. with Dana Andrews, Peggy Cummins,
Niall MacGinnis (Dr. Karswell), Maurice Denham, Athene
Seyler, Liam Redmond, Reginald Beckwith, Ewan Roberts, Peter
Elliott, Rosamund Greenwood, Brian Wilde, Richard Leech,
Lloyd Lamble, Peter Hobbes, Charles Lloyd-Pack, John Salew,
Janet Barrow, Percy Herbert, Lynn Tracy. The leader of a
devil cult conjures up demons to eliminate those who oppose
him. One of the best horror movies. It's remarkable how
much mythology and demonology the writers came up with con-
sidering the slightness of the story the film is based on. DEMON
is the closest thing to H. P. Lovecraft on film--and is as good
in its own way as some of his best stories--and bears more re-
lation to them than to the James' story. MacGinnis is a
memorable villain and gets, or makes, all the good lines.
CURSE OF THE DOLL PEOPLE (Mex) AI-TV/Calderon 1960
(LOS MUÑECOS INFERNALES. DEVIL DOLL MEN) D: Benito
Alazrahi. SP: Alfredo Salazar. PH: Enrique Wallace. Mus:
A. D. Conde. Ref: Indice. Pic: FM 18:10. COF 8:38. with
Ramon Gay, Elvira Quintana, Luis Aragon, Nora Veryan.
Miniature murderers, and a zombie that looks like a scarecrow
and isn't nearly as horrifying as what's done to it: A car runs
over it, tearing off its head, its chest is cut open, and its body
is burned.
CURSE OF THE FACELESS MAN UA/Vogue 1958 66m. D: Ed-
ward L. Cahn. SP: Jerome Bixby. P: Robett E. Kent. Ref:
FM 2:20. Pic: FM 8:17. with Richard Anderson, Elaine Ed-
wards, Adele Mara, Luis Van Rooten, Gar Moore. A man lies
in suspended animation 2000 years.
The CURSE OF THE FLY (B) Fox 1965 85m. D: Don Sharp.
SP: Harry Spalding. Sequel to THE FLY. P: Robert Lippert,
Jack Parsons. Ref: FFacts. Pic: FM 69:44. with Brian
Donlevy, George Baker, Carole Gray, Warren Stanhope.
Scientists experiment in teleportation.
The CURSE OF THE GHOST (J) Daiei 1969 color/scope 94m.
(YOTSUYA KAIDAN--OIWA NO BOREI) D: Issei Mori. Ref:
UFQ. A ghost causes a man to kill people.
CURSE OF THE GOLEM see IT!
CURSE OF THE HAUNTED FOREST see WEAPONS OF
VENGEANCE
CURSE OF THE HEADLESS HORSEMAN Kirt Films 1971 Ref:
V 5/12/71:203. COF 17:46. M/TVM'71. with Ultra Violet
(VALLEY OF THE HEADLESS HORSEMAN) "First horror
western."
The CURSE OF THE HINDOO PEARL Standard 1912 37m. Ref:
Bios 1912:141. Pearl brings death and disaster to its owners.
CURSE OF THE LAKE Vita 1912 16m. Ref: Bios 10/3/12.

White men lured to death at cursed lake by vision of Indian
maiden.

The CURSE OF THE LIVING CORPSE Fox 1964 84m. SP, D, P:
Del Tenney. PH: Richard L. Hilliard. Assoc P: Alan V.
Iselin. Ref: RVB. with Helen Waren, Robert Milli, Candace
Hilligoss. Tyrannical millionaire's corpse "returns from the
dead."

The CURSE OF THE MUMMY'S TOMB (B) Col/Hammer 1964
color 81m. P, D: Michael Carreras. SP: Henry Younger.
PH: Otto Heller. Mus: Carlo Martelli. Makeup: Roy Ashton.
with Fred Clark, Terence Morgan, Dickie Owen (the mummy),
Ronald Howard, Jeanne Roland, Jack Gwillim, Michael Ripper.
A pharaoh's tomb is violated. Fred Clark is interesting amidst
a lot of confusion.

CURSE OF THE OILY MAN (Malayan) Malay Films/Shaw 1958
(SUMPAH ORANG MINYAK) SP, D, Art D: P. Ramlee. PH:
A. B. Ali. See also THE OILY MAN. Ref: FEFN 4/4/58.
with Ramlee, Sri Dewi, S. Kamil, Marion Willis. "The Evil
One" gives a hunchback a ring which "transforms him into a
hideous oily man endowed with supernatural powers."

The CURSE OF THE SCARABEE RUBY Gaum/Urban-Eclipse 1914
42m. Ref: Bios 6/4/14. Lee. Evil spirit turns into girl.

CURSE OF THE STONE HAND (Mex?) ADP c1964 72m. D:
Jerry Warren. Ref: Orpheus 3:40. COF 7:46. with John Carra-
dine, Sheila Bon, Lloyd Nelson, Katherine Victor. Two stories:
Creepy moments in the suicide-club portion; nothing in the other.
Hilariously inconclusive conclusion.

CURSE OF THE SWAMP CREATURE AI-TV/Azalea 1966 color
80m. P, D: Larry Buchanan. SP: Tony Huston. PH: Ralph K.
Johnson. Art D: Jim Sullivan. Ref: RVB. M/TVM 11/68. with
John Agar, Francine York, Shirley McLine, Bill Thurman, Jeff
Alexander.

CURSE OF THE UNDEAD Univ 1959 79m. (AFFAIRS OF A
VAMPIRE. MARK OF THE WEST) D: Edward Dein. SP: E.
& Mildred Dein. PH: Ellis W. Carter. Makeup: Bud West-
more. P: Joseph Gershenson. Ref: FFacts. Orpheus 3:27. with
Eric Fleming, Michael Pate, Kathleen Crowley, Edwin Parker,
John Hoyt, Ed Binns, Bruce Gordon. A vampire in the Old
West. A window shade provides the one shock.

CURSE OF THE VAMPIRE see PLAYGIRLS AND THE VAMPIRE,
The/SON OF THE VAMPIRE, The

CURSE OF THE VAMPIRES (Fili-U. S.) Hemisphere 1970 Eastmancolor 90m. (CREATURES OF EVIL-Eng.) D: Gerardo De-
Leon. SP: B. Feleo, Pierre L. Salas. PH: Mike Acción. Mus:
Tito Arevalo. Art D: Ben Otico. Ref: Boxo 8/17/70. MFB.
with Amalia Fuentes, Eddie Garcia, Romeo Vasquez. CURSE
explores the dramatic possibilities of a horror-movie-soap-
opera about a close-knit family of vampires and comes up with
some richly ludicrous scenes. Simultaneously embarrassing
and endearing.

CURSE OF THE VOODOO (B) AA/Galaworld Films/Gordon Films
Inc. 1965 77m. (LION MAN. CURSE OF SIMBA. VOODOO
BLOOD DEATH?) D: Lindsay Shonteff. SP: Tony O'Grady,

Leigh Vance. Ref: COF 5:49. with Bryant Halliday, Dennis
Price, Lisa Daniely, Ronald Leigh Hunt. African curse follows
man from tribe's bush territory to London. One good shock at a
curtained window, a dreamlike park chase, but little else.
The CURSE OF THE WANDERING MINSTREL Walturdaw c1911
10m. Ref: Bios. Minstrel curses castle; his prophecy comes
true when the castle is invaded and its lord crushed under a
gateway.
CURSE OF THE WEREWOLF (B) Univ/Hammer 1961 Eastman-
color 91m. (THE WOLFMAN) D: Terence Fisher. SP: John
Elder. PH:Arthur Grant. Mus: Benjamin Frankel. Art D,
Sets: Bernard Robinson, Thomas Goswell. From the novel "The
Werewolf of Paris" by Guy Endore. Ref: FM 12:34-39. Pic:
FM 11:15. 19:41. with Oliver Reed, Clifford Evans, Yvonne
Romain, Catherine Feller, Anthony Dawson, Hira Talfrey, George
Woodbridge, Michael Ripper. Leisurely, rather dull horror
film. An alarming number of British phrases pop up for a story
set in Spain.
CURSE OF THE WRAYDONS (B) Ambassador 1946 94m.
(SECRET OF THE WRAYDONS. THE TERROR OF LONDON) D:
Victor Gover. SP: Owen George. From the play "Spring-
Heeled Jack, The Terror of London" by Slaughter. PH: S. Onions.
Ref: MFB'46:122. with Tod Slaughter, Bruce Seton, Andrew
Laurence. "Diabolical machine."
The CURSED POND (J) Toei 1968 85m. (KAIBYO NOROI NO
NUMA) D: Yoshihiro Ishikawa. Ref: Unij. Bltn#31 with Kotaro
Satomi, Royhei Uchida. Ghost story: cat-woman.
CURUCU, BEAST OF THE AMAZON Univ/Jewell 1956 color 76m.
SP, D: Curt Siodmak. PH: Rudolfo Icsey. Mus: Raoul Kraushaar.
Art D: Pierino Massenzi. SpFX: Howard A. Anderson. Ed:
Terry Morse. Ref: FDY. with Beverly Garland, John Bromfield,
Tom Payne, Harvey Chalk. "Mythical beast" scaring natives off
plantation at the headwaters of the Amazon. Badly-staged action;
lots of snakes.
CYBORG 2087 United 1966 87m. (MAN FROM TOMORROW) D:
Franklin Adreon. SP: Arthur C. Pierce. Eastmancolor. Mus:
Paul Dunlap. Art D: Paul Sylos, Jr. Ref: SF Film. with Michael
Rennie, Wendell Corey, Eduard Franz, Karen Steele. Cyborgs
travel back in time to prevent their own creation.
The CYCLOPS AA 1957 75m. SP, D, P: Bert I. Gordon. Ass't P:
Flora Gordon. Snake Fight Supervision: Ralph D. Helfer. Ref:
MFB'57:45. FM 14:17. Pic: FM 13:9. with Lon Chaney, Jr.,
James Craig, Gloria Talbott, Tom Drake. Expedition finds Cy-
clops in Mexican Valley. Clumsy and boring.
CYCLOTRODE X see CRIMSON GHOST, The

D-DAY ON MARS see PURPLE MONSTER STRIKES, The
D.O.A. see MONSTER AND THE GIRL, The
D.T.'S or THE EFFECT OF DRINK (B) Gaumont 1905 4m.
Drunk sees "demons and grotesque monsters." His bed turns

into a "dreadful monster."--Hist. Brit. Film.
DAGORA, THE SPACE MONSTER (J) Toho 1963 color 81m.
(DOGORA, UCHU DAIKAIJU DOGORA. SPACE MONSTER,
DOGORA) SP,D, Inoshiro Honda. PH: Hajime Koizumi. Ref:
V 8/4/65. with Hiroshi Koizumi, Yoko Fujiyama, Yosuke At-
suki. "Mutant cell from atomic radiation" floats in from space.
One of Toho's worst. Just a lot of running around.
DAI KOESU YONGKARI see MONSTER YONGKARI
DAI-SANJI SEKAI TAISEN see WORLD WAR III BREAKS OUT
DAIBOKEN see CRAZY ADVENTURE
DAIKAIJU BARAN see VARAN
DAIKYOJU GAMERA see GAMMERA--THE INVINCIBLE
DAIKOJU GAPPA see GAPPA
DAIMAJIN see MAJIN
DAIMAJIN GYAKUSHU see MAJIN STRIKES AGAIN
DAIMAJIN IKARU see RETURN OF MAJIN, The
DALEKS--INVASION EARTH 2150 A.D. (B) Cont/AARU (Amicus)
1966 Technicolor/scope 84m. (INVASION EARTH 2150 A.D.)
D: Gordon Flemyng. SP: Milton Subotsky. Add'l Dial: David
Whittaker. From the TV serial by Terry Nation. Sequel to DR.
WHO AND THE DALEKS. PH: John Wilcox. Mus: Bill McGuf-
fie. Art D: George Provis. SpFX: Ted Samuels. Electronic
Mus: Barry Gray. Ref: Shriek 4:53. MMF. with Peter Cush-
ing, Bernard Cribbins, Andrew Keir, Ray Brooks, Jill Curzon,
Roberta Tovey.
DAMA DE LA MUERTE, La see LADY AND DEATH, The
DAMA DI PICCHE, La see QUEEN OF SPADES (I-1913)
DAMA EN EL MUERTE, La see LADY AND DEATH, The
DAME DE PIQUE, La see QUEEN OF SPADES (1937/1965)
DAMNATION DE FAUST, La see FAUST (1897)
The DAMNATION OF DR. FAUST (F) 1904 15m. (LA DAMNA-
TION DU DOCTEUR FAUST) From the opera by Gounod. Ref:
Mitry II. DDC II: 383.
DAMNED, The see THESE ARE THE DAMNED
The DANCE OF FIRE Pathe 3m. 1909 Ref: Bios 1/20/10.
"Serpentine dancer" rises from crevice in the earth and dances
until a giant spider descends from above, causing her to sink
back.
DANCE OF COBRA TO PLAYING OF VEENA (India--Hindi) Chitra
1960 (NACHE NAGIN BAJE BEEN) D: Tara Harish. Ref:
FEFN 7/60. with Helen, Chandrasekhar. Girl cursed:
"Anyone who marries her will die of snake bite." Town boy
marries her, dies; "but the Queen of the Snake Empire restores
him from the dead."
DANCER AND THE VAMPIRE, The see VAMPIRE AND THE BAL-
LERINA, The
DANCES OF THE AGES Edison 1913 16m. Ref: Kinetogram
5/15/13. Bios 7/31/13: "Miniature dancers." with Duane
Wagar. Prehistoric to modern dance.
The DANCING BEETLE World 1915 Ref: MPW 24:142. MPN
3/27/15. Egyptian beetle's painful bite compels victim to
dance.
The DANCING DOLL Kalem 1915 40m. Ref: Lee. MPW

26:91. "A demented scientist" believes that life can be artificial-
ly created "in an inanimate object."

The DANCING POWDER Walturdaw 1908 8m. Powder makes
people dance.

The DANCING POWDER Pathe (F) 1911 7m. Ref: SilentFF.
"Valse Powder" prescribed by doctor makes everything it's ap-
plied to dance.

DANCING TABLOIDS (B) C&M 1909 8m. Ref: Bios 9/23/09.
Man buys "tabloids" which give user great energy.

DANGER: DIABOLIK (I-F) Para/Dino De Laurentiis--Marianne
Productions 1967 color 88m. (DIABOLIK. DIABOLIK CONTRE
L'INSPECTEUR GINKO-F) D: Mario Bava. SP: Bava, Dino
Maiuri, Adriano Baracco. Based on a story by Angela and
Luciana Guissani. PH: Antonio Rinaldi. Mus: Ennio Morri-
cone. Art D: Flavio Mogherini. Ref: MMF 18-19:21. with
John Phillip Law, Marisa Mell, Michael Piccoli, Adolfo Celi,
Terry-Thomas, Claudio Gora, Mario Donen. Laser torch;
"gold capsule" that allows Diabolik to simulate death.

DANGER VIENT DE L'ESPACE see DAY THE SKY EXPLODED,
The

DANGEROUS ADVENTURE see GAME OF DEATH, A

A DANGEROUS AFFAIR Col 1931 75m. D: Edward Sedgwick.
SP: Howard J. Green. PH: Teddy Tetzlaff. Ref: V 12/1/31.
Photoplay 11/31. with Jack Holt, Ralph Graves, Sally Blane,
Edward Brophy, William V. Mong, Charles Middleton, DeWitt
Jennings, Blanche Friderici, Esther Muir, Susan Fleming.
Lawyer murdered after reading of will; "ghost gang," "haunted
house," an "eerie," uninhabited mansion.

A DANGEROUS EXPERIMENT Victor 1913 30m. Ref: Lee.
"Soul-exchange."

DANGERS OF THE DEEP (By L. Jacobson) see SCARLET
STREAK, The

DANNY THE DRAGON (B) CFF/Ansus 1966 serial 10 episodes
SP, D: C. M. Pennington-Richards. SP: also Michael Barnes.
Based on a story by Henry Geddes. PH: John Coquillon. Mus:
Harry Robinson. Art D: Bernard Sarron. Ref: MFB'67:123.
with Sally Thomsett, Jack Wild, Jack Le White (Danny; voice by
Kenneth Connor). Danny the Dragon arrives on earth in an in-
visible ship.

DANS LE FILET DU SADIQUE see HORRORS OF SPIDER ISLAND

DANS LES GRIFFES DU MANIAQUE see DIABOLICAL DR. Z.,
The

DANSE MACABRE Macgowan 1922 11m. Based on the composition by Saint-Saens. Ref: MPW 57:529. with Adolph Bolm,
Olin Howland. Spectre of Death.

DANSE MACABRE (by E. A. Poe) see CASTLE OF BLOOD

DANTE'S INFERNO (I) Milano 1909 59m. (L'INFERNO) D:
Giuseppe de Liguoro. From Dante's "Hell." PH: Emilio
Proncarolo. Art D: F. Bertolini, A. Fadovan. Footage in
DANTE'S INFERNO (1924/1935) and HELLEVISION. Ref: SilentFF.
Mitry V:69. FM 67:11. with Salvatore Papa, A. Milta.

DANTE'S PURGATORIO Cinema Productions 1913 Ref: Bios
3/20/13. 7-headed beast.

DANZA MACABRA, La see CASTLE OF BLOOD

DARBY O'GILL AND THE LITTLE PEOPLE BV 1959 Techni-
color 93m. D: Robert Stevenson. SP: Lawrence Edward Wat-
kin. From stories by H. T. Kavanagh. P: Walt Disney. PH:
Winton C. Hoch. Mus: Oliver Wallace. Art D: Carroll Clark.
Sets: Emile Kuri, Fred MacLean. SpFX: Eustace Lycett, Peter
Ellenshaw. Animation: Joshua Meador. Ref: FFacts. FM 12:6.
COF 1:61. with Albert Sharpe, Janet Munro, Sean Connery,
Kieron Moore, Jimmy O'Dea, Estelle Winwood, Dennis O'Dea,
Jack MacGowran. Spirit horse (pookah); leprechauns; death
coach (Costa Bower); banshee. Fairly satisfying thanks to good
special effects; Janet Munro is appealing in a calculated way.

DAREDEVILS OF THE RED CIRCLE Rep 1939 serial 12 episodes D: William Witney, John English. Ref: Barbour. COF
11:26. Imagen. Pic: STI 3:10. with Charles Quigley, Herman
Brix (aka bruce Bennett), David Sharpe, Miles Mander, Charles
Middleton, C. Montague Shaw, Raymond Bailey, George Chesebro. Ray; mysterious waves; poison gas.

DARK, The see HORROR HOUSE

DARK BUTTERFLIES see BLACK BUTTERFLIES

DARK DREAMS 213 Releasing Organization 1971 75m. D: Roger
Guermontes. SP, P: Canidia Ference. Mus: Charles Morrow
Inc. Ref: V 6/2/71. with Tina Russell, Tim Long. Cult of
devil worshipers.

DARK EYES OF LONDON (novel by E. Wallace) see DEAD EYES
OF LONDON/HUMAN MONSTER, The

DARK INTRUDER Univ 1965 59m. D: Harvey Hart. SP: Barre
Lyndon. Made as pilot for TV show, "Black Cloak": shown on
the Alfred Hitchcock Hour. PH: John F. Warren. Mus D:
Stanley Wilson. Art D: L. S. Papez. Ref: COF 8:48. PM.
Orpheus 4:51. with Marck Richman, Gilbert Green, Leslie
Nielsen, Judi Meredith, Werner Klemperer. "Ancient Sumerian
gods" behind wave of murders in San Francisco in the 1890's.

The DARK MIRROR Para/Artcraft 1920 D: Charles Giblyn. Ref:
Exhibitors Herald: "Psychic influence." with Dorothy Dalton,
Pedro de Cordoba, Huntley Gordon. Gangster sees girl he thinks
is a ghost; drowns himself.

DARK SECRET (B) Nettleford 1949 85m. D: MacLean Roberts.
P: Ernest G. Roy. Ref: MFB'49:180. with Emrys Jones,
Dinah Sheridan, Irene Handle, Percy Marmont. Man's wife
possessed by spirit of murdered woman.

DARK SECRETS Para 1923 65m. D: Victor Fleming. SP: Edmund
Goulding. PH: Hal Rosson. Ref: MPN 27:469. with Dorothy
Dalton, Julia Swayne Gordon, Robert Ellis, Ellen Cassidy.
Mysterious Egyptian doctor cures woman, supposedly a cripple
for life, "with auto-suggestion and 'laying on of hands.' "

DARK SHADOWS see CURSE OF DARK SHADOWS
HOUSE OF DARK SHADOWS

The DARK TOWER (B) Warner 1943 D: John Harlow. Ref:
MFB'43:61. with Ben Lyon, Anne Crawford, David Farrar,
Herbert Lom, William Hartnell. Man controls tightrope walker
with hypnosis.

DARK TOWER (by Kaufman and Woollcott) see MAN WITH TWO

FACES
DARK WATERS UA/Astor 1944 90m. D: Andre de Toth. SP:
Joan Harrison, Marian Cockrell. Story: Frank and Marian
Cockrell. Add'l Dial: Arthur Horman. PH: Archie Stout, John
Mescall. Mus: Miklos Rozsa. Art D: Charles Odds. SpFX:
Harry Redmond. Ref: TBG. MPH 11/4/44. COF-A:36. with
Merle Oberon, Franchot Tone, Thomas Mitchell, Fay Bainter,
Rex Ingram, John Qualen, Elisha Cook, Jr., Alan Napier, Nina
M. McKinney, Eugene Borden. "Haunted" house; plot to drive
girl insane with noises, voices calling her, lights going on and
off. 99% predictable; 100% dull. Stupid ending.
DARKENED ROOMS Para 1929 silent & sound versions 63m.
D: Louis Gasnier. SP: Patrick Kearney, Melville Baker. From
Sir Philip Gibbs' novel. PH: Archie Stout. Ref: V 12/18/29.
COF-A:36. with Neil Hamilton, Evelyn Brent, Doris Hill,
David Newell, Wallace MacDonald, Gale Henry, Blanche Craig.
Spiritualism tricks exposed; pseudo-hypnotist; fake seances.
DARKEST AFRICA Rep 1936 serial (The HIDDEN CITY. KING
OF THE JUNGLELAND. BAT MEN OF AFRICA or BATMEN OF
AFRICA--'66 feature) D: B. Reeves Eason, Joseph Kane. SP:
Barney Sarecky, Ted Parsons, John Rathmell. Ref: MFB'37:
255. Pic: M&H 1:1, 4-7. STI 2:20. with Clyde Beatty, Lucien
Prival, Elaine Shepard, Edward McWade, Edmund Cobb,
Wheeler Oakman. "Batmen" patrol the Hidden City of Joba.
"Prehistoric reptiles"? Usual serial mess. The dialogue
("The bearers are becoming uneasy" "They would not dare lay
hands on a goddess of the Golden Bat") wasn't exactly designed
to be spoken by people, but the actors emphasize rather than dis-
guise the fact.
The DARLING OF PARIS Fox 1916 55m. From "The Hunchback
of Notre Dame" by Victor Hugo. Ref: FM 37:31.
The DARLING OF PARIS 1917 65m. D: J. Gordon Edwards.
From "The Hunchback of Notre Dame" by Victor Hugo. Ref:
MPN 15:1090. FM 37:31. with Theda Bara, John Webb Dillon.
DATE WITH DESTINY, A see MAD DOCTOR, The
DAUGHTER OF DR. JEKYLL AA 1957 71m. D: Edgar G.
Ulmer. SP, P: Jack Pollexfen. PH: John F. Warren. Mus:
Melvyn Leonard. Art D: Theobold Holsopple. with John Agar,
Gloria Talbott, Arthur Shields, John Dierkes, Martha Wentworth.
From "The Strange case of Dr. Jekyll and Mr. Hyde" by Robert
Louis Stevenson. Vampire-like, scientifically-created werewolf.
Fereydoun Hoveyda: "DAUGHTER OF DR. JEKYLL is worth all
the BRIDES OF DRACULA in the world." Andrew Sarris: "Any-
one who loves the cinema must be moved by DAUGHTER OF DR.
JEKYLL." Both statements perhaps should be taken with a grain
of salt. The movie hardly merits all the attention it gets.
DAUGHTER OF EVIL see ALRAUNE (1930)
DAUGHTER OF HORROR Exploitation/Int'l. Films. 1953 55m.
(DEMENTIA) SP, D, P: John Parker. PH: William C. Thompson.
Mus D: Ernest Gold. Mus sc: George Antheil. SpPhFX: Albert
Simpson. Assoc P: Bruno Ve Sota, Ben Roseman. Solo voice:
Marni Nixon. Narr. Ed McMahon Ref: V 12/28/55. MFB
'71. with Adrienne Barett, Ve Sota, Roseman, Debbie Ve Sota,

Richard Barron, Ed Hinkle. Sadism; psychopathic girl.
DAUGHTER OF HORROR see BLOB, The
DAUGHTER OF LIGHTNING (Fili) 1959 Tamarawa-Hollywood
(ANAK NG KIDLAT) D: Mario Barri.. Ref: FEFN 8/59.
Woman struck by lightning becomes pregnant. Daughter of
union, "potentially dangerous," has control of lightning and elec-
tricity.
DAUGHTER OF THE DRAGON Para 1931 70m. SP,D: Lloyd
Corrigan. SP: also Monte M. Katterjohn. Dial: Sidney Buch-
man. From "Daughter of Fu-Manchu" by Sax Rohmer. PH:
Victor Milner. Ref: FDY. London Times. with Anna May
Wong, Warner Oland, Sessue Hayakawa, Bramwell Fletcher,
Holmes Herbert, Frances Dade, Nicholas Soussanin. Ref: MPH
8/8/31. Trap doors; secret passages; hidden cellars, etc.
DAUGHTER OF THE MIND ABC-TV/Fox 1969 color 72m. P,D:
Walter Grauman. SP: Luther Davis, from the novel "The Hand
of Mary Constable" by Paul Gallico. PH: Jack Woolf. Mus:
Robert Drasnin. Art D: Jack Martin Smith, Philip Barber.
SpFX: L. B. Abbott, Art Cruickshank. Ref: TVG. RVB. with
Don Murray, Ray Milland, Gene Tierney, Barbara Dana, Edward
Asner, George Macready, John Carradine, Ivor Barry, Pamelyn
Ferdin. A scientist meets the spirit of his dead daughter.
DAUGHTERS OF DARKNESS (U.S.-Belg.-F-I-W.G.) Gemini/Maya
1971 color 87m. (Le ROUGE AUX LEVRES. ERZEBETH.
The PROMISE OF RED LIPS. The RED LIPS) SP,D: Harry
Kumel. SP: also Pierre Drouot, J. J. Amiel. PH: Edward
Van Der Enden. Mus: Francois De Roubiax. Ref: V/5/26/71.
12/8/71:24. MFB'71:203. Academy. with Delphine Seyrig,
Daniele Ouimet, John Karlen. A young couple encounters a
vampire woman. Stylish, silly. Bad to mediocre, but fairly
pleasant. The plot holds interest by not revealing its direction
too soon.
The DAWN OF FREEDOM Vita 1916 55m. D: Paul Scardon.
SP: William J. Hurlbut. Ref: MPN 14:1246. with Charles
Richman, Arline Pretty, Joseph Kilgour, James Morrison.
Man hypnotized into suspended animation.
DAY IT ALL HAPPENED, BABY, The (by R. Thom) see WILD
IN THE STREETS
The DAY MARS INVADED EARTH Fox/API 1962 scope 70m.
P,D: Maury Dexter. SP: Harry Spalding. PH: John Nickolaus,
Jr. Mus: Richard LaSalle.Art D: Harry Reif. Ref: FFacts.
Clarens. SM 8:8. with Kent Taylor, Marie Windsor, William
Mims, Betty Beall, Lowell Brown, Gregg Shank. Mysterious
connection between Mars rocket and strange happenings around
deserted estate where Mars project director resides.
DAY NEW YORK WAS INVADED, The see MOUSE THAT ROARED,
The
DAY OF SOULS, The (by C. T. Jackson) see SHOW, The
DAY OF THE ARROW (novel by P. Loraine) see EYE OF THE
DEVIL
DAY OF THE NIGHTMARE Governor 1965 89m. (DON'T
SCREAM, DORIS MAYS) D: John Bushelman. SP: Leonard Gold-
stein. PH: Ted Mikels. Mus: Andre Brummer. Ref: V 9/29/65.

RVB. with John Ireland, Elena Verdugo, John Hart, James Cross, Liz Renay. Supposedly murdered woman "returns from the dead" to seek revenge.

DAY OF THE TRIFFIDS (B) AA/Security 1963 color/scope 93m. (REVOLT OF THE TRIFFIDS. INVASION OF THE TRIFFIDS) D: Steve Sekely. SP: Philip Yordan, from the novel by John Wyndham. PH: Ted Moore, SpFX: Wally Veevers. Ref: Orpheus 3:28. with Howard Keel, Mervyn Johns, Kieron Moore, Nicole Maurey, Janette Scott. Carnivorous plants overrun the earth. A potpourri of loose ends, incomplete ideas, and occasional picturesque groupings of Triffids. Definitely not as good as the book, but not that inferior either.

DAY THAT SHADOW MOUNTAIN DIED, The see DEVIL-WOLF OF SHADOW MOUNTAIN

The DAY THE EARTH CAUGHT FIRE (B) Univ/Pax 1961 Dyaliscope 99m. (THE DAY THE SKY CAUGHT FIRE) P,D: Val Guest. SP: Guest, Wolf Mankowitz. PH: Harry Waxman. Mus: Stanley Black. Art D: Tony Masters. SpFX: Les Bowie. Ref: Orpheus 3:30. with Janet Munro, Leo McKern, Edward Judd, Michael Goodliffe, Arthur Christiansen, Reginald Beckwith, Renee Asherson, Edward Underdown, Austin Trevor. TVG: "Nuclear tests shift the earth's orbit and send it hurtling toward the sun." The plot gets lost in sub-plots, and vice versa. Then again, the plots are such that they should get lost.

DAY THE EARTH FROZE (Finnish-Russ)| Renaissance/Mosfilm 1959 ('63-U.S.) 67m. (SAMPO) D: Gregg Sebelious. P: Julius Strandberg. Narr: Marvin Miller. Ref: FM 8:15. Orpheus 4:37. A witch stops the sun and freezes the earth. Nonsensical dubbed mishmash.

The DAY THE EARTH STOOD STILL Fox 1951 92m. D: Robert Wise. SP: Edmund H. North, from the story "Farewell to the Master" by Harry Bates. PH: Leo Tover. Mus: Bernard Herrmann. Art D: Lyle Wheeler, Addison Hehr. Ref: FM 10:25. 13:7. 14:44. SM 8:32. Pic: FM 10:28. 16:42. with Michael Rennie, Patricia Neal, Hugh Marlowe, Sam Jaffe, Billy Gray, House Peters, Jr., James Seay, Drew Pearson, Francis Bavier, Frank Conroy, Lock Martin, Carleton Young, Tyler McVey, Robert Osterloh, Fay Roope, Edith Evanson. A man from outer space arrives on earth with a warning. The big, early-'50's s-f film doesn't hold up that well, though parts are still impressive.

The DAY THE FISH CAME OUT (B-Greek) Fox 1967 color 109m. SP,D,P: Michael Cacoyannis. PH: Walter Lassally. Mus: Mikis Theodorakis. Art D: Spyros Vassiliou. Ref: FFacts. MMF. with Tom Courtenay, Sam Wanamaker, Colin Blakely, Candice Bergen, Ian Ogilvy, William Berger, James Connolly, Patricia Burke. In the year 1972 two atom bombs and "the ultimate weapon" are lost on a Greek island.

DAY THE SKY CAUGHT FIRE, The see DAY THE EARTH CAUGHT FIRE, The

The DAY THE SKY EXPLODED (I-F) Excelsior/Royal-Lux 1958 ('61-U.S.) 80m. (LA MORTE VIENE DALLO SPAZIO-I. DANGER VIENT DE L'ESPACE-F. DEATH COMES FROM SPACE. DEATH COMES FROM OUTER SPACE) D: Paolo Heusch (William De

Lane Lea--Eng. version). SP: Marcello Coscia, A. Continenza.
Story: Virgilio Sabel. PH: Mario Bava. Mus: Carlo Rustichelli. Ref: FFacts. FM 2:23.26:4. with Paul Hubschmid, Fiorella
Mari, Madel(e)ine Fischer, Ivo Garrani, Sam Galter, Giacomo
Rossi-Stuart, Jean-Jacques Delbo. An explosion sends asteroids
out of their orbit. Hard-to-follow, or rather, hard-to-want-to-
follow dubbed mess.

DAY THE WORLD CHANGED HANDS see COLOSSUS--THE FOR-
BIN PROJECT

DAY THE WORLD ENDED American Releasing Corp/Golden State
1956 78m. D, P: Roger Corman. SP: Lou Rusoff. PH: Jock
Feindel. Mus: Ronald Stein. Exec P: Alex Gordon. Ref: V 12/29/
55. with Lori Nelson, Paul Birch, Richard Denning, Paul Blaisdell (monster), Adele Jergens, Touch Connors, Raymond Hatton,
Paul Dubov, Jonathan Haze. Seven people survive an atomic explosion. Poor early Corman. Remake: YEAR 2889?

A DAY WITH THE DEVIL (Mex) Posa Films 1945 (UN DIA
CON EL DIABLO) SP, D: Miguel Delgado. Story: Jaime Salva-
dor. PH: Gabriel Figueroa. Mus: R. Ramirez. Ref: Indice.
Lee. DDC II:342. with "Cantinflas," Susana Cora, Andres Soler,
Horned devil.

The DEAD ALIVE Gaumont 1916 55m. Ref: MPW 27:1189,1314.
MPN 13:1178. Hypnotism; crook forces twin sister of dead girl
to pose as her spirit.

The DEAD DON'T FORGIVE (Sp) Juro Films 1963 (LOS MUERTOS
NO PERDONAN) D: Julio Coll. PH: Julio Rojas. Ref: MMF.
9:16. COF 4:58. with Javier Escribá, Luis Prendes, Francisco Moran, Alberto Dalbes, May Heatherly, Antonio Casas, Irán
Eory. A student, through the use of the cards of Zener and an
old legend of the Middle Ages, discovers the man who killed his
father.

DEAD EYES OF LONDON (W.G.) Magna 1961 ('65-U.S.) 108m.
(DIE TOTEN AUGEN VON LONDON) D: Alfred Vohrer. SP:
Trygve Larsen. From "Dark Eyes of London" and "Testament
of Gordon Stuart" by Edgar Wallace. Ref: FIR'67:80. PM:
"Gang of gruesome blind men." Pic: MW 10:36-7. FM 17:11.19:
20. with Joachim Fuchsberger, Karin Baal, Dieter Borsche, Anna
Savo, Wolfgang Lukschy, Wolfgang Borschce. Ref: Boxo 11/29/
65.

The DEAD MAN WHO KILLED (F) Apex 1913 65m. (FANTOMAS
III. FANTOMAS: THE MYSTERIOUS FINGERPRINT. LE MORT
QUI TUE) Ref: MPW 19:1350. DDC II:339. Bios. Master
criminal's gloves made from human skin.

DEAD MAN'S EYES Univ 1944 64m. (Inner Sanctum series) D:
Reginald LeBorg. SP: Dwight V. Babcock. PH: Paul Ivano.
Mus: Paul Sawtell. Art D: John B. Goodman, Martin Obzina.
SpPH: John P. Fulton. Ref: FDY. with Lon Chaney, Jr., Jean
Parker, Paul Kelly, Thomas Gomez, Jonathan Hale, Eddie Dunn,
Acquanetta, George Meeker, Pierre Watkin, Edward Fielding.
Ref: COF 7:38. Pic: MadM 8:33. New cornea from stranger's
eyes grafted onto blind artist. Silly story, acting, comic relief.

DEAD MEN TELL Fox 1941 60m. D: Harry Lachman. SP: John
Larkin. Based on the character "Charlie Chan" created by Earl

Derr Biggers. PH: Charles Clarke. Ref: HR 3/21/41. Boxo 3/29/41: "Haunted treasure ship...ghostly thrills....Who is the ghost of Black Hook?" with Sidney Toler, Sheila Ryan, Sen Yung, Don Douglas, George Reeves, Truman Bradley, Ethel Griffies, Lenita Lane, Milton Parsons, Paul McGrath. Killer disguised as ghost of pirate frightens old woman to death.

DEAD MEN TELL NO TALES (B) Alliance/British Nat'l. 1938 80m. D: David MacDonald. From the book "The Norwich Victims" by Francis Beeding. Ref: PM. DDC II:445. III:262. FD 8/3/39. S&S'68:213. MFB 2/38. COF 16:22. NYT. SP: Walter Summers, Stafford Dickins, Emlyn Williams. with Williams, Marius Goring, Hugh Williams, Lesley Brook, Sara Seeger. Jekyll-Hyde-¹ike headmaster/hunchback commits "series of especially diabolical murders"; commits suicide by cutting his throat with a piece of glass.

DEAD MEN WALK PRC 1943 67m. D: Sam Newfield. SP: Fred Myton. PH: Jack Greenhalgh. Mus: Leo Erdody. Set Designer: Fred Preble. Makeup: Harry Ross. P: Sigmund Neufeld. Ref: V 12/31/42. HR 12/31/42. Pic: FM 21:30. with George Zucco (physician/vampire), Mary Carlisle, Nedrick Young, Dwight Frye, Fern Emmett, Robert Strange, Hal Price, Sam Flint. Physician's brother returns from the grave as a vampire.

DEAD OF LAUGHTER (Mex) Sotomayor 1957 (MUERTOS DE RISA) D: Adolfo Bustamante. SP: Fernando Galiana, Carlos Orellana. PH: A. Jimenez. Mus: S. Guerrero. Ref: Indice. FJA. Lee. with "Resortes," Maria Victoria, Armando Arriola, Luis Aragon. Giant spider; "ghosts"; "mummies."

DEAD OF NIGHT (B) Univ/Ealing 1945 107m. D: Basil Dearden (bus), Robert Hamer (mirror), Charles Crichton (golf), Alberto Cavalcanti (tower room, ventriloquist). SP: T.E.B. Clarke, John Baines, Angus MacPhail. From "Room in the Tower" and "The Bus Conductor" by E. F. Benson; "The Inexperienced Ghost" by H. G. Wells; and stories by John Baines and Angus MacPhail. PH: Jack Parker, H. Julius. Mus:Georges Auric. Art D: Michael Relph. Ref: Clarens. Pic: FM 23:26. COF 7:32. A:40. with Michael Redgrave, Mervyn Johns, Roland Culver, Mary Merrall, Googie Withers, Frederick Valk, Antony Baird, Sally Ann Howes, Miles Malleson, Esme Percy, Basil Radford, Naunton Wayne, Allan Jeayes, Magda Kun, Garry Marsh, Renee Gadd. The ventriloquism episode is the best short story horror movie I've seen. The comic golf sequence is out-of-place here but bright. The weak framing story leads up to a good nightmarish end. The other episodes range from poor to adequate.

The DEAD ONE Mardi Gras 1961 71m. Eastmancolor/Ultrascope P, D: Barry Mahon. PH: Mark Dennes. Ref: MFB'62:51. FM 10:13. Pic: FM 38:60. with Linda Ormond, John Macray, Monica Davis, Darlene Myrick, Clyde Kelley. Voodoo rituals, etc.

DEAD RISE, The see THERE ARE DEAD THAT RISE

The DEAD SECRET Monopol 1913 50m. From the story by Wilkie Collins. Ref: MPW'13:815. Bios 8/7/13. The Film Index. "Uncanny manifestations"; girl under hypnotist's influence.

The DEAD SPEAK (Mex) J. Luis Bueno 1935 (LOS MUERTOS HABLAN) D: Bustillo de Oro. (Gabriel Soria?) SP: Roberto Quigley. Story: Pedro Zapiain. PH: Jack Draper. Ref: Indice. NYT. FD 11/26/35. DDC II:64. with Julian Soler, Amalia de Ilisa, Manuel Noriega. "Drama based on the theory that the retina of the eye retains an image of the last thing seen by a person before death."

DEAD THAT WALK, The see ZOMBIES OF MORA TAU

DEADLY AUGUST NCB Int'l 1969 color 87m. Ref: M/TVM 8/69:10-A. with MacDonald Carey, Mary Murphy, Howard Duff. Space creature with disease fatal to humans runs amok in San Francisco.

The DEADLY BEES (B) Para/Amicus 1967 color 84m. D: Freddie Francis. SP: Robert Bloch, Anthony Marriott, from H. F. Heard's novel "A Taste for Honey" or "A Taste for Murder"? Mus: Wilfred Josephs. Ref: FFacts. FM 46:19. PM. with Suzanna Leigh, Frank Finlay, John Harvey, Michael Ripper, Katy Wild, Michael Gwynn, Guy Doleman, Frank Forsyth. Villain unleashes swarms of "specially bred bees."

DEADLY CITY, The (by P. Fairman) see TARGET(:)EARTH(!)

The DEADLY DIAPHANOIDS (I) Fanfare/Mercury/Manley/ Southern Cross 1965 color (I DIAFANOIDI PORTANO LA MORTE. DIAPHANOIDS, BRINGERS OF DEATH. WAR OF THE PLANETS I DIAFANOIDI VENGONO DA MARTE. I DIAFANOIDI VENGANO D'ALL MARTE) D: Antonio Margheriti (Anthony Dawson). SP: Ivan Reiner, Moretti. PH: Riccardo Pallottini. Ref: COF 9:45. Ital P. Boxo 4/7/69:112. with Tony Russell, Lisa Gastoni, Carlo Giustini, Massimo Serato, Michel Lemoine, Franco Nero, Moa Thai. Light/energy beings from Mars.

The DEADLY DREAM ABC-TV/Univ 1971 color 75m. D: Alf Kjellin. SP: Barry Oringer. PH: Jack Marta. Art D: Loyd S. Papez. Sets: Robert C. Bradfield. Ref: LATimes 9/27/71. with Lloyd Bridges, Janet Leigh, Leif Erickson, Carl Betz, Don Stroud, Richard Jaeckel, Philip Pine. Scientist tortured by "terrifying" nightmares.

THE DEADLY GASSES (F) 1916 (LES GAZ MORTELS) SP,D: Abel Gance. PH: Burel, Dubois. Ref: DDC II:384. Le Reve. with Leon Mathot, Maud Richard, "Pseudo-science."

DEADLY INVENTION, The see FABULOUS WORLD OF JULES VERNE, The

The DEADLY MANTIS Univ 1957 78m. (THE GIANT MANTIS) D: Nathan Juran. SP: Martin Berkeley. Story, P: William Alland. PH: Ellis W. Carter. Mus: Joseph Gershenson. Art D: Alexander Golitzen, Robert Clatworthy. Ref: FM 15:4.14:44. 42:58. Pic: FM 13:67. with Craig Stevens, Alix Talton, William Hopper, Donald Randolph, Pat Conway, Paul Smith. Giant prehistoric mantis returns to life. Sort-of-pleasant, thoroughly-formula '50's monster movie.

DEADLY RAY FROM MARS, The see FLASH GORDON CONQUERS THE UNIVERSE

A DEAL IN REAL ESTATE 1914 17m. Ref: Bios 5/28/14. Scheme to get mansion at reduced figure leads to report that the

115

place is haunted.
A DEAL WITH THE DEVIL Nordisk 1914 37m. Ref: Bios 5/28/
14. LC. Dream. Man makes bargain with devil: fame in ex-
change for ten years of his life.
DEATH Biorama 1911 5m. Ref: Bios 10/26/11. The Spirit of
Death wanders through the streets of a city.
DEATH (Austrian) 1921 (GEVATTER TOD) D: Heinz Hanus. SP:
Hans Berger, L. Gunther, from "Der Pate des Todes" by
Baumbach. PH: Hans Androschin, Eduard Hosch. Art D:
Berger. Ref: Osterr. with Armin Seydelmann, Artur Ranzen-
hofer (Death), Erika Wagner, Fritz StraBny, Louise Nerz.
DEATH AND THE GREEN SLIME see GREEN SLIME, The
DEATH BY WITCHCRAFT see TEMPTRESS, The
DEATH COMES FROM OUTER SPACE see DAY THE SKY EX-
PLODED, The
DEATH COMES FROM SPACE see DAY THE SKY EXPLODED,
The
DEATH COMES FROM THE DARK see BLIND MAN'S BLUFF
(1967)
DEATH CURSE OF TARTU Thunderbird Int'l. /Falcon 1967 87m.
SP, D: William Grefe. PH: Julio Chavez. Mus: Al Greene, Al
Jacobs. Makeup: Maria Del Russo. Ref: COF 12:6. Pic: FM
69:61. Mummified witch doctor returns to life, transforms him-
self into, successively, a shark, a snake, and an alligator to
revenge himself on the desecraters of his grave. with Fred
Pinero, Babette Sherrill, Mayra Christine, Sherman Hayes, Gary
Holtz.
DEATH FROM A DISTANCE Invincible 1935 65m. D: Frank
Strayer. SP: John W. Krafft. PH: M. A. Anderson. Ref:
FD 9/17/35. FJA. Boy's Cinema 8/24/35. with Wheeler Oak-
man, Russell Hopton, Robert Frazer, Lola Lane, Lee Kohlmar,
Lew Kelly, George Marion, Sr., Cornelius Keefe. While a lec-
ture is taking place in a darkened planetarium, a shot is fired and
a man is found dead. Solution to mystery: A ray from the star
Arcturus came through a telescope, setting off a cell which fired
the trigger of a gun.
DEATH FROM A TOP HAT (by C. Rawson) see MIRACLES FOR
SALE
DEATH HAS LAID AN EGG see PLUCKED
DEATH IN LOVE (Mex) Victoria Films 1950 (LA MUERTE EN
AMORADA) D: Ernesto Cortázar. SP: Fernando Galiana. PH:
Jack Draper. Mus: Manuel Esperon. Ref: Aventura: "Imitating
DEATH TAKES A HOLIDAY." with Miroslava Stern, Fernando
Fernandez, E. Issa, J. Reyes.
DEATH IN THE AIR see POSSIBILITIES OF WAR IN THE AIR
DEATH IN THE FULL MOON see WEREWOLF IN A GIRLS'
DORMITORY
DEATH IN THE GREEN SLIME see BATTLE BEYOND THE STARS
DEATH IN THE HAND (B) Five Star Films 1947 44m. D:
A. Barr-Smith. SP: Douglas Cleverdon, from the novel "Seven
Men" by Max Beerbohm. PH: Jo Jago, George Noble. Mus:
Albert Ferber. Ref: MFB'48:29. Brit. Fm.Ybk. '49/'50:227.
with Esme Percy, Ernest Jay, Carlton Hobbs, Cecile Chevrau.

Palmist predicts violent death for four train passengers.

DEATH IS CALLED MYRIAM   see   CAPTAIN FROM TOLEDO

DEATH ISLAND   see   ISLAND OF THE DOOMED

The DEATH KISS (Swedish) Great Northern 1916 (DODSKYSSEN.
LE CRIME DE L'INGENIEUR LEBEL-F.) D: Victor Sjostrom
(or Seastrom). Ref: EncicDS V.9:21. DDC II:308: Fantasy
film.

DEATH MAKES A DECREE (by P. Wylie) see CHARLIE CHAN IN
RENO

DEATH OF A CITIZEN (by D. Hamilton) see SILENCERS, The

The DEATH OF THE SUN (F) 1920 (LA MORT DU SOLEIL)
D: Germaine Dulac. Ref: SF in the Cinema:146. End-of-the-
world film.

DEATH ON THE FOUR POSTER (I-F) P. T. Cinematografica
1963 (CRIME IN THE MIRROR. SEXY PARTY. DELITTO
ALLO SPECCHIO) SP,D: Jean Josipovici. SP: also Giorgio
Stegani. PH: Raffaele Masciocchi. Mus: Marcello de Martino.
Makeup: Romolo de Martino. Art D: Mila. Ref: Ital P. MFB'65:
108. with Antonella Lualdi, Michel Lemoine, Luisa Rivelli,
Gloria Milland, Jose Greci, John Drew Barrymore. "Occult
experiment"; premonition of disaster.

DEATH PREDICTOR, The see WORLD WILL SHAKE, The

The DEATH RAY Pathe 1924 20m. Ref: MPN 30:1982, 2116.
Lee. NYT 11/3/24: H. Grindell-Matthews, English inventor,
directs his "death ray" at light bulb which illumines, then at
gunpowder which flares, then at rat which dies. "These illustrations were followed by hypothetical ones, such as what might happen to an airplane."

The DEATH RAY (B) Atlas 1924 (Q-Riosities series) D: Gaston
Quiribet. Ref: SF Film.

The DEATH RAY (Russ) Pathe/Goskino 1925 110m. (LUCH
SMERTI or LOUTCH SMERTI) D: Vladimir Kule(t)chov. SP:
Vsevolod Pudovkin. PH: Aleksandr Levitski. Ref: Imagen
(:1924). DDC II:308. Pic: Soviet Cinema: 286, 269, 250. with
Irena Kokhlova, Pudovkin, Vladimir Fogel, Porfiri Podobed.
Fascists & death ray.

DEATH RAY see MURDER AT DAWN

DEATH RAY MIRROR OF DR. MABUSE, The see SECRET OF
DR. MABUSE

DEATH RAYS OF DR. MABUSE see SECRET OF DR. MABUSE

The DEATH STONE OF INDIA Bison 1913 45m. Ref: MPW 17:
672. Before he dies, a priest of the Temple of Buddah curses
the sacred eye of the idol which a band of coolies steals. They
all die, the last casting the stone into the air where it hangs suspended until he falls to the ground when it drops on his breast.

DEATH TAKES A HOLIDAY Para 1934 78m. D: Mitchell Leisen.
SP: Gladys Lehman, Maxwell Anderson. Adap: Walter Ferris.
From the play by Alberto Casella. (STRANGE HOLIDAY. THE
STRANGE GUEST) PH: Charles Lang. Technical FX: Gordon Jen-
nings. Ref: Orpheus 3:45. Pic: FM 17:16. with Fredric March,
Evelyn Venable, Gail Patrick, Sir Guy Standing, Kent Taylor,
Henry Travers, Edward Van Sloan, Otto Hoffman, Katharine
Alexander, Helen Westley, G. P. Huntley.

DEATH TAKES A HOLIDAY ABC-TV 1971 color 75m. D: Robert Butler. SP: Rita Lakin. From the play by Alberto Casella, adapted by Walter Ferris. PH: Michael Margulies. Mus: Laurindo Almeida. Art D: Eugene Lourie. Ref: LAT 10/23/71. TVG 10/23/71. with Melvyn Douglas, Myrna Loy, Yvette Mimieux, Monte Markham, Bert Convy, Kerwin Mathews, Austin Willis, Maureen Reagan.

DEATH TRAVELS TOO MUCH (Sp-F-I) Epoca/Lux/Sagitario 1966 105m. (LA MUERTE VIAJA DEMASIADO) French episode: SP,D: Claude Autant-Lara. Italian episode: D: Giancarlo Zagni. SP: Zagni, T. Carpi. Spanish episode: D: José M. Forqué. SP: Forqué, J. de Armiñán, V. Coello, Marcelo Fondato. Ref: SpCinema'66. with Emma Penella, Leo Anchóriz, Pierre Brasseur, Alida Valli, Folco Lulli, Madame Sylvie, José L. Vázquez. Third of three stories ("The Crow"): A widow (Death) answers man's ad.

DEATH WATCH (by E. Wallace) see BEFORE DAWN

DEATHSHEAD VAMPIRE, The see VAMPIRE BEAST CRAVES BLOOD, The

DECIMA VITTIMA, La see TENTH VICTIM, The

DECOY Mono 1946 76m. D: Jack Bernhard. SP: Ned Young. Story: Stanley Rubin. PH: L. W. O'Connell. Mus D: Edward Kay. Ref: PM. V 9/9/46. with Jean Gillie, Edward Norris, Robert Armstrong, Sheldon Leonard, Herbert Rudley, Philip Van Zandt, Bert Roach, William Ruhl, William Self, Donald Kerr, Ray Teal. New drug revives executed murderer.

The DEFEAT OF SATAN Pathe 1909 14m. (LA DEFAITE DE SATAN) Ref: Bios 7/28/10. Mitry:138. Satan, after man's soul, transforms dice into frogs and spiders to make his love think he is a sorcerer.

DEFENSELESS AMERICA (by H. Maxim) see BATTLE CRY OF PEACE, The

DEL PALMA (book by P. Kellino) see LADY POSSESSED

DELITTO ALLO SPECCHIO see DEATH ON THE FOUR POSTER

DELUGE RKO 1933 70m. D: Felix Feist, Jr. SP: John Goodrich, Warren Duff, from a story by S. Fowler Wright. PH: Norbert Brodine, William B. Williams. Ref: FDY. PM. Pic: STI 3:50. Scenes of tidal wave flooding New York used also in S.O.S. TIDAL WAVE, DICK TRACY VS. CRIME INC., KING OF THE ROCKET MEN, JAMBOREE (1944). with Sidney Black- mer, Samuel S. Hinds, Edward Van Sloan, Peggy Shannon, Lois Wilson, Matt Moore, Fred Kohler. "Tale of the destruction of civilization by earthquakes and tornadoes."

DEMENTIA see DAUGHTER OF HORROR

DEMENTIA 13 AI/Filmgroup (U.S.-Ireland) 81m. (THE HAUNTED AND THE HUNTED-Eng) SP,D: Francis Coppola. PH: Charles Hannawalt. Art D: Albert Locatelli. P: Roger Corman. Mus: Ronald Stein. Ref: COF 4:4. 5:59. Pic: MW 4:8. with Luana Anders, William Campbell, Patrick Magee, Bart Patton, Bar- bara Dowling. Murder and violence in and around an old castle, prominently involving an axe, a wax figure, and even, eerily enough, a transistor radio. Still, not enough such props to make it work.

Demon

118

The DEMON (I) Ambrosio 1911 17m. From Lermontof's poem.
Ref: Bios 2/9/11. with Mme. Cemesnova-Moridgi, M. Navatzi.
Satan tempts woman.

DEMON, The see ONIBABA

The DEMON BARBER OF FLEET STREET (B) Select 1936 67m.
(SWEENEY TODD) P, D: George King. Ref: FD 10/11/39. with
Tod Slaughter, Bruce Seton, Eve Lister, Davina Craig. Barber is
a barber merely as a front. His real business is murder,
and he sells his victims to the owner of a pie shop. Slaughter
in good, jovial form.

DEMON DANS LA CHAIR, Le see DEMONIO, Il

DEMON DOCTOR, The see AWFUL DR. ORLOF, The/
JUGGERNAUT

The DEMON DOG (B) Hepworth 1911 7m. Ref: Bios 7/6/11.
Dream: Dog grows to giant size, pursues man.

The DEMON FROM DEVIL'S LAKE 1964 Ref: COF 6:51. with
Dave Heath. Space rays cause the animals aboard a spacecraft
to merge to form one single demon.

The DEMON IN THE BLOOD (Arg) 1964 EDELS/SADFO 102m.
(EL DEMONIO EN LA SANGRE) D: René Mujica. SP: Augusto
Roa Bastos, Tomás Eloy Martínez. PH: Ricardo Younis, Oscar
Melli. Mus: Rodolfo Arizaga. Art D: German Gelpi. Ref:
FM 33:8: "Horror film." Heraldo'64:174. with Rosita Quintana,
Ubaldo Martinez, Ernesto Bianco, Arturo García Buhr, Miguel
Segovia Wolf Ruvinski. Three stories: First: Manager hyp-
notizes boxer to kill. Second: Man believes he sees his dead wife.
Third: Person possessed by the devil.

The DEMON OF DUNKIRQUE Warwick/Ambrosio 1910 14m.
Ref: Bios 10/6/10. Half-man-half-devil-creature in bottle in
alchemist's laboratory grants wishes of man who releases him.

DEMON PLANET, The see PLANET OF THE VAMPIRES

DEMON SHADOW, The see ZUDORA

DEMONIAQUE (F) United Motion Picture Organization/Zodiaque
1956 ('58-U.S.) 97m. (LES LOUVES. SHE-WOLVES. DEMONI-
AC) SP, D: Luis Saslavsky. SP: also Boileau-Narcejac. PH:
Henry Thibault. Mus: Joseph Kosma. Ref: MFB'58:47. FD
3/10/58. A la DIABOLIQUE. New Yorker 3/15/58: "Spooky
old country house." Newsweek 3/17/58: "Cerebral fun in a house
of horrors"; clairvoyant girl. with Jeanne Moreau, Micheline
Presle, Francois Perier, Madeleine Robinson.

Il DEMONIO (I-F) Titanus-Vox/Marceau-Cocinor 1963 100m.
(LE DEMON DANS LA CHAIR-F) D: Brunello Rondi. SP:
Rondi, Ugo Guerra, Luciano Martino. PH: Carlo Bellero. Mus:
P. Piccioni. Ref: MFB'64:160. Pic: DDC II:313. with Daliah
Lavi, Frank Wolff, Lea Russo. Girl possessed by demon casts
spells.

DEMONIO AZUL, El see BLUE DEMON

DEMONIO AZUL CONTRA EL PODER SATANICON, El see BLUE
DEMON AGAINST THE SATANIC POWER

DEMONIO EN LA SANGRE, El see DEMON IN THE BLOOD, The

DEMONIO INFERNAL, El see INFERNAL FIEND, The

DEMONS OF THE SWAMP see GIANT LEECHES, The

DEMONYTE Film Releases 1913 45m. Ref: Bios 11/13/13.

Explosion of "terrific power."

DENARA E D'AMORE see MONEY AND LOVE
DENDAM PONTIANAK see REVENGE OF THE VAMPIRE
DENSO NINGEN see SECRET OF THE TELEGIAN
The DEPILATORY POWDER (F) Pathe 1908 7m. Ref: Lee.
   SilentFF.
DEPTHS, The see GHOST OF KASANE-GA-FUCHI (1957)
DEPTHS OF THE UNKNOWN see TIME TRAVELERS, The
DERNIER HOMME, Le see LAST MAN, The
DESCENT INTO THE MAELSTROM, A (by E. A. Poe) see RAVEN,
   The (1912)/WAR-GODS OF THE DEEP
DESERT PHANTOM Supreme 1936 60m. D: S. Roy Luby. SP:
   Earle Snell. Story: E. B. Mann. PH: Bert Longnecker. Ref:
   FD 3/21/36. with Johnny Mack Brown, Sheila Mannors, Karl
   Hackett, Hal Price, Ted Adams, Charlie King, Nelson Mc-
   Dowell. Hidden passages; paralytic who walks in his sleep ("This
   ghost-walking is plumb mysterious"). Terrible. Lacks even the
   usual pleasantness of a "B" western.
The DESERTERS AND THE NOMADS (Cz-I) Royal 1969 120m. (ZBE-
   HOVE A TULACI) D: Juro Jakubisco. Ref: V 5/28/69. Boxo 10/20/
   69. with Ferene Gejza. Death roams the world after an atomic war.
DESIRS DE VAMPIRE see PLAYGIRLS AND THE VAMPIRE, The
DESTIN EXECRABLE DE GUILLEMETTE BABIN, Le see
   GUILLEMETTE BABIN
DESTINATION INNER SPACE (TERROR OF THE DEEP) Magna/
   United 1966 Eastmancolor 83m. D: Francis Lyon. SP:
   Arthur C. Pierce. P: Earle Lyon. Ref: FFacts. Boxo 9/12/66.
   Pic: FMO 6:23, 40. 5:53. with Scott Brady, Sheree North, Gary
   Merrill, Mike Road, Wende Wagner, John Howard, Roy Bar-
   croft. Unidentified underwater object hatches amphibious crea-
   ture.
DESTINATION MOON UA/Eagle-Lion 1950 Technicolor sequence
   92m. D: Irving Pichel. SP: Robert Heinlein, Rip Van Ronkel,
   James O'Hanlon. From the book "Rocket Ship Galileo" or
   "Spaceship Galileo" by Heinlein. PH: Lionel Lindon. Mus:Leith
   Stevens. Art D: Ernest Fegte. P: George Pal. Ref: SF Film.
   FM 10:24.13:32.14:40.15:47. SM 2:24. with John Archer,
   Warner Anderson, Erin O'Brien-Moore, Dick Wesson, Tom
   Powers. Well-produced but fairly dull father of the '50's boom
   in s-f films.
DESTINATION SATURN see BUCK ROGERS
DESTINAZIONE LUNA see ROCKETSHIP X-M
DESTINY (BEYOND THE WALL) (G) Decla-Bioscop 1921 (DER
   MUDE TOD. THE WEARY DEATH. THE LIGHT WITHIN. THE
   THREE LIGHTS. BETWEEN WORLDS) D: Fritz Lang. SP: Lang,
   Thea von Harbou. PH: Erich Neitzschmann, Fritz Arno Wagner,
   Hermann Salfrank. Art D: Sets: Hermann Warm, Robert Herlth,
   Walter Rohrig. Ref: Orpheus 3:51. Clarens. Eisner. Pic: DDC
   III:195. with Bernhard Goetzke, Walter Janssen, Lil Dagover,
   Rudolf Klein-Rogge. Endless wall separates girl from Death; rein-
   carnation.
DESTINY see MAD DOCTOR, The/WOLF MAN, The
DESTINY'S SKEIN Lubin 1915 35m. Ref: MPN 7/24/15. LC. with

Tom Green, Ormi Hawley. SP, D: George Terwilliger. Man commits crimes during "fits of mental aberration"; remembers nothing.

DESTROY ALL MONSTERS see OPERATION MONSTERLAND

DESTROY ALL PLANETS see GAMERA VS. OUTER-SPACE MONSTER VIRUS

DESTRUCTION OF THE SPACE FLEET, The see ATTACK FROM SPACE

DESTRUCTOR DE MONSTRUOS, El see MONSTERS DEMOLISHER, The

The DESTRUCTORS Feature Film Corp. /United 1968(1966) color 97m. D: Francis D. Lyon. SP: Arthur C. Pierce, Larry E. Jackson. PH: Alan Stensvold. Mus: Paul Dunlap. P: Earle Lyon. Ref: V(d) 2/14/68. with Richard Egan, Patricia Owens, John Ericson, Michael Ansara, Joan Blackman, David Brian, Khigh Dhiegh, John Howard. Laser rubies; laser ray-gun.

The DETACHABLE MAN Pathe 1910 7m. Ref: Bios 9/22/10. A man is able to detach his limbs.

DETECTIVE LLOYD see LLOYD OF THE C.I.D.

DETECTIVES MGM 1928 silent 70m. D: Chester M. Franklin. SP: Robert Lord, Chester Dane. Ref: Photoplay 6/28. v 7/25/28. with Karl Dane, George K. Arthur, Tetsu Komai, Tenen Holtz, Clinton Lyle, Felicia Drenova, Polly Moran. Detectives, bellhops, and "spooks" in hotel.

DEUX CENT MILLE LIEUES SOUS LES MERS see 20,000 LEAGUES UNDER THE SEA (1907)

DEV BALA (India) Bharat 1938 152m. D: B. Apte. Ref: The Lighthouse 6/25/38. with Nil. "Black magic" vs. "heavenly weapons."

DEVDASI (India--Hindi) New Maharashta Pictures 1947 D: C. S. Bose. Mus: K. C. De. Ref: Filmindia 2/47. with Prithviraj, Monica Desai. Stone god returns woman to life.

The DEVIL Edison 1908. 17m. Ref: V&FI 9/12/08. Devil's sudden appearance frightens woman.

The DEVIL Powers 1910 8m. Ref: Bios 12/29/10. Man costumed as Mephistopheles accidentally frightens others.

The DEVIL New York Motion Picture 1915 55m. SP: Thomas H. Ince, from the novel by Charles Swickard and the play by Franz Molnar. Ref: MPN 3/20/15. with Bessie Barriscale, Arthur Maude. Devil tempts several people.

The DEVIL Associated Exhibitors /Pathe 1921. 70m. D: James Young. SP: Edmund Goulding. From Ferenc Molnar's "Az Ordög." PH: Harry Fischbeck. Art D: Charles O. Seessel. Ref: FM 67:10. V 1/21/21. LC. AFI. with George Arliss, Sylvia Breamer, Lucy Cotton, Mrs. Arliss, Edmund Lowe. Cross defeats devil.

The DEVIL AND DANIEL WEBSTER RKO 1941 109m. (ALL THAT MONEY CAN BUY. HERE'S A MAN. Present title from '52 reissue by Astor) P, D: William Dieterle. SP: Dan Totheroh, Stephen Vincent Benet, from the story by Benet. PH: Joseph August. Mus sc: Bernard Herrmann. Art D: Van Nest Polglase. Ed: Robert Wise. Ref: FM 10:26. RVB. COF 6:4. with Edward Arnold, Walter Huston, Simone Simon, Anne Shirley, James Craig,

Jane Darwell, Gene Lockhart, John Qualen, H. B. Warner, George Cleveland, Sonny Bupp, Jeff Corey, Carl Stockdale, Robert Emmet Keane, Fern Emmett, William Alland, Robert Strange, Alec Craig. A young farmer makes a deal with the devil for a box of gold and seven years of good luck. The acting is good, and there are some frightening scenes; but the overall effect leaves something (like real excitement) to be desired.

The DEVIL AND TOM WALKER Selig 1913 15m. D: Hardee Kirkland. SP: Edward McWade, from the story by Washington Irving. Ref: MPW'13:744. Bios 10/30/13. with Harry Lonsdale, William Stowell (devil). Tom Walker sells his soul to the devil for gold.

The DEVIL AS LAWYER Messter 1911 10m. Ref: Bios 10/5/11. "Satan appears in the role of justice, but he is but taking to himself his own."

DEVIL BAT PRC 1941 69m. (KILLER BATS) D: Jean Yarbrough. SP: John T. Neville. PH: Arthur Martinelli. Mus: David Chudnow. Art D: Paul Palmentola. Follow-up: DEVIL BAT'S DAUGHTER. Remade as THE FLYING SERPENT? Ref: FD 1/31/41. Pic: FM 2:48. 50:18. MadM 8:41. with Bela Lugosi, Dave O'Brien, Suzanne Kaaren, Guy Usher, Hal Price, Donald Kerr. Story: George Bricker. A mad doctor creates a giant bat.

DEVIL BAT'S DAUGHTER PRC 1946 66m. P,D: Frank Wisbar. SP: Griffin Jay. From a story by Leo J. McCarthy, Ern(e)st Jaeger. Follow-up to DEVIL BAT. PH: James S. Brown. Mus: Alexander Steinert. Art D: Edward Jewell. Makeup: Bud Westmore. Ref: FDY. MFB'47:49. Ad: "cursed by the brand of the vampires." with Rosemary LaPlanche, John James, Edward Cassidy, Eddie Kane, Monica Mars. The cast does some hilariously exaggerated double takes, and there are some double-take lines too: "Her father is Paul Carruthers? Then the girl's the Devil Bat's daughter!" "I used to dream I was a bat flying with him" "What man would want to know the secret of enlarging bats?"

DEVIL COMMANDS, The see WHEN THE DEVIL COMMANDS

DEVIL DIAMOND Ambassador 1937 Ref: MFB 6/30/37. with Kane Richmond, June Gale, Frankie Darro. Diamond brings misfortune to crooks.

DEVIL DIAMOND see DIAMOND WIZARD, The

DEVIL DOLL MGM 1936 79m. (The DEVIL-DOLL. The WITCH OF TIMBUKTU or The WITCH OF TIMBUCTOO) D, SP: Tod Browning. SP: also Erich von Stroheim, Guy Endore, Garrett Fort. PH: Leonard Smith. Mus: Franz Waxman. From the book "Burn, Witch, Burn" by A. A. Merritt. Art D: Cedric Gibbons. Ref: Imagen. FM 26:24. Academy. with Lionel Barrymore, Maureen O'Sullivan, Frank Lawton, Henry B. Walthall, Arthur Hohl, Pedro de Cordoba, Robert Greig, Rafaela Ottiano, Lucy Beaumont, Claire DuBrey, Grace Ford, Juanita Quigley, Rollo Lloyd, Sherry Hall, Robert Graves, Eily Malyon, Billy Gilbert, Edward Keane. Shivery scenes with miniature killer-dolls and a double-entendre field day for Barrymore as an old-lady toymaker. Diluted by a typical MGM sentimental subplot.

DEVIL DOLL (B) Gordon/Associated/Galaworld 1963 80m. D: Lindsay Shonteff. SP: Lance Z. Hargreaves, George Barclay, from a story by F. E. Smith. PH: Gerald Gibbs. Art D: Stan

Shields. Ref: FM-A'69:22. PM. with William Sylvester, Yvonne Romain, Bryant Haliday, Francis DeWolff, Karel Stepanek Sandra Dorne. Ventriloquist exercises hypnotic powers over his dummy. Film balances very dull Svengali plot with interesting soul-transference plot, tops everything off with a terrific ending.

DEVIL DOLL MEN see CURSE OF THE DOLL PEOPLE

DEVIL GIRL FROM MARS (B) Spartan/Danziger 1954 76m. D: David MacDonald. SP: John C. Maher, James Eastwood. PH: Jack Cox. Mus: Edwin Astley. SpFX: Jack Whitehead. Ref: MFB'54. Pic: FM 16:44. SM 5:20. with Patricia Laffan (Nyah), Hugh McDermott, Joseph Tomelty, Adrienne Corri, Peter Reynolds, Hazel Court, John Laurie, Sophie Stewart. A spaceship lands in the Scottish Highlands.

DEVIL IN A BOTTLE, The see LOVE, DEATH AND THE DEVIL

DEVIL INCARNATE, The see EVIL BRAIN FROM OUTER SPACE, The

DEVIL IS A WOMAN, The see VELVET VAMPIRE, The

DEVIL MEN FROM SPACE see SPACE DEVILS

DEVIL RIDES OUT, The (by D. Wheatley) see DEVIL'S BRIDE, The

DEVIL SAID NO, The see WHEN THE DEVIL COMMANDS

The DEVIL STONE Artcraft/Para 1917 65m. D: Cecil B. DeMille. Ref: MPW 35:90. Pic: FIR'66:213. with Wallace Reid, Tully Marshall, Hobart Bosworth, Gustav von Seyffertitz, Lillian Leighton, Ernest Joy, Geraldine Farrar. Cursed stone fatal to possessors.

The DEVIL, THE SERVANT, AND THE MAN 1910 Selig 17m. Ref: Bios 6/20/12. 10/6/10. The devil appears; man dreams he murders his wife.

The DEVIL WITHIN Fox 1921 75m. D: Bernard Durning. SP: Arthur J. Zellner. Story: George Allen England. PH: Don Short. Ref: MPW 53:588. with Dustin Farnum, Nigel De Brulier, Virginia Valli, Durning, Otto Hoffman. Witch puts curse on captain of ship.

DEVIL WOLF OF SHADOW MOUNTAIN Prin 1964 D: Gary Kent. SP: Gene Pollock. (DAY THAT SHADOW MOUNTAIN DIED?) Ref: MadM 9:41. Consumer Bulletin'64. with Johnny Cardoz (werewolf), Pollock. Man drinks from the track of a wolf in a stream and is transformed into a werewolf.

DEVIL WOMAN see ONIBABA

A DEVILISH DOCTOR Mutual (Majestic) 1913 8m. Ref: MPW'13: 776. Bios 12/18/13. Costume-party "devil" spreads terror; invention cures gout.

DEVILISH DR. MABUSE, The see SECRET OF DR. MABUSE

DEVILLED CRABS Jaxon 1917 Ref: MPW 34:880. Man trades soul for good time.

DEVILMAN STORY see SUPERARGO VS. THE ROBOTS

The DEVIL'S ANGEL Hiller 1920 55m. P,D: Lejaren a'Hiller. Ref: MPN 22:2625. AFI. with Helen Gardner, Templar Saxe, Peggy O'Neil. Hypnotism; psychic phenomena.

The DEVIL'S ASSISTANT Mutual 1917 SP,D,P: Harry Pollard. Story: F. Edward Hungerford. Ref: Clarens. with Margarita Fisher, Jack Mower. Vision of hell in heroine's dream: three-headed Cerberus, etc.

The DEVIL'S BILLIARD TABLE (F) Eclair 1910 5m. Ref: Lee.
    Bios 8/18/10. Man sells soul to win game.
DEVIL'S BONDMAN, The see SCORPION'S STING, The
The DEVIL'S BRIDE (B) Fox/Hammer 1967 color 95m. D:
    Terence Fisher. SP: Richard Matheson, from the novel "The
    Devil Rides Out" by Dennis Wheatley. PH: Arthur Grant. Mus sc:
    James Bernard. Art D: Bernard Robinson. SpFX: Michael Stain-
    er-Hutchins. Ref: MFB'68:102. PM. V 6/12/68. with Christopher
    Lee, Sarah Lawson, Charles Gray, N. Arrighi, Leon Greene,
    Patrick Mower, Gwen Ffrangcon-Davies. Two men arrive in
    London for a reunion with a young friend they find has taken up
    black magic. One of the few even half-decent horror movies in
    recent years. Well-structured for suspense. Lee a bit too much
    as a hero; Gray good as villain. There's a really chilling scene
    with a big spider.
DEVIL'S BROOD, The see HOUSE OF FRANKENSTEIN
The DEVIL'S CLAIM R-C 1920 55m. Ref: Lee. FD 5/16/20. with
    Colleen Moore, Sessue Hayakawa. Devil worshipers; Egyptian
    sorcerers; reincarnated evil spirits; talisman.
The DEVIL'S CASTLE (F) Melies 1896 (LE MANOIR DU DIABLE)
    Ref: FM 67:8. Bat transforms into devil; crucifix makes him dis-
    appear.
The DEVIL'S COMMANDMENT (I) RCIP/Titanus-Athena 1956
    ('63-U.S.) 79m. (I VAMPIRI. LUST OF THE VAMPIRE. The
    VAMPIRE OF NOTRE DAME) D: Riccardo Freda (Robert Hampton).
    SP: Piero Regnoli, Rik Sjostrom. PH: Mario Bava. Mus: Roman
    Vlad. Art D: Beni Montresor. Ref: Ital P. RVB. FanMo 6:31.
    Pic: FM 22:10. with Gianna Maria Canale, Antoine Balpetré,
    Carlo D'Angelo, Wandisa Guida, Paul Muller. Doctor injects girl's
    blood into countess to restore her youth.
The DEVIL'S DARLING Mutual 1915 35m. Ref: MPN 11/13/15.
    Clarens. with Francine Larrimore. Woman makes deal to deliver
    soul to satan.
The DEVIL'S ELIXIR (Austrian) Hugo-Held-Film 1921 50m.
    (ELEXIERE DES TEUFELS) D: Edmund Loewe. SP: H. Held,
    Reinhart Maur. PH: A. Russ. Story: E. T. A. Hoffmann. Ref:
    Osterr. with Karl Elfeld, Mario Mankoni, Julius Strobl, Lina
    Woiwoode, Rudolf Rudolfi (devil), R. Laa.
The DEVIL'S FIDDLER Apex 1914 60m. Ref: Lee. MPW 21:1016.
    Girl under spell dances self to death.
The DEVIL'S FOOT (B) Stoll 1921 20m. (Adventures of Sherlock
    Holmes series) D: Maurice Elvey. SP: William J. Elliott,
    from "The Adventure of the Devil's Foot" by Sir Arthur Conan
    Doyle. PH: Germain Burger. Ref: SilentFF. with Eille Norwood,
    Hubert Willis, Harvey Braban, Hugh Buckler. Original story: Three
    people are found dead, apparently frightened to death by "the
    Cornish Horror."
The DEVIL'S GARDEN F Nat 1920 75m. D: Kenneth Webb. SP:
    Webb, Whitman Bennett. Story: W. B. Maxwell. Ref: Exhibitors
    Herald. LC. Man haunted by the spectre of the man he killed.
DEVIL'S GARDEN, The see COPLAN SAVES HIS SKIN
The DEVIL'S GROTTO Pathe 1912 5m. Ref: Bios 4/25/12. Satan
    performs chemical experiments. "Weird faces in a crystal globe";

"spirit forms"; dragons.

The DEVIL'S HAND (F) Tobis-Continental 1942 ('46--U.S. as
CARNIVAL OF SINNERS) 80m. (LA MAIN DU DIABLE) D:
Maurice Tourneur. SP: Jean-Paul Le Chanois. PH: Armand
Thirard. From "La Main Enchantée" by Alfred de Musset. Mus:
Roger Dumas. Ref: DDC I:171. III:406, 503. TVG. with Pierre
Fresnay, Josseline Gaël, Marcelle Monthyl, Antoine Balpetré,
Palau, Noel Roquevert. A painter purchases the left hand of the
devil.

The DEVIL'S HAND Crown 1962 ('58) 71m. (NAKED GODDESS.
WITCHCRAFT) D: William J. Hole, Jr. SP: Jo Heims. PH:
Meredith Nicholson. Ref: MFB'67:93. COF 4:4. Lee. V(d)
3/24/59. Pic: HM 3:43. with Robert Alda, Linda Christian,
Neil Hamilton, Ariadne Welter, Jeannie Carmen, Julie Scott,
Diana Spears. Curio shop is front for voodoo cult.

The DEVIL'S LOCKSMITH (Austrian) Regent-Film 1919 (DER
TEUFELSSCHLOSSER) D: Franz Ferdinand. Ref: Osterr. with
Herr Ruibar, Ferdinand, Eugen Jensen (devil), Armin Seydelmann.
"Pact among some locksmiths with the devil."

The DEVIL'S LOVER (I) Nova Int'l 1971 color/scope D: Paolo
Lombardo. Ref: M/TVM'71: "Horror-sex." with Edmund Purdom, Rosalba Neri.

DEVIL'S MAN, The see SUPERARGO VS. THE ROBOTS

The DEVIL'S MASK Col 1946 66m. D: Henry Levin. SP: Charles O'Neal,
from the radio show "I Love a Mystery" by Carlton E. Morse. PH:
Henry Freulich Add'l Dial: Dwight V. Babcock. Mus D: Mischa Bakaleinikoff. Art D: Robert Peterson. Ref: FanMo 3:39: "Hypnotist, a
man who spoke from the grave, and a fiend who shrunk human heads."
with Anita Louise, Jim Bannon, Michael Duane, Mona Barrie, Barton Yarborough, Ludwig Donath, Thomas Jackson, Edward Earle.

The DEVIL'S MESSENGER Herts-Lion 1962 ('59) (U.S.-Swedish)
72m. (13 DEMON STREET or #13 DEMON STREET) D: Curt
Siodmak (U.S.-Herbert L. Strock). SP: Leo Guild, from "Girl in
Ice" and other stories by Siodmak. Ref: COF 4:4. FM 23:13-8:14.
Pic: HM 9:38. FM 21:7. FanMo 2:22. with Lon Chaney, Jr., Karen
Kadler, John Crawford, Michael Hinn. Devil has girl carry out
tasks in order to be admitted into the Dark World.

The DEVIL'S MISTRESS Emerson/Holiday/WGW 1968 color 66m.
SP, D: Orville Wanzer. PH: Teddy Gregory. Ref: Boxo 11/11/68.
4/7/69. with Joan Stapleton, Robert Gregory, Forrest Westmore-
land. Indian half-caste wreaks supernatural revenge on four outlaws who killed her husband, draining the life from them with her
"kisses."

The DEVIL'S MOTHER-IN-LAW 14m. Ref: Bios 4/14/10. Devil
marries girl, confines her mother to hell.

DEVILS OF DARKNESS (B) Fox 1964 Eastmancolor 88m. D:
Lance Comfort. SP: Lyn Fairhurst. PH: Reginald Wyer. Mus:
Bernie Fenton. Makeup: George Blackler. Ref: Shriek 2:53. with
William Sylvester, Hubert Noel, Tracy Reed, Carole Gray, Diana
Decker, Rona Anderson, Victor Brooks, Peter Illing, Brain Oulton,
Eddie Byrne. "Cult of vampires and devil worshippers."--PM.

The DEVIL'S OWN (B) Fox/Hammer 1966 color 90m. D: Cyril
Frankel. SP: Nigel Kneale, from the novel by Peter Curtis. (THE

WITCHES) PH: Arthur Grant. Mus sc: Richard Rodney Bennett.
Art D: Don Mingaye. Prod Des: Bernard Robinson. Ref: MFB'67:
14. PM. with Joan Fontaine, Kay Walsh, Duncan Lamont, Leonard
Rossiter, Gwen Ffrangcon-Davies, Martin Stephens, Alec McCowen,
Ingrid Brett. Schoolteacher, victim of witchcraft in Africa, returns
to England but the hex follows her.
The DEVIL'S PARTNER AI/Horon/Filmgroup 1962(1958) 61m.
    D: Charles Rondeau. SP: Stanley Clements, Laura Mathews. PH:
    Edward Cronjager. Mus: Ronald Stein, Art D: Daniel Haller. Ref:
    MFB'60:52. HM 9:40. with Edgar Buchanan, Edwin Nelson, Jean
    Allison, Richard Crane, Spencer Carlisle, Byron Foulger, Claire
    Carleton. Man invokes the devil with animal blood and incantations;
    transforms himself into a snake.
The DEVIL'S SONATA Skandinavia 1911 14m. Ref: Bios 11/2/11.
    "Weird violinist" exerts "magnetic" influence over girl.
The DEVIL'S THREE SINS 1908 Ref: MPW'08:243. Dream: Knight
    haunted by manifestations of the devil.
DEVIL'S TOUCH, The see SATAN'S SKIN
The DEVIL'S TOY Premo-Equitable 1916 55m. Ref: MPN 13:1616.
    SP: Edward Madden, Maurice Marks, from the poem "The Mills
    of the Gods" by Madden. with Adele Blood, Montagu Love, Edwin
    Stevens (the devil), Jack Halliday, Madge Evans. Visions of devil
    make man commit murder.
DEVJANI (India-Bengali) 1939 D: Phani Burma. Ref: Dipali 1/5/40.
    with N. Lahiri, C. Devi, M. Dutt. "War between the Gods and the
    demons. "
The DEVOURING ROCK (Malayan) Run Run Shaw (Malay Film Prod.)
    1959 124m. (BATU BELAH BATU BERTANGKUP. THE ROCK
    THAT OPENS AND CLOSES) SP, D: Jamil Sulong. PH: C. Ramachandra.
    Mus sc: O. Ahmad, P. Ramlee. Based on a folk tale. Art D:
    Mustafe Yassin. Ref: Orient. FEFN 11/58. "Haunted rock"
    opens and devours humans.
DEVTA (India-Hindi & Tamil versions) Narayanan 1956 color 178m.
    D: Pattanna. SP: K. V. Srinivas. Dial: M. Sharma. Mus: C.
    Ram(a)chandra. PH: K. Ghosh. Art D: A. K. Sekhar. Ref: FEFN
    9/21/56. Hunchback curses private who tries to steal magic stone.
    A goddess lifts the curse from him.
DHANWAN (India) Imperial 1937 130m. D: P. Atorthy. "Inspired
    by 'The Hunchback of Notre Dame' by Victor Hugo. " Ref: The
    Lighthouse 7/3/37. with Ratanbai, Hafeesjee.
DIA CON EL DIABLO, Un see DAY WITH THE DEVIL, A
The DIABOLICAL BOX Urbanora 1912 6m. Ref: Bios 1/25/12. Imp
    in box transforms itself into animal, man; terrifies witness.
DIABOLICAL DR. VOODOO see INCREDIBLY STRANGE
    CREATURES, The
The DIABOLICAL DR. Z U.S. Films (Joe Solomon)/Hesperia/
    Speva-Ciné Alliance (Sp-F) 86m. (MISS MUERTE-Sp. DANS
    LES GRIFFES DU MANIAQUE-F. MISS DEATH. MISS DEATH AND
    DR. Z. IN THE GRIP OF THE MANIAC) D: Jesus Franco (Henri
    Baum). 1965 SP: Franco, Jean-Claude Carrière. PH: Alejandro
    Ulloa. Mus: Daniel White. Art D: Antonio Cortés. Ref: Boxo
    5/15/67. MMF 13:64b. COF 10:48. SpCinema'66. Image et Son
    2/68. with Estella Blain, Howard Vernon, Mabel Karr, Fernando

Montes, Guy Mairesse. Doctor and daughter work "to convert man's will, making him good or bad, by means of an invention in the nerve centers"; produce robot creatures.

DIABOLICAL GAME (Mex) Azteca 1964 (JUEGO DIABOLICO) Ref: Lee. with Beto el Boticario, Paul Farell, Freddy Fernandez. Devil.

The DIABOLICAL HATCHET (Mex) c.1968 (LA HACHA DIABOLICA) Ref: Glut (Columbia). with Santo. Time travel? Living dead?

DIABOLICAL INVENTION, The see FABULOUS WORLD OF JULES VERNE, The

The DIABOLICAL MEETINGS (F-Sp) 1971 Garigliano/Lacj/General Int'l D: Jose Maria Elorrieta. Ref: M/TVM'71. with Spartaco Santoni, Krista Nell, Teresa Gimpera. "Black magic in modern setting."

DIABOLICAL PACT (Mex) Vergara c.1968 (PACTO DIABOLICO) From "The Strange Case of Dr. Jekyll and Mr. Hyde" by Robert Louis Stevenson. Ref: Don Glut (Columbia). FJA. with M. A. Alvarez, Regina Torne, John Carradine.

DIABOLICO DOTTOR SATANA, Il see AWFUL DR. ORLOF, The

DIABOLICO DOTTOR MABUSE, Il see THOUSAND EYES OF DR. MABUSE, The

DIABOLIK see DANGER: DIABOLIK

DIABOLIQUE (F) United Motion Picture Organization/Cinedis/ Filmsonor 1954 105m. (LES DIABOLIQUES. THE FIENDS--Eng.) D, SP: Henri-Georges Clouzot. SP: also Gerome Geronimi, Rene Masson, F. Grendel. From the book "Celle Qui N'Etait Plus" by Boileau-Narcejac. PH: A. Thirard. Mus: Georges van Parys. Ref: DDC III:328. with Simone Signoret, Vera Clouzot, Paul Meurisse, Charles Vanel, Noel Roquevert, Robert Dalban, Georges Poujouly. "Living corpse" scares woman to death. More successful as a mystery than a horror movie.

DIAFANOIDI..., I see DEADLY DIAPHANOIDS, The

DIAMOND, The see DIAMOND WIZARD, The

The DIAMOND FROM THE SKY American 1915 serial 30 episodes D: William Desmond Taylor, Jacques Jaccard. See also THE SEQUEL TO THE DIAMOND FROM THE SKY. Ref: CNW. with Lottie Pickford, Irving Cummings, William Russell, W. J. Tedmarsh. Sir Arthur Stanley finds a diamond in a meteorite.

DIAMOND HANDCUFFS MGM/Cosmopolitan 1928 60m. silent D: John P. McCarthy. SP: Carey Wilson, from "Pin Money" by Henry C. Vance. Adap: Willis Goldbeck. Continuity: Bradley King. Titles: Joe Farnham. Ref: V 7/11/28. Photoplay 6/28. with Conrad Nagel, Eleanor Boardman, Gwen Lee, Sam Hardy. Diamond brings death and disaster to possessors.

The DIAMOND MACHINE (F) American Continental 1956 92m. (VOUS PIGEZ?) D: Pierre Chevalier SP: Jacques Doniol-Valcroze. Ref: TVFFSB. FIR'68: From a novel by Peter Cheyney. with Eddie Constantine, Maria Frau, Yves Royan. An Italian scientist finds a way to make natural diamonds.

The DIAMOND MAKER, The Eclair (Univ) 1914 Ref: MPW 19:1158. Perfect artificial diamonds.

DIAMOND MAKER, The see MAKER OF DIAMONDS, The

The DIAMOND MAKERS (Univ (Rex) 1913 Ref: MPW'13:1100. Bhadon, an aged Hindoo alchemist, discovers the secret of making artificial

diamonds. He is stopped when his laboratory of chemical and elec-
trical furnaces is found.
The DIAMOND MASTER Univ 1929 silent serial 10 episodes D:
Jack Nelson. From a novel by Jacques Futrelle. Remake of THE
DIAMOND QUEEN. Ref: CNW. with Hayden Stevenson, Louise
Lorraine, Al Hart. Man invents machine which makes diamonds
from dust.
The DIAMOND MYSTERY Vita 1913 35m.Ref: Bios 10/2/13, 10/9/13.
with Charles Kent, Leah Baird. Inventor's machine destroyed;
"secret process" stolen.
DIAMOND OF DISASTER Than 1914 30m. D: Carroll Fleming. SP:
Phil Lonergan. Ref: Lee. MPW 22:250, 505. with J. S. Murray,
Ernest Ward, Morgan Jones. Diamond causes death, disaster.
The DIAMOND QUEEN Univ 1921 serial 18 episodes D: Ed Kull.
From a novel by Jacques Futrelle. Remade as THE DIAMOND
MASTER. Ref: CNW. with Eileen Sedgwick, George Chesebro.
Machine makes diamonds from dust.
The DIAMOND THIEVES Imp 1917 11m. Ref: MPW 31:739. Hindu
alchemist makes artificial diamonds.
The DIAMOND WIZARD (B) UA/Pallos 1954 (3-D) 83m. (THE
DIAMOND. DEVIL DIAMOND) D: Dennis O'Keefe, Montgomery
Tully. SP: John C. Higgins, from the novel "Rich is the Treasure"
by Maurice Proctor. PH: Arthur Graham. Mus: M. Seiber. Ref:
SF Film. V 7/12/54. with O'Keefe, Margaret Sheridan, Philip
Friend, Alan Wheatley, Francis de Wolff, Michael Balfour.
Organization of crooks manufactures perfect synthetic diamonds.
DIAPHANOIDS, BRINGERS OF DEATH see DEADLY DIAPHANOIDS,
The
DIARY OF A MADMAN UA/Admiral 1963 Technicolor 96m. D:
Reginald LeBorg. SP, P: Robert E. Kent. PH: Ellis W. Carter.
Mus: Richard LaSalle. Art D: Daniel Haller. From "The Horla"
by Guy de Maupassant. Ref: FM 24:58. with Vincent Price,
Nancy Kovack, Chris Warfield, Ian Wolfe, Stephen Roberts,
Elaine Devry, Lewis Martin. French magistrate is haunted by an
invisible being which lives on the evil of humans. --PM.
DIAVOLI DELLO SPAZIO, I see SPACE DEVILS
DIAVOLI DI SPARTIVENTO, I see WEAPONS OF VENGEANCE
DICK BARTON AT BAY (B) Eros/Hammer 1950 68m. D: Godfrey
Grayson. SP: Ambrose Grayson, from the BBC series. PH:
Stanley Clinton. Ref: MFB. COF-A:39. MMania 2:19. with Don
Stannard, Sebastian Cabot, Tamara Desni, Percy Walsh. Death
ray.
DICK BARTON--SPECIAL AGENT (B) Hammer-Marylebone 1948
70m. D: Alfred Goulding. SP: Goulding, Alan Stranks, based on
the radio serial by Edward J. Mason. PH: Stanley Clinton. Ref:
MFB'48:46. Brit. FmYbk'49/50. with Don Stannard, George
Ford, Jack Shaw, Gillian Maude. Sinister doctor plans to destroy
England with "germ bombs."
DICK BARTON STRIKES BACK (B) Eros/Exclusive 1949 73m.
D: Godfrey Grayson. SP: Ambrose Grayson, from the BBC series.
PH: Cedric Williams. Ref: MFB. COF-A:39: "Weapon with in-
credible power." with Don Stannard, Sebastian Cabot, Bruce
Walker. Atomic apparatus.

DICK TRACY Rep 1937 serial 15 episodes D: Ray Taylor, Alan
James. SP: Barry Shipman, George Morgan, Morgan Cox, Winston
Miller. PH: William Nobles, Edgar Lyons. Based on the cartoon
strip by Chester Gould. Mus sc: Harry Grey. REF: STI 1:56.
MFB'37: 69m. --feature. with Ralph Byrd, Kay Hughes, Smiley
Burnette, Lee Van Atta, John Picorri, Carleton Young, Francis X.
Bushman, John Dilson, Edwin Stanley, Byron Foulger. Man turned
into mindless being by operation. Destructive sound waves; ray on
aircraft.

DICK TRACY RETURNS Rep 1938 serial 15 episodes D: William
Witney, John English. SP: Barry Shipman, Franklyn Adreon, Ron
Davidson, Rex Taylor, Sol Shor. Based on the cartoon strip by
Chester Gould. PH: William Nobles. Mus sc: Alberto Colombo. Ref:
Barbour. The Serial. with Ralph Byrd, Lynn(e) Roberts, Charles
Middleton, John Merton, Jack Ingram, Reed Howes, Jerry Tucker.
New torpedo boat invention.

DICK TRACY MEETS GRUESOME RKO 1947 65m. (DICK TRACY'S
AMAZING ADVENTURE-Eng) D: John Rawlins. SP: Eric Taylor,
Robertson White. Story: William Graffis, Robert E. Kent. From
the comic strip by Chester Gould. PH: Frank Redman. Mus: Paul
Sawtell. with Boris Karloff, Ralph Byrd, Anne Gwynne, Edward
Ashley, Skelton Knaggs, Joseph Crehan, Milton Parsons, Lex Bark-
er, Sean McClory, Robert Bray, Robert Clarke, Ernie Adams,
Jason Robards, Bert Roach. Scientist's chemical composition halts
human movement temporarily. Above average on action, gimmicks;
Karloff in an exciting role.

DICK TRACY VS. CRIME, INC. Rep 1941 serial 15 episodes D:
William Witney, John English. SP: Ron Davidson, Norman S. Hall,
William Lively, Joseph O'Donnell, Joseph Poland. Based on the
cartoon strip by Chester Gould. Flood scenes from DELUGE. PH:
Reggie Lanning. Mus sc: Cy Feuer. SpFX: Howard Lydecker. Ref:
Barbour. STI I:57. ModM 4:39. Pic: TBG. (DICK TRACY VS.
PHANTOM EMPIRE) with Ralph Byrd, John Davidson, Kenneth
Harlan, Ralph Morgan, John Dilson, Robert Fiske, Jack Mulhall,
Robert Frazer, Anthony Warde, Jan Wiley, Howard Hickman,
Hooper Atchley, Michael Owen. "The Ghost," hooded menace with
a device which renders him invisible.

DICK TRACY'S AMAZING ADVENTURE see DICK TRACY MEETS
GRUESOME

DICK TRACY'S G-MEN Rep 1939 serial 15 episodes D: William
Witney, John English. SP: Barry Shipman, Franklyn Adreon, Rex
Taylor, Ron Davidson, Sol Shor. From the cartoon strip by Chester
Gould. PH: William Nobles. Mus sc: William Lava. Ref: Barbour.
FD 11/12/39. with Ralph Byrd, Irving Pichel, Ted Pearson,
Phylis Isley, Kenneth Terrell, Kenneth Harlan, Walter Miller.
Dead brought back to life.

DID YOU HEAR THE ONE ABOUT THE TRAVELLING SALESLADY?
Univ 1967 Technicolor /scope 96m. D: Don Weis. SP: John
Fenton Murray. Story: Jim Fritzell, Everett Greenbaum. PH:
Bud Thackery. Mus: Vic Mizzy. Art D: Alexander Golitzen, Robert
C. MacKichan. with Phyllis Diller, Joe Flynn, Bob Denver,
Jeanette Nolan. Inventor makes wood-burning car; "aphrodisiac
machine."

DIE! DIE! MY DARLING (B) Col/Hammer/17A 1965 Technicolor
105m. (FANATIC) D: Silvio Narizzano. SP: Richard Matheson,
from "Nightmare" by Anne Blaisdell. PH: Arthur Ibbetson. Mus:
Wilfred Josephs. Art D: Peter Proud. Ref: FFacts. with Tallulah
Bankhead, Stephanie Powers, Yootha Joyce, Donald Sutherland.
Religious fanatic rules over three servants in desolate English
mansion. Okay shocker. Exactly what you might expect from its
title and cast, but things do keep popping.
DIE, MONSTER, DIE! (B) AI 1965 Pathécolor/Pathéscope 80m.
(HOUSE AT THE END OF THE WORLD. MONSTER OF TERROR-
Eng) D: Daniel Haller. SP: Jerry Sohl, from "The Colour out of
space" by H. P. Lovecraft. PH: Paul Beeson. Mus: Don Banks.
Art D: Colin Southcott. Makeup: Jimmy Evans. SpFX: Wally
Veevers, Ernie Sullivan. Ref: FM 37:25. Boxo 11/1/65. Shriek
2:6. with Boris Karloff, Nick Adams, Suzan Farmer, Freda Jack-
son, Terence De Marney, Patrick Magee, Leslie Dwyer. Radiation
responsible for "strange occurences," grotesque animals about old
mansion. A real disaster. Nothing of the power of Lovecraft's
story is captured. Very weakly written and directed.
DIMANA GAJAH BERDIRI TEGAK see HAUNTED HOUSE (1957)
A DIME NOVEL DETECTIVE Lubin 1909 Ref: F Index 3/6/09.
Hypnotist hypnotizes girl; villain "bursts into atoms" at end.
DIMENSION 5 United 1966 Technicolor 84m. D: Franklyn Adreon.
SP: Arthur C. Pierce. PH: Alan Stensvold. Mus: Paul Dunlap.
Art D: Paul Sylos, Jr. P:Earle Lyon. Ref: MFB'67:139. with
France Nuyen, Jeffrey Hunter, Harold Sakata, Donald Woods, Linda
Ho. Espionage agent travels through time in an attempt to prevent
the destruction of Los Angeles.
DIMENSIONS IN DEATH see CASTLE OF BLOOD
DIMINISHING DRAFT, The (story by W. Kaempffert) see GIRL IN
HIS POCKET
THE DINOSAUR AND THE MISSING LINK Edison 1917 5m. P:
Willis O'Brien. Ref: FM 12:6.19:36.22:34.63:28. MPN 15:3015:
"New process of animating manikins." (THE DINOSAUR AND THE
MISSING BABOON) Cave men.
DINOSAURUS Univ/Fairview/Jack Harris 1960 color 85m. P, D:
Irvin S. Yeaworth, Jr. SP: Jean Yeaworth, Dan Weisburd. PH:
Stanley Cortez. Mus: Ronald Stein. Art D: Jack Senter. SpFX:
Tim Barr, Wah Chang, Gene Warren. Makeup: Don Cash. Sets:
Herman Schoenbrun. Ref: FFacts. with Paul Lukather, Ward
Ramsey, Gregg Martell, Alan Roberts. Lightning revives a cave
man and prehistoric animals.
DIO SERPENTE, Il see GOD SNAKE, The
DIRIGEABLE FANTASTIQUE, Le see FANTASTICAL AIRSHIP, The
DISCIPLES OF DRACULA see DRACULA, PRINCE OF DARKNESS
DISCO VOLANTE, Il see FLYING SAUCER, The (1964)
The DISEMBODIED AA 1957 65m. D: Walter Grauman. SP: Jack
Townley. PH: Harry Neumann. Mus: Marlin Skiles. Art D:
David Milton. Ass't D: Austen Jewell. with Paul Burke, Allison
Hayes, John E. Wengraf, Eugenia Paul. Woman uses voodoo to
lure man. Crude, unpleasant. Grade Triple-Z.
THE DISINTEGRATING RAY, Or THE ADVENTURES OF QUIQUE AND
ARTHUR THE ROBOT (Sp) Petruka 1966 scope 80m. (EL

RAYO DISINTEGRADOR, or AVENTURAS DE QUIQUE Y ARTURO EL ROBOT) SP, D: Pascual Cervera. Dial: José E. Aranguren. PH: Manuel Rojas. Mus: Carmelo A. Bernaola. Art D: S. Burman. Ref: SpCinema'66. with Peter Solis, María Balenciaga, Joaquín Nieto, José Luis Coll. Criminals steal ray from professor; latter lends boy his robot to get it back.

DISMEMBERED GHOST (J) Okura 1968 (KAIDAN BARABARA YUREI) D: Kinya Ogawa. Ref: Unij. Bltn 31: "Ghost story." with Reiko Akikawa, Miki Hayashi.

DISORIENTED MAN, The (novel by P. Saxon) see SCREAM AND SCREAM AGAIN

DISTILLED SPIRITS MinA 1915 12m. Ref: MPN 1/30/15. Drunkard beset by visions of devil, giants, "strange creatures."

DIXIEME VICTIME, La see TENTH VICTIM, The

DO GENTLEMEN SNORE? MGM 1928 short silent D: Arch Heath. P: Hal Roach. Ref: Photoplay 8/28. with Max Davidson. Plot to give house reputation of being haunted.

DO THE DEAD RETURN? see DRAMA OF THE CASTLE, A

DO THE DEAD TALK? 1919 Ref: Exhibitors Herald 12/20/19. Spirits materialize.

DO YOU KEEP A LION AT HOME? Brandon/Manley/Ceskoslovensky (Cz) 1963('67-U. S.) 81m. (MATE DOMA IVA? HAVE YOU A LION AT HOME?) D: Pavel Hobl. SP: S. Ochová, B. Sobotka. PH: J. Vojta. Mus: W. Bukovy. Ref: FFacts. COF 11:6. Modern Cz. Film. with Ladislav Ocenasek, Dagmar Kofronová. Sorcerer who casts evil spell over magicians; castle full of ghosts.

DO YOU LIKE WOMEN? (F-I) Kalfon/Les Films Number One-Francoriz-Federiz 1964 92m. (AIMEZ-VOUS LES FEMMES? -F) D: Jean Léon. SP: Roman Polanski. Dial: Gerard Brach. PH: Sacha Vierny. Mus: W. Swingle. Ref: MFB'64:163. La Prod. Cin. Fr. COF 6:56. with Edwige Feuillère, Guy Bedos, Sophie Daumer, Grégoire Aslan. From a story by Georges Bardawl. Asiatic sect's members consume a young woman every month during the period of the full moon.

DOCTEUR GOUDRON ET LE PROFESSEUR PLUME, Le see SYSTEM OF DR. TARR AND PROFESSOR FETHER, The

DOCTEUR RAMEAU, Le (by G. Ohnet) see MY FRIEND THE DEVIL

DOCTEUR TUBE, Le see MADNESS OF DR. TUBE, The

DR. BLOOD'S COFFIN (B) UA/Caralan 1961 Eastmancolor 92m. D: Sidney J. Furie. SP: Jerry Juran. Adap: James Kelly, Peter Miller. PH: Stephen Dade. Mus: Buxton Orr. Art D: Scott MacGregor. SpFX: Les Bowie, Peter Nelson. Ref: FFacts. PM. FM 13:10. Pic: FM 13:13.15:12.18:23. with Kieron Moore, Hazel Court, Ian Hunter, Fred Johnson, Kenneth J. Warren, Andy Alston. By removing the heart from a live body and transplanting it into the dead body of a gifted person, a young biochemist hopes to perpetuate the best brains and talents of mankind.

DR. BROMPTON-WATT'S AGE ADJUSTER Edison 1912 5m. Ref: Bios 6/20/12. Doctor's youth potion takes sixty years off a man's life.

DR. CADMAN'S SECRET see BLACK SLEEP, The

DR. CHARLIE IS A GREAT SURGEON Eclair (F?) 1911 7m. Ref: Bios 10/5/11. When Dr. Charlie replaces McTouch's stomach with a monkey's, the latter begins to cavort like a monkey.

DR. COPPELIUS (Sp-U. S.) Copelia/Hale 1966 color/Superpanorama
70 96m. (EL FANTASTICO MUNDO DEL DR. COPPELIUS. DR. ? ?
COPPELIUS! !. The MAGIC WORLD OF DR. COPPELIUS. The
FANTASTIC WORLD OF DR. COPPELIUS) D: Ted Kneeland; from
his ballet. SP: V. M. Tarruella. PH: C. Paniagua. Mus: L.
Delibes. Art D: Gil Parrondo. Ref: SpCinema'67. with Walter
Slezak, Claudia Corday, Carmen Rojas. Doctor creates "doll
without a soul." Pic: "Witch's brew: blood of a vampire."

DOCTOR CRIMEN see RESURRECTED MONSTER, The

DR. CYCLOPS Para 1940 Technicolor 75m. D: Ernest B. Schoedsack. SP: Tom Kilpatrick. PH: Henry Sharp, Winton C. Hoch.
Mus: Ernest Toch, Gerard Carbonara, Albert Hay Malotte. Art
D: Hans Dreier, Earl Hedrick. SpFX: Farciot Edouart, Wallace
Kelly. Ref: FDY. FM 10:26. 52:14. Pic: FM 7:24. 13:15, 35, 67.
with Albert Dekker, Janice Logan, Thomas Coley, Victor Kilian,
Charles Halton. Mad scientist reduces men and animals to the
size of puppets. Lots of special effects for the most part wasted on
dumb story.

DR. FAUSTUS (Polish) Ultra-Film 1937 (PAN TWARDOWSKI)
D: Henryk Szaro. Ref: NYT 9/25/37: "spooky incidents." with
Pan Brodniewicz. The devil fails to get his victim's soul, but the
hero must spend eternity as the man in the moon.

DR. FAUSTUS (B) Col 1967 color 92m. D: Richard Burton, Nevill
Coghill. SP: Coghill, from the play by Christopher Marlowe. PH:
Gabor Pogany. Mus: Mario Nascimbene. Prod Des: John De Cuir.
Costumes:Peter Hall. Ref:LATimes 3/15/68. 2/25/68. Skulls,
skeletons, cobwebs, apparitions of hell, etc. With Richard Burton,
Elizabeth Taylor, A. Teuber.

DOCTOR FRANKENSTEIN ON CAMPUS see FLICK

DR. FU MANCHU see MYSTERIOUS DR. FU-MANCHU, The

DR. GOLDFOOT AND THE BIKINI MACHINE AI 1965 Pathecolor/
scope 90m. D: Norman Taurog. SP: Elwood Ullman, Robert
Kaufman. Story: James Hartford. PH: Sam Leavitt. Mus sc:
Les Baxter Art D: Daniel Haller. Ref: FDY. COF 9:6. PM.
Pic: Shriek 4:65: "The Pit & The Pendulum" sequence. with
Vincent Price, Frankie Avalon, Dwayne Hickman, Susan Hart,
Jack Mullaney, Fred Clark, Vincent L. Barnett, Milton Frome,
Patti Chandler, Sally Sachse, Mary Hughes, China Lee. Machine
produces women.

DR. GOLDFOOT AND THE GIRL BOMBS (U. S. -I) AI/1966 AI/Italian
Int'l color 80m. (I DUE MAFIOSI DELL'F. B. I. DR. GOLDFOOT
AND THE LOVE BOMB. LE SPIE VENGONO DAL SEMIFREDDO.
SPIES COME FROM HALFCOLD. DR. GOLDFOOT AND THE "S"
BOMB) D: Mario Bava. SP: Louis Heyward, Robert Kaufman,
Castellano, Pipolo. Story: Fulvio Lucisano. PH: A. Rinaldi.
Ref: M/TVM 6/66. Annuario. FM 40:45. with Vincent Price,
Fabian, Franco Franchi, Ciccio Ingrassia, Laura Antonelli,
Francesco Mulè. Girl robots.

DR. GOUDRON'S SYSTEM see SYSTEM OF DR. TARR AND PRO-
FESSOR FETHER, The

DR. GROWEMQUICK'S FEEDING POWDER c. 1911 Walturdaw 10m.
Ref: Bios. Powder makes baby grow.

Doctor   132

DOCTOR HALLERS see OTHER, The (1930)
DR. HALLIN (Austrian) Lampel-Film 1921 SP,D: Alfred Lampel.
  SP: also J. C. Höger. Ref: Osterr. with Franz Herterich, Traute
  Carlsen, Karl Schöpfer, Paul Kronegg. Brain-transplanting.
DR. HEIDEGGER'S EXPERIMENT (by N. Hawthorne) see TWICE
  TOLD TALES
DR. JEKYLL AND MR. HYDE Selig 1908 (THE MODERN DR. JEKYLL
  reissue) Ref: Lee. FM 11:39. FanMo 1:64. MPW'08:194. '09:960.
DR. JEKYLL AND MR. HYDE (Danish) Nordisk 1909 (JEKYLL AND
  HYDE--Great Northern-'10-U.S. DEN SKAEBNESV ANGRE OP-
  FINDELSE) 17m. SP,D: August Blom. Ref: Clarens. Movie
  Monsters. FM 34:55 MPW 7:713. Bios 9/8/10. Mitry V:137.
  with Alwin Neuss, Oda Alstrup.
DR. JEKYLL AND MR. HYDE Than 1912 15m. D: Lucius Hender-
  son. Ref: Clarens. FM 11:39. MPW'12:87,152. Pic: FM 25:74.
  with James Cruze, Marguerite Snow, Harry Benham.
DR. JEKYLL AND MR. HYDE (Univ/Imp) 1913 33m. Ref: Bios '13:909.
  5/28/14:992. FM 11:39. with King Baggot, Jane Gail.
DR. JEKYLL AND MR. HYDE Kineto-Kinemacolor (B) 1913 30m.
  Ref: MF: 34:55.
DR. JEKYLL AND MR. HYDE Arrow 1920 Ref: FM 34:55. Comedy.
  with Hank Mann.
DR. JEKYLL AND MR. HYDE Pioneer 1920 40m. Ref: TBG. (DR.
  JEKYL AND MR. HYDE) with Sheldon Lewis. Poor-dream ending
  version of the story.
DR. JEKYLL AND MR. HYDE Para 1920 D: John S. Robertson. SP:
  Clara S. Berenger, from the story by Robert Louis Stevenson. PH:
  Roy Overbough. P: Louis B. Mayer. Ref: Clarens. Pic: COF 5:44.
  FM 11:33, 34. with John Barrymore, Brandon Hurst, Nita Naldi,
  George Stevens, Louis Wolheim, Charles Lane, Martha Mansfield
DR. JEKYLL AND MR. HYDE Standard 1925 Comedy. Ref: FM
  34:55.
DR. JEKYLL AND MR. HYDE Para 1932 90m. D: Rouben Mamoulian.
  SP: Percy Heath, Samuel Hoffenstein. PH: Karl Struss. From the
  story by Robert Louis Stevenson. Art D: Hans Dreier. Ref: FM
  11:32-6. 54:17. COF 16:26. Pic: DDC III:302. FM 19:42. 11:38, 68.
  41:7. with Frederic March, Miriam Hopkins, Rose Hobart, Tempe
  Piggott, Holmes Herbert, Halliwell Hobbes, Arnold Lucy, Edgar
  Norton. This may or may not be the best version of the tired old
  story (which wasn't much to begin with), but good it isn't. There
  are some impressive touches, mainly in the treatment of Hyde, but
  Hopkins is dull, and there are the usual obligatory time-filling
  scenes with Jekyll. Better than most of Mamoulian's early "classics."
DR. JEKYLL AND MR. HYDE MGM 1941 122m. P,D: Victor
  Fleming. SP: John Lee Mahin, from the Robert Louis Stevenson
  story. PH: Joseph Ruttenberg. Mus: Franz Waxman. Art D, Sets:
  Cedric Gibbons, Daniel Cathcart. SpFX: Warren Newcombe. Ref:
  Clarens. with Spencer Tracy (replacing Robert Donat in the title
  roles), Ingrid Bergman, Donald Crisp, Ian Hunter, Lana Turner,
  Barton MacLane, C. Aubrey Smith, Sara Allgood, Frances
  Robinson, Billy Bevan, Lumsden Hare, Peter Godfrey. Adequate
  version picks up somewhat after a very slow start. Bergman
  very appealing menaced by Hyde or in drunk, silly mood.

DR. JEKYLL AND MR. HYDE   see   HOUSE OF FRIGHT
DR. JEKYLL AND MR. HYDE DONE TO A FRAZZLE   Warner's
    1914   15m.   Comedy Ref: Lee. MPW 22:1077. Based on the
    story by Robert Louis Stevenson.
DR. JERKYLL AND MR. HYDE   see   NUTTY PROFESSOR, The
DOCTOR KNOWS-ALL   Itala 1911 10m. Ref: Bios 6/8/11.
    Mind-reading machine.
DR. MABUSE   (G) UFA/Ullstein-UCO der Decla-Bioscop 1922
    110m.   (Part I: DER SPIELER or THE GREAT GAMBLER) D:
    Fritz Lang.   SP: Lang, Thea von Harbou; from the novel by
    Norbert Jacques.   PH: Carl Hoffmann.   Art D: Stahl-Urach,
    Otto Hunte.   P: Erich Pommer. Ref: SilentFF. Eisner. TBG.
    Imagen. Pic: Bianco 7/8'68:88. MMF 13:17. with Rudolf
    Klein-Rogge, Paul Richter, Alfred Abel, Bernhard Goetzke, Aud
    Egede-Nissen, Lil Dagover, Anita Berber.   Probably the least
    of Lang's Mabuse films.   Excruciatingly dull.   With one great
    scene in which Mabuse hypnotizes another gambler.
DR. MABUSE   (G) 1922 (Part II: INFERNO, KING OF CRIME,
    or MENSCHEN DER ZEIT) For credits see Part I. Follow-up:
    THE TESTAMENT OF DR. MABUSE (Lang). Ref: Orpheus 2:19.
    Ghosts of victims haunt Mabuse.
DR. MABUSE VS. SCOTLAND YARD   (G) CCC 1964 90m.
    (SCOTLAND YARD JAGT DR. MABUSE. DIE SCHARLACHROTE
    DSCHUNKE) D: Paul May. SP: Ladisla(u)s Fodor. Story:
    Bryan Edgar Wallace. PH: Nenad Jovičić. Mus: Rolf Wilhelm.
    Ref: FIR'67. German Pictures. Pic: FM 30:10. with Peter
    Van Eyck, Walter Rilla, Dieter Borsche, Werner Peters, Klaus
    Kinski, Hans Nielsen, Sabine Bethmann.   Mabuse's spirit pos-
    sesses Prof. Pohland.
DR. MANIAC   see MAN WHO LIVED AGAIN, The
DOCTOR MAXWELL'S EXPERIMENT   Lubin 1913 17m. Ref:
    Bios 4/10/13. Lee. Operation makes crook honest man.
DR. MESNER'S FATAL PRESCRIPTION   Warwick 1910 12m. Ref:
    Bios 6/2/10. Husband hypnotizes wife, orders her to kill her-
    self.
DR. NICOLA, or THE HIDDEN TREASURE   (Danish) Nordisk 1909
    19m.   Ref: Bios 2/3/10. Mind-reader-hypnotist; "infernal
    machine."
DR. NICOLA IN TIBET   see   MYSTERY OF THE LAMA CONVENT,
    The
DR. NO   (B) UA/Eon 1962 Technicolor 111m. D: Terence
    Young. SP: Richard Maibaum, Johanna Harwood, Berkeley
    Mather, from the novel by Ian Fleming. PH: Ted Moore. Mus:
    Monty Norman. Ed: Peter Hunt. Ref: COF 4:4. Pic: FanMo 4:24.
    with Sean Connery, Ursula Andress, Joseph Wiseman, Jack
    Lord, Bernard Lee, Anthony Dawson, Lois Maxwell.   Atomic
    laboratory of Dr. No used to divert rockets off course.
DOCTOR OF DOOM   (Mex) AI-TV/Calderon 1962 90m. (LAS
    LUCHADORAS CONTRA EL MEDICO ASESINO) D: Rene Car-
    dona. SP: Alfredo Salazar. PH: Enrique Wallace. Mus:
    Antonio Diaz Conde. Ref: Indice. with Armando Silvestre, Lorena
    Velasquez, Roberto Cañedo, Martha "Guera" Solis, Irma
    Rodriguez, Chucho Salinas, Sonia Infante, Elizabeth Campbell.

Mad Doctor puts gorilla's brain into man's head. When that
doesn't work, he puts it in a lady wrestler's head. Not as good
as it sounds.

DOCTOR OF SEVEN DIALS see CORRIDORS OF BLOOD

DR. ORLOFF'S MONSTER (Sp-Austrian) AI-TV/Leo 1964 scope
88m. (EL SECRETO DEL DOCTOR ORLOFF-Sp. MISTRESSES
OF DR. JEKYLL. The BRIDES OF DR. JEKYLL) D: Jesus
Franco. SP: John Frank (Franco), Nick Frank, David Coll.
PH: Alfonso Nieva. Art D: J. A. de la Guerra. Ref: SpCinema
'65. with José Rubio, Agnes Spaak, Perla Cristal, Pastor
Serrador, Hugo Blanco. Andros, "human robot," guided by super-
sonic beams. Unwatchable.

DR. PHIBES see ABOMINABLE DR. PHIBES, The

DOCTOR POLLY Vita 1914 30m. Ref: MPW 19:1002. "Family
ghost" inhabits mansion.

DR. PYCKLE AND MR. PRIDE Standard 1925 20m. P: Joe Rock.
From "The Strange Case of Dr. Jekyll and Mr. Hyde" by Robert
Louis Stevenson. Set from THE HUNCHBACK OF NOTRE DAME
used. Ref: FM 34:55. with Stan Laurel.

DR. RAMEAU (novel by G. Ohnet) see MY FRIEND THE DEVIL

DR. RENAULT'S SECRET Fox 1942 58m. D: Harry Lachman.
SP: Robert Metzler, William Bruckner. From "Balaoo" by
Gaston Leroux? PH: Virgil Miller. Mus: David Raksin, Emil
Newman. Art D: Richard Day, Nathan Juran. Ref: Academy.
FDY. Pic: FM 17:10. with George Zucco, J. Carrol Naish,
Lynne Roberts, John Sheppard (aka Shepperd Strudwick), Mike
Mazurki, Jack Norton, Bert Roach, Eugene Borden, Arthur
Shields, Jean Del Val, Charles Wagenheim, Ray Corrigan
(gorilla). Doctor transforms ape into man. Routine.

DR. SATAN (Pakistani) Ideal Films 1959 (DR. SHAITAN) SP, D, P:
S. A. Aziz. Ref: FEFN XII:10-11, 12-13.2/60. with Talish
(Dr. Satan), Nayyar Sultana, Zurrain, N. Kardar. "Science-
fiction thriller."

DR. SATAN (India-Hindi) Bahra Bros. 1960 D: Shreeram. Ref:
FEFN 7/60. with S. Premnath, Sheikh Mukhtar. Doctor plans
to use atomic energy "for personal gains."

DR. SATAN AND BLACK MAGIC (Mex) Bruckner 1967 (VUELVE
EL DOCTOR SATAN-F. DR. SATAN Y LAMAGIA NEGRA-Mex)
D: Rogelio A. Gonzalez. Eastmancolor Ref: Cine Universal
2/10/68. MMF 18-19:15. with Joaquin Cordero (Dr. Satan),
Noe Murayama, Sonia Furio, Luz Maria Aguilar, Aurora Clavel.
The works: zombies, "The Devil King," warlock, death ray,
metal-into-gold formula.

DR. SATAN'S ROBOT see MYSTERIOUS DR. SATAN, The

DR. SHAITAN see DR. SATAN (1959)

DR. SKINUM Biog 1907 Ref: MPW'07:670. The doctor's
cabinet turns a girl three inches tall into a normal woman.

DR. SMITH'S AUTOMATON Pathe 1910 8m. Ref: Bios 7/21/10.
Unstoppable robot made of buckram and springs.

DR. STRANGELOVE or HOW I LEARNED TO STOP WORRYING
AND LOVE THE BOMB (U.S.-B) Col/Hawk 1964-3 93m.
D, P: Stanley Kubrick. SP: Kubrick, Terry Southern, Peter
George. From "Red Alert" by George (originally published as

"Two Hours to Doom" by 'Peter Bryant'). PH: Gilbert Taylor.
Mus: Laurie Johnson. Art D: Peter Murton. SpFX: Wally
Veevers. ED: Anthony Harvey. Makeup: Stuart Freeborn. Designer: Ken Adam. Ref: FFacts. COF 5:4. with Peter Sellers,
George C. Scott, Sterling Hayden, Keenan Wynn, Slim Pickens,
Peter Bull, Tracy Reed, James Earl Jones. "Doomsday" device
sets off nuclear explosions around the world. Scott is the hilarious highlight of an uneven film. Better on comedy than suspense,
of which there is much less than intended.

DR. TERROR'S GALLERY OF HORRORS American General 1967
Pathecolor/Totalvision (GALLERY OF HORRORS. RETURN FROM
THE PAST-TV) D: David L. Hewitt. SP: Gary Heacock, David
Prentiss. Story: Russ Jones. Art D: Ray Dorn. Ref: FM 43:6.
44:79. Pic: FM 46:21. MMania 2:32. with Lon Chaney, Jr.,
John Carradine, Rochelle Hudson, Roger Gentry, Vic McGee,
Gray Daniels, Mitch Evans (Count Alucard). PH: Austin Mc-
Kinney. Makeup: Jean Lister. (The BLOOD DRINKERS) Dracula,
Frankenstein's monster. Very shoddy, amateurish.

DR. TERROR'S HOUSE OF HORRORS c1943 National Roadshow
Compilation of scenes from THE GOLEM (1936), HISTOIRES
EXTRAORDINAIRES ("Black Cat" sequence), RETURN OF
CHANDU, VAMPYR, and WHITE ZOMBIE. Ref: COF 7:53. Pic:
WFC 4:47.

DR. TERROR'S HOUSE OF HORRORS (B) Para/Amicus 1964
Technicolor/scope 95m. D: Freddie Francis. SP: Milton
Subotsky. PH: Alan Hume. Mus: Elisabeth Lutyens. Art D:
Bill Constable. SpFX: Ted Samuels. Makeup: Roy Ashton. Ref:
FFacts. with Peter Cushing, Christopher Lee, Roy Castle,
Michael Gough, Neil McCallum, Ursula Howells, Peter Madden,
Katy Wild, Edward Underdown, Bernard Lee, Jeremy Kemp,
Donald Sutherland, Max Adrian, Frank Forsyth. Werewolf and
voodoo episodes creepy; others pretty weak, with vampire one
being least. Good pictorial effects.

DR. TRIMBALL'S VERDICT (B) Hepworth 1913 18m. Ref:
Bios 8/14/13. Skeleton takes form of doctor's murdered friend,
scares him to death.

DR. WHO AND THE DALEKS (B) Cont/AARU-Amicus 1965 Tech-
nicolor/scope 85m. D: Gordon Flemyng. SP: Milton Subotsky.
From the BBC-TV serial by Terry Nation. Sequel: DALEKS-
INVASION EARTH 2150 A.D. PH: John Wilcox. Mus: Malcolm
Lockye(a)r. Electronic Mus: Barry Gray. Art D: Bill Constable.
Sets: Scott Slimon. Makeup: Jill Carpenter. Ref: PM. with
Peter Cushing, Roy Castle, Jennie Linden, Roberta Tovey,
Geoffrey Toone. Eccentric scientist's time machine lands occu-
pants up on strange planet. Quaint, minimally-imaginative, low-
budget s-f.

DR. WRIGHT'S INVENTION (F) Pathe 1909 9m. (INVENTION
OF DR. WRIGHT) Ref: Lee. F Index 3/6/09. Device cures
the lame.

DR. X F Nat 1932 Technicolor 77m. D: Michael Curtiz. SP:
Robert Tasker, Earl Baldwin. PH: Richard Tower, Ray Renne-
han. Story: Howard W. Comstock, Allen C. Miller. Ref: FM
10:26. Pic: FM 7:41. MW 8:4-11. with Lionel Atwill, Fay

Wray, Preston Foster, Lee Tracy, John Wray, Mae Busch, Leila Bennett, Arthur Edmund Carewe, Harry Beresford, Willard Robertson, Harry Holman, Tom Dugan, Robert Warwick, George Rosener. Synthetic flesh! Silly; once in a while silly enough to be some fun; at any rate better than Curtiz's other early-Thirties horror hit MYSTERY OF THE WAX MUSEUM.

DOCTOR Z (India-Hindi) Baliwala Films 1960 Ref: FEFN 4/60. with Shakila, Hiralal, Mahipal. A scientist has perfected a fluid "which, when mixed with petrol, enables a car to be driven without a driver."

The DOCTOR'S EXPERIMENT 1908 (REVERSING DARWIN'S THEORY) Ref: Movie Monsters. Injection turns ape into man.

DOCTOR'S HORRIBLE EXPERIMENT, The see TESTAMENT OF DR. CORDELIER, The

The DOCTOR'S SECRET (F) Star/Melies 1909 13m. (HYDRO-THERAPIE FANTASTIQUE) Ref: Lee. Patient put in hydrotherapy machine blown apart, put back together by doctors. Standard Melies.

The DOCTOR'S SECRET (Dan) Nordisk 1915 Ref: MPW 25:1562. Cure for cancer.

DOCTORS WEAR SCARLET (by S. Raven) see BLOODSUCKERS

DODES O, De see ISLE OF THE DEAD, The (1913)

DODSKYSSEN see DEATH KISS, The

A DOG, A MOUSE AND A SPUTNIK (F) Films around the World/ Jean-Jacques Vital--Regina--Filmsonor 1957 92m. (A PIED, A CHEVAL ET EN SPOUTNIK. BY FOOT, HORSE AND SPUT-NIK. ROCKETFLIGHT WITH HINDRANCE. SPUTNIK) D: Jean Dréville. SP: J.-J. Vital. Adap: Noel-Noel, Vital, R. Rocca, Jacques Grello. PH: Andre Bac. Mus: Paul Misraki. Ref: Cinemundo 7/25/59:8. DDC III:132. FM 47:49. Pic: SM 4:12. with Noel-Noel, Denise Gray, Mischa Auer, Darry Cowl, Noel Roquevert. Russian professor and elderly Frenchman accidentally launched in sputnik into orbit.

The DOG FACTORY Edison 1904 Ref: SF Film. Sausages turned into dogs.

DOGORA see DAGORA

DOJOJI TEMPLE (J) Shochiku 1956 Eastmancolor 80m. (KYOKANOKO MUSUME DOJOJI) Ref: FEFN 6/22/56. with Utaemon Nakamura. Entertainer turned into white snake by the gods for killing a monk.

DOKUGA OKOKU see EVIL BRAIN FROM OUTER SPACE, The

DOKURO KYOJO see MASKED TERROR

The DOLL (G) 1919 (DIE PUPPE) D: Ernst Lubitsch. From the opera by Offenbach. Ref: Orpheus 3:48. SF Film. with Ossi Oswalda. Android.

DOLL, The see POUPEE, La (1962)

The DOLLAR-A-YEAR MAN Para 1921 60m. D: James Cruze. SP: Walter Woods. PH: Karl Brown. Ref: AFI. with Roscoe "Fatty" Arbuckle, Lila Lee, Winifred Greenwood, Edward Sutherland, J. M. Dumont. "Haunted" house.

The DOLL'S REVENGE WB&E 1907 Ref: MPW'07:124. A boy destroys a doll meant for his sister. The parts reassemble, and the doll grows to "alarming" size. Another doll appears,

and the two pull the boy apart and eat him.
DON JUAN (Austrian) Akkord 1954 Agfacolor 89m. (DON
  JUAN'S FAREWELL) Ed, D: H. Walter Kolm-Veltee. SP: Kolm-
  Veltee, A. Uhl, E. Henthaler. From the opera "Don Giovanni"
  by Mozart with libretto by L. daPonte from the play by G. Ber-
  tati. PH: W. Sohm, H. Fuchs. Art D: Hans Zehetner. Ref:
  Lee. MFB'56:71. with Cesare Danova, Hans von Borsody,
  Josef Meinrad. Ghostly voice from tomb.
DON JUAN AND FAUST (F) 1922 D: Marcel L'Herbier. Ref:
  DDC III:34. Pic: DDC III:227:eerie. with Philippe Hériat.
DON JUAN'S COMPACT Milano 1913 35m. Ref: Bios 3/20/13.
  Don Juan sells his soul to the devil for wealth and pleasure.
DON JUAN'S FAREWELL see DON JUAN
DONNA SCIMMIA, La see APE WOMAN, The
DONOVAN'S BRAIN UA/Dowling 1953 83m. SP, D: Felix Feist.
  PH: Joseph Biroc. Ed: Herbert L. Strock. P: Tom Gries.
  Ref: FDY. with Lew Ayres, Gene Evans, Nancy Olson, Steve
  Brodie, Tom Powers, Lisa K. Howard, John Hamilton. Scientist
  keeps dead millionaire's brain alive. From the novel by Curt
  Siodmak. See also BRAIN, The/LADY AND THE MONSTER,
  The.
DON'T CRY WOLF see CRAWLING HAND, The
DON'T PLAY WITH MARTIANS (F) UA/Fildebroc 1967 color
  85m. (COMME MARS EN CAREME. MARS EN CAREME. NE
  JOUEZ PAS AVEC LES MARTIANS. REGULAR AS CLOCKWORK.
  DON'T FOOL AROUND WITH MARTIANS. MARS AT LENT.
  MARS AT EASTER) Mus, D: Henri Lanoe. SP: Johanne Har-
  wood, from the story "Les Sextuplets de Locqmaria" by Michel
  Labry. PH: Rene Matchin. Ref: V 4/10/68. 5/8/68:121. 7/10/
  68:19. M/TVM 6/67. MMF 18-19:23. COF 13:27. Bianco
  11/68. Pic: FM 81:45. with Jean Rochefort, Macha Meril,
  Andre Vallardy, Haydee Politoff. Aliens; prehistoric monster.
DON'T SCREAM, DORIS MAYS see DAY OF THE NIGHTMARE
DOOM OF DRACULA see HOUSE OF FRANKENSTEIN
DOOMED (F) Pathe 1909 14m. Ref: MPW'09:265. Man with
  satanic hypnotic powers.
DOOMED Ambrosio 1917 20m. Ref: MPN 15:1719. Powder
  explodes when it touches water.
The DOOR WITH SEVEN LOCKS (F-W.G.) Leitienne/Rialto 1962
  96m. (DIE TUR MIT DEN SIEBEN SCHLOSSERN) D: Alfred
  Vohrer. SP: H. G. Peterson, Johannes Kai, from the story
  by Edgar Wallace. Remake of CHAMBER OF HORRORS (1940).
  Ref: FIR'66:240. "Replete with lurking fiends, nutty doctors
  experimenting in underground laboratories..." with Heinz Drache,
  Sabina Sesselman, Eddi Arent, Werner Peters, Adi Berber,
  Pinkaus Braun, Klaus Kinski, Hans Nielsen.
DOPO LA MORTE see AFTER DEATH
DOPPELANGER see JOURNEY TO THE FAR SIDE OF THE SUN
DORFGOLEM, Der see GOLEM'S LAST ADVENTURE, The
DORIAN GRAY see PICTURE OF DORIAN GRAY, The (Hung. -
  1917)/SECRET OF DORIAN GRAY, The
DORNROSCHEN see SLEEPING BEAUTY (1955)
DOS COSMONAUTAS A LA FUERZA see TWO COSMONAUTS

AGAINST THEIR WILL

DOS FANTASMAS Y UNA MUCHACHA see TWO GHOSTS AND A
GIRL

DOUBLE AFFAIR, The see SPY WITH MY FACE, The

DOUBLE DECEPTION (F) United Motion Picture Org. /Safra-
Speva /Henri Baum 1960 101m. (Les MAGICIENNES-F.
MISTERIUS-I. The ILLUSIONISTS. FRANTIC?) D: Serge
Friedman. SP: Francois Boyer, Bernard Revon, from a story
by Boileau-Narcejac. Ref: DDC II:314: fantasy. La Prod.Cin.
Fr. Boxo 7/29/63. with Alice and Ellen Kessler, Jacques
Riberolles, Jean Mercure, Ginette Leclerc. Man meets girl
who appears and disappears mysteriously; learns she has twin.
Later one dies, but he can't be sure which one.

DOUBLE DOOR Para 1934 70m. D: Charles Vidor. SP: Gladys
Lehman, Jack Cunningham. From the play by Elizabeth McFad-
den (and Hermine Kepac?). PH: Harry Fischbeck. Ed: James
Smith. Ref: FD 5/5/34. 5/2/34:12. TVK. FM 24:64. COF-A:
39. with Kent Taylor, Halliwell Hobbes, Evelyn Venable, Mary
Morris, Sir Guy Standing, Anne Revere, Colin Tapley, Virginia
Howell. "Haunted house" with secret doors, etc. Ad: "The
Female Frankenstein of Fifth Avenue."

DOUBLE DUBS Pathe (Starlight) 1916 Ref: MPN 13:1924. Two
men get revenge by playing ghosts, "haunting" those who stole
their sweethearts.

DOUBLE LIFE, A see CONVICTED BY HYPNOTISM

DOULOUREUSE ARCADIE (by P. de Mendelssohn) see MARIANNE
OF MY YOUTH

DOWN AMONG THE DEAD MEN (by C. E. Vulliamy) see THEY
ALL DIED LAUGHING

DOWN AND DIRTY c1969 color Ref: RVB. Man encounters cult
of devil-worshippers. (They watch a film with a werewolf in it.)

DRACULA Univ 1931 75m. D: Tod Browning. SP: Garrett
Fort. Dial: Dudley Murphy. From the play by Hamilton Deane
and John L. Balderston and the novel by Bram Stoker. PH: Karl
Freund. Art D: Charles D. Hall. Makeup: Jack Pierce. Ed:
Milton Carruth. P: Carl Laemmle. Ref: FM 9:27. 23:4. 27:66. 32:
69. Pic: FM 2:49. 9:23. 19:74. MW 4:43. with Bela Lugosi,
Helen Chandler, David Manners, Dwight Frye, Edward Van Sloan,
Frances Dade, Herbert Bunston, Charles Gerrard, Joan Stand-
ing, Michael Visaroff, Moon Carroll, Josephine Velez, Donald
Murphy. The opening sequences are the best of course, but the
rest is enjoyable too--if stagy--if only for the stagy performances
of Lugosi, Frye, and Van Sloan.

DRACULA (Spanish-language version of above) Univ 1931 D:
George Melford. Ref: Clarens. Pic: ModM 2:38. with Carlos
Villarias, Lupita Tovar, Barry Norton, Carmen Guerrero.

DRACULA (novel by B. Stoker) see ABBOTT AND COSTELLO MEET
FRANKENSTEIN /BAD FLOWER, The /BILLY THE KID VS.
DRACULA /BLOOD OF DRACULA /BLOOD OF DRACULA'S
CASTLE /BLOOD OF FRANKENSTEIN /BRIDES OF DRACULA /
DR. TERROR'S GALLERY OF HORRORS /EMPIRE OF DRACULA,
The /HORROR OF DRACULA /HOUSE OF DRACULA /HOUSE OF
FRANKENSTEIN /HOUSE ON BARE MOUNTAIN /JONATHAN /

NOSFERATU/ONE MORE TIME/RETURN OF DRACULA/SCALE
IN HI-FI/SCARS OF DRACULA/SON OF DRACULA/TASTE OF
BLOOD, A/TASTE THE BLOOD OF DRACULA/UNCLE WAS A
VAMPIRE/COUNT DRACULA/COUNTESS DRACULA and the fol-
lowing titles
DRACULA AND THE BOYS 1969 (DRACULA AND THE BOYS or
DOES DRACULA REALLY SUCK?) Ref: LA Times. RVB.
DRACULA HAS RISEN FROM THE GRAVE (B) WB-7A/Hammer
1968 Technicolor 92m. D: Freddie Francis. SP: John Elder.
PH: Arthur Grant. Mus: James Bernard. Art D: Bernard
Robinson. SpFX: Frank George. Ref: V(d) 11/11/68. with
Christopher Lee, Rupert Davies, Veronica Carlson, Michael
Ripper, Barbara Ewing. Monsignor bars Dracula's castle with
a cross.
DRACULA IN ISTANBUL (Turkish) 1952 (DRAKULA ISTANBULDA)
D: Mehmet Muhtar. SP: Umit Deniz. From Ali Riza Seyfi's
"The Impaling Voivode," adaptation of Stoker's "Dracula." P:
Turgut Demirag. Ref: FM 22:7. 23:43. 25:13. Pic: 26:61.
EncicDS IX:1180. with Atif Kaptan (Dracula).
DRACULA JAGT FRANKENSTEIN see DRACULA VS. FRANKEN-
STEIN
DRACULA PRINCE OF DARKNESS (B) Fox/Hammer 1965 Tech-
nicolor/scope 90m. (REVENGE OF DRACULA. DISCIPLES OF
DRACULA. DRACULA 3. The BLOODY SCREAM OF DRACULA-
Far East) D: Terence Fisher. SP: John Sansom, from an idea
by John Elder. Sequence from HORROR OF DRACULA. PH:
Michael Reed. Mus: James Bernard. Art D: Bernard Robinson.
Ref: Orpheus 3:34. COF 10:42. with Christopher Lee, Andrew
Keir, Barbara Shelley, Francis Matthews, Suzan Farmer, Charles
Tingwell, Thorley Walters. Count Dracula returns from the
dead. A bit noisy (thanks mainly to Bernard), but not too bad
thanks to some new shock ideas among the old and some small
(and on that level successful) attempts at characterization.
DRACULA '71' see COUNT DRACULA
DRACULA (THE DIRTY OLD MAN) Whit Boyd 1969 color SP, D,
P: William Edwards. PH: William Troiam. Makeup: Tony
Tierney. Ref: RVB. Warren. with Vince Kelly (Count Alucard
aka Dracula), Ann Hollis. Dracula hypnotizes a man who turns
into a werewolf called Irving Jekyllman.
DRACULA 3 see DRACULA, PRINCE OF DARKNESS
DRACULA VS. FRANKENSTEIN (SP-G-I) Prades/Eichberg 1969
color/70mm 81m. (DRACULA JAGT FRANKENSTEIN-G. El
HOMBRE QUE VINO DE UMMO or Los MONSTRUOUS DEL
TERROR-Sp. The MAN WHO CAME FROM UMMO) D: Tulio
Demicheli (and Hugo Fregonese?). SP: J. M. Alvarez. PH:
Godofredo Pacheco. Mus: R. Ferrer. Art D: A. Cofiño. Ref:
V 11/3/71:27. Fernsehen 5/70. SpCinema'71. with Michael
Rennie, Karin Dor, Craig Hill, Patty Shepard, Paul Naschy,
Angel del Pozo, Manuel de Blas. Mad scientist from another
planet revives Dracula, Frankenstein's monster, mummy, were-
wolf.
DRACULA VS. FRANKENSTEIN (1971) see BLOOD OF FRANK-
ENSTEIN

DRACULA'S COFFIN see BLOOD OF DRACULA'S CASTLE
DRACULA'S DAUGHTER Univ 1936 69m. D: Lambert Hillyer.
SP: Garrett Fort. From "Dracula" and "Dracula's Guest" by
Bram Stoker; suggested by Oliver Jeffries. PH : George
Robinson. Mus sc: Heinz Roemheld. Art D: Albert S. D'Agos-
tino. Special PH: John P. Fulton. Ref: Academy. RVB. with
Otto Kruger, Gloria Holden, Marguerite Churchill, Irving Pichel,
Edward Van Sloan, Nan Grey, E. E. Clive, Halliwell Hobbes,
Hedda Hopper, Billy Bevan, Gilbert Emery, Claude Allister,
Edgar Norton, Christian Rub, Eily Malyon, Gordon Hart, Fred
Walton, Paul Weigel, Hedwiga Reicher, Douglas Wood, Joseph E.
Tozer, Eric Wilton, George Kirby, William Schramm, Pietro
Sosso, Guy Kingsford, Douglas Gordon. Pic: FM 31:41.
DRACULA'S DAUGHTER proves that even a vampire can be a
sickly, sympathetic monster like The Wolf Man or Jekyll/Hyde.
If Holden (as the daughter) staring vacuously off into space isn't
silly enough, she's got an incredible-looking companion named
Sandor who is.
DRACULA'S LUST FOR BLOOD (CHIOSU ME. BLOOD-THIRSTY
EYES. LAKE OF DRACULA) (J) Toho 1971 D: M. Yamamoto.
Ref: V 6/30/71. M/TVM #7/71. with Mori Kishida.
DRACULA'S VAMPIRE LUST (Swiss) Monarex 1970 (DRACULAS
LUSTERNE VAMPIRE) D: Mario D'Alcala. PH: Hans Jura.
Ref: Fernsehen 5/71. cf. GUESS WHAT HAPPENED TO COUNT
DRACULA? with Des Roberts, Alon D'Armand, Ola Copa.
The DRAGON MURDER CASE F Nat 1934 68m. D: H. Bruce
Humberstone. SP: Robert N. Lee, F. Hugh Herbert. Adap: Rian
James. From the novel by S. S. Van Dine. PH: Tony Gaudio.
Ref: FDY. V 8/28/34. with Warren William (Philo Vance),
Lyle Talbot, Robert Warwick, Margaret Lindsay, Robert Mc-
Wade, Dorothy Tree, Robert Barrat, George E. Stone, George
Meeker, Etienne Girardot, Charles C. Wilson, Wilfred Lucas.
Pool supposedly haunted by dragon--murdered man's body found
with mysterious claw marks on it. Tepid mystery.
The DRAGON OF PENDRAGON CASTLE (B) Elstree 1950 52m.
P,D: John Baxter. SP: J. M. Smith, M. C. Borer. PH:
Arthur Grant. Ref: Lee. MFB'50:72. with Robin Netscher,
David Hannaford, Graham Moffatt, Leslie Bradley. Children
discover young sea dragon.
DRAGON'S BLOOD (I) Ferrigno 1957 color/scope 97m.
(SIGFRIDO. SIEGFRIED. SWORD AND THE DRAGON) D:
Giacomo Gentilomo. SP: Antonio Ferrigno, G. Constantini,
Gentilomo. PH: Carlo Nebiolo. Ref: Italin P. FM Ital P 28:18.
Orpheus 3:28. F Comment 48-9:83: German? with Rolf Tasna,
Katharina Mayberg, Sebastian Fischer, Ilaria Occhini. The
legend of Siegfried, who slays a dragon with a magic sword.
DRAKULA (Hung) 1921 D: Karoly Lajthay. Ref: A Magyar Film
Története. FIR'66:263.
A DRAMA OF THE CASTLE, or DO THE DEAD RETURN? (F)
1912 (UN DRAMA AU CHATEAU D'ACRE ou LES MORTS RE-
VIENNENT-ILS?) SP,D: Abel Gance. Ref: DDC II:416.
The DREAM CHEATER Hodkinson 1920 D: Ernest C. Warde.
From Honore de Balzac's "The Magic Skin, "Le Peau de

Chagrin, " or "The Wild Ass's Skin. " Ref: Exhibitors Herald.
with J. Warren Kerrigan.   Each wish on a magic skin shrinks it
and shortens man's life.
The DREAM DANCE Lubin 1915 30m. Ref: MPW 24:1986. Man
with bad dreams dies in his sleep.
DREAM KILLER, The see NIGHT WALKER, The
DREAM MACHINE, The see ELECTRONIC MONSTER, The
The DREAM OF AN OPIUM FIEND Melies 1908 Ref: MPW'08:
244. Dream: Glass sails to the moon; Diana becomes an "ugly
creature. "
The DREAM OF OLD SCROOGE   Cines (I?) 1910 11m. From
Dickens' "A Christmas Carol. " Ref: Bios 3/17/10. The three
ghosts in dream, etc.
DREAM OF OLWYN see WHILE I LIVE
The DREAM PILL Lubin 1910 8m. Ref: Bios 9/29/10. Pro-
fessor Swank's pill gives tramp wonderful dreams.
DREAMLAND (India) 1937 155m. D: V. Bhat. Ref: The Light-
house 8/21/37. with Jayant, S. Akhtar. "Magic wand used for
evil purposes. "
DREAMS IN THE WITCH-HOUSE, The (by H. P. Lovecraft) see
CRIMSON ALTAR, The
DROP OF WATER, A (by Chekhov) see BLACK SABBATH
DROPS OF BLOOD see MILL OF THE STONE WOMEN
DRUMS O'VOODOO Int'l Stageplays/Rbt. Mintz 1934 70m.
(LOUISIANA) D: Arthur Hoerl.   From a story by J. Augustus
Smith. Ref: FD 5/2/34.   Photoplay 9/34. with Smith, Morris
McKenny, Lionel Monagas, Edna Barr, Laura Bowman. Voodoo
woman casts spells with incantations and drums, strikes man
blind.
DRUMS OF FU-MANCHU Rep 1940 serial 15 episodes (also fea-
ture) D: William Witney, John English . SP: Sol Shor, Barney
Sarecky, Franklyn Adreon, Morgan Cox, Ron Davidson, Norman
S. Hall.   Based on the character created by Sax Rohmer. PH:
William Nobles. Mus sc: Cy Feuer. Ref: Barbour. Pic: MW 4:
23. with Henry Brandon (aka Henry Kleinbach), William Royle,
Olaf Hytten, Dwight Frye, John Merton, John Dilson, George
Cleveland, Wheaton Chambers, Lal C. Mehra, Luana Walters,
Gloria Franklin, Tom Chatterton. Ch. 2.   The Monster.
DRUMS OF JEOPARDY Truart/Hoffman 1923 D: Edward Dillon.
SP: Arthur Hoerl.   From a story by Harold McGrath. Remake:
DRUMS OF JEOPARDY (1931). Ref: AFI. V 3/19/24.
Clarens. LC. DDC III:9. with Elaine Hammerstein, Jack Mul-
hall, Wallace Beery, David Torrence. Emeralds supposedly ex-
ert sinister influence over owner.
DRUMS OF JEOPARDY Tiffany 1931 75m. (MARK OF TERROR
--United Screen Attractions reissue) D: George B. Seitz. SP:
Florence Ryerson.   From a story by Harold McGrath (first
filmed in '24). PH: Arthur Reed. Ed: Otto Ludwig. Art D:
Fay Babcock. Ref: FM 47:49. V 4/15/31. MPH 2/21/31.
Clarens. Photoplay 4/31: "Mystery melodrama satisfying to the
most bloodthirsty. " PM: "Weird, crazy doctor attempts to wipe
out a whole royal Russian family as vengeance for his daughter's
death. All the usual devices for thrill and horror. " with June

Collyer, Lloyd Hughes, Mischa Auer, Warner Oland, Clara
Blandick, Hale Hamilton, Ernest Hilliard, Wallace MacDonald.
DRUMS OF THE JUNGLE see POCOMANIA
2 [DUE] 5 MISSIONE HYDRA see +2 +5 MISSION HYDRA
DUE MAFIOSI CONTRO GOLDFINGER see AMAZING DR. G.,
The
DUE MAFIOSI DELL'F.B.I., I see DR. GOLDFOOT & THE GIRL
BOMBS
DUEL IN SPACE Reed/MCA-TV 1954 78m. From the "Rocky
Jones, Space Ranger" TV series. Ref: COF-A:40. TVG. with
Richard Crane, Robert Lyden.
The DUEL IN THE DARK Than 1915 Ref: MPN 3/27/15. with
Morris Foster, Flo LaBadie. Long-distance hypnotism.
DUEL OF THE GARGANTUAS see WAR OF THE GARGANTUAS
DUEL OF THE SPACE MONSTERS see FRANKENSTEIN MEETS
THE SPACEMONSTER
DUMMY OF DEATH see HYPNOSIS
The DUMMY TALKS (B) Alex/British Nat'l 1943 90m. D:
Oswald Mitchell. Ref: MFB'43:25. COF-A:40. with G. H.
Mulcaster, Jack Warner, Claude Hulbert, Beryl Orde. Mystery;
seance.
The DUNGEON OF HORROR Herts-Lion c1962 80m. (DUNGEONS
OF HORROR. The DUNGEON OF HARROW?) D: Pat Boyett.
Makeup,SP: Henry Garcia. PH: James Houston. Art D: Don
Russell. Ref: Orpheus 3:34. 4:37. COF-A:40, with Russ Harvey,
Helen Hogan, Bill McNulty, Maurice Harris, Russell, Lee
Morgan, Boyett. Wind-swept castle, mad count, cobwebs, tor-
ture chamber, leprous countess who goes insane and every night
relives her wedding night. But for the gleefully Grand Guignol
ending and the hero's encounter with the countess this would be
one of the worst.
The DUNWICH HORROR AI 1969 Movielab color 90m. D: Daniel
Haller. SP: Curtis Lee Hanson, Henry Rosenbaum, Ronald
Silkosky. From the story by H. P. Lovecraft. PH: Richard C.
Glouner. SpFX: Roger George. Exec P: Roger Corman. with
Sandra Dee, Dean Stockwell, Ed Begley, Sam Jaffe, Lloyd Boch-
ner, Barboura Morris, Beech Dickerson. The "Necronomicon"
and other names from Lovecraft make it to the screen, but Love-
craft doesn't. The film is ineptly staged, paced, and acted,
though there is one frightening bit of animation.
DUST OF EGYPT Vita 1915 D: George Baker. SP: Alan Camp-
bell. Ref: MPW 26:522. FIR'67:337. with Antonio Moreno,
Edith Storey, Hughie Mack, Cissy Fitzgerald. The mummy of an
Egyptian princess comes to life.
DWARF NOSE (Austrian) Astoria-Film 1921 (ZWERG NASE)
D: Ladislaus Tuszinsky. SP: Hans Berger, Tuszinsky, from the
fairy tale by Wilhelm Hauff. Ref: Osterr. with Herma Thun,
Fritz StraBny (witch) Rudi Merstallinger.
The DYBBUK (Polish/Yiddish) 1937 Geist 122m. (DYBUK)
D: Michael Waszynsky. Ref: FM 20:6. FD 2/1/38. Orpheus
3:42. From the play by S. An-ski. with A. Morewsky, R. Sam-
berg, M. Libman. Rabbi exorcises boy's spirit from girl.
THE DYBBUK (Israeli-G) Hiuni & Cohen 1968 color 90m. D:

Ilan Eldad (Ivan Lengiel), in collaboration with S. Friedman.
SP: Friedman, Eldad, from the play "Between Two Worlds" by
S. An-ski. PH: Goetz Neumann. Mus: Noam Sheriff. Art D:
Karl Schneider. Ref: V'68. with David Opatoshu, Tina
Wodetsky, Toty Lemkov, Peter Frye, Moti Barkan. Soul of de-
ceased bridegroom condemned to wanderings "between heaven
and hell. "

EARTH DEFENSE FORCE see MYSTERIANS, The
The EARTH DIES SCREAMING (B) Fox 1964 62m. D:
    Terence Fisher. SP: Henry Cross. Story: Harry Spalding.
    PH: Arthur Lavis. Art D: G. Povis. Exec P: Robert Lippert,
    Jack Parsons. Ref: COF 6:56. FFacts. PM. with Willard
    Parker, Virginia Field, Dennis Price, Vanda Godsell, Thorley
    Walters. Seven survivors of enemy attack battle enemy robots.
EARTH IN DANGER, The see ATOMIC RULERS OF THE WORLD
EARTH VS. THE FLYING SAUCERS Col 1956 83m. D: Fred F.
    Sears. SP: Raymond T. Marcus, George W. Yates, Story:
    Curt Siodmak. PH: Fred Jackman, Jr. SpFX: Ray Harry-
    hausen. From the book "Flying Saucers from Outer Space" by
    Donald E. Keyhoe. P: Charles Schneer. Exec P: Sam Katz-
    man. Pic: FM 12:18. 21:11. with Hugh Marlowe, Joan Taylor,
    Donald Curtis, Morris Ankrum, John Zaremba, Grandon
    Rhodes, Harry Lauter. Most stop-motion animation requires a
    willing suspension of disbelief in the viewer, but with the saucers
    in EARTH VS. it's more a matter of making an effort to realize
    that they are animated, their movements are so impeccably
    smooth. Unfortunately these totally believable saucers are al-
    most wasted on some of the most asinine, unbelievable charac-
    ters ever.
EARTH VS. THE GIANT SPIDER see SPIDER, The (1958)
The EARTHQUAKE ALARM Schultze 1909 5m. Ref: Bios
    10/21/09. Alarm rings five minutes before an earthquake.
EAST SIDE KIDS MEET BELA LUGOSI see GHOSTS ON THE
    LOOSE
EASY STREET Mutual 1917 25m. SP, D: Charles Chaplin. PH:
    William C. Foster, Rollie Totheroh. Ref: 70 Years. FIR'65:
    638. Pic: TBG. with Chaplin, Edna Purviance, Eric Camp-
    bell, Albert Austin, Mad doctor's formula turns man into a
    superman. Pretty much just mechanical knockabout. Not up to
    Chaplin's better shorts like THE PAWNSHOP.
EBIRAH see GODZILLA VS. THE SEA MONSTER
ECCE HOMO (by de Quincey) see HISTOIRES EXTRAORDINAIRES
    (1948)
ECHENME AL VAMPIRO see BRING ME THE VAMPIRE
EDGE OF RUNNING WATER, The (novel by W. Sloane) see WHEN
    THE DEVIL COMMANDS
EEGAH! Fairway Int'l 1962 Eastmancolor 90m. Story, D, P:
    Nicholas Merriwether. SP: Bob Wehling. PH: Vilis Lapenieks.
    Ref: FFacts. Boxo 8/20/62. Pic: FanMo 3:41. with Arch

Hall, Jr., Richard Kiel, Marilyn Manning, Ray Steckler. Prehistoric giant; cave of the mummies, etc. The movie that was
so cheap the budget wouldn't even allow for a broken window (just
the sound of a window breaking, over an empty space in a wall).
Thoroughly ridiculous.

The EFFECTIVE HAIR GROWER Lux 1908 Ref: MPW'08:549 Hair
tonic grows hair on maid's face, boy's chin.

The EFFECTS OF A ROCKET Itala 1911 7m. Ref: Bios 10/26/
11. Rockets fastened to man's coat tails send him on "meteoric
career."

EFFROYABLE SECRET DU DR. HICHCOCK, L' see HORRIBLE
DR. HICHCOCK, The

EGGHEAD'S ROBOT (B) CFF 1971 Eastmancolor 56m. D: Milo
Lewis. SP: Leif Saxon. PH: Johnny Coquillon. Mus sc & d:
Gordon Langford. Ref: MFB'71:95. with Keith Chegwin, Jeffrey
Chegwin, Roy Kinnear, Richard Wattis. Robot double of school-
boy.

The EGYPTIAN MUMMY Kalem 1913 8m. Ref: Bios 7/24/13.
Man impersonates mummy in mummy case.

The EGYPTIAN MUMMY Vita 1914 15m. D: Lee Beggs. SP:
A.A. Methley. Ref: LC. FIR'67:626. with Billy Quirk, Constance
Talmadge, Joel Day. Living mummy acts as matchmaker.

The EGYPTIAN MYSTERY Edison 1909 9m. Ref: MPW'09:61. Lady
frightened by power of pendant from Egyptian tomb which makes
anything the wearer's hands touch disappear.

EH? (play by H. Livings) see WORK IS A FOUR LETTER WORD

EIGHT BRAVE BROTHERS (J) Toei 1959 color/scope (SATOMI
HAKKEN-DEN--YOKAI NO RANBU) Part I: 58m. II: 57m. D:
Kokichi Uchida. SP: Shinji Kessoku. PH: Genya Washio. Based
on a well-known Japanese story. Ref:Unij.Bltn. #31. UFQ 6. with
Sentaro Fushimi, Kotaro Satomi, K. Onoue, Kensaku Hara.
Eight crystal globes emerge from the body of a dead dog that
fought a snake ("the daughter of a lord").

EIGHTH WONDER, The see KING KONG

EINSTEIN IS TO BLAME see MAN IN OUTER SPACE

EK SAAL PABLE (India) S.B. Films 1965 D: Dharam Kumar.
Ref: M/TVM 7/65. with Sayeeda Khan, Sujit Kumar. "Dead
man returns to the scene of the murder."

EL QUE MURIO DE AMOR see HE WHO DIES OF LOVE

The ELECTRIC BELT Cosmopolitan 1912 11m. Ref: Bios '12.
Belt makes man rush about energetically.

ELECTRIC BOOTS (F) Pathe 1911 8m. Ref: SilentFF. Bios
3/2/11. MPW'11:818. Boots accelerate actions of wearers.

The ELECTRIC CURRENT Pathe 1906 2m. Ref: V&FI 8/25/06.
Grocer electrifies his goods; current catches and holds thieves,
policemen.

The ELECTRIC DOLL (B) C&M 1914 8m. Ref: Bios 3/5/14.
Professor invents "human-like doll."

The ELECTRIC FANS Gaum 1910 5m. Ref: Bios 9/8/10. Fans
blow furniture out window.

The ELECTRIC GIRL Eclair 1914 15m. Ref: MPW 19:1428. Lee.
Electrified person attracts metal.

The ELECTRIC GOOSE Gaum 1905 D: Alf Collins. Ref: SF Film.

Electric shock machine restores Christmas dinner to life.
The ELECTRIC HOTEL (Sp) Pathe 1906 8m. (EL HOTEL ELEC-
TRICO) Ref: F Index 12/19/08. SF Film. "Mechanized
world of the future"-Imagen.
The ELECTRIC INSOLES Essanay 1910 8m. Ref: Bios 4/14/10.
Bill Smith has Dr. Wright's insoles placed in his shoes. When
he stands up, he can't stop his shoes from moving.
The ELECTRIC LAUNDRY Pathe 1912 1/2m. Ref: Bios 8/1/12.
Electric irons, soap, and brushes do the laundry.
The ELECTRIC LEG (B) Clarendon 1912 Ref: SF Film. Bios
11/7/12. One-legged professor invents electric leg.
ELECTRIC MAN, The (by H. J. Essex, S. Schwartz, and L.
Golos) see MAN MADE MONSTER
The ELECTRIC POLICEMAN (F) Gaum 1909 6m. Ref:
SilentFF. Wearer unable to stop "electric boots."
The ELECTRIC SERVANT (B) Urban 1909 D:Walter Booth.
Ref: SF Film. Robot.
ELECTRIC SNUFF (B) 1913 C&M 5m. Ref: Bios #352. Boy
buys snuff that has powerful effects.
The ELECTRIC VILLA Pathe 1911 7m. Ref: Bios 10/19/11.
Roast chicken comes to life; carpet moves; bottles empty them-
selves.
The ELECTRIC VITALISER (B) Kineto 1910 9m. (The ELEC-
TRIC VITALIZER) Ref: Bios 11/10/10. Brit.Cinema. D:
Walter R. Booth. Vitaliser resuscitates historical characters.
ELECTRICAL HOUSEBUILDING (B) Clarendon 1912 Ref: SF
Film. Bios 4/11/12.
The ELECTRICAL PHOTOGRAPHER (F) Melies 1908 (LA
PHOTOGRAPHIE ELECTRIQUE A DISTANCE) Ref: SF Film.
Takes pictures at long range.
The ELECTRICITY CURE (B) Hepworth 1900 Ref: SF Film.
The ELECTRIFIED PIG Cosmopolitan 1911 7m. Ref: Bios
4/20/11. Electrified pig upsets people and objects.
ELECTROCUTED Pathe 1907 Ref: V&FI 2/8/08. Electrician
adjusts electrodes, metal cap to cook's body to animate her.
ELECTRONIC LABYRINTH see THX 1138
The ELECTRONIC MONSTER (B) Col/Amalgamated 1957('60-
U.S.) 72m. (ESCAPEMENT. The DREAM MACHINE. ZEX.
ZEX, THE ELECTRONIC FIEND) D: Montgomery Tully. SP:
Charles Eric Maine, from his novel "The Man Who Couldn't
Sleep." PH: Bert Mason. Add'l Dial: J. MacLaren-Ross. Mus:
Richard Taylor. Assoc P: Jim O'Connolly. Ref: Orpheus 3:28.
MFB'58:45. PM. FM 26:4. with Rod Cameron, Mary Murphy,
Peter Illing, Meredith Edwards, Carl Jaffe. Invention has
"rows of dials which turn prerecorded fantasies into the brain
cells of mental patients." Dull.
The ELEVENTH DIMENSION Imp 1915 25m. P: Raymond L.
Shrock. Ref: Lee. MPN 7/17/15. Visions of cat; attempts
to restore the dead to life.
The ELEVENTH HOUR Fox 1923 80m. D: Bernard J. Durning.
SP: Louis Sherwin. PH: Don Short. Ref: NYT 8/28/23. AFI.
Motion Picture 11/23. with Charles Jones, Shirley Mason,
Alan Hale, June Elvidge, Nigel De Brulier, Fred Kelsey. Vial

of newly discovered explosive powerful enough to level New York City. Secret doors, secret panels.

ELEXIERE DES TEUFELS see DEVIL'S ELIXIR, The

The ELF KING; A NORWEGIAN FAIRY TALE Vita 1908 Ref: F Index. Cross dispels king and attendants.

ELIXIR OF BRAVERY Eclair 1910 7m. Ref: Bios 12/8/10. Patent elixir turns coward into brave man.

The ELIXIR OF LIFE (F) Pathe 1907 (THE ELIXIR OF STRENGTH) Ref: SilentFF. MPW'07:584. Prof. Rototo's elixir gives strength to hero.

The ELIXIR OF LIFE Gaum 1911 6m. Ref: Bios 11/9/11. Dr. Moyen discovers the secret of immortality.

ELIXIR OF LIFE Joker 1916 11m. D: Allen Curtis. SP: Harry Wulze. Ref: MPW 29:1559. with William Franey, Gale Henry, Lillian Peacock. Mummy brought to life.

The ELIXIR OF LONG LIFE Cines 1912 10m. Ref: Bios 10/10/12. Elixir has invigorating effect.

ELIXIR OF STRENGTH, The see ELIXIR OF LIFE, The (1907)

ELIXIR OF YOUTH Pathe 1910 9m. Ref: Bios 11/24/10. "Wiffles" buys an elixir that "transforms" him.

ELLA LOLA, A LA TRILBY Edison 1896 Ref: LC. From "Trilby" by George Du Maurier.

ELSTREE CALLING (B) British Int'l 1930 95m. D: Alfred Hitchcock, André Charlot, Jack Hulbert, Paul Murray. Sup: Adrian Brunel. SP: Val Valentine. PH: Claude Freise-Greene. Ref: SF Film. V 2/26/30. with Gordon Harker, Will Fyffe, Anna May Wong, Donald Calthrop, John Longden. TV apparatus.

ELUSIVE ISABEL Bluebird 1916 65m. D: Stuart Paton. SP: Raymond L. Shrock, from a story by Jacques Futrelle. Ref: MPN 13:3105. MPW'16. with Florence Lawrence, Harry Millarde, Paul Panzer, Sydney Bracey. Latin nations attempt to "bring about a compact whereby all the countries involved will secure complete control of the world." Inventor builds "mechanical and electrical contrivances."

The EMBALMER (I) Europix/Gondola 1964 ('66-U.S.) 83m. (Il MOSTRO DI VENEZIA. The MONSTER OF VENICE) D: Dino Tavella. PH: Mario Parapetti. Ref: FFacts. RVB. Boxo 7/25/66. with Maureen Brown, Elmo Caruso, Jean Mart, Viki Castillo. "Skeleton-clad" madman embalms women. A total bore, with a villain who is given one line ("Your beauty preserved forever!") and 36 variations on it, and a comic duo who are no threat to Franco and Ciccio.

The EMPEROR AND THE GOLEM (Cz) Artkino/State Film 1951 Agfacolor 95m. (The EMPEROR'S BAKER. CISARUV PEKAR, PEKARUV CISAR. CISARUV PEKAR, RELEKARUV CISAR. The GOLEM AND THE EMPEROR'S BAKER) D: Martin (Mac) Fric. SP: Fric, Jiri Brdecka, Jan Werich. PH: Jan Stallich, Bohumil Haba. Mus: Jan Kabas. Art D: Jan Zasvorka. Ref: MFB. DDC III:174. Pic: SM 4:28. FM-A'62:75. with Werich, Frantisek Cerny, Marie Vasova, Zdenek Stepanek. "Robot" with "unlimited power." Allegory; satire.

The EMPIRE OF DIAMONDS Perret-Pathe 1920 65m. SP, D: Leonce Perret. Story: V. Mandelstam. Ref: MPN 23:265. with

Robert Elliott, Lucy Fox, Leon Mathot, Henry G. Sell. "Artificial diamonds manufactured by a secret process so perfectly
that only the wear of years could prove their falsity."

The EMPIRE OF DRACULA (Mex) 1967 Vergara color (LAS
MUJERES DE DRACULA. EL IMPERIO DE DRACULA) D:
F. Curiel. SP: Ramon Obon. PH: Alfredo Uribe. Ref: FJA.
with Ethel Carrillo, Eric del Castillo, Cesar del Campo, Fernando Oses, Victor Alcocer, Lucha Villa.

The ENCHANTED KISS General 1917 20m. Ref: MPN 16:3487.
with Chet Ryan, Frances Parks. Dream: "Man who has found
the secret of remaining young by eating the flesh of a maiden
every year."

The ENCHANTED WREATH Warwick 1910 8m. Ref: Bios 9/15/
10. Imp with satanic powers makes girl disappear. "Forest
witch" brings her back.

The ENCHANTING SHADOW (Hong Kong) Shaw 1965 color 85m.
D: Li Han-Hsiang. SP: Wang Yueh-Ting. Ref: Boxo 8/30/65.
M/TVM 7/65. with Loh Tih, Chao Lei, Yang Chih-Ching,
Margaret Yong Jochling. Ghosts kill everyone daring to stay
overnight in a temple.

END OF AUGUST AT THE HOTEL OZONE (Cz) 1965 95m.
(KONEC SPRNA V HOTELU OZON. LATE AUGUST AT HOTEL
OZONE) D: Jan Schmidt. SP: Pavel Juracek. PH: Jiri Macak.
Mus: Jan Klusak. Ref: V 7/15/67. M/TVM 4/67. with Ondrej
Jariabek, Magda Seidlerova. Post-World-War-III.

END OF THE WORLD (Dan) Nordisk/Great Northern 1916 65m.
(VERLDENS UNDERGANG) D: August Blom. Ref: DDC II:368.
EncicDS'55. MPN 13:3093. Comet in earth's atmosphere.

END OF THE WORLD (F) Auten 1930 ('34-U.S.) 54m. D: Abel
Gance. From "The Imaginary World" by Camille Flammarion.
(LA FIN DU MONDE) PH: Jules Kruger. Mus: Ondes Martenot.
Art D: L. Meerson, J. Perrier. Ref: Imagen. COF 6:30.
FD 4/17/34. DDC II:307. III:37. Pic: DDC II:308. with
Gance, Victor Francen, Georges Colin, Jean D'Yd, Jeanne Brin-
deau. Comet approaches earth.

END OF THE WORLD see PANIC IN YEAR ZERO/WAKING UP
THE TOWN

ENEMY FROM SPACE (B) UA/Hammer 1957 84m. (QUATER-
MASS TWO-Eng) D: Val Guest. SP: Guest, Nigel Kneale.
Sequel to THE CREEPING UNKNOWN. Sequel: FIVE MILLION
YEARS TO EARTH. PH: Gerald Gibbs. Mus sc: James Bernard.
Ref: FDY. FM 14:46. COF 9:32. Pic: FM 18:43. with Brian
Donlevy, Vera Day, Bryan Forbes, Michael Ripper, Charles
Lloyd Pack, William Franklyn, John Van Eyssen, Percy Her-
bert, John Stuart, George Merritt, Michael Balfour. Govern-
ment project masks plot to take over earth. Fast-paced and ex-
citing; underrated, but maybe not as good as its sequel.

ENERGIZER Biog 1908 Ref: MPW'08:44. "Energizer" gives
man great strength.

The ENGINE OF DEATH Apex 1913 Ref: MPW'13:917. Powerful new explosive.

ENMASCARADO DE ORO CONTRA EL ASESINO INVISIBLE, El
see INVISIBLE MURDERER, The

ENOCH (by R. Bloch) see TORTURE GARDEN
ENSIGN PULVER see WALKING DEAD, The
ENTRE LAS REDES see BETWEEN THE NETS
EPIC HERO AND THE BEAST, The see SWORD AND THE
    DRAGON, The
EQUINOX Tonylyn/Harris 1971(1967) color 82m. SP,D: Jack
    Woods. Ref: Boxo 1/11/71. Pic: FM 80:22. with Edward
    Connell, Barbara Hewitt, Woods, Fritz Leiber. Demon pos-
    session; devil; other dimensions.
ERCOLE ALLA CONQUISTA DELLA ATLANTIDE see HERCULES
    AND THE CAPTIVE WOMEN
ERCOLE AL CENTRO DELLA TERRA see HERCULES IN THE
    HAUNTED WORLD
ERCOLE E LA REGINA DI LIDIA see HERCULES UNCHAINED
ERCOLE L'INVINCIBILE see HERCULES, THE INVINCIBLE
ERCOLE SFIDA SANSONE see HERCULES, SAMSON AND ULYSSES
ERDGEIST (play by F. Wedekind) see PANDORA'S BOX
ERIK THE GREAT see LAST PERFORMANCE, The
ERINNERUNGEN AN DIE ZUKUNFT see MEMORIES OF THE
    FUTURE
EROGAMI NO ONRYO see REVENGEFUL SPIRIT OF EROS, The
EROS EXPLODING see BIZARRE
The ERRATIC POWER (B) C&M 1910 7m. Ref: Bios 10/13/10.
    Professor electrifies wand; whatever it touches reverses itself.
ERZEBETH see DAUGHTERS OF DARKNESS
ESCALA EN HI-FI see SCALE IN HI-FI
ESCAMOTAGE D'UNE DAME CHEZ ROBERT HOUDIN see CON-
    JURING A LADY AT ROBERT HOUDIN'S
ESCAPE ABC-TV/Para 1971 color 72m. D: John L. Moxey.
    SP: Paul Playdon. PH: Al Francis. Art D: Walter M. Jeffries.
    Ref: TVG. LA Times 4/6/71. with Christopher George, Avery
    Schreiber, Marlyn Mason, William Windom, Gloria Grahame,
    William Schallert, Huntz Hall. Virus that could be the "origin
    of life" capable of reducing humans to robots.
ESCAPE FROM THE PLANET OF THE APES Fox 1971 Deluxe
    color/scope 97m. D: Don Taylor. SP: Paul Dehn. Based on
    characters created by Pierre Boulle. Third in the PLANET OF
    THE APES series. PH: Joseph Biroc. Mus: Jerry Goldsmith.
    Art D: Jack Martin Smith, William Creber. Ref: V 5/26/71.
    with Kim Hunter, Roddy McDowall, Bradford Dillman, Natalie
    Trundy, Eric Braeden, William Windom, Sal Mineo, Albert
    Salmi, Ricardo Montalban, Jason Evers. Too much plot, with
    too much of it talked out, all presupposing everyone's fascinated
    by human & ape histories. One bright scene with apes and
    oranges.
ESCAPEMENT see ELECTRONIC MONSTER, The
ESMERELDA Gaum 1906 D. V. Jasset. From "Notre Dame de
    Paris" by Victor Hugo. Ref: Mitry. Movie Monsters.
ESMERELDA (B) Master 1922 From "Notre Dame de Paris" by
    Victor Hugo. Ref: Movie Monsters.
ESPECTRO DEL ESTRANGULADOR, El see GHOST OF THE
    STRANGLER, The
ESPEJO DE LA BRUJA, El see WITCH'S MIRROR, The

149

Espionage

ESPIONAGE IN LISBON (I-F) 1965 Ref: TVG. with Brett Halsey, Marilu Tolo. Organization after scientist's electronic invention.

ESPIONAGE IN TANGIERS (Sp-I) Altantida/Dorica 1965 color/scope 97m. (MARC MATO, AGENTE S.007. S.007 SPIONAGGIO A TANGERI.) D: Gregg Tallas. SP: H. H. A. Curiel, J. L. M. Molla, Tallas, B. Lacasa, Del Grosso, J. L. J. Aloza. PH: R. Pacheco and A. Mancori. Mus: B. Ghiglia. Ref: SpCinema. Annuario. TVG. with Luis Davila, Jose Greci, Alberto Dalbes, Perla Cristal, Tomas Blanco. "Newly-invented disintegrator."

ESPIRITISMO see SPIRITISM

ESQUELETO DE LA SENORA MORALES, El see SKELETON OF MRS. MORALES, The

ESTADO CIVIL: MARTA (by J. J. A. Millan) see MARTA

ESTE NOITE ENCARNAREI NO TEU CADAVER see TONIGHT I WILL INCARDINATE YOUR BODY

ESTHER REDEEMED (B) Renaissance 1915 35m. SP, D: Sidney Morgan. From the play "The Wolfe Wife" by Arthur Bertram. Ref: Hist. Brit. Film. The Moral nature of a girl, "full of animal instincts and a predilection for crime," is altered by a surgical operation. with Julian Royce, William Brandon, Mona K. Harrison, Cecil Fletcher.

ESTRANHO MUNDO DE ZE DO CAIXAO, O see STRANGE WORLD OF ZE DO CAIXAO, The

ET MOURIR DE PLAISIR see BLOOD AND ROSES

The ETERNAL FEMININE Selig 1915 20m. Ref: MPW 9/25/15. Dream: A girl sees herself as ruler of the Clan Feminine in the Stone Age.

ETERNAL MUSIC (India) Sagar 1937 D: Hiren Bose. Ref: The Lighthouse 12/25/37. with Maya, Surendra. Scientist's invention "harnesses" sound waves.

EUGENIE...THE STORY OF HER JOURNEY INTO PERVERSION (G) Distinction/Video-Tel Int'l 1969 Eastmancolor 91m. D: Jesus Franco. SP: Peter Welbeck, from "Philosophy in the Boudoir" by the Marquis De Sade. PH: Manuel Merino. Mus Bruno Nicolai. P: Harry Alan Towers. Ref: V 8/5/70. with Marie Liljedahl, Maria Rohm, Jack Taylor, Christopher Lee. Sadistic cult;"blood drinking, sacrificial stabbings."

EVA See FACE OF EVE, The

EVE THE WILD WOMAN (I) 3 Star Films 1968 color (EVE LA VENERE SELVAGGIA) D: Robert Morris. SP: Ralph Zucker (aka Mario Pupillo), Mauri. PH: Mario Mancini. P: Zucker, Walter Brandi. Ref: Unitalia Films 12/68. with Brad Harris, Esmeralda Barros, Mark Farran, Marc Lawrence. Mad scientist's electronic devices "control" gorillas.

The EVIL BRAIN FROM OUTER SPACE (J) Shintoho/Manley-TV 1958-9 85m. (SUPER GIANT. SUPAH JAIYANTO #7, #8, & #9: UCHU KAIJIN SHUTSUGEN, THE DEVIL INCARNATE or AKUMA NO KESHIIN, and KINGDOM OF POISON MOTH or DOKUGA OKOKU ?) D: Chogi Akasaka? Ref: J Films '60:92. Imagen. with Ken Utsui, Junko Ikeuchi, Reiko Seto, Terumi Hoshi. Balazar, dying scientific genius of another galaxy, devises a way to keep his brain alive after his death. Memorable image: The brain of the alien floating down a river in a suitcase. Memorable lines: "To destroy the brain will be difficult--it's indestructible!" "I created you, Super Germ!"

The EVIL EYE Gaum 1909 6m. Ref: Bios 10/21/09. Witch casts spell on man who has refused her alms.

EVIL FORCE, The see 4-D MAN, The

EVIL FOREST, The see PARSIFAL (1951)

EVIL MIND, The see CLAIRVOYANT, The

The EVIL OF FRANKENSTEIN (B) Univ/Hammer 1964 Eastman-color 86m. D: Freddie Francis. SP: John Elder. PH: John Wilcox. Mus: Don Banks. Art D: Don Mingaye. SpFX: Les Bowie. Makeup: Roy Ashton. with Peter Cushing, Peter Woodthorpe, Kiwi Kingston (monster). Sandor Eles, Duncan Lamont, Katy Wild, Frank Forsyth. And with William Phipps, Steven Geray and Maria Palmer in added TV footage. Baron Frankenstein finds the monster preserved in glacial ice. Sluggish going.

The EVIL PHILTER Pathe 1909 Ref: MPW'09:851. Ugly hag gives man love potion in exchange for his soul; hideous creatures haunt him.

An EVIL POWER Selig 1911 17m. Ref: Bios 1/25/12. Girl under influence of hypnotist.

The EVIL POWER Rex 1913 30m. Ref: MPW'13:994. Bios 1/1/14. Dr. Kaishian hypnotizes young women; prevents them from leaving his house.

EVOCATION SPIRITE see RAISING SPIRITS

EVOLUTION 1925 52m. Documentary Ref: FD 7/19/25. Lee. MPW 75:432. "Reconstruction of prehistoric reptiles."

EX-DUKE, The (by E. P. Oppenheim) see PRINCE OF TEMPTERS, The

EXCURSION TO THE MOON see TRIP TO THE MOON, A (1902)

EXPEDITION MOON see ROCKETSHIP X-M

The EXPERIMENT Edison 1915 15m. Ref: MPN 2/27/15. LC. with Robert Brower, Bessie Learn. Experiment in hypnosis nearly proves fatal to man.

EXPERIMENT IN EVIL see TESTAMENT OF DR. CORDELIER, The

EXPERT'S OPINION (B) Para 1935 D: Ivar Campbell. Ref: Sound & Shadow 12/5/35. with Kim Peacock, Lucille Lisle. Demonstration of aerial gun, "possession of which assures any country military supremacy."

The EXPLOITS OF ELAINE Pathe 1914 serial 14 episodes. (THE CLUTCHING HAND) D: Louis Gasnier, George B. Seitz. Ref: CNW. TBG. DDC I:185. MPN 2/27, 3/6 & 4/10/15. with Pearl White, Sheldon Lewis, Arnold Daly, Creighton Hale, Floyd Buckley. Pic: PictHistCinema. Ch. 6. The Vampire. 9. The Death Ray. 13. The Devil Worshippers. "Vocaphone," suspended animation, "infra-red ray which causes instantaneous combustion of non-reflecting substances."--Brit. Film Ins. Dist. Cat'62.

The EXPLOSION OF FORT B2 (I) Picture Playhouse 1914 55m. Ref: MPN 2/27/15. Inventor's "powerful explosive" destroys fort.

EXTRAÑO CASO DEL DOCTOR FAUSTO, El see STRANGE CASE
  OF DR. FAUSTO, The
EXTRAÑO CASO DEL HOMBRE Y LA BESTIA, El see MAN AND
  THE BEAST, The
EXTRAORDINARY TALES see HISTOIRES EXTRAORDINAIRES
  (1931)
The EYE CREATURES AI-TV/Azalea 1965 color 80m. D:
  Larry Buchanan. Remake of INVASION OF THE SAUCERMEN.
  PH: Ralph K. Johnson. with John Ashley, Shirley McLine,
  Cynthia Hull, Warren Hammack, Chet Davis. Ref: ModM 2:19.
  Flying saucer lands on earth. Funny-you-should-ask-line:
  "Have you seen this picture before?" You're-a-poet-line: "The
  exertion and the liquor was just too much for his ticker." Ut-
  terly without redeeming value of any kind.
EYE OF THE CAT Univ/Schenck 1969 Technicolor 102m.
  (WYLIE) D: David Lowell Rich. SP: Joseph Stefano. PH: Rus-
  sell Metty, Ellsworth Fredricks. Mus: Lalo Schifrin. Art D:
  Alexander Golitzen, William D. DeCinces. with Michael Sarra-
  zin, Gayle Hunnicutt, Eleanor Parker, Laurence Naismith, Lin-
  den Chiles. Horde of cats used in murder plot.
EYE OF THE DEVIL (B) MGM/Filmways 1966 92m. (THIR-
  TEEN) D: J. Lee Thompson. SP: Robin Estridge, Dennis
  Murphy, from the novel "Day of the Arrow" by Philip Loraine.
  PH: Erwin Hillier. Mus: Garry McFarland. Ref: PM. Sat.Rev.
  12/2/67. with Deborah Kerr, David Niven, Donald Pleasence,
  Edward Mulhare, Flora Robson, Emlyn Williams, David Hem-
  mings, Sharon Tate, John Le Mesurier, Robert Duncan. Devil
  cult, human sacrifice.
EYES IN THE DARK Imp 1917 22m. D: Frank H. Crane. SP:
  Stuart Paton. Ref: MPW 32:320. Lee. Ruby with occult power;
  visions conjured up.
The EYES OF ANNIE JONES Fox/McCallum (B?) 1964 73m.
  D: Reginald LeBorg. SP: Louis Vittes. Story: Henry Slesar.
  PH: Peter Hennessy. Mus: Buxton Orr. P: Jack Parsons. Ref:
  FFacts. COF 9:32. with Richard Conte, Francesca Annis, Joyce
  Carey, Victor Brooks, Myrtle Reed. Girl speaks with dead
  woman's voice; has other supernatural powers.
EYES OF HELL, The see MASK, The (1961)
EYES OF SATAN Solax 1913 Ref: Lee. Conjuror makes skele-
  ton move.
EYES OF THE MUMMY (G) 1918 (DIE MUMIA MA. DIE AUGEN
  DER MUMIE MA) D: Ernst Lubitsch. UFA 55m. SP: Hans
  Kräly, Emil Rameau. PH: Alfred Hansen. (DIE AUGEN DER
  MUMMIR MA. THE EYES OF THE MUMMIE MA) Sets: Kurt
  Richter. Ref: DDC III:124. Shriek 1:63. MPW 57:613. The
  Lubitsch Touch. S&S Lubitsch index. with Pola Negri, Harry
  Liedtke, Emil Jennings, Max Laurence. Hypnotism; sect of
  mummy-worshippers; Egyptian religious fanatic who tries to
  drive woman mad by appearing as apparition.
EYES WITHOUT A FACE see HORROR CHAMBER OF DR.
  FAUSTUS, The

FBI CONTRO DR. MABUSE see RETURN OF DR. MABUSE, The
F. P. 1 (German version) Fox/Gaum 1932 90m. (F. P. 1 ANT-
WORTET NICHT. FLOATING PLATFORM #1 DOES NOT RE-
PLY) D: Karl Hartl. SP: Walter Reisch, Curt Siodmak, from
the novel by Siodmak. PH: Günther Rittau, Konstantin Tschet.
P: Erich Pommer. Ref: Imagen. with Peter Lorre, Hans Al-
bers, Sybille Schmitz, Paul Hartmann, H. Speelmanns, Werner
Schott. Landing platform for planes anchored in mid-Atlantic.
Pic: SM 6:26.
F. P. 1 (English version) English Dial: Robert Stevenson, Peter
MacFarland. with Conrad Veidt, Leslie Fenton, Jill Esmond,
George Merritt, Donald Calthrop, Francis L. Sullivan, Alexander
Field.
F. P. 1 (French version) with Charles Boyer, Danielle Parola, Jean
Murat, Pierre Brasseur, Marcel Vallée, Piere Piérade, Ernest
Ferny.
F. P. 1 (Spanish version)
FX 18 SECRET AGENT (Sp-F) 1965 color/scope 97m. (F. X.
18 AGENT SECRET) D: Maurice Cloche. (ORDEN: FX 18
DEBE MORIR. ORDER: FX 18 MUST DIE) SP: C. Plume,
J. Bollo, O. Cloche, from "Coplan Tente sa Chance" by Paul
Kenny. PH: P. Gueguen, J. J. Baena. Mus: Eddie Barclay.
Art D: R. Giordani. Ref: SpCinema'66. La Prod. Cin. Fr. with
Ken Clark, Jany Clair, Guy Delorme, Jacques Dacqmine. Man
transmits messages to Russian satellite from cave.
A FABLE MFR/Victor Ramos Jr. 1971 80m. D: Al Freeman,
Jr. SP: Leroi Jones, from his play "Slave." PH: Bruce
Sparks. Ref: V 5/19/71. with Freeman, Hildy Brooks, James
Patterson. Future war between blacks and whites in U. S.
The FABULOUS BARON MUNCHAUSEN (Cz) Manley/Gottwaldow
1962 color 83m. (BARON PRASIL. BARON MUNCHAUSEN.
THE ADVENTURES OF BARON MUNCHAUSEN) Art D, D: Karel
Zeman. SP: Joseph Kainar, Zeman. From a novel by Gottfried
Burger and engravings by Gustave Doré. PH: Jiri Tarantik. Mus:
Zdenek Liska. Sets: Zdenek Rozkopal. Ref: MFB'67:166. COF
7:54. Pic: FM 12:8. with Milos Kopecky, Jana Brejchova,
Rudolf Jelinek. Live action; animation; puppet. An astronaut
meets Munchausen on the moon. Sporadically very imaginative.
The FABULOUS WORLD OF JULES VERNE (Cz) WB/Ceskosloven-
sky 1958 ('61-U. S.) 83m. (VYNALEZ ZKAKY or WYNALEZ
ZKAZY. FACE THE FLAGS. THE DEADLY INVENTION. IN-
VENTION OF DESTRUCTION. INVENTION FOR DESTRUCTION.
THE DIABOLICAL INVENTION. WEAPONS OF DESTRUCTION.
JOURNEY OF THE JULES VERNE) SP, D: Karel Zeman. SP:
also Frantisek Hrubin. From "Face the Flags" or "For the
Flag" and "The Floating Island" by Jules Verne. PH: Jiri Tar-
antik. Mus: Zdenek Liska. Prologue Narr: Hugh Downs. Ref:
FFacts. DDC II:90. Orpheus 3:36. 4:38. with Lubor Tokos,
Arnost Navratil, Miroslav Holub. Submarines, flying machines,
deadly weapons, etc., in "Mystimation." Live action;
animation.

FACE, The see MAGICIAN, The (1958)
The FACE AT THE WINDOW (B) 1920 D: Wilfred Noy. Ref:
Lee. Brit. Cinema. with C. Aubrey Smith, Jack Hobbs, Gladys
Jennings. Dead revived.
The FACE AT THE WINDOW (B) 1932 D: Leslie Hiscott. Ref:
Lee. Brit. Cinema. with Raymond Massey, Claude Hulbert.
Dead revived.
The FACE AT THE WINDOW (B) Eros/Medallion-TV/Pennant
1939 66m. D: George King. SP: A. Rawlinson, from the play
by Brooke Warren. Ref: COF 9:32. DDC III:165. MFB'39:111.
with Tod Slaughter, Harry Terry (the face), John Warwick,
Marjorie Taylor, Aubrey Mallelieu. Professor's invention in-
tended to make recently dead person complete his last action.
Lots of nonsensical fun.
The FACE BEHIND THE MASK Col 1941 66m. D: Robert Florey.
SP: Paul Jarrico, Allen Vincent. Story: Arthur Levinson. PH:
Franz Planer. Mus D: M. W. Stoloff. Art D: Lionel Banks.
From a radio play by T. E. O'Connell. Ref: HR 4/14/43. Pic:
FM 19:55. 40:22. FMO 5:34. COF 5:17,19,22. with Peter Lorre,
Evelyn Keyes, Don Beddoe, George E. Stone, James Seay,
Charles Wilson, Frank Reicher, Ernie Adams, Lee Shumway.
Mask conceals man's horribly disfigured face.
A FACE IN THE FOG Victory 1936 64m. D: Robert Hill. SP:
Al Martin. From "The Great Mono Miracle" by Peter B. Kyne.
P: Sam Katzman. Ref: TVFFSB. COF 9:32. LC. FDY'36:254.
with June Collyer, Jack Mulhall, Lloyd Hughes, Lawrence Gray.
Bullets of frozen poison.
The FACE IN THE WINDOW Lubin 1908 Ref: F Index 12/19/08.
Mystic face appearing in window frightens clerk.
The FACE OF ANOTHER (J) Toho 1966 124m. (TANIN NO
KAO. I HAVE A STRANGER'S FACE) P,D: Hiroshi Teshiga-
hara. SP: K. Abe. PH: Hiroshi Segawa. Mus: Toru Takemitsu.
Ref: M/TVM 4/66. with Tatsuya Nakadai, M. Hira, Eiji
Okada, Machiko Kyo. Man burned in accident wears flesh-like
plastic mask.
The FACE OF EVE (B-Sp) Udastex/Hispamer 1968 94m.
(EVA) D: Jeremy Summers. SP: Peter Welbeck. PH: Manuel
Merino. Mus: Malcolm Lockyer. Art D: S. Ontañon. Ref:
MFB'70:105. with Robert Walker, Jr., Celeste Yarnall, Herbert
Lom, Christopher Lee, Fred Clark, Maria Rohm. Girl wields
strange power over Amazon River Indians.
FACE OF FEAR see FACE OF TERROR, The/PEEPING TOM
FACE OF FIRE (U.S.-Swedish) AA 1959 83m. (MANNEN UTAN
ANSIKTE) D: Albert Band. SP: Louis Garfinkle, from "The
Monster," short story by Stephen Crane. Ph, Art D: Edward
Vorkapich. Mus: Erik Nordgren. Ref: COF 9:32. Sweden I.
MadM 5:19. with Cameron Mitchell, Bettye Ackerman, James
Whitmore, Royal Dano, Lois Maxwell. Handyman's scarred face
frightens townsfolk.
The FACE OF FU MANCHU (B) 7A/Hallam/Anglo Amalgamated
1965 Technicolor/scope 96m. (MASK OF FU MANCHU) D:
Don Sharp. SP: Peter Welbeck. From novels by Sax Rohmer.
PH: Ernest Steward. Mus: Christopher Whelan. Art D: Frank

White. Ref: PM. Orpheus 3:32. with Christopher Lee, Nigel Green, Joachim Fuchsberger, Karin Dor, James Robertson Justice, Walter Rilla, Tsai Chin, Howard Marion Crawford. Fu Manchu attempts to gain control of a deadly drug.

FACE OF MARBLE Mono 1946 70m. D: William Beaudine. SP: Michel Jacoby. Story: William Thiele, Edmund Hartmann. PH: Harry Neumann. Mus: Edward Kay. Ref: FDY. with John Carradine, Robert Shayne, Claudia Drake, Willie Best, Maris Wrixon, Thomas E. Jackson, Rosa Rey. One of the wierdest horror movies ever: A doctor kills a dog and restores it to life. It seems to have developed rabies. It becomes transparent and walks through walls. Under a voodoo spell, it becomes a zombie. Finally, it develops "hemomania," turning, in effect, into a vampire!

The FACE OF TERROR (Sp) AI-TV/Yates/Documento 1959 81m. (LA CARA DEL TERROR. FACE OF FEAR) D: Isidoro M. Ferry (William Hole, Jr.--U.S.) SP: Monroe Maning. PH: Jose F. Aguayo. Mus: Jose Buenagu. Ref: MFB'64:133. MMF 9:16. with Lisa Gaye, Fernand(o) Rey, Virgilio Teixeira, Gerard Tichy. Dr. Taylor discovers a new method of plastic surgery.

The FACE OF THE MURDERER (Sp) Moncayo 1965 color/scope 86m. (EL ROSTRO DEL ASESINO) D: Pedro Lazaga. SP: Emilio Alfaro. Adap,Dial: Alfaro, J. M. Palacio, Lazaga. PH Victor Monreal. Mus: A. G. Abril. Art D: Teddy Villalba. Ref: SpCinema'66. with German Cobos, Paloma Valdés, Katia Loritz, Perla Cristal. Eight people take refuge in an isolated old hotel during a storm.

FACE OF THE SCREAMING WEREWOLF (Mex-U.S.) Warren (ADP)/Diana 1959 ('65-U.S.) 70m. (LA CASA DEL TERROR. HOUSE OF TERROR) D: Gilberto M. Solares (Jerry Warren-U.S.). Story: Solares. SP: Solares, Juan Garcia, F. de Fuentes. Mus: L. H. Breton. Ref: Indice. COF 7:46.9:32. MadM 2:49: (LA MOMIA). Pic: FM 9:12.11:8,22. MW 8:54: plot. with Lon Chaney, Jr. (mummy-werewolf), "Tin Tan," Yolanda Varela, Yerye Beirute, Oscar Ortiz de Pinedo, Consuelo Guerrero de Luna, Alfredo Barron, Raymond Gaylord.

FACE THE FLAGS (by J. Verne) see FABULOUS WORLD OF JULES VERNE, The

FACELESS MONSTER, The see NIGHTMARE CASTLE

FACTS IN THE CASE OF M. VALDEMAR, The (by E. A. Poe) see MASTER OF HORROR/TALES OF TERROR

FAHRENHEIT 451 (B) Univ/Anglo-Enterprise/Vineyard 1966 Technicolor 111m. (PHOENIX) SP,D: François Truffaut. SP: also Jean-Louis Richard. From the book by Ray Bradbury. Add'l Dial: David Rudkin, Helen Scott. PH: Nicolas Roeg. Mus: Bernard Herrmann. Art D: Syd Cain. Sets: Tony Walton. P: Lewis Allen. Ref: Orpheus 3:34. with Oskar Werner, Julie Christie, Anton Diffring, Cyril Cusack, Anna Palk, Jeremy Spenser, Gillian Lewis. Totalitarian society of the future forbids reading and burns books. Like most of Truffaut's movies, only partially successful, and, like most, episodic, and simply vacant where Truffaut has obviously tried hard to create mood.

FAIL SAFE Col/Youngsten-Lumet 1964 111m. D: Sidney Lumet.

SP: Walter Bernstein, from the novel by Eugene Burdick and
Harvey Wheeler. PH: Gerald Hirschfeld. SpFX: Storyboard,
Inc. Ref: FFacts. COF 6:56. with Henry Fonda, Dan O'Herli-
hy, Walter Matthau, Fritz Weaver, Frank Overton, Dom de
Louise, Russell Collins, Sorrell B(r)ooke, Edward Binns, Larry
Hagman, Russell Hardie, Dana Elcar. The U.S. accidentally
launches a nuclear attack on Moscow.
The FAIRY BOOKSELLER Pathe 1910 13m. Ref: Bios 12/1/10.
Dream: Beauty and the Beast; Puss in Boots; Bluebeard; ogre.
The FAIRY BOTTLE (B) C&M 1913 13m. Ref: Bios 3/20/13.
Evil spirit in bottle.
The FAIRY JEWEL (I?) Milano 1910 7m. Ref: Bios 2/9/11.
Fairy drowns hunter who is after gem.
FAIRY OF SINHALDWEEP (India) Paramount-India 1937 161m.
D: Kikubhai B. Desai. Ref: The Lighthouse 10/16/37. with
Navinchandra. Demon invulnerable through blood bath.
A FAKE DIAMOND SWINDLER Melies 1908 Ref: MPW'08:463.
Man claims to be able to produce diamonds with the electrical
apparatus in his laboratory.
The FAKER Col 1929 70m. silent D: Phil Rosen. SP: Howard
J. Green. PH: Teddy Tetzlaff. Art D: Harrison Wiley. Ed:
William Hamilton. P: Harry Cohn. Ref: AFI. Photoplay. with
Warner Oland, Jacqueline Logan, Charles Delaney, Fred Kelsey,
Gaston Glass, Flora Finch, Charles Mailes. Fake spiritualist.
The FAKIR'S SPELL Dreadnought (B?) 1914 D: Frank Newman.
Ref: Movie Monsters. with I. Newman. Ape.
The FALL OF A NATION Nat'l Drama Corp. 1916 88m. From
the novel by Thomas Dixon. Ref: NYT 6/7/16. European
forces invade America, reach Long Island unopposed.
The FALL OF THE HOUSE OF USHER (F) Epstein 1928 silent
55m. (LA CHUTE DE LA MAISON USHER) D: Jean Epstein.
Ass't D: Luis Bunuel. From "The Fall of the House of Usher"
and "The Oval Portrait" by Edgar Allan Poe. PH: Lucas Y.
Herbert. Sets: Pierre Kefer. Ref: SilentFF. FM 11:42. Pic:
DDC II:225. with Marguerite Abel Gance, Jean Debucourt,
Charles Lamyn.
The FALL OF THE HOUSE OF USHER Webber 1928 silent 20m.
SP: Melville Webber, from the story by Edgar Allan Poe. PH:
James Sibley Watson. Ref: SilentFF. FM 11:42. with Webber,
Herbert Stem, Hildegarde Watson. Good minor version of the
story.
The FALL OF THE HOUSE OF USHER (B) Gibraltor/Eros 1950
70m. PH, D: Ivan Barnett. SP: Kenneth Thompson, Dorothy
Catt, from the story by Edgar Allan Poe. Ref: MFB'51:106.
V 5/21/52. COF 9:32. with Gwendolyn Watford, Kay Tendeter,
Irving Steen. Man fears sister has been buried alive.
The FALL OF THE HOUSE OF USHER NBC-TV/Matinee Theater
1958 54m. Based on the story by Edgar Allan Poe. Adap:
Robert Esson. Ref: COF 9:32. TVFFSB. with Tom Tryon,
Marshall Thompson, Eduardo Cianelli.
FALL OF THE HOUSE OF USHER, The (by E. A. Poe) see
HOUSE OF USHER/HORROR
FALL X701, Der see FROZEN ALIVE

FANATIC   see   DIE! DIE! MY DARLING

FANTABULOUS   (I-F)   Pegaso/Summa-Procinex   1966 Eastman color   95m.   (FANTABULOUS, INC.)   D: Sergio Spina.   SP: O. Jemma, F. Colombo, Spina.   PH: Claudio Ragona.   Mus: Sandro Brugnolini.   Ref: Ital P. V. with Richard Harrison, Adolpho Celi, Judi West.   Emotions of hero and heroine short circuit apparatus intended to transform him into a superman.

FANTASIA...3   see   FANTASY...3

FANTASMA DE LA CASA ROJA, El   see   PHANTOM OF THE RED HOUSE, The

FANTASMA DE LA OPERETA, El   see   PHANTOM OF THE OPE-RETTA, The (1955/1959)

FANTASMA DE LAS NIEVES, El   see MONSTER OF THE VOL-CANOES, The

FANTASMA DEL CONVENTA, El see PHANTOM OF THE CONVENT, The

FANTASMA DI LONDRA, Il   see MONK WITH THE WHIP, The

FANTASMAS ASUSTADOS   see   FRIGHTENING GHOSTS

FANTASMAS BURLONES, Los   see   GHOST JESTERS, The

FANTASMAS EN BUENOS AIRES   see GHOSTS IN BUENOS AIRES

FANTASMI A ROMA   see   GHOSTS OF ROME

FANTASMI E LANDRI   see   GHOSTS AND THIEVES

FANTASTIC DISAPPEARING MAN, The   see   RETURN OF DRACULA

A FANTASTIC GHOST STORY (Korea)   Yun Bang Films   1968 color/scope   90m.   (GOE TAM)   D: Choe Joemyong.   SP: Hahn Youlim, Kim Kangyoon.   PH: Chung Woonkyo.   Ref: Korean Cinema '68.   with Nam Chungim, Moon Hee, Nam Kungwon, Nam Jin. 1. Baikran's sweetheart dies and appears to various people as a ghost without eyebrows.   2. In a dream Jinwoo sees a woman without a head.   3. A man sculpts a model of his dead wife and puts it in a coffin.

FANTASTIC LITTLE GIRL, The   see   INCREDIBLE SHRINKING MAN, The

FANTASTIC PUPPET PEOPLE, The   see   ATTACK OF THE PUP-PET PEOPLE

The FANTASTIC THREE   (I-W.G.-F-Yugos) Cinesecolo/Parnass/ Comptoir/Avala 1967 color/scope   (I TRE FANTASTICI SUPERMEN or I FANTASTICI TRE SUPERMEN-I.   The THREE FANTASTIC SUPERMEN)   D: Gianfranco Parolini (Frank Kramer). SP: Kramer, Marcello Coscia, Werner Hauff.   Mus: R. Cini, J. Fontana.   PH: F. Izzarelli.   Ref: Ital P. MFB '68:118.   with Tony Kendall, Brad Harris, Gloria Paul, Sabine Sun, Thomas Reiner, Patricia Carr.   Machine produces copies of people.

FANTASTIC VOYAGE   Fox   1966   Deluxe color/scope   100m. (MICROSCOPIA. STRANGE JOURNEY)   D: Richard Fleischer. SP: Harry Kleiner.   Adap: David Duncan.   PH: Ernest Laszlo. Story: Otto Klement, J. L. Bixby.   Mus: Leonard Rosenman. Art D: Jack Martin Smith, Dale Hennesy.   SpFX: L. B. Abbott, Art Cruickshank, Emil Kosa, Jr. Ref: FFacts.   Orpheus 3:34. with Stephen Boyd, Raquel Welch, Donald Pleasence, Arthur Kennedy, Arthur O'Connell, Edmond O'Brien, William Redfield, Barry Coe.   Experimental submarine with team of scientists takes lifesaving journey into a human body.   Moments of suspense

157   Fantastic

despite cardboard characters, wretched dialogue. The ending is
a real tear-jerker. Financially successful; so where are the
sequels--"Voyage through the Small Intestine" (a four-hour
movie), "The Northwest Nasal Passage, " etc. ?
FANTASTIC WORLD OF DR. COPPELIUS, The see DR. COP-
    PELIUS
The FANTASTICAL AIRSHIP (F) Melies 1906 (LE DIRIGEABLE
    FANTASTIQUE ou LE CAUCHEMAR D'UN INVENTEUR) Ref:
    SF Film. Mitry II. Dirigibles.
FANTASTICI TRE SUPERMEN, I see FANTASTIC THREE, The
FANTASTICO MUNDO DEL DR. COPPELIUS, El see DR. COP-
    PELIUS
FANTASY BAZAAR (India-Hindi) Basant 1959 150m. (MAYA
    BAZAAR) D: R. Mistry. Ref: FEFN XII:7-9. with Anita Guha,
    Mahipal. A lord's supernatural powers make everyone at a wed-
    ding "appear as the real demons they are. "
FANTASY OF THE MONASTERY, The see PHANTOM OF THE
    CONVENT, The
FANTASY... 3 (Sp) Pam Latina 1966 color /scope 82m.
    (FANTASIA... 3) SP, D: Eloy Germán de la Iglesia. SP: also
    F. M. Iniesta. PH: S. Crespo. Mus: F. G. Morcillo. Art D:
    E. T. de la Fuente. Ref: SpCinema'67. with Dianik Zurakowska,
    José Palacio, Tomas Blanco. 1: "The Maid of the Sea. " A
    siren becomes a woman. 2: "The Three Hairs of the Devil. "
    Tomasín must pull out the three gold hairs on the devil's chin.
    3: "The Wizard of Oz. "
FANTOMAS Fox 1920 serial 20 episodes D: Edward Sedgwick.
    Ref: Lee. CNW. Pic: DDC II:223. with Edna Murphy, Ed Rose-
    man, Eva Balfour, Johnny Walker, John Willard. Gold formula.
    Ch. 9. The Haunted Hotel.
FANTOMAS (F) Lopert-UA /Pac-Gaum 1964 ('66-U. S.) color /
    scope 104m. P, D: André Hunnebelle. SP: Jean Halain, Pierre
    Foucaud, from the novel by Pierre Souvestre and Marcel Allain.
    PH: Marcel Grignon, Jean Feyte. Mus: Michel Magne. Art D:
    P. -L. Boutie. Ref: V 12 /2 /64. FF. COF 9:41. Pic: FM 34:
    11. 46:38. with Jean Marais, Louis de Funes, Mylene Demongeot,
    Marie-Helene Arnaud, Jacques Dynam. "Fantomas molds masks
    using his unique method of duplicating human skin and makes plans
    to get a brain for the synthetic human being he has built. "
FANTOMAS AGAINST SCOTLAND YARD (F) Pac-Gaum-Fair 1967
    105m. (FANTOMAS CONTRE SCOTLAND YARD) D: André
    Hunnebelle. SP: Jean Halain, Pierre Foucaud. PH: R. C. For-
    get. Ref: V 4 /12 /67. with Jean Marais, Louis de Funes, Mylene
    Demongeot, Henri Serre. Haunted castle.
FANTOMAS STRIKES BACK (F-I) SNEG /Pac /Victory 1965
    color /scope 94m. (FANTOMAS SE DECHAINE or FANTOMAS
    REVIENT-F) D: André Hunnebelle. SP: Jean Halain, Pierre
    Foucaud. PH: Raymond Lemoigne. Mus: M. Magne. Art D:
    Max Douy. SpFX: Gil Delamare, G. Cogan, C. Carliez. Ref:
    MFB '68:102. COF 9:46. Pic: COF 15:46. DDC III:64. with
    Jean Marais, Louis de Funes, Mylene Demongeot, Robert Dalban.
    Kidnapped professors forced to develop a mind-controlling ray.
FANTOMAS: THE MYSTERIOUS FINGERPRINT see DEAD MAN

WHO KILLED, The
FANTOMAS III see DEAD MAN WHO KILLED, The
FANTOME DU MOULIN-ROUGE, Le see PHANTOM OF THE
  MOULIN ROUGE, The
FAREWELL TO THE MASTER (Story by H. Bates) see DAY THE
  EARTH STOOD STILL, The
The FAST EXPRESS Univ 1924 serial 15 episodes 4. The Haunt-
  ed House. D: William Duncan. SP: Frank H. Clark, from the
  novel "Crossed Wires" by Courtney Ryley Cooper. Ref: CNW.
  with William Duncan, Edith Johnson, Albert J. Smith, Harry
  Woods.
FATA MORGANA see LEFT-HANDED FATE
The FATAL APPETISER (B) Hepworth 1909 8m. Ref: Bios
  10/14/09. Dose of friend's medicine gives man remarkable
  appetite.
The FATAL HOUR Mono 1940 68m. (MR. WONG AT HEAD-
  QUARTERS) D: William Nigh. SP: Scott Darling. Story: Joseph
  West. From the Mr. Wong stories by Hugh Wiley. PH: Harry
  Neumann. Ref: MPH 1/20/40. with Boris Karloff, Grant
  Withers, Marjorie Reynolds, Charles Trowbridge, John Hamilton,
  Craig Reynolds, Jack Kennedy, Frank Puglia, Stanford Jolley,
  Jason Robards. "Remote control box to tune in radio at a dis-
  tance from the receiver" used in murder. The clever-murder-
  gimmick (which, at that, is probably lifted from some previous
  Monogram) comes as the only surprise after an incredible barrage
  of cliche lines and situations. You may find yourself saying the
  actors' lines before they do.
The FATAL NIGHT (B) Col/Anglofilm 1948 50m. D: Mario
  Zampi. SP: Gerald Butler, from "A Gentleman from America"
  by Michael Arlen. PH: Cedric Williams. Mus: Stanley Black.
  Ref: MFB'48:59. with Lester Ferguson, Jean Short, Leslie Armstrong, Brenda Hogan, Patrick Macnee. American spends night
  in English "haunted house."
The FATAL PACT Pathe 1912 7m. Ref: Bios 12/12/12. Gambler
  makes pact with "geni [sic] of terrible aspect" never to gamble
  again. He does and disappears.
The FATAL RING Pathe/Astra 1917 serial 20 episodes 6. Rays
  of Death. D: George B. Seitz. Ref: MPW 33:423. 34:136. MPN
  16:3859. Pic: TBG with Pearl White, Earle Fox, Warner Oland,
  Floyd Buckley. Liquid dissolves "any matter that comes within
  its rays."
FATICHE DI ERCOLE, Le see HERCULES
The FAUN Pathe 1908 Ref: F Index 12/26/08. Ugly faun; life-
  restoring philter; petrifying water.
FAUST (F) 1897 (sfa LA DAMNATION DE FAUST?) Melies?
  From Goethe. Ref: DDC III:502. Mitry II: 1898.
FAUST (F) Melies 1904 Ref: DDC II:383.
FAUST (F) 1907 Ref: Halliwell. Mitry II:52.
FAUST Edison 1909 17m. Ref: MPW'09:927. Bios 2/10/10.
FAUST (F) Eclair 1910 (sfa FAUST Melies '09?) From Goethe.
  Ref: DDC I:88. The Film Index, with Henry Andreani.
FAUST (I) Cines 1910 From Goethe. 16m. Ref: DDC III:462.
  SilentFF. Bios 6/2/10. Mitry V:7. with Fernanda Negri-Pouget.

FAUST (F) Pathe 1910 color 35m. From Goethe. Ref: The
  Film Index (1911?). Bios 11/3/10. Motography 7/11: German?
FAUST 1921 D: Frederick A. Todd. Ref: LC.
FAUST (G) UFA/MGM 1926 100m. D: F. W. Murnau. SP:
  Hans Kyser, from German folk tales. Titles: Gerhard Haupt-
  mann. PH: Carl Hoffmann. Art D: Walter Röhrig, Robert
  Herlth. Ref: SilentFF. Pic. DDC I:61. II:186. III:422. with
  Emil Jannings, Wilhelm Dieterle, Camilla Horn, Eric Barclay,
  Gösta Ekmann. Breathtaking images dominate (in the available
  shortened version).
FAUST (G) Divina 1960 color 133m. D: Peter Gorski. SP:
  Gustaf Grundgens. Ref: German Pictures. Orpheus 4:38. Boxo
  5/27/63. DDC II:358. with Elisabeth Flickenschildt, Will
  Quadflieg, Ella Buchi.
FAUST see BILL BUMPER'S BARGAIN/MISS FAUST/MARGUERITE
  OF THE NIGHT/RETURN TO YOUTH
FAUST AND MARGUERITE (F) Melies 1897 Ref: Mitry II. Pic:
  DDC I:51.
FAUST AND MARGUERITE Edison 1900 Ref: Niver. Skeleton;
  devil.
FAUST AND MARGUERITE (F) Gaum 1911 D: Jean Durand.
  Ref: Mitry II.
FAUST AND MEPHISTOPHELES (B) G. A. Smith 1898 Ref:
  Mitry II. DDC II:448.
FAUST AND THE DEVIL (I) Col 1948 87m. (LA LEGGENDA DI
  FAUST) D: Carmine Gallone. SP: Leopold Marchand. From the
  opera by Gounod. Mus: A. Cicognini. PH: V. Vich, A. Gallea.
  Ref: V 4/26/50. DDC I:417. II:415. COF 9:33. with Italo
  Tajo, Nelly Corradi, Gino Mattera.
FAUST AND THE LILY Biog 1913 8m. Ref: Bios 8/7/13. Bur-
  lesque of Goethe's "Faust."
FAUST FANTASY (B) 1935 color 50m. Ref: London Times
  3/14/35. with Dennis Hoey, Webster Booth, Ann Zeigler.
FAUST IN HELL (F) Melies/Star 1903 4m. (FAUST AUX ENFERS)
  From Berlioz. Ref: Mitry II.
FAUST XX (Rumania) Bucaresti 1966 85m. SP, D: Ion Popescu-
  Gopo. PH: Grigore Ionescu, Stefan Horvath. Mus: Stefan
  Niculescu. Ref: V 8/3/66. COF 10:50. with Emil Botta,
  Iurie Darie, Jorj Voicu. The devil has evolved a way of putting
  one mind or soul into another body.
FAUSTINA (Sp) Chapalo Films 1958 color SP, D: Jose Luis
  Saenz de Heredia. From Goethe's "Faust." PH: Alfredo Fraile.
  Ref: MMF 9:15. with Maria Felix, Fernando Gomez, Conrado
  San Martin, Fernando Rey, Elisa Montes, Jose Isbert.
FEAR IN THE NIGHT Para 1947 71m. SP, D: Maxwell Shane.
  Story: William Irish. Remake: NIGHTMARE (1956). PH: Jack
  Greenhalgh. Ref: MFB'47:63. COF 9:33. with Paul Kelly, De-
  Forest Kelley, Ann Doran, Kay Scott, Robert Emmett Keane, Jeff
  Yorke, Charles Victor. Man hypnotizes Vince Grayson to kill.
FEAR NO EVIL NBC-TV/Univ 1969 Technicolor 96m. D: Paul
  Wendkos. P, SP: Richard Alan Simmons. Story: Guy Endore.
  PH: Lionel Lindon. Mus: William Goldenberg. Sequel: RITUAL
  OF EVIL. Ref: TVG. RVB. with Louis Jourdan, Bradford Dillman,

Lynda Day, Marsha Hunt, Carroll O'Connor, Wilfrid Hyde-White, Kate Woodville. Woman finds she can bring dead fiance back in mirror. Not bad for a TV movie. Exciting ending.

FEAR OF THE SNAKE WOMAN (J) Toei 1968 83m. (KAIDAN HEBIONNA) D: Nobuo Nakagawa. Ref: Unij. Bltn 31. UFQ 42. with Akira Nishimura, Reiko Ohara. "Murdered young lady returns as snake."

FEARLESS FRANK see FRANK'S GREATEST ADVENTURE

The FEARLESS VAMPIRE KILLERS or PARDON ME, BUT YOUR TEETH ARE IN MY NECK (B) MGM/Cadre/Filmways 1967 Metrocolor/scope 98m. SP, D: Roman Polanski. SP: also Gerard Brach. PH: Douglas Slocombe. Mus: Krzysztof Komeda. Makeup: Tom Smith. Ref: FFacts. PM. Professor and assistant hunt down vampire. with Jack MacGowran, Polanski, Sharon Tate, Alfie Bass, Ferdy Mayne, Fiona Lewis, Iain Quarrier, Ronald Lacey. Likable at times, with some very funny bits, but far too long.

FEATHERTOP (F) Eclair/American Standard 1912 15m. From the story by Nathaniel Hawthorne. Ref: Bios'13. MPN 12:946. Scarecrow brought to life by witch.

FEATHERTOP (B?) Kinemacolor 1913 From the story by Hawthorne. Ref: Lee. MPW 16:281, 312.

FEATHERTOP see also LORD FEATHERTOP

FEDERAL AGENTS VS. UNDERWORLD, INC. Rep 1948 serial 12 episodes ('66 feature GOLDEN HANDS OF KURIGAL) D: Fred Brannon. SP: Sol Shor, Basil Dickey, William Lively, Royal Cole. Ref: Barbour. with Kirk Alyn, Rosemary LaPlanche, Roy Barcroft, Carol Forman, James Craven, Tristram Coffin, Bob Wilke, Dale Van Sickel, Tom Steele. Curse on those who possess hands; mind-controlling Oriental herb "dulls medicinal processes," makes "robots" of victims. Typical serial thrills; that is, not many.

FEE CARABOSSE, La see WITCH, The (1906)

FEMALE COBRA (Pakistani) Films Hayat 1959 118m. (NAGIN) D: Khalil Quaiser. Ref: FEFN 9/59. "Two dangerous supernatural reptiles disguise themselves as children," terrorize the countryside.

FEMALE FIEND see THEATRE OF DEATH

The FEMALE OF THE SPECIES Triangle-Kay Bee 1916 55m. Story: Russell E. Smith. Ref: MPN 14:4038. with Dorothy Dalton, Howard Hickman, Enid Markey. Operation restores man's memory.

FEMALE OF THE SPECIES, The (by H. C. McNeil) see BULLDOG DRUMMOND COMES BACK

FEMALE TRAP, The see NAME OF THE GAME IS KILL, The

FEMMES VAMPIRES, Les see QUEEN OF THE VAMPIRES, The

The FERRYMAN'S SWEETHEART Gaum 1909 14m. Ref: Bios 1/6/10. Ferryman dies when he sees vision of his lost sweetheart.

FETE A HENRIETTE, La see PARIS WHEN IT SIZZLES

FIEND WITHOUT A FACE (B) MGM/Amalgamated 1958 74m. D: Arthur Crabtree. SP: Herbert J. Leder, from Amelia Reynolds Long's "The Thought Monster." PH: Lionel Banes. Mus:

Frederic Lewis, Buxton Orr. P: John Croydon. Exec P:
Richard Gordon. Ref: FFacts. FM 2:16. Pic: FM 8:47. with
Marshall Thompson, Terence Kilburn, Kim Parker, Peter Madden, Michael Balfour, Kynaston Reeves. Scientist's evil thoughts
materialize as monsters. The action begins (finally) when the
fiends become visible. Their method of moving and killing
makes them one of the most fascinating of the late-'50's myriad
monsters.
FIENDISH GHOULS, The see MANIA
The FIENDISH TENANT Gaum 1910 7m. Ref: Bios 1/5/11.
Man takes apartment, extracts all his furniture and "several
human beings" from bag. When he leaves, he leaves behind a
cabinet which explodes when the landlord strikes it.
FIENDS, The see DIABOLIQUE
The FIENDS OF HELL (B) Apex 1914 60m. Ref: Lee. Moto-
graphy 12/26/14. Hypnotic medium; new kind of electric cur-
rent; metal stronger than steel that floats in the air; detective
with occult powers.
The FIERY HAND (B) Stoll 1923 25m. (Mystery of Dr. Fu-
Manchu series) D: A. E. Coleby. SP: Coleby, Frank Wilson,
from novels by Sax Rohmer. PH: D. P. Cooper, Phil Ross.
Art D: Walter W. Murton. Ref: SilentFF. with Harry Agar
Lyons, Joan Clarkson. "Haunted house."
FIFTEEN WIVES Invincible 1934 (THE MAN WITH THE ELEC-
TRIC VOICE-Eng) D: Frank Strayer. SP: Charles Belden,
Frederick Stephani. PH: M. A. Anderson. Ref: FJA. V 9/25/34.
SF Film. HR 10/3/34 with Conway Tearle, Natalie Moorhead,
Raymond Hatton, John Wray, Ralf Harolde ("the man..."). Man's
voice over radio shatters glass bowl containing lethal gas.
FIG LEAVES Fox 1926 80m. D: Howard Hawks. SP: Hope
Loring, Louis D. Lighton, from a story by Hawks. PH: Joseph
August. Two sequences in color. Art D: William Cameron Men-
zies. Ref: V 7/7/26. with George O'Brien, Olive Borden,
Andre de Beranger, Phyllis Haver, Heinie Conklin. Flatboat
drawn by dionsaur is the 8:40 local.
FIGHTING DEVIL DOGS Rep 1938 serial 12 episodes (Feature:
'43; '66-TORPEDO OF DOOM) D: William Witney, John English.
SP: Sol Shor, F. Adreon, B. Shipman, Ron Davidson. PH:
William Nobles. Ref: Barbour. Pic: FM 54:46. TBG. with
Herman Brix (aka Bruce Bennett), Lee Powell, Eleanor Stewart,
Montagu Love, Hugh Sothern, Sam Flint, Forrest Taylor, John
Picorri, Carleton Young, Tom London, John Davidson, Reed
Howes, Edmund Cobb. Electric torpedo; lightning gun. Eerie
special effects but not much else.
The FIGHTING GRINGO Red Feather-Univ 1917 55m. D: Fred
Kelsey. SP: Maud Grange. Story: H. W. Phillips. Ref:
MPN 15:2032. with Harry Carey, Claire Du Bray, George
Webb, T. D. Crittendon, Rex de Rosselli. Man with political
aspirations exercises hypnotic influence over girl.
FIGHTING LEGIONS, The see WEAPONS OF VENGEANCE
The FIGHTING MARINES Mascot 1935 serial 12 episodes D:
B. Reeves Eason, Joseph Kane. SP: Barney Sarecky, Sherman
Lowe. Story: R. Trampe, M. Geraghty, W. MacDonald. Ref:

Lee. Next Time. with Grant Withers, Ann Rutherford, Adrian Morris, Robert Warwick, George Lewis, Pat O'Malley, Victor Potel, Jason Robards, Robert Frazer, Frank Glendon, Donald Reed, Richard Alexander. Ray gun.

FIGHTING RANGER Barsky 1926 55m. D: Paul Hurst. Ref: AFI. with Al Hoxie. "Mysterious ghost of range."

FILLES POUR UN VAMPIRE, Des see PLAYGIRLS AND THE VAMPIRE, The

FINAL COUNT, The (by H. C. McNeil) see ARREST BULLDOG DRUMMOND

The FINAL WAR (J) Medallion-TV/Toho 1961 color 80m. (THE LAST WAR. SEKAI DAI SENSO) D: Shue Matsubayashi. SP: T. Yasumi, Takeshi Kimura. PH: Rokuro Nishigaki. SpFX: Eiji Tsuburaya. Ref: UFQ 15. COF 4:4.9:33. Pic: COF 3:55.4:59. with Frankie Sakai, Nobuko Otowa, Akira Takarada, Yumi Shirakawa, Y. Hoshi.

FINAL WAR, The see WORLD WAR III BREAKS OUT

FIRE see PYRO

The FIRE DETECTIVE Pathe 1929 silent serial 10 episodes D: Spencer G. Bennet, Thomas L. Storey. Ref: CNW. LC. with Gladys McConnell, Hugh Allan, Frank Lackteen. Ch. 7. The Ape Man.

FIRE MAIDENS FROM OUTER SPACE (B) Eros/Criterion/Topaz 1956 68m. (THE THIRTEENTH MOON OF JUPITER) SP,D: Cy Roth. PH: Ian Struthers. Art D: Scott MacGregor. Ref: MFB '56:104. SF Film. Pic: FM 18:17. WFC 4:51. with Anthony Dexter, Paul Carpenter, Susan Shaw, Sydney Tafler. Travelers to a moon of Jupiter are forced to remain by the female inhabitants. Film introduced classical music to s-f movies long before 2001. Otherwise it's what you'd expect from the title.

FIRE MONSTERS AGAINST THE SON OF HERCULES (I) Emb 1962 82m. (MACISTE CONTRO I MOSTRI. COLOSSUS OF THE STONE AGE. THE FIRE MONSTERS AGAINST MACISTE IN THE VALE OF WOE) SP,D : Guido Malatesta. SP: also Arpad De Riso. PH: Giuseppe La Torre. Ref: MFB. COF 9:33. Cavemen, sea monster, hydra-headed monster.

The FIRST FLYER Educ/Bray 1918 Ref: FM 63:28. The pterodactyl in prehistory.

FIRST MAN INTO SPACE (B) MGM/Amalgamated 1959 77m. (SATELLITE OF BLOOD) D: Robert Day. SP: John C. Cooper, Lance Z. Hargreaves. Story: Wyott Ordung. PH: Geoffrey Faithfull. Mus: Buxton Orr. P: John Croydon, Charles Vetter. Ref: Orpheus 3:26. FFacts. with Marshall Thompson, Marla Landi, Bill Edwards, Robert Ayres, Bill Nagy, Carl Jaffe. Test pilot exposed to gamma rays in outer space.

The FIRST MEN IN THE MOON (B) Gaum 1919 D: Jack Leigh. From the story by H. G. Wells. Ref: Brit.Cinema. FIR. with Bruce Gordon, Lionel D'Arragan, Heather Thatcher.

FIRST MEN IN THE MOON (B) Col 1965 Technicolor/scope 103m. D: Nathan Juran. SP: Nigel Kneale, Jan Read. From the story by H. G. Wells. PH: Wilkie Cooper. Mus: Laurie Johnson. Art D: John Blezard. SpFX: Ray Harryhausen. P: Charles Schneer. Ref: PM. with Edward Judd, Martha Hyer, Lionel

Jeffries, Miles Malleson, Paul Carpenter, Marne Maitland, Peter
Finch, Erik Chitty, Betty McDowall, Gladys Henson. Flight to
moon in 1899. The comedy is OK; it's just that there's too
much of it and not enough special effects.

FIRST MEN IN THE MOON see also TRIP TO THE MOON, A
    (1902)

FIRST SPACESHIP ON VENUS (Polish-E.G.) Crown/Defa-Film
    Polski 1958 ('63-U.S.) color/scope 94m. (MILCZACA
    GWIAZDA. PLANET OF THE DEAD. DER SCHWEIGENDE
    STERN. DER STILLE STERN. MOLCZACI KRZYDLA. THE
    SILENT STAR. SPACESHIP VENUS DOES NOT REPLY)
    SP, D: Kurt Maetzig. SP: also James Fethke, W. Kohlasse, J.
    Barckhausen, G. Reisch, G. Rucker, A. Stenbock-Fermor.
    From the novel"Planet of Death" or "Astronauts" or "Austronauci"
    by Stanislas Lem. PH: Joachim Hasler. Electronic Mus: Mas-
    kowski & Epper. Sets: A. Radzinowicz, A. Hirschmeier.
    SpFX: E. & V. Kunstmann, Jan Olejniczak, H. Grewald. Ref:
    Imagen. EncicDS IX. '55:330. SM 1:12. 2:9. FM 25:4. 26:4. Pic:
    FanMo 2:6. SM 5:9. with Yoko Tani, Günther Simon, I.
    Machowski, Oldrich Lukes, Kurt Rackelman. Set in 1970; robot,
    etc. Dubbing makes the going difficult.

FIRST STEPS TO THE MOON see STEPS TO THE MOON
FIRST WOMAN INTO SPACE see SPACE MONSTER

The FISHERMAN'S NIGHTMARE Pathe 1911 10m. Ref: Bios
    1/4/12. Angler dreams he's condemned by water nymphs to be
    grilled alive.

FIVE Col/Lobo 1951 93m. (FIVE--A STORY ABOUT THE DAY
    AFTER TOMORROW) SP, D, P: Arch Oboler. Ph, Ed: Sid Lubow,
    Ed Speigel, Louis Clyde Stoumen. Ref: FDY. with William
    Phipps, Susan Douglas, James Anderson, Charles Lampkin, Earl
    Lee. Five people left on earth after war.

FIVE DOOMED GENTLEMEN (F) 1920 (LES CINQ GENTLEMEN
    MAUDITS. THE FIVE ACCURSED GENTLEMEN) Remake:
    UNDER THE MOON OF MOROCCO. D: Luitz Morat. Ref: DDC III:
    251, 252. Sadoul:109. with André Luguet, Pierre Regnier, Yvonne
    Devigne.

The FIVE FRANC PIECE Selig 1916 35m. D: F. J. Grandon.
    Ref: LC. MPN 14:4042. with Edith Johnson, Charles Wheelock.
    Wireless torpedo.

FIVE GRAVES FOR A MEDIUM see TERROR CREATURES FROM
    THE GRAVE

FIVE MILLION YEARS TO EARTH (B) Fox/Hammer-7A color
    98m. (THE MIND BENDERS. QUATERMASS AND THE PIT-
    Eng) D: Roy Ward Baker. SP: Nigel Kneale, from his TV
    serial. PH: Arthur Grant. Mus: Tristram Cary. Art D: Bernard
    Robinson. SpFX: Bowie Films. Ref: Orpheus 4:38. FM 45:34.
    FFacts. Sequel to THE CREEPING UNKNOWN and ENEMY
    FROM SPACE. with James Donald, Andrew Keir, Barbara Shel-
    ley, Julian Glover, Maurice Good, James Culliford, Robert
    Morris. Martians invaded earth five million years ago, inter-
    bred with the ape inhabitants. It's easy to forgive an overly-
    convoluted plot when the convolutions generate so much suspense.
    Kneale evidently didn't want to leave anything of the original

serial out, which makes for some confusion of course but also for a more substantial, fully-detailed film.

FIVE ORANGE PIPS, The (By A. C. Doyle) see HOUSE OF FEAR (1945)

FIVE TALES OF HORROR (G) Oswald-Film 1919 (FUNF UNHEIM-LICHE GESCHICHTEN) SP, D: Richard Oswald. SP: also Robert Liebmann. From "The Black Cat" and "The System of Dr. Tarr and Professor Fether" by Edgar Allan Poe, "The Suicide Club" by Robert Louis Stevenson, "The Ghost" by R. Oswald, and stories by Liebmann and Anselma Heine. PH: Carl Hoffman. Ref: Fantastique. FIR'58:445. '61:466. '64:159. with Conrad Veidt (Death), Anita Berber, Reinhold Schünzel, Paul Morgan.

The FLAME BARRIER UA/Gramercy 1958 70m. (BEYOND THE FLAME BARRIER) D: Paul Landres. SP: Pat Fielder, George W. Yates. PH: Jack M(a)cKenzie. Ref: FM 11:6. FFacts. with Arthur Franz, Kathleen Crowley, Robert Brown, Vincent Padula, Rodd Redwing, Kaz Oran, Pilar Del Rey, Grace Mathews. Expedition searching for fallen satellite finds monster.

FLAME IN THE SKY see SATELLITE IN THE SKY

FLAMES (B) Butchers 1918 65m. D: Maurice Elvey. SP: Eliot Stannard, from the novel by Robert Hichens. Ref: Hist. Brit. Film. with Owen Nares, Margaret Bannerman, Edward O'Neill, Clifford Cobb. "Mystical exchange of souls between a good man and a corrupt one."

The FLAMING CLUE Vita 1920 D: Edwin L. Hollywood. SP: William B. Courtney. Story: F. Van Rensselaer Dey. Ref: MPW'20:136. with Harry T. Morey, Lucy Fox, Sidney Dalbrook, Eleanor Barry. Detective with a pocket periscope, a "subter-ranograph," a sound magnifying disc, an automatic typewriter, etc.

The FLAMING DISK Univ 1920 serial 18 episodes D: Robert F. Hill. Ref: CNW. Imagen. with Elmo Lincoln, Louise Lorraine, Lee Kohlmar, Ray Watson, Monty Montague. Lens "capable of melting iron and steel"; hero's brother under criminal's hypnotic influence. Ch. 14. The Purple Rays.

FLASH GORDON Univ 1936 serial 15 episodes (feature versions: ROCKET SHIP. SPACESHIP TO THE UNKNOWN. TV: SPACE SOLDIERS) SP, D: Frederick Stephani. SP: also Ella O'Neill, G. Plympton, B. Dickey. From the comic strip by Alex Raymond. PH: Jerry Ash, Richard Fryer. Ref: FM 10:32. SM 4:38. FanMo 1:38. ModM 4:38. Pic: FanMo 2:35. FM 34:15. SM 2:33. 3:31. 4:38. with Buster Crabbe, Jean Rogers, Charles Middleton, Frank Shannon, Priscilla Lawson, Richard Alexander, James Pierce, Duke York, Jr., Richard Tucker. Invisibility machine, ray guns, sea monsters, submarine city, winged men, city-in-the-sky, etc. Fun!

FLASH GORDON CONQUERS THE UNIVERSE Univ 1940 serial 12 episodes (Feature: DEADLY RAY FROM MARS, The. TV: SPACE SOLDIERS CONQUER THE UNIVERSE) D: Ray Taylor, Ford Beebe. SP: B. Dickey, G. Plympton, B. Shipman. From the comic strip by Alex Raymond. Ref: FM 10:32. with Buster Crabbe, Carol Hughes, Charles Middleton, Frank Shannon. Ch. 1. The Purple Death. 4. The Destroying Ray.

FLASH GORDON'S TRIP TO MARS Univ 1938 serial 15 episodes
(Features: Part I: PURPLE DEATH FROM OUTER SPACE. II:
PERIL FROM PLANET MONGO. MARS ATTACKS THE WORLD)
D: Ford Beebe, Robert Hill. SP: H. Dalmas, N. Hall, R.
Trampe, W. Gittens. (TV: SPACE SOLDIERS' TRIP TO MARS)
Ref: FM 10:32. FanMo 1:38. 3:36. Pic: SM 1:8. with Buster
Crabbe, Charles Middleton, C. Montague Shaw, Richard Alex-
ander, Beatrice Roberts. "The Nitron Lamp," "The Clay Peo-
ple," ray guns, death rays, etc.
FLASHMAN VS. THE INVISIBLE MEN (I-F) Zenith/Cinemato-
grafica 1966 color D: J. Lee Donan. SP: Ernesto Gastaldi.
PH: Floriano Trenker. Ref: Ital P'67: FLASHMAN CONTRE
LES HOMMES INVISIBLE or FLASHMAN. Mus: Franco Tamponi.
with John Heston, Seyna Seyn, Michaela Cendali, Paul Stevens,
Claudie Lang. Man concocts invisibility serum.
FLEMISH TALES (by P. Van Weigen) see MILL OF THE STONE
WOMEN
FLESH AND FANTASY Univ 1943 93m. (SIX DESTINIES. OB-
SESSIONS-F) D: Julien Duvivier. SP: Ernest Pascal, Ellis St.
Joseph, Samuel Hoffenstein. Story: "Lord Arthur Savile's Crime"
by Oscar Wilde. PH:Paul Ivano, Stanley Cortez. Mus:
Alexander Tansman, Charles Previn. Author: Laslo Vadnay.
Art D: John B. Goodman, Richard Riedel, Robert Boyle. Ref:
FDY. with Charles Boyer, Edward G. Robinson, Betty Field,
Edgar Barrier, Robert Benchley, Dame May Whitty, Robert Cum-
mings, Thomas Mitchell, Charles Winninger, C. Aubrey Smith,
Anna Lee, Marjorie Lord, Clarence Muse, Grace McDonald.
Pic: FM 48:47. Three stories of the supernatural. The first
two are routine, though the first ends with a nice touch.
FLESH AND THE FIENDS, The see MANIA
The FLESH EATERS Hansen 1964 92m. D: Jack Curtis. SP:
Arnold Drake. PH: Carson Davidson. SpFX: Roy Benson. Mus:
Julian Stein. Ed: Radley Metzger. Ref: COF 6:56. F&F 3/69.
Shriek 1:5. with Martin Kosleck, Barbara Wilkin, Byron
Sanders, Rita Morley, Ray Tudor. Small silvery creatures
consume flesh.
FLESH FEAST CineWorld/Viking Int'l 1970 color 72m. SP, D:
Brad F. Grinter. SP: also Thomas Casey. PH: Casey.Ref:
Boxo 11/9/70. with Veronica Lake, Phil Philbin, Heather
Hughes. Dr. Elaine Frederick employs flesh-eating maggots in
her rejuvenation operation, which she intends to perform on Adolf
Hitler (who is still alive).
FLICK (Canadian) Astral/Agincourt 1970 color 81m. (DR.
FRANKENSTEIN ON CAMPUS. FRANKENSTEIN ON CAMPUS-
Eng) D: Gil Taylor. SP: David Cobb, Taylor, Bill Marshall.
Updated version of Mary Shelley's "Frankenstein." PH: Jackson
Samuels. Mus: Paul Hoffert, Skip Prokop. Ref: V 4/22/70.
COF 17:4. with Robin Ward, Austin Willis, Kathleen Sawyer.
Victor Frankenstein experiments in remote brain-control.
FLICKAN OCH DJAVULEN see GIRL AND THE DEVIL, The
FLIEGENDE HOLLANDER, Der (by Wagner) FLYING DUTCHMAN,
The
FLIGHT BEYOND THE SUN see SPACE MONSTER

The FLIGHT THAT DISAPPEARED   UA /Harvard 1961 71m.
(The FLIGHT THAT VANISHED) D: Reginald LeBorg. SP:
Ralph & Judith Hart, Owen Harris. PH: Gil Warrenton. Mus:
Richard LaSalle. SpFX: Barney Wolff. P: Robert E. Kent. Ref:
FFacts. FM 13:62. SM 2:11. COF 9:36. with Craig Hill,
Paula Raymond, Dayton Lummis, Gregory Morton, Addison
Richards, John Bryant, Nancy Hale. Plane disappears into
another dimension.
FLIGHT TO A FAR PLANET see QUEEN OF BLOOD
FLIGHT TO FAME Col 1938 59m. (WINGS OF DOOM) D:
C. C. Coleman, Jr. SP: Michael Simmons. PH: Lucien
Ballard. Ed: James Sweeney. Ref: V. FDY. MFB'39:159.
with Charles Farrell, Jacqueline Wells, Hugh Sothern, Alex
D'Arcy, Jason Robards, Charles D. Brown, Addison Richards,
Selmer Jackson, Reed Howes. Electronic death ray shoots down
planes.
FLIGHT TO MARS Mono 1951 Cinecolor 72m. D: Lesley
Selander. SP: Arthur Strawn. PH: Harry Neumann. Mus:
Marlin Skiles. Art D: David Milton. P: Walter Mirisch. Ref:
FDY. Pic: FM 15:46. SM 2:8. with Marguerite Chapman,
Cameron Mitchell, Arthur Franz, John Litel, Morris Ankrum,
Robert Barrat, Edward Earle, Virginia Huston, Richard Gaines,
Lucille Barkley. No surprises at all. Dullest of the rocket-to-
the-moon or -Mars movies, and they're usually pretty dull.
FLIGHT TO THE SUN see STUDENT OF PRAGUE, The (1913)
FLIT (I) 1967 82m. (IL VOSTRO SUPER AGENTE. YOUR
SPECIAL AGENT FLIT. FLIT, IMBATIBLE SUPREMO) D:
Mauriano Laurenti. Ref: Heraldo 11 /6 /68. M /TVM 1 /68. with
Raimondo Vainello, Rafaella Carr(a). Extraterrestrial beings.
FLOATING ISLAND, The (by J. Verne) see FABULOUS WORLD OF
JULES VERNE, The
FLOATING PLATFORM #1 DOES NOT REPLY see F. P. 1
The FLORENTINE DAGGER WB 1935 70m. D: Robert Florey.
SP: Tom Reed. Story: Ben Hecht. Add'l Dial: Brown Holmes.
PH: Arthur Todd. Art D: Anton Grot, Carl Jules Weyl. Ref:
FDY. H'w'd in the Thirties. Pic: DDC II:359. with Donald Woods,
Margaret Lindsay, C. Aubrey Smith, Frank Reicher, Florence
Fair, Rafaela Ottiano, Paul Porcasi, Eily Malyon, Egon Brecher,
Henry Kolker. Herman Bing. Murderer's fire-scarred face hid-
den behind "realistic wax mask."
FLOWER OF YOUTH (F) Pathe c1907 5m. Ref: SilentFF.
MPW'08:104. Demon, ghosts, fairy; fire mazes.
FLOWERS FOR ALGERNON (by D. Keyes) see CHARLY
FLUCH DER GRUNEN AUGEN, Der see CAVE OF THE LIVING
DEAD
The FLY Fox 1958 Deluxe color /scope 94m. P, D: Kurt Neu-
mann. SP: James Clavell, from the novelette by George
Langelaan. Sequels: CURSE OF THE FLY. RETURN OF THE
FLY. PH: Karl Struss. Mus: Paul Sawtell. Art D: Lyle R.
Wheeler, Theobold Holsopple. Ref: FFacts. with Vincent Price,
Al (or David) Hedison, Patricia Owens, Herbert Marshall,
Kathleen Freeman, Eugene Borden. Pic: FM 21:12. Scientist
invents a matter transmitter. Poorly acted and directed.

Nevertheless there are those few unforgettable scenes. "See if
necessary"--Jean-Luc Godard.
The FLYING CLUE   Savoia   1914   45m.   Ref: Bios 5/21/14.
Inventor's machine's rays "fire explosives."
FLYING DISC MAN FROM MARS   Rep   1951   serial   12 episodes
('58 feature: MISSILE MONSTERS)   D: Fred C. Brannon.   SP:
Ron Davidson.   PH: Walter Strenge.   Ref: Barbour.   SM 5:50.   Pic:
FRO 3:27.   with Walter Reed, Lois Collier, Gregory Gay, James
Craven, Harry Lauter, Dale Van Sickel, Tom Steele, Jimmy
O'Gatty, Lester Dorr.   Plot line: "We must be realistic: It's the
only way we can bring earth under the domination of our Supreme
Dictator of Mars."
FLYING DISPATCH, The   see   POSSIBILITIES OF WAR IN THE AIR
The FLYING DUTCHMAN   FBO   1923   75m.   SP, D: Lloyd B.
Carelton.   From the opera "Der Fliegende Holländer" by Wag-
ner.   PH: Andra Barlatier.   Ref: MPN 28:559.   LC.   with Lawson
Butt, Lola Luxford, Edward Coxen.   "Phantom ship"; "phantom
gold"; "ghost"; "terrified villagers."
FLYING ELEPHANTS   Roach-Pathe   1927   22m.   D: Frank Butler.
Ref: BFI Dist. Cat. '62.   with Stan Laurel, Oliver Hardy, Jimmy
Finlayson, Leo Willis, Edna Marion, Viola Richard.   Stone Age
King Ferdinand decrees that all men 13 to 99 must marry or die.
The FLYING EYE   (B)   British Films/CFF 1955   54m.   SP, D: Wil-
liam Hammond.   SP: also Ken Hughes, Darrel Catling, from an
original story by John Newton Chase.   PH: Hone Glendenning.   Mus:
Arthur Wilkinson.   Ref: MFB.   with Geoffrey Sumner, Harcourt
Williams, David Hannaford, Julia Lockwood.   Model aircraft
operated by ground control carries "flying eye" television set.
FLYING EYE, The   see   CRAWLING EYE, The
FLYING HIGH   MGM   1931   78m.   Adap, D: Charles F. Reisner.
SP: A. P. Younger.   Add'l Dial: R. E. Hopkins.   PH: M. B.
Gerstad.   Ref: TVG.   V 12/15/31.   with Bert Lahr, Charlotte
Greenwood, Pat O'Brien, Charles Winninger, Hedda Hopper, Guy
Kibbee.   Musical-comedy: Cross between tractor and auto-gyro
breaks altitude record.
FLYING MACHINE, The   see   CONQUEST OF THE AIR, The
The FLYING SAUCER   Film Classics/Realart/Colon   1949   69m.
D, P: Mikel Conrad.   SP: Conrad, Howard Young.   PH: Philip
Tannura.   Mus: Darrell Calker.   Ref: FDY.   COF 9:36.   with
Conrad, Pat Garrison, Russell Hicks, Denver Pyle, Phil(l)ip
Morris, Virginia Hewitt, Gerry Owen.   Government agent sent
to Alaska to discover origin of "saucers."
The FLYING SAUCER   (I)   De Laurentiis   1964   93m.   (IL DISCO
VOLANTE.   The MARTIANS)   D: Tinto Brass.   SP: Rodolfo
Sonego.   PH: Bruno Barcarol.   Mus: Piero Piccioni.   Ref: Ital
P.   V 2/10/65.   COF 7:54.   with Alberto Sordi, Monica Vitti,
Eleanora Rossi-Drago, Silvana Mangano.   Eight people are ab-
ducted by Martians.
The FLYING SAUCERS   (Mex)   Mier & Brooks 1955 (LOS PLATOS
VOLADORES)   D: Julian Soler.   Ass't D: Alfonso Corona Blake.
SP: Carlos Orellana, Pedro de Urdimalas.   Story: Carlos León.
PH: Agustin M. Solares.   Mus: Manuel Esperon.   Art D: Jorge
Fernández, Rodolfo Benítez.   Ref: Indice.   Imagen.   FM 15:20.

31:20. Pic: FM 12:20. SM 4:30. with "Resortes," Andrés Soler, Adalberto Martinez, Evangelina Elizondo, Carlos Riquelme. "Robot," "saucers."

FLYING SAUCERS FROM OUTER SPACE (by D. E. Keyhoe) see EARTH VS. THE FLYING SAUCERS

The FLYING SERPENT PRC 1946 59m. D: Sherman Scott. SP: John T. Neville. Remake of DEVIL BAT? PH: Jack Greenhalgh. Mus: Leo Erdody. P: Sigmund Neufeld. Ref: FDY. Pic: FM 7:22. 14:42.16:8. with George Zucco, Ralph Lewis, Eddie Acuff, Henry Hall, Hope Kramer, Wheaton Chambers, James Metcalf, Terry Frost. Doctor guards lost treasure of Montezuma with "legendary prehistoric flying serpent" which drains the blood of its victims. The rest is none too good ("One thing is established--the criminal had wings"), but the ending sets some sort of record. The doctor sicks the bird on his enemies by planting feathers from it on them; he himself is caught with a feather in his hand at the end, and what does he do? He holds on to it and runs as the bird dives at him. Quick thinking.

FLYING SUPERSUB see ATRAGON

The FLYING TORPEDO Triangle 1916 SP, P: D. W. Griffith. D: Jack O'Brien. Ref: COF 16:18. MPN 13:1774. with Bessie Love, John Emerson. Southern California invaded by Asiatic hordes in flying torpedoes with "robot bombs."

FOG FOR A KILLER (B) Eternal 1962 68m. SP, D: Montgomery Tully. PH: James Harvey. Mus: Ken Thorne. Art D: John Earl. Ref: MFB'62:141. TVG. (OUT OF THE FOG) with Davis Sumner, Susan Travers, James Hayter, Jack Watson, George Woodbridge, Michael Ripper, Tony Quinn. Ex-convict the leading suspect in a series of full-moon murders.

FOG ISLAND PRC 1945 70m. D: Terry Morse. SP: Pierre Gendron, from the play "Angel Island" by Bernie Angus. PH: Ira Morgan. Art D: Paul Palmentola. Ref: FDY. TVG. COF 9:36. PM: "Horror film." Pic: FMO 6:15. with Lionel Atwill, George Zucco, Ian Keith, Veda Ann Borg, Jerome Cowan, Sharon Douglas, Jacqueline DeWitt. Once-rich man, framed on a charge of embezzlement, invites those responsible for his imprisonment to his private island, where he plans vengeance. Dull.

The FOG MURDERER (G) Waldemar-Schweitzer/Nora 1964 90m. (DER NEBELMORDER) D: Eugen York. SP: Walter Forster, Per Schwenzen. PH: Günter Haase. Mus: Herbert Jardzyk. Ref: German Pictures. with Hansjörg Felmy, Ingmar Zeisberg, Ralph Persson, Elke Arendt. "A devil in human form spreads fear and terror.... Murderer in nearby forest."

FOGHORN, The (by R. Bradbury) see BEAST FROM 20,000 FATHOMS, The

FOILED Kalem 1915 Ref: MPW 25:2234. with Ethel Teare. "Genii" turns man into skeleton.

FOLIE DU DOCTEUR TUBE, La see MADNESS OF DR. TUBE, The

The FOLLY OF SIN (Dan?) Great Northern 1916 55m. Ref: MPN 13:2218. with Joan Peterson, Charles Wieth, George Tolloway. Doctor discovers cancer cure.

FOOD OF THE GODS, The (by H. G. Wells) see VILLAGE OF THE

GIANTS

A FOOL AND HIS MONEY Col 1925 70m. D: Erle C. Kenton.
Adap: Douglas Z. Doty. Continuity: Dorothy Howell. Titles:
Walter Anthony. Ref: AFI. with Madge Bellamy, William
Haines, Stuart Holmes, Alma Bennett, Charles Conklin, Eugenie
Besserer. A writer buys a "haunted" castle.

FOOLS Cinerama/Translor 1970 Eastmancolor 93m. D: Tom
Gries. SP: Robert Rudelson. PH: Michael Hugo. Mus: Shorty
Rogers. Ref: HR 12/18/70. with Jason Robards, Katharine
Ross, Scott Hylands, Roy C. Jenson. Horror film actor watches
his vampire film in one sequence.

FOOLS IN THE DARK FBO 1924 75m. D: Al Santell. SP:
John Grey, Bertram Millhauser, from the latter's story "Peaceful Percy." PH: Leon Eycke, Blake Wagner. Ref: Wid's
6/28/24. NYT 8/18/24. with Tom Wilson, Matt Moore, Patsy Ruth
Miller, Charles Belcher, Bertram Grassby. "Skeleton" chases man
through "mystery house."

FOR THE FLAG (by J. Verne) see FABULOUS WORLD OF JULES
VERNE, The

FOR THE MASTERY OF THE WORLD Eclair 1914 45m. Ref:
MPW 22:1425. SF Film. Super-bomb exploded by wireless.

FORBIDDEN FEMININITY (I) Films Marbeuf 1963 color 87m.
(SEXY PROBITISSIMO-I. SEXY-SUPER INTERDIT or SEXY
INTERDIT-F) D: Marcello Martinelli. Mus: Lallo Gori. Ref:
Ital P'63. Index Cin. Française'65. Sketches include one
with Frankenstein's monster; cave-dweller; female cosmonaut
and Martians; vampire. with Karmela, Lilli de Saigon, Monique,
Joan Clair.

The FORBIDDEN FRUIT (F?) Pathe 1909 12m. Ref: Bios
2/7/10. A magician creates a castle for a peasant and his
wife and cautions them not to look under the cover of an immense dish in one of the rooms. After some time the wife
finally succumbs to curiosity and lifts the lid. An enormous frog
jumps out and chases the couple out of the castle.

FORBIDDEN GARDEN (novel by U. Curtiss) see WHAT EVER
HAPPENED TO AUNT ALICE

FORBIDDEN LAND, The see JUNGLE JIM IN THE FORBIDDEN
LAND

FORBIDDEN MOON MCA-TV/Roland Reed 1953 78m. From the
"Rocky Jones, Space Ranger" TV series. Ref: COF 9:36. with
Richard Crane, Robert Lyden.

FORBIDDEN PLANET MGM 1956 Eastmancolor/scope 98m.
D: Fred McLeod Wilcox. SP: Cyril Hume. Story: Irving Block,
Allen Adler. PH: George J. Folsey. See also INVISIBLE BOY,
The. Electronic Mus: Louis and Bebe Barron. Art D: Cedric
Gibbons, Arthur Lonergan. SpFX: A. Arnold Gillespie, Warren
Newcombe, Irving G. Ries, Joshua Meador. Ref: SM 8:32.
COF 9:36. FM 14:42.32:7. Pic: FM 14:46.19:45. with Walter
Pidgeon, Anne Francis, Warren Stevens, Jack Kelly, James
Drury, Leslie Nielsen, Earl Holliman, Richard Anderson, Bob
Dix, Harry Harvey, Jr., Morgan Jones, George Wallace. Space-
ship lands on the planet Altair-4 in the year 2200. Super-s-f,
with gadgets, special effects, color, amazing theories, sets,

electronic music; everything except drive and pace that could
have made it even more exciting. More a piece of production
than direction and writing, though the latter helps.

The FORBIDDEN ROOM Univ 1914 45m. Ref: Lee. MPW 20:
1830,1874. Girl hypnotized, ordered to kill; à la Edgar Allan
Poe.

FORBIN PROJECT, The see COLOSSUS-THE FORBIN PROJECT

The FORCES OF EVIL or THE DOMINANT WILL Leading Players
1914 45m. Ref: Lee. MPW 21:437. Woman under spell of
hypnotist.

The FOREMAN'S TREACHERY Edison 1913 34m. D: Charles
Brabin. Ref: Kinetogram 10/15/13. with Miriam Nesbitt,
Marc MacDermott, Charles Vernon. Man protects money in
ruined abbey by masquerading as ghost.

FORT ALESIA see GIANTS OF ROME

FORTUNE FAVORS THE BRAVE Gaston(?)Melies 1909 Ref:
MPW'09:809. Genie; lad who fights dragons.

FORTY-FIVE MINUTES FROM HOLLYWOOD Roach-Pathe 1926
22m. Ref: Don Glut. with Stan Laurel, Oliver Hardy, Jimmy
Finlayson. Dinosaurs in Hollywood.

FOU DU LABO 4, Le see MADMAN OF LAB 4, The

FOUND IN SPACE Zenith 1969 Astro-Color Ref: LA Times
1/22/69. S-f.

The 4-D MAN Univ/Fairview 1959 Deluxe color 85m. (The
EVIL FORCE-Eng. MASTER OF TERROR-'65 reissue. FOUR-
DIMENSIONAL MAN) D: Irvin (or Irwin)S. Yeaworth, Jr.
SP: Cy Chermak, Theodore Simonson. Story, P: Jack Harris,
Yeaworth. PH: Theodore J. Pahle. Mus sc & D: Ralph Car-
michael. Art D: William Jersey. SpFX: Barton Sloane. Makeup:
Dean Newman. Ref: FFacts. PM. COF 9. Orpheus 3:27. with
Robert Lansing, Lee Meriwether, James Congdon, Patty Duke,
Robert Strauss, Edgar Stehli, Jasper Deeter. Scientist dis-
covers that by regulating the electrical impulses of his brain he
can walk through walls.

400 TRICKS OF THE DEVIL, The see MERRY FROLICS OF
SATAN, The

FOUR MOODS (Taiwan) Blue Sky 1970 Technicolor 143m. (HSI,
NOU, AI, LUEH) D: Pai Ching Jui, King Hu, Lee Hsing, Li
Han Hsiang. Ref: V 10/14/70. with Tseng Cheng, Yueh Yang.
Four stories; three involving ghosts: "Joy": Scholar at first
frightened by pretty ghost. "Pleasure": Water-ghost. "Sorrow":
Bleeding gravestone.

The FOUR NIGHTS OF THE FULL MOON (Sp) Hispamer-Nec-
Documento 1964 (LAS CUATROS NOCHES DE LA LUNA LLENA)
D: Sobey Martin. PH: Juan Mariné. Ref: MMF 9:17. M/TVM
10/64. with Gene Tierney, Analia Gade, Dan Dailey, Perla
Cristal. "Superstition of the gypsies: woman possessed by evil
spirits must be killed and buried beneath rocks." The fourth
night the lover of the woman must remove the stones to know the
truth.

FOUR-SIDED TRIANGLE (B) UA/Astor/Hammer 1952 81m. SP,
D: Terence Fisher. SP: also Paul Tabori. From the novel by
William F. Temple. PH: Reginald Wyer. Mus: Malcolm Arnold.

Art D: J. Elder Wills. Ref: FDY.   Pic: FM 7:45.   with Barbara
Payton, Stephen Murray, James Hayter, John van Eyssen,
Kynaston Reeves, Percy Marmont.   Two scientists build a
machine which can duplicate anything.

The FOUR SKULLS OF JONATHAN DRAKE   UA/Vogue 1959   70m.
D: Edward L. Cahn.   SP: Orville Hampton.   PH: Maury Gertsman.   Mus: Paul Dunlap.   P: Robert E. Kent.   Pic: FM 29:50.
with Eduard Franz, Valerie French, Henry Daniell, Grant Richards, Paul Cavanagh, Lumsden Hare, Frank Gerstle, Paul Wexler, Howard Wendell.   A Jivaro witch doctor places a curse on
the Drake family.   Not as bad as it's supposed to be.

FOUR, THREE, TWO, ONE--DEATH   see   MISSION STARDUST

14 MILLION LEAGUES FROM THE EARTH   see   SKY SHIP, The

The FOX WOMAN   Mutual (Majestic) 1915   45m.   From the novel
by John Luther Long.   Ref: MPN 7/24/15.   MPW 25:726.   with
Elmer Clifton, Teddy Sampson.   Man's soul restored to him
when "fox woman/vampire" dies.

FRANCIS IN THE HAUNTED HOUSE   Univ 1956   80m.   D: Charles
Lamont.   SP: William Raynor, Herbert Margolis.   Based on the
character "Francis" [a talking mule] created by David Stern.
PH: George Robinson.   Mus D: Joseph Gershenson.   Art D:
Alexander Golitzen, Richard Riedel.   Ref: FDY.   with Mickey
Rooney, Virginia Welles, Paul Cavanagh, David Janssen, Richard
Deacon, James Flavin, Timothy Carey, Ramph Dumke.   Last in
the "Francis" series.   A laugh or two.   No thrills.

FRANKENSTEIN or The Modern Prometheus (by M. Shelley)   see
ABBOTT AND COSTELLO MEET FRANKENSTEIN/BLOOD OF
FRANKENSTEIN/BRIDE OF FRANKENSTEIN/CASINO ROYALE/
CURSE OF FRANKENSTEIN/DRACULA VS. FRANKENSTEIN/
FLICK/FORBIDDEN FEMININITY/GHOST OF FRANKENSTEIN/
HELLZAPOPPIN/HORROR OF FRANKENSTEIN, The/HOUSE OF
DRACULA/HOUSE OF FRANKENSTEIN/HOW TO MAKE A
MONSTER/I WAS A TEEN AGE FRANKENSTEIN/HOUSE ON
BARE MOUNTAIN/JESSE JAMES MEETS FRANKENSTEIN'S
DAUGHTER/LIFE WITHOUT SOUL/KISS ME QUICK/MUNSTER
GO HOME/NECROPOLIS/ONE MORE TIME/ORLAK/PHANTOM
OF THE OPERETTA(1955)/REVENGE OF FRANKENSTEIN/SON
OF FRANKENSTEIN/THREE ARE THREE/SHAME ON YOU and
the following titles

FRANKENSTEIN   Edison 1910   D: Searle Dawley.   From the novel
by Mary Shelley.   Ref: Film 9/67.   Bios 5/5/10.   Clarens.   FM
23:45.26:57.   FanMo 1:64.   COF 2:20.3:6.   with Charles Ogle.

FRANKENSTEIN   Univ 1931   71m.   D: James Whale.   SP:
Richard Schayer, Francis Edward Faragoh, Garrett Fort, Robert
Florey, John L. Balderston.   From the play by Peggy Webling and
the novel by Mary Shelley.   PH: Arthur Edeson.   Makeup: Jack
Pierce.   P: Carl Laemmle, Jr.   Ref: FM 2:31. 31:50.   MFB
'38:183.   COF 9:10.   FIR'64:512.   MMania 1:9.   Pic: FM 7:43.
10:24.13:34.19:41.   with Boris Karloff, Colin Clive, Dwight
Frye, Mae Clarke, Lionel Belmore, Frederick Kerr, John
Boles, Edward Van Sloan, Marilyn Harris, Otis Harlan.   One of
those you-know-it's-a-classic-because-it's-dull films.   Too-similar
imitations have killed whatever interest it originally had, if any.

FRANKENSTEIN BROTHERS, The see WAR OF THE GARGANTUAS
FRANKENSTEIN CONQUERS THE WORLD (J) AI/Toho-Benedict
1964 ('66-U.S.) color/scope 87m. (FUHARANKENSHUTAIN TAI
BARAGON or FRANKENSTEIN TAI BARAGON. FRANKENSTEIN
VS. THE GIANT DEVIL FISH. FRANKENSTEIN AND THE GIANT
LIZARD) D: Inoshiro Honda. SP: Kaoru Mabuchi. PH: Hajime
Koizumi. Art D: Takeo Kita. SpFX: Eiji Tsuburaya. Ref:
COF 11:6. Pic: Shriek 4:9. with Nick Adams, Tadao Takashima,
Kumi Mizuno, Takashi Shimura. Scientist combats giant terror-
izing Japan.
FRANKENSTEIN CREATED WOMAN (B) Fox/7A-Hammer 1966
color 92m. D: Terence Fisher. SP: John Elder. PH: Arthur
Grant. Mus: James Bernard. Art D: Don Mingaye, Bernard
Robinson. Makeup: George Partleton. SpFX: Les Bowie.
(FRANKENSTEIN MADE WOMAN) Ref: COF 2:7. MMF. with
Peter Cushing, Susan Denberg, Thorley Walters, Peter Madden,
Duncan Lamont.
FRANKENSTEIN DE SADE or HOLLOW MY WEENIE, DR. FRANK-
ENSTEIN 1969 Ref: FM 63:24.
FRANKENSTEIN MADE WOMAN see FRANKENSTEIN CREATED
WOMAN
FRANKENSTEIN LIVES AGAIN! see BRIDE OF FRANKENSTEIN
FRANKENSTEIN MEETS THE SPACEMONSTER AA/Vernon-Seneca
1965 (DUEL OF THE SPACE MONSTERS-Eng. MARTE INVADE
A PUERTO RICO. MARS ATTACKS PUERTO RICO) D: Robert
Gaffney. 78m. SP: George Garret. Original SP: Garret, John
Rodenbeck, R. H. W. Dillard. PH: Saul Midwall. Exec P: Alan
V. Iselin. Ref: FFacts. with James Karen, Nancy Marshall,
David Kerman, Lou Cutell, Robert Reilly (Col. Saunders/monster).
Doctor develops an "astro-robot."--Boxo 11/1/65. Ludicrous.
Unfortunately, too drawn-out to be very funny. A rock number
over a rocket launching is some historic first.
FRANKENSTEIN MEETS THE WOLF MAN Univ 1943 73m. D:
Roy William Neill. SP: Curt Siodmak. PH: George Robinson.
Mus D: H. J. Salter. Art D: John B. Goodman. SpPhFX: John
P. Fulton. P: George Waggner. Ref: FDY. Academy. Makeup:
Jack Pierce. Pic: FM 2:25. with Lon Chaney, Jr., Bela
Lugosi, Patric Knowles, Ilona Massey, Lionel Atwill, Maria
Ouspenskaya, Dennis Hoey, Dwight Frye, Harry Stubbs, Don
Barclay, Torben Meyer, Doris Lloyd, Jeff Corey, David Clyde,
Tom Stevenson, Cyril Delevanti. Fairly predictable.
FRANKENSTEIN MUST BE DESTROYED (B) WB/Hammer 1969
Technicolor 97m. D: Terence Fisher. SP: Bert Batt. Story:
Batt, Anthony Nelson Keys. PH: Arthur Grant. Mus: James
Bernard. Art D: Bernard Robinson. Makeup: Eddie Knight. Ref:
MFB'69:145. with Peter Cushing, Veronica Carlson, Thorley
Walters, Harold Goodwin. Baron Frankenstein moves into a
boarding house. Cushing and an all-out finale almost save blandly-
directed Hammer series entry.
FRANKENSTEIN 1970 AA/A-Z 1958 83m. D: Howard W. Koch.
SP: George W. Yates, Richard Landau. Story: Aubrey Schenck,
Charles A. Moses. PH: Carl E. Guthrie. Mus: Paul Dunlap.
Ref: FDY. with Boris Karloff, Don Barry, Jana Lund, Charlotte

Austin, Rudolph Anders, Tom Duggan, Mike Lane, John Dennis,
Norbert Schiller. TV crew invades Castle Frankenstein. Dismal.
FRANKENSTEIN ON CAMPUS see FLICK
FRANKENSTEIN TAI BARAGON see FRANKENSTEIN CONQUERS
THE WORLD
FRANKENSTEIN VS. THE GIANT DEVIL FISH see FRANKENSTEIN
CONQUERS THE WORLD
FRANKENSTEIN'S BLOODY TERROR see MARK OF THE WOLF-
MAN, The
FRANKENSTEIN'S DAUGHTER Astor/Layton 1958 85m. D:
Richard Cunha. SP: H. E. Barrie. PH: Meredith Nicholson.
Mus: Nicholas Carras. SpFX: Ira Anderson. Makeup: Harry
Thomas. Prod. Manager: Ralph Brooke. Ref: FFacts. Pic: FM
28:55. with John Ashley, Sandra Knight, Harold Lloyd, Jr.,
Wolfe Barzell, Voltaire Perkins, John Zaremba. Mad scientist
turns girl into a monster. Even below par for Astor.
FRANKENSTEIN'S MONSTER (I) 1920 (IL MOSTRI DI FRANKEN-
STEIN) Ref: FM 63:20.
FRANKESTEIN, THE VAMPIRE, & CO. (Mex) Calderon 1961
(FRANKESTEIN, EL VAMPIRO Y CIA) D: Benito Alazraki. SP:
Alfredo Salazar. PH: Enrique Wallace. Mus: G. C. Carrion. Art
D: J. R. Granada. Ref: Indice. with Manuel Valdes, José
Jasso, Nora Veryan (or Veyran), Roberto G. Rivera, Arturo
Castro.
FRANK'S GREATEST ADVENTURE AI/Jericho 1967 color 78m.
(FEARLESS FRANK) SP, D, P: Philip Kaufman. PH: Bill Butler.
Mus: Meyer Kupferman. Ref: V 5/3/67. Boxo 2/5/70. with
Jon Voight, Monique Van Vooren, Severn Darden, Nelson Algren,
Lou Gilbert. Man killed by gangsters, revived à la Frankenstein.
FRANTIC see DOUBLE DECEPTION
FRAU IM MOND see GIRL IN THE MOON
FRAUDULENT SPIRITUALISM EXPOSED Motograph 1913 45m.
Ref: Bios 10/30/13.
The FREAK OF FERNDALE FOREST Warwick (B?) 1910 9m.
Ref: Bios 10/27/10. Beggar transforms child into "hideous
beast."
FREAKS Joker 1915 15m. D: Allen Curtis. SP: Clarence
Badger. Ref: MPN 7/17/15. LC. with Max Asher, William
Franey, Gale Henry, Lillian Peacock. Actors "made up as
freaks.... The human skeleton is quite repelling."
FREAKS MGM 1931 61m. (NATURE'S MISTAKES. BARNUM.
THE MONSTER SHOW) D: Tod Browning. SP: Leon Gordon,
Willis Goldbeck. Add'l Dial: Edgar Allan Woolf, Al Boasberg.
PH: Merritt B. Gerstad. From the story "Spurs" by Tod Rob-
bins. Ref: FDY. with Wallace Ford, Leila Hyams, Olga Bac-
lanova, Roscoe Ates, Harry and Daisy Earles, Daisy and Violet
Hilton, Edward Brophy, Matt McHugh, Randion. FREAKS,
though it can't really be so simply categorized, turns from a
bizarre comedy into a bizarre horror movie and is effective
either way. But it's still difficult to know how to take it as a
whole.
FRECCIA D'ORO, La see GOLDEN ARROW, The
Der FREISCHUTZ (W.G.) 1968 Eastmancolor 127m. D: Joachim

Hess. PH: Hannes Schindler. Mus: Carl Maria von Weber. Ref:
MFB. with Tom Krause, Arlene Saunders. Man possessed by
devil.

FRENCH COUSINS, The see FROM EAR TO EAR

FRIDAY, THE 13TH (G) Terra-Film 1944 92m. (FREITAG,
DER 13) D: Erich Engels. SP: Just Scheu, Ernst Nebhut.
Mus: Ludwig Schmidseder. Ref: Deutscher. with Fritz Kampers,
Angelika Hauff, Fita Benkhoff, Rudolf Fernau. People spending
a night in a haunted salon disappear. "Haunted castle...ghost
and his gruesome goings-on!"

FRIGHT AA/Exploitation 1957 80m. (SPELL OF THE HYPNO-
TIST) P, D: W. Lee Wilder. PH: J. B. Contner. Mus: L.
Davies. SP: Myles Wilder. SpFX: Arthur Jackson. Ref: MFB
'58:46. RVB. COF 9:37. with Eric Fleming, Nancy Malone,
Dean L. Almquist, Frank Martin, Humphrey Davis. Psychiatrist
regresses woman into a former life.

The FRIGHTENED LADY (B) Hoffberg/British Lion 1940 80m.
(CASE OF THE FRIGHTENED LADY) D: George King. SP:
Edward Dryhurst. Ref: FIR'67:79. V 11/12/41. FD 11/12/41.
COF 16:22: horror. with Marius Goring, Pamela Dudley Ward,
Felix Aylmer, Torin Thatcher, Helen Haye, Ronald Shiner,
John Warwick, Patrick Barr. Homicidal maniac commits sever-
al murders at the manor of Lady Lebanon. From the story by
Edgar Wallace. See also CRIMINAL AT LARGE/INDIAN SCARF,
The.

FRIGHTENING GHOSTS (Arg) AAA 1951 72m. (FANTASMAS
ASUSTADOS) D: Carlos Rinaldi. SP: Maximo Aguirre. PH:
F. Boeniger. Mus: Tito Ribero. Ref: Historia del Cine
Argentino. with Susana Campos, Jorge Villoldo.

FRIGHTENING SECRET OF DR. HICHCOCK, The see HORRIBLE
DR. HICHCOCK, The

FRIGHTFUL HORSEMEN, The see KNIGHTS OF TERROR

FRILBY FRILLED Lubin 1916 SP, D: Edwin McKim. Burlesque
of George DuMaurier's "Trilby." Ref: MPN 13:3604. LC.
with David Don (Svengarlic), Patsy De Forest, George Egan.

FRISCOT DRINKS A BOTTLE OF HORSE EMBROCATION 1910
6m. Ref: Bios 10/20/10. Chemist's concoction makes stable
boy prance and gallop like horse.

FRISSON DES VAMPIRE, Le see VAMPIRE THRILLS

FROGGO AND DROGGO see GRAND DUEL IN MAGIC

FROLICS OF SATAN, The see MERRY FROLICS OF SATAN, The

FROLICSOME POWDERS (I?) Ambrosio 1908 9m. Ref: MPW
'08:401. Drug store's powder makes people happy.

FROM DEATH TO LIFE Rex 1911 Ref: Bios 10/5/11. Wife of
chemist/necromancer turned to stone accidentally by his petrifying acid.

FROM EAR TO EAR (F) Cinemation (Jerry Gross) 1970 DeLuxe
color 81m. (LES COUSINES. THE FRENCH COUSINS) D:
Louis Soulane(s). Mus: Clay Pitts. Ref: Film Bulletin 2/8/71,
6/71. RVB. COF 17:4. with Solange Pradel, Nichol Debonne,
Daniel Argence. Two cousins try to shock mute girl to death
with skeleton.

FROM HELL IT CAME AA 1957 71m. D: Dan Milner. SP:

Richard Bernstein. PH: Brydon Baker. Mus: Darrell Calker.
P: Jack Milner. Ref: TVG. with Tod Andrews, Tina Carver,
Gregg Palmer, Linda Watkins, John McNamara, Robert Swan.
Witch doctor puts chief's son to death. Soon after latter returns
as a tree. He wood. Very, very bad.
FROM LIFE TO DEATH see STUDENT OF PRAGUE, The (1913)
FROM MARS TO MUNICH Fox 1925 11m. Ref: MPN 31:1514.
Lee. Invisible visitor from Mars.
FROM THE BEYOND Eclair/American Standard 1913 35m. Ref:
MPW 18:158. Bios 4/23/14. Ghost returns to haunt ex-rival.
"Spirit photography."
FROM THE EARTH TO THE MOON WB-RKO 1958 Technicolor
100m. D: Byron Haskin. SP: Robert Blees, James Leicester,
from the book by Jules Verne. PH: Edwin B. DuPar. Mus:
Louis Forbes. Ref: FDY. with Joseph Cotten, George Sanders,
Debra Paget, Patric Knowles, Henry Daniell, Don Dubbins, Carl
Esmond, Melville Cooper, Ludwig Stossel, Morris Ankrum. Post-
Civil War rocket trip to moon. Cotten is good; Sanders and
Paget aren't. See also TRIP TO THE MOON, A (1902).
FROM THE ORIENT WITH FURY see AGENT 077, FROM THE
EAST WITH FURY
FROM THE OTHER SIDE (Sp) Agrupa 1966 scope 80m. (LA
OTRA ORILLA) Sp, D: José Luis Madrid. SP: also J. L.
Figueras. PH: A. G. Larraya. Mus: F. M. Tudó. Art D: M.
Infiesta. Ref: SpCinema'67. with Marisa de Leza, Luis Dávila,
A. G. Escribano. Life "prolonged for a few hours" for those
who die violent deaths: Characters leave their corpses. From the
work by José López Rubio.
FROZEN ALIVE (B-W.G.) Magna/Creole-Alfa 1964 63m. (DER
FALL X701) D: Bernard Knowles. SP: Evelyn Frazer. PH:
Robert Ziller. Art D: Jürgen Kiebach. Ref: FFacts. MFB'67:124.
TVG. with Mark Stevens, Marianne Koch, Delphi Lawrence,
Joachim Hansen, Walter Rilla, John Longden. Two scientists
plan to freeze a human being; suspended animation.
The FROZEN DEAD WB-7A/Goldstar (U.S.-B) 1967 95m. SP, D, P:
Herbert J. Leder. PH: Davis Boulton. Mus: Carlo Martelli.
Art D: Sean MacGregor. with Dana Andrews, Anna Palk, Philip
Gilbert, Karel Stepanek, Kathleen Breck, Basil Henson.Doctor
plans to revive Nazi corpses; "zombie butler"--PM.
The FROZEN GHOST Univ 1945 61m. (Inner Sanctum series)
D: Harold Young. SP: Luci Ward, Bernard Schubert. Story: Henry
Sucher, Harrison Carter. PH: Paul Ivano. Mus: Hans J. Salter.
Art D: John B. Goodman, Abraham Grossman(n). Ref: FDY. HM
8:18. COF 7:40. with Lon Chaney, Jr., Evelyn Ankers, Milburn
Stone, Tala Birell, Elena Verdugo, Martin Kosleck, Arthur Hohl,
Douglass Dumbrille. Suspended animation; murder by hypnotism.
Typically terrible Inner Sanctum series entry. Kosleck makes a
good villain.
FRUSTA E IL CORPO, La see WHAT!
FU MANCHU Y EL BESO DE LA MUERTE see BLOOD OF FU
MANCHU
FU MANCHU'S CASTLE see CASTLE OF FU MANCHU, The
FU MANCHU'S KISS OF DEATH see BLOOD OF FU MANCHU

FUEGO see PYRO
FUERZA DE LOS HUMILDES, La see STRENGTH OF THE
  HUMBLE, The
The FUGITIVE FUTURIST (B) 1924 9m. D: Gaston Quiribet.
  Ref: SilentFF. Inventor claims to have gadget which shows
  future.
FUHARANKENSHUTAIN TAI BARAGON see FRANKENSTEIN CON-
  QUERS THE WORLD
FULL OF SPIRITS Price 1920 22m. Ref: MPN 22:1080. Lee.
  with Mack Swain. Still of skeleton.
FUN IN A BUTCHER SHOP Edison 1901 D: Edwin S. Porter.
  Ref: Niver. SF Film. Dogs turned into sausages.
FUN WITH THE BRIDAL PARTY (F) Star /Melies 1908 Ref: F
  Index 9 /26 /08. "Ghost."
FUNF UNHEIMLICHE GESCHICHTEN see FIVE TALES OF
  HORROR /HISTOIRES EXTRAORDINAIRES (1931)
The FUNGI CELLARS (B) Stoll 1923 20m. (Mystery of Dr.
  Fu-Manchu series) SP, D: A. E. Coleby. SP: also Frank Wil-
  son. From novels by Sax Rohmer. PH: D. P. Cooper. Ref:
  SilentFF. with Harry Agar Lyons, Joan Clarkson, Humbertson
  Wright. Fu-Manchu produces a fungus which throws off poison-
  ous fumes.
FUNNICUS AND THE GHOST Eclair 1913 12m. (FUNNICUS'
  GHOSTS) Ref: Bios 4 /10 /13. 5 /15 /13. Man disguised as ghost
  terrifies owners of house.
FURANKENSHUTAIN NO KAIJU--SANDA TAI GAIRA see WAR OF
  THE GARGANTUAS
FURAT O BOMBA see BOMB WAS STOLEN, A
FURIA DEL HOMBRE LOBO, La see FURY OF THE WOLFMAN,
  The
FURY OF THE CONGO Col 1951 69m. D: William Berke. SP:
  Carroll Young. PH: Ira Morgan. Mus: Mischa Bakaleinikoff.
  Art D: Paul Palmentola. P: Sam Katzman. Ref: FDY. with
  Johnny Weissmuller, Sherry Moreland, Lyle Talbot, William
  Henry, George Eldredge. Jungle Jim encounters a maneating
  plant. Incredibly bad.
The FURY OF THE WOLFMAN (Sp) Maxper 1970 (LA FURIA DEL
  HOMBRE LOBO) D: Jose Maria Zabalza. Ref: V 5 /12 /71:143,
  with Perla Cristal, Veronica Lujan.

G-MEN NEVER FORGET Rep 1948 serial ('66 feature--CODE
  645) D: Fred Brannon, Yakima Canutt. SP: F. Adreon, B.
  Dickey, J. Duffy, S. Shor. PH: John MacBurnie. Mus D: Mort
  Glickman. SpFX: Howard and Theodore Lydecker. Ref: Glut.
  Barbour. with Clayton Moore, Roy Barcroft, Tom Steele, Ram-
  say Ames, Dale Van Sickel, Stanley Price, Ken Terrell, Eddie
  Acuff, Frank O'Connor, Edmund Cobb, Arvon Dale, Bob Wilke.
  Criminal's voice and face re-made to match police commission-
  er's exactly.
G-MEN VS. THE BLACK DRAGON Rep 1943 serial 15 episodes

('66 feature--BLACK DRAGON OF MANZANAR) D: William Wit-
ney. SP: R. Davidson, J. Poland, W. Lively, J. O'Donnell. PH:
Bud Thackery. Mus sc: Mort Glickman. SpFX: Howard Lydecker.
Ref: Barbour. Glut. Pic: STI 3:50. with Rod Cameron, Noel
Cravat, Maxine Doyle, C. Montague Shaw, Hooper Atchley,
Forbes Murray, George J. Lewis, Roland Got, Constance
Worth. Ray which destroys planes; explosive paint; man in
suspended animation disguised as mummy.

G THE VAMPIRE see GOKE

GABRIEL OVER THE WHITE HOUSE MGM/Cosmopolitan 1933
87m. (RINEHARD-Eng) D: Gregory La Cava. SP: Carey Wilson. Add'l Dial: Bertram Bloch. PH: Bert Glennon. Mus: William Axt. Ref: FDY. with Walter Huston, Karen Morley,
Franchot Tone, Arthur Byron, Dickie Moore, C. Henry Gordon,
David Landau, Samuel S. Hinds, Jean Parker, Claire DuBrey.
The President of the United States, inspired by a vision, attempts
to have himself made dictator of the country.

GAJ GOURI (India-Hindi) Prabhat 1958 D: Raja Thakur. SP:
G. D. Madgulkar. Dial: S. Joshi. PH: E. Mohammed. Ref:
Filmindia 1/59. FEFN '58/'59. with Sulochana, Ratnamala,
Nana Palsikar, Shahu Modak, Anant Marathe. Man uses magic
powers to become a giant; nearly destroys a city with giant mud
balls.

GALLERY OF HORRORS see DR. TERROR'S GALLERY OF HOR-
RORS

GALLOPING GHOSTS Pathe-Roach 1927 22m. Ref: DDC II:353.
MPN 3/3/28. LC. with James Finlayson, Ora Carew, Oliver
Hardy. Trail of stolen diamond leads to graveyard at midnight.

The GALVANIC FLUID or MORE LIQUID ELECTRICITY Vita 1908
8m. Sequel to LIQUID ELECTRICITY. Ref: MPW'08:103. Fluid
speeds people up.

GAMBARA TAI BARUGON see GAMERA VS. BARUGON

The GAMBLER AND THE DEVIL Vita 1908 8m. Ref: F Index.
10/3/08. Man gambles with devil for woman's life.

GAMBLING WITH THE GULF STREAM Hodkinson 1922 11m.
Ref: Lee. Shift in the Gulf Stream moves the polar ice cap to
England.

A GAME OF DEATH RKO 1945 80m. (DANGEROUS ADVENTURE)
D: Robert Wise. SP: Norman Houston, from the story "The Most
Dangerous Game" by Richard Connell. PH: J. Roy Hunt. with
John Loder, Audrey Long, Edgar Barrier, Russell Wade, Rus-
sell Hicks, Jason Robards, Noble Johnson, Robert Clarke, Gene
Stutenroth. Madman makes a sport of hunting people. The
original MOST DANGEROUS GAME is somewhat overrated but
better than this remake, which uses footage from it.

GAME OF MEN (Sp) Alfyega/Gasset. 1964 (JUEGO DE HOM-
BRES) SP,D: José Luis Gamboa. SP:also Lauro Olmo. PH:
Miguel F. Mila Mus: J. A. Buenagu. Art D: L. P. Espinosa.
Ref: SpCinema'64. with P. M. Sánchez, Antonio Brañas, Frank
Latimore, Laura Granados, Roberto Camardiel. A satellite fails
to land as planned on an interspace platform.

GAMERA see GAMMERA--THE INVINCIBLE

GAMERA VS. BARUGON (J) Daiei 1966 Eastmancolor 101m.

scope (GAMBARA TAI BARUGON. WAR OF THE MONSTERS-
TV. GODZILLA-DER DRACHE AUS DEM DSCHUNGEL-G) D:
Shigeo Tanaka. SpFX, SP: Fumi Takahashi. Ref: V 4 /27 /66.
with Kojiro Hongo, Kyoko Enami, Akira Natsuki. Giant opal
turns out to be egg.
GAMERA VS. GUIRON (J) Daiei 1969 color AI-TV (ATTACK
OF THE MONSTERS-TV) D: Noriaki Yuasa. SP: Fumi Taka-
hashi. PH: Akira Kitazaki. Ref: M /TVM 3 /69. TV FFSB. with
Nobuhiro Kashima (or Kajima), Christopher Murphy, M.
Akiyama. Giant turtle rescues two youngsters from monster.
GAMERA VS. GYAOS (J) AI-TV /Daiei 1967 Eastmancolor 87m.
(GAMERA TAI GYAOS. THE RETURN OF THE GIANT MON-
STERS-TV) D: Noriaki Yuasa. SP: Fumi Takahashi. PH:
K. Fujii. Mus: T. Yamaguchi. Ref: V 4 /19 /67. M /TVM
9 /68. with Kojiro Hongo, K. Ueda. M /TVM 9 /67: "Gamera
flies at Mach 3; Gyaos at Mach 3. 5. Gamera spits fire; Gyaos
puts it out with yellow smog. Gamera eats A-bombs; Gyaos
eats humans. "
GAMERA VS. JIGER (J) AI-TV /Daiei 1970 color /scope 83m.
(GAMERA TAI DAIMAJU JAIGA. GAMERA VS. MONSTER X-
TV) D: Noriaki Yuasa. SP: Fumi Takahashi. PH: Akira
Kitazaki. Mus: S. Kikuchi. Art D: Sho Inoue. Ref: UFQ.
TV FFSB. with Kelly Varis, T. Takakuwa. Monster bent on
ruining the Japan World Exposition.
GAMERA VS. OUTER-SPACE MONSTER VIRUS (J) AI-TV /Daiei
1968 color 75m. (GAMERA TAI VIRAS. GAMERA VS.
VIRAS. DESTROY ALL PLANETS-TV) D: Noriaka Yuasa. SP:
Fumi Takahashi. PH: Akira Kitazaki, K. Fujii, Y. Kaneko.
Ref: UFQ 40:5. TV FFSB. V 5 /22 /68. with Kojiro Hongo, Toru
Takatsuka, Peter Williams, Carl Clay, Michiko Yaegaki. "Squid-
like creatures" control Gamera's will.
GAMES Univ 1967 Technicolor 100m. D: Curtis Harrington.
SP: Gene Kearney. Story: George Edwards, Harrington. PH:
William A. Fraker. Mus D: Joseph Gershenson. Art D: Alex-
ander Golitzen, William D. DeCinces. Mus sc: Samuel Matlov-
sky. Sets: John McCarthy, James S. Redd. Makeup: Bud
Westmore, Ref: FFacts. LA Times 1 /26 /68. with Simone
Signoret, Katharine Ross, James Caan, Don Stroud, Kent Smith,
Estelle Winwood, Ian Wolfe, Florence Marly. Seances, appari-
tions, the occult; DRACULA playing on TV.
The GAMMA PEOPLE (B) Col /Warwick 1956   79m. SP, D:
John Gilling. SP: also John Gossage. Story: Louis Pollock.
PH: Ted Moore. Mus: George Melachrino. Art D: John Box.
Ref: FDY. Pic: FM 10:20. 19:68. with Eva Bartok, Paul
Douglas, Leslie Phillips, Walter Rilla, Martin Miller, Olaf
Pooley, Rosalie Crutchley. Invention turns people into either
geniuses or imbeciles. Weird conglomeration of genres that
doesn't work.
GAMMERA--THE INVINCIBLE (J) WEC /Daiei 1966 color /scope
88m. (DAIKAIJU GAMERA. GAMERA) D: Noriaki Yuasa. SP:
Fumi Takahashi. Ref: TVG. with Brian Donlevy, Albert Dek-
ker, John Baragrey, Eiji Funakoshi, Harumi Kiritachi. Giant
prehistoric turtle threatens the world.

GAMMO SANGO UCHU DAISAKUSEN   see BATTLE BEYOND THE
  STARS
GANG BUSTERS Univ 1942 serial 13 episodes D: Ray Taylor,
  Noel Smith. SP: M. Cox, Al Martin, Vic McLeod, G. Plymp-
  ton. with Kent Taylor, Irene Hervey, Robert Armstrong, Ralph
  Morgan, Richard Davies, Grace Cunard, John Gallaudet. Man
  brings criminals back to life; keeps them alive with certain cap-
  sules.
GAPPA--TRIPHIBIAN MONSTER (GAPPA. FRANKENSTEIN'S
  FLIEGENDE MONSTER--Germany) (J) Nikkatsu 1967 color/
  scope 90m. (DAIKYOJU GAPPA. MONSTER FROM A PRE-
  HISTORIC PLANET-TV) D: H. Noguchi. SP: Iwao Yamazaki,
  Ryuzo Nakanishi. PH: Muneo Ueda. Mus: S. Omori. Ref: J.
  Films'68. V 4/19/67. Pic: FM 52. with Tamio Kawaji,
  Yoko Yamamoto, Koji Wada, Yuji Odaka. Parents follow baby
  monster taken to Japan.
The GARDEN MURDER CASE MGM 1936 61m. D: Edwin L.
  Marin. SP: Bertram Millhauser, from the book by S. S. van
  Dine. PH: Charles Clarke. Mus: William Axt. Ref: Photoplay
  4/36. with Edmund Lowe, Gene Lockhart, Virginia Bruce,
  Benita Hume, Douglas Walton, Nat Pendleton, Kent Smith, H. B.
  Warner, Grant Mitchell, Frieda Inescort, Henry B. Walthall,
  Charles Trowbridge, Etienne Girardot. Murder by hypnotism.
GARGON TERROR, The see TEENAGERS FROM OUTER SPACE
GAS see GAS-S-S-S!
The GAS HOUSE KIDS IN HOLLYWOOD PRC-Eagle Lion 1947
  62m. D: Edward L. Cahn. SP: Robert E. Kent. PH: James
  Brown. Mus: Albert Glasser. Ref: PM. FDY. with Carl Swit-
  zer, Bennie Bartlett, Rudy Wissler, Tommy Bond, James Burke,
  Michael Whalen, Jan Bryant, Douglas Fowley. Haunted house.
GAS-S-S-S! AI 1970 Movielab color 79m. (GAS) P, D: Roger
  Corman. SP: George Armitage. PH: Ron Dexter. Ref: Boxo
  8/31/70. with Robert Corff, Elaine Giftos, Bud Cort, Country
  Joe and the Fish. Gas released from Alaskan defense plant
  causes everyone over 25 to die.
GASU-NINGEN DAI ICHI-GO see HUMAN VAPOR, The
The GATES OF THE NIGHT (F) Pathé Cinema 1946 Tricolor
  (LES PORTES DE LA NUIT)   D: Marcel Carné. SP: Jacques
  Prevert, from his ballet "Le Rendez-Vous." Mus: Joseph Kosma.
  Ref: Fowler. with Yves Montand, Nathalie Nattier. Man told by
  Destiny the date of his death.
GATO, El see CAT CREEPS, The (Sp)
GATO CON BOTAS, El see PUSS IN BOOTS
The GAUCHO AND THE DEVIL (Arg) TransAmerica 1952 color
  83m. (El GAUCHO Y EL DIABLO) D: Ernesto Remani. SP:
  J. M. F. Unsain. PH: Humberto Corell, A. y Vedia. from "The
  Imp in the Bottle" by Robert Louis Stevenson. Mus: Peter
  Kreuder. Ref: Cine Arg. Imparical Film 12/31/52. with Juan
  José Miguez, Elisa Christian Galvé, Francisco M. Allende.
GAVROCHE AND THE GHOSTS Eclair 1912 (GAVROCHE ET LES
  ESPRITS) Ref: Mitry II. D: Romeo Bosetti.
GAZ MORTELS, Les see DEADLY GASSES, The
GEANT DE THESSALIE, Le see GIANTS OF THESSALY

GEANTS DE ROME, Les see GIANTS OF ROME

GEBISSEN WIRD NUR NACHTS-HAPPENING DER VAMPIRE see VAMPIRE HAPPENING, The

GEHEIMNIS DER GELBEN MONCHE, Das see TARGET FOR KILLING

GEKKO KAMEN see CHALLENGING GHOST, The/LAST DEATH OF THE DEVIL, The/MONSTER GORILLA, The/MAN IN THE MOONLIGHT MASK

GENE AUTRY AND THE PHANTOM EMPIRE see PHANTOM EMPIRE, The

GENIE OF DARKNESS (Mex) AI-TV 1960 77m. (NOSTRADAMUS Y EL GENIO DE LA TINIEBLAS) D: F. Curiel. SP: C. Taboada, Alfredo Ruanova. Ref: FM 33:8. with German Robles, Domingo Soler. A new method of killing a vampire is introduced: steal the ashes from his coffin. Confusing at best. All too clear at worst.

GENIUS AT WORK RKO 1946 61m. (MASTER MINDS) D: Leslie Goodwins. SP: Robert E. Kent, Monte Brice. PH: Robert de Grasse. Mus D: C. Bakaleinikoff. Art D: Albert D'Agostino, Ralph Berger. SpFX: Vernon L. Walker. Ref: V 8/1/46. Pic: FM 9:25. with Bela Lugosi, Anne Jeffreys, Wally Brown, Alan Carney, Lionel Atwill, Marc Cramer, Ralph Dunn, Robert Clarke, Forbes Murray, Eddie Borden, Phil Warren. Criminal, the Cobra, has chamber of tortures with wax figures, torture instruments. Moronic.

GENOCIDE (J) Shochiku 1968 color/scope 90m. (KONCHU DAISENSO. WAR OF INSECTS) D: Kazui Nihonmatsu. SP: Susumu Takahisa. PH: S. Hirase. Mus: S. Kikuchi. Art D: T. Yoshino. Ref: UFQ 43. M/TVM 11/68. with Y. Kawazu, K. Sonoi. Woman breeds poisonous insects.

The GENTLE ART OF MURDER (F-I) Embassy/Transworld-Cosmas 1962 Dyaliscope 159m. (LE CRIME NE PAIE PAS. CRIME DOES NOT PAY) D: Gerard Oury. SP: Oury, J. C. Tacchella, P. Gordeaux. PH: Christian Matras. Mus: Georges Delerue. Ref: FFacts. with Michele Morgan, Jean Servais, Annie Girardot, Pierre Brasseur, Richard Todd, Danielle Darrieux, Gabriele Ferzetti, Edwige Feuillere, Rosanna Schiaffino, Louis de Funes. "The Mask": A man attends a funeral that turns out to be his own. Adap, Dial: Jean Aurenche, Pierre Bost. Based on "Italian Chronicles" by Stendhal. "The Man on the Avenue": A man is killed after seeing this movie. Adap, Dial: F. Dard.

GENTLEMAN FROM AMERICA, A see FATAL NIGHT, The

The GENTLEMAN IN THE HOUSE (G) Bavaria-Film 1940 88m. (DER HERR IM HAUS) SP, D: Heinz Helbig. SP: also Jacob Geis. Mus: Leo Leux. Ref: Deutscher. with Hans Moser, Leo Slezak, Maria Andergast, Hans Junkermann. "Spook-hunter" hit by "ghost of Napoleon" at seance.

GENTLEMAN, I HAVE KILLED EINSTEIN see I KILLED EINSTEIN, GENTLEMEN

GENUINE (G) Decla-Bioscop 1920 D: Robert Wiene. SP: Carl Mayer. PH: Willy Hameister. Sets: Cesar Klein. Ref: Orpheus 3:51. FM 10:26. Pic: DDC I:87, 299. with Fern Andra, Harald Paulsen, Ernst Gronau, H. H. von Twardowski. Old man buys

Oriental princess and imprisons her in glass case.
GEORGE WASHINGTON JONES Edison 1916 Ref: MPW 10/10/16.
Jones is frightened by a spiritualist's "ghosts."
The GERM Research Pictures 1923 D: P. S. McGreeney.
Author: C. S. Warnock. Ref: AFI. A scientist alters people's
personalities by eliminating germs from their blood.
The GERM OF MYSTERY Selig 1916 35m. D: William Robert
Daly. Ref: MPN 14:1101. with Guy Oliver, Fritzie Brunette,
Lillian Hayward. "A touch of Poe's spine-tingling horror...
huge, repulsive spider... super-explosive named Dynite."
GERMANIC LOVE Vogue (Mutual) 1916 11m. Ref: MPN 13:3111.
Lee. Professor tests love potion.
GET OFF MY FOOT (B) F Nat 1935 D: Monty Banks (William
Beaudine?). SP?: Frank Launder. Ref: Sound & S 12/5/35.
Brit. Cinema. with Max Miller, Chili Bouchier. "Ghost" of
murdered man returns.
GEVATTER TOD see DEATH (1921)
GEWISSEN, Das see CONSCIENCE, The
The GHASTLY ONES JER Pictures 1969 color 81m.   PH, D:
Andy Milligan. SP: Milligan, Hal Sherwood. Ref: V 1/15/69.
Film Bulletin 5/12/69. with Veronica Radbur, Maggie Rogers.
A will requires three couples to go to an old mansion on an is-
land, where they meet two old women and a hunchback who de-
vours live rabbits.
GHIDRAH, THE THREE-HEADED MONSTER (J) Cont/Toho
1965 color 85m. (CHIKYU SAIDAINO KESSEN. THE BIGGEST
FIGHT ON EARTH. MONSTER OF MONSTERS-GHIDORAH.
SANDAI KAIJU CHIKYU SAIDAI NO KESSEN. The GREATEST
BATTLE ON EARTH) D: Inoshiro Honda. SP: Shinichi Seki-
zawa. Mus sc: I. Ifukube. SpFX: Eiji Tsuburaya. Ref: Boxo
10/25/65. M/TVM 2/65. Orpheus 3:33. with Hiroshi Koizumi,
Takashi Shimura, Eiji Okada. Godzilla, Mothra, and Rodan meet
brand-new monster Ghidrah. Imaginative and amusing, in a
slight, silly way. The dubbing for once is a highlight ("Oh,
Godzilla, what terrible language").
The GHOST Biog 1911 8m. Ref: MPW'11:140,292. Bios 11/13/13.
Three crooks learn of a haunted house and each decides to play
the ghost.
The GHOST Univ (Victor) 1913 Ref: MPW'13:770. Two boys are
frightened away from a "haunted" country house by a thief dis-
guised as a ghost.
The GHOST Univ (Victor) 1913 15m. (sfa above?) Ref: MPW
17:845. Bios 12/4/13. with James Kirkwood, Gertrude
Robinson. Man makes bet he can stay the night in "haunted"
house, discovers den of thieves.
The GHOST Domino 1913 32m. Ref: Bios 2/19/14. St. Patrick
has a horrifying dream.
The GHOST Pathe 1914 45m. Ref: Motion Picture Magazine
5/14. Lee. with Crane Wilbur. "Ghost" scares villain to death.
The GHOST (I) Magna/Panda 1963 ('65-U.S.) Technicolor/scope
96m. (LO SPETTRO DE DR. HICHCOCK. The SPECTRE-Eng)
SP, D: Riccardo Freda (aka Robert Hampton). SP: also Oreste
Biancoli (aka Robert Davidson). PH: Raffaele Masciocchi. Mus:

Roman Vlad, Franco Mannino. Ref: FFacts. Sequel to The HORRIBLE DR. HICHCOCK, with Barbara Steele, Peter Baldwin, Elio Jotta, Harriet White, Umberto Raho. Husband fakes his own death, seeks revenge. -Boxo 11/22/65.

GHOST, The (by R. Oswald) see FIVE TALES OF HORROR

The GHOST AND MR. CHICKEN Univ 1966 Technicolor/scope 90m. D: Alan Rafkin. SP: James Fritzell, Everett Greenbaum. PH: William Margulies. Mus sc: Vic Mizzy. Mus D: Joseph Gershenson. Art D: Alexander Golitzen, George Webb. Ref: FFacts. Boxo 2/28/66. with Don Knotts, Joan Staley, Liam Redmond, Dick Sargent, Skip Homeier, Reta Shaw, Charles Lane, Harry Hickox, Philip Ober, Lurene Tuttle, George Chandler, Robert Cornthwaite, Cliff Norton, Eddie Quillan, Hal Smith, Ellen Corby, Nydia Westman, Hope Summers. "Haunted house"; portrait dripping blood, hidden staircase, etc. One or two good running gags.

The GHOST AND MRS. MUIR Fox 1947 104m. D: Joseph L. Mankiewicz. SP: Philip Dunne, from the book by R. A. Dick. PH: Charles Lang, Jr. Mus: Bernard Herrmann. Ref: FDY. with Rex Harrison, Gene Tierney, George Sanders, Edna Best, Vanessa Brown, Anna Lee, Robert Coote, Natalie Wood, Isobel Elsom. Haunted house; storm; maniacal laughing. Slow. See also STRANGER IN THE NIGHT.

The GHOST AND THE GUEST PRC 1943 62m. D: William Nigh. SP: Morey Amsterdam. Story: Milt Gross. PH: Robert Cline. Mus D: Lee Zahler. Ref: TVFFSB. MPH 5/15/43. with James Dunn, Florence Rice, Anthony Caruso, Mabel Todd, Renee Carson, Robert Bice. "Chiller": secret passages, stairways; coffin; hangman.

GHOST BEAUTY see TALE OF PEONIES AND STONE LANTERNS, A

The GHOST BREAKER Para 1914 60m. P: C. B. De Mille. Ref: MPN 22:1692. Lee. with H. B. Warner, Rita Sanwood. Fake ghosts.

The GHOST BREAKER Para 1922 55m. D: Alfred E. Green. SP: Jack Cunningham and Walter De Leon. PH: William Marshall. From the play by Paul Dickey and Charles W. Goddard. Ref: FD 9/17/22. FIR'66:230. AFI. with Wallace Reid, Lila Lee, Arthur Edmund Carewe, Snitz Edwards, J. Farrell MacDonald. A Kentuckian helps a Spanish senorita rid her castle of robbers posing as ghosts.

The GHOST BREAKERS Para 1940 85m. D: George Marshall. SP: Walt DeLeon, from the play by Paul Dickey and Charles W. Goddard. PH: Charles Lang. Ref: FDY. Pic: FM 15:39. 27:61. 32:16. with Bob Hope, Paulette Goddard, Richard Carlson, Paul Lukas, Anthony Quinn, Lloyd Corrigan, Noble Johnson, Virginia Brissac, Willie Best, Paul Fix, Tom Dugan, Pedro de Cordoba. Radio columnist finds ghosts and zombie in old castle. Third-rate gags for the most part. Bad as it is though, the Martin-and-Lewis remake (an almost-scene-for-scene, line-for-line remake) is even worse, lacking even the few effective chills this version has.

GHOST BREAKERS, The (by Dickey and Goddard) see SCARED

STIFF (1953)
The GHOST CAMERA (B) Favorite Films 1933 60m. D: Bernard Vorhaus. P: Julius Hagen. Ref: TVFFSB. Brit. Cinema. with Ida Lupino, John Mills, Henry Kendall. Ghost camera solves murder.
GHOST CAT MANSION see BLACK CAT MANSION
GHOST-CAT OF ARIMA PALACE (J) Daiei 1953 D, Ryohei Arai. Ref: Unij. Bltn. 31. with Takako Irie, Kotaro Bando. Ghost story. (KAIBYO ARIMA GOTEN)
GHOST-CAT OF GOJUSAN-TSUGI (J) Daiei 1956 D: Bin Kado. Ref: Unij. Bltn. 31. with Shintaro Katsu, Tokiko Mita. Ghost story. (KAIBYO GOJUSAN-TSUGI)
GHOST-CAT OF KARAKURI TENJO (J) Toei 1958 (KAIBYO KARAKURI TENJO) D: Kinnosuke Fukada. Ref: Unij. Bltn. 31. with Ryunosuke Tsukigata, Kyonosuke Nango. Ghost story.
GHOST-CAT OF NABESHIMA MANSION (J) Shintoho 1949 (NABESHIMA KAIBYODEN) D: Kunio Watanabe. Ref: Unij. Bltn. 31. with Denjiro Okochi, Michiyo Kogure. Ghost story.
GHOST-CAT OF OMA-GA-TSUJI (J) Daiei 1954 (KAIBYO OMA-GA-TSUJI) D: Bin Kado. Ref: Unij. Bltn. 31. with Takako Irie, Shintaro Katsu. Ghost story.
GHOST-CAT OF YONAKI SWAMP see NECROMANCY
GHOST-CAT WALL OF HATRED (J) Daiei 1958 88m. (KAIBYO NOROI NO KABE) D: Kenji Misumi. Ref: Unig. Bltn. 31. UFQ 46: 36. with Shintaro Katsu, Yoko Uraji. Demon cat in form of lady.
GHOST CATCHERS Univ 1944 67m. D: Edward L. Cline. SP, P: Edmund L. Hartmann. PH: Charles Van Enger. Mus: Edward Ward. Art D: John B. Goodman, Richard H. Riedel. Ref: FDY. with Ole Olsen, Chic Johnson, Leo Carrillo, Gloria Jean, Lon Chaney, Jr., Martha O'Driscoll, Kirby Grant, Walter Catlett, Walter Kingsford, Morton Downey, Mel Torme, Andy Devine, Tom Dugan, Tor Johnson, Edgar Dearing. House haunted by tap-dancing ghost.
GHOST CHASERS Mono 1951 69m. D: William Beaudine. SP: Bert Lawrence. PH: Marcel Le Picard. Art D: David Milton. with Leo Gorcey, Huntz Hall, Jan Kayne, Bernard Gorcey, Lloyd Corrigan, Billy Benedict, George Gorcey, Philip Van Zandt, Argentina Brunett. The Bowery Boys vs. a fake spiritualist in a haunted house.
The GHOST CLUB Gloria American 1914 Ref: LC.
GHOST CRAZY Mono 1944 64m. (MURDER IN THE FAMILY. CRAZY KNIGHTS) D: William Beaudine. SP: Tim Ryan. PH: Marcel Le Picard. P: Sam Katzman, Jack Dietz. Ref: COF 10: 36. FDY. with Billy Gilbert, Shemp Howard, Maxie Rosenbloom, Minerva Urecal, Jayne Hazard, John Hamilton, Bernie Sell. Girl inherits a haunted house.
The GHOST CREEPS Mono 1940 63m. (BOYS OF THE CITY-TV) D: Joseph H. Lewis. SP: William Lively. P: Sam Katzman. Ref: FD 7/22/40. with Bobby Jordan, Leo Gorcey, Dave O'Brien, Vince Barnett, Hally Chester, George Humbert, Sunshine Sammy, Frankie Burke, Minerva Urecal. House with secret passages; "ghost."
The GHOST FAKIRS Starlight 1915 Ref: MPW 24:1338. Two men

spend a night in a "haunted" house.

GHOST FROM THE POND (J) Toei 1959 (KAIDAN HITOTSU-ME JIZO) D: Kinnosuke Fukada. Ref: J. Films'60:96. with Tomisaburo Wakayama, S. Chihara.

The GHOST GOES GEAR (B) 1967 41m. SP, D: Hugh Gladwish (or Gladwich). PH: George Stevens. SP: also Roger Dunton. Ref: MFB. M/TVM 9/67. with Spencer Davis, Stevie Winwood, Lorne Gibson (ghost). Haunted house.

The GHOST GOES WEST (B) UA/London 1935 78m. (THE LAY-ING OF THE GLOURIE GHOST) D: René Clair. SP: Robert E. Sherwood, from the short story "Glowie Castle" or "Sir Tris-tram Goes West" by Eric Keoun. PH: Hal Rosson. P: Alexander Korda. Ref: FDY. with Robert Donat, Jean Parker, Eugene Pallette, Elsa Lanchester, Everly Gregg, Hay Petrie, Patricia Hilliard. Haunted castle. Generally uninspired, with scattered delightful moments.

The GHOST GOES WILD Rep 1947 66m. D: George Blair. SP: Randall Faye. Story: Faye, Taylor Caven. PH: John Alton. Mus: Morton Scott, Joseph Dubin. Ref: MFB'47:64. FDY. with James Ellison, Anne Gwynne, Edward Everett Horton, Stephanie Bachelor, Grant Withers, Lloyd Corrigan, Jonathan Hale, Charles Halton, Emil Rameau, Edward Gargan, William Austin. Haunted Hill Farm; seance; spirit accidentally conjured up.

GHOST GUNS Mono 1944 60m. (GHOST OF INDIAN SPRINGS) D: Lambert Hillyer. SP: Frank H. Young. Story: Bennet Cohen. PH: Marcel Le Picard. Mus: Edward Kay. Ref: MPH 11/18/44. with Johnny Mack Brown, Raymond Hatton, John Merton, Ernie Adams, Sarah Padden, Jack Ingram. Western: Hero makes killer confess by confronting him with ghost of sup-posed dead man.

The GHOST HOLIDAY WB&E 1907 Ref: MPW'07:458. Ghosts, skeletons leave graveyard; go out on the town.

GHOST HOUNDS Kalem 1917 Ref: MPW 31:1074. Thieves sen-tenced to spend night in haunted house: "ghosts, dancing skeletons," etc.

The GHOST HOUSE Para 1917 D: William C. DeMille. SP: Beulah Dix. PH: Paul Perry. Ref: MPN 16:2772. FIR'64:57. Bank robbers use "haunted" house.

GHOST IN THE CASTLE (G) Bavaria-Film 1944 (SPUK IM SCHLOSS) SP, D: Hans H. Zerlett. Mus: Leo Leux. Ref: Deutscher. DDC III:157. with Paul Kemp, Sonja Ziemann, Mar-got Hielscher, Albert Matterstock. Castle legend: "Midnight!--The witching hour! Ghosts are haunting, guests shudder..."

The GHOST IN THE GARRET Para 1921 55m. D: F. Richard Jones. Ref: Exhibitors Herald. FIR'68:412. AFI. SP: Wells Hastings, Fred Chaston. with Dorothy Gish, William Parke, Jr., Tom Blake, Porter Strong, Mrs. David Landau, Downing Clarke. A band of thieves has its headquarters in a "haunted" house.

GHOST IN THE INVISIBLE BIKINI AI 1966 Pathecolor/scope 82m. (BIKINI PARTY IN A HAUNTED HOUSE. BEACH PARTY IN A HAUNTED HOUSE. PAJAMA PARTY IN A HAUNTED HOUSE) D: Don Weis. SP: Elwood Ulmann, Louis Heyward. PH: Stanley Cortez. Mus: Les Baxter. Art D: Daniel Haller. Ref: FDY. MW

10:38. FM 37:48. 39:62. 63:24. with Boris Karloff, Basil Rathbone, Patsy Kelly, Deborah Walley, Tommy Kirk, Harvey Lembeck, Susan Hart, Aron Kincaid, Quinn O'Hara, Jesse White,
Nancy Sinatra, Claudia Martin, Francis X. Bushman, Benny
Rubin, Bobbi Shaw. Haunted house; chamber of horrors; mum-
my-man; Frankenstein-monster dummy. Yet another ghastly mess
from AI. Continuously embarrassing.

GHOST IN THE NIGHT see SPOOKS RUN WILD

The GHOST JESTERS (Mex) Sotomayor 1964 (LOS FANTASMAS
BURLONES) D: Rafael Baledon. SP: F. Galiana, F. Cordova.
PH: Raul M. Solares. Mus: R. Fuentes. Ref: Indice. Grafica
6-7 /66. with M. Lopez, "Tin Tan," "Resortes," "Clavillazo,"
"Loco" Valdes, Sonia Infante, Maria Eugenia San Martin. Bats,
skulls, etc.

GHOST MURDERER (J) Shochiku 1957 color /scope 71m.
(GINDA JUMON) D: Seiichi Fukuda. SP: S. Yasuda. PH: K.
Kataoka. Ref: FEFN 9 /27 /57. with K. Takada, J. Ban. Detective story about a murderer disguised as a "silver snake-car-
rying ghost."

GHOST MUSIC OF SHAMISEN (J) Toei 1962 (KAIDAN SHAMISEN-
BORI) D: Kokichi Uchide. Ref: Unij. Bltn. 31. with Ryuji
Shinagawa, N. Kitazawa. Ghost story.

GHOST OF BRAGEHUS (Swedish) Irefilm 1936 (SPOKET PA
BRAGEHUS) D: Tancred Ibsen, Ragnar Arvedson. SP: Fleming
Lynge. Ref: Lee. DDC II:228. with Adolf Jahr, Annalisa Ericson.

GHOST OF CHIBUSA ENOKI (J) Shintoho 1958 (KAIDAN
CHIBUSA ENOKI) D: Goro Katono. Ref: Unij. Bltn. 31. with
Katsuko Wakasugi, Keiko Hasegawa. Ghost story.

GHOST OF CHIDORI-GA-FUCHI (J) Toei 1956 66m. (KAIDAN
CHIDORI-GA-FUCHI. The SWAMP) D: Eiichi Koishi. Ref:
Unij. Bltn. 31. FEFN 10 /25 /57, 6 /29 /56. with Kinnosuke Naka-
mura, Yoshiko Wakamizu, S. Chihara. Ghost appears at night.

The GHOST OF CIRCLE X CAMP American Wild West 1912 19m.
(GHOSTS AT CIRCLE X CAMP) Ref: Bios 11 /14 /12. MPW 12:
1226. "Haunted" house.

GHOST OF DRAGSTRIP HOLLOW AI/Alta Vista 1959 65m. (The
HAUNTED HOTROD) D: William Hole, Jr. SP, P: Lou Rusoff.
PH: Gil Warrenton. Mus: Ronald Stein. Art D: Daniel Haller.
Ref: FDY. Orpheus 3:26. with Jody Fair, Paul Blaisdell, Russ
Bender, Henry McCann, Nancy Anderson, Kirby Smith, Martin
Braddock, Jack Ging. "Haunted house." The monster is bor-
rowed from AI's SHE CREATURE; the plot from AI's MOTOR-
CYCLE GANG; and the dialogue features plugs for AI pictures
(e.g., "They didn't use me in HORRORS OF THE BLACK MU-
SEUM"). The result is average for AI.

The GHOST OF FRANKENSTEIN Univ 1942 67m. D: Erle C.
Kenton. SP: W. Scott Darling. Story: Eric Taylor. PH: Milton
Krasner, Elwood Bredell. Mus sc: H. J. Salter. Art D: Jack
Otterson. Makeup: Jack Pierce. P: George Waggner. Ref:
Academy. FM 11:22. 48. 20. Pic: FM 4:60. MMania 1:40. with
Cedric Hardwicke, Lon Chaney, Jr., Ralph Bellamy, Evelyn
Ankers, Lionel Atwill, Bela Lugosi, Barton Yarborough, Doris
Lloyd, Leyland Hodgson, Olaf Hytten, Holmes Herbert, Lawrence

Grant, Brandon Hurst, Dwight Frye, Julius Tannen, Otto Hoffmann, Lionel Belmore, Harry Cording, Michael Mark, Dick Alexander, George Eldredge, Ernie Stanton. Plot to replace monster's brain with that of a learned man. A few twists but that's all. Quite a drop in quality in the Universal series from SON OF FRANKENSTEIN to this, which pretty much set the level for the rest of the series.

GHOST OF GOJUSAN-TSUGI (J) Daiei-Toei 1960 (KAIDAN GOJUSAN-TSUGI) D: Kokichi Uchide. Ref: Unij.Bltn.31. with Kokichi Takada, Hiromi Hanazono. Ghost story.

GHOST OF INDIAN SPRINGS see GHOST GUNS

GHOST OF JOHN HOLLING, The (story by E. Wallace) see MYSTERY LINER

GHOST OF KAGAMI-GA-FUCHI (J) Shintoho 1959 (KAIDAN KAGAMI-GA-FUCHI) D: Masaki Mori. Ref: Unij.Bltn.31. J.Films'60. with Noriko Kitazawa, Fumiko Miyata. Ghost story.

GHOST OF KASANE-GA-FUCHI (J) Shintoho 1957 57m. (KAIDAN KASANE-GA-FUCHI. The DEPTHS) D: Nobuo Nakagawa. SP: Y. Kawauchi. PH: Y.Hirano. Ref: Unij.Bltn.31. FEFN 7/5/57. with Katsuko Wakasugi, Takashi Wada, T. Tanba. Spirit of murdered man rises from sea to haunt killer.

GHOST OF KASANE-GA-FUCHI (J) Daiei 1960 (KAIDAN KASANE-GA-FUCHI) D: Kimiyoshi Yasuda. Ref: Unij.Bltn.31. with Ganjiro Nakamura, Yataro Kitagami. Ghost story.

The GHOST OF MUDTOWN Pathe 1910 9m. Ref: Bios 6/2/10. Village thrown into state of terror by "ghostly" visitant.

GHOST OF OLD MORRO KESE/Edison 1917 55m. D: Richard Ridgeley. SP: James Oppenheim. Ref: MPW 30:408. MPN 16: 118. Lee. with Mabel Trunnelle, Robert Conness, Helen Strickland. Old castle, hag, murders.

GHOST OF OTAMAGA-IKE (J) Shintoho 1960 (KAIBYO OTAMA-GA-IKE) D: Yoshihiro Ishikawa. Ref: Unij.Bltn.31. Toho Films'61. with Shozaburo Date, Yoichi Numata. Goblin cat haunts daughter of famous family.

GHOST OF RASHMON HALL, The see NIGHT COMES TOO SOON, The

The GHOST OF ROSIE TAYLOR American 1917 52m. Ref: SilentFF. D: Ed Sloman. SP: Elizabeth Mahoney. with Marion Lee, Helen Howard, Mary Miles Minter, Kate Price. House suspected of being haunted.

GHOST OF SAGA MANSION (J) Daiei 1953 (KAIDAN SAGA YASHIKI) D: Ryohei Arai. Ref: Unij.Bltn.31. with Takako Irie, Kotaro Bando. Ghost story.

The GHOST OF ST. MICHAEL'S (B) Ealing/ABFD 1940 82m. D: Marcel Varnel. Ref: MFB'41:13. with Peter Ustinov, Will Hay, Claude Hulbert. Comedy. "Phantom piping" of ghost heard before deaths.

The GHOST OF SEAVIEW MANOR 1913 17m. Ref: Lee. MPW 16:1137. Fake ghost.

The GHOST OF SELF Ess 1913 Ref: MPW 19:289. Lee. Ghost tries to reform evil man through apparitions.

The GHOST OF SLUMBER MOUNTAIN World 1919 P. Herbert M.

Dawley. SpFX: Willis O'Brien. Ref: MPW 40:32, 525. FM 12: 6. 19:36. Tricaratops, etc.

The GHOST OF SULPHUR MOUNTAIN American Wild West 1912 17m. Ref: Bios 9 /9 /12. Miners believe ghost of man haunts mountain.

GHOST OF THE GIRL DIVER (J) Shintoho 1960 (KAIDAN AMA YUREI) D: Goro Katono. Ref: Unij. Bltn. 31. with Juzaburo Akechi, Shinsuke Mikimoto. Ghost story.

GHOST OF THE MINE Eclair 1914 15m. Ref: MPW 22:1126. Lee. Girl spirit solves her murder.

GHOST OF THE HACIENDA 1913 Ref: MPW 17:1154. The Film Index. Girl disguised as ghost frightens bandits.

GHOST OF THE ONE-EYED MAN (J) Toei 1965 (KAIDAN KATAME NO OTOKO) D: Tsuneo Kobayashi. Ref: Unij. Bltn. 31. with Akira Nishimura, Sanae Nakahara. Ghost story.

GHOST OF THE OPERA (G) R. A. Stemmle c1940 (SPUK IM OPERNHAUS) Ref: Deutscher. "Horrifying experience"; girl prevents murder she saw in vision ("ghost-opera") from really happening.

GHOST OF THE RANCHO Pathe 1918 55m. D: William Worthington. SP: Jack Cunningham. Story: Arthur Gooden. Ref: MPW 37:882. with Bryant Washburn, Rhea Mitchell. Ghost posse.

The GHOST OF THE STRANGLER (Mex) SAyCN 1967 (EL ESPECTRO DEL ESTRANGULADOR) SP, D: Rene Cardona. Story: Rafael Travesi. PH: A. U. Jacones. Art D: A. A. Genner. (sfa SANTO CONTRA EL ESPECTRO?) Ref: Heraldo '71:7. FDY'67. LA Times 1 /30 /68. with Santo, Roberto Cañedo, Maria Duval, Carlos Lopez Moctezuma, Begonia Palacios.

GHOST OF THE TWISTED OAKS Lubin 1915 35m. D: Sidney Olcott. Story: Pearl Gaddis. Ref: LC. MPN 11 /20 /15. with Valentine Grant, Florence Wolcott, James Vincent. Voodooism; ghost.

The GHOST OF THE WHITE LADY (Dan?) Great Northern /Nordisk 1913 45m. (THE WHITE GHOST) Ref: Bios 11 /13 /13. MPW 19:473, 470. with Rita Sacchetto. Woman disguised as legendary ghost frightens man.

The GHOST OF TOLSTON'S MANOR Micheaux 1923 Ref: AFI.

The GHOST OF YOTSUYA (J) Shochiku 1949 (YOTSUYA KAIDAN, I & II) D: Keisuke Kinoshita. Ref: Unij. Bltn. 9 /65. with Ken Uehara, Kinuyo Tanaka.

The GHOST OF YOTSUYA (J) Shintoho 1956 (YOTSUYA KAIDAN) D: Masaki Mori. Ref: Unig. Bltn. 31. with Tomisaburo Wakayama, Akemi Tsukushi.

The GHOST OF YOTSUYA (J) Daiei 1959 (YOTSUYA KAIDAN) D: Kenji Misumi. Ref: Unij. Bltn. 31. with Kazuo Hasegawa, Yasuko Nakada.

The GHOST OF YOTSUYA (J) Shintoho 1959 color /scope 76m. (TOKAIDO YOTSUYA KAIDAN) D: Nobuo Nakagawa. SP: Masayashi Onuki, Yoshihiro Ishikawa. PH: Tadashi Nishimoto. Ref: UFQ 6. Unij. Bltn. 31. FM 23:11. Pic: FM 21:10. with Shigeru Amachi, K. Wakasugi, Junko Ikeuchi, Ryuzaburo Nakamura, N. Kitazawa. Spirit possesses man.

The GHOST OF YOTSUYA (J) Toei 1961 (KAIDAN OIWA NO

BOREI) D: Tai Kato. Ref: Unij. Bltn. 31. with Tomisaburo
Wakayama, Hiroko Sakuramachi.
GHOST OF YOTSUYA, The see ILLUSION OF BLOOD
GHOST PATROL Puritan 1936 60m. D: Sam Newfield. SP:
Wyndham Gittens. Ed, Story: Joseph O'Donnell. P: Sig
Neufeld, Leslie Simmonds. Ref: MFB '38:134. FD 9/10/36.
with Tim McCoy, Claudia Dell, Wheeler Oakman, Walter Miller,
Jim Burtis, Lloyd Ingraham, Slim Whitaker. Electric "radium-
tube" death ray shoots down planes. Western.
GHOST SHIP (B) Lippert/Anglo-Amalgamated 1952 74m. SP,
D, P: Vernon Sewell. PH: Stanley Grant. Exec P?: Herman
Cohen. Ref: MFB. with Hazel Court, Dermot Walsh, Hugh
Burden, John Robinson, Hugh Latimer. Couple suspect their new
yacht is haunted.
GHOST SHIP (J) Toei 1957 color/scope (YUREISEN, Parts I &
II) D. T. Matsuda, SP: K; Suzaki. PH: S. Kawasaki. Ref:
FEFN 7/19/57. Unij. Bltn. 6/65. with K. Nakamura, R. Otomo.
"Ghost ship appears and disappears as a symbol. "
GHOST STEPS OUT, The see TIME OF THEIR LIVES, The
GHOST STORIES see KWAIDAN
The GHOST STORY Vita 1907 P, D: J. Stuart Blackton. Ref: LC.
GHOST STORY (J) Toei 1957 (BANCHO SARAYASHIKI) Ref:
Japan, Autumn'57.
GHOST STORY see SPELLBOUND
A GHOST STORY IN PASSAGE (J) Toei 1958 85m (KAIDAN
DOCHU. GHOST STORY OF TWO TRAVELLERS. THE LADY
WAS A GHOST. A GHOST'S WARNING. From the Samurai Vaga-
bond (Tonosama Yajikita) series. D: Tadashi Sawashima. SP:
Tadashi Ogawa. PH: Makoto Tsuboi. Ref: FEFN'58. Unig. Bltn.
6/65. Toei Films. with Kinnosuke Nakamura, Kazuo Nakamura,
Hibari Misora, Satomi Oka. Two princes, chased by a ghostly
figure, run into a bandit gang.
GHOST STORY OF BOOBY-TRAP see GHOSTLY TRAP, The
GHOST STORY OF BROKEN DISHES AT BANCHO MANSION (J)
Toei 1957 (KAIDAN BANCHO SARAYASHIKI) D: Juichi Kono.
Ref: Unig. Bltn. 31. with Chiyonosuke Azuma, Hibari Misora.
Ghost story.
GHOST STORY OF DEVIL'S-FIRE SWAMP (J) Daiei 1963 (KAIDAN
ONIBI NO NUMA) D: Bin Kado. Ref: Unj. Bltn. 31. with
Kenzaburo Jo, Mieko Kondo. Ghost story.
GHOST STORY OF FUNNY ACT IN FRONT OF TRAIN STATION (J)
Toho 1964 (KIGEKI EKIMAE KAIDAN) D: Kozo Saeki. Ref:
Unij. Bltn. 31. with Frankie Sakai, Hisaya Morishige.
GHOST STORY OF KAKUI STREET (J) Daiei 1961 (KAIDAN
KAKUIDORI) D: Issei Mori. Ref: Unij. Bltn. 31. with Eiji
Funakoshi, Katsuhiko Kobayashi.
GHOST STORY OF STONE LANTERNS AND CRYING IN THE NIGHT
(J) Daiei 1962 (KAIDAN YONAKI-DORO) D: Katsuhiko Tasaka.
Ref: Unij. Bltn. 31. with Ganjiro Nakamura, Katsuhiko Kobayashi.
GHOST STORY OF TWO TRAVELLERS see GHOST STORY IN
PASSAGE, A
GHOST STORY OF WANDERER AT HONJO see SEVEN MYSTERIES
The GHOST TALKS Fox 1928 85m. sound D: Lew Seiler. SP:
Frederick H. Brennan, Harlan Thompson. Ed: Ralph Dietrich.

PH: George Meehan. From the play "Badges" by Max Marcin and
Edward Hammond. Ref: V 3/27/29. Pic: Photoplay 2/29.
AFI. with Helen Twelvetress, Charles Eaton, Stepin Fetchit,
Earle Foxe, Bess Flowers, Dorothy McGowan, Carmel Myers,
Joe Brown, Baby Mack, Arnold Lucy, Crooks responsible for
ghostly manifestations in "haunted" house.
The GHOST TIGER (Malayan) Keris Films 1959 (HANTU RIMAU)
D: B. N. Rao, L. Krishnan. Ref: FEFN 8/59, 7/59. with
Roomai Noor. "Tri-part thriller...tiger spirit."
GHOST TOWN LAW Mono 1942 65m. D: Howard Bretherton.
SP: Jess Bowers. PH: Harry Neumann. Ref: HR 3/25/42.
V 3/25/42. Boxo 4/4/42: "Ghost...thrills and chills."
with Buck Jones, Tim McCoy, Raymond Hatton, Charles King,
Virginia Carpenter. Mysterious band of killers hides out in
abandoned mine tunnels under ghost town. Western.
The GHOST TRAIN (B) 1927 D: Geza von Bolvary. From the
play by Arnold Ridley. Ref: Brit. Cinema. Halliwell. with Guy
Newall.
The GHOST TRAIN (B) Gaum/Gainsborough 1931 ('33-U.S.) 72m.
D: Walter Forde. From the play by Arnold Ridley. Ref: DDC I:
301. Photoplay 5/33: "It seems that on each anniversary of a
certain train wreck, a ghost train appears to roar by a little
village, sending inhabitants into frenzies of terror." with Jack
Hulbert, Cicely Courtneidge, Ann Todd, Cyril Raymond, Allan
Jeayes, Donald Calthrop.
The GHOST TRAIN (B) Gainsborough 1941 84m. D: Walter
Forde. Ref: COF 10:36.11:61. Brit. Cinema. with Wilfrid Law-
son, Carole Lynne, Arthur Askey, Richard Murdoch, Linden
Travers, Peter Murray-Hill. From the play by Arnold Ridley.
Ghost train haunts station.
GHOST VALLEY RKO 1932 61m. D: Fred Allen. SP: Adele
Buffington. PH: Ted McCord. Ref: FDY. Harrison's 6/4/32.
with Tom Keene, Mitchell Harris, Ted Adams, Merna Kennedy,
Harry Semels, Al Taylor. "Deals with ghosts and other mysteri-
ous doings." Western.
The GHOST WALKS Chesterfield 1935 67m. D: Frank Strayer.
SP: Charles Belden. PH: M. A. Anderson. Ed: Roland Reed.
Ref: FD 3/30/35. Photoplay 4/35. with John Miljan, June
Collyer, Henry Kolker, Eve Southern, Spencer Charters, Johnny
Arthur, Donald Kirke. Dress-rehearsal of new melodrama takes
place in "haunted" house. Terrible.
GHOST WOMAN (Taiwan) 1957 D: Sin Ta. Ref: FEFN 7/19/57.
with Ko Yu Shia, Wong Tai Chon.
GHOST YUKIJORO see SNOW GHOST
GHOSTLY FLOWERS see TALE OF PEONIES AND STONE
LANTERNS, A
GHOSTLY INN, The see HALFWAY HOUSE, The
The GHOSTLY TRAP (J) Daiei 1968 (KAIDAN OTOSHIANA.
GHOST STORY OF BOOBY-TRAP) D: Koji Shima. Ref:
Unij. Bltn. 31. M/TVM 9/69. with Mikio Narita, Mayumi Nagisa.
Businessman who commits murder driven insane by eerie events:
typewriter typing, etc.
GHOSTS (B) Hepworth 1912 7m. Ref: Bios 10/24/12. Ghost

stories; "ghosts."
GHOSTS Essanay 1912 Ref: Bios 12/5/12. MPW 13:1300.
"Haunted" house.
The GHOSTS Vita 1914(1913) 15m. (GHOSTS; or WHO'S AFRAID)
Ref: MPW 19:1414. Bios 6/25/14. D: W. J. Bauman. Mansion
supposedly haunted by ghost of old soldier; "ghoulish stories";
old ruin.
GHOSTS (B) Ivy Close 1914 19m. P, D: E. Neame. Ref: Bios
4/9/14. Haunted house.
The GHOSTS (Dan) 1914 (SPIRITISTEN. LES SPIRITES-F.) D:
Holger Madsen. Ref: DDC II:306, 315. Ghosts and spiritualism.
GHOSTS AND FLYPAPER Vita 1915 15m. P: Ulysses David.
Author: Louis B. Rose. Ref: Vitagraph News. with Anne
Schaefer, Marguerite Reid, Otto Lederer. Reputedly haunted
house; fake ghosts.
GHOSTS AND THIEVES (I) Jonia Films 1959 (FANTASMI E
LADRI) D: Giorgio Simonelli. Ref: FEFN 8/59. with Tina
Pica. "Aged eccentric refuses to be terrified by fake ghosts."
GHOSTS AT CIRCLE X CAMP see GHOST OF CIRCLE X CAMP,
The
GHOSTS! GHOSTS! (Swedish) c1943 (DET SPOKAR, DET SPOKAR)
Ref: Sweden I. with Sigge Fürst, Nils Poppe.
GHOSTS IN BUENOS AIRES (Arg) 1942 85m. (FANTASMAS EN
BUENOS AIRES) Argentina Sono Film D: Enrique Discépolo. PH:
Alberto Curchi. Ref: Imparcial Film 7/25/42. Heraldo
7/15/42. with Pepe Arias, Zully Moreno, Carlos Lagrotta.
Comedy-horror. "Spiritualistic sessions...ghosts."
GHOSTS IN ROME see GHOSTS OF ROME
GHOSTS IN THE NIGHT see GHOSTS ON THE LOOSE
GHOSTS-ITALIAN STYLE (I-F) MGM/Champion-Corona 1967
Technicolor 92m. (QUESTI FANTASMI) D: Renato Castellani.
SP: Castellani, Tonino Guerra, Adriano Baracco, De Barnardi.
From a play by Eduardo de Filippo. Dubbed by Ernest Pintoff.
PH: Tonino Delli Colli. Mus: Luis E. Bacalov. Art D: Piero
Poletto. Ref: V. Ital P. with Sophia Loren, Vittorio Gass-
man, Mario Adorf, Margaret Lee, Marcello Mastroianni (head-
less ghost). Reputedly haunted house; haunted castle.
GHOSTS OF BERKELEY SQUARE (B) British Nat'l 1947 90m.
D: Vernon Sewell. SP: James Seymour, from the book "NO
Nightingales" by S. J. Simon and C. Brahms. PH: Ernest
Palmer. Mus D: Hans May. Art D: Wilfred Arnold. Ref:
MFB'47:153. Dimmitt. Brit. FmYbk'49/'50. with Robert
Morley, Felix Aylmer, Ronald Frankau, Martita Hunt, Ernest
Thesiger, Harry Fine, James Hayter, Claude Hulbert, John
Longden, A. E. Matthews, Esme Percy, Abraham Sofaer, Wil-
frid Hyde-White. Two ghosts are condemned to haunt a castle
until it is visited by royalty. -TVG.
GHOSTS OF ROME (I) Lux 1961 color 105m. (FANTASMI A
ROMA. GHOSTS IN ROME. PHANTOM LOVERS) D: Antonio
Pietrangeli. SP: Ennio Flaiano, Pietrangeli, Ettore Scola,
S. Amidei, R. Maccari. Ref: DDC III:118. FM 12:10. with
Marcello Mastroianni, Sandra Milo, Vittorio Gassman, Belinda
Lee, Eduardo de Filippo. Phantoms haunt old Roman palace.

GHOSTS OF TWO TRAVELLERS AT TENAMONYA   (J)   Toho 1967
(TENAMONYA YUREI DOCHU)   D: Shue Matsubayashi. Ref:
Unij.Bltn. 31. with Makoto Fujita, Yumiko Nogawa. Ghost story.
GHOSTS ON PARADE see SPOOK WARFARE
GHOSTS ON THE LOOSE Mono 1943 65m. (GHOSTS IN THE
NIGHT-Eng. EAST SIDE KIDS MEET BELA LUGOSI) D: William
Beaudine. SP: Kenneth Higgins. PH: Mack Stengler. Mus: Ed-
ward Kay. P: Sam Katzman, Jack Dietz. Ref: FM 24:6. COF
10:36. FIR'64:580. with Bela Lugosi, Ava Gardner, Rick
Vallin, Leo Gorcey, Huntz Hall, Bobby Jordan, Minerva Urecal,
Wheeler Oakman, Stanley Clements, Billy Benedict, Jack Mul-
hall, Frank Moran. Supposedly haunted house and "the Katz-
man mob. "
The GHOST'S WARNING Edison 1911 17m. Ref: Bios 2/1/12.
Girl's ghost haunts castle.
GHOST'S WARNING, A see GHOST STORY IN PASSAGE, A
The GHOUL (B) Gaum 1933 73m. D: T. Hayes Hunter. SP:
Rupert Downing. Screen story: Roland Pertwee, J. H. Turner.
From the book by Frank King and Leonard Hines. PH: Gunther
Krampf. Art D: Alfred Junge. Ass't D: R. Lyons, John Croy-
don. Ref: MW 9:41. RVB. PM. Pic: MW 8:26. FM 2:28,
31.12:25.44:19. See also NO PLACE LIKE HOMICIDE. with
Boris Karloff, Anthony Bushell, Dorothy Hyson, Cedric Hard-
wicke, Ernest Thesiger, Ralph Richardson, D. A. Clarke-Smith,
Harold Huth, Kathleen Harrison. Mad Egyptologist rises from
the dead.
GHOUL IN A GIRLS' DORMITORY see WEREWOLF IN A GIRLS'
DORMITORY
GHOUL IN SCHOOL, The see WEREWOLF IN A GIRLS' DORMI-
TORY
The GIANT BEHEMOTH (B) AA/Artistes Alliance 1959 79m.
(BEHEMOTH, SEA MONSTER. The BEHEMOTH) SP, D: Eugene
Lourie. Story: Allen Adler, Robert Abel. PH: Ken Hodges.
Mus sc & d: Edwin Astley. Art D: Harry White. SpFX: Jack
Rabin, Louis DeWitt, Irving Block, Willis O'Brien, Pete Robin-
son (or Petterson). Makeup: Jimmy Evans. Ref: FFacts. Orpheus
3:27. FM 11:6. ModM 3:2. with Gene Evans, Andre Morell,
Leigh Madison, Jack MacGowran, John Turner, Maurice Kauf-
mann, Henry Vidon. Atomic particles affect sea creatures,
create gigantic monster. Resolutely routine.
The GIANT CLAW Col/Clover 1957 76m. (MARK OF THE CLAW)
D: Fred F. Sears. SP: Samuel Newman, Paul Gangelin. PH:
Benjamin H. Kline. Mus D: Mischa Bakaleinikoff. P: Sam Katz-
man. Ref: FDY. with Mara Corday, Jeff Morrow, Morris Ankrum,
Edgar Barrier, Robert Shayne, Louis D. Merrill, Morgan Jones.
Earth menaced by huge, clumsy-looking bird.
GIANT FROM THE UNKNOWN Astor 1958 77m. PH, D: Richard
E. Cunha. SP: Frank Taussig, Ralph Brooke. Mus: Harold
Glasser. Makeup: Jack Pierce? Assoc P: Marc Frederic. Ref:
HR 3/13/58. Pic: FM 7:22. with Buddy Baer, Morris Ankrum,
Bob Steele, Edward Kemmer, Sally Fraser. Giant encased in rock
300 years revives. Not as bad as some of Astor's pictures, but
then again nothing is as bad as some of Astor's pictures.

The GIANT GILA MONSTER Hollywood Pictures/McLendon 1959
75m. Story, D: Ray Kellogg. SP: Jay Simms. PH: Wilfred
Cline. Mus sc & d: Jack Marshall. Sets, Art D: Louis Cald-
well. SpPhFX: Ralph Hammeras, Wee Risser. Sound FX:
Milton Citron, James Richard. Makeup: Corinne Daniel. P: Ken
Curtis. Ref: sply. with Don Sullivan, Lisa Simone, Shug Fisher,
Jerry Cortwright, Yolanda Salas, Stormy Meadows. Monster
film turns sappily sentimental at the worst times.
The GIANT LEECHES AI 1959 65m. (DEMONS OF THE SWAMP
-Eng. ATTACK OF THE GIANT LEECHES. ATTACK OF THE
BLOOD LEECHES) D: Bernard Kowalski. SP: Leo Gordon. PH:
John Nickolaus, Jr. Mus sc & d: Alexander Laszlo. Art D:
Daniel Haller. P: Gene Corman. Exec P: Roger Corman. Ref:
RVB. FM 2:19. Pic: FM 7:10. FMO 4:34. with Michael Emmet,
Ken Clark, Bruno VeSota, Yvette Vicker, Jan Shepard, Gene
Roth, Tyler McVey, Jody Fair. Big leeches amok in the Ever-
glades. A few crude BEAST FROM HAUNTED CAVE-like thrills
and enough plot for 65 minutes.
GIANT MANTIS, The see DEADLY MANTIS, The
GIANT OF METROPOLIS (I) 7A/Centro 1961('63-U.S.) Eastman-
color 92m. (GIGANTE DI METROPOLIS. IL MISTERIO DI AT-
LANTIDE) D: Umberto Scarpelli. SP: Emmimo Salvi, Sabatino
Ciuffino, O. Palella, A. Molteni, G. Stafford. (METROPOLIS)
PH: Mario Sens. Mus: A. Trovajoli. Art D: G. Giovannisti.
Ref: FEFN 6/61. Orpheus 3:30. Pic: SM 4:13. 6:10. FM 67:57.
with Gordon Mitchell, Bella Cortez, Liana Orfei, Furio Meniconi.
In the year 10,000 B.C. a band of men attempts to reach
Metropolis. The effects and gimmicks aren't enough to save this
mess.
GIANT OF THE LOST TOMB see ATLAS AGAINST THE CZAR
GIANT OF THE VALLEY OF KINGS see SON OF SAMSON
GIANT YMIR, The see 20 MILLION MILES TO EARTH
GIANT'S CHALLENGE, The see CHALLENGE OF THE GIANT, The
GIANTS OF ROME (I-F) Devon/Radius/N.C. 1963 color (LES
GEANTS DE ROME, I GIGANTI DI ROMA-I. FORT ALESIA)
D: Antonio Margheriti (Anthony Dawson). SP: Martino, Castaldi.
PH: Fausto Zuccoli. Mus: Carlo Rustichelli. Ref: TVFFSB.
Ital P'64. TVG. with Richard Harrison, Ettore Manni,
Wandisa Guida, Renato Baldini, Piero Lulli, Philippe Hersent.
Caesar's most courageous legionnaires set out to destroy a
secret enemy weapon ("a colossal catapult").
GIANTS OF THESSALY (I-F) Medallion-TV/Alexandra-Lyre 1959
Eastmancolor/scope 82m. (I GIGANTI DELLA TESSAGLIA or
GLI ARGONAUTI-I. LE GEANT DE THESSALIE-F. The
ARGONAUTS) D: Riccardo Freda. SP: Masini, De Concini.
Mus: Carlo Rustichelli. Ref: Ital P'60. with Roland Carey, Ziva
Rodann, Moira Orfei, Massimo Girotti, Alberto Farnese. Witch,
flesh-eating monster.
GIBEL SENSATSY see LOSS OF SENSATION
GIFT OF GAB Univ 1934 70m. D: Karl Freund. SP:Rian James.
Lou Breslow, Story:Jerry Wald, Philip G. Epstein. PH: George
Robinson, Harold Wenstrom. Ref: FDY. with Boris Karloff
("The Phantom" in skit), Bela Lugosi, Edmund Lowe, Sterling

Holloway, Gloria Stuart, Roger Pryor, Binne Barnes, Andy De-
vine, Paul Lukas, Alexander Woollcott, Chester Morris, Ruth
Etting, Phil Baker, Victor Moore, Henry Armetta, Wini Shaw,
Edwin Maxwell, Douglas Fowley.
GIGANTE DI METROPOLIS see GIANT OF METROPOLIS
GIGANTES INTERPLANETARIOS see PLANETARY GIANTS
GIGANTES PLANETARIOS see PLANETARY GIANTS
GIGANTI DELLA TESSAGLIA, I see GIANTS OF THESSALY
GIGANTI DI ROMA, I see GIANTS OF ROME
GIGANTIS, THE FIRE MONSTER (J) WB/Toho 1955('59-U.S.)
    78m. (GOJIRA NO GYAKUSHU. GODZILLA'S COUNTERATTACK.
    THE RETURN OF GODZILLA. THE VOLCANO MONSTER.
    GODZILLA RAIDS AGAIN. COUNTERATTACK OF THE MONSTER)
    D: Motoyoshi Oda (or Odo); (U.S.-Hugo Grimaldi). SP:Takeo
    Murata, S. Hidaka. Story: S. Kayama. PH:S. Endo. SpPhFX:
    Akira Watanabe, H. Mukoyama, M. Shirota. Ref: FFacts. FM
    28:16.Orpheus 3:27. with Hiroshi Koizumi, Setsuko Wakayama,
    Mindru Chiaki.   Toho's least?
GILALA see X FROM OUTER SPACE, The
GILDERSLEEVE'S GHOST RKO 1944 63m. D: Gordon Douglas.
    SP: Robert E. Kent. PH: Jack Mackenzie. Mus: C. Bakaleinikoff.
    Art D: Albert D'Agostino, Carroll Clark. Ref: FDY. TVK. with
    Harold Peary, Marion Martin, Rich LeGrand, Amelita Ward,
    Freddie Mercer, Emory Parnell, Frank Reicher, Joseph Vitale,
    Margie Stewart. Haunted house, gorilla, invisible woman, mad
    scientist.
GILL WOMAN, The see VOYAGE TO THE PLANET OF PRE-
    HISTORIC WOMEN
GILL-WOMEN OF VENUS, The see VOYAGE TO THE PLANET
    OF PREHISTORIC WOMEN
GINDA JUMON see GHOST MURDERER
The GIRL AND THE DEVIL (Swedish) Scandia/Terra 1943 88m.
    (FLICKAN OCH DJAVULEN) D: Erik Faustman. Ref: S&S'46:30.
    Sweden I. with Hilda Borgström, Anders Ek. Witch, devil,
    satanism.
GIRL FROM BENEATH THE SEA see NIGHT TIDE
GIRL FROM 5000 A.D., The see TERROR FROM THE YEAR
    5000
The GIRL FROM SCOTLAND YARD Para 1937 62m. D: Robert
    Vignola. SP: Doris Anderson, Dore Schary. Story: Coningsby
    Dawson. Based on a character in Edgar Wallace's novel "The
    Square Emerald." PH: Robert Pittack. Ref: FD 6/4/37. FIR'67:
    77. TVK. with Karen Morley, Eduardo Ciannelli, Robert Bald-
    win, Katherine Alexander, Milli Monti, Lloyd Crane, Bud Flanagan,
    Lynn Anders. Madman invents radio-death-ray.
GIRL IN HIS POCKET (F) 7A-TV/Madeleine Films-SNEG-Contact
    1957 82m. (UN AMOUR DE POCHE. NUDE IN HIS POCKET)
    D: Pierre Kast. SP: France Roche, from the short story "The
    Diminishing Draft" by Waldemar Kaempffert. PH: Ghislain Cloquet.
    Mus: Marc Lanjean. Ref: FM 27:17. TVG. La Prod.Cin.Fr'57.
    with Jean Marais, Genevieve Page, Jean-Claude Brialy. Biology
    professor finds he can shrink people. Uninspired comedy.
GIRL IN ICE see DEVIL'S MESSENGER, The

The GIRL IN THE KREMLIN   81m.   D: Russell Birdwell.   SP:
Gene L. Coon, Robert Hill.   Story: DeWitt Bodeen, Harry Rus-
kin.   PH: Carl Guthrie.   Art D: Alexander Golitzen, Eric Orbom.
P: Albert Zugsmith.   Ref: FDY.   with Lex Barker, Zsa Zsa
Gabor, Maurice Manson, Jeffrey Stone, William Schallert, Aram
Katcher, Norbert Schiller, Kurt Katch, Gabor Curtiz.   Stalin's
face is transformed by plastic surgery. -TVG.
GIRL IN THE MOON   (G)   UFA   1929('31-U.S.) 120m. (FRAU IM
MOND.   BY ROCKET TO THE MOON)   Sequence in MAN IN
SPACE.   (WOMAN IN THE MOON) SP,D: Fritz Lang.   SP: also
Thea von Harbou.   PH: Kurt Courant, Oskar Fischinger, Otto
Kanturek.   Mus: Willy Schmidt-Gentner.   Art D: Otto Hunte, Emil
Hasler, Karl Vollbrecht.   SpFX: Konstantin Tschetwerikoff.   Tech-
nical consultants: Hermann Oberth,Willy Ley.   Ref: Imagen. Pic:
SM 1:3:46. 4:46. 5:23.   with Gerda Maurus, Willy Fritsch, Gustav
von Wangenheim, Klaus Pohl, Margaret Kuper.   The story of
the construction of a rocket and its voyage to the moon, the
construction more interesting than the voyage, which seems
trivial after the impressive beginning.   Very minor Lang. (Bit
with magazine, "Mond-Vampire").
The GIRL OF THE NILE   (G-U.S.)   UFA Int'l/Sidney Pink   1967
color D: Joe Lacy.   Ref: M/TVM 6/67. with Rory Calhoun, James
Philbrook, Nuria Torrey.   "Curse of ancient gods is visited on
members of an expedition to the desert."
The GIRL OF TIN   (I)   Scetr Film   1970   color 95m.   (LA
RAGAZZA DI LATTI.   The TIN GIRL)   D: Marcello Aliprandi.
SP: Aliprandi, F. Imbert, from a story by F. Leherissay.   PH:
G. De Giovanni.   Ref: V 7/28/71.   M/TVM 8/70.   with Sydne,
Roberto Antonelli, S. Rome.   Doctor Smack dominates the world;
robot girl; robot factory.
The GIRL UNDER THE SHEET   (I)   M. G.   Cine   1961 (La RAGAZ-
ZA SOTTO IL LENZUOLO)   D: M. Girolami.   Ref: FEFN 2/61.
with Chelo Alonso, Walter Chiari.   Ghosts.
The GIRL WHO DARED   Rep 1944 D: Howard Bretherton. SP:
John K. Butler.   From the book "Blood on Her Shoe" by Medora
Field.   PH: Bud Thackery.   Mus D: Morton Scott.   Art D: Russ
Kimball.   56m.   Ref: V 10/25/44.   MPH.   FDY.   with Lorna
Gray, Kirk Alyn, Veda Ann Borg, Grant Withers, Roy Barcroft,
John Hamilton, Willie Best, Peter Cookson, Vivian Oakland,
Tom London.   Ghost party, storm, secret panels, trap doors.
GIRL WHO STOLE THE EIFFEL TOWER, The see PARIS WHEN
IT SIZZLES
GIRLS OF SPIDER ISLAND   see   HORRORS OF SPIDER ISLAND
GIRLY   (B)   Cinerama 1970 Eastmancolor 101m.   (MUMSY,
NANNY, SONNY AND GIRLY)   D: Freddie Francis.   SP: Brian
Comfort, from a play by Maisie Mosco.   PH: David Muir.   Mus:
Bernard Ebbinghouse.   Art D: Maggie Pinhorn.   Ref: Film Bltn.
3/9/70.   with Ursula Howells, Michael Bryant, Pat Heywood,
Vanessa Howard, Robert Swann, Michael Ripper. Murder games
in "spooky" Gothic mansion.
GIVE US THE MOON   (B) Gainsborough 1944   D: Val Guest. Ref:
SF Film.   with Jean Simmons, Margaret Lockwood.   Vision of
postwar London.

The GLADIATOR   Col 1938 72m. D: Edward Sedgwick. SP:
   Charlie Melson, Arthur Sheekman, from a novel by Philip Wylie.
   Adap: James Mulhauser, Earle Snell. Add'l Dial: George Marion,
   Jr. PH: George Schneiderman. Mus D: Victor Young. Art D:
   Albert D'Agostino. Ref: MFB'38:238. FDY. COF 10:38. with
   Joe E. Brown, June Travis, Man Mountain Dean, Dickie Moore,
   Lucien Littlefield, Robert Kent. Professor develops a serum
   which gives a man great strength.
The GLADIATORS (Swedish) Sandrews 1969 Eastmancolor
   (GLADIATORERNA. The PEACE GAME)   D: Peter Watkins. SP:
   Watkins, Nicholas Gosling. PH: Peter Suschitzky. SpFX: Stig
   Lindberg. Narr: Keith Bradfield. Ref: F&F 3/70. with Arthur
   Pentelow, Frederick Danner. International Peace Games held in
   effort to avert world war.
GLAMIS CASTLE (B) 1926 short (HAUNTED CASTLES series)
   D: Maurice Elvey. Ref: Brit.Cinema. V 2/24/26.
GLEN AND RANDA   UMC 1971 94m. D: Jim McBride. SP:
   Lorenzo Mans, Rudolph Wurlitzer, McBride. PH: Alan Raymond.
   Art D: Gary Weist. Ref: LA Times 5/19/71. with Steven Curry,
   Shelley Plimpton, Garry Goodrow. Set in future after nuclear
   holocaust.
GLEN OR GLENDA Weiss 1953 (I LED TWO LIVES. TRANSVES-
   TITE. I CHANGED MY SEX. JAIL BAIT) SP,D: Edward D.
   Wood, Jr. Ref: FJA. FM 2:53. 41:23. FIR'64:580. WFC 3:53.
   with Bela Lugosi, Lyle Talbot, Dolores Fuller, Charles Crofts,
   Conrad Brooks, Daniel Davis. Lugosi, among skulls and skeletons,
   talks about mysticism.
GLI AMORI DI ERCOLE see LOVES OF HERCULES, The
GLI ARGONAUTI see GIANTS OF THESSALY
GLI ARTIGLI INVISIBILI DEL DR. MABUSE see INVISIBLE DR.
   MABUSE, The
GLI INVINCIBILI FRATELLI MACISTE see INVINCIBLE BROTHERS
   MACISTE, The
A GLIMPSE OF BYGONE DAYS (G) silent short Ref: FM 19:36. 63:
   28. Prehistory.
GLORIOUS TIMES IN THE SPESSART (W.G.) Constantin 1967
   color 105m. (HERRLICHE ZEITEN IM SPESSART. SPESSART
   ROCKETS) Third in the "Spessart" series. D: Kurt Hoffmann.
   SP: Guenter Neumann. PH: Richard Angst. Mus: Franz Grothe.
   Art D: Werner & Isabella Schlichting. Ref: V 11/8/67. M/TVM
   1/68. with Liselotte Pulver, Harald Leipnitz, Hans Richter,
   Kathrin Ackermann, Willy Millowitsch. Astronauts, rockets, &
   space ships.
GLORY OF LOVE, The (by Pan) see WHILE PARIS SLEEPS
GLOWIE CASTLE (story by E. Keoun) see GHOST GOES WEST,
   The
GO AND GET IT Neilan 1920 75m. D: Marshall Neilan, Henry
   Symonds. SP: Marion Fairfax. Ref: Lee. NYT 7/19/20. Pic:
   FM 52:50. with Pat O'Malley, Wesley Barry, Noah Beery, Bull
   Montana (gorilla). Dead convict's brain put into gorilla.
The GOD OF VENGEANCE Chariot 1914 60m. Ref: MPW 20:130.
   Lee. "Weird...East Indian sect of idol worshipers" out to "avenge
   their God. "

The GOD SNAKE (I) Arco Film 1970 color/scope (The SERPENT
GOD) D: Piero Vivarelli. Ref: M/TVM 9/70. V 5/12/71:39.
Voodoo and magic in the Caribbean. (IL DIO SERPENTE)
The GODDESS Vita 1915 serial 15 episodes D: Ralph Ince. Ref:
CNW. with Anita Stewart, Earle Williams, Paul Scardon. Girl
under the spell of a hypnotist.
GODDESS OF THE SEA (F?) Le Lion 1909 14m. Ref: MPW
'09:737. Bios 11/4/09. Shepherd trying to escape from goddess
drowns.
GODS AND THE DEAD, The see OF GODS AND THE DEAD
GODS HATE KANSAS, The (by J. Millard) see THEY CAME FROM
BEYOND SPACE
GOD'S WITNESS Than-Mutual 1915 50m. Ref: MPN 5/29/15. with
Florence La Badie, Morris Foster, Harris Gordon. Bolt of
lightning "photographs" death scene on pane of glass.
GODZILLA, KING OF THE MONSTERS (J) Embassy/Jewel/Toho
1954('56-U.S.) (GOJIRA) D: Inoshiro Honda (U.S.
version-Terry Morse). SP: Honda, Takeo Murata. PH:
Masao Tamai, Guy Roe. Mus: Akira Ifukube. SpFX: Eiji
Tsuburaya. Ref: FM 30:48. Pic: FM 9:15. with Raymond
Burr, Akira Takarada, Momoko Kochi, Takashi Shimura, S.
Sakai. From a story by S. Kayama. First of Toho's big-beast
films; otherwise unremarkable.
GODZILLA-DER DRACHE AUS DEM DSCHUNGEL see GAMERA
VS. BARUGON
GODZILLA RAIDS AGAIN see GIGANTIS
GODZILLA TAI MOTHRA see GODZILLA VS. THE THING
GODZILLA VS. THE GIANT MOTH see GODZILLA VS. THE
THING
GODZILLA VS. THE SEA MONSTER (J) Cont/Toho 1966 color/
scope 85m. (NANKAI NO DAI KETTO. BIG DUEL IN THE NORTH
SEA. EBIRAH, HORROR OF THE DEEP. FRANKENSTEIN UND
DIE UNGEHEUER AUS DEM MEER-G) D: Jun Fukuda. SP: S.
Sekizawa. SpFX: Eiji Tsuburaya. Ref: V. MMF 18-19:15. Pic:
FM 48:8. with Akira Takarada, Toru Watanabe. Godzilla,
Mothra, and Ebirah, a giant shrimp, meet.
GODZILLA VS. THE THING (J) AI/Toho 1964 Eastmancolor/
scope 90m. (MOSURA TAI GOJIRA. GODZILLA TAI MOTHRA.
GODZILLA VS. THE GIANT MOTH. MOTHRA VS. GODZILLA)
D: I. Honda. SP: S. Sekizawa. PH: Hajime Koizumi. Mus:
Akira Ifukube. Art D: Takeo Kita. SpFX D: Eiji Tsuburaya.
SpFX PH: S. Arikawa, M. Tomioka. SpFX Art D: Akira Watan-
abe. Ref: FFacts. Orpheus 3:33. with Akira Takarada, Yuriko
Hoshi, Hiroshi Koizumi, Yu Fujiki. Godzilla and Mothra meet.
GODZILLA'S COUNTERATTACK see GIGANTIS
GODZIRA NO MUSUKO see SON OF GODZILLA
GOE TAM see FANTASTIC GHOST STORY, A
GOG UA 1954 (3-D) color 85m. (GOG, THE KILLER) D:
Herbert L. Strock. SP: Tom Taggart. Story,P: Ivan Tors. PH:
Lothrop B. Worth. Ref: FDY. FM 14:42. Pic: FM 15:22. with
Richard Egan, Herbert Marshall, Constance Dowling, William
Schallert, John Wengraf, Philip Van Zandt. Machine tries to
sabotage missile base. Slow-moving, gadget-obsessed s-f.

GOGOLA (India) Indradhanush 1965 D: Balwant Dave. Ref:
M/TVM 6/65. with Azad, Tabassum. Sea monster terrorizes
Bombay.
GOJIRA see GODZILLA
GOJIRA NO GYAKUSHU see GIGANTIS
GOKE, BODY SNATCHER FROM HELL (J) Shochiku 1968 color/
scope 84m. (KYUKETSUKI GOKEMIDORO. G THE VAMPIRE)
D: Hajime Sato. SP: Susumu Takaku, K. Kobayashi. PH: Shizuo
Hirase. Mus: S. Kikuchi. Art D: T. Yoshino. Ref: UFQ 42.
M/TVM 9/68. with Hideo Ko, Teruo Yoshida, Tomomi Sato,
E. Kitamura, Masaya Takahashi. Creature from flying saucer
kills plane passengers, drinks their blood.
GOLD (G) UFA 1934 D: Karl Hartl. SP: Rolf E. Vanloo. PH:
Gunther Rittau, Otto Baecker, Werner Bohne. Mus: Hans-Otto
Borgmann. Sets: Otto Hunte. Ref: Imagen. Pic: FM 16:14.
DDC III:18. with Brigitte Helm, Michael Bohnen, Hans Albers,
Ernst Karchow, L. Dyers, F. Kayssler. Transmutation of lead
into gold.
GOLD (French version of above) UFA 1934 D: Serge de Poligny.
with Pierre Blanchar, Helm, Line Noro, Jacques Dumesnil,
Roger Karl, M. Fouchet.
GOLD AND LEAD (F) 1966 (L'OR ET LE PLOMB) D: Alain
Cuniot. From "Le Monde Comme Il Va" by Voltaire. PH: Y. Le
Masson. Mus: Michel Legrand. Ref: COF 10:48. F&F 10/66.
Bianco 7-8/66:124. La Prod. Cin. Fr. 9/65. with Cuniot, Em-
manuelle Riva, M. P. Fouchet, Jean Massin. Man from another
planet arrives to determine whether or not earth is worth saving.
GOLD BUG, The (by E. A. Poe) see MANFISH/RAVEN, The (1912)
The GOLDEN ARROW (I) MGM/Titanus 1962('64-U.S.) Techni-
color/scope 91m. (LA FRECCIA D'ORO) D: Antonio Margheriti.
SP: B. Vailati, A. Frassineti, Filippo Sanjust, G. Prosperi, G.
Arlorio. SP, D: (U.S.): George Higgins III. PH: Gabor Pogany.
Mus sc: Mario Nascimbene. Art D: F. Mogherini. SpFX:
Technicolor Italiana. Ref: Boxo 5/11/64. FFacts. with Tab
Hunter, Rossana Podesta, Renato Baldini, Dominique Boschero,
Gloria Milland. Monster, magic arrow, genii, magic carpet.
GOLDEN BAT (J) Toei 1966 color (OGON BATTO) D: Hajime
Sato. Based on the comic strip. Ref: Unij. Bltn. M/TVM 4/67.
with Shinichi Chiba, Wataru Yamakawa, H. Tsukuba. Golden
Batman awakes from a 10,000-year sleep.
The GOLDEN BEETLE (F) Pathe 1907 3m. Ref: SilentFF. The
"golden beetle" orders a magician to be consumed in the flames
of a brazier.
The GOLDEN BEETLE (I) Cines/Kleine c1911 60m. (LE
SCARABEE D'OR-F) Ref: Lee. DDC II:68. Killer with dual per-
sonality.
GOLDEN HANDS OF KURIGAL see FEDERAL AGENTS VS. UNDER-
WORLD, INC.
The GOLDEN MISTRESS UA 1954 82m. SP, D: Joel Judge. SP:
also Lew Hewitt. Technicolor PH: William C. Thompson. Mus:
Raoul Kraushaar. Ref: FDY. COF 10:38. with John Agar,
Rosemarie Bowe, Abner Biberman, Andre Marcisse. Voodoo
curse kills man who steals idol.

The GOLDEN POMEGRANATES (B) Stoll 1924 37m. (Further
Mysteries of Dr. Fu-Manchu series) Adap, P:Fred Paul. Based
on the character created by Sax Rohmer. PH:Frank Canham.
Art D: Walter W. Murton. Ref: SilentFF. with Harry Agar
Lyons, Paul, Humbertson Wright.

The GOLDEN SUPPER Biog 1910 Ref: MPN 13:1923. with Dorothy
West, Edwin August, Charles H. West. Girl, Camilla, in coma
buried as dead.

GOLDEN TREASURE, The see TINTIN & THE MYSTERY OF THE
GOLDEN FLEECE

GOLDFACE, THE FANTASTIC SUPERMAN (I-SP) Cineproduzioni /
Balcazar 1966 color /scope (GOLDFACE, IL FANTASTICO
SUPERMAN-I) D: Stanley Mitchell. SP: Balcazar, Molteni,
Fasan. PH: Carlo Fiore. Mus: Piero Umiliani. Ref: Ital P'67.
with Robert Anthony, Evy Mirandi, Micaela Pignatelli, Hugo
Pimentel, Big Mattews, Leontine May. Goldface assisted by
Lotario, "a huge half breed of Herculean strength."

GOLDFINGER (B) UA /Eon 1964 Technicolor 108m. D: Guy
Hamilton. SP: Paul Dehn, Richard Maibaum, from the novel
by Ian Fleming. PH: Ted Moore. Mus: John Barry. SpFX:
John Stears; ass't: Frank George. Ed: Peter Hunt. Ref: FFacts.
Pic: ModM 2:23. with Sean Connery, Gert Frobe, Honor Black-
man, Shirley Eaton, Harold Sakata, Bernard Lee, Austin Willis,
Lois Maxwell, Martin Benson, Bill Nagy, Nadja Regin, Varley
Thomas. Paralyzing gas; laser ray. One of the better James
Bond films.

GOLDSNAKE "KILLERS COMPANY" (I-F) Seven /Alexandra /Paris
Cannes 1966 color /scope (GOLDSNAKE "ANONIMA KILLERS")
D: Ferdinando Baldi. SP: Baldi, M. D. C. Martinez. PH: E.
F. Mallt. Ref: Ital P. with Stanley Kent, Yoko Tani, Annabella
Incontrera, Juan Cortes. "Atomic formula with which bombs of
a very small size can be made." Mus: C. Savina.

GOLDTOWN GHOST RIDERS Col 1953 59m. D: George Archain-
baud. SP: Gerald Geraghty. PH: William Bradford. Art D:
George Brooks. Mus: Mischa Bakaleinikoff. Ref: MFB. with Gene
Autry, Smiley Burnette, Gail Davis, Carleton Young, Kirk Riley.
Fake and real "ghost riders."

The GOLEM (G) Hawk /Bioscop 1914 (DER GOLEM UND WIE ER
AUF DIE WELT KAM. The MONSTER OF FATE-U.S. ALRAUNE
AND THE GOLEM?) D: Paul Wegener, Henrik Galeen. PH:
Guido Seeber. Art D: R. A. Dietrich, R. Gliese. Ref: Clarens.
MMF 13. MW 8:40.9:46: From the book by Gustav Meyrink.
DDC I:299. Pic: DDC I:57. with Wegener, Carl Ebert, Lyda
Salmonova. Tale of the legendary man of stone.

The GOLEM (Danish) 1916 D: Urban Gad. Ref: Film 9/67.

The GOLEM (G) UFA 1920 97m. (DER GOLEM, WIE ER IN
DIE WELT KAN) D: Paul Wegener, Carl Boese. SP: Wegener,
Henrik Galeen. PH: Karl Freund. Sets: Han Poelzig, Kurt
Richter. Costumes: Rochus Gliese. Ass't PH: Edgar G. Ulmer.
Ref: MMF. MW 8:42. EncicDS IX:1880. Pic: FM 7:8.16:29.28.
48. TBG. MW 10:45. with Wegener, Lyda Salmonova, Hans
Sturm, Lothar Muthel. Fairly interesting; but the sets are too
much the main thing. (The rock formations and tortuous stone

staircases are, and deserve to be, the real star.) And the acting
is silent-movie style.
The GOLEM (F-Cz) A-B/Metropolis 1935 (The LEGEND OF
   PRAGUE-Eng) Sequence in DR. TERROS'S HOUSE OF HORRORS
   (1943). SP,D: Julien Duvivier. SP: also Andre Paul-Antoine.
   PH: Vich, Stalich. Sets: Andreiev, Kopecky. Ref: FD 3/24/37.
   DDC I:48,191. with Harry Baur, Raymond Aimos, Roger Karl,
   Jany Holt, Gaston Jacquet. (LE GOLEM)
The GOLEM (F) ORTF 1966 (MASK OF THE GOLEM) D: Jean
   Kerchbron. SP: Kerchbron, Louis Pauwels. From the book by
   Gustav Meyrink. PH: Albert Schimel. Mus: Jean Wiéner. Art
   D: J. Gourmelin, A. Nègre. Makeup: R.Simon. Ref: MMF 15-16:
   14. Pic: FM 46:45. with André Reybaz (the golem), Pierre
   Tabard, Michel Etchevery. (LE GOLEM)
The GOLEM AND THE DANCING GIRL (G) Bioscop 1917 (DER
   GOLEM UND DIE TANZERIN) D: Paul Wegener. Ref: Clarens.
   with Wegener.
GOLEM AND THE EMPEROR'S BAKER, The see EMPEROR &
   THE GOLEM, The
The GOLEM'S LAST ADVENTURE (Austrian) Sascha-Film 1921
   (DES GOLEMS LETZTES ABENTEUER. DER DORFGOLEM) D:
   Julius Szomogyi. Ref: Osterr.
GOLIAT CONTRA LOS GIGANTES see GOLIATH AND THE GIANTS
GOLIATH AND THE BARBARIANS (I) AI/Alta Vista/Standard 1959
   Eastmancolor/scope 88m. (IL TERRORE DI BARBARI) D:
   Carlo Campogalliani. SP: G. Mangini, N. Stresa, G. Taffarel,
   Campogalliani. PH: Alberto Albertini. Mus (Ital): Carlo
   Innocenzi; (Amer) Les Baxter. Makeup: Romolo de Martino. Ref:
   FFacts. COF 10:39. with Steve Reeves, Chelo Alonso, Bruce
   Cabot,Arturo Dominici, Furio Meniconi, Andrea Checchi (Gori),
   G. Scotti. Giants, monsters.
GOLIATH AND THE DRAGON (I) AI 1961 color/scope 90m.
   (LA VENDETTA DI ERCOLE. VENGEANCE OF HERCULES) D:
   Vittorio Cottafavi. SP: M. Piccolo, Archibald Zounds, Jr. PH:
   Mario Montuori. Mus: Les Baxter. Ref: FFacts. with Mark
   For(r)est, Broderick Crawford, Phil(l)ipe Hersent, Eleanora
   Ruffo, Gaby Andre. See the blood diamond rise into the air!
   (on a string). Thrill to the bat-creature! (that looks like a teddy
   bear). Hear the horses' hoof-beats! (long after the horses have
   stopped).
GOLIATH AND THE GIANTS (I-Sp) Medallion-TV/Procusa-Filmar
   1962 color 100m. (GOLIAT CONTRA LOS GIGANTES-Sp)
   D: Guido Malatesta. PH: Alejandro Ulloa. SP: G. Parolini, G.
   Simonelli, Arpad de Riso, C. Seccia, Sergio Sollima. Ref:
   Maltin. TVG. with Brad Harris, Gloria Milland, Fernando
   Rey, Jose Rubio. Sea creatures; Amazons.
GOLIATH AND THE VAMPIRES (I) AI/Ambrosiana 1961('64-U.S.)
   Technicolor/scope 92m. (MACISTE CONTRO IL VAMPIRO-I.
   MACISTE CONTRE LE FANTOME-F. The VAMPIRES. GOLIATH
   AND THE ISLAND OF VAMPIRES. MACISTE AGAINST THE
   VAMPIRES. MACHISTE VS. THE VAMPIRES) D: Sergio Cor-
   bucci, Giacomo Gentilomo. SP: Corbucci, Duccio Tessari. PH:
   Alvaro Mancori. Mus: A. Lavagnino. Exec P: Dino De Laurentiis.

Ref: M/TVM 10/68. MadM 9:3. Orpheus 3:30. FanMo 2:63.
with Gordon Scott, Jacques Sernas, Gianna Maria Canale, Leonora
Ruffo, Edy Vessel. "The Vampire" transforms men into robot-
like creatures.

GONKS GO BEAT (B) Anglo-Amalgamated/Titan 1965 Eastman-
color 92m. D: Robert Hartford-Davis. SP: Jimmy Watson.
Based on a story by Hartford-Davis and Peter Newbrook. PH:
Newbrook. Ref: MFB'65:136. with Kenneth Connor, Frank
Thornton, Barbara Brown, Reginald Beckwith. The Great Galaxian
sends Wilco Rogers to earth to bring peace between Beatland and
Balladisle.

GOODY-GOODY JONES Selig 1912 8m. Ref: MPW 12:1058.
Pill makes man chase woman.

GOOFY GHOSTS Para-Christie Comedy 1928 silent D: Harold
Beaudine. Story: Sig Herzig. Ref: Lee. LC.

GORATH (J) Col/Toho 1962 color/scope 89m. (YOSEI GORASU)
D: Inoshiro Honda. SP: Takeshi Kimura. PH:Hajime Koizumi.
SpFX: Eiji Tsuburaya. Ref: UFQ 12. FM 28:18. SM 6:2,8. with
Ryo Ikebe, Jun Tazaki, Akihiko Hirata, Yumi Shirakawa, Takashi
Shimura, K. Mizano. In 1980 star-planet Gorath approaches
earth and melting snows unleash a prehistoric monster.

GORGO (B) MGM/King Bros. 1961 Technicolor 76m. (THE
NIGHT THE WORLD SHOOK) D: Eugene Lourie. SP: John
Loring, Daniel Hyatt. PH: F. A. Young. Mus: Angelo Lavag-
nino. SpFX: Tom Howard. Ref: FFacts. Pic: FM 11:24. with
Bill Travers, William Sylvester, Martin Benson, Bruce Seton,
Barry Keegan, Basil Dignam, Maurice Kaufmann, Thomas Duggan.
Prehistoric monster follows offspring to London. So-so.

The GORGON (B) Col/Hammer 1964 Technicolor 83m. D:
Terence Fisher. SP: John Gilling. PH: Michael Reed. Mus:
James Bernard. Art D: Bernard Robinson, Don Mingaye. SpFX:
Syd Pearson. Makeup: Roy Ashton. Ref: FFacts. with Barbara
Shelley, Christopher Lee, Peter Cushing, Richard Pasco, Michael
Goodliffe. Mere sight of monster turns villagers of Vandorf to
stone. Chilling atmosphere, but the story never develops.

The GORILLA F Nat 1927 80m. silent P,D: Alfred Santell. SP:
Al Cohn, James T. O'Donohoe, Henry McCarty. Titles: Al Boasberg, Sidney Lazarus. PH: Arthur Edeson. Ref: FDY. AFI.
with Charlie Murray, Claude Gillingwater, Walter Pidgeon, F.
Kelsey, Alice Day, Tully Marshall, Gaston Glass. From the play
by Ralph Spence. Gorilla loose in old mansion.

The GORILLA F Nat 1930 70m. sound D: Bryan Foy. SP:
B. Harrison Orkow, Herman Ruby. Ed: George Amy. PH:Sid
Hickox. From the play by Ralph Spence. Ref: Clarens. AFI.
with Walter Pidgeon, Roscoe Karns, Lila Lee, Joe Frisco, Harry
Gribbon, Purnell Pratt, Edwin Maxwell.

The GORILLA Fox 1939 59m. D: Allan Dwan. SP: Rian James,
Sid Silvers, from the play by Ralph Spence. PH: Edward Cron-
jager. Mus: David Buttolph. Art D: Richard Day, Lewis Creber.
Ref: PM. MFB'39:115. with Al, Harry, and Jimmy Ritz, Anita
Louise, Patsy Kelly, Lionel Atwill, Bela Lugosi, Joseph Calleia,
Edward Norris, Wally Vernon, Paul Harvey. Gorilla, "me-
chanical monster," secret passages, sliding panels.

GORILLA see APE, The
GORILLA AT LARGE Fox 1954 (3-D)/Panoramic/Technicolor 93m.
D: Harmon Jones. SP: L. Praskins, B. Slater. PH: Lloyd
Ahern. Mus D: Lionel Newman. Ref: "Horror"-V 5/5/54. with
Lee J. Cobb, Lee Marvin, Cameron Mitchell, Raymond Burr,
Anne Bancroft, Charlotte Austin, Warren Stevens. Murderous ape
on the loose in carnival. Bad all around. Leaves more loose
ends dangling than an explosion in a tinsel factory.
The GORILLA OF SOHO (W.G.) Constantin 1968 (Der GORILLA
VON SOHO) D: Alfred Vohrer. SP: Freddy Gregor. From the
works of Edgar Wallace. PH: Karl Löb. Ref: M/TVM 3/69.
Lee. German Film News. Filmkritik 9/68. with Horst Tappert,
Uschi Glas, Uwe Friedrichsen, Ilse Page. Killer disguised as
gorilla.
GORUNMIYEN ADAM ISTANBULDA see INVISIBLE MAN IN
ISTANBUL, The
GORY CREATURES, The see TERROR IS A MAN
GRAB DES DOKTOR CALIGARI, Das see MYSTERIES OF BLACK
MAGIC
GRAF VON CAGLIOSTRO, Der see CAGLIOSTRO (1920)
GRAFT Univ 1915 serial 20 episodes D: Richard Stanton. Ref:
CNW. MPN 13:876. with Robert Henley, Harry D. Carey,
Nanine Wright. Man who appears to be dead returns to life.
GRAND DUEL IN MAGIC (J) AI-TV/Toei 1967 86m. (MAGIC
SERPENT-TV. FROGGO AND DROGGO) D: Tetsuya Yamauchi.
SP: Masaru Igami. PH: Motonari Washio. Ref: J. Films'68.
MMF 18-19:15. TVFFSB. Pic: FM 48:9. with Hiroki Matsukata,
T. Ogawa, R. Otomo, B. Amatsu. Giant eagle; men transformed
into giant monsters battle each other.
GRANDFATHER FROST see JACK FROST
GRANDFATHER'S PILLS (F) Pathe 1908 9m. Ref: SilentFF.
MPW'08:532. Chemist's pills make grandchild strong, grand-
father young.
GRANT, POLICE REPORTER Kalem 1916 series D: Robert
Ellis. Ref: MPN 15:930,1259. MPW 31:738. with George Larkin,
Harry Gordon. Blinding ray; "micaphone" to listen to safe's
combination.
The GRASPING HAND (F) 1915 35m. (La MAIN QUI ETREINT.
MAX ET LA MAIN QUI ETREINT. MAX AND THE CLUTCHING
HAND) D: Louis Gasnier. Ref: FIR '65:282. DDC II:315. III:230.
with Max Linder. Ghost.
GRAVE ROBBERS (Mex) c1967 (PROFANADORES DES TUMBES)
Ref: Glut. with Santo, Gina Roland, Jorge Peral, Mario Orea.
GRAVE ROBBERS FROM OUTER SPACE see PLAN 9 FROM
OUTER SPACE
GRAVESIDE STORY, The see COMEDY OF TERRORS, The
GRAY DAME, The see GREY LADY, The
The GRAY HORROR Lubin 1915 40m. Ref: MPW 24:957. MPN
5/8/15. LC. Barrister and ward haunted by "frightful appari-
tion" in old mansion.
The GREAT ALASKAN MYSTERY Univ 1944 serial 13 episodes
(The GREAT NORTHERN MYSTERY) D: Ray Taylor, Lewis D.
Collins. SP: Maurice Tombragel, G. H. Plympton. PH:

William Sickner. Story: J. Foley. Ref: Academy. Pic: STI 5:
19. SM 5:11. with Ralph Morgan, Milburn Stone, Fuzzy Knight,
Marjorie Weaver, Edgar Kennedy, Samuel S. Hinds, Martin
Kosleck, Joseph Crehan, Anthony Warde, Jay Novello, Jack
Ingram, George Chesebro, Gibson Gowland. Peratron ray destroys
aircraft.

The GREAT BET (G) Piel 1916 (Die GROSSE WETTE) D:
Harry Piel. Ref: MPW'16:71. SF Film. In the year 2,000 an
American millionaire bets his fortune that he can live three days
with a "tricky automatic figure. "

GREAT CROONER, The (by C. B. Kelland) see MR. DODD TAKES
THE AIR

The GREAT GAMBINI Para 1937 71m. D: Charles Vidor. SP:
Frank Partos, Howard Young, Frederick Jackson. PH: Leon
Shamroy. Mus: Boris Morros. Art D: Albert D'Agostino. Ref:
FDY. COF 10:39. with Akim Tamiroff, Reginald Denny, William
Demarest, Edward Brophy, Marian Marsh, John Trent, Genevieve
Tobin, Lya Lys. Mind reader predicts murder.

GREAT GAMBLER, The see DR. MABUSE (Part I)

The GREAT GANTON MYSTERY Rex 1913 32m. Ref: Bios 8/28/13.
Murder; hypnotism.

The GREAT GERMAN NORTH SEA TUNNEL (B) Dreadnought
1914 D: Frank Newman. Ref: SF Film. "Underground invasion. "

The GREAT IMPERSONATION Univ 1935 67m. D: Alan Crosland.
SP: Frank Wead, Eve Greene. PH: Milton Krasner. From the
novel by E. Phillips Oppenheim. Ref: FDY. FD 12/14/35. RVB.
Motion Picture Reviews. Pic: MadM 10:44. with Edmund Lowe,
Valerie Hobson, Frank Reicher, Brandon Hurst, Lumsden Hare,
Spring Byington, Leonard Mudie, Claude King, Esteher Dale,
Murray Kinnell, Dwight Frye. Haunted baronial hall; ghostly
voice; secret panels; ghost rumors.

The GREAT LURE OF PARIS Feature Photoplay Co. 1913 45m.
Ref: MPW 18:783. Scientist uses superhuman powers to bring
girl to fame.-Lee.

GREAT MONO MIRACLE, The (by P. B. Kyne) see FACE IN THE
FOG, A

GREAT MYSTIC, The see STRANGE MR. GREGORY, The

GREAT NORTHERN MYSTERY, The see GREAT ALASKAN
MYSTERY, The

The GREAT PHYSICIAN Edison 1913 17m. D: Richard Ridgely.
SP: B. Merwin. Ref: Lee. MPW 13:1207. with Charles Ogle
(Death).

The GREAT RADIUM MYSTERY Univ 1919 serial 18 episodes
(The RADIUM MYSTERY) D: Robert F. Hill, Robert Broadwell.
Ref: CNW. Exhib. Herald. with Cleo Madison, Bob Reeves, Eileen
Sedgwick. "Mysterious tank which defies destruction. " Ch. 5. The
Torture Chamber.

The GREAT SECRET Serial Producing Co. 1917 serial 18 episodes P, D: Christy Cabanne. SP: Fred de Gresac. Ref: MPN
15:2685-6. CNW. with Francis X. Bushman, Beverly Bayne,
Tammany Young. Suspended animation.

The GREATER WILL Pathe (Gold Rooster) 1915 55m. Ref: MPN
12/25/15. with Cyril Maude, Lois Meredith. Hypnotism;

vision that makes man commit suicide.

GREATEST BATTLE ON EARTH, The see GHIDRAH

The GREATEST POWER Metro(Rolfe) 1917 55m. D: Edwin
   Carewe. SP: Albert S. LeVino. Story: Louis R. Wolheim. Ref:
   Lee. with Ethel Barrymore. Exonite, super-explosive.

The GREED OF WILLIAM HART (B) Eros/PSI/Ambassador/Hoff-
   berg 1948 80m. (HORROR MANIACS. CRIMES OF THE BODY
   SNATCHERS?) D: Oswald Mitchell. SP: John Gilling. PH:
   D. P. Cooper, S. Onions. Ref: MFB'48:46. COF 10:39. Film
   User 10/68. Brit. Fm. Ybk'49/'50. with Tod Slaughter, Henry
   Oscar, Denis Wyndham. Hubert Woodward, Jenny Lynn, Winifred
   Melville, Patrick Addison, Arnold Bell. "Ghouls" procure bodies
   for patron, Dr. Cox.

The GREEN ARCHER Pathe 1925 serial 10 episodes D: Spencer
   G. Bennet. From the book by Edgar Wallace. Ref: MW 5:48.
   CNW. with Allene Ray, Walter Miller, Frank Lackteen, Burr
   McIntosh. Appearance of masked figure in green signifies death.

The GREEN ARCHER Col 1940 serial 15 episodes D: James W.
   Horne; from the book by Edgar Wallace. PH: James S. Brown,
   Jr. SP: M. B. Cox, J. Cutting, J. A. Duffy, Horne. Ref:
   Barbour. MFB'58:114. with Victor Jory, Iris Meredith, James
   Craven, Robert Fiske, Dorothy Fay, Forrest Taylor, Jack
   Ingram. Castle; secret passage.

The GREEN ARCHER (W. G.) Copri Int'l/Casino 1961 95m.
   D: Jurgen Roland. SP: Wolfgang Menge, from the novel by Edgar
   Wallace. with Gert Frobe, Karin Dor, Charles Pallent. Murderer at large around creepy old house. Fair humor provides occasional relief from meandering plot.

The GREEN EYE OF THE YELLOW GOD Edison 1913 17m. D:
   Richard Ridgely. From the poem by J. Milton Hayes. Ref:
   Kinetogram 9/1/13: 1086. with Charles Ogle. Mad Carew dies
   mysteriously after stealing the eye of a Hindu idol.

GREEN EYED MONSTER Fox 1916 55m. SP, D: J. Gordon Edwards. SP: also Mary Murillo. Ref: MPN 13:256. with Robert
   B. Mantell, Stuart Holmes, Genevieve Hamper. Wife confronted
   by murdered husband's corpse dies of shock; later, murderer "un-
   covers the skeleton and collapses.... story of horror and death."

The GREEN GHOST (French-language version of UNHOLY NIGHT)
   MGM 1930 (Le SPECTRE VERT) 90m. D: Jacques Feyder.
   From the story by Ben Hecht. Ref: NYT. DDC II:341. III:251.
   with Georges Renavent, André Luguet. "Dead men" appear at
   seance.

The GREEN HORNET Univ 1940 serial 13 episodes D: Ford
   Beebe, Ray Taylor. SP: G. Plympton, B. Dickey, M. Wood, L.
   Margolies. PH: William Sickner, Jerry Ash. From the radio
   serial. Ref: Showmen's 12/2/39. FD 11/29/39. MPH 12/2/39.
   ModM 4:76. with Anne Nagel, Kenneth Harlan, Keye Luke, Anne
   Gwynne, Ann Doran, Wade Boteler, Joseph Crehan, Selmer Jack-
   son, Frederick Vogeding, Edward Earle, Guy Usher, Gordon
   Jones, Alan Ladd, Lane Chandler, Eddie Dunn, Edward Cassidy,
   Heinie Conklin. "Super-speed car"; gas-gun. -Glut.

The GREEN HORNET STRIKES AGAIN Univ 1940 serial 15
   episodes D: Ford Beebe, John Rawlins. From the radio serial.

PH: Jerome Ash. Ref: The Serial. with Warren Hull, Anne Nagel,
C. Montague Shaw, Nestor Paiva, Keye Luke, Wade Boteler,
Eddie Acuff, James Seay, Pierre Watkin, Eddie Dunn, John
Merton, Roy Barcroft, Lane Chandler, Pat O'Malley, Eddie
Parker, Ray Teal, Jason Robards, Walter Sande, Tristram Cof-
fin, Forrest Taylor, Jimmy O'Gatty. Powerful new anti-air-
craft bomb.
GREEN SLIME, The see BATTLE BEYOND THE STARS
GREEN SPOT MYSTERY, The see LLOYD OF THE C.I.D.
GREEN WOMAN, The see QUEEN OF BLOOD
GREGORY see STRANGE MR. GREGORY, The
GREY CART, The see PHANTOM CHARIOT, The (1958)
The GREY LADY (Dan?) Great Northern/Nordisk 1909 17m.
(The GRAY DAME) Ref: MPW'09:344. Bios 9/2/09. Legend
in noble English family that when the Grey Lady, a ghost, ap-
pears, the eldest son of the house dies. Sherlock Holmes is
sent for when a visitor decides to bring the legend to life.
Secret doors; subterranean dungeon.
GRIMM'S FAIRY TALES FOR ADULTS (W.G.) Cinemation 1969
color 76m. (GRIMM'S MARCHEN-FUR LUSTERNE PARCHEN)
SP,D: Rolf Thiele. Ref: Boxo 2/8/71. V 1/27/71. with
Marie Liljedahl, Ingrid Van Bergen, Walter Giller. Poisoned
apple; wicked Red Queen; cannibalistic thieves; Sleeping Beauty;
Snow White.
GRINSENDE GESICHT, Das see MAN WHO LAUGHS, The (1921)
GRIP OF THE STRANGLER see HAUNTED STRANGLER, The
GRITOS EN LA NOCHE see AWFUL DR. ORLOF, THE
GROSSE VERHAU, Der see BIG MESS, The
GROSSE WETTE, Die See GREAT BET, The
GROSSER GRAUBLAUER VOGAL, Ein see BIG GREY-BLUE BIRD,
A
The GRUESOME TWOSOME Mayflower 1968 P,D: Herschell G.
Lewis. Ref: LA Times 10/12/68. Photon 15:13. with Eliza-
beth Davis, Chris Martell, Gretchen Welles, Rodney Bedell.
Wigmaker's imbecile son scalps young women for her.
GUESS WHAT HAPPENED TO COUNT DRACULA? Merrick Int'l
1971 Movielab color Ref: Boxo 2/22/71. Exec P,D,SP:
Laurence Merrick. cf. DRACULA'S VAMPIRE LUST. with Des
Roberts (the count), Claudia Barron, John Landon, Robert
Branche, Sharon Beverly. Count takes up residence in Holly-
wood.
GUET-APENS A TEHERAN see TARGET FOR KILLING
GUGUSSE ET L'AUTOMATE see CLOWN AND THE AUTOMATON
GUILLEMETTE BABIN (F) 1947 (LE DESTIN EXECRABLE DE
GUILLEMETTE BABIN) D: Guillaume Radot. From works by
Maurice Garçon. Ref: DDC II:306. Pic: DDC II:229. Black
rites.
GUL BUKAWLI (Pakistani) Zaman 1961 color D: Munshi Dil.
Ref: FEFN 3/61. with Sudhir, Jamila, Nazar, Rakhshi. Art D:
Habib Shah. Monster, winged fairy-woman, magic flower.
GULBADAN (Pakistani) Super Hit Movies 1961 D: A. Hameed. Ref:
FEFN 2/61. with M. Nazir, Ejaz, Nazar. Princes and friends
vs. female genie and evil magician and his "magic flame."

GURU THE MAD MONK Nova Int'l/Maipix 1970 color 62m. SP,
  D, PH: Andy Milligan. Art D: Lillian Greneker. Ref: Boxo
  3/1/71. with Neil Flanagan, Judy Israel, Jacqueline Webb.
  Body-snatching; split personality; witch-like vampire; hunchback.
GUSTAVE THE MEDIUM (F) (GUSTAVE LE MEDIUM) 1921
  Ref: DDC I:239. with Georges Biscot.
GWANGI see VALLEY OF GWANGI, The
GWONJEE see VALLEY OF GWANGI, The
GYPSY MOON MCA-TV 1953 78m. Ref: COF 10:40. P: Roland
  Reed. From the "Rocky Jones, Space Ranger" TV series. with
  Richard Crane, Scotty Beckett, Sally Mansfield. The ruler of a
  gypsy moon offers to repair Rocky Jones' damaged space ship. -
  TVG.

H. G. WELLS' NEW INVISIBLE MAN see NEW INVISIBLE MAN,
  The
The H-MAN (J) Col/Toho 1958 Eastmancolor/scope 79m.
  (BIJOTO EKITAI-NINGEN) D: Inoshiro Honda. SP: Takeshi Kim-
  ura. Story: Hideo Kaijo. PH: H. Koizumi. Mus: Masaru Sato.
  Art D: Takeo Kita. SpFX: Eiji Tsuburaya. Ref: UFQ. Pic:
  FM 15:10. DDC III:128. with Yumi Shirakawa, Kenji Sahara,
  Akihiko Hirata, Mitsuru Sato. H-bomb testing creates beings made
  of water that subsist on humans. -TVG.
HABEAS CORPUS Roach-MGM 1928 D: Leo McCarey. with Stan
  Laurel, Oliver Hardy. A mad scientist hires Laurel and Hardy
  to steal bodies from the local cemetery.
HABITANTES DE LA CASA DESHABITADA, Los see INHABITANTS
  OF THE UNINHABITED HOUSE, The
HACHA DIABOLICA, La see DIABOLICAL HATCHET, The
The HAIR RESTORER WB&E 1907 Ref: MPW'07:393. Hair
  grown instantly on man; wife appears "covered in hair, resembling
  a bear."
The HAIR RESTORER Pathe 1909 8m. Ref: Bios 2/10/10.
  Hair restorer works quickly on man.
HAITI MOON (by C. Ripley) see BLACK MOON
HAKUSEN-MIDARE KURO-KAMI see WHITE FAN, The
HALF A LOAF... (J) Shochiku 1958 (YOKU) 106m. D: Heinosuke
  Gosho. Ref: FEFN 8/1/58. with J. Ban, Y. Todoroki. Doc-
  tor discovers the elixir of life.
HALF HUMAN (J) DCA/Toho 1955('58-U.S.) 95m. (JUJIN
  YUKI-OTOKO. The MONSTER SNOWMAN. THE SNOWMAN) D:
  Inoshiro Honda. SP: Takeo Murata. D (U.S. scenes): Kenneth G.
  Crane. Story: Shigeru Kayama. PH: Tadashi Imura. Mus:
  Masaru Sato. Art D: T. Kita. SpFX: Eiji Tsuburaya. Ref:
  FFacts. Pic: FM 15:11.16:9.18:18. with John Carradine, Mor-
  ris Ankrum, Russ Thorson, Akira Takarada, Momoko Kochi,
  Kenji (Ka)sahara. Hairy monster in the mountains of northern
  Japan.
The HALF WIT Lubin 1916 22m. D: Leon Kent. SP: Arthur
  Peterman. Ref: MPN 14:457. with L. C. Shumway, Helen Eddy,

George Routh.   Operation restores half-witted member of gang to
   normality.
The HALFWAY HOUSE (B) AFE Corp. /Ealing 1944 95m. (The
   GHOSTLY INN) D: Basil Dearden.   SP: Angus MacPhail, Diana
   Morgan.   Mus sc: Lord Berners.   P: Michael Balcon.   Assoc P:
   A. Cavalcanti.   Ref: MPH'44:1781.   COF 10:40.   NYT 8/13/45.
   with Francoise Rosay, Tom Walls, Mervyn Johns, Glynis Johns,
   Alfred Drayton, Esmond Knight, Richard Bird, Sally Ann Howes.
   Visitors to an inn witness inexplicable happenings: The landlord
   and his daughter cast no shadows or reflections; "last year's news-
   papers are strewn around untouched.... Inn and its landlord have
   been conjured up from the limbo of dead things. "
HALLEY'S COMMET (F) 1910 9m.   Ref: SilentFF.   Comet
   destroys city.
HALLUCINATION see THESE ARE THE DAMNED
HALLUCINATIONS DU BARON DE MUNCHAUSEN, Les see BARON
   MUNCHAUSEN'S DREAM
HAM AND THE EXPERIMENT Kalem 1915 12m.   Ref: MPN
   8/28/15.   MPW 25:1360.   Love potion injection.
HAM AND THE SAUSAGE FACTORY Kalem 1915 Ref: MPN
   2/13/15.   MPW 23:873.   Machine turns dogs into sausages.
HAMELIN (Sp) Prades 1967 color/scope 105m.   (The PIED
   PIPER OF HAMELIN) D: Luis María Delgado.   SP: R. P.
   Carpio.   PH: Godofredo Pacheco.   Mus: A. Waitzman.   Art D:
   Gil Parrondo.   Ref: SpCinema'68.   with Miguel Ríos, Margaret
   Peters, Luchy Soto.
HAMMER FOR THE WITCHES (Cz) Barrandov 1969 scope
   110m.   (KLADIVO NA CARODEJNICE)   SP, D: Otakar Vavra.
   Story: V. Kaplicky.   Mus: Jiri Srnka.   Sets: Karel Skvor.
   (WITCH HAMMER) Ref: V 4/8/70.   with Vladimir Smeral,
   Elo Romantcick.   Suspected witches tortured.
HAMMOND MYSTERY, The see UNDYING MONSTER, The
The HAND IN THE TRAP (Arg) Angel c1962 90m. (La MANO
   EN LA TRAMPA) SP, D: Leopoldo Torre Nilsson.   SP: also
   Ricardo Luna, Beatriz Guido.   PH: Alberto Etchebehere.   Mus:
   A. Stampone.   Ref: Boxo 8/5/63.   with Elsa Daniel, Francisco
   Rabal, Maria Rosa Gallo.   "Mystery which creates the eerie
   mood of an Edgar Allan Poe tale...horrifying climax...terrible
   secret in the family attic. "
The HAND OF A DEAD MAN (Sp) Albatros(s) 1963 (LA MANO
   DE UN HOMBRE MUERTO-Sp. Le SADIQUE-F) D: Jesus Franco.
   SP: J. Cobos, G. S. de Erice, Franco, P. Ballesteros.   Plot:
   David Kuhne.   PH: Godofredo Pacheco.   Mus: Daniel J. White.
   Sets: Andrés Vallvé.   Ref: SpCinema'64.   COF 4:48.   Pic: MW
   1:10.   with Howard Vernon, Paula Martel, Fernando Delgado,
   Ana Castor, Georges Rollin, Gogo Robins.   "In the Central Euro-
   pean village of Holpen there is a legend that when the moon is
   out the spirit of Baron Von Klaus comes out of a swamp and
   murders young women. "
HAND OF DEATH Fox/Associated Producers 1962 60m.   D: Gene
   Nelson.   SP, P: Eugene Ling.   PH: Floyd Crosby.   Mus: Sonny
   Burke.   Makeup: Bob Mark.   Ref: FFacts.   with John Agar, Roy
   Gordon, Paula Raymond, Steve Dunn, John Alonzo.   Scientist

turns into a monster whose touch is lethal.
HAND OF MARY CONSTABLE, The (novel by P. Gallico) see
   DAUGHTER OF THE MIND
HAND OF NIGHT, The see BEAST OF MOROCCO
The HAND OF PERIL Paragon 1916 55m. SP, D, P: Maurice
   Tourneur. Ref: MPW 27:2033. with House Peters. X-ray
   device makes wall transparent.
HAND OF THE GALLOWS see TERRIBLE PEOPLE, The
The HAND OF THE SKELETON (F) 1915 (La MAIN DU
   SQUELETTE) D: George Schneevoigt. Ref: DDC II:315. Ghost.
HANDS INVISIBLE Powers 1914 15m. Ref: MPW 19:1430. Lee.
   Hands repeat action of strangling wife.
HANDS OF A KILLER see PLANETS AGAINST US, The
HANDS OF A STRANGER aa/Glenwood-Neve 1962 86m. SP, D,
   P: Newton Arnold. P: also Michael DuPont. PH: Henry Cron-
   jager. Mus: Richard La Salle. From the novel "Les Mains D'
   Orlac" by Maurice Renard. Ref: FFacts. PM. Pic: FM 63:44.
   with Paul Lukather, Joan Harvey, James Stapleton, Irish McCalla,
   Ted Otis, George Sawaya, Barry Gordon, Sally Kellerman, David
   Kramer. Hands of unidentified corpse grafted onto arms of bril-
   liant young concert pianist. None of the "Hands of Orlac" adapta-
   tions is better than mediocre, and this may be the worst.
HANDS OF A STRANGLER see HANDS OF ORLAC, The (1961)
The HANDS OF ORLAC (Austrian) Pan-Film 1925 100m. (OR-
   LACS HANDE. Die UNHEIMLICHEN HANDE DES DR. ORLAK)
   D: Robert Wiene. SP: Louis Nerz. From the novel "Les Mains
   D'Orlac" by Maurice Renard. PH: G. Krampf. Sets: S. Wessely.
   Ref: FM 10:28. Imagen. Osterr. with Conrad Veidt, Fritz Kort-
   ner, Alexandra Sorina, Carmen Cartellieri, Paul Askonas, Fritz
   StraBny. Veidt's performance sole interest of dull film.
The HANDS OF ORLAC (B-F) Cont/Riviera Int'l Societe-Pendennis
   1964(1961) 105m. (HANDS OF A STRANGLER) D: Edmond T.
   Greville. SP: Greville, John Baines, from the novel "Les Mains
   D'Orlac" by Maurice Renard. PH: Desmond Dickinson, Jacques
   Lemare. Mus: Claude Bolling, Illona Kabos. Ref: FM 32:6.
   FFacts. with Mel Ferrer, Christopher Lee, Felix Aylmer, Basil
   Sydney, Donald Pleasence, Donald Wolfit, Dany Carrel, David
   Peel, Janina Faye, Lucille St.-Simon. A few impressive scenes
   lost among a lot of junk. Lee has a good role.
HANDS OF THE RIPPER (B) Hammer 1971 color 85m. D: Peter
   Sasdy. SP: L. W. Davidson. Story: Edward S. Shew. PH:
   Kenneth Talbot. Ref: V 10/13/71. with Eric Porter, Angharad
   Rees, Jane Merrow, Keith Bell, Dora Bryan, Norman Bird,
   Charles Lamb. Jack the Ripper returns "supernaturally" to force
   his daughter to murder for him.
HANDS OFF GRETEL (W. G.) Pohland 1970 color 82m.
   (HANSEL UND GRETEL VERLIEFEN SICH IM WALD) SP, D:
   F. J. Gottlieb. SP: also Heinz Freitag. PH: P. Schloemp, W.
   Dickman. Mus: Attila Zoller. Ref: MFB'71:96. with Barbara
   Klingered, Francy Fair, Dagobert Walter. Witch-countess (com-
   plete with the inscription "Dracula" over her fireplace).
The HANGING LAMP (F) Pathe 1908 5m. Ref: MPW'08:402. Wolf-
   like Demon.

HANGMAN OF LONDON, The see MAD EXECUTIONERS, The
HANGOVER SQUARE Fox 1945 77m. D: John Brahm. SP:
Barre Lyndon, from the book by Patrick Hamilton. Remade as
THE MAD MAGICIAN? PH: Joseph La Shelle. Mus: Bernard
Herrmann. SpFX: Fred Sersen. Ref: FDY. COF 9:60.10:40.
Pic: FM 24:36. with Laird Cregar, Linda Darnell, George
Sanders, Faye Marlowe, Glenn Langan, Alan Napier, Frederick
Worlock, Francis Ford. Pianist commits murders during men-
tal lapses.
HANNO CAMBIATO FACCIA see THEY'VE CHANGED FACES
HANSEL AND GRETEL Edison 1909 Ref: MPW'09:499. Bios
12/9/09. Witches
HANSEL AND GRETEL Century (Univ) 1923 22m. Ref: MPN
28:3000. Lee.
HANSEL AND GRETEL (Austrian) 1924 80m. (HANSEL UND
GRETEL) Ref: Osterr.
HANSEL AND GRETEL (G) Childhood 1954 ('65-U.S.) 52m.
(HANSEL UND GRETEL) Narr: Paul Tripp. Ref: COF 10:40.
DDC I:201.
HANSEL AND GRETEL see STORY OF HANSEL AND GRETEL,
The
HANSEL UND GRETEL see HANSEL AND GRETEL (1954)/STORY
OF HANSEL AND GRETEL, The
HANSEL UND GRETEL VERLIEFEN SICH IM WALD see HANDS
OFF GRETEL
HANTU RIMAU see GHOST TIGER, The
HAPPENING OF THE VAMPIRES see VAMPIRE HAPPENING, The
HAPPY NOW I GO see HER PANELED DOOR
HARAM ALEK see SHAME ON YOU
HARD TIMES FOR DRACULA see UNCLE WAS A VAMPIRE
HARD TIMES FOR VAMPIRES see UNCLE WAS A VAMPIRE
HARM MACHINE, The see AGENT FOR H.A.R.M.
HASHASHIN, THE INDIFFERENT (by G. Dillenback) see LOVE
DOCTOR, The
HATIM TAI (India-Hindi) Basant 1955 Ref: FEFN 4/13/56. with
Shakila, Jairaj. Girl under curse that will turn her to stone un-
less it is lifted.
HATIMTAI-KI-BETI (India-Hindi) Vakil 1955 Ref: FEFN
12/23/55. with Chitra, Mahipal. The devil sends evil spirits
to torment a beautiful princess.
HATTIE, THE HAIR HEIRESS Mutual (Falstaff) 1915 Ref: MPN
10/23/15. with Frances Keyes, Claude Cooper, Arthur Cunning-
ham. Tonic grows hair overnight.
HAUNTED Superba 1915 7m. Ref: MPN 1/23/15. Man haunted
by vision of dead man.
HAUNTED E. & R. Jungle Film Co. 1916 Ref: MPN 13:2552.
with Lillian Leighton, Ralph McComas. Chimpanzees' "ghostly
tricks" frighten newlyweds staying in bungalow.
HAUNTED see CURSE OF THE DEMON
HAUNTED AND THE HAUNTERS, The (story by E. Bulwer-Lytton)
see NIGHT COMES TOO SOON, The
HAUNTED AND THE HUNTED, The see DEMENTIA 13
The HAUNTED ATTIC Lubin 1914 10m. Ref: MPW 4/17/15:443.

Attic "haunted" by barber.

The HAUNTED BEDROOM (F) Urban-Eclipse 1907 5m. Ref:
MPW 1:622. Lee.

The HAUNTED BEDROOM Edison 1913 15m. Ref: SilentFF.
Bios 3/5/14. MPW 19:48: "Creepy." with Jack Strong, Mabel
Trunelle, Harry Linson. Ghost guards money in haunted room.

The HAUNTED BEDROOM Para 1919 55m. D: Fred Niblo. SP:
C. Gardner Sullivan. P: Thomas H. Ince. Ref: MPW 40:1689.
with Lloyd Hughes, Enid Bennett, Dorcas Mathews, Otto Hoffman,
Jack Nelson. "Haunted" bedroom; ghostly figures; chord played
on organ that opens secret door.

The HAUNTED BELL Imp (Univ) 1916 22m. D: Henry Otto.
SP: J. Grubb Alexander, from a story by Jacques Futrelle.
Ref: LC. MPW. with King Baggot, Edna Hunter, Joseph Smiley.
Woman believes sacred bell is haunted.

HAUNTED BY CONSCIENCE Kalem 1910 17m. Ref: MPW 7:207.
Ghost.

HAUNTED CAFE (G) Messter 1911 7m. Ref: SilentFF. A man
in a restaurant falls asleep and has an alarming dream in which
the waiter constantly vanishes and reappears, a girl materializes,
and the furniture spins round, vanishes and returns.

The HAUNTED CASTLE (F) Melies 1897 (Le CHATEAU HANTE)
Ref: DDC III:350. Mitry II: not sfa LE MANOIR DU DIABLE.

The HAUNTED CASTLE (B) 1897 D: G. A. Smith. Ref: Brit.
Cinema.

The HAUNTED CASTLE (F) Pathe 1908 12m. Ref: MPW'08:
424. Ghosts, witch.

The HAUNTED CASTLE (F) Pathe 1909 Ref: MPW'09:760.
Girl's suitors must get bouquet guarded by "ghost."

The HAUNTED CASTLE Educ 1922 11m. Ref: MPN 26:3253.

The HAUNTED CASTLE (B) UA/Alliance 1948 91m. (HAUNTED
HOUSE. JUST WILLIAM'S LUCK-U.S.) SP, D: Val Guest.
Based on a character created by R. Crompton. PH: Leslie Row-
son. Art D: Harry Moore. Art Supervisor: Andrew Mazzie. Ref:
MFB'48:3. Brit. Fm.Ybk'49/'50. COF 10:40. with William
Graham, Garry Marsh, A. E. Matthews, Michael Medwin, Michael
Balfour, Patricia Cutts, Jane Welsh, Hugh Cross, Kathleen
Stuart, Leslie Bradley. Kids plan to "haunt" old manor house,
scare occupants away.

HAUNTED CASTLE (J) Daiei 1969 color/scope 83m. (HIROKU
KAIBYODEN) D: Tokuzo Tanaka. SP: Shozaburo Asai. PH:
H. Imai. Mus: C. Watanabe. Art D: S. Ota. Ref: UFQ 48.
with Kojiro Hongo, Naomi Kobayashi, Mitsuyo Kamei, N. Oka.
Cat with supernatural powers becomes female demon that drinks
the blood of its victims. Uninspired but lively. Repetitious;
cheap effects and lots of blood.

HAUNTED CASTLE see SPOOK CASTLE OF SPESSART, The

HAUNTED CASTLES series see ASHRIDGE CASTLE/BADDESLEY
MANOR/BODIAM CASTLE/GLAMIS CASTLE/KENILWORTH
CASTLE/MISTLETOE BOUGH, The (1926)/TOWER OF LONDON
(1926/WARWICK CASTLE/WINDSOR CASTLE/WOODCROFT
CASTLE

The HAUNTED CAVE (J) Shintoho 1959 scope 87m. (AMA NO

BAKEMONO YASHIKI) D: Morihei Magatani. SP: Akira Sugi-
moto, Nao Akatsukasa. PH: Kagai Okado. Ref: UFQ 6. Unij.
Bltn. 31. with Bunta Sugawara, Yoko Mihara, Reiko Seto,
Masayo Banri, Yoichi Numata. Family under curse; ghost;
treasure in haunted cave.

The HAUNTED CHAMBER Anderson 1913 45m. Ref: Bios 9/4/13:
xxx.

The HAUNTED CURIOSITY SHOP (B) Paul 1899(1901?) (The
CURIOSITY SHOP) Ref: Hist. Brit. Film. SilentFF. Curio dealer
sees apparition which changes from woman to mummy to skeleton.

HAUNTED GOLD WB 1933 58m. D: Mack Wright. SP: Adele
Buffington. PH: Nick Musuraca. Ed: William Clemens. Ref:
Photoplay'33. FDY. with John Wayne, Sheila Terry, Erville
Anderson, Harry Woods, Otto Hoffman, Blue Washington. Wes-
tern. Sliding panels; haunted mine in ghost town.

HAUNTED HARBOR Rep 1944 serial 15 episodes (PIRATE'S
HARBOR) D: Spencer G. Bennet, Wallace Grissell. SP: R.
Cole, B. Dickey, J. Duffy, G. Nelson, J. Poland. PH: Bud
Thackery. Mus sc: Joseph Dubin. SpFX: Theodore Lydecker.
Based on a story by D. Douglas. Ref: MPH 8/26/44. FIR'68:
523. STI 3:16. with Kane Richmond, Kay Aldridge, Roy Bar-
croft, Oscar O'Shea, Forrest Taylor, Hal Taliaferro, George J.
Lewis, Kenne Duncan, Dale Van Sickel, Tom Steele, Bud Geary,
Robert Wilke, Marshall Reed, Edward Keane. "Sea monsters."

HAUNTED HEARTS Univ(Gold Seal) 1915 25m. D: W. T. Mc-
Culley. Ref: MPN 2/27/15. with Joe King, Cleo Madison.
Operation restores man's memory.

A HAUNTED HEIRESS Univ(Century) 1926 22m. Ref: FD
5/9/26. with Edna Marian. "Haunted house": Crooked lawyer
hires men to pose as ghosts to scare girl into selling her inherited house cheap.

The HAUNTED HILLS Educ 1924 11m. Ref: MPN 29:879. Lee.
with Jim Bemis. Mysterious events drive villain to death.

The HAUNTED HOMESTEAD Univ(Mustang) 1927 22m. D: William Wyler. SP: L. V. Jefferson. Ref: FD 4/3/27. Western.
"Old house suspected of being haunted...eccentric cornet player."

The HAUNTED HONEYMOON Hal Roach 1925 22m. (BILLY GETS
MARRIED) D: Fred Guiol. Ref: MPN 31:923. Lee. with Glenn
Tryon, Blanche Mehaffy, James Finlayson, George Rowe. Honey-
mooners in "haunted" house.

The HAUNTED HOTEL Vita 1907 8m. D: James Blackton? Ref:
MPW'07:62. Bios 5/28/14: "Trick film." DDC I:240.

The HAUNTED HOTEL Pathe 1913 20m. Ref: Bios 4/3/13.
"Strange happenings" in hotel.

The HAUNTED HOTEL (B) Kinekature 1918 11m. P: Fred Rains.
Ref: Hist. Brit. Film. DDC III:194. with Will Asher, Marion
Peake, Lupino Lane.

HAUNTED HOTROD see GHOST OF DRAGSTRIP HOLLOW

The HAUNTED HOUSE Lubin 1899 Ref: LC.

The HAUNTED HOUSE (F) 1907 (La MAISON HANTEE) D:
Segundo de Chomon. Ref: DDC I:403.

The HAUNTED HOUSE Imp 1911 17m. Ref: Bios 12/7/11.
MPW'11:644. Man attempts to convince villagers a house is

haunted; black cat, noises, etc.
The HAUNTED HOUSE (F?) Gaum 1911 13m. Ref: Bios 9/28/11.
Mitry II: 208: Feuillade: LA MAISON HANTEE. "Haunted"
house really headquarters for the band of "coiners."
The HAUNTED HOUSE Pathe 1912 8m. Ref: Bios 3/7/12.
From a Spanish inn peasants see a haunted house "turn thrice
around." Cats' faces appear at its windows; tongues of fire
appear on the chimneys.
The HAUNTED HOUSE Patheplay 1913 17m. Ref: Bios 6/4/14.
Afraid to pass a reputedly haunted house alone on her way to her
graduation, a little girl has her father accompany her.
The HAUNTED HOUSE Mutual (American) 1913 Ref: MPW 18:528.
Ethel Graham, the village belle, announces that she will marry
the first man that spends a night in the haunted house.
The HAUNTED HOUSE Kalem 1913 15m. Ref: SilentFF. MPW
16:403. Bios 7/3/13. with Edgar Davenport, Olive Temple.
Burglar risks ghost to get jewels in reputedly haunted house.
The HAUNTED HOUSE Triangle 1917 Ref: FD 9/20/17. Orpheus
2:19.
The HAUNTED HOUSE Frazee 1918 22m. D: Frank Borzage?
P, SP: Edwin A. Frazee. Ref: Lee. RVB. MPW 37:436.
"Mystical illusions" and "weird magic."
The HAUNTED HOUSE Metro 1921 22m. SP, D: Buster Keaton,
Eddie Cline. Ref: MPN 24:416. DDC II:315. Counterfeiters dress
up as ghosts in "haunted" house. Two or three prime Keaton
gags in one of his lesser shorts. The best has him directing
ghosts like traffic.
The HAUNTED HOUSE Fox 1922 22m. D: Erle Kenton. Ref:
LC.
The HAUNTED HOUSE F Nat 1928 65m. Silent. D: Ben Chris-
tensen. SP: Richard Bee, Lajos Biro. Titles: William Irish.
Ed: Frank Ware. PH: Sol Polito. From a play by Owen Davis.
Ref: V 12/19/28. Clarens. AFI. with Larry Kent, Thelma
Todd, Montagu Love, Chester Conklin, William V. Mong, Ed-
mund Breese, Barbara Bedford, Eve Southern, Flora Finch,
Sidney Bracy. Rainstorm; sliding panels; sleep-walking girl.
HAUNTED HOUSE (India) Shree Ranjit Film Co. 1932 (BHUTIO
MAHAL) Ref: Indian Cinematograph Year Book 1938, p. 159.
The HAUNTED HOUSE Mono 1940 70m. (The BLAKE MURDER
MYSTERY-Eng) D: Robert McGowan. SP: Dorothy Reid. Story:
Jack Leonard, Monty Collins. PH: Harry Neumann. Mus D:
Edward Kay. Art D: E. R. Hickson. Ref: FD 7/23/40. RVB.
MFB'48:156: "Sequences in a dark house may frighten children."
with Jackie Moran, Marcie Mae Jones, George Cleveland, Henry
Hall, Christian Rub, John St. Polis, Buddy Swan, Mary Carr,
Hooper Atchley, Clarence Wilson, Jessie Arnold. Newspaper
office boy and publisher's niece solve murder.
HAUNTED HOUSE (Malayan) Keris Films 1957 (RUMAH PUAKA.
DIMANA GAJAH BERDIRI TEGAK. WHERE THE ELEPHANT
STOOD) Ref: FEFN 11/15/57. with Maria Menado, M. Amin.
Relatives search dead miser's supposedly haunted house for his
fortune.
HAUNTED HOUSE see HAUNTED CASTLE, The (1948)

HAUNTED HOUSE OF HORROR, The see HORROR HOUSE
The HAUNTED HOUSE OF WILD ISLE 1915 25m. Ref: MPW 24:616
  MPN 5/1/15. with Anna Nilsson, Harry Millarde. The ghost of
  John Miller, a suicide, is said to haunt the house on Wild Isle.
The HAUNTED INN Cosmopolitan 1910 13m. Ref: Bios 1/20/10.
  Peasant passing by inn at night robbed by "ghosts."
HAUNTED ISLAND Powers 1911 15m. Ref: Bios 10/26/11.
  Creatures half-man, half-monkey.
The HAUNTED ISLAND Univ 1928 silent serial 10 episodes D:
  Robert F. Hill. Remake of THE BRASS BULLET. SP: George
  Morgan, Carl Krusada. From the story "Pleasure Island" by
  Frank R. Adams. Ref: CNW. with Jack Daughterty, Helen
  Foster, Grace Cunard. Ch. 4. The Haunted Room.
The HAUNTED LIFE OF A DRAGON-TATTOOED LASS (J)
  Nikkatsu 1970 color/scope (KAIDAN NOBORIRYU. TATTOOED
  SWORDSWOMAN. BLIND WOMAN'S CURSE) D: Teruo Ishii.
  SP: Ishii, Y. Sone. PH: S. Kitaizumi. Mus: H. Kaburagi. Art
  D: A. Satani. Ref: UFQ 50. with Meiko Kaji, Hoki Tokuda,
  Hideo Sunazuka, Toru Abe. Spirit; black-cat curse; hunchback
  who revives dead.
The HAUNTED MAN Walturdaw 1909 8m. Ref: Bios 12/9/09.
  Man haunted by his double.
The HAUNTED MANOR Gaum/Mutual 1916 Ref: FDY. MPW
  27:2082. Adventuress hides in secret chambers of an old
  house.
The HAUNTED MINE Mono 1946 52m. D: Derwin Abrahams.
  SP: Elizabeth Burbridge, Frank Young. PH: Harry Neumann.
  Ref: HR 3/27/46. MFB'47:115. with Johnny Mack Brown,
  Raymond Hatton, Claire Whitney, Linda Johnson, John Merton,
  Terry Frost. Western. Ghost town's mine "haunted" by dement-
  ed hermit with razor.
The HAUNTED PAJAMAS MGM 1917 55m. D: Fred J. Balshofer.
  Ref: MPN 15:4113. with Helen Ware, Ed Sedgwick, Harold Lock-
  wood, Carmel Myers, Paul Willis. Weaver becomes "someone
  else."
HAUNTED PALACE (B) Premier/Nell Gwynn Prod. 1948 SP,
  D: Richard Fisher. PH: Stanley Clinton. Ref: MFB'49. Docu-
  mentary feature. "Shaw Desmond, authority on ghosts, attempts
  to explain ghostly appearances."
The HAUNTED PALACE AI/LA Honda 1963 Pathecolor/scope
  85m. (The HAUNTED VILLAGE) P, D: Roger Corman. SP:
  Charles Beaumont, from the works of Edgar Allan Poe and "The
  Shadow over Innsmouth" and "The Case of Charles Dexter Ward"
  by H. P. Lovecraft. PH: Floyd Crosby. Mus: Ronald Stein.
  Art D: Daniel Haller. Ref: FFacts. PM. with Vincent Price,
  Debra Paget, Lon Chaney, Jr., Leo Gordon, Elisha Cook, Jr.,
  John Dierkes, Harry Ellerbe, Barboura Morris, Bruno VeSota,
  Milton Parsons, Guy Wilkerson. Joseph Curwen, burnt as a
  witch in 1765, returns from the dead 100 years later and takes
  over the mind and body of his descendant, Charles Dexter Ward.
The HAUNTED PICTURE GALLERY (B) 1899 D: G. A. Smith.
  Ref: Brit. Cinema
HAUNTED PLANET see PLANET OF THE VAMPIRES

The HAUNTED RANCH Mono 1943 D: Robert Tansey. SP:
Arthur Hoerl, Harriet Beecher. PH: Robert Cline. Ref: HR
5/18/43. FDY. with John "Dusty" King, Rex Lease, Glenn
Strange, David Sharpe, Max Terhune, Julie Duncan, Charles
King, Bud Osbo(u)rne, Snowflake. "Ghosts"; right tune played
on organ reveals treasure.

The HAUNTED RANGE Davis 1925 (The HAUNTED RANCH) D:
Paul Hurst. SP: Frank H. Clark. PH: Frank Cotner. Ref:
Photoplay 11/25. AFI: "Ghost of Haunted Ranch." with Ken
Maynard, Alma Rayford, Harry Moody, Al Hallett. Western.

The HAUNTED ROOM (F) Pathe 1911 8m. Ref: SilentFF. Bios
2/9/11. Ogre at window; glove's fingers become claws.

The HAUNTED SENTINEL TOWER Edison 1911 17m. Ref:
Bios 6/8/11. A guide tells the story of the ghost that haunts
the tower.

HAUNTED SPOOKS Pathe 1920 D?: Hal Roach. Ref: DDC III:
238. MPW'20:140. Haunted house, ghosts.

The HAUNTED STATION Kalem 1914 (#62 in The Hazards of
Helen series) D: J. P. McGowan, James Davis. SP: E. W.
Matlack. Ref: CNW. MPW 27:470. Apparent suicide's "ghostly"
appearances cause post to become known as "The Haunted
Station."

The HAUNTED STRANGLER (B) MGM/Amalgamated 1958 81m.
(GRIP OF THE STRANGLER) D: Robert Day. SP: Jan Read,
John C. Cooper. (STRANGLEHOLD) PH: Lionel Banes. Mus sc:
Buxton Orr. P: John Croydon. Pic: FM 2:30. Ref: PM. with
Boris Karloff, Anthony Dawson, Jean Kent, Elizabeth Allan,
Dorothy Gordon, Vera Day, Leslie Perrins. Jekyll-Hyde-like
killer. Weak thriller with poor attempts at "atmosphere."

HAUNTED VILLAGE, The see HAUNTED PALACE, The
HAUNTED WORLD see PLANET OF THE VAMPIRES

The HAUNTING (U.S.-B) MGM/Argyle 1963 scope 116m.
P,D: Robert Wise. SP: Nelson Gidding, from the novel "The
Haunting of Hill House" by Shirley Jackson. PH: Davis Boulton.
Mus: Humphrey Searle. Art D: Elliott Scott. SpFX: Tom How-
ard. Ref: Clarens. COF 4:18. with Richard Johnson, Julie
Harris, Claire Bloom, Russ Tamblyn, Valentine Dyall, Lois
Maxwell, Fay Compton, Diane Clare. Several well-calculated
scares and some rather powerful concepts of horror (the ghostly
hand, the writing on the wall) make The HAUNTING| one of the
best horror movies of recent years. Julie Harris is good
(though not great--as she can be, as in MEMBER OF THE WED-
DING) but she has too many soliloquys; and the supernatural is
too often subordinated to and is too dependent on facile character
analysis.

HAUNTING AT CASTLE MONTEGO, The see CASTLE OF EVIL

The HAUNTING CASTLE IN SALZKAMMERGUT (G) 1965
(SPUKSCHLOSS IM SALZKAMMERGUT) D: Hans Billian, Rolf
Olsen. PH: Karl LÖB. Ref: Germany. V 5/8/68.

HAUNTING SHADOWS Robertson-Cole 1920 D: Henry King. SP:
Eugene B. Lewis, from Meredith Nicholson's "The House of 1000
Candles." PH: Victor Milner. Ref: MPH 1/24/20. MPW 43:
632. with H. B. Warner, Edward Piel, Florence Oberle, Charles

French, Marguerite Livingston. Man must stay in "haunted" house every night for a year; "creaking stairways"; "mystery of ghostly visitations."

HAUNTING WINDS Powers (Univ) 1915 15m. D: Carl M. Le Viness. SP: Earl R. Hewitt. Story: G. E. Jenks. Ref: MPN 8/14/15. LC. with Sydney Ayres, Doris Pawn. A man who has accidentally killed is haunted by "moaning winds...swaying treetops, and banging doors."

HAUNTS FOR RENT Para (Bray-Gilbert) 1916 (HAUNTS FOR HIRE) Animation: L. M. Glackens. SP: C. Allan Gilbert. Ref: MPW 27:429. Live-action & animation. Girl agrees to marry the suitor who can stay in the haunted chamber of a road house overnight.

HAUS OHNE TUREN UND FENSTER, Das see HOUSE WITHOUT DOORS OR WINDOWS, The (1914)

HAUSER'S MEMORY NBC-TV/Univ 1970 color 96m. D: Boris Sagal. Mus: Bill Byers. SP: Adrian Spies, from a novel by Curt Siodmak. Makeup: Bud Westmore. Ref: RVB. TVG. with David McCallum, Susan Strasberg, Helmut Kautner, Leslie Nielsen, Robert Webber, Lilli Palmer. Scientist injects himself with the fluid from a German physicist's brain.

HAVE ROCKET, WILL TRAVEL Col 1959 76m. D: David Lowell Rich. SP: Raphael Hayes. PH: Ray Cory. Mus: Mischa Bakaleinikoff. Ref: FFacts. SM 4:6. COF 1:19.10:41. with Moe Howard, Larry Fine, Joe de Rita, Jerome Cowan, Annalisa. Robot, giant spider, death ray, Three Stooges.

HAVE YOU A LION AT HOME? see DO YOU KEEP A LION AT HOME?

The HAWK'S TRAIL Burston 1920 serial 15 episodes D: W. S. Van Dyke. Ref: Lee. CNW. with King Baggot, Rhea Mitchell, Grace Darmond. Crook with hypnotic powers.

HAXAN see WITCHCRAFT THROUGH THE AGES

HAY MUERTOS QUE NO HACEN RUDIO see THERE ARE DEAD THAT RISE

HAZAAR-RATEN (India) 1953 Ref: Filmfare 3/20/53. Magician "usurps throne with magical powers," hypnotism. Picture of horrible face.

HAZARDS OF HELEN, The see HAUNTED STATION, The

HE, SHE OR IT see POUPEE, La (1962)

HE WHO DIES OF LOVE (Mex) Artistas Asociados 1945 (EL QUE MURIO DE AMOR) D: Miguel Morayta. SP: Antonio Momplet, from "Avatar" by T. Gautier. PH: Ignacio Torres. Mus: M. Esperón. Ref: Aventura. with Julian Soler, Hilda Kruger, Fernando Cortés. Metempsychosis.

The HEAD (G) T-L/Rapid 1959 ('62-U.S.) 92m. (DIE NACKTE UND DER SATAN. A HEAD FOR THE DEVIL. The NAKED AND SATAN. The SCREAMING HEAD) SP, D: Victor Trivas. PH: Otto Reinwald, Kurt Rendel. Mus sc: W. Mattes, J. Lasry. Art D: Hermann Warm, B. Monden. SpFX: Theo Nischwitz. Ref: HM 5. Orpheus 3:26. FEFN 5/60. German Pictures. FFacts. Pic: FM 19:9. with Michel Simon, Horst Frank, Karin Kernke, Paul Dahlke, Dieter Eppler, Helmut Schmid, Christine Maybach. Doctor discovers serum which will keep decapitated

head alive.
HEAD OF JANUS see JANUSKOPF, Der
The HEAD OF PANCHO VILLA (Mex) Importadora 1955 79m.
  (La CABEZA DE PANCHO VILLA) Ref: Lee. FM 31:22.33:10.
  Pic: FM 12:9. with Luis Aguilar, Flor Silvestre, Jaime
  Fernandez, Pascual G. Pena.
HEAD THAT WOULDN'T DIE, The see BRAIN THAT WOULDN'T
  DIE, The
The HEADLESS GHOST (B) AI 1959 63m. D: Peter Graham
  Scott. SP: Kenneth Langtry, Herman Cohen. PH: John Wiles.
  Mus: Gerard Schurman. Prod. Man: Jim O'Connolly. Makeup:
  Jack Craig. P: Cohen. Ref: FFacts. with Richard Lyon, Liliane
  Scottane, David Rose, Clive Revill, Jack Ellen, Trevor Barnett.
  Haunted castle; ghost banquet. Dull, occasionally pleasant.
HEADLESS HORSEMAN Hodkinson 1922 D: Edward Venturini.
  From "The Legend of Sleepy Hollow" by Washington Irving.
  with Will Rogers.
The HEADLESS RIDER (Mex) Importadora 1957 (EL JINETE SIN
  CABEZA) 91m. Ref: FM 31:22. Lee still. TVG. with Luis
  Aguilar, Jaime Fernandez, Crox Alvarado, Pascual G. Pena, Flor
  Silvestre. Headless rider; men in skull-masks.
HEART FARM, The see MAN WHO WANTED TO LIVE FOREVER,
  The
HEART OF STONE see COLD HEART, The (1950)
The HEART OF THE PRINCESS MARSARI Than 1915 Ref: MPW
  24:1334. Man uses liquid air to commit murder, "meets with a
  still stranger death than did his victim."
HEARTS AND FLOWERS Majestic 1915 Ref: MPN 9/4/15.
  Man's memory restored by operation.
HEARTS ARE TRUMPS IN TOKYO FOR O.S.S. 117. see TERROR
  IN TOKYO
The HEATING POWDER Lubin 1908 7m. Ref: F Index 9/26/08.
  Powder invented that heats everything it touches.
HEAVEN SHIP, The see SKY SHIP, The
HEAVENS CALL, The see BATTLE BEYOND THE SUN
HEBA THE SNAKE WOMAN Excelsior 1915 Ref: Movie Monsters.
HEBIMUSUME TO HAKUHATSUMA see SNAKE GIRL AND THE
  SILVER-HAIRED WITCH, The
HECTOR SERVADAC (by J. Verne) VALLEY OF THE DRAGONS
The HEIR OF THE AGES Para(Pallas) 1917 55m. Ref: MPN 15:
  15:4112. with House Peters, Eugene Pallette, Adele Farrington.
  Cave men reincarnated.
HELL (J) Shintoho 1960 color/scope 100m. (JIGOKU.SINNERS TO
  HELL) D: Nobuo Nakagawa. SP: Nakagawa, Ichiro Miyagawa.
  PH: Mamoru Morita. Ref: UFQ 10. MW 3:6. with Shigeru
  Amachi, Yoichi Numata, Utako Mitsuya, Torahiko Nakamura.
  Scenes in hell of people being sawed in half, drowned in blood,
  turned into skeletons, etc.
HELL (by Dante) see DANTE'S INFERNO
HELL-CREATURES see INVASION OF THE SAUCERMEN
HELL-FACE (Mex) Clasa 1963 (El ROSTRO INFERNAL) Ref: FM
  29:46. Lee. with Jaime Fernandez, Rosa Carmina. Auto-
  matons.

HELL OF FRANKENSTEIN, The   see ORLAK, The HELL OF
FRANKENSTEIN
HELLEVISION Roadshow 1939 Footage from Italian DANTE'S
INFERNO. Ref: FM 67:11. FJA. Eccentric scientist's TV
invention tunes in on hell.
HELLO DOWN THERE Para 1969 Technicolor D: Jack Arnold.
SP: Frank Telford, John McGreevey. PH: Cliff Poland. Mus:
Jeff Barey. Exec P: Ivan Tors. Ref: PM. with Tony Randall,
Janet Leigh, Roddy McDowall, Merv Griffin, Jim Backus, Ken
Berry, Lou Wagner, Henny Backus, Bruce Gordon, Harvey Lem-
beck, Arnold Stang. Scientist's home located 90 feet under water.
HELL'S CREATURES see MARK OF THE WOLFMAN
HELLZAPOPPIN Univ 1941 82m. D: H. C. Potter. SP: Nat
Perrin, Warren Wilson. Suggested by the stage version. PH:
Elwood Bredell. SpPhFX : John P. Fulton. Ref: V 12/24/41.
Academy. with Ole Olsen, Chic Johnson, Robert Paige, Shemp
Howard, Jane Frazee, Martha Raye, Clarence Kolb, Mischa
Auer, Elisha Cook, Jr., Samuel S. Hinds, George Chandler,
Eddie Acuff, Angelo Rossitto. Invisibility; Frankenstein monster
in one sequence. Olsen and Johnson aren't too funny themselves,
but Herbert, Auer, Raye, and a lot of the sight gags are. Uni-
versal is to be commended for its great restraint in throwing in
only about 30 musical numbers.
HELP! (F) 1924 20m. (AU SECOURS!) SP,D: Abel Gance.
SP: also Max Linder. Ref: FIR'65:289. SilentFF. with Linder,
Gina Palerme. "Hair-raising experiences in a haunted castle."
HELP, I'M INVISIBLE (G) J.F.U. 1951 (HILFE, ICH BIN
UNSICHTBAR. ALAS I AM INVISIBLE!) D: E. W. Emo. Ref:
Deutsche Filme 1952. DDC III:232. with Theo Lingen, Arno
Assmann.
HENCRAKE WITCH Summit 1913 12m. Ref: Bios 6/19/13. Witch
turns squire into "ugly old dame."
HENKER VON LONDON, Der see MAD EXECUTIONERS, The
HENPECK'S NIGHTMARE Cosmograph 1914 8m. Ref: Bios
5/7/14. "Weird apparitions...psychic."
HENRIETTE see PARIS WHEN IT SIZZLES
HENRY ALDRICH HAUNTS A HOUSE Para 1943 73m. (HENRY
HAUNTS A HOUSE-Eng) D: Hugh Bennett. SP: Val Burton,
Muriel Bolton. Based on a character created by Clifford Gold-
smith. PH: Daniel L. Fapp. Mus sc: Gerard Carbonara. Art
D: Hans Dreier, Haldane Douglas. Ref: MFB'43:123. FDY.
COF 10:42. with James Lydon, John Litel, Charles Smith,
Jackie Moran, Lucien Littlefield, Mike Mazurki, Edgar Dearing,
Jack Gardner. High school student swallows scientist's new
chemical.
HENRY, THE RAINMAKER Mono/Mayfair 1949 64m. D: Jean
Yarbrough. SP: Lane Beauchamp, from the story "The Rain-
maker" by D. D. Beauchamp. PH: William Sickner. Ref: FDY.
with Walter Catlett, William Tracy, Mary Stuart, Barbara Brown,
Addison Richards, Robert Emmett Keane, William Ruhl. Man
uses science to make rain, can't stop it when it starts.
HENRY'S NIGHT IN 1969 color Ref: FVB. Man experiments in
invisibility.

HER DOLLY'S REVENGE   Lux   1909   5m.   Ref: Bios 10/21/09.
Little girl dreams her doll stabs her to death with scissors.
HER FATHER'S GOLD   Than (Mutual)   1916   55m.   Ref: MPN 13:
3092.   A reporter is sent to Florida to investigate reports of a
"water devil. " He is saved from death when the devil, "a non-
descript sea monster, " overturns the boat of a would-be assassin.
with Barbara Gilroy, Harris Gordon, William Burt, Louise Bates.
HER HEART IN HER THROAT   (by E. L. White) see UNSEEN, The
HER HUSBAND'S AFFAIRS   Col   1947   83m.   D: S. Sylvan Simon.
SP: Ben Hecht, Charles Lederer.   PH: Charles Lawton, Jr.
Mus: M. W. Stoloff. P: Raphael Hakim.   Ref: FDY. Film Digest
10:19. with Lucille Ball, Franchot Tone, Mikhail Rasumny, Larry
Parks, Edward Everett Horton, Gene Lockhart, Jonathan Hale,
Charles Trowbridge, Arthur Space, Selmer Jackson.   An inventor
invents a lather, a by-product of an embalming fluid, which pro-
vides an instant shave or grows hair where it didn't grow before.
Poorly directed comedy, with crummy dialogue, dull characters,
and fantastic situations that are unfunny with a vengeance.
HER INVISIBLE HUSBAND   (Univ Imp)   1916   Ref: MPN 13:1625.   MPW
27:1498.   Dream: "Malicious sorceress" gives man magic ring
which renders him invisible "without his knowing it. "
HER PANELED DOOR   (B)   A. B. P. C.   1950   84m.   (The WOMAN
WITH NO NAME-Eng) D: Ladislas Vajda.   SP: Vajda, Guy
Morgan, from the novel "Happy Now I Go" by Theresa Charles.
PH: Otto Heller.   Mus: Allan Gray.   Art D: Wilfred Arnold.
Ref: MFB'50:174.   TVG.   "Gothic tale": woman fears something
is behind mysterious paneled door.   "Nightmare dream sequence
in negative. " with Phyllis Calvert, Edward Underdown, Helen
Cherry, Richard Burton, James Hayter, Betty Ann Davies.
HER SURRENDER   Ivan   1916   55m.   SP, D: Ivan Abramson. Ref:
MPN 14:2053.   with Anna Nilsson, Wilmuth Merkyl, Harry Sping-
ler.   Blood boy gave her in transfusion makes girl love him.
HER TEMPTATION   Fox   1917   55m.   D: Richard Stanton.   SP: Nor-
ris Shannon.   Ref: MPN 15:2689.   with Gladys Brockwell, Bertram
Grassby, Ralph Lewis, James Cruze, Beatrice Burnham. Man
hypnotizes girl to make her think she committed murder.
HERCULE CONTRE LES VAMPIRES see HERCULES IN THE
HAUNTED WORLD
HERCULEAN LOVE see LOVES OF HERCULES, The
HERCULES   (I)   Embassy/O. S. C. A. R. -Galatea   1957   ('59-U. S.)
Eastmancolor/ Dyaliscope   107m.   (Le FATICHE DI ERCOLE.
The LABORS OF HERCULES) SP, D: Pietro Francisci.   SP: also
Ennio de Concini, Gaio Frattini. PH: Mario Bava. Mus: Enzo
Masetti.   Sets: Flavio Mogherini.   Ref: COF 10:42. F Facts. with
Steve Reeves, Sylva Koscina, Gianna Maria Canale, Ivo Garrani,
Arturo Dominici. The Cretan Bull; dragon; etc.
HERCULES AND THE BIG STICK   (F)   Gaum   1910   Ref: The Film
Index. Hydra; Nemean lion.
HERCULES AND THE CAPTIVE WOMEN   (I-F)   Woolner/SPA-
Comptoir   1961   ('63-U. S.)   Technicolor/scope   101m.   (ERCOLE
ALLA CONQUISTA DELLA ATLANTIDE-I. HERCULES IN THE
CONQUEST OF ATLANTIS) SP, D: Vittorio Cottafavi.   SP: also D.
Tessari, A. Continenza.   Story: Archibald Zounds.   PH: Carlo

Carlini.   Mus: Gino Marinuzzi.   Add'l mus: Gordon Zahler.   Ed:
(U.S.): Hugo Grimaldi.   Remade as The CHALLENGE OF THE
GIANT?   Ref: FFacts.   Orpheus 3:29.   with Reg Park, Fay
Spain, Ettore Manni, Ivo Garrani, Gian Maria Volonte.   Hercules
vs. the wicked queen of Atlantis.   Lesser Cottafavi.
HERCULES AND THE TEN AVENGERS   see   HERCULES VS. THE
GIANT WARRIORS
HERCULES IN THE HAUNTED WORLD   (I)   Woolner/SPA   1961('64-
U.S.) Technicolor/Totalscope   89m.   (ERCOLE AL CENTRO
DELLA TERRA-I.   HERCULE CONTRE LES VAMPIRES-F.   THE
VAMPIRES VS. HERCULES.   HERCULES AT THE CENTER OF
THE EARTH.   WITH HERCULES TO THE CENTER OF THE
EARTH.   HERCULES VS. THE VAMPIRES)   D: Mario Bava.
SP: Bava, A. Continenza, D. Tessari, Franco Prosperi.   PH:
Bava, Ubaldo Terzano.   Mus: Armando Trovajoli.   Ref: FM 23:
13.29:19.   COF 6:10.   FFacts.   Orpheus 3:30.   Pic: FM 26:13.
50:54.   with Reg Park, Christopher Lee, Leonora Ruffo,
Giorgio Ardisson, Ida Galli.   Hades; giant stone man, etc.
Lesser Bava.
HERCULES IN THE REGIMENT   (F?)   Pathe 1909   7m.   Ref:
Bios 11/18/09.   Bullets bounce off "invulnerable giant."
HERCULES IN THE VALE OF WOE   (I)   c1964   color (MACISTE
AGAINST HERCULES IN THE VALE OF WOE)   Ref: COF 17:28.
TVFFSB. TVG.   with Kirk Morris, Frank Gordon, Bice Valori,
Liana Orfei, Franco Franchi. Two fight promoters travel back in
time where they stage a battle between Hercules and Maciste.
HERCULES OF THE DESERT   (I)   Cineluxor 1964   color 90m.
(LA VALLE DELL'ECO TONANTE.   The VALLEY OF THE RE-
SOUNDING ECHO)   SP,D: Amerigo Anton.   SP: also De Rossi,
Moroni.   PH: Aldo Giordani.   Ref: Ital P. La Saison Cinem. with
Kirk Morris, Helène Chanel, Alberto Farnese, Spela Rozyn, Furio
Meniconi, Rosalba Neri.   "Echo-men" cause landslides and
avalanches.
HERCULES' PILLS (I) Maxima 1960 (LE PILLOLE DI ERCOLE)
D: Luciano Salce.   SP: Vighi, Baratti, Scola, Maccari.   PH:
Erico Menczer.   Mus: Armando Troviaoli.   Ref: Ital P'60.   DDC
II:70.   pic. with Sylva Koscina, Nino Manfredi, Vittorio de
Sica, Francis Blanche. Chinese doctor knows the secret of cer-
tain pills "which have an aphrodisiac effect on both men and
women."
HERCULES, PRISONER OF EVIL (I) AI-TV 1967 color 80m.
D: Antonio Margheriti (aka Anthony Dawson).   Ref: TVG.   M/TVM
3/67   with Reg Park, Ettore Manni, Maria Teresa Orsini,
Mireille Granelli.   Hercules defeats a monster.
HERCULES, SAMSON AND ULYSSES (I) MGM/I.C.D.   1963
('65-U.S.) Metrocolor 100m.   (ERCOLE SFIDA SANSONE)   SP,
D: Pietro Francisci.   PH: Silvano Ippoliti.   Mus: Angelo Lavag-
nino.   P: Joseph Fryd.   Ref: MFB'66:170.   F&F 11/66.   with
Kirk Morris, Richard Lloyd, Liana Orfei, Franco Fantasia. Sea
monster sequence. Funny at times, intentionally or not.
HERCULES, THE INVINCIBLE   (I) Metheus 1963   color (ERCOLE
L'INVINCIBILE), P,D: Al World.   SP: World, Kirk Mayor, Pat
Klein. PH:Claude Haroy.   Ref: MFB'67:7.   F&F 6/65.   with Dan

Vadis, Spela Rozin, Ken Clark. Dragon.
HERCULES UNCHAINED (I-F) WB-Embassy/Lux-Galatea 1959
Eastmancolor/Dyaliscope 101m. (ERCOLE E LA REGINA DI
LIDIA-I) SP, D: Pietro Francisci. SP: also Ennio de Concini.
PH: Mario Bava. Mus: Enzo Masetti. Ref: FFacts. FM 32:71.
COF 10:42. PM. with Steve Reeves, Sylva Koscina, Primo
Carnera, Sylvia Lopez, Sergio Fantoni. "Ogre of the Valley,"
beast-men, queen who disposes of lovers by embalming them,
etc.
HERCULES VS. THE GIANT WARRIORS (I-F) Alexander/Manley/
Cinematografica-Jacques Leitienne-Unicité 1964 Eastmancolor/
scope 94m. (Il TRIONFO DI ERCOLE. HERCULES AND THE
TEN AVENGERS. TRIUMPH OF HERCULES-TV) D: Alberto
De Martino. SP: R. Gianviti, A. Ferrau. PH: P. L. Pavoni.
Ref: MFB'65:59. Boxo 8/23/65. with Dan Vadis, Moira Orfei,
Marilu Tolo, Pierre Cressoy, Piero Lulli. Seven bronze giants
terrorize the kingdom of Micene (or Mycene). Zeus gives Her-
cules the strength to stop them.
HERCULES VS. THE MOONMEN (I-F) Nike/Comptoir 1964 color
88m. (MACISTE E LA REGINA DI SAMAR-I. MACISTE CONTRE
LES HOMMES DE PIERRE-F. MACISTE VS. THE STONE MEN)
SP, D: Giacomo Gentilomo. SP: also De Riso, Sangermano,
Scolaro. PH: O. Troiani. Ref: Ital P. COF 8:6. Pic: FM 34:
40-1. MMF 12:48g. with Alan Steel, Jany Clair, Jean Pierre
Honore, Delia D'Alberti, Mario Tamberlani. Strange beings who
came from the moon many centuries ago; their queen, who lies
in a state of "apparent death"; magic will-destroying potion; and,
of course, Hercules.
HERCULES VS. THE VAMPIRES see HERCULES IN THE HAUNTED
WORLD
HERCULES VS. ULYSSES (I-F) Embassy/CCM-Fides 1961 color/
Totalscope 98m. (ULISSE CONTRO ERCOLE-I. ULYSSES VS.
HERCULES. ULYSSES AGAINST THE SON OF HERCULES) SP, D:
Mario Caiano. SP: also André Tabet. PH: Alvaro Mancori. Mus:
A. Lavagnino. Art D: Piero Filippone. SpFX: Galliano Ricci.
Ref: MFB'64:108. DDC III:310. Embassy catalogue. with Georges
Marchal, Michael Lane, Dominique Boschero, Raffaella Carra,
Alessandra Panaro, Gabriele Tinti, Gianni Santuccio. "Cave-
dwellers," "half-man, half-birds."
HERE COMES THE BOOGIE MEN see YOU'LL FIND OUT
HERE'S A MAN see DEVIL AND DANIEL WEBSTER, The
HERENCIA MACABRA, La see MACABRE LEGACY, The
HERITAGE OF DRACULA, The see LESBIAN VAMPIRES
The HERITAGE OF THE CRYING WOMAN (Mex) Sonora Films 1946
(La HERENCIA DE LA LLORONA) SP, D: Mauricio Magdaleno.
Based on legend. PH: Jesus Hernandez. Mus: R. Ramirez. Ref:
Indice. with Paquita de Ronda, Florencio Castello, J.J.M.
Casado.
HERR ARNES PENGAR see SIR ARNE'S TREASURE (1919)
HERR ARNES PENNINGAR see SIR ARNE'S TREASURE (1954)
HERR DER WELT, Der see MASTER OF THE WORLD (1934)
HERR IM HAUS, Der see GENTLEMAN IN THE HOUSE, The
HERRIN DER WELT see MISTRESS OF THE WORLD

HERRIN VON ATLANTIS, Die   see LOST ATLANTIS
HERRLICHE ZEITEN IM SPESSART   see GLORIOUS TIMES IN THE
   SPESSART
HEXE, Die   see   WITCH, The (1954)
HEXEN BIS AUF BLUT GEQUALT   see   MARK OF THE DEVIL
HEXENTOTER VON BLACKMOOR, Der   see   WITCH-KILLER OF
   BLACKMOOR, The
HEXER, Der   see   MYSTERIOUS MAGICIAN, The
HIBERNATUS (F) 1969   Eastmancolor/Franscope   D: Edouard
   Molinaro.   SP: Jean Halain, Jacques Vilfrid, Jean-B. Luc,
   Louis de Funes, from the play by Luc.   Ref: V 9/24/69.   Uni-
   france 7/69.   with de Funes, Yves Vincent.   Girl's grandfather
   found frozen in ice in suspended animation.
HIDDEN CITY, The   see   DARKEST AFRICA
The HIDDEN CODE   Pioneer   1920   55m.   D: Richard Lestrange.
   Ref: MPN 22:1009.   with Grace Davidson, Ralph Osborne.   Hyp-
   nosis; new explosive.
HIDDEN DEATH   Gaum   1914   35m.   Ref: Bios 5/21/14.   A
   murderess becomes all powerful in a castle in the Middle Ages
   through the use of a machine which ultimately "compels her con-
   fession. "
The HIDDEN HAND   Pathe   1917   serial 15 episodes   Ref: MPN
   34:1110.   CNW.   with Doris Kenyon, Sheldon Lewis, Arline
   Pretty, Mahlon Hamilton.   New poison gas.
The HIDDEN HAND   WB   1942   68m.   D: Ben Stoloff.   SP:
   Anthony Coldeway, Raymond Shrock.   From the play "Invitation
   to a Murder" by Rufus King.   PH: Henry Sharp.   Art D: Stanley
   Fleischer.   Ref: V. HR.   with Craig Stevens, Elizabeth Frazer,
   Julie Bishop, Milton Parsons, Willie Best, Wade Boteler, Creigh-
   ton Hale, Monte Blue, Jack Mower.   Old woman put by doctor
   into state of suspended animation, buried in family vault, and then
   revived.   Sliding panels, secret passages.   subterranean river.
HIDDEN MENACE   (B)   Alliance   1938   56m.   (STAR OF THE
   CIRCUS-Eng)   D: Albert de Courville.   SP: Elizabeth Meehan,
   from the book "Program mit Truxa" by Henrich Seiler.   PH: C. F.
   Greene.   See also TRUXA.   Ref: Brit. Cinema. Dimmitt. DDC
   I:426.   FD 4/10/40.   with John Clements, Gene Sheldon, Otto
   Kruger, Gertrude Michael, Patrick Barr, Barbara Blair, Norah
   Howard.   Magician uses hypnotism to ruin tightrope act of rival
   for girl.
HIDDEN ROOM OF 1000 HORRORS   see   TELL-TALE HEART, The
   (1960)
The HIDEOUS SUN DEMON   Pacific Int'l/Realart/Clarke-King   1960
   (1955?)   74m.   (TERROR FROM THE SUN. BLOOD ON HIS LIPS-
   Eng.   THE SUN DEMON)   D, P: Robert Clarke.   SP: E. S.
   Seeley, Jr., and Doane Hoag, from the story "Strange Pursuit"
   by Clarke and Phil Hiner.   Ed, Co-D: Thomas Cassarino.   PH:
   John Morrill, Vilis Lapenieks, Jr., Stan Follis.   Mus: John
   Seely.   Ref: FM-A'69:29.   FFacts.   Pic: FM 2:21.18:21.   with
   Clarke, Patricia Manning, Nan Peterson, Del Courtney, Patrick
   Whyte.   Exposure to radioactive materials turns a physicist into
   a lizard-like creature.   Ludicrous.   Maybe one or two nice
   camera angles.

HIGH SPIRITS Cameo-Educ 1927 11m. Ref: FD 2/20/27. Oriental medium holds fake seance.

HIGH TREASON (B) Tiffany 1929 D: Maurice Elvey. SP: L'Estrange Fawcett, from the play by Pemberton Billing. Ref: FM 47:15. Imagen. SM 6: 31. Pic: SM 7:57. with Benita Hume, Jameson Thomas, Basil Gill, Raymond Massey, Rene Ray, Milton Rosmer. In 1940 the President of the United Nations averts world war by killing the leader of one bloc. "Channel Tunnel"; television.

HIGHLY DANGEROUS (B) Lippert/Two Cities 1950 88m. D: Roy Baker. SP: Eric Ambler. PH: David Harcourt. Mus: Richard Addinsell. Art D: Vetchinsky. Ref: MFB'51:204. V 9/10/51. with Dane Clark, Margeret Lockwood, Marius Goring, Naunton Wayne, Wilfrid Hyde-White, Olaf Pooley, Michael Hordern, Anthony Newley, Paul Hardtmuth. An Eastern European country is breeding germs to be used in bacteriological warfare "on a vast scale."

HIJA DE FRANKENSTEIN, La see SANTO AGAINST THE DAUGHTER OF FRANKENSTEIN

HILDE WARREN AND DEATH (G) Decla-Bioscop/May-Film 1917 (HILDE WARREN UND DER TOD) D: Joe May. SP: Fritz Lang. PH: Carl Hoffmann. Sets: S. Wroblewsky. Ref: DDC II:308. Fantastique. with Mia May, Hans Mierendorff. A woman meets Death at two points in her life.

HILFE, ICH BIN UNSICHTBAR see HELP, I'M INVISIBLE

HILLYBILLYS IN A HAUNTED HOUSE Woolner 1967 D: Jean Yarbrough. SP: Duke Yelton. 88m. with John Carradine, Lon Chaney, Jr., Basil Rathbone, Ferlin Husky, Joi Lansing, Linda Ho. Gorilla, skeletons, sliding panels.

HIMMELSKIBET see SKY SHIP, The

HIMMELSKIGET see SKY SHIP, The

The HINDOO'S CHARM Lubin 1912 18m. Ref: MPW 13:568. Lee. Wife's pin in clay figure felt by husband.

HINDU TOMBSTONE, The see INDIAN TOMB, The

HIPNOSIS see HYPNOSIS

HIRAM NA KAMAY see CLUTCHING HAND, The (1962)

HIROKU KAIBYODEN see HAUNTED CASTLE (1969)

HIS BROTHER'S GHOST PRC 1946 55m. D: Sam Newfield. SP: George Milton. P: Sigmund Neufeld. PH: Jack Greenhalgh. Ref: FDY. COF 10:42. with Buster Crabbe, Al (Fuzzy) St. John, Charles King, Bud Osborne. Man pretends to be twin brother's ghost.

HIS BROTHER'S KEEPER American (Pioneer) 1920 65m. D: Wilfrid North. SP: N. Brewster Morse. Ref: Lee. MPW 50:431. with Gladden James, Anne Drew. Thought transference; mind-control to commit murder.

HIS EGYPTIAN AFFINITY Nestor 1915 15m. SP, P: A. E. Christie. Ref: MPW 25:1379,1481. with Victoria Ford, Eddie Lyons. A princess returns to life after 3000 years and meets her reincarnated lover. He unwittingly brings back to life "the son of a shiek," who chases them.

HIS FIRST PLACE (B?) Warwick 1910 8m. Ref: Bios 9/15/10. Everyone in "electrical" store becomes connected to apparatus "with alarming results."

HIS PREHISTORIC PAST Keystone 1914 20m. SP, D: Charles
  Chaplin. Ref: SilentFF. NYT 3/31/19. with Chaplin, Mack
  Swain, Gene Marsh, Fritz Schade. Comedy set in prehistory.
HIS WONDERFUL LAMP (B) C&M 1913 8m. Ref: Bios 2/4/13.
  Professor invents magic lamp.
HISTOIRES EXTRAORDINAIRES (G) Hoffberg 1931('40-U.S.)
  (FUNF UNHEIMLICHE GESCHICHTEN. UNHEIMLICHE
  EESCHICHTEN. The LIVING DEAD-U.S. EXTRAORDINARY
  TALES. ASYLUM OF HORROR) SP, D: Richard Oswald. From
  "The Black Cat" and "The System of Dr. Tarr and Professor
  Fether" by Edgar Allan Poe and "The Suicide Club" by Robert
  Louis Stevenson. "Black Cat" sequence in DR. TERROR'S
  HOUSE OF HORRORS (1943). P: Gabriel Pascal. Ref: NYT
  12/17/40. FM 11:43. 47:60. COF 11:57. DDC III: 170,174.
  Pic: Le Surrealisme au Cinema 128a. with Paul Wegener,
  Eugen Klöpfer, Maria Koppenhöfer.
HISTOIRES EXTRAORDINAIRES (F) 1948 85m. SP, D: Jean
  Faurez. From "The Tell-Tale Heart" and "The Cask of
  Amontillado" by Edgar Allan Poe and "Ecce Homo" by De Quin-
  cey. Ref: FIR'61:470. FM 11:43. DDC III: 66,124,417,504.
  Art D: René Moulaert. with Jules Berry, Fernand Ledoux, Suzy
  Carrier, Olivier Hussenot, Jandeline.
HISTOIRES EXTRAORDINAIRES see TALES OF MYSTERY
  AND IMAGINATION
HOFFMANS ERZAHLUNGEN see TALES OF HOFFMAN (1914)
HOLD THAT GHOST Univ 1941 86m. D: Arthur Lubin. SP:
  Robert Lees, Frederic Rinaldo, John Grant. PH: Elwood Bre-
  dell, Joseph Valentine. Mus: H. J. Salter. Mus Numbers:
  Nick Castle. Art D: Jack Otterson. Ref: FDY. with Bud Abbott,
  Lou Costello, Richard Carlson, Evelyn Ankers, The Andrews
  Sisters, Joan Davis, Mischa Auer, Marc Lawrence, Shemp
  Howard, Russell Hicks, William Davidson. "Haunted" house.
HOLD THAT LINE Mono 1952 63m. D: William Beaudine. SP:
  Tim Ryan, Charles R. Marion. Story: Bert Lawrence. PH:
  Marcel LePicard. Mus: Edward J. Kay. Art D: Martin Obzina.
  Ref: V. FDY. with Leo Gorcey, Huntz Hall, David Gorcey,
  Bernard Gorcey, John Bromfield, Veda Ann Borg, Gil Stratton,
  Jr., Taylor Holmes, Mona Knox, Gloria Winters, David Condon,
  Bennie Bartlett, Francis Pierlot, Pierre Watkin. Superman
  potion.
HOLE, The see ONIBABA
A HOLE IN THE MOON (Israeli) 1964 (Un TROU DANS LA LUNE-
  F) D: U. Zohar. Ref: DDC III:109. Pic: Positif 71:45. Bur-
  lesque of KING KONG.
The HOLE IN THE WALL Metro 1921 77m. D, P: Maxwell
  Karger. SP: June Mathis. From a play by Fred Jackson. Art
  D: Joseph Calder. PH: Allen Siegler. Ref: MPW 53:588. Lee.
  AFI. with Alice Lake, Allan Forrest, Frank Brownlee, Claire
  DuBrey. Madame Mysteria, a medium, is killed in a train
  crash.
The HOLE IN THE WALL Para 1929 sound 65m. D: Robert
  Florey. SP: Pierre Collings, from the play by Fred Jackson.
  PH: George Folsey. Ref: TVG. Photoplay. FDY. AFI. with

Claudette Colbert, Edward G. Robinson, Donald Meek, David
Newell, Nellie Savage. Crooks masquerade as spiritualistic
mediums.

HOLIDAY FOR HENRIETTA see PARIS WHEN IT SIZZLES

HOLLYWOOD REVUE OF 1929 MGM 1929 130m. sound Tech-
nicolor sequences D: Charles Reisner. Dial: Al Boasberg,
Robert Hopkins. Ed: Wm. S. Gray, C. K. Wood. PH: John
Arnold, I. G. Ries, M. Fabian, J. M. Nickolaus. Art D:
Cedric Gibson, Richard Day. Ref: FDY. NYT 8/15/29. AFI.
with John Gilbert, Norma Shearer, Joan Crawford, Bessie Love,
Lionel Barrymore, Stan Laurel, Oliver Hardy, Nils Asther,
Marion Davies, William Haines, Buster Keaton, Marie Dressler,
Charles King, Polly Moran, Gus Edwards, Karl Dane, George K.
Arthur, Conrad Nagel, Jack Benny. During the singing of Gus
Edwards' "Lon Chaney Will Get You If You Don't Watch Out"
"there comes to view a good many figures of characters of Mr.
Chaney's past performances."

HOMBRE INVISIBLE ATACA, El see INVISIBLE MAN ATTACKS,
The

HOMBRE LOBO, El see MARK OF THE WOLFMAN, The

HOMBRE QUE LOGRO SER INVISIBLE, El see NEW INVISIBLE
MAN, The

HOMBRE QUE VINO DE UMMO, El see DRACULA VS. FRANKEN-
STEIN

HOMBRE SIN ROSTRO, El see MAN WITHOUT A FACE, The

HOMBRE Y EL MONSTRUO, El see MAN AND THE MONSTER,
The

HOMBRE Y LA BESTIA, El see MAN AND THE BEAST, The

HOMICIDAL Col 1961 87m. (HOMICIDE-Belgium) D, P: William
Castle. SP: Robb White. PH: Burnett Guffey. Mus: Hugo
Friedhofer. Art D: Cary Odell. Ref: FFacts. FM 13:64. with
Glenn Corbett, Patricia Breslin, James Westerfield, Jean Arless,
Eugenie Leontovich, Alan Bunce, Richard Rush, Hope Summers.
Woman returns to the old mansion she lived in as a child and
becomes involved in a mystery. Poor.

HOMME A LA TETE DE CAOUTCHOUC, L' see MAN WITH THE
RUBBER HEAD, The

HOMME AUX FIGURES DE CIRE, L' see MAN OF THE WAX
FIGURES, The

HOMME DANS LA LUNE, L' see ASTRONOMER'S DREAM, The

HOMME QUI RIT, L' see MAN WHO LAUGHS, The (1909)

HOMME QUI VENDIT SON AME AU DIABLE, L' see MAN WHO
SOLD HIS SOUL TO THE DEVIL, The (1920/1943)

HOMMES VEULENT VIVRE, Les! see MAN WANTS TO LIVE!

HOMUNCULUS (G) Deutsch-Bioscop 1916 serial six feature-length
episodes (DIE RACHE DES HOMUNKULUS) SP, D: Otto Rippert.
SP: also Robert Neuss. PH: C. Hoffmann. Art D: R. Dietrich.
Ref: MMF. Film. 9/67. Orpheus 2:33. COF 2:20. 7:32. DDC
II:315, 368. III:257, 287, 337. HOMUNCULUS, DER FUHRER.
with Olaf Föns (Homunculus), Aud E. Nissen, Theodor Loos,
Lupu Pick. Doctor creates android.

HOODOO RANCH Action 1926 60m. D: William Bertram. Ref:
AFI. Western. "Haunted" ranch house. with Buddy Roosevelt.

HOP FROG (F) Continental Warwick 1910 (HOP FROG, THE
JESTER) D: Henri Desfontaines. From the story by Edgar Allan
Poe. Ref: Bios 2/24/10. DDC II:68. A jester throws oil on and
sets fire to his tormentors, who are dressed in monkey costumes.
See also MASQUE OF THE RED DEATH.

HOP HARRIGAN Col 1946 serial 15 episodes D: Derwin Abra-
hams. SP: G. H. Plympton, Ande Lamb. From the comic strip
by J. Blummer and the radio show. PH: Ira H. Morgan. P: Sam
Katzman. Ref: Lee. Academy. SF Film. Barbour. Pic: M&H
1:25. with William Bakewell, John Merton, Ernie Adams, Anthony
Warde, Jackie Moran, Jack Buchanan, Jim Diehl, Jennifer Holt.
Ch. 2. The Secret Ray. 9. Dr. Tobor's Revenge. "Destructive
Fusion Force"; inventor's new motor.

HOP O' MY THUMB (F) Gaum 1912 30m. From the Perrault
fairy tale. Ref: Bios 11/13/13. Giant.

The HOPE DIAMOND MYSTERY Kosmik Films 1921 serial 15
episodes D: Stuart Paton. Ref: CNW. MPW 48:889. with Grace
Darmond, William Marion, Boris Karloff, George Chesebro.
Diamond has sinister influence for 400 years.

HORLA, The (by G. De Maupassant) see DIARY OF A MADMAN

HORRIBLE DOCTEUR ORLOF, L' see AWFUL DR. ORLOF, The

The HORRIBLE DR. HICHCOCK (I) Sigma III/Panda 1962('65-
U.S.) Technicolor/scope 88m. (76m-U.S.) L'ORRIBILE SE-
GRETO DEL DOTTOR HICHCOCK-I. L'EFFROYABLE SECRET
DU DR. HICHCOCK-F. RAPTUS, THE SECRET OF DR. HICH-
COCK. The TERROR OF DR. HICHCOCK-Eng. The FRIGHTEN-
ING SECRET OF DR. HICHCOCK) Sequel: The GHOST (1963).
D: Riccardo Freda (aka Robert Hampton). SP: Julyan Perry (aka
Ernesto Gastaldi). (The HORRIBLE SECRET OF DR. HICHCOCK)
PH: Raffaele Masciocchi. Mus: Roman Vlad. Art D: Franco Fuma-
galli. Ref: Orpheus 3:32. COF 10:42. Clarens. Pic: COF 5:50.
FM 27:11. with Barbara Steele, Robert Flemyng, Montgomery
Glenn, Harriet White. Old mansion, ghosts, necrophilia, pre-
mature burial.

HORRIBLE HYDE Lubin 1915 D: Jerold Hevener. Based on "The
Strange Case of Dr. Jekyll and Mr. Hyde" by Robert Louis
Stevenson. SP: E. Sargent. Ref: MPN 8/14/15. FM 34:55.
Actor poses as Mr. Hyde.

THE HORRIBLE SEXY VAMPIRE Amati 1971 (I) Ref: V 5/12/71:63.

The HORROR F. P. Pictures/Stanley c1933. D: Bud Pollard.
Ref: FJA. Hirsute monster, hunchback, snake, Indian mystic.

HORROR (SP-I) AI-TV/Columbus-Llama-Titanus 1963 (The
BLANCHEVILLE MONSTER-TV) D: Alberto de Martino. SP:
Jean Grimaud, Gordon Wilson. From "The Fall of the House of
Usher" and "Berenice" or "The Premature Burial" by Edgar
Allan Poe. PH: Alejandro Ulloa. Mus: Francis Clark. Ref:
MMF 9:17. MW 1:12. Pic: COF 7:7. with Gérard Tichy, Leo
Anchoriz. Joan Hills, Irán Eory, Richard Davis, Helga Liné.
Girl buried prematurely in cataleptic state. Long on ominous si-
lences and sinister glances, short on plot and character. Awk-
wardly dubbed ("Emily's buoyant, young, and jovial").

HORROR AND SEX (Mex) Calderon c1969 Eastmancolor (HORROR
Y SEXO) D: Rene Cardona. SP: Cardona and Rene Cardona, Jr.

PH: Raul Solares. Mus: Antonio Diaz (Conde?). with Armando
Silvestre, Noelia Noel, Jose Elias Moreno. A scientist puts a
gorilla's heart into his son's body. When that doesn't work out
too well, he puts in a girl's heart. The boy becomes a monster
and runs around tearing girls' clothes off. He is shot, falls from
a tall building, and onlookers sympathize "Poor madman" and
"Very sad." So cheap that extras in crowd scenes don't have
voices when they open their mouths.
HORROR CASTLE Manley/Zodiac/Gladiator/Atlantica (I) 1963
('65-U.S.) Eastmancolor/Totalscope 83m. (LA VERGINE DI
NORIMBERGA, CASTLE OF TERROR-Eng) D: Antonio Margheriti, G. Green, Edmond T. Greville. From "The Virgin of
Nuremberg" by Frank Bogart. Mus: Riz Ortolani. Art D: Ot-
tavio Scotti. Ref: FFacts. MW 1:9. with Christopher Lee,
Rossana Podesta, Georges Riviere, Lucille St. Simon. German
count's bride frightened by mysterious events in castle. Bloody,
with cheap shocks, music. "The Punisher"'s origin makes inter-
esting story at end. (TERROR CASTLE)
The HORROR CHAMBER OF DR. FAUSTUS (F-I) Lopert/Champs-
Elysées--Lux 1959 ('62-U.S.) 92m. (Les YEUX SANS VISAGE-F.
OCCHI SENZA VOLTO-I. EYES WITHOUT A FACE. HOUSE OF
DR. RASANOFF. Das SCHRECKENS DES DR. RASANOFF-G.)
D: Georges Franju. SP: Boileau-Narcejac, Jean Redon, Claude
Sautet, Franju. Dial: Pierre Gascar; from the novel by Redon.
PH: Eugen Shuftan. Mus: Maurice Jarre. Art D: Auguste Capelier.
Ref: FFacts. COF 3:4.11:24. FM 9:16. Pic: FanMo 5:23. with
Alida Valli, Edith Scob, Pierre Brasseur, Juliette Mayniel. Surgeon
kidnaps girls in order to transplant their facial skin for a new
visage for his disfigured daughter. Some stray breathtaking images,
but the dubbing pretty much ruins the English version.
HORROR FROM BEYOND, The see BLOOD THIRST
HORROR HOTEL (B) T-L/Medallion/Vulcan 1960 ('63-U.S.) 76m.
(CITY OF THE DEAD) D: John Moxey. SP: George Baxt. Story:
Milton Subotsky. PH: Desmond Dickinson. Mus: Douglas Gamley,
Ken Jones. Art D: John Blezard. SpFX: Cliff Richardson. Ref:
FFacts. FM 12:8. PM. with Christopher Lee, Betta St. John,
Valentine Dyall, William Abner, Patricia Jessel, Venetia Stevenson.
College girl disappears in New England town where Puritans have been
burned for making pacts with the devil. One well-edited sequence of
witch suddenly appearing in road. Mainly just sinister faces peering
through fog.
HORROR HOUSE (U.S.-B) AI/Tigon 1970 Movielab color 83m.
(The DARK. The HAUNTED HOUSE OF HORROR) SP, D: Michael
Armstrong. Add'l material: Peter Marcus. PH: Jack Atcheler.
Mus: Reg Tilsely. Art D: H. Pearce. Ref: V 4/29/70. Pic: COF
15:48. with Frankie Avalon, Jill Haworth, Richard O'Sullivan,
Dennis Price. Maniac loose in "haunted" house.
HORROR ISLAND Univ 1941   60m. D: George Waggner. SP: Maurice
Tombragel, Victor McLeod. Story: Alex Gottlieb. PH: Elwood
Bredell. Mus: H. J. Salter, Charles Previn. Art D: Jack Otterson.
Ref: FDY COF 10:42. Pic: HM 5:22. with Leo Carrillo, Dick Foran,
Peggy Moran, Hobart Cavanaugh, Fuzzy Knight, John Eldredge,
Walter Catlett, Ralf Harolde, Iris Adrian, Emmett Vogan, Lewis

Howard. Treasure hunters in "haunted" castle are warned to leave by The Phantom. Ghostly voices, noises. Sometimes pleasant. Nothing good but nothing really bad either. Howard fairly amusing as bored playboy.

HORROR IN THE MIDNIGHT SUN see INVASION OF THE ANIMAL PEOPLE

HORROR MAN, The see TELL-TALE HEART, The (1960)

HORROR MANIACS see GREED OF WILLIAM HART, The

HORROR OF DRACULA (B) Univ/Hammer 1958 Technicolor 82m. (DRACULA-Eng.) D: Terence Fisher. SP: Jimmy Sangster. Based on the novel "Dracula" by Bram Stoker. Sequence in DRACULA, PRINCE OF DARKNESS. PH: Jack Asher. Mus: James Bernard. Art D: Bernard Robinson. Makeup: Phil Leakey. Ass't D: Robert Lynn. Ref: FM 14:6. Clarens. Pic: FM 8:16.18:45. with Christopher Lee, Peter Cushing, Michael Gough, John van Eyssen, Valerie Gaunt, Miles Malleson, Melissa Stribling, Carol Marsh. Easily Hammer's best horror movie. Designed for speed, action, and suspense, with Lee's Dracula exciting and original. Good on all counts: score, script, direction, acting. See also BAD FLOWER, The.

The HORROR OF FRANKENSTEIN (B) EMI/Hammer 1970 color 95m. SP, D: Jimmy Sangster. SP: also Jeremy Burnham. PH: Moray Grant. Mus: James Bernard. Makeup: Tom Smith. with Ralph Bates, Kate O'Mara, Veronica Carlson, Dennis Price. Dr. Victor Frankenstein succeeds in bringing a tortoise back to life.

The HORROR OF IT ALL (B) Fox/Associated Producers 1964 75m. D: Terence Fisher. SP: Ray Russell. PH: Arthur Lavis. Exec P: Robert Lippert. Ref: FFacts. PM. MW 1:9. COF 6:52, 56.10:42. Pic:FM 31:11. with Pat Boone, Erica Rogers, Dennis Price, Andree Melly, Valentine Dyall, Erik Chitty, Jack Bligh. Spooky, isolated house; vampirish "Natalia"; maniac, etc. Lame farce.

HORROR OF MALFORMED MEN (J) Toei 1969 color/scope 99m. (KYOFU KIKEI NINGEN) D: Teruo Ishii. SP: Ishii, M. Kakefuda. PH: S. Akatsuka. Ref: UFQ 47. with Teruo Yoshida, Minoru Oki. Web-fingered man transforms island into menagerie of artificially-created freaks.

HORROR OF PARTY BEACH Fox/Iselin-Tenney 1964 82m. (IN-VASION OF THE ZOMBIES) D, P: Del Tenney. SP: Richard Hilliard. Mus: Bill Holmes. Ref: Orpheus 4:36. FFacts. with John Scott, Alice Lyon, Allen Laurel, Marilyn Clark. Zombie-like creatures who live on blood do away with extras while the hero races for sodium for some reason. Inconceivably bad.

HORROR OF THE BLOOD MONSTERS Independent Intl 1971 Movielab color 85m. (CREATURES OF THE PREHISTORIC PLANET) D, P: Al Adamson. SP: Sue McNair. Mus: Mike Belarde. Narr: Theodore. Ref: RVB. FM 80:48. Boxo 4/5/71. with John Carradine, Robert Dix, Vicki Volante. Vampire-killings sweep the world.

HORROR STORY, A see THREE ARE THREE

HORROR Y SEXO see HORROR AND SEX

HORRORS DEL BOSQUE NEGRO, Los see SHE-WOLF, The

HORRORS OF BLOOD ISLAND see BEAST OF BLOOD

HORRORS OF SPIDER ISLAND (G-Yugos) Pacemaker/Intercontinental-Rapid 1959 ('66-U.S.) 82m. (EIN TOTER HING IM NETZ. IN HET

NET VAN DE SADIST. Le MORT DANS LE FILET-F. DANS LE
FILET DU SADIQUE-Belg. GIRLS OF SPIDER ISLAND. IT'S HOT
IN PARADISE) SP, D: Fritz Böttger (aka Jamie Nolan). Mus: Willy
Mattes, Karl Bette. Ref: Imagen. COF 8:6. Boxo 4/4/63.11/29/65.
DDC II:314. FM 11:14.34:24. German Pictures. Pic: Le Sur-
realisme au Cinema 96e. with Helga Frank, Harald Maresch, Alex
D'Arcy, Barbara Valentin, Reiner Brand. Man attacked by giant
spider becomes blood-thirsty monster.
HORRORS OF THE BLACK MUSEUM (B) AI/Carmel/Anglo-Amal-
gamated 1959 Eastmancolor/scope 95m. D: Arthur Crabtree.
SP: Aben Kandel, Herman Cohen. PH: Desmond Dickinson. Mus:
Gerard Schurmann. ArtD: Wilfred Arnold. P: Cohen. Ref:
Clarens. FM 9:7. Pic: FM 7:13. with Michael Gough, June Cunning-
ham, Shirley Ann Field, Beatrice Varley, Austin Trevor, Nora
Gordon. To get story material a journalist commits horrible
crimes. Traces of Jekyll and Hyde and zombiism. Utter nonsense
seasoned with a few sadistic thrills.
HOT ICE (B) Apex/Present Day 1952 85m. SP, D: Kenneth Hume.
From "A Weekend at Thrackley" by Alan Melville. PH: Ted Lloyd.
Mus: Ivor Slaney. Ref: MFB. with Barbara Murray, John Justin,
John Penrose, Ivor Barnard, Michael Balfour. Man invites guests
to his spooky mansion to add their diamonds and gems to his collec-
tion.
HOT WATER Lloyd/Pathe 1924 57m. D: Sam Taylor, Fred
Newmeyer. SP: Taylor, John Grey, Tommy Gray, Tim Whelan.
PH: Walter Lundin. Ref: Wid's 10/25/24. FD 11/2/24: Imitates
ONE EXCITING NIGHT "with a spook...thrills and screams."
with Harold Lloyd, Jobyna Ralston, Charles Stevenson, Josephine
Crowel.
HOTEL ELECTRICO, El see ELECTRIC HOTEL, The
The HOUND OF BLACKWOOD CASTLE (W.G.) Rialto 1967
(DER HUND VON BLACKWOOD CASTLE) D: Alfred Vohrer.
From a story by Edgar Wallace. Ref: Germany. M/TVM 5/68.
Film 3/68. Bianco 11/68. with Heinz Drache, Karin Baal,
Uta Levka, Siegfried Schurenberg.
The HOUND OF THE BASKERVILLES (G) 1914 (DER HUND VON
BASKERVILLE) D: Rudolf Meinert. Sets: Hermann Warm. Ref:
Germany. EncicDS.
The HOUND OF THE BASKERVILLES (F) Pathe 1914 45m.
(Le CHIEN DES BASKERVILLE) Ref: DDC II:106. MPN 3/6/15.
Motography 3/6/15.
The HOUND OF THE BASKERVILLES (G) Vitascop 1917
(DER HUND VON BASKERVILLE) D: Richard Oswald. PH:
Werner Brandes? Ref: FIR'61:411. Germany: 1920?
The HOUND OF THE BASKERVILLES (B) FBO/Stoll 1921 64m. D:
Maurice Elvey. SP: William J. Elliott. PH: G. Burger. Art
D: Walter W. Murton. Ref: SilentFF. LC. with Eille Norwood,
Hubert Willis, Allen Jeayes, Lewis Gilbert, Betty Campbell,
Mme. D'Esterre.
The HOUND OF THE BASKERVILLES (B-G) Erda-Film 1929
(DER HUND VON BASKERVILLE) D: Richard Oswald. SP:
Herbert Juttke, Georg C. Klaren. Ref: Deutsche. Halliwell.
with Carlyle Blackwell (Sherlock Holmes), George Seroff, Fritz Rasp.

The HOUND OF THE BASKERVILLES (B) First Anglo 1931 72m.
D: V. Gareth Gundry. SP: Edgar Wallace, from the book by Sir
Arthur Conan Doyle. PH: Bernard Knowles. Ed: Ian Dalrymple.
Ref: FDY. Brit. Cinema. DDC I:90. with John Stuart, Henry
Hallett, Heather Angel, Reginald Bach, Robert Rendel, Fred
Lloyd, Wilfred Shine, Sybil Jane.

The HOUND OF THE BASKERVILLES (G) German Bavaria Films
1936 (DER HUND VON BASKERVILLE) D: Carl Lamac. Ref:
Lee. Halliwell. with Fritz Rasp.

The HOUND OF THE BASKERVILLES Fox 1939 80m. D: Sidney
Lanfield. SP: Ernest Pascal, from the book by Sir Arthur Conan
Doyle. PH: J. Peverell Marley. Mus: Cyril Mockridge. Art
D: Richard Day, Hans Peters. Ref: Clarens. ModM 3:5. with
Basil Rathbone, Nigel Bruce, Richard Greene, Lionel Atwill,
Wendy Barrie, John Carradine, Barlowe Borland, Beryl Mercer,
E. E. Clive, Nigel de Brulier, Mary Gordon, Morton Lowry,
Ralph Forbes, Eily Malyon, Ivan Simpson, Ian MacLaren, John
Burton. Mediocre version of Doyle's tale of the "ghost-hound."
Nothing much happens until the last 20 minutes.

The HOUND OF THE BASKERVILLES (B) UA /Hammer 1959
Technicolor 84m. D: Terence Fisher. SP: Peter Bryan, from
the book by Sir Arthur Conan Doyle. PH: Jack Asher. Mus:
James Bernard. Art D: Bernard Robinson. Ref: Clarens. with
Peter Cushing, Christopher Lee, Marla Landi, Andre Morell,
Miles Malleson, David Oxley, Francis de Wolff, John Le Mesurier.
Cushing is an energetic Holmes, but the film is even weaker than
the '39 version.

HOUNDS OF ZAROFF, The see MOST DANGEROUS GAME, The

An HOUR BEFORE THE DAWN Famous Players 1913 45m. D:
J. Searle Dawley. Ref: The Film Index. with House Peters.
Scientist killed by explosive ray.

HOUR OF THE WOLF (Swedish) Lopert /Svensk 1968 88m.
(VARGTIMMEN) SP, D: Ingmar Bergman. PH: Sven Nykvist. Mus:
Lars Johan Werle. Art D: Marik Vos-Lundh. SpFX: Evald Anders-
son. Ref: FFacts. Newsweek: "werewolf" story. PM: "The demonic
world of a tormented artist." with Max Von Sydow, Liv Ullmann,
Erland Josephson, Ingrid Thulin.

HOUSE AND THE BRAIN, The (short story by E. Bulwer-Lytton)
see NIGHT COMES TOO SOON, The

HOUSE AT THE END OF THE WORLD see DIE, MONSTER, DIE /
TOMB OF LIGEIA

HOUSE BEHIND THE HEDGE, The see UNKNOWN TREASURES

HOUSE IN MARSH ROAD, The see INVISIBLE CREATURE, The

The HOUSE IN THE WOODS (B) Archway /Edict 1957 62m.
SP, D: Maxwell Munden. Mus: Larry Adler. From the short story
"Prelude to Murder" by Walter C. Brown. Ref: FEFN 2 /14 /58.
COF 10:42. FFATF. with Michael Gough, Patricia Roc, Ronald
Howard. Ghost of murdered woman returns.

The HOUSE OF A 1000 CANDLES Selig 1915 D: T. N. Heffron.
SP: Gilson Willets, from the novel by Meredith Nicholson. Ref:
MPW 25:1327. MPN 8 /21 /15: "Eerie atmosphere." with Harry
Mestayer, Grace Darmond, George Backus. House with secret
panels, etc. See also HAUNTING SHADOWS.

HOUSE OF DARK SHADOWS MGM 1970 Metrocolor 97m. D: Dan
Curtis. SP: Sam Hall, Gordon Russell. PH: Arthur Ornitz.
Based on the "Dark Shadows" TV series. Prod.des: Trevor
Williams. Mus: Robert Cobert. Ref: V 9/2/70. with Jonathan
Frid, Grayson Hall, Joan Bennett, Kathryn Leigh Scott.
Vampire.
HOUSE OF DARKNESS (B) Broder/Int'l Motion Picture 1948 ('54-
Realart-U.S.) 77m. D: Oswald Mitchell. SP: John Gilling, from
a novel by Betty Davies. PH: Cyril Bristow. Mus: George
Melachrino. Ref: Brit. Fm. Ybk. '49/'50. MFB'48:73. COF
10:44. with Laurence Harvey, Leslie Brooks, John Stuart, Les-
ley Osmond. Through suggestion a man kills his stepbrother in
haunted house. He then fears his dead brother haunts him.
HOUSE OF DR. RASANOFF see HORROR CHAMBER OF DR.
FAUSTUS, The
HOUSE OF DOOM see BLACK CAT, The (1934)
HOUSE OF DRACULA Univ 1945 67m. D: Erle C. Kenton. SP:
Edward T. Lowe. PH: George Robinson. Mus: Edgar Fairchild.
Art D: John B. Goodman, Martin Obzina. SpFX: John P. Fulton.
Makeup: Jack Pierce. P: Paul Malvern. Exec P: Joseph Gershen-
son. Ref: Academy. Clarens. FM 43:50. COF 7:40. Pic: FM
2:19. 14:46. 19:41. 20:20. with Lon Chaney, Jr., John Carradine,
Onslow Stevens, Ludwig Stossel, Jane Adams, Lionel Atwill,
Glenn Strange, Martha O'Driscoll, Skelton Knaggs, Dick Dickin-
son, Gregory Muradian. Frankenstein's monster! Dracula!
Hunchbacked nurse! And the Wolf Man is cured! A real mess.
Enough silly little twists to keep things moving though.
The HOUSE OF FEAR Lubin 1914 35m. Ref: Bios 4/23/14:
"Real ghosts... mystifying."
HOUSE OF FEAR Univ 1939 67m. D: Joe May. SP: Peter
Milne, from a book by Wadsworth Camp and the play "The Last
Warning" by Thomas Fallon. PH: Milton Krasner. Ref: MPH
6/10/39. FD 6/5/39. with Irene Hervey, William Gargan, Alan Dine-
hart, Walter Woolf King, El Brendel, Dorothy Arnold, Robert Coote,
Harvey Stephens, Jan Duggan, Tom Dugan, Don Douglas. Theatre
haunted by murder victim's "ghost."
HOUSE OF FEAR Univ 1945 69m. P, D: Roy William Neill. SP:
Roy Chanslor, from "The Five Orange Pips" by Sir Arthur Conan
Doyle. PH: Virgil Miller. Mus: Paul Sawtell. Art D: John B.
Goodman, Eugene Lourie. Ref: FDY. with Basil Rathbone, Nigel
Bruce, Gavin Muir, Dennis Hoey, Holmes Herbert, Aubrey Mather,
Paul Cavanagh. Old house, coffins, mysterious disappearances.
Fairly atmospheric Sherlock Holmes film. Bruce has a nice solo
scene.
HOUSE OF FRANKENSTEIN Univ 1944 70m. (The DEVIL'S
BROOD. DOOM OF DRACULA) D: Erle C. Kenton. SP: Edward
T. Lowe. Story: Curt Siodmak. PH: George Robinson. Mus:
H. J. Salter. Art D: John B. Goodman, Martin Obzina. SpFX:
John P. Fulton. Ref: Academy. FM 11:22. 23:41. Pic: FM 20:19.
with Boris Karloff, Anne Gwynne, Lon Chaney, Jr., J. Carrol
Naish, Elena Verdugo, John Carradine, Peter Coe, Lionel At-
will, Sig Ruman(n), George Zucco, Phil(l)ip van Zandt, Julius
Tannen, Olaf Hytten, Frank Reicher, Brandon Hurst, Glenn

Strange, Charles Miller, Dick Dickinson, George Lynn, Michael
Mark, Belle Mitchell, Eddie Cobb.   Frankenstein's monster!
Dracula! Hunchback! The Wolf Man! Repellent mixture of horror
and sentimentality.
HOUSE OF FRIGHT   (B)   AI/Hammer   1960   Eastmancolor/
Megascope 89m.   (The TWO FACES OF DR. JEKYLL.
JEKYLL'S INFERNO.   DR. JEKYLL AND MR. HYDE) D:
Terence Fisher.   SP: Wolf Mankowitz, from Robert Louis
Stevenson's "The Strange Case of Dr. Jekyll and Mr. Hyde." PH:
Jack Asher. Mus sc: Monty Norman, David Heneker.   Art D:
Bernard Robinson.   Makeup: Roy Ashton.   Ref: F Facts. Orpheus
3:27.   FM 11:38.13:62.   with Paul Massie, Dawn Addams, Chris-
topher Lee, David Kossoff, Francis de Wolff, Joe Robinson.
Slightly different but still one of the weakest versions of the
Jekyll and Hyde story.
HOUSE OF FRIGHT   see   BLACK SUNDAY
The HOUSE OF HATE   Pathe   1918   serial 20 episodes.   Ch. 6.
Liquid Fire Apparatus Tested with Thrilling Results.   7. Deadly
Germs Play Part in Thrilling Serial. Ref: CNW. MPW 36:434. D:
George B. Seitz.   with Pearl White, Antonio Moreno, Peggy
Shanor, Floyd Buckley.   "The Terror" attempts to kill girl with
germs.
The HOUSE OF HORROR   F Nat 1929   65m.   part-talking and
silent versions D: Ben Christensen. SP: Richard Bee, William
Irish. PH: Ernest Haller, Sol Polito. P: R. Rowland. Ref:
Clarens. FDY. FM 23:24. with Thelma Todd, Louise Fazenda,
Chester Conklin, Emile Chautard, Michael Visaroff, Dale Fuller,
William V. Mong, William Orlamond, Tenen Holtz. Old house
with secret panels, etc.
HOUSE OF HORRORS   Univ 1946 65m.   (JOAN MEDFORD IS
MISSING-Eng.)   D: Jean Yarbrough. SP: George Bricker. Story:
Dwight V. Babcock. PH: Maury Gertsman. Mus: H. J. Salter.
Art D: John B. Goodman, Abraham Grossman. Ref: FDY. Pic:
HM 4:12. with Robert Lowery, Virginia Grey, Rondo Hatton,
Bill Goodwin, Martin Kosleck, Alan Napier. Sculptor sends "The
Creeper" out to silence unfriendly critics. Junk.
The HOUSE OF MYSTERY (F?)   Pathe 1911 8m. Ref: Bios 1/4/12.
Burglar in villa attacked by automata and mechanical policemen.
HOUSE OF MYSTERY   Mono 1934 62m.   D: William Nigh. SP:
Albert DeMond, from the play by Adam Hull Shirk. Ed: Carl
Pierson. P: Paul Malvern. Ref: LC. TVFFSB. COF 10:44.
MPH'34. with Ed Lowry, Verna Hillie, Mary Foy. "Unseen
monster seeks vengeance" when sacred Indian temple is despoiled.
HOUSE OF MYSTERY   Mono/Associated British/ABPC (B) 1939
('41-U.S.) 74m.   D: Walter Summers. SP: Doreen Montgomery.
From the book "At the Villa Rose" by A. E. W. Mason. PH:
Claude Friese-Greene. Ref: Dipali 3/17/39.   V6/4/41.   MFB
'39:155. with Ken(n)eth Kent, Judy Kelly, Walter Rilla, Clifford
Evans, Martita Hunt.   "Hooded murderer" strikes during seance.
HOUSE OF MYSTERY   (B)   Independent Artists 1961 56m. (The
UNSEEN) SP, D: Vernon Sewell. PH: Ernest Steward. Art D:
Jack Shampan. Mus: Stanley Black. P: Julian Wintle, Leslie
Parkyn. Ref: FM 22:13.   Film Review. FEFN 5/61.   MFB'61:

82. with Jane Hylton, Peter Dyneley, Nanette Newman, Maurice
Kaufmann, Colin Gordon, John Merivale. "A young couple go to
look at a strangely cheap old house--and the occupant tells them
the reason for the low price, a story of ghostly mysteries. "
HOUSE OF MYSTERY see MAKING THE HEADLINES/NIGHT
  MONSTER
HOUSE OF SECRETS Batcheller/Chesterfield 1929 sound 60m.
  D: Edmund Lawrence. SP: Adeline Leitzbach, from a novel by
  Sydney Horler. PH: G. Webber, G. Peters, L. Lang, I. Brown-
  ing. Ed: Selma Rosenbloom. Ref: V. FD 5/26/29. AFI. with
  Joseph Striker, Marcia Manning, Elmer Grandin, Herbert War-
  ren, Edward Roseman. Great scientist (played by "the guy who
  apes Chaney") murders his housekeeper "in the noble cause of
  experimentation.... Mysterious and spooky house... terrifying happenings. "
HOUSE OF SECRETS Batcheller/Chesterfield 1936 70m. D:
  Roland Reed. SP: John Krafft. Based on the novel "Hawk's Nest"
  by Sydney Horler. Ref: NYT 2/22/37. with Sidney Blackmer,
  Holmes Herbert, Leslie Fenton, Syd Saylor, Muriel Evans, Noel
  Madison, Ian MacLaren. MPH 11/7/136: Man seeking to claim
  inheritance of ancestral home "runs into amazing and fearsome ex-
  periences. With all the weird twists common to a terror drama. "
  Ed: Dan Milner. PH: M. A. Anderson 2/24/37.
HOUSE OF SILENCE Lasky/Para 1918 D: Donald Crisp. SP:
  Margaret Turnbull, from a novel. Ref: FIR'66:227. MPH
  10/7/39:17: "Mystery story of a haunted house. " with Wallace
  Reid, Ann Little, Winter Hall, Ernest Joy.
HOUSE OF SILENCE, The see SILENT HOUSE, The
HOUSE OF TERROR see FACE OF THE SCREAMING WEREWOLF
HOUSE OF TERRORS (J) Toei 1965 scope 81m. (KAIDAN
  SEMUSHI OTOKO. HOUSE OF TERROR) D: Hajime Sato. SP:
  Hajime Takaiwa. PH: Shoe Nishikawa. Ref: Unij. Bltn. 31. with
  Akira Nishimura, Y. Kusunoki, Yoko Hayama. Hunchback,
  haunted house, and the "strange compulsion to murder which
  comes upon those who stay there. "
HOUSE OF THE BLACK DEATH 1965 80m. Ref: TVFFSB. with
  Lon Chaney, Jr., John Carradine, Andrea King, Tom Drake.
  "Disciple of black magic holds people captive in old house. "
HOUSE OF THE DAMNED Fox/A.P.I. 1963 scope 62m. P,D:
  Maury Dexter. SP: Harry Spalding. PH: John Nickolaus, Jr.,
  Mus: Henry Vars. Art D: Harry Reif. Ref: FFacts. MW 10:26.
  COF 4:4. with Ronald Foster, Merry Anders, Richard Kiel,
  Richard Crane, Erika Peters. Giant; headless woman; legless
  man, etc., in isolated mansion.
The HOUSE OF THE LOST COURT Para/Edison 1915 55m.
  Ref: MPN 5/29/15. D: Charles J. Brabin. From the novel by
  Mrs. C. M. Williamson. with Gertrude McCoy, Viola Dane,
  Duncan McRae. Oriental poison makes man appear to be dead.
HOUSE OF THE SEVEN GABLES Edison 1910 From the book by
  Nathaniel Hawthorne. Ref: Bios 12/15/10. Curse on house.
HOUSE OF THE SEVEN GABLES Univ 1940 89m. D: Joe May.
  SP: Lester Cole, Harold Greene, from the book by Nathaniel
  Hawthorne. PH:Milton Krasner. Ref: FDY. with Vincent Price,

George Sanders, Margaret Lindsay, Nan Grey, Alan Napier,
Cecil Kellaway, Gilbert Emery, Miles Mander, Edgar Norton,
Charles Trowbridge. Curse hangs over the house of the Pyncheon
family. Smooth but unexciting; frequently hampered by lousy
dialogue.

HOUSE OF THE SEVEN GABLES (by N. Hawthorne) see TWICE
TOLD TALES

HOUSE OF THE TOLLING BELL Pathe 1920 D, P: J. Stuart
Blackton. Story: Edith S. Tupper. Ref: Exhibitors Herald. with
Bruce Gordon, May McAvoy, William Jenkins. "Brimming with
ghostly and eerie effects.... Ghosts that roam... hands that apparently come out of the air..."

HOUSE OF USHER AI/Alta Vista 1960 Pathecolor/Scope 82m.
(The MYSTERIOUS HOUSE OF USHER) D, P: Roger Corman. SP:
Richard Matheson, from "The Fall of the House of Usher" by
Edgar Allan Poe. PH: Floyd Crosby. Mus: Les Baxter. Art
D: Daniel Haller. Ref: Orpheus 3:28. Pic: FM 8:18.9:28-33. NY
Herald Tribune: "Walks conscientiously in Poe's stylistic steps."
NY Times: "Ignored the author's style." with Vincent Price,
Mark Damon, Myrna Fahey, Harry Ellerbe. Visitor becomes en-
meshed in the mysteries of an evil old mansion.

HOUSE OF WAX WB 1953 88m. Warnercolor/3-D (Das KABINETT
DES PROFESSOR BONDI-G.) D: Andre de Toth. SP: Crane
Wilbur. From the play "Waxworks" by Charles S. Belden. PH:
Bert Glennon, Peverell Marley. Mus: David Buttolph. Art D:
Stanley Fleischer. Ref: Clarens. FM 14:6. Pic: FM 11:11.19:70.
with Vincent Price, Frank Lovejoy, Phyllis Kirk, Carolyn Jones,
Charles Bronson, Roy Roberts, Paul Picerni, Paul Cavanagh,
Dabbs Greer, Philip Tonge. Mad proprietor of wax museum uses
human bodies for wax displays. Better, surprisingly, than its
famous, once-rare original, MYSTERY OF THE WAX MUSEUM,
though not that much better. See also CHAMBER OF HORRORS
(1966).

The HOUSE OF WHISPERS Brunton-Hodkinson 1920 D: Ernest C.
Warde. SP: Jack Cunningham. PH: Arthur L. Todd. Ref: Exhibitors Herald. MPN 10/2/20. with J. W. Kerrigan, Joseph
J. Dowling, Fritzi Brunette, Fred C. Jones. Apartment house
"haunted" by whispers which frighten tenants; secret staircases;
crooks.

The HOUSE ON BARE MOUNTAIN Olympic Int'l 1962 62m.
(NIGHT ON BARE MOUNTAIN?) D: R. L. Frost. SP: Denver
Scott. PH: Greg Sandor. color/scope Mus: Pierre Martel.
Ref: Imagen. MW 3:6. MMF. with Jeffrey Smithers (Count
Dracula), Bob Cresse, Laura Eden, Angela Webster, Hugh Can-
non (Krakow, the werewolf), Warren Ames (Frankenstein monster).
Monsters turn out to be hoaxes.

HOUSE ON HAUNTED HILL AA/Susian 1958 P, D: William Castle.
SP: Robb White. PH: Carl E. Guthrie. 75m. Mus: Von Dexter.
Art D: David Milton. Ref: Clarens. Pic: FM 8:68.16:7. with
Vincent Price, Carol Ohmart, Richard Long, Alan Marshal,
Elisha Cook, Jr., Julie Mitchum, Leona Anderson. Fair haunted-
house movie, with more small chills than most of its type. Best
prop is a tinkling of chandelier.

The HOUSE ON HOKUM HILL Beauty (Mutual) 1916 Ref: MPN
13:3934. with John Sheehan, Carol Holloway, John Steppling,
John Gough. Writer of thrillers uses "patented plot machine" to
devise plots.
The HOUSE THAT DRIPPED BLOOD (B) Cinerama/Amicus 1970
Eastmancolor 101m. D: Peter Duffell. SP, story: Robert Bloch.
From "Method for Murder," "Waxworks," "Sweets to the Sweet,"
and "The Cloak" by Bloch. PH: Ray Parslow. Art D: Tony
Curtis. Makeup: Harry and Peter Frampton. Ref: Boxo 3/8/71.
with Peter Cushing, Christopher Lee, Ingrid Pitt, Denholm Elliott, Jon Pertwee, Nyree Dawn Porter, Tom Adams, John
Bryans (Stoker). Pertwee is very capable in the low-comedy vampire tale, "The Cloak," the best of the four stories. The other
three just have their moments, the best perhaps a comic-shock
scene with a psychiatrist, cleverly adapted from CAT PEOPLE, in
"Method for Murder." Poor framing story.
HOUSE THAT SCREAMED, The see BOARDING SCHOOL, The
The HOUSE THAT WOULD NOT DIE ABC-TV/Aaron Spelling 1970
color 72m. D: John L. Moxey. SP: Henry Farrell, from the
novel "Ammie, Come Home" by Barbara Michaels. PH: Fleet
Southcott. Mus sc: Laurence Rosenthal. Art D: Tracy Bousman.
Ref: LA Times, TVG. with Barbara Stanwyck, Richard Egan,
Michael Anderson, Jr., Katherine Winn, Doreen Lang. Old
house seems to be occupied by ghosts.
The HOUSE WITH NOBODY IN IT Rialto/Gaum 1915 D: Richard
Garrick. SP: Dr. Clarence J. Harris. Ref: MPW 9/18/15:2014,
2017, 2036. with Ivy Troutman, Bradley Barker, Frank Whitson.
"Mysterious flashes" from house "lead to reports that the house
is haunted."
The HOUSE WITHOUT DOORS OR WINDOWS (G) 1914 (DAS HAUS
OHNE TUREN UND FENSTER) D: Stellan Rye. Ref: DDC II:
308: fantasy film. Pic: DDC I:299.
The HOUSE WITHOUT DOORS OR WINDOWS (G) 1921 D:
Friedrich Feher. Ref: Lee. FIR'61:567. Clarens. CALIGARI
influence.
HOW AWFUL ABOUT ALLAN ABC-TV/Aaron Spelling 1970 color
72m. D: Curtis Harrington. SP: Henry Farrell, from his book.
PH: Fleet Southcott. P: George Edwards. Mus: Laurence Rosen-
thal. Ref: RVB. with Julie Harris, Joan Hackett, Kent Smith,
Robert H. Harris, Anthony Perkins. Hooded figure haunts man.
Script seems just a lot of raw material no one bothered to work
out. Harris and Perkins are totally wasted; Hackett makes the
best of a bad situation.
HOW DO YOU DOOO? PRC 1945 81m. D: Ralph Murphy. SP:
Joseph Carole, Harry Sauber. PH: B. H. Kline. Mus D: How-
ard Jackson. Art D: Edward C. Jewell. Ref: MFB'46. with
Bert Gordon, Harry von Zell, Cherly Walker, Ella Mae Morse,
Claire Windsor, Frank Albertson, Keye Luke, Charles Middleton,
Matt McHugh, Thomas Jackson, Leslie Denison, James Burke,
Francis Pierlot, Fred Kelsey. Man apparently dead--victim of
doctor's experiments in curing heart disease--turns up alive at
end.
HOW LOVE CONQUERED HYPNOTISM see STRANGE CASE OF

PRINCESS KHAN, The
HOW THEY WORK IN CINEMA (F) Eclair 1911 Ref: The Film
Index. MPN 9:394. Electrical devices, robot-cast used in mak-
ing film.
HOW TO BE LUCKY (F?) Pathe 1910 10m. Ref: Bios 4/21/10.
Dr. Puffem's "Back-Straightener" removes hunchback's hump.
HOW TO KILL A LADY see TARGET FOR KILLING
HOW TO MAKE A MONSTER AI/Sunset 1958 75m. D: Herbert L.
Strock. SP: P: Herman Cohen. SP: also Kenneth Langtry. PH:
Maury Gertsman. Mus: Paul Dunlap. Ref: FDY. FM 2:16. with
Robert H. Harris, Paul Brinegar, Gary Conway, Gary Clarke,
John Ashley, Walter Reed, Morris Ankrum, Paul Maxwell,
Robert Shayne, Malcolm Atterbury. Pic: FM 10:12. Props and
monsters from past AI productions: the She Creature, the Cat
Girl, the Three-eyed Mutant, the Teenage Frankenstein and
Teenage Werewolf. Slightly different; more-than-slightly bad.
Roger Corman was whipping them out just as fast at AI about
the same time Cohen was; so when you see one of AI's grade-C
horrors from that era you may not know whether it's Corman or
Cohen.
HOW TO STEAL THE CROWN OF ENGLAND (I) Fida 1966 color/
scope (COME RUBARE LA CORONA D'INGHILTERRA or
ARGOMAN SUPERDIABOLICO-I. SUPERMAN LE DIABOLIQUE-
F) D: Terence Hathaway. SP: Verde, Flamini. PH: Tino San-
toni. Mus: Piero Umiliani. Ref: Ital P'67. with Roger Browne,
Dominique Boschero. Diamond from meteorite that absorbs solar
energy and makes any object as malleable as wax; robot ("modern
electric dragon"); force that can stop plane engines.
HOW TO SUCCEED WITH GIRLS see PEEPING PHANTOM, The
HOW WE STOLE THE ATOMIC BOMB (I) Five/Fono Roma/Copro
1966 color/scope (COME RUBAMMO LA BOMBA ATOMICA)
D: Lucio Fulci. SP: Continenza, Gianviti, Sollazzo. PH: Fausto
Rossi. Mus: Lallo Gori. Ref: Ital P'67. with Franco Franchi,
Ciccio Ingrassia, Julie Menard, Eugenia Litrel, Youssef Wahby,
Adel Adham. Dr. Si works in a lab in the middle of the Egyptian
desert trying to revive mummies with atomic energy. Other char-
acters include James Bomb, Derek Flit, and Modesty Bluff.
HSI, NOU, AI, LUEH see FOUR MOODS
The HUMAN DUPLICATORS (U.S.-I?) AA/Woolner/Crest/
Indipendenti Regionali 1964 Deluxe color 80m. (AGENTE
SPAZIALE K 1. SPACE AGENT K 1) D: Hugo Grimaldi. SP:
Arthur C. Pierce. PH:Monroe Askins. Ref: V 5/19/65.
Annuario. COF 10:44. TVG. with George Nader, George Mac-
ready, Barbara Nichols, Dolores Faith, Richard Kiel, Richard
Arlen, Hugh Beaumont, Tommy Leonetti. Humans duplicated by
androids in invasion plot.
The HUMAN MONSTER (B) Mono/Argyle/Pathe 1939 73m. SP,
D: Walter Summers. SP: also John Argyle, Patrick Kirwin. From
"Dark Eyes of London" by Edgar Wallace. PH: Bryan Langl(e)y. Ref:
FDY. FM 45:29. FMO 2:13. Pic: FM 19:46. TBG. with Bela
Lugosi (Dr. Orloff), Leslie Banks, Greta Gynt, Hugh Williams,
Edmon Ryan, Wilfred Walter. Series of mysterious drownings.
HUMAN RELATIONS see RoGoPaG

The HUMAN VAPOR (J) Brenco-AA/Toho 1960 ('64-U.S.) color/ scope 80m. (GASU-NINGEN DAI ICHI-GO) D: I. Honda. SpFX: Eiji Tsuburaya. Ref: COF 10:44. FEFN 1/61. Pic: FM 22:13. 26:11. with Tatsuya Mihashi, Kaoru Yachigusa, Yoshio Tsuchiya. Convict can vaporize at will.

The HUNCHBACK AND THE DANCER (G) Helios 1920 (DER BUCKLIGE UND DIE TANZERIN) D: F. W. Murnau. SP: Carl Mayer. Sets: Robert Neppach. Ref: S&S Index to the Films of F. W. Murnau. with Sacha Gura. "Apparently inspired by, or similar to, Reinhardt's SUMURUN."

The HUNCHBACK OF CEDAR LODGE Balboa 1914 45m. Ref: MPW 21:838. Lee. Ghost story--haunted library.

The HUNCHBACK OF NOTRE DAME Univ 1923 D: Wallace Worsley. SP: P. Poore Sheehan, Edward T. Lowe, from "Notre Dame de Paris" by Victor Hugo. Set used in DR. PYCKLE AND MR. PRIDE. PH: Robert S. Newhard, Tony Korn- man. Art D: E. E. Sheeley, Sydney Ullman. Ref: Clarens. FM 8:25.11.14. 15:34.17:31. with Lon Chaney, Patsy Ruth Miller, Norman Kerry, Ernest Torrence, Brandon Hurst, Tully Marshall, Raymond Hatton, Nigel de Brulier. Chaney's impress- ive presence as the hunchback interrupts the dull solemnities too infrequently.

The HUNCHBACK OF NOTRE DAME RKO 1939 114m. D: Wil- liam Dieterle. SP: Sonya Levien, Bruno Frank. From the novel by Victor Hugo. (QUASIMODO-F) PH: Joseph August. Mus: Alfred Newman. Art D: Van Nest Polglase. SpFX: Vernon L. Walker. Ref: FDY. with Charles Laughton, Sir Cedric Hardwicke, Maureen O'Hara, Thomas Mitchell, Edmond O'Brien, Alan Marshal(l), Walter Hampden, Katherine Alexander, Minna Gombell, Arthur Hohl, George Tobias, George Zucco, Harry Davenport, Fritz Leiber, Rod La Rocque, Spencer Charters, Helen Whitney, Etienne Girardot.

The HUNCHBACK OF NOTRE DAME (India-Hindi) 1954 (BADSHAH) D: Amiya Chakrabarty. From the novel by Victor Hugo. Ref: Thought 11/13/54. with K. N. Singh, Usha Kiron, Pradeep, Agha, Ulhas (hunchback).

The HUNCHBACK OF NOTRE DAME (F) AA/Paris-Hakim 1956 Technicolor/scope 103m. (NOTRE DAME DE PARIS) D: Jean Delannoy. SP: Jean Aurenche, Jacques Prevert, from the novel by Victor Hugo. PH: Michael Kelber. Mus: Georges Auric. P: Robert and Raymond Hakim. Ref: FDY. Pic: FM 23:65. with Anthony Quinn, Gina Lollobrigida, Jean Danet, Alain Cuny, Jean Tissier, Robert Hirsch.

HUNCHBACK OF NOTRE DAME, The (by V. Hugo) see DHANWAN/ DARLING OF PARIS, The (1916/1917)/NAV JAWAN/RETURN TO MANHOOD

HUND VON BASKERVILLE, Der see HOUND OF THE BASKER- VILLES, The (1917/1929/1936)

HUND VON BLACKWOOD CASTLE, Der see HOUND OF BLACK- WOOD CASTLE, The

The HUNDRED MONSTERS (J) Daiei 1968 color 79m. (YOKAI HYAKU MONOGATARI. The HUNDRED GHOST STORIES) D: Kimiyoshi Yasuda. SP: Tetsuo Yoshida. PH: Y. Takemura. Mus:

C. Watanabe. Art D: Y. Nishioka, Shigeru Kato. Ref: UFQ
41. M/TVM 3/68. with Jun Fujimaki, Miwa Takada, Mikiko
Tsubouchi, Takashi Kanda, Yoshio Yoshida. 100 spirits from
story-teller's stories haunt brothel.

HUNDRED YEARS TO COME, The see THINGS TO COME

HURRAH FOR ADVENTURE! (Sp-F) P.C. Día/CICC Films Bor-
derie 1970 color/scope 82m. (¡ VIVA LA AVENTURA!)
D: Francis Rigaud. Dial J. Vilfrid. SP: Rigaud, Vilfrid,
C. Viriot. PH: J. Gelpí. Mus: G. G. Segura. Art D: R.
Calatayud. Ref: SpCinema'71. with Roger Pierre, María José
Alfonso, Jean-Marc Thibault, Milo Quesada. International or-
ganization's "electronic machine" controls people's behavior.

HURRICANE ISLAND Col 1951 70m. Super Cinecolor D: Lew
Landers. SP: David Mathews. PH: Lester White. P: Sam
Katzman. Mus D: Mischa Bakaleinikoff. Ref: FDY. with Jon
Hall, Marie Windsor, Marc Lawrence, Romo Vincent, Edgar
Barrier, Nelson Leigh, Don Harvey, Rick Vallin, Lyle Talbot,
Alex P. Montoya. Chieftess with supernatural powers grows old
instantly at end. Fountain of Youth. Yet another Katzman dud.

HURRY! KURAMA! (J) Toho 1956 90m. (SHIPPU! KURAMA
TENGU) Ref: FEFN 6/29/56. with K. Arashi, D. Ohkochi, C.
Ogi. "Temple priest uses hypnotism to make his enemies pow-
erless."

HURRY UP, PLEASE (F) Pathe 1908 Ref: F Index 11/14/08.
Invention controls speed of action.

HUSH, HUSH, SWEET CHARLOTTE Fox 1965 134m. (CROSS
OF IRON. WHAT EVER HAPPENED TO COUSIN CHARLOTTE?)
D, P: Robert Aldrich. SP: Lukas Heller, Henry Farrell. Ref:
PM. COF 4:57. with Bette Davis, Olivia de Havilland, Agnes
Moorehead, Joseph Cotten, Cecil Kellaway, Victor Buono, Mary
Astor, William Campbell, Wesley Addy, Bruce Dern, George
Kennedy, Dave Willock, Ellen Corby, Frank Ferguson, Helen
Kleeb. Gothic horror: decaying Louisiana mansion; recluse who
sees apparitions of dead lover, etc. Acceptable; overlong at-
tempt to repeat WHAT EVER HAPPENED TO BABY JANE's
success.

HUSN KA CHOR (India) Wadia Bros. 1953 SP, D: J. B. H. Wadia.
Based on "The Arabian Nights." Dial: Wadia, Tahir Lucknavi.
PH: A. Wadadekar. Mus: B. C. Rani. Ref: Filmfare 9/18/53.
with Usha Kiron, Sharda, B. Raje. Bewitched Moon Fairy, enchanted palace, magic mirror, flying horse, flying carpet,
magic wish box.

HYDE PARK CORNER (B) Pathe/Grosvenor 1935 85m. D:
Sinclair Hill. SP: Selwyn Jepson. PH:Cyril Bristow. Ass't PH:
Jack Asher. From the play by Walter Hackett. Ref: TVG. with
Gordon Harker, Donald Wolfit, Eric Portman, Gibb McLaughlin,
Binnie Hale. Effect of curse from dying man's lips spans three
centuries. Unwatchable.

HYDROTHERAPIE FANTASTIQUE see DOCTOR'S SECRET, The
(1909)

The HYENA OF LONDON (I) Geos Film 1964 (La JENA DI
LONDRA) SP, D: Henry Wilson. PH:Griffith Hugh. Mus: Frank
Mason. Ref: Ital P'64. with Bernard Price, Diana Martin, Tony

Kendall, Anthony Wright. Professor studying criminology injects liquid from the brain of dead criminal into his own brain and becomes criminal.

The HYPERBOLOID OF ENGINEER GARIN (Russ) 1965 D: M. Berdicevski. SP: I. Manevic, A. Ginzburg. Ref: RVB. F&F 11/66. MMF 15-16:35. with V. Safonov, N. Klimova. In the Twenties a madman sets out to conquer the world with a death ray.

HYPNOSIS (Sp-I-W.G.) Procusa/Domiziana/Germania 1963 (HIPNOSIS-Sp. NUR TOTE ZEUGEN SCHWEIGEN-G. DUMMY OF DEATH-Eng) D: Eugenio Martin. SP: Giuseppe Mangione, Martin, G. M. Burgos, F. Niewel, G. Schmidt. PH: Francisco Sempere. Mus: Roman Vlad. Art D: Ramiro Gomez. Ref: MMF 9:17, 21. MFB'66:62. "The opening scene involving the dummy, hypnotism, and an X-ray machine which shows Magda's heart almost stopping under hypnosis promises well..." with Eleonora Rossi-Drago, Götz George, Jean Sorel, Massimo Serato, Heinz Drache, Werner Peters, Mara Cruz, Hildegarde Kneff. Ventriloquist's dummy seems to have strange power.

The HYPNOTIC CHAIR Majestic 1912 Ref: MPW 14:1082. Chair paralyzes with electricity.

The HYPNOTIC CURE Lubin 1909 Ref: F Index 6/26/09. Bios 9/2/09. Hypnotist cures rheumatism.

The HYPNOTIC EYE AA/Penguin 1960 77m. HypnoMagic D: George Blair. SP: Gitta and William Woodfield. PH: Archie Dalzell. Mus: Marlin Skiles. SpFX: Milton Olsen. Makeup: E. LaVigne, T. Lloyd. Hypnological D: Gil Boyne. Ref: FFacts. TVG. Pic: FM 10:8. 21:15. with Jacques Bergerac, Merry Anders, Allison Hayes, Marcia Henderson, James Lydon, Eric Nord, Fred Demara, Lawrence Lipton. A stage hypnotist makes beautiful women mutilate themselves. Something less than hypnotic.

The HYPNOTIC MONKEY Kalem 1915 15m. D: Al Santell. Ref: MPW 25:880. with Lloyd Hamilton, Bud Duncan. Dream: Hypnotist turns man into monkey and back into man.

The HYPNOTIC SPRAY Gaum 1909 6m. Ref: Bios 10/7/09. Vendor's spray makes everyone do boy's bidding.

The HYPNOTIC VIOLINIST Warner's 1914 45m. Ref: Lee. MPW 22:706. "Pyschic power" steals doctor's wife.

The HYPNOTIC WIFE (F?) Pathe 1909 Ref: MPW'09:321. Wife casts hypnotic spell over husband.

HYPNOTISEUR, Der see SVENGALI (1914)

HYPNOTISM (I?) Lux 1910 11m. Ref: Bios 10/13/10. Girl commits robbery under influence of hypnotist.

The HYPNOTIST (B) Merton Park 1956 SP, D: Montgomery Tully, from the play by Falkland Cary. PH: Philip Grindrod. Mus sc: Trevor Duncan. Art D: Wilfred Arnold. Ref: FEFN 12/21/56. British Film Catalogue. with Roland Culver, Patricia Roc, Paul Carpenter, William Hartnell. "Murder by remote control": Pilot undergoing hypnotic treatments is suspect in murder case.

HYPNOTIST, The (by T. Browning) see LONDON AFTER MID-MIDNIGHT

HYPNOTIZED World Wide 1933 70m. Story, D: Mack Sennett.
Story: also Arthur Ripley. SP: J. A. Waldron, Harry McCoy,
E. Rodney, Gene Towne. PH: John W. Boyle, George Unholz.
Ed: William Hornbeck, Francis Lyon. Ref: NYT 1/16/33. FDY.
with George Moran, Charles Mack, Ernest Torrence, Charles
Murray, Wallace Ford, Maria Alba, Marjorie Beebe, Herman
Bing, Alexander Carr, Luis Alberni, Matt McHugh. The evil
Professor Limberly hypnotizes members of a circus troupe in
his search for $500,000 in sweepstake winnings.
HYSTERIA (B) MGM/Hammer 1964 86m. D: Freddie Francis.
SP, P: Jimmy Sangster. PH: John Wilcox. Mus: Don Banks.
Ref: MFB'65:110. MPH. V. with Robert Webber, L. Goldoni,
Anthony Newlands, Jennifer Jayne, Maurice Denham, Sue Lloyd,
Peter Woodthorpe. Sounds and voices torment amnesia victim.
"Macabre melodrama"-MFB.

I ACCUSE (F) 1918 (J'ACCUSE) SP, D: Abel Gance. Ref: NYT
10/10/21. FM-A'62:32. Pic: DDC II:379. Men rise from the
graveyards of World War I to march on the world.
I ACCUSE (F) 1937 (J'ACCUSE) SP, D: Abel Gance. SP: also
Steve Passeur. Ref: DDC III:60. Pic: DDC II:473. Moderately
effective remake of the silent version.
I AM CURIOUS TAHITI Hollywood Int'l 1970 65m. Ref: Enter-
tainment Today 11/4/70. Machine, the "transducer," enables
girl spy to see through walls.
I AM LEGEND (novel by R. Matheson) see LAST MAN ON EARTH,
The (1964)/OMEGA MAN, The
I BELIEVE Cosmotofilm 1917 75m. Adap, P: George L. Tucker.
Ref: MPN 16:114. with Milton Rosmer. Man revived from dead by
professor lacks soul.
I BURY THE LIVING UA/Maxim 1958 76m. D: Albert Band.
SP: Louis Garfinkle. PH: Frederick Gately. Mus: Gerald Fried.
Visual Design: E. Vorkapich. Ref: FFacts. with Richard
Boone, Theodore Bikel, Peggy Maurer, Robert Osterloh, Russ
Bender, Cyril Delevanti, Matt Moore. A cemetery manager finds
that someone dies every time he sticks a black pin into a chart
of the reserved plots. Nifty idea provides a little suspense
before the unsatisfying conclusion.
I CHANGED MY SEX see GLEN OR GLENDA
I DIDN'T RAISE MY BOY TO BE A SOLDIER see I'M GLAD MY
BOY GREW UP TO BE A SOLDIER
I DRINK YOUR BLOOD Cinemation 1971 DeLuxe color/scope
SP, D: David Durston. PH: Jacques Demarecaux. Mus: Clay
Pitts. Ref: RVB. with Bhaskar, Jadine Wong. People become
killers after consuming rabid blood.
I EAT YOUR SKIN Cinemation 1971(1964) SP, D, P: Del Tenney.
(ZOMBIES) PH: Francois Farkas. Mus: Lon E. Norman. Make-
up:Guy Del Russo. Ref: RVB. with William Joyce, Heather
Hewitt. Voodoo priest forces mad doctor to continue making
zombies. (VOODOO BLOOD BATH)

I HAVE A STRANGER'S FACE see FACE OF ANOTHER, The
I, JUSTICE (Cz) Czech State Film/Sebor-Bor 1968 90m. (JA,
SPRAVEDLNOST) SP,D: Zhynek Brynych. SP: also Milos
Macourek, Miroslav Nanus. PH: Josef Vanis. Ref: V 7/24/68.
A doctor discovers that his patient is Hitler. with Karel Hoger,
Fritz Dietz, Jiri Vrstala.
I KILL, YOU KILL (I-F) Metropolis/Gulliver 1965 (LO UCCIDO,
TU UCCIDI) SP,D: Gianni Puccini. SP:also Filippo Sanjust,De
Concini, Boschi. PH: Marcello Gatti. Ref: Ital P. with E.
Riva, Jean-Louis Trintignant, Dominique Boschero, Margaret Lee,
Luciana Paluzzi. "Fullmoon": Woman suffers from "sexual
lycanthropy," choosing a different man each of the seven nights
after the full moon. "Bitter Games": "Three children cause all
the 'bad' people they know to die mysteriously."
I KILLED EINSTEIN, GENTLEMEN (Cz) Czech State Film 1970
Eastmancolor 95m. (ZABIL JSEM EINSTEIN A, PANOVE)
SP,D: Oldrich Lipsky. SP: also Josef Nesvadba, Milos Macourek.
PH: Ivan Slapeta. Art D: Jindrich Goetz. Ref: V 9/30/70.
with Jiri Sovak, Jana Brejchova, L. Lipsky, Iva Janzurova. When
it is discovered that atom bombs have robbed women of their
child-bearing power, scientists are sent back in time via a time
machine to kill Einstein.
I LED TWO LIVES see GLEN OR GLENDA
I LOVE A MYSTERY Col 1944 68m. D: Henry Levin. SP:
Charles O'Neal, from the radio show by Carlton Morse. PH:
Burnett Guffey. Art D: George Brooks. Ref: FDY. COF 11:36.
Pic: FanMo 3:39. with Jim Bannon, Nina Foch, George Mac-
ready, Barton Yarborough, Carole Mathews, Lester Matthews,
Gregory Gay(e), Frank O'Connor, Joseph Crehan, Ernie Adams,
Kay Dowd. Crooks employ Oriental "black magic" in attempt to
drive man to suicide. Unremarkable. See also DEVIL'S MASK,
The/UNKNOWN, The (1946)
I LOVE YOU, I KILL YOU (G) 1971 color D: Uwe Brandner. Ref:
VVoice 6/17/71. 4/13/72. Benevolent totalitarianism totally con-
trolls utopian society of the near future.
I LOVE YOU, I LOVE YOU (F) Fox/Parc-Fox Europa 1968 East-
mancolor 92m. (JE T'AIME, JE T'AIME) D: Alain Resnais. SP:
Jacques Sternberg. PH: Jean Boffety. Mus: K. Penderecki. Ref:
V 5/15/68. with Claude Rich, Olga Georges-Picot, Anouk Fer-
jac, Van Doude. Man becomes subject of time-machine experi-
ment. Very dull, with stray brief moments of life.
I MARRIED A MONSTER FROM OUTER SPACE Para 1958 78m.
D,P: Gene Fowler,Jr. SP: Louis Vittes. PH: Haskell Boggs.
SpFX: John P. Fulton. Makeup: Charles Gemora. Ref: FFacts.
with Gloria Talbott, Tom Tryon, Ken Lynch, John Eldredge,
Valerie Allen, Maxie Rosenbloom, Alan Dexter, Jean Carson,
Peter Baldwin. A monster from outer space that kills little dogs
can't be all bad. Another picture that supposedly isn't as bad as
its title that isn't--quite. The monster dies a nastily-timed death
(just after he has discovered emotion).
I MARRIED A WEREWOLF see WEREWOLF IN A GIRLS'
DORMITORY
I MARRIED A WITCH UA-Paramount 1942 76m. D,P: René Clair.

SP: Marc Connelly, Robert Pirosh, from "The Passionate Witch" by Thorne Smith, completed by Norman Matson, and the Rodgers and Hart play. PH: Ted Tetzlaff. Mus sc: Roy Webb. Art D: Hans Dreier, Ernst Fegte. SpPhFX: Gordon Jennings. Makeup: Wally Westmore. Ref: V 10/19/42. Pic: DDC I:208. II:247. with Fredric March, Veronica Lake, Susan Hayward, Cecil Kellaway, Robert Benchley, Elizabeth Patterson, Eily Malyon, Robert Greig, Emory Parnell, Wade Boteler, Peter Leeds, Chester Conklin, Lee Shumway, Monte Blue, Billy Bevan, Reed Hadley. Girl burned as witch places curse on all male descendants of the House of Wooley. Irritatingly conventional character types. Occasional bright writing (including an hilarious election montage). Benchley and Kellaway have the best scenes.

I SAW WHAT YOU DID Univ 1965 82m. D, P: William Castle. SP: William McGivern, from the novel "Out of the Dark" by Ursula Curtiss. PH: Joseph Biroc. Mus: Van Alexander. Ass't D: Terry Morse, Jr. Ref : FD 5/14/65. V(d) 5/12/65. COF 8:6. Kids' telephone prank ("I saw what you did and I know who you are") unnerves man who has just committed murder. Fairly effective, if mechanical, shocker, which sometimes makes the mistake of telegraphing its shocks. with Joan Crawford, John Ireland, Leif Erickson, Sarah Lane, Patricia Breslin, John Archer , John Crawford.

I SLEPT WITH A GHOST (Mex) Nuevo Mundo/Modesto Pascó 1946 (YO DORMI CON UN FANTASMA) D: Jaime Salvador. PH: Raul M. Solares. Ref: Indice: 1947. Aventura. with "Resortes, " Eduardo Casado, Rafael Alcayde. Comic ghost story.

I, THE BODY see MORIANNA

I WALKED WITH A ZOMBIE RKO 1943 69m. D: Jacques Tourneur. SP: Curt Siodmak, Ardel Wray. Story: Inez Wallace. P: Val Lewton. PH: J. Roy Hunt. Ed: Mark Robson. Ref: MMF 18:99. COF 7:30. 11:61. 15:22. Pic: WFC 3:49. with James Ellison, Frances Dee, Tom Conway, Edith Barrett, Christine Gordon, James Bell, Sir Lancelot, Darby Jones. Voodoo turns a woman into a zombie. Eerily beautiful scenes alternate with dull, melodramatic ones. Music is put to several good uses.

I WAS A TEENAGE FRANKENSTEIN AI/Santa Rosa 1957 72m. (TEENAGE FRANKENSTEIN-Eng) D: Herbert L. Strock. SP: Kenneth Langtry. PH: Lothrop Worth. Mus: Paul Dunlap. Ass't D: Austen Jewell. P: Herman Cohen. Ref: FDY. FM 12:26-31. Pic: FM 9:19. with Whit Bissell, Phyllis Coates, Robert Burton, Gary Conway, George Lynn. Some of the lines (e. g., the doctor to his monster: "Speak! You have a civil tongue in your head! I ought to know; I sewed it there") hint that this was supposed to be a satire. And some of the turns of plot are so nonsensical they seem to be intended humorously. (E. g., The doctor plans to take the monster apart, place the pieces in separate boxes, and smuggle it into England.) But it's pretty miserable, satire or not.

I WAS A TEENAGE WEREWOLF AI/Sunset 1957 76m. D: Gene Fowler, Jr. SP: Ralph Thornton. PH: Joseph LaShelle. P: Herman Cohen. Ref: FDY. Pic: FM 9:19, 68. 14:67. with Michael

Landon, Yvonne Lime, Whit Bissell, Guy Williams, Robert
Griffin, Vladimir Sokoloff, Malcolm Atterbury, Eddie Marr,
Louise Lewis, S. John Launer, Dorothy Crehan. You can't
argue with a title like that. Surprisingly, there's one well-done
chase sequence and a camera trick or two.

ICE   David C. Stone   1970   135m.   SP, D: Robert Kramer.   P:
American Film Institute.   PH: Robert Machover.   Ref: V 5/6/70.
Political unrest in the United States in the near-future.

IDO ZERO DAISAKUSEN   see LATITUDE ZERO

IDOL, The (story by M. Brown) see   MAD GENIUS, The

IF ALL THE WOMEN IN THE WORLD   see KISS THE GIRLS &
MAKE THEM DIE

IF ONE COULD SEE INTO THE FUTURE (I)   Ambrosio   1911 Ref:
The Film Index.   Death personified.

IKARIE XB-1   see VOYAGE TO THE END OF THE UNIVERSE

IL NE FAUT PAS PARIER SA TETE AVEC LE DIABLE   see
TALES OF MYSTERY AND IMAGINATION

ILE D'EPOUVANTE   see   ISLAND OF TERROR (1913)

ILE DES MORTS, L'   see ISLE OF THE DEAD   (1913)

I'LL SEE YOU IN HELL (I) Verdestella 1960   (TI ASPETTERO'
ALL'INFERNO.   I'LL WAIT FOR YOU IN HELL)   D: Piero
Regnoli.   SP: Regnoli, Dario Serra, Arpad de Riso. Ref: Bianco.
FEFN 4/60. with John Drew Barrymore, Eva Bartok, Massimo
Serato, Moira Orfei. One jewel thief on the run kills another,
and the latter seemingly returns to haunt his killer.

ILLUSION OF BLOOD (J)   Toho   1965   Eastmancolor/scope 104m.
(YOTSUYA KAIDAN.   The YOTSUYA GHOST STORY.   The GHOST
OF YOTSUYA) D: Shiro Toyoda.   SP: Toshio Yazumi.   Story:
N. Tsuruya.   PH: Hiroshi Murai.   Mus: Toru Takemitsu.   Ref:
Screen World'67. Unij. Bltn. 31.   with Tatsuya Nakadai, Mariko
Okada, Junko Ikeuchi, Kanzaburo Nakamura Masao Mishima.

ILLUSIONISTS, The   see   DOUBLE DECEPTION

The ILLUSTRATED MAN   WB-7A   1969   Technicolor/scope 103m.
D: Jack Smight.   SP: Howard B. Kreitsek, from Ray Bradbury's
"The Illustrated Man" ("The Veldt," "The Last Night of the
World," and "The Long Rain").   PH: Philip Lathrop.   Mus:Jerry
Goldsmith.   Art D: Joel Schiller.   Sets: Marvin March.   SpFX:
Ralph Webb.   Skin illustrations designer: James E. Reynolds.
Ref: V(d) 2/14/69. with Rod Steiger, Claire Bloom, Robert
Drivas, Don Dubbins, Jason Evers, Tim Weldon. Skin drawings
on a man come to life to tell three stories.   A poor choice of ma-
terial for Smight since he hasn't proved yet that he can tell one
story.   Really bad.

ILS   see THEM(1970)

ILYA MOUROMETZ   see   SWORD AND THE DRAGON, The

ILYA MUROMETS   see   SWORD AND THE DRAGON, The

I'M GLAD MY BOY GREW UP TO BE A SOLDIER   V-L-S-E--Selig
1915 60m.   D: Frank Beal.   SP: Gilson Willets. Version of the
song "I Didn't Raise My Boy To Be a Soldier."   Ref: MPW 26:
2090.   LC.   with Harry Mestayer, Eugenie Besserer, Guy Oliver.
Foreign power invades the United States.

IM SCHLOSS DER BLUTIGEN BEGIERDE see   CASTLE OF LUST,
The

IM STAHLNETZ DES DR. MABUSE see RETURN OF DR. MABUSE, The

The IMAGINARY VOYAGE (F) de Maré 1925 62m. (LE VOY-AGE IMAGINAIRE. A MIDSUMMER DAY'S DREAM) SP, D: René Clair. PH: Jimmy Berliet, A. Morin. Sets: Robert Gys. Ref: SilentFF. FM 10:26. with Jean Borlin, Dolly Davis, Albert Préjean, Maurice Schutz. Bluebeard; clutching hands; evil fairy; "alligafrog." Very minor Clair. Intermittently interesting.

IMAGINARY WORLD, The (by C. Flammarion) see END OF THE WORLD('30)

IMMEDIATE DISASTER see STRANGER FROM VENUS

The IMMORAL MR. TEAS Padram 1958 D: Russ Meyer. Ref: SF Film. Anaesthetic enables man to see through clothes.

The IMMORTAL ABC-TV/Para 1969 color 72m. D: Joseph Sargent. SP: Robert Specht, from the book "The Immortals" by James Gunn. PH: Howard Schwartz. Mus: Dominic Frontiere. Mus D: Leith Stevens. Ref: RVB. TVG 9/18/69. with Christopher George, Ralph Bellamy, Carol Lynley, Barry Sullivan, Jessica Walter. Science-fiction.

The IMP ABROAD Victor 1914 15m. Ref: Bios. "Imp" elopes with heiress, "discomfits" her parents by returning to "his Satanic form."

IMP IN THE BOTTLE, The (by R. L. Stevenson) see GAUCHO AND THE DEVIL, The/BOTTLE IMP, The/IMP OF THE BOTTLE, The/LOVE, DEATH AND THE DEVIL

The IMP OF THE BOTTLE Edison 1909 12m. Ref: MPW'09:729. Bios 1/13/10. From "The Imp in the Bottle" by Robert Louis Stevenson. "Terrible little imp" in bottle grants wishes; person damned who dies with bottle in his possession.

IMPALING VOIVODE, The (by A. R. Seyfi) see DRACULA IN ISTANBUL

IMPERIO DE DRACULA, El see EMPIRE OF DRACULA, The

The IMPOSSIBLE VOYAGE (F) Melies/Star 1904 20m. (VOYAGE A TRAVERS L'IMPOSSIBLE. WHIRLING THE WORLDS) Ref: DDC III:349. SilentFF. COF 6:31. SF Film. Band of explorers journeys to the sun by train.

IN HET NET VAN DE SADIST see HORRORS OF SPIDER ISLAND

IN LIKE FLINT Fox 1967 DeLuxe color/scope 114m. Sequel to OUR MAN FLINT. D: Gordon Douglas. SP: Hal Fimberg. PH: William Daniels. Mus: Jerry Goldsmith. SpFX: L. B. Abbott, Art Cruickshank, Emil Kosa, Jr. Ref: FFacts. with James Coburn, Jean Hale, Lee J. Cobb, Anna Lee, Steve Inhat, Yvonne Craig, Erin O'Brien, Andrew Duggan, Herb Edelman, Eve Bruce, Thordis Brandt. Girls frozen into suspended animation.

IN PREHISTORIC DAYS Biog 1913 D: D. W. Griffith. Ref: Lee. LC.

IN ROOM THREE (Hung) 1919 (A-III-ES) D: A. Korda. Ref: Sarris.

IN ROOM THREE (Hung) Danubia/Muveszfilm 1937 82m. (IN ROOM III. A III-ES. III-ES SZOBABAN) D: Stephen Szekely. Ref: NYT 4/2/38. with Paul Javor. FD 4/18/38: "Jeno Torzs, as a magician, sets out to avenge the dead girl. He employes hypnotism, illusions..."

IN THE BOGIE MAN'S CAVE (F) Melies/Star 1908 Ref: MPW
'08:45. The Bogie man decides to fry a boy for dinner.
Gnomes, fairy.
IN THE DIPLOMATIC SERVICE Quality-Metro 1916 55m. SP,
D: Francis X. Bushman. Story: John C. Clymer, Hamilton
Smith. Ref: MPN 14:2713. with Bushman, Beverly Bayne,
William Davidson. Working model of anti-aircraft gun "that will
revolutionize warfare" employs electricity.
IN THE GRIP OF A CHARLATAN Kalem 1913 17m. Ref: Bios
6/12/13. Girl kept prisoner of fakir with hypnotic powers.
IN THE GRIP OF THE MANIAC see DIABOLICAL DR. Z, The
IN THE GRIP OF THE VAMPIRE Gaum 1912 Author: Leonce
Perret. Ref: MPW 14:1308. Girl's guardian, the "vampire,"
gives her drug which makes her go insane. Scientist hypnotizes
her with "cinematographic images" to bring her to her reason.
IN THE LONG AGO Selig 1913 D: Colin Campbell. SP: Lanier
Bartlett. Ref: The Film Index. with Wheeler Oakman, Tom
Santschi. Spell of sleep.
IN THE NEXT ROOM F Nat 1930 70m. D: Edward Cline. Dial:
James A. Starr. SP: Harvey Gates. From the play by Eleanor
Robson Belmont and Harriet Ford and the book "The Mystery
of the Boule Cabinet" by Burton E. Stevenson. PH: John Seitz.
Ref: PM. Dimmitt. New Yorker. AFI. with DeWitt Jennings,
C. Allister, Jack Mulhall, Alice Day, Crauford Kent, John St. Polis,
Lucien Prival. Mysterious murders in old house, clutching
hands, secret staircase, "cataleptic lady in gauze."
IN THE POWER OF THE HYPNOTIST Warner's 1913 45m. D:
Sidney Olcott. Ref: Lee. MPW 18:499. with Olcott, Gene
Gauntier.
IN THE SECRET SERVICE (story by J. Swerling) see BEHIND
THE MASK
IN THE STEEL CABINET OF DR. MABUSE see RETURN OF DR.
MABUSE, The
IN THE STEEL NET OF DR. MABUSE see RETURN OF DR.
MABUSE, The
IN THE TOILS OF THE DEVIL (I) Milano 1913 40m. Ref:
MPW 16:993. Pact with the devil.
IN THE YEAR 2889 see YEAR 2889
IN THE YEAR 2,000 Solax 1912 Ref: SF Film. Lee. Women
rule.
IN THE YEAR 2,014 Joker 1914 13m. Ref: Bios 4/30/14. Lee.
Women rule.
IN ZULULAND 1915 Ref: MPW 9/25/15. with Mattie and John
Edwards. "Daughters disguise as ghosts" to frighten man out
of marrying their mother.
INAFFERRABILE MR. INVISIBLE, L' see MR. INVISIBLE
INCANTESIMO TRAGICO see TRAGIC SPELL, The
INCIDENT FROM DON QUIXOTE (F) Star/Melies 1908 Pic: F
Index 10/17/08. Suit of armor transforms into giant spider.
INCONNU DE SHANDIGOR, L' see UNKNOWN MAN OF SHANDI-
GOR, The
The INCREDIBLE FACE OF DR. B (Arg?) c1961 82m. Ref:
TVFFSB. COF 10:46. with Erich del Castillo, Elsa Cardenas.

Man "cursed with eternal life."

INCREDIBLE, FANTASTIC, EXTRAORDINARY (Braz) Chadler 1969 color (INCREDIBLE, FANTASTICO, EXTRAORDINARIO) D: Adolph o Chadler. Ref: V 4/29/70:167. with Cyl Farney Sonia Clara, Glauche Rocha. "Horror drama."

The INCREDIBLE PETRIFIED WORLD Governor/G.B.M. 1960 (1958) 70m. P, D: Jerry Warren. SP: John W. Steiner. PH: Victor Fisher. Mus: Josef Zimanich. Art D: Marvin Herbert. Ref: FFacts. FM 15:14. with John Carradine, Phyllis Coates, Robert Clarke, Allen/Windsor, Sheila Noonan (aka Sheila Carol), George Skaff, Harry Raven, Lloyd Nelson. Four people find themselves trapped in a network of caves at the bottom of the sea. One of the dullest movies ever, with lots of padding to make it to feature length. Jerry Warren's greatest sin this time is wasting Sheila Carol, who was an actress as well as a presence in BEAST FROM HAUNTED CAVE.

The INCREDIBLE SHRINKING MAN Univ 1957 81m. D: Jack Arnold. SP: Richard Matheson. PH: Ellis W. Carter. From "The Shrinking Man" by Matheson. Unfilmed sequel: THE FAN- TASTIC LITTLE GIRL. Mus: Joseph Gershenson. Art D: Alexander Golitzen, Robert Clatworthy. SpFX: Clifford Stine. P: Al Zugsmith. Ref: Clarens. B. Warren. FM 14:46.13:40. with Grant Williams, Paul Langton, Randy Stuart, April Kent, Raymond Bailey, William Schallert. Man passes through a mysterious fog, begins to shrink. In the latter half high adven- ture takes over from shallow humanitarianism, and the movie really comes to life. The sure-fire effects overcome overscor- ing and even the dumber dialogue. Overrated but not by much; the best s-f film on industriousness.

The INCREDIBLE TWO-HEADED TRANSPLANT AI/John Lawrence- Mutual General 1971 Movielab color 85m. (The INCREDIBLE TRANSPLANT) Ed, D: Anthony Lanza. SP: Lawrence, James Gordon White. PH: Jack Steely, Glen Gano, Paul Hipp. Mus: John Barbar. Art D: Ray Markham. Ref: Film Bltn 2/22/71. LA Times 4/16/71. with Bruce Dern, Pat Priest, Casey Kasem, Berry Kroeger, Larry Vincent. Two-headed killer.

INCREDIBLE WEREWOLF MURDERS, The see MALTESE BIPPY, The

The INCREDIBLY STRANGE CREATURES WHO SUDDENLY STOPPED LIVING AND BECAME CRAZY MIXED-UP ZOMBIES Fairway 1962 color 81m. (TEENAGE PSYCHO MEETS BLOODY MARY. DIABOLICAL DR. VOODOO?) D: Ray Steckler. SP: Gene Pollock, Robert Silliphant. (The INCREDIBLY MIXED-UP ZOMBIE) PH: Joseph Mascelli. Ref: ModM 3:8. COF 8:6. Orpheus 3:32. Pic: FanMo 6:18. with Cash Flagg (aka Steckler), Carolyn Brandt. Gypsy fortune teller in carnival hypnotically controls dis- figured creatures.

INCUBUS (U. S. -Esperanto) Daystar 1967 SP, D: Leslie Stevens. PH: Conrad Hall. P: Antony M. Taylor. Ref: V. with William Shatner, Milos Milos. "Evil demons vs. good in the mythical land of Nomen Tuum."

The INDESTRUCTIBLE MAN AA 1956 70m. D, P: Jack Pollexfen. SP: Vi (or Vy) Russell, Sue Bradford. PH: John Russell, Jr.

Mus D: Albert Glasser.   Art D: Ted Holsopple.   Ref: FDY. with
Lon Chaney, Jr., Casey Adams, Robert Shayne, Marian Carr,
Ross Elliott, Kenneth Terrell, Marvin Ellis, Stuart Randall. An
executed killer is brought back to life.   Not too swell.
The INDESTRUCTIBLE MR. JENKS Kalem 1913 8m.   Ref: Bios
5/29/13.   Man's experiments make him indestructible.
The INDIAN CHIEF AND SEIDLITZ POWDER (B) c1901 2m.
Ref: SilentFF. Chemist's powders cause Indian to swell and float
above shop.
An INDIAN LEGEND Broncho (Mutual) 1912 Ref: MPW 14:69. Lee.
Spirit of Indian girl haunts lake.
The INDIAN SCARF (W.G.) Constantin 1963 90m. (DAS IN-
DISCHE TUCH) D: Alfred Vohrer. SP: H. G. Petersson, George
Hurdalek, from Edgar Wallace's "The Frightened Lady." PH:
Karl Löb. Mus: Peter Thomas. Ref: German Pictures. FIR
'66:240. '67:82. with Heinz Drache, Corny Collins, Ady Ber-
ber, Klaus Kinski, Hans Nielsen, Siegfried Schürenberg. Grue-
some spider, secret passages, portrait with peep-holes, unex-
plained fantasy touches. Bad mystery, pleasant actors.
The INDIAN TOMB (G) May 1921 (Two parts in U.S.:
MYSTERIES OF INDIA and ABOVE ALL LAW. DAS INDISCHE
GRABMAL. The HINDU TOMBSTONE) D: Joe May. SP: Thea
von Harbou, Fritz Lang. Ref: MPW 8/5/22. S&S Lang index.
with Conrad Veidt, Lya de Putti, Mia May, Olaf Föns, Bernhard
Goetzke. Prince plans to entomb wife alive.   Yogi-magic.
INDISCHE TUCH, Das see INDIAN SCARF, The
INDISCREET LETTERS Le Lion 1909 6m. Ref: Bios 10/7/09.
X-rays show contents of envelope.
INEXPERIENCED GHOST, The (by H. G. Wells) see DEAD OF
NIGHT
The INFERNAL FIEND (Mex) c1960 (EL DEMONIO INFERNAL)
Ref: FM 31:22. Pic: COF 3:54: of man putting mask over scarred
face.
INFERNO see DR. MABUSE (Part II)
INFERNO, The (by Dante) see DANTE'S INFERNO/MACISTE IN
HELL/TOO MUCH CHAMPAGNE
INFERNO IN SPACE MCA-TV 1954 From the "Rocky Jones,
Space Ranger" TV series.
INFIERNO DE FRANKENSTEIN, El see ORLAK
INGAGI Congo Pictures 1931 silent 75m. D: William Campbell.
SP: Adam Hull Shirk. Ref: PM. LC. FDY. Rampaging gorillas
abduct women.
The INHABITANTS OF THE UNINHABITED HOUSE (Sp) Guión, P.C.
1959 (LOS HABITANTES DE LA CASA DESHABITADA) D: Pedro
L. Ramirez. SP: Vicente Coello. PH: Emilio Toriscot. Mus:
Contreras. Ref: SpCinema'59. with Tony Leblanc, Luz Márquez,
Fernando Rey, Manuel G. Bur. Old house; pair trying to drive
woman out of her mind by frightening her.
The INHERITANCE (B) Rank/Two Cities 1947 103m. D: Charles
Frank. SP: Ben Travers, from "Uncle Silas" by Sheridan Le
Fanu. PH: Robert Krasker. Mus: Alan Rawsthorne. Art D:
Ralph Brinton. Ref: MFB 47:144. Brit. Fm. Ybk. '49/'50. with
Jean Simmons, Derrick De Marney, Katina Paxinou, Esmond

Knight, John Laurie, Derek Bond, George Curzon, Guy Rolfe.
Girl's "nightmarish experiences" in old house; locked room
where murder occurred.

INHUMAINE, L' see LIVING DEAD MAN, The

The INNER BRUTE Ess 1915 25m. Ref: MPN 7/3/15. Son whose
mother was frightened by a tiger "inherits the instincts" of a
tiger.

The INNER MIND Selig 1911 17m. Ref: MPW 10:549. Lee. Hyp-
notist-detective. "Weird," "uncanny."

An INNOCENT SINNER Kalem 1915 40m. Ref: MPN 5/8/15. with
Katherine La Salle, Guy Coombs. Villainous doctor with hypnotic
powers.

The INNOCENTS (B) Fox/Achilles 1961 99m. (SUSPENSE-I)
scope D, P: Jack Clayton. SP: Truman Capote, William Archibald,
John Mortimer. PH: Freddie Francis. From "The Turn of the
Screw" by Henry James. Mus: Georges Auric. Art D: Wilfred
Shingleton. Ref: Clarens. with Deborah Kerr, Michael Redgrave,
Peter Wyngarde, Martin Stephens, Pamela Franklin, Megs
Jenkins. THE INNOCENTS may have a questionable, cheap-
Gothic basis in the repressed-governess's-imagination-or-is-it-
really-a-ghost? ambiguity--the weakness originates in James's
story, one of his less convincing ones--but Francis's photography
and Clayton's direction make the movie look so good that it hardly
matters. The photography is about the richest and most sophisti-
cated use of black-and-white I've seen, and the movie is much
more varied visually than dramatically. Much of the dialogue is
affected, unsubtly-subtle, and redundant.

INSECT WOMAN see WASP WOMAN

INSIDE THE EARTH (F) Pathe 1910 8m. Ref: Lee. MPW 7:142.

INSIDIOUS DR. FU-MANCHU, The see MYSTERIOUS DR. FU-
MANCHU, The

The INSPIRATIONS OF HARRY LARRABEE General 1917 45m.
D: Bertram Bracken. From a novelette by Howard Fielding.
Ref: MPN 15:2030. with Clifford Gray, Margaret Landis,
Winifred Greenwood, William Ehfe, Frank Brownlee. A doctor
restores a dead girl to life with the "pulmoter."

INSTANTANEOUS NERVE POWDER (F) Pathe 1909 5m. Ref:
F Index 5/8/09. Powder makes grouch happy.

INTERNATIONAL HOUSE Para 1933 65m. D: Edward Sutherland.
SP: Walt DeLeon, Francis Martin. From a story by Lou Heifetz
and Neil Brant. PH: Ernest Haller. Ref: FDY. Pic: DDC I:65.
with W. C. Fields, Bela Lugosi, Rudy Vallee, Cab Calloway,
Baby Rose Marie, Sterling Holloway, Franklin Pangborn, Col.
Stoopnagle and Budd, Lumsden Hare, Edmund Breese, Peggy Hopkins Joyce, Stuart Erwin, Sari Maritza, George Burns, Gracie
Allen. TV invention (the "radioscope") brings in radio perform-
ers. Lugosi crushes a phone bare-handed. Gracie Allen: "Will
you write me your autograph?" Fields: "I'd like to write your
epitaph."

INTERPLANETARY TOURISTS (Mex) c1960 (TURISTAS INTER-
PLANETARIOS) Ref: FM 33:8. with Viruta, Capulina.

INTERPLANETARY WEDDING (I) Latium 1910 (MATRIMONIO
INTERPLANETARIO) SP, D: Enrico Novelli. Ref: Lee. DDC III:483.

The INTRIGUE Para/Pallas 1916 D: Frank Lloyd. Ref: SF
Film. MPN 14: 2056. MPW 29:2101. X-ray gun invention a
"contrivance that would end European war....kills all in reach
over miles."
The INTRUDER Allied 1933 D: Albert Ray. SP:Frances
Hyland. PH: Harry Neumann, Tom Galligan. with Monte Blue,
Lila Lee, Gwen Lee, Sidney Bracy, Mischa Auer (wild man),
Harry Cording, William B. Davidson, Wilfred Lucas. MPH
1/14/33: "Terror...murder...party terrorized by weird jungle
noises...group of skeletons in a cave...fanatical Wild Man."
Photoplay 5/34: "Crazy Robinson Crusoe and his man Ingagi."
INVADER FROM MARS Fox/Edward L. Alperson 1953 Cinecolor
/3-D 77m. SP: Richard Blake, Art D,D: William Cameron
Menzies. Art D: also Boris Leven. PH: John Seitz. Mus:
Raoul Kraushaar. SpPhFX: Jack Cosgrove. Makeup: Gene Hibbs.
Special Makeup: Anatole Robbins. Ass't D: Ben Chapman. Ref:
Clarens. SM 1:8. Photon 21:22-24. Pic: FM 34:58. with
Helena Carter, Arthur Franz, Jimmy Hunt, Leif Erickson,
Hillary Brooke, Morris Ankrum, Max Wagner, Janine Perreau,
Bill Phipps, Milburn Stone, John Eldredge, Robert Shayne.
INVADERS FROM MARS abounds with hideous, nightmarish
ideas about parents who turn into zombies, people who disappear
into holes in the sand, Martians who drill into people's brains,
and a brainy creature who directs it all; all perfectly
calculated to scare the hell out of kids. The music, boy's-
nightmare sets, and ingenious psychological/emotional tricks in
the editing (including an almost brilliant flashback montage)
carry the show and give force to the ideas. Only the fastidious
will hold the acting and the logic of the script against the movie.
The INVADERS FROM OUTER SPACE (Sp) Acra Films 1967 71m.
(JAVIER AND THE INVADERS FROM SPACE) D: Guillermo Ziener.
SP: Carlos Serrano, Rafael Henríquez. PH: J. L.Alcaine. Mus:
Luis de Pablo. Art D: Pablo Gago. Ref: SpCinema'68. with
Angel Aranda, José María Prada, Mairata O'Wisiedo, Manuel
F. Aranda. Strange gasses surround the earth's surface,
"paralyzing humanity." Martian space ships begin to land.
INVADERS FROM SPACE (J) Medallion/Manley-TV/Shintoho
1956 83m. (SUPER GIANT. SPACEMAN CONTRO I VAMPIRI
DELLO SPAZIO-I? SUPAH JAIYANTO #1 &#2. The STEEL-
MAN FROM OUTER SPACE and RESCUE FROM OUTER SPACE?
The APPEARANCE OF SUPER GIANT?) Ref: Bianco. Imagen.
FEFN. Super-Giant pamphlet. with Ken Utsui, Junko Ikeuchi.
The Emerald Planet in the Marpet Gallaxy sends an emissary to
warn the earth of an imminent invasion by the Salamander Men.
INVADERS FROM THE PLANETS see ATOMIC RULERS OF THE
WORLD
INVADERS FROM THE SPACESHIP see PRINCE OF SPACE, The
INVASION (B) AI-TV/Merton Park 1966 80m. D: Alan Bridges.
SP: Roger Marshall. Story: Robert Holmes. PH: James Wilson.
Mus: Bernard Ebbinghouse. Art D: Scott MacGreg(g)or. SpFX:
Ronnie Whitehouse, Jack Kine, Stan Shields. Ref: MFB. with
Valerie Gearon, Edward Judd, Yoko Tani, Tsai Chin, Barrie
Ingham. Interplanetary travelers make a forced landing on earth.

Drab, and very slow to get started.

INVASION DE LOS VAMPIROS, La see INVASION OF THE
VAMPIRES

INVASION EARTH 2150 A.D.   see   DALEKS-INVASION EARTH
2150 A.D.

INVASION FROM A PLANET see INVASION OF THE NEPTUNE
MEN

INVASION FROM THE MOON see MUTINY IN OUTER SPACE

INVASION OF ASTRO-MONSTER   (J)   Maron/Toho 1965 color/
scope 96m. (KAIJU DAISENSO. BATTLE OF THE ASTROS.
INVASION OF PLANET X. MONSTER ZERO) D: Inoshiro Honda.
SP: Shinichi Sekizawa.   PH: Hajime Koizumi. SpFX: Eiji
Tsuburaya. Ref: MMF. Pic: FM 47:18. with Nick Adams, Akira
Takarada, Akira Kubo, Jun Tazaki. Plus Ghidrah, Godzilla,
and Rodan.

INVASION OF MARS see ANGRY RED PLANET, The

INVASION OF THE ANIMAL PEOPLE (U.S.-Swedish) ADP 1960
('62-U.S.) Sp,D: Jerry Warren and Virgil Vogel.
(TERROR IN THE MIDNIGHT SUN. SPACE INVASION OF LAP-
LAND. HORROR IN THE MIDNIGHT SUN) Ref: FM 8:16.26:4.
Orpheus 3:29. COF 4:4. with John Carradine, Barbara Wilson,
Robert Burton. Mountain-dwellers are terrorized by huge
monsters.

INVASION OF THE BODY SNATCHERS AA 1956 scope 80m. (THEY
CAME FROM ANOTHER WORLD) D: Don Siegel. SP: Daniel
Mainwaring, from "The Body Snatchers" by Jack Finney. PH:
Ellsworth Fredricks. Mus: Carmen Dragon. Art D: Edward
Haworth. Ass't D: Richard Maybery, Bill Beaudine. P: Walter
Wanger. Ref: MMF 18-19:99. FM 14:46.15:40. with Dana
Wynter, Kevin McCarthy, King Donovan, Carolyn Jones, Sam
Peckinpah, Dabbs Greer, Pat O'Malley, Whit Bissell, Richard
Deacon, Larry Gates, Jean Willes. Seedpods from outer space
become doubles of humans and replace them. A basically good
story is cheapened by overexcited music and acting. The
details are horrific, but they're thrown at you a little too gleefully sometimes and seem silly. And much of the dialogue,
ranging from "realistic" small-talk to earth-shaking pronounce-
ments ("It's a malignant disease that's spreading throughout the
country"), is faintly embarrassing.

INVASION OF THE BODY STEALERS (B) Tigon/Sagittarius 1969
Eastmancolor 91m. (The BODY STEALERS. THIN AIR)
D: Gerry Levy. SP: Mike St. Clair, Peter Marcus. PH: Johnny
Coquillon. Mus: Reg Tilsley. Art D: Wilfred Arnold. Ref:
MFB'69:170. M/TVM 4/69. Pic: FM 63:13. with George
Sanders, Maurice Evans, Patrick Allen, Neil Connery, Hilary
Dwyer, Robert Flemyng, Allan Cuthbertson. Parachutist dis-
appears into mysterious red mist. The characters keep saying
"It's preposterous," but it's no use--it is preposterous, and
without a budget for special effects it isn't enjoyably so.

INVASION OF THE GARGON see TEENAGERS FROM OUTER
SPACE

INVASION OF THE HELL CREATURES see INVASION OF THE
SAUCERMEN

INVASION OF THE NEPTUNE MEN (J) Medallion/Manley-TV/Toei
1961 scope 74m. (UCHU KAISOKU-SEN. SPACE CHIEF.
SPACE GREYHOUND. INVASION FROM A PLANET) D: Koji
Ota. SP: Shin Morita. PH: S. Fujii. Ref: UFQ 14. M/TVM
7/61. with Shinichi Chiba, Shinjiro Ebara, Mitsue Komiya,
Ryuko Minakami. Unpolished dubbed dialogue makes the con-
fusion and running about bearable: "What a situation is now con-
fronting the world!" "Hooray for the electro-barrier!" etc.
INVASION OF THE SAUCERMEN AI/Malibu 1957 68m. (HELL
CREATURES-Eng. SPACEMEN SATURDAY NIGHT. INVASION
OF THE HELL CREATURES) Remake: The EYE CREATURES. D:
Edward L. Cahn. SP: Al Martin, Robert Gurney, Jr., from
the story "The Cosmic Frame" by Paul Fairman. PH: Frederick
E. West. Ref: FDY. MMF 13:45. FM 2:16. with Steve Ter-
rell, Raymond Hatton, Gloria Castillo, Frank Gorshin, Russ
Bender, Scott Peters, Ed Nelson, Lyn Osborn, Douglas Hender-
son, Jason Johnson, Kelly Thorsden. Teenagers vs. space men.
Offbeat, sometimes grisly, with strange bits of humor.
INVASION OF THE STAR CREATURES AI 1959 (1961) 70m.
(The STAR CREATURES) D: Bruno VeSota. SP: Jonathan Haze.
PH: Basil Bradbury. Electronic Mus: Jack Cookerly, Elliott
Fisher. Makeup: Joseph Kinder. Ref: FFacts. Pic: FM 20:8.
with Bob Ball, Frankie Ray, Gloria Victor, Dolores Reed, Mark
Ferris. Plant-like creatures invade earth. More than twice as
funny as BEAUTY AND THE ROBOT.
INVASION OF THE TRIFFIDS see DAY OF THE TRIFFIDS
INVASION OF THE VAMPIRES (Mex) AI-TV/Tele-Talia 1961
78m. (LA INVASION DE LOS VAMPIROS) SP, D: Miguel
Morayta. PH: Raul M. Solares. Mus: L. H. Breton. Art D:
Manuel Fontanals. Ref: Indice. FM 57:12. Pic: COF 11:40.
with Tito Junco, David Reynoso, "Mantequilla," Carlos Agosti,
Erna Martha Bauman. Well, there are some atmospheric shots of
fog-shrouded coffins. But mostly there's dialogue like "This
town is full of stupid men--champions of stupidity--class A
morons" and other things too swell to mention.
INVASION OF THE ZOMBIES see HORROR OF PARTY BEACH/
SANTO AGAINST THE ZOMBIES
INVASION, U.S.A. Col 1952 74m. D: Alfred E. Green. SP:
Robert Smith. Story: Smith, Franz Spencer. PH: John L. Rus-
sell. SpPhFX: Jack Rabin. P: Smith, Al Zugsmith. Ref: FDY.
with Peggie Castle, Gerald Mohr, Dan O'Herlihy, Noel Neill,
Phyllis Coates, Edward G. Robinson, Jr., Aram Katcher. Man
envisions invasion of U.S. Draggy.
INVENCIBLE HOMBRE INVISIBLE, El see MR. INVISIBLE
INVENTION OF DESTRUCTION see FABULOUS WORLD OF JULES
VERNE, The
INVENTION OF DR. WRIGHT see DR. WRIGHT's INVENTION
INVENTIONS OF AN IDIOT Lubin 1909 5m. Ref: F Index 5/1/09.
"Flymobile," hair remover, hair restorer.
The INVENTOR (F?) Pathe 15m. Ref: Bios 9/29/10. An artisan
invents a material that cannot be punctured.
The INVENTOR BRICOLO Roach 1914 Ref: Lee. COF 6:31.
The INVENTOR'S PERIL Lubin 1915 25m. D: Joseph Smiley. Ref:

MPN 6/5/15. Motography 6/5/15. with Lulu Leslie, Jack Standing. Man invents wireless telephone.

The INVENTOR'S SECRET Biog 1911 8m. Ref: Bios 11/30/11.1/29 /14. Inventor makes "patent automatic figure."

The INVENTOR'S SECRET (I) Cines 1911 35m. Ref: Bios '12:61. Naval officer invents powerful new explosive which blows up house.

The INVENTOR'S SON (B?) Kinemacolor 1911 Ref: SF Film. diamonds manufactured.

The INVINCIBLE BROTHERS MACISTE (I) IFESA 1964 color/ scope (GLI INVINCIBILI FRATELLI MACISTE) SP, D: Roberto Mauri. SP: also Mulargia. PH: Romolo Garroni. Mus: F. Di Stefano. Ref: Ital P. with Richard Lloyd, Claudie Lange, Tony Freeman, Anthony Steffen, Ursula Davis. Underground city; will-destroying potion; superman potion.

INVINCIBLE INVISIBLE MAN, The see MR. INVISIBLE

INVINCIBLE SPACEMAN see ATOMIC RULERS OF THE WORLD

INVISIBLE AGENT Univ 1942 81m. D : Edwin L. Marin. SP: Curt Siodmak. Based on ideas in "The Invisible Man" by H. G. Wells. PH: Lester White. Mus D: Charles Previn. Art D: Jack Otterson. P: Frank Lloyd. Assoc P: George Waggner. Ref: FDY. COF 5:22. with Ilona Massey, Jon Hall, Peter Lorre, J. Edward Bromberg, Albert Basserman, Sir Cedric Hardwicke, John Litel, Holmes Herbert. Drug renders American agent invisible.

INVISIBLE AVENGER Rep 1958 60m. D: James Wong Howe, John Sledge. SP: George Bellak, Betty Jeffries. PH: Willis Winford, Joseph Wheeler. Mus: Edward Dutreil. Ref: FFacts. with Richard Derr, Mark Daniels, Helen Westcott, Jeanne Neher, Dan Mullin. Oriental mystic instructs Lamont Cranston in the art of making himself invisible.

INVISIBLE AVENGER, The see INVISIBLE MAN, The (1954)

The INVISIBLE BOY MGM/Pan 1957 85m. (S.O.S. SPACE-SHIP-G.) D: Herman Hoffman. SP: Cyril Hume. Story: Edmund Cooper. Character, Robby the Robot, from FORBIDDEN PLANET. PH: Harold Wellman. Mus: Les Baxter. Art D: Merrill Pye. Ref: FDY. Pic: FM 12:19. with Richard Eyer, Diane Brewster, Philip Abbott, Harold J. Stone, Robert H. Harris, Michael Miller. Rather intriguing monster-computer story. No FORBIDDEN PLANET though.

The INVISIBLE CREATURE (B) AI-TV/Eternal 1960 70m. (The HOUSE IN MARSH ROAD) D: Montgomery Tully. SP, P: Maurice Wilson. Story: L. Meynell. PH: James Harvey. Mus sc: John Veale. Art D: John G. Earl. Ref: MFB'61:9. with Tony Wright, Sandra Dorne, Patricia Dainton, Sam Kydd, Olive Sloane, Geoffrey Denton. Poltergeist haunts house. Not too hot.

The INVISIBLE DR. MABUSE (W.G.) Manley-TV/CCC 1962 89m. (DIE UNSICHTBAREN KRALLENDES DES DR. MABUSE. GLI ARTIGLI INVISIBILI DEL DR. MABUSE-I. The INVISIBLE HORROR) D: Harald Reinl. SP: Ladislas Fodor. P, Idea: Arthur Brauner. PH: Ernst W. Kalinke. Mus: Peter Sandloff. Art D: Gabriel Pellon, Oskar Pietsch. SpFX: K. L. Ruppel.

Invisible

Ref: COF 11:37. Bianco 12/62. with Lex Barker, Karin Dor, Werner Peters, Wolfgang Preiss, Siegfried Lowitz, Alan Dijon. Pic: FMO 5:29. Invisibility machine.

INVISIBLE FLUID AM&B 1908 Ref: Niver. MPW'08:531. Fluid causes objects and people to disappear.

INVISIBLE GHOST Mono 1941 65m. (The PHANTOM KILLER) D: Joseph Lewis. SP: Helen and Al Martin. PH: Marcel Le Picard. Mus: Lange and Porter. P: Sam Katzman. Ref: FDY. with Bela Lugosi, Polly Ann Young, John McGuire, Ottola Nesmith, Ernie Adams, Betty Compson, Fred Kelsey, Jack Mulhall, Clarence Muse. Man under wife's hypnotic spell. A few surprisingly good comic moments, surprising because the rest is, as might be expected, so bad.

INVISIBLE HORROR, The see INVISIBLE DR. MABUSE, The

INVISIBLE HOST, The (by G. Bristow, B. Manning) see NINTH GUEST, The

The INVISIBLE INFORMER Rep 1946 57m. D: Philip Ford. SP: Sherman Lowe. Story: G. D. Adams. PH: William Bradford. Mus D: Mort Glickman. Art D: James Sullivan. Ref: COF 11: 37. FD 9/18/46: "Horror film." MPH 8/24/46: "Eerie atmosphere of lurking danger." with Linda Stirling, William Henry, Adele Mara, Gerald Mohr, Tristram Coffin, Peggy Stewart, Cy Kendall. Madman attempts to kill girl.

INVISIBLE INVADERS UA/Premium 1959 67m. D: Edward L. Cahn. SP: Samuel Newman. PH: Maury Gertsman. Art D: William Glasgow. Makeup: Phil Scheer. SpFX: Roger George. P: Robert E. Kent. Ref: FFacts. with John Agar, Jean Byron, Robert Hutton, Paul Langton, John Carradine, Philip Tonge, Hal Torey. Invaders from the moon enter the bodies of dead earthmen. Flaw-ridden. Poor special effects.

INVISIBLE KILLER PRC 1940 63m. D: Sherman Scott. SP: Joseph O'Donnell. Story: Carter Wayne. PH: Jack Greenhalgh. Mus D: Fred Preble. Ref: Showmen's 2/10/40. with Grace Bradley, Roland Drew, William Newell, Jeanne Kelly, Ernie Adams. Murders "contrived by an ingenious device in a telephone which causes two chemicals to combine when the receiver is lifted."

The INVISIBLE MAN Univ 1933 71m. D: James Whale. SP: Philip Wylie, R. C. Sherriff, from H. G. Wells' novel and "The Murderer Invisible" by Wylie. PH: Arthur Edeson, John Mescall. SpFX: John P. Fulton. P: Carl Laemmle. with Claude Rains, Henry Travers, Gloria Stuart, William Harrigan, Una O'Connor, E. E. Clive, Dudley Digges, Holmes Herbert, Forrester Harvey, Harry Stubbs, Merle Tottenham, Donald Stuart, John Carradine, Dwight Frye. Ref: FM 48:6. Pic: FM 16:25. Although the film is in large part a comedy (and a good one) the power than an invisible man would have is frighteningly conveyed.

The INVISIBLE MAN (J) Toho 1954 (TOMEI NINGEN. The INVISIBLE AVENGER) D: Motoyoshi Oda. SpFX: Eiji Tsuburaya. Ref: Unij. Bltn. with Seizaburo Kozu, Miki Sanjo.

INVISIBLE MAN (J) Toei 1958 (TOMEI KAIJIN) D: Tsuneo Kobayashi. Ref: Imagen. with Susumu Namishima, Y. Ito. A man becomes invisible.

The INVISIBLE MAN (Mex) Chapultepec 1961 (LOS INVISIBLES)
D: Jaime Salvador. SP: R. G. Bolaños. PH: Jose O. Ramos.
Mus: A. D. Conde. Ref: Indice. Imagen. FM 33:8. (The IN-
VISIBLE MEN) with Viruta, Capulina, Eduardo Fajardo, Martha
Elena Cervantes, Rosa M. Gallardo, José Jasso, Chucho Salinas.
Art D: R. G. Granada.
INVISIBLE MAN, The see INVISIBLE TERROR, The
INVISIBLE MAN, The (by H. G. Wells) see ABBOTT AND COS-
TELLO MEET FRANKENSTEIN/ABBOTT AND COSTELLO MEET
THE INVISIBLE MAN/INVISIBLE AGENT/INVISIBLE MAN
RETURNS, The/INVISIBLE THIEF/INVISIBLE MAN'S REVENGE,
The/NEW INVISIBLE MAN, The
The INVISIBLE MAN ATTACKS (Arg) Argentina Sono Films 1967
color 80m. (El HOMBRE INVISIBLE ATACA) D, P: Martin
Mentasti. SP: Sergio De Cecco. PH: Ricardo Younis. Mus:
R. Arizaga. Ref: Cine Argentino. Heraldo'68:321. with
Martin Karadagian, Gilda Lousek, Tristán. Art D: L. D.
Pedreira.
An INVISIBLE MAN GOES THROUGH THE CITY (G) Ariel Film
1933 (EIN UNSICHTBAR GEHT DURCH DIE STADT. DIE WELT
IST MEIN! THE WORLD IS MINE! MASTER OF THE WORLD)
D: Harry Piel. Ref: FJA. FM 13:30. with Fritz Odemar, Piel,
Ernst Rothemuend, Walter Steinbeck. Fare leaves cabbie suit-
case containing invisibility equipment.
The INVISIBLE MAN IN ISTANBUL (Turkish) 1956 (GORUN-
MIYEN ADAM ISTANBULDA) D: Lüftü Akad. Ref: Lee. FM 22:
7. with Atif Kaptan.
INVISIBLE MAN IN MEXICO, The see NEW INVISIBLE MAN, The
The INVISIBLE MAN RETURNS Univ 1940 81m. D: Joe May.
SP: Curt Siodmak, Lester Cole. Story: May, Siodmak. PH:
Milton Krasner. Mus sc: H. J. Salter, Frank Skinner. Art D:
Jack Otterson, Martin Obzina. Based on H. G. Wells' "The In-
visible Man." SpPhFX: John P. Fulton. Ref: Academy. V 1/10/
40. with Sir Cedric Hardwicke, Vincent Price, Nan Grey, John
Sutton, Cecil Kellaway, Alan Napier, Forrester Harvey, Harry
Stubbs, Ivan Simpson, Edward Fielding, Matthew Boulton, Billy
Bevan, Bruce Lester, Mary Gordon, Leyland Hodgson, Dave
Thursby, George Kirby, Ernie Adams. A man uses invisibility
to hunt for his brother's murderer.
The INVISIBLE MAN'S REVENGE Univ 1944 77m. P,D: Ford
Beebe. SP: Bertram Millhauser. Based on H. G. Wells' "The
Invisible Man." PH: Milton Krasner. Art D: John B. Goodman.
SpFX: John P. Fulton. Ref: Academy. Pic: FM 2:25.20:20. with
John Carradine, Jon Hall, Gale Sondergaard, Alan Curtis, Evelyn
Ankers, Lester Matthews, Ian Wolfe, Halliwell Hobbes, Billy
Bevan, Leon Errol, Doris Lloyd, Leyland Hodgson, Cyril
Delevanti, Skelton Knaggs, Guy Kingsford, Jim Aubrey. Invisible
man kills doctor who fails to return him to visibility. Mediocre.
INVISIBLE MEN, The see INVISIBLE MAN, The (1961)
The INVISIBLE MONSTER Rep 1950 serial 12 episodes (The
PHANTOM RULER. SLAVES OF THE INVISIBLE MONSTER-'66
feature) D: Fred C. Brannon. SP: Ronald Davidson. PH:Ellis
W. Carter. Mus: Stanley Wilson. SpFX: Howard and Theodore

Lydecker.   Ref: Barbour.   ModM 4:39.   with Richard Webb,
Aline Towne, John Crawford, Dale Van Sickel, Tom Steele, Ed
Parker, Frank O'Connor, Lane Bradford, Stanley Price, George
Meeker, Bud Wolfe, Marshall Reed.   Villain uses light ray and
new kind of chemically-treated clothing to become invisible.
The INVISIBLE MURDERER   (Mex) Panamericana/Pelimex 1964
   (EL ENMASCARADO DE ORO CONTRA EL ASESINO INVISIBLE)
   D: Rene Cardona.   PH: Raul M. Solares.   Mus: S. Guerrero.
   Ref: Indice. Imagen.   with Ana Bertha Lepe, Guillermo Murray,
   El Enmascarado de Oro, Carlos Agosti.   Formula for invisibility;
   "machine capable of killing from a great distance."
The INVISIBLE POWER   Kalem   1914   Ref: MPW 22:842.   Lee.
   Girl under man's hypnotic influence.
The INVISIBLE RAY   Frohman   1920   serial   15 episodes D: Harry
   Pollard.   SP: Guy McConnell.   Ref: NYT 2/22/20.   CNW.   with
   Ruth Clifford, Sidney Bracy, Jack Sherrill, Ed Davis.   Mineralo-
   gist discovers a new force.
The INVISIBLE RAY   Univ   1936   81m.   D: Lambert Hillyer.   SP:
   John Colton.   Story: Howard Higgins, Douglas Hodges.   PH:
   George Robinson, John P. Fulton. Ref: Clarens. Pic: FM 16:31.
   19:40.   SM 2:30.   DDC III:42.   with Bela Lugosi, Boris Karloff,
   Frances Drake, Frank Lawton, Beulah Bondi, Frank Reicher,
   Walter Kingsford, Nydia Westman, George Renavent, Violet
   Kemble Cooper, Etta McDaniel, Winter Hall.   Scientist's slightest
   touch means death after he absorbs powerful dose of radiation.
   One of the better Karloff-Lugosi co-starrers.   It's actually
   moderately enjoyable.
INVISIBLE SWORDSMAN   (J) 1970 79m.   (TOMEI KENSHI) D:
   Yoshiyuki Kuroda.   Ref: UFQ 49:36.   M/TVM 8/69: INVISIBLE
   SWORDSMAN STRIKES AGAIN.   Invisible swordsman; Death per-
   sonified.
The INVISIBLE TERROR   (W.G.) R&B/Aero/Konsul 1963 90m.
   (DER UNSICHTBARE.   The INVISIBLE MAN) SP, D: Raphael
   Nussbaum.   SP: also Wladimir Semitjof.   PH: Michael Mars-
   zalek.   Mus: Jean Thomé.   Ref: German Pictures.   COF 11:38.
   M/TVM 6/63.   with Hanaes Hauser, Ellen Schwiers, Hannes
   Schmidhauser, Hans Borsody, Ivan Desny, Ilse Steppat.   Drug
   makes objects and people invisible.
INVISIBLE TERROR   see   MONSTER FROM THE SURF
INVISIBLE THIEF   (F) Pathe 1909 6m.   D: Ferdinand Zecca?
   From H. G. Wells' "The Invisible Man."   Ref: MPW'09:65.
   SilentFF.   BFI Dist. Cata. '62.   Young man makes himself in-
   visible.
The INVISIBLE WOMAN   Univ   1940   72m.   D: Edward Sutherland.
   SP: Robert Lees, F. Rinaldo, Gertrude Purcell.   Story: Curt
   Siodmak, Joe May.   PH: Elwood Bredell.   Mus: Charles Previn.
   Art D: Jack Otterson. Ref: FDY.   with Virginia Bruce, John
   Barrymore, John Howard, Oscar Homolka, Anne Nagel, Charlie
   Ruggles, Edward Brophy, Donald MacBride, Margaret Hamilton,
   Shemp Howard, Maria Montez, Mary Gordon, Thurston Hall,
   Charles Lane.   Hypodermic solution plus machine will render
   humans invisible.
INVISIBLES, Los   see INVISIBLE MAN, The (1961)

INVITATION TO A MURDER (by R. King)   see HIDDEN HAND, The (1942)

IO, DORIAN GRAY see SECRET OF DORIAN GRAY, The

The IRON CLAW Pathe 1916 serial 20 episodes D: Edward Jose. From stories by Arthur Stringer. Ref: MPN 13:1322, 3112. 14:635. Pic: DDC II:223. with Sheldon Lewis, Creighton Hale, Pearl White, Harry Fraser, J. E. Dunn. Ghosts; ray projector; fluid that ages, kills villain instantly. Ch. 10. The Living Dead. 12. The Haunted Canvas.

The IRON CLAW Col 1941 serial 15 episodes D: James W. Horne. SP: B. Dickey, G. H. Plympton, J. A. Duffy, C. R. Condon, J. Stanley, Arthur Stringer. Ref: Barbour. Pic: FM 17:17. with Charles Quigley, Joyce Bryant, Forrest Taylor, Walter Sande, Norman Willis, John Beck, Hal Price, Charles King, James Morton. Grotesque-looking villain, "The Claw."

IS CONAN DOYLE RIGHT? Pathe 1923 Documentary Ref: NY Times 10/3/23: The film shows "several ways of producing the more common spiritualistic manifestations and phenomena, ectoplasm, slate writing and other evidences of supernatural power."

ISABEL (Canadian) Para/Quest 1968 Technicolor 108m. SP, D, P: Paul Almond. PH: Georges Dufaux. Mus: Harry Freedman. Ref: V 7/24/68. Sat. Review 8/17/68. with Genevieve Bujold, Mark Strange, Gerard Parkes, Elton Hayes. Heroine encounters apparitions, mysterious noises, etc. Lots of ambiguity, but none that anybody could care about. Everything is kept just vague enough so that you can't tell when the director is lost.

ISHIMATSU TRAVELS WITH GHOSTS (J) Toho 1959 (MORI NO ISHIMATSU YUREI DOCHU) D: Kozo Saeki. Ref: Japanese Films '60. with Frankie Sakai, Kaoru Yachigusa.

ISIS (F) 1910 Ref: The Film Index. MPW 7:1247. A prince rejects the sweetheart that the moon goddess, Isis, selects for him.   Isis punishes him by taking human form, enchanting him, and leaving him to the torment of frustrated love.

ISLA DE LA MUERTE, La see ISLAND OF THE DOOMED

ISLA DE LOS DINOSAUR(I)OS, La see ISLAND OF THE DINOSAURS, The

ISLAND OF DR. MOREAU, The (by H. G. Wells) see ISLAND OF LOST SOULS/TERROR IS A MAN

ISLAND OF LOST SOULS Para 1932 74m. D: Erle C. Kenton. SP: Waldemar Young, Philip Wylie, from "The Island of Dr. Moreau" by H. G. Wells. PH: Karl Struss. Ref: FM 2:51. 10:26. 11:4. Pic: FM 2:45. 10:27. 11:8. 16:25. with Charles Laughton, Bela Lugosi, Richard Arlen, Kathleen Burke, Leila Hyams, Arthur Hohl, Stanley Fields, Tetsu Komai, Paul Hurst, Joe Bonomo, Hans Steinke, George Irving. Scientist's experiments in turning animals into humans results in half-human monsters. Laughton isn't quite the whole show, but his (to say the least) distinctive interpretation of a mad scientist, smirking and chuckling lewdly and indulgently, steals it away from the horde of monster-men and probably the most horrendously sadistic (offscreen) moment ever. In the movies' annals of mad scientists, Laughton is one of the most memorably, flamboyantly mad of all, topping maybe even Lugosi in MURDERS IN THE RUE MORGUE and Thesiger in

in BRIDE OF FRANKENSTEIN. Between Laughton and the beast-
men Richard Arlen is, fortunately, lost.
ISLAND OF LOST WOMEN WB/Jaguar 1959 66m. D: Frank W.
Tuttle. SP: Ray Buffum. Story: Prescott Chaplain. PH: John
Seitz. Mus: Raoul Kraushaar. Art D: Jack Collis. Ref: FFacts.
Lee. with Jeff Richards, John Smith, Venetia Stevenson, Alan
Napier, Gavin Muir. Powerful radar screen; deadly rays; flame-
throwing pistol.
The ISLAND OF SURPRISE Vita 1916 55m. P: Paul Scardon.
SP: Cyrus T. Brady. Ref: MPN 13:718. with Eleanor Woodruff,
William Courtenay, Anders Randolf, Julia Swayne Gordon. Man
struck by lightning loses memory.
ISLAND OF TERROR (F) SCE/Kleine/Urbanora 1913 30m. (ILE
D'EPOUVANTE) ?: Joe Hamman. Ref: DDC III. Bios 12/4/13.
Maniac doctor conducts "gruesome experiments."
ISLAND OF TERROR (B) Univ/Planet 1966 color 89m. (NIGHT
OF THE SILICATES. NIGHT THE CREATURES CAME. The
CREEPERS. The NIGHT THE SILICATES CAME) D: Terence
Fisher. SP: Edward A. Mann, Al(l)an Ramsen. PH: Reg Wyer.
Mus sc & d: Malcolm Lockyear. Art D, SpFX: John St. John
Earl. Electronic FX: Barry Gray. Exec P: Richard Gordon,
Gerald A. Fernback. Ref: FFacts. FM 42:8. MW 9:31. PM.
with Peter Cushing, Niall MacGinnis, Edward Judd, Eddie Byrne,
Sam Kydd, Carole Gray. Scientist attempting to create an organ-
ism to combat cancer breeds monsters. Some very effective
scenes which are what nightmares are made of: deadly silicates
falling from trees, through skylights, etc. A lot of trite dialogue
with an occasional nice line.
ISLAND OF THE BURNING DAMNED see NIGHT OF THE BIG HEAT
The ISLAND OF THE DINOSAURS (Mex) Calderon 1966 (LA
ISLA DE LOS DINOSAUR(I)OS) D: Rafael Portillo. Ref: MMF
18-19:15. M/TVM 7/66. 8/66. with Armando Silvestre, Elsa
Ca(r)denas, Crox Alvarado, Regina Torne, Roberto Cañedo, Tito
Junco. Prehistoric man.
ISLAND OF THE DOOMED (G-Sp) AA/Tefi(Theumer)-Orbita
1966 color/scope 88m. (LA ISLA DE LA MUERTE-Sp. The
BLOOD SUCKERS-Eng. DEATH ISLAND. Le BARON VAMPIRE-F.
MANEATER OF HYDRA-TV) D: Mel Welles. SP: Ira Meltcher,
E. V. Theumer. PH: Cecilio Panigua. Mus: A. G. Abril. Art
D: F. Canet. Ref: SpCinema'67. with Cameron Mitchell, Elisa
Montés, George Martin, Kay Fischer, Rolf V. Naukoff, Hermann
Nehlsen. Vampire tree feeds on human blood.
ISLE OF MYSTERY, The (by J. Verne) see MYSTERIOUS ISLAND
(1951)
The ISLE OF THE DEAD (Dan) 1913 (DE DODES O. L'ILE DES
MORTS-F) D: Wilhelm Gluckstadt. Ref: Mitry V: 197. DDC II:
315. Ghost.
ISLE OF THE DEAD RKO 1945 72m. D: Mark Robson. SP:
Ardel Wray, Joseph Mischel. PH: Jack Mackenzie. Mus: Leigh
Harline. Art D: Albert D'Agostino, Walter E. Keller. P: Val
Lewton. Ref: Clarens. Pic: FM 36:64. FanMo 2:52. with Boris
Karloff, Ellen Drew, Marc Cramer, Katherine Emery, Helen
Thimig, Alan Napier, Jason Robards, Skelton Knaggs. Premature

burial; hints of vampirism ("vorvolaka"). An almost oppressive atmosphere of death pervades the film to create a strange, claustrophobic sort of horror. Toward the end there are moments of horror of a more familiar, comfortable sort. Karloff is fine in an unusual role in one of the best of the Lewtons.

ISLE OF THE SNAKE PEOPLE see SNAKE PEOPLE, The

ISLE MYSTERIEUSE, L' (by J. Verne) see MYSTERIOUS ISLAND (1929)

ISMAIL YASSINE AND THE GHOST (UAR) 1954 (AFRITET ISMAIL YASSINE) D?: Hassan el Saifi. Ref: Sadoul. Index des Films Egyptiens 1953-55:103. Ghost.

ISOLA STREGATA DEGLI ZOMBIES, L' see VOODOO ISLAND

The ISOLATED HOUSE Pathe-Victory 1915 40m. Based on the character Sherlock Holmes created by Sir Arthur Conan Doyle. Ref: MPN 7/17/15. MPW 25:904. Roger of Baskerville imprisons Lord and Lady Baskerville in a "submersible house." "Pocket wireless."

ISOTOPE MAN, The (by C. E. Maine) see ATOMIC MAN, The

IT! WB-7A/Gold Star 1967 color 95m. (CURSE OF THE GOLEM. ANGER OF THE GOLEM) SP,D,P: Herbert J. Leder. PH: David Boulton. Mus: Carlo Martelli. Art D: Sean MacGregor. Ref: LA Times 1/26/68. FFacts. PM. COF 10:47. with Roddy McDowall, Jill Haworth, Paul Maxwell, Noel Trevarthen, Aubrey Richards, Russell Napier. An assistant curator of a museum learns the secret of bringing the Golem to life.

IT CAME FROM BENEATH THE SEA Col 1955 78m. (MONSTER FROM BENEATH THE SEA) D: Robert Gordon. SP: Hal Smith, George W. Yates. PH: Henry Freulich. Mus: Mischa Bakaleinikoff. SpFX: Ray Harryhausen. P: Charles Schneer. Exec P: Sam Katzman. Ref: FM 46:76. Pic: FM 15:8. with Faith Domergue, Kenneth Tobey, Ian Keith, Donald Curtis, Harry Lauter, Del Courtney. H-bomb experiments drive giant octopus up from the depths of the sea. It's a long, dull wait for the monster, which is fairly impressive when it finally does something.

IT CAME FROM OUTER SPACE Univ 1953 (3-D) 80m. D: Jack Arnold. SP: Harry Essex. Story: Ray Bradbury. PH:Clifford Stine. Mus D: Joseph Gershenson. Art D: Bernard Herzbrun, Robert Boyle. SpPH: David Horsley. P: William Alland. Ref: V 5/21/53. FM 14:46. 20:47. SM 8:32. Pic: SM 1:21. FM 13:32. with Richard Carlson, Barbara Rush, Charles Drake, Russell Johnson, Joe Sawyer, Dave Willock, George Eldredge, Edgar Dearing. Beings from outer space land in the Arizona desert. Cloddish acting and writing sink some potentially interesting ideas. Plenty of dud lines: "When are you going to stop being a badge and start being a human being?" "A strange man--and odd"--"More than odd. Individual and lonely" "Is it reasonable for something to stay alive after hitting earth that hard?"--"It's reasonable because it's true."

IT CONQUERED THE WORLD AI/Sunset 1956 68m. P,D: Roger Corman. SP: Lou Rusoff. PH: Frederick E. West. Mus: Ronald Stein. Remake: ZONTAR. Ref: MFB'56:141. Pic: FM 2:4. with Beverly Garland, Peter Graves, Lee Van Cleef, Dick

Miller, Jonathan Haze, Russ Bender, Sally Fraser, Charles B. Griffith, Kareen Kadler, Paul Blaisdell. Scientist aids being from outer space in its plot to conquer the world. Okay early Corman looks even better now thanks to ZONTAR.

IT HAPPENED HERE (B) Lopert 1966 (1958) 95m. SP, D, P: Kevin Brownlow, Andrew Mollo. PH: Peter Suschitsky. Ref: COF 6:56. PM. with Pauline Murray, Sebastian Shaw, Fiona Leland. What might have happened if Germany had conquered England during World War II.

IT HAPPENS EVERY SPRING Fox 1949 89m. D: Lloyd Bacon. SP: Valentine Davies, Shirley Smith. PH: Joe MacDonald. Ref: FDY. with Ray Milland, Paul Douglas, Jean Peters, Alan Hale, Jr., Ray Collins, Ed Begley, Ted de Corsia, Jessie Royce Landis, Bill Murphy, Gene Evans, Ray Teal, Grandon Rhodes. Chemistry professor discovers serum that makes baseballs jump by bats. Fairly entertaining comedy.

IT STALKED THE OCEAN FLOOR see MONSTER FROM THE OCEAN FLOOR

IT! THE TERROR FROM BEYOND SPACE UA/Vogue 1958 68m. (IT! THE VAMPIRE FROM BEYOND SPACE) D: Edward L. Cahn. SP: Jerome Bixby. PH: Kenneth Peach, Sr. Mus: Paul Sawtell, Bert Shefter. Art D: William Glasgow. P: Robert E. Kent. Ref: FFacts. FM 2:20. with Marshall Thompson, Shawn Smith, Ann Doran, Paul Langton, Dabbs Greer, Kim Spalding, Robert Bice, Ray (Crash) Corrigan, Richard Benedict. Blood-drinking monster loose on board spaceship. The monster isn't very frightening, though there are a few tense moments in the latter half.

IT WAS NOT IN VAIN (Yugos) Jadran Film c1967 (NIJE BILO UZALUD) SP, D: Nikola Tanhofer. PH: Slavko Zalar. Mus: Milo Cipra. Ref: Jadran Film. with Mira Nikolić, Boris Buzancic, Zvonimir Rogoz, Antun Vrdoljak. A fortune teller rules over a swamp with curses that come true. Her son is thought to be dead and a ghost.

ITALIAN CHRONICLES (by Stendhal) see GENTLE ART OF MURDER, The

ITCHING PALMS FBO/R-C Pictures 1923 65m. D:James W. Horne. From the play "When Jerry Comes Home" by R. Briant. Art D: W. L. Heywood. Ed: J. Wilkinson. Ref: Motion Picture 11/23. AFI. with Tom Gallery, Virginia Fox, Tom Wilson, Victor Potel. Haunted house.

IT'S A GIFT Pathe 1923 11m. P: Hal Roach. with Snub Pollard. Gasoline substitute; flying car. Fairly amusing comedy.

"IT'S ALIVE!" AI-TV/Azalea 1968 color 80m. SP, D, P: Larry Buchanan. PH: Robert Alcott. SpFX: Jack Bennett. Ref: RVB. M/TVM 4/68. TVG. with Tommy Kirk, Shirley Bonne, Annabelle Macadams, Carveth Austerhouse. Mad farmer discovers prehistoric masasaurus ("Isn't it a magnificent creature!") near his farm. By trying several tricks with the camera, Buchanan proves he can't do any of them competently. And he subjects his actors to long, unpleasant, embarrassing scenes.

IT'S ALWAYS DARKEST BEFORE THE DAWN see VAMPIRE, The (UA-1957)

IT'S GREAT TO BE ALIVE Fox 1933 D: Alfred Werker. SP:
Paul Perez. Dial: Arthur Kober. Story: John Swain. PH:
Robert Planck. Remake of the 1924 LAST MAN ON EARTH.
Ref: FDY. with Edward Van Sloan, Herbert Mundin, Edna May
Oliver, Robert Greig, Emma Dunn, Gloria Stuart, Raul Roulien.
A disease kills off most of the men on earth.
IT'S HOT IN PARADISE see HORRORS OF SPIDER ISLAND
IT'S ONLY MONEY Para/York/Lewis 1962 83m. D: Frank
Tashlin. SP: John Fenton Murray. PH: W. Wallace Kelley.
Mus: Walter Scharf. Ref: V 11/21/62. COF 11:40. with
Jerry Lewis, Zachary Scott, Joan O'Brien, Jesse White, Jack
Weston, Barbara Pepper, Francine York, Milton Frome, Del
Moore, Ted de Corsia, Doodles Weaver, Dick Whittinghill.
Radio-controlled electronic lawnmowers.
I'VE LIVED BEFORE Univ 1956 82m. D: Richard Bartlett. SP:
William Talman, Norman Jolley. PH: Maury Gertsman. Mus
D: Joseph Gershenson. Mus sc: Herman Stein. with Jock
Mahoney, Leigh Snowden, Ann Harding, John McIntire, Jerry
Paris, Raymond Bailey, April Kent, Phil Harvey, Brad Morrow,
Simon Scott. Man believes he has lived another life in another
time. Alternates between the clinical and the melodramatic
pretty dull either way.
IVORY TRAIL, The see JUNGLE MYSTERY

J'ACCUSE see I ACCUSE (1918/1937)
JA, SPRAVEDLNOST see I, JUSTICE
JACK AND THE BEANSTALK Edison 1902 10m. D: Edwin S.
Porter Ref: Niver. MPW 14:961.
JACK AND THE BEANSTALK Lubin 1903 Ref: LC.
JACK AND THE BEANSTALK Edison 1912 Ref: MPW'12:140.
Bios'12. Ogre, ogre's giant wife, magic harp, golden eggs.
JACK AND THE BEANSTALK Fox 1917 SP, D: C. M. and S. A.
Franklin. Ref: NYT 7/31/17. with Francis Carpenter, Vir-
ginia Lee.
JACK AND THE BEANSTALK WB/Exclusive 1952 Super Cine-
color 78m. D: Jean Yarbrough. SP: Nat Curtis. Story: Pat
Costello. Add'l Comedy: Felix Adler. PH: George Robinson.
Mus sc & d: Heinz Roemheld. Mus Sup: Raoul Kraushaar. Art
D: McClure Capps. Ref: HR 4/3/52. TVG. with Bud Abbott,
Lou Costello, Buddy Baer, Barbara Brown, Dorothy Ford,
William Farnum, James Alexander. Giant, talking harp, goose
that lays golden eggs. Fairly embarrassing mixture of comedy
and songs. At least it wasn't called ABBOTT AND COSTELLO
MEET JACK AND THE BEANSTALK.
JACK ARMSTRONG Col 1947 serial 15 episodes D: Wallace
Fox. SP: A. Hoerl, L. Clay, R. Cole, L. Swabacker. From
the radio show. PH: Ira H. Morgan. P: Sam Katzman. Ref:
Barbour. SF Film. Pic: M&H 1:20. with John Hart, Rose-
mary LaPlanche, Joe Brown, Jr., Jack Ingram, Eddie Parker,
Hugh Prosser, John Merton, Charles Middleton, Gene Stutenroth,

Russ Vincent, Wheeler Oakman, Pierre Watkin, Claire James.
"Aeroglobe." Ch. 1. Mystery of the Cosmic Ray. 5. The
Space Ship. 11. The Cosmic Annihilator.
JACK FROST (Russ) Emb/Gorky 1965 Pathecolor 79m.
(MOROZKO. GRANDFATHER FROST) D: Alexander Row. SP:
Mikhail Volpin, Nikolai Erdman. PH: D. Surensky. Mus: N.
Budashkin. Art D: A. Klopotovsky. Ref: FFacts. with Natasha
Sedykh, Alexander Khvylya, Eduard Izotov, Yuri Millyar. Grem-
lin that changes man's head into a bear's; old witch; walking
trees; magic, flying clubs; magic sceptre which causes girl to
fall into trance.
JACK O'LANTERN (by G. Goodchild) see CONDEMNED TO DEATH
JACK O'LANTERN MURDERS, The see CONDEMNED TO DEATH
JACK SPRATT AND THE SCALES OF LOVE Ess 1915 15m.
Ref: MPN 12/4/15. LC. with Victor Potel, Margaret Joslin.
Newlyweds buy "Thino" and "Fato" at drug store. A few hours
after finishing the bottles, the wife weighs 290 pounds, the hus-
band 85.
JACK THE GIANT KILLER UA 1962 Technicolor/Fantascope
94m. SP, D: Nathan Juran. SP: also Orville Hampton. PH:
David S. Horsley. Mus: Paul Sawtell. Art D: Fernando Carrere,
Frank McCoy. SpFX: Howard A. Anderson. Makeup: Charles
Gemora. Mus: also Bert Shefter. P: Edward Small. Assoc P:
Robert E. Kent. Ref: FFacts. PM. with Kerwin Mathews, Judi
Meredith, Torin Thatcher, Walter Burke, Roger Mobley, Don
Beddoe, Anna Lee, Tudor Owen, Dayton Lummis. Pic: FM
21:13. A'64:40. Tentacled sea monster; wizard, giant, spell,
etc. Good special effects, color. The sea monster is especially
impressive.
JACK THE RIPPER Para/Emb/Mid-Century 1959 color sequence
88m. (B) (The RETURN OF JACK THE RIPPER) D, P, PH:
Monty Berman, Robert Baker. SP: Jimmy Sangster. Story:
Peter Hammond, Colin Craig. Mus: Jimmy McHugh, Pete Rugolo.
Ref: FFacts. Orpheus 3:27. Pic: FM 15:9. with Lee Patterson,
Eddie Byrne, Betty McDowall, Ewen Solon, John Le Mesurier,
George Rose, George Woodbridge, The Montparnasse Ballet.
Rather dull re-telling of the story of London's phantom killer.
JACK THE RIPPER (Sp) 1971 D: Jose Luis Madrid. Ref:
V 10/6/71:6.
The JADE BOX Univ 1930 serial 10 episodes D: Ray Taylor.
silent & sound versions Ref: FD 2/23/30. CNW. with Monroe
Salisbury, Francis Ford, Jack Perrin, Eileen Sedgwick.
"Phantom in black"; evil spirits of oriental cult.
The JADE MASK Mono 1945 D: Phil Rosen. SP: George Calla-
han. Based on the character "Charlie Chan" created by Earl
Derr Biggers. PH: Harry Neumann. Art D: Dave Milton. Ref:
HR 2/21/45. V 2/21/45. with Sidney Toler, Mantan Moreland, Ed-
win Luke, Hardie Albright, Ralph Lewis, Frank Reicher, Dorothy
Granger, Jack Ingram, Lester Dorr, Henry Hall. "Mystery house,"
hidden rooms, walking "dead men," secret formula for making
wood as durable as steel.
JAGGA DAKU see BANDIT, The
JAIL BAIT see GLEN OR GLENDA

JALOPY AA 1953 62m. D: William Beaudine. SP: Tim Ryan,
Jack Crutcher. Add'l Dial: Bert Lawrence. PH: Harry
Neumann. Mus: Marlin Skiles. Ref: COF 11:40. V 3/25/53.
with Leo Gorcey, Huntz Hall, Bernard Gorcey, Bob Lowry,
Richard Benedict. A Bowery Boy's chemical formula acts as a
love potion or a super car-fuel.
JAMBOREE see DELUGE/SON OF KONG
JAMES BOND see SUPER DIABOLICAL
JAMES TONT, OPERATION D.U.E. (I-F) Panda/Cineurop 1966
color (JAMES TONT, OPERAZIONE D.U.E.) D: Bruno Corbucci.
SP: Corbucci, E. Donati, L. Carpentieri, Vighi, Guerra,
Pellevant. PH: Sandro D'Eva. Mus: Bruno Canfora. Ref:
Ital P'66. with Lando Buzzanca, France Anglade, Furio Meni-
coni, Claudie Lange, Loris Gizzi, Mirko Valentin. Phial of
hormones makes man age rapidly.
JANAK NANDINI (India-Bengali) Radha Films 1939 D: Phani
Burma. PH: P. Das. Ref: Dipali 1/13/39. with A. Chaudhuri,
Sushil Roy, Robi Roy. Curse: "Ahalya turned into stone for in-
fidelity."
JANNE VANGMAN OCH DEN STORA KOMETAN see JOHNNY
VENGMAN AND THE BIG COMET
Der JANUSKOPF (G) Decla-Bioscop/Lippow 1920 (JANUS-FACED.
HEAD OF JANUS. LOVE'S MOCKERY) D: F. W. Murnau. SP:
Hans Janowitz, from "The Strange Case of Dr. Jekyll and Mr.
Hyde" by Robert Louis Stevenson. PH: Carl Hoffmann, Karl
Freund. Art D: Heinrich Richter. Ref: S&S'68:213. FM 11·32,
36.14:4.34:44. with Conrad Veidt, Bela Lugosi, Margarete
Schlegel.
The JAPANESE MASK Pathe-Aetna 1915 40m. Ref: Motography
6/12/15. MPN 6/5/15. Superstition that whoever looks at
mask will not die a natural death.
A JAPANESE PEACH BOY Edison 1910 15m. Ref: Bios 3/24/
10. Ogres in cavern capture boy and his mother; huge snake
turns into magic wand.
JARDINS DU DIABLE, Les see COPLAN SAVES HIS SKIN
JASON AND THE ARGONAUTS (U.S.-B) Col/BLC/Morningside/
World Wide 1963 Technicolor/Super Dynamation 90m. (JASON
AND THE GOLDEN FLEECE) D: Don Chaffey. SP: Jan Read,
Beverly Cross. PH: Wilkie Cooper. Mus: Bernard Herrmann.
SpFX: Ray Harryhausen. P: Charles Schneer. Ref: FFacts.
Pic: ModM 1:78. with Todd Armstrong, Nancy Kovack, Gary
Raymond, Laurence Naismith, Niall MacGinnis, Michael Gwynn,
Douglas Wilmer, Jack Gwillim, Honor Blackman, Nigel Green,
John Crawford. Jason vs. harpies, skeletons, Hydra, etc.
Harryhausen's animated harpies deserve a movie of their own.
This one won't do.
JAVIER AND THE INVADERS FROM SPACE see INVADERS FROM
OUTER SPACE, The
THE JEALOUS PROFESSORS Lux 1910 7m. Ref: Bios 2/10/10.
Professors' potions turn each other into a monkey and a toad.
JE T'AIME, JE T'AIME see I LOVE YOU, I LOVE YOU
JEKYLL AND HYDE see DR. JEKYLL AND MR. HYDE (1910)
JEKYLL'S INFERNO see HOUSE OF FRIGHT

JENA DI LONDRA, La see HYENA OF LONDON, The
JESSE JAMES MEETS FRANKENSTEIN'S DAUGHTER Emb /Circle
   1966 color 82m. (JESSE JAMES MEETS FRANKENSTEIN)
   D: William Beaudine. SP: Carl K. Hittleman. PH:Lothrop Worth.
   Mus: Raoul Kraushaar. P: Carroll Case. Ass't D: Howard Koch,
   Jr. Ref: Screen World'67. Orpheus 3:34. MW 8:16. with John
   Lupton, Cal Bolder, Narda Onyx, Estelita, Steven Geray, Jim
   Davis.   Female mad doctor keeps the "last living artificial
   brain" of Dr. Frankenstein around, just in case. The worst
   western cliches are combined with the worst horror cliches.
   ("You are no longer Hank Tracy. You are Igor.")
The JEWEL OF ALLAH Eclair 1914 15m. Ref: MPW 22:1681.
   Lee. with Edna Payne, Stanley Walpole. Jewel from meteorite
   heals blindness.
JEWEL OF DEATH 1916 22m. D: M. J. Fahrney. SP: James
   Dayton. Ref: MPW 31:416. Lee. with William Clifford, Bud
   Osborne.   Magic idol eye.
JEWEL OF SEVEN STARS, The (by B. Stoker) see BLOOD FROM
   THE MUMMY'S TOMB
JIGOKU see HELL
JIM HOOD'S GHOST Mustang /Univ 1926 22m. D: John O'Brien.
   SP: William Lester. Ref: MPW'26:48. Lee. Western. Twin
   brother pretends to be ghost of other twin to get confession.
JINETE SIN CABEZA, El see HEADLESS RIDER, The
JINETES DEL TERROR, Los see KNIGHTS OF TERROR
JINKO EISEI TO JINRUI NO HAMETSU see ATTACK FROM
   SPACE
JITTERBUGS Fox 1943 74m. D: Mal St. Clair. SP: Scott Dar-
   ling. PH: Lucien Andriot. SpPhFX: Fred Sersen. Ref: FDY.
   with Stan Laurel, Oliver Hardy, Vivian Blaine, Bob Bailey,
   Douglas Fowley, Noel Madison, Lee Patrick, Robert Emmett
   Keane, Charles Halton, Anthony Caruso, Jimmy Conlin, Sid
   Saylor, Francis Ford, Chick Collins. "Gas pills" cause taker
   to inflate and float in air.
JOAN MEDFORD IS MISSING see HOUSE OF HORRORS
JOHNNY VENGMAN AND THE BIG COMET (Swedish) Europa 1955
   (JANNE VANGMAN OCH DEN STORA KOMETEN. The BIG
   COMET) D: Bengt Palm. PH: Ingvar Borild. Ref: FJA. FM
   12:20.15:3,20.16:43 Pic: FM 17:17. with Adolf Jahr, Karl-Erik
   Flens, Sten Gester, Carl-Gustaf Lindstedt, Märta Dorff, Birgitta
   Olzon, Lasse Krantz. s-f comedy. Robot.
JOLLY BAD FELLOW, A see THEY ALL DIED LAUGHING
JONATHAN (W. G.) Iduna /Obelisk 1970 color SP, D: Hans W.
   Geissendörfer.   Based on the novel "Dracula" by Bram Stoker.
   Mus: Dr. Roland Kovac. PH: Robby Müller. Ref: Fernsehen
   6 /70. Atlas 2 /71. with Jürgen Jung, P. A. Krumm, Arthur
   Brauss.   Count Dracula pursues a young couple.
JONES' NIGHTMARE, or The LOBSTER STILL PURSUED HIM
   Acme 1911 Ref: Bios 2 /16 /11. Giant lobster pursues man in
   his dream.
JOUEUR D'ECHECS see CHESS PLAYER, The (1926/1938)
JOURNEY BENEATH THE DESERT (F-I) Emb /CCM-Titanus 1961
   95m. (ANTINEA, L'AMANTE DELLA CITTA SEPOLTA-I.

QUEEN OF ATLANTIS. LOST KINGDOM. ATLANTIS, CITY
BENEATH THE DESERT) D: Edgar Ulmer, Giuseppi Masini,
Frank Borzage. Based on the novel "L'Atlantide" by Pierre
Benoit. Ref: Orpheus 3:31. with Haya Harareet, Rod Fulton,
Georges Riviere, Gabriele Tinti, Gian Maria Volonte. Two men
discover the lost continent of Atlantis beneath the Sahara Desert.
A real bore.
JOURNEY INTO THE UNKNOWN see WIZARD OF MARS, The
JOURNEY OF THE JULES VERNE see FABULOUS WORLD OF
JULES VERNE, The
JOURNEY THAT SHOOK THE WORLD, The see THOSE
FANTASTIC FLYING FOOLS
JOURNEY TO PLANET FOUR see ANGRY RED PLANET, The
JOURNEY TO THE BEGINNING OF TIME (Cz) New Trends/Gottwal-
dov 1955('66-U. S.) color 80m. (CESTA DO PRAVEKU.
JOURNEY TO A PRIMEVAL AGE. VOYAGE TO PREHISTORIC
TIMES) Art D, SP, D: Karel Zeman. SP: also J. A. Novotny.
PH: Vaclav Pazdernik, Antonin Horak. Mus: Emil F. Burian.
Ref: Imagen. COF 11:7. V 9/2/70. Pic: MMF 15-16:59.
EncicDS V: plate 6. with V. Bejval, P. Herrman, Z. Hustak,
J. Lukas. Four boys discover a land of cave men and dinosaurs
(tyrannosaurus, stegosaurus, etc.).
JOURNEY TO THE BOTTOM OF THE SEA see VOYAGE TO THE
BOTTOM OF THE SEA
JOURNEY TO THE CENTER OF THE EARTH (F) Pathe 1909
9m. (VOYAGE AU CENTRE DE LA TERRE. JOURNEY TO THE
MIDDLE OF THE EARTH) D: Segundo de Chomon. Ref: Bios
1/13/10. Four friends set out to walk to the center of the
earth.
JOURNEY TO THE CENTER OF THE EARTH Fox 1959 DeLuxe
color/scope 132m. (A TRIP TO THE CENTER OF THE EARTH)
D: Henry Levin. SP: Walter Reisch, Charles Brackett. Based on
the novel by Jules Verne. PH: Leo Tover. Mus sc: Bernard
Herrmann. Art D: Lyle Wheeler, Franz Bachelin, Herman A.
Blumenthal. Sets: Walter M. Scott, Joseph Kish. SpFX: L.
B. Abbott, James B. Gordon Emil Kosa, Jr. Ref: FFacts.
Orpheus 3:27. PM. Pic: FM 8:20. with Pat Boone, James Mason,
Arlene Dahl, Diane Baker, Alan Napier, Peter Ronson, Robert
Adler, Alan Caillou. Explorers into caverns in the earth dis-
cover the lost island of Atlantis, dinosaurs, etc. Fun with color-
ful sets, effects.
JOURNEY TO THE CENTER OF TIME 1968 color D: David L.
Hewitt. SP: David Prentiss. PH: Robert Caramico. Ref: B.
Warren. TVG. with Scott Brady, Gigi Perreau, Anthony Eisley,
Abraham Sofaer, Austin Green, Andy David, Lyle Waggner.
People lost in time encounter aliens, dinosaurs, etc.
JOURNEY TO THE FAR SIDE OF THE SUN (B) Univ/Century 21
1969 Technicolor 101m. (DOPPELGANGER) D: Robert Parrish.
SP: Gerry and Sylvia Anderson, Donald James. PH:John Read.
Mus sc & d: Barry Gray. Art D: Bob Bell. Visual FX D: Derek
Meddings. SpFX PH: Harry Oakes. Ref: MFB'69:240. Screen
World. with Ian Hendry, Roy Thinnes, Patrick Wymark, Lynn
Loring, Herbert Lom. A "negative earth" is discovered on the

other side of the sun.   The effects almost carry the rest, which
is miserable.   Just about everyone has been killed by the end of
the movie.
JOURNEY TO THE MIDDLE OF THE EARTH see JOURNEY TO THE
   CENTER OF THE EARTH (1909)
JOURNEY TO THE SEVENTH PLANET   (U.S.-Swedish) AI 1962
   sequences in Eastmancolor/scope 80m.   SP,D,P: Sidney Pink.
   SP: also Ib Melchior.   PH: Age Wiltrup.   Cinemagic Mus: Ib
   Glindemann.   SpFX: Bent Barford.   Ref: FFacts.   with John Agar,
   Greta Thyssen, Ann Smyrner, Mimi Heinrich,Carl Ottosen.
   Evil being materializes the thoughts of visitors to Uranus in the
   year 2001.   Weak direction, acting defeat an idea or two.   Com-
   plete with theme song.
JOURNEY WITH GHOST ALONG TOKAIDO ROAD   (J)   Daiei   1969
   color (ALONG WITH GHOSTS)   D: Kimiyoshi Yasuda.   SP: Tetsuo
   Yoshida.   PH: Hiroshi Imai.   Mus:H. Watanabe.   Ref: B. Warren.
   Cinefantastique.   with Kojiro Hongo, Pepe Hozumi, Masami
   Furukido.   Ghosts and samurai.
JUAN AND JUNIOR IN A DIFFERENT WORLD (Sp) Ronte 1970 color
   89m.   (JUAN Y JUNIOR EN UN MUNDO DIFERENTE)   D: Pedro
   Ole.   SP, Story: Olea, J. A. Porto. Story: also J. G. Atienza.
   PH: Manuel Rojas.   Art D: W. Burman.   Ref: SpCinema'71.   with
   Juan Pardo, Antonio "Junior" Morales, Maribel Martin, Conchita
   Rabal.
JUDEX (F)   1916   serial 12 episodes   D: Louis Feuillade.   Follow-
   up: THE NEW MISSION OF JUDEX.   Ref: COF 9:39.   DDC II:
   308,339.   Pic: Pict. Hist. Cinema   DDC II:338.   with Yvette
   Andreyor, René Cresté.
JUDEX (F)   1933   D: Maurice Champreux.   From the work of
   Arthur Bernede and Louis Feuillade.   PH:Georges Raulet.   Mus:
   Francois Gailhard.   Ref: FJA.   COF 9:39.   with Réné Ferté,
   Marcel Vallee, Mihalesco, Jean Lefebvre, René Navarre,
   Costantini.
JUDEX Cont/Comptoir Francais-Filmes 1963 (F-I) 96m.   (L'UOMO
   IN NERO-I)   D: G. Franju.SP: Francis Lacassin, Jacques
   Champreux.   Ref: COF 5:51.9:38.   Pic: FM 27:8.   Based on
   scenarios by Louis Feuillade, Arthur Bernede.   PH: Marcel
   Fradetal.   Mus: Maurice Jarre.   with Channing Pollock, Francine
   Berge, Edith Scob, Sylva Koscina, Michel Vitold.   TV-spy ap-
   paratus; "human flies." A few impressive scenes, and one
   startling, memorable burst of Jarre music.
JUEGO DIABOLICO   see   DIABOLICAL GAME
JUEZ SANGRIENTO, El see WITCH-KILLER OF BLACKMOOR, The
JUGGERNAUT (THE DEMON DOCTOR) (B) Grand National 1936
   70m.   D: Henry Edwards.   SP: Cyril Campion, H. Fowler
   Mear, H. Fraenkel.   From the book by Alice Campbell.   Ref:
   MPH 10/17/36.   COF 1:45.   FDY.   with Boris Karloff, Gibb Mc-
   Laughlin, Morton Selten, Anthony Ireland.   Doctor kills patient
   with hypodermic injection for money for work on paralysis.
JUIF POLONAIS, Le (by Erckmann-Chatrian) see BELLS, The (1926)
JUJIN YUKI-OTOKO see HALF HUMAN
JULES VERNE'S MYSTERIOUS ISLAND   see   MYSTERIOUS ISLAND
   (1961)

JULES VERNE'S ROCKET TO THE MOON   see THOSE FANTASTIC
FLYING FOOLS
JULIANA DO AMOR PERDIDO   see   LOST LOVE JULIANA
JUMBO   see ZAMBO THE APE MAN
The JUNGLE   Lippert/Modern Theatres Ltd. /Voltaire 1952 74m.
P, D: William Berke.   SP: Carroll Young.   PH: Clyde de Vinng.
Ref: MFB'53:24.   TVG. with Rod Cameron, Marie Windsor, Cesar
Romero, Sulochana.   A hunting party encounters mammoths in
India.   Pretty Bad.
JUNGLE CAPTIVE   Univ   1945   63m.   D: Harold Young.   SP: Dwight
V. Babcock, M. Coates Webster.   Follow-up to CAPTIVE WILD
WOMAN and JUNGLE WOMAN.   '52 Realart reissue as WILD
JUNGLE CAPTIVE.   PH: Maury Gertsman.   Mus: Paul Sawtell.
Art D: John B. Goodman, Robert Clatworthy.   Ref: Clarens.   Pic:
FM 24:37. 45:58. 46:44.   with Otto Kruger, Vicky Lane, Amelita
Ward, Phil Brown, Jerome Cowan, Rondo Hatton, Eddie Acuff,
Ernie Adams.   A biochemist attempts to restore an ape woman
to life.
JUNGLE JIM   Col   1948   73m.   D: William Berke.   SP: Carroll
Young.   PH: Lester White. Mus D: Mischa Bakaleinikoff.   P: Sam
Katzman.   Ref: FDY. with Johnny Weissmuller, Virginia Grey,
George Reeves, Lita Baron, Rick Vallin, Holmes Herbert. Ad:
sea serpent.
JUNGLE JIM IN THE FORBIDDEN LAND   Col   1952   65m.   (The
FORBIDDEN LAND) D: Lew Landers.   SP: Samuel Newman.   PH:
Fayte Browne.   Mus: Mischa Bakaleinikoff.   P: Sam Katzman.   Ref:
FDY.   Pic: FM 13:68. 14:27.   with Johnny Weissmuller, Angela
Greene, Lester Matthews, Jean Willes, William Tannen, George
Eldredge.   Jim encounters the Giant People in The Forbidden
Land.   And yet another Katzman dud.
The JUNGLE LOVERS   Selig   1915   40m.   D: Lloyd B. Carleton.
SP: James Oliver Curwood.   Ref: MPN 9/18/15.   MPW 9/18/15.
A scientist's cave is filled with inflammable gasses from which he
is perfecting a "high explosive." A stray bullet "explodes the
powerful compound."
JUNGLE MANHUNT   Col   1951   66m.   D: Lew Landers.   SP: Samuel
Newman.   PH: William W(h)itney.   Mus: Mischa Bakaleinikoff.
P: Sam Katzman.   Ref: FDY.   FM 19:36.   with Johnny Weissmuller,
Sheila Ryan, Rick Vallin, Bob Waterfield, Lyle Talbot. Jungle
Jim meets dinosaurs from ONE MILLION B. C.
JUNGLE MOON MEN   Col/Sirius   1955   70m.   D: Charles S. Gould.
SP: Joe Pagano, Dwight V. Babcock.   P: Sam Katzman.   Ref: FDY.
with Johnny Weissmuller, Jean Byron, Myron Healey, Bill Henry,
Helene Stanton, Ed Hinton.   Pygmy Moon Men capture Johnny
Weissmuller.   Katzman cranks out another dud.
JUNGLE MYSTERY   Univ   1932   serial D: Ray Taylor.   SP: E.
O'Neill, G. Plympton, B. Dickey, G. Morgan.   Based on "The
Ivory Trail" by Talbot Mundy.   Ref: FJA.   with Noah Beery, Jr.,
Tom Tyler, Cecilia Parker, William Desmond, Carmelita Geraghty.
Ape-man.
JUNGLE QUEEN   (India) Chitra   1956   D: Nari Ghadiali.   SP: P.
Dehlvi.   PH: Suleman and Manzoor.   Mus: N. Bazmi.   Art D:
I. M. Sheikh.   Ref: FEFN 7/13/56.   with Nadia, John Cavas,

Habib. "Secret weapon" renders victim powerless with hysterical
laughter.
JUNGLE WOMAN Univ 1944 54m. D: Reginald LeBorg. SP:
Henry Sucher, Bernard Schubert, Edward Dein. Follow-up to
CAPTIVE WILD WOMAN. Follow-up:JUNGLE CAPTIVE. PH:
Jack Mackenzie. Art D: John B. Goodman, Abraham Grossman.
Ref: FDY. HM 8:43. with Evelyn Ankers, Acquanetta, J. Carrol
Naish, Lois Collier, Samuel S. Hinds, Milburn Stone, Douglass
Dumbrille, Alec Craig, Pierre Watkin, Christian Rub, Richard
Davis, Heinie Conklin, Beatrice Roberts, Edward Clark. An ape
is transformed into a woman.
JUNIOR "G" MEN OF THE AIR Univ 1942 serial 12 episodes D:
Ray Taylor, Lew Collins. SP: P. Huston, G. Jay, G. H. Plymp-
ton. Add'l Dial: Brenda Weisberg. Ref: Showmen's 5/30/42. with
Billy Halop, Lionel Atwill, Frank Albertson, Huntz Hall, Bernard
Punsley, Gabe Dell, Noel Cravat, John Bagni, Eddie Foster,
David Gorcey, Frankie Darro, Jack Arnold, Jay Novello, Pat
O'Malley, Guy Kingsford, Jimmy O'Gatty, Hugh Prosser, Guy
Usher, Billy Benedict. Inventor's "airplane muffler" lost; farm
"equipped with an amazing array of intricate devices and electric-
eye operated openings."
JUNKET 89 (B) CFF/Balfour 1971 Eastmancolor 56m. D: Peter
Plummer. SP: David Ash. PH: Tony Imi. Mus: Harry Robinson.
Art D: Chris Cook. Ref: MFB'71:99. with Stephen Brassett, John
Blundell, Linda Robson. "Instant Transportation Machine" trans-
ports boy to South Sea Island
JUST IMAGINE Fox 1930 113m. SP, D: David Butler. Mus D:
Arthur Kay. Ed: Irene Morra. Costumes: Sophie Wachner,
Dorothy Tree, Alice O'Neill. Story, Dial: DeSylva, Brown, and
Henderson. PH: Ernest Palmer. Ref: Clarens. Pic: SM 1:56. FM
47:49. 81:26-33. DDC II:310. AFI. with El Brendel, Maureen
O'Sullivan, John Garrick, Frank Albertson, Hobart Bosworth,
Mischa Auer, Ivan Linow, Wilfred Lucas, Joseph Girard, Joy-
zelle. s-f-musical set in New York in 1980. Art D: Stephen
Goosson, Ralph Hammeras.
JUST WILLIAM'S LUCK see HAUNTED CASTLE, The (1948)

KAATHAVARAAYAN (India-Tamil) R. R. Pictures 1959 170m. D:
Ramanna. Ref: FEFN XII: 5-6. with S. Ganesan, M. N. Rajam.
"Consort of a god and her son cursed to be born on earth."
KABINETT DES DR. CALIGARI, Das see CABINET OF DR.
CALIGARI, The
KABINETT DES PROFESSOR BONDI, Das see HOUSE OF WAX
KAHAN-HAI-MANZIL (India) Wadia 1940 PH: M. A. Rehman.
Ref: Dipali 3/8/40. with Illa Devi, Minoo, Radhi Rani. "Fights
of the Aryans and the Santhals in pre-historic days."
KAIBYO ARIMA GOTEN see GHOST-CAT OF ARIMA PALACE
KAIBYO GOJUSAN-TSUGI see GHOST-CAT OF GOJUSAN-TSUGI
KAIBYO KARAKURI TENJO see GHOST-CAT OF KARAKURI
TENJO

KAIBYO KOSHINUKE DAISODO see WEAK-KNEED FROM FEAR
OF GHOST-CAT
KAIBYO NOROI NO KABE see GHOST-CAT WALL OF HATRED
KAIBYO NOROI NO NUMA see GHOST-CAT SWAMP OF HATRED
KAIBYO OKAZAKI SODO see TERRIBLE GHOST-CAT OF
OKAZAKI
KAIBYO OMA-GA-TSUJI see GHOST-CAT OF OMA-GA-TSUJI
KAIBYO OTAMA-GA-IKE see GHOST OF OTAMAGE-IKE
KAIBYO RANBU see PHANTOM CAT, The
KAIBYO YONAKI NUMA see NECROMANCY
KAIDAN see KWAIDAN
KAIDAN AMA YUREI see GHOST OF THE GIRL DIVER
KAIDAN BANCHO SARAYASHIKI see GHOST STORY OF BROKEN
DISHES AT BANCHO MANSION
KAIDAN BARABARA YUREI see DISMEMBERED GHOST
KAIDAN BOTAN DORO see TALE OF PEONIES & STONE
LANTERNS, A
KAIDAN CHIBUSA ENOKI see GHOST OF CHIBUSA ENOKI
KAIDAN CHIDORI-GA-FUCHI see GHOST OF CHIDORI-GA-FUCHI
KAIDAN DOCHU see GHOST STORY IN PASSAGE, A
KAIDAN FUKAGAWA JOWA see SAD GHOST STORY OF FUKA-
GAWA
KAIDAN GOJUSAN- TSUGI see GHOST OF GOJUSAN-TSUGI
KAIDAN HEBIONNA see FEAR OF THE SNAKE-WOMAN
KAIDAN HITOTSU-ME JIZO see GHOST FROM THE POND
KAIDAN HONJO NANA FUSHIGI see SEVEN MYSTERIES
KAIDAN IJIN YUREI see CAUCASIAN GHOST
KAIDAN KAGAMI-GA-FUCHI see GHOST OF KAGAMI-GA-FUCHI
KAIDAN KAKUIDORI see GHOST STORY OF KAKUI STREET
KAIDAN KASANE-GA-FUCHI see GHOST OF KASANE-GA-FUCHI
KAIDAN KASENEGAFUCHI see MASSEUR'S CURSE
KAIDAN KATAME NO OTOKO see GHOST OF THE ONE-EYED
MAN
KAIDAN NOBORIRYU see HAUNTED LIFE OF A DRAGON-TAT-
TOOED LASS, The
KAIDAN OIWA NO BOREI see GHOST OF YOTSUYA, The (1961)
KAIDAN ONIBI NO NUMA see GHOST STORY OF DEVIL'S-FIRE
SWAMP
KAIDAN OTOSHIANA see GHOSTLY TRAP, The
KAIDAN SAGA YASHIKI see GHOST OF SAGA MANSION
KAIDAN SEMUSHI OTOKO see HOUSE OF TERRORS
KAIDAN SHAMISEN-BORI see GHOST MUSIC OF SHAMISEN
KAIDAN YONAKI-DORO see GHOST STORY OF STONE LANTERNS
KAIDAN YUKIJORO see SNOW GHOST
KAIDAN ZANKOKU MONOGATARI see CRUEL GHOST LEGEND
KAII UTSONOMIYA TSURITENJO see WEIRD DEATH-TRAP AT
UTSUNOMIYA
KAIJU DAISENSO see INVASION OF ASTRO-MONSTER
KAIJU SOKOGEKI see OPERATION MONSTERLAND
KAIJU SOSHINGEKI see OPERATION MONSTERLAND
KAITEI DAISENSO see WATER CYBORGS
KAITEI GUNKAN see ATRAGON
KALABOG AND BOSYO (Fili) Sampaguita 1959 (KALABOG EN

BOSYO) D: Tony Cayado. Ref: FEFN 6/59.9/59. with Dolphy,
Barbara Perez, Tito Galla, Eddie Arenas. Mad doctor concocts
hair lotion which makes men hate women.

KALKOOT (India) Sudha Pictures 1935 (KISMAT-KI-BHUL) D:
D. K. Kale. Imitation of THE MUMMY (1932). PH: Sirpotdar.
Ref: The Moving Picture Monthly 5/35.6/35. with Nyampally,
Godse, Lobo. Kalkoot tortures people with his supernatural powers.

KALOSZE SZCZESCIA see LUCKY BOOTS

KALTE HERZ, Das see COLD HEART, The (1923/1923/1929/
1950)

KAMLA (India-Hindustani) Laxmi 1946 Dial: M. Nazir. PH: Jal
Mistry. Mus: G. Dutt. Ref: Filmindia 1/47. with Lila Desai,
Agha, Gulab. Evil spirit leaves madman/hero when his "skull
is opened. "

KARATE A TANGIER POUR AGENT 27 see MARK DONEN AGENT
27

The KARATE KILLERS MGM/Arena 1967 Metrocolor D: Barry
Shear. SP: Norman Hudis. Story, P: Boris Ingster. From "The
Man from U.N.C.L.E." TV series. PH: Fred Koenekamp. Mus:
Gerald Fried. Art D: George W. Davis, James W. Sullivan.
Ref: MFB'67:141. with Robert Vaughn, David McCallum, Curt
Jurgens, Joan Crawford, Herbert Lom, Telly Savalas, Terry-
Thomas, Kim Darby, Diane McBain, Jill Ireland, Leo G. Car-
roll, Danielle De Metz, Philip Ahn, Frank Arno. Process for
extracting gold from sea water; midget planes.

KARNSTEIN CURSE, The see TERROR IN THE CRYPT

KASHI TO KODOMO see PITFALL, The

KDO CHCE ZABIT JESSII see WHO KILLED JESSIE ?

KEEPERS, The see BRAIN EATERS, The

KEEPERS OF THE EARTH see BRAIN EATERS, The

KELLY OF THE SECRET SERVICE Principal 1936 69m. D:
Robert Hill. SP: Al Martin. From the story "On Irish Hill" by
Peter B. Kyne. PH: William Hyer. Ed: Dan Milner. P: Sam
Katzman. Ref: FD 7/22/36. with Lloyd Hughes, Sheila Manors,
Fuzzy Knight, Syd Saylor, Jack Mulhall, Forrest Taylor. Sci-
entist's invention "to keep enemy battle fleets from American
shores" is stolen.

KEMEK GHM 1970 Technicolor 90m. SP, D: Theodore Gershuny.
PH: Enzo Barboni. Mus: John Lewis & the Modern Jazz Quar-
tet. Sets: Flavio Mogherini. Ref: V 9/16/70. with Helmut
Schneider, Alexandra Stewart, David Hedison. Owner of international drug company searches for mysterious new drug. People
"controlled" by forces outside themselves.

KENILWORTH CASTLE (B) 1926 short (HAUNTED CASTLES
series) D: Maurice Elvey. Ref: Brit. Cinema. V 2/24/26.

KESSEN NANKAI NO DAIKAIJU see SPACE AMOEBA

The KEY OF LIFE Edison 1910 16m. Ref: Lee. MPW 7:1118,
1125. Kitten reincarnated as a "human kitten"/cat-woman via
Hindu charms.

KHUBSURAT BALA (India) Sansar Movietone 1934 D: D. N.
Madhok. PH: D. Khosla. SP: M. R. Kapur. Ref: Dipali
5/11/34. with M. Kale, Ekbal. Woman driven to suicide
brought back to life by the supernatural powers of a "sadhu. "

The KIDNAPPED STOCKBROKER Vita 1915 25m. D: William Humphrey. Ref: LC. MPN 9/11/15. "Haunted" house.

The KID'S CLEVER Univ 1929 silent 50m. D: William J. Craft. SP: Ernest S. Pagano(?), Jack Foley. Story: Vincent Moore. Titles: Albert DeMond. Art D: Chas. D. Hall. Ed: Chas. Craft. PH: Al Jones. Ref: V 5/15/29. Lee. AFI. with Glenn Tryon, Kathryn Crawford, Russell Simpson, George Chandler, Joan Standing, Stepin Fetchit, Lloyd Whitlock. Auto deriving power from air runs on land & sea.

KIGANJO NO BOKEN see ADVENTURES OF TALKA MAKAN

KIGEKI EKIMAE KAIDAN see GHOST STORY OF FUNNY ACT IN FRONT OF TRAIN STATION

KILL, BABY, KILL (I) Europix/F.U.L. 1966 Eastmancolor 83m. OPERAZIONE PAURA. CURSE OF THE DEAD. OPERA-TION FEAR) D: Mario Bava. PH: Antonio Rinaldi. SP: Bava, R. Migliorini, Roberto Natale. Mus: Carlo Rustichelli. Art D: Sandro Dell'Orco. Dubbing D: John Hart. Ref: MFB'67:104. V 10/30/68. with Giacomo Rossi Stuart, Erika Blanc, Max Lawrence, Fabienne Dali, Piero Lulli. Baroness haunts people to death with apparition of her dead child. Cumbersome dubbed dialogue and distracting little zooms and reverse zooms dissipate good shock gimmicks involving a doorway, a staircase, and even a bouncing ball. The cobwebs are more elaborate than ever.

KILLER APE Col 1953 68m. D: Spencer G. Bennet. SP: Arthur Hoerl, Carroll Young. P: Sam Katzman. Ref: FDY. FanMo 1:32. with Johnny Weissmuller, Nestor Paiva, Carol Thurston, Max Palmer, Nick Stuart. Drug that paralyzes minds and bodies; man-ape descended from apes and natives; baby dinosaur. Another in Katzman's seemingly endless series of duds.

KILLER AT LARGE Col 1936 54m. (POKER FACE. KILLER ON THE LOOSE) D: David Selman. SP:Harold Shumate. Story: Carl Clausen. PH: Allen G. Siegler. Ref: V 10/28/36. with Mary Brian, Russell Hardie, Betty Compson, Thurston Hall, Henry Brandon, Lon Chaney, Jr. (coffin man), Lee Shumway. "Spook material": Murderer in wax storeroom pretends to be wax dummy. Cemetery scene.

KILLER BATS see DEVIL BAT

KILLER 77, ALIVE OR DEAD (I-Sp) Adelphia Compagnia/Balcazar 1966 (SICARIO 77, VIVO O MORTO) D: Mino Guerrini. SP: Guerrini, Balcazar, Vaughan, Ciuffini, Bolzoni. PH: Aldo Scavarda. Ref: Ital P'66. with Robert Mark, Alicia Brandet, Monica Randall. Secret weapon; "psycho-hypnotic treatment."

The KILLER SHREWS McLendon 1959 70m. D: Ray Kellogg. SP: Jay Simms. PH: Wilfred Cline. Mus: H. Bluestone, E. Cadkin. Art D: Louis Caldwell. Ref: FFacts. Pic: FM 7:18. with James Best, Ingrid Goude, Ken Curtis, Baruch Lumet. Scientist creates really big shrews. Not too good.

KILLERS FROM SPACE RKO/Planet 1953 71m. P,D: W. Lee Wilder. SP: Bill Raynor. PH: William Clothier. Story: Myles Wilder. Mus: Manuel Compinsky. Ref: Clarens. Pic: FM 2:10. with Peter Graves, Barbara Bestar, James Seay, Shep Menken, Frank Gerstle, John Merrick. Space invaders bring a man back to life.   Graves at his worst in silly film.

KILLERS OF THE CASTLE OF BLOOD   see SCREAM OF THE
DEMON LOVER

The KILLING BOTTLE   (J)   Toho/Takarazuka   1967   color/scope
93m.   (ZETTAI ZETSUMEI)   D: Senkichi Taniguchi.   SP: S.
Sekizawa.   PH: Takao Saito.   Ref: Japanese Films'68.   with
Nick Adams, Tatsuya Mihashi, Kumi Mizuno, Makoto Sato, Jun
Tazaki, Yoshio Tsuchiya.   Contents of bottle expand thousands of
times, suffocating victim.

KING DINOSAUR   Lippert/Zingor   1955   63m.   D: Bert I. Gordon.
SP: Tom Gries.   From "The Beast from Outer Space" by
Gordon and Al Zimbalist.   Narr: Marvin Miller.   Ref: FM 14:
17.   Pic: FM 19:35.   SM 1:53.   with Bill Bryant, Wanda Curtis,
Douglas Henderson.   Dinosaurs are discovered on the planet
Nova.   Auteur Gordon's style (awkward, subtly alternating the
dull and the silly, presenting the most asinine material straight-
forwardly) is noticeable even in this early, "prehistoric" effort.

KING KONG   RKO   1932   100m.   D: Merian C. Cooper, Ernest B.
Schoedsack.   SP: Ruth Rose, James Creelman.   Story: Edgar
Wallace, Merian C. Cooper.   PH: Edward Lindon.   Mus: Max
Steiner.   SpFX: Willis O'Brien.   Art D: Carroll Clark, Al Herman.   Exec P: David O. Selznick.   (The 8TH WONDER OF THE
WORLD.   The 8TH WONDER.   CREATION)   Ref: Clarens.   FM
10:26.   FM 27.22:31.   Pic: FM 13:15.18:41.19:42.25:42.   with
Fay Wray, Robert Armstrong, Bruce Cabot, Frank Reicher, Sam
Hardy, Noble Johnson, James Flavin, Victor Long.   Still easily
the best stop-motion animation movie, though far from being the
great movie some would have it.   O'Brien's LOST WORLD has
more exciting scenes of animation but is weaker overall.   Good
immediate build-up to the first appearance of Kong, but it takes
too long to build up to the build-up.

KING KONG   (Indi-Hindi)   Santosh   1962   color   142m.   D: Babubhai
Mistri.   Ref: M/TVM 8/62.   Lee (Collier).   with Kum Kum,
Dara Singh.   "Actioner featuring wrestler Dara Singh."

KING KONG ESCAPES!   (J)   Univ/Toho   1967   color/scope   96m.
(KINGUKONGU NO GYAKUSHU.   KING KONG'S COUNTERAT-
TACK.   REVENGE OF KING KONG)   D: I. Honda.   SpFX: Eiji
Tsuburaya.   Ref: V 6/26/68.   M/TVM 4/67.   PM.   with Akira
Takarada, Mie Hama, Rhodes Reason, Linda Miller, Eisei
Amamoto (Dr. Who).   King Kong vs. a robot Kong.

KING KONG VS. GODZILLA   (J)   Univ/Toho   1963   color/scope
90m.   (KING KONG TAI GODZILLA.   KINGUKONGU TAI
GOJIRA.   KING KONG VS. PROMETHEUS.   KING KONG VS.
FRANKENSTEIN)   D: Inoshiro Honda.   SP: Shinichi Sekizawa.
PH: Hajime Koizumi.   Idea: Willis O'Brien.   SpFX: Eiji
Tsuburaya.   D (U.S.): Thomas Montgomery.   SP (U.S.): Paul
Mason, Bruce Howard.   Ref: FFacts.   FM 39:60.   COF 4:4.
with Tadao Takashima, Mie Hama, Kenji Sahara, James Yagi.
Weird combination of slapstick monster battles and funny dubbing
("Find me a genuine monster, whether he exists or not" "Oh!
Godzilla is roasting King Kong"), on the one hand, and eerie
music, dark-blue backgrounds and horror scenes with an octo-
pus, on the other.

King   270

KING KONG'S COUNTERATTACK   see   KING KONG ESCAPES!
KING OF CRIME   see   DR. MABUSE (Part II)
The KING OF ILLUSIONISTS   Gaum   1911   9m.   Ref: Bios 3/9/11.
    Prof. Barnum materializes spirit which grows to gigantic pro-
    portions.
KING OF THE CONGO   Col   1952   serial 15 episodes (The MIGHTY
    THUNDA)   D: S. G. Bennet, W. A. Grissell.   SP: G. H.
    Plympton, R.Cole, A. Hoerl, from the "Thunda" comic maga-
    zine.   PH: William Whitley.   P: Sam Katzman.   Ref: The
    Serial.   Pic: M&H 1:27.   with Buster Crabbe, Gloria Dea,
    Leonard Penn, Jack Ingram, Rusty Wes(t)coatt, Rick Vallin,
    William Fawcett.   Cave men, rock people, magnetic rocks that
    grip man.
KING OF THE CRIMINALS   see   SUPERARGO VS. THE ROBOTS
KING OF THE JUNGLELAND   see   DARKEST AFRICA
KING OF THE KONGO   Mascot   1929   serial   sound & silent ver-
    sions Ch. 4. Gorilla Warfare.   D: Richard Thorpe.   Ref: The
    Informal Film Club.   Mus: Lee Zahler.   with Walter Miller,
    Jacqueline Logan, Richard Tucker, Boris Karloff.   A secret
    service agent, searching for his missing brother in the Congo,
    encounters many perils, including a dinosaur.
KING OF THE MOUNTIES   Rep   1942   serial   D: William Witney.
    SP: R. Davidson, J. Poland, W. Lively, J. O'Donnell, T. Ca-
    van.   Based on a character created by Zane Grey.   Sequel to
    KING OF THE ROYAL MOUNTED   PH: Bud Thackery.   Mus sc:
    Mort Glickman.   SpFX: Howard Lydecker.   Ref: Barbour.   D.
    Glut.   with Allan Lane, Abner Biberman, Nestor Paiva, Jay
    Novello, Duncan Renaldo, Douglass Dumbrille, Gilbert Emery,
    Russell Hicks, Peggy Drake, George Irving, William Bakewell,
    Francis Ford, Anthony Warde.   Flying wing/saucer.
KING OF THE ROCKET MEN   see   LOST PLANET AIRMEN
KING OF THE ROYAL MOUNTED   Rep   1940   serial (The YUKON
    PATROL--feature version)   D: William Witney, John English.
    SP: F. Adreon, S. Shor, B. Sarecky, N. S. Hall, J. Poland.
    PH: W. Nobles.   Mus sc: Cy Feuer.   Based on a character cre-
    ated by Zane Grey.   Ref: Barbour.   MPH 8/17/40.   HR 10/15/
    42.   with Allan Lane, Robert Strange, Herbert Rawlinson, John
    Davidson, John Dilson, Lucien Prival, Norman Willis.   Sequel:
    KING OF THE MOUNTIES.   "Compound X" from mine has mag-
    netic qualities "valuable in depth bomb composition."
KING OF THE WILD   Mascot   1931   serial 12 episodes (BIMI-Arg.)
    D: Richard Thorpe.   SP: W. Gittens, F. Beebe.   PH: Ben
    Kline, E. Kull.   Mus D: Lee Zahler.   Ref: STI 2:33.   FM 46:9.
    with Walter Miller, Boris Karloff, Nora Lane, Dorothy Christy,
    Tom Santschi.   Ape-man.   Also with Victor Potel, Mischa Auer.
KING OF THE ZOMBIES   Mono   1941   67m.   D: Jean Yarbrough.
    SP: Edmund Kelso.   PH: Mack Stengler.   Mus: Edward Kay.
    Art D: Charles Clague.   Ref: FDY.   TVG.   with Dick Purcell,
    Joan Woodbury, John Archer, Mantan Moreland, Guy Usher,
    Mme. Sul-Te-Wan, Lawrence Criner.   Professor turns people
    into zombies.   Mantan Moreland seems to have improvised a
    bit: he has all the good lines.   Someone remarks on the sound
    of voodoo drums: "What are those drums?"   Moreland: "Well,

it ain't Gene Krupa. " He becomes a zombie and joins the others
("Move over, I'm one of the boys") and ends up leading the group
("Company, halt!") Thanks to his witty asides, this is probably
Monogram's best horror movie, which, admittedly, isn't saying
an awful lot.

KING ROBOT   see   MY SON. THE VAMPIRE

KING OF THULE   see   LURED BY A PHANTOM

KING SCATTERBRAIN'S TROUBLES   (F?)   Pathe   1908   Ref:
V&FI 7/25/08.   Wizard curses king: Every time clock strikes,
ghosts attack him.

KING TUT-ANKH-AMEN'S EIGHTH WIFE   Max Cohen   1923   55m.
(The MYSTERY OF TUT-ANKH-AMEN'S EIGHTH WIFE)   Story,
D: Andrew Remo.   SP: George M. Merrick, Cohen.   PH: John
Bitzer.   Ref: AFI.   Curse on those who violate tombs of
Pharoahs.

KINGDOM IN THE SAND   see   CONQUEROR OF ATLANTIS

KINGDOM OF POISON MOTH   see   EVIL BRAIN FROM OUTER
SPACE, The

The KINGDOM OF THE FAIRIES   (F)   Melies   1903   (Le ROY-
AUME DES FEES)   Ref: Mitry:35.   Halliwell.   Sorcerer's curse,
demons, haunted castle.

KING'S ROW   see   MAN FROM 1997, The

KINGUKONGU NO GYAKUSHU   see   KING KONG ESCAPES!

KINGUKONGU TAI GOJIRA   see   KING KONG VS. GODZILLA

KISMAT-KI-BHUL   see   KALKOOT

KISS AND KILL   see   BLOOD OF FU MANCHU

The KISS FROM BEYOND THE GRAVE   (Mex)   Delta   1962   (EL
BESO DE ULTRATUMBA)SP, D: Carlos Toussaint.   SP: also C.
Ravelo, A. R. de Aguilar.   PH: Jorge Stahl, Jr.   Mus: S.
Guerrero.   Ref: Indice.   M/TVM 8/62: "Horror." with Ana
Bertha Lepe, Sergio Jurado, Enrique Lucero, Magdo Donato.
"Does love exist beyond the grave?"

KISS ME QUICK   Fantasy Films   1964   color   Ref: FM 63:24.
Pic: MW 5:20.   with Jackie DeWitt, Althea Currier, Frank Coe
(Frankenstein monster).   Vampire; mummy?

KISS OF THE VAMPIRE   (B)   Univ/Hammer   1963   Eastmancolor
88m.   (KISS OF EVIL-TV)   D: Don Sharp.   SP: John Elder.   PH:
Alan Hume.   Mus: James Bernard.   SpFX: Les Bowie.   Makeup:
Roy Ashton.   Ref: FFacts.   COF 4:4.   PM.   with Noel Willman,
Clifford Evans, Edward de Souza, Jennifer Daniel, Isobel Black;
Carl Esmond (in TV footage).   In Bavaria a honeymoon couple
falls into the clutches of a society of vampires.   Moderately good.
Novel ending and some fresh concepts in vampirism.

KISS THE GIRLS AND MAKE THEM DIE   (I-U. S.)   Col/de Laurentiis
1966 Technicolor   106m.   (OPERAZIONE PARADISO.   OPERA-
TION PARADISE.   IF ALL THE WOMEN IN THE WORLD.
RAMDAM A RIO.   SI TUTTE LE DONNE DEL MONDO)   D: Henry
Levin.   SP: Jack Pulman, Dino Maiuri.   PH: Aldo Tonti. Mus:
Mario Nascimbene.   SpFX: Augie Lohman.   Ref: M/TVM 7/66.
with Michael Connors, Dorothy Provine, Raf Vallone, Margaret
Lee, Terry-Thomas, Beverly Adams, Jack Gwillim, Senya Seyn,
Marilu Tolo, Nicoletta Machiavelli.   Millionaire develops process
for freezing women in giant plastic cubes, thawing them out later.

KISSES FOR MY PRESIDENT WB/Pearlayne 1964 113m. P, D:
Curtis Bernhardt. SP: Claude Binyon, Robert G. Kane. PH:
Robert Surtees. Mus: Bronislau Kaper. Ref: FM 27:9. COF
6:56. with Polly Bergen, Fred MacMurray, Edward Andrews,
Arlene Dahl, Eli Wallach, Anna Capri. The first woman presi-
dent takes office in 1970.

KISSING PILLS Lubin 1912 17m. Ref: Bios 2/22/12. MPW
'12:144. Prof. Newton invents pills which make user want to
kiss.

The KITE Kay-Bee 1915 25m. Ref: MPW 24:981. Inventor's
"electric kite" detects approaching storms.

KLADIVO NA CARODEJNICE see HAMMER FOR THE WITCHES

KLAUN FERDINAND A RAKETA see ROCKET TO NOWHERE

KNIFE IN THE BODY, The (by R. Williams) see MURDER
CLINIC, The

KNIGHT OF THE NIGHT (F) Telouet-Zodiaque 1953 90m. (LE
CHEVALIER DE LA NUIT) SP, D: Robert Darène. SP: also
Jean Anouilh. Ref: DDC II:4. La Prod. Cin. Fr. with Jean-
Claude Pascal, Renee Saint-Cyr, Max Dalban, Louis de Funes.
Old manor; storm; old man who has discovered the secret of
separating the good and bad personalities of man.

The KNIGHT OF THE SNOWS (F?) Pathe 1912 22m. Ref: Bios
1/2/13. The magician Alcofribas summons the Prince of Darkness. A baron sells him his soul in exchange for preventing a
wedding from taking place. Talisman, "evil creatures."

KNIGHTS OF TERROR (Sp-F-I) Hispamer/Radius/Tibre 1964
color/scope 86m. (Los JINETES DEL TERROR. The TERROR
RIDERS. The FRIGHTFUL HORSEMEN) D: Mario Costa. SP: N.
Lillo, E. Fallete. PH: Julio Ortas. Art D: T. Villalba. Ref:
M/TVM 2/65. SpCinema'65. COF 12:36. with Tony Russel(l),
Scilla Gabel, Pilar Clemens, Tony Soler. Bandits in horror
masks plunder villages.

KNOCKOUT DROPS (J) Toho 1957 59m. (TOKYO NO TEKISASU-
JIN) D: Motoyoshi Oda. SP: Shinichi Sekizawa. PH: I. Ashida.
Ref: FEFN 9/27/57. with M. Minami, E. H. Elic. A Texan's
only possession when he arrives in Tokyo is a patent medicine
which gives him "supernatural" strength.

KOHRAA (India) Geetanjali Pictures 1964 (KOHRAH) D: Biren
Naug. Ref: N/TVM/6/64. Shankar's 4/19/64. with W. Rehman. Dead woman who continues to cast her shadow; old witch
who is striving to bring her dead pet back to life; ghostly voices.

KOIYA KOI NASUNA KOI see LOVE NOT AGAIN

KONCHU DAISENSO see GENOCIDE

KONEC SRPNA V HOTELU OZON see END OF AUGUST AT THE
HOTEL OZONE

KONGA (U.S.-B) AI/Cohen/Merton Park 1961 Eastmancolor/
SpectaMation 90m. D: John Lemont. SP: Herman Cohen,
Aben Kandel. PH: Desmond Dickinson. Mus: Gerard Schur-
mann. Ref: Clarens. Pic: FM 13:65.15:2. with Michael Gough
Margo Johns, Jess Conrad, Claire Gordon, Austin Trevor, Vanda
Godsell. A scientist turns a chimpanzee into a gigantic monster.
Crude, simple-minded. About as good as you would expect a
Herman Cohen version of KING KONG to be.

KONGO MGM 1932 85m. D: William Cowen. SP: Leon Gordon.
Remake of WEST OF ZANZIBAR. From a play by Chester De-
Vonde and Killman Gordon. PH: Harold Rosson. Ref: FDY.
COF 12:36. Pic: TBG. with Walter Huston, Lupe Velez, Con-
rad Nagel, C. Henry Gordon, Virginia Bruce, Mitchell Lewis,
Forrester Harvey. Horror film with voodoo, sadism.
KOPPELIA see COPPELIA (1912)
KORKARLEN see PHANTOM CHARIOT, The (1958)
KOSMITCHESKY REIS see COSMIC VESSEL
KOTETSU NO KYOJIN see ATOMIC RULERS OF THE WORLD
KRAKATIT (Cz) Artkino 1947 D: Otakar Vavra. From a book
by Karel Capek. Ref: DDC III:319. Lee. SF Film. with
Florence Marly. Demon from hell; atomic explosion set off by
radio beam.
KRONOS Fox/Regal 1957 78m. D, P: Kurt Neumann. SP:
Lawrence Goldman. Assoc P, Story: Irving Block. Assoc P:
also Jack Rabin, Louis De Witt. PH: Karl Struss. Mus: Paul
Sawtell, Bert Shefter. Art D: Theobold Holsopple. Ref: FDY.
Pic: FM 10:18. with Jeff Morrow, Barbara Lawrence, John
Emery, Morris Ankrum, Richard Harrison, Robert Shayne.
Monster from outer space stores up "pure energy." Not nearly
as funny as THE GIANT CLAW.
KUNWARI OR WIDHWA (India) Luxmi 1938 D: Pandit Sudarshan,
Profulla Roy. Ref: Dipali 1/21/38. with Z. Khatoon, R. P.
Kapoor. Magician hypnotizes woman.
KURONEKO see BLACK CAT (1968)
KWAIDAN Cont/Toho (J) 1964 color 164m. (KAIDAN. GHOST
STORIES. WEIRD TALES) D: Masaki Kobayashi. SP: Yoko Mizuki.
From stories by Lafcadio Hearn; "selections from Koizumi
Yagumo." YUKI-ONNA (WOMAN OF THE SNOW) episode (29m.)
released in Europe as separate film. PH: Yoshio Miyajima. Mus:
Toru Takemitsu. Art D: Shigemasa Toda. Ref: Unij. Bltn. 31. FIR
'66:261. MFB'68:186. with Michiyo Aratama, Keiko Kishi, Tak-
ashi Shimura, Tatsuya Nakadai, Tetsuo Tamba. Four ghost
stories about vampiric snow-woman, spirit in teacup, etc.
"Hoichi the Earless" is a good, full-bodied story. The other
three are rather routine, and the atmospheric effects aren't
strong enough to carry them.
KYOFU KIKEI NINGEN see HORROR OF MALFORMED MEN
KYOKANOKO MUSUME DOJOJI see DOJOJI TEMPLE
KYUKETSU DOKUROSEN see LIVING SKELETON
KYUKETSU GA see VAMPIRE MOTH, The
KYUKETSUKI GOKEMIDORO see GOKE

L.A. 2017 NBC-TV 1970-1 color 75m. Teleplay: Philip Wylie.
"The Name of the Game" episode shown as feature at Trieste.
Ref: TVG. V 7/21/71. with Sharon Farrell, Barry Sullivan,
Severn Darden, Paul Stewart, Edmond O'Brien, Louise Latham.
"Subterranean world."
LABORS OF HERCULES, The see HERCULES

LADIES AND GENTLEMEN (I-F) RPA/Dear/du Siecle 1965
SP,D: Pietro Germi. SP: also Vincenzoni, Scarpelli, Age. PH:
A. Parolin. Ref: Ital P. with Virna Lisi, Gastone Moschin,
Alberto Lionello, Nora Ricci, Franco Fabrizi. After a man is
hurt in a car crash "there takes place in him what could be
described as a type of biological mutation which gives him an
acute vision of reality."

LADRO DI BAGDAD, Il see THIEF OF BAGHDAD, The (1960-F-I)

LADRON DE CADAVERES, El see BODY SNATCHER, The (1956)

The LADY AND DEATH (Chilean) Chile Films 1946 (La DAMA
EN EL MUERTE. La DAMA DE LA MUERTE) D: Carlos Hugo
Christensen. SP: Cesar Tiempo. PH: Alfredo Traverso. Mus:
Jorge Andreani. Art D: Jean de Bravura. From "The Suicide
Club" by Robert Louis Stevenson. Ref: S&S'46:123. Historia del
Cine Chileno. Pic: S&S'46:124. with Carlos Cores, Juan Corona,
Carlos Morris.

LADY AND THE DRAGON, The see BEAUTY AND THE DRAGON

The LADY AND THE MONSTER Rep 1944 86m. (The TIGER
MAN) D: George Sherman. SP: Frederick Kohner, D. Lussier,
from the novel "Donovan's Brain" by Curt Siodmak. PH: John
Alton. Mus sc: Walter Scharf. Art D: Russell Kimball. Ref:
FDY. SM 6:28. Pic: TBG. with Erich Von Stroheim, Richard
Arlen, Vera Hruba Ralston, Sidney Blackmer, Helen Vinson,
Mary Nash, Lola Montes, Juanita Quigley. A scientist keeps a
brain alive after death. A good script dully directed. Oddly,
Von Stroheim's most powerful line is simply "Instruments!" It's
the way he says it.

LADY BEWARE see THIRTEENTH GUEST, The

A LADY CALLED ANDREW (Sp) Izaro 1970 color/scope 96m.
(UNA SEÑORA LLAMADA ANDRES) SP,Story,D: Julio Buchs.
SP: also R. J. Salvia, J. M. de Arozamena, de Urrutia. Story:
also E. Szel, Leon Klimovsky, F. de Urrutia. PH: Rafael Pacheco. Mus: A. Algueró. Art D: J. P. Cubero. Ref: SpCinema
'71. with Carmen Sevilla, Juan Luis Galiardo, José Sacristán,
Helga Liné. Cupid's electronic brains "control the sentimental
processes of humans."

LADY IN A CAGE Para/A.E.C. 1964 93m. D: Walter Grauman. SP,P: Luther Davis. PH: Lee Garmes. Art D: Rudolph
Sternad. Ref: FFacts. Boxo 6/1/64. with Olivia de Havilland,
Ann Sothern, Jeff Corey, James Caan, Jennifer Billingsley,
Rafael Campos, William Swan, Scat Man Cruthers, Pic: COF
4:56. Hoodlums terrorize wealthy woman trapped in her private
elevator. Crude, with violence so elaborately calculated to
shock it's comical.

LADY MORGAN'S VENGEANCE (I) Morgan Film 1966 (La VEN-
DETTA DI LADY MORGAN) D: Max Hunter. SP: Jean Grimaud.
Story: Edward Duncan. PH: D. Troy. Ref: Annuario. with
Gordon Mitchell, Erika Blanc, Paul Muller, Barbara Nelly.
Madwoman returns from the dead.

A LADY OF SPIRITS Edison 1914 Ref: MPW 20:1146. with
Harry Gripp (the ghost), William Wadsworth.

LADY OF THE SHADOWS TERROR, The (1963)

LADY POSSESSED Rep 1952 87m. D: William Spier, Roy Kellino.

SP: Pamela Kellino, James Mason, from the book "Del Palma"
by P. Kellino. PH: Karl Struss. Mus: Nathan Scott. Art D:
Frank Arrigo. P: Mason. Ref: FDY. with June Havoc, James
Mason, Fay Compton, Steven Geray, Stephen Dunne. Woman
believes man's wife's spirit possesses her.
LADY WAS A GHOST, The see GHOST STORY IN PASSAGE, A
LAKE OF DRACULA see DRACULA'S LUST FOR BLOOD
LAMA NEL CORPO, La see MURDER CLINIC, The
LAND UNKNOWN Univ 1957 78m. D: Virgil Vogel. SP: W.
Robson, Laszlo Gorog. Story: Charles Palmer. PH: Ellis
Carter. Art D: Alexander Golitzen, Richard Riedel. SpFX:
Roswell A. Hoffman, Jack Kevan, Orien Ernest, Fred Knoth.
P: William Alland. Ref: FDY. Pic: FM 2:17.19:33.60:57. with
Jock Mahoney, Shawn Smith, William Reynolds, Douglas Kennedy,
Phil Harvey. Expedition to the South Pole discovers land of
dinosaurs. Routine, with at least an attempt at a plot. A few of
the dinosaurs have become more believable characters than the
humans by the film's end.
The LAST CHILD ABC-TV/Aaron Spelling 1971 color 75m. D:
John Moxey. SP: Peter S. Fischer. PH: Arch Dalzell. Mus:
Laurence Rosenthal. Art D: Paul Sylos. Ref: TVG. LAT 10/5/
71. with Van Heflin, Michael Cole, Harry Guardino, Janet Mar-
golin, Edward Asner, Kent Smith. In the future a population-
control law dictates that a baby must be killed.
The LAST DEATH OF THE DEVIL (J) Toei 1959 (GEKKO KAMEN.
MOONLIGHT MASK--THE LAST DEATH OF THE DEVIL. MAN
IN THE MOONLIGHT MASK) D: Shoichi Shimazu. Ref: Japanese
Films'60. with Fumitake Omura.
LAST GOLEM, The see PRAGUE NIGHTS
The LAST HOUR (B) Nettlefold/Butchers 1930 75m. D: Walter
Forde. Ref: SF Film. From the play by Charles Bennett. with
Stewart Rome, Wilfred Shine, Richard Cooper. Plans for death
ray.
The LAST LOOK (F?) Pathe 1909 10m. Ref: Bios 9/23/09.
Solution to murder mystery lies in the theory that the retina of
a dead man's eye retains an impression of the last thing he saw.
The LAST MAN (F) Dovidis-Annouchka 1969 color 82m.
(Le DERNIER HOMME) SP, D: Charles Bitsch. PH: Pierre Lhomme.
Ref: V 4/9/69. M/TVM 5/69. with Jean-Claude Bouillor,
Corinne Brill, Sophia Torkell. Three people survive an atomic
war.
The LAST MAN ON EARTH Fox 1924 80m. D: Jack Blystone.
Story: Donald W. Lee, John D. Swain. PH: Allan Davey. Re-
makes: IT'S GREAT TO BE ALIVE. The LAST MAN ON
EARTH (1933). Ref: NYT 12/13/24. AFI. with Earle Foxe,
Derelys Perdue, Grace Cunard, Gladys Tennyson, Pauline
French. In the year 1960 all males (but one) over 14 fall vic-
tim to a plague.
The LAST MAN ON EARTH (Spanish-language version of IT'S
GREAT TO BE ALIVE) Fox 1933 (EL ULTIMO VARON SOBRE LA
TIERRA) D: James Tinling. Ref: NYT 6/12/33. with Rosita
Moreno, Raoul Roulien, Mimi Aguglia, Romualdo Tirado, Carmen
Rodriguez. The Council of the League of Nations must decide

which country will supply the mate for the last man on earth, survivor of a world-wide epidemic.

The LAST MAN ON EARTH (U.S.-I) AI/Alta Vista/Assoc. Producers/La Regina 1964 86m. (VENTO DI MORTE or L'ULTIMO UOMO DELLA TERRA-I. The NIGHT CREATURES. NIGHT PEOPLE. NAKED TERROR) D: Sidney Salkow. D: (Ital. version) Ubaldo Ragona. SP: Logan Swanson, William Leicester, from the novel "I am Legend" by Richard Matheson. PH: Franco Delli Colli. Mus sc: Paul Sawtell, Bert Shefter. Art D: G. Giovannini. Makeup: Piero Mecacci. P: Robert L. Lippert. Ref: Orpheus 3:27. FanMo 5:33. MW 2:24. with Vincent Price, Franca Bettoia, Giacomo Rossi-Stuart. Victims of world-wide plague become vampires, menace one man who is immune. Lackluster production and direction defeat fairly faithful adaptation of book. Exciting concluding chase.

The LAST MOMENT Goldwyn 1923 70m. D: J. Parker Read. SP: J. Clarkson Miller. Story: Jack Boyle. PH: J. Taylor. Ref: AFI. with Henry Hull, Doris Kenyon, Louis Wolheim, Louis Calhern, Jerry Peterson ("The Thing"), Mickey Bennett. Brutal sea captain enforces order on ship with caged, ape-like monster, "The Thing."

LAST NIGHT OF THE WORLD, The (by R. Bradbury) see ILLUSTRATED MAN, The

LAST OF THE WARRENS Supreme 1936 60m. SP, D: Robert N. Bradbury. PH: S. Roy Luby. Ref: FD 7/2/36. COF 13:58. with Bob Steele, Margaret Marquis, Charles King, Charles French, Lafe McKee. Western. Hero returns disguised as ghost after being wounded, scares villain.

The LAST PERFORMANCE Univ 1927 sound & silent versions (ERIK THE GREAT) D: Paul Fejos. SP: James Creelman. Titles: Walter Anthony, Tom Reed. PH: Hal Mohr. Ref: AFI. PM. with Mary Philbin, Conrad Veidt, Anders Randolf, George Irving, Leslie Fenton. Magician with hypnotic powers. Pretty slow going except for a few spectacular camera tricks and a macabre climax.

LAST TOMB OF LIGEIA see TOMB OF LIGEIA

LAST WAR, The see FINAL WAR, The

The LAST WARNING Univ 1929 silent 90m. D: Paul Leni. SP: Alfred A. Cohn, from the play by Thomas Fallon; the book by Wadsworth Camp. Remade as HOUSE OF FEAR (1939). P: Carl Laemmle. Ref: NYT 1/7/29. Clarens. COF 15:22. FM 37:49. DDC II:309. Pic: DDC III:201, 221. with Laura LaPlante, Montagu Love, Roy D'Arcy, John Boles, Bert Roach, Mack Swain, George Summerville, D'Arcy Corrigan, Charles K. French, Fred Kelsey. Theatre haunted by spiders, bats, and "ghosts." One of the last and one of the liveliest, most exciting silent horror movies, WARNING is a talkie in spirit, with all sorts of ingenious "sound effects" with props and titles. Leni's fund of visual tricks with props and camera seems limitless. (One of the cleverest is a woman who becomes a "ghost" by walking through some thick cobwebs.)

LAST WILL OF DR. MABUSE, The see TESTAMENT OF DR. MABUSE (G-1932)

The LAST WOMAN ON EARTH Filmgroup 1960 71m. (WORLD
WITHOUT WOMEN) P, D: Roger Corman. SP: Robert Towne.
PH: Jack Marquette. Mus: Ronald Stein. Eastmancolor? /Vita-
Scope Ref: FFacts. Orpheus 3:27. with Anthony Carbone,
Betsy Jones-Moreland, Edward Wain. Three people find that
they're the last people on earth.
LATE AUGUST AT HOTEL OZONE see END OF AUGUST AT THE
HOTEL OZONE
The LATEST STYLE AIRSHIP (F) Pathe 1908 Ref: V&FI 7/11/08.
Boxes plus bike become airplane.
The LATIN QUARTER (B) Brit. Nat'l. 1945 80m. SP, D: Vernon
Sewell. PH: Gunther Krampf. From the play "L'Angoise" by
Pierre Mills and C. Vylars. Ref: Brit. Fm. Ybk'47/'48. MFB
'46:2. with Derrick de Marney, Frederick Valk, Joan Green-
wood, Beresford Egan, Joan Seton, Valentine Dyall, Martin
Miller, Lily Kann. Seance reveals girl's murderer, who en-
cased her in statue.
LATITUDE ZERO (J) Nat'l General/Toho 1969 color/scope 106m.
(IDO ZERO DAISAKUSEN) D: Insohiro Honda. SP: Ted Sherdeman, Shinichi Sekizawa. PH: Taiichi Kankura. Mus: Akira
Ifukube. Art D: T. Kita. SpFX: Eiji Tsuburaya. Ref: UFQ 46.
with Joseph Cotten, Cesar Romero, Akira Takarada, Richard
Jaeckel, Patricia Medina, Masumi Okada. Scientific organiza-
tion located 11 miles below the surface of the Pacific Ocean.
Fun effects and monsters (especially a lion-vulture and some bat-
like beasts), dull plot, and wretched acting, especially by Romero,
who seems to be alternately taking it seriously and just having
fun and is bad either way.
LAUGHING AT DANGER FBO/Truart 1924 65m. D: James W.
Horne. PH: Wm. Marshall. SP: Frank H. Clark. Ref: MPN
30:3185. AFI. with Joe Girard, Rich. Talmadge, Joe Harring-
Ton, Eva Novak. Death Ray. -Lee.
LAUGHING POWDER (I?) Aquila 1911 7m. Ref: Bios 3/16/11.
Powder makes people laugh.
The LAW OF FEAR FBO 1928 60m. D: Jerome Storm. SP:
Ethel Hill. Story: William F. Dugan. silent Ref: MPN 3/10/28.
with Ranger, Jane Reid, Al Smith, Sam Nelson. "Horribly
grotesque makeup of hunchback too exaggerated."
LAWS OF SATAN'S CASTLE, The see HELL
LAYING OF THE GLOURIE GHOST, The see GHOST GOES WEST,
The
LEAVES FROM SATAN'S BOOK (Dan) Nordisk 1919 (BLADE AT
SATANS BOG) D: Carl Dreyer. SP: Edgar Hoyer, from the
novel by Marie Corelli. PH: George Schneevoight. Art D:
Dreyer, Axel Bruun, Jens G. Lind. Ref: Lee. DDC II:8. with
Helge Nissen, Halvard Hoff. Satan enters into four villains.
LEBENDE BUDDHAS see LIVING BUDDHAS
LEBENDEN DES DR. MABUSE, Die see SCREAM AND SCREAM
AGAIN
The LEECH WOMAN Univ 1960 77m. (The LEECH) D: Edward
Dein. SP: David Duncan. Story: Ben Pivar, Francis Rosenwald,
PH: Ellis Carter. Mus: Irving Gertz. Art D: Alexander Golit-
zen, Robert Clatworthy. Makeup: Bud Westmore. P: Joseph
Gershenson. Ref: FFacts. Orpheus 3:27. with Gloria Talbott,

Grant Williams, Coleen Gray, Phil(l)ip Terry, John Van Dreelen, Kim Hamilton, Arthur Batanides. Woman's rejuvenation formula requires hormone from male pineal glands. Unpleasant. Evidently there's something in the formula that transforms into lipstick.

LEFT-HANDED FATE (Sp-W.G.) FISA 1966 color/scope 87m. (FATA MORGANA) SP,D: Vicente Aranda. SP: also G. Suárez. PH: A. G. Larraya. Mus: A. P. Olea. Art D: P. Gago. Ref: SpCinema'67. M/TVM 5/67. with Teresa Gimpera, M. Bennet, A. Dalbes. "Collective fear" makes inhabitants of city abandon it.

LEGALLY DEAD Univ 1923 60m. D: William Parke. SP: Harvey Gates. Story: Charles Furthman. PH: Richard Fryer. Ref: AFI. Wid's 8/4/23. with Milton Sills, Claire Adams, Margaret Campbell, Joseph Girard, Robert Homans, Edwin Sturgis, Brandon Hurst. A drug, injected into his heart, revives an executed man from the dead.

LEGEND OF A GHOST (F) Pathe 1907 17m. (La LEGENDE DU FANTOME) D: Segundo de Chomon. Ref: DDC I:403. MPW '08:463. Ghost's voice from grave; woman who battles "demons, dragons, and vampire" in hell.

LEGEND OF CAGLIOSTRO (F?) Gaum 1912 32m. Ref: Bios 8/15/12. Cagliostro predicts Marie Antoinette's death.

LEGEND OF PRAGUE, The see GOLEM, The (1935)

The LEGEND OF SLEEPY HOLLOW Kalem 1908 14m. From the story by Washington Irving. Ref: MPW 2:467.

The LEGEND OF SLEEPY HOLLOW Eclair/American Standard 1912 12m. (SLEEPY HOLLOW) From the story by Washington Irving. Ref: MPW 12: 427. Bios 11/14/12: "Headless spectre."

LEGEND OF SLEEPY HOLLOW, The (by W. Irving) see HEADLESS HORSEMAN, The

LEGEND OF THE BEAR'S WEDDING see MARRIAGE OF THE BEAR

The LEGEND OF THE LAKE (I?) Cines 1911 10m. Ref: Bios 3/28/12. Man hears legend that fairy, Morgane, vowed vengeance on murderers of young man; sees it apparently come to life.

The LEGEND OF THE LONE TREE Vita 1915 15m. D: Ulysses Davis. Ref: MPN 1/16/15. LC. with Myrtle Gonzalez, Alfred D. Vosburgh. Murderer cursed by tribe's medicine man "turns into a tree."

LEGEND OF THE PHANTOM TRIBE Bison 1914 30m. Ref: MPW 19:1090. Lee. Witchcraft brings tribe to life.

The LEGEND OF THE UNDINES (F) Pathe 1910 8m. (La LEGENDE DES ONDINES) Ref: Bios 5/11/11. Mitry II:139. Siren lures knight into the sea.

LEGEND OF THE WITCHES (B) Negus-Fancey 1969 87m. Semidocumentary SP,D: Malcolm Leigh. PH: Robert Webb. Ref: F&F 3/70. MFB'70:87.

LEGENDE DES ONDINES, La see LEGEND OF THE UNDINES, The
LEGENDE DU FANTOME, La see LEGEND OF A GHOST
LEGGENDA DI FAUST, La see FAUST AND THE DEVIL
The LEMON GROVE KIDS MEET THE MONSTERS Morgan-Steckler

c1966 DeLuxe color D, P: Ray Steckler.   SP: Ron Haydock, Jim
Harmon. Ref: RVB. Modesto Bee. Ape?, mummy?

The LEOPARD AVENGER (F?) Lux 1912 22m. Ref: Bios
2/6/13. Chemist discovers the secret of making diamonds.

The LEOPARD LADY Pathe 1928 silent 65m. D: Rupert Julian.
SP: Beulah Marie Dix. From the play by E. C. Carpenter. PH:
John Mescall. Supervision: Bertram Millhauser. Ref: MPN
3/10/28. with Jacqueline Logan, Alan Hale, Robert Armstrong,
Dick Alexander. Man trains pet ape to kill, à la "Murders in
the Rue Morgue." "Touch of gruesomeness to the opening
scenes."

The LEOPARD MAN RKO 1943 66m. D: Jacques Tourneur. P:
Val Lewton. SP: Ardel Wray, Edward Dein. From the novel
"Black Alibi" by Cornell Woolrich. PH: Robert de Grasse. Mus:
Roy Webb. Art D: Albert D'Agostino, Walter E. Keller. Ed:
Mark Robson. Ref: FDY. COF 7:30. FM 23:25.24:4.26:8. with
Dennis O'Keefe, Margo, Jean Brooks, Isabel Jewell, James Bell,
Abner Biberman, Richard Martin. Leopard spreads terror when it
escapes from a traveling show in New Mexico. Classic horror
scenes distinguish routine mystery, which isn't much of a mystery
since there aren't very many characters. About as good as the
book.

The LEPRECHAWN Edison 1908 Ref: F Index 9/26/08. Lepre-
chawn(sic); witch-woman curses man.

LESBIAN VAMPIRES (G-Sp) Telecine/Fenix 1970 (VAMPYROS
LESBOS--DIE ERBIN DES DRACULA-G. El SIGNO DEL VAM-
PIRO-Sp. The SIGN OF THE VAMPIRE) D: Jesus Franco (aka
Franco Manera). Ref: Fernsehen 5/71. V 5/12/71:143. with
Dennis Price, Susann Korda, Paul Müller, Ewa Stroemberg,
Soledad Miranda. (The HERITAGE OF DRACULA)

LET THERE BE LIGHT American-Flying A 1915 25m. D: William Bertram. Ref: MPN 10/23/15. with Helen Rosson, Charles
Newton, E. Forrest Taylor. Inventor perfects "electric ray, for
illumination purposes."

LET'S KILL UNCLE Univ 1966 Technicolor 92m. P, D: William
Castle. SP: Mark Rodgers, from a novel by Rohan O'Grady. PH:
Harold Lipstein. Mus: Herman Stein. Art D: Alexander Golitzen, William DeCinces. Ref: PM. with Nigel Green, Linda
Lawson, Mary Badham, Pat Cardi, Nestor Paiva. Boy and girl
join forces to kill uncle before he kills them in order to inherit
the boy's money. "Spooky hotel," "tarantula island."

LET'S NOT LOSE OUR HEADS (I) Galatea 1959 (NON PER-
DIAMO LA TESTA) D: Mario Mattoli. PH: Gabor Pogany.
Ref: Ital P'59. with Ugo Tognazzi, Franca Valeri, Carlo Campa-
nini. Mad scientist wants to kill man and use his brain to study.

LET'S SCARE JESSICA TO DEATH Para 1971 color 89m. D:
John Hancock. SP: Norman Jones, Ralph Rose. PH: Bob
Baldwin. Mus: Orville Stoeber. Electronic Mus: Walter Sear. Ref:
V(d) 8/20/71. "New England Gothic horror"; ghostly house,
vampire. with Zohra Lampert, Barton Heyman, Kevin O'Connor.

LIBERXINA 90 (Sp) Formentera/Nova 1971 90m. Sp, D: Carlos
Duran. SP: also Joaquin Jorda. PH: Juan Amoros. Mus: Luis
de Pablo. Art D: J. A. Soler. Ref: V 9/8/71. with Serena

Vergano, William Pirie, Romy, Edward Meeks. "Sci-fi adventure": "Chemical substance capable of wiping clean man's mind of all Establishment conditioning."

LICENSE TO KILL (F) Florida Films/Chaumiane/Filmstudio 1964 95m. (NICK CARTER VA TOUT CASSER. NICK CARTER CASSE TOUT, SERVICE SECRET) D: Henry Decoin, P. Senne. SP: Jean Marcillac, Andre Haguet (or Huguet), Andre Legrand, based on the character created by John R. Corryell. Ref: FIR'68. TVG. with Eddie Constantine, Daphne Dayle, Paul Frankeur, Vladimir Inkijinoff, Yvonne Monlaur, Charles Belmont. Chinese spies seize Professor Formentor's anti-flight weapon.

LICENSED TO KILL see SECOND BEST SECRET AGENT IN THE WHOLE WIDE WORLD, The

LIEBE MUSS VERSTANDEN SEIN! see LOVE HAS ITS REASONS!

LIEBE, TOD UND TEUFEL see LOVE, DEATH AND THE DEVIL

LIFE IN THE NEXT CENTURY (F?) Lux 1909 5m. D: Gerard Bourgeois. Ref: Bios 2/24/10. SF Film   Life in the year 2010 A.D.

LIFE WITHOUT SOUL Ocean 1915 55m. D: Joseph W. Smiley. SP: Jessie J. Goldberg, from the novel "Frankenstein" by Mary Shelley. Ref: MPW 12/4/15. MPN 12/11/15. with Percy Darrell Standing (the creature), Lucy Cotton, Pauline Curley, Jack Hopkins, George DeCarlton, William W. Cohill, David McCauley, Violet De Biccari. Medical student creates "near-human" being.

LIGEIA (by E. A. Poe) see TOMB OF LIGEIA

The LIGHT THAT KILLS Gaum 1913 Ref: Lee. MPW 16:1072. "A Rays" heal; too much causes inventor's death.

LIGHT WITHIN, The see DESTINY

LIGHTNING BOLT Woolner/Seven-Balcazar (I-Sp) 1966 color/ scope 96m. (OPERAZIONE GOLDMAN. OPERATION GOLDMAN) D: Antonio Margheriti (aka Anthony Dawson). SP: P. C. Balcazar, J. De La Loma. PH: Riccardo Pallottini. Mus: Riz Ortolani. Ref: Ital P. FFacts. Pic: FM 60:30. with Anthony Eisley, Wandisa Leigh, Diana Lorys, Fulco Lulli. Millionaire plans to conquer world with laser cannon.

LILA DE CALCUTTA (by J. Bruce) see SHADOW OF EVIL

The LIMPING MAN Powers (B) 1931 53m. (CREEPING SHADOWS-Eng) D: John Orton. From a play by Will Scott. Ref: Harrison's 8/27/32. Brit. Cinema. with Franklin Dyall, Margot Grahame, Arthus Hardy, Lester Matthews. Old mansion, mysterious screams, secret panel, tunnel.

The LIMPING MAN (B) Pathe British 1936 72m. SP, D: Walter Summers. From a play by Will Scott. PH: Bryan Langley. Ref: V 11/18/36. with Francis L. Sullivan, Hugh Wakefield, Iris Hoey, Leslie Perrins. "The good and the bad brother who are twins, the scientific criminologist, the old house, the furtive butler, the secret passages..."

LION MAN see CURSE OF THE VOODOO

The LION'S BREATH Nestor 1916 11m. D; Horace Davey. SP: Al Christie. Story: Ruth Snyder. Ref: Lee. MPW 27:1532. with Neal Burns, George French. "UV Rays" give hero attributes of lion.

The LION TONIC (I) Cines 1912 6m. Ref: Bios 10/17/12. Lee. Chemist's tonic causes wife to grow; turns dog into lion.

The LIQUID AIR (F) Gaum-Kleine 1909 8m. Ref: MPW'09:539.
Inventor's liquid air has temperature of 140 below zero.
LIQUID ELECTRICITY, or THE INVENTOR'S GALVANIC FLUID
Vita 1907 8m. Sequel: The GALVANIC FLUID. Ref: SilentFF.
MPW'08:103. Prof. Watt sprays fluid on people, who instantly
move with lightning speed.
LIQUID LOVE (B) C&M 1913 7m. Ref: Bios 9/11/13. Professor
Brainwave discovers the elixir of love.
LITTLE RED RIDING HOOD (F) Melies 1901 (Le PETIT CHAPERON
ROUGE) Ref: Mitry II.
LITTLE RED RIDING HOOD (F) Pathe 1907 5m. Ref: MPW 1:622.
LITTLE RED RIDING HOOD Majestic 1911 Ref: MPW 10:926.
with Mary Pickford. Dream.
LITTLE RED RIDING HOOD (B) C&M 1911 8m. Ref: Bios 269.
LITTLE RED RIDING HOOD Ess 1911 11m. Ref: Bios 1/18/12.
MPW 10:556, 903. with Eva Prout.
LITTLE RED RIDING HOOD Edison/KESE 1917 8m. Ref: MPW
34:127.
LITTLE RED RIDING HOOD Blanton 1921 11m. Ref: Lee.
LITTLE RED RIDING HOOD Selznick 1922 Ref: Lee.
LITTLE RED RIDING HOOD Special Century 1925 22m. Ref:
Lee. MPN 26:2110. with Baby Peggy.
LITTLE RED RIDING HOOD (F) 1929 (Le PETIT CHAPERON
ROUGE) SP, D: Alberto Cavalcanti. Ref: DDC I:337. Lee.
Sadoul. with Catherine Hessling, Jean Renoir
LITTLE RED RIDING HOOD See TOM THUMB AND LITTLE RED
RIDING HOOD VS. THE MONSTERS
LITTLE RED RIDING HOOD AND THE MONSTERS see TOM
THUMB AND LITTLE RED RIDING HOOD VS. THE MONSTERS
The LITTLE RED SCHOOLHOUSE Arrow 1923 70m. D: John G.
Adolfi. SP: J. S. Hamilton, from the play by Hal Reid. PH:
George F. Webber. Ref: AFI. Bolt of lightning sketches
murderer's face on window.
The LITTLE SHOP OF HORRORS AA/Santa Clara/Filmgroup
1960 70m. (The PASSIONATE PEOPLE EATER) P, D: Roger
Corman. SP: Charles Griffith. PH: Archie Dalzell. Art D:
Daniel Haller. Ref: FFacts. Orpheus 3:29. with Jonathan Haze,
Jackie Joseph, Mel Welles, Wally Campo, Jack Nicholson,
Richard Miller, Myrtle Vail. Plant in flower shop needs meat
for nourishment, in fact demands it ("Feed me!"). Funniest
three-day movie ever. Joseph, Miller, and Nicholson (as a giddy
masochist) have some memorable comic moments. And the plant
doesn't get all the good lines.
LITTLE SNOW WHITE (F) Pathe 1910 18m. (LITTLE SNOW-
DROP) From "Snow White" by the Bros. Grimm. Ref: Bios
5/19/10. SilentFF. Poisoned apple, magic mirror, etc.
LIVE MAN's TOMB (I) Itala 1912 35m. Ref: Bios 9/19/12.
Woman throws man's body down shaft into dungeon, believing him
dead. Later she sees him in lantern's light and thinks it's his
ghost.
LIVER EATERS, The see SPIDER BABY
LIVING BUDDHAS (G) 1924 (LEBENDE BUDDHAS. BUDDHAS
LEBENDE) SP, D: Paul Wegener. SP: also Hans Sturm. Ref:

Lee. DDC II:414. Deutsche. with Wegener, Asta Nielsen, K.
Haack, Carl Ebert, Max Pohl, Sturm, Gregori Chmara. A
fantasy of the Snow Land.

The LIVING COFFIN (Mex) AI-TV c1964 (SCREAM OF DEATH)
with Gaston Santos, Mary Duval. A girl is fearful of being buried alive. -TVG.

The LIVING DEAD Gaum 1911 14m. Ref: Bios 9/28/11. Twin
sister impersonates dead countess.

The LIVING DEAD (B) First Division/Alliance/BIP 1934 65m.
(SCOTLAND YARD MYSTERY) D: Thomas Bentley. SP: Frank
Miller, from the play by Wallace Geoffrey. PH: James Wilson.
Art D: David Raunsley. Ref: FJA. MPH 1/11/36. HR 1/9/36.
FD 6/4/35. with Gerald Du Maurier, George Curzon, Leslie
Perrins, Belle Chrystall, Grete Natzler, Henry Victor, Frederick Peisley. Dr. Masters defrauds the World Insurance Co. with
the aid of a serum that produces "complete catalepsy." In an
attempt to escape from the police he gives himself a dose of the
serum. A bullet smashes his bottle of anti-toxin, and Masters
is doomed to remain one of the living dead.

LIVING DEAD, The see HISTOIRES EXTRAORDINAIRES (1931)

The LIVING DEAD MAN (F) 1923 (L'INHUMAINE) D: Marcel
L'Herbier. Art D: Fernand Léger, R. Mallet-Stevens, Alberto
Cavalcanti. Ref: DDC I:151. II:379. III:217. with Eve Francis,
Jaque Catelain, Georgette Leblanc. A singer, poisoned by a
jealous Maharajah, is saved by an engineer's dangerous labora-
tory experiment.

The LIVING GHOST Mono 1942 61m. (The WALKING NIGHT-
MARE) D: William Beaudine. SP: Joseph Hoffman. Story:
Howard Dimsdale. PH: Mack Stengler. Mus D: Frank Sanucci.
Ref: FDY. Lee. with James Dunn, Joan Woodbury, Paul Mc-
Vey, Minerva Urecal, Vera Gordon, J. Farrell MacDonald,
Norman Willis, George Eldredge, Harry Depp. Fluid paralyzes
brain, leaving living corpse.

The LIVING HEAD (Mex) AI-TV/Cinematografica, A.B.S.A. 1961
(La CABEZA VIVIENTE) D: Chano Urueta. SP: Adolfo Portillo.
Story: Federico Curiel. PH: Jorge Stahl, Jr. Mus: G. C.
Carrion. Ref: Indice. with Abel Salazar, German Robles, Ana
Luisa Peluffo, Antonio Raxell, Mauricio Garcés. Living head in
league with mummy. Inconsistent and poorly dubbed, but even if
it weren't it would still be terrible.

The LIVING IDOL MGM (U.S.-Mex) 1956 Eastmancolor/scope
101m. SP, D: Albert Lewin. Assoc D: Rene Cardona. Ref:
FM 2:14. PM. MFB'58:22. with Steve Forrest, Liliane Mon-
tevecchi, James Robertson Justice, Eduardo Noriega. Professor
believes girl is reincarnation of an Indian princess sacrificed to
a jaguar god.

LIVING SKELETON (J) Shochiku 1968 scope 81m. (KYUKETSU
DOKUROSEN) D: Hiroki Matsuno. SP: K. Shimoiizaka, K.
Kobaysashi. PH: M. Kato. Mus: N. Nishiyama. Art D: K.
Morita. Ref: UFQ 43. with Kikko Matsuoka, Akira Nishimura.
Phantom ship, necrophilia, woman disguised as ghost.

LIZZIE MGM/Bryna 1957 D: Hugo Haas. SP: Mel Dinelli, from
"The Bird's Nest" by Shirley Jackson. PH: Paul Ivano. Mus:

Leith Stevens. Art D: Rudi Feld. Ref: FDY. with Eleanor Park-
er, Richard Boone, Joan Blondell, Johnny Mathis, Michael
Mark(s). Hypnosis reveals girl has two personalities.
LLEGARON LOS MARCIANOS   see   TWELVE-HANDED MEN OF
MARS, The
LLORONA, La   see   CRYING WOMAN, The (1933/1959)
LLOYD OF THE C. I.D.   (B) Mutual (Universal) 1931 serial 12
episodes (The GREEN SPOT MYSTERY-feature. DETECTIVE
LLOYD) SP, D: Henry Macrae. Ref: LC. MPH 9/3/32. with
Jack Lloyd, Wallace Geoffrey, Muriel Angelus, Janice Adair,
Emily Fitzroy, Lewis Drayton, Gibb McLaughlin. Death ray,
"Manor Ghost," secret panels, Egyptian tomb.
LO UCCIDO, TU UCCIDI   see   I KILL, YOU KILL
LOBA, La   see SHE-WOLF, The
The LOBSTER NIGHTMARE Walturdaw (Vita?) 1910 8m. Ref:
Bios 2/2/11. Dream. Huge lobster, imps torment man in hell.
LOCH NESS MYSTERY, The   see   SECRET OF THE LOCH
LOCK YOUR DOORS   see   APE MAN, The
LOCURA DEL TERROR   see   MADNESS FROM TERROR
The LODGER--A STORY OF THE LONDON FOG   (B) Gainsborough
/Amer-Anglo 1926 D: Alfred Hitchcock. SP: Hitchcock, Eliot
Stannard. PH: Baron Ventimiglia. Art D: C. W. Arnold, Ber-
tram Evans. Ed: Ivor Montagu. Ref: SilentFF. COF 6:43.
FIR'66:233. with Ivor Novello, Malcolm Keen, Arthur Chesney,
Marie Ault. Based on the book by Marie Belloc-Lowndes.
The LODGER Fox 1944 84m. D: John Brahm. SP: Barre
Lyndon, from the book by Marie Belloc-Lowndes. PH: Lucien
Ballard. Mus: Hugo Friedhofer. Art D: James Basevi, John
Ewing. Ref: Clarens. COF 9:60. Pic: Pict.Hist.Cinema. with
Laird Cregar, Merle Oberon, George Sanders, Sir Cedric Hard-
wicke, Sara Allgood, Aubrey Mather, Queenie Leonard, Doris
Lloyd, Lumsden Hare, Frederick Worlock, Billy Bevan, Skelton
Knaggs, Forrester Harvey. Cregar as Jack the Ripper is every-
thing, but that's more than enough.
LODGER, The (by M. Belloc-Lowndes) see MAN IN THE ATTIC /
PHANTOM FIEND, The
LOKIS (Polish) Polski State 1970 color 100m. (The BEAR) SP, D:
Janusz Majewski, from the story by Prosper Merimee. PH: S.
Matyjaskiewicz. Mus: W. Kilar. Ref: V 9/9/70. M/TVM 6/70:
40. with Josef Duriasz, Edmund Fetting. A witch-like character
believes the son of a woman attacked by a bear is part animal.
LOKIS combines the beauty of the Polish countryside with unsettling
intimations of folkloric evil lying dormant behind the beauty. It
is perhaps the best horror film--and is just about the only one of
any real quality--since the HAUNTING, and the last scene, a
sudden, subdued chill, is a perfect example of a horror movie
working through intimation rather than revelation.
LOKIS (by P. Merimee) see MARRIAGE OF THE BEAR
LOLA World 1916 (WITHOUT A SOUL) From the play by Owen
Davis. Ref: MPN 14:3171. with Clara Kimball Young, James
Young, Alec Francis. Daughter of doctor who invented life-
restoring machine brought back to life by it.
LONDON AFTER MIDNIGHT MGM 1927 75m. SP, D, P: Tod

Browning. SP: also Waldemar Young. From Browning's story
"The Hypnotist. " PH: Merritt B. Gerstad. Remade as MARK
OF THE VAMPIRE. Titles: Joe Farnham.   Art D, Sets: Cedric
Gibbons, Arnold Gillespie. Ed: Harry Reynolds. Ref: RVB.
WFC 4:55. V 12/14/27.   FM 69:27. 80:6.   Pic: FM 8:33.14:7.
MW 10:13. with Lon Chaney, Marceline Day, Henry B.
Walthall, Percy Williams, Conrad Nagel, Polly Moran, Edna
Tichenor, Claude King, Jules Cowles, Andy McClellan. Vampires
turn out to be pawns in a scheme to catch a murderer.

The LONG HAIR OF DEATH (I) Cinegai 1964 100m. (I LUNG-
HI CAPELLI DELLA MORTE) D: Antonio Margheriti (aka Anthony
Dawson). SP: Robert Bohr. Story: Margheriti, Julian Berry
(aka Ernesto Gastaldi). PH: Richard Thierry (aka Riccardo
Pallottini). Mus: Carlo Rustichelli. Ref: MFB'67:142. Pic:
FM 42:2. COF 15:49. with Barbara Steele, George Ardisson,
Halina Zalewska. Robert Rains. Adele Karnestein put to death
for using black magic; spirit in dummy.

LONG RAIN, The (by R. Bradbury) see ILLUSTRATED MAN, The

LOOKING FORWARD Than 1910 17m. Ref: The Film Index. Potion makes man sleep 100 years; he awakes to find women
dominant.

LOONIES ON BROADWAY see ZOMBIES ON BROADWAY

LORD ARTHUR SAVILE'S CRIME (F) 1921 (Le CRIME DE LORD
ARTHUR SAVILE) D: René Hervil. See also FLESH AND
FANTASY. From the story by Oscar Wilde. Ref: DDC III:38.
Original story: Man told by palmist he'll commit murder.

LORD FEATHERTOP Edison 1908 From "Feathertop" by
Nathaniel Hawthorne. Ref: F Index 12/5/08. Witch endows
scarecrow with life.

LOSS OF SENSATION (Russ) 1935 (GIBEL SENSATSY) D: A.
Andrievski. Ref: Musee Du Cinema. "Political s-f...robot
kills inventor. "

LOST ATLANTIS (F) Nero-Film 1932 (ATLANTIS. L'ATLANTIDE.
DIE HERRIN VON ATLANTIS. MISTRESS OF ATLANTIS) D:
G. W. Pabst. SP: Ladislaus Vayda, Hermann Oberländer.
From "L'Atlantide" by Pierre Benoit. PH Eugen Shuftan,
Ernst Koerner. Mus: Wolfgang Zeller. Art D: Erno Metzner.
Ref: Imagen. FIR'64:101, 109.   COF 6:30. DDC III:30, 334.
Pic: DDC I:5 8, 90. with Brigitte Helm, Jean Angelo, Pierre
Blanchar, Georges Tourel, Odette Florelle. The lost continent
of Atlantis.

LOST ATLANTIS (English version of above) 1932 Ref: FIR'64:109.
with Brigitte Helm, John Stuart, Gibb McLaughlin, Florelle,
Gustav Diessl.

LOST ATLANTIS (German version) 1932 (DIE HERRIN VON
ATLANTIS) Ref: FIR'64:109. with Helm, Diessl, Heinz Kling-
enberg, Tela Tschai, Vladimir Sokoloff, Florebelle, Mathias
Wieman.

The LOST CITY Super-Serial/Regal 1935 serial 12 episodes
D: Harry Revier. (LOST CITY OF THE LIGURIANS) Ref:
Photoplay 11/35. Menville. SM 6:6. STI 1:19. SF Film.
FD 2/20/35. ModM 3:22. Pic: ModM 2:53. FM 63:55. with
Kane Richmond, William (Stage) Boyd, Claudia Dell, Ralph
Lewis, Josef Swickard. Mad doctor in lost jungle city uses

super-scientific devices to change natives into zombies.

LOST CITY OF THE JUNGLE Univ 1946 serial 13 episodes D:
Ray Taylor, Lewis D. Collins. SP: J. Poland, T. Gibson, P.
Huston. PH: Gus Peterson. Ref: COF 8:46. Lee. Academy. with
Lionel Atwill, Keye Luke, Russell Hayden, Jane Adams, John
Miljan, John Eldredge, John Gallaudet, Gene Stutenroth, Arthur
Space, Ralph Lewis, Frank Lackteen, Sam Flint, Luke Chan,
George Eldredge, Mauritz Hugo, Jimmy Aubrey, Wheaton
Chambers. New element for A-bombs; metal defense against
A-bombs.

LOST CONTINENT Lippert 1951 82m. D: Sam Newfield. SP:
Richard Landau. Story: Carroll Young. PH: Jack Greenhalgh.
Mus: Paul Dunlap. Art D: Paul Sylos. SpFX: Augie Lohman.
P: Sigmund Neufeld. Ref: FDY. Pic: FM 19:32. with Cesar
Romero, Hillary Brooke, Chick Chandler, John Hoyt, Whit
Bissell, Hugh Beaumont, Acquanetta, Sid Melton, Murray Alper.
Searching for a lost missile, an expedition discovers a land of
dinosaurs. Not-too-bad, formula dinosaur picture.

The LOST CONTINENT (B) Fox/Hammer/7A 1968 color 89m.
(LOST ISLAND) P,D: Michael Carreras. SP: Michael Nash, from
the novel "Uncharted Seas" by Dennis Wheatley. PH: Paul Benson.
Mus Sup: Philip Martell. Art D: Arthur Lawson. SpFX: Robert
Mattey. Ref: V. FM 48:7. PM. with Eric Porter, Nigel Stock,
Hildegarde Neff, Suzanna Leigh, Jimmy Hanley, Neil McCallum,
Michael Ripper, Victor Maddern. Giant jellyfish, prehistoric
sharks, deadly seaweed, etc. Shoddy s-f version of STAGE-
COACH, with the outcasts relating their various dull histories
and running into comically repulsive monsters. Despite some
bizarre elements, no more interesting than its lost-island
predecessors.

LOST EMPRESS (By S. Ornitz) see SECRETS OF THE FRENCH
POLICE

LOST FACE (Cz) Czech State Film 1964 scope 85m.
(ZTRACENA TVAR. The BORROWED FACE) D: Pavel Hobl. SP:
Hobl, Josef Nesvadba. PH: Jiri Vojta. Ref: Continental Fm.Rev.
9/65. Imagen. M/TVM 6/65. with Vlastimil Brodsky, Jana
Brejchova, Fred Delmare. Young doctor transplants faces from
one body to another.

LOST ISLAND see LOST CONTINENT, The (1968)

LOST KINGDOM see JOURNEY BENEATH THE DESERT

LOST LOVE JULIANA (Braz) MGM/Entrefilmes-Vera Cruz-Bras-
continental 1969 Eastmancolor 94m. (JULIANA DO AMOR PER-
DIDO) Mus,D: Sergio Ricardo. SP: Ricardo, Roberto Santos.
PH: Dib Lufti. Art D: C. Cruz. Ref: V. 10/14/70. with Mario
do Rosario, Macedo Neto. Fisherman's daughter converted into
a "voodoo Cinderella"; man bewitched by her "sorcerous charm."

The LOST MISSILE UA 1958 70m. Story,D: Lester William
Berke. SP: Jerome Bixby, John McPartland. PH: Kenneth Peach.
Mus: Gerald Fried. Art D: William Ferrari. Ref: Ffacts. TVG.
with Robert Loggia, Ellen Parker, Larry Kerr, Philip Pine,
Selmer Jackson, Joe Hyams, Bill Bradley. Radioactive missile
from another planet circles the earth.

The LOST PLANET Col 1953 serial 15 episodes D: Spencer G.

Bennet.   SP: G. H. Plympton, A. Hoerl.   PH: W. Whitley.
P: Sam Katzman. Ref: Barbour. with Judd Holdren, Vivian
Mason, Ted Thorpe, Forrest Taylor, Michael Fox, Gene Roth,
Leonard Penn, Nick Stuart, I. Stanford Jolley, Pierre Watkin.
Pic: FanMo 1:41. SM 3:36. Ch. 2. Trapped by the Axial Pro-
peller. 3. Blasted by the Thermic Disintegrator. 4. The Mind
Control Machine. 5. The Atomic Plane. 7. Snared by the
Prysmic Catapult. 9. The Hypnotic Ray Machine. 11. Dr. Grood
Defies Gravity. 12, Trapped in a Cosmic Jet. 14. In the Grip
of the De-thermo Ray.
LOST PLANET AIRMEN Rep 1949 (feature version of KING OF
THE ROCKET MEN, 12-episode serial) D: Fred C. Brannon.
SP: R. Cole, S. Shor, W. Lively. Scenes from DELUGE. PH:
Ellis W. Carter. Ref: Barbour. Pic: M&H 1:26. ModM 1:69.
SM 7:42. with Tristram Coffin, Mae Clarke, Don Haggerty,
House Peters, Jr., James Craven, I. Stanford Jolley, Ted
Adams, Stanley Price, Dale Van Sickel, Tom Steele David
Sharpe, Eddie Parker, Frank O'Connor. Scientist plans to con-
quer world with deadly new weapon.
The LOST SHADOW (G) UFA/Wegener Film Union 1921 64m.
(Der VERLORENE SCHATTEN) D: Rochus Gliese. SP: Paul
Wegener.   PH: Karl Freund. Art D: Kurt Richter. Ref: Fan-
tastique. with Wegener, Hannes Sturm, Lyda Salmonova.
Violinist sells his shadow to "the evil one" for a magic violin.
The LOST SOUL Or The DANGERS OF HYPNOSIS (Austrian) 1923
Astra-Film 80m. (Das VERLORENE IÇH or GEFAHREN DER
HYPNOSE) D: Hugo Werner-Kahle. SP: L. Thoma, J. Malina.
PH: R. Mayer, H. Pebal. Ref: Osterr. with Werner-Kahle,
Paul Kronegg, Annemarie Steinsieck.
LOST VALLEY, The see VALLEY OF GWANGI, The
LOST WOMEN see MESA OF LOST WOMEN
LOST WOMEN OF ZARPA see MESA OF LOST WOMEN
The LOST WORLD F Nat 1925 110m. D: Harry Hoyt. SP:
Marion Fairfax. From the book by Sir Arthur Conan Doyle.
PH: Arthur Edeson. SpFX: Willis O'Brien. Ref: Imagen. FM
10:26. 29:39. DDC III:403. with Bessie Love, Wallace Beery,
Lewis Stone, Lloyd Hughes, Arthur Hoyt, George Bunny, Bull
Montana (missing link), Virginia Brown Faire. Lost world of
dinosaurs. Some spectacular special-effects scenes overshadow
routine adventure-story framework.
The LOST WORLD Fox/Saratoga 1960 DeLuxe color/scope 98m.
SP,D,P: Irwin Allen. SP: also Charles Bennett. PH: Winton
Hoch. Mus: Paul Sawtell, Bert Shefter. Art D: Duncan Cramer,
Walter M. Simonds. Ref: FM 10:41. COF 6:55. with Michael
Rennie, Jill St. John, Claude Rains, David Hedison, Fernando
Lamas, Jay Novello, Richard Haydn, Ray Stricklyn, Ian Wolfe.
From the book by Sir Arthur Conan Doyle. Lots of second-rate
dinosaurs and other obstacles; little suspense.
The LOST WORLD OF SINBAD (J) AI/Toho 1964 Pathecolor/
scope 93m. (SAMURAI PIRATE DAITOZOKU. 7TH WONDER
OF SINBAD) D: Senkichi Taniguchi. SP: Shinichi Sekizawa,
Takeshi Kimura. SpFX: Eiji Tsuburaya. Mus: Masaru Sato.
Ref: V 3/17/65. COF 2:47. with Toshiro Mifune, Makoto Sato.

Witch hypnotically turns people into stone. Numerous camera
tricks fail to save the movie. Poor.
LOTTA COIN'S GHOST Ham Comedies 1915 12m. Ref: SilentFF.
MPN 4/24/15. MPW 24:439. with Marin Sais, Lloyd Hamilton,
Bud Duncan. Mrs. Coin dresses as ghost to frighten burglars.
LOU COSTELLO AND HIS 30 FOOT BRIDE see 30 FOOT BRIDE
OF CANDY ROCK, The
LOUISIANA see DRUMS O'VOODOO
LOUP DES MALVENEUR, Le see WOLF OF THE MALVENEURS,
The
LOUP-GAROU, Le see WEREWOLF, The (1923)
LOUTCH SMERTI see DEATH RAY, The (1925)
LOUVES, Les see DEMONIAQUE
LOVE AND GOODFELLOWSHIP PILLS (F?) Pathe 1910 10m. Ref:
Bios 7/7/10. Max Linder buys pills that make him embrace
every girl he meets.
LOVE AND SCIENCE Eclair 1912 17m. Ref: Bios 5/23/12.
Scientist perfects phone invention that enables one to see person
at other end of line.
LOVE BIRDS Univ 1934 61m. D: William Seiter. SP: Dale Van
Every, Clarence Marks. PH: Norbert Brodine. Ref: MPH 4/21/
34. FD 5/4/34: "An amusing ghost scene." with ZaSu Pitts,
Slim Summerville, Mickey Rooney, Emmett Vogan, Maude Eburne,
Dorothy Christy, Clarence Wilson.
The LOVE CAPTIVE Univ 1934 65m. D: Max Marcin. SP: Karen
de Wolf. PH: Gilbert Warrenton. Ref: FD 6/7/34. with Nils
Asther, Robert Greig, Gloria Stuart, Paul Kelly, Alan Dinehart,
Renee Gadd, Addison Richards, John Wray. Hypnotic doctor uses
his powers to take another man's girl.
LOVE, DEATH AND THE DEVIL (G) UFA 1934 100m. (LIEBE,
TOD UND TEUFEL. The DEVIL IN A BOTTLE) D: Heinz Hil-
pert, Reinhart Steinbicker. SP: K. Heuser, P. von Felinau, L.
Gravenstein, from "The Imp in the Bottle" by Robert Louis
Stevenson. Mus: Theo Mackeben. Ref: Deutscher. FD 5/31/35.
with Käthe von Nagy, Brigitte Horney, Albin Skoda, Erich Ponto.
Bottle makes wishes come true at the price of the owner's soul
unless he can sell it at a lower price than he paid for it.
The LOVE DOCTOR Vita 1917 55m. D: Paul Scardon. From
the story "Hashashin, the Indifferent" by George Dillenback.
Ref: MPN 16:2949. with Earle Williams, Corinne Griffith, Patsy
DeForest. Doctor transfers brain cells from girl who loves him
to girl he loves.
The LOVE DOCTORS Sigma III 1969 D: Bon Ross. SP: Louis
Garfinkle. Ref: Film Bltn. 12/69. with Ann Jannin, Frank
Mahalan. Robot provides sexual satisfaction.
The LOVE DOPE MGM/Ralph Hertz 1917 11m. Ref: MPN 15:2863.
Comedy. Love tablets promote love.
LOVE FROM A STRANGER (B) UA/Trafalgar 1936 86m. (A
NIGHT OF TERROR) D: Rowland V. Lee. From the play by
Frank Vosper and the story by Agatha Christie. SP: Frances
Marion. PH: Philip Tannura. Ref: FD 4/21/37. V 1/27/37.
"Macabre story of a suave gentleman who marries women for their
money and murders them... gruesome." Pic: TBG. with Basil

Rathbone, Ann Harding, Bruce Seton, Binnie Hale, Donald Calthrop.

LOVE FROM A STRANGER Eagle-Lion 1947 81m. D: Richard Whorf. SP: Philip MacDonald, from a play by Frank Vosper and a story by Agatha Christie. PH: Tony Gaudio. Mus sc: Hans J. Salter. Art D: Perry Smith. PhFX: George J. Teague. Sp ArtFX: Jack R. Rabin. Ref: V 11/5/47. MFB'48:97: For "Horror lovers." Storms, strange noises. with Sylvia Sidney, John Hodiak, Ann Richards, John Howard, Isobel Elsom, Philip Tonge, Frederick Worlock, Billy Bevan, Donald Kerr, Phyllis Barry. Husband secretly digs wife's grave in cellar.

LOVE FROM OUT OF THE GRAVE Film D'Art 1913 25m. Ref: Bios 11/6/13. Artist haunted by apparition of wife's lost lover.

The LOVE GERMS Lubin 1909 8m. Ref: F Index 1/30/09. Scientist discovers "love germs."

LOVE HAS ITS REASONS! (G) UFA 1933 84m. (LIEBE MUSS VERSTANDEN SEIN!) D:Hans Steinhoff. Ref: Deutscher. with Rose Barsony, Theo Lingen. Remote-control "robot doll" dances. It turns out to be girl instead of inventor's doll.

LOVE ITALIAN STYLE see SUPER DIABOLICAL

The LOVE MAGNET Kalem 1916 11m. Ref: MPN 14:2400. Magnet attracts women, mermaids.

The LOVE MICROBE AM&B 1907 12m. Ref: Niver. MPW'07:526. Microbes, "tinted red on the screen just as the professor sees them," turn housekeeper from vixen to angel.

LOVE NOT AGAIN (J) Toei 1962 scope/color 100m. (KOIYA KOI NASUNA KOI. The MAD FOX. LOVE, THY NAME BE SORROW) D: Tomu Uchida. SP: Yoshitaka Yoda. PH: Teiji Yoshida. Ref: J. Films '63. FIR'62:474. UFQ 17. with Hashizo Okawa, Michiko Saga, Sumiko Hidaka. "Yasuna is rescued by a white fox whose daughter transforms herself in the shape of Kuzunoha who gives birth to a boy child."

The LOVE OF A SIREN (I) Cines 1911 10m. Ref: Bios 2/29/12. Siren's spell lures boy to death.

LOVE SPOTS Planet 1914 10m. Ref: Bios 4/23/14. Tonic makes user feel romantic.

LOVE, THY NAME BE SORROW See LOVE NOT AGAIN

The LOVE WANGA Hoffberg 1941 61m. Ref: Lee. V 1/7/42. Black magic, zombies, love charm.

The LOVE WAR ABC-TV/Aaron Spelling 1970 color 72m. D: George McGowan. SP: Q. Trueblood, David Kidd. Mus: Dominic Frontiere. SpPhFX: Howard A. Anderson Co. Ref: RVB. TVG. with Lloyd Bridges, Angie Dickinson, Dan Travanty, Harry Basch, Allen Jaffe, Bill McLean. Six beings from two warring planets take human form and use earth as a battleground.

LOVE WITHOUT QUESTION Jans-Rolfe 1920 65m. P,D: B. A. Rolfe. Adap: Violet Clark. From the novel "The Abandoned Room" by C. Wadsworth Camp. Ref: MPW 44:141. with Olive Tell, James W. Morrison, Mario Marjaroni, Ivo Dawson, Charles Mackay, George S. Stevens. A man is killed in a "haunted" room.

LOVER OF THE MOON (F) 1905 (AMANT DE LA LUNE. REVE A LA LUNE. A MOONLIGHT DREAM-Eng.) D: Ferdinand Zecca,

Gaston Velle. Ref:Imagen.   DDC II:383. SF Film. Drunk travels
to moon on chimney.
LOVE'S MOCKERY   see JANUSKOPF, Der
LOVES OF COUNT IORGA   AI/Erica 1970 Movielab color   90m.
(released as   COUNT YORGA-VAMPIRE. VAMPIRE) Sequel:
The RETURN OF COUNT YORGA.   SP,D: Bob Kelljan. PH:
Arch Archambault. Mus: William Marx. Art D: Bob Wilder.
SpFX: James Tannenbaum. Makeup: M. Rogers, M. Dental-
smith. Narr: George Macready. with Robert Quarry, Roger
Perry. Vampire count moves to California. Some imaginative,
well-staged sequences. Acting ranges from good (Quarry) to
amateur.
The LOVES OF HERCULES (I-F) Grandi Schermi Italiani-Contact
1959 Technicolor/scope (GLI AMORI DI ERCOLE-I. HERCULEAN
LOVE) D: Carlo Bragaglia. SP: Continenza, Doria. Mus: Carlo
Innocenzi. Ref: Ital P. FEFN 7/60. with Jayne Mansfield,
Mickey Hargitay, Moira Orfei, Massimo Serato. Cave of the
many-headed hydra! Cyclops! Forest of trees that once were
men! The usual junk!
LOVE'S POTION   Powers   1911   6m. Ref: Bios 10/5/11. Dr.
Bunyan concocts effective love potion.
LUANA (I) Primex 1968 Eastmancolor/scope 88m. (LUANA,
LA FIGLIA DELLA FORESTA VERGINE. LUANA, DAUGHTER
OF THE VIRGIN FOREST) D: Bob Raymond. SP: L. Road. PH:
Mario Capriotti. Mus: S. Cipriani. Ref: MFB'69:174. with Mei
Chen, Evi Marandi, Glenn Saxon. "Powerful drug" extracted
from carnivorous plant; villain "assimilated by the carnivorous
cabbage."
LUCH SMERTI see DEATH RAY, The (1925)
LUCHADORAS CONTRA EL MEDICO ASESINO, Las see DOCTOR
OF DOOM
LUCHADORAS CONTRA EL ROBOT ASESINO, Las see WRESTLING
WOMEN VS. THE MURDERING ROBOT, The
LUCHADORAS CONTRA LA MOMIA, Las see WRESTLING WOMEN
VS. THE AZTEC MUMMY, The
LUCKY BOOTS (Polish) Film Polski 1958 100m. (KALOSZE
SZCZESCIA) D: A. Bohdziewicz. Ref: Film Polski '58/'59.
with M. Gella, Z. Zintel. "Magic galoshes" carry owners across
time and space.
LUCKY STAR (by O. Rutter) see ONCE IN A NEW MOON
LUDOT-VORNIMAC see MAGIC SWORD, The (1950)
LUFT-TORPEDO, Das see AIR TORPEDO, The (1913)
LUGOSI MEETS A BROOKLYN GORILLA see BELA LUGOSI
MEETS A BROOKLYN GORILLA
LUKE'S DOUBLE Pathe (Phunphilm) 1916 Ref: MPN 13:2560. Man
reading "The Strange Case of Dr. Jekyll and Mr. Hyde" falls
asleep, dreams he has a double who torments him.
LUNATIC ASYLUM Educational Film Exchanges/Lupino Lane 1925
17m. Ref: SilentFF. Doctor hypnotizes young man, who later
floats up into the air.
LUNE A UN METRE, La see ASTRONOMER'S DREAM, The
LUNGA NOTTE DI VERONIQUE, La see VERONIQUE'S LONG
NIGHT

LUNGHI CAPELLI DELLA MORTE, I see LONG HAIR OF DEATH, The
LURED BY A PHANTOM (F) Gaum 1910 12m. (Le ROI DE THULE. KING OF THULE) Ref: Mitry II:204. Bios 9/15/10. The Film Index. King follows visions of his dead wife into the sea.
The LURKING VAMPIRE (Arg) c1959 (EL VAMPIRO ACECHA or EL VAMPIRO AECHECHA) From a story by William Irish. Ref: COF 4:38. FM 18:4. MMF 9:18. with Nestor Zarvade, Blanca del Prado, Abel Salazar.
LUST FOR A VAMPIRE (B) Hammer 1971 Technicolor 95m. D: Jimmy Sangster. SP: Tudor Gates. Based on characters created by J. Sheridan Le Fanu. Sequel to The VAMPIRE LOVERS. PH: David Muir. Mus sc: Harry Robinson. Art D: Don Mingaye. Makeup: George Blackler. Ref: MFB'71:25. with Ralph Bates, Barbara Jefford, Suzanna Leigh, Erik Chitty, Yutte Stensgaard (Mircalla). Vampire reincarnated. (TO LOVE A VAMPIRE)
The LUST OF THE AGES Ogden 1917 55m. Ref: MPN 16:1665. "Liquid fire" destroys metal.
LUST OF THE VAMPIRE see DEVIL'S COMMANDMENT, The
LYCANTHROPE, Le see WEREWOLF IN A GIRLS' DORMITORY
LYCANTHROPUS see WEREWOLF IN A GIRLS' DORMITORY

M.A.R.S. see RADIO-MANIA
MA FEMME EST UNE PANTHERE See MY WIFE IS A PANTHER
MACABRE AA 1958 73m. P, D: William Castle. SP Robb White, from Theo Durrant's book "The Marble Forest." PH: Carl Guthrie. Mus: Les Baxter. SpFX: Jack Rabin, Louis DeWitt, Irving Block. Ref: FFacts. PM. with William Prince, Jim Backus, Christine White, Ellen Corby, Voltaire Perkins, Philip Tonge, Susan Morrow. A doctor is told that his daughter has been buried alive. Bad acting, unsympathetic characters, and weak use of flashbacks.
The MACABRE LEGACY (Mex) 1939 (La HERENCIA MACABRA) Ref: Indice. NY Times. D: Jose Bohr. P: Roberto Gallardo. "Gruesome thrills."
The MACABRE TRUNK (Mex) Ezet/Distripel 1936 (EL BAUL MACABRO) D: Miguél Zacarías. SP: A. Galindo. Story: J. M. Dada. PH: Alex Phillips. Ref:NYT 11/30/37. Indice. El Cine Grafico'41:93. with Ramón Pereda, Manuel Noreiga, René Cardona, Esther Fernandez, Carlos López Chaflán. "Gruesome atmosphere." Doctor seeks to cure wife by transfusing the blood of young women into her.
MACARIO (Mex) Azteca 1960 Sp, D: Roberto Gavaldon. SP: also Emilio Garballido. From B. Traven's story "The Third Guest." PH: Gabriel Figueroa. Mus: Raul Lavista. Art D: Manuel Fontanals. 91m. SpFX: Juan M. Ravelo. Pic: DDC II:426. with Ignacio Lopez Tarso, Pina Pellicer, Jose Galvez, Jose L. Jiminez, Sofia Infante. A peasant encounters the devil, God, and

Death.
MACHISTE, STRONGEST MAN IN THE WORLD   see   MOLEMEN
  VS. THE SON OF HERCULES
MACHT DER FINSTERNIS, Die see POWER OF DARKNESS, The
MACISTE AGAINST HERCULES IN THE VALE OF WOE   see
  HERCULES IN THE VALE OF WOE
MACISTE AGAINST THE VAMPIRE see   GOLIATH AND THE
  VAMPIRES
MACISTE ALL CORTE DELLO CZAR see   ATLAS AGAINST THE
  CZAR
MACISTE ALL'INFERNO see   WITCH'S CURSE, The
MACISTE ALLA CORTE DEL GRAN KHAN see SAMSON AND
  THE 7 MIRACLES OF THE WORLD
MACISTE AND THE NIGHT QUEEN see MOLEMEN AGAINST THE
  SON OF HERCULES
MACISTE CONTRE LE FANTOME see   GOLIATH AND THE VAM-
  PIRES
MACISTE CONTRE LES HOMMES DE PIERRE see HERCULES VS.
  THE MOONMEN
MACISTE CONTRO I MOSTRI see   FIRE MONSTERS AGAINST
  THE SON OF HERCULES
MACISTE CONTRO IL VAMPIRO see   GOLIATH AND THE VAM-
  PIRES
MACISTE E LA REGINA DI SAMAR see HERCULES VS. THE
  MOONMEN
MACISTE IN HELL   (I) Excelsior/Olympia 1925 ('31-U.S.) D:
  Guido Brignone. From "The Inferno" by Dante. SpFX: Segundo
  de Chomon. Ref: DDC I:404. Bianco 4/64. FM 67:12. with
  Bartolomeo Pagano. Satan as huge demon frozen in lake of ice,
  with Brutus, Cassius and Judas in his three mouths.
MACISTE IN KING SOLOMON'S MINES (I) Panda 1964 (MACISTE
  NELLE MINIERE DI RE SALOMONE) color/scope D: Martin
  Andrews. SP: Piero Regnoli. PH: Luciano Trasatti. Ref: Ital
  P. with Reg Park, Wandisa Guida, Dan Harrison, Leonard G.
  Eliot. "Fazira, having recourse to magic, has his will-power
  destroyed."
MACISTE IN THE LAND OF THE CYCLOPS see ATLAS IN THE
  LAND OF THE CYCLOPS
MACISTE, L'UOMO PIU FORTE DEL MONDO see MOLEMEN VS.
  THE SON OF HERCULES
MACISTE NELLA TERRA DEI CICLOPI see ATLAS IN THE LAND
  OF THE CYCLOPS
MACISTE NELLA VALLE DEI RE see SON OF SAMSON
MACISTE-THE MIGHTY see SON OF SAMSON
MACISTE VS. THE STONE MEN see HERCULES VS. THE MOON-
  MEN
MACISTE VS. THE VAMPIRE see GOLIATH AND THE VAMPIRES
MacNAB VISITS THE COMET (F) Lux 1910 Ref: Bios 5/26/10.
  "Maidens" discovered on Halley's Comet.
MACUMBA LOVE UA 1960 Eastmancolor 86m. (MACUMBA,
  L'ISOLA DEI VAMPIRI-I) P,D: Douglas Fowley. SP: Norman
  Graham. PH: Rudolfo Icsey. Mus: Enrico Simonetti. Ref:
  FFacts. COF 17:31. with Walter Reed, Ziva Rodann, June

Wilkinson, William Wellman, Jr. Wealthy woman on small island off South America under hypnotic influence of voodoo queen.
MAD ABOUT MONEY (B) Morgan 1938 78m. D: Melville
  Brown. Ref: MFB'38. SF Film. with Ben Lyon, Wallace
  Ford, Harry Langdon, Lupe Velez, Jean Collin. Musical-comedy
  about two movie producers who buy up options on a new color
  process. "In addition there are some surprising 'effects' intro-
  duced by Len Lye, including a rocket trip to Saturn with a ballet
  of the stars, and the trial of a modern composer by the ghosts
  of past musicians."
The MAD DOCTOR Para 1941 88m. (DESTINY. A DATE WITH
  DESTINY) D: Tim Whelan. SP: Howard Green. PH: Ted
  Tetzlaff. Mus sc: Victor Young. Art D: Hans Dreier, Robert
  Usher, SpFX: Gordon Jennings. Ref: Academy. FM 23:26.
  HR: "Horror melodrama." with Basil Rathbone, Martin Kosleck,
  Ellen Drew, John Howard, Ralph Morgan, Billy Benedict, Vera
  Vague (aka Barbara Allen), Hugh Sothern, James Seay, Edward
  Earle, George Chandler, Philip Morris, Eddie Dunn, Wanda Mc-
  Kay, Douglas Kennedy, Henry Victor. A Viennese doctor mar-
  ries wealthy women and then kills them. Rathbone and Kosleck
  as the villains make a good team, but the movie is still pretty
  dull.
MAD DOCTOR OF BLOOD ISLAND (U.S.-Fili) Hemisphere 1969
  color 85m. Follow-up to BRIDES OF BLOOD. D: Eddie
  Romero, Gerardo de Leon. Ref: LA Times 1/9/70. Pic: FM
  63:9,11. with John Ashley, Angelique Pettyjohn. Giant terrorizes island natives.
The MAD DOCTOR OF MARKET STREET Univ 1942 61m. D:
  Joseph Lewis. SP: Al Martin. PH: Jerome Ash. Mus D:
  H. J. Salter. Art D: Jack Otterson. Ref: HM 7:17. FDY.
  Pic: FMO 6:10. with Lionel Atwill, Una Merkel, Nat Pendle-
  ton, Claire Dodd, Anna Nagel, Hardie Albright, John Eldredge,
  Noble Johnson, Milton Kibbee, Ray Mala. A doctor experiment-
  ing in suspended animation brings a native princess out of a
  coma after a heart attack. Novel cast wasted on trite material.
The MAD EXECUTIONERS (W.G.) Para/CCC/Omnia/Vogel 1963
  ('65-U.S.) 92m. (Der HENKER VON LONDON. The HANGMAN
  OF LONDON) D: Edwin Zbonek. SP: R. A. Stemmle. From
  Bryan Edgar Wallace's "White Carpet." PH: Richard Angst.
  Ref: COF 8:6. Maltin. with Wolfgang Preiss, Chris Howland,
  Harry Riebauer, Rudolph Fernau. A deranged scientist-killer is
  tried by mysterious "executioners" in mausoleum.
MADE FOR LOVE Producers Distributing Corp. 1926 80m. D:
  Paul Sloane. P: Cecil B. DeMille. SP: Garrett Fort. PH:
  Arthur Miller. Art D: Max Parker. Ref: AFI. with Leatrice
  Joy, Edmund Burns, Ethel Wales, Bertram Grassby, Brandon
  Hurst, Frank Butler. Curse on Egyptian tomb.
MAD FOX, The See LOVE NOT AGAIN
The MAD GENIUS WB 1931 81m. D: Michael Curtiz. SP: J.
  Grubb Alexander, Harvey Thew. From the story "The Idol" by
  Martin Brown. PH: Barney McGill. Ref: Clarens. COF 17:
  28. with John Barrymore, Marian Marsh, Donald Cook, Charles
  Butterworth, Luis Alberni, Frankie Darro, Boris Karloff.

Hypnotism, madness. Very weak. Not redeemed by spectacular, grotesque ending. None of Curtiz's ventures into horror were much.

The MAD GHOUL Univ 1943 65m. D: James P. Hogan. SP: Paul Gangelin, Brenda Weisberg. Story: Hans Kraly. PH: Milton Krasner. Mus D: H. J. Salter. Art D: John B. Goodman, Martin Obzina. Ref: FDY. with David Bruce, Evelyn Ankers, George Zucco, Robert Armstrong, Turhan Bey, Milburn Stone, Rose Hobart, Addison Richards, Charles McGraw, Andrew Tombes. A doctor discovers a poison which causes a state of "death in life." Not bad--for Forties Universal.

MAD LOVE MGM 1935 83m. D: Karl Freund. SP: John Balderston, Guy Endore, P. J. Wolfson. PH: Gregg Toland, Chester Lyons. From the novel "Les Mains D'Orlac" by Maurice Renard. Mus: Dmitri Tiomkin. Ref: Academy. FM 17:13. 10:28. Pic: COF 5:15. FM 31:62. with Peter Lorre, Colin Clive, Frances Drake, Ted Healy, Edward Brophy, Keye Luke, Isabel Jewell, Henry Kolker, Harold Huber, Ian Wolfe, Charles Trowbridge, Sara Haden, Murray Kinnell, Rollo Lloyd, Hooper Atchley, Sam Ash, Otto Hoffman, Frank Darien, Robert Emmett Keane, Carl Stockdale, Billy Gilbert, Clarence H. Wilson, Sara Padden. A mad surgeon grafts the hands of a guillotined knife-thrower onto the wrists of an injured concert pianist. A bad script awkwardly directed by Freund. Bits and pieces here and there in Lorre's performance and the editing.

The MAD MAGICIAN Col 1954 3-D 73m. D: John Brahm. SP: Crane Wilbur. Remake of HANGOVER SQUARE? PH: Bert Glennon. Mus: Emil Newman, Arthur Lange. Art D: Frank Sylos. Ref: COF 10:40. TVG. FDY. with Vincent Price, Eva Gabor, Mary Murphy, Patrick O'Neal, Jay Novello, John Emery, Lenita Lane. A magician kills his employer with a buzz saw. Not much.

MAD MONK, The see RASPUTIN, THE MAD MONL

The MAD MONSTER PRC 1942 77m. (The MAD MONSTERS) D: Sam Newfield. SP: Fred Myton. PH: Jack Greenhalgh. Mus: David Chudnow. P: Sigmund Neufeld. Ref: ModM 4:16. HR 5/6/42. V 6/2/42. Pic: FMO 4:38. MW 9:29. with George Zucco, Anna Nagel, Johnny Downs, Glenn Strange (Petro, the creature), Robert Strange, Sarah Padden, Mae Busch, Reginald Barlow, Henry Hall, Edward Cassidy. A scientist, by transfusing the blood of a wolf into a man, creates a "werewolf."

MAD MURDERER AND SEX, The see WRESTLING WOMEN VS. THE MURDERING ROBOT, The

MADAM WHITE SNAKE (or MADAME WHITE SNAKE) (Hong Kong-Chinese-J) Shaw/Toho 1956 ('65-U.S.) Eastmancolor 105m. (BYAKU FUJIN NO YOREN. The BEWITCHED LOVE OF MADAME PAI.) D: Shiro Toyoda. SP: Toshio Yasumi. PH: Mitsuo Miura. Mus: Ikuma Dan. Art D: R. Mitsubayashi. SpFX: Eiji Tsuburaya. Ref: FEFN 7/13/56. Rep. Gen'63. Toho Films'60. COF 10:48. with Shirley Yamaguchi, Ryo Ikebe, Kaoru Yachigusa. Two snake spirits engage in a battle of black magic with evil monks.

The MADMAN OF LAB 4 (F) Gaum Int'l 1967 color 90m. (Le

FOU DU LABO 4) D: Jacques Besnard. SP: Jean Halain, from
a book by Rene Cambon. PH: Raymond Lemoigne. Ref: V 1/17/
68. with Jean Lefebvre, Maria Latour, Pierre Brasseur, Ber-
nard Blier. A man invents a gas which makes people love each
other.
MADMEN OF MANDORAS Crown 1964 74m. (The AMAZING
MR. H. RETURN OF MR. H) D: David Bradley. SP: Richard
Miles, Steve Bennett. PH: Stanley Cortez. Ref: MMF 9:96b.
Orpheus 3:37. FM 27:3,44. COF 5:4. with John Holland,
Walt Stocker, Scott Peters, Nestor Paiva, Carlos Rivas, Audrey
Caire. A group of fanatics on the island of Mandoras has kept
the head of Hitler alive.
MADMEN'S TRIAL (Russ) Mosfilm 1962 color/scope 115m.
SP,D: Grigori Roshal. Ref: FEFN 4/61. Imagen. with Irina
Skobtseva, Vasili Livanov, Victor Jojriakov. A physicist dis-
covers a power capable of destroying the will of human beings
for miles around.
MADNESS FROM TERROR (Mex) Sotomayor 1960 (LOCURA DEL
TERROR. MADNESS BY TERROR) D: Julian Soler. SP: J.M.F.
Unsain, A. Varela, Jr. PH: Raul M. Solares. Mus: C. Zar-
zosa. Ref: Indice. Pic: FanMo 3:41. with "Tin Tan," S.
Furio, David Silva, Manuel Valdes. Huge spider, monster.
The MADNESS OF DR. TUBE (F) Les Films D'Art/Louis Nalpas
1915 (Le DOCTEUR TUBE. STORY OF A MADMAN. La FOLIE
DU DOCTEUR TUBE) SP,D: Abel Glance. PH: Wentzel.
Ref: DDC II:306. Clarens. SF in the cinema. Pic: DDC
I:151. with Albert Dieudonne. A scientist experiments in
breaking up light waves.
MADRID IN THE YEAR 2000 (Sp) Madrid Film 1925 (MADRID
EN EL ANO 2000) SP,D: Manuel Noriega. PH: A. Macasoli.
Ref: Imagen. with Roberto Iglesias, Roberto Rey, Javier
Rivera, Amelia Sanz Cruzado, Juan Nadal.
MAGIC CAR, The see BIG WORLD OF LITTLE CHILDREN, The
MAGIC CARTOONS Gaum/Kleine 1909 6m. Ref: MPW'09:319.
A doctor discovers the secret of spontaneous generation and
makes a germ which goes through a series of transformations.
The MAGIC CHRISTIAN (B) Grand 1969 Technicolor 95m.
D: Joseph McGrath. SP: Terry Southern, McGrath, Peter
Sellers. Based on the book by Southern. PH: Geoffrey Uns-
worth. Mus: Ken Thorne. SpVisual FX: Wally Veevers. Ref:
RVB. MFB. with Christopher Lee (ship's vampire), Peter
Sellers, Ringo Starr, Wilfrid Hyde-White, Leonard Frey,
Laurence Harvey, Spike Milligan, Roman Polanski, Raquel Welch,
Hattie Jacques, John Le Mesurier, Victor Maddern, Ferdy
Mayne, Dennis Price, Edward Underdown. Pretty bad as a
whole, but there are three or four genuinely funny routines.
The MAGIC ELIXIR (I) Cines 1912 6m. Ref: MPW 14:692.
Elixir makes people invulnerable to weapons.
The MAGIC FACE Col 1951 88m. D: Frank Tuttle. SP,P:
Mort Briskin, Robert Smith. PH: Tony Braun. Mus: H. B.
Gilbert. Art D: E. Stolba. Ref: V 8/1/51. with Luther
Adler, Patricia Knight, R. Wanka, Ilka Windish. A man kills
Hitler and takes his place.

The MAGIC FOUNTAIN Davis 1961 Eastmancolor/scope 78m.
P,D: Allan David. SP: John Lehmann, from "The Water of
Life" by the Bros. Grimm. Mus: Steve Allen. Ref: Boxo
4/27/64. with Sir Cedric Hardwicke, Hans Conreid, Buddy
Baer, Peter Nestler. Curse on castle; dwarf that turns
princes into ravens.
The MAGIC GLASS (B) Hepworth 1914 12m. Ref: SilentFF
with Eric Desmond. Professor invents liquid that when poured
on glasses allows him to see through solid objects.
MAGIC ISLAND, The (by W. Seabrook) see WHITE ZOMBIE
The MAGIC MIRROR (F) Pathe 1908 8m. D: Ferdinand
Zecca. Ref: The Film Index. Inventor puts fluid on mirror
and his double emerges.
MAGIC REPORT see WITCHCRAFT'70
MAGIC SERPENT see GRAND DUEL IN MAGIC
MAGIC SHAVING POWDER Walturdaw 1909 9m. Ref: Bios 12/9/
09. Man buys powder which removes hair by means of pair of
bellows.
The MAGIC SKIN Victor 1913 35m. From Balzac's "Le Peau
de Chagrin," "The Wild Ass's Skin," or "The Magic Skin."
Ref: Bios 5/7/14. MPW 19:50,84. with J. Warren Kerrigan.
Skin shrinks as owner's soul shrinks.
The MAGIC SKIN Kleine-Edison 1915 55m. SP,D: Richard
Ridgely. From Balzac's "Le Peau de Chagrin," "The Wild
Ass's Skin," or "The Magic Skin." Ref: MPN 10/23/15.
MAGIC SKIN, The (by Balzac) see DREAM CHEATER, The/
SINISTER WISH, The/SLAVE OF DESIRE/WILD ASS' SKIN, The
The MAGIC SWORD (B) Paul c1902 3m. Ref: Hist.Brit.Film.
Ghost, witch, ogre, magic cauldron, good fairy.
The MAGIC SWORD (Yugos) Ellis/Avala/Zvezda Film 1950
(LUDOT-VORNIMAC) 95m. SP,D: Voja Nanovic. Ref: MPH
3/15/52. with Rade Markoovich, M. Zhivanovich. "Steel
giant."
The MAGIC SWORD UA 1962 color 80m. (ST. GEORGE AND
THE 7 CURSES. ST. GEORGE AND THE DRAGON) D,P:
Bert I. Gordon. SP: Bernard Schoenfeld. PH: Paul Vogel.
Makeup: Dan Striepeke. Ref: FanMo 1:61. FM 12:4. 13:22.
14:20. with Basil Rathbone, Estelle Winwood, Vampira, Gary
Lockwood, Anne Helm, Liam Sullivan, Danielle de Metz,
Angelo Rossit(t)o. Ogre, dragon, "vampire-witch," evil sor-
cerer, etc. Gordon's big one isn't much better than his little
ones.
The MAGIC VOYAGE OF SINBAD (Russ) Filmgroup/Artkino/Mosfilm
1946 (SADKO) 79m. D: Alexandre Ptouchko. SP: K. Isayev. Based
on Rimsky-Korsakoff's opera. SpFX: S. Mulin. Ref: DDC III:428.
Pbk. with Edward Stolar, Anna Larion, Laurence Astan. Legendary
Phoenix casts hypnotic spell.
The MAGIC WEAVER (Russ) AA/Mossilm 1960 ('65-U.S.) 87m.
(MARIA, THE WONDERFUL WEAVER) D: Alexander Row. Ref:
PM. FEFN 7/60. with N. Myshkova, M. Kuznetsov. "Sea
king" holds child's mother captive in sea.
MAGIC WORLD OF DR. COPPELIUS, The see DR. COPPELIUS.
MAGICAL MATCHES Urbanora 1912 5m. Ref: Bios 4/4/12.
Matches form skeleton which takes its head in its arms and

disappears.
The MAGICIAN MGM 1926 71m. SP,D: Rex Ingram. Based
on the novel by Somerset Maugham. PH: John F. Seitz. Also
based on the career of Aleister Crowley. Ed: Grant Whytock.
Ref: Clarens. FM 14:4.22:25. AFI. with Alice Terry, Paul
Wegener, Stowitts, Ivan Petrovich, Firmin Gémier, Gladys
Hamer. Magician who creates human life; hypnotism.
The MAGICIAN (Swedish) Janus/Svensk 1958 102m. (ANSIKTET.
The FACE) SP,D: Ingmar Bergman. PH: Gunnar Fischer. Mus:
Erik Nordgren. Art D: P. A. Lundgren. Ed: Oscar Rosander.
Ref: Orpheus 4:37. FFacts. TVG. with Max von Sydow,
Ingrid Thulin, Gunnar Bjornstrand, Bibi Andersson, Bengt Ekerot.
Pic: FM 19:10. Mesmerist claims to have supernatural powers.
A little comedy, a little horror; otherwise the usual lethargic
Bergman. "See"-Eric Rohmer. "Not worth bothering about"-
Jean-Luc Godard.
MAGICIAN, The (1965) see MYSTERIOUS MAGICIAN, The
MAGICIENNES, Les see DOUBLE DECEPTION
The MAGNETIC EYE Lubin 1908 5m. Ref: MPW'08:83,481.
Man's eye attracts or repels people or objects.
The MAGNETIC FLUTE (F?) Pathe 1912 5m. Ref: Bios
5/2/12. Flute turns people and objects like tops.
A MAGNETIC INFLUENCE Urbanora 1912 8m. Ref: Bios 5/2/12.
Girl under spell of hypnotist.
MAGNETIC KITCHEN (F) 1908 (CUISINE MAGNETIQUE) D:
Segundo de Chomon. Ref: DDC I:404. Imagen. "Totally
mechanized future."
MAGNETIC MONSTER UA 1953 75m. SP,D: Curt Siodmak.
SP: also Ivan Tors. Footage from GOLD. PH: Charles van
Enger. Mus: Blaine Sanford. Art D: George Van Marter.
Ref: FM 14:44. Clarens. with Richard Carlson, King
Donovan, Jean Byron, Jarma Lewis, Harry Ellerbe, Leonard
Mudie, Byron Foulger, John Zaremba, Frank Gerstle, John
Vosper, Kathleen Freeman. Everything in hardware store mag-
netized by radioactive source that doubles its power every twelve
hours.
The MAGNETIC MOON MCA-TV 1954 From the "Rocky Jones,
Space Ranger" TV series. with Richard Crane, Sally Mansfield.
MAGNETIC REMOVAL (F?) Pathe 1908 12m. Ref: MPW'08:
547. Invention's magnetic powers dismantle house.
The MAGNETIC SQUIRT Le Lion 1909 8m. Ref: Bios 7/15/09.
Scientist discovers magnetic fluid that makes lame walk.
The MAGNETIC UMBRELLA Pathe (F) 1911 6m. Ref: Silent-
FF. Bios 11/30/11. Scientist's potion renders umbrella mag-
netic.
MAGNETIC VAPOR Lubin 1908 6m. Ref: MPW'08:497. Vapor
gives magnetic powers to user.
The MAGNETIZED MAN (F) Gaum 1907 Ref: MPW 1:622. Lee.
The MAGNIFICENT 6-1/2 (B) CFF/Century 1967 Eastmancolor
serial 6 episodes SP,D: Harry Booth. SP: also Glyn Jones.
PH: Arthur Wooster. Mus: Ivor Slaney. Art D: Peter Proud.
Ref: MFB'68:181. with Len Jones, Ian Ellis, Lionel Hawkes,
George Woodbridge, Peter Madden. Ch. 1. Ghosts and Ghoulies.

Boy initiated into gang by spending hour in haunted house.
The MAGUS (B) Fox/Blazer 1968 Deluxe color/scope 116m.
D: Guy Green. SP: John Fowles, from his novel. PH: Billy
Williams. Mus: John Dankworth. Art D: William Hutchinson.
Prod.Des: Don Ashton. Ref: MFB '69:269. with Michael
Caine, Anthony Quinn, Candice Bergen, Anna Karina, Julian
Glover, Jerome Willis, Corin Redgrave. Villa haunted by ghosts
and fauns.
MAID AND THE MARTIAN, The see PAJAMA PARTY
MAIN DU DIABLE, La see DEVIL'S HAND, The (1942)
MAIN DU SQUELETTE, La see HAND OF THE SKELETON, The
MAIN ENCHANTEE, La (by A. de Musset) DEVIL'S HAND,
The (1942)
MAIN QUI ETREINT, La see GRASPING HAND, The
The MAIN STREET KID Rep 1948 64m. D: R. G. Springsteen.
SP: Jerry Sackheim, from a radio play by Caryl Coleman.
Mus D: Morton Scott. Ref: PM. FDY. with Al Pearce, Janet
Martin, Adele Mara, Roy Barcroft, Byron S. Barr. Man struck
by lightning finds he can read others' minds.
MAINS D'ORLAC, Les (by M. Renard) see HANDS OF A STRANGER
/HANDS OF ORLAC, The (1925/1964)/MAD LOVE
MAISON HANTEE, La see HAUNTED HOUSE, The (1907/1911
Gaum)
MAITRE DE TEMPS, Le see MASTER OF TIME, The
MAJIN (J) Daiei 1966 color/scope 84m. (DAIMAJIN. MAJIN,
THE HIDEOUS IDOL. MAJIN, MONSTER OF TERROR-TV) D:
Kimiyoshi Yasuda. SP: Tetsu(r)o Yoshida. Sequels: MAJIN
STRIKES AGAIN. THE RETURN OF MAJIN. PH: F. Morita.
Mus: Akira Ifukube. Art D: H. Okuda. Ref: FFacts'68.
V 8/14/68. COF 11:46. with Miwa Takada, Yoshihiko Aoyama,
Ryutaro Gomi. Legend in medieval Japan that an immense idol in the
form of a man in ancient armor would one day come to life.
MAJIN NO TSUME see CLAWS OF SATAN
MAJIN STRIKES AGAIN (J) Daiei 1966 (DAIMAJIN GYAKUSHU)
D: Issei Mori, Yoshiyuki Kuroda. Sequel to MAJIN. Ref:
Unij.Bltn. with Hideki Ninomiya, Masahide Iizuka.
MAJIN, THE HIDEOUS IDOL see MAJIN
The MAKER OF DIAMONDS, or, FORTUNE OR MISFORTUNE Vita
1909 (The DIAMOND MAKER) Ref: SF Film. F Index 6/19/09.
Chemist makes diamonds.
MAKING SAUSAGES (B) Smith 1898 Ref: SF Film. Cats and
dogs turned into sausages.
MAKING THE HEADLINES Col 1938 60m. (HOUSE OF MYSTERY.
ALL WERE ENEMIES) D: Lewis D. Collins. SP: Howard J.
Green, Jefferson Parker. PH: James S. Brown. Ref: FD 4/1/38:
"Wild scurrying in and out of a mysterious spooky mansion." FD
1/6/38. Boxo 2/5/38. MPH 1/8/38. with Jack Holt, Beverly
Roberts, Craig Reynolds, Gilbert Emery, Tom Kennedy, John
Wray, Tully Marshall. Ref: MFB'38:74.
MALDICION DE LA LLORONA, La see CURSE OF THE CRYING
WOMAN, The
MALDICION DE LA MOMIA AZTECA, La see CURSE OF THE
AZTEC MUMMY, The

MALDICION DE LOS KARNSTEIN, La   see   TERROR IN THE
CRYPT

MALDICION DE NOSTRADAMUS, La   see CURSE OF NOSTRA-
DAMUS, The

MALE VAMPIRE   see   VAMPIRE MAN

MALEDICTION DE BELPHEGOR, La   see   CURSE OF BELPHEGOR,
The

MALEFICES   see   WITCHCRAFT   (1961)

MALENKA   (Sp-I) Triton-Victory/Cobra-Felix 1968 color/scope 94m.
(La NIPOTE DEL VAMPIRO-I.   The NIECE OF THE VAMPIRE)
SP,D: Amando de Ossorio.   PH: Fulvio Testi.   Mus: Carlo
Savina.   Ref: SpCinema.   M/TVM 8/68.   V 5/8/68:143. with
Anita Ekberg, John Hamilton, Diana Lorys, Julian Ugarte,
Adriana Ambesi.   The Count of Wolduck Castle possesses the
secret of immortality.   Secret passages; woman condemned to
death for practicing witchcraft. (The VAMPIRE'S NIECE)

MALIKA SALOMI   (India) Comedy Pictures 1953 SP,D: Mohamed
Hussein.   Based on "She" by H. Rider Haggard.   PH: V Kamat.
Mus: Iqbal, K. Dayal.   Ref: Filmfare 5/15/53. with Rupa Var-
man, Krishna Kumari, Kamran, Sheikh, Shafi, Nanda, Kamal
Mohan, Helen.   A woman waits 2,000 years for her lover's re-
birth.

MALIKMATA (Fili?) Palaris/Fernando Poe c1967 D: Richard
Abelardo.   Ref: FJA still: "Exciting vampire story." with
Sylvia Rosales.

The MALTESE BIPPY MGM 1969 Metrocolor/scope 92m.
(The INCREDIBLE WEREWOLF MURDERS.   The STRANGE
CASE OF...!#*%?   D: Norman Panama.   SP: Everett Freeman,
Ray Singer.   PH: William H. Daniels.   Mus: Nelson Riddle.
Makeup: William Tuttle.   Prod Man: Kurt Neumann. Ref: LA
Times.   with Dan Rowan, Dick Martin, Carol Lynley, Julie
Newmar, Mildred Natwick, Fritz Weaver, Robert Reed, Dana
Elcar, Arthur Batanides, Pamela Rodgers, Maudie Prickett.
Werewolves; dream with Dracula-type.

MAMY WATTA   see CAGE, The

MAN Yankee/Comet 1911 Ref: Bios 11/14/11. Love in prehistory; spiritualism.

The MAN (India) 1968 (AADMI) Ref: Shankar's 8/18/68. with
Dilip Kumar, Manoj Kumar.   "Fable and miracle, ghost story
and psychological kink are thrown in for good measure....Dis-
embodied voices and miracle cure play their part in overcoming
the homicidal streak in the hero."

The MAN ABC-TV 1971 Ref: TVG.   "James Earl Jones as the
nation's first black President."

MAN ALIVE RKO 1945 70m.   (The AMOROUS GHOST) D: Ray
Enright.   SP: Edwin Blum.   Story: Jerry Cady, John Battle.
PH: Frank Redman. Mus sc: Leigh Harline. Art D: Albert
D'Agostino, Al Herman. SpFX: Vernon L. Walker. Ref: TVK.
FDY.   with Pat O'Brien, Ellen Drew, Adolphe Menjou, Jason
Robards, Rudy Vallee, Fortunio Bonanova, Joseph Crehan, Min-
na Gombell, Jonathan Hale, Jack Norton. Husband thought dead
returns and plays ghost to haunt a suitor away from his wife.

MAN AND HIS MATE   see ONE MILLION B.C.

The MAN AND THE BEAST (Arg) Sono 1951 80m. (El HOMBRE
Y LA BESTIA. El SENSACIONAL Y EXTRAÑO CASO DE EL
HOMBRE Y LA BESTIA. EL EXTRAÑO CASO DEL HOMBRE Y
LA BESTIA) D: Mario Soffici. SP: Ulises Petit de Murat,
from "The Strange Case of Dr. Jekyll and Mr. Hyde" by Robert
Louis Stevenson. PH: Antonio Merayo. Mus: Silvio Vernazza.
Ref: Cine Arg. FM 2:14. with Soffici, Ana Maria Campoy,
Olga Zubarry, Jose Cibrian, Rafael Frontura.

The MAN AND THE MONSTER (Mex) AI-TV/Cinematografica,
A.B.S.A. 1958 (El HOMBRE Y EL MONSTRUO) D: Raphael
Baledon. SP: Alfredo Salazar. PH: Raul M. Solares. Mus:
G. C. Carrion. Story: Raul Zenteno. P: Abel Salazar. Ref:
Indice. FM 29:44. Pic: FMO 1:33. with Salazar, Enrique
Rambal, Marta Roth, A. Baledon, Jose Chavez, Carlos Suarez,
Mary Vela, Ofelia Guilmain. A man sells his soul to the devil
so he can play the piano. Sure.

MAN BEAST Associated producers/Warren (Favorite Films) 1956
P,D: Jerry Warren. SP: B. Arthur Cassidy. PH: Victor Fisher.
Mus D: Josef Zimanich. Assoc P: Ralph Brooke. Ref: MFB
'61:9. TVG. Pic: FM 22:72.54:44. with Rock Madison,
Virginia Maynor, Tom Maruzzi, Lloyd Nelson, George Skaff.
Member of mountain-climbing expedition somehow related to the
Yeti. Some eerie scenes at night with flares distinguish the
usual (terrible) Warren pic.

A MAN CALLED DAGGER MGM 1967 color 82m. D: Richard
Rush. SP: James Peatman, Robert S. Weekley. Ref: MPH
12/20/67. LA Times 5/10/68. with Paul Mantee, Terry Moore,
Jan Murray, Sue Ann Langdon, Eileen O'Neill, Maureen Arthur,
Leonard Stone, Richard Kiel. Mastermind plots to take over
world with aid of mind-controlling devices.

MAN EATER OF KUMAON see BRIDE AND THE BEAST, The

The MAN FROM BEYOND Houdini 1921 75m. D: Burton King.
SP: Harry Houdini, Coolidge Streeter. PH: Frank Zucker, I. B.
Ruby, Harry Fischbeck, A. G. Penrod, L. Dunmyre, L. D.
Littlefield. Ref: AFI. Segment in DAYS OF THRILLS &
LAUGHTER. with Nita Naldi, Arthur Maude, Luis Alberni,
Houdini. Man encased in ice for 100 years in suspended anima-
tion. Ridiculous plot choked with subtitles and florid dialogue.
Hardly anything happens.

MAN FROM MARS, The see RADIO-MANIA

The MAN FROM 1957 WB-TV 1947 56m. From the "King's Row"
TV series. Host: John Conte. Ref: TVFFSB. COF 17:30.
with James Garner, Jacques Sernas, Gloria Talbott, Charles
Ruggles. Being from the beyond; book which foretells the future.

The MAN FROM PLANET ALPHA (J) 1966 Ref: LA Times'67.
S-f-musical-comedy.

The MAN FROM PLANET X UA 1951 70m. D: Edgar G. Ulmer.
P,SP: Aubrey Wisberg, Jack Pollexfen. PH: John L. Russell.
Mus: Charles Koff. Art D: Angelo Scibetti. Ref: Clarens. TVG.
with Robert Clarke, Margaret Field, Raymond Bond, William
Schallert, Roy Engel, Charles Davis. Creature from another
planet arrives on earth. Atmospheric.

MAN FROM THE FIRST CENTURY see MAN IN OUTER SPACE

MAN FROM TOLEDO, The see CAPTAIN FROM TOLEDO
MAN FROM TOMORROW see CYBORG 2087
MAN FROM U.N.C.L.E., The see KARATE KILLERS, The/ONE
  OF OUR SPIES IS MISSING/SPY IN THE GREEN HAT, The/
  SPY WITH MY FACE, The
The MAN FROM YESTERDAY (B) Renown/Int'l Motion Pictures
  1949 68m. D: Oswald Mitchell. SP: John Gilling. PH: Cyril
  Bristow. Ref: MFB'49. TVFFSB. with John Stuart, Henry
  Oscar, Marie Burke, Laurence Harvey, Gwyneth Vaughan.
  Woman wants spiritualist to put her in touch with her dead
  fiancé.
The MAN IN BLACK (B) Eros/Hammer 1949 75m. D: Francis
  Searle. SP: John Gilling. PH: Cedric Williams. P: Antnony
  Hinds. Ref: COF 17:30. MFB'50:10. with Valentine Dyall,
  Betty Ann Davies, Sheila Burrell, Sidney James. Old mansion;
  spirit; man who simulates death.
The MAN IN HALF MOON STREET Para 1944 92m. D: Ralph
  Murphy. SP: Charles Kenyon. From "The Man Who Could
  Cheat Death" by Barre Lyndon. Adap: Garrett Fort. Ref: FDY.
  TVG. PH: Henry Sharp. Mus sc: Miklos Rozsa. Art D: Hans
  Dreier, Walter Tyler. with Helen Walker, Nils Asther, Edmond
  Breon, Paul Cavnagh, Reinhold Schunzel, Morton Lowry, Matthew
  Boulton, Brandon Hurst, Forrester Harvey. Scientist searching
  for secret of eternal youth needs fresh glands from other bodies.
  Rather dull.
MAN IN OUTER SPACE (Cz) AI-TV 1961 85m. (MUZZ
  PRVNIHO STOLETI. MAN OF THE FIRST CENTURY. MAN
  FROM THE FIRST CENTURY. EINSTEIN IS TO BLAME) D:
  Oldrich Lipsky (William Hole, Jr.--U.S.). SP: Munro Manning.
  Ref: MMF 2:46. FJA. SM 8:7. TVG. with Milos Kopecky,
  Radevan Lukavsky. Repairman accidentally launched on spacecraft
  winds up in the earth of the future. A few funny scenes.
MAN IN THE ATTIC Fox 1953 82m. D: Hugo Fregonese. SP:
  Barre Lyndon, Robert Presnell, Jr. From "The Lodger" by
  Marie Belloc-Lowndes. PH: Leo Tover. Art D: Lyle Wheeler,
  Leland Fuller. Ref: FDY. COF 9:60. Pic:TBG. with Jack
  Palance, Constance Smith, Frances Bavier, Rhys Williams, Sean
  McClory, Lilian Bond, Isabel Jewell. Jack the Ripper.
MAN IN THE DARK Col 1953 68m. D: Lew Landers. SP: George
  Bricker, Jack Leonard. Adap: William Sackheim. Story: Tom
  Van Dycke, Henry Altimus. PH: Floyd Crosby. Art D: John
  Meehan. Ref: FDY. Remake of THE MAN WHO LIVED TWICE.
  with Edmond O'Brien, Audrey Totter, Ted de Corsia, Horace
  McMahon, Dayton Lummis, Shepard Menken. Operation makes
  man lose memory and criminal instincts.
The MAN IN THE MOON (F) Gaum 1909 Ref: MPW 5:99. 5m.
  Balloon takes man into space.
MAN IN THE MOON (B) T-L/Allied-Excalibur 1960 98m. D:
  Basil Dearden, Norman Harrison. SP: Dearden, Michael Relph.
  PH: Harry Waxman. Mus: Philip Green. Art D: Jack Maxted.
  Prod des: Don Ashton. Ref: FFacts. SM 2:12. V 11/16/60:
  "Spoof of science fiction." with Kenneth More, Shirley Anne
  Field, Norman Bird, Michael Hordern, Charles Gray, Noel

Purcell, Jeremy Lloyd.
MAN IN THE MOONLIGHT MASK (J) Toei 1958 scope (GEKKO
KAMEN. The MOONBEAM MAN) 102m. D: Tsuneo Koyayashi.
SP: Yasuhiro Kawauchi. PH: Ichiro Hoshijima. Ref: FEFN
10/3/58. UFQ 2. See also CHALLENGING GHOST, The. LAST
DEATH OF THE DEVIL, The. MONSTER GORILLA, The. with
Fumitake Omura, Junya Usami, Hiroko Mine, Mitsue Komiya.
"H-O-Joe Bomb" secrets; "Skull Mask"; Gekko Kamen, a super-
being from outer space.
The MAN IN THE TRUNK Fox 1942 71m. D: Mal St. Clair. SP:
John Larkin. PH: Glenn MacWilliams. Ref: FDY. with Lynne
Roberts, George Holmes, Raymond Walburn, J. Carrol Naish,
Eily Malyon, Milton Parsons, Matt McHugh, Theodore von Eltz,
Syd Saylor, Douglas Fowley, Tim Ryan. Bookmaker's ghost re-
turns to track down his murderer.
The MAN IN THE WHITE CLOAK (Dan) Greta Northern 1913 45m.
Ref: MPW 16:945. Lee. Spectre; the supernatural.
The MAN IN THE WHITE SUIT (B) Univ/Ealing 1951 85m.
SP, D: Alexander MacKendrick. SP: also Roger MacDougall,
John Dighton. PH: Douglas Slocombe. Mus: Benjamin Frankel.
Art D: Jim Morhan. P: Michael Balcon. Ref: FDY. FM 12:24.
with Alec Guinness, Joan Greenwood, Ernest Thesiger, Cecil
Parker, Michael Gough, Howard Marion Crawford, Duncan La-
mont, Harold Goodwin, Colin Gordon. Scientist invents cloth
that won't tear or soil. Good British comedy, with some in-
spired comic moments.
MAN, INC. (Canadian) 1970 NFB D: Jacques Languirand. Ref:
M/TVM 6/70:41. with Don Francks, Patricia Collins. Story of
man from Genesis to the year 2001.
MAN MADE MONSTER Univ 1941 59m. (ATOMIC MONSTER.
The MYSTERIOUS DR. R) D: George Waggner. SP: Joseph West,
from the story "The Electric Man" by H. J. Essex, Sid Schwartz,
and Len Golos. PH: Elwood Bredell. Mus sc: H. J. Salter. Ref:
FDY. HM 6:18. COF 6:20. Pic: FM 2:12. 7:45. 11:2. 69:42.
FMO 6:9. with Lon Chaney, Jr., Lionel Atwill, Anne Nagel,
Frank Albertson, Samuel S. Hinds, William Davidson, Frank
O'Connor, Byron Foulger, Russell Hicks. After a series of ex-
periments a man finds himself invulnerable to electric shock.
80% unimproved cliches. Chaney is electrifying but not too
good. A good de-electrocution scene. Mentioned in The OWL
AND THE PUSSYCAT.
The MAN MONKEY (F) Pathe 1909 7m. Ref: F Index. Hyp-
notist replaces man's brain with monkey's brain.
The MAN MONKEY (B) C&M 1911 7m. (A BAG OF MONKEY
NUTS) Ref: Bios 11/12/11. "Monkey nuts" make man act like
monkey.
MAN OF A THOUSAND FACES Univ 1957 scope 122m. D:
Joseph Pevney. SP: R. Wright Campbell, Ivan Goff, Ben
Roberts. Story: Ralph Wheelright. PH: Russell Metty. Mus:
Frank Skinner. Art D: Alexander Golitzen, Eric Orbom. Ref:
V 7/16/57. with James Cagney (Lon Chaney), Dorothy Malone,
Jane Greer, Jim Backus, Robert Evans, Marjorie Rambeau,
Roger Smith (Lon Chaney, Jr.), Celia Lovsky, Jeanne Cagney,

Jack Albertson, Simon Scott, Clarence Kolb, Philip Van Zandt, Hank Mann, Snub Pollard. Scenes from Chaney's PHANTOM OF THE OPERA, MIRACLE MAN, HUNCHBACK OF NOTRE DAME recreated. You wouldn't have thought that Lon Chaney's life could become one of Universal's glossy soapers, but it did. Still, often interesting. Cagney very good.

The MAN OF MYSTERY Vita 1917 55m. Ref: MPN 15:274. with E. H. Sothern, Charlotte Ives, Vilda Varesi. Man caught in "intense heat and sulphur fumes of an eruption of Mt. Vesuvius" finds himself twenty years younger and cured of his deformity.

MAN OF THE FIRST CENTURY see MAN IN OUTER SPACE

The MAN OF THE WAX FIGURES (F) 1913 (L'HOMME AUX FIG-URES DE CIRE) D: Maurice Tourneur. Ref: COF 16:18. Orpheus 2:20. DDC II:308: Fantasy.

The MAN THEY COULD NOT HANG Col 1939 D: Nick Grinde. SP: Karl Brown. Story: George Sayre, Leslie White. PH: Benjamin Kline. Mus: M. W. Stoloff. Ref: Clarens. FM 2:32. ModM 1:24. with Boris Karloff, Lorna Gray, Robert Wilcox, Roger Pryor, Ann Doran, Don Beddoe, Charles Trowbridge, James Craig, Byron Foulger. Man restored to life seeks revenge on those responsible for his death. Routine at best.

The MAN THEY COULDN'T ARREST (B) Gainsborough 1931 72m. D: T. Hayes Hunter. SP: Hunter, Angus MacPhail. Dial: Arthur Wimperis. PH: Leslie Rowson. Based on the story by "Seamark." Ref: NYT 3/14/33. with Hugh Wakefield ("The Ghost"), Gordon Harker, Garry Marsh, Nicholas Hannen, Dennis Wyndham. An inventor's wireless apparatus enables him to listen in on the conferences of a murderous gang of jewel thieves.

MAN WANTS TO LIVE! (F-I) Societe Nouvelle-Romana 1961 110m. (LES HOMMES VEULENT VIVRE!) D, P: Leonide Moguy. PH: André Villard. Mus: Joseph Kosma. Art D: Rino Mondellini. Ref: La Prod. Cin. Fr. 7/61. DDC III:62, 327. with Claudio Gora, John Justin, Yves Massard, Jacqueline Huet, Death ray.

MAN WHO CAME FROM UMMO, The see DRACULA VS. FRANKENSTEIN

MAN WHO CHANGED HIS MIND, The see MAN WHO LIVED AGAIN, The

MAN WHO CHEATED LIFE, The see STUDENT OF PRAGUE, The (1926)

MAN WHO COLLECTED POE, The (by R. Bloch) see TORTURE GARDEN

The MAN WHO COULD CHEAT DEATH (B) Para/Cadogan/Ham-mer 1959 Technicolor 83m. D: Terence Fisher. SP: Jimmy Sangster, from the book by Barre Lyndon. See also The MAN IN HALF MOON STREET. PH: Jack Asher. Mus: Richard Bennett. Art D: Bernard Robinson. with Anton Diffring, Hazel Court, Christopher Lee. Protagonist remains young through gland operation every ten years. -PM.

The MAN WHO COULD WORK MIRACLES (B) UA/London 1936 82m. D: Lothar Mendes. SP: H. G. Wells. PH: Maurice Forde, Bernard Browne. P: Alexander Korda. Ref: FD 2/24/37.

Brit. Cinema. FM 10:26. with Roland Young, Ralph Richard-
son, George Zucco, George Sanders, Joan Gardner, Ernest
Thesiger, Lady Tree, Sophie Stewart, Bernard Nedell. Clerk
becomes ruler of world and commands earth to stand still.
MAN WHO COULDN'T SLEEP, The (by C. E. Maine) see ELEC-
TRONIC MONSTER, The
The MAN WHO HAUNTED HIMSELF (B) Warner-Pathe/EMI/As-
sociated British 1970 Technicolor 94m. SP, D: Basil Dearden.
SP: also Michael Relph, from a novel by Anthony Armstrong.
PH: Tony Spratling. Mus: Michael J. Lewis. Art D: Albert
Witherick. SpFX: Tommy Howard. Ref: V 7/29/70. with Roger
Moore, Hildegard Neil, Thorley Walters, Charles Lloyd Pack,
John Carson. Man dies for a few moments on operating table,
enabling his "other self" to escape.
The MAN WHO LAUGHS (F) 1909 (L'HOMME QUI RIT) from
Hugo. Ref: DDC III:503.
The MAN WHO LAUGHS (Austrian) Olympic Film 1921 90m.
(Das GRINSENDE GESICHT) D: Julius Herzka. SP: Louis Nerz,
from the book by Hugo. PH: Eduard Hosch. Art D: Ladislaus
Tuszynsky. Ref: Osterr. with Franz Hobling, Nora Gregor,
Lucienne Delacroix, Anna Kallina, Eugen Jensen, A. Seydelmann,
Fritz StraBny.
The MAN WHO LAUGHS Univ 1928 silent 90m. D: Paul Leni.
SP: J. Grubb Alexander, from the novel by Victor Hugo. PH:
Gilbert Warrenton. P: Carl Laemmle. Ref: Clarens. SilentFF.
Pic: FM 2:2. 16:11. 21:15. 29:17. 80:46. with Conrad Veidt, Mary
Philbin, Olga Baclanova, Brandon Hurst. A child whose face
has been horribly disfigured joins a travelling circus. After a
good, plotty beginning the film settles down into a lot of long, dull
takes in which nothing much happens.
The MAN WHO LAUGHS (I-F) Sanson/CIPRA 1965 (L'UOMO
CHE RIDE) SP, D: Sergio Corbucci. SP: also Rossetti, Ronconi,
PH: Enzo Barboni. Mus: Piero Piccioni. From Hugo's novel.
P: Joseph Fryd. Ref: Ital P: COF 9:46. SP: also Filippo San-
just, Issaverdens, Bertolotto. with Jean Sorel, Ilaria Occhini,
Edmund Purdom, Lisa Gastoni, Linda Sini.
The MAN WHO LIVED AGAIN (B) Univ/Gaum 1936 61m. (The
MAN WHO CHANGED HIS MIND. DR. MANIAC. The BRAIN-
SNATCHER) D: Robert Stevenson. SP: Sidney Gilliat, L. Du-
Garde Peach. Story: John Balderston. PH: Jack Cox. Ref: FDY.
COF 1:45. FM 2:34. 48:50. Pic: MW 2:18. with Boris Karloff,
Anna Lee, John Loder, Frank Cellier, Lyn Harding, Cecil
Parker, Donald Calthrop. Doctor transplants brains from one
body to another.
The MAN WHO LIVED TWICE Col 1936 73m. Remake: MAN IN
THE DARK. D: Harry Lachman. SP: Tom Van Dycke, Arthur
Strawn, Fred Niblo, Jr. Story: Van Dycke, Henry Altimus. PH:
James Van Trees. Ref: FDY. COF 17:31. Pic: FM-A'69:29.
with Ralph Bellamy, Isabel Jewell, Ward Bond, Marian Marsh,
Thurston Hall, Henry Kolker, Willard Robertson. Operation
eliminates man's criminal tendencies and all memory of his past.
The MAN WHO MADE DIAMONDS (B) First Nat'l 1937 73m.
D: Ralph Ince. Ref: MFB'37. with Noel Madison, Lesley

Brook, George Galleon, Wilfrid Lawson. High tension cable provides power for making artificial diamonds.

The MAN WHO RECLAIMED HIS HEAD Univ 1934 80m. Remake:
STRANGE CONFESSION. D: Edward Ludwig. SP: Jean Bart,
from the play by Jean Bart. PH: Merritt Gerstad. Ref: FDY.
Photoplay 3/35. FM 47:15. with Claude Rains, Lionel Atwill,
Joan Bennett, Baby Jane, Henry O'Neill, Wallace Ford, Gilbert
Emery, Henry Armetta, Lawrence Grant, Rollo Lloyd, F.
Gottschalk. Man carries around sinister hatbox supposedly containing head.

The MAN WHO SAW TOMORROW Para 1922 80m. D: Alfred E.
Green. SP: Frank Condon, Will Ritchey. PH: Alvin Wyckoff.
Story: Perley Poole Sheehan, F. Condon. Ref: MPN 26:2433.
Lee. AFI. with Alec Francis, Leatrice Joy, Eva Novak,
Theodore Roberts, Thomas Meighan. Man sees future with hypnotism.

The MAN WHO SOLD HIS SOULD TO THE DEVIL (F) 1920
(L'HOMME QUI VENDIT SON AME AU DIABLE) D: Pierre
Caron. PH: Andre A. Dantan. Ref: DDC II:10, 308: Fantasy.

The MAN WHO SOLD HIS SOUL TO THE DEVIL (F\ 1943 90m.
(L'HOMME QUI VENDIT SON AME AU DIABLE) D: J.-P. Paulin. Ref: Rep.Gen'47:263. DDC II:55. III:251. with André
Luguet, Jean-Jacques Delbo, M. Alfa, Robert Le Vigan (devil),
Larquey, J. Perrier, M. Goya. A banker, on the brink of
committing suicide out of despair, makes a pact with the devil.
His bank becomes a great success, but he must use the money to
do evil.

The MAN WHO THOUGHT THINGS (Dan) Palladium/Asa 1969
97m. (MANDEM DER TAENKTE TING) D: Jens Ravn. SP:
Ravn, Henrik Stangerup, from a book by V. Holst. PH: W.
Leszczynski. Mus: Per Noergaard. Ref: V 5/21/69. with
Preben Neergaard, Lotte Tarp, John Price. Man wills cigars,
brandy, double of doctor into existence; needs brain operation to
keep living things alive.

The MAN WHO TURNED TO STONE Col/Clover 1957 71m.
(The PETRIFIED MAN) D: Leslie Kardos. SP: Raymond T.
Marcus. PH: Benjamin H. Kline. Mus D: Ross DiMaggio.
Art D: Paul Palmentola. P: Sam Katzman.Ref: FDY. with Ann
Doran, Victor Jory, Charlotte Austin, William Hudson, Paul
Cavanagh, Tina Carver, Jean Willes, Victor Varconi,
Friedrich Ledebur, George Lynn, Barbara Wilson. Group perpetuates itself by transferring the vitality of young women into
its veins. Not bad--for a Katzman dud.

The MAN WHO WANTED TO LIVE FOREVER (Canadian-U.S.)
ABC-TV/Palomar 1970 color 72m. (The ONLY WAY OUT IS
DEAD. The HEART FARM) D: John Trent. SP: Henry Denker.
PH: Marc Champion. Ref: V 11/17/71. TVG. RVB. with
Burl Ives, Stuart Whitman, Sandy Dennis, Jack Creley, Ron
Hartman, Tom Harvey.

The MAN WHO WOULDN'T DIE Fox 1942 65m. D: Herbert
Leeds. SP: Arnaud D'Usseau, from Clayton Rawson's "No
Coffin for the Corpse." PH: Joseph P. MacDonald. Art D:
R. Day, Lewis Creber. Ref: FDY. with Lloyd Nolan, Marjorie

Weaver, Richard Derr, Henry Wilcoxon, Billy Bevan, Robert Emmett Keane, Jeff Corey, Francis Ford, Olin Howland. Man buried as dead returns. Scientist experiments in prolonging life. The kind of mystery in which nobody makes a move without someone's spying on them.

The MAN WITH NINE LIVES Col 1940 73m. (BEHIND THE DOOR-Eng) D: Nick Grinde. SP: Karl Brown, Harold Shumate. PH: Benjamin Kline. Ref: Clarens. FM 2:34. Pic: FM 56:13. with Boris Karloff, Jo Ann Sayers, Roger Pryor, Stanley Brown, John Dilson, Byron Foulger, Hal Taliaferro, Charles Trowbridge, Ernie Adams. Machine restores the dead to life. One of the worst in Karloff's Columbia series.

MAN WITH THE ELECTRIC VOICE, The see FIFTEEN WIVES

The MAN WITH THE IRON HEAD (B) C&M 1912 7m. Ref: Bios 5/9/12. Hammers bounce harmlessly off man's "iron head."

MAN WITH THE MAGNETIC EYES (B) British Foundation 1945 52m. SP, D: Ron Haines. PH: Stanley Fletcher. From a novel by Roland Daniel. Ref: MFB'45:70. with Robert Bradfield, Henry Norman, Joan Carter. Bogus count hypnotizes with magnetic eyes.

The MAN WITH THE RUBBER HEAD (F) Melies/Star 1902 3m. (L'HOMME A LA TETE DE CAOUTCHOUC) Ref: SilentFF. Scientist attaches bellows to head and inflates it.

MAN WITH THE YELLOW EYES, The see PLANETS AGAINST US, The

MAN WITH TWO FACES F Nat 1934 72m. (The MYSTERIOUS MR. CHAUTARD) D: Archie Mayo. SP: Tom Reed, Niven Busch, from "Dark Tower" by George S. Kaufman and Alexander Woollcott. PH: Tony Gaudio. Ref: Photoplay. FDY. with Louis Calhern, Mary Astor, Edward G. Robinson, Ricardo Cortez, Mae Clarke, Henry O'Neill, John Eldredge. Villain keeps woman under hypnotic spell.

The MAN WITH TWO LIVES Mono 1942 65m. D: Phil Rosen. SP: Joseph Hoffman. PH: Harry Neumann. Mus D: Frank Sanucci. Ref: V 3/9/42. HR 3/9/42. with Edward Norris, Marlo Dwyer, Eleanor Lawson, Frederick Burton, Addison Richards, Edward Keane, Hugh Sothern, Anthony Warde, Ernie Adams, Kenneth Duncan, Jack Ingraham, George Kirby. Killer's soul transmigrated at death into another body.

MAN WITH X-RAY EYES, The see X, THE MAN WITH X-RAY EYES

The MAN WITHOUT A BODY (B) Eros/Filmplays Ltd. 1957 80m. D: W. Lee Wilder, Charles Saunders. SP: William Grote. PH: Brendan Stafford. Mus: Robert Elms. Pic: FanMo 2:34. with Robert Hutton, George Coulouris, Julia Arnall, Nadja Regin, Kim Parker, Tony Quinn, Michael Golden (Nostradamus). Fancy directorial touches wasted on story which reaches awesome heights of ludicrousness ("You know it's odd this head living on your dead assistant's body. Quick thinking, doctor").

MAN WITHOUT A BODY, The see THING THAT COULDN'T DIE, The

The MAN WITHOUT A FACE (Mex) Azteca 1950 (EL HOMBRE
SIN ROSTRO) SP, D: J. Bustillo Oro. PH: Jorge Stahl, Jr.
Mus: Raul Lavista. Ref: FM 31:22. FDY'51. Laclos. Lee.
with Fernando Galiana, Carmen Molino.

The MAN WITHOUT A SOUL (B) London 1916 D: George Loane
Tucker. Ref: Hist. Brit. Film. with Barbara Everest (or Everett),
Milton Rosmer, Edward O'Neill, Kitty Cavendish, Hubert Willis,
Charles Rock. "Man brought back from the dead totally lacking
in moral sense."

The MAN WITHOUT DESIRE (B) Atlas-Biograph 1923 60m.
P, D: Adrian Brunel. Story: Monckton Hoffe. SP: Frank Fowell.
PH: Henry Harris. Ref: COF 16:31. SilentFF. NYT 1/13/24.
with Ivor Novello, Nina Vanna, Sergio Mari, Brunel. Hero put
into hypnotic sleep by scientist for 200 years.

The MANCHURIAN CANDIDATE UA 1962 126m. D: John Frank-
enheimer. SP: George Axelrod, from the novel by Richard Con-
don. PH: Lionel Lindon. Mus: David Amram. Prod Des:
Richard Sylbert. Sets: George R. Nelson. SpFX: Paul Pollard.
PH FX: Howard Anderson Co. Ed: Ferris Webster. Ass't D:
Joseph Behm. Exec P: Howard W. Koch. See also The PSYCHO
LOVER. with Frank Sinatra, Laurence Harvey, Janet Leigh,
Angela Lansbury, Henry Silva, James Gregory, Leslie Parrish,
John McGiver, Khigh Dhiegh, James Edwards, Lloyd Corrigan,
Whit Bissell, Mickey Finn, Robert Burton, Douglas Henderson,
Barry Kelly, Reggie Nalder, Helen Kleeb, Bess Flowers, Harry
Holcomb, James Yagi. American brainwashed, ordered to kill
in Communist plot against U.S. Offbeat, sometimes brilliant
political s-f becomes a little too strange when it tries (as the
book tries too) to make the unloveable Raymond human. Powerful, spectacular violence is somehow mixed with misanthropic
humor, somehow to the advantage of both.

MANDEM DER TAENKTE TING see MAN WHO THOUGHT
THINGS, The

MANDRAKE see ALRAUNE (1928/1930/1952)

MANDRAKE LA FILLE SANS AME see ALRAUNE (1952)

MANDRAKE, THE MAGICIAN Col 1939 serial 12 episodes D:
Sam Nelson, Norman Deming. SP: J. F. Poland, B. Dickey,
Ned Dandy. Based on the King Features comic by Lee Falk and
Phil Davis. PH: Ben Kline. Ref: Barbour. FD 5/11/39: "New
death-dealing machine." with Warren Hull, Doris Weston, Don
Beddoe, George Chesebro, George Turner, Ernie Adams, Al
Kikume.

MANEATER OF HYDRA see ISLAND OF THE DOOMED

MANFISH UA 1956 DeLuxe color 76m. (CALYPSO) P, D: W.
Lee Wilder. SP: Joel Murcott. From "The Tell-Tale Heart"
and "The Gold Bug" by Edgar Allan Poe. Story: Myles Wilder.
PH: Charles S. Wellborn. Mus sc & d: Albert Elms. with
Victor Jory, Lon Chaney, Jr., John Bromfield, Barbara Nichols,
Vincent Chang. "The Tell-Tale Heart" figures fleetingly and in-
geniously in this otherwise very poor adventure film as tell-tale
bubbles from a drowning man's body.

MANGU (India-Hindustani) Sheikh Mukhtar Prod. 1955 D: N. A.
Ansari. SP: Takir Luckowi. Lyrics: Majrooh Sultanpuri. PH:

S. Srivastava. Ref: Filmindia 4/55. with Nigar Sultana, Mukhtar, Sheila Ramani, Mukri, Ansari, Baby Shashi. A crook invents a serum which makes the person injected with it his slave for a short time.

MANHATTAN SHAKEDOWN (Canadian) Columbia/Central 1938 57m. D: Leon Barsha. Ref: MFB'38. with John Gallaudet, Rosalind Keith. "Climax takes place in strange house where a hooded villain renders the protagonists unconscious by tapping them on the neck with an electric stick."

MANHUNT IN SPACE MCA-TV 1954 From the "Rocky Jones, Space Ranger" TV series. with Richard Crane, Sally Mansfield. Invisible space ship.

MANHUNT OF MYSTERY ISLAND Rep 1945 serial 15 episodes (CAPTAIN MEPHISTO AND THE TRANSFORMATION MACHINE- '66 feature) D: Yakima Canutt, S. G. Bennet, Wallace Grissell. SP: A. Demond, B. Dickey, A. Duffy, A. James, G. Nelson, J. Poland. Ref: Barbour. STI 3:17. with Richard Bailey, Linda Stirling, Roy Barcroft, Kenne Duncan, Forrest Taylor, Forbes Murray, Jack Ingram, Dale Van Sickel, Tom Steele, Edward Cassidy, Lane Chandler. "Transformation Chair" re-arranges the molecular structure of a man's blood so that he can become "at will an exact counterpart of the original Mephisto." "Radi-atomic Power Transmitter."

MANI DELL'ALTRO, Le see HANDS OF ORLAC, The (1964)

MANIA (B) Valiant-Pacemaker/Eros/Regal Int'l 1960 97m. (The FLESH AND THE FIENDS. The FIENDISH GHOULS) SP,D: John Gilling. SP: also Leon Griffiths. P: Monty Berman, Bob Baker. with Donald Pleasence, Peter Cushing, June Laverick, Dermot Walsh, George Rose, Ian Fleming. Grave robbers supply bodies for experiments in reworking of the Burke and Hare story. Cushing and Rose are good, Pleasence is even better in other-wise shoddy production. Spectacularly well-acted for what it is.

MANIAC Roadshow 1934 70m. (SEX MANIAC) D: Dwain Esper. SP: Hildegarde Stadie. From "The Black Cat" by Edgar Allan Poe. Ref: FD 1/7/36. FIR'62:62. with Phyllis Diller. Mad scientist.

MANNEN UTAN ANSIKTE see FACE OF FIRE

MANO DE UN HOMBRE MUERTO, La see HAND OF A DEAD MAN, The

MANO EN LA TRAMPA, La see HAND IN THE TRAP, The

MANOIR DU DIABLE, Le see DEVIL'S CASTLE, The

MANOIR MAUDIT, Le see TOMB OF TORTURE

MANOS--THE HANDS OF FATE c1966 color 65m. Ref: TVFFSB. Emerson with Tom Neyman, John Reynolds. Family in desert comes across cult of "Night People" that defaces beautiful woman with a "burning hand."

MAN'S GENESIS 1912 Ref: Bios 8/29/12. FM 63:28. Prehistoric village.

The MANSTER (U.S.-J) Lopert/Shaw-Breakston 1962 (1960) 72m. D: George Breakston, Kenneth G. Crane. SP: Walter Sheldon, from the story "Nightmare" by Breakston. (The SPLIT) PH: David Mason. Mus: Hirooki Ogawa. Ref: FM 25:4. PM. Orpheus 3:29. FFacts. with Peter Dyneley, Jane Hylton,

Satoshi Nakamura. A Japanese scientist splits a man's person-
ality. Really crummy; almost nauseating at times.
MANTIS IN LACE Boxoffice Int'l 1968 color 73m. D: William
Rotsler. SP, P: Sanford White. PH:Leslie Kovacs. Mus: Frank
Coe. Sets: Frank Borass. Makeup:Mike Welson. Ref: FJA.
Boxo 9/2/68. with Susan Stewart, Steve Vincent, M. K. Evans,
Pat Barrington, Vic Lance. Woman under LSD commits cleaver
murders.
MANUGANG NI DRAKULA, Mga see SECRETS OF DRACULA, The
MANUSCRIPT FOUND IN SARAGOSSA see SARAGOSSA MANU-
SCRIPT, The
MANUTARA see VULTURE, The
MANY GHOST CATS see PHANTOM CAT, The
MARBLE FOREST, The (by T. Durrant) see MACABRE
MARC MATO, AGENTE S.007 see ESPIONAGE IN TANGIERS
MARCA DE SATANAS, La see MARK OF SATAN, The
MARCA DEL HOMBRE LOBO, La see MARK OF THE WOLFMAN,
The
MARCA DEL MUERTO, La see MARK OF DEATH, The
MARCH OF MONSTERS, The see OPERATION MONSTERLAND
MARCH OF THE WOODEN SOLDIERS MGM 1934 73m. (RE-
VENGE IS SWEET) D: Gus Meins, Charles R. Rogers. From
the operetta "Babes in Toyland" by Glen McDonough and Victor
Herbert. PH: Nick Grinde. Ref: FD 11/12/34. Movie Comedy
Teams. Pauline Kael: "Horror scenes at end" with the Bogeymen.
Pic: TBG. with Stan Laurel, Oliver Hardy, Charlotte Henry,
Johnny Downs, Henry Brandon, Marie Wilson, Angelo Rossitto,
Dick Alexander. SP: Grinde, Frank Butler. Mixture of comedy,
horror, and music is pretty good fun.
MARGUERITE OF THE NIGHT (F-I) Del Duca Film 1955
(MARGUERITE DE LA NUIT) D: Claude Autant-Lara. SP:
Ghislaine Autant-Lara, Gabriel Aout, from a story by Pierre
MacOrlan based on the "Faust" legend. PH: Jacques Natteau.
Mus: Lucien Cloerec Ref: Le Surrealism au Cinema. with Yves
Montand, Michele Morgan, Palau.
MARIA MARTEN see MURDER IN THE RED BARN
MARIA, THE WONDERFUL WEAVER see MAGIC WEAVER, The
MARIANNE OF MY YOUTH (F-G) United Motion Picture Organiza-
tion/Royal/Filmsonor-Regina-Allfram 1954 ('59-U.S.) 105m.
(MARIANNE. MARIANNE DE MA JEUNESSE) SP,D: Julien
Duvivier From the novel "Sorrowful Arcadia" or "Douloureuse
Arcadie" by Peter de Mendelssohn. PH: L. H. Burel. Mus sc:
Jacques Ibert. Sets: Jean D'Eaubonne. Ref: DDC III:46. FFacts.
Pic: DDC II:162. with Marianne Hold, Pierre Vaneck, Adi
Berber, Isabella Pia. Female phantom haunts castle.
MARIPOSAS NEGRAS see BLACK BUTTERFLIES
MARK DONEN AGENT 27 (I-Sp-G) CA. PI./Agata/Planet 1966 90m.
(KARATE A TANGIER POUR AGENT 27. MARK DONEN AGENTE
27. MARK DONEN AGENTE ZETA 7) SP,D: Giancarlo Romitelli.
SP: also Ennio De Concini, R. Veller. PH: G. Mancori. Ref:
Annuario. with Lang Jeffries, Laura Velanzuela, Carlo Hinter-
man, Mitsouko. A German scientist has developed a weapon that
uses the sun's rays.

The MARK OF DEATH (Mex) Alameda 1962 (La MARCA DEL
MUERTO) SP, D: Fernando Cortes. SP: also A. Varela, Jr.
PH: Jose O. Ramos. Mus: G. C. Carrion. Story: J. M. F.
Unsain. Ref: FM 33:10, 12. Pic: FM 38:39: man in horror make-
up. with Fernando Casanova, Sonia Furio, E. Espino.
The MARK OF SATAN (Mex) Clasa 1958 (La MARCA DE SATANAS)
Ref: FM 31: 22: fantasy. Lee still: man in disguise. with Luis
Aguilar, Flor Silvestre, Crox Alvarado, Pascual G. Pena.
MARK OF TERROR see DRUMS OF JEOPARDY
MARK OF THE CLAW see GIANT CLAW, The
MARK OF THE DEVIL (W. G. -B) Atlas 1970 color (BRENN;
HEXE, BRENN. HEXEN BIS AUF BLUT GEQUALT) D:
Michael Armstrong. Mus: Michael Holm. Ref: Fernsehen
2/70. COF 15:16. V 5/20/70. with Herbert Lom, Herbert
Fux, Ingeborg Schöner, Gaby Fuchs. Witchcraft, torture, witch-
finder.
MARK OF THE VAMPIRE MGM 1935 85m. (VAMPIRES OF
PRAGUE) D: Tod Browning. SP: Guy Endore, Bernard Schu-
bert. Remake of LONDON AFTER MIDNIGHT. PH: James Wong
Howe. Art D: Cedric Gibbons. Ed: Ben Lewis. P: E. J. Man-
nix. Ref: Academy. RVB. FM 46:76. COF 17:60. Pic: MW
9:27. with Lionel Barrymore, Elizabeth Allan, Bela Lugosi,
Lionel Atwill, Jean Hersholt, Henry Wadsworth, Donald Meek,
Jessie Ralph, Ivan Simpson, Leila Bennett, Carol (or Carroll)
Borland, Holmes Herbert, June Gittelson, Michael Visaroff,
Franklyn Ardell, Eily Malyon, Zeffie Tilbury, Rosemary Glosz,
Baron Hesse, Egon Brecher, Christian Rub, Robert Greig,
Torben Meyer. Mystery-horror: The mystery doesn't work
(clever as the finale is), but the horror does--astonishingly well.
Howe's photography and the unusual sound effects give the vampire
scenes a cold, beautiful sense of unearthliness that goes far beyond
the usual fog-and-cobweb atmospherics of similar movies. The
only thing wrong with these sequences is that they're often too
tantalizingly brief, though well-alternated for pace with the
mystery-comedy scenes. Lugosi is grand throughout, though a
bit differently in the last scene. Breathtaking special effects.
MARK OF THE VAMPIRE see VAMPIRE, The (1957-UA)
MARK OF THE WEST see CURSE OF THE UNDEAD
The MARK OF THE WOLFMAN (Sp) Maxper 1967 color /70mm /3-d /
Hi-Fi Stereo 133m. (La MARCA DEL HOMBRE LOBO or EL
HOMBRE LOBO-Sp. Der WOLFSMENSCH or Die VAMPIRE DES
DR. DRACULA-G. HELL'S CREATURES-Belg. FRANKEN-
STEIN'S BLOODY TERROR-U. S.) D: Enrique L. Eguiluz. SP:
Jacinto Molina. PH: Emilio Foriscot. Mus: Angel Arteaga. Art
D: J. L. R. Ferrer. Ref: SpCinema. Film 4/68, 2/69. with
Manuel Manzaneque, Aurora de Alba, Jose Nieto, Dianik
Zurakowska, Paul Naschy, Diane Konopka, Julian Ugarte. The
Wolfman's bite turns a man into a werewolf. Vampires. The
old props look better in 3-D (the cobwebs should get top billing)
but nothing could help the plot which argues, at great length, that
lycanthropy is incurable. (There's no end to such surprises.)
Very bad.
MAROONED Col 1969 Technicolor 134m. D: John Sturges.

SP: Mayo Simon, from Martin Caidin's novel. PH: Daniel Fapp.
Prod Des: Lyle R. Wheeler. SpFX: Butler-Glouner-Robinson.
Ref: V 11/19/69. with Gregory Peck, Richard Crenna, David
Janssen, James Franciscus, Gene Hackman, Lee Grant, Nancy
Kovack, Mariette Hartley, Scott Brady, Walter Brooke. Lunar
rocket fails to fire for reentry to earth's gravity.
The MARRIAGE OF PSYCHE AND CUPID 1914 30m. Ref: MPW
20:944. Psyche visits Proserpine, "queen of the underworld."
MARRIAGE OF THE BEAR (Russ) Amkino/Mezhrabpom-Russ 1926
94m. (LEGEND OF THE BEAR'S WEDDING) D: Konstantin V.
Eggert. SP: A. Lunacharsky. From Prosper Merimee's "Lokis."
PH: E. Tisse, P. Ermolov. Ref: FD 12/23/28. Lee. with
Eggert, Vera Malanovskaya. Man-bear. "Weird...morbid."
MARS AT EASTER see DON'T PLAY WITH MARTIANS
MARS AT LENT see DON'T PLAY WITH MARTIANS
MARS ATTACKS PUERTO RICO see FRANKENSTEIN MEETS
THE SPACEMONSTER
MARS ATTACKS THE WORLD see FLASH GORDON'S TRIP TO
MARS
MARS EN CAREME see DON'T PLAY WITH MARTIANS
MARS, GOD OF WAR see VENUS AGAINST THE SON OF
HERCULES
MARS NEEDS WOMEN AI-TV/Azalea 1964 color 80m. SP, D:
Larry Buchanan. PH: Robert C. Jessup. Ref: RVB. TVG.
with Tommy Kirk, Byron Lord, Yvonne Craig. Mars is in need
of five women for its genetic experiments.
MARS PROJECT see CONQUEST OF SPACE
MARTA (Sp-I) Atlantida/Cinemar 1971 color 100m. SP, D:
J. A. N. Conde. SP: also J. J. A. Millan, Lopez Aranda.
From the story "Estado Civil: Marta" by Millan. PH: Ennio
Guarnierri. Mus: Piero Piccione. Art D: R. Calatayud. Ref:
V. with Marisa Mell, Stephen Boyd, Jesus Puente, Isa Miranda.
"Horrific innuendo." Madman keeps dead wife's body in suit of
armor. Torture chamber.
MARTE, DIO DELLA GUERRA see VENUS AGAINST THE SON OF
HERCULES
MARTE INVADE A PUERTO RICO see FRANKENSTEIN MEETS
THE SPACEMONSTER
A MARTIEN IN PARIS (F) 1960 (Un MARTIAN A PARIS) SP, D:
Jean-Daniel Daninos. Dial: Jacques Vilfrid. Ref: Imagen. SM
2:11. DDC III:39. with Darry Cowl, Nicole Mirel, Henri Vil-
bert, Gisèle Grandré.
MARTIANS, The see FLYING SAUCER, The (1966)
MARTIANS ARRIVED, The see TWELVE-HANDED MEN OF
MARS, The
MARTIEN DE NOEL, Le see CHRISTMAS MARTIAN, The
A MARVELLOUS CURE (Dan?) Nordisk 7m. Ref: Bios 2/10/10.
Hair restorer.
A MARVELLOUS INVENTION (F?) Gaum 1911 5m. Ref: Bios
12/28/11. Prof. Boffo's invention for accelerating movement
gets town into "marvellous state of activity."
The MARVELLOUS PEARL (I) Cines 1909 12m. Ref: Bios
9/9/09. A pearl casts a spell on the lord of the district. He

follows it to the sea and is drowned.
MARZIANI HANNO DODICI MANI, I see TWELVE-HANDED MEN
OF MARS, The
MASCHERA DEL DEMONIO, Le see BLACK SUNDAY
The MASK Rex 1913 Ref: MPW 18:1153. Lee. Dual personality.
The MASK WB/Beaver-Champion 1961 3-D 83m. (The EYES
OF HELL) (Canadian) P,D: Julian Roffman. SP: Frank Taubes,
Sandy Haber. PH: Herbert S. Alpert. Mus: Louis Applebaum.
Art D: David S. Ballou, Hugo Wuehtrich. SpFX & 3-D: Herman
S. Townsley, Charles W. Smith, James B. Gordon. Ref:
Shriek 4:15. FFacts. PM. with Paul Stevens, Claudette
Nevins, Bill Walker, Anne Collings, Martin Lavut, Paul Nevins,
Ray Lawlor. Ancient ritual mask allows the wearer to see into
his subconscious. The story is a weak framework for the 3-D
sequences, which aren't too amazing themselves.
The MASK OF DESTINY (J) Shochiku 1955 color 105m.
(SHUZENJI MONOGATARI. The MASK AND DESTINY) D:
Noboru Nakamura. SP: Toshio Yasumi, from the play by Kido
Okamoto. PH: Toshio Ubukata. Mus D: Toshiro Mazuzumi.
Art D: Kisaku Itoh. Ref: Orient. HR 1/2/57. with Teiji Taka-
hashi, Chikaga Awashima, Keiko Kishi. Mask seems to foretell
death.
The MASK OF DIJON PRC/Western Television 1946 73m. (The
MASK OF DILJON) D: Lew Landers. SP: Griffin Jay, Arthur
St. Claire. PH: Jack Greenhalgh. Art D: Edward Jewell. SpFX:
Ray Mercer. Ref: FDY. with Erich von Stroheim, Jeanne Bates,
Edward Van Sloan, William Wright, Mauritz Hugo. Villain uses
hypnotism on robber, newsboy. Except for a bizarre ending al-
most totally undistinguished. Von Stroheim bad in a Lugosi-like
role as a "stubborn egomaniac" of a magician.
The MASK OF FU MANCHU MGM 1932 72m. D: Charles
Brabin, Charles Vidor. SP: Edgar Allan Woolf, Irene Kuhn, John
Willard. PH: Gaetano Gaudio. From stories by Sax Rohmer.
Ref: Clarens. Pic: SM 4:20. COF 14:4. FMO 3:9. with Boris
Karloff, Lewis Stone, Karen Morley, Charles Starrett, Myrna
Loy, Jean Hersholt, Lawrence Grant, David Torrence. Ray
machine, diabolical tortures, etc. Gosh-wow torture scenes and
special effects in the middle of a half-hearted, serial-like story.
Alligators, snakes, and spiders put to good, grisly use. The in-
gredients of the zombie-serum are especially ghastly.
MASK OF FU MANCHU, The see FACE OF FU MANCHU, The
MASK OF THE DEMON see BLACK SUNDAY
MASK OF THE GOLEM see GOLEM, The (1966)
The MASKED MARVEL Rep 1943 serial 12 episodes (feature
SAKIMA AND THE MASKED MARVEL) D: Spencer Bennet. SP:
R. Cole, R. Davidson, B. Dickey, J. Duffy, G. Nelson,
G. Plympton, J. Poland. PH: Reggie Lanning. Mus sc: Mort
Glickman. SpFX: Howard Lydecker. Ref: Barbour. FIR'68:316.
with Tom Steele, William Forrest, Louise Currie, Anthony
Warde, Kenneth Harlan, Eddie Parker, Dale Van Sickel, Robert
Wilke, Ernie Adams, Howard Hickman, Herbert Rawlinson,
Forbes Murray, George Pembroke, Roy Barcroft, Tom London,
Sam Flint, Edward Van Sloan, Frank O'Connor. Nitrolene,

powerful new explosive; model of TV-periscope that permits sub-
marine to fire torpedoes without showing periscope. The usual
"We have very effective ways of persuading people"-type serial.
MASKED TERROR (J) Shochiku 1957 color/scope 105m.
(DOKURO KYOJO) D: Seiichi Fukuda. SP: I. Nagae. Story:
K. Nomura. PH: K. Kataoka. Ref: FEFN 12/27/57. with
Kokichi Takada, J. Ban, O. Ichikawa. Detective rescues "spell-
bound" princess and defeats band of skull-masked terrorists.
MASKS OF THE DEVIL MGM 1928 silent 68m. P,D: Victor
Seastrom. SP: Frances Marion, Svend Gade. Ref: V 11/28/28:
"A variation of the Dorian Gray theme." From a story by Jakob
Wasserman, "Die Masken Erwin Reiners." with John Gilbert,
Frank Reicher, Polly Ann Young, Ralph Forbes, Alma Rubens,
Theodore Roberts. Titles: Marian Ainslee, Ruth Cummings.
PH: Oliver Marsh. Art D: Cedric Gibbons. Ass't D: Harold S.
Bucquet. Ref: AFI. Man sees himself as devil in mirror as he
progresses in wickedness.
MASQUE OF THE RED DEATH (U.S.-B) AI/Alta Vista/Anglo-
Amalgamated 1964 Technicolor P,D: Roger Corman. SP: Charles
Beaumont, R. Wright Campbell. From "The Masque of the Red
Death" and "Hop Frog" by Edgar Allan Poe. See also A SPEC-
TRE HAUNTS EUROPE. PH: N. Roeg. Mus: David Lee. Art D:
Robert Jones. Ref: Clarens. COF 6:53. with Vincent Price,
Hazel Court, Jane Asher, David Weston, Patrick Magee, Nigel
Green, Skip Martin, Julian Burton. Satan powerless before the
Red Death. A few good scenes, sets, but otherwise ponderous.
MASQUERADE UA 1965 Eastmancolor 102m. (SHABBY TIGER)
D: Basil Dearden. SP: Ralph and William Goldman. From Vic-
tor Canning's "Castle Minerva." PH: Otto Heller. Mus: Philip
Green. Prod Des: Don Ashton. Ref: COF 7:46: "'Homage' to
Corman set in spooky castle." V 4/21/65: "Eerie castle."
with Jack Hawkins, Michel Piccoli, Cliff Robertson, Bill Fraser,
Charles Gray, John Le Mesurier, Felix Aylmer. Spy-spoof.
MASSEUR'S CURSE (J) Daiei 1970 color/scope 82m. (KAIDAN
KASENEGA-FUCHI) D: Kimiyoshi Yasuda. SP: S. Asai. PH:
T. Hayashi. Mus: H. Kaburagi. Art D: A. Naitô. Ref: UFQ
50. with Ritsu Ishiyama, Maya Kitajima, Reiko Kasahara. Woman
turns into "horrible monster."
The MASTER KEY Univ 1945 serial 13 episodes D: Ray Taylor,
Lewis D. Collins. SP: J. O'Donnell, G. H. Plympton, A. Lamb.
Story: Jack Natteford, Dwight V. Babcock. PH: W. Sickner,
M. Gertsman. Ref: Lee. Academy. with Jan Wiley, Dennis
Moore, Addison Richards, Byron Foulger, Sarah Padden, George
Lynn, Russell Hicks, Roland Varno, John Eldredge, Ernie Adams,
George Chesebro, Gene Stutenroth, Lee Shumway, Dick Alexander,
John Merton. Machine extracts gold from sea water.
MASTER KEY, The see MASTER MYSTERY, The
The MASTER MIND 1920 65m. D: Kenneth Webb. Ref: NYT
9/13/20. with Lionel Barrymore, Gypsy O'Brien, Ralph Kellard,
Bradley Barker. Man telepathically forces secret out of person
he is seeking revenge on.
MASTER MINDS Mono 1949 64m. D: Jean Yarbrough. SP:
Charles Marion. Add'l Dial: Bert Lawrence. PH: Marcel Le

Picard. Mus D: Edward Kay. Art D: Dave Milton. Ref:
HR 11/30/49. with Glenn Strange (Atlas), Jane Adams, Alan
Napier, Minerva Urecal, Leo, Bernadd, and David Gorcey,
Huntz Hall, Gabe Dell, Billy Benedict, Skelton Knaggs, Bennie
Bartlett. Pic: TBG. Mad scientist puts Bowery Boy's brain
into monster by means of electrical vibrations.

MASTER MINDS see GENIUS AT WORK

The MASTER MYSTERY Octagon 1919 serial 15 episodes D: Burton King. Ref: CNW. FM 17:7. 31:73. ModM 3:21. FanMo
4:63. 5:37. with Harry Houdini, Marguerite Marsh, Ruth Stone-
house, William Pike. Automaton turns out to be man with super
powers.

MASTER OF HORROR (Arg) US Films/Sono 115m. (61m. -U.S.)
(OBRAS MAESTRAS DEL TERROR. SHORT STORIES OF TER-
ROR. MASTERWORKS OF TERROR. MASTERPIECES OF HOR-
ROR) 1960 ('65-U.S.) D: Enrique Carreras. SP: Luis Penafil.
Adap: Rodolfo M. Taboada. From "The Facts in the Case of M.
Valdemar," "The Cask of Amontillado," and "The Tell-Tale
Heart" by Edgar Allan Poe. PH: Américo Hoss. Mus: Victor
Schlichter. Art D: Mario Vanarelli. Ref: FFacts. FIR'61:473.
Heraldo 8/3/60. FM 33:8. COF 9:6. Argentine Films'60.
Pic: FM 67:54. Exec P: Jack H. Harris. with Narcisco Ibanez
Menta, Carlos Estrada, Inés Morano, Narcisco Ibanez Serrador,
Mercedes Carreras, Lilian Valmar.

MASTER OF TERROR see DIE, MONSTER, DIE!/4-D MAN, The

MASTER OF THE WORLD (Dan?) Film Releases of America 1914
45m. Ref: Lee. MPW 20:1691,1744. Gold made.

MASTER OF THE WORLD (G) Ariel 1934 (DER HERR DER
WELT) D: Harry Piel. (RULER OF THE WORLD) Ref: FD
12/17/35. FM 13:30. NYT 12/16/35. with Walter Janssen,
Sybille Schmitz, Walter Franck, S. Schuerenberg. Displaced
workers are given jobs pushing buttons controlling the function-
ing of their robot successors. Death rays.

MASTER OF THE WORLD AI 1961 color 104m. D: William
Witney. SP: Richard Matheson. From Jules Verne's "Master of
the World or A Tale of Mystery and Marvel" and "Robur, the
Conqueror." Mus: Les Baxter. PH: Gil Warrenton. Art D:
Daniel Haller. SpFX: Tim Barr, Wah Chang, Gene Warren.
PhFX: Ray Mercer. Sp Props & FX: Pat Dinga. Ref: FFacts.
PM. with Vincent Price, Henry Hull, Charles Bronson, David
Frankham, Richard Harrison, Mary Webster, Vito Scotti,
Wally Campo, Ken Terrell. Mad inventor proposes to enforce
peace on the world by threatening to destroy it with his flying
ship. Fairly enjoyable.

MASTER OF THE WORLD see INVISIBLE MAN GOES THROUGH
THE CITY, An

The MASTER OF TIME (F-Braz) UA/Films 13-Barreto 1969
(Le MAITRE DE TEMPS) D: Jean D. Pollet. SP: Pollet, Pierre
Kast. P: Claude Lelouch, Luis-Carlos Barreto. Ref: V 4/29/70:
73: "Sci fi." RVB.

The MASTER PHYSICIAN (Dan?) Nordisk 1916 40m. Ref: Pictures and the Picturegoer 7/15/16. with Gunner Tolnas,
George Weith. "A modern Faust story."

MASTERPIECES OF HORROR see MASTER OF HORROR
MASTERS OF VENUS (B) CFF/Wallace 1962 serial 8 episodes
(128-minute feature version) D: Ernest Morris. SP: Michael
Barnes. Story: H. B. Gregory. Adap: Mary Borer. PH: Reg
Wyer. Mus: Eric Rogers. Art D: Norman Arnold. Ref: MFB.
MMF 8:53. SM 8:7. with Norman Wooland, Ferdy Mayne,
Amanda Coxell, Robin Stewart. Descendants of Atlantis inhabit
Venus.
MASTERWORKS OF TERROR see MASTER OF HORROR
MATANGO see ATTACK OF THE MUSHROOM PEOPLE
MATE DOMA IVA? See DO YOU KEEP A LION AT HOME?
MATRIMONIO INTERPLANETARIO see INTERPLANETARY WED-
DING
MAX AND THE CLUTCHING HAND see GRASPING HAND, The
MAX ET LA MAIN QUI ETREINT see GRASPING HAND, The
MAX HYPNOTIZED (F) 1910 9m. (MAX HYPNOTIZE) Ref:
DDC III:230. Bios 12/1/10. 10/23/13. FIR'65:276. with Max
Linder. Two servants order their hypnotized master to commit a
murder.
MAYA BAZAAR see FANTASY BAZAAR
MAYA MANIDHAN (India-Tamil) Southern 1958 Ref: FEFN 6/13/58.
'58-59. with Sriram. Killer hiding in dispensary discovers
"magic concoction which can make him invisible."
The MAZE Mono(AA) 1953 3-D 81m. Art D, D: William Camer-
on Menzies. SP: Dan Ullman. From the novel by Maurice San-
doz. PH: Harry Neumann. Mus: Marlin Skiles. P: Walter
Mirisch. Ref: Clarens. with Richard Carlson, Veronica Hurst,
Katherine Emery, Michael Pate, Lilian Bond, Hillary Brooke,
Robin Hughes. Mutant, frog-like monster inhabits Scottish castle.
Supposedly a sleeper classic on the order of INVADERS FROM
MARS, The MAZE in reality looks suspiciously like a dull, run-
of-the-mill horror movie.
MEASURE FOR MEASURE Lubin 1909 15m. Ref: Bios 10/7/09.
"New and highly destructive submarine mine" causes "terrific ex-
plosion."
MECHANICAL BUTCHER (F) Lumiere 1898 Ref: SF film.
Steam-driven machine turns pig into ham, bacon, etc.
The MECHANICAL HUSBAND LCC 1910 Ref: SF Film. Robot.
The MECHANICAL LEGS (F) Gaum 1908 Ref: SF Film. Legless
cripple gets pair of mechanical legs.
The MECHANICAL MAN Univ Joker) 1915 15m. Ref: SF Film.
MPN 7/3/15. with "Phroso," Max Asher. Robot.
MECHANICAL MARY ANNE (B) Hepworth 1910 D: Lewin Fitzhamon.
Ref: SF Film. Robot.
MEDEA (I-G-F) Planfilm/Rosima Anstalt-San Marco-Janus-Les
Films Number One-Fernsehen 1969 color 110m. Mus, SP, D:
Pier Paolo Pasolini. PH: Ennio Guarnieri. Ref: V 3/11/70.
Ital P'69. with Maria Callas, Laurent Terzieff, Massimo Girot-
ti. Witch-like woman; centaur; sadism; cannibalism.
The MEDICINE OF THE FUTURE (F?) Lux 1912 7m. Ref:
Bios 2/6/13. Inventor's machine makes people more energetic.
The MEDIUM (B) MGM 1934 D: Vernon Sewell. From a play by
José Levy. Ref: Brit. Cinema. Lee. "Horrific." Psychic powers.

The MEDIUM Trans-Film-Lopert 1951 80m. SP, D: Gian Carlo
Menotti, from his opera. Co-D:Alexander Hammid. PH: Enzo
Serafin. Ref: FDY. Pic: FM 28:8. with Marie Powers, Anna
Maria Alberghetti, Leo Coleman. Fake Spiritualist visited by unknown force. If you haven't heard English-language opera,
imagine the dialogue of CAT PEOPLE or The MUMMY'S GHOST
set to music or the leads singing, "Hello! What a surprise! Do
come in." Anyway, a well-done medium story is rare.
The MEDIUM'S NEMESIS Mutual(Than) 1913 17m. Ref: MPW
'13:882. Bios 12/18/13. At a seance conducted by "Princess
Ozeb" a man who thinks he has murdered is confronted by the
"spirit" of his supposed victim.
MEDUSA vs. THE SON OF HERCULES (I-SP) Bistolfi/Copercines
1962 color/Totalscope (PERSEE L'INVINCIBLE-I. PERSEO
L'INVINCIBLE, PERSEO Y MEDUSA, or El VALLE DE LOS
HOMBRES DE PIEDRA-SP. The VALLEY OF THE STONE MEN.
PERSEUS THE INVINCIBLE. PERSEUS AGAINST THE MON-
STERS) D: Alberto de Martino. SP: Martino, Guerra, Gastaldi,
from an idea by E. G. Conti. Mus: Carlo Franci. Ref: MMF
8:71. SpCinema'64. TVFFSB. Pic: MMF 8:48n. with Richard
Harrison, Anna Ranalli, Arturo Dominici, Leo Anchoriz, Elisa
Cegani. Perseus vs. the stone men.
MEET JOHN DOE WB 1941 123m. D, P: Frank Capra. SP: Robert
Riskin, from a story by Richard Connell and Robert Presnell.
PH: George Barnes. Mus sc: Dmitri Tiomkin. Art D: Stephen
Goosson (or Gooson). SpFX: Jack Cosgrove. Montage FX:
Slavko Vorkapich. Ed: Daniel Mandel. Ref: Academy. with Gary
Cooper, Barbara Stanwyck, Edward Arnold, Walter Brennan, Spring
Byington, James Gleason, Gene Lockhart, Rod La Rocque, Irving
Bacon, Regis Toomey, J. Farrell Macdonald, Warren Hymer, Har-
ry Holman, Pierre Watkin, Andrew Tombes, Sterling Holloway,
Mike Frankovich, Harry Davenport, Ann Doran, Bennie Bartlett,
Charles Trowbridge, Edward Earle, Forrester Harvey, Bess
Flowers, Wyndham Standing, Guy Usher, Frederick Vogeding,
Fritzi Brunette, Eddie Cobb, Kenneth Harlan, Frank Moran,
Forbes Murray, George Pembroke, Paul Panzer, Maris Wrixon,
Jack Mower, Tom Wilson, John Hamilton, William Forrest, Selmer Jackson. o An industrialist uses "John Doe Clubs" and their
national hero in an attempt to seize political power in the United
States. The affirmations of life in Capra's movies have a remarkable, saving self-consciousness about them, as summed up in a
line in MEET JOHN DOE: "You've heard it all before." The
major accomplishment of Capra and his writers was that they made
you think that this was your last, best chance to hear it, that this
was the ultimate statement on the brotherhood of man and the goodness of life. This quality comes through in the performances of
the players, especially, in JOHN DOE, in that of Arnold, who
seems to be the ultimate in evil. Cooper too is unusually good,
but Arnold dominates, which is perhaps a weakness of the film.
MEET THE GHOSTS see ABBOTT AND COSTELLO MEET FRANK-
ENSTEIN
MEETING AT MIDNIGHT see BLACK MAGIC (1944)
MELODY IN THE DARK (B) Adelphi/Advent 1948 67m. D: Robert

Melody 316

Jordan Hill. SP: Hill, John Guillermin. PH: Jo Jago. Ref:
MFB'49:60. with Ben Wrigley, Eunice Gayson, Richard Thorpe.
Woman inherits haunted mansion from uncle.
The MELODY OF DOOM Selig 1915 25m. D: Frank Beal. SP:
W. E. Wing. Ref: MPN 8/7/15 with Eugenie Besserer, Wil-
liam Sheerer, Fred Huntley. Certain tune played on violin ter-
rifies adventuress Zara, ultimately kills her.
MEMOIRS OF A PHYSICIAN (by Dumas) see BLACK MAGIC (1949)
MEMORIES OF THE FUTURE (G) Constantin-Terra 1970 92m.
(CHARIOTS OF THE GODS) SP,D: Harald Reinl, from the books
"Memories of the Future" and "Back to the Stars" by Erich von
Daeniken. Commentary: Wilhelm Roggersdorf. (ERINNERUNGE-
NAN DIE ZUKUNFT) Ref: V 5/13/70. Documentary probes the
question of whether, long ago, earth was visited by beings from
other planets.
MENACE FROM OUTER SPACE MCA-TV 1954 From the "Rocky
Jones, Space Ranger" TV series. with Richard Crane, Maurice
Cass.
MEN MUST FIGHT MGM 1933 72m. D: Edgar Selwyn. SP:
C. Gardner Sullivan, from the play by Reginald Lawrence and
S. K. Lauren. PH: George Folsey. Ref: FDY. NYT 3/11/33.
with Diana Wynward, Lewis Stone, Phillips Holmes, May Robson,
Ruth Selwyn, Robert Young, Robert Greig, Hedda Hopper, Donald
Dillaway, Mary Carlisle, Luis Alberni. Hostilities between the
U.S. and the "Eurasian states" in 1970.
MEN WITH STEEL FACES see PHANTOM EMPIRE
MENSCHEN DER ZEIT see DR. MABUSE (Part II)
MEPHISTO AND THE MAIDEN Selig 1909 15m. Ref: V&FI IV:
18:9. Lee. Friar trades soul for two hours with girl.
The MEPHISTO WALTZ Fox 1971 115m. D: Paul Wendkos. SP:
Ben Maddow, from the novel by Fred Mustard Stewart. DeLuxe
color PH: William Spencer. Mus: Jerry Goldsmith. Art D: Rich
Hamen. SpFX: Howard A. Anderson. with Alan Alda, Jacqueline
Bisset, Barbara Parkins, Brad Dillman, William Windom, Curt
Jurgens, Kathleen Widdoes, Lilyan Chauvin, Khigh Dhiegh, Berry
Kroeger. Through witchcraft a man's soul enters another body.
MEPHISTO'S SON (F) Pathe 1906 19m. Ref: V&FI 10/13/06.
Cross repels devil's son.
MERMAIDS AND SEA ROBBERS (J) Shochiku 1959 (NINGYO
SHOTEN) D: Seiichiro Uchikawa. From a novel by A. Hino.
Ref: Shochiku Selected Films, 1959. with Kyoko Izumi, Tatsuya
Mihashi. "Mystery craft" operated by mermaid and her lover.
The MERMAIDS OF TIBURON Filmgroup 1962 Eastmancolor/scope
(AQUA-SEX) SP,D,P: John Lamb. Mus sc: Richard LaSalle.
Ref: Boxo 6/25/62. with Diane Webber, George Rowe, Timothy
Carey, Jose Gonzalez-Gonzalez. Mermaids lure man to his death.
Dull.
The MERRY FROLICS OF SATAN (F) Melies/Star 1905 18m.
(Les QUATRE CENTS FARCES DU DIABLE. The 400 TRICKS OF
THE DEVIL. The FROLICS OF SATAN) Ref: V&FI 10/13/06.
70 years. F&F 11/68:63. Inventor's submarine and balloon-car;
alchemist Satan's "weird" laboratory; woman who appears and
turns into "hideous monster"; horse that turns into "mythical

monster"; carriage that travels in space; man who's roasted on a
spit in hell.
MESA OF LOST WOMEN Howco/M. Gordon, W. Perkins 1952 69m.
(LOST WOMEN. LOST WOMEN OF ZARPA) SP, D: Herbert Tevos.
D: also Ron Ormond. PH: Gil Warrenton, Karl Struss. Mus:
Hoyt Curtin. Ref: MFB'54:88. with Jackie Coogan, Allan Nixon,
Richard Travis, Mary Hill. A doctor who refuses to aid another
doctor in creating a race of superwomen and 8-foot-high spiders is
driven mad.
MESSAGE FROM MARS (Australian) 1909 Ref: Lee.
MESSAGE FROM MARS (B) Urban 1913 60m. SP, P: Wallett
Waller. From the play by Richard Ganthon(e)y. Ref: Imagen.
RVB. with Charles Hawtrey, Holman Clark, Hubert Willis.
A MESSAGE FROM MARS Metro 1921 65m. P: Maxwell Karger.
SP: Arthur Zellner, Arthur Maude. From the play by Richard
Ganthon(e)y. Ref: Exhibitors Herald. AFI. with Bert Lytell,
Raye Dean, Leonard Mudie, Frank Currier, Maude Milton,
Gordon Ash. PH: Arthur Martinelli. The shadowy form of a
messenger from Mars stalks through the streets and points out to a
man the needs of the poor.
METEMPSYCHO see TOMB OF TORTURE
METEMPSYCHOSIS (F) 1907 (METEMPHYCHOSE) Ref: DDC II:
383. Mitry II:52.
METEMPSYCHOSIS (I) 1913 (METEMPSICOSI) Ref: DDC III:38.
Mitry II:81:1920. with Hesperia.
METEOR MONSTER see TEENAGE MONSTER
METHOD FOR MURDER (by R. Bloch) see HOUSE THAT DRIPPED
BLOOD, The
METROPOLIS (G) Para/UFA 1926 D: Fritz Lang. SP: Lang, Thea
von Harbou. PH: Karl Freund, Günther Rittau. Art D: Otto Hunte,
Erich Kettelhut, Karl Vollbrecht. SpFX: Eugen Shuftan. Costumes:
Anne Willkomm. P: Erich Pommer. Ref: SilentFF. FM 12:18.
36:51. SM 6:34. 7:26. 8:10. Pic: TBG. DDC I:61. II:29, 401. III:30.
with Brigitte Helm, Alfred Abel, Gustave Froehlich, Rudolf Klein-
Rogge, Heinrich George, Fritz Rasp. City of the future: robo-
trix, subterranean city of workers, etc. Tremendous special ef-
fects and exciting cinematic concepts, all leading up to a dismay-
ingly bland concluding moral. The creation of the robotrix is one
of the most impressive scenes in film history.
METROPOLIS see GIANT OF METROPOLIS
METZENGERSTEIN (by E. A. Poe) see TALES OF MYSTERY AND
IMAGINATION
MEURTRE EN 45 TOURS see MURDER at 45 R. P. M
MEXICAN SPITFIRE SEES A GHOST RKO 1942 70m. D: Leslie
Goodwins. SP: Monte Brice, Charles Roberts. PH: Russell
Metty. Ref: V 5/5/42. HR 5/5/42. with Lupe Velez, Leon
Errol, Charles "Buddy" Rogers, Minna Gombell, John Maguire,
Mantan Moreland, Marten Lamont, Donald MacBride, Elisabeth
Risdon, Don Barclay. Saboteurs make house's inhabitants think
it's haunted.
MICROSCOPIA see FANTASTIC VOYAGE
MIDI MINUIT (F) Planfilm/Albertine 1969 color 105m. SP, D:
Pierre Philippe. PH: Pierre Villemin. Ref: V 7/1/70: "Horror,"

with Sylvie Fennac, Beatrice Arnac. Sadist tears up victims with gloves with claws on them.

MIDNIGHT Imp 1916 11m. SP: E. J. Clawson. Ref: MPW 31: 246, 275. Girl who leads priest to dying man turns out to be a ghost.

MIDNIGHT AT MADAME TUSSAUD'S (B) 1936 62m. D: George Pearson. Ref: TVFFSB. Brit. Cinema. with Charles Oliver, James Carew, Bernard Miles, William Hartnell. In the Chamber of Horrors.

A MIDNIGHT BELL F Nat 1921 D: Albert Ray. Ref: NYT 8/8/21. MPH. with Charles Ray, Donald MacDonald. On a dare a man spends a night in a "haunted" church.

MIDNIGHT MANHUNT Para 1945 81m. D: William C. Thomas. SP: David Lang. PH:Fred Jackman, Jr. Mus sc: Alexander Lazslo. Art D: F. Paul Sylos. Sets: Ray Berk. (ONE EXCITING NIGHT) Ref: HR 6/8/45: "Semi-spooky." with George Zucco, William Gargan, Leo Gorcey, Ann Savage, Paul Hurst, Don Beddoe, Charles Halton, George E. Stone, Robert Barron. Murder committed in wax museum.

MIDNIGHT MENACE (B) ABFD/Grosvenor 1937 78m. D: Sinclair Hill. SP: G. H. Moresby-White. Story: Roger MacDougall, Alexander Mackendrick. PH: Cyril Bristow. Ref: MFB'37. V 7/14/37 SF Film. with Charles Farrell, Fritz Kortner, Margaret Vyner, Danny Green, Billy Bray. London bombed by a fleet of pilotless radio-controlled planes.

A MIDNIGHT SCARE Crystal 1914 8m. Ref: Bios? Ghost stories lead to practical joke.

THE MIDNIGHT SPECTER (I) Talia 1915 (Lo SPETTRO DI MEZZANOTTE) Ref: Lee.

MIDNIGHT WARNING Mayfair/Weeks 1933 60m. D: Spencer G. Bennet. Story: Norman Battle. Adap: J. T. Neville. PH: Jules Cronjager. Redone as non-horror film SO LONG AT THE FAIR (1950). Ref: TVFFSB: "Haunted hotel room." V 3/14/33. 1/20/ 33: "Telescope spectacle.. grisly stuff in a mortuary." Photoplay 4/33: "Horror picture." with Claudia Dell, William Boyd, John Harron, Huntley Gordon, Hooper Atchley, Lloyd Ingraham, Henry Hall, Art Winkler, Lloyd Whitlock.

MIDSTREAM Tiffany-Stahl 1929 sound & silent versions 90m. D: James Flood. SP: Frances Guihan. Dial, Titles: Frederick Hatton, Fanny Halton. Story: Bernice Boone. PH: Jackson Rose. Mus: Hugo Riesenfeld. Ref: AFI. with Ricardo Cortez, Claire Windsor, Montagu Love, Larry Kent, Helen Jerome Eddy. A financier undergoes a rejuvenation operation.

MIDSUMMER DAY'S DREAM, A see IMAGINARY VOYAGE, The

MIDWICH CUCKOOS, The (novel by J. Wyndham) see VILLAGE OF THE DAMNED

The MIGHTY GORGA Western Int'l 1970 color 83m. D: David Hewitt. SP: Jean Hewitt, David Prentiss. P: Robert O'Neil. Ref: B. Warren. with Anthony Eisley, Scott Brady, Kent Taylor, Megan Timothy. Legendary 50-ton gorilla; dinosaurs.

MIGHTY JOE YOUNG RKO 1949 94m. (MR. JOE YOUNG OF AFRICA. PANIK UM KING KONG-G.) D: Ernest B. Schoedsack. SP: Ruth Rose. PH: J. Roy Hunt. Mus: Roy Webb. SpFX:

Willis O'Brien. Ass't SpFX: Ray Harryhausen. P: Merian C.
Cooper, John Ford. Art D: James Basevi. Ref: FDY. FM
10:26. with Terry Moore, Ben Johnson, Robert Armstrong,
Frank McHugh, Douglas Fowley, Paul Guilfoyle, Nestor Paiva,
Regis Toomey, James Flavin. More like SON OF KONG than
KING KONG: cute ape; ridiculous, uninvolving story. Best
scene (a throwaway) just has giant Joe twiddling his thumbs on
the back of a truck. (Though there are some votes for his grand
entrance supporting a piano.)
MIGHTY THUNDA, The see KING OF THE CONGO
MILCZACA GWIAZDA see FIRST SPACESHIP ON VENUS
MILL OF THE STONE WOMEN (I-F) Parade /Galatea /CEC /Vanguard
/FARO /Explorer 1960 ('63-U.S.) color /Dyaliscope 94m.
(Il MULINO DELLE DONNE DI PIETRA-I. Le MOULIN DES
SUPPLICES-F. DROPS OF BLOOD-Eng. MILL OF THE STONE
MAIDENS) SP, D: Giorgio Ferroni. SP: also R. Del Grosso, Ugo
Liberatore, G. Stegani. From a short story in "Flemish Tales"
by Peter Van Weigen. PH: P. Pavoni. Mus: Carlo Innocenzi.
Art D: Arrigo Equini. Ref: FEFN 3/60. FFacts. DDC I:270. COF
5:59. Orpheus 3:29. FM 10:10.12:13. Pic: COF 4:10. with Pierre
Brice, Scilla Gabel, Dany Carrel, Wolfgang Preiss, Liana Orfei.
Professor needs young girls to keep daughter alive; uses their
bodies as statuary. Not without interest.
$1,000,000 DUCK BV 1971 Technicolor 91m. D: Vincent
McEveety. SP: Roswell Rogers, from a story by Ted Key. PH:
William Snyder. Mus: Buddy Baker. Art D: J. B. Mansbridge,
Al Roelofs. Ref: V 6/16/71. with Dean Jones, Sandy Duncan,
Joe Flynn, James Gregory, Jack Kruschen, Arthur Hunnicutt,
Virginia Vincent. A duck exposed to radiation lays eggs with
yolks of solid gold. Usual ungodly Disney comedy, four laughs
maximum. Whatever comic talent Sandy Duncan has was checked
at the gate.
The MILLION EYES OF SU-MURU (B) AI /Sumuru 1967 Techni-
color /scope (SUMURU) D: Lindsay Shonteff. SP: Kevin
Kavanagh. Story: Peter Welbeck. From characters created by
Sax Rohmer. PH: John Von Kotze. Mus sc & d: Johnny Scott.
Art D: Scott MacGregor. Ref: FFacts. COF 17:60. with
Frankie Avalon, George Nader, Shirley Eaton, Wilfrid Hyde-
White, Klaus Kinski, Patti Chandler, Salli Sachse, Maria Rohm.
Plot by world-wide organization of women to enslave mankind;
Kubra Mortis gun that turns its victims into stone; torture
chamber.
MILLS OF THE GODS, The (poem by E. Madden) see DEVIL'S
TOYS, The
The MIND BENDERS (B) AI /Novus /Anglo-Amalgamated 1963
98m. (The PIT) D: Basil Dearden. SP: James Kennaway. PH:
Denys Coop. Art D: James Morahan. P: Michael Relph. Ref:
MFB'63:31. with Dirk Bogarde, Mary Ure, John Clements,
Norman Bird, Michael Bryant. Man given Jekyll-Hyde personality
by "reduction of sensation" experiments." Pretty dull.
MIND BENDERS, The see FIVE MILLION YEARS TO EARTH
The MIND OF MR. SOAMES (B\ Amicus 1969 Technicolor 98m.
D: Alan Cooke. SP: John Hale, Edward Simpson, from Charles

Eric Maine's novel. PH: Billy Williams. Ref: MFB. with
Terence Stamp, Robert Vaughn, Donal Donnelly, Nigel Davenport, Scott Forbes. Surgery releases John Soames from the
coma he has been in since birth. In the trite conflict between
the instructional and the instructional-plus-recreational methods of
teaching, SOAMES bears an unhealthy resemblance to CHARLY
("He's a person, not just a subject for your experiments"),
though the recreation scenes are amusing. The ending is almost a direct steal from REBEL WITHOUT A CAUSE.

MINGLING SPIRITS Nestor 1916 Ref: MPN 13:406. with Lee
Moran, Eddie Lyons, Betty Compson. Man scares spiritualistic
mother-in-law away by dressing sandwich man as devil.

The MINOTAUR Vita 1910 16m. Ref: MPW 6:703. Theseus and
the Minotaur.

The MINOTAUR (I) UA/Illiria Film 1960 Technicolor/Totalscope
95m. (TESEO CONTRO IL MINOTAURO. The WILD BEAST OF
CRETE. The WARLORD OF CRETE. THESEUS AND THE
MINOTAUR) D: Silvio Amadio. SP: S. Continenza, G. P.
Callegari. English-language Adap: Daniel Mainwaring. PH: Aldo
Giordani. Mus: Carlo Rustichelli. Art D: Piero Poletto. Ref:
FFacts. Orpheus 3:29. with Bob Mathias, Rosanna Schiaffino,
Alberto Lupo, Rik Battaglia, Suzanne Loret, Milo Malagoli (the
Minotaur). Theseus slays the Minotaur in his labyrinth. A real
nothing.

MIO AMICO JECKYLL, Il see MY FRIEND, DR. JEKYLL

The MIRACLE (B) Stoll 1923 21m. (Mystery of Dr. Fu-
Manchu series) SP: A. E. Coleby, Frank Wilson. PH: D. P.
Cooper. Ref: SilentFF. with Harry Agar Lyons, Joan Clark-
son, Stacey Gaunt, Wilson, Humbertson Wright, Fred Paul.
Based on the character created by Sax Rohmer.

MIRACLE FROM MARS see RED PLANET MARS

The MIRACLE OF TOMORROW (G) Piel 1923 D: Harry Piel
Ref SF Film. Electrically-controlled robot.

The MIRACLE RIDER Mascot 1935 serial 15 episodes (El
RAYO-Mex) D: Armand Schaefer, B. Reeves Eason. SP:
J. Rathmell. Story: B. Sarecky, W. Totman, G. Geraghty.
Ref: FIR'57:396. Next Time. Pic: FanMo 2:40. with Tom
Mix, Joan Gale, Charles Middleton, Jason Robards, Edward
Earle, Ernie S. Adams, George Chesebro. Villain Zaroff after
Indian land rich in mineral necessary to his "X-94," super-
explosive.

MIRACLES DO HAPPEN (B) 1939 D: Maclean Rogers. Ref:
SF in the Cinema. Brit.Cinema. with Jack Hobbs. Synthetic
Milk!

MIRACLES FOR SALE MGM 1939 71m. D: Tod Browning. SP:
Harry Ruskin, Marion Parsonnet, James E. Grant. From the
book "Death from a Top Hat" by Clayton Rawson. PH: Charles
Lawton. Art D: Cedric Gibbons. Makeup: Jack Dawn. Ed:
F. Y. Smith. Ref: NYT 8/10/39. Academy. FM 22:40:
Magician's "weirdly phosphorescent eyes." with Robert Young,
Florence Rice, Henry Hull, Astrid Allwyn, Gloria Holden,
Frank Craven, Lee Bowman, Cliff Clark, Walter Kingsford,
Frederick Worlock, William Demarest, Charles Lane, Richard

Loo, John Picorri, Suzanne Kaaren, Edward Earle, Truman
Bradley, Phillip Terry, Eddie Acuff, John Davidson. A man is
found dead in a devil's circle.

The MIRROR OF LIFE (F) Pathe 1909 5m. Ref: Bios 1/20/10.
Beggar shows couple two mirrors, in which they see themselves
grow old and withered.

MISADVENTURES OF MERLIN JONES BV 1963 Technicolor
88m. D: Robert Stevenson. SP: Tom & Helen August. Story:
Bill Walsh. Sequel: The MONKEY'S UNCLE. P: Walt Disney.
Ref: FFacts. COF 5:4. Pic: HM 9:31. with Tommy Kirk,
Annette Funicello, Leon Ames, Stu Erwin, Connie Gilchrist.
Brain machine gives high-school genius the power to read minds.

The MISER'S REVERSION Than 1914 50m. Ref: Bios 6/25/14.
Dream: Miser reverts to ape.

MISS DEATH see DIABOLICAL DR. Z, The

MISS DEATH AND DR. Z see DIABOLICAL DR. Z, The

MISS FAUST (F) Pathe 1909 color 10m. Adaptation of "Faust"
legend. Ref: V&FI IV:22:7. Lee. Miss Faust sells soul for
youth, beauty.

MISS JEKYLL AND MADAME HYDE Vita 1915 Ref: FM 34:55.
Lee. with Helen Gardner, Paul Scardon (the devil). Satan chains
soul of villain.

MISS MUERTE see DIABOLICAL DR. Z, The

MISS PINKERTON F Nat 1932 75m. D: Lloyd Bacon. From
a story by Mary Roberts Rinehart. Adap: Niven Busch, Lillie
Hayward. Add'l Dial: Robert Tasker. PH: Barney McGill. Ed:
Ray Curtis. Ref: FDY. NYT. with Joan Blondell, George Brent,
Mae Madison, John Wray, Ruth Hall, Alan Lane, C. Henry Gor-
don, Donald Dillaway, Elizabeth Patterson, Blanche Friderici,
Mary Doran, Holmes Herbert, Lucien Littlefield, Nigel de Brulier.
"Spiritistic housekeeper," "cloaked man with the clutching fingers,"
shadows, creaking doors, howling wind.

MISS SHUMWAY CASTS A SPELL (F) Metzger & Woog 1962
color/scope 91m. (UNE BLONDE COMME CA! or MISS SHUM-
WAY JETTE UN SORT-F. MISS SHUMWAY GOES WEST) WB-
7A-TV D: Jean Jabely. From a novel by James Hadley Chase.
SP: Félicien Marceau. Adap: Jabely, Jacques Robert. Ref:
Imagen. TVFFSB. with Taïna Béryl, Jess Hahn, Robert
Manuel, Harold Kay, Rene Lefè(b)vre. Myra Shumway possesses
supernatural powers.

MISS TRILLIE'S BIG FEET Novelty 1915 Ref: MPN 10/16/15.
with Edith Thornton, Joe Burke. Hypnotist "Svengali" attempts
to hypnotize woman.

MISSILE BASE AT TANIAK see CANADIAN MOUNTIES VS.
ATOMIC INVADERS

MISSILE MONSTERS see FLYING DISC MAN FROM MARS

MISSILE TO THE MOON Astor 1958 78m. D: Richard Cunha.
SP: Vincent Fotre, H. E. Barrie. Remake of CAT-WOMEN OF
THE MOON. PH: Meredith Nicholson. Mus: Nicholas Carras.
SpFX: Ira Anderson. Visual FX: Harold Banks. Ref: FFacts.
with Richard Travis, Cathy Downs, Michael Whalen, K. T.
Stevens, Gary Clarke, Laurie Mitchell, Tania Velia, Lisa
Simone. Expedition to the moon finds women, rock creatures,

and a giant spider or two. Even worse than the original, if that's possible.

The MISSING GUEST Univ 1938 68m. D: John Rawlins. SP: Charles Martin, Paul Perez, from Erich Philippi's "Secret of the Blue Room." PH: Milton Krasner. Ref: MFB'38:261. with Paul Kelly, Constance Moore, William Lundigan, E. Stanley, Selmer Jackson, Harlan Briggs, Pat C. Flick, Hooper Atchley, Thomas Carr, Leonard Sues, John Harmon, Allen Fox, Guy Usher, Patrick J. Kelly. V 9/14/38: "Attempted spook mystery is localed in a haunted house as full of prop noises as a Hallowe'en ghost walk. There are enough sliding panels, hidden stairways, phantom voices and clutching hands to make a satire to end all whodunits."

MISSING HEAD The see STRANGE CONFESSION

The MISSING LINK WB 1927 80m. D: Charles Reisner. SP: Reisner, Darryl F. Zanuck. PH: J. D. Jennings. Ref: LC. FD 5/22/27. with Syd Chaplin, Sam Baker (the missing link), Ruth Hiatt, Crauford Kent, Tom McGuire.

The MISSING MUMMY Kalem 1915 Ref: MPW 26:2425. with Bud Duncan, Charles Inslee, Ethel Teare. Man disguised as mummy.

MISSION APOCALYPSE see 087 "MISSION APOCALYPSE"

MISSION MARS AA/Sagittarius-Red Ram 1968 Berkey-Pathe color 87m. (RED PLANET MARS) D: Nicholas Webster. SP: Mike St. Clair. Story: Aubrey Wisberg. PH: Cliff Poland. Mus: Berge Kalajian, Gus Pardalis. Prod Des: Hank Aldrich. SpFX: Haberstroh Studios. Ref: V(d) 9/23/68. FM 52:18. with Darren McGavin, Nick Adams, George DeVries, Heather Hewitt, Shirley Parker. Astronauts find a city and "monsters" on Mars.

MISSION STARDUST (Sp-G-I) Times/Aitor-Theumer-P.E.A. 1968 color/scope 95m. (ORBITA MORTAL-Sp. 4,3,2,1 MUERTE-So. America. MORTAL ORBIT. OPERATION STARDUST) D: Primo Zeglio. SP: K. H. Volgeman, F. de Urrutia. PH: Manuel Merino. Mus: Marcello Giombini, A. G. Abril. Art D: J. P. Cubero. Ref: SpCinema. Boxo 11/11/68. Heraldo'68:323. with Lang Jeffries, Essy Persson, Gianni Rizzo, Luis Dávila, John Karelson, Pinkas Braun, Joachim Hansen. Private company lands spaceship on the moon.

MISSIONE APOCALISSE see 087 "MISSION APOCALYPSE"
MISSIONE PIANETA ERRANTE see PLANET ON THE PROWL
MISSIONE SPECIALE LADY CHAPLIN see OPERATION LADY CHAPLIN

MR. BIDDLE'S CRIME WAVE Univ-Hope/NBC-TV c1959 49m. Ref: TVFFSB. with Roddy McDowall, Pat Crowley, Shari Lewis. "Telefeature": Chemist invents "chemical that eats everything."

Mr. DODD TAKES THE AIR WB 1937 85m. D: Alfred E. Green. SP: William Wister Haines, Elaine Ryan, from "The Great Crooner" by Clarence Budington Kelland. PH: Arthur Edeson. Mus & Lyrics: Harry Warren, Al Dubin. Art D: Robert Haas. P: Mervyn LeRoy. Ref: NYT 8/12/37. with Kenny Baker, Frank McHugh, Alice Brady, Gertrude Michael, Jane Wyman, John Eldredge, Harry Davenport. Invention "cures" broken radios; operation turns inventor, a baritone, into a tenor.

MR. DRAKE'S DUCK (B) UA/Fairbanks-Angel 1951 77m. (The
ATOMIC DUCK) SP, D: Val Guest. Story: Ian Messiter. PH: Jack
Cox. Mus sc: Bruce Campbell. Art D: Maurice Carter. Ref:
HR 8/10/51. with Douglas Fairbanks, Jr., Yolande Donlan,
Howard Marion-Crawford, Wilfrid Hyde-White, Reginald Beckwith,
Jon Pertwee, A. E. Matthews. Duck that lays uranium eggs.
MISTER FREEDOM (F) O. P. E. R. A. /Rond-Point 1968 color 110m.
SP, D: William Klein. PH: Pierre Lhomme. Mus: Serge Gains-
bourg. Art D: J. Dugied, A. Piltant. Ref: MFB'69:51. with
John Abbey, Delphine Seyrig, Philippe Noiret, Catherine Rouvel,
Donald Pleasence, Yves Montand, Sabine Sun. The ultimate
weapon destroys France.
MR. INVISIBLE (G-Sp-I-Monaco) Carsten/P. C. Dia/Edo 1970
color/scope 98m. (MISTER UNSICHTBAR-G. El INVENCIBLE
HOMBRE INVISIBLE-Sp. L'INAFFERRABILE MR. INVISIBLE-I.
The INVINCIBLE INVISIBLE MAN) D: Antonio Margheriti
(Anthony Dawson). SP: M. Eller, L. Marquina. PH: Alejandro
Ulloa. Mus: C. Savina. Art D: A. Cofiño, A. Crugnola. Ref:
SpCinema'71. V 5/12/71. M/TVM 5/70. with Dean Jones,
Philippe Leroy, G. Moschin, Ingeborg Schoener. Indian potion
which renders things invisible; scientist's anti-flu serum.
MR. JARR'S MAGNETIC FRIEND Vita 1915 15m. Ref: LC.
MPN 4/17/15. D: Harry Davenport. Man magnetized by
dynamo.
MR. JOE YOUNG OF AFRICA see MIGHTY JOE YOUNG
MR. KRANE NBC-TV 1957 54m. Ref: TVFFSB. with Sir
Cedric Hardwicke, John Hoyt, Peter Hansen. In 1962 a race from
another world gives earth a life-or-death ultimatum.
MR. SARDONICUS Col 1962 89m. D, P: William Castle. SP:
Ray Russell, from his "Sardonicus." PH: Burnett Guffey. Mus:
Von Dexter. Art D: Cary Odell. Ref: FFacts. TVG. with Guy
Rolfe, Oscar Homolka, Ronald Lewis, Audrey Dalton, Erika
Peters, James Forrest, Vladimir Sokoloff, Lorna Hanson. Paraly-
sis freezes baron's face into hideous grin.
MR. SERVADAC'S ARCH see ON THE COMET
MR. SMITH GOES GHOST Toddy c1950 Ref: FJA poster: "You'll
quiver." with "Pigmeat" Markham, Lawrence Criner, Johnny
Taylor, Florence O'Brien.
MR. STEINWAY (by R. Bloch) see TORTURE GARDEN
MISTER UNSICHTBAR see MR. INVISIBLE
MR. WONG, DETECTIVE Mono 1938 68m. D: William Nigh.
SP: Houston Branch. Based on Hugh Wiley's "James Lee Wong"
stories. Ref: Hollywood Spectator. with Boris Karloff, Grant
Withers, Evelyn Brent, Lucien Prival, John Hamilton, George
Lloyd. "Little glass balls, filled with a deadly gas and so
delicately constituted that certain sound vibrations will shatter
them."
MR. WONG AT HEADQUARTERS see FATAL HOUR, The
MISTERIO DE LAS NARANJAS AZULES, El see MYSTERY OF THE
BLUE ORANGES, The
MISTERIO DEL ROSTRO PALIDO, El see MYSTERY OF THE
GHASTLY FACE, The
MISTERIO DEL CUARTO AMARILLO, El see MYSTERY OF THE

YELLOW ROOM, The (1947)
MISTERIO DI ATLANTIDE, Il see GIANT OF METROPOLIS
MISTERIOS DE ULTRATUMBA see BLACK PIT OF DR. M
MISTERIOS DELA MAGIA NERA, Los see MYSTERIES OF BLACK
  MAGIC
MISTERIOSO TIO SYLAS, El see MYSTERIOUS UNCLE SILAS, The
MISTERIUS see DOUBLE DECEPTION
MISTERO DEI TRE CONTINENTI, Il see MISTRESS OF THE
  WORLD
The MISTLETOE BOUGH (B\ Clarendon 1904 8m. Mus: Sir
  Henry Bishop. Ref: SilentFF. The bride vanishes at a wedding
  celebration. Thirty years later the groom has a vision of her
  leaving a chest. He rushes to the chest, pries it open, and finds
  her skeleton.
The MISTLETOE BOUGH (B) 1926 short (HAUNTED CASTLES
  series) D: C. C. Calvert. Ref: V 2/24/26. Brit. Cinema.
MISTRESS OF ATLANTIS see LOST ATLANTIS
MISTRESS OF THE WORLD (I-F-G) Continental/Franco London/CCC
  1960 color 100m. Part I/90m.-Part II (Il MISTERO DEI TRE
  CONTINENTI-I. Les MYSTERES D'ANGKOR-F. HERRIN DER
  WELT-G.) D: William Dieterle. SP: Jo Esinger, M. G.
  Petersson. PH: Richard Angst. Mus: Roman Vlad. Art D: Willy
  Schatz, Helmut Nentwig. Ref: Bianco'61. German Pictures 63/64.
  with Martha Hyer, Carlos Thompson, Micheline Presle, Gino
  Cervi, Sabu, Lino Ventura, Wolfgang Preiss, Georges Rivière,
  Carl Lange, Hans Nielsen, Charles Regnier, Rolf von Nauckhoff,
  Jean Claude Michel, Carlo Giustini. Professor's invention con-
  trols the world's magnetic fields.
MISTRESSES OF DR. JEKYLL see DR. ORLOFF'S MONSTER
A MODERN BLUEBEARD (Mex) Alsa Films 1946 (El MODERNO
  BARBA-AZUL) SP, D: Jaime Salvador. Story: Victor Trivas.
  PH: Agustin Jimenez. Art D: Ramon Rodriguez. Makeup: A.
  Garibay. Ass't D: Alfonso Corona Blake. Ref: FM 31:19. Indice.
  with Buster Keaton, Angel Garasa, Virginia Serret, Fernando
  Soto, "Mantequilla," Jorge Mondragon. Man takes trip to
  "moon": lunar inhabitants really lunatics.
MODERN DR. JEKYLL, The see DR. JEKYLL AND MR. HYDE
  (1908)
The MODERN PIRATES (B?) Alpha 1906 Ref: SF Film. Armored
  car.
The MODERN SPHINX American 1916 33m. D: Charles Bennett.
  Ref: MPW 27:1189. with Winifred Greenwood, Edward Coxen,
  Robert Klein, George Field, Nan Christy, Charles Newton. An
  Egyptian astrologer "puts his daughter to sleep for 3,000 years."
  Reincarnated in the present, she has a tragic love affair, takes
  poison, and dies. "Her father reawakens her in Egypt."
A MODERN YARN (F) Pathe 1911 6m. Ref: Bios 5/30/12. Man
  in car travelling along ocean floor encounters "big fish, oysters,
  crabs and sea-anemones."
MOJU see BLIND BEAST, The
MOLCZACI KRZYDLA see FIRST SPACESHIP ON VENUS
The MOLE PEOPLE Univ 1956 78m. D: Virgil Vogel. SP:
  Laszlo Gorog. PH: Ellis Carter. Mus D: Joseph Gershenson.

Art D: Alexander Golitzen, Robert E. Smith.   SpPH: Clifford
Stine.   P: William Alland.   Ref: FDY.   PM. with John Agar,
Cynthia Patrick, Hugh Beaumont, Alan Napier, Dr. Frank Baxter,
Nestor Paiva, Rodd Redwing, Robin Hughes, Phil Chambers.
Sumerian city dropped hundreds of feet below ground-level by an
earthquake about 3,000 B.C. survives to the present day. The
plot is more than a little embarrassing but provides for creepy
scenes of the mole people wriggling up through sand to kidnap
people.
MOLEMEN VS. THE SON OF HERCULES   (I)   Interfilm-Leone
1961 color/scope 97m.   (MACISTE, L'UOMO PIU FORTE DEL
MONDO.   MACHISTE, STRONGEST MAN IN THE WORLD.   The
STRONGEST MAN IN THE WORLD.   MACISTE AND THE NIGHT
QUEEN)   Story, D: Antonio Leonviola.   SP: Marcello Baldi,
G. Mangione, PH: Alvaro Mancori.   Mus: Armando Trovaioli.
Ref: MFB'64:75.   Pic: FM 22:10. with Mark For(r)est, Moira
Orfei, Paul Wynter, Raffaella Carrà, Gianni Garko, Graziella
Granata, Enrico Glori.   Underground kingdom; molemen, crea-
tures that live in the dark.
MOLTEN METEOR, The   see   BLOB, The
MOMIA, La   see   AZTEC MUMMY, The/FACE OF THE SCREAM-
ING WEREWOLF
MOMIA ATZECA, La   see   AZTEC MUMMY, The
MOMIA ATZEKA CONTRA EL ROBOT HUMANO, La   see   ROBOT
VS. THE AZTEC MUMMY, The
MOMIE DU ROI, La   see   MUMMY OF THE KING OF RAMSEES,
The
MONCH MIT DER PEITSCHE, Der   see   MONK WITH THE WHIP,
The
MONDE COMME IL VA, Le (by Voltaire)   see   GOLD AND LEAD
MONDE TREMBLERA, Le   see   WORLD WILL SHAKE, The
MONEY AND LOVE (I)   Capitani/Cines   1936   (DENARA E
D'AMORE)   D: Guido Brignone.   SP: Luigi Bonelli, Ivo Perilli.
Ref: FD 3/22/37. with Elsa Merlini, Amedeo Mazzari, Maurizio
D'Ancora, E. Roveri.   A girl falls into a trance.   She is pro-
nounced dead and is relegated to a tomb.   Her trance terminates,
and she disappears.
MONEY TO BURN   Fox 1922 55m.   D: Rowland V. Lee.   SP: Jack
Strumwasser.   PH: David Abel.   Ref: AFI. with William Russell,
Sylvia Breamer, Hallam Cooley, Harvey Clark.   "Lucky" Garrity
buys a "haunted" country estate.
The MONITORS   Commonwealth United/Bell & Howell   1969 Techni-
color 92m.   D: Jack Shea.   SP: Myron J. Gold, from a novel by
Keith Laumer.   PH: William Zsigmond.   Mus: Fred Kaz.   Art D:
Roy Henry.   Ref: TVFFSB.   RVB.   Boxo 11/10/69. with Guy
Stockwell, Susan Oliver, Avery Schreiber, Larry Storch, Ed
Begley, Keenan Wynn, Sherry Jackson, Alan Arkin, Shepperd
Strudwick, Xavier Cugat, Stubby Kaye, Jackie Vernon, Everett
Dirksen.   Monitors from another world control earth.
The MONK WITH THE WHIP   (W.G.)   Rialto/Constantin 1968
(Der MONCH MIT DER PEITSCHE-G.   Il FANTASMA DI LONDRA-
I.) color   D: Alfred Vohrer.   SP: Alex Berg.   PH: Karl Löb.   Ref:
Bianco 9/68. with Joachim Fuchsberger, Ursula Glas, Grit

Böttcher, Ilse Page, Tilly Lauenstein.

A MONKEY BITE (F) Pathe 1911 7m. Ref: Bios 10/26/11.
Victims of monkey's bite act like monkeys.

MONKEY BUSINESS Fox 1952 97m. D: Howard Hawks. SP:
Ben Hecht, I.A.L. Diamond, Charles Lederer. Story: Harry
Segall. PH: Milton Krasner. Mus sc: Leigh Harline. Ref: FDY.
with Cary Grant, Ginger Rogers, Marilyn Monroe, Charles
Coburn, Hugh Marlowe, Robert Cornthwaite, Larry Keating,
Douglas Spencer, Esther Dale, George Winslow. Professor discovers rejuvenation serum. Erratically amusing. Ginger Rogers
in a badly misconceived role. Only an auteur-inclined critic would
call this Hawks' "greatest comedy." Fairly good.

MONKEY PLANET (novel by P. Bouille) see PLANET OF THE
APES

The MONKEY TALKS Fox 1927 D: Raoul Walsh. SP: L. G.
Rigby. Ref: FMO 5:9. FM 52:42. Photoplay 4/27. Makeup:
Jack Pierce. A man steals a vaudeville performer's "man-
monkey," " a strange little man," and substitutes a real simian.
"The real monkey--a murderous beast--slinks into the dressing
room of the girl whom the talking monkey had loved." with Olive
Borden, Jacques Lerner, Don Alvarado, Ted McNamara.

The MONKEY'S PAW (B) Magnet 1915 45m. From the story by
W. W. Jacobs. Ref: Hist.Brit.Film. with Jack Lawson.

The MONKEY'S PAW (B) Selznick 1923 55m. D: Manning Haynes.
SP: Lydia Hayward. From W. W. Jacobs' story.

The MONKEY'S PAW RKO 1932 56m. D: Wesley Ruggles. SP:
Louise Parker, Graham John. From W. W. Jacobs' story. PH:
Leo Tover. Ref: FDY. with C. Aubrey Smith, Ivan Simpson,
Louise Carter, Bramwell Fletcher, Herbert Bunston, Winter
Hall. Harrison's 11/26/32: "Mother wishes for return of dead
son....subsequent knocking on the door..."

The MONKEY'S PAW (B) Butcher's/Kay Film 1948 64m. SP, D,
Norman Lee. SP: also Barbara Toy. From the story by W. W.
Jacobs. PH: Bryan Langley. Mus D: Stanley Black. Ref:
MFB'48:92. Brit.Fm.Ybk. '49/'50. with Milton Rosmer, Michael
M. Harvey, Norman Shelley, Joan Seton, Megs Jenkins, Alfie
Bass, Hay Petrie, Sydney Tafler, Mackenzie Ward.

MONKEY'S PAW, The (by W. W. Jacobs) see SPIRITISM

The MONKEY'S UNCLE BV 1965 87m. D: Robert Stevenson.
SP: Tom and Helen August. PH: Edward Colman. Sequel to
MISADVENTURES OF MERLIN JONES. Ref: COF 7:46. with
Tommy Kirk, Annette, Arthur O'Connell, Cheryl Miller, Leon
Ames, Frank Faylen, Connie Gilchrist. Highschool genius in-
vents bicycle-driven aircraft.

The MONOCLE (F) Les Films Cocinor-Laetitia 1964 (Le
MONOCLE RIT JAUNE. "The MONOCLE" GIVES A SICKLY SMILE)
D: Georges Lautner, SP: M. Renault, J. Robert, A. Kantoff.
PH: Maurice Fellous. Mus: M. Magne. Ref: La Prod.Cin.Fr.
7/64. with Paul Meurisse, Robert Dalban, Marcel Dalio,
Barbara Steele. Radio-steered junk.

The MONOLITH MONSTERS Univ 1957 77m. D: John Sherwood.
SP: Robert Fresco, Norman Jolley. Story: Jack Arnold, Fresco.
PH: Ellis Carter. Mus: Joseph Gershenson. Art D: Alexander

Golitzen, Bob Smith. SpFX: Clifford Stine. P: Howard Christie.
Ref: FDY. with Grant Williams, Lola Albright, Phil Harvey,
Les Tremayne, Trevor Bardette, William Flaherty, Harry Jackson, William Schallert. PM: "Meteor deposit grows into giant
obelisks that crash, splinter--then each piece starts shooting
up.... The rocks absorb the silicon in humans, and they turn to
stone." One of the best-conceived of the late-Fifties' movie
monsters (though the special-effects execution isn't quite equal to
the conception), the monolith "monsters" are really just a new
form of natural disaster like a hurricane or a flood.
MONOPOLE CAPITALISM, The (by Baran and Sweezy)   see BIG
   MESS, The
The MONOPOLIST Pathe 1915 50m. Ref: MPN 8/21/15.   Inven-
   tion will "increase the speed of all merchant vessels."
The MONSTER (F) Melies/Star 1903 (Le MONSTRE) Ref: DDC
   III:352. Living skeleton.
The MONSTER MGM 1925 80m. D: Roland West. Titles: C.
   Gardner Sullivan. PH: Hal Mohr. Ed: A. Carle Palm. SP:
   Willard Mack, Albert Kenyon. From the play by Crane Wilbur.
   Ref: NYT 2/16/25. V 2/18/25. FM 8:26.24:8. TBG. Pic:
   FM 23:75.54:37. MW 10:13. AFI. with Lon Chaney, Gertrude
   Olmstead, Edward McWade, Walter James. George Austin, Hal-
   lam Cooley, Charles Sellon, Johnny Arthur. Dr. Ziska gets sub-
   jects for vivisection by arranging auto accidents on a lonely
   stretch of road near his underground laboratory.
MONSTER, The (story by S. Crane)   see FACE OF FIRE
MONSTER A GO-GO B.I.&L. 1965 Ref: FJA poster. Pic: FM
   36:9. with Phil Morton, June Travis, George Perry, Lois
   Brooks.   Ten-foot-tall man-monster.
MONSTER AMONG THE GIRLS, The see WEREWOLF IN A
   GIRLS' DORMITORY
A MONSTER AND A HALF (I) Adelphia 1964 (Un MOSTRO...E
   MEZZO) SP, D: Steno. SP: also Continenza. PH: C. Santoni.
   Ref: Ital P. with Franco Franchi, Ciccio Ingrassia, Margaret
   Lee.   Plastic surgery gives thief face of well-known gangster.
The MONSTER AND THE APE Col 1945 serial 15 episodes D:
   Howard Bretherton. SP: S. Lowe, R. K. Cole. PH: L. W. O'
   Connell. Ref: Barbour. STI 4:49. ModM 3:22. Pic: FanMo
   7:16. with Robert Lowery, George Macready, Ralph Morgan,
   Carole Mathews, Willie Best, Jack Ingram, Anthony Warde,
   Eddie Parker, Stanley Price. Robot, gorilla, "electronic ener-
   gizer" with fatal rays.
The MONSTER AND THE GIRL Para 1941 65m. (D.O.A.) D:
   Stuart Heisler. SP: Stuart Anthony. PH: Victor Milner. Ref:
   FDY. FM 66:20. with Ellen Drew, Rod Cameron, Robert Paige,
   Paul Lukas, Joseph Calleia, George Zucco, Onslow Stevens,
   Gerald Mohr, Phillip Terry, Marc Lawrence, Tom Dugan, Willard Robertson, Minor Watson. "Mangle Murderer" is an ape
   with the brain of a man executed for murder. Combination of
   dumb melodrama, cheap gangster movie, and dumb shocker fails
   thoroughly as any one of the three or as a whole. The horror
   plot seems tacked on. "Nobody does" line: "I don't wanna get
   mangled!"

MONSTER BARAN, The see VARAN

MONSTER FROM A PREHISTORIC PLANET see GAPPA

MONSTER FROM BENEATH THE SEA, The see IT CAME FROM BENEATH THE SEA

MONSTER FROM GREEN HELL DCA 1957 71m. (BEAST FROM GREEN HELL. CREATURE FROM GREEN HELL) D: Kenneth Crane. SP: Louis Vittes, Endre Bohen. PH: Ray Flin. SpFX: Jess Davison. SpPhFX: Jack Rabin, Louis DeWitt. P: Al Zimbalist. Ref: FM 2:64. FDY. with Jim Davis, Barbara Turner, Eduardo Ciannelli, Vladimir Sokoloff, Robert E. Griffin, Joel Fluellen, Tim Huntley. Radiation-affected insects become monsters. Dull, shoddily-made s-f.

MONSTER FROM MARS see ROBOT MONSTER

MONSTER FROM THE EARTH'S END (novel by M. Leinster) see NAVY VS. THE NIGHT MONSTERS, The

MONSTER FROM THE MOON see ROBOT MONSTER

MONSTER FROM THE OCEAN FLOOR Lippert/Palo Alto 1954 64m. (IT STALKED THE OCEAN FLOOR) D: Wyott Ordung. SP: William Danch. PH: Floyd Crosby. Mus: Andre Brumer. P: Roger Corman. Ref: MFB'56:33. FM 15:10. 27:17. with Anne Kimbell, Stuart Wade, Ordung, Dick Pinner. Miniature submarine vs. octopus-like sea monster. Very talky. But only one memorable line: "She's pretty and she's got a head on her shoulders, among other things." Totally terrible.

MONSTER FROM THE SURF AI-TV/US Films/Favorite Films 1965 70m. (SURF TERROR. INVISIBLE TERROR. BEACH GIRLS AND THE MONSTER) D: Jon Hall. SP: Joan Gardner. Mus: Frank Sinatra, Jr. Ref: MW 10:9. with Hall, Sue Casey, Walker Edmiston, Dale Davis, Read Morgan. Murders apparently committed by sea creature. Terrible. Half the movie is dull surfing footage. One of the very worst.

MONSTER FROM THE UNKNOWN WORLD see ATLAS IN THE LAND OF THE CYCLOPS

The MONSTER GORILLA (J) Toei 1959 scope 60m. (GEKKO KAMEN. MOONLIGHT MASK. MAN IN THE MOONLIGHT MASK) D: Satoru Ainoda. Ref: J. Films'60. FEFN 6/59. Pic: SM 8:5. with Fumitake Kimura, Yaeko Wakamizu. Gekko Kamen combats "assorted monsters."

MONSTER IN THE NIGHT see MONSTER ON THE CAMPUS

The MONSTER KILLS Tiffany 1931 69m. (MURDER AT MID-NIGHT-TV) D: Frank Strayer. SP: Strayer, W. Scott Darling. PH: William Rees. Ref: FDY. MPH 7/18/31:33. with Alice White, Aileen Pringle, Hale Hamilton, Clara Blandick, Brandon Hurst, Leslie Fenton, Robert Ellis. One funny gag and one twist don't save a poor mystery. It's not as bad as it seems it will be at first, but it's bad enough. There is no real "monster."

MONSTER LIVES AGAIN, The see RESURRECTED MONSTER, The

The MONSTER MAKER PRC 1944 62m. D: Sam Newfield. SP: Martin Mooney, Pierre Gendron. Story: Lawrence Williams. PH: Robert Cline. Mus sc: Albert Glasser. Art D: Paul Palmentola. P: Sigmund Neufeld. Ref: HR 3/6/44. V 3/6/44. COF-A:47. 17:18-20. Pic: FM 29:60. HM 9:37. with J. Carrol Naish, Ralph Morgan, Wanda McKay, Tala Birell, Terry Frost,

Glenn Strange, Sam Flint. Russian doctor injects acromegaly germs into victims, creates monsters.

MONSTER MEETS THE GORILLA, The see BELA LUGOSI MEETS A BROOKLYN GORILLA

MONSTER OF FATE, The see GOLEM, The (1915)

The MONSTER OF HIGHGATE PONDS CFF/Halas & Batchelor 1960 (B) 59m. (The CREATURE FROM HIGHGATE POND) D: Alberto Cavalcanti. SP: Mary Cathcart Borer. Story: Joy Batchelor. PH: Frank North. Mus: Francis Chagrin. Model animation: Vic Hotchkiss. Ref: MFB'61:83. FanMo 6:31. with Ronald Howard, Terry Raven, Michael Wade, Rachel Clay, Roy Vincente (monster), Michael Balfour, Philip Latham. Egg from Malaya hatches into monster.

The MONSTER OF LONDON CITY (W. G.) PRO/Manley/CCC-Omnia-Gloria 1964 ('67-U.S.) 87m. (Das UNGEHEUER VON LONDON CITY) D: Edwin Zbonek. SP: R. A. Stemmle. Story: B. Edgar Wallace. PH: Siegfried Hold. Mus: Martin Böttcher. Art D: H. J. Kiebach, E. Schomer. Makeup: H. Stamm, I. Haas. Ref: V 8/2/67. FIR'67:85. German Pictures. with Hansjörg Felmy, Marianne Koch, Dietmar Schönherr, Hans Nielsen, Kai Fischer. "While the actor Richard Sand plays the part of Jack the Ripper on the stage of the Edgar Allan Poe Theatre at London Whitechapel, a series of murders which recall those of Jack the Ripper is enacted."

MONSTER OF MONSTERS-GHIDORAH see GHIDRAH

The MONSTER OF PIEDRAS BLANCAS DCA/Vanwick/Filmservice 1961(1958) 71m. D: Irvin Berwick. SP: Haile Chace. PH: Philip Lathrop. Art D: W. Woodworth. Ref: MFB'62:54. with Les Tremayne, Jeanne Carmen, John Harmon, Don Sullivan, Forrest Lewis. Lighthouse keeper suspects legendary monster lurks in nearby cave. Not much.

MONSTER OF THE OPERA see VAMPIRE OF THE OPERA, The

The MONSTER OF THE SHADOW (Mex) Importadora/Cub-Mex 1954 92m. (El MONSTRUO EN LA SOMBRA) D: Zacarias Urquiza. SP: A. P. Delgado. Story: F. B. Caignet. PH: Gabriel Figueroa. Mus: G. C. Carrion. Ref: Indice. FM 31:22: fantasy. with Eduardo Noriega, Martha Roth, Jaime Fernandez.

MONSTER OF THE SHADOWS see WARNING SHADOWS

The MONSTER OF THE VOLCANOES (Mex) Grovas-Cinematografica 1962 (EL MONSTRUO DE LOS VOLCANES. El FANTASMA DE LAS NIEVES) D: Jaime Salvador. SP: Federico Curiel, Alfredo Ruanova. PH: E. Carrasco. Art D: S. L. Mena. Ref: M/TVM 5/62. Indice. with Joaquin Cordero, Ana B. Lepe, Victor Alcocer, Andres Soler, Antonio Raxell, David Hayat, Jose Chavez. cf. THE TERRIBLE SNOW GIANT.

MONSTER OF THE WAX MUSEUM see NIGHTMARE IN WAX

MONSTER OF VENICE see OMICRON

MONSTER OF VENICE, The see EMBALMER, The

MONSTER ON THE CAMPUS Univ 1958 76m. (MONSTER IN THE NIGHT. STRANGER ON THE CAMPUS) D: Jack Arnold. SP: David Duncan. PH: Russell Metty. Mus D,P: Joseph Gershenson. Art D: Alexander Golitzen. SpPH: Clifford Stine. Makeup: Bud Westmore. Ref: FFacts. FM-A'69:35. TVG. with

Monster   330

Arthur Franz, Joanna Moore, Troy Donahue, White Bissell,
Judson Pratt, Phil Harvey, Helen Westcott, Ross Elliott. Strange
substance turns living things into the species from which they
stemmed.   The ending is a bit different. Everything else is the
same.
MONSTER ON THE HILL   see   TEENAGE MONSTER
MONSTER SHOW, The see   FREAKS
MONSTER SNOWMAN, The see   HALF HUMAN
The MONSTER STRIKES (Fili) People's Pictures 1959 (PUSANG
ITEM) D: Cirio H. Santiago. Ref: FEFN XII: #5-6. with John-
ny Monteiro, Cynthia Zamora, Laura Delgado, Carol Varga.
Half-man, half-cat monster killed once has been cursed to "live
and die 9 times like a cat. "
The MONSTER THAT CHALLENGED THE WORLD   UA /Gramarcy
1957 83m. D: Arnold Laven. SP: Pat Fielder.   Story: David
Duncan. PH: Lester White. Underwater PH: Scotty Welbourne.
Mus: Heinz Roemheld.   Art D: James Vance. P: Jules Levy,
Arthur Gardner. Ref: Clarens. PM. with Tim Holt, Audrey
Dalton, Hans Conreid, Casey Adams, Mimi Gibson, Gordon Jones,
Marjorie Stapp, Jody McCrea, William Swan, Charles Tannen,
Hal Taggert, Milton Parsons. California earthquakes provide
hatching conditions for the eggs of a giant prehistoric snail.
The usual.
The MONSTER WALKS Mayfair /Action 1932 63m. (The MONSTER
WALKED) D: Frank Strayer. SP: Robert Ellis. PH: Jules Cron-
jager. Ref: MFB'41:167. Clarens. Photoplay 4 /32. with Rex
Lease, Vera Reynolds, Mischa Auer, Sheldon Lewis, Martha
Mattox, Sidney Bracy, Sleep 'n' Eat (aka Willie Best). "Creepy"
house, doctor experimenting with apes, murderer on the loose.
MONSTER WANGMAGWI (Korea) Century 1967 80m. (WANGMAGWI)
D: Hyukjin Kwon. SP: Hayong Byun. PH: Changyong Ham. SpFX:
Soonjai Byun. Ref: Korea Cinema 1967. with Kungwon Nam,
Haekyung Kim, Unjin Hahn, Hikap Kim. Monster 500x human size
sent by race from outer space to conquer world.
MONSTER WHO LIVED AGAIN, The see   RESURRECTED
MONSTER, The
MONSTER WITH GREEN EYES, The see PLANETS AGAINST US,
The
MONSTER WITH YELLOW EYES, The see PLANETS AGAINST
US, The
MONSTER YONGKARI (Korea) AI-TV /Toei-Kuk Dong 1967 100m.
(DAI KOESU YONGKARI. YONGARY-MONSTER FROM THE DEEP
-TV) D: Kiduck Kim. SP: Yunsung Suh. PH: K. Nakagawa,
I. Byon. Ref: Korea Cinema. with Yungil Oh, Chungim Nam,
Soonjai Lee, Moon Kang. Earthquake in China releases monster
which eats tanks, buildings, and ice plant and drinks gasoline
from gas trucks.
MONSTER ZERO see INVASION OF ASTRO-MONSTER
MONSTERS CRASH PAJAMA PARTY Brandon c1965 45m. Ref:
Photon. Orpheus 3:40. with Don Brandon. Haunted house, mad
doctor, man in were-wolf mask, gorilla, vampirish woman.
The MONSTERS DEMOLISHER (Mex) AI-TV 1960 (NOSTRA-
DAMUS Y EL DESTRUCTOR DE MONSTRUOS. NOSTRADAMUS

AND THE DESTROYER OF MONSTERS. El DESTRUCTOR DE
MONSTRUOS) SP, D: Federico Curiel. SP: also C. Taboada.
Ref: FM 33:8. with Jermon Robles, Julio Aleman, Domingo
Soler. Professor combats vampire Nostradamus. A spider web
turns into a magic mirror; but don't expect much else.
MONSTERS FROM THE MOON see ROBOT MONSTER
MONSTERS OF THE NIGHT see NAVY VS. THE NIGHT
    MONSTERS, The
MONSTRE AU FILLES, Le see WEREWOLF IN A GIRLS'
    DORMITORY
MONSTRE AU MASQUE, Le see ATOM AGE VAMPIRE
MONSTRE AUX YEUX VERTS, Le see PLANETS AGAINST US,
    The
MONSTROSITY Emerson 1964 70m. (The ATOMIC BRAIN-TV)
    D: Joseph Mascelli. Ref: V 12/16/64. FM 26:15. TVG. with
    Erika Peters, Judy Bamber, Frank Gerstle, Frank Fowler,
    Marjorie Eaton. Scientist hired to put elderly woman's brain in
    young girl's body produces zombies.
MONSTRUO DE LA MONTANA HUECA, El see BEAST OF HOL-
    LOW MOUNTAIN, The
MONSTRUO DE LOS VOLCANES, El see MONSTER OF THE
    VOLCANOES, The
MONSTRUO EN LA SOMBRA, El see MONSTER OF THE
    SHADOW, The
MONSTRUO RESUCITADO, El see RESURRECTED MONSTER,
    The
MONSTRUOUS DEL TERROR, Los see DRACULA VS. FRANKEN-
    STEIN
MOON PILOT BV 1962 Technicolor 98m. (MOON PILOTS)
    D: James Neilson. SP: Maurice Tombragel. Story: Robert
    Buckner. PH: William Snyder. Mus sc: Paul Smith. Art D:
    Carroll Clark, M. A. Davis. SpFX: Eustace Lycett. Ref:
    FFACTS. FM 13:62. with Tom Tryon, Brian Keith, Edmond
    O'Brien, Dany Saval, Kent Smith, Bob Sweeney, Tommy Kirk,
    Simon Scott, Bert Remsen, Nancy Kulp, Cheeta, William Hudson,
    Girl from outer space sent from friendly planet to correct defect
    in U.S. moon rocket.
MOON ZERO TWO (B) WB/Hammer 1969 Technicolor 100m. D:
    Roy Ward Baker. SP, P: Michael Carreras. Story: G. Lyall,
    F. Hardman, M. Davidson. PH: Paul Beeson. Mus: Don Ellis.
    Art D: Scott MacGregor. SpFX: Les Bowie. SpPhFX: Kit West,
    Nick Allder. Ref: Boxo 2/5/70. MFB. with James Olson,
    Catherina Von Schell, Adrienne Corri, Bernard Bresslaw, Neil
    McCallum, Michael Ripper, Sam Kydd. Men on Mars and the
    moon in the year 2021. A little of everything (including some
    cliches borrowed from westerns) poorly slapped together.
MOONBEAM MAN, The see MAN IN THE MOONLIGHT MASK
MOONLIGHT DREAM, A see LOVER OF THE MOON
MOONLIGHT MASK See CHALLENGING GHOST, The/LAST
    DEATH OF THE DEVIL, The/MONSTER GORILLA, The
MOONSHINE MOUNTAIN Dominant c1967 Eastmancolor 90m.
    P, D: Herschell Gordon Lewis. SP: Charles Glore. Ref: Miami
    Herald 12/16/67. with Chuck Scott, Adam Sorg, Jeffrey Allen,

Bonnie Hinson. Sheriff Potter keeps "Half-human, ape-like Basham" to kill revenuers who approach his giant still.

The MOONSTONE Selig 1909 17m. From the novel by Wilkie Collins. F Index 6/12/09. Hypnotic trance.

The MOONSTONE Urbanora 1911 22m. From the novel by Wilkie Collins. Ref: Bios 9/28/11. 10/9/13. Misfortune follows the one who steals the jewel of the Moon God. Sleepwalker; "mysterious hand."

The MOONSTONE World 1915 D: Frank Crane. From the novel by Wilkie Collins. Ref: MPN 6/26/15. COF 11:61. with Eugene O'Brien, Elaine Hammerstein.

The MOONSTONE Mono 1934 62m. D: Reginald Barker. SP: Adele Buffington. PH: Robert Planck. P: Paul Malvern. From the novel by Wilkie Collins. Ref: MPH 8/11/34. V 9/18/34: "Shrieking wind, eerie cries." with David Manners, Claude King, Phyllis Barry, Gustav von Seyffertitz, Herbert Bunston, Olaf Hytten, John Davidson, Jameson Thomas. Oriental drug makes user walk in sleep.

MOONSTRUCK (F) Pathe 1909 12m. Ref: F Index. Dream: Little moonmen.

MORE LIQUID ELECTRICITY see GALVANIC FLUID, The

MORELLA (by E. A. Poe) see TALES OF TERROR

MORI NO ISHIMATSU YUREI DOCHU see ISHIMATSU TRAVELS WITH GHOSTS

MORIANNA (Swedish) Hakim-Mondial/Bison 1965 ('68-U.S.) 100m. (90m. -U.S.) (MORIANERNA. I, THE BODY) SP,D: Arne Mattsson. SP: also Per Wahloo. From a novel by Jan Ekström. PH: Max Vihlen. Mus: George Riedel. Art D: Doa Sivertaer. Ref: FFacts. Shriek 4:49: "Horror thriller." with Anders Henriksson, Lotte Tarp, Heinz Hopf, Eva Dahlbeck. Man appears from darkness "like an avenging ghost."

MOROZKO see JACK FROST

MORT DANS LE FILET, Le see HORRORS OF SPIDER ISLAND

MORT DU SOLEIL, La see DEATH OF THE SUN, The

MORT QUI TUE, Le see DEAD MAN WHO KILLED, The

MORT VIVANT, Le see LIVING DEAD MAN, The

MORTAL ORBIT see MISSION STARDUST

MORTE HA FATTO L'UOVO, La see PLUCKED

MORTE VIENE DALLO SPAZIO, La see DAY THE SKY EXPLODED, The

MORTMAIN Vita 1915 55m. Ref: MPN 9/4/15. with Robert Edeson, Donald Hall. Man dreams he loses his hand and has one grafted on in its place.

MORTS-REVIENNENT-ILS, Les? See DRAMA OF THE CASTLE, A

The MOST DANGEROUS GAME RKO 1932 70m. (The HOUNDS OF ZAROFF) P,D: Irving Pichel, Ernest B. Schoedsack. PH: Henry Gerrard. From the short story by Richard Connell. SP: James Creelman. Mus: Max Steiner. Art D: Carroll Clark. Makeup: Wally Westmore. P: Merian C. Cooper. Exec P: David O. Selznick. Ref: MMF 6:47. Pic: FM-A'64:59. COF 16:45. with Joel McCrea, Fay Wray, Robert Armstrong, Leslie Banks, Hale Hamilton, Noble Johnson, Steve Clemento. Big-game hunter arranges shipwrecks off an island in the Malay Archipelago to provide human game for hunting. Not quite the master suspense thriller it's reputed to be but it has some excitement and Banks' performance. See also BLACK FOREST, The/BLOODLUST/COP-LAN SAVES HIS SKIN/GAME OF DEATH, A

MOST DANGEROUS MAN ALIVE Col 1961(1958) 82m. (The STEEL MONSTER) D: Allan Dwan. SP: James Leicester, Phillip Rock. Story: Rock, Michael Pate. PH: Carl Carvahal. Mus: Louis Forbes. Ref: FM 13:64. FFacts. with Ron Randell, Debra Paget, Elaine Stewart, Anthony Caruso, Morris Ankrum, Gregg Palmer, Tudor Owen. An escaped convict is turned into a steel-man by an experimental cobalt bomb explosion. His feats of strength are impressive, but all anybody else gets to do is say things like, "Maybe bullets and electricity won't stop him, but gas might."

MOST DANGEROUS MAN IN THE WORLD, The see CHAIRMAN, The

MOST UNUSUAL WOMAN, A see APE WOMAN, The

MOSTRA DI VENEZIA see OMICRON

MOSTRI DI FRANKENSTEIN, Il see FRANKENSTEIN'S MONSTER

MOSTRO DAGLI VERDI, Il see PLANETS AGAINST US, The

MOSTRO DI VENEZIA, Il see EMBALMER, The

MOSTRO...E MEZZO, Un see MONSTER AND A HALF, A

MOSURA see MOTHRA

MOSURA TAI GOJIRA see GODZILLA VS. THE THING

MOTHER GETS THE WRONG TONIC (B) C&M 1913 7m. Ref: Bios 8/28/13. Chemist's "buck-up" formula makes woman prance about like horse.

MOTHER GOOSE Edison 1909 5m. Ref: MPW'09:133. "Large spider of most ferocious aspect" frightens Miss Muffet and picks up a small boy.

MOTHER-IN-LAW WOULD FLY (B) Walturdaw 1909 9m. Ref: Bios 12/9/09. Motor and propeller added to bed make it fly.

MOTHER RILEY MEETS THE VAMPIRE see MY SON THE VAMPIRE

MOTHRA (J) Col/Toho 1962 Eastmancolor /scope 100m. (MOSURA) D: Inoshiro Honda (Eng. version: Lee Kresel). SP: Shinichi Sekizawa. From the short story "Shukan Asahi" by S. Nakamura. PH: Hajime Koizumi. SpFX: Eiji Tsuburaya. Ref: Clarens. with Frankie Sakai, Kyoko Kagawa, Hiroshi Koizumi, Ken Uehara. Giant caterpillar turns into a giant moth. Not as amusing as Toho's later, more-obviously-intentional comedies.

MOTHRA VS. GODZILLA see GODZILLA VS. THE THING

MOTOR CAR OF THE FUTURE (G) Messter 1910 5m. Ref: Bios 2/23/11. SF Film. Car leaps over train, sea, mountains, etc.

The MOTOR CHAIR (I) Itala 1911 6m. Ref: Bios 7/27/11. Inventor's chair-on-wheels runs "by its own motive power."

The MOTOR VALET (B?) Alpha 1906 D: Arthur Cooper. Ref: SF Film. Robot.

MOULIN DES SUPPLICES, Le see MILL OF THE STONE WOMEN

MOUSE ON THE MOON (B) Lopert 1963 Eastmancolor 85m. (A ROCKET FROM FENWICK) D: Richard Lester. SP: Michael Pertwee. Follow-up to The MOUSE THAT ROARED. PH: Wilkie Cooper. Mus: Ron Grainer. Art D: John Howell. Ref: Orpheus

3:29. FFacts. with Margaret Rutherford, Bernard Cribbins, Ron
Moody, Terry-Thomas, Michael Crawford, David Kossoff, John Le
Mesurier. The Duchy of Grand Fenwick enters the space race
and lands a rocket on the moon.

The MOUSE THAT ROARED (B) Columbia/Highroad 1959 East-
mancolor by Pathe 83m. (The DAY NEW YORK WAS INVADED)
D: Jack Arnold. SP: Stanley Mann, Roger MacDougall, from the
novel by Leonard Wibberley. PH: John Wilcox. Mus sc & d:
Edwin Astley. Ref: handbill. with Peter Sellers, Jean Seberg,
William Hartnell, David Kossoff, Leo McKern, Austin Willis,
Colin Gordon. The Duchy of Grand Fenwick declares war on the
United States. Moderately amusing.

MOVEITE, A NEW HUSTLING POWDER (B) Walturdaw 1910 5m.
Ref: Bios 12/15/10. Inventor's powder makes burglar "gyrate
in an extraordinary manner."

MRS. DEATH (Mex) Col c1968 color (La SEÑORA MUERTE) Ref:
D. Glut. Pic: FM 80:23. with John Carradine, "Frankestein,"
Miguel A. Alvarez, Regina Torne.

MRS. SMITHERS' BOARDING SCHOOL Biog 1907 12m. Ref:
MPW'07:62. Two pupils dressed as ghosts frighten teacher.

MUDE TOD, Der see DESTINY (1921)

MUERTE ENAMORADA, La see DEATH IN LOVE

MUERTE SE LLAMA MYRIAM, La see CAPTAIN FROM TOLEDO

MUERTE VIAJA DEMASIADO, La see DEATH TRAVELS TOO
MUCH

MUERTE VIVIENTE, La see SNAKE PEOPLE, The

MUERTOS DE RISA see DEAD OF LAUGHTER

MUERTOS HABLAN, Los see DEAD SPEAK, The

MUERTOS NO PERDONAN, Los see DEAD DON'T FORGIVE, The

MUJER Y LA BESTIA, La see WOMAN AND THE BEAST, The

MUJERES DE DRACULA, Las see EMPIRE OF DRACULA, The

MUJERES VAMPIROS, Las see SAMSON VS. THE VAMPIRE
WOMEN

MULHER DE TODES, A see WOMAN OF EVERYONE, The

MULINO DELLE DONNE DI PIETRA, Il see MILL OF THE STONE
WOMEN

MUMIA MA, Die see EYES OF THE MUMMY

The MUMMY (B?) Urban 1911 16m. Ref: Bios 9/14/11. Professor dreams mummy comes to life.

The MUMMY Than 1911 17m. Ref: MPW 8:546. Lee. Electricity
turns a mummy into a girl.

The MUMMY (F) Pathe 1911 9m. Ref: Bios 2/15/12. Professor
Darnett discovers a fluid which returns the dead to life. His
assistant impersonates a mummy as part of a plan to marry the
professor's daughter.

The MUMMY Univ 1932 72m. D: Karl Freund. SP: John Balderston. Story: Nina Putnam, Richard Schayer. See also KALKOOT.
PH: Charles Stumar. Makeup: Jack Pierce. Ref: Clarens. with
Boris Karloff, Zita Johann, David Manners, Arthur Byron, Edward Van Sloan, Bramwell Fletcher, Noble Johnson, Leonard
Mudie, Henry Victor. Egyptian mummy Im-ho-tep revived from
the dead. Slow but atmospheric.

The MUMMY (B) Univ/Hammer 1959 Technicolor (TERROR OF

THE MUMMY-Eng.) D: Terence Fisher. SP: Jimmy Sangster.
PH: Jack Asher. Mus: Frank Reizenstein. Art D: Bernard
Robinson. Makeup: Roy Ashton. Ref: FM 42:17. FFacts. with
Peter Cushing, Christopher Lee, Yvonne Furneaux, Eddie Byrne,
Felix Aylmer, Raymond Huntley, John Stuart. Mummy of high
priest menaces the Banning family.

MUMMY, The see AZTEC MUMMY, The

MUMMY LOVE FBO-Standard 1926 22m. D: Joe Rock. Ref:
MPW 78:797. with Neely Edwards, Alice Ardell. "Ghostly and
spooky gags" in mummy vault. Exploring party escapes dressed
as mummies.

The MUMMY OF THE KING OF RAMSEES (F) Lux 1909 10m.
(La MOMIE DU ROI) D: Gerard Bourgeois. Ref: Mitry II.
Bios 7/22/09. An elderly professor brings the mummy of a
king back to life.

MUMMY STRIKES The see AZTEC MUMMY, The

MUMMY'S BOYS RKO 1936 68m. D: Fred Guiol. SP: Jack
Townley, Charles Roberts, Philip Epstein. Story: Townley, Lew
Lipton. PH: Jack MacKenzie. Ed: John Lockert. Ref: FDY.
Motion Picture Reviews. with Bert Wheeler, Robert Woolsey,
Moroni Olson, Willie Best, Frank M. Thomas, Frank Lackteen,
Mitchell Lewis, Francis McDonald, Barbara Pepper. Egyptian
tomb with curse hanging over those who desecrate it; fake living
mummy; bats. Weak plot sparked by some funny bits.

The MUMMY'S CURSE Univ 1944 62m. D: Leslie Goodwins.
SP: Bernard Schubert, Dwight V. Babcock, Leon Abrams.
PH: Virgil Miller. Mus: Paul Sawtell. Art D: John B. Goodman.
Ref: Clarens. FM 11:22. COF 7:40. with Lon Chaney, Jr.,
Virginia Christine, Peter Coe, Kay Harding, Martin Kosleck,
Kurt Katch, Addison Richards, Holmes Herbert, William Farnum.
Kharis and Ananka turn up in the Louisiana bayou. New setting,
same old plot for the mummy story. Very poor.

The MUMMY'S GHOST Univ 1944 61m. D: Reginald LeBorg. SP:
Griffin Jay, Brenda Weisberg, Henry Sucher. PH: William Sick-
ner. Mus: H. J. Salter. Art D: John B. Goodman, Abraham
Grossman. Makeup: Jack Pierce. Ref: Academy. with John Car-
radine, Lon Chaney, Jr., Ramsay Ames, Robert Lowery, Barton
MacLane, Claire Whitney, George Zucco, Frank Reicher, Harry
Shannon, Emmett Vogan, Lester Sharpe, Oscar O'Shea, Jack
Rockwell, Bess Flowers, Caroline Cooke, Eddy Waller, Fay
Holderness, Ivan Triesault, Anthony Warde, Peter Sosso, Martha
MacVicar. Kharis back in America. This one has its moments,
unlike the others in the Chaney mummy series. The writers
have an inside joke when a radio announces, "Dr. X, the mad
doctor of Market Street."

The MUMMY'S HAND Univ 1940 67m. D: Christy Cabanne. SP:
Griffin Jay, Maxwell Shane. PH: Elwood Bredell. Ref: Clarens.
FM 14:6. Pic: FM 69:43. with Dick Foran, Peggy Moran, Wal-
lace Ford, Eduardo Ciannelli, George Zucco, Cecil Kellaway,
Charles Trowbridge, Tom Tyler (the mummy), Si(e)gfried Arno,
Harry Stubbs, Michael Mark, Leon Belasco. Archaeologists
seek tomb of royal Egyptian princess. Trivial but pleasant; Zucco
overdoes it. The archaeological deductions are fairly interesting.

The MUMMY'S SHROUD (B) Fox/7A/Hammer 1967 Technicolor
by DeLuxe 90m. SP, D: John Gilling. Story: John Elder. PH:
Arthur Grant. Mus: Don Banks. Prod Des: Bernard Robinson.
Art D: Don Mingaye. SpFX: Bowie Films. Makeup: George Par-
tleton. Narr: Peter Cushing. Ref: FFacts. FM 46:24. with
Andre Morell, John Phillips, Elizabeth Sellars, Michael Ripper,
Catherine Lacey, Eddie Powell (Prem, the mummy). Defilers
of Egyptian tomb cursed with death.

The MUMMY'S TOMB Univ 1942 61m. D: Harold Young. SP:
Griffin Jay, Henry Sucher. Story: Neil P. Varnick. Scenes
from The MUMMY'S HAND. PH: George Robinson. Mus: H. J.
Salter. Art D: Jack Otterson. Makeup: Jack Pierce. Ref:
Clarens. Egyptian priest sicks mummy on enemies. Worst of
the Universal series. Nothing but cliches. with Lon Chaney,
Jr., Dick Foran, Elyse Knox, John Hubbard, George Zucco,
Wallace Ford, Turhan Bey, Virginia Brissac, Cliff Clark,
Mary Gordon, Frank Reicher, Emmett Vogan.

MUMSY, NANNY, SONNY AND GIRLY see GIRLY

MUNCHAUSEN see ADVENTURES OF BARON MUNCHAUSEN,
The

MUNDO DE LOS VAMPIROS, El see WORLD OF THE VAMPIRES,
The

MUNECOS INFERNALES, Los see CURSE OF THE DOLL PEO-
PLE

MUNSTER, GO HOME Univ 1966 Technicolor 96m. D: Earl
Bellamy. SP: G. Tibbles, Joe Connelly, Bob Mosher. From
"The Munsters" TV series. PH: Benjamin Kline. Mus: Jack
Marshall. Art D: Alexander Golitzen, John Lloyd. Makeup: Bud
Westmore. Ref: PM. FFacts. COF 10:6. FM 32:12. 41:54.
with John Carradine, Yvonne DeCarlo, Al Lewis, Butch Patrick,
Debbie Watson, Hermione Gingold, Terry-Thomas, Bernard
Fox, Cliff Norton, Thelma Ritter. Munsters, descendants of
Frankenstein; vampirish daughter; werewolf.

MURDER AT DAWN Big Four 1932 55m. (DEATH RAY) D:
Richard Thorpe. SP: Barry Barringer. PH: Edward Kull. Ed:
Fred Bain. P: Burton King. Ref: V 4/5/32. Photoplay 4/32.
with Jack Mulhall, Josephine Dunn, Mischa Auer, Martha Mattox, Crauford Kent, Marjorie Beebe, Phillips Smalley, Frank
Ball, Eddie Boland. Professor's death ray that uses power
developed from sunlight; old country house; trap doors; "faces at
windows, falling bodies, weird happenings."

MURDER AT 45 R.P.M. (F) MGM/Cite-Films 1960 105m.
(MEURTRE EN 45 TOURS) D: Etienne Perier. SP: Albert
Valentin, Dominique Fabre, Perier. PH:Marcel Weiss. Ref:
V 6/15/60. Maltin. with Danielle Darrieux, Michael Auclair,
Jean Servais. Composer killed in car crash seems to be haunt-
ing his wife.

MURDER AT MIDNIGHT see MONSTER KILLS, The

MURDER BY INVITATION Mono 1941 67m. D: Phil Rosen.
SP: George Bricker. PH: Marcel Le Picard. Ref: FD 6/30/41.
V 7/30/41. with Wallace Ford, Sarah Padden, Marian Marsh,
Gavin Gordon, Minerva Urecal, Dave O'Brien, Lee Shumway,
John James. Hooded knife-thrower eliminating heirs to spinster's

fortune; sliding panels, hidden passageways, secret doors.
MURDER BY PROXY (by B. E. Wallace) see PHANTOM OF
SOHO, The
MURDER BY TELEVISION Cameo-Imperial 1935 60m. D: Clifford
Sanforth. P: William M. Pizor. Ref: RVB. Pic: STI 8:53. with
Bela Lugosi, June Collyer, Huntley Gordon, George Meeker,
Charles K. French. Prof. Houghland invents a revolutionary
television tube.
MURDER BY THE CLOCK Para 1931 D: Edward Sloman. SP:
Henry Myers, from the book by Rufus King. Ref: NYT. Pic:
TBG. with Lilyan Tashman, William Boyd, Regis Toomey,
Irving Pichel, Sally O'Neil, Lenita Lane, Blanche Friderici,
Willard Robertson. Man restored to life by drug is killed again.
Secret passages, clutching hands.
The MURDER CLINIC (I-F) Europix/Leone-Orphee 1966 color
75m. (La LAMA NEL CORPO-I. Les NUITS DE L'EPOUVANTE-
F. The BLADE IN THE BODY) D, P: Elio Scardamaglia (aka
Michael Hamilton). SP: Julian Berry (aka E. Gastaldi), Alberto
De Martino (aka Martin Hardy). PH: Marcello Masciocchi. From
"The Knife in the Body" by Robert Williams. Mus: Franco De
Masi. Ref: MMF. MFB'69:103. Ital P. with William Berger,
Françoise Prevost, Mary Young, Barbara Wilson, Harriet White,
Philippe Hersent. Woman disfigured in quicklime is kept by Dr.
Vance in locked room; "monster" armed with razor roams
gloomy corridors.
MURDER IN THE AIR WB 1940 55m. D: Lewis Seiler. SP:
Raymond Shrock. PH: Ted McCord. Art D: Stanley Fleisher.
Ref: PM. FDY. with John Litel, Ronald Reagan, Lya Lys,
James Stephenson, Eddie Foy, Jr., Robert Warwick. "The in-
ertia projector" stops mechanical devices in motion.
MURDER IN THE BLUE ROOM Univ 1944 61m. D: Leslie Good-
wins. SP: I. A. L. Diamond, Stanley Davis, from Erich Philip-
pi's "Secret of the Blue Room." Ref: MPH. with Anne Gwynne,
Donald Cook, John Litel, Grace McDonald, Betty Kean, June
Preisser, Regis Toomey, Emmett Vogan, Ian Wolfe. "Mansion
encrusted with a legend of being haunted because of a murder
committed 20 years previously in its blue room.... secret pas-
sages, sliding panels, irrelevant ghost."
MURDER IN THE FAMILY see GHOST CRAZY
MURDER IN THE GILDED CAGE (play by S. Spewack) see SECRET
WITNESS
MURDER IN THE RED BARN (B) MGM/Olympic 1935 67m.
(MARIA MARTEN or The MURDER IN THE RED BARN. MUR-
DER IN THE OLD RED BARN) D: Milton Rosmer. SP: Randal
Faye. Ref: FD 8/19/36: "Sequences have a gruesome touch as
vivid as the sordid scenes in FRANKENSTEIN." V 9/2/36.
NYT 8/19/36: "Fiend in human form." with Tod Slaughter,
Eric Portman, Sophie Stewart, Dennis Hoey, Noel Dainton, Ann
Trevor. Slaughter, in his film debut, is disappointingly sub-
dued (for him it's subdued), though his occasional audacious
hypocrisy ("Don't you trust me, Maria?") is winning. For com-
pletists only.
MURDERER INVISIBLE, The (by P. Wylie) see INVISIBLE Man,

The (1933)

MURDERERS FROM ANOTHER WORLD (Mex) 1971 (ASESINOS DE
OTROS MUNDOS) D: Rubén Galindo. PH: Raul M. Solares. Ref:
Cinelandia 9/25/71. with Santo, Sasha Montenegro, Carlos
Agosti, Carlos Suárez, Juan Gallardo. Santo vs. "strange and
powerful creatures."

MURDERER'S COMMAND (Sp-G-Portuguese) Hispamer/A.V./Ger-
mania 1966 color/scope 86m. (COMANDO DE ASESINOS)
SP, D: Julio Coll. SP: also José Huici. Story: A. Andrade.
PH: Mario Pacheco. Mus: J. L. Alonso. Sets: T. Villalba. Ref:
SpCinema'67. with Peter van Eyck, Antonio Vilar, Letitia
Roman, Mikaela. "A professor has discovered a new kind of
steel, which even though thin, is invulnerable."

MURDERER'S ROW Col 1966 Technicolor 108m. D: Henry
Levin. SP: Herbert Baker, from the novel by Donald Hamilton.
PH: Sam Leavitt. Mus: Lalo Schifrin. SpFX: Danny Lee. Ref:
FFacts. COF 11:6. with Dean Martin, Ann-Margret, Karl Mal-
den, Camilla Sparv, James Gregory, Beverly Adams. Mad doc-
tor intends to use the helio-beam, super weapon, on Washington,
D.C. Follow-up to THE SILENCERS.

MURDERER'S TIME IS SHORT, The see COPLAN SAVES HIS
SKIN

The MURDERING MITE (J) Daiei 1957 (TOMEININGEN TO
HAIOTOKO. The TRANSPARENT MAN AND THE FLY MAN)
D: Mitsuo Murayama. SP: H. Takaiwa. PH: H. Murai.Ref:
FEFN 8/9/57. 8/23/57. COF 4:58. Pic: COF 3:19. with
Ryuji Shinagawa, Y. Kitahara, Junko Kano. Killer can make him-
self as small as a fly with the "transparency ray."

MURDERS IN THE RUE MORGUE Rosenberg 1914 SP: Sol A.
Rosenberg. Ref: FM 11:42.

MURDERS IN THE RUE MORGUE Univ 1932 75m. D, Adap:
Robert Florey. SP: Tom Reed, Dale van Avery. Dial: John
Huston. From the story by Edgar Allan Poe. PH: Karl Freund.
Art D: Charles D. Hall. SpFX: John P. Fulton. Ref: COF 15:21.
with Bela Lugosi, Sidney Fox, Leon Ames (aka Leon Waycoff),
Bert Roach, Brandon Hurst, Noble Johnson, D'Arcy Corrigan,
Arlene Francis, Herman Bing, Torben Meyer. Number of women
found dead with traces of gorilla blood in their veins. Lugosi
(florid prose and incredible delivery) and the art director (arty
fog and stylized rooftops) have a field day, but the crazy power
of the film fades quickly when Lugosi is offscreen too long, and
the last half hour, wasted on trivial matters and bad comic relief, is strictly ho-hum. Lugosi, as bizarrely hammy as he is,
is almost matched by a gorilla that sniggers.

MURDERS IN THE RUE MORGUE (U.S.-B) AI 1971 Movielab
color 87m. D: Gordon Hessler. SP: Christopher Wicking,
Henry Slesar, from the story by Poe. PH: Manuel Berenguer.
Prod Des: José Luis Galicia. Mus sc & d: Waldo de los Rios.
Ref: V. with Jason Robards, Jr., Christine Kaufmann, Herbert
Lom, Adolfo Celi, Michael Dunn, Lilli Palmer, Maria Perschy,
José Calvo, Peter Arne.

MURDERS IN THE RUE MORGUE (by E. A. Poe) see PHANTOM
OF THE RUE MORGUE/RAVEN, The (1912/SHERLOCK HOLMES

IN THE GREAT MURDER MYSTERY
MURDERS IN THE ZOO   Para 1933 66m.   D: Edward Sutherland.
    SP: Philip Wylie, Seton Miller. PH: Ernest Haller. Ref: FDY.
    Photoplay 7/33: "Horror." with Lionel Atwill, Charles Ruggles,
    Randolph Scott, Harry Beresford, Kathleen Burke, Gail Patrick,
    John Lodge, Edward McWade. Bizarre murders. Drab thriller.
The MUSEUM OF HORROR (Mex) Sotomayor 1963 75m. (El
    MUSEO DEL HORROR) D: Rafael Baledon. SP: J. M. F. Un-
    sain. PH: Raúl M. Solares. Mus: Sergio Guerrero. Art D:
    J. R. Granada. Ref: Heraldo 5/31/67. with Julio Aleman,
    Patricia Conde, Joaquín Cordero, Carlos López Moctezuma,
    Sonia Infante, David Reynoso. Insane ex-actor converts girls
    into exhibits for a museum.
MUSEUM SPOOKS; or, DREAMS IN A PICTURE GALLERY (B)
    Walturdaw 1910 6m. Ref: Bios 1/27/10. While gentleman
    sleeps in art gallery, figures step from paintings and dance
    around him.
The MUSGRAVE RITUAL (F) SFFCE 1913 Ref: LC. From the
    Sherlock Holmes story by Sir Arthur Conan Doyle.
The MUSGRAVE RITUAL (B) Stoll 1922 21m. From the Sherlock
    Holmes story by Sir Arthur Conan Doyle. (Further Adventures
    of Sherlock Holmes series) Adap: George Ridgewell. PH: A. H.
    Moses. Art D: W. W. Murton. Ref: SilentFF. with Eille Nor-
    wood, Hubert Willis, C. Boyne.
MUSGRAVE RITUAL, The (by A. C. Doyle) see SHERLOCK
HOLMES FACES DEATH
MUTINY IN OUTER SPACE   Woolner (U.S.-I?) 1964 85m.   (IN-
    VASION FROM THE MOON. SPACE STATION X. AMMUTINA-
    MENTO NELLO SPAZIO-I. SPACE STATION X-14) D: Hugo
    Grimaldi. SP: Arthur C. Pierce. Ref: TVFFSB. COF 5:51.
    6:51. Orpheus 3:33. Pic: MW 2:25. with William Leslie,
    Dolores Faith, Pamela Curran, Richard Garland, Harold Lloyd,
    Jr. Space station contaminated with a deadly fungus. Ref:
    Boxo 11/22/65.
MUZZ PRVNIHO STOLETI see MAN IN OUTER SPACE
MY BLOOD RUNS COLD WB 1965 104m. P,D: William Conrad.
    SP: John Mantley. PH: Sam Leavitt. Mus: George Duning. Ref:
    PM. FDY. with Troy Donahue, Joey Heatherton, Barry Sullivan,
    Jeanette Nolan. Young man tries to convince heiress that she is
    the reincarnation of his long-dead mistress. What you might ex-
    pect a Troy Donahue-Joey Heatherton horror movie to be, only
    more so.
MY FRIEND DEATH (J) Toho 1961 95m. (YUREI HANJO-KI)
    D: Kozo Saheki. SP: Naoshi Izumo. PH: Hideo Ito. Mus: H.
    Matsui. Ref: Toho Films'61. with Frankie Sakai, Kyoko Kaga-
    wa, Ichiro Arishima, Kingoro Yanagiya. Undertaker's assistant
    strikes up a friendship with Death.
MY FRIEND, DR. JEKYLL (I) Union/MG-Cei Incom 1960 (Il MIO
    AMICO JECKYLL. MY FRIEND JECKYLL. MY PAL, DR.
    JEKYLL) SP,D: M. Girolami. SP: also Scarnicci, Tarabusi.
    From "The Strange Case of Dr. Jekyll and Mr. Hyde" by
    Stevenson. PH: Luciano Trasatti. Ref: Imagen. Ital P. FM
    17:6. COF 7:46. with Ugo Tognazzi, Abbe Lane, Raimondo

Vianello, Carlo Croccolo. Professor invents machine which trans-
fers personalities from one person to another.
MY FRIEND THE DEVIL   Fox   1922   100m.   D: Harry Millarde.
SP: Paul H. Sloane, from the novel "Dr. Rameau" or "Le Docteur
Rameau" by Georges Ohnet. PH: J. Ruttenberg.   Ref: MPN 26:
1165.   AFI.   with Charles Richman, Ben Grauer, Alice May,
Robert Frazer, William Tooker.   Boy calls on God to kill step-
father; lightning strikes his mother.
MY MAID IS TOO SLOW (F?)   Eclair 1910 8m. Ref: Bios 4/14/10.
Hawker's battery attached to woman makes her fly about.
MY PAL, DR. JEKYLL   see   MY FRIEND, DR. JEKYLL
MY SON, THE HERO   (I-F)   UA/Cides-Ariane   1961 ('63-U.S.) Tech-
nicolor 111m.   (I TITANI or ARRIVANO I TITANI-I. The
TITANS, SONS OF THUNDER-Eng.)   SP,D: Duccio Tessari. SP:
also Ennio de Concini.   PH: Alfio Contini.   Mus: Carlo Rustichel-
li. Art D: Ottavio Scotti.   SpFX: Joseph Natanson. Ref: MFB'63:
98.   Film Review 63/4.   FFacts.   Pic:Shriek 4:33.   with Pedro
Armendariz, Giuliano Gemma, Antonella Lualdi, Jacqueline Sas-
sard, Ingrid Schoeller.   Gorgon, Cyclops, Pluto's helmet of invisibility.
MY SON THE VAMPIRE (B)   Blue Chip-Bell-Renown 1952 74m.
(MOTHER RILEY MEETS THE VAMPIRE. VAMPIRES OVER
LONDON. OLD MOTHER RILEY MEETS THE VAMPIRE) D, P:
John Gilling. SP: Val Valentine.   Art D: Bernard Robinson. Ref:
FanMo 5:46.   COF 8:24.   MFB'52:112.   FM 35:66. 41:23   Pic: FM
28:7.   Lugosi's scenes cut, intended for film that was to be
called KING ROBOT.   with Bela Lugosi (Baron Von Housen,
"vampire"), Arthur Lucan, Hattie Jacques, Richard Wattis, Dora
Bryan, Charles Lloyd Pack.   Robot; machine that can "blow up
200 battleships"; Arc Control that reverses the action momentarily.
Really mixed up.   There are a few malapropisms that could be
considered funny, and it's always nice to see Lugosi as a vampire.
MY WIFE IS A PANTHER (F)   UFA Comacuco-Francis Lopez 1961
85m.   (MA FEMME EST UNE PANTHERE)   D: Raymond Bailly.
SP: Gérard Carlier.   PH: Walter Wottitz.   Mus: Lopez.   Ref:
Rep.Gen'61.   with Jean Richard, Jean Poiret & Serault, Silvana
Blasi, Jean-Max, Marcel Lupovici.   A colonel's wife, through
metempsychosis, has been reincarnated as a panther, capable of
assuming human form at will.
MY WORLD DIES SCREAMING   see   TERROR IN THE HAUNTED
HOUSE
MYRTE AND THE DEMONS (B-Holland)   European Art Union/Gyles
Adams   1949 73m.   D, P: Paul Schreiber.   SP: Adams.   PH: Bert
Haanstra.   Mus: Marinus Adam.   Ref: MFB'51:281.   with Myrte,
John Moore, Sonia Gables.   Wood demons are jealous of girl and
seek to destroy her, turning her playmates to stone.
MYSTERE DE LA CHAMBRE JAUNE, Le   see MYSTERY OF THE
YELLOW ROOM, The (1948)
MYSTERE DE LA VILLA ROSE, Le   see MYSTERY AT THE VILLA
ROSE (1931)
MYSTERE SAINT-VAL, Le   see SAINT-VAL MYSTERY, The
MYSTERES D'ANGKOR, Les   see   MISTRESS OF THE WORLD

MYSTERES DE LA VIE ET DE LA MORT see MYSTERIES OF
LIFE AND DEATH
The MYSTERIANS (J) RKO-MGM/Toho 1957 ('59-U.S.) East-
mancolor/scope 89m. (CHIKYU BOEIGUN. EARTH DEFENSE
FORCE) D: Inoshiro Honda. SP: Takeshi Kimura. Story: Jojiro
Okami. Adap: S. Kayama. PH: Hajime Koizumi. Mus: Akira If-
ukube. Art D: Teruaki Aba. SpFX: Eiji Tsuburaya. Ref: PM.
FFacts. with Kenji Sahara, Yumi Shirakawa, Takashi Shimura.
Visitors from outer space bent on carrying off earth women to
improve their race. Slow start, fast finish.
MYSTERIES FROM BEYOND THE GRAVE see BLACK PIT OF
DR. M
MYSTERIES OF BLACK MAGIC (Mex) ALFA/APO/TEC 1957
(Los MISTERIOS DE LA MAGIA NERA. Das GRAB DES DOK-
TOR CALIGARI-G. RETURN FROM THE BEYOND?)   D:
Miguel M. Delgado. SP: Ulises Petit de Murat. PH: Victor
Herrera. Mus: Jose de la Vega. Art D: G. Gerszo. Ref: COF
10:46. RVB. MadM 3:9. Indice. with Nadia Haro Oliva, Carlos
Riquelme, Aldo Moni, Lulu Parga, Carlos Ancira. Woman tries
to communicate with her dead husband through black magic.
MYSTERIES OF INDIA see INDIAN TOMB, The
MYSTERIES OF LIFE AND DEATH (F) 1923 (MYSTERES DE LA
VIE ET DE LA MORT) Ref: DDC II:306. Spiritualism.
The MYSTERIES OF MYRA   Pathe 1916 serial 15 episodes
3. The Mystic Mirrors. 9. The Invisible Destroyer. 10. Levita-
tion. 11. The Fire-Elemental. 12. The Elixir of Youth. 13. Witch-
craft. 14. Suspended Animation. 15. The Thought Monster.
D: Theodore and Leo Wharton. Ref: CNW. MPN 13:2720, 3625,
4083. with Jean Sothern, Howard Estabrook, Allen Murnane,
M. W. Rale, Bessie Wharton. "Remarkable photographic effects."
Vampire?; plant that emits poisonous gas; hypnotizing machine;
black magic, used to slow heroine's heartbeat; machine that col-
lects thought waves in jar.
MYSTERIES OF THE FRENCH POLICE see SECRETS OF THE
FRENCH POLICE
MYSTERIOUS AUTOMATON OF DR. KEMPELEN, The (by H.
Dupuy-Mazuel) see CHESS PLAYER, The (1926)
The MYSTERIOUS CONTRAGRAV Gold Seal 1915 30m. D: Henry
McRae. Ref: Motography 4/10/15. MPN 4/10/15. MPW 24:32.
Antigravity device.
The MYSTERIOUS DOCTOR WB 1943 57m. D: Ben Stoloff. SP:
Richard Weil. PH: Henry Sharp. Art D: Charles Novi. Ref:
FDY. with Eleanor Parker, John Loder, Lester Matthews, Matt
Willis, Creighton Hale, Bruce Lester, Forrester Harvey, Clyde
Cook, DeWolf Hopper, Jack Mower, Crauford Kent. Headless
ghost terrorizes a lonely English village. Bad mystery with a
good makeup job and an odd lot of fog in a cave.
The MYSTERIOUS DR. FU-MANCHU Para 1929 sound and silent
versions 80m. (DR. FU MANCHU. The INSIDIOUS DR. FU-
MANCHU) D: Rowland V. Lee. SP: Florence Ryerson, Lloyd
Corrigan, based on the character created by Sax Rohmer. Comedy
Dial: George Marion, Jr. PH: Harry Fischbeck.Ref: V 7/24/29:
"Mysterious passages, ghostly apparitions." AFI. Pic: TBG. with

Warner Oland, O. P. Heggie, Jean Arthur, Claude King, Noble Johnson, Neil Hamilton. William Austin, Tully Marshall.

MYSTERIOUS DR. R, The see MAN MADE MONSTER

The MYSTERIOUS DR. SATAN Rep 1940 serial 15 episodes ('66 feature DR. SATAN'S ROBOT) D: William Witney, John English. SP: S. Shor, J. Poland, R. Davidson, N. S. Hall, F. Adreon. PH: William Nobles. Ref: Barbour. STI 3:36. with Eduardo Ciannelli, Robert Wilcox, C. Montague Shaw, William Newell, Ella Neal, Charles Trowbridge, Jack Mulhall, Edwin Stanley, Bud Geary, Archie Twitchell, Kenneth Terrell. Mad doctor plans to create army of robots.

MYSTERIOUS HOUSE OF USHER, The see HOUSE OF USHER

MYSTERIOUS INVADER, The see ASTOUNDING SHE MONSTER, The

MYSTERIOUS ISLAND MGM 1929 95m. Technicolor 90% sound SP, D: Lucien Hubbard, Maurice Tourneur, Ben Christiansen, Carl Pierson. From the novel "Mysterious Island" or "L'Isle Mysterieuse" by Jules Verne. PH: Percy Hilburn. Art D: Cedric Gibbons. SpFX: James Basevi, Louis H. Tolhurst, Irving Ries. Mus: Broones & Lange. Ref: Clarens. FM 10:26. Pic: FM 39:54. with Lionel Barrymore, Jane Daly, Harry Gribbon, Montagu Love, Snitz Edwards, Gibson Gowland, Lloyd Hughes. People aboard submarine encounter dragon, tiny human-like creatures.

MYSTERIOUS ISLAND (Russ) 1941) D: E. Penzline, B. Chelintzev. SP: Chelintzev, M. P. Kalinine. From the novel by Jules Verne. PH: M. B. Belskine. SpFX: M. F. Karukov. Ref: MMF 15-16:35. Bianco 7-8'66. RVB. with M. V. Commisarov, A. S. Krasnopolski, P. I. Klansky.

MYSTERIOUS ISLAND Col 1951 serial 15 episodes. D: Spencer G. Bennet. SP: L. Clay, R. Cole. G. H. Plympton. From Jules Verne's "The Isle of Mystery." PH: Fayte Browne. P: Sam Katzman. Ref: Barbour. with Richard Crane, Marshall Reed, Leonard Penn (Capt. Nemo), Karen Randle, Gene Roth, Hugh Prosser, Terry Frost, Rusty Wescoatt.

MYSTERIOUS ISLAND (B) Col/Ameran 1961 Eastmancolor/Super-Dynamation 101 m. (JULES VERNE'S MYSTERIOUS ISLAND) D: Cy Endfield. SP: Crane Wilbur, John Prebble, Dan Ullman. From Verne's novel. PH: Wilkie Cooper. Mus: Bernard Herrmann. P: Charles Schneer. SpFX: Ray Harryhausen. Ref: FM 13:68. Clarens. with Michael Craig, Joan Greenwood, Michael Callan, Gary Merrill, Herbert Lom[Nemo], Nigel Green. Electric super-gun, giant crabs, giant bees, etc. Lesser Harryhausen.

MYSTERIOUS ISLAND (by Verne) see 20000 LEAGUES UNDER THE SEA (1916)

The MYSTERIOUS MAGICIAN (W. G.) 1965 (Der HEXER. The MAGICIAN. The WIZARD) D: Alfred Vohrer. SP: Herbert Reinecker, H. G. Petersson. From "The Ringer" by Edgar Wallace. Ref: FIR. TVK. with Joachim Berger, Heinz Drache, Eddi Arent, Sophie Hardy, Siegfried Lowitz. Phantomlike avenger seems to have returned from the dead.

MYSTERIOUS MR. CHAUTARD, The see MAN WITH TWO FACES, The

The MYSTERIOUS MR. M Univ 1946 serial 13 episodes D: Lewis D.

343   Mysterious

Collins, Vernon Keays. SP: J. Poland, P. Huston, B. Shipman.
PH: Gus Peterson. Ref: FD 8/5/46. Academy. with Jack Ingram,
Jane Randolph, Richard Martin, Pamela Burke, Dennis Moore,
Byron Foulger, Virginia Brissac, Joseph Crehan, John Hamilton,
Mauritz Hugo, George Eldredge, Anthony Warde, Donald Kerr,
Emmett Vogan, Jr. Hypnotic injections; plans for new type of
battery-less submarine motor.
The MYSTERIOUS MR. WONG Mono 1935 60m. D: William
Nigh. SP: Lew Levinson, Nina Howatt. From "The 12 Coins of
Confucius" by Harry Keeler. PH: Harry Neumann. Ref:
V 3/13/35. FD 1/15/35. Pic: COF 8:24. with Bela Lugosi,
Wallace Ford, Arline Judge, Luke Chan, Lee Shumway, Lotus
Long, Robert Emmet O'Connor. Madman mandarin divises
horrible tortures for victims.
The MYSTERIOUS MRS. M Bluebird 1916 55m. Ref: MPW
31:908. MPN 15:757. with Harrison Ford, Mary MacLaren,
Willie Marks. Fortune teller prophesies that she and customer
will die soon. He begins to believe her when he receives word
that she has died.
The MYSTERIOUS RETORT (F) Melies 1906 3m. Ref: V&FI
12/15/06. Dream. "Devil's messenger," large green reptile
with crocodile-like head; "huge grimacing face in spider web."
MYSTERIOUS SATELLITE, The see WARNING FROM SPACE
The MYSTERIOUS STRANGER (F) Eclipse 1911 10m. Ref: Lee.
MPW 10:903. Girl struck by lightning revived.
The MYSTERIOUS STRANGER Ess 1913 17m. Ref: Bios 8/28/13.
Hypnotist gives man visions which haunt him.
The MYSTERIOUS UNCLE SILAS (Arg) Efa 1947 (El MISTERIOSO
TIO SYLAS) D: Carlos Schliepper. SP: Jorge Jantus, from
Sheridan Le Fanus "Uncle Silas." SP: also Leon Mirlas. PH:
Roque Funes. Mus: Juan Ehlert. Art D: Juan M. Concado. Ref:
Historio del Cine Argentino. with Elisa Galve, Francisco de
Paula, Elsa O'Connor, Ricardo Galache.
MYSTERIOUS WORLD OF JULES VERNE, The see STOLEN AIR-
SHIP, The
MYSTERY (India) 1965 (RAAZ) Ref: M/TVM 10/65. Shankar's
2/12/67. with Sapru, Johar, Harindranath Chattopadhyaya,
Rajesh Khanna, Babita, Khanna, Rahul. "Ghost," "creepiness...
haunted temples, and faces in the dark."
MYSTERY AT THE VILLA ROSE (B) Auten 1930 sound 100m. D:
Leslie Hiscott. From the novel "At the Villa Rose" by A. E. W.
Mason. P: Basil Dean. Ref: NYT. with Austin Trevor, Richard
Cooper, Francis Lister, John Hamilton, Norah Baring. Seance,
murder, woman interested in spiritualism.
MYSTERY AT THE VILLA ROSE (F) Haik 1931 (Le MYSTERE DE
LA VILLA ROSE) From A. E. W. Mason's "At the Villa Rose."
Ref: NYT 1/11/32. DDC III:38, 315, 356. with Simone Vaudry,
Leon Mathot, Helene Manso, Jean Mercanton. Elderly woman's
interest in spiritualism makes her easy prey for jewel thieves.
MYSTERY IN THE MINE (B) CFF/Merton Park/Film Producers
Guild 1958 serial 8 episodes D: James Hill. SP: Hill, Dallas
Bower. Story: Peter Ling. Mus: Max Saunders. PH: John
Wiles. Ref: MFB'59:138. with Ingrid Cardon, Howard Greene,

David Rose.   Scientist intends to use "space mirror" to conquer the world.

MYSTERY LINER   Mono   1934   62m.   (The GHOST OF JOHN HOLLING)   D: William Nigh.   SP: Wellyn Totman.   PH: Archie Stout.   From a story by Edgar Wallace.   P: Paul Malvern.   Ref: Photoplay 4/34.   FD 2/28/34.   FIR'67: 77.   Monogram pamphlet: "Ghost-ridden ship." with Noah Beery, Astrid Allwyn, Gustav von Seyffertitz, Edwin Maxwell, Cornelius Keefe, Ralph Lewis, Zeffie Tilbury, George Cleveland, Olaf Hytten.   A radio-controlled ship, operated by an S505 radio tube, leaves port.

The MYSTERY MIND   Supreme (Pioneer) 1920 serial 15 episodes   D: William Davis, Fred Sittenham.   Ref: CNW. Lee. with J. Robert Pauline, Peggy Shanor, Paul Panzer, Ed Rogers.   Ape-man, hypnotism.   Ch. 5. Thought Waves. 7. The Nether World. 9. Dual Personality. 12. The Temple of the Occult. 13. The B(l)inding Ray.

MYSTERY MOUNTAIN   Mascot 1934 serial   D: Otto Brower, B. Reeves Eason.   Story: S. Lowe, B. Sarecky, Eason.   Continuity: Ben Cohen, A. Schaefer.   Ref: Next Time. D. Glut. TBG.   with Ken Maynard, Syd Saylor, Verna Hillie, Edmund Cobb.   "The mysterious Rattler" makes masks that perfectly match the faces of the other leading characters.

The MYSTERY OF EDWIN DROOD   Univ 1935 86m.   D: Stuart Walker.   SP: John Balderston, Gladys Unger, Leopold Atlas, Bradley King, from the unfinished work by Charles Dickens.   PH: George Robinson.   FD 3/20/35: "Creepy murder melodrama... one of those stormy and spooky nights." ModM 3:68.   RVB: Footage from FRANKENSTEIN.   MPH 12/15/34: Rains as Jekyll-Hyde type.   with Claude Rains, Heather Angel, J. M. Kerrigan, David Manners, Valerie Hobson, Douglass Montgomery, E. E. Clive, Zeffie Tilbury, Frances L. Sullivan, Walter Kingsford, Forrester Harvey, Ethel Griffies.

The MYSTERY OF GRAYSON HALL   Eclair 1914 30m.   Ref: MPW 22:643, 714.   Detective impersonates murdered man, "haunts" killer.

The MYSTERY OF HIDDEN HOUSE   Vita 1914 30m.   Ref: MPW 20:102.   Girl with dual personality possessed by souls of "Moina" and "Robina."

MYSTERY OF ISLINGTON, The   see SKELETON OF MRS. MORALES, The

MYSTERY OF LIFE   Univ 1931 62m.   D: George Cochrane.   SP: H. M. Parshley.   Ref: FDY. V 7/7/31.   MPH 7/11/31:33.   FJA: Animated dionsaur sequence.   Pic: FM 19:32.   Documentary.

The MYSTERY OF LOST RANCH   Vita 1925 60m.   D: Harry S. Webb, Tom Gibson.   Continuity: George Hull.   Story: Barr Cross.   Ref: AFI.   with Pete Morrison.   A scientist tests his death ray on birds and wild animals.   Western.

MYSTERY OF MARIE ROGET   Univ 1942 61m.   (PHANTOM OF PARIS)   D: Phil Rosen.   SP: Michel Jacoby.   From the story by Poe.   PH: Elwood Bredell.   Mus: H. J. Salter.   Art D: Jack Otterson.   Ref: FDY.   with Maria Montez, Patric Knowles, John Litel, Maria Ouspenskaya, Charles Middleton, Lloyd Corrigan, Edward Norris, Frank Reicher, Reed Hadley, Bill Ruhl.

Woman's body found, face clawed off as if by animal; brain
snatched from body in morgue; references to "Murders in the Rue
Morgue." Perfunctory characterization and comic relief dull the
mystery, which becomes intriguing near the end, way too late.
The MYSTERY OF SOULS   (I) Itala 1911 50m. Ref: Bios 12/28/11.
   5/14/14. Girl under influence of hypnotist aids him in crime.
The MYSTERY OF THE BLUE ORANGES (Sp-F) Procusa/AdPC
   1965 color 74m.   (El MISTERIO DE LAS NARANJAS AZULES.
   TIN TIN. TINTIN ET LES ORANGES BLEUES-F.) D: Philippe
   Condroyer. SP: F. Go(n)zalvez, A. Barret, A. G. Rico. (TIN-
   TIN AND THE BLUE ORANGEA) PH: Jean Badal. Mus: Antoine
   Duhamel. Art D: R. Gomez, P. L. Thevenet. Ref: M/TVM
   3/65. COF 7:54. SpCinema'66. with Jean Pierre Talbot, Jean
   Bouise, Felix Fernandez. "French scientist finds a way of in-
   ducing oranges to grow in sand."-SpC.
MYSTERY OF THE BLUE ROOM see SECRET OF THE BLUE
   ROOM
MYSTERY OF THE BOULE CABINET, The (book by B. E. Steven-
   son) see IN THE NEXT ROOM/PURSUING VENGEANCE, The
MYSTERY OF THE CASTLE Film Releases/Anderson's 1913 45m.
   Ref: Bios 12/18/13: "weird adventures."
MYSTERY OF THE DEATH HEAD (Dan?) 1914 Ref: Lee. LC.
The MYSTERY OF THE FATAL PEARL American Kineto 1914
   80m. Ref: MPW 19:730. Lee. Possessors of stolen pearl die.
The MYSTERY OF THE GHASTLY FACE (Mex) Alcayde 1935
   (El MISTERIO DEL ROSTRO PALIDO) D: J. Bustillo Oro. PH:
   A. Jimenez. Mus: F. Ruiz. Ref: Indice. Aventura: "In the man-
   ner of Gaston Leroux." NYT 1/4/37: "nocturnal horror." Doctor
   goes mad trying to "solve the mystery of life." with Carlos
   Villarias, Joaquin Busquets, Beatriz Ramos, Rene Cardona,
   Miguel Arenas, Manuel Noriega, Natalia Ortiz.
The MYSTERY OF THE GLASS COFFIN Eclair/Tyler c1912 50m.
   Ref: Bios. Count discovers preserved body of Indian princess in
   coffin.
The MYSTERY OF THE HAUNTED HOTEL Than 1913 17m. Ref:
   MPW 18:420. Bios 1/29/14. "Ghost."
The MYSTERY OF THE LAMA CONVENT (Dan) Great Northern
   1909 (DR. NICOLA IN TIBET) Ref: Bios 11/18/09. Monks can
   "call back to life a dead person."
The MYSTERY OF THE SLEEPING DEATH Kalem 1914 30m.
   Ref: MPW 21:1549. Lee. DDC III:408. with Tom Moore. Re-
   incarnation; curse of living death.
The MYSTERY OF TEMPLE COURT Vita 1910 15m. Ref: Bios
   6/9/10. Murdered woman appears to man in dream and points
   to closet where her body is hidden.
MYSTERY OF THE 13TH GUEST Mono 1943 61m. (The 13TH
   GUEST) D: William Beaudine. SP: Tim Ryan, Arthur Hoerl,
   Charles Marion. From Armitage Trail's "The Thirteenth Guest."
   PH: Mack Stengler. Art D: David Milton. Ref:HR 10/7/43:
   "Blood-curdling...horrific." V 10/7/43. with Dick Purcell,
   Helen Parrish, Tim Ryan, Frank Faylen, John Duncan, Paul Mc-
   Vey, Addison Richards, Lloyd Ingraham. Members of family
   mysteriously murdered in old mansion.

MYSTERY OF THE WAX MUSEUM WB 1933 72m. Technicolor
(WAX MUSEUM) D: Michael Curtiz. SP: D. Mullaly, Carl Erick-
son, from the play "Waxworks" by Charles S. Belden. PH: Ray
Rennahan. Ref: MPH 1/7/33. COF-A:62. COF 16:26. Pic:
TBG. with Lionel Atwill, Fay Wray, Glenda Farrell, Holmes
Herbert, Arthur Edmund Carewe, Gavin Gordon, Allen Vincent,
Frank McHugh, Edwin Maxwell, Pat O'Malley, DeWitt Jennings,
Thomas Jackson, Matthew Betz. Not worth seeing for any
qualities it has (it doesn't have any), but worth seeing as a
novelty: It's the strangest sensation to see a color horror
movie from the early '30's. There's disappointingly little hor-
ror--more mystery and comedy--and the attempts at horror are
so awkward they're laughable, though the famous unmasking
scene is still fairly effective. Glenda Farrell stands out in a
generally crudely-acted film. (Fay Wray, Vincent, and Gordon
are worst.) Good with bad lines, she's even better with good
lines, such as Riskin's in LADY FOR A DAY.
The MYSTERY OF THE YELLOW ROOM Realart/Mayflower 1919
SP, D: Emile Chautard. From the book by Gaston Leroux. Ref:
Exhibitors Herald. MPN 20:2684. NYT 10/19/19. with Ethel G.
Terry, George Cowl.
The MYSTERY OF THE YELLOW ROOM (F) Osso 1930 D: Marcel
L'Herbier. Ref: FD 5/31/31. DDC III:227, 309, 528. London
Times: "laboratory, complete with its black cat and half-witted
assistant.... The architecture of the house belongs to the realm
of nightmare." with Roland Toutain, Marcel-Vibert. From
Leroux's book.
The MYSTERY OF THE YELLOW ROOM (Arg) Film Andes/Pyada
1947 (El MISTERIO DEL CUARTO AMARILLO) 82m. D: Julio
Saraceni. SP: Ariel Cortazzo, from Leroux's book. PH: Jose M.
Beltran. Mus: Juan Ehlert. Ref: Hist. Cine Arg. with Santiago
Gomez Cou, Herminia Franco.
The MYSTERY OF THE YELLOW ROOM (F) 1948 (Le MYSTERE
DE LA CHAMBRE JAUNE) From Leroux's book. Ref: DDC II:
11. III:36. with Marcel Herrand, Gaston Modot, Lucien Nat,
Janine Darcey, Arthur Devère.
The MYSTERY of 13 Burston 1919 serial 15 episodes Ref: Lee.
CNW. D: Francis Ford. with Nigel de Brulier (aka Brouiller),
Ford, Rosemary Theby, Pete Girard. Weird "glow" effects.
Ch. 9. The Phantom House.
MYSTERY OF TUT-ANKH-AMEN'S EIGHTH WIFE, The see KING
TUT-ANKH-AMEN'S EIGHTH WIFE
MYSTERY PLANE see SKY PIRATE
The MYSTERY RIDER Univ 1928 serial 10 episodes silent D:
Jack Nelson. Ref: CNW. with William Desmond, Derelys Perdue,
Sid Saylor, Tom London. Heroine's father produces rubber from
mesquite plant's sap. "The Claw" has big "claw-like, clutching
hand."
The MYSTERY SHIP Univ 1917 serial 18 episodes D: Harry Harvey,
Henry McRae. Ref: Lee. CNW. with Nigel de Brulier, Ben
Wilson, Neva Gerber, Duke Worne. Super light-ray, death ray,
helmet that enhances the senses.
MYSTERY SQUADRON Mascot Master 1933 serial 12 episodes

SP, D: Colbert Clark. D: also David Howard. SP: also Howard,
B. Sarecky, W. Gittens. Story: S. Lowe, A. Martin. Ref: Next
Time. D. Glut. SF Film. death ray? with Bob Steele, Jack
Mulhall, Guinn "Big Boy" Williams, Lucile Brown. Radio-con-
trolled miniature plane.
The MYSTIC MGM 1925 77m. D: Tod Browning. PH: Ira
Morgan. Art D: Cedric Gibbons, H. Libbert. Ed: Frank Sullivan.
SP: Waldemar Young. Ref: NYT 8/31/25. FM 22:40. AFI. with
Aileen Pringle, Conway Tearle, Mitchell Lewis, Robert Ober,
David Torrence, DeWitt Jennings. Fake clairvoyant frightened by
"ghost. "
The MYSTIC CIRCLE MURDER Merit/Continental 1938 69m. SP, D:
Frank O'Connor. Ref: FD 8/13/39. 4/18/38: aka RELIGIOUS
RACKETEERS. Film World'51/2: "Deals with the supernatural,
fake spiritualists, mediums, and mind-reading charlatans."
with Betty Compson, Robert Fiske, Arthur Gardner, Helen Le
Berthon, Madame Harry Houdini, David Kerman.
The MYSTIC HOUR Art Dramas/Apollo 1917 55m. D: Richard
Ridgely. Ref: MPN 15:3622. with Charles Hutchinson, Alma
Hanlon, John Sainapolis. Man "obsessed with the desire for the
death" of another man dreams he murders him. In the morning
he finds him dead.
The MYSTIC MIRROR (G) UFA 1928   silent D, PH: Carl Hoffmann.
Ref: V 10/17/28. with Fritz Rasp, Felicitas Malten, Rina de
Kigoure. Mystic mirror in old castle tells the future when the
moon is out. Villain sees himself strangled in it.
The MYSTIC SWING Edison 1900 1m. D: Edwin S. Porter. Ref:
Niver. Magician makes woman and skeleton appear and disappear.
The MYSTICAL MAID OF JAMASHA PASS American 1912 16m.
(The MYTH OF JAMASHA PASS) Ref: Bios 5/23/12. with J.
Warren Kerrigan. Maid disappears through rock and lures men
to death.

N. P. (I) Zeta-A-Elle 1971 color 106m. SP, D: Silvano Agosti.
PH: Nicola Dimitri. Mus: Nicola Piovani. Art D: Isabella
Genoese. Ref: V 8/4/71: "Futuristic. " with Francisco Rabal,
Irene Papas, Ingrid Thulin. A tycoon holds "complete industrial
automation in the palm of his hand. "
NA KOMETE see ON THE COMET
NABESHIMA KAIBYODEN see GHOST-CAT OF NABESHIMA
MANSION
NACHE NAGIN BAJE BEEN see DANCE OF COBRA TO PLAYING
OF VEENA
NACHT DES GRAUENS, Eine see TWELFTH HOUR, The
NACHTE DES GRAUENS see NIGHT OF TERROR (1916)
NACHTS, WENN DRACULA ERWACHT see COUNT DRACULA
NACKT SIND SEINE OPFER see X+YY-FORMULA OF EVIL
NACKTE UND DER SATAN, Die see HEAD, The
NAGIN see FEMALE COBRA
NAIDRA, THE DREAM WORKER Than 1914 Ref: MPW 22:1524.

Lee. Man dreams he makes beautiful woman with alchemist's formula.

NAKED AND SATAN, The see HEAD, The

NAKED EVIL Gibralter/Protelco 1966 (B) 79m. SP,D: Stanley Goulder. From the play "The Obi" by Jon Manship White. PH: Geoffrey Faithfull. Mus sc & d: Bernard Ebbinghouse. Art D: George Provis, Denys Pavitt. Exec P: Stephen Pallos, Richard Gordon, Gerald A. Fernback. Ref: MFB'69:148. COF 9:45. ModM 3:8. with Anthony Ainley, Richard Coleman, Suzanna Neve, Olaf Pooley, Basil Dignam. Black-magic cult in present-day England.

NAKED GODDESS see DEVIL'S HAND, The (1962)

The NAKED GUN Associated Film Releasing Corp. 1957 69m. D: Edward Dew. SP: Ron Ormond, Jack Lewis. Mus: Walter Green. Ref: MPH'57:266. LC. with Willard Parker, Mara Corday, Barton MacLane, Tom Brown, Veda Ann Borg, Chick Chandler, Jody McCrea, Billy House, Morris Ankrum, Bill Phillips. Treasure cursed by Indian sorcerer. "Grim conclusion." Western.

NAKED TERROR see LAST MAN ON EARTH, The (1964)

The NAKED VAMPIRE (F) Films ABC 1969 color 90m. (La VAM-PIRE NUE) D: Jean Rollin. PH: Jean-Jacques Renon. Mus: Y. Géraud, F. Tusques. Ref: MMF 24:51. V 4/29/70. with Christine François, Olivier Martin, Ly Letrong.

NAME OF THE GAME, The see L.A. 2017

The NAME OF THE GAME IS KILL (The FEMALE TRAP-TV) Fanfare/Poore & Todd 1968 Eastmancolor 88m. D: Gunnar Hellstrom. SP: Gary Crutcher. PH: William Szigmond. Mus sc & d: Stu Phillips. Art D: Ray Markham. Ref: MFB'69:242: "Horror film." with Jack Lord, Susan Strasberg, Co(l)lin Wilcox, Tisha Sterling, T. C. Jones, Mort Mills. MPH 4/10/68: "Chiller...gloomy atmosphere." "Psychotic household in the Southwest."-PM.

NAN IN FAIRYLAND (B) C&M 1912 19m. Ref: SilentFF. The giant's children decide to eat Nan for dinner.

NAN OF THE NORTH Arrow 1921 serial 15 episodes D: Duke Worne. Ref: CNW. with Ann Little, Joseph W. Girard, Leonard Clapham, Hal Wilson. Substance Titano from meteorite is source of unlimited energy.

NANBANJI NO SEMUSHI-OTOKO see RETURN TO MANHOOD

NANKAI NO DAI KETTO see GODZILLA VS. THE SEA MONSTER

NANKAI NO DAIKAIJU see SPACE AMOEBA

NARUKAMI see BEAUTY AND THE DRAGON

NATHANIEL HAWTHORNE'S TWICE TOLD TALES see TWICE TOLD TALES

The NATION'S PERIL Lubin-V.L.S.E. 1915 55m. SP,D: George Terwilliger. SP: also Harry Chandlee. Ref: MPW 26: 1675. LC. with Earl Metcalfe (or Melcalfe), Ormi Hawley, William H. Turner. In 1918 the ruler of a "foreign nation" de-cides to attack the United States. Air torpedo invention.

NATURE FAKIRS Kalem 1907 8m. Ref: MPW'07:472,475. "Enormous chicken-like creature termed a 'Dingbat'" attacks professor and assistant.

NATURE GIRLS ON THE MOON Jer/Luna 1960 (NUDE ON THE
    MOON. NUDES ON THE MOON) Ref: MMF 8:31. Members of
    nudist colony on moon hypnotize two astronauts who land there.
NATURE'S MISTAKES see FREAKS
NAUGHTY GIRL (India) Ranjit 1934 SP, D: Chandulal Shah. Ref:
    Dipali 1/11/35. with Gohar, Ghory, Dixit. Professor of
    hypnotism draws girl to him with his "hypnotic power."
NAV JAWAN (India) Wadia 1937 136m. D: Aspi. From "The
    Hunchback of Notre Dame" by Hugo. Ref: The Lighthouse
    3/13/37: "An attempt is made to portray Quasimodo." with
    Harischchandra.
NAVE DE LOS MONSTRUOUS, La see SHIP OF THE MONSTERS,
    The
NAVIGATION BY WIRELESS (B?) Danube 1912 6m. Ref: Bios
    2/1/12. Prof. Wirth invents wireless-operated vessels.
The NAVY VS. THE NIGHT MONSTERS Realart/Standard Club
    1965 color 87m. (The NIGHT CRAWLERS. MONSTERS OF THE
    NIGHT-Eng.) SP, D: Michael A. Hoey. From the book "Monster
    from the Earth's End" by Murray Leinster. PH: Stanley Cortez.
    Mus: Gordon Zahler. SpFX: Edwin Tillman. Art D: Paul Sylos.
    P: George Edwards. Assoc P: Madelynn Broder. Ref: FM 49:42.
    FanMo 3:41. SM 5:8. Pic: FMO 5:28. MFB'67:78. with Anthony
    Eisley, Mamie Van Doren, Pamela Mason, Bill Gray, Bobby Van,
    Walter Sande, Phillip Terry, Russ Bender.   Well-distributed
    mystifying details (probably from the book) have nothing to support
    them in the acting, direction, or dialogue ("It's hard to imagine--
    carnivorous trees that walk on their roots").
NE JOUEZ PAS AVEC LES MARTIANS see DON'T PLAY WITH
    MARTIANS
NEAL OF THE NAVY Pathe 1915 serial 14 episodes D: W. M.
    Harvey. Ref: MPW 9/18/15. MPN 9/4/15. with Lillian Lor-
    raine, William Conklin, William Courtleigh, Jr. , Ed Brady.
    Apeman/slave cuts rope ladder with his teeth, twists iron bars,
    etc.
The NEANDERTHAL MAN UA/Global 1953 78m. D: E. A.
    Dupont. SP: Aubrey Wisberg, Jack Pollexfen. PH: Stanley Cortez.
    Mus: Albert Glasser. Art D: Walter Koestler. SpFX: Jack Rabin,
    David Commons. Ref: FDY. Pic: FM 29:59. 43:67. with Robert
    Shayne, Doris Merrick, Richard Crane, Joy Terry, Beverly
    Garland, Robert Long. Doctor turns housecat into sabre-toothed
    tiger. A real dog. The saber-tooth looks suspiciously like your
    run-of-the-mill tiger, with tusks only for close-ups. The doctor
    is so ill-natured you hardly notice it when he turns into the
    Neanderthal man.
The NECKLACE OF RAMESES Edison 1914 Ref: Bios 4/2/14.
    Curse prevents jewel thief from getting rid of necklace from
    mummy.
NECKLACE OF THE DEAD (Dan) Nordisk 1910 17m. Ref: The
    Film Index. Bios 12/1/10. Girl nearly buried alive.
NECROMANCERS, The (novel by H. Benson) see SPELLBOUND
NECROMANCY (J) Daiei 1957 (KAIBYO YONAKI-NUMA. GHOST-
    CAT OF YONAKI SWAMP) D: Katsuhiko Tasaka. SP: T. Tami-
    kado. Story: A. Yamazaki. PH: S. Takeda. Ref: FEFN 6/28/57.

Unij. Bltn. 31.   with S. Katsu, T. Chiba, T. Hosokawa, T. Mita.
Cat's spirit possesses woman.
The NECRONOMICON   (G)   AI(Trans American)/Constantin/Aquila
1967 Eastmancolor 83m. (NECRONOMICON--GETRAUMTE
SUNDEN. SUCCUBUS) D: Jesus Franco. SP: Pier A. Caminneci.
PH: Franz Lederle, Georg Herrero. Ref: FM 50:9. FFacts.
Boxo 4/28/69. Film 4/68. with Janine Reynaud, Jack Taylor,
Adrian Hoven, Howard Vernon, Nathalie Nord, Caminneci. Night
club performer haunted, goaded into murder by "emissary of the
devil."
NECROPOLIS   (I)   Cosmoseion/Q Productions 1970 color 120m.
SP, D: Franco Brocani. PH: Ivan Stoinov. Mus: G. Bryars. Art
D: Peter Steifel. SpFX: A. Gola. Ref: MFB'71:55. with Viva
Auder, Tina Aumont, Pierre Clémenti, Nicoletta Machiavelli.
Frankenstein's monster, the devil, the Minotaur "in the person
of King Kong."
NEEL KAMAL (India) 1968 Ref: Shankar's 10/13/68. "Raaj Kumar,
a princely ghost who comes back to earth after centuries to make
life hell on earth for Waheeda Rehman....He loved her centuries
ago and was buried alive, and she, presumably, jumped a few
centuries to marry Manjo Kumar."
NEST IN A FALLING TREE (by J. Crowley) see NIGHT DIGGER,
The
NEST OF SPIES (Sp-I) Leda/Meteor 1967 color 106m. (NIDO DE
ESPIAS) D: Frank G. Carroll. Story, SP: J. A. Cabezas, J.
Comas, Aldo Cristiani. PH: M. H. Sanjuán. Mus: Gianni Ferri.
Art D: Luis Argüello. Ref SpCinema'68. with Gordon Scott,
Alberto Dalbes, Delfy Maurenn, Man Dean, Ted Carter, Silvia
Solar. Prof. McCorm, inventor of the laser beam, is kidnapped.
"Everything ends successfully, with the help of the discovered
ray."
NET, The (novel by J. Pudney) see PROJECT M-7
NEUTRON BATTLES THE KARATE ASSASSINS (Mex) TEC c1962
72m. Ref: TVFFSB: "s-f." with Wolf Rubinski.
NEUTRON, THE BLACK-MASKED (Mex) TEC 1963 80m. (NEUTRON
AND THE BLACK MASK. NEUTRON, EL ENMASCARADO
NEGRO) SP, D: Federico Curiel. Story: Alfredo Ruanova. PH:
Fernando Colin. Ref: TVFFSB. FM 29:44. Lee. with Julio Ale-
man, Wolf Rubinski, Armando Silvestre, Beto el Boticario,
Claudio Brook, Rosita Arenas. Neutron battles the villainous
elements after a neutron bomb formula.
NEUTRON TRAPS THE INVISIBLE KILLERS (Mex) TEC 1964 78m.
Ref: TVFFSB.
NEUTRON VS. THE AMAZING DR. CARONTE (Mex) TEC 1960 83m.
(NEUTRON CONTRA EL DOCTOR CARONTE) Ref: TVFFSB.
COF 10:45. Pic: FM 29:46. Lee still: monster-men.
NEUTRON VS. THE DEATH ROBOTS (Mex) TEC/Commonwealth
1961 80m. (Los AUTOMATAS DE LA MUERTE. ROBOTS OF
DEATH. NEUTRON AGAINST THE DEATH ROBOTS) SP, D:
Federico Curiel. Story: Alfredo Ruanova. PH: Fernando Colin.
Ref: TVFFSB. FM 29:44. Pic: FM 22:12. with Wolf Rubinski,
Rosita Arenas, Julio Aleman, Armando Silvestre, Claudio Brook,
Beto el Boticario. Dr. Caronte uses human blood to nourish a

master brain created with the brains of three dead scientists.
NEUTRON VS. THE MANIAC (Mex) TEC-Harold Goldman 1962 81m.
(NEUTRON AND THE COSMIC BOMB) Ref: TVFFSB. Imagen:
others in series include El TESTAMENTO DEL DR. CARONTE
and FRENTE A FRENTE. Neutron and Dr. Caronte fight for
control of cosmic bombs.
NEVER BET YOUR HEAD ON THE DEVIL see TALES OF
MYSTERY AND IMAGINATION
NEW ADVENTURES OF BATMAN AND ROBIN, The see BATMAN
& ROBIN
NEW ADVENTURES OF DR. FU-MANCHU, The see RETURN OF
DR. FU-MANCHU, The
The NEW EXPLOITS OF ELAINE Pathe 1915 serial 10 episodes
D: George B. Seitz. Ref: MPW 4/17/15. MPN 4/17/15, 6/5/15,
6/12/15. CNW. with Pearl White, Creighton Hale. House
haunted by strange noises; underground passages; wireless phone;
"the Sphymograph."
The NEW INVISIBLE MAN (Mex) Calderon 1957 94m. (El
HOMBRE QUE LOGRO SER INVISIBLE. The INVISIBLE MAN IN
MEXICO-Eng. H. G. WELLS' NEW INVISIBLE MAN) D: Alfredo
B. Cravenna. SP: J. A. de Castro. Story: Alfredo Salazar. PH:
Raul M. Solares. Mus: A. D. Conde. Ref: Indice. MFB '62:40.
Imagen. with Arturo de Cordova, Ana Luisa Peluffo, Augusto
Benedico, Raul Meraz. A man accused of murder becomes in-
visible.
The NEW JONAH (F?) Pathe 1909 7m. Ref: Bios 10/14/09.
"Immense, scaly, web-footed monster."
The NEW MICROBE (I) Cines 1912 7m. Ref: Bios 12/26/12. Prof.
Thynne discovers the microbe that produces weakness.
The NEW MISSION OF JUDEX (F) Gaum 1917 serial 12 episodes
(La NOUVELLE MISSION DE JUDEX) D: Louis Feuillade. Follow-
up to JUDEX (1916). Ref: COF 9:39. Pic: DDC II:223.III:225.
with André Brunelle, Marcel Lévesque. Ch. 3. Hypnotized--the
Bewitched Woman. 4. The Trap Room-Room of a 1000 Traps.
5. The Haunted Forest. 7. The Dead Hand.
The NEW PAIN KILLER (F) Gaum/Kleine 1909 6m. Ref: F Index
5/8/09. Spray renders body immune to pain.
NEW TRIP TO THE MOON (F) Pathe 1908 (NUEVO VIAJE A LA
LUNA) D: Segundo de Chomon. Ref: Imagen.
NEW YORK TO PARIS BY MOTOR (G) Melies 1908 (RAID NEW
YORK-PARIS EN AUTOMOBILE) Ref: SF Film. Cars cross
Alaska, the ocean bed, Siberia.
The NEWSBOY'S CHRISTMAS DREAM (B) C&M 1913 30m. Ref:
Bios 10/30/13. Dream: "Fearful monster, breathing flames
and dating from the stone age."
NIBELUNGEN, The see SIEGFRIED (1923/1967)
NIBELUNGENLIED, Das see SIEGFRIED (1923/1967)/TREASURE
OF THE PETRIFIED FOREST, The
NIBELUNGHI, I see SIEGFRIED (1912)
NICK CARTER CASSE TOUT see LICENSE TO KILL
NICK CARTER IN PANAMA see PHANTOM RAIDERS
NICK CARTER VA TOUT CASSER see LICENSE TO KILL
NICK WINTER AND THE SOMNABULIST THIEF (F?) Pathe 1911

12m. Ref: Bios 8/24/11.   Girl steals under hypnotic influence of maid.

NIDO DE ESPIAS see NEST OF SPIES

NIECE OF THE VAMPIRE, The see MALENKA

NIGHT CALLER FROM OUTER SPACE see BLOOD BEAST FROM OUTER SPACE

NIGHT CALLERS, The (novel by F. Crisp) see BLOOD BEAST FROM OUTER SPACE

The NIGHT COMES TOO SOON (B) British Animated-Federated/M.C. 1947 57m. (The GHOST OF RASHMON HALL) D: Denis Kavanagh. SP: Pat Dixon, from Bulwer-Lytton's "The Haunted and the Haunters, or The House and the Brain." PH: Ray Densham. Ref: MFB'48:16. FJA. with Valentine Dyall, Anne Howard, Alec Faversham, Howard Douglas, Beatrice Marsden. Dr. Clinton finds a crystal and a book (which belonged to a necromancer) under the flooring of a haunted house. He shatters the crystal and the ghosts depart. One of the people he is telling the story to says he doesn't believe it. Whereupon the doctor vanishes to the sound of breaking glass.

NIGHT CRAWLERS, The see NAVY VS. THE NIGHT MONSTERS, The

NIGHT CREATURES (B) Univ/Hammer/Major 1962 Technicolor 81m. (CAPTAIN CLEGG-Eng.) D: Peter Graham Scott. SP: John Elder. Add'l Dial: Barbara S. Harper. PH: Arthur Grant. Mus: Don Banks. Art D: Bernard Robinson, Don Mingaye. Ref: FFacts. COF 3:36. with Peter Cushing, Oliver Reed, Yvonne Romain, Milton Reid, Michael Ripper, Patrick Allen, Derek Francis, Martin Benson, Jack MacGowran. In 18th-century England ghostly "marsh phantoms" hinder the investigation of a smuggling ring.

NIGHT CREATURES, The see LAST MAN ON EARTH, The (1964)

The NIGHT DIGGER (B) MGM/Yongestreet-Tacitus 1971 Metrocolor 110m. D: Alastair Reid. SP: Roald Dahl, from "Nest in a Falling Tree" by Joy Crowley. PH: Alex Thomson. Mus: Bernard Herrmann. Art D: Anthony Pratt. Ref: V 5/19/71. with Patricia Neal, Pamela Brown, Nicholas Clay, Yootha Joyce. Psychopath loose in old dark house.

NIGHT GALLERY NBC-TV/Univ 1969 Technicolor 95m. D: Boris Sagal, Stephen Spielberg, Barry Shear. SP, Narr: Rod Serling. PH: Richard Batcheller, William Margu(i)lies. Mus sc: William Goldenberg. Art D: Howard E. Johnson. Ref: RVB. with Joan Crawford, Richard Kiley, Roddy McDowall, Barry Sullivan, Ossie Davis, George Macready, Sam Jaffe, Tom Bosley, Barry Atwater. Stories of the supernatural: ghostly portrait, etc.

The NIGHT HAS A THOUSAND EYES Para 1948 80m. D: John Farrow. SP: Barre Lyndon, Jonathan Latimer, from a novel by Ernst Lothar. Remake of The CLAIRVOYANT. Story: Cornell Woolrich. PH: John F. Seitz. Mus: Victor Young. Art D: Hans Dreier, Franz Bachelin. Ref: FDY. with Edward G. Robinson, Gail Russell, Virginia Bruce, Luis van Rooten, John Lund, William Demarest, Richard Webb, Jerome Cowan, Onslow Stevens. A man discovers he has clairvoyant powers. Fairly intriguing but too infrequently imaginative. And too many of Young's violins.

NIGHT HAS EYES, The see TERROR HOUSE
A NIGHT IN THE CHAMBER OF HORRORS Eclair 1914 15m.
Ref: Bios 2/26/14. "Grand Guignol.... The chamber receives
another figure to its collection. "
NIGHT IS THE PHANTOM. see WHAT!
NIGHT KEY Univ 1937 67m. D: Lloyd Corrigan. SP: Tristram
Tupper, John Moffitt. Story: William Pierce. PH: George
Robinson. Mus D: Lou Forbes. Art D: Jack Otterson. SpFX:
John P. Fulton. Ref: FD 4/21/37. FM 2:31. HM 8:19. MFB'37.
Pic: FM 23:58. 56:26. with Boris Karloff, Ward Bond, Warren
Hull, Samuel S. Hinds, Jean Rogers, Alan Baxter, Hobart
Cavanaugh, George Cleveland, Frank Reicher, Edwin Maxwell,
Ralph Dunn, Monte Montague, Tom Hanlon. A man invents an
"invisible ray" alarm.
NIGHT LIFE OF THE GODS Univ 1935 73m. (PRIVATE LIFE OF
THE GODS) D: Lowell Sherman. SP: Barry Trivers, from the
book by Thorne Smith. PH: John Mescall. P: Carl Laemmle, Jr.
Ref: FD 2/23/35.   PM. FM 10:26. with Alan Mowbray, Irene
Ware, Florine McKinney, Richard Carle, Gilbert Emery, Douglas
Fowley, William Boyd, Henry Armetta, Robert Warwick. Half-
mad scientist finds a way to turn people into statues.
NIGHT MONSTER Univ 1942 70m. (HOUSE OF MYSTERY-Eng)
D: Ford Beebe. SP: Clarence Young. PH: Charles Van Enger.
Mus D: H. J. Salter. Art D: Jack Otterson, Richard Riedel.
Ref: FDY. S&S'68:213. FM 14:6. Pic: FM 37:41. FMO 6:14.
with Lionel Atwill, Bela Lugosi, Irene Hervey, Ralph Morgan,
Leif Erickson, Nils Asther, Don Porter, Fay Helm, Frank
Reicher, Doris Lloyd, Cyril Delevanti. A skeleton is "willed
into existence" through yogi magic, in a startling scene. Better-
than-average, for Universal in the Forties that is. Omnipresent
blood stains are left unexplained.
NIGHT MUST FALL MGM 1937 115m. D: Richard Thorpe. SP:
John Van Druten, based on the play by Emlyn Williams. PH:
Ray June. Mus sc: Edward Ward. Art D: Cedric Gibbons. Ref:
FD 4/22/37. with Robert Montgomery, Rosalind Russell, Dame
May Whitty, Alan Marshall, Merle Tottenham, Kathleen Harrison,
Matthew Boulton, Eily Malyon, Beryl Mercer, E. E. Clive.
Murderer carries victim's head around in hatbox. Overrated.
NIGHT MUST FALL (B) MGM 1964 99m. D: Karel Reisz.
SP: Clive Exton. Based on the play by Emlyn Williams. PH:
Freddie Francis. Mus: Ron Grainer. Art D: Timothy O'Brien.
Ref: RVB. with Albert Finney, Mona Washbourne, Susan Hamp-
shire, Sheila Hancock. Psychopathic axe-murderer carries
head around in hatbox.
The NIGHT MY NUMBER CAME UP (B) Cont/Ealing 1954 94m.
D: Leslie Norman. SP: R. C. Sherriff. PH: Lionel Banes.
Mus: Malcolm Arnold. P: Michael Balcon. Ref: V 3/30/55.
with Michael Redgrave, Alexander Knox, Sheila Sim, Denholm
Elliott, Ursula Jeans, Michael Hordern, Alfie Bass, George
Rose, Victor Maddern.   Naval officer has a dream--in which
eight people die in a plane crash--which seems to be coming
true.
NIGHT OF ANUBIS see NIGHT OF THE LIVING DEAD

NIGHT OF BLOODY HORROR   Howco-Int'l/Cinema IV 1969 color
   90m.   Ref: Film Bltn.1/12/70.   SP,D,P: Joy N. Houck, Jr.
   SP: also Robert A. Weaver. with Gerald McRaney, Gaye Yellen.
   Man has spells during which he fears he commits brutal murders.
NIGHT OF DARK SHADOWS   see   CURSE OF DARK SHADOWS
NIGHT OF HORROR   see   NIGHT OF TERROR (1916)
NIGHT OF HORROR IN THE MENAGERIE, A   see NIGHT OF
   TERROR (1916)
A NIGHT OF MAGIC   (B\ Berkeley Films 1944 56m. D: Herbert
   Wynne. SP: Ewesley Bracken. PH: W. Richards. Ref: MFB'44:
   114. with Billy Scott, Marion Olive (the mummy), Robert Grif-
   fith. Musical: A man dreams that his uncle sends him a sar-
   cophagus with a 3000-year-old Egyptian mummy in it. He opens
   it and finds her alive.
NIGHT OF TERROR (G) 1916 (NACHTE DES GRAUENS. NIGHT OF
   HORROR. A NIGHT OF HORROR IN THE MENAGERIE) D:
   Arthur Robison. Ref: DDC III:257. RVB. Orpheus 3:47. F&F
   6/58. with Werner Krauss, Emil Jannings, Lupu Pick. A night
   among the "grey people of superstition." Vampire-film fore-
   runner.
NIGHT OF TERROR Col 1933 D: Benjamin Stoloff. SP: Beatrice
   Van, William Jacobs, from the story "The Public Be Damned" by
   Willard Mack. PH: Joseph Hilton. Ref: FDY. FM 2:48. Pic:
   WFC 3:52. FM 67:55. with Bela Lugosi, Wallace Ford, Matt
   McHugh, Sally Blane, Gertrude Michael, Tully Marshall, George
   Meeker, Edwin Maxwell. Man returns from the dead at the end
   to warn audience not to reveal the plot. Almost lively and fast
   enough to obscure the fact that it's thoroughly mediocre.
NIGHT OF TERROR, A   see LOVE FROM A STRANGER (1936)
NIGHT OF THE BIG HEAT (B) 1967 Maron/Planet 94m. color
   D: Terence Fisher. SP: Ronald Liles, from a novel by John
   Lymington. Add'l Dial: Pip & Jane Baker. PH: Reg Wyer. Mus:
   Malcolm Lockyer. Art D: Alex Vetchinsky. P: Tom Blakeley. Ref:
   MFB. with Christopher Lee, Peter Cushing, Patrick Allen,
   Sarah Lawson, Jane Merrow, Percy Herbert, William Lucas. In-
   vaders from other world need heat to survive. The s-f-suspense
   structure, borrowed from better of its type, is dully filled in
   with unintentionally funny characterizations and unintriguing details.
   The moronic ending is stolen from DAY OF THE TRIFFIDS'
   equally moronic ending.
NIGHT OF THE BLOOD BEAST AI/Balboa 1958 65m. (The
   CREATURE FROM GALAXY 27) D: Bernard Kowalski. SP: Martin
   Varno. Story, P: Gene Corman. PH:John Nicholaus (or Nickolaus), Jr.
   Mus: Alexander Laszlo. Art D: Daniel Haller. Exec P: Roger
   Corman. Ref: FFacts. FM 2:6,19. with Michael Emmet, Angela
   Greene, Ed Nelson, Tyler McVey, John Baer. Creature from
   outer space plants fertilized seedlings in man's bloodstream.
   (Is this the first pregnant man?) Rather humdrum movie for such
   an unusual premise.
NIGHT OF THE DEMON   see   CURSE OF THE DEMON
NIGHT OF THE EAGLE   see BURN, WITCH, BURN
NIGHT OF THE FLESH EATERS see NIGHT OF THE LIVING DEAD

NIGHT OF THE FULL MOON (India) 1965 D: Kishore Sahu.
(POONAM KI RAAT) Ref: Shankar's Weekly 4/18/65. Mother
India 6/65. "Haunted house... singing ghost, ghost of woman
miserly man killed long ago... black cat which will curdle the
blood of any average rat who goes to this movie."
NIGHT OF THE GHOULS AA/Atomic Productions 1958 (REVENGE
OF THE DEAD) SP,D,P: Edward D. Wood, Jr. Ref: FM 3.31:61.
Orpheus 4:35. RVB. Pic: FM-A'69:28. Unreleased. with Tor
Johnson, K. Duncan, Vampira, Valda Hansen, Criswell, Lon
Chaney, Jr. Dr. Acula, the White Ghost, the Dead Man, etc.
Ref: FanMo 5:40.
The NIGHT OF THE HUNTER UA 93m. D: Charles Laughton.
SP: James Agee, from the novel by Davis Grubb. PH: Stanley
Cortez. Mus: Walter Schumann. Ed: Robert Golden.Ref: FDY.
with Robert Mitchum, Shelley Winters, Lillian Gish, James
Gleason, Evelyn Varden, Peter Graves, Don Beddoe, Gloria
Castillo, Billy Chapin, Sally Jane Bruce, Mary Ellen Clemons,
Cheryl Callaway. Artiness blights the edges of this now-classic
shocker of a psychopathic killer after two children, but Mitchum's
menace and eerie poetic-atmospheric images of death and evil
dominate the weaker elements.
NIGHT OF THE LIVING DEAD Cont 1968 90m. (NIGHT OF THE
FLESH EATERS. NIGHT OF ANUBIS) D, PH:George A. Romero.
SP: John A. Russo. Ref: V 10/16/68. with Judith O'Dea, Russell Streiner, Duane Jones, Karl Hardman. Recently dead bodies
return as cannibals. No characters, no plot, just gore as graphic
as in the horror comics of the Fifties, though the makers may
not care to admit their origins. The best case yet for the "suggestion" theory of horror. If the movie has anything for people
I think it's only because Romero is totally unrestrained, and the
only social significance it has is its popularity, a rather unpleasant
significance at that. Lewis and Friedman's similarly-unrestrained
BLOOD FEAST films, forerunners of Romero's, might have gar-
nered the critical acclaim of the latter if Lewis and Friedman had
taken the trouble to make them passable technically, but how were
they to know that a total lack of taste would someday be con-
sidered an artistic merit?
NIGHT OF THE SILICATES see ISLAND OF TERROR (1966)
The NIGHT OF THE SPECTERS (I) 1913 (La NOTTE DEGLI
SPETTRI) Volsca Ref: Lee (Scognamillo).
NIGHT OF THE WITCHES Medford/Matchpoint 1970 DeLuxe color
SP,D: Keith Erik Burt (aka Keith Larsen?). SP: also Vincent
Fotre. PH: Herb Thiess. Ref: Boxo 1/4/71. COF 17:4. with
Burt, Ron Taft. Horror-comedy: Preacher gets mixed up with
witch cult.
NIGHT OF VIOLENCE (I) DMC 1965 SP,D: Roberto Mauri. SP:
also Mulargia. PH: Vitaliano Natalucci. Ref: Ital P. with Al-
berto Lupo, Marilu Tolo, Lisa Gastoni, Helène Chanel. "Man
who had been near Hiroshima when the atom bomb was dropped
presents a visage of such monstrosity that nothing human can be
recognized in it."
NIGHT ON BARE MOUNTAIN see HOUSE ON BARE MOUNTAIN, The
NIGHT PEOPLE see LAST MAN ON EARTH, The (1964)

NIGHT SLAVES ABC-TV /Bing Crosby 1970 color 72m. D: Ted
Post. SP: Robert Specht, Everett Chambers, from the novel by
Jerry Sohl. PH: Robert Hauser. Mus: Bernardo Segall. Art D:
Howard Hollander. Ref: TVG. RVB. with James Franciscus, Lee
Grant, Leslie Nielsen, Scott Marlowe, Andrew Prine, Tisha
Sterling, John Kellogg, Victor Izay, Russell Thorson. Man
awakens during the night to see his wife and other townspeople
silently board trucks and leave town. S-f-suspense.

NIGHT STAR, GODDESS OF ELECTRA see WAR OF THE ZOMBIES

NIGHT THE CREATURES CAME see ISLAND OF TERROR (1966)

NIGHT THE SILICATES CAME, The see ISLAND OF TERROR (1966)

The NIGHT THE WORLD EXPLODED Col /Clover 1957 64m. D:
Fred F. Sears. SP: Luci Ward, Jack Natteford. PH: Benjamin
Kline. Mus D: Ross DiMaggio. Art D: Paul Palmentola. Ref:
FDY. PM. with Kathryn Grant, William Leslie, Tristram Coffin,
Terry Frost, Raymond Greenleaf. Machine called the photometer
predicts earthquakes by recording rising pressures within the
earth.

NIGHT THE WORLD SHOOK see GORGO

NIGHT TIDE AI /Virgo /Filmgroup 1963 (1961) 84m. (GIRL FROM
BENEATH THE SEA) SP, D: Curtis Harrington. PH: Vilis
Lapenieks. Mus: David Raksin. Ref: F&F 7 /67. Orpheus 3:29.
A sailor meets a carnival girl who believes she is descended
from The Sea People, who kill under the spell of the full moon.
Slight, but interesting for the stray homages to past horror
movies (for "Sea People" read "Cat People, " etc.) with Dennis
Hopper, Gavin Muir, Linda Lawson, Luana Anders.

The NIGHT VISITOR UMC-Glazier 1971 Eastmancolor 102m.
(SALEM COME TO SUPPER) D: Laslo Benedek. SP: Guy Elmes,
from a story by Samuel Roecca. PH: Henning Kristiansen. Mus:
Henry Mancini. Art D: Viggo Bentzon. P: Mel Ferrer. Ref: HR
2 /11 /71: "Gothic horror. " with Max von Sydow, Trevor Howard,
Liv Ullman, Per Oscarsson, Rupert Davies, Andrew Keir. Man
escapes from prison to commit hatchet murder.

The NIGHT WALKER Univ 1964 86m. (The DREAM KILLER)
D, P: William Castle. SP: Robert Bloch. PH: Harold Stein. Mus:
Vic Mizzy. Makeup: Bud Westmore. Ref: Orpheus 3:32. FFacts.
with Robert Taylor, Barbara Stanwyck, Hayden Rourke, Rochelle
Hudson, Lloyd Bochner, Judith Meredith, Tetsu Komai. A few
unsettling ideas about dreams in the framework of the usual it's-
all-a-plot plot. The prologue is promising, but the idea behind
the shock scenes and Stanwyck's screams seems to be that the
louder the more terrifying.

The NIGHTCOMERS (B) K-L-K 1971 96m. D: Michael Winner.
SP: Michael Hastings, inspired by Henry James' "The Turn of
the Screw. " PH: Robert Paynter. Mus: Jerry Fielding. Ref:
V 9 /8 /71: "Atmospheric Thriller. " with Marlon Brando,
Stephanie Beacham, Thora Hird, Harry Andrews, Anna Palk.

NIGHTMARE UA 1956 89m. SP, D: Maxwell Shane, from a novel
by Cornell Woolrich. PH: Joseph Biroc. Mus sc & D: H. B.
Gilbert. Art D: Frank Sylos. Remake of FEAR IN THE NIGHT.
Ref: V 5 /11 /56. with Edward G. Robinson, Kevin McCarthy,
Connie Russell, Rhys Williams, Gage Clarke, Barry Atwater.

Man hypnotized to kill.
NIGHTMARE (B) Univ/Rank/Hammer 1964 83m. D: Freddie
Francis. SP, P: Jimmy Sangster. PH: John Wilcox. Mus: Don
Banks. Boxo 5/4/64. V 4/22/64. with David Knight, Moira
Redmond, Jennie Linden, Brenda Bruce. Eerie house with
shadows, noises, phantom-like woman in white.
NIGHTMARE see DIE! DIE! MY DARLING/MANSTER, The
NIGHTMARE ALLEY Fox 1947 112m. D: Edmund Goulding.
SP: Jules Furthman, from the novel by William Lindsay
Gresham. PH: Lee Garmes. Mus sc: Cyril Mockridge. Art D:
Lyle Wheeler, J. Russell Spencer. SpPhFX: Fred Sersen. P:
George Jessel. Ref: FDY. HR 10/9/47: "realistic horror." with
Tyrone Power, Joan Blondell, Coleen Gray, Helen Walker, Mike
Mazurki, Ian Keith, Julia Dean, Taylor Holmes, James Flavin,
Roy Roberts, James Burke, Henry Hall, Gene Stutenroth, George
Chandler, Emmett Lynn. Spiritualist sees vision of dead girl.
NIGHTMARE CASTLE (I) AA/Emmeci 1965 105m. (AMANTI
D'OLTRETOMBA. The FACELESS MONSTER-Eng.) SP, D: Mario
Caiano (aka Allen or Allan Grunewald). SP: also Fabio De
Agostini. PH: Enzo Barboni. Mus: Ennio Morricone. Art D:
Massimo Tavazzi. Ref: MFB'70:10. FFacts. with Barbara Steele,
Paul Miller, Helga Line, Rik Battaglia. Ghostly, "vampiric"
gardener; mad scientist who injects dead wife's blood into his
assistant, making her beautiful. Notable mainly for Morri-
cone's wildly romantic renditions of "Sweet Genevieve." (He
uses the melody much as Victor Young used it in The SUN SHINES
BRIGHT. Coincidence?)
NIGHTMARE IN WAX Crown/Paragon Int'l/Productions Enterprises
1969 Pathecolor 95m. (MONSTER OF THE WAX MUSEUM)
D: Bud Townsend. SP, Exec P: Rex Carlton. Exec P: also Her-
bert Sussan (or Susaan). Ref: LA Times 5/22/69. Boxo 8/25/69.
with Cameron Mitchell, Anne Helm, Scott Brady, Berry Kroeger,
Victoria Carroll. "Wax figures" are really living persons,
paralyzed and kept alive by injections.
NIGHTS OF PRAGUE see PRAGUE NIGHTS
NIJE BILO UZALUD see IT WAS NOT IN VAIN
The NINE AGES OF NAKEDNESS (B) Token Films 1969 Eastman-
color SP, D: G. Harrison Marks. PH: Terry Maher. Mus sc & D:
Peter Jeffries. Narr: Charles Gray. Ref: MFB'69:218. with
Marks, Max Wall, June Palmer. Stone Age sequence; futuristic
sequence; "Frankenstein Marks" sequence.
1984 (B) Col 1956 91m. D: Michael Anderson. SP: William Temple-
ton, Ralph Bettinson, from the novel by George Orwell. PH:
C. Pennington Richards. Mus sc: Malcolm Arland. Art D:
T. Verity. Ref: FDY. Pic: SM 3:30. with Edmond O'Brien,
Michael Redgrave, Jan Sterling, Donald Pleasence, Michael
Ripper, David Kossoff, Mervyn Johns, Patrick Allen, Ewen
Solon, Kenneth Griffith. Future police state. Pleasence's electri-
fying bit makes the rest of the movie look duller than it actually
is.
NINGYO SHOTEN see MERMAIDS AND SEA ROBBERS
The NINTH GUEST Col 1934 65m. D: Roy William Neill. SP:
Garnett Weston, from the play by Owen Davis and the novel "The

Invisible Host" by Gwen Bristow and Bruce Manning. Ref: PM:
"Gruesome...horrible."FD 3/3/34.   V 3/6/34: "Shivery." TVG.
with Donald Cook, Genevieve Tobin, Hardie Albright, Edward
Ellis, Edwin Maxwell, Vince Barnett, Samuel S. Hinds. Eight
guests at a penthouse party hear a mysterious radio voice tell
them that each is marked for death.

NIOBE   Famous Players 1915 55m.   Ref: MPW 4/17/15. MPN
4/17/15. with Hazel Dawn, Charles Abbe. Woman turned into
stone is restored to life by electric wires.

NIPOTE DEL VAMPIRO, La   see MALENKA

NIPPON TANJO see   THREE TREASURES, The

The NITWITS RKO 1935 81m.   D: George Stevens. SP: Fred
Guiol, Al Boasberg. Story: Stuart Palmer. PH: Edward Cron-
jager. Ref: FD 6/5/35: "Electric chair for making persons tell
what is actually on their minds." with Bert Wheeler, Robert
Woolsey, Betty Grable, Hale Hamilton, Evelyn Brent, Fred
Keating, Erik Rhodes, Willie Best, Arthur Treacher, Charles
Wilson.

NO BLADE OF GRASS (U.S.-B) MGM 1970 Metrocolor 97m. D,P:
Cornel Wilde. SP: Sean Forestal, Jefferson Pascal, from the
novel by John Christopher. PH: H. A. R. Thomson. Art D:
Elliot Scott.   Ref: Boxo 11/30/70. V 11/4/70. with Nigel
Davenport, Jean Wallace, Patrick Holt, John Hamill. Virus
mutates into organism deadly to crops.

NO COFFIN FOR THE CORPSE (by C. Rawson) see MAN WHO
WOULDN'T DIE, The

NO HAUNT FOR A GENTLEMAN (B) Apex/Anglo-Scottish 1952
58m. D: Leonard Reeve. Ref: MFB'52:115. TVFFSB. with Sally
Newton, Jack McNaughton, Anthony Pendrell. Owner of country
house persuades Elizabethan ghost to frighten mother-in-law away.

NO MORE BALD HEADS (F) Pathe c1908 Ref: SilentFF. 2m. Fast-
working hair restorer.

NO NIGHTINGALES (book by Simon & Brahms) see GHOSTS OF
BERKELEY SQUARE

NO PLACE LIKE HOMICIDE (B) Emb/New World 1961 87m. (WHAT
A CARVE UP!) D: Pat Jackson. SP: Ray Cooney, Tony Hilton,
from the book "The Ghoul" by Frank King and Leonard Hines.
PH,P: Monty Berman. P: also Robert Baker. Mus:Muir Mathieson.
Art D:·Ivan King. Ref: FFacts. FM 25:4. with Kenneth Connor,
Sidney James, Shirley Eaton, Donald Pleasence, Dennis Price,
Michael Gough, Valerie Taylor, George Woodbridge, Michael
Gwynn. Relatives gather at a gloomy mansion for the reading of
a will.   A storm causes a power shortage and leaves the house
in darkness.

NO PLACE TO HIDE   (U.S.-Fili) AA 1955 DeLuxe color 71m.
Story,D,P: Josef Shaftel. SP: Norman Corwin. PH: Gilbert
Warrenton.Mus: H. B. Gilbert. Ref: MFB'58:37. with David
Brian, Marsha Hunt, Celia Flor, Manuel Silos. New "ultra-
malignant" bacteria strain contained in pellets.

NO SURVIVORS, PLEASE (W.G.) Albin/Schorcht 1963 (DER CHEF
WUNSCHT KEINE ZEUGEN) 95m. D: Hans Albin, Peter Berneis.
SP: Berneis. PH: Heinz Schnackertz. Mus: Hermann Thieme.
Art D: Tibor Rednas. Ref: MFB'65:90. German Pictures 63/4:

"Supernatural beings which have assumed the physical entities
and positions of three influential earthly personalities are
systematically inciting East and West into an atomic war."
with Maria Perschy, Robert Cunningham, Uwe Friedrichsen,
Gustavo Rojo, Rolf v. Nauckhoff, Karen Blanguernon.
NOCHE DE WALPURGIS, La   see   WEREWOLF'S SHADOW
NON PERDIAMO LA TESTA   see LET'S NOT LOSE OUR HEADS
NON-STOP, NEW YORK (B) Gaum   1937   D: Robert Stevenson.
SP: Roland Pertwee, J. C. Orton, from the book "Sky Steward"
by Ken At(ti)will. PH: M. Greenbaum. Ref: SF Film:
"Transatlantic flight." FDY.with John Loder, Anna Lee, Francis
Sullivan, Athene Seyler, Fran Cellier.
NOOR-E-YAMAN (India) Wadia 1935 D: J. B. H. Wadia. Sequel to
LAL-E-YAMAN. Ref: Dipali 9/6/35. with Feroze Dastur,
Sharifa. "Fantastic story...The home of the demon horrifies
the audience....trick scenes."
NORWICH VICTIMS, The (book by F. Beeding)   see DEAD MEN
TELL NO TALES
NOSFERATU, A SYMPHONY OF HORROR   (G) Prana 1922 (NOS-
FERATU, EINE SYMPHONIE DES GRAUENS. NOSFERATU THE
VAMPIRE. TERROR OF DRACULA. DRACULA. NOSFERATU,
A SYMPHONY OF TERROR) D: F. W. Murnau. SP: Henrik
Galeen, from the novel "Dracula" by Bram Stoker. PH: Fritz
Arno Wagner. Art D: Albin Grau. See also The TWELFTH HOUR.
Ref: Eisner. FM 10:28.41:66. COF 4:26. Pic: COF-A:20. with
Max Schreck (Dracula/Orlock), Alexander Granach, Gustav von
Wangenheim, G. Schroeder, Ruth Landshoff, G. H. Schnell,
John Gottowt, Gustav Botz, Max Nemetz, Wolfgang Heinz, Albert
Venohr, Herzfeld, Hardy von François, Heinrich Witte. NOS-
FERATU, the great silent horror movie, has had little or no
competition from sound horror movies.   Nosferatu (Dracula) is unearthly enough as he appears in stills: bald, skull-like head; un-
naturally rigid posture; long, clawlike fingers. But his movements are what give the film its memorable nightmare images.
(One of the most nightmarish is his hypnotic stare which remains
fixed on the heroine as his body mechanically turns to go for
her, as if his eyes had independent life.) His features and
movements, grotesque exaggerations of human features and movements, are the horror of NOSFERATU.   Schreck in the role is
less an actor giving a performance than an embodiment of ideas
of visual horror, and Murnau has about the best ideas of any
director (in this, FAUST, and SUNRISE) of what to do with film
on the visual level.
NOSFERATU   see also THEY'VE CHANGED FACES
NOSTRADAMUS Y EL DESTRUCTOR DE MONSTRUOUS see MONSTER
DEMOLISHER, The
NOSTRADAMUS Y EL GENIO DE LA TINIEBLAS   see   GENIE OF
DARKNESS
NOT OF THIS EARTH AA/Los Altos 1957 67m. (Il VAMPIRO DEL
PIANETA ROSSO-I.) D, P: Roger Corman.   SP: Charles Griffith,
Mark Hanna. PH: John Mescall.   Mus: Ronald Stein. SpFX:
Paul Blaisdell. Ref: FM 19:77. FDY. with Beverly Garland, Paul
Birch, Morgan Jones, Richard Miller, Jonathan Haze, Gail Ganley.

Emissary from a planet of beings who live on blood arrives on
earth. Okay early Corman.

NOTHING VENTURE (B) Baxter 1947 73m. D: John Baxter.
SP: Geoffrey Orme. PH: Jo Jago. Ref: MFB'48:30. with Terry
Randal, Patric Curwen, Michael Aldridge. Crooks attempt to
steal plans of inventor's "secret ray."

NOTRE DAME Patheplay 1913 45m. (NOTRE DAME DE PARIS
-Eng) From Hugo's novel "Notre Dame de Paris." Ref: Bios
10/16/13.

NOTRE-DAME DE PARIS (F) Pathe 1911 45m. D: Albert
Capellani. Ref: FM 37:31. The Film Index. SilentFF. Bios 9/21/
11. with Stacia Napierkovska, Henry Krauss, Claude Garry,
René Alexandre. From "Notre Dame de Paris" by Hugo.

NOTRE DAME DE PARIS (by V. Hugo) see ESMERELDA (1906/
1922)/HUNCHBACK OF NOTRE DAME, The (1923/1939/1956)

NOTTE DEGLI SPETTRI, La see NIGHT OF THE SPECTERS, The

NOUVELLE AVENTURE DE LEMMY CAUTION, Une see
ALPHAVILLE

NOUVELLE MISSION DE JUDEX, La see NEW MISSION OF JUDEX,
The

A NOVICE AT X-RAYS (F) Melies 1898 (Les RAYONS ROENTGEN)
Ref: SF Film. Skeleton leaves its body.

NUDE IN HIS POCKET see GIRL IN HIS POCKET

NUDE...SI MUORE see YOUNG, THE EVIL AND THE SAVAGE, The

NUDE UND SATAN, Die see HEAD, The

NUDES ON THE MOON see NATURE GIRLS ON THE MOON

NUIT DES VAMPIRES, La see CAVE OF THE LIVING DEAD

NUIT TERRIBLE, Une see TERRIBLE NIGHT, A

NUITS DE L'EPOUVANTE, Les see MURDER CLINIC, The

#13 DEMON STREET see DEVIL'S MESSENGER, The

NUOVA AVVENTURA DI LEMMY CAUTION, Una see ALPHA-
VILLE

NUR TOTE ZEUGEN SCHWEIGEN see HYPNOSIS

NURSERY RHYME MURDERS, The see AND THEN THERE WERE
NONE/TEN LITTLE INDIANS

NURSIE AND KNIGHT Than 1912 17m. Ref: Bios 1/2/13. Boy slays
dragon in dream.

NUTTY, NAUGHTY CHATEAU (F) 1963 color 102m. (CHATEAU EN
SUEDE) D: Roger Vadim. SP: Vadim, Claude Choblier, from a
play by Françoise Sagan. PH: Armand Thirard. Mus: Raymond
Le Senechal. Ref: UA catalog. with Monica Vitti, Curt Jurgens,
Jean-Claude Brialy, Sylvie, Jean-Louis Trintignant, Françoise
Hardy. Ghosts haunt mysterious castle.

The NUTTY PROFESSOR Para 1963 Technicolor 107m. SP,D:
Jerry Lewis. SP: also Bill Richmond. (DR. JERKYLL AND MR.
HYDE) From "The Strange Case of Dr. Jekyll and Mr. Hyde" by
Stevenson. PH: W. Wallace Kelley. Mus: Walter Scharf.
SpPhFX: Paul K. Lerpae. Ref: FFacts. FM 12:8. with Jerry
Lewis, Stella Stevens, Del Moore, Skip Ward, Kathleen Free-
man, Howard Morris, Milton Frome, Buddy Lester, Marvin
Kaplan, Henry Gibson, Les Brown & his band. A chemical po-
tion transforms Julius Kelp into Buddy Love. "See by all
means"--Jean-Luc Godard. Much better than most of Lewis's

features. Possibly better than any of the straight versions of
Jekyll and Hyde. Hilarious in spots.
NYLON NOOSE (W. G.) Monachia/Urania/Medallion-TV 1963 83m.
(Die NYLONSCHLINGE) D: Rudolf Zehetgruber. SP: Fred
Ignor, Thomas Engel. PH: Otto Ritter. Mus: Walter Baumgart-
ner. Ref: German Pictures. Pic: FM 37:2. with Richard Goodman, Laya Raki, Dietmar Schönherr, Helga Sommerfeld, Adi
Berber, Gustav Knuth. Mummy-filled catacombs, doctor trying
to transfer mummies' preservative substance to humans, etc.
As is usual with German horrors, six subplots are sometimes
advanced in the course of a single conversation. And action-
suspense scenes are staged as if they were just being squeezed
into dead spots between chats. Which effectively renders the
movie one long dead spot.
The NYMPHS' BATH (F) Gaum 1909 6m. Ref: Bios 12/9/09.
Daphnis "struggles with ghosts."
NYOKA see PERILS OF NYOKA

087 "MISSION APOCALYPSE" (I-Sp) Nike/Estela 1966 (087 "MIS-
SIONE APOCALISSE or MISSIONE APOCALISSE"-I. MISSION
APOCALYPSE) D: James Reed. SP: Reed, A. Sangermano.
PH: J. Ortas. Ref: Ital P. Annuario. with Arthur Hansel,
Pamela Tudor, Moa Thai, Harold Bradley, Eduardo Fajardo. A
criminal group founds a missile base for the construction of an
invulnerable weapon.
O. K. CONNERY see OPERATION KID BROTHER
002 OPERATION MOON see TWO COSMONAUTS AGAINST THEIR
WILL
002 OPERAZIONE LUNA see TWO COSMONAUTS AGAINST THEIR
WILL
OSS 117 TAKES A VACATION (F-Braz) Cocinor/Films Number One-
Vera Cruz 1969 color 92m. (OSS 117 PREND DES VACANCES)
SP, D: Pierre Kalfon. SP: also Josette Bruce, Pierre Philippe,
from the book by Bruce. PH: Etienne Becker. Ref: V 2/25/70.
with Luc Merenda, Elsa Martinelli, Edwige Feuillere, Genevieve
Grad, Norma Bengall. Secret weapons.
OBEAH Arcturus Pictures 1935 75m. SP, D: F. Herrick Herrick.
PH: Harry W. Smith. Ed: Leonard Weiss. Ref: FD 2/13/35.
with Phillips H. Lord, Jeane Kelly, Alice Wesslar. Lost explorer
under spell of high priestess's voodoo curse.
OBI, The (play by J. M. White) see NAKED EVIL
The OBLONG BOX (U. S. -B) AI 1969 Eastmancolor by Berkey
Pathe 91m. D, P: Gordon Hessler. SP: Laurence Huntingdon,
from a story by Edgar Allan Poe. Add'l Dial: Christopher Wicking.
PH: John Coquillon. Mus: Harry Robinson. Ref: MFB. with Vincent
Price, Christopher Lee, Hilary Dwyer, Alastair Williamson, Peter
Arne, Harry Baird, Rupert Davies, Sally Geeson, Ivor Dean, Uta
Levka, James Mellor, Hira Talfrey, Hedgar Wallace. Witch doc-
tor's capsule makes madman appear to be dead.
OBRAS MAESTRAS DEL TERROR see MASTER OF HORROR

OBSESSIONS see FLESH AND FANTASY
OCCHI SENZA VOLTO see HORROR CHAMBER OF DR. FAUSTUS, The
The OCCULT American/Flying A 1913 Charles D. Myers. Ref: Bios 1/22/14. Lee. "Hypnotic influence."
The OCEAN WAIF Int'l/Golden Eagle 1916 55m. SP: Frederick Chapin. Ref: MPN 14:3012. with Doris Kenyon, Carlisle Blackwell, Fraunie Fraunholz. Girl plays ghost in supposedly haunted house.
OCTAVE OF CLAUDIUS, The (by B. Pain) See BLIND BARGAIN, A
The OCTOBER MOTH (B) Independent Artists 1959 53m. SP,D: John Kruse, Ref: Lee. Brit.Cin. with Lee Patterson, Peter Dyneley. TVFFSB: "Horror." Mad killer, isolated house.
ODYSSEY, The see ULYSSES
OEYAMA SHUTEN DOJI see OGRE IN MT. OE, The
OF GODS AND THE DEAD (Braz) Daga/Rosenberg 1969 East-mancolor 129m. (OS DEUSES E OS MORTOS) SP,D: Ruy Guerra. SP: also Paulo Jose, Flavio Imperio. PH: Dib Lutfi. Mus: Milton Nascimento. Ref: V 7/8/70. VVoice 6/17/71: The GODS AND THE DEAD. Supernatural creatures take on human form, mingle with humans.
OFF ON A COMET (by J. Verne) see ON THE COMET/VALLEY OF THE DRAGONS OFF
OFFICER 444 Davis 1926 serial 10 episodes. 6. The Radio Ray. D: Ben Wilson, Francis Ford. Ref: TBG. CNW. with Wilson, Neva Gerber, Jack Mower, Phil Ford, Al Ferguson. Criminal's formula, "Haverlyite," gives victims mean, criminal natures.
OFFICIAL SECRET (play by J. Dell) see SPIES OF THE AIR
OGON BATTO see GOLDEN BAT
The OGRE IN MT. OE (J) Daiei 1960 color (OEYAMA SHUTEN DOJI) D: Tokuzo Tanaka. SP: Fuji Yahiro. PH:Hiroshi Imai. Ref: UFQ 9. with Kazuo Hasegawa, Raizo Ichikawa, Shintaro Katsu, Kojiro Hongo, Fujiko Yamamoto, Tamao Nakamura. Japan is overrun with apparitions, witches, and wizards. The prime minister is haunted by monsters in the form of a huge ox and a flying goblin.
OH, BOY! (B) A.B.P.C. 1938 76m. D: Albert De Courville. Ref: MFB'38. with Albert Burdon, Mary Lawson, Bernard Nedell, Jay Laurier. A mysterious scientist presents a timid chemist with an elixir which makes him strong and self-confident and which, unexpectedly, causes him to revert gradually to a baby.
OH, GRANDMOTHER'S DEAD! (I) Cristaldi/Vides 1969 color (TO', E MORTA LA NONNA! WELL, GRANDMA'S DEAD) SP,D: Mario Monicelli. SP: also Malerba, Montagnanq. PH: Luigi Kuveiller. Mus: Piero Piccioni. Ref: Ital P. with Sirena Adgemova, Valentina Cortese, Carole Andre. Dead woman communicates with the living through a tele-printer. Seances.
OH, THAT TONIC! (I) Lux 1910 4m. Ref: Bios 199:35. Vendor's tonic makes woman rush away madly.
OH! WHAT AN APPETITE Ess 1908 Ref: V&FI 8/29/08. Dr. Makem-eat's medicine gives man appetite for anything.
OH YOU SKELETON Selig 1910 Ref: The Film Index. Maid chased by skeletons.

OH! YOU UNBREAKABLE DOLL (F) Lux 1913 8m. Ref: Bios
5/15/13. Scientist invents unbreakable doll.
OHATARI TANUKI GOTEN see BADGER PALACE, The
The OILY MAN (Malayan) Keris Films 1958 see also CURSE OF
THE OILY MAN. Ref: FEFN 11/28/58.
The OILY MAN STRIKES AGAIN (Malayan) Keris Films 1958
Technical adviser: a witch doctor. Ref: FEFN 11/28/58. See
also CURSE OF THE OILY MAN.
The OLD DARK HOUSE Univ 1932 70m. D: James Whale. SP:
Benn Levy. Dial: R. C. Sherriff. From the book "Benighted"
or "The Old Dark House" by J. B. Priestley. PH: Arthur
Edeson. P: Carl Laemmle, Jr. Ref: FM 2:31. 23:4. 12:24. 66:35.
FDY. FMO 3:11. COF 11:15. 14:17. Pic: TBG. DDC II:306.
COF 16:19. with Boris Karloff, Melvyn Douglas, Charles
Laughton, Gloria Stuart, Lilian Bond, Ernest Thesiger, Eva
Moore, Raymond Massey, Brember Wells, John Dudgeon.
Travellers are forced to spend the night at an old mansion in-
habited by a weird family. A good old-dark-house movie,
bizarrely comic. Good, eccentric characters (e.g., an old man
who happily cackles "I could die any minute") are found for so
many in the cast it's disappointing they didn't find one for
Laughton. A few forgettable, embarrassing "romantic" moments.
Better than the book.
The OLD DARK HOUSE (B) Col/Hammer 1963 86m. D: William
Castle. SP: Robert Dillon. From the novel "Benighted" or
"The Old Dark House" by J. B. Priestley. PH: Arthur Grant.
Mus: Benjamin Frankel. Art D: Bernard Robinson. SpFX: Les
Bowie. Drawings by Charles Addams. Ref:FFacts. with Tom
Poston, Robert Morley, Joyce Grenfell, Janette Scott, Fenella
Fielding, Mervyn Johns, Peter Bull. Mysterious murderer loose
in Femm Hall. Listless, undirected. Some but not nearly enough
clever little gimmicks.
OLD MOTHER RILEY MEETS THE VAMPIRE see MY SON THE
VAMPIRE
OLD SCROOGE (I) Cines 12m. From "A Christmas Carol" by
Charles Dickens. Ref: Bios 12/1/10.
The OLD SHOEMAKER (F) Gaum 1909 14m. Ref: Bios 11/14/09.
Fear and visions of victim drive murderer mad.
An OLD-TIME NIGHTMARE Powers 1911 Ref: MPW'11:778. Bios
3/14/12. Dream: Huge birds menace boy.
The OLDEST PROFESSION IN THE WORLD (F-I-W.G.) Jack H.
Harris/VIP Films/Athos/Les Films Gibé-Francoriz-Rizzoli-
Rialto 1966 Eastmancolor 115m. (98m.-U.S.) (L'AMORE AT-
TRAVERSO I SECOLI-I.) "Prehistoric Era" sketch: D: Franco
Indo-vina. SP: Ennio Flaiano. with Michele Mercier, G. Tinti.
"Anticipation"-Year 2000 sketch: SP, D: Jean-Luc Godard. with
Anna Karina, Jacques Charrier, Marilu Tolo, Jean-Pierre Leaud.
Slight, with nice color changes. D: (other sketches) Claude
Autant-Lara, Philippe deBroca, Mauro Bolognini, Michael
Pfleghar. PH: Pierre Lhomme. Mus: Michel Legrand. also with
Elsa Martinelli, Jeanne Moreau, Raquel Welch.
The OMEGA MAN WB 1971 Technicolor 98m. D: Boris Sagal.
SP: John William, Joyce H. Corrington, from the book "I am

Legend" by Richard Matheson. PH: Russell Metty. Mus: Ron
Grainer. Art D: Arthur Loel, Walter M. Simonds. Ref: V(d)
7/30/71. with Charlton Heston, Anthony Zerbe, Rosalind Cash,
Paul Koslo. Man fears he is the "last man on earth. "

OMICRON (I) Manley/Lux-Ultra-Vides 1963 (MOSTRA DI
VENEZIA. MONSTER OF VENICE) SP, D: Ugo Gregoretti. PH:
Carlo Di Palma. Mus: Piero Umiliani. Ref: Bianco 9/63.2/64.
Heraldo 9/8/65. COF 4:57. Ital P. with Renato Salvatori,
Rosemary Dexter, Gaetano Quartaro, Mara Carisi. Spirit-like
inhabitant of the planet Ultra dwells in a man's body.

ON BORROWED TIME MGM 1939 99m. D: Hal Bucquet. SP:
Alice Duer Miller, Frank O'Neill, Claudine West, from the
play by Paul Osborne and Lawrence Watkin. PH: Joseph Rutten-
berg. Ref: Clarens. with Lionel Barrymore, Sir Cedric Hardwicke,
Beulah Bondi, Una Merkel, Bobs Watson, Henry Travers, Nat
Pendleton, Ian Wolfe, Phillip Terry, Truman Bradley, Grant
Mitchell, Eily Malyon. Death trapped up a tree.

ON HER MAJESTY'S SECRET SERVICE UA 1969 Technicolor/scope
130m. D: Peter Hunt. SP: Richard Maibaum, from the book by
Ian Fleming. PH: Michael Reed. Mus: John Barry. Art D: Bob
Laing. SpFX: John Stears. Ref: V 12/17/69. with George Laz-
enby (James Bond), Diana Rigg, Telly Savalas, Gabriele Ferzetti, Bernard Lee, Lois Maxwell, Bessie Love. Villain hypnotizes
international beauties and plans to send them back to their native
lands with germs that will destroy all vegetable life. Pretty
tedious until the last half-hour-or-so of dazzling spectacle.

ON IRISH HILL (by P. B. Kyne) see KELLY OF THE SECRET
SERVICE

ON THE BEACH UA 1959 134m. D, P: Stanley Kramer. SP: John
Paxton, from the novel by Nevil Shute. PH: Giuseppe Rotunno.
Mus: Ernest Gold. Art D: Fernando Carrere. Prod Des: Rudolph Sternad. SpFX: Lee Zavit(t)s. Ref: FFacts. FM 9:7.
with Gregory Peck, Anthony Perkins, Ava Gardner, Fred
Astaire, Donna Anderson, Guy Doleman, John Tate. The last
people on earth face certain death by radioactive air pollution
after a third world war.

ON THE COMET (Cz) Czech State/Barrandov c1969 color 85m.
(NA KOMETE, MR. SERVADAC'S ARCH) SP, D: Karel Zeman,
from the book "Off on a Comet" by Jules Verne. PH: Rudolf
Stahl. Mus: Lubos Fiser. Art D: Jiri Hlupy. Ref: M/TVM 12/
68. V. with Emil Horvath, Magda Vasarykova. Prehistoric
animals.

ON TIME Truart 1924 65m. SP: Garrett Fort. Story: Al Cohn. PH:
Wm. Marshall. Ref: Lee. LC. AFI. D: Henry Lehrman. Ed:
Ralph Spence. with Billie Dove, Stuart Holmes, Chas. Clary,
Tom Wilson, Richard Talmadge. Mad doctor attempts to put
gorilla's brain into man's head.

ON TO MARS see ABBOTT AND COSTELLO GO TO MARS

ONCE IN A NEW MOON (B) 1935 D: Anthony Kimmins. From the
book "Lucky Star" by Owen Rutter. Ref: FM 47:16. FJA.
Brit. Cinema. with John Clements, Rene Ray. A piece of
England breaks off, floats into space, and becomes known as
"Upper Shrimpton, a satellite of the earth. "

ONCE UPON A TIME (Cz) c1921 40m. (SOVEREIGN GOOSE PIE)
Czecho-Slovakia Films Ref: SilentFF. with Theodor Pistek. A
shoemaker's son is taken to a witch's castle and put to sleep for
seven years.

ONE ARABIAN NIGHT see SUMURUN

ONE BODY TOO MANY Para 1944 75m. D: Frank McDonald. SP:
Maxwell Shane, Winston Miller. PH: Fred Jackman. Art D: F.
Paul Sylos. Ref: V 10/18/44: "Horror whodunit." with Jack
Haley, Lucien Littlefield, Lyle Talbot, Bela Lugosi, Jean Parker,
Blanche Yurka, Douglas Fowley, Fay Helm, Bernard Nedell,
Dorothy Granger. Trap doors, secret panels, storm, etc. Lugosi
has a small but very amusing comedy role in this otherwise
thoroughly routine horror-comedy as a butler whose cups of
poisoned coffee, are continually declined by the house guests.

ONE EXCITING NIGHT UA 1922 120m. SP, D: D. W. Griffith.
PH: Hendrick Sartov. Art D: Charles M. Kirk. Story: Irene
Sinclair. PH: Hendri(c)k Sartov. Mus sc synchronized: Albert
Pesce. Ref: Clarens. AFI. S&S'46:82. Pic: DDC II:466. with
Carol Dempster, Henry Hull, Morgan Wallace, Porter Strong,
Irma Harrison, Margaret Dale, Grace Griswold. Cloaked, hooded
menace lurks behind secret panels and doors of old house.

ONE EXCITING NIGHT see MIDNIGHT MANHUNT

ONE FRIGHTENED NIGHT Mascot 1935 68m. D: Christy Cabanne. SP: Wellyn Totman. Story: Stuart Palmer. PH: William
Nobles, Ernest Miller. Ed: Joseph Lewis. Ref: Next Time. Photoplay 7/35. FDY. with Mary Carlisle, Arthur Hohl, Hedda Hopper,
Wallace Ford, Lucien Littlefield, Regis Toomey, Rafaela Ottiano,
Charles Grapewin, Evalyn (or Evelyn) Knapp, Fred Kelsey,
Clarence Wilson. Black-shrouded killer, secret passages, "creepy
music," "wildly storming night." An old millionaire gathers his
relatives together to read them his will.

ONE GLORIOUS DAY Para 1922 56m. (SOULS BEFORE BIRTH)
D: James Cruze. SP: A. B. Baringer, Walter Woods. PH: Karl
Brown. Ref: AFI. NYT 1/30/22. with Lila Lee, Will Rogers,
Alan Hale, John Fox. A professor interested in "spiritism" puts
himself in a trance and sends his spirit out of his body. An unborn
spirit enters him and the professor's spirit wanders about searching for its owner.

ONE HOUR BEFORE DAWN. Pathe 1920 D: Henry King. Ref: NYT
7/12/20: "Creepy scenes." Exhibitors Herald. From "Behind
Red Curtains," novel by Mansfield Scott. with H. B. Warner.
A hypnotist commands the hero to kill a man an hour before dawn:
An hour before dawn the hero dreams of killing the man. Next
morning the man is found dead.

100 CRIES OF TERROR (Mex) AI-TV/México Films 1964 (CIEN
GRITOS DE TERROR) D: Ramón Obon. PH: A. M. Solares. Mus:
Rafael Carrión. Ref: Aventura. TVG. with Ariadna Welter, George
Martinez, Joaquin Cordero, Ofelia Montesco, Alicia Caro. Two
stories: A man plans to murder his wife. A man is locked in a
mausoleum.

ONE HUNDRED YEARS AFTER (F) Pathe 1911 13m. Ref: Bios
10/5/11. A young scientist who has perfected a means of sus-
pending life puts himself to sleep for 100 years and awakens in

the year 2011.

100 YEARS HENCE   see AIRSHIP, The

ONE MILLION B.C.   UA 1940 80m. (CAVE MAN. MAN AND
HIS MATE-Eng. BATTLE OF THE GIANTS) D: Hal Roach, Hal
Roach, Jr., D. W. Griffith. SP: Mickell Novak, George Baker,
Joseph Frickert. Remake: ONE MILLION YEARS B.C. Special
effects footage used in: JUNGLE MANHUNT. ROBOT MONSTER.
TARZAN'S DESERT MYSTERY. TWO LOST WORLDS. VALLEY
OF THE DRAGONS. PH: Norbert Brodine. Mus: Werner R.
Heymann. Art D: Charles D. Hall. SpFX: Roy Seawright. Ref:
Clarens. FM 10:26.11:20.19:36.28:78.42:57. COF 6:18. Narr:
Conrad Nagel. with Victor Mature, Carole Landis, Lon Chaney,
Jr., Nigel de Brulier, John Hubbard, Jean Porter. Cave men
vs. prehistoric animals. Mediocre; inferior even to O'Brien's
lesser monster films like SON OF KONG and MIGHTY JOE
YOUNG.

ONE MILLION DOLLARS Rolfe-Metro 1915 55m. D: John W.
Noble. Ref: MPN 11/27/15. LC. with William Faversham,
Henry Bergman, Charles Graham. Detective projects his astral
body "into the presence of those he suspects."

ONE MILLION YEARS B.C. (B) Fox/7A-Hammer 1966 Technicolor by DeLuxe 100m. D: Don Chaffey. (ONE MILLION B.C.)
SP, P: Michael Carreras. PH: Wilkie Cooper. Mus: Mario Nascimbene. Art D: Bob Jones. SpFX: George Blackwell. SpVisual
FX: Ray Harryhausen. Remake of ONE MILLION B.C. Ref: PM.
COF 8:46. with Raquel Welch, John Richardson, Martine Beswick. Percy Herbert, Robert Brown. Rock people, shell people,
and dinosaurs. No better or worse than the original.

ONE MORE TIME (B) UA/Chrislaw--Trace-Mark 1969 DeLuxe
color 93m. Follow-up to SALT AND PEPPER. D: Jerry Lewis.
SP: Michael Pertwee. PH: Ernest W. Steward. Mus sc & D:
Les Reed. SpFX: Terry Witherington. Ref: MFB. FM 63:22.
with Sammy Davis, Jr., Peter Lawford, Percy Herbert,
Glyn Owen, Allan Cuthbertson, Christopher Lee (Dracula), Peter Cushing (Dr. Frankenstein). And Frankenstein's
monster.

ONE NIGHT...BY CHANCE (F) 1964 (Un SOIR...PAR HASARD)
D: Ivan Govar. SP : Pierre Sabatier, from a story by R. Collard.
PH: Pierre Levent. Adap: Govar, André Allard. Ref: Trieste
bulletin. M/TVM 10/64: "s-f spy." with A. Stroyberg, Pierre
Brasseur, Jean Servais.

ONE OF OUR SPIES IS MISSING MGM/Arena 1966 Metrocolor
91m. D: E. Darrell Hallenbeck. SP: Howard Rodman. Story:
Henry Slesar. From "The Man from U. N. C. L. E." TV series.
PH: Fred Koenekamp. Mus: Gerald Fried. Title theme: Jerry
Goldsmith. Ref: MFB'66:126. with Robert Vaughn, David Mc-
Callum, Leo G. Carroll, Maurice Evans, Vera Miles, Ann Elder,
Dolores Faith, Cal Bolder. Scientist's rejuvenation formula works
on man.

ONE SPOOKY NIGHT Pathe/Sennett 1923 Ref: LC

1000 YEARS FROM NOW see CAPTIVE WOMEN

ONE TOO EXCITING NIGHT (B) Hepworth 1912 Ref: Suspense in the
Cinema. 15m. A man buys a reputedly haunted country house.

"Apparition in a sheet."
ONE WAY STREET   F Nat 1925 70m. D: John F. Dillon. SP:
Arthur Statter, Mary Scully. P, Adap: Earl Hudson. PH: Arthur
Edeson. Story: Beale Davis. Ref: AFI. Lee.   LC. with Dorothy
Cumming, Ben Lyon, Anna Q. Nilsson, Marjorie Daw, Lumsden
Hare. Woman rejuvenated by monkey glands.
ONESIME AUX ENFERS see SIMPLE SIMON AND THE DEVIL
ONESIME ET LA MAISON HANTEE see SIMPLE SIMON & THE
HAUNTED HOUSE
ONESIME HORLOGER see SIMPLE SIMON WATCHMAKER
ONIBABA (J) Toho 1965 scope 105m. (The HOLE. The DEMON.
DEVIL WOMAN) SP,D: Kaneto Shindo. PH: K. Kuroda. Mus:
H. Hayashi. Ref: Shriek 3:50. M/TVM. with Nobuko Otowa,
Kei Sato. Mother attempts to frighten her daughter away from
man. Slight tale takes too long to tell, though the punch line is
good. Moderately interesting.
ONLY A COFFIN see ORGIES OF DR. ORLOFF, The
ONLY WAY OUT IS DEAD, The see MAN WHO WANTED TO LIVE
FOREVER, The
ONNA KYUKETSUKI see VAMPIRE MAN
OPERACION LADY CHAPLIN see OPERATION LADY CHAPLIN
OPERATION ATLANTIS (I-Sp) Splendor/Fisa 1965 color/scope
88m. (AGENT S03, OPERATION ATLANTIS. AGENTE 003,
OPERACION ALTANTIDA-Sp.) D: Doménico Paolella (aka Paul
Fleming). SP: Victor Auz. Story: Vic Powell. PH: F. Sánchez,
Marcello Masciocchi. Mus: Theo Usuelli. Ref: Ital P. SpCinema
'67. with John Ericson, Berna Rock, Erika Blanc (or Blank),
Beni Deus, José Manuel Martin, María Granada. Chinese atomic
station in Africa behind legend that "descendants of the survivors
of Atlantis" inhabit a "New Atlantis."
OPERATION COUNTERSPY (I-F-Sp) Cineproduzioni/Copernic/Bal-
cazar 1965 color/scope 111m. ("ASSO DI PICCHE,"
OPERAZIONE CONTROSPIONAGGIO-I. AS DE PIC, OPERACION
CONTRAESPIONAJE-Sp. "ACE OF SPADES"--COUNTER-ES-
PIONAGE OPERATION. ACE OF PIC, OPERATION COUNTER
ESPIONAGE) SP,D: Nick Nostro. SP: also G. Simonelli, A.
Balcazar. Story: G. Maggi. Dial: J. A. de la Loma. PH:
Franco Delli Colli. Mus: Franco Pisano. Art D: J. A. Soler.
Ref: Ital P'65. SpCinema'67. with George Ardisson, Joaquin
Diaz, Leontine May, Helene Chanel, Lena Von Martens. Mad-
man who attempts to use secret installation to destroy world
vaporized by hero.
OPERATION FEAR see KILL, BABY, KILL
OPERATION GOLDMAN see LIGHTNING BOLT
OPERATION KID BROTHER (I) UA 1967 Technicolor/scope 104m.
(O.K. CONNERY-I) D: Alberto de Martino. SP: Paul Levy,
Frank Walker. PH: A. Ulloa. Mus: Ennio Morricone, Bruno
Nicolai. SpFX: Gagliano. Ref: MFB. with Neil Connery, Daniela
Bianchi, Adolfo Celi, Bernard Lee, Anthony Dawson, Lois Max-
well. Rare form of Tibetan hypnosis; master criminal who begins
demagnetizing the dynamos in Europe.
OPERATION LADY CHAPLIN (I-F-Sp) Fida/Roitfeld/Sincronia 1966
color/scope 102m. (MISSIONE SPECIALE LADY CHAPLIN-I.
OPERACION LADY CHAPLIN-Sp) D: Alberto De Martino. SP: S.

Continenza, M. Coscia, H. de Diego. PH: A. Ulloa. Art D:
Ramiro Gómez. Ref: Ital P. SpCinema'67. with Daniela Bianchi,
Ken Clark, Jacques Bergerac, Helga Liné, Mabel Karr, Philippe
Hersent, Tómas Blanco. Spongy substance in villa laboratory
"swells up enormously in water."

OPERATION MONSTERLAND (J) Toho 1968 color/scope 89m.
(KAIJU SOKOGEKI. KAIJU SOSHINGEKI. DESTROY ALL MON-
STERS. The MARCH OF MONSTERS) D: I. Honda. SP: Honda,
Kaoru Mabuchi. PH: Taiichi Kankura. Mus: Akira Ifukube. Art D:
Takeo Kita. SpFX: Eiji Tsuburaya. Ref: UFQ 42. M/TVM 5/68.
with Akira Kubo, Jun Tazaki, Yukiko Kobayashi, Kyoko Ai,
Kenji Sawara. And Ghidrah, Godzilla, Son of Godzilla, Mothra,
Rodan, Varan, etc. In the same enjoyable slapstick spirit as
GHIDRAH.

OPERATION PARADISE see KISS THE GIRLS AND MAKE THEM
DIE

OPERATION POKER (I-Sp) Wonder/Alcocer 1965 color/scope D:
Osvaldo Civirani. SP: Roberto Gianviti. PH: Alfonso Nieva. Ref:
Ital P'65. with Roger Browne, Jose Greci, Sancho Gracia,
Carol Brown, Helga Linè. (OPERAZIONE POKER) "Device per-
mits one to see through solid objects."

OPERATION STARDUST see MISSION STARDUST
OPERATION, WANDERING PLANET see PLANET ON THE PROWL
OPERATION WHITE SHARK see A.D.3 OPERATION WHITE
WHALEFISH

OPERAZIONE PARADISO see KISS THE GIRLS AND MAKE THEM
DIE

OPERAZIONE PAURA see KILL, BABY, KILL
OR ET LE PLOMB, L' see GOLD AND LEAD
ORBITA MORTAL see MISSION STARDUST
ORDEN: FX 18 DEBE MORIR see FX 18 SECRET AGENT
ORDER: FX 18 MUST DIE see FX 18 SECRET AGENT
ORDOG, Az (by F. Molnar) see DEVIL, The (1921)
ORFEU DA CONCEICAO (by V. de Moraes) see BLACK ORPHEUS
ORGASMO see PARANOIA
The ORGIES OF DR. ORLOFF (Sp) Hispamer 1966 89m. (SOLO
UN ATAUD. ONLY A COFFIN) SP, D: Santos Alcocer. Story:
E. Jarnes. (Les ORGIES DU DOCTEUR ORLOFF-F) PH: Emilio
Foriscot. Mus: Ramon Femenia. Sets: Teddy Villalba. Ref: MMF
18-19:104. SpCinema'67. with Howard Vernon, Danielle Godet,
María Saavedra, Adolfo Arlés, José Bastida. Castle, coffin,
disappearing body, etc.

ORGY OF BLOOD see BRIDES OF BLOOD
ORGY OF THE DEAD Astra 1966 color (REVENGE OF THE DEAD.
ORGY OF THE VAMPIRES) D, P: A. C. Stevens. SP: Edward D.
Wood, Jr. PH: Robert Caramico. Ref: Positif 98:66. with Cris-
well, Fawn Silver, Pat Barringer. Mummy, werewolf, banshee,
Prince and Princess of Darkness terrorize couple in forest.

ORIENTAL BLACK ART (F) Melies 1908 Ref: V&FI 9/12/08.
Two spirits leave and return to woman's body; magician appears
in bubble, frightens natives.

The ORIENTAL MYSTIC Vita 1909 6m. Ref: Bios 7/22/09.
Turkish Mystic appears and disappears in mirrors, frightening
woman.

ORLACS HANDE see HANDS OF ORLAC, The (1925)
ORLAK, THE HELL OF FRANKENSTEIN (Mex) 1961 (ORLAK, EL
   INFIERNO DE FRANKENSTEIN. The HELL OF FRANKEN-
   STEIN. El INFIERNO DE FRANKENSTEIN) D: Rafael Baledon.
   SP: Carlos Taboada, Alfredo Ruanova. Ref: FM 31:18. MadM
   5:27. FJA. Pic: SM 5:33. with Joaquin Cordero, Armando
   Calva. Dr. Carlos Frankenstein brings an executed murderer
   back to life to help him in his experiments. Mummy, vampires,
   zombies, witches?
ORLOFF AND THE INVISIBLE MAN (F-Sp) Celia/Mesquiriz 1970
   (ORLOFF Y EL HOMBRE INVISIBLE-Sp. ORLOFF ET L'HOMME
   INVISIBLE-F.) D: Pierre Chevalier. Ref: V 5/12/71:143:
   "Horror sci-fi." with Howard Vernon, Elisabeth del Rio.
ORPHEUS (F) Paulve 1950 SP, D: Jean Cocteau. PH: Nicolas
   Hayer. Mus: Georges Auric. Art D: D'Eaubonne. Costumes:
   Marcel Escoffier. Ref: Gilson's "Jean Cocteau." COF 5:41. with
   Jean Marais, François Périer, Maria Casarès, Marie Déa,
   Pierre Bertin, Juliette Gréco. Poet brought back to life by
   Death; Underworld entered through mirrors. Eerie, exquisite
   fantasy, with a haunting performance by Maria Casarès.
ORRIBILE SEGRETO DEL DOTTOR HICHCOCK, L' see HORRIBLE
   DR. HICHCOCK, The
OS DEUSES E OS MORTOS see OF GODS AND THE DEAD
The OTHER (G) Vitascop 1913 (Der ANDERE) D: Max Mach.
   From a play by Paul Lindau. Remade in 1930. Ref: Fantastique.
   Orpheus 2:34. DDC I:290. with Albert Basserman, Emmerich
   Hanus, Reilly Ridon, Otto Collot. Dr. Hallers has a split per-
   sonality.
The OTHER (G) Tobis 1930 (Der ANDERE   Le PROCUREUR
   HALLERS or DR. HALLERS-F.) D: Robert Wiene. Remake of
   '13 The OTHER. Mus: Pasqualle Perris. Ref: NYT 1/15/32. DDC
   II:309. III:454. with Fritz Kortner, Hermine Sterler, Ursula von
   Diemen, Eduard von Winterstein, Kaethe von Nagy, Heinrich
   George. A district attorney's personality undergoes an abrupt
   change every night at ten.
The OTHER FU-MANCHU (Sp) 1945 (El OTRO FU-MANCHU) Cien-
   fuegos SP, D: Ramón Barreiro. PH:Cesar Benitez. Ref: MMF 9:14.
   with Rosita Yarza, Adela Esteban, Alicia Torres, Candida Lopez.
   Fu-Manchu steals a magic shell from a tea merchant's shop. A
   mysterious cult is also after the shell.
OTHER ONE, The see BACK FROM THE DEAD
The OTHER SELF Lubin 1915 30m. D: Leon D. Kent. SP: J. L.
   Lamothe. Ref: MPN 5/29/15. Hypnosis gives girl split per-
   sonality.
The OTHER SELF (Austrian) Sascha-Film 1918 66m. (Das ANDERE
   ICH) D: Fritz Freisler. SP: Ladislaus Tuszinsky. Ref: Osterr.
   with Raoul Aslan, Fritz Kortner, Magda Sonja. Professor
   separates a soul from its body.
OTOKO TO ONNA NO SHINWA see STAR OF ADAM
OTRA ORILLA, La see FROM THE OTHER SIDE
OUANGA see POCOMANIA
OUR HEAVENLY BODIES (G) (WUNDER DER SCHOPFUNG.
   WONDERS OF THE UNIVERSE) Ref: FJA. SM 1:3: "A German

trip around the Solar System via ethership. "
OUR MAN FLINT   Fox 1966 color   107m. D: Daniel Mann. SP:
Hal Fimberg, Ben Starr. Sequel: IN LIKE FLINT. PH: Daniel L.
Fapp. Mus: Jerry Goldsmith. Ref: FFacts. COF 10:6. with James
Coburn, Lee J. Cobb, Gila Golan, Russ Conway, Rhys Williams,
Sigrid Valdis, Benson Fong, Edward Mulhare. An organization
that has learned the secret of controlling the weather creates a
series of natural catastrophes.   Device in watch revives agent
after he stops his heart.
OUT OF THE DARK (novel by U. Curtiss) see I SAW WHAT YOU
DID
OUT OF THE DARKNESS see TEENAGE CAVEMAN
OUT OF THE FOG see FOG FOR A KILLER
OUT OF THIS WORLD   MCA-TV 1954 From the "Rocky Jones,
Space Ranger" TV series.   with Richard Crane, Ian Keith.
OUTLAW PLANET see PLANET OF THE VAMPIRES
OUTSIDER, The see BATTLE OF THE WORLDS, The
OVAL PORTRAIT, The (by E. A. Poe) see FALL OF THE HOUSE
OF USHER, The (1928-F)
OVER MY DEAD BODY see BRAIN, The
OWANA, THE DEVIL WOMAN Nestor 1913 Ref: Bios 12/11/13. 17m.
Indian bridegroom transformed into pony.

P. T. BARNUM'S ROCKET TO THE MOON see THOSE FANTASTIC
FLYING FOOLS
PACT WITH THE DEVIL (I) 1949 (PATTO COL DIAVOLO) D: Luigi
Chiarini. SP: Corrado Alvaro. Ref: DDC II:353.
PACTO DIABOLICO see DIABOLICAL PACT
PAGAL (India-Hindi) Ranjit Movietone 1941 D: A. R. Kardar. Ref:
Dipali 2/14/41. with Charlie, Khatoon. Girl injected by doctor
with serum "develops signs of insanity. "
PAINTING THE TOWN Univ-Jewel 1927 70m. D: W. J. Craft.
P: Carl Laemmle. SP,D(?): Harry O. Hoyt. SP: also Vin Moore.
Titles: Albert De Mond. PH Al Jones. Ref: AFI. with Glenn
Tryon, Patsy Ruth Miller, Charles Gerrard, Sidney Bracey,
Monte Collins. "Wonder car" capable of going 150 miles an hour
and "stopping in two car lengths. "
PAJAMA PARTY AI 1964 color 82m.   (The MAID AND THE MAR-
TIAN) D: Don Weis. SP: Louis M. Heyward. PH: Floyd Cros-
by. Ref: MW 1:12. COF 6:56. with Tommy Kirk, Annette, Elsa
Lanchester, Buster Keaton, Dorothy Lamour, Harvey Lembeck,
Jesse White, Ben Lessey, Frankie Avalon, Don Rickles. Martian
with powers of telepathy and levitation.   Not totally worthless:
Keaton looks funny when someone drops a pail of water on him.
PAJAMA PARTY IN A HAUNTED HOUSE see GHOST IN THE IN-
VISIBLE BIKINI
PAKT MIT DEM SATAN, Der See COLD HEART, The (1923-Sauer)
The PALACE OF THE ARABIAN NIGHTS (F) Melies/Star 1905 (Le
PALAIS DES MILLE ET UNE NUITS) Ref: Mitry:37. Sorcerer,
enchanted sword, genie of fire, ghosts, dragon, stone monsters.

PAN TWARDOWSKI see DR. FAUSTUS (1937)
PANDORA'S BOX (G) Nero Film 1928 100m. (Die BUESCHSE
    DER PANDORA) silent D: G. W. Pabst. SP: Ladislaus Vayda,
    from two plays by Frank Wedekind, "Erdgeist" and "Buesche der
    Pandora." PH: Gunther Krampf. Art D: Andreiev and Hesch.
    Ref: Eisner. SilentFF. Orpheus 2:20. DDC III:213. Pic: EncicDS
    II:plate CLXVI. Positif 99:42. with Louise Brooks, Gustav Diessl
    (Jack the Ripper), Fritz Kortner, Franz (or Francis) Lederer,
    Siegfried Arno.
PANIC see TELL-TALE HEART, The (1960)
PANIC AT MADAME TUSSAUD'S (B) Exclusive /Van Dyke 1949
    51m. (PANIC IN A WAX MUSEUM) D: Peter Graham Scott. SP:
    Roger Proudlock. PH: S. D. Onions. Ref: MFB'49. with Patricia
    Owens, Harry Fine, Francis Clare, Harry Locke. Fight in the
    Chamber of Horrors.
PANIC IN YEAR ZERO AI /Alta Vista 1962 93m. (SURVIVAL. END
    OF THE WORLD) D: Ray Milland. SP: Jay Simms, John Morton.
    PH: Gil Warrenton. Mus: Lex Baxter. Art D: Daniel Haller. P:
    Lou Rusoff, Arnold Hoagland. Ref: PM. FFacts. Orpheus 4:37.
    with Ray Milland, Jean Hagen, Frankie Avalon, Scott Peters,
    Russ Bender, O. Z. Whitehead, Richard Garland, Richard Bakal-
    yan. A city is nuclear bombed, and anarchy reigns among the
    survivors. The script is characterized by confusion and disorder
    too.
PANIC ON THE AIR Col 1936 60m. D: D. Ross Lederman. SP:
    Harold Shumate. Story: Theodore A. Tinsley. PH: Benjamin
    Kline. Ref: SF Film. MPH 5/2/36. with Lew Ayres, Florence
    Rice, Benny Baker, Edwin Maxwell, Charles Wilson, Murray
    Alper, Robert Emmet Keane. Inventor's high-frequency "trans-
    ceiver" interrupts radio broadcasts.
PANNA DEGLI AEROMOBILI, La see BREAKDOWN OF THE
    AEROMOBILES, The
PANTHER GIRL OF THE KONGO Rep 1955 serial 12 episodes
    ('66 feature The CLAW MONSTERS) D: Franklyn Adreon. SP:
    Ronald Davidson. PH: Bud Thackery. Ref: Barbour. with Phyllis
    Coates, Myron Healey, Arthur Space, Archie Savage, Mike
    Ragan. A chemist enlarges crawfish to gigantic proportions.
    Fistfights and gun battles.
PAPA GASPARD; or, THE GHOST OF THE ROCKS. Le Lion/
    Brockliss 1909 12m. Ref: Bios 12/23/09. Miser guards fortune
    in cave by posing as ghost.
PARADISO (B) c1962 (PARADISIO) Ref: SF Film. Lee. with
    Arthur Howard. X-ray glasses.
PARANOIA (I-F) Tritone-S. N. C. 1969 color /scope 91m. (ORGASMO)
    D: Umberto Lenzi. SP: Lenzi, Ugo Moretti, Marie Sollenville.
    PH: Guglielmo Mancori. Ref: MFB'70:15. with Carroll Baker,
    Lou Castel, Colette Descombes, Tino Carraro. Woman held
    prisoner in her villa: lights going on and off, toad in tray, other
    shock devices. Shock twist ending doesn't redeem tired BABY
    JANE-GASLIGHT attempts at suspense.
PARANOIAC (B) Univ /Hammer 1963 80m. D: Freddie Francis. SP:
    Jimmy Sangster. PH: Arthur Grant. Mus: Elisabeth Lutyens.
    SpFX: Les Bowie. Ref: FFacts. with Janette Scott, Oliver Reed,

Sheila Burrell, Liliane Brousse, Alexander Davion, Maurice Denham. Eleanor Ashby's dead brother appears to have returned to haunt the Ashby estate. Nothing remarkable, but the tensions among the principles keep things alive, and there are one or two eerie scenes.

PARDE KE PEECHEY (India-Hindi) Em. CeR Films 1971 Ref: Shanker's 4/25/71. "Vaults joined by automatic devices; a flying villain (batman [sic]-type). "

PAREMA, CREATURE FROM THE STAR-WORLD (Austrian) Cartellieri-Film 1922 55m. (PAREMA, DAS WESEN AUS DER STERNENWELT) SP, D: Mano Ziffer-Teschenbruck. SP: also Hans Hinays. PH: Rudolf Mayer. Ref: Osterr. with Carmen Cartellieri, Viktor Kutschera, Karl Götz. Alchemy, artificial diamonds.

PARIS PLAYBOYS Mono-AA 1954 62m. D: William Beaudine. SP: Elwood Ullman, Edward Bernds. PH: Harry Neumann. Mus: Marlin Skiles. Ref: HR 3/3/54. TVG. with Leo Gorcey, Huntz Hall, Bernard Gorcey, Steven Geray, John Wengraf, Bennie Bartlett. Bowery Boy's sour-cream-plus formula acts as super-explosive.

PARIS QUI DORT see CRAZY RAY, The

PARIS WHEN IT SIZZLES Para 1964 Technicolor 110m. (The GIRL WHO STOLE THE EIFFEL TOWER) D: Richard Quine. SP: George Axelrod. Based on a screenplay, "Holiday for Henriette," "La Fete a Henriette," or "Henriette" by Julien Duvivier and Henri Jeanson. PH: Charles Lang, Jr. Mus: Nelson Riddle. SpPhFX: Paul K. Lerpae. Makeup: Frank McCoy. Ref: FFacts. FM 32:71. TVG. Pic: FM 31:59. with William Holden, Audrey Hepburn, Noel Coward, Gregoire Aslan, Marlene Dietrich, Tony Curtis, Mel Ferrer, and the voices of Fred Astaire and Frank Sinatra. Vampire bit; Dr. Jekyll and Mr. Hyde sequence.

PAROXISMUS see VENUS IN FURS

PARSIFAL (I) Ambrosio 1912 Ref: The Film Index. DDC III:427. Bios 10/30/13. MPW 14:1307. Mitry V:28. Two "magicians" try to kill knights. Magic looking-glass, vision, angel. From Wagner.

PARSIFAL (Sp) Huguet 1951 (The EVIL FOREST) SP, D: Daniel Mangrané. D: also Carlos S. de Osma. PH: Cecilio Paniagua. Art D: Jose Caballero. with Ludmil(l)a Tcherina, Gustavo Rojo, Carlo Tamberlani. Based on the musical drama by Wagner.

PASI SPRE LUNA see STEPS TO THE MOON

PASSIONATE PEOPLE EATER, The see LITTLE SHOP OF HORRORS, The

PASSPORT TO PIMLICO (B) Eagle Lion/Balcon 1949 72m. D: Henry Cornelius. SP: T. E. B. Clarke. PH: Lionel Barnes. Mus D: Georges Auric. Art D: Roy Oxley. Ref: FD 10/10/49. with Stanley Holloway, Betty Warren, Barbara Murray, Jane Hylton, Raymond Huntley, Sidney Tafler, Hermione Baddeley, Margaret Rutherford. Residents of a section of London find documents which show that they are really citizens of Burgundy.

PATE DES TODES, Der (by Baumbach) see DEATH (1921)

PATHALA BHAIRAVI (India-Tamil) Vijaya Productions 1951 D: K. V. Reddy. Dial & Songs: Tanjore Ramayyah Das. Ref: Filmindia 7/51. with N. D. Rama Rao, S. V. Ranga Roo, "C.S.R.,"

Malathi. A wicked necromancer in search of a talisman, through his supernatural powers, discovers that it is deposited in a temple deep inside the earth. He sends young Ramu down after it. A goddess "cured of her crocodile body" warns Ramu of the magician's schemes. Ramu kills him and with the talisman builds a dream palace. The wizard's disciple brings him back to life. He regains the talisman and magically transports Ramu to his realm. Ramu's friend brings him magic slippers and a cloak which renders him invisible, and the magician is defeated.

(PATHE TRICK FILM-title unknown) (F) Pathe c1908 15m. Ref: Silent FF. Two men undress and reveal themselves as skeletons; a flower girl transforms herself into a goblin.

PATTO COL DIAVOLO see PACT WITH THE DEVIL

The PAWNS OF MARS Vita 1915 45m. D: Theodore Marston. SP: Donald Buchanan. Ref: MPN 2/24/15. MPW 4/17/15. with Dorothy Kelly, James Morrison. Rays explode bombs from a distance.

PEACE GAME, The see GLADIATORS, The

PEACEFUL PERCY (by B. Millhauser) see FOOLS IN THE DARK

PEACH BOY (J) Toei 1956 87m. (TAKARAJIMA ENSEI) Ref: FEFN 8/3/56. with K. Enomoto, A. Kishii, K. Masuda. A youth battles "the king of the demons" on an island.

PEACOCK FEATHER, The (by L. Moore) see PENNIES FROM HEAVEN

The PEARL FISHER (F) Pathe 1907 9m. Ref: MPW'07:652. A fisherman, after seeing a vision of the "queen of the deep," dives into the ocean, swims through "subterranean caverns and past weird and curious fish," and reaches mysterious halls full of plants and sea monsters.

PEARL OF DEATH Univ 1944 75m. D, P: Roy William Neill. SP: Bertram Millhauser. From "Adventure of the Six Napoleons" by Sir Arthur Conan Doyle. PH: Virgil Miller. Mus D: Paul Sawtell. Art D: John B. Goodman, Martin Obzina. Ref: FM 69:66. HR 8/25/44: "Horror." with Basil Rathbone, Nigel Bruce, Evelyn Ankers, Ian Wolfe, Miles Mander, Dennis Hoey, Mary Gordon, Holmes Herbert, Rondo Hatton (the Creeper). One of Rathbone's better Sherlock Holmes mysteries.

PEAU DE CHAGRIN, Le (by Balzac) see DREAM CHEATER, The / MAGIC SKIN, The (1913/1915) /SINISTER WISH, The /SLAVE OF DESIRE /WILD ASS'S SKIN, The

PECCATORI DELLA FORESTA NERA, I see BURNING COURT, The

The PEEPING PHANTOM 1964 (HOW TO SUCCEED WITH GIRLS) Ref: MMW 9:50. Lee: Orpheus 3:33. FM 31:13. Phantom-of-the-Opera-like monster.

PEEPING TOM (B) Powell 1959 Eastmancolor (FACE OF FEAR-TV) D, P: Michael Powell. SP: Leo Marks. PH: Otto Heller. Mus: Brian Easdale. Ref: Clarens. with Carl Boehm, Moira Shearer, Anna Massey, Shirley Anne Field, Michael Goodliffe, Esmond Knight. Man obsessed by people's expressions of fear becomes a murderer. Mediocre.

PENDULUM, The see SNAKE PIT, The

PENNIES FROM HEAVEN Col 1936 90m. D: Norman Z. McLeod. SP: Jo Swerling. Story: William Rankin, Katherine Moore. From "The Peacock Feather" by Leslie Moore. PH: Robert

Pittack. Mus & Lyrics: Arthur Johnston, John Burke. Ed: John Rawlins. Ref: FD 11/16/36. Dimmitt. with Bing Crosby, Madge Evans, Edith Fellows, Donald Meek, Louis Armstrong, John Gallaudet, Nydia Westman. "Haunted" house converted into cafe.

PEONIES AND STONE LANTERNS (J) Toei 1955 (BOTAN-DORO) D: Akira Nobuchi. Ref: Unij. Bltn. 31. FEFN 10/25/57: "Ghost thriller." with Chiyonosuke Azuma, Yuriko Tashiro.

PEPITO AND THE MONSTER (Mex) Roma 1957 (PEPITO Y EL MONSTRUO) SP, D: Story: Joselito Rodriguez. SP: also C. G. Dueñas. Story: also Dueñas, J. R. Mas. PH: Ezequiel Carrasco. Mus: S. Guerrero. Ref: Indice. FM 29:46. Pic: FM 7:10. 9:12, 15. FMO 1:30-1. with Pepito Romay, Titana Romay, Yerye Bierute, Martha Rangel.

PER PIACERE, NON SPARATE COL CANNONE see PLEASE, DON'T FIRE THE CANNON

PERCY (B) Anglo-Emi/Welbeck 1971 Technicolor 103m. D: Ralph Thomas. SP: Hugh Leonard. Based on the novel by Raymond Hitchcock. Add'l Material: Terence Feely. PH: Ernest Steward. Ref: MFB'71:56. with Hywel Bennett, Denholm Elliott, Elke Sommer, Britt Ekland, Tracy Reed, Sue Lloyd, Patrick Mower. Surgeon Sir Emmanuel Whitbread achieves the first penis transplant.

PERCY PIMPERNICKEL, SOUBRETTE Kalem 1914 D: Albert Hale. Ref: SF Film. MPW 22:223. Women dominant in the year 1950.

The PERFECT WOMAN (B) Two Cities/Eagle-Lion 1949 89m. D: Bernard Knowles. SP: George Black, Knowles. Dial: J. B. Boothroyd. From the play by Wallace Geoffrey and Basil John Mitchell. PH: Jack Hildyard. Mus: Arthur Wilkinson. Art D: J. Elder Wills. Ref: SM 4:6. FDY. with Patricia Roc, Nigel Patrick, Stanley Holloway, Miles Malleson, Irene Handl. A scientist gives his robot the appearance of a woman.

PERIL FROM PLANET MONGO see FLASH GORDON'S TRIP TO MARS

PERILS OF NYOKA Rep 1942 serial 15 episodes ('66 feature NYOKA AND THE LOST SECRETS OF HIPPOCRATES. NYOKA AND THE TIGERMAN) D: William Witney. SP: R. Davidson, N. S. Hall, W. Lively, J. O'Donnell, J. Poland. PH: Reggie Lanning. Ref: Barbour. The Serial. with Kay Aldridge, Clayton Moore, William Benedict, Lorna Gray, Charles Middleton, Tristram Coffin, Forbes Murray, Robert Strange, George Pembroke, John Davidson, Ken Terrell, Kenneth Duncan, John Bagni, George Renavent, George Lewis, Arvon Dale. Trained killer gorilla; operation on man to erase memories.

PERILS OF PARIS, A TALE OF TERROR (THE TERROR OF FAILURE) FBO 1924 65m. (TERROR-F.) D: Edward José. SP: Gerard Bourceois. with Pearl White, Robert Lee, Henry Bandin, Arlette Marchall. Inventor tests "radio-minium." Tired attempts at thrills.

The PERILS OF PAUL Keefe-Arrow 1920 22m. Ref: MPN 22:2491. SP: William Keefe. Ouija boards, "spirit world."

PERILS OF PAULINE Pathe 1914 serial 20 episodes D: Louis Gasnier, Donald MacKenzie. Ref: Lee. CNW. SilentFF. with Pearl White, Crane Wilbur, Edward José. Pic: TBG. Paul Panzer.

Germs compel victim to go into water.
The PERILS OF PAULINE Univ 1933 serial 12 episodes D: Ray
Taylor. SP: Ella O'Neill, B. Dickey, G. Plympton, J. Foley.
Story: Charles W. Goddard. Ref: Boy's Cinema 4/7/34.
Academy. with Evalyn Knapp, John Davidson, Robert Allen, Frank
Lackteen. Prof. Hargrove attempts to find the formula for a
poison gas which destroyed an ancient civilization. He finds a
related explosive with some power left. "Walking mummy"
frightens men.
The PERILS OF PAULINE Univ 1967 color 107m. D: Herbert
B. Leonard, Joshua Shelley. SP: Albert Beich. Story: Charles
W. Goddard. PH: Jack A. Marta. Mus: Vic Mizzy. Art D:
Alexander Golitzen, John T. McCormack. Ref: FFacts. FM 46:
63. with Pat Boone, Pamela Austin, Edward Everett Horton,
Terry-Thomas, Kurt Kasznar, Vito Scotti, Aram Katcher,
Hamilton Camp, Doris Packer. '25 PHANTOM OF THE OPERA
set used. Madman plans to put Pauline into suspended animation
in block of ice.
PERPETUAL MOTION SOLVED (B?) Hilarity 5m. Ref: Bios
6/4/14. Homemade car "defies every known law of gravitation."
PERRY GRANT, AGENT OF IRON (I) GV/Fono 1966 color
(PERRY GRANT, AGENTE DI FERRO) D: Lewis King. SP:
Poggi, Del Grosso. PH: Memmo Mancori. Ref: Ital P'66. with
Peter Holden, Marilù Tolo, Jack Stuart, Seyna Seyn, Umberto
D'Orsi. Electro-magnetic ray destroys electronic equipment set
up in subterranean passage of the Colosseum.
PERSEE L'INVINCIBLE see MEDUSA VS. THE SON OF HERCULES
PERSEO L'INVINCIBLE see MEDUSA VS. THE SON OF HERCULES
PERSEO Y MEDUSA see MEDUSA VS. THE SON OF HERCULES
PERSEUS AGAINST THE MONSTERS see MEDUSA VS. THE SON
OF HERCULES
PERSEUS THE INVINCIBLE see MEDUSA VS. THE SON OF
HERCULES
PETER'S EVIL SPIRIT (F) Urban-Eclipse 1914 8m. Ref: SilentFF.
Satanic tramp beseiges man, who is suddenly surrounded by
flames.
PETIT CHAPERON ROUGE, Le see LITTLE RED RIDING HOOD
(1901/1929)
PETRIFIED MAN, The see MAN WHO TURNED TO STONE, The
PHAEDRA (F) Pathe 1909 15m. Ref: Bios 3/24/10. Sea monster.
The PHANTOM (F) Pathe 1910 12m. Ref: Bios 6/16/10. The God
of Phantoms changes a girl into an ugly old witch; she bewitches
a student.
The PHANTOM Col 1943 serial 15 episodes Ch. 5. The Ghost Who
Walks. D: B. Reeves Eason. SP: M. B. Cox, V. McLeod, S.
Lowe, L. J. Swabacker. PH: James S. Brown, Jr. Ref: Barbour.
D. Glut. The Serial. with Tom Tyler, Kenneth MacDonald, Frank
Shannon, Jeanne Bates, Ace the Wonder Dog, Guy Kingsford,
Ernie Adams, John Bagni. The mysterious Phantom, according
to the legend, is a ghost "who never dies."
PHANTOM APE, The see PHANTOM OF THE RUE MORGUE
The PHANTOM BARON (F) 1943 (Le BARON FANTOME) 99m.
SP, D: Serge de Poligny. Dial: Jean Cocteau. Adap: Poligny,

Louis Chavance. PH: Roger Hubert. Mus: Louis Beydts. Art D:
Krauss. Ref: Gilson. Rep.Gen. '47. COF 5:38: "Atmospheric."
with Odette Joyeux, Jany Holt, Alain Cuny, Alerme, André
Lefaur, P. Dorian. An old baron disappears suddenly from his
castle. Ten Years later a woman discovers the baron's corpse lying near his treasure in a secret dungeon.

PHANTON CART, The see PHANTOM CHARIOT, The (1939)

The PHANTOM CAT (J) Toei 1956 73m. (KAIBYO RANBU. MANY
GHOST CATS. "Mito Komon" series) D: Masamitsu Igayama.
Ref: Unij.Bltn. 31. FEFN 8/17/56: "Pet cat turns into figure of
deceased maid," fights villains. with Ryunosuke Tsukigata, Shino-
bu Chihara, H. Tomiya.

The PHANTOM CHARIOT (Swedish) Svensk 1919 70m. (KORKARLEN.
THY SOUL SHALL BEAR WITNESS. THE STROKE OF MID-
NIGHT-U.S.) SP,D: Victor Sjöström. PH: J. Julius. Art D:
Alexander Bako. Ref: SilentFF. Pic: Pict.Hist.Cinema NYT
6/5/22. with Victor Sjöström, Hilda Borgström. The man who
dies last on New Year's eve drives the death cart all year as
the penalty for his evil. From Lagerlöf.

The PHANTOM CHARIOT (F) Col/Transcontinental 1939 (La CHAR-
RETTE FANTOME. The PHANTOM CART) SP,D: Julian Duvivi-
er. From "La Charretier de la Mort" by Selma Lagerlöf. PH:
J. N. Kruger. Dial: Alexandre Arnoux. Mus: Jacques Ibert. Ref:
NYT 5/28/40. DDC. V 3/20/40. with Pierre Fresnay, Marie
Bell, Louis Jouvet, Palau, Robert Le Vigan, Mila Parely.
Death's chariot, skeleton horse.

The PHANTOM CHARIOT (Swedish) Nordisk/Agascope 1958
(KORKARLEN. The PHANTOM CARRIAGE. The GREY CART)
D: Arné Mattsson. SP: Rune Lindström. From the novel by
Selma Lagerlöf. Ref: Beranger. with George Fant, Ulla Jacobs-
son, Anita Björk, Edvin Adolphson, Bengt Brunskog.

PHANTOM CITY F Nat 1928 silent D: Albert Rogell. SP: Adele
Buffington. P: Harry J. Brown. Ref: Photoplay 8/28. with Ken
Maynard, James Mason, Eugenia Gilbert, Jackie Coombs, Jack
McDonald. Western. Black-robed phantom haunts town.

The PHANTOM CREEPS Univ 1939 serial 12 episodes (The
SHADOW CREEPS) D: Saul Goodkind, Ford Beebe. SP: G.
Plympton, B. Dickey, Mildred Barish. Story: Willis Cooper.
PH: Jerry Ash. Ref: STI 1:19. FM 9:6.28:16. V. Pic: FanMo
5:36. MW 9:29. ModM 3:20. with Bela Lugosi, Robert Kent,
Regis Toomey, Edward Van Sloan, Eddie Acuff, Edwin Stanley,
Roy Barcroft, Forrest Taylor, Charles King, Willard Parker,
George Melford, Hooper Atchley, Lane Chandler. Huge robot;
"devisualizer belt"; chemical (from meteorite) that causes
suspended animation.

The PHANTOM EMPIRE Mascot 1935 serial 12 episodes (RADIO
RANCH and MEN WITH STEEL FACES-'40 feature versions.
GENE AUTRY AND THE PHANTOM EMPIRE) D: B. Reeves Ea-
son, Otto Brower. SP: W. MacDonald, G. Geraghty, H. Freed-
man. Ref: Imagen. FM 15:20. SM 6:6. FanMo 5:37. Pic: FM
16:44. ModM 3:23. with Gene Autry ("Flash Gordon"-Spain;
Gene Autry-U.S.), Frankie Darro, Smiley Burnette, Dorothy
Christy, Wheeler Oakman, Charles K. French, Edward Piel, Sr.,

Jack Carlyle. Lost civilization discovered below Texas Ranch. Robots (used in CAPT. VIDEO).

The PHANTOM FIEND (B) Olympic 1935 67m. (The LODGER) D: Maurice Elvey. SP: Miles Mander, Paul Rotha, from the play "The Celebrated Lodger" and the book "The Lodger" by Marie-Belloc Lowndes. Ref: FDY. PH: S. Blythe, Basil Emmott, William Luff. with Ivor Novello, Elizabeth Allan, W. E. Bascomb, Jack Hawkins, Kynaston Reeves, Barbara Everest. The story of Jack the Ripper.

The PHANTOM FOE   Pathe 1920 serial 15 episodes D: Bertram Millhauser. Ref: CNW. Lee. Pic: TBG. DDC II:223. with Juanita Hansen, William N. Bailey, Warner Oland, Harry Semels. Ch. 9. The Mystic Summons. Giant foot, hypnotism.

PHANTOM 45'S TALK LOUD (story by J. Chadwick) see RIM OF THE CANYON

PHANTOM FROM SPACE UA/Planet 1953 72m. D, P: W. Lee Wilder. SP: Bill Raynor, Myles Wilder. PH:William Clothier. Mus: William Lava. SpFX: Alex Welden. PhFX: Howard Anderson. Ref: FDY. Pic: SM 3:10. with James Seay, Noreen Nash, Ted Cooper, Rudolph Anders, Harry Landers, Jim Bannon, Michael Mark. Invisible being from space lands on earth. Fairly effective considering budget limitations.

PHANTOM FROM 10,000 LEAGUES American Releasing Corp. (AI) 1956 75m. D: Dan Milner. SP: Lou Rusoff. Story: Dorys Lukather. PH: B. Baker. Mus: Ronald Stein. P: Dan & Jack Milner. Ref: FDY. with Kent Taylor, Cathy Downs, Michael Whalen, Helene Stanton, Philip Pine. Monster guards uranium deposit in sea. Not too swell.

PHANTOM HONEYMOON Hallmark 1919 D: J. Searle Dawley. Ref: Exhibitors Herald. Prof. Juno P. Tidewater, who devotes his time to "exploding" ghost stories, investigates Denmore Castle and is startled by the appearance of three ghosts.

PHANTOM KILLER Mono 1942 61m. D: William Beaudine. SP: Karl Brown. Remake of The SPHINX. PH: Marcel Le Picard. Ref: Showmen's 8/22/42: "Jekyll and Hyde personality." with Dick Purcell, Joan Woodbury, John Hamilton, Warren Hymer, Mantan Moreland, J. Farrell MacDonald, Kenneth Harlan, George Lewis, Karl Hackett, Harry Depp. Deaf and dumb man indicted for murder.

PHANTOM KILLER, The see INVISIBLE GHOST

The PHANTOM LIGHT Bison 1914 30m. Ref: Lee. Indian haunted by spirit of brother he killed.

PHANTOM LOVERS see GHOSTS OF ROME

PHANTOM MEETS THE RETURN OF DR. MABUSE, The see RETURN OF DR. MABUSE, The

PHANTOM MELODY Univ 1920 D: Douglas Gerrard. Ref: Exhibitors Herald. with Monroe Salisbury. A count, struck by lightning and buried alive, regains consciousness in the tomb.

PHANTOM OF CRESTWOOD RKO 1932 77m. SP,D: J. Walter Ruben. SP: also Bartlett Cormack. PH: Henry Gerrard. P: David O. Selznick. Ref: TVK. Harrison's 10/22/32: "Floating Faces," screams, secret doors, subterranean tunnels, thunderstorm. with Ricardo Cortez, Karen Morley, Anita Louise, H. B. Warner,

Pauline Frederick, Sam Hardy, Skeets Gallagher, Robert Mc-
Wade, Gavin Gordon, Ivan Simpson, George E. Stone. A
woman assembles a group of her extortion victims at a deserted
country house.
The PHANTOM OF SOHO (W.G.-B) Producers Releasing Org./CCC
1963 ('67-U.S.) 97m. scope (Das PHANTOM VON SOHO) SP:
Ladisla(u)s Fodor. From Bryan Edgar Wallace's novel "Murder
by Proxy." D: F. J. Gottlieb. PH: Richard Angst. Mus:
Martin Böttcher. Art D: H. J. Kiebach, E. Schomer. Ref:
MFB'68:43. German Pictures. COF 9:31. V 8/2/67: "Some
crude horrific elements." FIR'67:82. with Dieter Borsche, Hans
Söhnker, Barbara Rutting, Elisabeth Flickenschildt, Helga
Sommerfeld, Werner Peters, Hans Nielsen. "Phantom" kills
several Londoners.
PHANTOM OF PARIS see MYSTERY OF MARIE ROGET
PHANTOM OF THE AIR Univ 1933 serial 12 episodes D: Ray
Taylor. SP: Ella O'Neill, B. Dickey, G. Plympton. Ref: Lee.
MPH 6/10/33:41. with Tom Tyler, William Desmond, Gloria
Shea, LeRoy Mason. Ground-control device for plane.
PHANTOM OF THE CIRCUS see CIRCUS OF HORRORS
The PHANTOM OF THE CONVENT (Mex) FESA/Clasa 1934 82m.
(El FANTASMA DEL CONVENTA. The FANTASY OF THE
MONASTERY) SP,D: Fernando de Fuentes. SP: also Juan Bus-
tillo Oro. Story: J. Pezet, de Fuentes,Oro. PH:Ross Fisher.
Mus: Max Urban. Ref: Indice. FM 29:46. NYT 4/22/35. with
Enrique del Campo, Carlos Villatoro, Martha Roel, Paco
Martinez. "Night spent in an old monastery dreaming of the
ghosts of the departed monks." "Mummies"?
PHANTOM OF THE FERRIS WHEEL see PYRO
The PHANTOM OF THE MOULIN ROUGE (F) Fernand 1925 80m.
(Le FANTOME DU MOULIN ROUGE) SP,D: René Clair. Ass't D:
G. Lacombe. PH: Jimmy Berliet, Louis Chair. Art D: Robert Gys.
Ref:SilentFF. with George Vaultier, Jose Davert, Albert Prejean.
Doctor releases man's spirit from his body.
The PHANTOM OF THE OPERA Univ 1925 ('30 part-talking reis-
sue in which Chaney did not speak) Technicolor sequences D:
Rupert Julian. SP: Raymond Shrock, Elliot Clawson, from the
novel by Gaston Leroux. PH: Charles van Enger, Virgil Miller,
Milton Bridenbecker. Ass't D: Edward Sedgwick. Art D: Dan Hall.
Set used in The BLACK CASTLE, '67 PERILS OF PAULINE, etc.
Ref: Clarens. FM 8:28. 9:34-45. 10:26. 14:6. 40:44. A'64:24. 46:63.
with Lon Chaney, Mary Philbin, Norman Kerry, Snitz Edwards,
Gibson Gowland, John St. Polis, Arthur Edmund Carewe, John
Miljan. Someone (Leroux? Julian?) got the inspired idea of
matching the spectacular horror of Chaney's Phantom against
ballet dancers' pirouetting and fluttering among the gargoyles as
an expression of giddy fear. The non-Phantom, non-dancer scenes
are pretty dull but can be gotten through.
The PHANTOM OF THE OPERA Univ 1943 95m. Technicolor
D: Arthur Lubin. SP: Eric Taylor, Samuel Hoffenstein, from
the novel by Gaston Leroux. PH: Hal Mohr, W. Howard Greene.
Mus sc & d: Edward Ward. Art D: John B. Goodman, Alexander
Golitzen. P: George Waggner. Ref: Academy. FM 10:44-49. COF

5:46. with Nelson Eddy, Susanna Foster, Claude Rains, Edgar
Barrier, Leo Carrillo, Jane Farrar, J. Edward Bromberg, Hume
Cronyn, Miles Mander, Fritz Leiber, Paul Marion, Fritz Feld,
Frank Puglia, Steven Geray, Nicki Andre, Kate Lawson, Cyril
Delevanti, Wheaton Chambers, Belle Mitchell, Renee Carson,
Lane Chandler, Stanley Blystone, Jim Mitchell, John Walsh, Dick
Bartell, Beatrice Roberts. Uninspired remake, the production
values and Rains all that distinguish it from a Universal '40's
programmer.

The PHANTOM OF THE OPERA (B) Univ/Hammer 1962 color 84m.
D: Terence Fisher. SP: John Elder. From Leroux's novel. PH:
Arthur Grant. Mus: Edwin Astley. Art D: Bernard Robinson, Don
Mingaye. Makeup: Roy Ashton. Ref: FFacts. with Herbert Lom,
Heather Sears, Thorley Walters, Edward De Souza, Michael
Gough, Marne Maitland, Michael Ripper, Miles Malleson. Third
major version of the horror story, as if we even needed a
second.

PHANTOM OF THE OPERA, The (by G. Leroux) see SANTO AGAINST
THE STRANGLER

The PHANTOM OF THE OPERETTA (Arg) Gral. Belgrano 1955
70m. (El FANTASMA DE LA OPERETA) D: Enrique Carreras.
SP: Jose Dominianni, Manuel Rey, Alfredo Ruanova. PH: Alfredo
Traverso. Mus: Victor Slister. Art D: Oscar Lagomarsino. Ref:
Esto Es 7/5/55. Cine Argentine. with Amelita Vargas, Alfredo
Barbieri, Tono Andreu, Gogo Andreu, Ines Fernandez. Satire on
horror films with a vampire-type and a Frankenstein-monster-
type.

The PHANTOM OF THE OPERETTA (Mex) Brooks & Enriquez
1959 90m. (El FANTASMA DE LA OPERETA) D: Fernando
Cortes. SP: Gilberto M. Solares, Juan Garcia. Story: Alfredo
Ruanova. Mus: Manuel Esperon. Ref: FM 31: 18. FEFN 3/61.
Indice. Pic: MadM 2:53. with "Tin Tan," Ana Luisa Peluffo,
Antonio Brillas, Eduardo Alcaraz. Whole horde of phantoms.

The PHANTOM OF THE RED HOUSE (Mex) Chapultepec 1954
(El FANTASMA DE LA CASA ROJA) D: Miguel M. Delgado. SP:
R. P. Pelaez. Story: C. Lesser. PH: Raul Martinez Solares. Mus:
Jose de la Vega. Ref: Indice. TVG. TVFFSB. with Alma Rosa
Aguirre, Raul Martinez, Anthony Espino, "Clavillazo," Che
Reyes, Victor Alcocoer. Dead man watches as his heirs murder
each other.

PHANTOM OF THE RUE MORGUE WB 1954 3-D 84m. (The
PHANTOM APE) D: Roy Del Ruth. SP: Harold Medford, James
Webb. From "Murders in the Rue Morgue" by Edgar Allan Poe.
PH: J. Peverell Marley. Mus: David Buttolph. Art D: Bertram
Tuttle. Warnercolor Ref: Clarens. with Karl Malden, Claude
Dauphin, Patricia Medina, Steve Forrest, Dolores Dorn,
Anthony Caruso, Merv Griffin, Erin O'Brien-Moore, Paul
Richards, Charles Gemora, Henry Kulky. Mad killer on the loose
in Paris. So-so.

The PHANTOM PLANET AI/Four Crown 1961 82m. D: William
Marshall. SP, P: Fred Gebhardt. PH: Elwood J. Nicholson. Mus:
Hayes Pagel. Art D: Bob Kinoshita. Ed: Hugo Grimaldi, Don
Wolfe. Makeup: Dave Newall. Ref: FFacts. with Coleen Gray,

Dean Fredericks, Anthony Dexter, Dolores Faith, Francis X.
Bushman, Al Jarvis, Richard Kiel (Solarite). The planet is an
asteroid that moves when someone waves his hand over a little
gadget. The monsters attack in orange crates. A space girl
tells the hero that the unusual fruit he is eating is "the equivalent
of your breadfruit." It's like that.
PHANTOM RAIDERS Lowe's Inc. 1940 70m. (NICK CARTER IN
PANAMA) D: Jacques Tourneur. SP: William Lipman. Story:
Jonathan Latimer. PH: Clyde De Vinna. Ref: NYT 6/24/40.
with Walter Pidgeon, Florence Rice, Joseph Schildkraut, John
Carroll, Donald Meek, Nat Pendleton, Steffi Duna, Cecil Kella-
way, Matthew Boulton, Alec Craig, Dwight Frye. Radio that
explodes bombs by remote control is used to sink ships. Every-
thing a dumb, fun B-picture should be.
PHANTOM RULER, The see INVISIBLE MONSTER, The
The PHANTOM SIRENS Urban-Eclipse/Kleine 1909 Ref: F Index
7/3/09. Sirens' spell lures fishermen.
The PHANTOM SPEAKS Rep 1945 69m. D: John English. SP:
John K. Butler. PH: William Bradford. Art D: Russell Kimball.
Ref: FDY. with Richard Arlen, Stanley Ridges, Lynne Roberts,
Jonathan Hale, Tom Powers, Pierre Watkin, Marian Martin, Ralf
Harolde. An executed killer returns from the dead as a spirit
that takes over a scientist's body, spirit-possession being the
film's explanation of insanity. Can't-argue-with-that line: "It's
not hard to die. It's the coming back that's hard." Arguable: "I've
got a will that's better than yours." The action is as crude as the
script.
The PHANTOM THIEF Col 1946 64m. D: D. Ross Lederman. SP:
Richard Weil, Richard Wormser. Story: G. A. Snow. Mus D:
Mischa Bakaleinikoff. PH: George B. Meehan, Jr. Art D:
Robert Peterson. Ref: HR 7/1/46. with Chester Morris (Bos-
ton Blackie), Jeff Donnell, Richard Lane, Dusty Anderson,
George E. Stone, Marvin Miller, Wilton Graff, Murray Alper,
Forbes Murray, Frank Sully, Joseph Crehan. A chauffeur is
stabbed during a seance conducted by a phony spiritualist.
The PHANTOM VIOLIN Univ 1914 Ref: Lee. DDC II:371: D:
Francis Ford. Madman hides in crypt.
The PHANTOM WITNESS Than 1915 45m. SP: Philip Lonergan.
Ref: MPW 27:442. with Kathryn Adams. Ghost of ward poisoned
by guardian incriminates latter.
PHAROAH'S CURSE UA/Bel Air 1957 66m. D: Lee Sholem.
SP: Richard Landau. PH: William Margulies. Mus: Les Baxter.
P: Howard W. Koch. Ref: FDY. with Mark Dana, Ziva Rodann,
Diane Brewster, Terence De Marney, Ralph Clanton, Kurt Katch,
George Neise. Archaeological expedition encounters centuries-
old monster guarding Egyptian tomb.
PHILOSOPHIE DANS LE BOUDOIR, La see BEYOND LOVE AND
EVIL
PHOENIX see FAHRENHEIT 451
PHOTOGRAPHIE ELECTRIQUE A DISTANCE, La see ELEC-
TRICAL PHOTOGRAPHER, The
PHOTOGRAPHING A GHOST (B) G. A. Smith 1898 1m. Ref:
Hist. Brit. Film. A box labelled "ghost" contains the "ghost of a

'swell' ".

PIANETA DEGLI UOMINI SPENTI, Il see BATTLE OF THE
    WORLDS, The
PIANETI CONTRO DI NOI, I see PLANETS AGAINST US, The
PICTURE MOMMY DEAD Emb 1966 Pathecolor 88m. (COLOR
    MOMMY DEAD) D, P: Bert I. Gordon. SP: Robert Sherman.
    PH: Ellsworth Frederick(s). Ref: COF 12:6. Boxo 9/12/66.
    with Don Ameche, Martha Hyer, Zsa Zsa Gabor, Susan Gordon,
    Maxwell Reed, Wendell Corey, Signe Hasso, Anna Lee, Kelly
    Corcoran. A girl is haunted by visions of her dead mother.
The PICTURE OF DORIAN GRAY New York Motion Picture
    1913 D: Phillips Smalley. Ref: FIR'66:222. Bios 9/25/13. with
    Wallace Reid, Lois Weber.
The PICTURE OF DORIAN GRAY Than 1915 30m. Ref: MPN
    7/24/15. with Harris Gordon, A. Howard, Helen Fulton.
The PICTURE OF DORIAN GRAY (Russ) 1915 (PORTRET DORI-
    ANA GREJA) D: Meyerhold, Vsevolod. Ref: Cahiers 220:114.
    DDC II:315. EncicDS IX:1341.
The PICTURE OF DORIAN GRAY (B) Neptune 1916 45m. D, P: Fred
    W. Durrant. From the book by Oscar Wilde. Ref: Hist. Brit.
    Film. with Henry Victor, Sidney Bland, Jack Jordan, A. B.
    Imeson.
The PICTURE OF DORIAN GRAY (Hung) 1917 (AZ ELET
    KIRALYA. DORIAN GRAY) D: Alfred Deesy. Ref: A Magyar.
    with Bela Lugosi?
The PICTURE OF DORIAN GRAY (G) 1917 (Das BILDNIS DES DORI-
    AN GRAY) D: Richard Oswald. Ref: DDC III:504. EncicDS VII:
    1421.
The PICTURE OF DORIAN GRAY MGM 1945 SP, D: Albert Lewin.
    Technicolor sequence 110m. From the book by Oscar Wilde.
    PH: Harry Stradling. Mus: Herbert Stothart. Art D: Cedric
    Gibbons, Hans Peters. Ref: Clarens. with George Sanders,
    Hurd Hatfield, Donna Reed, Angela Lansbury, Peter Lawford,
    Miles Mander, Billy Bevan, Lilian Bond, Douglas Walton, Rich-
    ard Fraser, Lowell Gilmore, Mary Forbes, Morton Low(e)ry,
    Moyna M(a)cGill, Robert Greig. Portrait of a young man reflects
    his gradual corruption, while he remains youthful in appearance.
    Lewin's camera is always over-emphasizing the obvious: Half
    the film is shot from behind a sinister-looking cat statuette.
    There are two other great distractions: We want to see the por-
    trait; and Sanders' (Wilde's) epigrams are so witty we'd rather
    listen to them and forget the rest. Haunting "Little Yellow Bird"
    theme. At least the movie does things and doesn't just sit
    around.
PICTURE OF DORIAN GRAY, The (by O. Wilde) see SECRET OF
    DORIAN GRAY, The
The PIED PIPER OF HAMELIN (B) Clarendon 1907 Ref: Hist.
    Brit. Film
The PIED PIPER OF HAMELIN Than 1911 Ref: MPW'11:174, 226.
The PIED PIPER OF HAMELIN (F) Pathe 1911 15m. Ref: Bios
    3/28/12.
The PIED PIPER OF HAMELIN Edison 1913 17m. D: George
    Lessey. Ref: Bios 10/16/13. Edison Kinetogram 8/5/13. with
    Herbert Prior, Robert Brower.

The PIED PIPER OF HAMELIN 1917 11m. Ref: LC
The PIED PIPER OF HAMELIN (G) 1917 (Der RATTENFANGER VON
    HAMELN) D: Paul Wegener. SP: Henrik Galeen. Art D: Rochus
    Gliese. Ref: DDC II:414. Clarens. with Wegener, Lyda Salmonova,
    Wilhelm Diegelmann, Jakob Tiedtke.
The PIED PIPER OF HAMELIN Crest /Int'l Film Distributors
    1957 color 90m. D: Bretaigne Windust. SP, Lyrics: Irving Taylor,
    Hal Stanley. PH: William E. Snyder. Mus: Edvard Grieg. SpFX:
    Jack Rabin, Irving Block, Louis DeWitt. Based on the legend and
    the poem by Robert Browning. with Van Johnson, Claude Rains,
    Jim Backus, Lori Nelson, Kay Starr, Doodles Weaver. Piper
    lures children of town into mountain cave with his magic music.
    Abysmal. Totally static. There is a bit where two of the comic
    relief knock their heads together to underscore a rhyme that is
    a high point of sophisticated comedy.
PIED PIPER OF HAMELIN, The see HAMELIN
PIFFKINS' PATENT POWDER Warwick 1910 5m. Ref: Bios
    10 /20 /10. Compound makes hair disappear.
PIGSTY (I-F) Cinematografica-I Film Dell'Orso /CAPAC 1969
    color /scope D: Pier Paolo Pasolini. Ref: M /TVM 6 /69. with
    Pierre Clementi, Jean-Pierre Leaud, Anne Wiazemsky. "Princi-
    pals devoured by animals in two-episode chiller. "
PIKOVAJA DAMA see QUEEN OF SPADES (1916)
PILGRIM PROJECT, The (novel by H. Searls) see COUNTDOWN
PILLOLE DI ERCOLE, Le see HERCULES' PILLS
PILLOW OF DEATH Univ 1945 55m. (Inner Sanctum series)
    D: Wallace Fox. SP: George Bricker. Story: Dwight V. Babcock.
    PH: Jerome Ash. Mus: Frank Skinner. Art D: John B. Goodman,
    Abraham Grossman. Ref: MFB'45:154. Clarens. COF 7:40. with
    Lon Chaney, Jr. , Brenda Joyce, Rosalind Ivan, J. Edward Brom-
    berg, Wilton Graff, George Cleveland, Fern Emmett, J. Farrell
    MacDonald. "Ghost" that accuses man of murder; seance; "ap-
    parition"; secret room. Inconsistent medium sometimes recalls
    what he has said in trances, sometimes doesn't. One or two pos-
    sible moments of interest, but only possible and only moments.
PIN MONEY (by H. Vance) see DIAMOND HANDCUFFS
PIQUE DAME see QUEEN OF SPADES (1927 /1937 /1960)
PIRATE'S HARBOR see HAUNTED HARBOR
PIRATES OF 1920: A FORECAST OF THE WARS OF THE FUTURE
    (B) C&M 1911 15m. D: Dave Aylott, A. E. Coleby. PH:
    J. H. Martin. Ref: SilentFF. Bios 2 /2 /11. Pirate aircraft robs
    ship.
PIT, The see MIND BENDERS, The
The PIT AND THE PENDULUM (F) Warwick 1910 11m. (Le PUITS
    ET LE PENDULE) D: Henri Desfontaines. From the story by
    Edgar Allan Poe. Ref: DDC II:68. Bios 4 /21 /10. The Grand
    Tribunal orders Digo to suffer in the Chamber of Horrors.
The PIT AND THE PENDULUM Solax 1913 50m. D: Alice Guy
    Bla(n)ché. From the story by Edgar Allan Poe. Ref: Bios
    10 /23 /13. FIR'61:464. DDC II:480. with Darwin Karr, Blanche
    Cornwall, Fraunie Fraunholz.
The PIT AND THE PENDULUM AI /Alta Vista 1961 Technicolor /
    scope 85m. D, P: Roger Corman. SP: Richard Matheson, from

the story by Edgar Allan Poe. PH: Floyd Crosby. Mus: Les
Baxter. Art D: Daniel Haller. Ref: Clarens. FM 13:66. 14:8-15.
COF 1:52. PM. with Vincent Price, John Kerr, Barbara Steele,
Luana Anders, Anthony Carbone. In the 16th Century an English-
man arrives at a Spanish castle to investigate the mysterious
death of his sister. Very bad on acting, dialogue, plot; very good
on shock scenes.

PIT AND THE PENDULUM, The (by E. A. Poe) see AVENGING
CONSCIENCE, The /DR. GOLDFOOT & THE BIKINI MACHINE /
RAVEN, The (1912) / SNAKE PIT, The

The PITFALL (J) Teshigara (or Teshigahara) Productions 1962
(KASHI TO KODOMO) D: Hiroshi Teshigahara. SP: Kobo Abe. PH:
Hiroshi Segawa. Ref: S&S'63:124. M /TVM 9 /62. Japan. with
H. Igawa, K. Miyahara, Mus: T. Takemitsu. Murder victims
return as ghosts to torment their enemies.

PITONG PASIKLAB SA BAHAY NA TISA (Fili) RTG /Imperial Pictures 1963 D: Luis San Juan. Ref: M /TVM 9 /63. with Gloria
Sevilla. The owner of a haunted house disappears.

A PLACE OF ONE'S OWN (B) Univ /Eagle-Lion /Gainsborough 1945
D: Bernard Knowles. SP: Brock Williams, from a book by Sir
Osbert Sitwell. PH: Stephen Dade. Ed: Charles Knott. Ref: MFB
'45:46. Dimmitt. with James Mason, Margaret Lockwood,
Dennis Price, Barbara Mullen, Dulcie Gray, Helen Haye, Moore
Marriott, Ernest Thesiger. Mus D: Louis Levy. Girl possessed
by spirit of dead woman.

PLACER SANGRIENTO see BLOODY PLEASURE

PLAGUE OF THE ZOMBIES (B) Fox /Hammer 1966 Technicolor
(The ZOMBIE. The ZOMBIES) D: John Gilling. SP: Peter Bryan.
PH: Arthur Grant. Mus : James Bernard. Art D: Bernard Robinson.
Ref: Clarens. PM. Orpheus 3:34. MW 5:14. with Andre Morell,
Diane Clare, Jacqueline Pearce, Brook Williams, John Carson,
Alex Davion, Michael Ripper. Squire who studied voodoo and black
magic in Haiti returns to Cornish village.

The PLAGUE SPOT Vita 1915 15m. D: Theodore Marston. Ref:
MPW'15:2234. Cure for plague.

PLAN 9 FROM OUTER SPACE DCA 1958 (1956) 79m. (GRAVE
ROBBERS FROM OUTER SPACE) SP, D: Edward D. Wood, Jr.
PH: William C. Thompson. Mus: Gordon Zahler. Ref: FFacts.
FM 24:67. A'69:24. with Bela Lugosi, Vampira, Tor Johnson.
Lyle Talbot, Gregory Walcott, Mona McKinnon, Joanna Lee. Aliens
begin to resurrect the dead of the earth. Really bad.

PLANET OF BLOOD see PLANET OF THE VAMPIRES /QUEEN OF
BLOOD

PLANET OF DEATH (by S. Lem) see FIRST SPACESHIP ON VENUS

PLANET OF EARTH, The see BATTLE OF THE WORLDS, The

PLANET OF EXTINGUISHED MEN, The see BATTLE OF THE
WORLDS, The

PLANET OF TERROR see PLANET OF THE VAMPIRES /QUEEN
OF BLOOD

PLANET OF THE APES Fox 1968 color /scope 112m. D: Franklin J. Schaffner. SP: Rod Serling, Michael Wilson. From the
novel (also known as "Monkey Planet") by Pierre Bouille. PH:
Leon Shamroy. Mus: Jerry Goldsmith. Art D: Jack Martin Smith,

William Greber. SpFX: L. B. Abbott, Art Cruickshank, Emil
Kosa, Jr. Makeup: John Chambers. Sequels: BENEATH THE
PLANET OF THE APES. ESCAPE FROM THE PLANET OF THE
APES. with Charlton Heston, Roddy McDowall, Kim Hunter,
Maurice Evans, James Whitmore, James Daly, Linda Harrison.
Astronauts land on planet where apes are rulers and humans are
hunted and caged. The ape makeup is the star, and some of the
actors (especially Hunter and McDowall) under it are good too,
but too often brutal action has to be resorted to to keep the plot
(a patchwork of old "Twilight Zone" 's) going.
PLANET OF THE DAMNED see PLANET OF THE VAMPIRES
PLANET OF THE DEAD see FIRST SPACESHIP ON VENUS
PLANET OF THE VAMPIRES (U. S. -I-Sp-G) 1965 AI /Italian
Int'l /Castilla /Omnia Technicolor /scope 86m. (TERRORE
NELLO SPAZIO-I. TERROR EN EL ESPACIO-Sp. PLANET OF
TERROR. PLANET OF BLOOD. The DEMON PLANET-TV.
HAUNTED PLANET HAUNTED WORLD. OUTLAWED PLANET.
PLANET OF THE DAMNED) D: Mario Bava. SP: Bava, Ib
Melchior, Louis Heyward, Alberto Bevilacqua, R. Salvia, A.
Roman, C. Cosulich. PH: Antonio Rinaldi. Mus: Gino Marinuzzi.
Ref: FM 34:10. M /TVM 9 /65. Orpheus 3:34. FM 32:70. 36:9. 37:
48. Clarens. with Barry Sullivan, Norma Bengell, Angel Aranda,
Evi Marandi, Franco Andrei. Astronauts on strange planet
beset by spirit-like beings in search of inhabitable bodies. Strong
on atmosphere, weak on everything else.
PLANET OF THE VAMPIRES see QUEEN OF BLOOD
PLANET ON THE PROWL (I) Mercury /Manley /Southern Cross 1965
color (MISSIONE PLANETA ERRANTE. OPERATION, WANDER-
ING PLANET. WAR BETWEEN THE PLANETS) D, P: Antonio
Margheriti (aka Anthony Dawson). P: also Joseph Fryd. SP:
Ivan Reiner, Moretti. PH: Riccardo Pallottini. Mus: F. Lavagnino.
Ref: Ital P. COF 9:45. with Giacomo Rossi Stuart, Ombretta
Colli, Halina Zalewska, Peter Martell, Enzo Fiermonte, Renato
Baldini, Archie Savage, Furio Meniconi, Isarco Ravaioli. Waves
affecting earth's weather are found to be coming from a wander-
ing planet.
PLANET OUTLAWS see BUCK ROGERS
PLANETA BURG see STORM PLANET
PLANETARY GIANTS (Mex) America 1963 (GIGANTES PLANE-
TARIOS. GIGANTES INTERPLANETARIOS) D: Alfredo B. Cra-
venna. PH: Alfredo Uribe. Ref: Imagen. with Guillermo Murray,
Lorena Velazquez, José Gálvez, Adriana Roel, Rogelio Guerra,
Irma Lozano. Death ray.
The PLANETS AGAINST US (F-I) Comptoirs Français /Vanguard-
P.C. 1961 85m. (Le MONSTRE AUX YEUX VERTS-F. Il
MOSTRO DAGLI VERDI or I PIANETI CONTRO DI NOI-I.
HANDS OF A KILLER-Eng. The MONSTER WITH GREEN EYES.
The MONSTER WITH YELLOW EYES. The MAN WITH THE
YELLOW EYES) D: Romano Ferrara. SP: Ferrara, Piero Pierot-
ti. Story: M. Rendina. PH: P. L. Pavoni. Mus: A. Trovajoli.
Art D: A. Visone. Ref: MFB'65:138. Orpheus 3:34. MW 8:54.
Pic: FM 30:9. with Jany Clair, Michel Lemoine, Maria Pia Luzi,
Otello Toso. The UN and NASA investigate a man with magnetic

powers. Sluggish. A few interesting scenes showing the con-
struction of robots.
PLATOS VOLADORES, Los see FLYING SAUCERS, The
The PLAYGIRLS AND THE VAMPIRE (I) Fanfare /Gordon /Nord
Film Italiana 1960 ('64-U. S.) 85m. (Des FILLES POUR UN
VAMPIRE-F. L'ULTIMA PREDA DEL VAMPIRO-I. DESIRS DE
VAMPIRE-Belg. The VAMPIRE'S LAST VICTIM. CURSE OF
THE VAMPIRE-TV) SP, D: Piero Regnoli. PH: Ugo Brunelli.
Mus sc: Aldo Piga. Art D: Giuseppe Ranieri. Ref: MFB'65:11.
TVFFSB. FM 12:13. Orpheus 3:30. Pic: FM 26:15. with Lyla
Rocco, Walter Brandi (vampire), Maria Giovannini, Alfredo Riz-
zo, Tilde Damiani. Nobleman's vampire twin preys on group of
showgirls staying at his castle.
PLAYTIME (F) Specta /Prodis 1966 color 145m. D: Jacques Tati.
SP: Tati, Jacques Lagrange. PH: Jean Badal, Andreas Winding.
Mus: Francis Lemarque. Art D: Eugène Roman. Eng. Dial: Art
Buchwald. Ref: Imagen. V 12 /27 /67. F&F. with Tati, Barbara
Dennek, Yves Barsacq. World of the future with people living in
glass houses.
PLEASE, DON'T FIRE THE CANNON (I-Sp) Nike /Fenix 1965 color
(PER PIACERE, NON SPARATE COL CANNONE) D: Mario
Caiano. SP: Tojodor, Continenza. PH: Julio Ortas. Mus sc:
Angel O. Piña. Ref: Ital P. with Frank Wolff, Rossella Como,
Claudio Gora, Gerard Landry. New radar apparatus intercepts
any kind of missile and changes its trajectory.
PLEASURE ISLAND (by F. R. Adams) see HAUNTED ISLAND
(1928) /BRASS BULLET, The
PLEINS FEUX SUR L'ASSASSIN see SPOTLIGHT ON A MURDERER
The PLOT Vita 1914 30m. D: Robert Gaillord, Maurice Costello.
Ref: MPN 1 /2 /15. with Estelle Mardo, Gaillord. Reporter hyp-
notized, ordered to kill Russian ambassador to the United States.
PLUCKED (I-F) (U-M)Summa /Azimut-Les Films Corona 1967
Movielab color 105m. (La MORTE HA FATTO L'UOVO-I. DEATH
HAS LAID AN EGG. A CURIOUS WAY TO LOVE) SP, D:Giulio
Questi. SP: also Franco Arcalli. PH: Dario Di Palma. Mus sc:
Bruno Mader(n)a. Art D: Sergio Canevari. Ref: Film Bltn
9 /29 /69. MFB'69:104. Ital P'67. with Gina Lollobrigida, Jean-
Louis Trintignant, Ewa Aulin. Subplot: "radioactive accident
creates mutated headless chickens."
PLUS VIEUX METIER DU MONDE, Le see OLDEST PROFESSION
IN THE WORLD, The
POCOMANIA Lenwal 1939 65m. D, P: Arthur Leonard. Story:
George Terwilliger. (OUANGA. DRUMS OF THE JUNGLE) Ref:
Showmen's 12 /9 /39. FD 12 /14 /39. Sarris. Movie Monsters.
with Nina Mae McKinney, Jack Carter, Ida James. A woman
"invokes voodooism" in an attempt to gain control of a Jamaican
plantation.
POE'S TALES OF TERROR see TALES OF TERROR
The POISON AFFAIR (F) Gqum /Franco-London Film 1955 Techni-
color 110m. (L'AFFAIRE DES POISONS. The CASE OF POI-
SONS-TV) SP, D: Henri Decoin. SP: also Georges Neveux, Albert
Valentin. PH: Pierre Montazel. Mus: Rene Cloerec. Ref: Lee.
V 12 /28 /55. TVFFSB. DDC III:226. with Anne Vernon, Danielle

Darrieux, Viviane Romance, Paul Meurisse, Albert Remy. Black Mass, torture, clairvoyant.

POISONED WATERS Univ (Nestor) 1913 Ref: MPW'13:1102. Eaedy, a Greek witch, curses Roma's fountain so that whoever bathes there becomes beautiful and whoever drinks dies. A girl, Zarus, suffering from unrequited love of Yuro, drinks from the waters and dies. Yuro's true love, Roma, dies of fright when the spirits of love's suicides arise from the fountain at midnight. Yuro too drinks and dies.

POKER FACE see KILLER AT LARGE

The POLICE OF THE FUTURE (F) Gaum 1909 9m. Ref: Bios 6/9/10. The police of the future have a "special aeroplane."

POLIDOR AT THE DEATH CLUB (I) Pasquali 1912 11m. (POLIDOR AL CLUB DELLA MORTE. POLIDOR, A MEMBER OF THE DEATH CLUB) Ref: Bios 1/2/13. SilentFF.

POLTERGEIST, The (play by F. Harvey) see THINGS HAPPEN AT NIGHT

PONTIANAK see VAMPIRE, The (1957-Malayan)

PONTIANAK GUA MUSANG see VAMPIRE OF THE CAVE, The

PONTIANAK KEMBALI see VAMPIRE RETURNS, The

POONAM KI RAAT see NIGHT OF THE FULL MOON

POPDOWN (B) New Realm/Fremar 1968 color 54m. SP,D,P: Fred Marshall. PH: Oliver Wood. Ref: MFB. with Diane Keen, Jane Bates, Marshall, Zoot Money, Richard LeClare. Two visitors from another world observe life on earth.

PORT SINISTER RKO 1953 65m. (BEAST OF PARADISE ISLAND --'57 reissue) D: Harold Daniels. SP,P: Aubrey Wisberg, Jack Pollexfen. PH: William Bradford. Ref: FDY. with Anne Kimball, House Peters, Jr., James Warren, Lynne Roberts, Paul Cavanagh, William Schallert, Robert Bice. Two scientists checking reports of volcanic eruptions in the Caribbean are attacked by huge crabs. One of the lesser giant-crab films.

PORTES DE LA NUIT, Les see GATES OF THE NIGHT, The

PORTRET DORIANA GREJA see PICTURE OF DORIAN GRAY, The

POSSESSED, The (by C. Turney) see BACK FROM THE DEAD

POSSIBILITIES OF WAR IN THE AIR (B) Urban/Warwick 1910 15m. (The FLYING DISPATCH. DEATH IN THE AIR) D: Charles Urban. Ref: Bios'12:862. Confused story about revenge via blimps and aircraft of the then-future. Good special effects.

La POUPEE (F) Lumiere 1899 From the opera by Edmond Audrian and E. T. A. Hoffman's "The Sandman." Ref: SF Film. Android.

La POUPEE (B) Milton 1920 D: Meyrick Milton. From the opera by Offenbach. Ref: SF Film. with Flora Le Breton. Android.

La POUPEE (F) 1962 Eastmancolor/scope 100m. (The DOLL. HE, SHE OR IT) Procinex D: Jacques Baratier. SP: Jacques Audiberti, Baratier. PH: Raoul Coutard. Mus: Joseph Kosma. Ref: V 5/9/62. COF 4:58. with Sonnie Teal, Zbigniew Cybulski, Catherine Millinaire. Scientist discovers way to duplicate objects.

POWER (I) Aquarius Audiovisual 1971 (1965) 85m. (Il POTERE) SP, D: Augusto Tretti. PH: Ubaldo Marelli. Mus: E. T. Manzoni. Art D: Guido Bassi. Ref: V(d) 9/22/71. Five episodes. First: The Stone Age.

The POWER MGM/George Pal 1968 Metrocolor/scope 108m. D: Byron

Haskin. SP: John Gay, from the novel by Frank M. Robinson.
PH: Ellsworth Fredericks. Mus: Miklos Rozsa. Art D: George W.
Davis, Merrill Pye. SpFX: J. McMillan Johnson, Gene Warren.
Ref: LA Times 4/3/68. with George Hamilton, Suzanne
Pleshette, Richard Carlson, Yvonne De Carlo, Earl Holliman,
Gary Merrill, Arthur O'Connell, Nehemiah Persoff, Ken Murray,
Michael Rennie, Barbara Nichols, Celia Lovsky, Aldo Ray, Miiko
Taka, Beverly Hills. Science-fiction-mystery involving person
with superhuman powers. Good effects; poorly-told story.
The POWER GOD Davis 1925 serial 15 episodes D: Ben Wilson.
Ref: CNW. Story: Rex Taylor, Harry Haven. with Wilson, Neva
Gerber, Mary Brooklyn. Ch. 3. The Living Dead. Electrical
device runs train.
The POWER OF DARKNESS (G) Neumann 1922 72m. (Die MACHT
DER FINSTERNIS) D: Robert Wiene. Ref: Lee. V 10/31/28.
From Leo Tolstoy's play. Man has strange power over women.
POWER OF THE WHISTLER Col 1945 66m. D: Lew Landers. SP:
Aubrey Wisberg. Suggested by the CBS radio program "The
Whistler." PH: L. W. O'Connell. Art D: John Datu. Ref: PM.
FDY. with Richard Dix, Janis Carter, Jeff Donnell, Tala Birell,
John Abbott, Murray Alper. Cards foretell death for homicidal
maniac.
PRAGUE NIGHTS (Cz) Feix-Broz 1968 102m. (NIGHTS OF PRAGUE)
SP: Jiri Brdecka. Ref: Ceskoslovensky 10/1/68. M/TVM
3/69, 6/69. with Josef Abrham. Three stories: 1. "The Bread
Shoes." D: Evald Schorm. PH: Frantisek Uldrych. The Devil.
2. "The Poisoned Poisoner." D: Milos Makovec. PH: Jan Kalis.
3. "The Last Golem." D: Brdecka. When Rabbi Low refuses to
bring the golem back to life, Rabbi Chaim begins modeling a new
golem's head. He completes his golem, a giant compared to Low's,
with the aid of demons.
PREHISTORIC HAYSEEDS (Australian) 1923 Ref: Lee.
PREHISTORIC MAN (F) Urban-Eclipse 1908 Ref: FM 19:36. Pictures
of prehistoric man and monster come to life.
The PREHISTORIC MAN (B) Stoll 1925 50m. SP: A. E. Coleby.
PH: D. P. Cooper. Art D: Walter W. Murton. Ref: SilentFF.
with Harry Agar Lyons, W. G. Saunders, George Robey. Pre-
historic Britain.
PREHISTORIC PEEPS (B) Hepworth 1905 D: Lewis Fitzhamon. Based
on works by E. T. Reed in "Punch" magazine. Ref: Mitry II. Lee.
PREHISTORIC PLANET see QUEEN OF BLOOD
PREHISTORIC PLANET WOMEN see WOMEN OF THE PREHISTORIC
PLANET
PREHISTORIC POULTRY c1917 short Staged by Willis O'Brien. Ref:
Lee (Classic Film Collector 30:55).
PREHISTORIC SOUND, The see SOUND OF HORROR
PREHISTORIC VALLEY see VALLEY OF THE DRAGONS
PREHISTORIC WOMEN UA-Eagle-Lion 1951 70m. Cinecolor SP, D:
Gregg Tallas. SP: also Sam X. Abarbanel. PH: Lionel Lindon.
Mus: Raoul Kraushaar. Art D: Jerome Pycha, Jr. Pic: FM 38:36.
HM 5:19. with Laurette Luez, Mara Lynn, Alan Nixon, Joan
Shawlee, Johann Peturrson (the giant). 20,000 B.C.: cave women,
"winged dragon," etc. Not one of the really good ones. One of the

10 best of '55: Alain Resnais.
PREHISTORIC WOMEN (B) Fox/Hammer-7A 1966 color 91m. (SLAVE
GIRLS-Eng) D, P: Michael Carreras. SP: Henry Younger. PH:
Michael Reed. Mus: Carol Martelli. Art D: Robert Jones. Ref:
MMF. Boxo 2/13/67. with Carll White, Martine Beswick, Edina
Ronay, Michael Latimer, Yvonne Horner. Tribe of prehistoric
jungle women keep men in slavery.
PREHISTORIC WORLD see TEENAGE CAVEMAN
PRELUDE TO MURDER (story by C. Brown) see HOUSE IN THE
WOODS, The
The PREMATURE BURIAL AI/Filmgroup 1962 Pathecolor/scope
D, P: Roger Corman. SP: Charles Beaumont, Ray Russell, from
"Berenice" or "The Premature Burial" by Edgar Allan Poe. PH:
Floyd Crosby. Mus: Ronald Stein. Art D: Daniel Haller. Ref:
Clarens. with Ray Milland, Hazel Court, Richard Ney, Heather
Angel, Alan Napier, John Dierkes, Richard Miller. A man has a
dread of being buried alive.
PREMATURE BURIAL, The (by E. A. Poe) see CRIME OF DR.
CRESPI, The/HORROR/RAVEN, The (1912)
The PRESIDENT'S ANALYST Para 1967 color 103m. (T. P. A.)
SP:D: Theodore J. Flicker. PH: William A. Fraker. Mus: Lalo
Schifrin. Art D: Hal Pereira, Al Roelofs. Ass't D: Kurt Neumann.
Ref: V 12/20/67. with James Coburn, Godfrey Cambridge, Sev-
ern Darden, Joan Delaney, Pat Harrington, Eduard Franz, Walter
Burke, Will Geer, William Daniels, Arte Johnson. Words fed into
automaton via plug in heel.
The PRICE OF SILENCE Sunrise 1921 65m. D: F. L. Granville.
PH: Leland Lancaster. Ref: AFI. with Peggy Hyland, Campbell
Gullan, Tom Chatterton, Dorothy Grodon. "Ghost": Lightning
sketches picture of murder scene on window.
The PRIEST AND THE BEAUTY (J) Daiei 1960 color 80m. (ANCHIN
TO KIYOHIME) D: Koji Shima. SP: Hideo Oguni. PH: Joji Obara.
Ref: UFQ 10. with Raizo Ichikawa, Ayako Wakao, Yoko Uraji,
Akihiko Katayama, Ikuko Mori, Akio Kobori. Priest in coma after
being struck by lightning sees woman jump into river and trans-
form into ugly serpent.
The PRIMITIVE INSTINCT Kalem 1914 30m. D: George Melford.
Ref: MPW 21:930. Lee. with Marin Sais. Dream: cave men.
The PRIMITIVE MAN Biog 1913 (WAR OF THE PRIMAL TRIBES)
Ref: FIR'68:524. Niver. Dream: cave men, dinosaurs.
The PRIMROSE RING Lasky 1917 55m. D: Robert Leonard. Based
on a book by Ruth Sawyer. SP: Marion Fairfax, C. Carr. Ref:
MPW 32:818. with Mae Murray, Tom Moore. Nurse in children's
hospital tells story of "giant ogre."
The PRINCE OF DARKNESS AM&B 1902 Ref: Niver. Spectre of
Death frightens man to death.
The PRINCE OF DARKNESS (I?) Aquila 1914 Ref: LC
The PRINCE OF SPACE (J) Toei/Manley 1959 scope 57m.-Part I.
64m. -Part II. (YUSEI OJI. INVADERS FROM THE SPACESHIP.
SPACE PRINCE) D: Eijiro Wakabayashi. SP: Shin Morita. PH:
Masahiko Iimura. Ref: UFQ 5. MW 8:54. J. Films'60:96. with
Tatsuya Umemiya, Ushio Skashi, Nobu Yatsuna, Ken Sudob, Joji
Oka, Hiroko Mine, Takashi Kanda. The Prince of Space vs. an

"extraterrestrial dictator." Usual loony Japanese super-hero epic.
PRINCE OF TEMPTERS F Nat 1926 90m. D: Lothar Mendes.
SP: Paul Bern. PH: Ernest Haller. From "The Ex-Duke" by E.
Phillips Oppenheim. Ref: AFI. FM 26:11. Photoplay 12/26. with
Lois Moran, Lya de Putti, Ben Lyon, Ian Keith (the devil), Mary
Brian, J. Barney Sherry, Olive Tell, Sam Hardy. The devil, in
the guise of a renegade monk, tries to ruin a young man with the
help of a "vamp."
The PRINCESS AND THE FISHERMAN (F) Gaum 1909 15m. Ref:
12/23/09. A witch-like woman gives a fisherman a princess and
a castle; but he must return to her when he hears the sound of a
bugle. He fails to return when he hears it, and the castle, with
the princess and him in it, sinks into the sea.
The PRINCESS AND THE MAGIC FROG Fantasy Films c1966 Ref:
S Union 1/30/71. Evil sorcerer.
The PRINCESS IN THE VASE AM&B 1908 Ref: Niver. MPW'08:145.
with D. W. Griffith. Dream: Smoke from cremated Egyptian
princess returns to life.
PRIVATE LIFE OF THE GODS see NIGHT LIFE OF THE GODS
PRIVATE PROPERTY (story by N. Houston) see ROYAL ROMANCE,
A
PRIVILEGE (B) Univ 1967 color D: Peter Watkins. SP: Norman
Bogner, from a story by Johnny Speight. PH: Peter Suschitsky.
Mus: Mike Leander. Art D: Bill Brodie. Ref: PM. with Paul
Jones, Jean Shrimpton, Mark London, Max Bacon. In England in
the near future a rock star is used by the government to manipu-
late the population.
PROCESO DE LAS BRUJAS, El see WITCH-KILLER OF BLACK-
MOOR, The
PROCUREUR HALLERS, Le see OTHER, The (1930)
PROFANADORES DES TUMBES see GRAVE ROBBERS
The PROFESSOR AND HIS WAXWORKS WB&E 1907 11m. Ref: V&FI
92:10. Wax figures come to life.
PROFESSOR BRIC-A-BRAC'S INVENTIONS (F) Pathe 1908 Ref:
V&FI 7/11/08. Magnet attracts everything.
PROFESSOR CREEPS Dixie Nat'l 1942 63m. D: William Beaudine.
SP: Roy Clements, Jed Buell, William Crowley. Story: Robert
Edmunds. PH: Arthur Martinelli. Ref: HR 2/20/42. with F. E.
Miller, Mantan Moreland, Florence O'Brien, Arthur Ray. Mad
professor, gorilla, magic.
PROFESSOR HOSKINS PATENT HUSTLER Imperial 1914 7m. Ref:
Bios 1/29/14. "Trick...Marvellous effect on the public."
PROFESSOR OLDBOY'S REJUVENATOR 1914 10m. Ref: Bios
5/28/14. Invention restores youth to all.
PROFESSOR PIECAN'S DISCOVERY (B) C&M 1910 10m. Ref: Bios
6/9/10. Professor discovers fluid which makes cowards brave.
PROF. PUDDENHEAD'S PATENTS (B) Urban-Eclipse 1909 7m.
Futuristic flight series, including The AEROCAB AND VACUUM
PROVIDER. Ref: SF Film. MPW'09:319.
PROFESSOR ROUFF'S GREAT DISCOVERY (F) Pathe 1911 14m. Ref:
Bios 9/7/11. Professor discovers new and deadly drug.
PROFESSOR WEISE'S BRAIN SERUM INJECTOR Lubin 1909 5m. Ref:
F Index 6/12/09. Bios 8/5/09.

PROF. WISEGUY'S TRIP TO THE MOON Powers 1916 7m. Ref: LC.

PROFESSOR ZANIKOFF'S EXPERIENCES OF GRAFTING (F?) Lux 1909 5m. Ref: Bios 2/17/10. Professor shows his pupils his method of "curing various physical defects."

The PROFESSOR'S ANTI-GRAVITATIONAL FLUID (B) Hepworth 1908 Ref: SF Film. Fluid makes fish and hat fly into sky.

The PROFESSOR'S LOVE TONIC Ess 1909 Ref: F. Index 1/16/09. Tonic incites passion.

The PROFESSOR'S SECRET (F) Gaum 1908 10m. Ref: MPW'08:328. Injection causes people to revert to monkeys.

PROGRAM MIT TRUXA (book by H. Seiler) see HIDDEN MENACE/ TRUXA

PROHIBITION Prohibition Film 1915 65m. Ref: MPN 4/17/15. with Thurlow Bergan, Charles Trowbridge. Visions of Mephistopheles and "the Demon of Rum" appear to victims of drink. Allegorical scenes show "the Drink Octopus sapping the blood of its grovelling victims."

PROJECT M-7 (B) Two Cities/Univ 1953 86m. D: Anthony Asquith. SP: William Fairchild, from the novel "The Net" by John Pudney. PH: Desmond Dickinson. Aerial PH: Stanley Grant. Mus: Benjamin Frankel. Ref: FDY. Pic: SM 3:12. with Phyllis Calvert, James Donald, Robert Beatty, Herbert Lom, Noel Willman, Maurice Denham. New high-speed jet aircraft, the M-7.

PROJECT MOONBASE Lippert/Galaxy 1953 63m. D: Richard Talmadge. SP: Robert Heinlein, Jack Seaman. PH: Willard Thompson. Mus: H. B. Gilbert. Prod Des: Jerome Pycha, Jr. Ref: HR 8/28/53. FM 15:46. Pic: SM 3:13. The movie's big scene is "the first wedding on the moon." The rest is what you would expect of an early-Fifties cheapie. with Donna Martell, Hayden Ro(u)rke, James Craven, Ross Ford, Barbara Morrison.

PROJECT X Para 1968 Technicolor 97m. D, P: William Castle. SP: Edmund Morris, based on novels by Leslie F. Davies. PH: Harold Stine. Mus: Van Cleave. Art D: Hal Pereira, Walter Tyler. Ref: V 6/26/68. PM. with Christopher George, Greta Baldwin, Henry Jones, Monte Markham, Keye Luke, Harold Gould, Philip E. Pine. In the year 2118 a team of scientists performs laser-beam examinations of the mind of a scientist who has just returned from Sino-Asia with knowledge of a secret attack. Messy, involved storyline, with a few interesting sequences.

The PROJECTED MAN (B) Univ/Protelco-M.L.C. 1966 Technicolor/ scope 90m. (77m.-U.S.) D: Ian Curteis. SP: John C. Cooper, Peter Bryan. Story: Frank Quattrocchi. PH: Stanley Pavey. Mus sc & d: Kenneth V. Jones. Art D: Peter Mullins. SpFX: Flo Nordhoff, Robert Hedges, Mike Hope. P: Maurice Foster, John Croydon. Exec P: Richard Gordon, Gerald A. Fernback. Ref: FFacts. PM. with Bryant Haliday, Norman Wooland, Derek Farr, Tracey Crisp, Mary Peach, Derrick De Marney, Ronald Allen, Sam Kydd. Project to transform matter into energy and back.

The PROJECTIONIST Maron/Maglan 1970(1968) Technicolor 88m. SP, D, P, Ed: Harry Hurwitz. PH: Victor Petrashevic. Mus: Igo Kantor, Erma E. Levin. Ref: Boxo 2/8/71: clips from the FLASH GORDON serials, CITIZEN KANE. V 11/11/70: "Science

Promise

fiction hoopla." with Chuck McCann, Ina Balin, Rodney Danger-
field, Jara Kohout. Projectionist sees himself as Captain Flash,
defender of a scientific mastermind and his daughter.
PROMISE OF RED LIPS, The see DAUGHTERS OF DARKNESS
The PROPHETESS OF THEBES (F) Melies/Star 1908 Ref: MPW'08:
351. Vision: A king sees himself assassinated.
PSYCHO Para/Shamley 1960 109m. D, P: Alfred Hitchcock. SP:
Joseph Stefano. PH: John L. Russell. From the book by Robert
Bloch. Mus: Bernard Herrmann. Art D: Joseph Hurley, Robert
Clatworthy, George Milo. SpPhFX: Clarence Champagne. Ed:
George Tomasini. Ref: Clarens. COF 6:42. Pic: DDC III:44.
with Anthony Perkins, Vera Miles, John Gavin, Martin Balsam,
John McIntire, Janet Leigh, Frank Albertson, Patricia Hitchcock,
Vaughn Taylor, Simon Oakland, Lurene Tuttle. Sinister house,
rotting corpse, bizarre murders, etc. Good shocker. The best
scenes are in the old house and a jail cell. Raymond Durgnat:
"PSYCHO is only a potpourri of CHARLEY'S AUNT, BLUEBEARD,
SWEENEY TODD, "Oedipus Rex," and THE LAUREL AND HARDY
MURDER CASE."
The PSYCHO LOVER Medford/Isley 1970 color 75m. SP, D, P:
Robert V. O'Neal. Ref: Boxo 8/24/70. with Lawrence Montaigne,
Joanne Meredith, Frank Cuva. A man's mistress tells his psy-
chiatrist about the movie The MANCHURIAN CANDIDATE, in which
a person is brainwashed to kill. The psychiatrist directs the man
to kill his wife.
The PSYCHOPATH (B) Para/Amicus 1966 color/scope 83m.
(SCHIZOID) D: Freddie Francis. SP: Robert Bloch. PH: John
Wilcox. Mus: Elisabeth Lutyens. Art D: Bill Constable. SpFX:
Ted Samuels. Ref: PM. Boxo 5/9/66. MMF. Orpheus 4:37. with
Alexander Knox, Thorley Walters, Patrick Wymark, Frank For-
syth, Colin Gordon, Margaret Johnston, John Standing, Judy Hux-
table, Don Borisenko. A widow lives with her "strange son and
hundreds of dolls in a deranged world."
PUBLIC BE DAMNED, The (story by W. Mack) see NIGHT OF TERROR
PUFNSTUF Univ 1970 Technicolor 98m. D: Hollingsworth Morse. SP:
John Fenton Murray, Si Rose, from the TV show. PH: Kenneth
Peach. Mus: Charles Fox. Art D: Alexander Golitzen, Walter S.
Herndon. Ref: V 6/3/70. with Jack Wild, Billie Hayes, Martha
Raye, Mama Cass. Strange island harbors witches, ambulatory
trees, a big spider, and a huge, clumsy bat. Skull's voice an imi-
tation of Karloff. Wretched story and topical jokes; funny costumes.
Film fails when it tries to be clever; succeeds brilliantly when it
tries to be stupid.
PUITS ET LE PENDULE, Le see PIT AND THE PENDULUM, The
(1910)
PULGARCITO see TOM THUMB (1958)
The PULVERIZER (F) Pathe 1909 9m. Ref: F. Index 6/12/09.
Scientist's powder pulverizes anything.
PUNISHMENT PARK AI/Chartwell-Francoise 1970 color SP, D, Ed:
Peter Watkins. PH: Joan Churchill. Mus: Paul Motian. Ref:
VVoice 6/17/71. V 6/30/71. with Paul Alelyanes, Carmen
Argenziano. Political repression in the near future in the United
States.

PURITAN PASSIONS Hodkinson/Film Guild 1923 77m. SP, D: Frank
Tuttle. SP: also A. Creelman. PH: Fred Waller. From "The
Scarecrow or The Glass Truth" by Percy MacKaye. Ref: AFI.
Clarens. NYT 10/15/23. with Glenn Hunter, Mary Astor, Osgood
Perkins, Frank Tweed, Maude Hill. Satan brings scarecrow to
life.
PURPLE CLOUD, The (novel by M. P. Shiel) see WORLD, THE
FLESH, AND THE DEVIL, The
PURPLE DEATH FROM OUTER SPACE see FLASH GORDON'S
TRIP TO MARS
The PURPLE MONSTER STRIKES Rep 1945 serial 15 episodes ('66
feature: D-DAY ON MARS) D:Spencer G. Bennet, Fred Brannon.
SP: R. Cole, A. DeMond, B. Dickey, L. Perkins, J. Poland,
B. Sarecky. PH: Bud Thackery. Ref: Barbour. FM 15:47. TVG.
with Dennis Moore, Linda Stirling, Roy Barcroft (the purple
monster), James Craven, Bud Geary, John Davidson, Emmett
Vogan, George Carleton, Kenne Duncan, Wheaton Chambers,
Anthony Warde, Ken Terrell. A Martian plans the invasion of
earth.
The PURPLE NIGHT Knickerbocker 1915 45m. D: S. E. V.
Taylor. Ref: MPN 9/25/15. with Florence Rockwell, Noah
Beery, Lionel Adams, Richard Carlyle. Inventor's explosive
destroys house.
The PURSUING VENGEANCE Unity-Sales 1916 55m. D: Martin
Sabine. From "The Mystery of the Boule Cabinet" by Burton E.
Stevenson. Ref: MPN 13:3598. with Sheldon Lewis. Boule cabi-
net drawer containing crook's loot coated with "poison whose
slightest touch means instant death."
PUSANG ITEM see MONSTER STRIKES, The
PUSS IN BOOTS (Mex) Rodriguez 1961 90m. color (El GATO
CON BOTAS) SP, D: Roberto Rodriguez. Story: S. M. Esquival.
From the fairy tale by Perrault. Ref: FM 33:10. Lee. with Rafael
Munoz, Humberto Dupeyron, Ogre, "ghoulish creatures."
PUSS, PUSS (F) Gaum 1909 color 6m. Ref: Bios 10/7/09. Fairy
transforms cat into beautiful girl.
PYRO-MAN WITHOUT A FACE (U.S.-Sp) AI/Esamer 1963 Pana-
color (FUEGO-Sp. FIRE. PHANTOM OF THE FERRIS WHEEL.
WHEEL OF FIRE. PYRO-THE THING WITHOUT A FACE) 99m.
D: Julio Coll. SP: Sid Pink, Louis de Los Arcos, Richard Meyer.
Mus: Jose Sola. Ref: FM 12:8. Orpheus 3:37. 4:38. TVFFSB. with
Barry Sullivan, Martha Hyer, Sherry Moreland, Hugo Pimentel.
Man horribly burned in fire seeks revenge. Bad melodrama.

Q PLANES see CLOUDS OVER EUROPE
QUANDO LE DONNE AVEVANO LA CODA see WHEN WOMEN HAD
TAILS
QUASIMODO see HUNCHBACK OF NOTRE DAME, The (1939)
QUATERMASS AND THE PIT see FIVE MILLION YEARS TO
EARTH
QUATERMASS EXPERIMENT, The see CREEPING UNKNOWN, The

QUATERMASS TWO   see   ENEMY FROM SPACE
QUATRE CENTS FARCES DU DIABLE, Les   see MERRY FROLICS
   OF SATAN, The
QUEEN OF ATLANTIS   see JOURNEY BENEATH THE DESERT /
   SIREN OF ATLANTIS
QUEEN OF BLOOD AI 1966 Pathecolor 80m. (PLANET OF BLOOD-
   TV. PREHISTORIC PLANET. FLIGHT TO A FAR PLANET.
   PLANET OF VAMPIRES. PLANET OF TERROR. The GREEN
   WOMAN) SP, D: Curtis Harrington.   From the story "The Veiled
   Woman." PH: Vilis Lapenieks. Mus:Leonard Moreland.   Art D:
   Albert Locatelli. Makeup: William Condos.   P: George Edwards.
   Assoc P: Stephanie Rothman. Ref: FFacts. MW 7:13.9:48.
   Orpheus 4:37.   FM 27:9.35:77. COF 11:48. Boxo 2/28/66. Pic:
   FM 45:61. with Basil Rathbone, Florence Marly, Judi Meredith,
   John Saxon, Dennis Hopper, Forest J Ackerman, Terry Lee,
   Robert Porter, Don Eitner. A vampire-woman is the only sur-
   vivor of an alien ship which crash-lands on Mars.
The QUEEN OF HEARTS   (B) Stoll 1923   22m. (Mystery of Dr.
   Fu-Manchu series) SP: A. E. Coleby, Frank Wilson. Based on
   the character created by Sax Rohmer. PH: D. P. Cooper. Ref:
   SilentFF. with Harry Agar Lyons, Fred Paul, Humbertson Wright,
   Joan Clarkson. Dr. Petrie and an eminent British surgeon perform
   a secret operation on Fu-Manchu.
QUEEN OF OUTER SPACE   AA   1958 DeLuxecolor /scope 80m. D:
   Edward Bernds. SP: Charles Beaumont, from a story by Ben
   Hecht.   PH: William Whitley. Mus sc: Marlin Skiles. Art D:
   David Milton. Ref: FDY TVG. with Zsa Zsa Gabor, Eric Fleming,
   Laurie Mitchell, Paul Birch, Dave Willock, Kathy Marlowe, Lisa
   Davis, Tania Velia, Lynn Cartwright. (QUEEN OF THE UNIVERSE)
   A rocket crash-lands on Venus. Its crew finds a civilization of
   women. Drab s-f.
The QUEEN OF SPADES (G) Deutsche Biograph 1910   15m. From
   the story by Pushkin. Gambler attempting to learn secret of win-
   ning frightens countess to death, later learns secret from vision
   of her. Ref: Bios 12/22/10.
QUEEN OF SPADES   (Russ) 1910 D: Gontcharov. From the story
   by Pushkin. Ref: Cahiers 220:114.
QUEEN OF SPADES   (F) Eclipse 1912 15m. Ref: Lee. Suicide club:
   Reporter joins, draws wrong card.
QUEEN OF SPADES   (I)   Celio/Kleine/Societa-Italiana 1913 (La
   DAMA DI PICCHE)   From the story by Pushkin. Ref: LC.DDC
   III:38. Mitry V: 51. with Leda Gys, Hesperia.
QUEEN OF SPADES   Fidelity   1913   Ref: LC. From Pushkin's
   story.
QUEEN OF SPADES (Russ) Pathe/Russian Art Film Co.   1916
   (PIKOVAJA DAMA) D: Protazanov. From Pushkin's story. P:
   Joseph N. Ermolieff. Ref: Cahiers 220:114. Orpheus 2:20. DDC
   II:229. EncicDS IX:1341.
QUEEN OF SPADES (Hung) 1921 D: Paul Fejos. From Pushkin. Ref:
   DDC II:324.
QUEEN OF SPADES   Aywon From Pushkin's story. Ref: FDY. Orphe-
   us 2:20.
QUEEN OF SPADES (G) Phoebus-Film 1927 (PIQUE DAME)

D: Alexander Rasumny. From Pushkin. Ref: Deutsche. with
Rudolf Forster, Alexandra Schmitt.
QUEEN OF SPADES (F) 1937 ('44-U.S.) Hoffberg-Brill (PIQUE
DAME) D: Fedor Ozep. SP: Bernard Zimmer, from Pushkin's
story. Ref: MPH. NYT. DDC III:122. with Pierre Blanchar,
Palau, Andre Luget, Abel Jacquin, Camille Bert. Even in
death Countess Tomski keeps the secret of the cards.
QUEEN OF SPADES (B) Mono 1949 95m. D: Thorold Dickinson.
SP: Rodney Ackland, Arthur Boys, from Pushkin's story. PH:
Otto Heller. Mus: Georges Auric. Art D: William Kellner. Ref:
HR 9/26/50. FM 23:26. Pic: DDC II:115. with Anton Walbrook,
Edith Evans, Ronald Howard, Anthony Dawson, Miles Malleson,
Athene Seyler, Michael Medwin. A Russian Army captain learns of
a countess who sold her soul for the secret of winning at cards.
When she dies, her dead voice says she will tell him the secret.
QUEEN OF SPADES (Russ) Artkino/Mosfilm 1960 Sovcolor 100m.
(PIQUE DAME) SP,D: Roman Tikhomirov. SP: also G. & S. Vas-
siliev, P. Vesibram, B. Yaroustovski. From Pushkin's story and
Tschaikowsky's opera. PH: E. Svetlanov. Ref: V 12/20/61:
"Eerie." with Oleg Stirjanov, Olga Krassina. Man frightens
countess to death.
QUEEN OF SPADES (F) Paris-Cité 1965 (La DAME DE PIQUE)
D: Léonard Keigel. SP: J. Green, E. Jourdan, from Pushkin's
story. PH: Alain Levent. Mus: Franz Schubert. Ref: La Prod
Cin Fr 9/65. COF 10:48. Pic: DDC III: 463. with Dita Parlo,
Jean Negroni, Katharina Renn. Satanic character shows countess
secret of the "three winning cards." Ghosts.
QUEEN OF THE NORTH WOODS Pathe 1929 serial 10 episodes
silent D: Spencer G. Bennet, Thomas L. Storey. Ref: CNW. Pic:
FM 38:42. TBG. with Ethlyne Clair, Walter Miller. Ch.1. The
Wolf Devil's Challenge. Ch.3. Devil Worshippers.
QUEEN OF THE SEA Fox 1918 70m. Ref: NYT 9/2/18. with
Annette Kellermann, Hugh Thompson. Mermaids, demons,
Master of Storms, etc.
QUEEN OF THE UNIVERSE see QUEEN OF OUTER SPACE
The QUEEN OF THE VAMPIRES (F) ABC/Selsky 1967 100m.
(La REINE DES VAMPIRES. Le VIOL DU VAMPIRE. Les FEMMES
VAMPIRES) SP,D: Jean Rollin. PH: Guy Leblond, Antoine Harispe.
Mus: Y. Géraud, F. Tusques. Ref: MMF 24:50. Cinema'68:18.
with Solange Pradel, Nicole Romain, Jacqueline Sieger, Bernard
Letrou, Urusle Pauly.
QUELQU'UN DERRIERE LA PORTE see SOMEONE BEHIND THE
DOOR
QUESTI FANTASMI see GHOSTS-ITALIAN STYLE/THESE GHOSTS
The ? MOTORIST (B) Paul 1906 3m. Ref: SilentFF. Pic: Hist.Brit.
Film. Motorist drives off into space and around Saturn's rings.
QUICK-CHANGE MESMERIST (F) Urban-Eclipse 1908 Ref: The Film
Index. Convict under influence of hypnotist.
A QUIET PLACE IN THE COUNTRY (I-F) Lopert/PEA-LPAA 1968
Technicolor 106m. (Un TRANQUILLO POSTO DI CAMPAGNA)
Story,SP,D: Elio Petri. SP: also Luciano Vincenzoni. Story:
also Tonino Guerra. PH: Luigi Kuveiller. Mus: Ennio Morricone.
Ref: Ital P'68. with Franco Nero, Vanessa Redgrave, Georges

Geret. Mysterious noises, seance.

R. F. D. 1000000 B. C.   see RURAL DELIVERY, MILLION B. C.
RAAT ANDHERI THI (India) 1967 Ref: Shankar's 2/19/67. with
    Sheikh Mukhtar. Spy movie: X-ray glasses that permit wearer to
    see through walls.
RAAZ see MYSTERY
RACE MEMORIES (F) Pathe 1913 30m. Ref: MPW 18:350, 520. with
    Lillian Wiggins. Love in prehistory and the present.
RACE SUICIDE Farnham 1916 65m. SP, D, George W. Terwil-
    liger. Ref: MPN 13:718. with Ormi Hawley, Earl Metcalfe.
    Stone age sequence.
RACHE DES DR. FU MANCHU, Die see BLOOD OF FU MANCHU
RACHE DES HOMUNKULUS, Die see HOMUNCULUS
RACING MAD Educ 1928 22m. D: Stephen Roberts. Ref: MPN
    1/28/28. with Al St. John, Phil Dunham. "Half auto, half
    airplane" wins race.
RADAN see RODAN
RADAR MEN FROM THE MOON Rep 1952 serial 12 episodes ('66
    feature-RETIK, THE MOON MENACE) See also COMMANDO
    CODY. D: Fred Brannon. SP: R. Davidson. PH: John MacBurnie.
    Ref: Barbour. TVG. Pic: SM 5:16. with George Wallace, Aline
    Towne, Roy Barcroft, William Bakewell, Clayton Moore, Tom
    Steele, Dale Van Sickel, Noel Cravat, Dick Cogan. Commando
    Cody battles a madman out to conquer the world. Death ray.
RADAR PATROL VS. SPY KING Rep 1950 serial 12 episodes D:
    Fred C. Brannon. SP: R. Cole, W. Lively, S. Shor. PH: Ellis
    W. Carter. Mus: Stanley Wilson. SpFX: Howard and Theodore
    Lydecker. Ref: Barbour. The Serial. with Kirk Alyn, Jean Dean,
    Anthony Warde, George J. Lewis, John Merton, Tristram Coffin,
    John Crawford, Dale Van Sickel, Tom Steele, Eddie Parker,
    Forbes Murray, Frank O'Connor, Arvon Dale, Harold Goodwin.
    Hypnotic serum; "Gamma ray tubes"; "ultra-ray camera" that
    develops charred paper; Auto-Monitor that steers truck by remote
    control; Electro-Annihilator, explosive device; radar-beam
    neutralizer.
RADIO DETECTIVE Univ 1926 serial 10 episodes D: William Crin-
    ley, William Craft. Ref: CNW. with Jack Dougherty, Margaret
    Quimby, Jack Mower, Howard Enstedt and the Boy Scouts. Ref:
    Photoplay 6/26. Invention called "Evansite" that would revolu-
    tionize radio.
RADIO KING Univ 1922 serial 10 episodes D: Robert F. Hill. SP:
    Robert Dillon. Ref: Lee. with Roy Stewart, Louise Lorraine, Al
    Smith, Sidney Bracey. 8. The Master Wave. Radio invention.
RADIO-MANIA Hodkinson 1923 65m. (The MAN FROM MARS.
    M.A.R.S.) "3-D"-like Teleview. Titles: Joseph W. Farnham.
    D: Roy William Neill. PH: George Folsey. SP: Lewis Allen
    Browne. Ref: AFI. Motion Picture 11/23. FDY. Lee. MPN 28:
    558. with Grant Mitchell, Margaret Irving, W. H. Burton. Dream:
    Martians with huge heads and ears and small bodies.

RADIO PARADE OF 1935 (B) 1934 D: Arthur Woods. Ref: SF Film. Brit. Cinema. with Fred Conyngham, Claude Dampier, Will Hay. Color TV.

RADIO PATROL Univ 1937 serial 12 episodes D: Ford Beebe, Cliff Smith. SP: W. Gittens, N. S. Hall, R. Trampe. Based on the newspaper feature by E. Sullivan and C. Schmidt. Ref: V 9/15/37. Boy's cinema 2/5/38. with Grant Withers, Adrian Morris, Catherine Hughes, Frank Lackteen, Montague Shaw, Harry Davenport, Wheeler Oakman, Jack Mulhall. Hypnotized slaves, flexible steel, "trick machine."

RADIO RANCH see PHANTOM EMPIRE

RADIUM MYSTERY, The see GREAT RADIUM MYSTERY, The

RADON see RODAN

RAECHER, Der see AVENGER, The

RAGAZZA DI LATTI, La see GIRL OF TIN, The

RAGGI MORTALI DEL DR. MABUSE, I see SECRET OF DR. MABUSE

RAH, RAH, RAH Vita 1916 12m. D: Lawrence Semon. Story: Semon, Graham Baker. Ref: MPN 14:3332. LC. with Hughie Mack, James Aubrey, Patsy de For(r)est. Robbers and actors loose in "haunted" house.

RAID NEW YORK-PARIS EN AUTOMOBILE, La see NEW YORK TO PARIS BY MOTOR

RAINMAKER, The (by D. D. Beauchamp) see HENRY, THE RAINMAKER

RAISING SPIRITS (F) Melies 1899 (EVOCATION SPIRITE) Ref: Mitry II.

The RAJAH'S CASKET (F) Pathe 1906 Part-color 9m. Ref: V&FI 6/23/06:9, 12. Wizard has rajah's casket carried off on dragon.

RAKE'S PROGRESS, The (by W. Hogarth) see BEDLAM

RALPH BENEFITS BY PEOPLE'S CURIOSITY (F) Pathe 1909 5m. Ref: MPW '09:321. People who look through machine/toy see strange transformations.

RAMADAL (Fili) Premiere 1958 D: Efren Reyes. SpFX: Alejandro Marcelino. Ref: FEFN 8/29/58: "Invisible man." Based on the comic strip. with Reyes, Cynthia Zamora, M. de Leon, Jose Garcia.

RAMAR AND THE SAVAGE CHALLENGES ITC/Rudolph Flothow 1953 ('64 feature) From the "Ramar of the Jungle" TV series. Ref: TVFFSB. TVG. with Jon Hall. 83m. A woman believes she's bewitched.

RAMDAM AND THE UNKNOWN TERROR ITC/Rudolph Flothow c1953 ('64 feature) 83m. From the "Ramar of the Jungle" TV series. Ref: TVFFSB. TVG. with Jon Hall, Ray Montgomery. "Unknown terror" causes tribal unrest.

RANDAM A RIO see KISS THE GIRLS AND MAKE THEM DIE

RAMPER DER TIERMENSCH see STRANGE CASE OF CAPTAIN RAMPER, The

RANDIN AND CO. (I) Ambrosio 1913 36m. Ref: Bios 7/3/13. Drug makes man appear to be dead.

The "RAPID" POWDER (F) Pathe 1910 4m. Ref: Bios 1/5/11. Thief steals powder which gives people energy.

RAPPAC(C)INI'S DAUGHTER (by N. Hawthorne) see TWICE TOLD

TALES
RAPSODIA SATANICA see SATANIC RHAPSODY
RAPTUS, THE SECRET OF DR. HICHCOCK see HORRIBLE DR.
     HICHCOCK, The
RASPUTIN, THE MAD MONK (B) Fox/Hammer 1965 Technicolor/
     scope 91m. (The MAD MONK) D: Don Sharp. SP: John Elder.
     PH: Michael Reed. Mus: Don Banks. Art D: Don Mingaye. Prod.
     Des: Bernard Robinson. Ref: MFB'66:63. COF 7:50. with Chris-
     topher Lee, Barbara Shelley, Richard Pasco, Francis Matthews,
     Suzan Farmer, Renee Asherson, Derek Francis. Rasputin keeps
     girl under hypnotic spell.
RATMAN'S NOTEBOOKS (by S. Gilbert) see WILLARD
RATTENFANGER VON HAMELN, Der see PIED PIPER OF
     HAMELIN, The (1917)
RAVAGED (F) Transatlantic 1969 color 88m. (La ROSE ECORCHEE.
     The BLOOD ROSE. The BURNT ROSE) SP,D: Claude Mulot.
     SP: also Edgar Oppenheimer, Jean Carriaga. PH: Roger Fellous.
     Mus: Jean-Paul Dorsay. SpFX: Guy Delecluse. Ref: Cont. Fm. Rev.
     4/70. MFB. with Philippe Lemaire, A. Duperey, Howard Vernon.
     Man wants doctor to graft another face to his wife's, which was
     scarred in a fire. Lush music, weird little atmospheric bits, and
     senseless bursts of brutality, all of which adds up to nothing but
     a small bore.
The RAVEN Eclair/American Standard 1912 30m. From Edgar
     Allan Poe's "The Gold Bug   "The Black Cat," "Murders in the
     Rue Morgue," "The Pit and the Pendulum," "A Descent into the
     Maelstrom," "The Raven," and "Buried Alive" or "The Premature
     Burial." Ref: Bios 1/2/13. FIR '61:463. with Guy Oliver. Black
     cat, poet's wife "Lenore," morgue, "ghastly figure," visions of
     raven.
The RAVEN Ess 1915 70m. From a play by George C. Hazelton and
     the life and works of Edgar Allan Poe. Ref: FM 11:42. FD
     11/25/15. FIR'61:465-6. MPW 26:1507. MPN 11/27/15. with
     Henry B. Walthall, Wanda Howard. Poe kills "dream self" in
     vision, thinks he sees spirit of "Leonore." Death, ghost.
The RAVEN Univ 1935 62m. D: Louis Friedlander (aka Lew
     Landers). SP: David Boehm. From the story by Edgar Allan
     Poe. PH: Charles Stumar. Ref: Clarens. ModM 1:41-50. with
     Bela Lugosi, Boris Karloff, Irene Ware, Lester Matthews, Inez
     Courtney, Samuel S. Hinds, Ian Wolfe, Spencer Charters, Arthur
     Hoyt. Mad doctor equips his home with torture devices (pendulum,
     diminishing room, etc.). Sometimes hilarious, always ludicrous
     Universal "classic," with unforgettable exchanges between Karloff
     and Lugosi: "Maybe if a man is ugly, he does ugly things"--
     "You are saying something profound" and many others!
The RAVEN AI/Alta Vista 1963 Pathecolor/scope D, P: Roger
     Corman. SP: Richard Matheson. Based on Poe's story. PH: Floyd
     Crosby. Mus: Les Baxter. Art D: Daniel Haller. Crow Trainer:
     Moe Disesso. SpFX: Pat Dinga. Ref: Clarens. FM 32:6. COF
     3:11. with Vincent Price, Peter Lorre, Boris Karloff, Hazel
     Court, Olive Sturgess, Jack Nicholson, Connie Wallace. Comedy.
     Magicians, talking corpses, etc. Not nearly as funny as the '35
     version.

RAYO DISINTEGRADOR, El see DISINTEGRATING RAY, The
RAYON INVISIBLE, Le see CRAZY RAY, The
RAYONS MORTELS DU DOCTEUR MABUSE, Les see SECRET OF
   DR. MABUSE
RAYONS ROENTGEN, Les see NOVICE AT X-RAYS, A
RE DEI CRIMINALI, Il see SUPERARGO VS. THE ROBOTS
The READER OF MINDS Than 1910. 30m. SP: Philip Lonergan. Ref:
   Ref: MPW 22: 1434. Lee. Mind-reading machine.
REAR CAR, The (play by E. E. Rose) see RED LIGHTS
REBELLION DE LOS FANTASMAS, La see REVOLT OF THE
   GHOSTS, The
RED ALERT see DR. STRANGELOVE
The RED CLUB American 1914 60m. Ref: Bios 2/19/14:xvii:
   Picture of mystical paraphernalia.
RED HANGMAN, The see BLOODY PIT OF HORROR
The RED HOUSE UA/Thalia 1947 100m. SP, D: Delmar Daves. From
   the novel by G. A. Chamberlain. PH: Bert Glennon. Mus:
   Miklos Rozsa. Art D: McClure Capps. Ref: RVB. TVG. with
   Edward G. Robinson, Lon McCallister, Judith Anderson, Allene
   Roberts, Julie London, Rory Calhoun, Ona Munson, Harry
   Shannon, Arthur Space, Walter Sande. Old house with evil secret;
   supposedly haunted woods.
RED LIGHTS Goldwyn/Cosmopolitan 1923 70m. D: Clarence Badger.
   SP: Carey Wilson, from the play "The Rear Car" by Edward E.
   Rose. PH: Charles Berquist. Ref: FDY. Wid's 9/8/23. with
   Ray Griffith, Marie Prevost, Alice Lake, Lionel Belmore, Jean
   Hersholt, Johnny Walker. An inventor's "red light" speaks by a
   combination of electricity and radio."
RED LIPS, The see DAUGHTERS OF DARKNESS
The RED MILL MGM/Cosmopolitan 1927 80m. D: William Goodrich.
   SP: Frances Marion. Titles: Joe Farnham. PH: Hendrik Sartov.
   Art D: Cedric Gibbons, Merrill Pye. From the play by Victor
   Herbert and H. M. Blossom. Ref: AFI. PM. "Haunted" mill.
RED PLANET MARS UA/Melaby 1952 87m. (MIRACLE FROM
   MARS) D: Harry Horner. SP: Anthony Veiller, John L. Balderston.
   from Balderston's play "Red Planet." PH: Joseph Biroc. Mus:
   David Chudnow. Art D: Charles D. Hall. Ref: Clarens. TVG.
   with Peter Graves, Andrea King, Bayard Veiller, Walter Sande,
   Marvin Miller, Herbert Berghof, Morris Ankrum, House Peters,
   Bill Kennedy, Gene Roth, Vince Barnett. With the aid of a "hy-
   drogen tube, " a scientist establishes contact with Mars. Incredibly,
   fascinatingly bad in its messagey (in more ways than one) and up-
   lifting way. Raises hysterically irresponsible plotting to the level
   of art (or something).
RED PLANET MARS see MISSION MARS
RED ROSES OF PASSION Boxoffice Int'l/Amalfi 1969 85m. SP, D:
   Joe Sarno. PhFX: Anthony Lover. Ref: Boxo 1/20/69. with
   Laurene Claire, Helena Clayton. A girl falls under the evil spell
   of a mystic, who keeps Pan, God of Love, "hidden behind a cur-
   tain" in her "seance studio."
The REGENERATION OF MARGARET Ess 1916 35m. D: Charles
   J. Brabin. Ref: MPN 13:4090. with W. Howard, Ernest Maupa(i)n.
   Operation cures baby of birth defects.

REGRESO DEL MONSTRUO, El see RETURN OF THE MONSTER,
The
REGULAR AS CLOCKWORK see DON'T PLAY WITH MARTIANS
The REINCARNATE (Canadian) Int'l Film Distributor/Meridian 1971
color 122m. D: Don Haldane. SP, P: Seelig Lester. PH: Norman
Allin. Mus: Milan Kymlicka. SpFX: Wally Gentleman. Art D:
Harry Maxfield. Ref: V 5/5/71. with Jack Creley, Jay Rey-
nolds, Trudy Young. Lawyer, member of cult, convinces artist
to "accept his brain via ancient ritual."
REINCARNATION, The see CRIMSON ALTAR, The
The REINCARNATION OF A SOUL Univ (Powers) 1913 Ref: MPW
'13:990. with Edwin August. When a bolt of lightning strikes a
thief, he is reincarnated.
The REINCARNATION OF KARMA Vita 1912 30m. Ref: Bios
2/20/13. The Film Index. Spell that brings death; transforma-
tion into snake.
REINE DES VAMPIRES, La see QUEEN OF THE VAMPIRES, The
REJSEN TIL MARS see SKY SHIP, The
The REJUVENATION OF DAN H&W 1913 8m. Ref: Bios 11/20/13:
"Wonderful pills."
The REJUVENATORS Passing Show Comedies 1918 15m. Ref:
SilentFF. Dr. Young's rejuvenation process is highly effective.
RELIGIOUS RACKETEERS see MYSTIC CIRCLE MURDER, The
REMOTE CONTROL MGM 1930 62m. D: Malcolm St. Claire,
Nick Grinde, Edward Sedgwick. Art D: Cedric Gibbons. SP:
Sylvia Thalberg, Frank Butler. Dial F. Hugh Herbert, Robert E.
Hopkins. PH: Merritt B. Gerstad. Ed: Harry Reynolds. From a
play by Clyde North, Albert C. Fuller, and Jack Nelson. Ref:
AFI. V 12/8/30. with William Haines, John Miljan, Russell
Hopton, Polly Moran, Edward Brophy, J. C. Nugent, Charles King,
Mary Doran. Prof. Kruger, supposed authority on the occult,
gives instructions to his "ghost gang" via a radio clairvoyant pro-
gram.
RENDEZ-VOUS, Le see GATES OF THE NIGHT
RENFREW OF THE ROYAL MOUNTED (by L. Erskine) see SKY
BANDITS
RENFREW RIDES THE SKY see SKY BANDITS
The REPTILE (B) Fox/Hammer 1966 color 90m. (The REPTILES)
D: John Gilling. SP: John Elder. PH: Arthur Grant. Mus: Don
Banks. Art D: Bernard Robinson, Don Mingaye. Ref: PM. F&F
4/66. with Noel Willman, Jennifer Daniel, Ja(c)queline Pearce,
Ray Barrett, Michael Ripper, John Laurie, Marne Maitland,
Charles Lloyd Pack, George Woodbridge. Old mansion, girl who
can turn into a snake, "serpentine mystic." Hammer at its flimsi-
est. Elder doesn't even bother to attempt to work out a plot to
string the events on; he just maneuvers the characters from one
cheap shock to another. The blatancy of his contrivances in the
climactic scenes is almost breathtaking.
REPTILICUS (U.S.-Danish) AI/Cinemagic color 1962 81m. D, P:
Sidney Pink. SP: Pink, Ib Melchior. PH: Aage Wiltrup. Mus sc &
d: Sven Gyldmark. Ref: FFacts. FM 10:13-14. with Carl
Ottosen, Ann Smyrner, Mimi Heinrich, Dirk Passer, Asbjorn
Andersen. Prehistoric monster's tail grows a new body. A few

fair lab scenes, otherwise nil.

REPULSION (B) Royal/Compton/Tekli 1965 105m. SP,D: Roman
Polanski. SP: also Gerard Brach. PH: Gilbert Taylor. Mus:
Chico Hamilton. Art D: Seamus Flannery. Ref: Clarens. TVG.
with Catherine Deneuve, Yvonne Furneaux, John Fraser, Ian
Hendry, Patrick Wymark, Renee Houston. Mad girl beset by apparitions, some of them ingenious, phenomenally effective as
fright devices, though the movie's quieter moments are less
effective.

RESCUE FROM OUTER SPACE see INVADERS FROM SPACE

RESCUED IN MID AIR (B) c1906 Ref: SilentFF. Professor rescues
woman from steeple with airship with flapping wings.

RESIDENCIA, La see BOARDING SCHOOL, The

The RESIDENT PATIENT (B) Stoll 1921 22m. D: Maurice Elvey.
From the story by Doyle. (Adventures of Sherlock Holmes series)
Ref: SilentFF. with Eille Norwood, Hubert Willis, Mme.
D'Esterre, C. Pitt Chatham. Man lives in state of fear until
one day he is found hanged.

The RESURRECTED MONSTER (Mex) Internacional Cinematografica
1952 (El MONSTRUO RESUCITADO. The REVIVED MONSTER.
The MONSTER WHO LIVED AGAIN. The MONSTER LIVES
AGAIN. DR. CRIMEN-I.) D: Chano Urueta. PH: Victor Herrera.
Mus: Raul Lavista. Ref: Aventura. Bianco 8/62. Indice. FM
29:45. MadM 4:31. Pic: FM 29:43.A'69:18. MW 4:53. with
Miroslava, Carlos Navarro (or Novarro), Jose Maria Rivas,
Alberto Mariscal, Fernando Wagner. "A la Mary Shelley."
Scientist brings dead body back to live, gives his "zombie" new
brain.

The RESURRECTION OF ZACHARY WHEELER Vidtronics/Robert
Stabler 1971 Technicolor 100m. D: Robert Wynn. SP: Jay Simms,
Tom Rolf. PH: Bob Boatman. Mus: Marlin Skiles. Ref: V 11/17/71.
with Leslie Nielsen, Bradford Dillman, James Daly, Angie
Dickinson, Robert J. Wilke, Jack Carter, Don Haggerty, Lee
Giroux. Senator in auto accident given "massive transplants" at
mysterious medical center.

RETIK, THE MOON MENACE see RADAR MEN FROM THE MOON

RETORNO A LA JUVENTAD see RETURN TO YOUTH

RETURN FROM THE BEYOND Medallion-TV 1961 79m. (Mex?)
Ref: TVFFSB: "s-f." with Elsa Cardenas, Jaime Fernandez.

RETURN FROM THE BEYOND see MYSTERIES OF BLACK MAGIC

RETURN FROM THE PAST see DR. TERROR'S GALLERY OF
HORRORS

RETURN OF CAPTAIN AMERICA see CAPTAIN AMERICA

RETURN OF CAPTAIN MARVEL see ADVENTURES OF CAPTAIN
MARVEL, The

RETURN OF CHANDU Principal/Victory 1934 76m. (CHANDU'S
RETURN) D: Ray Taylor. SP: Barry Barringer. See also CHANDU
ON THE MAGIC ISLAND. Sequence in DR. TERROR'S HOUSE OF
HORRORS (1943). Ref: STI 1:18.2:41. COF 8:52. Film World
'51/2. Photoplay 1/35. Pic: FM 9:16. with Bela Lugosi, Maria
Alba, Lucien Prival, Joseph Swickard, Clara Kimball Young,
Phyllis Ludwig. "Spooky music," "ghost drums," fourth dimen-
sion, genii, magic charms, "self-steering automobiles."

The RETURN OF COUNT YORGA AI 1971 Movielab color 96m.
(CURSE OF COUNT YORGA. The ABOMINABLE COUNT YORGA)
SP,D: Bob Kelljan. SP: also Yvonne Wilder. Sequel to LOVES
OF COUNT IORGA. Scenes from The VAMPIRE LOVERS. PH:
Bill Butler. Mus: Bill Marx. Art D: Vince Cresceman. Ref:
V 8/11/71. with Robert Quarry, Mariette Hartley, Roger
Perry, Y. Wilder, George Macready, Walter Brooke. The Count
takes up residence near an orphanage.

The RETURN OF DR. FU-MANCHU Para 1930 71m. (The NEW
ADVENTURES OF DR. FU-MANCHU) D: Rowland V. Lee. SP:
Florence Ryerson, Lloyd Corrigan. From stories by Sax Rohmer.
PH: A. J. Stout. Ref: FDY. Pic: COF 8:14. with Warner Oland,
Tetsu Komai, Jean Arthur, O. P. Heggie, Neil Hamilton, William
Austin, Evelyn Hall. Fu-Manchu is killed, then resurrected.

The RETURN OF DR. MABUSE (G) CCC/Ajay 1961 (IM STAHL-
NETZ DES DR. MABUSE. FBI CONTRO DR. MABUSE-I. IN THE
STEEL NET OF DR. MABUSE. IN THE STEEL CABINET OF DR.
MABUSE. The PHANTOM MEETS THE RETURN OF DR. MA-
BUSE) D: Harald Reinl. SP:Ladisla(u)s Fodor, Marc Behm. Ref:
FM 21:10. Orpheus 3:37. MFB'70:81. German Pictures 63/64.
FJA. with Gert Froebe, Daliah Lavi, Lex Barker, Ady Berber
(Sandro), Wolfgang Preiss (Dr. Mabuse). Narcotic which turns its
victims into robots; ray-gun.

The RETURN OF DR. X WB 1939 61m. D: Vincent Sherman. SP:
Lee Katz, from a story by William J. Makin. PH: Sid Hickox. Art
D: Esdras Hartley. Ref: Academy. with Humphrey Bogart, Rose-
mary Lane, Dennis Morgan, Wayne Morris, Lya Lys, John Litel,
Olin Howland, Huntz Hall, Creighton Hale, Charles Wilson, Joseph
Crehan, Jack Mower, Howard Hickman, Glen(n) Langan, DeWolf
Hopper, John Ridgely, John Harron, Ed Chandler, Virginia Brissac,
Ian Wolfe, George Reeves. Man brought back from the dead.
Mediocre.

The RETURN OF DRACULA UA/Gramercy 1958 77m. (CURSE OF
DRACULA-TV. The FANTASTIC DISAPPEARING MAN-Eng.) D:
Paul Landres. SP: Pat Fielder. PH: Jack M(a)cKenzie. Mus:
Gerald Fried. P:Jules Levy, Arthur Gardner. Ref: MFB'58:154.
FFacts. with Francis Lederer, Norma Eberhardt, John Wengraf,
Ray Stricklyn, Norbert Schiller, Gage Clark, Hope Summers.
Count Dracula attempts to found a colony of vampires in California.
Film quickly becomes routine after a promising opening scene.

RETURN OF FRANKENSTEIN, The see BRIDE OF FRANKENSTEIN
RETURN OF GIANT MAJIN, The see RETURN OF MAJIN, The
RETURN OF GODZILLA, The see GIGANTIS
RETURN OF JACK THE RIPPER, The see JACK THE RIPPER

The RETURN OF MAJIN (J) Daiei 1966 (DAIMAJIN IKARU. The
RETURN OF GIANT MAJIN-TV) Sequel to MAJIN. D: Kenji
Misumi. SP: Tetsuo Yoshida. SpFX: Yoshiyuki Kuroda. Ref: Unij.
Bltn. TVFFSB. with Kojiro Hongo, Shiho Fujimura, Taro Marui.

The RETURN OF MAURICE DONNELLY Vita 1915 35m. D: William
Humphrey. Author: W. A. Lathrop. Ref: LC. MPN 4/17/15. with
Leo Delany, Leah Baird, Anders Randolph. A doctor restores a
dead man to life with the aid of electricity.

RETURN OF MR. H, The see MADMEN OF MANDORAS

The RETURN OF RICHARD NEAL Ess/Edw. T. Lowe, Jr. 1915 40m. Ref: MPN 4/10/15. Motography 4/10/15. with Francis X. Bushman, Bryant Washburn, Nell Craig, Ernest Maupin. Girl under influence of hypnotist.

RETURN OF THE APEMAN Mono 1944 60m. D: Phil Rosen. SP: Robert Charles. PH: Marcel Le Picard. Mus: Edward Kay. Ref: FDY. FM 46:48. Pic: FMO 1:37. MadM 9:39. HM 8:49. 9:21. with Bela Lugosi, John Carradine, George Zucco, Frank Moran, Judith Gibson, Michael Ames, Mary Currier, Ed Chandler. Two scientists discover a method for reviving the dead, test it out on a prehistoric ape. Utterly ridiculous. Probably Monogram's worst.

RETURN OF THE FLY Fox/Associated Producers 1959 79m. scope SP, D: Edward L. Bernds. Sequel to The FLY. PH: Brydon Baker. Mus: Paul Sawtell, Bert Shefter. Ref: Clarens. FM 15:4. PM. with Vincent Price, Brett Halsey, David Frankham, Dan Seymour, John Sutton, Danielle de Metz. Scientist experiments with a matter transmitter. Unpleasant mess. If the FLY hardly merited a follow-up, this merited one (CURSE OF THE FLY) even less.

RETURN OF THE GIANT MONSTERS, The see GAMERA VS. GYAOS

The RETURN OF THE MONSTER (Mex) Azteca 1960 (El REGRESO DEL MONSTRUO) Ref: FM 29:45. Lee. with Luis Aguilar, Pascual Pena. Doctor makes deal with witch: She makes him powerful, and he brings her monster-son back to life and finds her a new body.

The RETURN OF THE TERROR F Nat/Vitaphone 1934 65m. D: Howard Bretherton. SP: Peter Milne, Eugene Solow. From Edgar Wallace's play, "The Terror." Ref: V 7/17/34. Lee. Ad: "It will grow icicles on your heart." with Mary Astor, Lyle Talbot, John Halliday, J. Carrol Naish, Irving Pichel, Frank Reicher, Etienne Girardot, Frank Conroy, Maude Eburne, Charles Grapewin, Howard Hickman, Edmund Breese, Phil(l)ip Morris. Super x-ray machine. "Chilling mystery" in a sanitarium. -Photoplay 9/34.

RETURN OF THE TIME TRAVELERS, The see TIME TRAVELERS, The

RETURN OF THE VAMPIRE Col 1944 69m. D: Lew Landers. Story & SP: Griffin Jay, Kurt Neumann, Randall Faye. PH: John Stumar, L. W. O'Connell. Mus sc: Mario Tedesco. Art D: Lionel Banks. SpFX: Aaron Nadley. Ref: FDY. S&S '68:213. with Bela Lugosi, Nina Foch, Miles Mander, Frieda Inescort, Matt Willis, Gilbert Emery, Ottola Nesmith, Roland Varno, Billy Bevan. Vampire, werewolf, etc. Disappointing. Merely adequate, humdrum plot. Same old vampire talk. One good disappearing trick.

RETURN TO MANHOOD (J) Daiei 1957 78m. (NANBANJI NO SEMUSHI -OTOKO) D: Torajiro Saito. SP: Akira Fushimi. PH:H. Imai. Story: Katsumi Mizoguchi. Ref: FEFN 7/26/57. with Achako Hanabashi, Shunji Sakai. Satire on Hugo's "The Hunchback of Notre Dame": Alcohol gives a warrior a hunchback.

RETURN TO THE HORRORS OF BLOOD ISLAND see BEAST OF BLOOD

RETURN TO YOUTH (Mex) Reforma Films 1953 (RETORNO A LA JUVENTUD) D: Bustillo Oro. PH: R. M. Solares. Ref: Aventura. with Enrique Rambal, Rosario Granados, Andres Soler, Carlos

Reve

Lopez Moctezuma. Mus: Raul Lavista. "Combination of "Don Juan Tenorio," "Faust," and "Dorian Gray"."

REVE D'UN ASTRONOME, Le see ASTRONOMER'S DREAM, The

The REVELATION Kay-Bee 1913 15m. Ref:MPW 18:67. Lee. Dream: Cave men.

REVENANT, Le see APPARITION, The

REVENGE IS SWEET see MARCH OF THE WOODEN SOLDIERS

REVENGE OF DRACULA see DRACULA, PRINCE OF DARKNESS

REVENGE OF KING KONG see KING KONG ESCAPES

The REVENGE OF FRANKENSTEIN (B) Col/Hammer 1958 Technicolor 91m. D: Terence Fisher. SP: Jimmy Sangster. PH: Jack Asher. Mus: Leonard Salzedo. Art D: Bernard Robinson. Ref: Clarens. PM. with Peter Cushing, Francis Matthews, Eunice Gayson, Michael Gwynn, Lionel Jeffries, Oscar Quitak, John Stuart, Charles Lloyd Pack. Baron Frankenstein, saved from the guillotine by a hunchbacked accomplice, builds an unhandicapped body in which to transplant the brain of his rescuer. Offbeat little horror drama is probably Hammer's best Frankenstein. Fair to good.

REVENGE OF KING KONG see KING KONG ESCAPES

REVENGE OF THE BLOOD BEAST see SHE BEAST

REVENGE OF THE COLOSSAL MAN see WAR OF THE COLOSSAL BEAST

REVENGE OF THE CREATURE Univ 1955 82m. D: Jack Arnold. SP: Martin Berkeley. Sequel to CREATURE FROM THE BLACK LAGOON. PH: Charles S. Welbourne. Mus D: Joseph Gershenson. Art D: Alexander Golitzen, Alfred Sweeney. P: William Alland. Ref: FDY. with John Agar, John Bromfield, Lori Nelson, Nestor Paiva, Robert B. Williams, Dave Willock, Charles Cane, Grandon Rhodes. The creature from the Devonian should have faded into oblivion instead of being given another movie. Nerve-wracking music and childish dialogue.

REVENGE OF THE DEAD see NIGHT OF THE GHOULS/ORGY OF THE DEAD

REVENGE OF THE VAMPIRE (Malayan) Keris Films 1957 (DENDAM PONTIANAK) D:B. N. Rao. Mus sc: Zubir Said. Sequel to The VAMPIRE (Keris'57). Ref: FEFN 8/9/57. 8/23/57. 9/13/57. with Maria Menado (girl, mutate, vampire), M. Maarof. Vampires, ghosts, and demons.

REVENGE OF THE VAMPIRE see BLACK SUNDAY

REVENGE OF THE ZOMBIES Mono 1943 61m. (The CORPSE VANISHED-Eng.) D: Steve Sekely. SP: Edmund Kelso, Van Norcross. PH: Mack Stengler. Mus D: Edward Kay. Art D: David Milton. Ref: Photon 21:11. MW 6:14. with John Carradine, Gale Storm, Robert Lowery, Mantan Moreland, Bob Steele, Veda Ann Borg, Mauritz Hugo, Mme. Sul-Te-Wan. A scientist plans to create an army of zombies.

The REVENGEFUL SPIRIT OF EROS (J) Shochiku 1930 (EROGAMI NO ONRYO) D: Yasujiro Ozu. SP: Kogo Noda. PH: Hideo Shigehara. Ref: RVB (Film Comment). Ghost comedy.

REVERSING DARWIN'S THEORY see DOCTOR'S EXPERIMENT, The

REVIVED MONSTER, The see RESURRECTED MONSTER, The

The REVOLT OF THE GHOSTS (Mex) Prod.de Peliculas 1946 (La REBELLION DE LOS FANTASMAS) D: A. F. Bustamente. PH:

Solares. Ref: Aventura. with Gilbert Roland, Amanda Ledesma.
Comic ghost story.

REVOLT OF THE ROBOTS see AELITA

REVOLT OF THE TRIFFIDS see DAY OF THE TRIFFIDS

REVOLT OF THE ZOMBIES Academy 1936 65m. (REVOLT OF
THE DEMONS) D: Victor Halperin. SP: V. Halperin, Rollo
Lloyd, Howard Higgin. P: Edward Halperin. PH: Arthur
Martinelli. Mus D: Abe Meyer. Art D: Leigh Smith. SpFX: Ray
Mercer. Ref: FD 6/5/36. Photon 21:11. with Dean Jagger,
Dorothy Stone, Roy D'Arcy, Robert Noland, George Cleveland,
Fred Warren, Carl Stockdale, Teru Shimada. Regiment of dead
Indo-Chinese soldiers revived to aid France in World War I.

REVOLTE DES VIVANTS, La see WORLD WILL SHAKE, The

RFKOPIS ZNALEZIONY SARAGOSSIE see SARAGOSSA MANU-
SCRIPT, The

The REWARD OF THE FAITHLESS Bluebird 1917 55m. SP, P:
Rex Ingram. Story: E. Magnus Ingleton. Ref: MPN 15:1092. with
Betty Schade, Wedgewood Nowell, Claire Du Bray, Nicholas
Dunaew. Princess in trance, entombed as dead, returns as "ghost"
to frighten man who tried to kill her.

RICH IS THE TREASURE (novel by M. Procter) see DIAMOND
WIZARD, The

RIDDLE OF THE GREEN UMBRELLA Kalem 1914 D: Kenean Buel.
Ref: The Film Index. with James Ross, Alice Joyce. Vocophone,
detectophone, recordophone.

The RIDER OF THE SKULLS Col (Mex) c1966 (El CHARRO DE LAS
CALAVERAS) Ref: FJA. with Dagoberto Rodriguez, David Silva,
Pascual Pena. Werewolf.

RIDERS TO THE STARS UA 1954 82m. D: Richard Carlson.
SP: Curt Siodmak. PH: Stanley Cortez. Art D: Jerome Pycha, Jr.
P: Ivan Tors. Ref: FDY. SM 1:15. FM 14:42. TVG. with Carlson,
Herbert Marshall, William Lundigan, Martha Hyer, Dawn Addams,
Lawrence Dobkin, George Eldredge, King Donovan, James K.
Best. A rocket is sent into space to capture a meteor.

RIDING ON AIR RKO 1937 71m. D: Edward Sedgwick. SP:
Richard Macaulay, Richard Flournoy. Mus sc: Arthur Morton.
PH: Al Gilks. SpFX: Fred Jackman. Ref: FD 6/28/37. MFB.
with Joe E. Brown, Guy Kibbee, Florence Rice, Harlan Briggs,
Andrew Tombes, Clem Bevans. Radio-ray device controls and
guides airplanes.

RIFIFI IN AMSTERDAM (SP-I) Procensa/Claudia 1967 color/scope
90m. (RIFIFI EN AMSTERDAM) D: Terence Hathaway. SP:
L. M. Batistrada, A. Crispino, R. C. de Turnes. PH: E. M.
Medina. Mus: P. Umiliani. Ref: SpCinema'68. M/TVM 5/68.
with Roger Browne, Aida Power, Umi Raho. Secret agents attempt
to destroy deadly atomic ray.

The RIGHT TO BE HAPPY Bluebird 1916 60m. D: Rupert Julian.
From "A Christmas Carol" by Charles Dickens. SP: E J. Clawson.
Ref: MPN 14:4236. with Julian (Scrooge), John Cook, Claire Mc-
Dowell.

RIM OF THE CANYON Col 1949 70m. D: John English. SP:
John K. Butler, from the story "Phantom 45's Talk Loud" by J.
Chadwick. PH: William Bradford. Mus Sup: Paul Mertz. Mus D:

Mischa Bakaleinikoff. Art D: Harold MacArthur. with Gene
Autry, Nan Leslie, Thurston Hall, Clem Bevans, Walter Sande,
Jock O'Mahoney, Alan Hale, Jr., Amelita Ward, "Champion."
Ref: PM: Ghost story/western. HR: 10/14/49: Girl claims
ghost talked to her.

RINEHARD see GABRIEL OVER THE WHITE HOUSE

RING AROUND SATURN see BEAST OF HOLLOW MOUNTAIN

The RING OF DUCHESS ANN (Polish) 1970 Ref: M/TVM 6/70: "Boys
break time barrier."

RING OF TERROR Ashcroft-States Rights/Playstar 1962 D: Clark
L. Paylow. SP: Lewis Simeon, G. J. Zinnamon(?). PH:Brydon
Baker. Mus:James Cairncross. Makeup: Roland Ray. Ref: FM
13:12. with George Mather, Austin Green, Esther Furst, Joseph
Conway. Cemetery custodian recalls story: Medical-college stu-
dent must open crypt and take ring from corpse.

RINGER, The (by E. Wallace) see MYSTERIOUS MAGICIAN, The

The RISK (B) Boulting 1960 81m. (SUSPECT-Eng.) D, P: Roy
Boulting, John Boulting. SP: Nigel Balchin, from his novel
"A Sort of Traitors." Add'l Dial: R. Boulting, Jeffrey Dell.
PH: Max Greene. Art D: Albert Witherick. Ref: MFB'60:167.
TVG. with Peter Cushing, Tony Britton, Virginia Maskell, Ian
Bannen, Donald Pleasence, Raymond Huntley, Thorley Walters,
Spike Milligan, Kenneth Griffith, Basil Dignam, John Payne, Brian
Oulton, Sam Rydd, Margaret Lacey, Murray Melvin. A scientist
discovers a new virus which can combat plague.

RITUAL OF EVIL NBC-TV 1970 color 96m. D: Robert Day. SP:
Robert Presnell, Jr. Based on characters created by Richard Alan
Simmons. Sequel to FEAR NO EVIL. PH: Lionel Lindon. Mus:
William Goldenberg. Art D: William B. DeCinces. SpPhFX:
Mobile Color FX. Ref: TVG. RVB. with Louis Jourdan, Anne
Baxter, Diana Hyland, John McMartin, Wilfrid Hyde-White, Carla
Borelli. Witch, supernatural.

RIVAL TO SATAN (F) Pathe 1910 (RIVAL DE SATAN) D: Gerard
Bourgeois. Ref: Bios 1/19/11. Mitry II. Satan, in the form of
a Hindu prince, tries to win the hand of a woman.

ROAD TO HONG KONG (U.S.-B)UA/Melnor 1961 91m. (ROAD TO
THE MOON) SP, D: Norman Panama. SP: also Melvin Frank.
Mus: Robert Farnon. Art D: Sidney Cain, Bill Hutchinson. SpFX:
Wally Veevers, Ted Samuels. Ref: FFacts. SM 3:12. with Bing
Crosby, Bob Hope, Dorothy Lamour, Joan Collins, Robert Mor-
ley, Peter Sellers, Felix Aylmer, Peter Madden, Bill Nagy, Robert
Ayres, Robin Hughes, Victor Brooks, Frank Sinatra, Dean Mar-
tin, David Niven, Jerry Colonna. Drug that cures amnesia;
rocket fuel formula; flight to planet Plutonium. One of the least
of the "Road" pictures.

The ROADSIDE INN (F) Melies c1913 4m. Ref: Bios. Three attendants frighten man by dressing one as ghost & putting "spooky-
looking dummy" in his bed.

The ROBBER-CATCHING MACHINE (F) Eclair 1911 7m. Ref: Bios
6/29/11. Magnetic devices catches robbers.

ROBERT, THE DEVIL, or FREED FROM SATAN'S POWER (F)
Gaum-Lux 1910 17m. Ref: Bios 5/12/10. Devil, evil spirits.

ROBINSON CRUSOE OF CLIPPER ISLAND Rep 1936 serial

(ROBINSON CRUSOE OF MYSTERY ISLAND-feature. S.O.S.
CLIPPER ISLAND-Eng.) D: Mack V. Wright, Ray Taylor. SP:
M. Geraghty, B. Shipman, J.Rathmell. Story: M. Cox, W.
Miller, L. Swabacker. PH: W.Nobles. Mus sup: Harry Grey.
Ref: Barbour. MFB 8/31/37. with Mala, Rex, Buck, Mamo
Clark, Herbert Rawlinson, Selmer Jackson, John Piccori, George
Chesebro, George Cleveland. Electronic engine makes volcano
erupt.

ROBINSON CRUSOE ON MARS Para/Devonshire 1964 Technicolor
109m. scope D: Byron Haskin. SP: Ib Melchior, John C. Higgins.
Idea from Defoe's "Robinson Crusoe." PH: Winton C. Hoch.
Mus: Van Cleave. Art D: Hal Pereira, Arthur Lonergan. Ref:
PM. Clarens. with Paul Mantee, Vic Lundin, Adam West.
Member of two man rocket crew survives crash-landing on
Mars, struggles to survive alone.   Though slow at times this is
one of the better s-f movies of the Sixties, with suspense and
some exciting special effects.

ROBOT HUMANO, El see ROBOT VS. THE AZTEC MUMMY, The
ROBOT MONSTER Astor/3-D Pictures 1953 3-D 63m. D: Phil
Tucker. SP: Wyott Ordung. (MONSTER FROM MARS. MONSTER(S)
FROM THE MOON) PH: Jack Greenhalgh. Mus: Elmer Bernstein.
Scenes from ONE MILLION B.C. Exec P:Al Zimbalist. Ref: MFB
'54:180. FM 14:6.15:10.19:36.31:73. FanMo 1:26. Pic: FM-A'64:
44. MadM 5:51. FM 28:45. with George Nader, Claudia Barrett,
Selena Royle, Gregory Moffett. Robots land on earth.

ROBOT OF REGALIO MCA-TV 1954 From the "Rocky Jones,
Space Ranger" TV series. with Richard Crane, James Lydon.

The ROBOT VS. THE AZTEC MUMMY (Mex) AI-TV/Calderon 1957
(La MOMIA ATZEKA CONTRA EL ROBOT HUMANO. El ROBOT
HUMANO) D: Rafael Portillo. Story,SP: Alfredo Salazar. Story:
also Guillermo Calderon. PH:Enrique Wallace. Mus: A. D.
Conde. Ref: Indice. with Ramon Gay, Rosita Arenas, Crox Alvarado, Luis Aceves Castañeda, Angel D'Esteffani. This has
everything: 1. A mummy. 2. A robot. 3. A rattlesnake pit.
4. A mad doctor. 5. Remote-control hypnotism. 6. Gangsters.
7. A person with a disfigured face. 8. Body-snatching. 9. Death
by radium. 10. Uninterrupted stupidity.

ROBOTS OF DEATH see NEUTRON AND THE DEATH ROBOTS
ROBSON'S REVOLVING HEEL PADS Graphic 1909 6m. Ref:
Bios 8/26/09. Pads in boots make feet move in circles.

ROBUR, THE CONQUEROR (by J. Verne) see MASTER OF THE
WORLD (1961)

ROCK-A-BYE BABY! (by N. Lessing and M. Davidson) see
ARTISTS AND MODELS

ROCK THAT OPENS AND CLOSES, The see DEVOURING ROCK,
The

ROCKET AND ROLL see ABBOTT AND COSTELLO GO TO MARS
ROCKET ATTACK U.S.A. Exploit 1960 68m. D,P: Barry
Mahon. PH: Mike Tabb. Ref: FFacts. with John McKay, Monica
Davis, Daniel Kern. World War III begins with a Russian rocket
attack on New York City.

ROCKET FROM FENWICK, A see MOUSE ON THE MOON
ROCKET MAN Fox/Panoramic 1954 79m. D: Oscar Rudolph. SP:

Lenny Bruce, Jack Henley. Story: George W. George, George F. Slavin. PH: John Seitz. Ref: FDY. with Charles Coburn, Anne Francis, George Winslow, Spring Byington, John Agar, Emory Parnell, Stanley Clements, Beverly Garland, Don Haggerty. "Space gun" turns crooks honest.

ROCKET SHIP see FLASH GORDON

ROCKET SHIP GALILEO (book by R. Heinlein) see DESTINATION MOON

ROCKET TO NOWHERE (Cz) Brandon/Barrandov 1962 79m. (KLAUN FERDINAND A RAKETA. CLOWN FERDINAND AND THE ROCKET) D: Jindrich Polak. SP: Ota Hofman, Polak. PH: Jan Kalis. Mus: Evzen Illin. Ref: Imagen. with Jiri Vrstala, E. Hrabetova, H. Bor, V. Horka. Friendly robot captures clown and children.

ROCKET TO THE MOON see CAT-WOMEN OF THE MOON/ THOSE FANTASTIC FLYING FOOLS

ROCKETFLIGHT WITH HINDRANCE see DOG, A MOUSE AND A SPUTNIK, A

ROCKETSHIP X-M Lippert 1950 78m. (EXPEDITION MOON. DESTINAZIONE LUNA-I.) SP,D,P: Kurt Neumann. PH: Karl Struss. Mus: Ferde Grofé. Art D: Theobold Holsopple. SpFX: Jack Rabin, I. A. Block. Ref: FDY. Pic: SM 4:31. with Lloyd Bridges, Osa Massen, John Emery, Noah Beery, Jr., Hugh O'Brian, Morris Ankrum. Moon rocket out of control lands on Mars. Melodramatic but occasionally interesting.

The ROCKING HORSE WINNER (B) Rank/Univ 1949 90m. SP,D: Anthony Pelissier. From the story by D. H. Lawrence. PH: Desmond Dickinson. Mus: William Alwyn. Art D: Carmen Dillon. P: John Mills. Ref: HR 6/8/50. Brit.Cinema. with Valerie Hobson, John Howard Davies, Mills, Hugh Sinclair. Boy able to pick race winners riding rocking horse eventually dies from the strain. Fascinating horror story becomes unconvincing film which takes itself too seriously.

ROCKY JONES, SPACE RANGER see BEYOND THE MOON/COLD SUN, The/CRASH OF MOONS/BLAST OFF/DUEL IN SPACE/ FORBIDDEN MOON/GYPSY MOON/INFERNO IN SPACE/MAG-NETIC MOON/MANHUNT IN SPACE/MENACE FROM OUTER SPACE/OUT OF THIS WORLD/ROBOT OF REGALIO/SILVER NEEDLE IN THE SKY

RODAN (J) DCA/King Bros./Toho 1956 ('58-U.S.) 99m. (RADON. RADAN) (RODAN, THE FLYING MONSTER) D: Inoshiro Honda. SP: T. Kimura, Takeo Murata. Story: Takashi Kuronuma. PH: Isamu Ashida. Art D: Tatsuo Kita. SpFX: Eiji Tsuburaya. Narr: David Duncan. Ref: FFacts. FM 28:15. with Kenji Sahara, Yumi Shirakawa. Giant winged monster, smaller creatures called Meganuron. Picture tries for heart-tugging ending à la SON OF KONG, but only proves it isn't easy to work up sympathy for giant birds.

RoGoPaG (I-F) 1962 125m. (HUMAN RELATIONS) Arco-Cineriz-Lyre Ref: Imagen. DDC III:118. COF 7:49. 20-minute sketch "Le Nouveau Monde": SP,D: Jean-Luc Godard. PH: Jean Rabier. with Alexandra Stewart, Jean-Marc Bory. Atomic explosion changes world.

ROGUES GALLERY PRC 1945 60m. D: Albert Herman. SP: John
T. Neville. PH: Ira Morgan. Mus D: Lee Zahler. Art D: Paul
Palmentola. Ref: Film World '51/52. MFB'45:109. with Frank
Jenks, Robin Raymond, H. B. Warner, Edward Keane, Davison
Clark, Milton Kibbee, Gene Stutenroth, George Kirby. Girl
reporter and photographer employ device which picks up conver-
sations without using radio waves.

ROI DE THULE, Le see LURED BY A PHANTOM

ROMA CONTRO ROMA see WAR OF THE ZOMBIES

The ROMANCE OF ELAINE Pathe 1915 serial 12 episodes D:
George B. Seitz. Ref: MPW 24:2109, 2178. 25:904. MPN 7/31/15.
9/11/15. with Lionel Barrymore, Pearl White, Creighton Hale.
Ch. 7. The Death Cloud. 8. The Searchlight Gun. 11. The Disappearing Helmet. Super-torpedo; "special wireless apparatus";
poisonous gas that paralyzes temporarily.

The ROMANCE OF THE MUMMY (F) Pathe 1910 14m. Ref: Bios
1/5/11. From the book by Theophile Gautier. Lord Evandale
falls asleep before the mummy of a queen of Egypt. He dreams
that he is in ancient Egypt and is the object of the queen's affections. When he awakens he meets and marries a girl who "has
the features of the dead queen."

ROMAN'S AWAKENING, The see BACK TO LIFE AFTER 2000
YEARS

ROOM IN THE TOWER (story by E. F. Benson) see DEAD OF NIGHT

ROOM TO LET (B) Hammer 1950 68m. D: Godfrey Grayson. SP:
Grayson, John Gilling, from the BBC feature by Margery Alling-
ham. PH: Cedric Williams. Mus: Frank Spencer. P: Anthony
Hinds. Ref: MFB. with Jimmy Hanley, Valentine Dyall, Merle
Tottenham, Charles Hawtrey. The story of Jack the Ripper is told
in a series of flashbacks.

ROSALIE AND SPIRITUALISM (F) Pathe-Lux 1911 (ROSALIE FAIT
DU SPIRITISME) D: Romeo Bosetti. Ref: Mitry II.

ROSE ECORCHEE, La see RAVAGED

ROSEMARY'S BABY Para 1968 color 134m. SP, D: Roman
Polanski. PH: William Fraker. Mus: Christopher Komeda. Art D:
Joel Schiller. From the novel by Ira Levin. P: William Castle.
Ref: LATimes. V 5/29/68. with Mia Farrow, John Cassavetes,
Maurice Evans, Sidney Blackmer, Ruth Gordon, Ralph Bellamy,
Patsy Kelly, Angela Dorian, Elisha Cook, Jr. , Emmaline Henry,
Wendy Wagner, Hope Summers, Philip Leeds. Couple's neighbors
in New York City apartment house practice witchcraft. Long and
slow, but with an intermittently frightening use of the everyday to
bring the horror closer to home. Diluted by Ruth Gordon's performance, which is a little too emphatically everyday.

ROSTRO DEL ASESINO, El see FACE OF THE MURDERER, The

ROSTRO INFERNAL, El see HELL-FACE

ROUGE AUX LEVRES, Le see DAUGHTERS OF DARKNESS

A ROYAL ROMANCE Col 1930 71m. D: Erle C. Kenton. Art D:
Harrison Wiley. Ed: Gene Havlick. SP: Norman Houston, from
the story "Private Property" by Houston. PH: Ted Tetzlaff. Ref:
AFI. PM: "ghost thrills." FD 4/27/30: "Starts off as a mystery
thriller with creeps and shivers galore...spooky scenes." with
William Collier, Jr. , Pauline Starke, Clarence Muse, Ann Brody,

Walter P. Lewis, Betty Boyd, Eugenie Besserer, Bert Sprotte.
A young writer buys a haunted castle in a mythical Balkan king-
dom and "marries the princess who had been doing the haunting."
ROYAUME DES FEES, Le see KINGDOM OF THE FAIRIES, The
RUBBER HEELS (F) Pathe 1908 4m. Ref: F Index 12/12/08. Store-
bought rubber heels bounce man high in the air.
The RUBBER MAN Lubin 1909 5m. Ref: MPW'09:771. Bios 12/30/09.
Rubber automaton.
RUBEZAHL'S MARRIAGE (G) Wegener 1916 (RUBEZAHLS HOCH-
ZEIT) SP, D: Paul Wegener. Art D: Rochus Gliese. Ref: DDC
II:414. Fantastique. with Wegener, Lyda Salmonova, Marianne
Niemeyer. Orpheus 3:47: A phantom giant releases a storm on a
family picnicking in the mountains.
RULER OF THE WORLD see MASTER OF THE WORLD (1934)
The RULING PASSION Fox 1916 55m. D: Joseph Mackay. SP, P:
Herbert Brenon. Ref: MPN 13:866. with Claire Whitney, Stephen
Grattan, Edward Boring. Indian prince casts hypnotic spell on wife
of English officer.
RUMAH PUAKA see HAUNTED HOUSE (1957)
RURAL DELIVERY, MILLION B.C.   Edison c1918 Ref: FM 63:28:
RFD 1000000 B.C. SpFX: Willis O'Brien.
RUUSUJEN AIKA see TIME OF ROSES

S-A FURAT O BOMBA see BOMB WAS STOLEN, A
S. 007 SPIONAGGIO A TANGERI see ESPIONAGE IN TANGIERS
S.O.S. COAST GUARD Rep 1937 serial 12 episodes (69m. feature-
1942) D: William Witney, Alan James. SP: M. Cox, R. Davidson,
J. Rathmell, B. Shipman, F. Adreon. PH: W. Nobles. Mus:
Raoul Kraushaar. Ref: Barbour. Pic: FM 18:17. with Bela
Lugosi, Ralph Byrd, Maxine Doyle, Herbert Rawlinson, Richard
Alexander, John Piccori (or Picorri), Thomas Carr, Lawrence
Grant, Carleton Young, George Chesebro, Ranny Weeks. Mad
scientist plans to sell deadly new gas to foreign power.
S.O.S. CLIPPER ISLAND see ROBINSON CRUSOE OF CLIPPER
ISLAND
S.O.S. INVASION (Sp) I.M.T. 1969 color/scope 87m. D: Silvio F.
Balbuena. SP: J. L. N. Bassó. PH: Alfonso Nieva. Mus: M.
Buendia. Ref: SpCinema'70. with Jack Taylor, Mara Cruz, Diana
Sorel, José María Tasso. Unearthly beings in the ruins of an old
castle create robot girls.
S.O.S. SPACESHIP see INVISIBLE BOY, The
S.O.S. TIDAL WAVE Rep 1939 60m. D: John Auer. SP: Maxwell
Shane, Gordon Kahn. Story: James Webb. PH: Jack Marta.
Flood scenes from DELUGE. Ref: PM. FDY. with Ralph Byrd,
George Barbier, Kay Sutton, Frank Jenks, Marc Lawrence,
Dorothy Lee, Oscar O'Shea, Donald Barry. Fake television broad-
cast depicts tidal wave sweeping over New York, "Orson Welles'
Mars broadcast having suggested that the voters could thus be
duped."
The SABLE LORCHA Triangle 1915 D: Lloyd Ingraham. P: D. W.

Griffith. SP: Chester B. Clapp. From the novel by Horace Hazeltine. Ref: MPN with Tully Marshall, Thomas Jefferson, Elmer Clifton. Scientist's compound renders person temporarily unconscious.

The SACRED ORDER (B) Stoll 1923 20m. SP: A. E. Coleby, Frank Wilson. From a story by Sax Rohmer. PH: D. P. Cooper. Ref: SilentFF. with Harry Agar Lyons, Fred Paul, Humbertson Wright, Joan Clarkson. (Mystery of Dr. Fu-Manchu series)

SAD GHOST STORY OF FUKAGAWA (J) Daiei 1952 (KAIDAN FUKA- GAWA JOWA) D: Minoru Inuzuka. Ref: Unij. Bltn. 31. with Mitsuko Mito, Yuji Hori.

SADIQUE, Le see HAND OF A DEAD MAN, The

The SADIST (Swedish) Flamingo 1966 (TRAFRACKEN. The COF- FIN) 90m. SP, D: Lars Magnus Lindgren. Based on a novel by Jan Ekström. PH: Tony Forsberg. Mus: Bo Nilsson. Ref: MFB 69:129. with Gunnar Björnstrand, Essy Persson, Catrin Wester- lund. Private clinic run by sadist; doctor who plays "sinister chords on the organ"; undertakers looking for fresh corpses.

SADKO see MAGIC VOYAGE OF SINBAD, The

SAGA OF THE VIKING WOMEN AND THEIR VOYAGE TO THE WATERS OF THE GREAT SEA SERPENT, The see VIKING WOMEN & THE SEA SERPENT, The

SAINT AGAINST THE VAMPIRE WOMEN, The see SAMSON VS. THE VAMPIRE WOMEN

ST. GEORGE AND THE DRAGON Edison 1910 Ref: LC.

ST. GEORGE AND THE DRAGON (I) Milano 1912 color 45m. Ref: MPW 12:933.

SAINT GEORGE AND THE DRAGON see MAGIC SWORD, The (1962)

SAINT GEORGE AND THE 7 CURSES see MAGIC SWORD, The (1962)

SAINT OF MT. KOYA, The (by K. Izumi) see TEMPTRESS, The

The SAINT, THE DEVIL AND THE WOMAN Than 1916 60m. D: Frederick Sullivan. Ref: MPN 14:1893. with Florence LaBadie, Ethyle Cooke. Satanic Spaniard hypnotizes heiress.

The SAINT-VAL MYSTERY (F) 1945 95m. (Le MYSTERE SAINT- VAL) D: René Le Hénaff. Ref: Rep. Gen'47:370. with Fernandel, Pierre Renoir, A. Rignault, Arlette Guttinguer. "Mystification of an apprentice detective in a strange manor where six people are murdered in the course of a night. Vexed at having been played with, after seeing these pseudo-cadavres return in perfect health, the detective catches the author of this sinister farce."

SAIR-E-PARISTAN see SHAN-E-KHUDA

SAKIMA AND THE MASKED MARVEL see MASKED MARVEL, The

SALEM COME TO SUPPER see NIGHT VISITOR, The

SALOME CRAZE Phoenix 1909 8m. Ref: MPW'09:67. Liquid spray causes people to dance.

The SALOON-KEEPER'S NIGHTMARE (F) Gaum 1908 7m. Ref: MPW'08. Satan torments man.

SAMPO see DAY THE EARTH FROZE

SAMSON AND THE 7 MIRACLES OF THE WORLD (I-F) AI-Panda/ Gallus-Agiman 1961 Technicolor by Pathe/scope 95m. (80m.-U.S.) D: Riccardo Freda. SP: Oreste Biancoli, Duccio Tessari. PH: Riccardo Pallottini. Mus: Carlo Innocenzi; (U.S.) Les Baxter. Ref: FFacts: MACISTE ALLA CORTE DEL GRAN KHAN-I. with

Gordon Scott, Yoko Tani, Helene Chanel. Samson, buried alive
in an underground vault, creates an earthquake in escaping from
his tomb.
SAMSON IN THE WAX MUSEUM (Mex) AI-TV /Panamericana 1963
   (El SANTO EN EL MUSEO DE CERA) D: Alfonso Corona Blake.
   SP: F. Galiano, Julius Porter. PH: Jose O. Ramos. Mus: S.
   Guerrero. Ref: Indice. Imagen. with Santo, Norma Mora, Fernando Oses, Jose Luis Jimenez. A mad doctor and wax figures
   of Frankenstein's monster, Quasimodo, Landru, The Phantom of
   the Opera(?), The Abominable Snowman(?). How do you criticize
   a movie in which the hero engages in three wrestling matches and
   the mad doctor is drowned in a vat of soapsuds?
SAMSON VS. THE GIANT KING see ATLAS AGAINST THE CZAR
SAMSON VS. THE VAMPIRE WOMEN (Mex) AI-TV /Panamericana
   1961 89m. (El SANTO VS. LAS MUJERES VAMPIROS-Arg. Las
   MUJERES VAMPIROS. El SANTO CONTRA LAS VAMPIRAS. El
   SANTO CONTRA LAS MUJERES VAMPIROS. The SAINT AGAINST
   THE VAMPIRE WOMEN. SUPERMAN CONTRE LES FEMMES
   VAMPIRES-F.) D: Alfonso Corona Blake. SP: Rafael Travesi.
   Story: Travesi, A. Orellana, Fernando Oses. PH: Jose O. Ramos.
   Mus: Raul Lavista. Art D: Roberto Silva. Ref: Aventura. M /TVM
   1 /62. with Santo, Lorena Velazquez, Maria Duval, Oses. Ridicu-
   lous heroics of superhero Samson alternate with atmospheric se-
   quences with the vampire women.
SAMURAI PIRATE DAITOZOKU see LOST WORLD OF SINBAD, The
SANAD FUUNROKU (J) Toei 1963 color /scope 100m. D: Tai
   Kato. Ref: M /TVM 6 /63. with Kinnosuke Nakamura, M. Watanabe.
   Two clans, battling for supremacy in 17th-century Japan, employ
   magicians, one of which received his powers from a stone from
   outer space.
SANDAI KAIJU CHIKYU SAIDAI NO KESSEN see GHIDRAH
SANDMAN, The (by E. T. A. Hoffmann) see POUPEE, La (1899)
SANGRE DE NOSTRADAMUS, La see BLOOD OF NOSTRADAMUS,
   The
SANGRE DE VIRGENES see BLOOD OF THE VIRGINS
SANTA CLAUS (Mex) Calderon 1959 D: Rene Cardona. SP: Car-
   dona, Adolpho Portillo. PH: Raul M. Solares. Mus: A. D. Conde.
   Ref: Indice. FM 29:43. with Jose Elias Moreno, Cesare Queza-
   das, Nora Veryan, Jose Luis Aguirre. Santa Claus vs. a demon.
SANTA CLAUS CONQUERS THE MARTIANS Emb 1964 color 80m.
   D: Nicholas Webster. SP: Glenville Mareth. PH: David Quaid. Art
   D: Maurice Gordon. Ref: PM. FFacts. with John Call, Leonard
   Hicks. Martians kidnap Santa and two children. Sure.
SANTO AGAINST BLUE DEMON IN ATLANTIS (Mex) c1968 Sotomayor
   (SANTO CONTRA BLUE DEMON EN LA ATLANTIDA) D: Julian
   Soler. SP: G. Travesi. Ref: RVB. with Jorge Rado, Rafael
   Banquells, Agustin M. Solares.
SANTO AGAINST THE BARON BRAKOLA (Mex) Vergara 1965
   (SANTO CONTRA EL BARON BRAKOLA. SANTO VERSUS THE
   BARON BRAKOLA) D: Jose Diaz Morales. Ref: Imagen. M /TVM
   9 /65: vampire. with Santo, Fernando Oses, Susana Robles,
   Andrea Palma, Mercedes Carreño.
SANTO AGAINST THE DAUGHTER OF FRANKENSTEIN (Mex)

Calderon 1971 (SANTO CONTRA LA HIJA DE FRANKENSTEIN.
La HIJA DE FRANKENSTEIN) D: Miguel M. Delgado. Ref: Cinelandia 9/25/71. with Santo, Gina Romand, Anel, Sonia Fuentes,
Jorge Casanova. Santo vs. Ursus, monster created by Frankenstein's daughter. Mummies? Vampires?

SANTO AGAINST THE DIABOLICAL BRAIN (Mex) Azteca c1963
(SANTO CONTRA EL CEREBRO DIABOLICO. El CEREBRO DEL
MAL) Ref: TVG. with Santo.

SANTO AGAINST THE KING OF CRIME (Mex) Azteca 1962 (SANTO
CONTRA EL REY DEL CRIMEN) D: Federico Curiel. Ref: Lee.
Imagen. with Fernando Casanova, Ana Berthe Lepe, Rene Car-
dona. FJA still: lab.

SANTO AGAINST THE STRANGLER (Mex) Clasa 1964 (SANTO
CONTRA EL ESTRANGULADOR) From "The Phantom of the
Opera" by Gaston Leroux. Ref: Imagen. with Santo, Alberto Váz-
quez, Maria Duval.

SANTO AGAINST THE ZOMBIES (Mex) TEC/Panamericana 1961
85m. (El SANTO CONTRA LOS ZOMBIES. SANTO CONTRA LOS
MONSTRUOS. INVASION OF THE ZOMBIES-TV) SP, D: Benito
Alazraki. PH: Jose O. Ramos. Mus: Raul Lavista. Story: An-
tonio Orellana, Fernando Oses. Ref: Indice. Heraldo 2/7/68.
COF 4:4.11:37. TVG. with Santo, Lorena Velazquez, Armando
Silvestre, Jaime Fernandez, Carlos Agosti, Dagoberto Rodriguez,
Irma Serrano, Ramon Bugarini. A mad scientist plans to conquer
the world with an army of zombies.

SANTO AND BLUE DEMON AGAINST THE MONSTERS (Mex) Sotomayor c1969 color (El SANTO Y BLUE DEMON CONTRA LOS
MONSTRUOS) D: Gilberto Martinez Solares. Ref: M/TVM 3/69:10.
RVB. with "Resortes," Heydi Blue. Frankenstein-monster-type,
vampire, werewolf, mummy, Cyclops.

SANTO AND DRACULA'S TREASURE (Mex) Calderon c1969 color
85m. (El VAMPIRO Y EL SEXO) D: Rene Cardona. SP: Alfredo
Salazar. Mus: Sergio Guerrera. with Santo, Noelia Noel, Aldo Monti,
Roberto G. Rivera, Carlos Agosti, Pili Gonzalez, Alberto Rojas.
Reincarnation machine allows girl to relive another girl's story
and her encounter with Count Alucard (aka Dracula). Not even
any attempt at atmosphere as in earlier Santos. Highlight has the
Count stamping new additions to his chorus line of vampire
women with a bat-ring.

SANTO ATTACKS THE WITCHES (Mex) Vergara 1964 (SANTO ATACA
LAS BRUJAS. ATACAN LAS BRUJAS) D: Jose Diaz Morales. SP:
Rafael Travesi, Fernando Oses. Ref: Lee. TVG. with Santo,
Lorena Velazquez, Ramon Bugarini, Maria Eugenia San Martin,
Oses, Crox Alvarado, Lobo Negro.

SANTO CONTRA EL ESPECTRO see GHOST OF THE STRANGLER,
The

SANTO CONTRA LAS MUJERES VAMPIROS, El see SAMSON VS.
THE VAMPIRE WOMEN

SANTO CONTRA LAS VAMPIRAS, El see SAMSON VS. THE VAM-
PIRE WOMEN

SANTO EN EL MUSEO DE CERA, El see SAMSON IN THE WAX
MUSEUM

The SARAGOSSA MANUSCRIPT (Polish) Contemporary/Polski 1964

125m. Dyaliscope (RFKOPIS ZNALEZIONY SARAGOSSIE. MANU-
SCRIPT FOUND IN SARAGOSSA) D: Wojciech Jerzy Has. SP:
Tadeusz Kwiatkowski, from a book by Jan Potocki. Ref: M/TVM
3/65. Positif 71:40: "Succubi, cablistes." MFB'67:6. F&F 3/67:
"Supernaturally obliging Moorish girls...stress on horror."
COF 2:50. with Zbigniew Cybulski, Kazimierz Opalinski, Iga
Cembryzska, Joanna Jedryka. Good but fairly easy comedy-ad-
venture for listening to their strange stories; then there's a dull
half hour or so where not much happens and no interesting new
characters are introduced; then everything starts to connect, and
the various stories overlap and intrude on each other, and there
are stories within stories, and you're as confused as the hero yet
caught up in the comic deliriousness of the confusion.
SARDONICUS see MR. SARDONICUS
SARMISTHA (India-Bengali) Kali Films   1939 D: Naresh Mitter. Ref:
Dipali 1/5/40. with A. Cowdhury, Chitra, Mitter. "War be-
tween Gods and demons."
SASAYAKU SHIBIJIN see WHISPERING DEAD BEAUTY
SATAN Monopol/Ambrosio 1912 40m. (SATAN; or THE DRAMA OF
HUMANITY) Ref: Bios 1/16/13. MPW'13:1115. FM 67:12. Satan
through the ages.
The SATAN BUG   UA   1965   color   114m. (STATION THREE-UL-
TRA SECRET-F.) D,P: John Sturges. SP: James Clavell, Edward
Anhalt, from the book by A. MacLean. PH: Robert Surtees. Mus:
Jerry Goldsmith. Ref: PM. with George Maharis, Richard Base-
hart, Anne Francis, Dana Andrews, Edward Asner, Frank Sutton,
John Larkin, Richard Bull, Russ Bender, Simon Oakland, Harry
Lauter. Ultimate weapon in germ warfare stolen from government
laboratory in southern California.
SATAN DEFEATED (F) Pathe 1911 12m. Ref: MPW 8:492. Satan's
face changes into horrible masks.
SATANA (I)   1911 D: Luigi Maggi. SP: Guido Volante. Ref: DDC
II:315. Mitry II. Pic: DDC III:285: Devil gleefully approaching
victim. with Antonio Grisanti, Mario Bonnard.
SATANAS (G) 1919 D: F. W. Murnau. PH: Karl Freund. Ref:
Orpheus 3:50. FIR'63:96. with Conrad Veidt (satan). Tale of the
devil.
SATANIC RHAPSODY (I) 1915 tinted (RAPSODIA SATANICA) Ref:
VVoice. with Lyda Borelli. A woman sells her soul to the devil
to regain her youth.
SATANIK (Sp-I) Copercines/Rodiacines 1968 color/scope 80m.
D: Piero Vivarelli. SP: E. M. Brochero. PH:S. Ippoliti. Mus:
Manuel Parada. Ref: SpCinema'69. with Magda Konopka, Julio
Peña, Armando Calvo. Woman drinks professor's formula and
becomes young and beautiful.
SATANISTS, The see WITCHCRAFT'70.
SATAN'S CASTLE (I?) Ambrosio 1913 Ref: MPW 19:98. Soldier of
fortune makes pact with devil and becomes master of castle. Satan
returns to claim his soul. Spirit of man haunts castle.
SATAN'S FIVE WARNINGS (Sp) Nave 1938 (Las CINCO ADVERTENCI-
AS DE SATANAS) D: I. Socias. Ref: NYT 1/14/39. with Felix
de Pomes, Pastora Peña, Julio Peña, Luis Villasial. A tale of the
devil.

SATAN'S FIVE WARNINGS (Mex) 1945 141m. (Las CINCO AD-
VERTENCIAS DE SATANAS) D: Julian Soler. PH: Jorge Stahl.
Mus: R. Ramirez. P: Abel Salazar. Ref: Aventura. with Salazar,
Fernando Soler, Mária Elena Marques.

SATAN'S FIVE WARNING (Sp-Portugese) Hispamer/Francisco de
Castro 1969 color/scope 104m. (Las CINCO ADVERTENCIAS DE
SATANAS) SP, D: Jose Luis Merino. SP: also M. Simoes. Story:
E. J. Poncela. PH: de Castro. Mus: J. L. Navarro. Art D:
E. T. de la Fuente. Ref: SpCinema'70. with Arturo Fernández,
Cristina Galbo, Eduardo Fajardo, Luis Felipe. Satan give Félix
Coimbra four warnings about his life, but withholds the fifth.

SATAN'S SATELLITES see ZOMBIES OF THE STRATOSPHERE

SATAN'S SISTER see SHE BEAST

SATAN'S SKIN (B) Tigon/Chilton 1970 color 93m. (The BLOOD ON
SATAN'S CLAW. The DEVIL'S TOUCH) D: Piers Haggard. SP:
Haggard, Robert Wynne-Simmons. PH: Dick Bush. Mus: Marc
Wilkinson. Art D: Arnold Chapkis. Makeup: Eddie Knight. Ref:
MFB'71:57. with Patrick Wymark, Linda Hayden, Anthony Ain-
ley, James Hayter, Michele Dotrice. Witch-cult, "devil skin."

SATAN'S SMITHY (F) Pathe 1908 8m. Ref: MPW'08:263. Satan lures
blacksmith to hell.

SATAN'S TREASURE (F) Melies/Star 1902 3m. (Le TRESOR DE
SATAN) Ref: SilentFF. Thief chased by men who leap out when he
opens Satan's treasure chest.

SATELLITE IN THE SKY (B) WB/Fridelta 1956 Warnercolor/scope
85m. (FLAME IN THE SKY) Mus: Albert Elms. D of SpFX:
Wally Veevers. D: Paul Dickson. SP: John Mather, J. T.
M(a)cIntosh, Edith Dell. Art D: Erik Blakemore. Ref: FDY. with
Kieron Moore, Thea Gregory, Barry Keegan, Lois Maxwell,
Donald Wolfit, Bryan Forbes, Jimmy Hanley, Carl Jaffe, Walter
Hudd, Robert O'Neil. A rocket is sent into space to explode an
experimental bomb. The everyday problems of the Men of
Progress, continued from BREAKING THE SOUND BARRIER, and
even sillier here. Brilliant dialogue ("So that's the bomb"). Bad
all around.

SATI SAVITRI (India) East India Film Co. 1933 Ref: Sound & Shadow
3/33. Tortures of hell.

SATI VIJAYA (India-Hindustani) M. & K. Prods. 1948 D: K. J.
Parmar. SP: V. R. Mehta, from the "Ramayana." PH: N. M.
Adhikari. Mus: Desai. Dial: Pt. Anuj. Ref: Filmindia 10/48.
with Ratnamala, Kishore Kumari, Pt. Ramchandra Shastri, Kanta
Kumari. A king's son travels to the bottom of the ocean to war
with the serpent king of Patal. A bridge across the ocean is constructed.

SATOMI HAKKEN-DEN see EIGHT BRAVE BROTHERS

The SAUSAGE MACHINE Biog 1897 Ref: SF Film. Turns dogs into
sausages.

The SAVAGE F Nat 1926 63m. D: Fred Newmeyer. SP: Ernest
Pascal. Ref: Photoplay 10/26. V 8/4/26. Pic: COF 6:38. with
May McAvoy, Ben Lyon. Scientist plants man on island as "miss-
ing link" to fool other scientist. Dinosaur.

SAVED BY A SCENT Powers 1915 (The Mysterious Lady Baffles and
Detective Duck series) D: Allen Curtis. SP: Clarence Badger.

Ref: MPN 8/7/15. with Max Asher. An inventor's "smello-graph" sends limburger fumes "through the thickest wall."

The SAVING OF FAUST (F) Pathe 1911 8m. Faust in purgatory allowed to see modern Babylon.

SAVITRI Bombay Talkies (India) 1938 D: Franz Osten. SP: N. Pal. Ref: Dipali 1/21/38. with D. Rani, Ashok(e) Kumar. Wife brings dead husband back to life.

SAVITRI SATYAVAN (India) Madans 1933 Ref: Sound & Shadow 1/33. with T. P. Rajalaxmi. Kingdom of death and its denizens.

SCALE IN HI-FI (Sp) Documento-Izaro 1963 (ESCALA EN HI-FI) D: Isidoro Martinez-Ferry. SP: Martinez-Ferry, G. Quintana, Juan Cobos. PH: F. Sempere. Mus: Waldo de los Rios. Ref: SpCinema'64. Pic: MMF 8:64d. with Arturo Fernández, Cassen, Germaine Damar, José Rubio. Sketch: A nightmare in the castle of Count Dracula.

SCARABEE D'OR, Le see GOLDEN BEETLE, The

SCARECROW, The (by P. MacKaye) see PURITAN PASSIONS

SCARED MGM 1933 78m. SP, D: Elliot Nugent. From the play "Whistling in the Dark" by Lawrence Gross and E. C. Carpenter. PH: Norbert Brodine. Ref: FD 1/28/33. with Ernest Truex, Una Merkel, Edward Arnold, John Miljan, C. Henry Gordon, Johnny Hines, Joseph Cawthorn, Nat Pendleton, Tenen Holtz. "Spooky suspense": Crime writer falls into hands of racketeers. Mildly amusing.

SCARED SILLY Tuxedo Educational 1927 25m. Ref: FD 11/6/27. with Johnny Arthur. "Spook" helps Hindu who stages spiritualistic seances.

SCARED STIFF Pathe/Roach 1926 25m. D: James W. Horne. Ref: MPW 80:52. with Clyde Cook, Eileen Percy, Stuart Holmes. Old dark house, eccentric scientist, gorilla.

SCARED STIFF Para 1953 108m. D: George Marshall. SP: Herbert Baker, Walter de Leon, from the play "Ghost Breakers" by Paul Dickey and Charles W. Goddard. Ref: FDY. with Dean Martin, Jerry Lewis, Carmen Miranda, Lizabeth Scott, Dorothy Malone, Frank Fontaine, Percy Helton, George Dolenz, William Ching, Tom Powers, Bing Crosby, Bob Hope. Zombie and ghost haunt old castle on island. Perhaps the difference between this and GHOST BREAKERS can best be shown by comparing each version's version of the same joke: In GHOST BREAKERS: "Zombies--walking around not seeing, not hearing"--"Like democrats." In SCARED STIFF: "Zombies--no will of their own"--"Just like husbands."

SCARED TO DEATH Lippert/Golden Gate/Screen Guild 1947 Natural-color 65m. D: Christy Cabanne. SP: W. J. Abbott. Remake of The 13th GUEST? PH: Marcel Le Picard. Mus sc: Carl Hoefle. Art D: Harry Reif. Makeup: Roland Ray. Ref: FMO 2:14. FDY. Pic: FanMo 3:60. with Bela Lugosi, George Zucco, Joyce Compton, Douglas Fowley, Roland Varno, Angelo Rossit(t)o. Woman who dies of fright; hypnotic trance; telepathy. Ridiculous narrative device which has woman's corpse tell the story seems to have been added to cover up the disjointedness of the film. Everything's inept --staging, acting, comedy relief. The highly excitable music alone would have ruined a better picture.

The SCARLET CLAW Univ 1944 74m. SP, D, P: Roy William Neill.

SP: also Edmund L. Hartmann. Based on characters created by
Sir Arthur Conan Doyle. Story: Paul Gangelin, Brenda Weisberg.
PH: George Robinson. Mus D: Paul Sawtell. Art D: John B. Good-
man, Ralph M. DeLacy. SpPH: John P. Fulton. Ed: Paul Landres.
Ref: FDY. Pic: COF 13:30. with Basil Rathbone, Nigel Bruce,
Arthur Hohl, Ian Wolfe, Paul Cavanagh, Miles Mander, Kay
Harding, David Clyde, Victoria Horne, Gerald Hamer. Sherlock
Holmes investigates tales of a Canadian marsh monster. Okay.
The SCARLET CLUE Mono 1945 65m. D: Phil Rosen. SP: George
Callahan. From Earl Derr Biggers' "Charlie Chan" stories.
PH: William Sickner. Mus D: Edward Kay. Art D: David Milton.
Ref: RVB. V 4/19/45. Pic: FM 5:12. with Sidney Toler, Mantan
Moreland, Benson Fong, Virginia Brissac, Jack Norton, Robert
Homans, Ben Carter. Poison capsules exploded by radio beams;
murderer in horror-mask.
The SCARLET CRYSTAL Red Feather 1917 55m. SP: J. Grubb
Alexander. Ref: MPW 31:905. Lee. with Betty Schade, Herbert
Rawlinson. Crystal shows "scenes of horror."
SCARLET EXECUTIONER, The see BLOODY PIT OF HORROR
SCARLET HANGMAN, The see BLOODY PIT OF HORROR
The SCARLET STREAK Univ 1925 serial 10 episodes D: Henry
McRae. From the story "Dangers of the Deep" by Leigh Jacobson.
Ref: CNW. LC. with Jack Daugherty, Lola Todd, Albert J.
Smith. Ch. 4. The Death Ray. "The Scarlet Ray," "machine so
powerful its inventor felt it might put an end to all warfare."
SCARS OF DRACULA (B) EMI/Hammer 1970 color 96m. D: Roy
Ward Baker. SP: John Elder. PH: Moray Grant. Mus: James
Bernard. Ref: MFB. with Christopher Lee, Christopher Matthews,
Jenny Hanley, Michael Gwynn. Farmers march on Castle Dracula
when a girl is found dead.
SCHARLACHROTE DSCHUNKE, Die see DR. MABUSE VS. SCOT-
LAND YARD
SCHATTEN see WARNING SHADOWS
SCHIZOID see PSYCHOPATH, The
SCHLANGENGRUBE UND DAS PENDEL, Die see SNAKE PIT, The
SCHNEEWITTCHEN UND DIE SIEBEN ZWERGE see SNOW WHITE
AND ROSE RED
SCHRECKENS DES DR. RASANOFF, Das see HORROR CHAMBER
OF DR. FAUSTUS, The
SCHWARZE ABT, Der see BLACK ABBOT, The
SCHWARZE MANN, Der (novel by A. Machard) see WEREWOLF, The
(1932)
SCHWARZE PANTHER VON RATANA, Der see BLACK PANTHER OF
RATANA
SCHWEIGENDE STERN, Der see FIRST SPACESHIP ON VENUS
A SCIENTIFIC MOTHER Falstaff/Mutual 1915 Ref: MPN 5/15/15.
Motography 5/8/15. Mother brings child up scientifically: At
the age of two he's as tall as a child of ten.
The SCORPION'S STING Victor 1916 (B) 35m. (The DEVIL'S BOND-
MAN?) D: Percy Nash? Ref: MPN 13:3605. Brit.Cinema. with
George Bellamy, Fay Temple. Ex-convict sells soul to devil.
SCOTLAND YARD Fox 1930 65m. D: William K. Howard. PH: George
Schneiderman. Art D: Duncan Cramer. SP: Garrett Fort. From

the play by Denison Clift. Ref: AFI. PM: "Straining credibility
because of impossible achievements of plastic surgery. "
V 10/22/30. with Edmund Lowe, J. Carrol Naish, Arnold Lucy,
Joan Bennett, Lumsden Hare, Donald Crisp, Georges Renavent,
David Torrence, Halliwell Hobbes. French plastic surgeon uses
locket picture of English nobleman as model for new face for
crook.

SCOTLAND YARD   Fox 1941 68m. D: Norman Foster. SP: Samuel
G. Engel, John Balderston, from the play by Denison Clift. PH:
Virgil Miller. Mus D: Emil Newman. Art D: Richard Day, Lewis
Creber. Ref: V 1/8/41. with Nancy Kelly, Edmund Gwenn,
John Loder, Henry Wilcoxon, Melville Cooper, Gilbert Emery,
Lilian Bond, Leo G. Carroll, Eugene Borden, Jimmy Aubrey,
Lester Matthews, Doris Lloyd. Through plastic surgery a man
is able to masquerade as a woman's husband.

SCOTLAND YARD JAGT DR. MABUSE   see DR. MABUSE VS.
SCOTLAND YARD

SCOTLAND YARD MYSTERY   see LIVING DEAD, The (1934)

SCREAM AND SCREAM AGAIN (B) AI/Amicus 1970 Movielabcolor
94m. (SCREAMER. Die LEBENDEN DES DR. MABUSE-G.)
D: Gordon Hessler. SP: Christopher Wicking, from the novel
"The Disorientated Man" by Peter Saxon. PH: John Coquillon.
Art D: Bill Constable. Ref: V 2/11/70. with Vincent Price,
Peter Cushing, Alfred Marks, Christopher Lee, Judy Huxtable,
Uta Levka. Superhuman vampire; mad doctor perfecting system of
limb and brain transplanting. Terribly contrived and structured.
Hessler's direction is so sloppy it's hard to tell when the actors
are supposed to be funny and when they're supposed to be menac-
ing.

SCREAM OF DEATH   see LIVING COFFIN, The

SCREAM OF FEAR (B) Col/Hammer 1961 81m. (A TASTE OF
FEAR) D: Seth Holt. SP, P: Jimmy Sangster. PH: Douglas Slo-
combe. Mus: Clifton Parker. Art D: Bernard Robinson. Ref:
Orpheus 3:30. with Susan Strasberg, Ann Todd, Christopher Lee,
Ronald Lewis. Corpse keeps appearing and disappearing about
villa. Overrated shocker. Maybe one or two effective jolts.

SCREAM IN THE NIGHT   Selznick 1919 D: Burton King, Leander
De Cordova. Story: Charles A. Logue. PH: William Reinhart,
A. A. Cadwell. Ref: MPN 20:3202. Exhibitors Herald 9/20/19:
"Out of the jungle came beautiful Darwa, the victim of a crazed
scientist's Great Experiment to prove the Darwinian theory of the
origin of the human race. " with Ruth Budd, Ralph Kellard.

SCREAM OF THE DEMON LOVER (I) New World/Eureka 1970
(KILLERS OF THE CASTLE OF BLOOD. ALTAR OF BLOOD?
sfa The CASTLE WITH THE FIERY GATES?) P,D: J. L.
Merino. SP: E. Colombo. PH: E. Di Cola. Ref: Boxo. Photon
21:10. with Jeffrey Chase, Jennifer Harvey. "Matter regeneration
experiments, " disfigured killer.

SCREAMER   see SCREAM AND SCREAM AGAIN

SCREAMING   see CARRY ON SCREAMING

SCREAMING HEAD, The   see HEAD, The

The SCREAMING SHADOW Hallmark 1920 serial 15 episodes D: Duke
Worne. PH: King Gray. Ref: SilentFF. SP: Harvey Gates, J. Grubb

Alexander. Exhibitors Herald: "Founded upon the scientific discovery that the substitution of monkey glands prolongs human
life." with Ben Wilson, Neva Gerber, William Dyer, Joseph W.
Girard, William Carroll. "The Black Seven" tries to obtain the
secret of eternal life.

SCREAMING SKULL AI 1958 70m. D: Alex Nicol. SP: John
Kneubuhl. PH: Frank Crosley. Mus: Ernest Gold. Makeup:
Don Robertson. Ref: FFacts. Pic: FM 69:44. Woman terrorized
by apparitions. with John Hudson, Peggy Webber, Russ Conway,
Nicol, Toni Johnson. Unconvincingly developed melodrama, with
a few nice shock effects.

SCROOGE (B) 1901 D: Walter R. Booth. Ref: Brit. Cinema.

SCROOGE (B) Big Features 1913 50m. D: Leedham Bantock. SP:
Sir Seymour Hicks. with Hicks. From Dickens' "A Christmas
Carol."

SCROOGE (B) Para/Twickenham 1935 67m. D: Henry Edwards.
SP: H. Fowler Mear, Sir Seymour Hicks, from "A Christmas
Carol" by Charles Dickens. PH: S. Blythe, William Luff. Ref:
FDY, with Hicks, Donald Calthrop, Philip Frost, Eve Gray, Robert
Cochrane.

SCROOGE (B) 1970 Nat'l General Technicolor/scope 111m. D: Ronald
Neame. SP, Mus: Leslie Bricusse. PH: Oswald Morris. Art D:
Bob Cartwright. Prod Des: Terry Marsh. SpPhFX: Jack Mills.
SpFX: Wally Veevers. Ref: MFB. with Albert Finney, Alec
Guinness, Edith Evans, Kenneth More, Laurence Naismith, Roy
Kinnear, Mary Peach, Kay Walsh.

SE LE PASO LE MANO (Mex) Apolo Films 1952 D: Julian Soler.
PH: Jose Ramos. Mus: Jose de la Vega. Ref: Aventura. with
Abel Salazar, Mart(h)a Roth, Andrés Soler. Rejuvenation "in the
style of MONKEY BUSINESS."

The SEA BAT MGM 1930 silent and sound versions 90m. D:
Wesley Ruggles. SP: Bess Meredyth, John Howard Lawson. Titles:
Philip J. Leddy. Story: Dorothy Yost. PH: Ira Morgan. Art D:
Cedric Gibbons. Ref: AFI. with Raquel Torres, Charles Bickford,
Nils Asther, George F. Marion, John Miljan, Boris Karloff,
Gibson Gowland, Mack Swain, Edmund Breese. Native voodoo
rites, "monstrous sea bat."

The SEA HOUND Col 1947 serial 15 episodes D: Walter B. Eason,
Mack Wright. SP: G. H. Plympton, L. Clay, A. Hoerl. PH:
Ira H. Morgan. Mus D: Mischa Bakaleinikoff. Ref: The Serial.
with Buster Crabbe, James Lloyd, Pamela Blake, Robert Barron,
Hugh Prosser, Rick Vallin, Jack Ingram, Milton Kibbee, Emmet
Lynn, William Fawcett. Giant man-eating plant.

SEA RAIDERS Univ 1941 serial 13 episodes D: Ford Beebe, John Raw-
lins. SP: C. U. Young, Paul Huston, PH: William Sickner. Ref:
Showmen's 7/19/41. with Billy Halop, Huntz Hall, Bernard
Punsley, Gabe Dell, Hally Chester, Reed Hadley, Dick Alexander,
Ernie Adams, John Merton, Forrest Taylor, Eddie Parker,
House Peters, Jr. "Special type of bomb with a time device";
inventor's "torpedo boat."

The SEAL OF SOLOMON (Malayan) Shaw 1958 (AZIMAT) SP:
Rolf Bayer. PH: L. M Seong. Mus D: Dick Abel. Art D: Y. H.
Lip. Ref: FEFN 4/4/58. with Pancho Magalona, Saloma, Tita

Doran. A playboy buys a magic skin from an old man in a curio shop. Every time he makes a wish the skin shrinks and someone dies.

SEANCE DE SPIRITISME see SPIRITUALISTIC SEANCE, A (1910)

SEANCE MYSTERY, The (by N. Parker) see SINISTER HANDS

The SEARCH FOR BRIDEY MURPHY Para 1956 scope 84m. D: Noel Langley. PH: John F. Warren. Mus Sup: Irwin Talbot. P: W. Lee Wilder. Ref: TVK. FDY. From the book by Morey Bernstein. with Louis Hayward, Teresa Wright, Nancy Gates, Kenneth Tobey, Richard Anderson, Walter Kingsford. Housewife under hypnosis recalls a previous life.

SEARCH, THE SCIENTIFIC DETECTIVE Biog 1914 Ref: MPW 21:730. Lee. Hat makes wearer invisible.

The SECOND BEST SECRET AGENT IN THE WHOLE WIDE WORLD (B) Embassy/Alistair 1965 color 97m. (LICENSED TO KILL) D: Lindsay Shonteff. SP: Howard Griffiths, Shonteff. PH: Terry Maher. Mus sc & d: Bertram Chappell. Sequel: WHERE THE BULLETS FLY. Ref: SF Film. MFB'65:137. COF 10:6. with Tom Adams, Karel Stepanek, Veronica Hurst, Peter Bull, Francis De Wolff, Judy Huxtable. Plastic-surgery double; fake anti-gravity machine.

SECONDS Para 1966 106m. D: John Frankenheimer. SP: Lewis John Carlino, from the novel by David Ely. PH: James Wong Howe. Mus: Jerry Goldsmith. Art D: Ted Haworth. Ref: PM. with Rock Hudson, Salome Jens, John Randolph, Will Geer, Jeff Corey, Richard Anderson, Murray Hamilton, Khigh Dheigh, Edgar Stehli. A middle-aged man gets a second chance at life through the services of a secret organization. Episodic, though a few of the episodes are pretty powerful.

SECRET AGENT FIREBALL (I-F) AI/Devon-Radius 1965 color/scope 89m. (Lie SPIE UCCIDONO A BEIRUT) D: Martin Donan. SP: Julian Berry. PH: Richard Thierry. Mus: Carlo Savina. Ref: V 2/2/66. FD 1/5/66. with Richard Harrison, Dominique Boschero, Wandisa Guida. Ball-point laser ray.

SECRET AGENT 777 OPERATION MYSTERY (I) Protor Film 1965 (AGENTE SEGRETO 777 OPERAZIONE MISTERO) D: Henry Bay. SP: Arpad De Riso, Nino Scolaro. PH: A. Albertini. Ref: Anuario. with Mark Damon, Mary Young, Seyna Seyn, Lewis Jourdan, Stanley Kent. Prof. Keller has discovered a method for restoring the dead to life.

SECRET AGENT X-9 Univ 1937 serial 12 episodes D: Ford Beebe, Cliff Smith. SP: W. Gittens, N. S. Hall, R. Trampe, L. Swabacker. PH: Dick Fryer. Based on the comic strip. Ref: HR 11/9/36. LC. Lee: Fantasy elements. with Scott Kolk, Jean Rogers, Monte Blue, Henry Brandon, Lon Chaney, Jr., Ed Parker, Tom Steele, Eddy C. Waller. Ch. 2. The Ray that Blinds.

SECRET AGENT X-9 Univ 1945 serial D: Ray Taylor, Lewis D. Collins. SP: J. O'Donnell, H. C. Wire. Based on the comic strip. PH: M. Gertsman, E. Miller. Ref: Lee: Fantasy elements. Academy. with Lloyd Bridges, Keye Luke, Jan Wiley, Samuel S. Hinds, Benson Fong, George Lynn, Edmund Cobb, Gene Stutenroth, Mauritz Hugo, Stan Jolley, Luke Chan, George Eldredge,

John Merton, George Chesebro.
SECRET BRIDE OF CANDY ROCK, The   see THIRTY FOOT BRIDE
OF CANDY ROCK, The
SECRET FILE OF THE TELEGIAN see SECRET OF THE TELEGIAN
The SECRET KINGDOM (B) Stoll 1926 70m. SP: Alicia Ramsay.
   PH: Percy Strong. Art D: W. W. Murton. Ref: SilentFF. with
   Matheson Lang, Stella Arbenia, Lilian Oldland. Inventor's ma-
   chine enables man to read others' thoughts.
SECRET OF DR. ALUCARD, The see TASTE OF BLOOD, A
The SECRET OF DR. CHALMERS (I-Sp)Roma/Filmardis 1970
   color/scope 86m. (Il SEGRETO DEL DR. CHALMERS. L'UOMO
   CHE VISSE DUE VOLTE. TRANSPLANTE DE UN CEREBRO.
   BRAIN TRANSPLANT) SP,D: Juan Logar. SP: also G. Marcelli.
   PH: A. Modica. Mus: G. Robuschi. Art D: A. G. Sanabria. Ref:
   V 5/12/71:143. SpCinema'71. M/TVM 5/70. with Eduardo Fa-
   jardo, Silvia Dionisio, Frank Wolff, Nuria Torray, Simón Andreu.
   "Middle-aged judge whose brain has been replaced by that of a
   20-year-old goes mad."
SECRET OF DR. MABUSE (I-G-F) Manley-TV/Serena--Filmkunst--
   Criterion-Franco 1964 (I RAGGI MORTALI DEL DR. MABUSE-I.
   Les RAYONS MORTELS DU DOCTEUR MABUSE-F. DEATH RAYS
   OF DR. MABUSE. The DEVILISH DR. MABUSE? The DEATH
   RAY MIRROR OF DR. MABUSE) D: Hugo Fregonese. SP:
   Ladislas Fodor. Mus: Carlos Diernhammer. Ref: Orpheus 3:38.
   FM 22:10. DDC II:108. 394. M/TVM 10/64.9/67. with Peter Van
   Eyck, Werner Peters, Leo Genn, Yvonne Furneaux, Yoko Tani,
   O. E. Hasse. Death ray; spirit.
The SECRET OF DORIAN GRAY (G-B-I) AI/Terra-Commonwealth
   United-Sargon 1970 Movielab color 95m. (DORIAN GRAY. IO,
   DORIAN GRAY) D: Massimo Dallamano. SP: Dallamano,
   M. Co(a)scia. PH:Otello Spila. Mus: P. DeLuca, Carlos Pes.
   Art D: Maria Ambrosino. P: Harry Alan Towers. Ref: MFB.
   M/TVM 11/69. V 11/18/70. From "The Picture of Dorian
   Gray" by Oscar Wilde. with Helmut Berger, Richard Todd,
   Herbert Lom, Marie Liljedahl, Margaret Lee, Maria Rohm,
   Isa Miranda, Eleonora Rossi-Drago.
The SECRET OF FYLFOT (J) Toei 1968 scope/color (SHINOBI NO
   MANJI) D: Norifumi Suzuki. SP: Kan Saji, Ryunosuke Ono. Story:
   Futaro Yamada. PH: Juhei Suzuki. Mus: Harumi Ibe. Art D: K.
   Horiike. Ref: UFQ 40. with Isao Natsuyagi, Hiroko Sakuramachi,
   Tatsuo Endo, Kenji Ushio. "When the Shogun Tokugawa III is in
   bed with a girl, she turns into a monster. The court believes she
   is Ninja Magic, used to frighten the lord off women so that there
   will be no heirs."
The SECRET OF MY SUCCESS (B) MGM 1965 Metrocolor 105m. SP,
   D,P: Andrew Stone. P: also Virginia Stone. PH: Davis Boulton.
   Mus: Lucien Cailliet, Derek New, Joao Laurenco, C. Stone. Ref:
   MFB. with Shirley Jones, Stella Stevens, Honor Blackman, James
   Booth, Lionel Jeffries, Amy Dolby. Three spisodes, second in-
   volving "a horde of technically realistic giant spiders."--Christian
   Science Monitor.
The SECRET OF PANCHO VILLA (Mex) Luis Manrique 1954 96m.
   (El SECRETO DE PANCHO VILLA) D: Rafael Baledon. SP: Ramon

Obon. PH: A. M. Solares. Mus: S. Guerrero. Ref: Indice. FM
31:23. Pic: FM 33:10: skeleton. with Alicia Caro, Pascual
Garcia Pena, Fernando Oses, Victor Alcocer.

SECRET OF THE BLUE ROOM Univ 1933 60m. (MYSTERY OF THE
BLUE ROOM) D: Kurt Neumann. SP: William Hurlbut, from the
book by Erich Philippi. PH: Charles Stumar. Mus: Heinz Letton.
Art D: Stanley Fleischer. P: Carl Laemmle, Jr. Ref: FDY. FM
24:64. with Paul Lukas, Onslow Stevens, Edward Arnold, Russell Hopton, Elizabeth Patterson, Lionel Atwill, Gloria Stuart,
William Janney, Robert Barrat. A detective, the third person to
die in a "haunted room," died with a look of horror on his face;
windy night prompts "ghost story." Secret panel, passage,
screams, etc. Secondary mysteries distract from and complicate
the main one, which is very dull. The murderer is easy to guess
halfway through. Fun to spot the sets from other Universal horror movies. Remakes: The MISSING GUEST. MURDER IN THE
BLUE ROOM.

SECRET OF THE CHATEAU Univ 1934 67m. D: Richard Thorpe.
SP: Albert DeMond. Story: Lawrence Blockman. Continuity: Harry
Behn. PH: Robert Planck. P: Carl Laemmle, Jr., L. L. Ostrow.
Ref: FD 1/8/35. V 2/5/35. with Claire Dodd, Clark Williams,
Osgood Perkins, Alice White, Jack LaRue, George E. Stone,
DeWitt Jennings, Helen Ware, Frank Reicher, Olaf Hytten.
Ghost rumor; old legend that the tolling of a bell in an old tower
heralds death.

SECRET OF THE GOLDEN HILL (India-Tamil) Padmini 1957
(THANAMALAI RAHASYAM) D, P: B. R. Pantulu. Story: C.
Annamalai, Lakshmanan. Dial: P. Neelakantan. Ref: FEFN
8/2/57. with S. Ganesan, M. V. Kajamma (or Rajamma). Sorcerer casts spell on parents of boy reared by elephants.

The SECRET OF THE HAND (F?) Lux 1910 17m. Ref: Bios 11/17/10.
Secret Chinese society has man's hand cut off and sent to his
friends.

SECRET OF THE KING (Dan) Nordisk 1916 35m. Ref: Pictures and
the Picturegoer 6/17/16. "Mysterious ring which, separated from
the trinket it is attached to, brings certain death to the wearer.
Romantic Egyptian scenes."

SECRET OF THE LOCH (B) Gaum 1934 (The LOCH NESS
MYSTERY) D: Milton Rosmer. Story: Charles Bennett, Billie
Bristow. Technical D: J. Elder-Wills. Ref: Brit Cinema. PM.
MPH 6/16/34:82. with Seymour Hicks, Nancy O'Neil, Gibson
Gowland, Frederick Peisley, Rosamund John. A newspaperman
investigates reports of a monster in a lake in the highlands of
Scotland.

SECRET OF THE MOUNTAIN LAKE (Russ) Gala c1952 70m. D: A.
Row. Ref: MFB. with Knarik Saroyan, Romik Pagosya. Fisherman's tale visualized: Maiden ventures into lair of Mountain Fiend.

SECRET OF THE SUBMARINE American (Mutual) 1916 serial 15 episodes D: George Sargent. Ref: CNW. NYT 5/4/16. Motion Picture
Magazine '16: 86. with Juanita Hansen, Tom Chatterton, William
Tedmarsh. Inventor's secret process whereby submarine draws
oxygen from sea water and is thus able to remain submerged
indefinitely.

SECRET OF THE TELEGIAN (J) Toho 1960 color/scope 86m.
(DENSO NINGEN. SECRET FILE OF THE TELEGIAN. The
TELEGIANS) D: Jun Fukuda. SP: S. Sekizawa. PH:Kazuo Yamada.
SpFX: Eiji Tsuburaya. Ref: UFQ 9. TVFFSB. COF 4:56. SM 4:12.
Pic: FM 28:8. with Koji Tsuruta, Tadao Nakamaru, Yumi Shira-
kawa, Akihiko Hirata, Seizaburo Kawaza. A scientist turns men
into monsters by substituting electricity for blood.
SECRET OF THE WRAYDONS see CURSE OF THE WRAYDONS
SECRET OF THE YELLOW MONKS, The see TARGET FOR KILL-
ING
The SECRET OF TREASURE ISLAND Col 1938 serial D: Elmer Clif-
ton. Ass't D: Adrian Weiss. SP: G. Rosener, Clifton, G. Mer-
rick, L. Ron Hubbard. PH: Edward Linden, Herman Schopp.
SpFX: Ken Peach, Earl Bun. Ref: Barbour. Lee. Pic: TBG: of
"The Ghost." with Don Terry, Grant Withers, Hobart Bosworth
(Dr. X), William Farnum, George Rosener, Dave O'Brien, Yakima
Canutt, Gwen Gaze. Death ray.
The SECRET ORCHARD 1915 Ref: MPW 9/18/15. with Blanche Sweet.
"Personality which is the result of pre-natal influence" underlies
woman's outer personality.
The SECRET ROOM Kalem 1915 25m. D: Tom Moore. Ref: MPN
2/27/15. LC. with Moore, Marguerite Courtot, Robert Ellis. Mad
doctor plans to transfer man's soul to body of his imbecile son.
SECRET WITNESS Col 1931 (TERROR BY NIGHT) D: Thornton Free-
land. SP: Samuel Spewack, from his novel "Murder in the Gilded
Cage." PH: Robert Planck. Ref: FD 12/20/31. MPH 10/17/31.
NYT. Photoplay 12/31.2/32. with Una Merkel, William Collier,
Jr., ZaSu Pitts, Purnell Pratt, Clyde Cook(e), Paul Hurst, Nat
Pendleton, Ralf Harolde, Clarence Muse, Hooper Atchley. Trained
ape commits series of murders.
SECRET WORLD OF DR. LAO, The see 7 FACES OF DR. LAO, The
SECRETO DE LOS FRAILES AMARILLOS, El see TARGET FOR
KILLING
SECRETO DE PANCHO VILLA, El see SECRET OF PANCHO VILLA,
The
SECRETO DEL DOCTOR ORLOFF, El see DR. ORLOFF'S MONSTER
The SECRETS OF DRACULA (Fili) 1964 (Mga MANUGANG NI
DRAKULA) Ref: M/TVM 2/64:41.
SECRETS OF SEX see BIZARRE
SECRETS OF THE FRENCH POLICE RKO 1932 59m. (MYSTERIES
OF THE FRENCH POLICE) D: Edward Sutherland. SP: Samuel
Ornitz, Robert Tasker. From the book "Lost Empress" by Ornitz
and "Secrets of the Surete" by H. Ashton-Wolfe. Ref: Photoplay
1/33. script: "Terrifying spectre: tremendous car driven by hor-
rible hunched figure." Harrison's 11/19/32: "The villain puts the
heroine on a slab, pricks her arm, and starts to draw the blood
from her body, his purpose being to drain all the blood from her,
and then to cover her body with some plaster, so as to make a
statue of her, as he was shown to have done with another woman."
PH: Al Gilks. with Frank Morgan, Lucien Prival, Julia Gordon,
John Warburton, Murray Kinnell, Gregory Ratoff, Christian Rub.
Cats embalmed in cellar; parabolic mirror used to hypnotize.
SEDDOK see ATOM AGE VAMPIRE

SEE MY LAWYER Robertson-Cole 1921 70m. D: Al Christie.
SP: W. Scott Darling, from the play by Max Marcin. PH: A.
Nagy, A. Phillips. Ref: AFI. with T. Roy Barnes, Grace Darmond, Lloyd Whitlock, Eugenie Ford, Jean Acker. Formula "produces an indestructible paving block."

The SEED OF MAN (I) S.R.L. /Polifilm 1969 101m. (Il SEME DELL'
UOMO) SP, D: Marco Ferreri (or Ferrari). SP: also Sergio
Bazzini. PH: Mario Vulpiani. Mus: Teo Usuelli. Ref: Ital P'69.
with Marco Margine, Anne Wiazemsky, Annie Girardot. Warfare
and plague devastate earth.

SEGRETO DEI FRATI GIALLI, Il see TARGET FOR KILLING

SEGRETO DEL DR. CHALMERS, Il see SECRET OF DR. CHAL-
MERS, The

SEI DONNE PER L'ASSASSINO see BLOOD AND BLACK LACE

SEKAI DAI SENSO see FINAL WAR, The

SELECTIONS FROM KOIZUMI YAGUMO see KWAIDAN

SELTSAME GESCHICTE DES BRANDNER KASPAR, Die see STRANGE
STORY OF BRANDNER KASPAR, The

SEME DELL'UOMO, Il see SEED OF MAN, The

SEÑORA LLAMADA ANDRES, Una see LADY CALLED ANDREW, A

SENORA MUERTE, La see MRS. DEATH

SENSACIONAL Y EXTRANO CASO DE EL HOMBRE Y LA BESTIA
see MAN AND THE BEAST, The

SEPT CHATEAUX DU DIABLE, Les see 7 CASTLES OF THE
DEVIL, The

SERENADE FOR TWO SPIES (W.G.-I) Modern Art /Metheus 1965
color /scope 87m. (SERENADE FUR ZWEI SPIONE-G.) SP, D:
Michael Pfleghar. SP: also Klaus Munro. From a book by K. H.
Günther. PH: Ernst Wild. Ref: MFB '68:183. with Hel(l)mut
Lange, Tony Kendall, Barbara Lass. Laser gun stolen and re-
trieved.

SERGEANT DEADHEAD, THE ASTRONAUT AI 1965 Pathecolor /
scope 89m. D: Norman Taurog. SP: Louis M. Heyward. PH: Floyd
Crosby. Mus: Les Baxter. Ref: V 8/11/65. with Frankie Avalon,
Deborah Walley, Cesar Romero, Fred Clarke, Gale Gordon,
Buster Keaton, Eve Arden, Reginald Gardiner, Harvey Lembeck,
Pat Buttram, John Ashley, Donna Loren, Romo Vincent, Bobbi
Shaw, Patti Chandler, Salli Sachse, Luree Holmes, Mary Hughes.
Orbiting in missile alters soldier's personality. Embarrasingly bad
at times; routinely bad the rest of the time.

SERPENT GOD, The see GOD SNAKE, The

SERPENT ISLAND Medallion-TV 1954 65m. D?, P: Bert Gordon.
Ref: TVFFSB. TVG. with Sonny Tufts, Mary Munday. Treasure
hunters in the Caribbean witness voodoo rites and a fight with a
giant snake.

SERPENT MAN, The see SNAKE MAN, The

The SERPENTS Vita 1912 17m. Ref: MPW 12:316. Lee. with
Ralph Ince, Edith Storey, Helen Gardner. Story of cave men.

The SEQUEL TO THE DIAMOND FROM THE SKY American (Mutual)
1916 serial 4 episodes D: Edward Sloman. Ref: MPN 14:3863.
CNW. with William Russell, Charlotte Burton, William Tedmarsh.

SERVICE SECRET see LICENSE TO KILL

SETTE NANI ALLA RISCOSSA see 7 DWARFS TO THE RESCUE, The

SETTING BACK THE HANDS OF TIME (F) Pathe 8m. Ref: Bios
3/3/10. Professor discovers powder which makes people and
objects "young." 1909

SETU BANDHAN (India) Hindustani Film Co. 1932 Ref: The Lighthouse 8/21/37. P,D: D. Phalke. Ocean bridge constructed.

The 7 CASTLES OF THE DEVIL (F) 1901 (Les SEPT CHATEAUX
DU DIABLE) D: Ferdinand Zecca. Ref: Mitry II. DDC II:382.
Orpheus 2:20: 1920's?

The 7 DWARFS TO THE RESCUE (I) Childhood/Victor 1950 ('65-
U.S.) 84m. (SETTE NANI ALLA RISCOSSA. SNOW WHITE PRIN-
CESS) SP,D,P: P. W. Tamburella. PH: Aldo Giordani. Ref: La
Production Italienne '50/'51. with Georges Marchal, Rossana
Podesta, Roberto Risso, Ave Ninchi. Evil prince of darkness,
spells.

The 7 FACES OF DR. LAO   MGM 1964 color 100m. (The SECRET
WORLD OF DR. LAO) D, P: George Pal. SP: Charles Beaumont,
from Charles G. Finney's novel "The Circus of Dr. Lao." PH:
Robert Bronner. Mus: Leigh Harline. Art D: George W. Davis,
Gabriel Scognamillo. SpVisualFX: Paul Byrd, Wah Chang, Jim
Danforth, Ralph Rodine, Robert R. Hoag. Makeup: William Tuttle.
Ref: FFacts. FM 13:10. 29:53. 49:44. with Tony Randall (Medusa,
Pan, Dr. Lao, etc.), Barbara Eden, Arthur O'Connell, John
Ericson, Noah Beery, Jr., Lee Patrick, Minerva Urecal, John
Qualen, Royal Dano, John Doucette, Frank Cady, Douglas Fowley.
Travelling circus with seer, magician, sea serpent, etc., visits
the town of Abalone. Several of Randall's best roles; good effects.

SEVEN FOOTPRINTS TO SATAN F Nat 1929 60m. silent & synchro-
nized sound versions D: Ben Christensen. SP: Richard Bee. Titles:
William Irish. From the novel by A. A. Merritt. PH:Sol Polito.
Ed: Frank Ware. P: Richard Rowland. Ref: AFI. FDY. Photoplay.
FM-A'62:31. COF 16:31. Pic: FM 23:76. 66:22. COF 17:24. 6:33.
with Thelma Todd, Creighton Hale, William V. Mong, Sheldon
Lewis, Sojin, DeWitt Jennings, Harry Tenbrook, Angelo Rossitto.
Gorillas, dwarfs, sliding panels, "weird characters."

7 KEYS TO BALDPATE Artcraft 1917 D: Hugh Ford. From the
book by Earl Derr Biggers. Ref: MPN 16:1856. with Elda Furry,
Joseph Smiley, Purnell Pratt, George Cohan.

7 KEYS TO BALDPATE Para 1925 85m. SP: Wade Boteler,
Frank Griffin. From Biggers' book and the play by George
M. Cohan. PH: Jack MacKenzie. D: Fred Newmeyer.
Ref: AFL FD 11/8/25: "Thrills, scares." NYT
11/3/25: "Haunted house." with Edith Roberts, William Orlamond,
Crauford Kent, Anders Randolf, Ned Sparks, Wade Boteler,
Fred Kelsey, Douglas MacLean. From Biggers' book.

7 KEYS TO BALDPATE RKO 1929 80m. sound. Art D: Max
Ree. D: Reginald Barker. SP: Jane Murfin. From the play by
by George M. Cohan and the book by Earl Derr Biggers. PH:
Edward Cronjager. Ref: AFI. FDY. Pic: Pict Hist Talkies. with
Richard Dix, Miriam Seegar, Lucien Littlefield, Margaret
Livingston, DeWitt Jennings, Crauford Kent, Nella Walker.
"Haunted" hotel.

7 KEYS TO BALDPATE RKO 1935 80m. D: William Hamilton,
Edward Kelly. SP: Anthony Veiller, Wallace Smith, from the play

by George M. Cohan and the book by Earl Derr Biggers. PH:
Robert de Grasse. Ref: LC. FD 11/30/35: "Author comes to the
closed Baldpate Inn for quiet, only to find the place run over with
crooks and spooks." with Eric Blore, Gene Raymond, Emma Dunn,
Grant Mitchell, Margaret Callahan, Moroni Olson, Harry Beresford, Henry Travers, Erin O'Brien-Moore, Walter Brennan,
Murray Alper, Philip Morris.

7 KEYS TO BALDPATE RKO 1947 68m. D: Lew Landers. SP:
Lee Loeb. Based on Biggers' book. PH: Jack MacKenzie. Mus
sc: Paul Sawtell. Art D: Albert S. D'Agostino, L. O. Croxton.
Ref: RVB. with Phillip Terry, Jacqueline White, Eduardo Cian-
nelli, Margaret Lindsay, Arthur Shields, Jimmy Conlin, Richard
Powers, Jason Robards.

SEVEN MEN (novel by M. Beerbohm) see DEATH IN THE HAND
SEVEN MYSTERIES (J) Shintoho 1957 (KAIDAN-HONJO NANA
FUSHIGI. GHOST STORY OF WANDERER AT HONJO) D: Goro
Katono. SP: O. Hayashi, N. Akasaka. PH:H. Suzuki. Ref: FEFN
7/12/57. Unij Bltn 31. with H. Hayashi, J. Akechi. S.
Amachi. "Ghost story...Chief ghost turns into a badger when
cornered and helps a warrior's son avenge the death of his
father."

The SEVEN REVENGES (I) Embassy/Adelphia/Fryd 1963 color Ref:
COF 6:51. 7:58. V 6/13/61. with Ed Fury, Elaine Stewart.
Monster.

The SEVEN SWANS Para 1917 D: J. Searle Dwaley. From the fairy
tale by Hans Christian Andersen. Ref: FIR'64:624. with Marguerite Clark, Richard Barthelmess, William Danforth. Evil witch
casts spell over seven swans.

The SEVENTH SEAL Janus (Swedish) 1957 105m. (Det SJUNDE
INSEGLET) Ref: COF 1:56. TVG. SP, D: Ingmar Bergman. PH:
Gunnar Fischer. Mus: Eric Nordgren. with Max von Sydow, Gunnar Bjornstrand, Bengt Ekerot (Death), Nils Poppe, Bibi Andersson, Inga Gill, Maud Hansson (witch). Returning home from the
crusades during the Middle Ages, a knight meets the figure of
Death. "Masterpiece"--Jacques Demy, Eric Rohmer. One of
Bergman's better movies--there is actually a little life to a few
scenes--but by no stretch of imagination could it be called good.

The SEVENTH VICTIM RKO 1943 71m. D: Mark Robson. SP:
DeWitt Bodeen, Charles O'Neal. PH: Nicholas Musuraca. Mus:
Roy Webb. P: Val Lewton. Ref: COF 11:57. with Tom Conway,
Jean Brooks, Isabel Jewell, Kim Hunter, Evelyn Brent, Hugh
Beaumont, Chef Milani, Wally Brown, Elizabeth Russell, Erford
Gage, Ben Bard, Feodor Chaliapin, Mary Newton. A girl encounters devil-worshippers in New York City. SEVENTH VICTIM
almost successfully unites the separate strains of horror and
melodrama in the Lewton series, and the last chilling, numbing
scene does unite them, briefly, in what is perhaps the most effective instance of suggested horror in any Lewton movie. There
is the usual quota of lines to make you flinch, and the leads are
dull, but for once the moodiness (here mainly talk about failure
and unhappiness) is integral to the horror. Jean Brooks is not
one of the dull leads, and her attractively melancholic "presence"
dominates.

The 7th VOYAGE OF SINBAD Col/Morningside 1958 Technicolor
89m. D: Nathan Juran. SP: Kenneth Kolb. PH: Wilkie Cooper.
Mus: Bernard Herrmann. Art D: Gil Parrendo. SpFX: Ray
Harryhausen. P: Charles H. Schneer. Ref: Clarens. FM 23:8.
ModM 4:13. with Kerwin Mathews, Kathryn Grant, Richard Eyer,
Torin Thatcher, Virgilio Teixeira. Sinbad vs. Cyclops, roc,
dragon, skeleton, etc. Better-than-average Harryhausen. The non-
animation scenes are awkwardly directed by Juran.

SEVENTH WONDER OF SINBAD see LOST WORLD OF SINBAD, The
SEX KITTENS GO TO COLLEGE see BEAUTY AND THE ROBOT
SEX MANIAC see MANIAC
SEX MONSTER see WRESTLING WOMEN VS. THE MURDERING
ROBOT, The
SEX RITUALS OF THE OCCULT Occult Films 1971 Ref: RVB:
Horror. color Ref: Boxo 9/13/71: E-7
SEXO FUERTE, El see STRONGER SEX, The
SEXTON BLAKE: THE JEWEL THIEVES (F) Gaum 1909 Ref: Bios
3/24/10. "Weird looking place"; secret chamber; "revolver
actuated by a timepiece."
SEXTUPLETS DE LOCQMARIA, Les (by M. Labry) see DON'T
PLAY WITH MARTIANS
SEXY PARTY see DEATH ON THE FOUR POSTER
SEXY PROBITISSIMO see FORBIDDEN FEMININITY
SEXY-SUPER INTERDIT see FORBIDDEN FEMININITY
SFIDA DE KING KONG, La see WHITE PONGO
SFIDA DEI GIGANTI, La see CHALLENGE OF THE GIANT, The
SH! THE OCTOPUS WB 1937 D: William McGann. SP: George
Bricker. PH: Arthur Todd. From a play by Ralph Murphy and
Donald Gallager. Ref: FD 12/28/37. with Hugh Herbert, Allen
Jenkins, John Eldredge, Marcia Ralston, George Rosener. "De-
serted lighthouse, trap doors, octopus that kills, eerie lights,
hidden death ray."
SHABBY TIGER see MASQUERADE
The SHADOW (B) Globe 1933 ('36-U.S.) 63m. D: George A. Cooper.
SP: H. Fowler Mear, Terrance Egan. PH: Sydney Blythe. Story:
Donald Stuart. Ref: FD 6/27/36. Brit Cinema. with Elizabeth
Allan, Reggie Ogen, Henry Kendall. Masked, cloaked killer
skulks around old dark house shooting people before they reveal
his name.
The SHADOW Col 1940 serial 15 episodes D: James W. Horne. SP:
J. Poland, N. Dandy, J. O'Donnell. From the "Shadow" radio
show and "Shadow Magazine" stories by Maxwell Grant. PH: James
S. Brown, Jr. Ref: Barbour. MPH 12/16/39. 1/13/40. Pic:
STI 3:47. FanMo 6:46-7. with Victor Jory, Veda Ann Borg,
Roger Moore, Robert Fiske, J. Paul Jones, Jack Ingram. "The
Black Tiger," villain, speaks through electrified head of cat
statuette.
SHADOW CREEPS, The see PHANTOM CREEPS, The
SHADOW OF CHINATOWN Victory 1936 serial & 65-minute feature
(YELLOW PHANTOM) D: Robert F. Hill. SP: I. Bernstein, B.
Dickey. Author: Rock Hawkey. Dial: W. Buchanan. PH: Bill Hyer.
Sets: Fred Preble. P: Sam Katzman. Ref: RVB. STI 1:18. COF
12:59. MFB 6/30/37. with Bela Lugosi, Herman Brix (aka

Bruce Bennett), George Brent?, Joan Barclay, Luana Walters,
Charles King, Forrest Taylor, George Chan. Mad scientist, slid-
ing panels, trap doors, long distance hypnotism by means of a
machine, "control of personality."
SHADOW OF EVIL (F-I) 7A/P.A.C. --C.I.C.C. /DaMa 1964 color/
scope 115m. SP,D: André Hunnebelle. SP: also Pierre Foucaud,
R. Borel, M. Lebrun, R. Caron, P. Rondard. PH:Raymond
Lemoigne. Based on the novel "Lila de Calcutta" by Jean Bruce.
Mus: Michel Magne. Art D: René Moulaert. (BANCO A BANG-
KOK POUR O.S.S. 117) Ref: MFB'66:184. with Kerwin Mathews,
Robert Hossein, (Anna Maria) Pierangeli. Organization intent
on wiping out masses with plague spread by rats.
The SHADOW OF THE BAT (Mex) 1966 Vergara (La SOMBRA DEL
MURCIELAGO) D: Federico Curiel. SP: Jesus Velazquez. Ref:
Lee. Pic: FM 67:55. with Blue Demon, Jaime Fernandez, Martha
Romero, Jesus Velazquez.
The SHADOW OF THE CAT (B) Univ/BHP 1961 79m. D: John Gilling.
SP: George Baxt. PH: Arthur Grant. Mus: Mikis Theodorakis.
Art D: Bernard Robinson. Ref: FM 47:62. ModM 3:30. with Andre
Morell, Barbara Shelley, Freda Jackson, William Lucas, Alan
Wheatley, Catherine Lacey, Vanda Godsell, Kynaston Reeves.
Woman's murder seen through eyes of cat.
SHADOW OF THE EAGLE   Mascot 1932 serial SP,D: Ford Beebe.
SP: also C. Clark, W. Gittens. PH: Benjamin Kline, V. Scheurich.
Ref: SF Film. Next Time. with John Wayne, Dorothy Gulliver,
Edward Hearn, Walter Miller, Pat O'Malley, Edmund Burns, Ivan
Linow, Ernie S. Adams, Roy D'Arcy, Bud Osborne, Yakima
Canutt. Anti-aircraft ray.
The SHADOW OF THE EAST Fox 1924 75m. D: George Archainbaud.
Ref: MPN 29:757. Lee. with Frank Mayo, Norman Kerry, Evelyn
Brent, Joseph Swickard. SP: F. & F. Hatton. Spectre of Indian
girl haunts man.
SHADOW ON THE LAND ABC-TV/Screen Gems 1968 color (U.S.)
D: Richard C. Sarafian. SP:Nedrick Young. Created by: Sidney
Sheldon. PH: Fred Koenekamp. Mus: Sol Kaplan. Ref: RVB. TVG.
with Jackie Cooper, John Forsythe, Carol Lynley, Janice Rule,
Gene Hackman, Marc Strange, Myron Healey. ISF, a CIA-type
organization which seized power during a national emergency, plans
to take over complete power in the U.S. in the event of another
emergency. Confused. Tries to mix the topical and the futuristic
with action and trite drama.
SHADOW OVER INNSMOUTH, The (by H. P. Lovecraft) see HAUNT-
ED PALACE, The
SHADOW VS. THE 1000 EYES OF DR. MABUSE, The see
THOUSAND EYES OF DR. MABUSE, The
A SHADOWED SHADOW Joker 1916 SP: Jack Byrne. Ref: MPN
14:2869,3498. Fake ghosts.
SHADOWS IN THE NIGHT Col 1944 67m. D: Eugene Forde. SP:
Eric Taylor. From the "Crime Doctor" radio show. PH: James
S. Brown, Jr. Art D: John Datu. Ref: MPH 8/5/44. with
Warner Baxter, Nina Foch, George Zucco, Minor Watson, Edward
Norris, Charles Halton, Jeanne Bates, Lester Matthews, Charles
Wilson. "Stormy, eerie night"; hypnotic gas that makes woman

walk in her sleep; "haunting apparitions."

SHAIL BALA (India) Ranjit 1932 Ref: Sound & Shadow 8/32. with Miss Gohar, Bhagwandas. Guru's black magic causes deaths of children.

SHAME (Swedish) Svensk/Cinematograph 1968 94m. (SKAMMEN) SP, D: Ingmar Bergman. PH: Sven Nykvist. Ed: Ulla Ryghe. Ref: V. PM. with Liv Ullmann, Max von Sydow, Gunnar Bjornstrand, Hans Alfredson, Sigge Furst. In 1971 a couple takes refuge on an island from a civil war on the mainland. Bergman tries to make a movie again, ends up with another closet drama that should have stayed in the closet. His films aren't "deep"; it just seems that they must be since they have nothing on the surface.

SHAME ON YOU (Egyptian) Studio Guiza 1953 (HARAM ALEK) D: Issa Karama. Ref: Ciné Nouvelles 9/55:43. Cinema in the Arab Countries. with Ismail Yassine. Comedy with a Frankenstein-monster-type, a mummy and a werewolf.

SHAN-E-KHUDA (India) Bhavnani 1934 (SAIR-E-PARISTAN) Ref: Moving Picture Monthly 5/34:3. with Miss Bibbo, Master Nisar, S. Nayampally, P. Jairaj. Monster.

SHANKAR-PARVATI (India-Hindustani) Ranjit 1944 Story, D: Chaturbbuj Doshi. Dial, Songs: Pandit Indra. PH: D. K. Ambre. Mus: Jnan Dutt. Art D: S. A. Wahab. Ref: Filmindia 4/44. with Kamla Chatterjee, Sadhona Bose, Aroon. Tarakasur, a demon in Hindu mythology, can only be destroyed by someone born explicitly for that purpose.

SHAPE OF THINGS TO COME (by H. G. Wells) see THINGS TO COME

SHARAD OF ATLANTIS see UNDERSEA KINGDOM, The

SHE Edison 1908 17m. From the book by H. Rider Haggard. Ref: F Index 11/14/08.

SHE Than 1911 30m. From the novel by H. Rider Haggard. Ref: MPW 10:598. with James Cruze, Marguerite Snow.

SHE (B) Barker 1916 D: Lisle Lucoque. SP: Nellie E. Lucoque. From the Haggard novel. Ref: Hist Brit Cinema. Brit. Cinema. with Alice Delysia, Henry Victor, Jack Denton, Sidney Bland, Blanche Forsythe.

SHE Fox 1917 60m. D: Kenean Buel. SP: Mary Murillo. From Haggard's novel. Ref: MPW 32:354, 679. with Valesha Suratt.

SHE (B) Lee-Bradford/Samuelson 64m. D: Leander Cordova. SP: Walter Summers. From Haggard's novel. PH: Sidney Blythe. Art D: Heinrich Richter. Ref: SilentFF. NYT 5/25/25:21. Pic: COF 7:55. Brit Cinema. with Betty Blythe, Carlyle Blackwell, Marjorie Statler. The white queen of an African race possesses the secret of eternal youth. 1925

SHE RKO 1935 95m. D: Irving Pichel, Lansing Holden. SP: Dudley Nichols, Ruth Rose. Lansing Holden. From Haggard's novel. PH: J. Roy Hunt. P: Merian C. Cooper. Ref: FDY. COF 7:55. with Randolph Scott, Nigel Bruce, Helen Gahagan, Helen Mack, Gustav von Seyffertitz, Samuel S. Hinds, Noble Johnson, Lumsden Hare.

SHE (B) MGM/7A-Hammer 1965 Metrocolor/scope 106m. D: Robert Day. SP: David Chantler, from the novel by H. Rider Haggard. PH: Harry Waxman. Mus: James Bernard. Art D: Robert Jones. SpFX: Bowie Films Ltd. Ref: FDY. PM: Magic fire of immortality, lost kingdom. with Ursula Andress, Christopher Lee, Peter Cushing, Bernard Cribbins, John Richardson, Andre Morell. Lumbering spectacle. Hammer at its biggest and dullest.

SHE (by H. R. Haggard) see COLUMN OF FIRE/MALIKA SALOMI/ VENGEANCE OF SHE

SHE BEAST (I-Yugoslav) Europix/Leith 1965 74m. (La SORELLA DI SATANA. SATAN'S SISTER. REVENGE OF THE BLOOD BEAST-Eng.) D: Mike Reeves. SP: Michael Byron. PH: G. Gengareli. Mus: Ralph Ferraro. Ref: FFacts. MMF. RFB. Boxo 7/25/66. F&F 11/66. with Barbara Steele, John Karlsen, Jay Riley, Richard Watson, Mel Welles, Ian Ogilvy. She beast restored to life after 200 years at bottom of lake.

SHE CREATURE AI 1957 77m. D: Edward L. Cahn. SP: Lou Rusoff. PH: Frederick E. West. Mus: Ronald Stein. Art D: Don Ament. P: Alex Gordon. Remake: CREATURES OF DESTRUC-TION. Ref: FDY. with Marla English, Chester Morris, Tom Conway, Cathy Downs, Lance Fuller, Frieda Inescort, Ron Randell, Jack Mulhall, Paul Blaisdell, Frank Jenks, Bill Hudson, El Brendel, Paul Dubov. Sideshow hypnotist, with assistant's aid, can call prehistoric monster up from sea. Veteran actors Morris and Conway make the most of their scenes together, and the film isn't so bad that it deserves a Buchanan remake.

SHE DEMONS Astor/Screencraft 1958 77m, Sp, D: Richard Cunha. SP: also H. E. Barrie. PH: Meredith Nicholson. Mus: N. Carras. SpFX: David Koehler. Makeup: Carlie Taylor. Prod Man: Ralph Brooke. Assoc P: Marc Frederic. Ref: FFacts. with Irish Mccalla, Tod Griffin, Victor Sen Yung, Gene Roth. Party shipwrecked on island encounters escaped Nazi war criminal experimenting in scar tissue replacement. Par for Astor; i.e, abominable.

SHE DEVIL Fox/Regal 1957 77m. SP, D, P: Kurt Neumann. SP: also Carroll Young. From "The Adaptive Ultimate" by John Jessel. PH: Karl Stuuss. Mus: Paul Sawtell, Bert Shefter. Ref: FDY. FM 52:13. with Mari Blanchard, Jack Kelly, Albert Dekker, John Archer, Blossom Rock, Paul Cavanagh. A tuberculosis victim is injected with a serum which makes her indestructible. Lesser Neumann. Prod Des: Theobold Holsopple. Makeup: Louis Hippe. also with X. Brands, Tod Griffin. Regalscope. Unpalatable mixture of s-f, soap opera, and predestination ("She was meant to die"). An impossible script: situations, characterizations, and lines are all awkward. But it's pointless to worry about each little thing when everything's wrong.

SHE FREAK Crest/Sonney-Friedman 1967 color 87m. (ALLEY OF NIGHTMARES) Ed, D: Byron Mabe. Sp, P: David Friedman. PH: Bill Troiano. Mus: Billy Allen. Makeup: Harry Thomas. Ref: COF 12:7. B. Warren. LAT 10/14/67. with Claire Brennan, Lee Raymond, Lynn Courtney. Ending a la FREAKS.

SHE SHALL HAVE MUSIC (B) Twickenham 1935 D: Leslie Hiscott. Ref: SF Film. with Claude Dampier. TV wristwatch.

The SHE-WOLF (Mex) Sotomayor 1964 (La LOBA. Los HORRORS DEL BOSQUE NEGRO) D: Rafael Baledon. SP: Ramón Obón. PH: Raul M. Solares. Mus: Raul Lavista. Ref: Indice. COF 8:48. Pic: FM 57:11. with Kitty de Hoyos, Joaquin Cordero, Jose Elias

Moreno, Crox Alvarado, Roberto Cañedo, Ramon Bugarini. Werewolf.

SHE-WOLF OF LONDON Univ 1946 61m. (The CURSE OF THE ALLENBYS-Eng.) D: Jean Yarbrough. SP: George Bricker. Story: Dwight V. Babcock. PH: Maury Gertsman. Mus D: William Lava. Art D: Jack Otterson, Abraham Grossman. Ed: Paul Landres. Ref: FDY. MFB'47:113. Pic: MadM 10:40. with June Lockhart, Don Porter, Lloyd Corrigan, Martin Kosleck, Sara Haden, Eily Malyon, Dennis Hoey, Frederic(k) Worlock. Girl convinced she is wolf-woman. Dull, totally undistinguished.

SHE-WOLVES see DEMONIAQUE

SHEIKH CHILLI (India-Hindi) Jyoti 1956 152m. D: R. Thakur. SP: Dhananjay. Dial: P. Indra. PH: D. Dadich. Mus: Vinod. Ref: FEFN 8/3/56. with Shyama, Bhagwan. Barber's uncle, turned into donkey by curse, finds he has supernatural powers.

SHER-E-JUNGLE see ZAMBO THE APE MAN

SHERLOCK HOLMES Ess 1916 80m. D: Arthur Berthelet. SP: H. S. Sheldon. From the play by William Gillette. Ref: MPN 13:3268. with Gillette, Marjorie Kay, Ernest Maupain, Edward Fielding.

SHERLOCK HOLMES Goldwyn 1922 D: Albert Parker. SP: Marion Fairfax. From the play by William Gillette, stories by Sir Arthur Conan Doyle. Ref: MPN 25:2880. with John Barrymore, Roland Young, Carol Dempster, Hedda Hopper, Gustav von Seyffertitz, William H. Powell, Reginald Denny, David Torrence, Lumsden Hare, Louis Wolheim. "Terrifying climax--with lights and shadows, secret panels, dark stairways."

SHERLOCK HOLMES (play by W. Gillette) see ADVENTURES OF SHERLOCK HOLMES, The

SHERLOCK HOLMES AND THE SECRET WEAPON Univ 1942 68m. (SHERLOCK HOLMES FIGHTS BACK) D: Roy William Neill. SP: Edward T. Lowe, Edmund L. Hartmann, W. Scott Darling. PH: Les White. Mus D: Charles Previn. Art D: Jack Otterson. From "The Adventure of the Dancing Men" by Sir Arthur Conan Doyle. Ref: FDY. with Basil Rathbone, Lionel Atwill, Nigel Bruce, Holmes Herbert, Kaaren Verne, Dennis Hoey, Mary Gordon, Paul Fix, Philip Van Zandt. "Secret bomb sight."-TVG. Routine.

SHERLOCK HOLMES AND THE SPIDER WOMAN see SPIDER WOMAN, The

SHERLOCK HOLMES BAFFLED AM&B 1903 Ref: Niver. Orpheus 4:61. Man disappears, reappears magically.

SHERLOCK HOLMES FACES DEATH Univ 1943 68m. D, P: Roy William Neill. SP: Bertram Millhauser, from "The Musgrave Ritual" by Sir Arthur Conan Doyle. PH: Charles Van Enger. Mus D: H. J. Salter. Art D: John B. Goodman, Harold MacArthur. Ref: FDY. FIR'68:463. with Basil Rathbone, Nigel Bruce, Dennis Hoey, Halliwell Hobbes, Milburn Stone, Gavin Muir, Olaf Hytten, Frederic(k) Worlock, Mary Gordon, Peter Lawford. "Who first shall find it better were dead/Who next shall find it perils his head/The last to find it defies dark powers." Fairly intriguing plot, some humor--and determined attempts at atmosphere: A clock strikes 12 or 13 every few minutes or so.

SHERLOCK HOLMES FIGHTS BACK see SHERLOCK HOLMES AND
  THE SECRET WEAPON
SHERLOCK HOLMES IN THE GREAT MURDER MYSTERY (Dan)
  Crescent 1908 From Edgar Allan Poe's story "Murders in the
  Rue Morgue" and the "Sherlock Holmes" stories by Sir Arthur
  Conan Doyle. Ref: The Film Index. Orpheus 4:61. Pic: Pict
  Hist Cinema. In a trance Sherlock Holmes discovers a murderer
  to be a gorilla.
SHIBIJIN MANSION (J) Daiei 1954 (SHIBIJIN YASHIKI) D: Ryohei
  Arai. Ref: Unij Bltn 31: ghost story. with Yataro Kurokawa,
  Kazuko Fushimi.
The SHIELDING SHADOW Astra/Pathe 1916 serial 15 episodes
  D: Louis Gasnier, Donald Mackenzie. SP: George B. Seitz.
  Ref: MPN 14:1724. Lee. with Grace Darmond, Ralph Kellard,
  Leon Bary. Shadow "with burning eyes" that protects heroine;
  hypnotism; cloak of invisibility.
SHIKARI (India) 1964 Eastmancolor Ref: Shankar's 1/12/64.
  with K. N. Singh, Ajit, Ragini, Helen. A doctor creates a
  "King Kong" (or "Dracula") with the aid of drugs and chemicals.
  It kills many and destroys villages /before it is stopped.
SHINOBI NO MANJI see SECRET OF FYLFOT, The
SHINPAN YOTSUYA KAIDAN see YOTSUYA GHOST STORY NEW
  EDITION
The SHIP OF THE MONSTERS (Mex) Sotomayor 1959 (La NAVE
  DE LOS MONSTRUOS) D: Rogelio Gonzalez. SP: J. M. F. Un-
  sain, A. Varela. PH: Raul M. Solares. Mus: S. Guerrero. Ref:
  Indice. Pic: FM 17:17, 30. FanMo 4:48. with Lalo Gonzalez, Ana
  Berthe Lepe, Lorena Velazquez, "Piporro." "Spider creature,"
  robot with "flame ray."
SHIPPU! KURAMA TENGU see HURRY! KURAMA!
SHOCK Fox 1946 70m. D: Alfred Werker. SP: Eugene King.
  Story: Albert DeMond. Add'l Dial: Martin Berkeley. PH: Glen
  McWilliams, Joe MacDonald. Mus: David Buttolph. SpFX: Fred
  Sersen. Ref: FM 25:16. FDY. with Vincent Price, Lynn Bari,
  Reed Hadley, Charles Trowbridge, Renee Carson, Pierre Watkin,
  Selmer Jackson. Man attempts to destroy woman's mind with
  drugs and hypnotism. Grade-Z melodrama, a composite of bits
  and pieces of several familiar Z plots. Really dull.
SHOCK see CREEPING UNKNOWN, The
SHONEN TANTEIDAN see BOY DETECTIVES, The
SHONEN TANTEIDAN-KABUTOMUSHI NO YOKI & TETTO NO
  KAIJIN see TWENTY FACES
SHOOTING IN THE HAUNTED WOODS (F) Gaum 1909 Ref: MPW
  6:65. Dream.
The SHOW MGM 1927 D: Tod Browning. SP: Waldemar Young.
  from the novel "The Day of Souls" by Charles T. Jackson. Ed:
  Errol Taggart. Ref: FDY. Photoplay 4/27: "Strange and deadly
  reptile resembling a gila monster." FM 22:41. with John Gil-
  bert, Renee Adoree. "The Spider Woman," "the living arm of
  Cleopatra," "the Half Woman," "the Bodiless Head."
SHREE GANESH JANMA (India) K Pictures 1951 D: Jayant Desai.
  SP: B. Shukla. Mus: M. Dey, K. Prakash. Ref: Filmcritic
  8/51. with Trilok Kapur, Ulhas, Nirupa Roy, A. Shah. The god

Shiva beheads Kumar, his son. Bhagwan replaces Kumar's head with the head and trunk of an elephant and brings him back to life.

A SHRIEK IN THE NIGHT Allied/M. H. Hoffman 1933 65m. D: Albert Ray. SP: Frances Hyland. Story: Kurt Kempler. PH: Harry Neumann, Tom Galligan. Ed: L. R. Brown. Ref: FDY. FIR'68:127. Harrison's 6/17/33: "Spooky situations." Photoplay 6/33. V 7/25/33: "Melo trick consists of having the murder victim's screams burst out at frequent intervals." V 3/17/33. with Lyle Talbot, Purnell Pratt, Harvey Clark, Arthur Hoyt, Louise Beavers, Clarence Wilson.

The SHRINE OF SEVEN LAMPS (B) Stoll 1923 20m. (Mystery of Dr. Fu-Manchu series) SP: A. E. Coleby, Frank Wilson. PH: D. P. Cooper. From the stories by Sax Rohmer. Ref: SilentFF. with Harry Agar Lyons, Fred Paul, Humbertson Wright, Joan Clarkson.

SHRINKING MAN, The (novel by R. Matheson) see INCREDIBLE SHRINKING MAN, The

SHUK RAMBHA (India) Desai/Patel 1953 D: Dhirubhai Desai. SP: K. R. Brahmbhat, D. K. Kane. Dial: V. Mehrotra. Mus: M. Dey. Ref: Filmfare 6/12/53. with Anjali Devi, Bharat Bhushan, Raj Kumar, Dilip. "Immortal" parrot cursed to be born as mortal.

SHUKAN ASAHI (story by S. Nakamura) see MOTHRA

The SHUTTERED ROOM (B) 7A/Troy-Schenck 1967 Technicolor 99m. D: David Greene. SP: D. B. Ledrov, Nathaniel Tanchuck, from a story by H. P. Lovecraft and August Derleth. PH: Ken Hodges. Mus sc: Basil Kirchin. Art D: Brian Eatwell. Ref: MFB'67:109. HR 1/23/68. Pic: FM 46:19. with Gig Young, Carol Lynley, Oliver Reed, Flora Robson, Charles Lloyd Pack, Bernard Kay. Unseen presence watches intruders from its cage.

SHUZENJI MONOGATARI see MASK OF DESTINY, The

SI TUTTE LE DONNE DEL MONDO see KISS THE GIRLS & MAKE THEM DIE

SIAMO QUATTRO MARZIANI see TWELVE-HANDED MEN OF MARS, The

SICARIO 77, VIVO O MORTO see KILLER 77, ALIVE OR DEAD

SIDEREAL CRUISES (F) FIC 1942 95m. (CROISIERES SIDERALES) D: Andre Zwoboda. SP: Pierre Guerlais. Adap, Dial: Pierre Bost. PH: Isnard. Mus: Georges Van Parys. Art D: Henri Mahe. Ref: Rep.Gen'47. Bianco 7-8'66:121. RVB. with Madeleine Sologne, Jean Marchat, Julien Carette, Robert Arnoux, Jean Daste. Supposed inhabitants of Venus interrupt inter-sidereal cruise taken by earthlings.

The SIEGE OF SYRACUSE (I-F) Para/Galatea-Glover-Lyre 1959 ('62-U.S.) Eastmancolor/Dyaliscope 96m. (L'ASSEDIO DI SIRA-CUSA) D: Pietro Francisci. SP: Francisci, Ennio DeConcini, Giorgio Graziosi. PH: Carlo Carlini. Mus: F. Lavagnino Ref: FJA pbk. with Rossano Brazzi, Tina Louise, Gino Cervi, Sylvia Koscina, Alberto Farnese. The "burning glasses" of Archimedes harness the energy of the sun's rays and destroy ships.

SIEGFRIED (I) Ambrosio 1912 (I NIBELUNGHI) D: Mario Caserini. From Wagner. Ref: Mitry V:28. DDC I:331. Film Kunst 48:19.

SIEGFRIED (G) UFA 1923 95m. Part I of The NIBELUNGEN.
(SIEGFRIEDS TOD) SP,D: Fritz Lang. SP: also Thea von Har-
bou. PH: Carl Hoffmann, Günther Rittau, Walter Ruttman.
Based on "Das Nibelungenlied." Art D: Otto Hunte, Eric Kettel-
hut, Karl Vollbrecht. Ref: FM 26:20. M&H 2:22. SilentFF. with
Rudolf Klein-Rogge, Paul Richter, Margarete Schön. The story
of Siegfried and the dragon. Uninteresting except for some pic-
torial effects. Most of Siegfried's heroic deeds are standard.
Things really don't get going until (non-fantasy) part two, KRIEM-
HILD'S REVENGE, which builds to a shattering climax.
SIEGFRIED (Fili) c1963 Ref: FM 28:18. Film Comment 48-9:83.
Lee.
SIEGFRIED (W.B.-Yugos) CCC/Avala 1967 color/scope (The
TERRIBLE QUICK SWORD OF SIGFRIED. SIEGFRIED VON
XANTEN. WHOM THE GODS WISH TO DESTROY) Part I of
The NIBELUNGEN or SONG OF NIBELUNGEN. 91m. SP,D:
Harald Reinl. SP: also H. G. Petersson, Ladislas Fodor.
Based on "Das Nibelungenlied." PH: Ernst W. Kalinke. Mus:
Rolf Wilhelm. Art D: A. Schulz, W. & I. Schlichting. Ref: MFB
'69:197. M&H 2:25. with Uwe Beyer, Maria Marlow, Karin Dor,
Herbert Lom, Hans von Borsody, Rolf Henninger, Skip Martin,
Dieter Eppler.
SIEGFRIED see DRAGON'S BLOOD
SIEGFRIED AND THE DRAGON see DRAGON'S BLOOD
SIEGFRIED UND DAS SAGENHAFTE LIEBESLEBEN DER NIBELUNG-
EN see TERRIBLE QUICK SWORD OF SIEGFRIED, The
SILENCERS TOD see SIEGFRIED (1923)
SIGFRIDO see DRAGON'S BLOOD
SIGMA III see AGENT SIGMA 3-MISSION GOLDWATHER
SIGN OF THE VAMPIRE, The see LESBIAN VAMPIRES
SIGNALS--AN ADVENTURE IN SPACE (E.G.-Polish) DEFA 1971
color/70mm 90m. (SIGNALE--EIN WELTTRAUMABENTEUER)
D: Gottfried Kolditz. Ref: V 7/21/71. M/TVM 6/71. with
Piotr Pavlovski, Yevgeni Sharikov, Iurie Darie. "In the middle
of the next century a spaceship loses its bearings."
SIGNO DEL VAMPIRO, El see LESBIAN VAMPIRES
SILENCE OF HELEN MC CORD, The see SPIRAL STAIRCASE,
The
The SILENCERS Col 1966 Pathecolor 103m. D: Phil Karlson.
SP: Oscar Saul, from the books "The Silencers" and "Death
of a Citizen" by Donald Hamilton. PH: Burnett Guffey. Mus:
Elmer Bernstein. See also The AMBUSHERS, MURDERER'S ROW
First in the Matt Helm series. Ref: V 2/9/66. COF 10:6.
with Dean Martin, Stella Stevens, Victor Buono, Daliah Lavi,
Robert Webber, Arthur O'Connell, Richard Devon, James
Gregory, Nancy Kovack, Roger C. Carmel, Cyd Charisse,
Beverly Adams, Frank Gerstle. Lasers; plan to divert U.S.
missiles.
The SILENT ACCUSER (F) Pathe 1913 55m. Ref: Bios 12/18/13.
TV-Telephone.
The SILENT CASTLE (F) Gaum 1912 17m. "Based on "Sleeping
Beauty." Ref: Bios 7/4/12. Sorcerer casts spell of motionless-
ness over all in castle.

The SILENT COMMAND Univ/Laemmle 1915 50m. SP, D: Robert
Leonard. Ref: MPN 6/5/15. Motography 6/5/15. with Ella
Hall, Harry Carter, Alan Forrest. Doctor attempts to hypno-
tize girl into killing her father.

SILENT DEATH see VOODOO ISLAND

SILENT EVIDENCE (B) Gaum 1922 D: Charles Calvert. Ref:
SF Film. Brit Cinema. "Wireless-vision" apparatus.

The SILENT HOUSE (B) Butchers 1929 silent 95m. (The
HOUSE OF SILENCE) D: Walter Forde. P: Archibald Nettlefold.
Ref: MMF 18-19:34-7. Brit Cinema. with Frank Perfitt, Arthur
Pusey, Mabel Poulton, Gibb McLaughlin, Arthur Stratton.
Secret panel for concealing corpses; hypnotism; snake pit;
clutching hands. "Grand-Guignolesque."

The SILENT MYSTERY Silent Mystery Corp. /Burston 1918 serial
15 episodes D: Francis Ford. Ref: CNW. Lee. with Ford,
Rosemary Theby, Mae Gaston, Elsie Van N(e)ame. Invisible
power seems to pursue those who stole jewel from Egyptian
mummy.

The SILENT PERIL Bison 1914 30m. Ref: MPW 22:828. Lee.
"Powerless boat"; "alien" electrical wave.

SILENT STAR, The see FIRST SPACESHIP ON VENUS

The SILENT STRANGER Univ 1916 SP: Frank Smith. Ref: MPN
14:949. with King Baggot, Irene Hunt. A dead girl is restored
to a man by satan "with the stipulation that he must not laugh
or smile." He smiles, and she dies.

The SILVER BUDDHA (B) Stoll 1923 20m. (Mystery of Dr. Fu-
Manchu series) SP: A. E. Coleby, Frank Wilson. Based on
Sax Rohmer's stories. PH: D. P. Cooper. Ref: SilentFF. with
Harry Agar Lyons, Joan Clarkson, Fred Paul, Humbertson
Wright.

SILVER NEEDLE IN THE SKY MCA-TV 1954 From the "Rocky
Jones, Space Ranger" TV series. with Richard Crane.

The SILVER STREAK RKO 1934 72m. D: Thomas Atkins. SP:
Roger Whately, H. W. Hanemann. PH: J. Roy Hunt. Mus D:
Max Steiner. Art D: Van Nest Polglase, Perry Ferguson. PhFX:
Vernon Walker. Ref: SF Film. MPH 12/8/34. with Sally
Blane, Charles Starrett, Hardie Albright, William Farnum, Irving
Pichel, Theodore Von Eltz, Guinn Williams, Edgar Kennedy,
Murray Kinnell. Streamlined train makes 2,000-mile dash.

SILVERY DUST (Russ) 1951 Ref: Menville: Life 11/11/54: An
American scientist has developed a radioactive substance capable
of wiping out vast areas of the world.

SIMON, KING OF THE WITCHES Fanfare 1971 Eastmancolor
91m. D: Bruce Kessler. SP: Robert Phippeny. PH: David Butler.
Mus: Stu Phillips. Art D: Dale Hennesy. Ref: V 4/7/71. with
Andrew Prine, Brenda Scott, Ultra Violet. Warlock calls on dark
forces to cause man's death.

SIMPLE SIMON AND THE DEVIL (F) 1912 8m. (ONESIME AUX
ENFERS? SIMPLE SIMON IN HELL?) D: Jean Durand. Ref:
Bios 10/3/12. Lee. Dream: Man surrenders his soul to the
devil.

SIMPLE SIMON AND THE HAUNTED HOUSE (F) Gaum 1913
(ONESIME ET LA MAISON HANTEE) D: Jean Durand. Ref: Mitry II.

SIMPLE SIMON AND THE SUICIDE CLUB (F) Gaum 1913   7m.
Ref: Bios 3/5/14.
SIMPLE SIMON WATCHMAKER (F) 1912 (ONESIME HORLOGER)
Ref: FFF. Laclos: 188. DDC II:308. III:392. FanMo 5:40. with
Gaston Modot. Man tampers with clock to speed time.
SINBAD, ALI BABA AND ALADDIN (India) 1965 D, P: P. N. Arora.
SpFX: Eiji Tsuburaya. Ref: Shankar's 5/23/65. Pic: Mother
India 6/65:69. with Bhagwan, Pradeep Kumar, Sayeeda Khan,
Helen. Fire-breathing, Tyrannosaurus-like monster; genie;
magic sword; flying carpet.
SINEWS OF THE DEAD Gaston Melies 1914 Ref: MPW 21:990.
Lee. Graft from dead strangler drives man insane.
SINGED WINGS Para 1922 70m. D: Penrhyn Stanlaws. SP:
Ewart Adamson, Edfrid A. Bingham. Based on a novel by
Katharine Burt. Ref: Lee. MPN 26:3942. with Bebe Daniels,
Conrad Nagel, Adolphe Menjou, Ernest Torrence. Curse; witch
on broomstick.
SINHASAN (India) Himalaya Pictures 1934 D: Gajanan Jagirdar.
SP: P. Shivkumar. PH: D. Khosla. Art D: N. M. Kelkar. Ref:
Moving Picture Monthly 7/34. with S. Kumari, Indumati.
Criminal who uses black magic and hypnosis; man who's brought
back from the dead.
SINISTER HANDS Kent 1932 65m. (The SEANCE MYSTERY) D:
Armand Schaeffer. SP: Norton Parker, from his "The Seance
Mystery." Ref: Harrison's 8/20/32. with Jack Mulhall,
Mischa Auer, Phyllis Barrington, Crauford Kent, Lloyd Ingra-
ham, Fletcher Norton, Bess Flowers. A wealthy man is killed
at a seance.
SINISTER HANDS see SUCKER MONEY
SINISTER HOUSE see WHO KILLED 'DOC' ROBBIN?
The SINISTER MONK (W.G.) 1965 85m. (Der UNHEIMLICHE
MONCH) D: Harald Reinl. SP: J. Joachim Bartsch, Fred
Denger. PH: Ernest W. Kalinke. Mus: Peter Thomas. Ref:
FIR'67:85. M/TVM 4/66. with Deiter Eppler, S. Lowitz, Uta
Levka, Ursula Glas, Eddi Arent, Karin Dor, Harald Leipnitz.
A fiend masked in a monk's hood spreads terror. The person
who did the music should be bludgeoned severely: He has one
good theme, unfortunately realizes it, and won't let go of it. A
hooded character with a gigantic whip occasionally enlivens the
usual plot-heavy mess.
SINISTER SPACESHIP, The see ATTACK FROM SPACE
The SINISTER WISH (G) Tobis-film 1939 100m. (Der UNHEIM-
LICHEN WUNSHCE) D: Heinz Hilpert. SP: Kurt Heuser, from
Balzac's "The Wild Ass's Skin" or "The Magic Skin" or "Le
Peau de Chagrin." Mus: Wolfgang Zeller. Ref: Deutscher. with
Olga Tschechowa, Käthe Gold, Elisabeth Flickenschild, Ewald
Balser. Young man owns animal-skin which fulfills all his
wishes--but his life loses all interest.
SINNERS IN SILK MGM 1924 70m. D: Hobart Henley. SP:
Carey Wilson. Story: Benjamin Glazer. PH: John Arnold. Art
D: Richard Day. Ref: AFI. with Adolphe Menjou, Eleanor Board-
man, Conrad Nagel, Jean Hersholt, John Patrick, Hedda Hopper,
Virginia Lee Corbin. An aging roué undergoes rejuvenation surgery.

SINNERS TO HELL see HELL

SINS OF THE FLESHAPOIDS Film-Makers 1966-67 44m. SP, D,
P: Mike Kuchar. Ref: Boxo 4/7/69. with Bob Cowan, Donna
Kerness, George Kuchar, Maren Thomas. Robots a million
years from now.

SIR ARNE'S TREASURE (Swedish) Svenska 1919 80m. (HERR ARNES
PENGAR) D: Mauritz Stiller. SP: Stiller, Gustaf Molander,
from the novel by Selma Lagerlöf. PH: J. Julius. Art D: H.
Dahlström, A. Bakö. Ref: Lee. SilentFF. Pic: Pict Hist
Cinema. with Erik Stocklassa, Bror Berger, Richard Lund.
Shepherd cursed, frozen in sea.

SIR ARNE'S TREASURE (Swedish) 1954 (HERR ARNES PENNINGAR)
SP, D, Gustaf Molander. Ref: Sweden I. Lee. with Bibi Andersson, Bengt Eklund, Ake Grönberg, Ulla Jacobsson. Shepherd
cursed, frozen in sea. From the novel by Selma Lagerlöf.

SIR TRISTAM GOES WEST (story by E. Keoun) see GHOST GOES
WEST, The

SIRE DE MALETROIT'S DOOR, The (by R. L. Stevenson) see
STRANGE DOOR, The

SIREN OF ATLANTIS UA 1948 75m. (ATLANTIS. QUEEN OF
ATLANTIS) D: Gregg Tallas. SP: Rowland Leigh, Robert
Lax. From "L'Atlantide" by Pierre Benoit. PH: Karl Struss.
Mus D: Heinz Roemheld. Art D: Lionel Banks. Ref: FDY. COF
6:5. with Maria Montez, Dennis O'Keefe, Jean-Pierre Aumont,
Henry Daniell, Morris Carnovsky, Alan Nixon. Foreign Legion-
naires stumble upon the famous lost continent.

SITUATION OF GRAVITY, A (story by S. Taylor) see ABSENT-
MINDED PROFESSOR, The

SIX DESTINIES see FLESH AND FANTASY

SIX HOURS TO LIVE Fox 1932 80m. D: William Dieterle. SP:
Bradley King. From "Auf Wiedersehen" by Gordon Morris and
Morton Barteaux. PH: John Seitz. Ref: Photoplay 12/32. FDY.
with Warner Baxter, Irene Ware, John Boles, Edwin Maxwell,
Miriam Jordan, George Marion, Beryl Mercer, Halliwell Hobbes,
John Davidson, Edward McWade. A scientist invents a ray that
revives the dead for six hours.

SIX INCHES TALL see ATTACK OF THE PUPPET PEOPLE

The SIX NAPOLEONS (B) Stoll 1922 22m. (Further Adventures of
Sherlock Holmes series) Adap: George Ridgewell, from "Ad-
venture of the Six Napoleons" by Sir Arthur Conan Doyle. PH:
Alfred H. Moses. Art D: W. W. Murton. Ref: SilentFF. Re-
make: PEARL OF DEATH. with Eille Norwood, Hubert Willis,
Mme. D'Esterre.

SIX WOMEN FOR THE MURDERER See BLOOD AND BLACK LACE

SJUNDE INSEGLET, Det see SEVENTH SEAL, The

SKAEBNESVANGRE OPFINDELSE, Den see DR. JEKYLL & MR.
HYDE (1910)

SKAMMEN see SHAME

The SKELETON Vita 1910 7m. Ref: MPW 6:216, 228. Bios 4/21/10.
Skeleton frightens police officers, performs stunts.

The SKELETON OF MRS. MORALES (Mex) Alfa 1959 (El ESQUELETO
DE LA SEÑORA MORALES) D: Rogelio Gonzalez, Jr. SP: Luis
Alcoriza, from "The Mystery of Islington" by Arthur Machen.

PH: Victor Herrera. Mus: Raul Lavista. Ref: Heraldo'63:2.
Lee. with Arturo de Cordova, Amparo Rivelles, Elda Peralta,
Guillermo Orea, Rosenda Monteros, Luis Aragon. Man keeps
private museum of skeletons and embalmed animals.
SKELETON ON HORSEBACK (Cz) Laemmle Imports/Moldavia
Films 1939 78m. D: Hugo Haas. Titles: Fannie Hurst. From
Karel Capek's "White Sickness." Ref: Time 2/19/40. FD
2/7/40. with Haas, Zdenek (or Zdanek) Stepanek, Vaclav Vydra,
Bedrich Karen. A doctor discovers a cure for the leprous epi-
demic which is slowly killing off the human race.
SKELLEY'S SKELETON American 1916 11m. Ref: MPN 13:3111.
"Ghost house," "skeleton head,' magician, "visit to the forest by
torch light."
SKIES ABOVE, The see SKY ABOVE HEAVEN
The SKIVVY'S GHOST (F?) Lux 1912 Ref: MPW 11:804. Bios
2/29/12. Couple disturbed by rumors of ghosts in their house.
The SKULL (B) Para/Amicus 1965 Technicolor/scope 83m. D:
Freddie Francis. SP: Milton Subotsky. From "The Skull of the
Marquis de Sade." by Robert Bloch. PH: John Wilcox. Mus:
Elisabeth Lutyens. Art D: Bill Constable. SpFX: Ted Samuels.
Ref: PM. with Peter Cushing, Patrick Wymark, Jill Bennett,
Christopher Lee, Nigel Green, April Olrich, Michael Gough,
George Coulouris, Patrick Magee, Peter Woodthorpe, Maurice
Good, Frank Forsyth, Anna Palk. A collector is offered the skull
of the Marquis de Sade.
SKULLDUGGERY Univ 1970 Technicolor/scope D:Gordon Douglas.
SP: Nelson Gidding, from the book "Ye Shall Know Them" or
"You Shall Know Them" by Vercors. PH: Robert Moreno. Ref:
V 3/18/70. with Burt Reynolds, Roger C. Carmel, Susan Clark,
Pat Suzuki, Chips Rafferty, Alexander Knox, Paul Hubschmid,
Wilfrid Hyde-White, Rhys Williams. A safari into the jungles of
New Guinea finds a tribe of half-human missing links called the
Tropis.
SKY ABOVE HEAVEN (F-I) Gaumont/S.N.E.-Galatea 1964 color/
scope 105m. (Le CIEL SUR LA TETE or STADE ZERO-F. Il
CIELO SULLA TESTA-I. The SKIES ABOVE. SKY BEYOND
HEAVEN) SP,D: Yves Ciampi. SP: also Jean Raymond, Maurice
Aubergé, Alain Fatou, Jean Chapot. PH: Edmond Sechan. Mus:
Jacques Loussier. Ref: M/TVM 11/64.8/65. La Prod Cin Fr
11/64. Heraldo 3/8/67. DDC I:417. TVG. with André Smagghe,
Marcel Bozzufi, Henri Piegay, Jean Dasté, Yvonne Monlaur. A
radioactive satellite from outer space falls into orbit around the
earth. Just a lot of philosophizing, arm-waving, and running
around (i.e., nothing happens).
SKY BANDITS Mono/Criterion 1940 (1938) D: Ralph Staub. (REN-
FREW RIDES THE SKY. RENFREW OF THE ROYAL MOUNTED
IN SKY BANDITS) SP: Edward Halperin, from "Renfrew of the
Royal Mounted" by Laurie Erskine. P: Phil Goldstone. Ref: PM.
LC. STI 2:40. with James Newill, Louise Stanley. "The mystery
ray makes a reappearance in this story of vanishing airplanes."
-PM.
SKY BEYOND HEAVEN see SKY ABOVE HEAVEN
The SKY BIKE (B) 1968 CFF 62m. Eastmancolor D: Charles Frend.

Ref: M/TVM 4/68. with Liam Redmond, William Lucas, Ellen
McIntosh. Man invents bicycle with flapping wings.

The SKY PARADE Para 1936 70m. D: Otho Lovering. SP:
Brian Marlow, Byron Morgan, Arthur J. Beckhard, from "Air
Adventures of Jimmie Allen," radio sketches by Robert M. Burtt
and Willfred G. Moore. PH: William Mellor. Ref: V 4/22/36.
FD 4/1/36. with Jimmie Allen, William Gargan, Katherine De-
Mille, Kent Taylor, Grant Withers, Sid Saylor, Robert Fiske,
Bennie Bartlett, Georges Renevant, Wheaton Chambers, Lucien
Prival, Pat O'Malley, Frank Faylen. Automatic flying control
for airplanes.

SKY PIRATE Mono 1939 60m. D: George Waggner. SP: Paul
Schofield, Joseph West. Based on "Tailspin Tommy" by Hal
Forrest. (MYSTERY PLANE-Eng.) P: Paul Malvern. Ref: MPH
2/25/39. MFB'39:116. Hollywood Spectator: "New device for
the automatic dropping of bombs from an airplane through the
use of radio beams." with John Trent, Jason Robards, Milburn
Stone, Marjorie Reynolds, Lucien Littlefield, Polly Ann Young,
George Lynn.

The SKY RANGER Pathe 1921 serial 15 episodes D, P: George
B. Seitz. Ref: CNW. Lee. MPW 49:993. with Seitz, June
Caprice, Spencer Bennet, Harry Semels, Joe Cuny. "Powerful
light," hypnotism, silent plane. Ch. 6. The Crystal Prism.

The SKY SHIP (Dan) Nordisk/Tower 1917 ('20-U.S.) (HIMMEL-
SKIBET or HIMMELSKIGET. A QUATORZE MILLIONS DE LIEUES
DE LA TERRE-F. FOURTEEN MILLION LEAGUES FROM THE
EARTH. A TRIP TO MARS. REJSEN TIL MARS. The HEAVEN
SHIP) D: Holger Madsen. SP:Ole Olsen. Ref: DDC II:307, 308.
III:511. SF Film. SM 1:3. EncicDS'55:326. Le Surrealisme au
Cinema. Rocket ship to Mars.

The SKY SKIDDER Univ 1929 (1928) 60m. silent D: Bruce Mitchell.
SP: Val Cleveland. PH: William Adams. Ref: Photoplay 3/29.
LC. with Al Wilson, Helen Foster, Wilbur McGaugh. Inventor
wins race with "new flying gas."

The SKY SPLITTER Bray 1922 11m. Ref: SM 1:3. Lee. Scientist exceeds speed of light and sees events of past fifty years.

SKY STEWARD (by K. At(ti)will) see NON-STOP, NEW YORK

The SLAUGHTER OF THE VAMPIRES (I) Pacemaker/Mercur(y)
1962 84m. (La STRAGE DEI VAMPIRI. CURSE OF THE
BLOOD GHOULS) SP, D: Roberto Mauri. PH: Ugo Brunelli. Mus:
Aldo Piga. Art D: Giuseppe Ranieri. Ref: MFB'67:47. with
Walter Brandi, Dieter Eppler, Alfredo Rizzo, Graziella Granata,
Paolo Solvay. Two newlyweds encounter vampires on the out-
skirts of Vienna.-TVG. Very dull, with a lot of old-horror-
movie music and a nauseatingly romantic vampire ("She's no
more the Louise you knew").

SLAVE (play by L. Jones) see FABLE, A

SLAVE GIRLS see PREHISTORIC WOMEN (1966).

SLAVE OF DESIRE Goldwyn 1923 80m. D: George Baker. From
Balzac's "The Magic Skin" or "The Wild Ass's Skin" or "Le
Peau de Chagrin." Ref: Lee. with Bessie Love, Carmel Myers,
George Walsh.

SLAVES OF THE INVISIBLE MONSTER see INVISIBLE MONSTER, The

The SLEEPER (F) Pathe 1909 10m. Ref: MPW'09:809. Bios 10/7/
09. Hypnotist puts woman into trance that lasts for months.
SLEEPING BEAUTY (F) Pathe 1902 (La BELLE AU BOIS DOR-
MANT) D: Ferdinand Zecca. '03 Lubin pirated version. Ref:
V&FI 1:3:8. Mitry II. Lee.
SLEEPING BEAUTY (B) Hepworth 1912 17m. D, PH: Elwin Neame.
From the fairy tale by Charles Perrault. Ref: SilentFF. Bios
12/19/12. DDC I:440. III:33. with Ivy Close. Witch's curse.
SLEEPING BEAUTY Venus/Warner's 1913 45m. (The SLEEPING
BEAUTY) From the Perrault fairy tale. Ref: Bios 11/13/13:
576. MPW 17:430.
SLEEPING BEAUTY (HK) MP & GI 1961 D: Tang Huang. Ref:
FEFN 8/60.4/61. with Yeh Fung, Lai Chen, Liu En-chia.
Sorceress ruins man financially when he leaves her for another
girl.
The SLEEPING BEAUTY (Russ) Lenfilm/Royal 1964 Sovcolor 87m.
D, P: A. Dudko, K. Sergeyev. SP: Sergeyev, I. Shapiro, from
the story by Perrault. PH: A. Nazarov. Mus: P. I. Tschaikov-
sky. Art D: T. Vassilkovskaia, V. Oulitko. Ref: MFB. Boxo
6/27/66. COF 10:48. with Alla Sizova, Yuri Soloyov. Ballet:
Wicked fairy casts spell of "endless sleep."
SLEEPING BEAUTY (G) Childhood 1955 ('65-U.S.) color 70m.
(DORNROSCHEN) SP, D, P: Fritz Genschow. Narr: Paul Tripp.
SP: also R. Stobrawa, H. Weichert. From the Bros. Grimm.
PH: G. Huttula. Mus: H.-J. Wunderlich. Art D: O. Reysser,
W. Volkmer. Ref: MFB'71:163. FD 10/27/65. with Karin
Hardt, F. Genschow, Angela von Leitner. Witch curses princess
to sleep 100 years.
SLEEPING BEAUTY see BEAUTY OF THE SLEEPING WOODS/
SILENT CASTLE, The
SLEEPY HOLLOW see LEGEND OF SLEEPY HOLLOW, The (1912)
The SLIME PEOPLE Hansen 1963 60m. D: Robert Hutton. SP:
Vance Skarstedt. PH: William Troiano. Mus: Lou Froman. P:
Joseph Robertson. Ref: RVB. FM 27:11. Pic: FMO 2:26. with
Susan Hart, Robert Hutton, Robert Burton, Les Tremayne. Pre-
historic creatures, disturbed by nuclear tests, invade Los
Angeles.
The SLINGSHOT KID FBO 1927 60m. D: Louis King. P: Joseph P.
Kennedy. Continuity: Oliver Drake. Story: John Twist, Jean
Dupont. PH:Roy Eslick, William Nobles. Ref: AFI. Western.
with Buzz Barton, Frank Rice, Jeanne Morgan, Buck Connors.
Heroes play ghost to scare gang.
SLUMBERLAND Vita 1908 Ref: F Index 12/19/08. Dream: Menac-
ing gnomes.
The SMILING GHOST WB 1941 77m. D: Lewis Seiler. SP: Kenneth
Gamet, Stuart Palmer. PH: Arthur Todd. Ref: V 8/12/41. with
Wayne Morris, Brenda Marshall, Alexis Smith, Alan Hale, Lee
Patrick, David Bruce, Helen Westley, Willie Best, Charles
Halton, Richard Ainley, Clem Bevans. Murders supposedly com-
mitted by ghost. Dull, sometimes pleasant horror-comedy, with
all the expected cliches. Bright line: "Why, she's got enough
brains for two people" "Yes, she's just the girl for you."
SMOKED GLASSES (by W. Foster) see BLIND MAN'S BLUFF (1936)

SMUGGLER'S COVE   Mono 1948 66m. D: William Beaudine. SP:
Tim Ryan, Edmond Seward. Story: Talbert Josselyn. PH:
Marcel Le Picard. Art D: David Milton. Ref: TVG. FDY. with
Leo Gorcey, Huntz Hall, Gabriel Dell, Billy Benedict, David
Gorcey, Bennie Bartlett, Martin Kosleck, Amelita Ward, Gene
Stutenroth, William Ruhl, Emmett Vogan. "Haunted" house with
secret passages, sliding panels, "staring faces."

The SNAKE GIRL AND THE SILVER-HAIRED WITCH (J) Daiei
c1969 (HEBIMUSUME TO HAKUHATSUMA) D: Noriaki Yuasa.
Ref: UFQ 43. with Y. Matsui, Y. Hamada. Girl possessed by
spirit of snake.

The SNAKE MAN (F) Lux 1910 (The SERPENT MAN) Ref: MPW
6:533, 600. Bios 3/31/10. A man turns himself into a snake.

The SNAKE PEOPLE (U.S.-Mex) Vergara 1968 (La MUERTE
VIVIENTE. ISLE OF THE SNAKE PEOPLE) D: Juan Ibanez. SP:
Jack Hill, Luis Enrique Vergara. PH: Raul Dominguez. Ref:
TVG. RVB. TVFFSB. with Boris Karloff, Julissa, Charles East.
Voodoo/snake cult.

The SNAKE PIT (W.G.) Hemisphere/Constantin 1967 ('70-U.S.)
color 85m. (Die SCHLANGENGRUBE UND DAS PENDEL. The
PENDULUM. The SNAKE PIT AND THE PENDULUM. The
TORTURE CHAMBER OF DR. SADISM. BLOOD DEMON-U.S.)
D: Harald Reinl. SP: Manfred R. Köhler, from "The Pit and
the Pendulum" by Edgar Allan Poe. PH: Ernst W. Kalinke. Mus:
Peter Thomas. Art D: G. Pellon, W. M. Achmann. Ref: MMF
18-19:6. V 5/8/68. Heraldo '68:209. Bianco 11/68. M/TVM
9/69. with Christopher Lee, Lex Barker, Karin Dor, Carl
Lange, Vladimir Medar, Christiane Rucker, Dieter Eppler.

The SNAKE WOMAN (B) UA/Caralan 1960 68m. (TERROR OF THE
SNAKE WOMAN) D: Sidney J. Furie. SP: Orville Hampton. PH:
Stephen Dade. Mus sc: Buxton Orr. Makeup: Freddie Williamson.
Ref: FFacts. PM. with John McCarthy, Susan Travers, Hugh
Moxey, Geoffrey Danton, Arnold Marle. Herpetologist keeps his
wife from going insane by giving her injections of snake venom.
She dies giving birth to a literally cold-blooded baby.

The SNOW CREATURE UA 1953   70m. D, P: W. Lee Wilder. SP:
Myles Wilder. PH:Floyd Crosby. Mus sc & d: Manuel Compinsky.
Art D: Frank Sylos. SpFX: Lee Zavitz. Pic: HM 4:36. with Paul
Langton, Rudolph Anders, William Phipps, Teru Shimada,
Darlene Fields, Leslie Denison, Robert Bice, Rusty Westcott
(or Wescoatt). Expedition to the Himalayas discovers Yeti. Combines elements of KING KONG and WEREWOLF OF LONDON but
doesn't contribute any new ones. Fairly effective treatment of
the monster--obscured by shadows, snow, glass--in an otherwise
undistinguished shocker.

SNOW CREATURE, The see ABOMINABLE SNOWMAN, The
SNOW DEVILS see SPACE DEVILS

SNOW GHOST (J) Daiei 1968 color 80m. (KAIDAN YUKIJORO.
YUKIONNA. GHOST YUKIJORO) D: Tokuzo Tanaka. SP: Fuji
Yahiro. PH: Chishi Makiura. Mus: Akira Ifukube. Art D: Akira
Naito. Ref M/TVM 5/70:29. UFQ 41. Unij Bltn 31. with Shiho
Fujimura, Akira Ishihama, Machiko Hasegawa, Mizuho Suzuki,
Taketoshi Naito. A ghost appears out of a snowstorm and freezes

a man to death with her stare.
SNOW MAN, The   see HALF HUMAN
SNOW WHITE Lubin 1903 Ref: Lee. LC.
SNOW WHITE Powers 1913 50m. From the Bros. Grimm. Ref:
    Bios 7/10/13.
SNOW WHITE Educ 1916 45m. Ref: MPN 14:3672. Wicked step-
    mother "wants to get rid of Snow White."
SNOW WHITE Para 1916 70m. D: J. Searle Dawley. PH: H. L.
    Broening. From the fairy tale by the Bros. Grimm.   Ref:
    MPN 15:113. with Creighton Hale, Marguerite Clark.
SNOW WHITE Rex 1917 35m. Ref: MPW 31:2158.
SNOW WHITE see LITTLE SNOW-WHITE/SNOW WHITE AND ROSE
    RED
SNOW WHITE AND ROSE RED   Childhood/Schonger 1955 ('66-U.S.)
    color 76m. (G) (SCHNEEWITTCHEN UND DIE SIEBEN ZWERGE.
    SNOW WHITE) D: Erich Kobler. SP: Konrad Lustig, Walter
    Oehmichen; Eng. version: Anne and Milton DeLugg. PH: Wolf
    Schwan. Art D: Gunther Strupp. Narr: Paul Tripp. Mus: C.
    Steuber, F. Miller. Ref: TVG. MFB'71:82. Enchanted forest in-
    habited by a wicked dwarf with magical powers.
SNOW WHITE AND THE THREE STOOGES Fox/Chanford 1961
    DeLuxe color 107m. D: Walter Lang. SP: Elwood Ullman, Noel
    Langley, from a story by Charles Wick and the fairy tale by the
    Bros. Grimm. PH: Leon Shamroy.   Art D: Jack Martin Smith,
    Maurice Ransford. SpPhFX: L. B. Abbott, Emil Kosa, Jr. Ref:
    FFacts. with Carol Heiss, Moe Howard, Larry Fine, Joe De
    Rita, Edson Stroll, Patricia Medina, Guy Rolfe, Buddy Baer,
    Edgar Barrier, Peter Coe, Lisa Mitchell, Owen McGivney, Sam
    Flint, Blossom Rock. Witch, poisoned apple, etc.
SNOW WHITE PRINCESS see 7 DWARFS TO THE RESCUE, The
The SNOWMAN AM&B 1908 Ref: Niver. Snowman comes to life,
    frightens man.
SO SAAL BAAD (India) 1967 Ref: Shankar's 3/19/67. with Feroz(e)
    Khan, Kum Kum. "Ghost which keeps on singing at odd hours and
    vanishes into blank walls"; ax-wielding character; old palace.
The SOAP BUBBLES OF TRUTH (F) Pathe 1910 7m. Ref: Bios
    8/11/10. Bubbles from bottom of well predict miser will die at
    hand of thief.
SOLD TO SATAN Lubin 1916 35m. SP: R. P. Rifenborich, Jr. Ref:
    MPW 27:1011, 1314, 1317. with Edward Sloman(satan), LC.
    Shumway. A man sells his soul to the devil for youth and
    money.
The SOLE SURVIVOR CBS-TV/Cinema Center 1970 color D: Paul
    Stanley. SP: G. Trueblood. PH: James Crabbe.   Mus: Paul Glass.
    Art D: Craig Smith. Ref: RVB. with Vince Edwards, Richard
    Basehart, William Shatner, Alan Caillou, Patrick Wayne.
    Ghosts of men killed in plane crash in desert doomed to stay
    near plane until their bodies are recovered.
The SOLITARY ATTACKS (Sp-F) PAI/CFdPdF 1968 color/scope
    96m. (El SOLATARIO PASA AL ATAQUE) D: Ralph Habib.
    SP: André Haguet. Dial: M. Lebrun. PH: M. F. Mila. Mus:
    B. Gerard. Ref: SpCinema'69. with Roger Hanin, Jean Lefe(b)vre,
    Teresa Gimpera, Gerard Tichy. "New type of ray which disinte-

grates planes in the air."
SOLO UN ATAUD see ORGIES OF DR. ORLOFF, The
SOMBRA DEL MURCIELAGO, La see SHADOW OF THE BAT, The
SOMBRA, THE SPIDER WOMAN see BLACK WIDOW, The
SOME GIRLS DO (B) Rank 1969 color 93m. D: Ralph Thomas. SP:
    David Osborn, Liz Charles-Williams. Based on the character
    "Bulldog Drummond" created by Sapper. PH: Ernest Steward.
    Mus: Charles Blackwell. Art D: Edward Marshall. SpFX:
    Kit West. Ref: MFB'69:61. V(d) 1/27/69. with Richard Johnson,
    Daliah Lavi, Beba Loncar, James Villiers, Maurice Denham,
    Robert Morley, Virginia North. "Infrasonic ray machine" which
    destroys planes; girl robots.
SOME MUST WATCH (novel by E. L. White) see SPIRAL STAIR-
    CASE, The
SOMEONE AT THE DOOR (B) Hammer 1950 65m. D: Francis
    Searle. SP: A. R. Rawlinson, from a play by Major C. Christie
    and Miss Dorothy C. Christie. PH: W. Harvey. Mus: F. Spencer.
    Art D: Denis Wreford. Ref: MFB'50:88. P: Anthony Hinds. with
    Yvonne Owen, Michael Medwin, Hugh Latimer, Garry Marsh.
    Old mansion with sliding panels, priest-holes, etc.
SOMEONE BEHIND THE DOOR (F-I) Medusa/Lira 1971 color
    (QUELQU'UN DERRIERE LA PORTE-F.) D: Nicola Gessner.
    Ref:M/TVM'71. V 5/12/71:79. with Charles Bronson, Anthony
    Perkins, Jill Ireland. "Doctor transfers personality of amnesiac
    to himself so he can kill his own wife."
SOMETHING ALWAYS HAPPENS Para 1928 silent 50m.   Ed:
    Verna Willis. SP, D: Frank Tuttle. SP: Raymond Cannon, Florence
    Ryerson. Titles: Herman Mankiewicz. PH: J. Roy Hunt. Ref:
    AFI. PM. FDY. with Esther Ralston, Noble Johnson (The
    Thing), Neil Hamilton, Sojin, Roscoe Karns, Mischa Auer,
    Charles Sellon, Lawrence Grant, The Mysterious Feet (as them-
    selves). "Haunted house, several perambulating ghosts, seven
    or eight Chinamen and a Blue Sapphire...Blood will curdle joy-
    ously."-PM.
SOMETHING IS CRAWLING IN THE DARK (I) Akla S.p.A. 1970
    color/scope D: Mario Colucci. Ref: M/TVM 9/70. with Farley
    Granger, Lucia Bose. "Eight persons seek shelter during a
    storm in an old country house with a nightmarish atmosphere."
SOMETHING WEIRD Mayflower 1968 color 83m. D: Herschell G.
    Lewis. P, SP: James F. Hurley. Ref: Spectre 19:5. with Tony
    McCabe, Elizabeth Lee, William Brooker. An engineer burned
    by loose high tension wire finds he can read minds. An ugly
    witch restores his scarred face in exchange for love.
A SON-IN-LAW'S NIGHTMARE (F) Pathe 1913 9m. Ref: Bios
    4/4/12. Dream: Man thinks he murdered mother-in-law; her
    head chases him.
SON OF DR. JEKYLL Col 1951 76m. D: Seymour Friedman.
    SP: Jack Pollexfen, Mortimer Braus, from "The Strange Case
    of Dr. Jekyll and Mr. Hyde" by Stevenson. PH: Henry Freulich.
    Mus sc: Paul Sawtell. Art D: Walter Holscher. Makeup: Clay
    Campbell. Ref: FDY. TVG. with Louis Hayward, Jody Lawrence,
    Alexander Knox, Gavin Muir, Lester Matthews, Paul Cavanagh,
    Rhys Williams, Doris Lloyd, James Logan. The son of Dr.

Jekyll tries to prove his father was a serious scientist. As Jekyll-and-Hyde movies go, not bad.

SON OF DRACULA Univ 1943 78m. D: Robert Siodmak. SP: Eric Taylor. Story: Curt Siodmak. PH: George Robinson. Mus: H. J. Salter. Art D: John B. Goodman, Martin Obzina. SpFX: John P. Fulton. Makeup: Jack Pierce. Ref: Academy. COF 6:24. with Lon Chaney, Jr., Robert Paige, Louise A(l)britton, Evelyn Ankers, Frank Craven, J. Edward Bromberg, Samuel S. Hinds, Adeline De-Walt Reynolds, Patrick Moriarty, Etta McDaniel, George Irving, Jack Rockwell, Robert Dudley, Walter Sande, Cyril Delevanti, Charles Bates, Sam McDaniel. Okay story and effects; bad acting, production, and dialogue ("Let me take you away from all this"). One girl becomes a vampire through her morbidness, a cautionary thought for horror movie fans.

SON OF FLUBBER BV 1962 100m. D: Robert Stevenson. SP: Bill Walsh. P: Walt Disney. PH: Edward Colman. Sequel to The ABSENT-MINDED PROFESSOR. From a story by Samuel Taylor and the Danny Dunn books. Mus: George Bruns. SpFX: Peter Ellenshaw, Eustace Lycett, Robert A. Mattey. Ref: FFacts. with Fred MacMurray, Nancy Olson, Tommy Kirk, Keenan Wynn, Ed Wynn, Bob Sweeney, Elliot(t) Reid, Joanna Moore, Leon Ames, Ken Murray, Charlie Ruggles, William Demarest, Paul Lynde, Stu Erwin, Edward Andrews, Forrest Lewis, James Westerfield, Alan Carney, Jack Albertson, Lee Giroux. Machine creates miniature artificial storms, shatters glass over wide area of town, and ultimately grows giant vegetables over same area; "flubbergas" enables football players to bounce across field. Hideous close-ups and strained, unpleasant "comic" performances. MacMurray has an embarrassing speech on why he teaches America's youth ("Even if they fall flat on their faces, they're still going forward").

SON OF FRANKENSTEIN Univ 1939 93m. D, P: Rowland V. Lee. SP: Willis Cooper. PH: George Robinson. Mus sc: Frank Skinner. Art D: Jack Otterson, Richard Riedel. Sets: R. A. Gausman. Ref: Academy. MFB'39:21: "Karloff is again the monster, a part in which it is impossible to give a bad performance'." with Bela Lugosi, Boris Karloff, Basil Rathbone, Lionel Atwill, Josephine Hutchinson, Emma Dunn, Donnie Dunagan, Gustav von Seyffer-titz, Edgar Norton, Perry Ivins, Lawrence Grant, Lionel Belmore, Michael Mark, Caroline Cooke, Lorimer Johnson, Tom Ricketts. The doctor's son encounters the monster. Competent, elaborate horror movie tries for "A," winds up a good "B." Atmospheric, with the acting, story and production all better-than-average.

SON OF GODZILLA (J) Toho 1967 color/scope 86m. (GODZIRA NO MUSUKO) (FRANKENSTEINS MONSTER JAGEN GODZILLAS SOHN -Germany) D: Jun Fukuda. SP: Shinichi Sekizawa, Kazue Shiba, PH: Kazuo Yamada. Mus: Masaru Sato. Art D: Takeo Kita. SpFX: Eiji Tsuburaya, Sadamasu Arikawa. Ref: UFQ 40. with Tadao Takashima, Akira Kubo, Beverly (or Bibari) Maeda, Akihiko Hirata, Kenji Sahara.

SON OF INGAGI Sack/Hollywood Productions 1939 66m. SP, D: Richard C. Kahn. SP: also Spencer Williams. Ref: Showmen's 1/20/40. with Alfred Grant, Daisy Bufford, Laura Bowman, Zack Williams. "Young bride at the mercy of ape-man monster" from the jungle.

SON OF KONG RKO 1933 60m. (The SON OF KONG) D: Ernest
B. Schoedsack. SP: Ruth Rose. (JAMBOREE) PH: Eddie Linden,
Vernon Walker, J. O. Taylor. Mus: Max Steiner. SpFX: Willis
O'Brien. Ref: Clarens. FM 10:26. 22:31. 24:37. with Robert Arm-
strong, Helen Mack, Frank Reicher, John Marston, Victor Wong,
Noble Johnson, Lee Kohlmar, Clarence Wilson. Silly but fun.
Played for laughs and tears. The son is too tame; if they had
taken him to New York, he would have ridden the subway rather
than wrecked it.

SON OF SAMSON (I-F) Medallion/Gallus-Jolly 1960 Technicolor
90m. scope (MACISTE NELLA VALLE DEI RE-I. MACISTE-
THE MIGHTY-Eng. GIANT OF THE VALLEY OF KINGS) D:
Carlo Campogalliani. SP: Oreste Biancoli, Ennio De Concini.
PH: Riccardo Pallottini. Mus: Carlo Innocenzi. Ref: FFacts.
with Mark Forest, Chelo Alonso, Angelo Zanolli, Vira Silenti.
Queen Smedes keeps a young hunter in a hypnotic state by means
of a magic potion.

A SON OF SATAN Micheaux 1924 65m. Ref: AFI. with Andrew S.
Bishop, Ida Anderson. "Haunted" house.

SON OF THE VAMPIRE (Malayan) Malay/Shaw 1958 (ANAK PON-
TIANAK. CURSE OF THE VAMPIRE) D: Ramon Estella. SP:
Abdul Razak. Ref: FEFN 11/22/57. 2/28/58: Shaw's "latest
vampire series." with Hasimah, Haj Sattar, Dayang Sofia, Jins
Shashudin. "Demons include Pontianak (vampire), Anak Pontianak
(son of the vampire), the Polong (bodiless creature), and the
Hnatu (snake devil)."

SON OF ZAMBO (India) Bhawnani 1939 Sequel to ZAMBO. Ref:
Dipali 9/1/39. 6/30/39. with Bimla Kumari, S. Devi, Fatty
Prasad.

SON OF NIBELUNGEN see SIEGFRIED (1967)

The SONG OF THE SIREN (Mex) Caricolor Films 1946 (EL CANTO
DE LA SIRENA) SP, D: Norman Foster. PH: Jack Draper. Mus:
Manuel Esperon. Ref: Indice. Lee LATimes 6/15/49. with Julian
Soler, Rosita Diaz, Virginia Serret, Tito Junco. Siren's song
bewitches men.

SONGOKU see ADVENTURES OF SUN WU KUNG, The

SONHO DE VAMPIROS, Um see VAMPIRE'S DREAM, A

SONS OF THUNDER see MY SON, THE HERO

SOPHY AND THE FAKER Ess 1915 Ref: MPN 6/5/15. with Harry
Todd, Victor Potel, Ben Turpin. "Magic electric belt."

The SORCERER (F) Discina 1944 103m. (SORTILEGES. WITCH-
CRAFT) D: Christian-Jaque. SP: Jacques Prevert. From the
novel "Le Cavalier de Rion Clair" by Claude Boncompain. Ref:
S&S'46:50. DDC III:213. PH: Louis Page. with Fernand Ledoux,
Renée Fauré. Witchcraft; the supernatural.

The SORCERER, THE PRINCE AND THE GOOD SPIRIT (F)
Melies 1900 (Le SORCIER, LE PRINCE ET LE BON GENIE) Ref:
Mitry II.

THE SORCERERS (B) AA/Tigon-Curtwell-Global 1967 color 85m.
SP, D: Michael Reeves. SP: also Tom Baker. PH: Stanley Long.
Mus sc & d: Paul Ferris. Art D: Tony Curtis. Idea: John Burke.
Ref: MFB'67:109. PM. with Boris Karloff, Catherine Lacey, Ian

Ogilvy, Susan George, Ivor Dean, Peter Fraser, Elizabeth Ercy.
A professor of hypnosis and his wife find that through the use of
light and sound waves they are able to control their subject at
any distance and also experience his bodily sensations.

SORCERESS OF THE STRAND (F) Eclair 1910 11m. Ref: Bios
5/19/10. Witch transformed into maiden curses, drowns fisher-
lad.

SORCIER, LE PRINCE ET LE BON GENIE, LE see SORCERER,
THE PRINCE AND THE GOOD SPIRIT, The

SORELLA DI SATANA, La see SHE BEAST

SORROWFUL ARCADIA (Novel by P. de Mendelssohn) see
MARIANNE OF MY YOUTH

The SORROWS OF SATAN (B) Samuelson 1917 D, P: Alexander But-
ler. From the novel by Marie Corelli. Ref: Hist Brit Film. with
Owen Nares, Gladys Cooper, Lionel D'Aragon, Cecil Humphreys.
"Eerie melodrama with a prologue and an epilogue in Hell."

The SORROWS OF SATAN Para 1926 100m. D, P: D. W. Grif-
fith. SP: Forrest Halsey, from the novel by Marie Corelli.
Ref: AFI. Clarens. Adap: John Russell, George Hull. From
"The Sorrows of Satan; or The Strange Experience of One
Geoffrey Tempest, Millionaire" by MC. Ed, Titles: Julian
Johnson.   PH: Harry Fischbeck, Arthur DeTitta.   Art D:
Chas. Kirk. Miniatures: Fred Waller, Jr. with Adolphe
Menjou, Ricardo Cortez, Carol Dempster, Lya de Putti, Dorothy
Hughes, Ivan Lebedeff, Nellie Savage, Lawrence D'Orsay. Slow
and dull, with interminable lingering close-ups. Highlighted by
very effective horror scenes of the devil's huge, winged shadow-
figure pursuing Cortez.

SORT OF TRAITORS, A (by N. Balchin) see RISK, The

SORTILEGES see SORCERER, The

The SOUL OF A MONSTER Col 1944 61m. D: Will Jason. SP:
Edward Dein. PH:Burnett Guffey. Mus D: Mischa Bakaleinikoff.
Art D: George Brooks, Lionel Banks. Ref: FDY. with George
Macready, Rose Hobart, Jim Bannon, Jeanne Bates. A dying
man is saved by a woman's supernatural powers. Lots of talk,
all bad: "Monsters live, saints die" "It isn't fair that Ann should
carry my cross" "The man who walks with evil walks alone."
One imitation-Lewton suspense scene (with an el), clumsily done.
One clever camera trick with a mirror.

The SOUL OF PHYRA Domino 1915 30m. Ref: MPN 6/19/15.
Indian high priest mystically summons maiden back to India to
be sacrificed. Her husband later hears her soul "calling him"
and dies.

SOULS BEFORE BIRTH see ONE GLORIOUS DAY

The SOUL'S CYCLE Centaur 1916 55m. D: Ulysses Davis. Ref:
MPN 13:1019. with Margaret Gibson, Roy Watson (the devil).
Man reincarnated as lion; deal with the devil.

SOUND OF HORROR (Sp) Zurbano 1965 91m. (El SONIDO PREHISTOR-
ICO. SOUND FROM A MILLION YEARS AGO. The PREHISTORIC
SOUND) D: Jose Conde. SP: San-X-Abar Banel, G. Sacristan.
PH: Manuel Berenguer. Mus: Luis de Pablo. Art D: P. Espinosa,
Gil Parrondo. Ref: SpCinema. with Arturo Fernandez, Soledad

Miranda, Antonio Casas, James Philbrook, Ingrid Pitt. Treasure hunters come across invisible prehistoric animal.

SOUS LA LUNE DU MAROC   See UNDER THE MOON OF MOROCCO

SOVEREIGN GOOSE PIE   see   ONCE UPON A TIME

SPACE AGENT Kl   see HUMAN DUPLICATORS, The

SPACE AMOEBA (J) Toho 1969 color/scope 84m. (NANKAI NO DAIKAIJU. KESSEN NANKAI NO DAIKAIJU. YOG-MONSTER FROM SPACE) D: Inishiro Honda. SP: Ei Ogawa. Mus: Akira Ifukube. Art D: Takeo Kita. Ref: UFQ 49. with Akira Kubo, Kenji Sahara, Yukiko Kobayashi, Yu Fujiki. The space between Mars and Jupiter is inhabited by colonies of giant amoeba-like creatures.

SPACE CHIEF   see INVASION OF THE NEPTUNE MEN

The SPACE CHILDREN Para 1958 69m. D: Jack Arnold. SP: Bernard Schoenfeld. Story: Tom Filer. PH: Ernest Laszlo. Mus: Van Cleave. Art D: Hal Pereira, Roland Anderson. SpFX: John P. Fulton. P: William Alland. Ref: FFacts. PM. Pic: HM 1:13. FM-A'69:30. with Michael Ray, Adam Williams, Peggy Webber, Jackie Coogan, Sandy Descher, Russell Johnson, John Crawford, Larry Pennell, Raymond Bailey. Being from outer space empowers children of the world to stop launching of nuclear armed satellite.

SPACE DEVILS (I) Mercury/Manley/Southern Cross 1965 color (I DIAVOLI DELLO SPAZIO. SNOW DEVILS. DEVIL MEN FROM SPACE) D, P: Antonio Margheriti (aka Anthony Dawson). P: also Joseph Fryd. SP: Sinclair, Finger, Moretti. PH: Riccardo Pallottini. Mus: F. Lavagnino. Ref: COF 9:45. Ital P. with Giacomo Rossi Stuart, Ombretta Colli, Renato Baldini, Archie Savage, Furio Meniconi, Peter Martell, Halina Zalewska, Enzo Fiermonte, Isarco Ravaioli. Abominable Snowmen prove to be survivors of the planet Aytia.

SPACE FLIGHT IC-1 (B) Fox 1965 65m. D: Bernard Knowles. SP: Harry Spalding. P: Robert Lippert, Jack Parsons. PH: Geoffrey Faithfull. Mus: Elisabeth Lutyens. Ref: PM. COF 9:6. with Bill Williams, John Cairney, Linda Marlowe, Kathleen Breck. Space flight to Earth Two in the year 2015.

SPACE GREYHOUND   see INVASION OF THE NEPTUNE MEN

SPACE INVASION OF LAPLAND see INVASION OF THE ANIMAL PEOPLE

SPACE MEN see ASSIGNMENT-OUTER SPACE

SPACE MEN APPEAR IN TOKYO see WARNING FROM SPACE

SPACE MONSTER AI-TV/Burt Topper 1964 80m. (FIRST WOMAN INTO SPACE. FLIGHT BEYOND THE SUN) SP, D: Leonard Katzman. Ref: TVG. V 6/9/65. Orpheus 3:34. ModM 3:8. with Russ Bender, Francine York, James B. Brown, Baynes Barron. Four scientists set out to explore space. Poor. The movie switches plots midway, but it doesn't help.

SPACE MONSTER, DOGORA see DAGORA

SPACE PRINCE see PRINCE OF SPACE, The

SPACE SOLDIERS see FLASH GORDON

SPACE SOLDIERS CONQUER THE UNIVERSE   see FLASH GORDON CONQUERS THE UNIVERSE

SPACE SOLDIERS' TRIP TO MARS see FLASH GORDON'S TRIP TO

MARS
SPACE STATION X see MUTINY IN OUTER SPACE
SPACE STATION X-14 see MUTINY IN OUTER SPACE
SPACE THING Pussycat Films/B&B 1968 D: B. Ron Elliott.
    P: David F. Friedman. Ref: LAT 9/28/68: "Buck Rogers for
    adults." RVB. with "April Playmate," Bart Black. SP: "Cosmo
    Politan."
SPACEMASTER X-7 Fox/Regal 1958 Regalscope 71m. D: Edward
    Bernds. SP: George W. Yates, Daniel Mainwaring. PH: Brydon
    Baker. Mus: Josef Zimanich. Makeup: Robert Littlefield. Ref:
    FFacts. with Bill Williams, Robert Ellis, Moe Howard, Lyn
    Thomas, Paul Frees, Gregg Martell, Jesse Kirkpatrick. Organ-
    ism from outer space called Blood Rust.
SPACEMEN SATURDAY NIGHT see INVASION OF THE SAUCER-
    MEN
SPACESHIP GALILEO (by R. Heinlein) see DESTINATION MOON
SPACESHIP TO THE UNKNOWN see FLASH GORDON
SPACESHIP VENUS DOES NOT REPLY see FIRST SPACESHIP ON
    VENUS
SPACEWAYS (B) Lippert/Hammer 1953 76m. D: Terence Fisher.
    SP: Paul Tabori, Richard Landau. From the radio play by
    Charles Eric Maine. PH: Reg Wyer. Mus: Ivor Slaney. Art D:
    J. Elder Wills. P: Michael Carreras. Ref: Bianco. Clarens.
    with Howard Duff, Eva Bartok, Alan Wheatley, Andrew Osborn,
    Michael Medwin, Cecile Chevreau, David Horne, Hugh Moxey.
    Rocket successfully launched into space. A carnival of cliches
    in plot and dialogue. Usual dull early-Fifties non-monster s-f.
The SPANIARD'S CURSE (B) British Lion 1958 D: Ralph Kemplen.
    SP: Kenneth Hyde. From the book "Assize of the Dying" by Edith
    Pargeter. PH:Arthur Grant. Art D: Tony Masters. Ref: Brit
    Cinema. MFB'58:92. Film Review '59/'60. with Tony Wright,
    Susan Beaumont, Basil Dignam, Lee Patterson, John Watson,
    Jack McNaughton, Brian Oulton. Before he is executed, a man
    pronounces the dreaded "Assize of the Dying." Later the jurors
    who sentenced him die one by one.
SPEAK, SPEAK! (painting by J. Millais) see VISION, The
The SPECKLED BAND (B) SFFCE 1912 35m. From the Sherlock
    Holmes story "Adventure of the Speckled Band" by Sir Arthur
    Conan Doyle. Ref: LC. Bios 9/18/13. Murder in country house.
The SPECKLED BAND (B) Stoll 1923 22m. (Last Adventures of
    Sherlock Holmes series) From Doyle's "Adventure of the Speckled
    Band." PH: Alfred Moise. Art D: W. W. Murton. Ref: SilentFF.
    with Eille Norwood, Hubert Willis, Mme. D'Esterre.
The SPECKLED BAND First Division 1931 (B) D: Jack Raymond.
    SP: W. Lipscomb. From Doyle's "Adventure of the Speckled
    Band." PH: F. A. Young. Ref: MFB'38:198. 88m. with Raymond
    Massey, Lynn Harding, Athole Steward, Nancy Price. "The
    screams, dark old houses and malevolent Indian servants are as
    creepy as ever."
The SPECTER (F) Pathe 1908 8m. Ref: V&FI 7/4/08:10,13. Cob-
    bler haunted by ghost of man he murdered.
The SPECTER OF JAGO (I) Aquila 1912 (Lo SPETTRO DI JAGO)
    Ref: DDC III:241. D: Alberto Carlo Lolli.

The SPECTER OF THE VAULT (I) Riviera 1915 (Lo SPETTRO DEL
   SOTTERRANEO) D: Ubaldo Maria Del Colle. Ref: Lee.
The SPECTRE (F) Pathe 1910 15m. Ref: Bios 9/1/10. Innkeeper
   haunted by visions of man he killed.
SPECTRE, The see GHOST, The (1963)
A SPECTRE HAUNTS EUROPE (Russ) 1921 (Un SPECTRE ERRE A
   TRAVERS L'EUROPE-F.) D: Vladmir R. Gardin. From Edgar
   Allan Poe's "Masque of the Red Death." Ref: DDC II:418. FIR
   '61:466.
SPECTRE VERT, Le see GREEN GHOST, The
SPEED Para 1917 11m. Ref: Lee. LC. Scientist invents speed powder
   for typist.
SPEEDING HOOFS Rayart 1927 60m. D: Louis Chaudet. PH:Eddie
   Linden. Ref: AFI. Western. with Dick Hatton. Gang of thieves
   spreads rumor that ranch is haunted.
The SPEEDING VENUS Producers Distributing Corp. 1926 70m.
   D: Robert Thornby. Adap: Finis Fox. From "Behind the Wheel"
   by Welford Beaton. PH : Georges Benoit. Ref: AFI with Priscilla
   Dean, Robert Frazer, Dale Fuller, Charles Sellon. "Gearless
   motor invention."
The SPELL Vita 1913 27m. Ref: Bios 9/11/13. 10/2/13. with Mary
   Chapelson. Girl under hypnotist's spell. Seance.
The SPELL Powers 1913 35m. Ref: Bios 11/6/13. Girl under hyp-
   notist's spell.
SPELL OF THE HYPNOTIST Helios 1912 Ref: MPW 11:528. Lee.
   Hypnotist causes murder.
SPELL OF THE HYPNOTIST see FRIGHT
SPELLBOUND (B) UA/Pyramid 1940 ('45-U.S.) 82m. (60m. -U.S.)
   (The SPELL OF AMY NUGENT-U.S. GHOST STORY) D: John
   Harlow. SP: Miles Malleson. From the novel "The Necromancers"
   by Hugh Benson. Ref: MPH 2/17/45. PM. V 1/29/41. with
   Derek Farr, Vera Lindsay, Hay Petrie, Felix Aylmer, Gibb
   McLaughlin, Joyce Redman, Frederick Leister. Spiritualism;
   demon possession; apparition.
SPESSART ROCKETS see GLORIOUS TIMES IN THE SPESSART
SPETTRO DE DR. HICHCOCK, Lo see GHOST, The (1963)
SPETTRO DEL SOTTERRANEO, Lo see SPECTER OF THE
   VAULT, The
SPETTRO DI JAGO, Lo see SPECTER OF JAGO, The
SPETTRO DI MEZZANOTTE, Lo see MIDNIGHT SPECTER, The
SPETTRO VENDICATORE see AVENGING SPECTER, The
The SPHERE (I) Europa/Algor 1971 D: Gianni Poggi. Ref: M/TVM
   6/71. with Beatrice Pellegrino, Guido Coderin. Time machine.
The SPHINX Mono 1933 70m. D: Phil Rosen. SP: Albert DeMond.
   Remade as PHANTOM KILLER. PH: G. Warrenton. Ref: Fir'68:
   127. Harrison's 7/15/33. Clarens. with Lionel Atwill, Sheila
   Terry, Luis Alberni, Robert Ellis, Lucien Prival, Paul Fix,
   Paul Hurst, Lillian Leighton, Hooper Atchley, Wilfred Lucas.
   Harrison's: "A gripping murder mystery of the horror brand":
   The twin brother of a deaf mute is a murderer.
The SPIDER Fox 1931 D: William Cameron Menzies, Kenneth Mac-
   Kenna. SP: Barry Conners, Philip Klein, from a play by
   Fulton Oursler, Lowell Brentano. Ed: Al DeGaetano. Ref:

NYT. PM. Pic: FanMo 5:22? with Edmund Lowe, Lois Moran,
Purnell Pratt, Warren Hymer, George E. Stone, Earle Fox, El
Brendel. "Voice from beyond the grave," magic, trap doors,
sliding panels, clutching hands, shadows, hypnotist.

The SPIDER AI 1958 72m. (EARTH VS. THE GIANT SPIDER.
L'ARAIGNEE VAMPIRE-F.) D: Bert I. Gordon. SP: George
W. Yates, Lazslo Gorog. PH: Jack Marta. Mus: Albert Glasser.
SpFX, P: Gordon. Spider Handler: Jim Dannaldson. Ref: FFacts.
FM 2:20. 14:19. 27:16. 35:29. with Ed Kemmer, June Kenny,
Skip Young, Gene Roth, June Jocelyn, Mickey Finn, Sally
Fraser. A giant spider terrorizes a community. A few shocks;
otherwise the usual giant-spider antics.

SPIDER, The see SPIDER RETURNS, The /SPIDER'S WEB, The

SPIDER BABY American General 1968 (1965) (ATTACK OF THE
LIVER EATERS. The LIVER EATERS. CANNIBAL ORGY, or
THE MADDEST STORY EVER TOLD) SP, D: Jack Hill. PH: Alfred
Taylor. Mus: Ronald Stein. Ref: RVB. LATimes 1/12/68.
MMania 3:35. with Lon Chaney, Jr., Carol Ohmart, Quinn Re-
decker, Mantan Moreland.

A SPIDER IN THE BRAIN (I) Itala 1912 8m. Ref: Lee. MPW 14:
977. Big spider that crawled in person's ear located by x-ray.

The SPIDER RETURNS Col 1941 serial 15 episodes D: James W.
Horne. SP: J. A. Duffy, G. H. Plympton, M. B. Cox,
L. E. Taylor, J. Cutting, H. Fraser. Based on "The
Spider" magazine stories. PH: James S. Brown, Jr. Ref: Bar-
bour. SF in the cinema. Showmen's 5/10/41. Pic: TBG. with
Warren Hull, Mary Ainslee, Dave O'Brien, Kenneth Duncan, Joe
Girard. Ch. 10. The X-Ray Belt. Villainous Gargoyle's "diabol-
ical tortures"; electrical gadget that operates machines by re-
mote control.

The SPIDER WOMAN Univ 1944 62m. D, P: Roy William Neill. SP:
Bertram Millhauser. Based on the characters created by Sir
Arthur Conan Doyle. PH: Charles Van Enger. Mus D: H. J.
Salter. Art D: John B. Goodman, Martin Obzina. Ref: FDY.
TVG. with Basil Rathbone, Nigel Bruce, Gale Sondergaard,
Arthur Hohl, Dennis Hoey, Mary Gordon. Sherlock Holmes dis-
covers the bizarre method of murder behind a series of apparent
suicides. Above average Holmes mystery-horror.

The SPIDER WOMAN STRIKES BACK Univ 1946 59m. D: Arthur
Lubin. SP: Eric Taylor. PH: Paul Ivano. Mus D: Milton Rosen.
Art D: John B. Goodman, Abraham Grossman. Ref: FDY. Pic:
HM 4:24. with Gale Sondergaard, Kirby Grant, Hobart Cavanaugh,
Rondo Hatton, Brenda Joyce, Milburn Stone, Tom Daly. "Blind"
woman extracts blood from nurse, feeds it and black widows to
plant, and extracts poison from plant. Thoroughly ridiculous and
incredible. All-time favorite bad line: Gale Sondergaard reas-
sures her intended victim: "It won't really be dying because you'll
be living on in this plant."

SPIDERS FROM HELL (Mex) Col c1966 (ARAÑAS INFERNALES)
D: Federico Curiel. SP: Adolfo Portillo. Ref: Lee. D. Glut. with
Blue Demon, "Frankestein," Martha Elena Cervantes, Ramon
Bugarini, Fernando Oses. Flying saucer, giant spider, creatures
from another planet.

The SPIDER'S WEB Col 1938 serial 15 episodes D: Ray Taylor,
   James W. Horne. SP: Robert E. Kent, B. Dickey, G. Plymp-
   ton, M. Ramson. Based on "The Spider" magazine stories. PH:
   Allen G. Siegler. Ref: Barbour. Showmen's 10/29/38: "Death-
   ray gun." Pic: TBG. with Warren Hull, Iris Meridith (or
   Meredith), Kenneth Duncan, Nestor Paiva, Richard Fiske,
   Charles C. Wilson ("The Octopus"), Forbes Murray, Marc
   Lawrence, Donald Douglas.
SPIE AMANO I FIORI, Le see SPY WHO LOVED FLOWERS, The
SPIE UCCIDONO A BIERUT, Lie see SECRET AGENT FIREBALL
SPIE VENGONO DAL SEMIFREDDO, Le see DR. GOLDFOOT
   AND THE GIRL BOMBS
SPIELER, Der see DR. MABUSE (Part I)
SPIES COME FROM HALFCOLD see DR. GOLDFOOT AND THE
   GIRL BOMBS
SPIES LOVE FLOWERS see SPY WHO LOVED FLOWERS, The
SPIES OF THE AIR (B) 1939 78m. D: David MacDonald. SP:
   A. R. Rawlinson, Bridget Boland. From the play "Official
   Secret" by Jeffrey Dell. Mus?: Brian Langley. Ed: David
   Lean. Ref: TVG. Showmen's 8/12/39. with Basil Radford,
   Barry K. Barnes, Roger Livesey, Joan Marion, Felix Aylmer,
   Henry Oscar, John Turnbull. "Secret plane" flown.
SPIFFKINS EATS FROGS (F) Lux 1912 8m. Ref: MPW 14:596,660.
   ...and becomes frog-like.
The SPIRAL STAIRCASE RKO 1946 83m. D: Robert Siodmak.
   SP: Mel Dinelli, from the novel "Some Must Watch" by Ethel
   Lina White. (The SILENCE OF HELEN McCORD) PH: Nicholas
   Musuraca. Mus sc: Roy Webb. Art D: Albert S. D'Agostino,
   Jack Okey. SpFX: Vernon L. Walker. Ref: MPH. FDY. P: Dore
   Schary. with Dorothy McGuire, George Brent, Ethel Barrymore,
   Kent Smith, Sara Allgood, Elsa Lanchester, Rhonda Fleming,
   Gordon Oliver, Rhys Williams, James Bell. Old house, stormy
   night, murder seen through killer's eyes. Imaginatively staged
   killings and fantasy sequence added to a lot of dull psychology
   and plot diversions.
The SPIRIT (F) Gaum 1908 9m. Ref: MPW'08:354. Medium,
   spiritualism.
The SPIRIT IS WILLING Para 1967 (1966) Technicolor 94m. D,P,
   William Castle. SP: Ben Starr, from the book "The Visitors" by
   Nathaniel Benchley. PH: Hal Stine. Mus sc & d: Vic Mizzy.
   SpFX: Lee Vasque. SpPhFX: Paul K. Lerpae. Process PH:
   Farciot Edouart. Ref: FFacts. FM 42:53. with Sid Caesar,
   Vera Miles, Barry Gordon, John McGiver, Cass Daley, Jill
   Townsend, Mary Wickes, Jesse White, Nestor Paiva, Doodles
   Weaver, Jay C. Flippen, John Astin, Harvey Lembeck. House
   haunted by three ghosts. Wretchedly-directed TV-style comedy
   with the same music over every scene, comic or otherwise.
   The script may have had something, but no one will ever know.
SPIRIT OF THE DEAD see CRIMSON ALTAR, The
The SPIRIT OF THE LAKE (I) Cines 1909 10m. Ref: Bios 3/24/10.
   Sea nymphs and "little Undina"; apparition; bewitched knight.
The SPIRIT OF THE SWORD (F) Pathe 1910 8m. Ref: Bios 4/21/10.
   Soldier's magic sword frightens innservant sent to fetch it.

The SPIRIT OF '23 C.B.C. 1922 25m. Pic: MPN 26:2174: skeleton.

SPIRIT WORLD OR THE RAJAH'S RUBY Kenilworth 1927 Author: Arthur B. Reeves. Ref: LC. Lee.

A SPIRITED ELOPEMENT Edison 1915 Ref: MPN 2/20/15. with William Wadsworth, Viola Dane. "Ghosts."

SPIRITISM (I) 1920 (SPIRITISMO) Ref: DDC I:221. with Francesca Bertina.

SPIRITISM (Mex) AI-TV/Calderon 1961 (ESPIRITISMO) D: Benito Alazaraki. SP: Rafael Travesi. Inspired by "The Monkey's Paw" by W. W. Jacobs. PH: Enrique Wallace. Mus: Antonio Diaz Conde. Ref: Aventura. with José Luis Jiminez, Nora Veryan, Carmen Gonzalez, Antonio Bravo.

SPIRITISTEN see GHOSTS, The (Dan-1914)

SPIRITUALISM EXPOSED (B) 1913 D: Charles Raymond. Ref: Brit Cinema.

SPIRITUALIST, The see AMAZING MR. X, The

SPIRITS OF THE DEAD see TALES OF MYSTERY AND IMAGINA-TION

A SPIRITUALISTIC CONVERT (F) Pathe 1912 7m. Ref: Bios 4/8/12. Maid impressed by seance studies book of mystic signs, succeeds in spinning objects around.

A SPIRITUALISTIC MEETING (F) Melies 1906 4m. Ref: V&FI 9/29/06. Seance, "ethereal bodies."

SPIRITUALISTIC SEANCE (F) Pathe 1908 5m. Ref: MPW'08:424. Scientist can "confer with spirits." "Huge form" materializes at seance.

A SPIRITUALISTIC SEANCE (F) Gaum 1910 7m. (SEANCE DE SPIRITISME) Leonce Perret. Ref: Bios 2/9/11. Mitry II:229. Man under table makes those at seance think spirits are present.

A SPIRITUALISTIC SEANCE (F) Pathe 1911 6m. Ref: Bios 10/5/11. Man who denounces spiritualism beset by spirits.

SPLIT, The see MANSTER, The

SPOKAR, DET SPOKAR, Det see GHOSTS! GHOSTS!

SPOKET PA BRAGEHUS see GHOST OF BRAGEHUS

SPOOK BUSTERS Mono 1946 68m. D: William Beaudine. SP: Edmund Seward, Tim Ryan. PH: Harry Neumann. Mus D: Edward Kay. Ref: HR 8/15/46. V 8/15/46. MFB'47:40. with Leo Gorcey, Huntz Hall, Douglass Dumbrille, Bobby Jordan, Gabe Dell, Billy Benedict, David Gorcey, Charles Middleton, Bernard Gorcey, Richard Alexander. Mad doctor, supposedly haunted country house.

The SPOOK CASTLE OF SPESSART (G) Exportfilm 1960 color/ scope 104m. (Das SPUKSCHLOSS IM SPESSART. HAUNTED CASTLE) D: Kurt Hoffmann. First in the "Spessart" series. Ref: German Pictures. Heraldo'62:92. DDC III:46. Pic: FM 18:11. with Liselotte Pulver, Hubert von Meyerinck, Curt Bois, George Thomalla. SP: Heinz Pauck, L. Enderle.

SPOOK CHASERS AA 1957 61m. D: George Blair. SP: Elwood Ullman. Ass't D: Austen Jewell, Lindsley Parsons, Jr. PH: Harry Neumann. Mus: Marlin Skiles. Art D: Dave Milton. Ref: MFB'58:118. with Huntz Hall, Stanley Clements, David Gorcey, Robert Sha(y)ne, Percy Helton, Darlene Fields. The Bowery boys are haunted by a pair of "ghosts."

SPOOK HOUSE see BEWARE, SPOOKS!

The SPOOK RAISERS Kalem 1915 Ref: MPN 7/24/15. MPW
7/20/15. with Ethel Teare. Two men set up a fake "ghost em-
porium" for seances.

SPOOK RANCH Univ 1925 64m. D: Edward Laemmle. PH: Harry
Neumann, SP: R. L. Shrock, Edward Sedgwick. Ref: AFI. FD
4/26/25. Photoplay 7/25: "Touches that are reminiscent of
Griffith's ONE EXCITING NIGHT, including the negro comedy
character." with Hoot Gibson, Tote DuCrow, Ed Cowles,
Helen Ferguson, Robert McKim, Frank Rice, Bandits
after gold mine hold girl and her father at supposedly haunted
ranch.

SPOOK SPOOFING 1927 25m. Ref: MPH 1/14/28. with Our
Gang. "Spooky devices" in graveyard.

SPOOK WARFARE (J) Daiei 1968 color/scope 79m. (YOKAI
DAISENSO. GHOSTS ON PARADE) D: Yoshiyuki Kuroda. SP:
Tetsuro Yoshida. PH: Hiroshi Imai. Mus: Shigeru Ikeno. Art D:
S. Ota, S. Kato. Ref: UFQ. M/TVM 11/68. with Yoshihiko Aoy-
ama, Akane Kawasaki. Blood-sucking monster Daimon who once
ruled over ancient Babylon awakens 4,000 years later.

SPOOKS (F?) Pathe 1912 15m. Ref: Bios 7/4/12. Man has ghostly
visions of dead brother.

SPOOKS Mermaid 1922 D: Jack White, Robert Kerr. Ref: MPW
55:663. Lee. with Lige Conley. Prize for person who spends
night in wax museum.

SPOOKS Bray 1927 25m. D: Robert B. Wilcox. A. McDougall
Alley Comedy. Ref: LC.

SPOOKS see CHRONICLES OF BLOOM CENTER

SPOOKS AND SPASMS Vita 1917 11m. Ref: LC.

SPOOKS DO THE MOVING (F) Pathe 1908 Ref: F Index 10/3/08.
Students, in order to steal their furniture, frighten old couple
by masquerading as ghosts.

SPOOKS RUN WILD Mono/Banner 1941 D: Phil Rosen. SP: Carl
Foreman, Charles Marion. (GHOST IN THE NIGHT-Eng.) PH:
Marcel Le Picard. Add'l Dial: Jack Hanley. Art D: David
Milton. P: Sam Katzman. Ref: FDY. ModM 1:32. Pic: FM
41:32. FanMo 3:60. with Bela Lugosi, Dave O'Brien, Leo
Gorcey, David Gorcey, Huntz Hall, Bobby Jordan, George Pem-
broke, Dennis Morgan, Guy Wilkerson, Angelo Rossit(t)o.
"Haunted" house; magician suspected of being vampirish killer.

A SPOOKY ROMANCE Century 1923 25m. SP,D: Al Herman.
Ref: LC.

SPOTLIGHT ON A MURDERER (F) Champs-Elysées 1960 (PLEINS
FEUX SUR L'ASSASSIN) D: Georges Franju. Ref: Unifrance
1/61. with Pierre Brasseur. Three murders are committed in
a medieval castle. "Dark corridors, squeaking doors and moaning
wind, classic devices of the horror film, are scientifically ex-
ploited by Franju."

SPRING-HEELED JACK, THE TERROR OF LONDON (play by T.
Slaughter) see CURSE OF THE WRAYDONS

SPUK IM OPERNHAUS see GHOST OF THE OPERA

SPUK IM SCHLOSS see GHOST IN THE CASTLE

SPUKSCHLOSS IM SALZKAMMERGUT   see HAUNTING CASTLE IN
   SALZKAMMERGUT, The
SPUKSCHLOSS IM SPESSART, Das see SPOOK CASTLE OF SPES-
   SART, The
SPURS (story by T. Robbins) see FREAKS
SPUTNIK see DOG, A MOUSE AND A SPUTNIK, A
The SPY IN THE GREEN HAT MGM/Arena 1966 Metrocolor D:
   Joseph Sargent. SP: Peter Allan Fields. Story: David Victor.
   From "The Man from U.N.C.L.E." TV series. PH: Fred
   Koenekamp. Mus: Nelson Riddle. Art D: George W. Davis, James
   W. Sullivan. Ref: MFB'67:47. P: Boris Ingster. with Robert
   Vaughn, David McCallum, Jack Palance, Janet Leigh, Letitia
   Roman, Eduardo Ciannelli, Allen Jenkins, Jack La Rue, Leo G.
   Carroll, Ludwig Donath, Joan Blondell, Frank Puglia, Maxie
   Rosenbloom, Vince Barnett, Elisha Cook, Jr. Plot to divert the
   Gulf Stream; "sonic destruction mechanism."
SPY IN YOUR EYE (I) AI/Publitalia 1965 color 88m. (BERLINO,
   APPUNTAMENTO PER LE SPIE) D: Vittorio Sala. SP: Ferrara,
   Bolzoni, Marcuzzo, Baraceo. PH: F. Zuccoli. Mus: Riz Orto-
   lani. Ref: COF 10:6. Ital P. with Pier Angeli, Brett Halsey,
   Dana Andrews. Laser death-ray; "electronic eyeball."
The SPY RING Univ 1938 61m. D: Joseph Lewis. SP: George
   Waggner. PH: Harry Neumann. Ref: TVK. TVG. FDY. with
   Jane Wyman, Leon Ames, William Hall, Ben Alexander, Don
   Barclay, Robert Warwick, Jack Mulhall, Egon Brecher. In-
   ventor's device transforms a machine-gun into an anti-aircraft
   weapon.
SPY SMASHER Rep 1942 serial 12 episodes ('66 feature SPY
   SMASHER RETURNS) D: William Witney. SP: R. Davidson, N. S.
   Hall, J. Poland, W. Lively, J. O'Donnell. PH: Reggie Lanning.
   Based on the "Whiz" comics character. Ref: Barbour. FIR'68:
   316. SF Film. Pic: FanMo 5:58. M&H 1:23. ModM 4:63. COF
   3:40. with Kane Richmond, Sam Flint, Marguerite Chapman, Hans
   Schumm, Tristram Coffin, Georges Renavent, Tom London, Crane
   Whitley, John James, Robert Wilke. "Bat plane," death ray that
   knocks out plane motors. Pretty dull serial.
The SPY WHO LOVED FLOWERS (I) Romana 1966 (Le SPIE AMANO
   I FIORI. SPIES LOVE FLOWERS) SP,D: Umberto Lenzi. PH: A.
   Tiezzi. Ref: Ital P. Annuario. with Roger Browne, Emma
   Danieli, Dan Vargas, Yoko Tani. An electronic weapon, the
   gamma electrometre, is stolen from a secret laboratory.
The SPY WITH MY FACE MGM/Arena 1964 Metrocolor 86m.
   D: John Newland. SP: Clyde Ware, Joseph Calvelli. First seen
   as "The Double Affair" on "The Man from U.N.C.L.E." TV
   show. PH: Fred Koenekamp. Mus: Morton Stevens. Ref: MFB
   '67:142. COF 10:6. with Robert Vaughn, David McCallum,
   Senta Berger, Leo G. Carroll, Sharon Farrell, Paula Raymond,
   Jan Arvan, Michele Carey. Secret agent turned into exact double
   of Napoleon Solo through plastic surgery. Midget-robots.
The SPY'S RUSE Kalem 1915 Ref: MPN 1/1/16. with Marguerite
   Courtot, R. A. Bennett, Harry Edwards, Electric torpedo-
   deflector invention.
SQUARE EMERALD, The (novel by E. Wallace) see GIRL FROM
   SCOTLAND YARD, The

STADE ZERO see SKY ABOVE HEAVEN
The STAGE IS CLEARED FOR MARIKA (G) Europa 1958 color
93m. (BUHNE FREI FUR MARIKA) D: Georg Jacoby. Mus:
Franz Grothe. Ref: German Pictures'58. with Marika Rökk,
Johannes Heesters, Carla Hagen, Harald Juhnke. Musical. Sketch:
The first rocket from the moon to earth.
STAR CREATURES, The see INVASION OF THE STAR CREATURES
STAR OF ADAM (J) Toho 1969 (OTOKO TO ONNA NO SHINWA)
D: Hideo Onchi. Survivors of nuclear war on earth sent on photon
rocket to another planet.
STAR OF INDIA Blanché 1913 60m. Ref: MPW 18:1342. Lee. Pos-
sessors of stolen stone die horrible deaths.
STAR OF THE CIRCUS see HIDDEN MENACE
The STAR ROVER Metro-Shurtleff 1920 70m. D: Edward Sloman.
SP: A. S. LeVino. From the novel by Jack London. PH:
Jackson Rose. Art D: Edward Shulter. Ref: MPN 22:4157.
V 1/21/21. with Courtenay Foote, Thelma Percy, Jack Car-
lysle. Man accused of murder, subjected by police to the third
degree, lives through previous incarnations on earth.
STARK MAD WB 1929 sound 70m. Titles: Francis Powers. D:
Lloyd Bacon. SP: Harvey Gates. PH: Barney McGill. Story:
Jerome Kingston. Ref: AFI. V 7/3/29. Pic: Pict Hist Talkies.
MPH/MPW 12/1/28:33. with Louise Fazenda, Irene Rich,
Claude Gillingwater, H. B. Warner, Jacqueline Logan, H. B.
Walthall, Lionel Belmore, Andre Beranger. "Deserted temple,
chained ape, lunatics, and eerie atmosphere. "
START SOMETHING Univ 1928 silent 25m. (Keeping Up with the
Joneses series) Ref: MPN 1/14/28. A fortune teller predicts a
family will have a "mysterious visitor" at midnight. As the hour
approaches they hear "weird noises and see strange sights" in
the house.
STATION THREE ULTRA-SECRET see SATAN BUG, The
STEEL MONSTER, The see MOST DANGEROUS MAN ALIVE, The
STEELMAN FROM OUTER SPACE, The see INVADERS FROM
SPACE
STEPS TO THE MOON (Rumanian) 1963 (PASI SPRE LUNA. FIRST
STEPS TO THE MOON) D: Ion Popesco-Gopo. Ref: M/TVM
8/64. COF 6:30.8:49: STEPS TOWARDS THE MOON: "The
story begins in the future, as the hero rushes out of a space-
port to keep a date on the moon. " Stone Age, the devil, the
ancient winged bulls of Assyria, etc. Comedy-documentary.
STILLE STERN, Der see FIRST SPACESHIP ON VENUS
STING OF DEATH Thunderbird Int'l 1967 76m. D: William Grefe.
SP: Al Dempsey. Makeup: Harry Kerwin. Ref: F&F 10/68.
COF 12:7. with Neal (or Neil) Sedaka, Joe Morrison, Valerie
Hawkins, John Vella. Lab assistant changes himself into half-
man, half-jellyfish creature.
The STOLEN AIRSHIP (Cz-I) Barrandov/Gottwaldov-Ponti 1966
color 105m. (UKRADENA VZDUCHOLOD) Part I of serial "The
Mysterious World of Jules Verne." SP,D: Karel Zeman. SP:
also Radovan Kratky. Based loosely on Jules Verne's "Two
Years' Vacation." PH: Josef Novotny. Mus: Jan Novak. Art D:
Jaroslav Krska. Ref: V 10/1/69. M/TVM 7/66.2/67. Pic:

Continental Film Review 11/67. with Michael Pospisil, Hanus
Bor, Jan Cizek. Captain Nemo; flying machine.
STOLEN FACE (B) Lippert/Exclusive 1952 71m. D: Terence Fisher.
P: Anthony Hinds. SP: Richard Landau, Martin Berk(e)ley. PH:
Walter Harvey. Mus: Malcolm Arnold. Ref: MPH'52:1389.
TVG. MFB'52:81. with Paul Henreid, Lizabeth Scott, Andre
Morell, Mary MacKenzie, Arnold Ridley, John Wood. A plastic
surgeon remakes a woman's face into the image of the girl he
loved and lost.
The STOLEN VOICE World 1915 50m. Ref: MPN 8/14/15. Lee.
with Robert Warwick, Frances Nelson. Voice lost through hypnosis.
The STONE FLOWER (Russ) Artkino/Moscow Film Studio c1946
D: Alexandre Ptushko. SP: P. Bazhov, I. Keller. PH: F. Prov-
orov. Mus sc: L. Schvarts. Ref: MFB'47:69. with V. Druzhnikov,
T. Makarova. A stone-cutter is in bondage to the Mistress of
the Copper Mountains in her magic palace.
STORM PLANET (Russ) New Realm 1962 (PLANETA BURG.
COSMONAUTS ON VENUS-Eng.) SP,D: Pavel Klushantsev. SP:
also Alexander Kazantsev. PH: Arkady Klimov. See also VOY-
AGE TO THE PLANET OF PREHISTORIC WOMEN. Ref: Clarens.
MFB'65:77. Pic: SM 8:7. with Kyunna Ignatova, Gennadi Vernov,
Georgi Zhonov. U.S. version: SP,D: John Sebastian. Mus:
Ronald Stein. Assoc P: Stephanie Rothman. P: George Edwards.
Pathecolor. VOYAGE TO A PREHISTORIC PLANET. with Basil
Rathbone, Faith Domergue. Venusian dinosaurs; robot.
STORY OF A MADMAN see MADNESS OF DR. TUBE, The
The STORY OF HANSEL AND GRETEL (G) c1924 23m. (HANSEL
UND GRETEL) From "Hansel and Gretel" by the Bros. Grimm.
Ref: SilentFF.
The STORY OF MANKIND WB/Cambridge 1957 color 100m.
SP,D,P: Irwin Allen. SP: also Charles Bennett. From the book
by H. W. Van Loon. PH: Nicholas Musuraca. Mus: Paul Saw-
tell. Art D: Art Loel. Ref: FM 19:36. 67:12. V 10/23/57.
with Vincent Price, Peter Lorre, Ronald Colman, Dennis Hopper,
Sir Cedric Hardwicke, Henry Daniell, Francis X. Bushman, John
Carradine, Hedy Lamarr; Groucho, Harpo and Chico Marx; Vir-
ginia Mayo, Agnes Moorehead, Charles Coburn, Cesar Romero,
Marie Wilson, Helmut Dantine, Edward Everett Horton, Reginald
Gardiner, Marie Windsor, George E. Stone, Cathy O'Donnell,
Franklin Pangborn, Melville Cooper, Nick Cravat, Anthony Dex-
ter, Melinda Marx, Don Megowan, Marvin Miller, Leonard
Mudie, Tudor Owen, Ziva Rodann, Harry Ruby, William Schallert,
Abraham Sofaer, Bobby Watson. Super-H-bomb, Pleistocene man,
the devil, and the Spirit of Mankind. A big mess.
STORY OF UGETSU, The see UGETSU MONOGATARI
The STORY WITHOUT A NAME Para 1924 80m. (aka WITHOUT WARN-
ING?) D: Irvin Willat. SP: Victor Irvin. PH: Harold Rosson.
Story: Arthur Stringer. Ref: Wid's 9/27/24. NYT 10/6/24.
FD 10/26/24. AFI: "Triangulator" emits "death rays." with
Agnes Ayres, Antonio Moreno, Tyrone Power, Frank Currier,
Louis Wolheim, Maurice Costello, Ivan Linow, Jack Bohn. For-
eign spies steal an inventor's plans for a death ray.
STRAGE DEI VAMPIRI, La see SLAUGHTER OF THE VAMPIRES, The

STRAIT-JACKET Col 1963 89m. D,P: William Castle. SP: Robert
Bloch. PH: Arthur Arling. Mus: Van Alexander. Art D: Boris
Leven. SpFX: Richard Albain. Makeup: Ben Lane. Ref: FFacts.
with Joan Crawford, Diane Baker, Leif Erickson, Rochelle
Hudson, Howard St. John , George Kennedy, Edith Atwater. A
woman is a suspect in a series of ax murders.

STRANGE ADVENTURE Mono 1933 60m. D: Phil Whitman. SP:
Lee Chadwick. Story: Arthur Hoerl. PH: Leon Shumway. Ref:
Harrison's 2/18/33: "Spookiness." FDY. with William V.
Mong, Regis Toomey, June Clyde, Lucille LaVerne, Jason
Robards, Eddie Phillips, Dwight Frye. A millionaire is mur-
dered by a mysterious hooded killer.

STRANGE ADVENTURE OF DAVID GRAY, The see VAMPYR

STRANGE CARGO 1929 sound SP,D: Benjamin Glazer. SP: also
Melchior Lengyel. Ref: Photoplay 4/29: "Spooks have come to
the talkies." NYT 2/18/29. with Russell Gleason, June Nash,
Frank Reicher, Lee Patrick, George Barraud, Claude King,
Ned Sparks, Andre Beranger. Seance, Hindu mystic, etc.

The STRANGE CASE OF CAPTAIN RAMPER F Nat/Defu (G) 1927
79m. (RAMPER DER TIERMENSCH) D: Max Reichmann. SP:
Kurt J. Braun, Paul Wegener, from the play "Ramper" by Max
Mohr. PH: F. Weinmann, H. Körner. Art D: Leopold Blonder.
Ref: PM. SilentFF. EncicDS IX:1881. Pic: FM 17:33. with
Wegener (Capt. Ramper), Max Schreck ("The Thin One"),
Emilie Kurz, Mary Johnson, Kurt Gerron, George D. Gurtler,
Karl Ballhaus, Dillo Lombardi, Raimondo van Riel. Arctic ex-
plorer dropped from his airship in Greenland lives there for
ten years and turns into a wild animal.

The STRANGE CASE OF DR. FAUSTO (Sp) Hersua Interfilms 1969
color/scope 82m. (El EXTRAÑO CASO DEL DOCTOR FAUSTO)
SP,D: Gonzalo Suárez. PH: Carlos Suárez. Mus: S. Pueyo. Art
D: A. Corazón. Ref: SpCinema'70. with G. Suárez, Teresa
Gimpera, Charo López, Emma Cohen. Dr. Fausto is plagued by
beings which try to prevent him from discovering a key to under-
standing the world.

STRANGE CASE OF DR. JEKYLL AND MR. HYDE, The (story by
Robert Louis Stevenson) see ABBOTT AND COSTELLO MEET
DR. JEKYLL AND MR. HYDE/DAUGHTER OF DR. JEKYLL/
DIABOLICAL PACT/DR. JEKYLL AND MR. HYDE/DR. JEKYLL
AND MR. HYDE DONE TO A FRAZZLE/DR. PYCKLE AND
MR. PRIDE/HORRIBLE HYDE/HOUSE OF FRIGHT/JANUS-
KOPF , Der/LUKE'S DOUBLE/MAN AND THE BEAST, The/MY
FRIEND DR. JEKYLL/NUTTY PROFESSOR, The/SON OF DR.
JEKYLL/TESTAMENT OF DR. CORDELIER, The/UGLY DUCK-
LING, The/WHEN QUACKEL DID HYDE

The STRANGE CASE OF DR. RX Univ 1942 66m. D: William
Nigh. SP: Clarence Upson Young. PH: Elwood Bredell. Mus D:
H. J. Salter. Art D: Jack Otterson. Ref: V 3/27/42. HR 3/27/
42. HM 8:18. Pic: FMO 6:11,12. with Lionel Atwill, Patric
Knowles, Anne Gwynne, Mantan Moreland, Shemp Howard,
Samuel S. Hinds, Mona Barrie, Paul Cavanagh, John Gallaudet,
Leyland Hodgson. Mystery with horror scenes: Dr. RX intends
to switch hero's and ape's brains ("He's going to be smart--and

457   Strange

you'll be...not so smart"). The mystery's solution is interest-
ing, but nothing else is.
STRANGE CASE OF...!#* ?   See MALTESE BIPPY
The STRANGE CASE OF PRINCESS KHAN Selig 1915 25m. (HOW
  LOVE CONQUERED HYPNOTISM) D: Edward J. LeSaint. Story:
  James Oliver Curwood. Ref: MPN 1/9/15. Motography 1/9/15.
  with Stella Razeto, Jack McDonald, Guy Oliver. Girl under spell
  of hypnotist.
STRANGE CONFESSION Univ 1945 62m. (The MISSING HEAD)
  D: John Hoffman. SP: M. Coates Webster. (Inner Sanctum series)
  PH: Maury Gertsman. Mus: Frank Skinner. Remake of The
  MAN WHO RECLAIMED HIS HEAD. Ref: COF 7:40. FDY. Pic:
  HM 8:46. Ref: FM 11:23. From a play by Jean Bart. with Lon
  Chaney, Jr., Brenda Joyce, Milburn Stone, Lloyd Bridges,
  Addison Richards, Mary Gordon, George Chandler, Wilton
  Graff, Jack Norton, Christian Rub. Fugitive shows attorney
  bag, hints head is in it.
The STRANGE DEATH OF ADOLF HITLER Univ 1943 72m.
  D: James Hogan. SP: Fritz Kortner. Story: Kortner, Joe May.
  PH: Jerome Ash. Mus sc: H. J. Salter. Art D: John B. Good-
  man, Ralph DeLacy. Ref: V 8/26/43. with Ludwig Donath, Gale
  Sondergaard, George Dolenz, Kortner, Ludwig Stossel, Ivan
  Triesault, Rudolph Anders, Kurt Katch, Kurt Kreuger, Hans
  Schumm, Hans von Twardowsky. Plastic surgery allows a Nazi
  official to impersonate Hitler.
The STRANGE DOOR Univ 1951 80m. D: Joseph Pevney. SP:
  Jerry Sackheim. From the story "The Sire de Maletroit's Door"
  by Robert Louis Stevenson. PH: Irving Glassberg. Mus D:
  Joseph Gershenson. Art D: Bernard Herzbrun, Eric Orbom.
  Ref: FDY. with Boris Karloff, Charles Laughton, Sally Forrest,
  Michael Pate, Richard Stapely, Alan Napier, Paul Cavanagh.
  Tyrant gets revenge by imprisoning family of his dead sweet-
  heart. Sluggish quasi-horror film. Laughton gives life to a few
  scenes.
STRANGE EXPERIMENT (B) 1937 72m. D: Albert Parker.
  Ref: TVFFSB. FJA. with Alastair Sim, Donald Grey, Ann
  Wemyss. "Doctors test dangerous brain operation that will re-
  form the most hardened criminal."
STRANGE GUEST, The see DEATH TAKES A HOLIDAY
STRANGE HOLIDAY PRC/Elite 1946 54m. SP,D: Arch Oboler, from
  his radio play "This Precious Freedom." PH: Robert Surtees.
  Mus sc: Gordon Jenkins. Art D: Bernard Herzbrun. Ref: FM
  47:16. FDY. TVG. with Claude Rains, Gloria Holden, Martin
  Kosleck, Barbara Bates, Milton Kibbee, Helen Mack. After
  World War II an American returns from a vacation to find the
  Nazis in control of the country.
STRANGE HOLIDAY see DEATH TAKES A HOLIDAY
STRANGE IMPERSONATION Rep 1946 68m. D: Anthony Mann.
  SP: Mindret Lord. From a story by Anne Wigton and Lewis
  Herman. PH: Robert W. Pittack. P: William Wilder. Ref: HR
  2/26/46. with Brenda Marshall, William Gargan, Hillary
  Brooke, George Chandler, Ruth Ford, H. B. Warner, Lyle
  Talbot, Mary Treen. New anesthetic causes horrible nightmares.

STRANGE JOURNEY see FANTASTIC VOYAGE
The STRANGE MR. GREGORY Mono 1946 64m. (The GREAT
MYSTIC. GREGORY) D: Phil Rosen. SP: Charles S. Belden.
Story: Myles Connolly. PH: Ira Morgan. Mus D: Edward J.
Kay. Ref: HR 12/31/45. V 1/17/46. Showmen's '45. with
Edmund Lowe, Jean Rogers, Don Douglas, Frank Reicher, Robert
Emmett Keane, Jonathan Hale, Fred Kelsey, Jack Norton, Tom
Leffingwell. Suspended animation permits a stage magician to
be buried as dead "and to leave the tomb at his convenience."
STRANGE OBSESSION, The see WITCH IN LOVE, The
STRANGE PEOPLE Chesterfield 1933 63m. D: Richard Thorpe.
SP: Jack Townley. PH: M. A. Andersen. Ref: V 3/10/33.
Harrison's 7/1/33: "Eerie." Photoplay 6/33: "A rather obvious
mixture of several horror pictures you have seen lately, with the
set from The OLD DARK HOUSE used bodily." with Hale
Hamilton, John Darrow, Gloria Shea, Wilfred Lucas, Lew Kelly,
Michael Visaroff, Jack Pennick, Walter Brennan, Stanley Blystone, Frank Glendon. NYT 6/17/33: "The twelve members of
the jury which sentenced an innocent man to death are summoned
at midnight to the murdered man's house....Rain, shadows and
the half-human sounds the wind makes when it whistles around
the gables of a house at night; stairs that creak and floors that
groan; the stifled screams of women who imagine they can see the
silhouette of a man hanging dead on the balcony; and the look on
the face of a corpse when it tumbles out from behind a
screen..."
STRANGE PURSUIT see HIDEOUS SUN DEMON, The
The STRANGE STORY OF BRANDNER KASPAR (G) Bavaria-Film
1949 104m. (Die SELTSAME GESCHICTE DES BRANDNER KAS-
PAR) D: Josef von Baky. SP: Erna Fentsch, from a story by
Franz von Kobell and the Bühnenstück "Der Brandner Kaspar
Schaut ins Paradies." Mus: Alois Melichar. Ref: Deutscher. with
Paul Hörbiger, Carl Wery, Ursula Lingen, Georg Thomalla.
"Death in person" visits an old hunter on the latter's birthday.
STRANGE TALES see TALES OF MYSTERY AND IMAGINATION
The STRANGE UNKNOWN Lubin 1915 45m. SP: William H. Ratter-
man. Ref: MPW 26:1153. with L. C. Shumway, George Routh,
Helen Eddy, Dorothy Barrett, Melvin Mayo. Drug that deprives
woman of her senses; haunted house; woman's ghost.
STRANGE WORLD OF PLANET X see COSMIC MONSTER(S), The
The STRANGE WORLD OF ZE DO CAIXAO (Braz) Iberia 1968
80m. (O ESTRANHO MUNDO DE ZE DO CAIXAO) D: Jose
Mojica Marins. Ref: M/TVM 6/69. V 5/7/69:208. with
Marins, Luiz Person, Iris Bruzzi. Three horror stories: 1. Doll
maker who uses human eyes for his creations. 2. "Hunchback
sex maniac." 3. "Strange professor who collects horrors."
STRANGER FROM VENUS Princess--TV 1954 (B) 76m. (IMMEDIATE
DISASTER. VISITOR FROM VENUS. The VENUSIAN) Ref: Brit
Cinema: D: Burt Balaban. COF 11:36. FM 24:4. FFF. with
Patricia Neal, Helmut Dantine, Derek Bond.
STRANGER IN THE NIGHT c1955 56m. From "The Ghost and Mrs.
Muir" by R. A. Dick. Ref: TVG. with Joan Fontaine, Michael
Wilding, Elsa Lanchester, Tom Conway. An attractive widow

takes a cottage by the sea only to find that it's haunted by the ghost
of s sea captain.
STRANGER ON THE CAMPUS see MONSTER ON THE CAMPUS
STRANGER ON THE THIRD FLOOR RKO 1940 63m. D: Boris Ingster.
SP: Frank Partos. PH: Nicholas Musuraca. Mus sc: Roy Webb.
Art D: Van Nest Polglase, Albert D'Agostino. SpFX: Vernon L.
Walker. Ref: FM 17:13. 30:20. COF 5:14. 16:22. V 8/30/40:
"Eerie drama settles into the horror groove." Pic: COF 5:22.
with Peter Lorre, Charles Halton, Elisha Cook, Jr., Ethel Grif-
fies, John McGuire, Margaret Tallichet, Cliff Clark, Alec Craig,
Paul McVey, Frank Yaconelli, Robert Dudley, Frank O'Connor,
Bud Osborne, Emory Parnell, Don Kerr. A psychopathic killer
is on the loose, and an innocent man faces execution for his
crimes. Lighting, sharply drawn minor characters, Webb's ef-
fective mood music, and Lorre's powerful performance distinguish
a familiar story. Lorre's choicest line is, "I want a couple of
hamburgers and I'd like them raw."
STRANGLEHOLD see HAUNTED STRANGLER, The
STRANGLER OF BENGAL, The see STRANGLERS OF BOMBAY,
The
The STRANGLER OF BLACKMOOR CASTLE (G) Manley-TV/CCC/
Gloria 1963 89m. (Der WURGER VON SCHLOSS BLACKMOOR)
D: Harald Reinl. SP: Ladislas Fodor, Gustav Kampendonk. Story:
Bryan Edgar Wallace. PH: E. W. Kalinke. Mus: Oskar Sala.
Ref: FIR'67:83. German Pictures. Pic: COF 9:31. with Karin
Dor, Ingmar Zeisberg, Dieter Eppler, Hans Nielsen. Masked
killer loose in old English castle.
STRANGLER OF THE SWAMP PRC 1945 60m. SP,D: Frank Wis-
bar. Story: Wisbar, Leo McCarthy. PH: James S. Brown. Art
D: Edward C. Jewell. Ref: FDY. with Robert Barrat, Rosemary
LaPlanche, Blake Edwards, Charles Middleton (the ghost), Effie
Parnell, Frank Conlan. Condemned man curses those responsi-
ble for hanging him. The film, supposedly a sleeper, is, in the
wrong way. It's a little better (maybe) than Wisbar's DEVIL
BAT'S DAUGHTER, but less interesting.
STRANGLER'S MORGUE see CRIMES OF STEPHEN HAWKE, The
The STRANGLERS OF BOMBAY (B) Col/Hammer 1959 81m.
(The STRANGLER OF BENGAL) D: Terence Fisher. SP: David
Z. Goodman. MegaScope PH: Arthur Grant. Mus: James Ber-
nard. Art D: Bernard Robinson, Don Mingaye. Ref: MMF 1:37.
Brit Cinema. Orpheus 3:27. with Allan Cuthbertson, Guy Rolfe,
Marne Maitland, Jan Holden. Indian cult attempts to drive
British from trading station. Brutal, with the most evil, blood-
thirsty cult on film. Bernard's score almost as exciting as his
score for HORROR OF DRACULA. Better-than-average Hammer.
STREAMLINE EXPRESS Mascot-Republic 1935 D: Leonard Fields.
SP: Fields, David Silverstein, Olive Cooper. Ref: SF Film.
MPH 9/14/35. with Evelyn Venable, Victor Jory, Esther
Ralston, Ralph Forbes, Sidney Blackmer, Erin O'Brien-Moore,
Vince Barnett. Streamline train.
STREETS OF GHOST TOWN Col 1950 54m. D: Ray Nazarro. SP:
Barry Shipman. PH: Fayte Browne. Art D: Charles Clague. Ref:
MFB'54. HR 8/9/50. with Charles Starrett, Smiley Burnette,

George Chesebro, Mary Ellen Kay, Frank Fenton, Jack Ingram.
"Spooky things happen" in ghost town; bandits hide loot in tunnel.
STREGA DE SIVIGLIA, Il see WITCH OF SEVILLE, The
STREGA IN AMORE, La see WITCH IN LOVE, The
STREGHE, Le see WITCHES, The
The STRENGTH OF THE HUMBLE (Mex) Cub-Mex c1955 90m.
  (La FUERZA DE LOS HUMILDES) Ref: FM 31:23: fantasy. with
  Columba Dominguez, Roberto Cañedo, Joaquin Cordero.
A STRIKE IN THE MAKE-YOUNG BUSINESS (F) Eclair 1911 Ref:
  The Film Index. MPW 8:901. A man undergoes mechanical treat-
  ment to make him younger, but a strike reverses the machinery.
STROKE OF MIDNIGHT, The see PHANTOM CHARIOT, The (1919)
A STRONG TONIC Ref: MPW'09:891, 960. 1909 A man buys a drug-
  store tonic which makes him strong.
The STRONGER MIND Selig 1912 17m. Ref:MPW 12:448. Hypnotic
  detective.
The STRONGER SEX (Mex) Clasa 1945 (El SEXO FUERTE. Las
  SUPER-HEMBRAS. SUPER FEMALES) D: E. G. Muriel. SP:
  H. G. Landero. PH: A. M. Solares. Story: Miguel Morayta.
  Ref: Indice. FM 31:19. with Mapy Cortes, José Pidal. Kingdom
  of the future where women reign.
STRONGEST MAN IN THE WORLD, The see MOLEMEN VS. THE
  SON OF HERCULES
The STUDENT OF PRAGUE or A BARGAIN WITH SATAN (G)
  Apex/Bioscop 1913 (Der STUDENT VON PRAG. FROM LIFE TO
  DEATH, or FLIGHT TO THE SUN) D: Stellan Rye. SP: Hanns
  Heinz Ewers, From the story "William Wilson" by Edgar Allen
  Poe. PH: Guido Seeber. Art D: Robert A. Dietrich, K. Richter.
  Ref: Clarens. Pic: Pict Hist Cinema. with Paul Wegener, John
  Gottowt, Greta Berger, Lyda Salmonova, Lother Körner. A stu-
  dent signs away his mirrored reflection to a mysterious man.
The STUDENT OF PRAGUE (G-Austrian) Sokal-Film 1926 (Der
  STUDENT VON PRAG. The MAN WHO CHEATED LIFE) SP, D:
  Henrik Galeen. From a novel by H. H. Ewers and the story
  "William Wilson" by Edgar Allan Poe. PH: Günther Krampf,
  Erich Nitzschmann. Art D: Hermann Warm. Ref: Clarens.
  Osterr. Pic: Pict Hist Cinema. with Conrad Veidt, Agnes
  Esterhazy, Werner Krauss, Ferdinand von Alten, Eliza La
  Porta.
The STUDENT OF PRAGUE (G) 1935 D: Arthur Robison. From
  the story "William Wilson" by Edgar Allan Poe. Mus: Theo
  Mackeben. Ref: DDC I:63. III:269. S&S'68:213. Pic: Le Sur-
  realisme au Cinema. with Anton Walbrook.
A STUDIO SATIRE Beauty 1916 Ref: MPN 14:794. with Orral
  Humphrey, Jo Taylor. Actor's "Dreamo Pills" make director
  and writer cast him in "more congenial part."
A STUDY IN TERROR (B) Col/Compton-Tekli-Sir Nigel 1965
  color 95m. (FOG) D: James Hill. SP: Donald and Derek Ford.
  Based on characters created by Sir Arthur Conan Doyle. PH:
  Desmond Dickinson. Mus: John Scott. Art D: Alex Vetchinsky.
  SpFX: Wally Veevers. Exec P: Herman Cohen. Ref: MMF. PM.
  with John Neville, Donald Houston, John Fraser, Anthony
  Quayle, Robert Morley, Adrienne Corri, Barbara Windsor,

Frank Finlay, Cecil Parker, Kay Walsh, Edina Ronay, Charles
Regnier, Patrick Newell, Peter Carsten, John Cairney. Sherlock
Holmes discovers the identity of Jack the Ripper.

The SUBMARINE EYE Submarine Films 1917 90m. PH: Harold
Sintzenith. Ref: NYT 5/28/17: "Inverted periscope attached to the
side of a boat by which objects beneath the surface of the ocean
may be seen." MPN 15:3791. with Edith Conway, Lindsey Hall,
Lillian Cook, Chester Barnett.

SUCCUBUS see NECRONOMICON, The

SUCKER MONEY Kent/Hollywood 1933 70m. (SINISTER HANDS)
D: Dorothy Reid, Melville Shyer. SP, P: Willis Kent. From a
magazine story by Elinor Glyn. Ed: S. Roy Luby. Ref: Photoplay 7/33. NYT. TVFFSB. TVG. Harrison's 5/13/33: "The
heroine, who had been hypnotized by the villain, comes out of
the trance when the villain dies." with Mischa Auer, Mae
Busch, Mona Lisa, Phyllis Barrington, Ralph Lewis. Seance;
two murders; fake descriptions of wanderings of spirits in other
world.

The SUICIDE CLUB AM&B 1909 5m. Ref: F Index 5/8/09. Bios
6/22/11.

The SUICIDE CLUB (B) Apex/British & Colonial 1914 P: Maurice
Elvey. Ref: DDC II:189. Brit Cinema. with Elisabeth Risdon.

SUICIDE CLUB, The (by R. L. Stevenson) see FIVE TALES OF
HORROR/HISTOIRES EXTRAORDINAIRES (1931)/LADY AND
DEATH, The/TROUBLE FOR TWO

SULOCHANA see TEMPLE BELLS

SUMPAH ORANG MINYAK see CURSE OF THE OILY MAN

SUMPAH PONTIANAK see VAMPIRE'S CURSE, The

SUMURU see MILLION EYES OF SUMURU, The

SUMURUN (G) F Nat/Union-Film-UFA 1920 (ONE ARABIAN
NIGHT) D: Ernst Lubitsch. SP: Hans Kraly; an adaptation of
the pantomime "Sumurun" by F. Freksa and V. Hollander. See
also The HUNCHBACK AND THE DANCER. PH: Theodor Spar-
kuhl. Art D: Kurt Richter, Ernö Metzner. Ref: Orpheus 3:48.
NYT 10/3/21. with Lubitsch (hunchback), Paul Wegener, Pola
Negri, Jenny Hasselquist, Harry Liedtke, Jakob Tiedtke, Aud
Egede Nissen.

SUN DEMON, The see HIDEOUS SUN DEMON, The

SUPAH JAIYANTO see ATOMIC RULERS OF THE WORLD/ATTACK
FROM SPACE/EVIL BRAIN FROM OUTER SPACE, The/IN-
VADERS FROM SPACE

SUPER DIABOLICAL (I) European Incorporation 1965 (I SUPER-
DIABOLICI. AMORE ALL'ITALIANA. LOVE ITALIAN STYLE)
SP, D: Steno. SP: also Luzi, Scarnicci, Tarabusi. PH: Carlo
Carlini. Ref: Ital P. Annuario. with Walter Chiari, Raimondo
Vianello, Paolo Panelli, Vivi Bach, Paolo Carlini. "Operation
Goldballs": The "red ray" makes James Bond begin to speak
"with an effeminate voice." "Wedding Present": A couple receives
a tape recorder as a wedding gift. They play a tape on which
the voice of a friend says that the machine "will immediately
blow up. It does."

SUPER-FEMALES see STRONGER SEX, The

El SUPER FLACO (Mex) Alfa 1957 D: Miguel Delgado. SP: Carlos

Orellana. Story: G. Gerszo. PH: J. O. Ramos. Mus: Federico
Ruiz. Ref: Indice. FJA still: monster. with Evangelina Elizondo,
Alfonso Iglesias "Pompin," Wolf Rubinsky, Alfredo Varela, Jr.,
José jasso.

SUPER GIANT see ATOMIC RULERS OF THE WORLD/ATTACK
FROM SPACE/EVIL BRAIN FROM OUTER SPACE, The/IN-
VADERS FROM SPACE

SUPER GIANT AGAINST THE SATELLITES see ATTACK FROM
SPACE

The SUPER HE-MAN (Mex) 1958 80m. (El SUPERMACHO) D:
Alejandro Galindo. SP: F. Cordova, Raul de Anda. Story:
Rafael Travesi. PH: R. Solano. Mus: S. Guerrero. Ref: Indice.
Lee. with Manuel Valdes, Sonia Furio. A scientist turns a man
into a superman.

SUPER-HEMBRAS, Las see STRONGER SEX, The

SUPER-HOOPER-DYNE LIZZIES Pathe/Sennett 1925 25m. D: Del
Lord. SP: Frank Capra, Jefferson Moffitt. Ref: Lee. MPN
31:2968. with Andy Clyde, Billy Bevan. Cars run on hot air from
radio speakers.

SUPER SCIENTIST (Mex) Posa Films 1948 (El SUPER-SABIO) D:
Miguel Delgado. SP: Jaime Salvador, Iñigo de Martino. Story:
J. B. Luc, Alex Joffe. PH: Raul M. Solares. Mus: Gonzalo
Curiel. Ref: Indice. Lee. DDC I:317. with Cantinflas, Perla
Agui(l)ar, Carlos M. Baena, Jose Pidal, Alfredo Varela, Jr.,
Alejandro Cobe. Synthetic gasoline; formulae for preserving
roses.

SUPER SLEUTH RKO/Edward Small 1937 75m. D: Ben Stoloff.
SP: Gertrude Purcell, Ernest Pagano, from a play by Harry
Segall. Contributing writers: Arthur Sheekman, Bertram Millhauser, Mark Kelly, Joseph Anthony. Ref: MFB 7/31/37.
V 7/14/37. Nealon. FD 7/13/37. Academy: "Horror...spine-
tickling...weird, semilighted wax-museum showing methods of
execution and torture." with Jack Oakie, Ann Sothern, Eduardo
Ciannelli, Alan Bruce, Edgar Kennedy, Joan Woodbury, Paul
Guilfoyle, Willie Best, Paul Hurst, Bradley Page, George Rosener, Fred Kelsey, Philip Morris. Egotistical mystery writer
becomes real detective, receives poison pen letters.

SUPER SPEED Rayart 1925 60m. D: Albert Rogell. SP: J. W.
Grey. H. R. Symonds. Ref: AFI. with Reed Howes, Mildred
Harris, Sheldon Lewis, Charles Clary. "Revolutionary super-
charger."

SUPERARGO VS. DIABOLICUS (I-Sp) 1966 Liber/SEC/Balcazar
87m. (SUPERARGO CONTRO DIABOLICUS) D: Nick Nostro. SP:
Balcazar, Giarda. PH: Francisco Marin. Ref: Ital P. SpCinema
'68. with Ken Wood, Gerard Tichy, Loredana Nusciak, Monica
Randal. Wrestling champion Superargo vs. master criminal
Diabolicus, who has "produced a gold isotope."

SUPERARGO VS. THE ROBOTS (I-Sp) GV/SEC/Izaro 1966 color
80m. (Il RE DEI CRIMINALI-I. SUPERARGO EL GIGANTE-Sp.
SUPERARGO AND THE FACELESS GIANTS. KING OF THE
CRIMINALS. DEVILMAN STORY. The DEVIL'S MAN) D: Paolo
Binachini (aka Paul Maxwell). SP: Julio Buchs. PH: Godofredo
Pacheco. Mus: Berto Pisano. Ref: Ital P'67. SpCinema'69. MFB

'69:100. (SUPERDRAGO E I GIGANTI SENZA VOLTO-I) Cinema
'68:114. with Ken Wood, Guy Madison, Liz Barrett, Diana
Lorys, Thomas Blanco. Artificial brain; hypnotic villain; robots
with electric batteries instead of hearts.
SUPERDIABOLICI, I see SUPER DIABOLICAL
SUPERGIRL (W.G.) Thome 1970 100m. D: Rudolf Thome. SP:
    Thome, Max Zihlmann. PH: A. Beato. Ref: V 3/31/71. FM
    52. with Iris Berben, Marquard Bohm, Jess Hahn. Creature
    from another planet.
SUPERHOMBRE, El see SUPERMAN, The
SUPERMACHO, El see SUPER HE-MAN, The
The SUPERMAN (Mex) Luis Manrique 1946 (El SUPERHOMBRE)
    D: Chano Urueta. SP: Antonio Monsell. PH: Ignacio Torres. Mus:
    Jorge Perez. Story:Hugo Thilgmann. Ref: Indice. Lee. HR
    9/9/46. LA Times 8/10/48. with Enrique Herrera, Luis Man-
    rique, Susana Cora. Blow on head gives man dual personality.
SUPERMAN Col 1948 serial 15 episodes (88-minute feature) D:
    Spencer G. Bennet, Thomas Carr. SP: A. Hoerl, Lewis Clay,
    R. Cole. Based on "Superman" and "Action" comics and the
    "Superman" radio show. PH: Ira H. Morgan. P: Sam Katzman.
    Ref: Barbour. with Kirk Alyn, Noel Neill, Tommy Bond, Carol
    Forman, George Meeker, Jack Ingram, Pierre Watkin, Terry
    Frost, Charles King, Charles Quigley, Herbert Rawlinson. For-
    rest Taylor, Stephen Carr, Rusty Wescoatt. Ch. 3. The Reducer
    Ray.
SUPERMAN (India-Hindi) Mukul Pictures 1960 D: Anant Thakur.
    Ref: FEFN 9/60. with Nirupa Roy, Neeta, Jairaj, Tiwari.
    "Science-fictioner dealing with drugs for invisibility and super-
    human powers."
SUPERMAN see ATOM MAN VS. SUPERMAN
SUPERMAN AND THE MOLE MEN Lippert 1951 58m. (SUPER-
    MAN AND THE STRANGE PEOPLE-Eng.) D: Lee Sholem. SP:
    Richard Fielding. Shown as "Unknown People," episodes 25 and
    26 of the "Superman" or "Adventures of Superman" series, on
    TV. PH: Clark Ramsey. SpFX: Ray Mercer. Ref: V 12/12/51.
    MFB'52:132. MW 10:23. STI 2:46. FM 14:29. Pic: MW 10:23.
    with George Reeves, Phyllis Coates, Jeff Corey, Walter Reed,
    J. Farrel MacDonald, Stanley Andrews.
SUPERMAN CONTRE LES FEMMES VAMPIRES see SAMSON VS.
    THE VAMPIRE WOMEN
SUPERMAN FLIES AGAIN Whitney Ellsworth 1954-56 77m. D:
    Thomas Carr, George Blair. Combination of three "Superman"
    or "Adventures of Superman" TV shows shown in theatres. SP:
    David Chantler. Ref: lee. with George Reeves, Noel Neill, John
    Hamilton, Jack Larson, Robert Shayne.
SUPERMAN LE DIABOLIQUE see HOW TO STEAL THE CROWN
    OF ENGLAND
SUPERNATURAL Para 1933 60m. D: Victor Halperin. SP: Harvey
    Thew, Brian Marlowe. Story: Garnett Weston. PH: Arthur
    Martinelli. P: Edward Halperin. Dial D: Sidney Salkow. Ref:
    Clarens. TVK. with Carole Lombard, Randolph Scott, Vivienne
    Osborne, Alan Dinehart, H. B. Warner, Beryl Mercer, William
    Farnum, Willard Robertson, George Burr M(a)cAnnan, Lyman

Williams. Executed murderess' spirit takes possession of girl.
Needlessly complicated plot fails to obscure dumb premise and
travels through a lot of elaborate contrivances to arrive at
nothing. Crudely sentimental. The acting, all ominous looks and
pauses, provides some laughs.

SUPERNATURAL POWER (F) Pathe 1912 7m. Ref: Bios 4/4/12.
Seance disrupted by "spirits."

SUPERSONIC SAUCER (B) CFF/British Lion 1955 50m. D: S. G.
Fergusson. Ref: FEFN 4/13/56. SF Film. with Fella Edmonds,
Marcia Monolescue, Gillian Harrison. Friendly visitor from
space.

SUPERSPEED Col 1935 56m. D: Lambert Hillyer. SP: Harold
Shumate. PH: Benjamin Kline. Ref: FD 12/2/35. with Norman
Foster, Florence Rice, Mary Carlisle, Charles Grapewin,
Arthur Hohl, Robert Middlemass, George McKay. Crooks conniv-
ing against inventor of superspeed device damage test car.

SUR UN AIR DE CHARLESTON see CHARLESTON

A SURE CURE Crystal 1914 Ref: MPW 19:718. Bottled medicine
makes lazy people active.

SURF TERROR see MONSTER FROM THE SURF

The SURGEONS' EXPERIMENT Majestic 1914 30m. Ref: MPW
20:116. Lee. with Paul Scardon. Operation makes crook honest.

A SURGICAL OPERATION AND ITS AFTER EFFECTS (F) Pathe
1909 8m. Ref: Bios 9/16/09. Man more sprightly than ever after
having leg amputated.

A SURPRISING POWDER (I) Cines 1909 Ref: MPW'09:922. Professor's powder encourages romantic feelings.

SURVIVAL see PANIC IN YEAR ZERO

SUSPECT, The see RISK, The

SUSPENSE see INNOCENTS, The

SVENGALI (Austrian) Wiener Kunstfilm 1914 58m. (Der HYPNO-
TISEUR) D: Luise Kolm, Jakob Fleck. From "Trilby" by George
du Maurier. Ref: Osterr. with Frl. Nording, Ferdinand Bonn.

SVENGALI (B) 1922 11m. (Tense Moments with Great Authors
series) From "Trilby" by George Du Maurier. Ref: Halliwell.
Clarens.

SVENGALI (G) Terra-Film 1927 D: Gennaro Righelli, H. Grund.
SP: Max Glass, from "Trilby" by George Du Maurier. Art D:
Hans Jacoby. Ref: Deutsche. Fantastique. Germany. with Paul
Wegener, Anita Dorris, André Mattoni, Alexander Granach.

SVENGALI WB 1931 D: Archie Mayo. SP: J. Grubb Alexander,
from the novel "Trilby" by George Du Maurier. PH: Barney
McGill. Ref: Clarens. with John Barrymore, Marian Marsh,
Carmel Myers, Luis Alberni, Donald Crisp, Lumsden Hare,
Bramwell Fletcher, Paul Porcasi. "Some of the sequences are
startling: Svengali, his eyes a blank white, stands at the window
and casts his spell over the rooftops to the room where Trilby
lives."--Pauline Kael.

SVENGALI (B) MGM/Alderdale 1954 color 82m. SP, D: Noel Lang-
ley. From "Trilby" by George Du Maurier. PH:Wilkie Cooper.
Mus D: William Alwyn. Art D: Fred Pusey. Ref: FM 7:6.
FDY. with Donald Wolfit, Hildegarde Neff, Terence Morgan,
Derek Bond, David Kossoff, Noel Purcell, Alfie Bass, Harry

Secombe, Peter Illing, David Oxley, Toots Pound, Michael
Craig, Marne Maitland.

SWAMP, The   see GHOST OF CHIDORI-GA-FUCHI

SWAMP OF THE LOST MONSTER (Mex) AI-TV c1965 (The SWAMP
OF LOST SOULS) D: Raphael Baledon. SP: Ramon Obon. P:
Alfred Ripstein, Jr. Ref: TVG. TVFFSB. with Gaston Santos,
Manola Saavedra, Manuel Dondi. Just another western-horror-
mystery-comedy-musical. The monster looks like a big mouse.
The film steals a trick from NIGHT OF TERROR.

SWEENEY TODD (B) 1928 D: Walter West. Ref: Brit Cinema. with
Harry Lorraine.

SWEENEY TODD see DEMON BARBER OF FLEET STREET, The

SWEET SOUND OF DEATH (U.S.-Sp-W.G.) Gala 1965 85m. D:
Javier Setó. SP: Setó, Paul Diez. Eng Dial: John Hart. PH:
Frank Sanchez. Mus: G. S. Segura. P: Sidney W. Pink. Ref:
MFB'66:76. M/TVM 5/67. with Dianik, Sun Sanders, Daniel
Blum. Spirit of girl tries to convince man that he too is dead. He
eventually joins her in death.

SWEET, SWEET RACHEL ABC-TV 1971 color 72m. D: Sutton
Roley. SP: Anthony Lawrence. PH: James Crabbe. Mus:
Laurence Rosenthal. Art D: Paul Sylos. Ref: RVG. TVG:
"ESP, terror." with Alex Dreier, Stefanie Powers, Pat Hingle,
Brenda Scott, Chris Robinson, Steve Inhat. Psychic uses his
telepathic powers to commit murder.

SWEET TO BE KISSED, HARD TO DIE (I) Phoenix 1971 color
D: Emilio Miraglia. Ref: M/TVM #6/71. with Anthony Steffen,
Marina Malfatti, Erika Blanck. Lord sees "strange apparitions"
after returning to his castle.

The SWEETNESS OF SIN (F) E.G.E. 1968 color (La TOUR DE
NESLE) D,P: Leo Joannon. From a play by Alexandre Dumas.
Ref: RVB. Horror/Fantasy. with Mario-Ange Anies, Terry
Torday, Veronique Vendell. Wife of Louis X believed to be
vampire-witch.

SWEETS TO THE SWEET (by R. Bloch) see HOUSE THAT DRIPPED
BLOOD, The

SWISS MADE (Swiss) Yersin-Maeder-Murer 1969 Ektachrome
100m. D: Yves Yersin, Fritz Maeder, Fredy Murer. SP: Yersin,
Michel Contat. PH: W. Lesniewicz. Ref: V 10/22/69. with Henri
Noverraz, Elsa Skorecka. Three episodes: First takes place in
1980; third in 2069 when robots are exploring Switzerland, which
is run by computers.

The SWORD AND THE DRAGON (Russ-Yugos) Valiant 1956
('60-U.S.) 3-D 83m. (ILYA MOUROMETZ. The BEAST. The
EPIC HERO AND THE BEAST-Eng. ILYA MUROMETS) D:
Alexander Ptushko. SP: V. Kotochnev. PH: B. Travkin. Based
on the Russian folk character Ilya Mourometz (or Muromets).
Ref: V 9/29/60. Orpheus 3:28. with Andrei Abrikosov, Boris
Andreav. Demons, devils, dragons.

SWORD AND THE DRAGON   see DRAGON'S BLOOD

The SWORD AND THE KING Vita 1909 17m. Ref: Bios 9/9/09.
Old hag's curse: ghost haunts king.

SYLVIE AND THE PHANTOM (F) Discina 1946 (SYLVIE ET LE
FANTOME) D: Claude Autant-Lara. Ref: S&S'46:48, 51. Show-

men's 10/21/50. with Jacques Tati ("the phantom"). Man killed in duel haunts castle. "Ghost scares."

The SYSTEM OF DR. TARR AND PROFESSOR FETHER (F) A.C.A.D. /Eclair 1912 (1909?) 25m. (Le SYSTEME DU DOC-TEUR GOUDRON ET DU PROFESSEUR PLUME. Le DOCTEUR GOUDRON ET LE PROFESSEUR PLUME. DR. GOUDRON'S SYSTEM) D: Robert Saidrean (Maurice Tourneur?). From the story by Edgar Allan Poe. PH: Victorin Jasset. Ref: FM 11:42. DDC II:306. FIR'61. Bios 11/20/13. with M. Gouget (or Gougat). "Horror," "Grand Guignol": Lunatics take over asylum, perform "operation" on director.

SYSTEM OF DR. TARR AND PROFESSOR FETHER, The (by E. A. Poe) see FIVE TALES OF HORROR/HISTOIRES EXTRAORDI-NAIRES (1931)

THX 1138 WB/American Zoetrope 1971 Technicolor 88m. D: George Lucas. SP: Lucas, Walter Murch. Based on Lucas's short film THX 1138 4EB or ELECTRONIC LABYRINTH. PH: Dave Meyers, Albert Kihn. Mus: Lalo Schifrin. Art D: Michael Haller. Exec P: Francis Ford Coppola. Ref: V 3/17/71. with Robert Duvall, Donald Pleasence, Don Pedro Colley, Maggie McOmie, Ian Wolfe, Johnny Weissmuller, Jr. A computer-ruled future civili-zation is policed by robots. THX has a new, original look and sound to it, but it's too original and disorienting for its own good. Words are muffled, mumbled, overlapped, and crushed under music; the film leaves you with an overall aural and visual im-pression and not much else (except an exciting chase and an exactly-right, ambiguous ending).

T.P.A. see PRESIDENT'S ANALYST, The

TAILSPIN TOMMY see SKY PIRATE, The

TAKAMARU AND KIKUMARU (J) Shochiku 1959 color/scope 139m. (TAKAMARU KIKUMARU) D: Santaro Marune. SP: Ryuta Mine, Noburo Mizukami. PH: Kiyomi Kuroda. Ref: UFQ 5; FEFN XII: 12-13. with Kinshiro Matsumoto, K. Hananomoto, Hiroshi Nawa, Kiki Hojo, Kyoko Izume. "Death's-Head Castle," villain "skilled in the art of sorcery," submarine called "Black Whale," giant frog.

TAKARAJIMA ENSEI see PEACH BOY

TALE OF MYSTERY AND MARVEL, A (by J. Verne) see MASTER OF THE WORLD (1961)

A TALE OF PEONIES AND STONE LANTERNS (J) Daiei 1968 color/scope 89m. (KAIDAN BOTAN DORO. BOTAN-DORO. GHOST BEAUTY. GHOSTLY FLOWERS. The BRIDE FROM HADES) D: Satsuo Yamamoto. SP: Yoshitaka Yoda. PH: C. Makiura. Mus: S. Ikeno. Ref: V 7/24/68. M/TVM 5/68.6/68. Unij Bltn 31. UFQ 42. with Kojiro Hongo, Miyoko Akaza, M. Ogawa, Takashi Shimura. A young man meets two ghosts during the O-bon festival.

TALES OF HOFFMAN (G) 1914 (HOFFMANS ERZAHLUNGEN) D: Richard Oswald. From the opera by Offenbach.Ref: SF Film. Fantastique. with Alice Scheel-Hechy. Automaton in first of three

stories.
TALES OF HOFFMAN (B) Powell-Pressburger/British Lion/London
  1951 Technicolor 127m. SP, D, P: Michael Powell, Emeric Press-
  burger. From the opera by Offenbach. PH: Christopher Challis.
  Mus: Jacques Offenbach. Conductor: Sir Thomas Beecham. Art
  D: Arthur Lawson. Prod Des: Hein Heckroth. Ref: TVG. FDY. with
  Robert Rounseville, Robert Helpmann, Moira Shearer, Ludmilla
  Tcherina, Pamela Brown. Three acts. I: Hoffman has a love af-
  fair with a life-size doll. II: A witch steals Hoffman's shadow.
TALES OF MYSTERY AND IMAGINATION (F-I) AI/Marceau-Cocinor
  --P.E.A. 1968 Berkey Pathe color 120m. (HISTOIRES EXTRA-
  ORDINAIRES. 3 STEPS TO DELIRIUM. STRANGE TALES.
  SPIRITS OF THE DEAD. TROIS PAS DAN L'ETRANGE-F. TRE
  PASSI NEL DELIRIO-I.) From stories by Edgar Allan Poe. 1:
  "Metzengerstein": SP, D: Roger Vadim. SP: also Pascal Cousin.
  PH: Claude Renoir. Mus: Jean Prodromides. Art D: Jean
  Forester. with Jane Fonda, Peter Fonda, James Robertson
  Justice, Francoise Prevost, Serge Marquand. 2: "William Wil-
  son": SP, D: Louis Malle. Dial: Daniel Boulanger. PH: Tonino
  Delli Colli. Mus: Diego Masson. Art D: G. Uhry, C. Leva.
  with Brigitte Bardot, Alain Delon, Umberto D'Orsi. 3: "Toby
  Dammit" or "Il Ne Faut Pas Parier Sa Tete avec le Diable"
  or "Never Bet Your Head on the Devil." SP, D: Federico Fellini.
  SP: also Bernardino Zapponi. PH: Giuseppe Rotunno. Mus: Nino
  Rota. Art D: P. Tosi. SpFX: Joseph Nathanson. with Terence
  Stamp, Salvo Randone. Eng Narr: Vincent Price. Ref:FFacts.
  V 5/8/68. 6/5/68.
TALES OF TERROR AI 1962 Pathecolor/scope (POE'S TALE OF
  TERROR) D, P: Roger Corman. SP: Richard Matheson, from
  "Morella," "The Black Cat," "The Cask of Amontillado," and
  "The Facts in the Case of M. Valdemar" by Edgar Allan Poe.
  PH: Floyd Crosby. Mus: Les Baxter. Art D: Daniel Haller. Ref:
  Clarens. PM. COF 5:24. Three episodes involving ghosts,
  mesmerism, etc. The first and third sections have their shock
  moments, but the first gets too silly and the third gets to be too
  long. The second is best, hilarious at times, and intentionally so.
TALES OF THE PALE MOON AFTER THE RAIN see UGETSU
  MONOGATARI
The TALISMAN (Swedish) Svensk c1947 83m. D: Gustaf Mollander.
  SP: K.-R. Gierow. PH: Ake Dahlquist. Mus: Lars-Eric Larsson.
  Ref: MFB 7/31/49. with Elvin Adolphson, Inga Tidblad. Man's
  soul doomed to be damned if he can't sell talisman for less than
  he paid for it.
TALKED TO DEATH Lubin 1909 Ref: F Index 3/20/09. Old maid
  literally talks people to death.
TANIN NO KAO see FACE OF ANOTHER, The
TARANTULA Univ 1955 80m. D: Jack Arnold. SP: Martin Berkeley,
  Robert Fresco. PH: George Robinson. Mus: Joseph Gershenson.
  Art D: Alexander Golitzen, Alfred Sweeney. Makeup: Bud West-
  more. P: William Alland. Ref: Clarens. with John Agar, Mara
  Corday, Leo G. Carroll, Nestor Paiva, Ross Elliott. Biochemist
  experimenting with artificial nutrients responsible for unleashing
  giant spider on countryside. One of Universal's better s-f-

Target

monster epics of the Fifties.
TARGET EARTH AA/Abtcon 1954 75m. (TARGET: EARTH!) D:
Sherman A. Rose. SP: William Raynor, from "The Deadly City"
by Paul Fairman. PH: Guy Roe. Art D: James Sullivan. P: Herman
Cohen. Ref: FDY. FM 12:20. Pic: FanMo 5:37. with Richard Den-
ning, Virginia Grey, Kathleen Crowley, Arthur Space, Whit Bis-
sell, House Peters, Jr. People in deserted city battle invading
robots. Mediocre at best.
TARGET FOR KILLING (Austrian-I) Intercontinental/PEA 1966
color 102m. (Das GEHEIMNIS DER GELBEN MONCHE. The
SECRET OF THE YELLOW MONKS. HOW TO KILL A LADY.
WIETOTET MAN EINE DAME? GUET-APENS A TEHERAN.
COME SI UCCIDE UNA SIGNORA? Il SEGRETO DEI FRATI GIAL-
LI. COMO SE MATA A UNA SENORA? El SECRETO DE LOS
FRAILES AMARILLOS) D: Manfred Köhler. SP: Anatol Bratt.
PH: Siegfried Hold. Mus: M. Giombini. Ref: Film Kunst 49: F4.
MFB. TVG. with Stewart Granger, Karin Dor, Curt Jurgens,
Rupert Davies, Adolfo Celi, Klaus Kinski, Erika Remberg. New
form of brainwashing, "electro-psychic massage," is key to or-
ganization's power.
TARGETS Para/Saticoy 1968 Pathecolor 90m. (BEFORE I DIE)
SP,D,P: Peter Bogdanovich. Story: Bogdanovich, Polly Platt.
PH: Laszlo Kovacs. Prod Des: Miss Platt. Ref: V(d) 5/6/68.
S&S'68:188-9. COF 15:25. with Boris Karloff (Byron Orlok),
Tim O'Kelly, Sandy Baron, Bogdanovich, Nancy Hsueh, James
Brown, Monte Landis. The film contrasts the realistic horror of
a psychotic sniper with screen horror. (Karloff plays an aging
horror movie actor.) Bogdanovich keeps the more sensational
elements of the script pretty well under control, though the di-
rector's hand is a little too evident at times, and some scenes
seem almost posed for stills they're so carefully "composed."
The script's powerful conceptions, though sometimes bordering
on silliness, overcome some of the less-well-staged and -acted
scenes.
TARZAN VS. IBM see ALPHAVILLE
TARZAN'S DESERT MYSTERY RKO 1943 70m. D: William Thiele.
SP: Edward T. Lowe. Story: Carroll Young. Based on the char-
acter created by Edgar Rice Burroughs. PH: Harry Wild, Russ
Harlan. Mus sc: Paul Sawtell. Art D: Hans Peters, Ralph Berger.
Ref: V 12/8/43. FM 13:58.19:36:scenes from ONE MILLION
B.C.? with Johnny Weissmuller, Otto Kruger, Johnny Sheffield,
Joseph Sawyer, Lloyd Corrigan, Robert Lowery, Frank Puglia,
Philip van Zandt. Huge spider, prehistoric monsters, carnivor-
ous plant. So-so Tarzan film.
TASTE FOR HONEY, A or TASTE FOR MURDER, A (novel by
H. F. Heard) see DEADLY BEES, The
A TASTE OF BLOOD Ajay/Creative 1967 Eastmancolor 120m.
(The SECRET OF DR. ALUCARD) D,P: Herschell G. Lewis. SP:
Donald Stanford. Ass't D: Louise Downe. with Bill Rogers,
Thomas Wood, Ted Schell, Gail Janis, Elizabeth Wilkinson, Otto
Schlesinger (Howard Helsing). A man drinks from a bottle of
Dracula's blood and turns into a vampire. A movie can do quite
a bit in 120 minutes. It can at least do something. A TASTE OF

BLOOD proves that a movie can, if it tries, do absolutely nothing in two hours. Nothing 24 times a second for 120 minutes is an awful lot of nothing. There have been few, if any, worse movies.

A TASTE OF EVIL ABC-TV Aaron Spelling 1971 color 75m. D: John Moxey. SP: Jimmy Sangster. PH: Arch Dalzell. Mus: Robert Drasnin. Art D: Paul Sylos. Ref: LATimes 10/12/71. with Barbara Stanwyck, Barbara Parkins, Roddy McDowall, William Windom, Arthur O'Connell, Bing Russell. A young woman back home after seven years in a mental institution is beset by "apparitions."

TASTE OF FEAR, A see SCREAM OF FEAR

TASTE THE BLOOD OF DRACULA (B) WB/Hammer 1969 color D: Peter Sasdy. SP: John Elder. PH: Arthur Grant. Mus: James Bernard Ref: MFB. with Christopher Lee, John Carson, Roy Kinnear, Michael Ripper, Geoffrey Keen, Gwen Watford, Peter Sallis, Ralph Bates. A man mixes his blood with the dried blood of Dracula to bring him back to life.

TATTOOED SWORDSWOMAN see HAUNTED LIFE OF A DRAGON-TATTOOED LASS, The

TAUSEND AUGEN DES DR. MABUSE, The see THOUSAND EYES OF DR. MABUSE, The

TEACHER WAS A SEXPOT see BEAUTY AND THE ROBOT

TEENAGE CAVEMAN AI/Malibu 1958 65m. (PREHISTORIC WORLD OUT OF THE DARKNESS-Eng.) D, P: Roger Corman. SP: R. Wright Campbell. PH: Floyd Crosby. Mus: Albert Glasser. Superama Ref: FFacts. with Robert Vaughn, Leslie Bradley, Robert Shayne, Jonathan Haze, Darrah Marshall, Frank de Kova, Beech Dickerson. Cave men turn out to be survivors of an atomic war.

TEENAGE FRANKENSTEIN see I WAS A TEENAGE FRANKEN-STEIN

TEENAGE MONSTER Howco/Marquette 1957 65m. (METEOR MONSTER-TV. MONSTER ON THE HILL) D, P: James Marquette. Ref: COF 12:33. Pic: FM 30:54. with Anne Gwynne, Stuart Wade, Gloria Castillo, Charles Courtney, Gilbert Perkins (the monster), Frank Davis. Teen-ager horribly deformed when meteorite crashes to earth. An indescribable mixture of horror and pathos. The loving son/monster's last word before falling to his death is, "Mama!" How touching.

TEENAGE PSYCHO MEETS BLOODY MARY see INCREDIBLY STRANGE CREATURES, The

TEENAGE ZOMBIES Governor/G.B.M. 1960 (1958) 73m. D, P: Jerry Warren. SP: Jacques Lecotier. PH: Allen Chandler. Mus D: Erich Bromberg. Makeup: Jean Morrison. Ref: FFacts. FM 15:14. with Don Sullivan, Steve Conte, Katherine Victor, Jay Hawk. Six teenagers discover a mysterious island and a plot to drop zombie pellets into America's water supply. Half the film is riotous dialogue ("The army will be very grateful to you kids"); the other half is just monotonous walking around and bad acting. The whole film is a bad joke.

TEENAGERS FROM OUTER SPACE WB 1959 86m. (INVASION OF THE GARGON. The GARGON TERROR-Eng.) SP, D, P, PH, Ed, SpFX, Mus: Tom Graeff. Ref: FFacts. A spaceship carrying alien youth and a monster lands on earth. with David Love, Dawn Anderson, Bryan Grant. Disappointing considering all the talent involved.

TELEGIANS, The see SECRET OF THE TELEGIAN

TELEPHONE, The (by F. G. Snyder) see BLACK SABBATH

TELEVISION FOLLIES (B) Benstead 1933 D: Geoffrey Benstead. Ref: SF Film. with George Carney. TV apparatus.

TELEVISION SPY Para 1939 58m. (The WORLD ON PARADE) D: Edward Dmytryk. SP: Horace McCoy, William R. Lipman, Lillie Hayward. Story: Endre Bohem. PH: Harry Fischbeck. Art D: Hans Dreier, Franz Bachelin. Ref: TVK. FD 10/13/39. with William Henry, Judith Barrett, Anthony Quinn, Richard Denning, John Eldredge, William Collier, Sr., Dorothy Tree, Morgan Conway, Minor Watson, Byron Foulger. Spies go after a TV invention capable of transmitting two thousand miles.

The TELL-TALE HEART 1928 SP, D: Charles Klein. From the story by Edgar Allan Poe. PH: Leo(n) Shamroy. Ref: SilentFF. FM 11:42. with Otto Matiesen, Darvas. Murderer haunted by throbbing of victim's heart.

The TELL-TALE HEART DuWorld (B) 1934 52m. (A BUCKET OF BLOOD) D: Brian Desmond Hurst. SP: David Greene, from the story by Edgar Allan Poe. Ref: FDY. FM 11:43. Photoplay 9/34. FD 6/21/34. with Norman Dryden, Yolande Terrell, John Kelt, Thomas Shenton. Youth slowly goes mad, to the point of killing an old man whose ugly eye haunts him.

The TELL-TALE HEART (B) Brigadier 1960 81m. (The HORROR MAN. PANIC-I. HIDDEN ROOM OF 1000 HORRORS-'65 reissue) D: Ernest Morris. SP: Brian Clemens, Elden Howard, from the story by Poe. PH: Jimmy Wilson. Mus: Tony Crombie, Bill Le Sage. Ref: Orpheus 3:28. Consumer Bulletin. RVB. MW 1:10. FFacts. Pic: COF 3:53. Brit Cinema. with Laurence Payne, Adrienne Corri, Dermot Walsh, Selma Vaz Dias. Man haunted by beating of dead man's heart. A real bore.

TELL-TALE HEART, The (by E. A. Poe) see AVENGING CON-SCIENCE, The /HISTOIRES EXTRAORDINAIRES (1948)/MANFISH/ MASTER OF HORROR

TELLTALE REFLECTIONS (F?) Gaum-Kleine 1909 Ref: MPW'09: 693. Hypnotic-mirror invention reflects thoughts in people's minds.

TEMPI DURI PER I VAMPIRI see UNCLE WAS A VAMPIRE

TEMPLE BELLS (India) Imperial 1934 (SULOCHANA) D: Chaudhury. Ref: Dipali 6/15/34. with Chanda, Zilloo, Hadi. A man invents an elixir for reviving the dead.

TEMPLE TOWER Fox 1930 58m. D: Donald Gallagher. SP: Llewellyn Hughes. From a story by H. C. McNeil. Remake: BULL-DOG DRUMMOND'S SECRET POLICE. PH:Charles G. Clarke. Ed: Clyde Carruth. Ref: Photoplay 4/30. V 5/14/30. NYT. with Henry B. Walthall, Kenneth MacKenna, Ivan Linow, Marceline Day. Trap doors, fog, "masked monster," "mysterious gadgets."

TEMPS DE MOURIR, Le see TWICE UPON A TIME

The TEMPTATIONS OF JOSEPH Kineto 1914 22m. Ref: Bios 4/23/14: ix. "Amorous mummy awakens to the terror of its antiquarian owner."

The TEMPTATION OF ST. ANTOINE (F) C1898 Melies/Star

(La TENTATION DE SAINT ANTOINE) 1m. Ref: SilentFF. St.
Antoine is tempted by visions (through skull he holds, etc.) of
young women.
The TEMPTATIONS OF SATAN Warner's 1914 75m. D: Herbert
Blache. Ref: MPW 22:644. with Binnie Burns, Joseph Lovering,
James O'Neil (Satan). Satan sends out helpers to tempt woman.
The TEMPTRESS (J) Nikkatsu 1957 color/scope 87m. (BYA-
KUYA NO YOJO. DEATH BY WITCHCRAFT) D: Eisuke Takizawa.
SP: Toshio Yazumi. PH: Minoru Yokoyama. From the novel
"Saint of Mt. Koya" by Kyoka Izumi. Art D: Takashi Matsuyama.
Ref: UFQ. FEFN 8/9/57. with Yumeji Tsukioka, Ryoji Hayama,
Tadashi Kobayashi, Ichijiro Ohya. Temptress-witch turns travel-
ler into ox.
TEN LITTLE INDIANS (B) 7A/Tenlit 1965 92m. D: George Pol-
lock. SP: P. Yeldman (or Yeldham), Peter Welbeck. Remake of
AND THEN THERE WERE NONE. From Agatha Christie's book
(also called "10 Little Niggers" or "The Nursery Rhyme Mur-
ders"). PH: Ernie Steward. Mus sc & d: Malcolm Lockyer.
Art D: Frank White. Ref: RVB. FFacts. Pic: Shriek 4:64. with
Hugh O'Brian, Shirley Eaton, Wilfrid Hyde-White, Fabian, Leo
Genn, Stanley Holloway, Daliah Lavi, Dennis Price, Mario Adorf.
Multiple murder in isolated castle.
TENAMONYA YUREI DOCHU see GHOSTS OF TWO TRAVELLERS
AT TENAMONYA
The TENDERFOOT'S GHOST Frontier 1913 17m. Ref: Bios
12/11/13. Apparition proves robber's undoing.
TENTATION DE SAINT ANTOINE, La see TEMPTATION OF ST.
ANTOINE, The
The TENTH VICTIM (I-F) Embassy/Champion-Concordia 1965
color 90m. (La DECIMA VITTIMA-I. La DIXIEME VICTIME-F.)
SP,D: Elio Petri. SP: also Ennio Flaiano, Tonino Guerra,
Giorgio Salvoini (or Salvione). From the book by Robert Sheck-
ley. PH: G. Di Venanzo. Mus: Piero Piccioni. P:Carlo Ponti.
Ref: MMF. PM. with Marcello Mastroianni, Ursula Andress,
Elsa Martinelli, Massimo Serato, Salvo Randone. In the 21st
century war has been outlawed but killing has been legalized.
Intermittently effective.
TERRIBLE GHOST-CAT OF OKAZAKI (J) Daiei 1954 (KAIBYO
OKAZAKI SODO) D: Bin Kado. Ref: Unij Bltn 31. with
Takako Irie, Kotaro Bando.
TERRIBLE GIGANTE DE LAS NIEVES, El see TERRIBLE SNOW
GIANT, The
A TERRIBLE NIGHT (F) Melies 1896 1m. (Une NUIT TERRIBLE)
Ref: SilentFF. "A man preparing to retire for the night is
disturbed by a very large beetle."
The TERRIBLE PEOPLE Pathe 1928 silent serial 10 episodes
D: Spencer G. Bennet. Ref: LC. CNW. Lee. with Allene Ray,
Walter Miller, Wilfred North. "Ghost," villain with hairy, claw-
like hands.
The TERRIBLE PEOPLE (G) R&B 1960 95m. (Die BANDE DES
SCHRECKENS. HAND OF THE GALLOWS) D: Harald Reinl.
SP: Joachim Bartsch, Wolfgang Schnitzler. Ref: FIR. COF 10:40.
From a book by Edgar Wallace. with Joachim Fuchsberger, Eddi

Arent, Karin Dor, Fritz Rasp, Chris Howland, Elizabeth
Flickenschildt. Condemned criminal vows to return from the
grave for revenge. Dull, with one good comedy routine. You
need a map to get through these long German mystery-horror
films.
The TERRIBLE QUICK SWORD OF SIEGFRIED (G) Atlas/Hermes
Synchron 1970 color (SIEGFRIED UND DAS SAGENHAFTE
LIEBESLEBEN DER NIBELUNGEN) D: Adrian Hoven. SP: Al de
Ger. Ref: Fernsehen 5/71. M/TVM Spring'71. with Raimund
Harmstorf, S. Danning.
TERRIBLE QUICK SWORD OF SIGFRIED, The see SIEGFRIED
(1967)
The TERRIBLE SNOW GIANT (Mex) Grovas-Cinematografica 1962
(El TERRIBLE GIGANTE DE LAS NIEVES) D: Jaime Salvador.
SP: Federico Curiel, Alfredo Ruanova. PH: E. Carrasco. Mus:
S. Guerrero. Art D: S. L. Mena. Ref: Indice. FJA poster.
with Joaquin Cordero, Ana Berthe Lepe, Andres Soler, David
Hayat, Jose Chavez, Jose Eduardo Perez, Elizabeth Dupeyron.
TERRIFIED Crown 1964 (1962) 66m. D: Lew Landers. SP:
Richard Bernstein. PH: Curt Fetters. Mus: Michael Andersen. Art
D: Rudi Feld. Ref: MFB'64:179. FanMo 3:54. COF 4:5. with
Rod Lauren, Steve Drexel, Harry Lauter, Stephen Roberts,
Barbara Luddy, Denver Pyle. Hooded killer; ghost town's
"haunted house." Uninspired, dull.
TERROR FBO 1928 silent 55m. D: Louis King. Continuity: F. H.
Clark. Titles: Helen Gregg. Story: Wyndham Gittens. PH: Nick
Musuraca. Ref: AFI. with Tom Tyler, Jane Reid, Al Ferguson,
Frankie Darro. Western. "Apparitions" seen about deserted
house.
The TERROR WB 1928 sound 90m. Titles: Joseph Jackson. Ed:
Thomas Pratt, Jack Killifer. D: Roy Del Ruth. SP: Harvey
Gates. From the play by Edgar Wallace. PH: Barney McGill.
Ref: AFI. Clarens. Pic: FM 41:31. Photoplay 10/28. with May
McAvoy, Louise Fazenda, Edward Everett Horton, Alec B. Fran-
cis, Holmes Herbert, John Miljan, Otto Hoffman, Joseph Girard.
Criminal in black hood stalks heroine through secret tunnels and
passageways.
The TERROR (B) Alliance/Associated British/Mycroft 1938
('41-U.S.) 73m. D: Richard Bird. SP: William Freshman, from
Edgar Wallace's play. PH: Walter Harvey. Ref: V 8/6/41.
FIR'67:78. S&S'68:212. MFB'38:132. TVG. with Wilfrid Lawson,
Bernard Lee, Arthur Wontner, Alastair Sim, Henry Oscar, Linden Travers, Iris Hoey, John Turnbull. Monk's Hall Priory is
reputed to be haunted. When the daughter of the owner arrives,
"ghostly manifestations reach their height. An organ is heard
at dead of night, a monk walks, maniacal laughter is heard..."
The TERROR AI/Filmgroup 1963 Pathecolor/Vistascope 81m.
(CASTLE OF TERROR. LADY OF THE SHADOWS) D, P: Roger
Corman. SP: Leo Gordon, Jack Hill. PH: John Nickolaus. Ex-
teriors: Monte Hellman. Mus: Arnold Stein. Art D: Daniel Haller. Ref: PM. COF 4:5. Orpheus 3:31. Clarens. with Boris Karloff, Jack Nicholson, Sandra Knight, Richard Miller, Jonathan
Haze. Young French soldier meets girl who seems to be under

some strange spell. Another of Corman's three-day pictures
but, unlike LITTLE SHOP OF HORRORS, it looks it.
TERROR see PERILS OF PARIS
TERROR, The (play by E. Wallace) see RETURN OF THE TER-
ROR, The
TERROR ABOARD Para 1933 69m. D: Paul Sloane. SP:
Manuel Seff, Harvey Thew. PH: Harry Fischbeck. From a story
by Robert Presnell. Ref: FDY. TVFFSB: "Horror." with John
Halliday, Charlie Ruggles, Neil Hamilton, Shirley Grey, Verree
Teasdale, Jack LaRue, Leila Bennett, Thomas Jackson, William
Janney, Paul Hurst, Clarence Wilson, Paul Porcasi. Harrison's
4/15/33: "It should sicken even the most morbid follower of
horror melodramas, for there is one killing after another. One
man is poisoned; another is shot; a woman is shoved into a re-
frigerator; a man is incited into killing another man and then
himself; another man is stabbed; and as a final stroke of homi-
cidal genius, a boat-load of sailors are thrown into the sea and
drowned."
TERROR BY NIGHT see SECRET WITNESS
TERROR CASTLE see HORROR CASTLE
TERROR CREATURES FROM THE GRAVE Pacemaker/IEC/MBS
Cinematografica (I) 1965 ('67-U.S.) D: Mario Pupillo (aka Ralph
Zucker). SP: Romano Migliorini, Roberto Natale. PH: Carlo Di
Palma. Mus: Aldo Piga. (CINQUE TOMBE PER UN MEDIUM.
FIVE GRAVES FOR A MEDIUM. TOMBS OF HORROR. COF-
FIN OF TERROR) Ref: MMF. Orpheus 4:37. with Barbara
Steele, Walter Brandi, Marilyn Mitchell, Alfredo Rizzo (aka
Alfred Rice).
TERROR EN EL ESPACIO see PLANET OF THE VAMPIRES
TERROR FROM THE SUN see HIDEOUS SUN DEMON, The
TERROR FROM THE YEAR 5000 AI 1958 (TERROR FROM 5000
A.D. The GIRL FROM 5000 A.D. CAGE OF DOOM-Eng.)
SP, D, P: Robert J. Gurney, Jr. PH: Arthur Florman. Ed: Dede
Allen. Prod Co-ordinator: Mark Hanna. Ref: FFacts. FM 2:6.
TVG. with Joyce Holden, Ward Costello, John Stratton, Frederic
Downs. An archaeologist finds that the statuette sent him by a
friend was made in the year 5000 A.D. Fairly pleasant for a
while until the plot bogs down. The monster hypnotizes people
with her fingernails.
TERROR HOUSE (B) PRC/Pathe Pictures 1942 70m. (The
NIGHT HAS EYES) D: Leslie Arliss. From a book by Alan
Kennington. PH, lighting: Gunther Krampf. Art D: Duncan
Sutherland. Ref: V 5/6/43. with James Mason, Wilfrid Law-
son, Mary Clare, Tucker McGuire, Joyce Howard. Shock leads
man to kill animals during full moon. Skeleton, ESP. Tepid
for a good two-thirds, the film suddenly becomes hideous in
cleverly-calculated ways near the end. Mason (as usual) is good
at times, not-so-good at others.
TERROR IN THE CRYPT (Sp-I) AI-TV/Alta Vista/Hispamer-
Mec 1963 82m. (La MALDICION DE LOS KARNSTEIN-Sp.
La CRIPTA E L'INCUBO-I. CATHARSIS. The KARNSTEIN
CURSE. CRYPT OF HORROR) D: Camillo Mastrocinque (aka
Thomas Miller). SP: María del Carmen Martínex Román, José

L. Monter.   Story: Ernesto Gastaldi (aka Julian Berry),
Valeri (aka Bohr).   From "Carmilla" by Sheridan Le Fanu.
PH: Julio Ortas. Mus: C. Savina.   Art D: Teddy Villalba.   Ref:
SpCinema'65.   MFB'65:8.   FM 8:16.   COF-A:32. 6:10.   Orpheus
3:33.   with Christopher Lee, José Campos, Adriana Ambessi,
José Villasante, Vera Valmont.   Witch-vampire reincarnated in
girl.   Effective as a mystery, with a few good horror scenes,
but slow-building.

TERROR IN THE HAUNTED HOUSE   Howco 1961 (1958) (MY
   WORLD DIES SCREAMING) D: Harold Daniels. SP: Robert C.
   Dennis. PH: Frederick West. Mus: Darrell Calker. Art D:
   Leslie Thomas. Ref: FM 14:3.   Orpheus 3:27.   Pic: MW 4:14.
   with Gerald Mohr, Cathy O'Donnell, William Ching, John Qualen,
   Barry Bernard. A man takes his bride to an old mansion.
   Thoroughly routine mystery-horror.

TERROR IN THE MIDNIGHT SUN   see INVASION OF THE ANIMAL
   PEOPLE

TERROR IN THE STREETS   (J) Toho 1970 color/scope 76m.
   (AKUMA GA YONDEIRU) D: Michio Yamamoto. Ref: UFQ 50.
   "Horror story about a girl shadowed by an invisible man."

TERROR IN TOKYO (F-I) P.A.C./Victory 1966 color/scope
   101m. (A TOUT COUER A TOKYO POUR O.S.S. 117. HEARTS
   ARE TRUMPS IN TOKYO FOR O.S.S. 117) D: Michel Boisrond.
   SP: Terence Young, Pierre Foucaud, from a novel by Jean Bruce.
   PH: M. Grignon. Dial: Marcel Mithois. Mus: M. Magne.
   SpFX: Gil Delamare, Claude Carliez. Ref: MFB'67:155.
   M/TVM 9/66. with Frédérick Stafford, Marina Vlady, Henri
   Serre.   Secret weapon destroys organization's base.

TERROR IS A MAN (U.S.-Fili) Valiant/Lynn-Romero/Premiere
   1959 89m. (BLOOD CREATURE. The GORY CREATURES.
   CREATURE FROM BLOOD ISLAND) D: Gerardo de Leon. SP:
   Harry Paul Harber. Inspired by "The Island of Dr. Moreau"
   by H. G. Wells. PH: Emmanuel I. Rojas. Mus: A. Auelino.
   Art D: Vicente Bonus. P: Eddie Romero, Kane Lyn(n). Ref:
   MFB'65:59.   FEFN 6/59. XII:10-11. S&S'68:213.   FM 37:57.
   with Francis Lederer, Greta Thyssen, Richard Derr, Oscar
   Keesee, Lilia Duran. A doctor attempts to speed up the process-
   es of evolution, experiments in changing a panther into a man.
   Silly and slow.

TERROR OF DR. HICHCOCK, The see HORRIBLE DR. HICHCOCK,
   The

TERROR OF DRACULA see NOSFERATU

TERROR OF LONDON, The see CURSE OF THE WRAYDONS

The TERROR OF THE AIR (B) Hepworth 1914 45m. Ref: Brit
   Cinema. DDC III:33. with Tom Powers, Violet Hopson,
   Stewart Rome.   Invention explodes underground mines.

TERROR OF THE DEEP see DESTINATION INNER SPACE

TERROR OF THE KIRGHIZ (I-Tunisian) c1969 D: Antonio
   Margheriti (aka Anthony Dawson). Ref: RVB. Photon 21. with
   Reg Park, Mireille Granelli, Ettore Manni, Maria Teresa Orsini
   (witch).   Werewolf.

TERROR OF THE MAD DOCTOR see TESTAMENT OF DR.
   MABUSE (1962)

TERROR OF THE MUMMY see MUMMY, The (1959)
TERROR OF THE SNAKE WOMAN see SNAKE WOMAN, The
TERROR OF THE TONGS (B) Col/Hammer 1961 Eastmancolor
80m. D: Anthony Bushell. SP: Jimmy Sangster. PH: Arthur
Grant. Mus sc: James Bernard. Art D: Bernard Robinson. Make-
up: Roy Ashton. Ref: FFacts. with Christopher Lee, Geoffrey
Toone, Yvonne Monlaur, Marne Maitland, Ewen Solon, Milton
Reid, Charles Lloyd Pack. Another Hammer blood-and-thunder
horror melodrama, but less effective than The STRANGLERS OF
BOMBAY. Lee has some choice lines.
TERROR ON BLOOD ISLAND see BRIDES OF BLOOD
TERROR OVER HOLLYWOOD (by R. Bloch) see TORTURE
GARDEN
TERROR RIDERS, The see KNIGHTS OF TERROR
TERROR STRIKES, The see WAR OF THE COLOSSAL BEAST
TERRORE see CASTLE OF BLOOD
TERRORE DI BARBARI see GOLIATH AND THE BARBARIANS
TERRORE NELLO SPAZIO see PLANET OF THE VAMPIRES
The TERRORNAUTS (B) Embassy/Amicus 1967 Pathecolor
75m. D: Montgomery Tully. SP: John Brunner, from the novel
"The Wailing Asteroid" by Murray Leinster. PH: Geoffrey
Faithful(l). Mus sc: Elizabeth Lutyens. Art D: Bill Constable.
SpFX: Ernest Fletcher-Bowie Films. Ref: Boxo 10/23/67.
V 10/18/67. with Max Adrian, Simon Oates, Charles Hawtrey,
Zena Marshall, Frank Forsyth, Patricia Hayes. Project that
seeks to communicate with beings on other planets; robot creatures.
Mediocre s-f.
TERZO OCCHIO Il see THIRD EYE, The
TESEO CONTRO IL MINOTAURO see MINOTAUR, The (1960)
TESORO DELLA FORESTA PIETRIFICATA, Il see TREASURE OF
THE PETRIFIED FOREST, The
The TESTAMENT OF DR. CORDELIER (F) RTF/Sofirad 1959
95m. (Le TESTAMENT DU DOCTEUR CORDELIER. EXPERI-
MENT IN EVIL. The DOCTOR'S HORRIBLE EXPERIMENT-TV)
Story, SP, D, P: Jean Renoir. From "The Strange Case of Dr.
Jekyll and Mr. Hyde" by Robert Louis Stevenson. PH: Georges
Leclerc. Mus: Joseph Kosma. Art D: M.-L. Dieulot. Ed: Renée
Lichtig. Pic: FM 17:13. Ref: FM 34:55. with Jean-Louis
Barrault (Dr. Cordelier/Opale), Teddy Bilis, Jean Topart, Michel
Vitold, Micheline Gary, Gaston Modot. "Masterpiece"-Eric
Rohmer. Barrault is amusing as Opale, but the story is talky and
poorly developed. Renoir's great films (DAY IN THE COUNTRY,
RULES OF THE GAME) weren't in the field of fantasy.
The TESTAMENT OF DR. MABUSE (G) Nero/Constantin 1932
(Das TESTAMENT VON DOKTOR MABUSE. LAST WILL OF
DR. MABUSE. CRIMES OF DR. MABUSE) SP, D, P: Fritz
Lang. SP: also Thea von Harbou. Remade under the same title.
Follow-up: The THOUSAND EYES OF DR. MABUSE. Follow-up
to DR. MABUSE. PH: Fritz Arno Wagner. Mus: Hans Erdmann.
Art D: Karl Vollbrecht, Emil Hasler. Ref: COF 5:50. DDC
II:306. Imagen. London Times 9/24/34. Pic: TBG. with
Rudolf Klein-Rogge, Oscar Beregi, Theodor Loos, Klaus Pohl,
Gustav Diessl, Theo Lingen, Ludwig Stossel, Paul Bernd, Camilla

Spira. Dr. Mabuse's spirit takes possession of Prof. Baum. Lots
of super-serial-like thrills and cinematic excitement, marred by
a bad subplot about one criminal trying to go straight. Bravura
scenes, great gimmicks.

The TESTAMENT OF DR. MABUSE (French version of above) 1932
(Das TESTAMENT VON DR. MABUSE. Le TESTAMENT DU DR.
MABUSE) SP, Dial: A. René-Sti, with Klein-Rogge, Beregi, Jim
Gérald, Thomy Bourdelle, Maurice Maillot, Raymond Cordy,
Daniel Mendaille, René Ferté.

The TESTAMENT OF DR. MABUSE (W.G.) CCC 1962 88m. (Das
TESTAMENT DES DR. MABUSE. TERROR OF THE MAD DOC-
TOR) D: Werner Klinger. SP: Ladislas Fodor, R. A. Stemmle.
Story: Thea von Harbou. Remake of Lang's film. PH: Albert
Benitz. Mus: Raimund Rosenberger. Art D: Helmut Nentwig,
P. Markwitz. Ref: MFB'65:10. with Gert Frobe, Senta Berger,
Helmut Schmid, Charles Regnier, Walter Rilla, Wolfgang
Preiss, Ann Savo, Harald Juhnke. Mabuse employs hypnotism
in his schemes.

TESTAMENT OF DR. MABUSE, The see THOUSAND EYES OF
DR. MABUSE, The

TESTAMENT OF GORDON STUART (by E. Wallace) see DEAD
EYES OF LONDON

TESTAMENT OF ORPHEUS, or DON'T ASK ME WHY (F) Cinédis
1962 (1960) 79m. (Le TESTAMENT D'ORPHEE) SP, D: Jean
Cocteau. PH: R. Pontoiseau. Ed: M. -J. Yoyotte. Ref: COF 5:
48. Pic: FM 17:32. DDC I:443. with Cocteau, Edouard Dermit,
Maria Casares, Jean Marais, Yul Brynner, Jean-Pierre Leaud,
Pablo Picasso, Charles Aznavour, Michel Lemoine. A scientist
breaks a man out of the space-time continuum. Inventive and
absorbing except for a talky stretch in the middle.

TESTING A SOLDIER'S COURAGE (F) Gaum 1910 8m. Ref: Bios
4/7/10. Lieutenant shoots at "ghost" haunting his room.

TEUFELSSCHLOSSER, Der see DEVIL'S LOCKSMITH, The

THANAMALAI RAHASYAM see SECRET OF THE GOLDEN HILL

THARK, THE HAUNTED HOUSE (B) B&D 1933 78m. D: Tom
Walls. From a play by Ben Travers. Ref: MFB'45:46: reissue.
with Walls, Ralph Lynn, Claude Hulbert, Robertson Hare. Sir
Hector and his nephew Ronald rid Thark Manor, "a weird and
ghostly mansion, " of its "ghost. "

THAT RIVIERA TOUCH (B) Rank/Continental 1966 ('68-U. S.) 98m.
D: Cliff Owen. SP: S. C. Green, R. M. Mills, Peter Blackmore. PH: Otto Heller. Mus: Ron Goodwin. Ref: LATimes
6/5/68. MFB'66: 77. HR 6/5/68. with Eric Morecambe, Ernie
Wise, Suzanne Lloyd, Paul Stassino, Michael For(r)est, George
Pastell. "Haunted" villa complete with creepy caretaker, trap
doors, ect.

THAT'S THAT Univ 1928 25m. Ref: MPN 3/17/28. Radio-controlled plane.

THAT'S THE SPIRIT Univ 1924 11m. Ref: FD 9/7/24. with Bert
Roach. "Spooks, spirits, spirit-photograph bug, skeletons, flying chickens with humans' skulls. "

THEATRE OF DEATH (B) Hemisphere/Pennea 1966 Technicolor/
scope 91m. (FEMALE FIEND. BLOOD FIEND-U. S.) D: Samuel

Gallu. SP: Ellis Kadison, Roger Marshall. PH: Gilbert Taylor.
Mus: Elisabeth Lutyens. Ref: FM 38:45. S Union 8/15/68. Film
3/68. with Christopher Lee, Julian Glover, L. Goldoni, Jenny
Till, Ivor Dean, Evelyn Laye. Paris is the scene of a series of
"vampire" murders.
THEIR BIG MOMENT   RKO   1934 68m. D: James Cruze. SP:
Marion Dix, Arthur Caesar, from a play by Walter Hackett.
PH: Harold Wenstrom. Ref: Photoplay 10/34. FDY. with ZaSu
Pitts, Slim Summerville, William Gaxton, Bruce Cabot, Kay
Johnson, Ralph Morgan, (J.) Huntl(e)y Gordon. Fake magician
gets into real seance.
THEM! WB   1954 94m. D: Gordon Douglas. SP: George W. Yates,
Jim Sherdeman. PH: Sid Hickox. Mus: Bronislau Kaper. Art D:
Stanley Fleischer. Ref: Clarens. FM 14:46.10:25. with James
Whitmore, Edmund Gwenn, Joan Weldon, James Arness,
Onslow Stevens, Sandy Descher, Sean McClory, Fess Parker,
Olin Howlin. Atomic testing creates giant ants. Intriguing s-f-
mystery. There are of course some lines to wince at, and the
ants look kind of spindly if left out in the open too long; but
aspects of ant-life are well-exploited for plot purposes, and the
movie features perhaps the best use of the brief, educational
filmstrip, that favorite feature of fifties monster movies.
THEM (F) 1970 (ILS) D: Jean-Daniel Simon. Ref: V 5/12/71:74.
M/TVM 8/70. with France Delahalle, Michael Duchaussoy,
Charles Vanel, Alexandra Stewart. Inventor's device explores
the subconscious.
THERE ARE DEAD THAT RISE (Mex)   As Films   1946 (HAY
MUERTOS QUE NO HACEN RUDIO. sfa The DEAD RISE?) D:
H. G. Landero. PH: Victor Herrera. Mus: A. Rosales. Ref:
Aventura. HM 3:34. with Germán Valdes, "Tin Tan," Marcelo
Chavéz. Ghost comedy "à la TOPPER."
THESE ARE THE DAMNED (B) Col/Hammer/Swallow 1961 ('65-
U.S.) 87m. (The DAMNED-Eng. HALLUCINATION-I.) Hammer-
scope D: Joseph Losey. SP: Evan Jones, from the novel "The
Children of Light" by H. L. Lawrence. PH: Arthur Grant. Mus:
James Bernard. Art D: Bernard Robinson. P: Anthony Hinds.
Ref: Clarens. COF 10:32. with Macdonald Carey, Shirley Ann
Field, Viveca Lindfors, Oliver Reed, Alexander Knox, Brian
Oulton, Barbara Everest. A couple flee from the woman's brother
into a cave of scientifically reared children. -PM.
THESE GHOSTS (I) 1954 (QUESTI FANTASMI) SP: Giuseppe
Marotta. P: Gustavo Lombardo. See also GHOSTS-ITALIAN
STYLE. Ref: DDC III:243, 320.
THESEUS AND THE MINOTAUR see MINOTAUR, The (1960)
THEY ALL DIED LAUGHING (B) Cont/Michael Balcon/Pax 1963
90m. (A JOLLY BAD FELLOW-Eng.) D: Don Chaffey. SP:
Robert Hamer, Donald Taylor, from the novel "Down among the
Dead Men" by C. E. Vulliamy. PH: Gerald Gibbs. Mus: John
Barry. Ref: Brit Cinema. Boxo 6/1/64. with Leo McKern,
Janet Munro, Dennis Price, Miles Malleson, Leonard Rossiter,
Jerome Willis. Chemist's serum makes takers laugh and cavort
before they die.
THEY CAME FROM ANOTHER WORLD see INVASION OF THE

BODY SNATCHERS
THEY CAME FROM BEYOND SPACE (B) Embassy/Amicus 1966
Pathecolor 85m. D: Freddie Francis. From "The Gods Hate
Kansas" by Joseph Millard. PH: Norman Warwick. Mus: James
Stevens. Art D: Don Mingaye, Scott Slimon. SpFX: Bowie Films.
Ref: MFB. with Bernard Kay, Jennifer Jayne, Robert Hutton,
Michael Gough, Maurice Good, Frank Forsyth, Katy Wild. A
meteorite shower falls on a farm.
THEY CREEP IN THE DARK (story by K. Brown) see APE MAN,
The
THEY'VE CHANGED FACES (I) Garigliano 1971 Eastmancolor 90m.
(HANNO CAMBIATO FACCIA) SP, D: Corrado Farina. SP: also
Giulio Berruti. PH: A. Parolin. Mus: A. Tommasi. Ref:
V 9/1/71: Updating of NOSFERATU. with Giuliano Disperati,
Geraldine Hooper, Adolfo Celi (Boss/Nosferatu). The hero kills
Nosferatu "who, however, is not dead."
The THIEF AND THE PORTER'S HEAD (I) Milano 1912 7m. Ref:
Bios 5/15/13. A doctor restores a man's head with the aid of
electricity.
The THIEF IN THE DARK Fox 1928 54m. Ed: Jack Dennis.
D: Albert Ray. Story: Andrew Bennison, Ray, Kenneth Hawks.
Titles: William Kernell. SP: C. Graham Baker. PH: Arthur
Edeson. Ref: AFI. V 6/13/28. Photoplay 6/28. with George
Meeker, Doris Hill, Gwen Lee, Marjorie Beebe. "Spooky": Fake
spiritualists; "haunted" house with hidden panels, secret passages.
The THIEF OF BAGDAD Fairbanks 1924 140m. D: Raoul Walsh.
SP: Lotta Woods. Story: Elton Thomas. PH: Arthur Edeson. Art
D: William Cameron Menzies. Ref: SilentFF: The THIEF OF BAGH-
DAD. FM 10:26. Pic: M&H 1:2. with Douglas Fairbanks, Snitz
Edwards, Charles Belcher, Anna May Wong, Etta Lee, Brandon
Hurst, Sojin. V 3/26/24: Vale of dragons, valley of fire, in-
visible cloak, magic rope, magic carpet. Fun.
THIEF OF BAGDAD (India-Hindi) 1934 Paramount Movietone
D: D. M. Madhak. SP: K. B. Desai. PH: V. M. Vyas. Mus:
D. Sharma. Ref: Moving Picture Monthly 3/34/60. Dipali 4/6/34:
"Poor imitation" of the Fairbanks THIEF. with Miss Moti, Master
Shiraz, Ali, Mansoor.
The THIEF OF BAGDAD (B) UA/London 1940 Technicolor 106m.
D: Michael Powell, Ludwig Berger, Tim Whelan. SP: Lajos
Biro, Miles Malleson. PH: Georges Périnal, Osmond Borradaile.
Mus: Miklos Rozsa. SpFX: Lawrence Butler. (THIEF OF BAGH-
DAD) Ref: Clarens. FM 12:6. with Sabu, Conrad Veidt, June
Duprez, Mary Morris, John Justin, Rex Ingram, Malleson, Hay
Petrie, Allan Jeayes, Morton Selten. Evil magician, giant spider,
flying horse, deadly living statue, etc. Lush, elaborate fantasy-
spectacle is moderately good thanks to a few highly impressive
sequences (spider, statue). Some of the effects in the other big
sequences are kind of tacky, and the extravagance, in the sets,
color, story, and music, while appealing at times, is more a matter of quantity than quality or imagination. Filmindia 9/48: "To
catalogue all the historical anachronisms and incongruities rampant
in this film would fill volumes.... Some of the harem ladies wear
Spanish mantillas. You see even Sikhs in the streets of Bagdad in

the times of Haroun-al-Rashid, several centuries before the Sikh religion was born! That the Western audiences lap up all such incongruous nonsense is not surprising because to them all Orientals are the same.... Sabu, as the thief, looks as ugly as ever."

The THIEF OF BAGDAD (F-I) MGM/Titanus-Lux/Compagnie Cinematographique 1960 Eastmancolor/scope 96m. (IL LADRO DI BAGDAD. The THIEF OF BAGHDAD) D: Arthur Lubin. SP: B. Vailati, F. Sanjust, A. Frassinetti. PH: Tonino Delli Colli. Mus: Carlo Rustichelli. SpFX: Tom Howard. Ref: FFacts. PM. with Steve Reeves, Georgia Moll, Arturo Dominici, Edy Vessel. Invisible giant, faceless men, magic potion, winged horse.

THIEF OF BAGHDAD (India-Tamil) 1960 Southern Movies 185m. (BAGHDAD THIRUDAN) D: T. P. Sundaram. Ref: FEFN 7/60. with M. N. Rajam, T. S. Balaiah. Disinherited prince recovers father's throne.

The THIEVING HAND Vita 1908 5m. Ref: V&FI 2/1/08. An artificial hand is "imbued" with dishonest instincts.

THIN AIR see INVASION OF THE BODY STEALERS

The THING RKO/Winchester 1951 87m. (The THING FROM ANOTHER WORLD-Eng.) P: Howard Hawks. D: Hawks, signed by Christian Nyby. SP: Charles Lederer, from the story "Who Goes There?" by John W. Campbell, Jr. PH: Russell Harlan. Mus: Dmitri Tiomkin. Art D: Albert D'Agostino, John J. Hughes. SpFX: Donald Stewart. SpPhFX: Linwood Dunk. Ref: FM 11:31.12: 40-50.13:70-83.14:6,46. with Margaret Sheridan, Kenneth Tobey, Robert Cornthwaite, Douglas Spencer, James Young, Dewey Martin, William Self, Eduard Franz, James Arness (the thing), Paul Frees, John Dierkes, Norbert Schiller. Vampire-like alien found frozen in Arctic ice returns to life at research station. Tense, suspenseful s-f/horror, the tension and suspense deriving from simple things like a geiger counter and dripping water. Like Hawks' other good films, strong on setting, atmosphere, ensemble playing. One of Tiomkin's more evocative, less aggravating scores. Each biological detail about the monster is calculated for maximum ghoulishness.

The THING THAT COULDN'T DIE Univ 1958 69m. (The THING THAT COULD NOT DIE. The MAN WITHOUT A BODY) D, P: William Cowan. SP: David Duncan, from his story, "The Water Witch." PH: Russell Metty. Mus D: Joseph Gershenson. Art D: Alexander Golitzen, Eric Orbom. Special PH: Clifford Stine. Ref: FFacts. FM 2:17. Orpheus 3:26. with Andra Martin, William Reynolds, Carolyn Kearney, Robin Hughes, Forrest Lewis. 400-year-old-living head hypnotizes people to do its bidding. Cloddishly written and directed. Several unintentionally funny scenes, like the girl's bringing the head downstairs for the body, etc.

THINGS HAPPEN AT NIGHT (B) Renown/Alliance 1947 79m. D: Francis Searle. SP: St. John L. Clowes, from the play "The Poltergeist" by F. Harvey. PH: Leslie Rowson. Mus: George Melachrino. Art D: Harry Moore. Ref: MFB'48:172. Brit Fm Ybk '49/'50. Dimmitt. with Garry Marsh, Olga Linda, Beatrice Campbell, Robertson Hare, Gordon Harker. A poltergeist takes

possession of a person's body.
THINGS TO COME. The HUNDRED YEARS TO COME. WHITHER
MANKIND) D: William Cameron Menzies. SP: H. G. Wells, from
MANKIND) D: William Cameron Menzies. SP: H. G. Wells, from
his writings. PH: Georges Périnal. Mus: Arthur Bliss. Art D:
Vincent Korda. SpFX: Ned Mann, Harry Zech. P: Alexander
Korda. Costumes: René Hubert, John Armstrong. Ref: FM
10:24.12:24. Clarens. Moving Picture Monthly 3/34. with
Raymond Massey, Ralph Richardson, Cedric Hardwicke, Derrick
de Marney, Pearl Argyle, Edward Chapman, Allan Jeayes,
Patricia Hilliard, Margaretta Scott. The decline of civilization
after a second World War. Ludicrous acting, dialogue, plot.
And the special effects aren't nearly good enough to save it.
THINNEN STOUT (Beauty (Mutual) 1916 Ref: MPN 13:3604. with
Orral Humphrey, Lucille Ward, John Gough. "Reducing special-
ist" reduces man to skeleton.
The THIRD EYE (B) Graham-Wilcox 1928 D: Maclean Rogers. Ref:
SF Film. with Hayford Hobbs. TV apparatus.
The THIRD EYE (I) Panda 1965 (Il TERZO OCCHIO) SP,D:
James Warren. SP: also Craig, Young. Story: Gilles De Reys.
PH: S. Deaves. Ref: Ital P. M/TVM 12/65. with Franco Nero,
G. Pascal, Diana Sullivan, Olga Sunbeauty. Madman keeps dead
fiancée's embalmed body in his bed. He believes that her sister
is her reincarnation.
THIRD GUEST, The (by B. Traven) see MACARIO
The THIRD ROUND (B) Astra-Nat'l 1925 65m. (BULLDOG DRUM-
MOND'S THIRD ROUND) SP,D: Sidney Morgan. PH:Bert Cann.
From the story by H. C. McNeil. Remade as BULLDOG DRUM-
MOND'S PERIL. Ref: SilentFF. with Jack Buchanan, Betty
Faire, Allan Jeayes. Man invents method of manufacturing
diamonds.
THIRTEEN see EYE OF THE DEVIL
The THIRTEEN CLUB AM&B 1905 Ref:Niver. Club members
flout superstitions and die. Skeletons replace them.
13 DEMON STREET see DEVIL'S MESSENGER, The
THIRTEEN GHOSTS Col 1960 88m. D, P: William Castle. SP:
Robb White. PH: Joseph Biroc. Mus: Von Dexter. Art D: Cary
Odell. Color SpFX: Butler-Glouner, Inc. Ref: FFacts. PM.with
Charles Herbert, Martin Milner, Jo Morrow, Rosemary De
Camp, Donald Woods, Margaret Hamilton, John van Dreelen.
A boy is overjoyed when his father is willed a haunted house.
Routine Castle. Some good wind and candle tricks.
13 WOMEN RKO 1932 75m. D: George Archainbaud.SP: Bartlett
Cormack, from the novel by Tiffany Thayer. PH:Leo Tovar. Ed:
Charles L. Kimball. Ref: Harrison's 10/8/32. Photoplay 10/32.
TVG. Pic: TBG. with Irene Dunne, Myrna Loy, Ricardo Cortez,
Jill Esmond, Florence Eldredge, Kay Johnson, Julie Haydon,
C. Henry Gordon, Blanche Friderici. "Mental suggestion": A
woman, in league with a swami, writes 12 letters to her hated
ex-classmates at a girls' school, predicting their deaths.
The THIRTEENTH CHAIR Pathe 1919 SP,D: Leonce Perret. From
the play by Bayard Veiller. Ref: MPN 20:819,1695. with Yvonne
Delva,Creighton Hale, Marie Shotwell, Christine Mayo, Suzanne

Colbert, George Deneubourg. Marc McDermott, Walter Law,
Man in 13th chair at seance murdered.
The THIRTEENTH CHAIR MGM 1929 sound and silent versions
75m. Titles: Joe Farnham. D, P: Tod Browning. SP: Elliot
Clawson, from the play by Bayard Veiller. PH: Merritt B.
Gerstad. Ref: AFI. FM 22:42. Clarens. withConrad Nagel, Leila
Hyams, Margaret Wycherly, Holmes Herbert, Mary Forbes,
Bela Lugosi, John Davidson, Moon Carroll, Lal Chand Mehra,
Helene Millard. Spiritualistic medium aids in solving murder.
The THIRTEENTH CHAIR MGM 1937 66m. D, P: George Seitz.
SP: Marion Parsonnet, from the play by Bayard Veiller. PH:
Charles Clarke. Art D: Cedric Gibbons. Mus sc: David Snell.
Ref: FD 5/4/37. with Dame May Whitty, Madge Evans, Lewis
Stone, Elissa Landi, Thomas Beck, Henry Daniell, Ralph Forbes,
Holmes Herbert, Heather Thatcher, Charles Trowbridge, Robert
Coote, Lal Chand Mehra. Photoplay 7/37: "Two seances played
in complete darkness give this murder mystery an eerie, ghost-
ly effect. "
The THIRTEENTH GUEST Mono 1932 65m. (LADY BEWARE)
D: Albert Ray. SP: Arthur Hoerl, Francis Hyland. From a
story by Armitage Trail. See also MYSTERY OF THE THIR-
TEENTH GUEST. SCARED TO DEATH. Ref: Harrison's. Photo-
play 11/32. MFB 3/38:74: "To add to the horrors of the situa-
tion screams and moans are heard at intervals. " V 9/6/32:
"Cobwebby house... masked figure at an electric switch which
tolls the victims. " TVG. Pic: TBG. with Ginger Rogers, Lyle
Talbot, J. Farrell MacDonald, Frances Rich, James Eagles, Ed-
die Phillips, Paul Hurst, William Davidson, Crauford Kent.
The 13TH HOUR MGM 1928 53m. silent Ed: Dan Sharits.
SP, D: Chester M. Franklin. SP: also Douglas Furber, Edward
T. Lowe, Jr., Titles: Wellyn Totman. Art D: Eugene Hornbostel.
Ref: AFI. PH:Max Fabian. From a play by Franklin and Douglas
Furber. Ref: FD 12/11/127: "Spooky situations, weird atmos-
phere. " Photoplay 3/28: "Trapdoors, secret panels and under-
ground passages. " V 11/30/27: "Instrument which shows him
what's going on in the next room. " with Lionel Barrymore, Fred
Kelsey, Polly Moran, Charles Delaney, Jacqueline Gadsdon.
THIRTEENTH MOON OF JUPITER, The see FIRE MAIDENS OF
OUTER SPACE
The THIRTY FOOT BRIDE OF CANDY ROCK Col 1959 75m.
(LOU COSTELLO AND HIS 30 FOOT BRIDE. The SECRET
BRIDE OF CANDY ROCK) D: Sidney Miller. SP: Rowland
Barber, Arthur Ross. Story: Lawrence Goldman. PH:Frank
G. Carson. Mus: Raoul Kraushaar. SpFX: Jack Rabin, Irving
Block, Louis DeWitt. Ref: FD 8/6/59. Orpheus 3:27. Ref:
FFacts. with Lou Costello, Dorothy Provine, Gale Gordon,
Jimmy Conlin, Robert Burton, Will Wright, Peter Leeds, Joey
Faye, Doodles Weaver. Electronic gadget turns woman into
giant. Lots of gimmicks, a few of them amusing.
THIS IS NOT A TEST 1962 Ref: RVB. Take One II:6:11. with
Seamon Glass, Mary Morlas. Atomic attack on U.S.
THIS ISLAND EARTH Univ 1955 Technicolor 89m. (WAR OF
THE PLANETS) D: Joseph Newman. SP: Franklin Coen, Edward

O'Callaghan. From the book by Raymond F. Jones. PH: Clifford Stine. Mus: Herman Stein. Art D: Alexander Golitzen, Richard Riedel. P: William Alland. Ref: FDY. Clarens. FM 2:16.14:42. with Jeff Morrow, Faith Domergue, Rex Reason, Lance Fuller, Russell Johnson, Robert Nichols, Douglas Spencer. Scientist builds "interociter," communicates with beings from the planet Metaluna. Episodic, but the episodes are fairly intriguing. Changes speed midway from too slow to too fast. Good use of colored rays and other special-effect gadgets. Raymond Durgnat: "The meteors (which we have characterized as "phallic-sadistic") are also globes (feminine); Metaluna (the body of the dead mother) is inhabited by a hierarchy of fathers (with Brack as "elder sibling")..."

THIS PRECIOUS FREEDOM (by A. Oboler) see STRANGE HOLIDAY

THIS SAME GARDEN (by R. Bell) see WHILE I LIVE

THIS TIME TOMORROW see TIME TRAVELERS, The

THOSE FANTASTIC FLYING FOOLS (B) AI/Anglo/Towers 1967 Eastmancolor 95m. (BLAST OFF. JOURNEY THAT SHOOK THE WORLD. P. T. BARNUM'S ROCKET TO THE MOON. JULES VERNE'S ROCKET TO THE MOON. ROCKET TO THE MOON) D: Don Sharp. SP: Dave Freeman. Story: Peter Welbeck. PH: Reg Wyer. Mus: Patrick John Scott. Art D: Frank White. Inspired by the writings of Jules Verne. SpFX: Les Bowie, Pat Moore. Ref: FFacts. PM. with Burl Ives, Troy Donahue, Gert Frobe, Lionel Jeffries, Edward de Souza, Klaus Kinski, Derek Francis, Allan Cuthbertson, Terry-Thomas, Hermione Gingold, Daliah Lavi, Dennis Price. New explosive; planned rocket-to-moon. Leaden, uninspired comedy.

THOSE WHO DARE Creative 1924 70m. D: John B.O'Brien. Adap: Frank Beresford. Story: I. W. Irving. Ref: AFI. with John Bowers, Marguerite De La Motte, Joseph Dowling, Claire McDowell, Spotiswoode Aitken, Sheldon Lewis. Leader of mutinous ship's crew practices voodoo.

THOUGHT MONSTER, The (by A. R. Long) see FIEND WITHOUT A FACE

The THOUSAND EYES OF DR. MABUSE (W. G.-I) CCC/Omnia 1960 103m. (Die TAUSEND AUGEN DES DR. MABUSE or DIE AUGEN DES DR. MABUSE-G. Il DIABOLICO DOTTOR MABUSE-I. The TESTAMENT OF DR. MABUSE. The SHADOW VS. THE 1000 EYES OF DR. MABUSE The ONE THOUSAND EYES OF DR. MABUSE) SP,D: Fritz Lang. SP: also Heinz Wuttig. Idea: Jan Fethge. Follow-up to Lang's The TESTAMENT OF DR. MABUSE. PH: Karl Lo(e)b. Mus: Gerhard Becker. Sets: Erich Kettelhut, Johannes Ott. Ref: Imagen. MFB'62:137. TVK. DDC I: 63?,395.II:400. TBG. with Peter Van Eyck (Henry Travers), Dawn Addams, Wolfgang Preiss, Gert Fro(e)be, Andrea Checci, Howard Vernon, Werner Peters, Jean-Jacques Delbo, Linda Sini. TV "eyes"; girl under doctor's hypnotic power; "psychic"; remote-control door-opener; gun that fires steel needles. Dull dialogue, unimaginative plot. Enlivened only by some fast action near the end.

1000 L SPOOK, The (B) 1907 D: Walter Booth. Ref: Brit Cinema

The THREE AGES Metro 1923 70m. D: Buster Keaton, Eddie Cline.

SP: Clyde Bruckman, Jean Havez, Joseph Mitchell. PH: William
McGann, Elgin Lessley. Technical D: Fred Gabourie. Ref: David
Robinson's "Buster Keaton." with Keaton, Wallace Beery,
Margaret Leahy, Joe Roberts, Oliver Hardy, Lilian Lawrence.
Stone Age sequence: cave men, dinosaur. Other ages: Roman
and modern. One of Keaton's second-best features (and that's
very good), with some of his most amazing acrobatic feats and
funniest bits and a lion that's almost as funny as The Giant Claw.
The only trouble with the intentionally-episodic structure is that
you go in one era and out the other just as the comedy gets
going good.

THREE ARE THREE (Sp) CdC/Victory/CyC/Madrid/Fotofilm 1955
one section in color (TRES ERAN TRES. TIAPACA) SP, D:
Eduardo G. Morato. PH: G. y. Pahissa. Art D: Villalba. Ref:
Imagen. MMF 9:17. FM 63:24. with Manolo Morán, Antonio
Riquelme, Gustavo Re, Manuel Arbó (monster), Antonio Casas.
Sketch: "A Horror Story" or "Una de Miedo": Parody of "Frank-
enstein" and the horror films of Universal.

THREE CASES OF MURDER (B) Associated Artists 1954 99m. D:
Wendy Toye, David Eady, George More O'Ferrall. SP: Ian
Dalrymple, Donald Wilson, Sidney Carroll. PH: Georges Périnal.
Art D: Paul Sheriff. Ref: FDY. FM 17:32. with Orson Welles,
Alan Badel, Elizabeth Sellars, Eddie Byrne, John Gregson,
Arthur Wontner, Andre Morell, Zena Marshall. Three episodes.
1. "In the Picture": Ghostly happenings in an art gallery.

THREE DATES WITH DESTINY (Sp) Union 1953 (TRES CITAS CON
EL DESTINO) D: Florian Rey. PH: Ricardo Torres. Ref: Lee.
Spanish "Anuario" '55. with Jorge Mistral, Antonio Vilar,
Narcisco Menta, Manuel Arbo. Accursed diamond brings bad
luck.

THREE FACES OF FEAR, The see BLACK SABBATH
THREE FACES OF TERROR, The see BLACK SABBATH
THREE FANTASTIC SUPERMEN, The see FANTASTIC THREE, The
THREE LIGHTS, The see DESTINY
THREE STEPS TO DELIRIUM see TALES OF MYSTERY AND
IMAGINATION

The THREE STOOGES IN ORBIT Col/Normandy 1962 87m. D:
Edward Bernds. SP: Elwood Ullman. Story, P: Norman Maurer.
PH: W. F. Whitley. Mus: Paul Dunlap. Art D: Don Ament. Ref:
FFacts. with Moe Howard, Larry Fine, Joe De Rita, Emil Sit-
ka, Nestor Paiva, Edson Stroll, George Neise. Eccentric pro-
fessor believes Martian spies are after his new invention.
A mess, but there are a few laughs anyway.

The THREE STOOGES MEET HERCULES Col/Normandy 1962 89m.
D: Edward Bernds. SP: Elwood Ullman. Mus: Paul Dunlap. Ref:
FFacts. with Moe Howard, Larry Fine, Joe De Rita, Vicki
Trickett, Quinn Redeker, Samson Burke, Mike McKeever, Emil
Sitka, Gregg Martell, Gene Roth. The Stooges travel in a time
machine back to ancient Greece. A few laughs.

3000 A.D. see CAPTIVE WOMEN

The THREE TREASURES (J) Toho 1958 color 182m. (NIPPON
TANJO) D: Hiroshi Inagaki. SpFX: EIji Tsuburaya. SP: Ryuzo

Kikushima. Ref: Unij Bltn 11/64. J Films'60. Pic: FM 22:75.
with Toshiro Mifune, Toshio Yasumi, Takashi Shimura, Akira
Takarada, Jun Tazaki, Kyoko Kagawa. Dragon.
THREE WAX MEN see WAXWORKS
The THREE WISHES Gaum 1915 8m. Ref: MPN 1/9/15. Goblin
grants three wishes to aged couple.
THREE'S COMPANY (B) British Lion/Douglas Fairbanks, Jr.
1953 78m. D: Charles Saunders. SP: John Cresswell. Story:
Hester Holland. PH: J. Wilson, B. Stafford. Art D: Norman
Arnold. Ref: MFB'53:125. with Basil Sydney, Elizabeth Sellars,
George Benson, Fairbanks, Jr., Constance Cummings. "The
Scream," third of three stories: "A ghostly scream waits for
its murder still to be committed when a man and his perfidious
wife buy the house it inhabits."
THRONE OF FIRE, The see WITCH-KILLER OF BLACKMOOR,
The
THROUGH SOLID WALLS Univ 1916 22m. D: Walter Morton.
SP: E. J. Clawson (or Clauson). Ref: MPN 14:2714. SF Film.
with Marc Fenton, Peggy Custer. Machine enables person to
see through walls.
THROUGH THE AGES Martin 1914 18m. Ref: Bios 5/14/14. Dream:
Stone Age.
THROUGH THE CENTURIES Selig 1914 18m. Ref: Bios 5/7/14.
Two scientists on an expedition in Egypt find a princess in a
trance in a catacomb.
THROUGH THE LOOK-ING GLASS see VELVET VAMPIRE, The
THUNDA see KING OF THE CONGO
THY SOUL SHALL BEAR WITNESS see PHANTOM CHARIOT, The
(1919)
TI ASPETTERO'ALL'INFERNO see I'LL SEE YOU IN HELL
TIAPACA see THREE ARE THREE
TIBBET-KAJADU see YANGRILLA
TIGER (by Max Brand) see TIGER TRUE
The TIGER LILY Vita 1913 45m. Ref: The Film Index. Tigress
reincarnated.
TIGER MAN, The see LADY AND THE MONSTER, The
TIGER TRUE Univ 1921 55m. P: J. P. McGowan. SP: George
C. Hull, from the novel "Tiger" by Max Brand. Ref: V 2/4/21.
LC. with Frank Mayo, Fritzi Brunette. "The Baboon," "supposed
to be invested with supernatural strength," masquerades as
"Whitey," "a paralytic-stricken old man."
TILLIE OF NINE LIVES La Salle 1917 11m. Ref: MPN 15:3800. A
girl is poisoned and "dynamited" and still lives.
TIME FLIES (B) Gainsborough 1944 D: Walter Forde. Ref: s-f in
the Cinema. Brit Cinema. with Felix Aylmer, Tommy Handley,
Evelyn Dall, George Moon. Time machine called a "Time Ball."
The TIME MACHINE MGM/Galaxy 1960 Metrocolor 103m. D, P:
George Pal. SP: David Duncan. From the novel by H. G. Wells.
PH: Paul C. Vogel. Mus: Russell Garcia. Art D: George W.
Davis, William Ferrari. Sets: Henry Grace, Keough Gleason.
SpPhFX: Gene Warren, Tim Barr. Makeup: William Tuttle. Ref:
FFacts. with Rod Taylor, Alan Young, Yvette Mimieux, Sebastian
Cabot, Whit Bissell. A London scientist travels far into the

future. Good color, story, gimmicks, effects. Probably Pal's
best film.
TIME OF ROSES (Finnish) Filminor 1969 90m. (RUUSUJEN AIKA)
SP, D: Risto Jarva. SP: also P. von Bagh, J. Pakkasvirta. PH:
Artii Peippo. Ref: M/TVM 8/69. Boxo 9/7/70. V 10/15/69.
with Arto Tuominen, Tarja Markus. Political s-f, set in the
year 2012.
The TIME OF THEIR LIVES Univ 1946 82m. (The GHOST STEPS
OUT) D: Charles T. Barton. SP: Val Burton, Walt DeLeon,
Bradford Ropes. Add'l Dial: John Grant. PH: Charles Van Enger.
Mus sc & d: Milton Rosen. Art D: Jack Otterson, Richard
Reidel. SpPH: D. S. Hurley, Jerome Ash. Ref: FDY. with Bud
Abbott, Lou Costello, Marjorie Reynolds, Rex Lease, Donald
MacBride, Binnie Barnes, John Shelton, Gale Sondergaard,
Robert Barrat, Anne Gillis. A seance draws two ghosts; one
plays a harpsichord to frighten a man. The effects are good but
can't save the rest. A few mild laughs.
TIME TRAP see TIME TRAVELERS, The
The TIME TRAVELERS AI 1964 color 82m. (DEPTHS OF THE
UNKNOWN? THIS TIME TOMORROW. TIME TRAP. The
RETURN OF THE TIME TRAVELER) SP, D: Ib Melchior. Story:
Melchior, David Hewitt. PH: William Zsigmond. Mus: Richard
Lasalle. Art D: Ray Storey. SpFX: Hewitt. Ref: FanMo 5:33.
Orpheus 3:29,36. FFacts. with Preston Foster, Merry Anders,
Forrest J Ackerman, Philip Carey, John Hoyt, Joan Woodbury,
Stephen Franken. Scientists travel 107 years into the future.
Mixed-up combination of The FLY, WORLD WITHOUT END,
WHEN WORLDS COLLIDE, and CREATION OF THE HUMAN-
OIDS. Effects and ending are only plusses.
The TIMES ARE OUT OF JOINT (F) Gaum 1910 Ref: The Film
Index. D: Emile Cohl. A fast clock accelerates time.
TIMESLIP see ATOMIC MAN, The
TIMIDITY VANQUISHED (F) Pathe 1910 6m. (La TIMIDITE VAIN-
CUE) SP, D: Max Linder. Ref: SilentFF. with Linder. Nasal
injection of pepper and water turns timid man into bully.
TIN GIRL, The see GIRL OF TIN, The
TIN HATS MGM 1926 80m. Story, D: Edward Sedgwick. Con-
tinuity: Albert Lewin. Titles: Ralph Spence. Adap: Lew Lipton,
Donald W. Lee. PH: Ben Reynolds. Art D: Cedric Gibbons,
F. Hope. Ref: AFI. with Conrad Nagel, Claire Windsor, George
Cooper, Bert Roach, Eileen Sedgwick. Castle with "mysterious
doors, traps...ghost in ancestral armor."
The TINGLER Col 1959 80m. D, P: William Castle. SP: Robb
White. PH: Wilfrid M. Cline. Mus: Von Dexter. Ref: Clarens.
with Vincent Price, Judith Evelyn, Darryl Hickman, Philip
Coolidge, Patricia Cutts. A doctor discovers a creature,
created by fear, at the base of the spine. Ineffective shocker.
TINTIN AND THE MYSTERY OF THE BLUE ORANGES see
MYSTERY OF THE BLUE ORANGES, The
TINTIN AND THE MYSTERY OF THE GOLDEN FLEECE (F) 1961
color/scope D: Jean-Jacques Vierne. SP: Andre Barret. PH:
Raymond Lemoigne. Art D: P. Ancellin. Ref: La Prod Cin Fr
11/61. with Tintin, Marcel Bozzufi, Georges Wilson, Charles

Vanel, Milou. Pills put into fuel make boat go at incredible speed.

TINTIN ET LES ORANGES BLEUES see MYSTERY OF THE BLUE ORANGES, The

'TIS NOW THE VERY WITCHING TIME OF NIGHT Edison 1909 8m. Ref: MPW '09:385. Bios 11/11/09. A man bets that he can sleep a night in a haunted house. He encounters bats, witches, skeletons, "toothless hags, " etc.

TITANI, I see MY SON, THE HERO

TITANS, The see MY SON, THE HERO

TO DIE WITH PLEASURE see BLOOD AND ROSES

TO', E MORTA LA NONNA! see OH, GRANDMOTHER'S DEAD!

TO HEX WITH SEX RAF/August Films 1970 Eastmancolor 86m. D, P: Simon Nuchtern. SP: Nuchtern, Arthur Littman. Ref: Film Bltn 1/26/70. with Stefen Peters, Paula Shaw, Jack Taylor. A man sells his soul to a female devil in return for eternal youth.

TO LOVE A VAMPIRE see LUST FOR A VAMPIRE

TOBOR THE GREAT Rep 1954 77m. D: Lee Sholem. SP: Philip MacDonald. PH: John L. Russell. Art D: Gabriel Scognamillo. Ref: FDY. FM 12:20. with Charles Drake, Karin Booth, Billy Chapin, Steven Geray, Henry Kulky, Robert Shayne, Lyle Talbot. Dull gimmicks, dumb "boy and his robot" plot.

TOBY DAMMIT see TALES OF MYSTERY AND IMAGINATION

TOD ROBBINS (by C. Robbins) see UNHOLY THREE, The (1925/1930)

TODESKUSS DES DR. FU MAN CHU, Der see BLOOD OF FU MANCHU

TOKAIDO YOTSUYA KAIDAN see GHOST OF YOTSUYA, The (1959)

TOKYO NO TEKISASU-JIN see KNOCKOUT DROPS

TOM THUMB 1909 17m. Ref: MPW'09:353. "Vicious old giant" intends to cut boys' heads off.

TOM THUMB (F) Pathe 1912 12m. Ref: Bios 5/23/12. A huge fish swallows Tom Thumb.

TOM THUMB (Mex) AI-TV/Childhood 1958 color 85m. (PULGARCITO) SP, D: Rene Cardona. SP: also A. L. Portillo. From the fairy tale by Perrault. PH: J. O. Ramos. Mus: Raul Lavista. Narr: Paul Tripp. Ref: PM. RVB. M/TVM 10/67: "Horrible ogre." with Cesare Quezadas, Maria Elena Marqués, Jose Elias Moreno (ogre).

TOM THUMB AND LITTLE RED RIDING HOOD VS. THE MONSTERS (Mex) Rodriguez 1960 Eastmancolor/scope 90m. (CAPURCITA Y PULGARCITO CONTRA LOS MONSTRUOS. LITTLE RED RIDING HOOD. LITTLE RED RIDING HOOD AND THE MONSTERS. LITTLE RED RIDING HOOD AND TOM THUMB AGAINST THE MONSTERS) SP, D: Roberto Rodriguez. SP: also Sergio Magaña. Story: Adolfo Portillo, F. M. Ortiz. PH: Rosalio Solano. Mus: Raul Lavista. Ref: Indice. FM 33:10. COF 14:49. M/TVM 5/63. with Maria Garcia, José Moreno, Rafael Muñoz.

TOMB OF LIGEIA (U. S. -B) AI/Alta Vista--Anglo-Amalgamated 1964 Eastmancolor/scope 79m. (HOUSE AT THE END OF THE WORLD. LIGEIA. LAST TOMB OF LIGEIA) D, P: Roger Corman.

SP: Robert Towne, from "Ligeia" by Edgar Allan Poe. PH:
Arthur Grant. Mus: Kenneth V. Jones. Art D: Colin Southcott.
Ref: FM 32:68. Shriek 1:18. Clarens. with Vincent Price,
Elizabeth Shepherd, John Westbrook, Derek Francis, Richard
Vernon. Ref: Orpheus 3:31. COF 7:36. PM. A widower is ob-
sessed with the idea that his first wife is not really dead.
TOMB OF TORTURE (I-G) Trans-Lux/Filmar/Virginia/FDC/
Richard Gordon 1963 ('66-U.S.) 87m. (METEMPSYCHO. Le
MANOIR MAUDIT-F.) SP,D: Antonio Boccacci. SP: also Giorgio
Simonelli. Ref: FFacts'66. Bianco 6/63. Pic: FMO 6:22. with
Elizabeth Queen, Annie Albert, Marco Mariani, Enny Eco,
Adriano Micatoni. A girl is haunted by nightmares of the murder
of a girl who looks like her. Poor.
TOMBS OF HORROR see TERROR CREATURES FROM THE
GRAVE
TOMEI KAIJIN see INVISIBLE MAN (1958)
TOMEI KENSHI see INVISIBLE SWORDSMAN
TOMEI NINGEN see INVISIBLE MAN, The (1954)
TOMEI NINGEN ARAWARU see TRANSPARENT MAN, The
TOMEI NINGEN TO HAI OTOKO see MURDERING MITE, The
TOMMY AND THE POWDER (F) Lux 1910 7m. Ref: Bios 4/14/10.
Professor's powder makes lazy people active.
TOMORROW AT SEVEN RKO 1933 60m. D: Ray Enright. SP:
Ralph Spence. PH: Charles Schoenbaum. Ref: NYT. Harrison's
7/8/33: "The usual props such as lights going out, windows
suddenly opening, shadow on the wall, mysterious figures prowl-
ing around, are used to get eerie effects." with Chester Morris,
Vivienne Osborne, Allen Jenkins, Frank McHugh, Henry
Stephenson, Grant Mitchell, Charles Middleton, Cornelius Keefe,
Oscar Apfel. Murder in an old Louisiana mansion.
TOMORROW YOU DIE see CRAWLING HAND, The
TONIGHT I WILL INCARDINATE YOUR BODY (Sp) c1965? (ESTE
NOITE ENCARNAREI NO TEU CADAVER) D?: Pereira. Ref:
FJA folder. with Mina Monte, Arlete Brasulin, Oswaldo de
Souza, Roque Rodriguez, Antonio Marins, Tina Wholers, William
Morgan, Nivaldo de Lima, Nadia Tell, Palito (Death). Hand from
the grave that drags man in; hordes of snakes, spiders.
TONOSAMA YAJIKITA see GHOST STORY IN PASSAGE, A
TOO MUCH ELIXIR OF LIFE Alhambra 1915 D: Bruce Mitchell.
SP: Anthony Coldeway. Ref: MPW 26:338. MPN 10/16/15. Pro-
fessor thinks he has revived mummy with elixir.
TOO MUCH CHAMPAGNE Vita 1908 Ref: MPW'08:147. V&FI
2/29/08: Scenes from "Dante's Inferno." Dream: Satan spirits
clubman away. Imps chase him in the "Devil's Woods."
TOMORROW (B) Rank/Lowndes 1970 Technicolor 95m. SP,D: Val
Guest. PH: Dick Bush. Mus: Hugo Montenegro. SpFX: John
Stears. Ref: V 9/16/70. with Olivia Newton-John, Benny Thomas,
Vic Cooper. An "Alphoid" is detailed to track down a tonsaliser
which causes a powerful vibration on earth and sterility of sound
in outer space.
TOPPER RETURNS UA 1941 85m. D: Roy Del Ruth. SP: Jonathan
Latimer, Gordon Douglas. PH: Norbert Brodine. Ref: FDY. ModM
1:31. with Roland Young, Billie Burke, Joan Blondell, Carole

Landis, Dennis O'Keefe, Patsy Kelly, H. B. Warner, Eddie
"Rochester" Anderson, George Zucco, Donald MacBride, Rafaela
Ottiano, Trevor Bardette. Mystery-horror-comedy of the eerie-
old-house type.
TORGUS, THE COFFIN MAKER (G) Union-Film der UFA 1920
D: Hans Kobe. SP: Carl Mayer. PH: Karl Freund. Art D:
Robert Neppach. Ref: DDC I:300. III:170. Fantastique. with Eugen
Klöpfer, Maria Leiko. An old woman receives a coffin containing
a body.
THE TORMENT; or THE SCIENTIST'S SECRET (F) Eclair 1912
36m. Ref: Bios 4/4/12. Chemical formula causes terrific ex-
plosion.
TORMENTED   AA/Cheviot 1960 75m. D, P: Bert I. Gordon. SP:
George W. Yates. P: also Joseph Steinberg. PH: Ernest Laszlo.
Mus: Albert Glasser. Art D: Gabriel Scognamillo. SpFX: Herman
Townsley. SpVisualFX: B. I. and Flora Gordon. Ref: FFacts.
FM 10:40.14:20. with Richard Carlson, Juli Reding, Susan
Gordon, Gene Roth. Man haunted by female ghost. Though one
of Gordon's better pictures, it's still no great shakes.
TORPEDO OF DOOM see FIGHTING DEVIL DOGS
TORPILLE AERIENNE, La see AIR TORPEDO, The (1912)
TORRE DE LOS SIETE JOROBADOS, La see TOWER OF THE
SEVEN HUNCHBACKS, The
TORTURE CHAMBER OF DR. SADISM, The see SNAKE PIT, The
TORTURE DUNGEON Mishkin/Constitution 1970 color 80m. SP, D,
PH: Andy Milligan. SP: also John Borske. Sets: James Fox.
Makeup: Walter Terry. Ref: Boxo 1/12/70. with Jer(r)emy
Brooks, Susan Cassidy. One of the most inept, amateurish
movies ever made, with a score only this picture deserves,
odd-sounding dialogue ("Decadence--the mother of invention"),
no continuity, and no acting. In one memorably absurd scene
a poor, hunchbacked ex-beggar describes how his mother had
two men jump on his back and break his spine, to make him
"look more like a beggar." ("Mother was happy. I was miser-
able.")
TORTURE GARDEN (B) Col/Amicus 1968 Technicolor 93m.
D: Freddie Francis. SP: Robert Bloch, from his stories "The
Man Who Collected Poe," "Enoch," "Terror over Hollywood"
and "Mr. Steinway." PH: Norman Warwick. Mus sc: Don Banks,
James Bernard. Art D: Don Mingaye, Scott Slimon. Ref:
FFacts. FM 46:20. SF Film. with Burgess Meredith, Jack
Palance, Beverly Adams, Peter Cushing, Robert Hutton, Michael
Ripper, Maurice Denham, Ursula Howells, Niall MacGinnis,
Hedger Wallace (Edgar Allan Poe). Four episodes involving
robots, spirits, and a cat that craves human heads.
TORTURE SHIP Producers Pictures 1939 56m. D: Victor Hal-
perin. PH: Jack Greenhalgh. Ref: Showmen's 9/9/39.
FD 11/22/39. with Lyle Talbot, Irving Pichel, Jacqueline
Wells, Sheila Bromley, Wheeler Oakman, Leander de Cordova,
Skelton Knaggs, Russel(l) Hopton. A scientist seeks to "cure"
criminals by "gland inductions."
TOTEN AUGEN VON LONDON, Die see DEAD EYES OF LONDON
TOTER HING IM NETZ, Ein see HORRORS OF SPIDER ISLAND

TOTER SUCHT SEINEN MORDER, Ein see BRAIN, The
TOTO IN HELL (I) Excelsa-Ponti 1955 (TOTO ALL'INFERNO)
D: Camillo Mastrocinque. PH: L. Tonti. SP: Mastrocinque,
S. Continenza, V. Metz-Nelli, Tuddo, Mangini, De Curtis.
Ref: Unitalia Film 4/55. with Toto, Maria Frau, Dante Maggio.
A man commits suicide and descends to hell, where the devil
"asks for his definite condemnation."
TOTO IN THE MOON (I-Sp) Maxima/Variety/Montfluor 1958
(TOTO NELLA LUNA) SP, D: Steno. SP: also Continenza,
Scuola. Ref: Ital P'58. with Toto, Sylva Koscina, Ugo Tognazzi,
Sandra Milo. Inhabitants of the moon invade the earth and
create doubles of people.
TOTO SHEIK (I) Manenti 1950 (TOTO SCEICCO) PH: Mario Al-
bertelli. Mus: Fragna, Montagnini. Ref: La Production Italienne
'50/'51. with Toto, Tamar(r)a Lees, Laura Gore, Mario Cas-
tellani, Ada Dondini. The Queen of Atlantis turns men into gold
statues by kissing them.
The TOUCH OF MELISSA Para (Col?)/Dundee 1971 Ref: FJA.
V 9/1/71:20. D: Don Henderson. with Robert Easton, Lew Lorn,
J. J. Fox Woman uses witchcraft to remain young.
TOULA'S DREAM (F) Pathe 1908 Ref: MPW'08:217. Dream: Cook
frightened by ugly, grimacing head in pan and other apparitions.
TOUR DE NESLE, La see SWEETNESS OF SIN, The
TOWER OF LONDON (B) 1926 short (HAUNTED CASTLES series)
D: Maurice Elvey. Series directors include: Bert Cann and Hugh
Croise. Ref: Brit Cinema. V 2/24/26. Series actors include:
Godfrey Tearle, I. Jeans, Isobel Elsom, John Stuart, Betty
Faire.
TOWER OF LONDON Univ 1939 D, P: Rowland V. Lee. SP:
Robert N. Lee. PH: George Robinson. Mus: Charles Previn.
Art D: Jack Otterson. Ref: Clarens. with Basil Rathbone, Boris
Karloff, Barbara O'Neil, Ian Hunter, Vincent Price, Nan Grey,
John Sutton, Leo G. Carroll, Rose Hobart, Miles Mander, Lionel
Belmore, Ronald Sinclair, Ralph Forbes, G. P. Huntley, Donnie
Dunnagan. Club-footed executioner commits series of murders.
Fairly interesting mixture of history and horror.
TOWER OF LONDON UA/Admiral 1963 79m. D: Roger Corman.
SP: Leo Gordon, James B. Gordon, Amos Powell. PH: Floyd
Crosby. P: Gene Corman. Ref: FFacts. with Vincent Price,
Bruce Gordon, Michael Pate, Joan Freeman, Robert Brown.
Richard III, murder, nightmares, torture, and general villainy.
TOWER OF TERROR (B) Mono 1941 62m. D: Lawrence Huntington.
SP: John Reinhardt. PH: Walter Harvey. Mus: E. Benson. Ref:
FD 7/3/42: "Horror meller." MFB'41:131. S&S '68:212: horror.
TVG. with Michael Rennie, Movita, Wilfrid Lawson, John Long-
den, George Woodbridge. Crazed lighthouse keeper mistakes
woman for his dead wife, plans to bury her in grave.
The TOWER OF THE SEVEN HUNCHBACKS (Sp) 1944 (La TORRE
DE LOS SIETE JOROBADOS) D: Edgar Neville. SP: Emilio
Carrere. Art D: Shild, Simont and Canet. Ref: MMF 9:14.
DDC III:466. with Isabel de Pomes, Julia Lajos, Manolita Morán.
Criminal band of hunchbacks uses "haunted" house as its base of
operations. Doctor's niece falls under ringleader's hypnotic
influence.

The TOY BOX   Boxoffice Int'l 1971   85m.   SP,D: Ron Garcia. PH:
H. P. Edwards. Ref: Boxo 8/16/71. LATimes 8/6/71. Man
from another world collects humans to sell on his planet, Arcon.
Arcons devour human brains "to experience human depravity."

TRACK OF THE VAMPIRE   see   BLOOD BATH

TRAFRACKEN   see   SADIST, The

The TRAGEDIES OF THE CRYSTAL GLOBE   Edison 1915   45m.
D: Richard Ridgely. Ref: MPN 7/3/15. LC. with Robert Conness,
Mabel Trunelle, Bigelow Cooper. Girl under Oriental mystic's
hypnotic influence sees herself die three times in previous incarnations.

TRAGIC SPELL (I) Epic/Lux 1951 95m. (INCANTESIMO
TRAGICO) D: Mario Segui (or Sequi). PH: Piero Portalupi.
Ref: V 1/23/52. Unitalia 12/51. with Maria Felix, Rossano
Brazzi, Charles Vanel, Massimo Serato, Emma Gramatica.
Treasure's curse brings death.

TRAIL OF THE OCTOPUS Hallmark 1919 serial 15 episodes
D: Duke Worne. SP: J. Grubb Alexander. Ref: Exhibitors Her-
ald. MPN 20:1892, 3345. CNW. with Ben Wilson, Neva Gerber,
William Dyer, Howard Crampton. Ch. 10. The Ape Man. Ad:
"Mysterious eyes that terrify."

TRANCE   see   ANITA (1920)

TRANQUILLO POSTO DI CAMPAGNA, Un   see   QUIET PLACE IN
THE COUNTRY, A

TRANSATLANTIC TUNNEL (B) Gaum 1935 94m. (The TUNNEL)
D: Maurice Elvey. SP: Curt Siodmak. Dial: Clemence Dane, L.
DuGarde Peach.   From "Der Tunnel" by Bernhard Kellermann.
PH: G. Krampf. Ref: SM 6:31. Clarens. New Yorker 11/2/35.
with Richard Dix, Leslie Banks, Walter Huston, George Arliss,
Madge Evans, C. Aubrey Smith, Helen Vinson, Basil Sydney,
Jimmy Hanley. A tunnel is constructed to link the U.S. and
England.

The TRANSPARENT MAN (J) Daiei 1949 (TOMEI NINGEN ARA-
WARU) D: Shinsei Adachi. Ref: Unij Bltn. with Chizuri Kita-
gawa, Takiko Mizunoe.

TRANSPARENT MAN AND THE FLY MAN, The   see MURDERING
MITE, The

TRANSPLANTE DE UN CEREBRO   see   SECRET OF DR.
CHALMERS, The

TRANSVESTITE   see GLEN OR GLENDA

The TRAP CLOSES AT BEIRUT (I-Monaco-F) Metheus-Rapid-
C.L.dC 1966 (La TRAPPOLA SCATA A BEIRUT-I.) SP,D:
Manfred Kohler. SP: also M. Sirko. PH: Rolf Kästel. Mus:
Ennio Morricone. Ref: Annuario. with Frederick Stafford,
Genevieve Cluny, Kim Arden, Chris Howland, H. Leipnitz. A
gang intends to use a scientist's fertilizing device to destroy the
earth.

TRAPPED BY TELEVISION Col 1936 63m. (CAUGHT BY TELE-
VISION) D: Del Lord. SP: Lee Loeb, Harold Buchman. Story:
Sherman Lowe, Al Martin. Ref: FD 6/16/36. SF Film. with
Thurston Hall, Lyle Talbot, Mary Astor, Nat Pendleton, Robert
Strange, Marc Lawrence. An inventor perfects a television send-
ing and receiving apparatus.

TRAUMA   Parade 1962 92m. SP,D: Robert Malcolm Young. PH:
Jacques Marquette. Ed: Harold Dennis. Ref: FJA. with John
Conte, Lynn Bari, Ruby Borner, Lorrie Richards. Gloomy mansion has strange effect on girl trying to recover memory of past
horrors.

TRE FANTASTICI SUPERMEN, I see FANTASTIC THREE, The

TRE PASSI NEL DELIRIO see TALES OF MYSTERY AND
IMAGINATION

TRE VOLTI DELLA PAURA, I see BLACK SABBATH

The TREASURE OF CIBOLA Kalem 1916 (The Girl from 'Frisco
series # 6) Ref: MPN 14:1723. Heroine plays ghost to scare
others.

The TREASURE OF THE PETRIFIED FOREST (I) Asteria-Olga
Chart 1965 (Il TESORO DELLA FORESTA PIETRIFICATA) D:
Emimmo Salvi. SP: Salvi, L. Tosi, A. Antonelli, B. Ilforte.
From the Nibelungen. PH: M. Parapetti. Ref: M/TVM 7/65.
Annuario. with Gordon Mitchell, E. Bianchi, Pamela Tudor, Ivo
Payer.

The TREE OF HAPPINESS (F) Pathe 1910 7m. Ref: Bios 5/26/10.
Robbers fall victim to genie.

The TREMBLING HOUR Univ 1919 70m. D: George Siegmann. Ref:
Exhibitors Herald 11/15/19. with Kenneth Harlan, Helen Eddy.
A "sudden crash" can turn a man into a killer and make him
lose his memory. Suspected of murder, he has the victim's
twin brother pose as the victim's ghost to force a confession
out of the killer.

TRES CITAS CON EL DESTINO see THREE DATES WITH DES-
TINY

TRES ERAN TRES see THREE ARE THREE

TRESOR DE SATAN, Le see SATAN'S TREASURE

The TRICK BOX (F) Melies/Star 1903 1m. (La BOITE A MALICE)
Ref: SilentFF. with Melies. Girl assisted into scientist's magic
box vanishes.

TRICK FOR TRICK Fox 1933 67m. D: Hamilton MacFadden. SP:
Howard Green. From a play by Vivian Crosby, Shirley Warde,
and Harry Gribble. PH: L. W. O'Connell. Ref: Photoplay
6/33: "More or less a sequel for CHANDU." with Ralph Morgan, Victor Jory, Sally Blane, Luis Alberni, Tom Dugan, John
George, Edward Van Sloan, Herbert Bunston, Willard Robertson.
A magician gathers murder suspects at his gloomy mansion to
witness a seance. "During the seance at which Morgan brings
back the "spirit" of the dead girl, Jory is killed."-Harrison's
4/22/33.

TRIFLING WOMEN MGM 1922 SP,D: Rex Ingram. PH: John
Seitz. Remake of 1916 non-horror BLACK ORCHIDS. Ref:
Clarens. with Barbara LaMarr, Ramon Novarro, Lewis Stone,
Edward Connelly. Strange castle, satanism, necromancer,
necrophilia.

TRILBY (Danish) Nordisk 1908 D: A. R. Nielsen. P: Ole Olsen.
Ref: DDC II:8. Lee. From the book by George Du Maurier.

TRILBY (Austrian-Hung) 1912 50m. D: Luise and Anton Kolm,
Jakob Fleck, Claudius Veltée. From the book by Du Maurier.
Ref: Osterr. with Frau Galafrès-Hubermann, Paul Askonas.

TRILBY (B) Standard 1912   Ref: RVB. From Du Maurier's book.
TRILBY Vitascope 1913   Ref: Lee. MPW 15:1155. From Du
     Maurier's book.
TRILBY (B) London 1914 From Du Maurier's book. P: Harold
     Shaw. Ref: SilentFF. with Sir Hubert Tree, Viva Birkett, Philip
     Merivale.
TRILBY World 1915   D: Maurice Tourneur. From the novel by
     George Du Maurier. Ref: Clarens. with Wilton Lackaye, Clara
     Kimball Young.
TRILBY F Nat 1923 90m. D: James Young. PH: Georges Benoit.
     SP: Richard Tully, from the book by George Du Maurier. Ref:
     AFI. Halliwell. DDC III:6. with Creighton Hale, Arthur-Ed-
     mund Carewe, Andrée Lafayette, Wilfred Lucas, Gertrude Olm-
     stead.
TRILBY (by G. Du Maurier) see ELLA LOLA A LA TRILBY/FRIL-
     BY FRILLED/SVENGALI
TRILOGY OF TERROR (F-Braz) PNF/Galasy/Franco-Brazilian
     1968 (TRILOGIA DE TERROR) D: Jose Mojica Marins, Ozualdo
     Candeias, Luis Person. Ref: V 5/7/69:208: "Horror." with
     Vany Miller, Mario Lima, Lucy Rangel, Regina Celia, Lima Du-
     arte, Cacilda Lanuza.
TRIONFO DI ERCOLE, Il see HERCULES VS. THE GIANT WAR-
     RIORS
TRIONFO DI MACISTE, Il see TRIUMPH OF THE SON OF
     HERCULES
TRIP ON THE CHANNEL TUNNEL, A see TUNNELING THE
     ENGLISH CHANNEL
TRIP TO A STAR (F) Pathe 1906 8m. (Le VOYAGE DANS UNE
     ETOILE. VOYAGE AUTOUR D'UNE ETOILE. AROUND A STAR.
     VOYAGE AROUND A STAR) D: Gaston Velle. Ref: DDC II:383.
     Menville. SF Film. V&FI 8/11/06. Astronomer travels to star
     in soap bubble.
TRIP TO A STAR (I) 1906 (VOYAGE TO A STAR) D: Gaston Velle.
     Remake of Velle's French TRIP TO A STAR. Ref: Lee. SF
     Film.
A TRIP TO DAVY JONES' LOCKER (F) Pathe c1910 11m. Ref:
     SilentFF. Spectre, spirits, demons.
A TRIP TO JUPITER (F) Pathe 1907 10m. (VOYAGE A LA
     PLANETE JUPITER) D: Segundo de Chomon. Ref: Menville.
     SM 1:3. DDC I:404. The Film Index. MPW'09:263. A king
     dreams he journeys to Jupiter on a ladder and meets the King
     of Jupiter.
A TRIP TO MARS Edison 1910 5m. Ref: Bios 4/7/10. SM 1:3.
     A professor's two powders, mixed, defy the law of gravity, al-
     lowing him to float to Mars. He meets a half-human Martian
     and tree monsters.
TRIP TO MARS, A see SKY SHIP, The/TRIP TO THE MOON, A
     (1902)
TRIP TO THE CENTER OF THE EARTH, A see JOURNEY TO THE
     CENTER OF THE EARTH (1959)
TRIP TO THE CENTER OF THE MOON (I) 1905 (VIAGGO AL
     CENTRO DELLA LUNA) Ref: DDC I:331. with Mario Caserini.
A TRIP TO THE MOON (F) Melies/Star 1902 color 15m. (VOYAGE

TO THE MOON. EXCURSION TO THE MOON) D: Georges Melies.
PH: Lucien Tainguy. From Jules Verne's "From the Earth to
the Moon" and H. G. Wells' "First Men in the Moon." Featured
in The GREAT MELIES and AROUND THE WORLD IN 80 DAYS.
Ref: FM 13:32. V&FI 2/1/08. SF Film. Imagen. SM 1:3.
COF 6:30. Lee: 1903 Lubin pirated version called A TRIP TO
MARS. Explorers on the moon find mushrooms, acrobatic
moonmen, and dancing women. Amusing, if a little repetitive,
Melies.
A TRIP TO THE MOON (F) 1903 (Un VOYAGE DANS LA LUNE)
D: Segundo de Chomon. Ref: Menville. DDC I:404: 1909?
TRIP TO THE MOON, A see ASTRONOMER'S DREAM, The
TRIUMPH OF HERCULE S, The see HERCULES VS. THE GIANT
WARRIORS
TRIUMPH OF THE SON OF HERCULES (I) Embassy/York 1963
87m. (Il TRIONFO DI MACISTE) D: Amerigo Anton. Ref:
Embassy catalogue. Lee. with Kirk Morris, Cathia Caro, Carla
Colo, Ljuba Bodin. The "monstrous Yuri Men in the Temple of
the Mountain of Thunder."
TROG (B) WB 1970 Technicolor 91m. D: Freddie Francis. SP:
Aben Kandel. Story: John Gilling, Peter Bryan. Footage from
The ANIMAL WORLD. PH: Desmond Dickinson. Mus: John
Scott. Art D: Geoffrey Tozer. P: Herman Cohen. with Joan
Crawford, Michael Gough, Robert Hutton, Bernard Kay, John
Hamill, Thorley Walters, Maurice Good. An anthropologist dis-
covers the missing link.
TROIS PAS DANS L'ETRANGE see TALES OF MYSTERY &
IMAGINATION
TROLLENBERG TERROR, The see CRAWLING EYE, The
TROMBA, THE TIGER MAN (G) Lippert 1949 ('52-U.S.) 62m.
(TROMBA) D: Helmut Weiss. SP: Weiss, Elisabeth Zimmer-
mann. PH: Werner Krien. Mus: Adolf Steimel. Ref: V 11/19/52.
Lee. DDC III:21,58. with René Deltgen, Gustav Knuth,Angelika
Hauff, Adrian Hoven. Lion tamer hypnotizes cats, gets power
from drug.
TRONO DI FUOCO, Il see WITCH-KILLER OF BLACKMOOR, The
TROU DANS LA LUNE, Un see HOLE IN THE MOON, A
TROUBLE FOR TWO MGM 1936 75m. D: J. Walter Ruben.
SP: Manuel Seff, Edward Paramore, Jr. From "The Suicide
Club" and "Young Man with the Cream Tarts" by Robert Louis
Stevenson. PH: Charles Clarke. Ref: FD 6/1/36. "Eerie."
Motion Picture Reviews: "The idea of a secret society which
deals out death is too blood-chilling for children." with Robert
Montgomery, Rosalind Russell, Frank Morgan, Reginald Owen,
Louis Hayward, E. E. Clive, Walter Kingsford, Ivan Simpson,
Robert Greig, Pedro de Cordoba.
TRUXA (G) Tobis-Magna 1936 From "Program Mit Truxa" by
Heinrich Seiler. See also The HIDDEN MENACE. Ref: NYT
7/26/37. Deutscher. with La Jana, Peter Elsholtz, Rudolf
Klein-Rogge. Illusionist-hypnotist.
TUKO SA MADRE CACAO (Fili) LVN 1958 D: Richard Abelardo.
Ref: FEFN 8/29/58.9/5/58 .D:with Nita Javier, Willie Sotelo,
Hector Reyes, Vic Diaz, Elena Balmori. "Mad scientist discovers

a serum which increases the size of animals to huge proportions."
TUMANNOCT' ANDROMED   see CLOUD OF ANDROMEDA, The
TUNNEL, Der (by B. Kellermann) see TRANSATLANTIC TUNNEL/
    TUNNEL, The
The TUNNEL (G) Bavaria-Film 1933 (Der TUNNEL) D: Curtis
    Bernhardt. Ref: Menville. Imagen. with Paul Hartman, Ferdinand
    Marian, Otto Wernicke, Attila Hörbiger. From "Der Tunnel" by
    Bernhard Kellermann. Underwater tunnel.
The TUNNEL   (French-language version of above) 1933 Ref: Lee.
    V 1/9/34. with Jean Gabin, Madeleine Renaud, Gustaf Gründ-
    gens. Tunnel beneath the Atlantic Ocean.
TUNNELING THE CHANNEL UNDER THE SEA   (F) Melies/Star
    1907 (Le TUNNEL SOUS LA MANCHE ou LE CAUCHEMAR
    FRANCO-ANGLAIS. TUNNELING THE ENGLISH CHANNEL.
    A TRIP ON THE CHANNEL TUNNEL) Ref: Menville. MPW'07:
    331. SF Film.
TUR MIT DEN SIEBEN SCHLOSSERN, Die see DOOR WITH 7
    LOCKS, The
TURSISTAS INTERPLANETARIOS see INTERPLANETARY
    TOURISTS
TURN OF THE SCREW, The (by H. James) see INNOCENTS, The
    and NIGHTCOMERS, The
'TWAS EVER THUS Pallas Comedy 1916 45m. Ref: Pictures
    and the Picturegoer 6/24/16. with Elsie Janis. "The art of
    love-making from the prehistoric down to the present day."
TWEEDLEDUM BECOMES A HERCULES (I) Ambrosio 1912 8m.
    Ref: Bios 7/4/12. Prof Force's electrical treatment gives
    Tweedledum super-human strength.
TWEEDLEDUM'S ITCHING POWDER (I) Ambrosio 1910 7m. Ref:
    Bios 10/6/10. Man who has itching powder poured down his
    back scratches himself against objects, bringing down balcony
    and house.
The TWELFTH HOUR (G) Deutsche Film-Produktion 1921 (1930)
    90m. (Die ZWOLFTE STUNDE. Eine NACHT DES GRAUENS)
    D: Dr. Waldemar Ronger. Ref: Deutsche. "Record of the mak-
    ing of NOSFERATU."
12 COINS OF CONFUCIUS, The (by H. Keeler) see MYSTERIOUS
    MR. WONG, The
The TWELVE GOLD MEDALLIONS (Hong-Kong Chinese) 1970 East-
    mancolor/scope D: Cheng Kang. Shaw Ref: M/TVM 8/70:41.
    VVoice 4/15/71. with Chin Pin(g), Yueh Hua. VV: "Actors
    levitate, fly, or catapult through the ceiling....Characters can
    split trees with their bare hands, stop waterfalls with a power-
    ful stare, and cause instant death with a tap on the chest."
The TWELVE-HANDED MEN OF MARS (I-Sp) Dario/Epoca 1964
    95m. (SIAMO QUATTRO MARZIANI or I MARZIANI HANNO
    DODICI MANI-I. LLEGARON LOS MARCIANOS-Sp. The MAR-
    TIANS ARRIVED) SP,D: Franco Castellano. D: also G.
    Pipol(l)o. SP: also G. Mocchia, L. Martin. PH: Alfio Contini.
    Mus: Ennio Morricone. Ref: M/TVM'63. SpCinema'66. Ital P.
    with Paolo Panelli, Carlo Croccolo, Enzo Garinei, Alfredo
    Landa, Magali Noel, Umberto D'Orsi, Margaret Lee, Franco
    Franchi, Ciccio Ingrassia. Four Martians carry out different

495   12

assignments on earth.
12 TO THE MOON Col 1960 74m. D: David Bradley. SP: DeWitt
Bodeen. PH: John Alton. Mus: Michael Andersen. Art D: Rudi
Feld. SpFX: Howard A. Anderson, E. Nicholson, P: Fred Geb-
hardt. Ref: FFacts. PM. with Tom Conway, Francis X. Bush-
man, Robert Montgomery, Jr., John Wengraf, Cory Devlin,
Anna-Lisa, Phillip Baird. Invisible (saves money) moonmen
start a cold war by freezing North America. Just plain dumb.
The TWENTIETH CENTURY TRAMP Edison 1902 D: Edwin S.
Porter. Ref: SF Film. Bicycle-balloon.
2889 see YEAR 2889
TWENTY FACES (J) Toei 1957 113m. (SHONEN TANTEIDAN-
KABUTOMUSHI NO YOKI & TETTO NO KAIJIN) D: Hideo
Sekigawa. SP: T. Ogawa. Story: R. Edogawa. Idea: N. Nezu.
PH: H. Fukushima. Ref: FEFN 5/31/57. with Eiji Okada, Jun
Usami, Kyoko Koga. An escaped convict known as "The Man with
Twenty Faces" uses "robot beetles, man-made monsters and other
weird devices" to steal atomic secrets.
TWENTY MILLION DOLLAR MYSTERY, The see ZUDORA
20 MILLION MILES TO EARTH Col/Morningside 1957 82m. D:
Nathan Juran. (The GIANT YMIR) SP: Robert Williams, Chris-
topher Knopf. Story: Charlott Knight. PH: Irving Lippman, Carlos
Ventimiglia. Mus: Mischa Bakaleinikoff. SpFX: Ray Harryhausen.
P: Charles Schneer. Ref: Clarens. with William Hopper, Joan
Taylor, Frank Puglia, John Zaremba, Arthur Space, Jan Arvan.
Rocket returns to earth from Venus carrying specimen of
Venusian animal life. Fairly eerie until the monster grows and
becomes the standard giant menace.
2001: A SPACE ODYSSEY (B) MGM 1968 Metrocolor/Cinerama/
scope 160m. SP, D, P: Stanley Kubrick. SP: also Arthur C.
Clarke. PH: Geoffrey Unsworth. Add'l PH: John Alcott. Prod
Des: Tony Masters, Harry Lange, Ernie Archer. SpFX: Wally
Veevers, Douglas Trumbull, Con Pederson, Tom Howard. Ed:
Ray Lovejoy. with Keir Dullea, Gary Lockwood, William Sylvester, Douglas Rain, Margaret Tyzack, Daniel Richter, Leonard
Rossiter, Robert Beatty, Sean Sullivan, Ann Gillis, Glenn Beck,
Frank Miller, Danny Grover, John Jordan, John Ashley, Scott
Mackee. Scientists find a strange slab on the moon. The parts
don't quite fit together, and the ending doesn't work (It's too
simple coming after such a complicated buildup); but 2001 con-
tains some of the most impressive scenes in s-f-film history
and some astonishingly convincing special effects. (You may find
it hard to believe it wasn't all shot on location.)
2069 A.D.-A SENSATION ODYSSEY 1969 D: Cam Sopetsky. PH:
Vic Goss. Ref: RVB. LATimes. with Harvey Foster. Time
travel into the past.
The 27TH DAY Col/Romson 1957 75m. D: William Asher. SP:
John Mantley. Scenes from EARTH VS. THE FLYING SAUCERS.
PH: Henry Freulich. Mus: Mischa Bakaleinikoff. Art D: Ross
Bellah. Ref: Clarens. with Gene Barry, Valerie French, George
Voskovec, Arnold Moss, Paul Birch, Ed Hinton, Friedrich
Ledebur, Stefan Schnabel. A visitor from space gives people of
five nationalities capsules capable of destroying human life. Dull.

20,000 LEAGUES UNDER THE SEA (F) Melies/Star 1907 (DEUX
CENT MILLE LIEUES SOUS LES MERS ou LE CAUCHEMAR
D'UN PECHEUR. UNDER THE SEAS) Ref: Menville. Mitry II.
Giant fish, etc.
20,000 LEAGUES UNDER THE SEA Univ 1916 105m. SP,P:
Stuart Paton. From "20,000 Leagues under the Sea" and
"Mysterious Island" by Jules Verne. See also The CROSS-
EYED SUBMARINE. Ref: NYT 12/25/16. Ghosts, etc. Very
long and very dull.
20,000 LEAGUES UNDER THE SEA BV 1954 Technicolor/scope
122m. D: Richard Fleischer. SP: Earl Felton, from the novel
by Jules Verne. Art D: John Meehan. SpFX: Ub Iwerks. Ed:
Elmo Williams. Ref: COF 5:23. FDY. with James Mason (Captain Nemo), Kirk Douglas, Peter Lorre, Paul Lukas, Robert J.
Wilke, Carleton Young, Ted de Corsia, Percy Helton, Ted
Cooper, J. M. Kerrigan. "Phantom submarine," giant squid,
atomic base. Long and not as dull as the '16 version but dull
enough. Lots of cheap humor. Lorre is wasted; Douglas is at
his worst; and even Mason isn't that good. The lighted sub
barreling through the water at night is an eerie effect.
TWICE TOLD TALES UA/Admiral 1963 Technicolor 119m.
(The CORPSE-MAKERS. NATHANIEL HAWTHORNE'S TWICE
TOLD TALES) D: Sidney Salkow. SP,P: Robert E. Kent. From
"Dr. Heidegger's Experiment," "The House of the 7 Gables,"
and "Rappac(c)ini's Daughter" by Hawthorne. PH: Ellis W.
Carter. Mus: Richard La Salle. Art D: Franz Bachelin. SpFX:
Milton Olsen. Ref: FFacts. Orpheus 3:31. FM 22:9. with
Vincent Price, Sebastian Cabot, Brett Halsey, Beverly Garland,
Richard Denning, Mari Blanchard, Abraham Sofaer, Joyce
Taylor, Edith Evanson, Jacqueline De Wit, Floyd Simmons. Gene
Roth. Elixir of youth, skeletal strangling hand, etc.
TWICE UPON A TIME (F) Prodis/Filmsky-Licorne 1969 color
82m. (Le TEMPS DE MOURIR) SP,D: Andre Farwagi. SP:
also Alain Morineau. PH: Willy Kurant. Mus: Karel Trow. Art D:
Jean-Claude Gallouin. Ref: V 3/18/70. 4/29/70. with Anna
Karina, Jean Rochefort. Futuristic.
TWIN PAWNS Acme 1920 SP,D: Leonce Perret. From the novel
"The Woman in White" by Wilkie Collins. PH: Alfred Ortlieb.
Ref: SilentFF. with Mae Murray, J. W. Johnston. Man frightens
girl with weak heart to death.
TWISTED NERVE (B) Nat'l General/Boulting 1968 Eastmancolor
118m. SP,D: Roy Boulting. SP: also Leo Marks, from an idea
by Marshall & Jeremy Scott. PH: Harry Waxman. Mus: Bernard
Herrmann. Art D: Albert Witherick. Ref: V(d) 12/11/68.
LATimes: "Horror." PM. with Hayley Mills, Hywel Bennett,
Billie Whitelaw, Phyllis Calvert, Frank Finlay, Thorley Walters,
Russell Napier. Psychopath commits grisly murders. Compared
to PSYCHO and NIGHT MUST FALL as a "shocker."
TWO BOOBS Starlight 1915 Ref: MPN 5/1/15. with James
Aubrey, Walter Kendig. Two men spend a night in a haunted
house.
TWO COSMONAUTS AGAINST THEIR WILL (Sp-I) Agata/Ima 1966
scope 89m. (Dos COSMONAUTUS A LA FUERZA-Sp. 002

OPERAZIONE LUNA-I.   002 OPERATION MOON.   TWO RELUC-
TANT ASTRONAUTS) D: Lucio Fulci. SP: V. Metz, J. L.
Dibildos, A. Sollazzo. PH: T. Santoni. Mus: C. Gori. Art D:
A. Cofiño. Ref: SpCinema'67. with Franco Franchi, Ciccio
Ingrassia. The Russians launch a space ship from a space base.
TWO COUSINS Lubin 1908 16m. Ref: MPW'08:64-5 Woman
under spell of hypnotist.
TWO CRAZY BUGS Gaston(?)Melies 1908 Ref: V&FI 8/29/08. Two
spiritualists produce a "grotesque bug," a white sheet in human
form, a female apparition, and "spooks."
TWO FACES OF DR. JEKYLL, The see HOUSE OF FRIGHT
TWO GHOSTS AND A GIRL (Mex) Sotomayor 1958 (Dos FANTAS-
MAS Y UNA MUCHACHA) D: Rogelio A.Gonzalez. Story,SP:
F. Galiana. Story: also A. Tato. PH: Raul M. Solares. Mus:
S. Guerrero. Ref: Indice. TVG. with "Tin Tan," Ana L. Peluffo,
Manuel Valdez, Luis Aldas, Miguel Manzano.
TWO HOURS TO DOOM (by P. Bryant) see DR. STRANGELOVE
TWO LOST WORLDS Eagle-Lion 1951 62m. D: Norman Dawn.
SP: Norman Hubbard. Story: Tom Hubbard, Phyllis Barker. PH:
Harry Neumann. Art D: D. Hall. P: Boris Petroff. Scenes
from ONE MILLION B.C. Ref: FDY. FM 10:26.19:36. with James
Arness, Gloria Petroff, Laura Elliott, William Kennedy. Prehis-
toric beasts roam about mysterious island.
TWO MAFIOSI AGAINST GOLDGINGER see AMAZING DR. G, The
The TWO NATURES WITHIN HIM Selig 1915 40m. D: Thomas
Santschi. SP: Jules Goodman. Ref: MPN 5/22/15. with Santschi,
Bessie Eyton, Franklin Paul. Blow on head gives man dual
personality.Operation cures him.
TWO ON A GUILLOTINE WB 1965 107m. D, P: William Conrad.
SP: John Kneubahl, Henry Slesar. PH: Sam Leavitt. Mus: Max
Steiner. Ref: FM 32:52. FDY. COF 7:46. with Connie Stevens,
Cesar Romero, Dean Jones, Virginia Gregg, Parley Baer, Con-
nie Gilchrist, John Hoyt. A girl learns that she will inherit her
father's old mansion if she spends seven nights in it.
2+5: MISSION HYDRA (I) Golden 1966 (2+5 MISSIONE HYDRA) SP,
D: Pietro Francisci. SP: also Curti. Story: F. P. Girolami. PH:
Silvano Ippoliti, Giulio Albonico. Mus: Nico Fidenco. Ref: Ital P.
Annuario.with Leonora Ruffo, Ant(h)ony Freeman, Kirk Morris,
Gordon Mitchell, Roland Lesafrre, Leontine Snell. A spaceship
from the planet Hydra is found on Roman countryside.
The TWO POWDERS (I) Cines 1912 7m. Ref: Bios 7/25/12. A
quack's powder causes people to rush about madly.
TWO RELUCTANT ASTRONAUTS see TWO COSMONAUTS AGAINST
THEIR WILL
TWO SOULED WOMAN, The see UNTAMEABLE, The
2000 MANIACS Boxoffice Spectaculars 1964 Eastmancolor 84m.
SP,D,PH: Herschell G. Lewis. Mus: Larry Wellington. P:David
Friedman. Ref: RVB. COF 6:56. with Connie Mason,Thomas
Wood, Jeffrey Allen. Townsfolk massacred 100 years earlier in
Civil War reappear to wreak vengeance. More Lewis-Friedman
gore and sadism. The direction is so incompetent that you can't
tell the intent of a scene unless it's supposed to make you retch.
And there is some question as to whether there were 2000 maniacs

or 2000 just sounds better than 20.

2000 YEARS LATER WB-7A 1969 Technicolor 80m. SP,D,P: Bert Tenzer. PH: Mario Di Leo. Mus: Stu Phillips. Mus Sup: Igo Kantor. Art D: Myke Haller. Sets: Henry Reif. Ref: PM. with Terry-Thomas, Edward Everett Horton, Pat Harrington, Lisa Seagram, John Abbott, Monti Rock, III, Casey Kasem, Tenzer, Rudi Gernreich, Milton Parsons. A Roman soldier is preserved in suspended animation 2000 years.

TWO WEEKS TO LIVE RKO 1942 76m. D: Mal St. Clair. SP: Michael L. Simmons, Roswell Rogers. PH: Jack Mackenzie. Ref: SF Film. Showmen's 2/6/43. with Lum and Abner (or Chester Lauck and Norris Goff), Franklin Pangborn, Irving Bacon, Kay Linaker, Herbert Rawlinson, Ivan Simpson, Rosemary LaPlanche, Charles Middleton, Luis Alberni, Tim Ryan, Oscar O'Shea, Edward Earle. HR 2/3/43: "Haunted house... Jekyll and Hyde potion-taking, complicated by a tame gorilla... rocket ship to Mars."

TWO YEARS' VACATION (by J. Verne) see STOLEN AIRSHIP, The

The TWONKY UA 1953 72m. SP,D,P: Arch Oboler. Story: Henry Kuttner. PH: Joseph Biroc. Ref: FDY. with Hans Conreid, Gloria Blondell, Billy Lynn, Janet Warren, William Phipps, Trilby Conreid. A creature from outer space takes over a television set.

The TYROLESE DOLL (F) Pathe 1911 15m. Ref: Bios 2/1/12. A toymaker invents an automatic doll.

UFO see UNIDENTIFIED FLYING OBJECTS

U.S. see SHADOW ON THE LAND

UCHU DAIKAIJU DOGORA see DAGORA

UCHU DAIKAIJU GUIRARA see X FROM OUTER SPACE, The

UCHU DAISENSO see BATTLE IN OUTER SPACE

UCHU KAIJIN SHUTSUGEN see EVIL BRAIN FROM OUTER SPACE, The

UCHU KAISOKU-SEN see INVASION OF THE NEPTUNE MEN

UCHUJIN TOKYO NI ARAWARU see WARNING FROM SPACE

UCHUTEI TO JINKO EISEI NO GEKITOTSU see ATTACK FROM SPACE

UGETSU MONOGATARI (J) Daiei 1953 98m. (The STORY OF UGETSU. TALES OF THE PALE MOON AFTER THE RAIN) D: Kenji Mizoguchi. SP: Matsutaro Kawaguchi, Giken Yoda. From a novel by Akinari Uyeda. PH: Kazuo Miyagawa. Mus sc: Fumio Hayasaka. Art D: Kisaku Ito. P: Masaichi Nagata. Ref: Orient. with Machiko Kyo, Mitsuko Mito, Kinuyo Tanaka, Masayuki Mori, Sakae Ozawa. Two parts. I: "Asaji Ga Yado": Husband away seven years returns home to find his wife has died and become a ghost. II: A ghost appears to a man as a beautiful woman. "Masterpiece"--Jean-Luc Godard, Eric Rohmer.

The UGLIEST QUEEN ON EARTH (F) Gaum 1909 12m. Ref: Bios 2/24/10. An ugly queen orders all mirrors and reflecting

kingdom broken or hidden.   She sees her reflection in the exe-
cutioner's axe and falls dead.
The UGLY DUCKLING (B) Hammer 1959 84m. D: Lance Comfort.
SP: Sid Colin, Jack Davies.   Based on "The Strange Case of Dr.
Jekyll and Mr. Hyde" by Robert Louis Stevenson. PH: Michael
Reed. Mus: Douglas Granley. Art D: Bernard Robinson. Ref:
MFB'59:125. with Bernard Bresslaw, Reginald Beckwith, Jon
Pertwee, Richard Wattis, Michael Ripper.   Moronic Henry Jekyll
finds his grandfather's long-lost secret formula and transforms
himself into slick Teddy Hyde.
UKRADENA VZDUCHOLOD see STOLEN AIRSHIP, The
ULISSE CONTRO ERCOLE see HERCULES VS. ULYSSES
ULTIMA PREDA DEL VAMPIRO, L' see PLAYGIRLS AND THE
VAMPIRE, The
ULTIMO UOMO DELLA TERRA, L' see LAST MAN ON EARTH,
The (1964)
ULTIMO VARON SOBRE LA TIERRA, El see LAST MAN ON
EARTH, The (Sp-1933)
ULTRAMAN (J) Toho 1967 D: Hajime and Eiji Tsuburaya. Ref:
Unij Bltn. Pic: COF 12:46-7: monster. with Satoshi Furuya,
Shoji Kobayashi.
ULYSSE ET LE GEANT POLYPHEME see ULYSSES & THE
GIANT POLYPHEMUS
ULYSSES (U.S.-I) Para/Lux 1955 color 104m. D: Mario Camerini.
SP: Hugh Gray, Ben Hecht, Ennio de Concini, Irwin Shaw, Franco
Brusati, Ivo Perilli, Camerini. From "The Odyssey" by Homer.
PH: Harold Rosson. Mus: A. Cicognini. Art D: F. Mogherini.
SpPhFX: Eugen Shuftan. P: Carlo Ponti, Dino de Laurentiis. Ref:
FM 12:6. V 6/23/55. with Kirk Douglas, Silvano Mangano,
Anthony Quinn, Rossana Podesta, Sylvie. One-eye giant Polyphe-
mus, The Sirens, Circe the enchantress.
ULYSSES AGAINST THE SON OF HERCULES see HERCULES VS.
ULYSSES
ULYSSES AND THE GIANT POLYPHEMUS (F) Melies/Star 1905
(ULYSSE ET LE GEANT POLYPHEME) Ref: DDC III:352.
ULYSSES VS. HERCULES see HERCULES VS. ULYSSES
UN SOIR...PAR HASARD see ONE NIGHT...BY CHANCE
UNA DE MIEDO see THREE ARE THREE
UNCHARTED SEAS (novel by D. Wheatley) see LOST CONTINENT,
The (1968)
UNCLE JOSH IN A SPOOKY HOTEL Edison 1900 1m. Ref: Niver.
Ghost appears and disappears.
UNCLE JOSH'S NIGHTMARE Edison 1900 2m. Ref: Niver. Ghost
appears and disappears.
UNCLE SILAS (book by S. Le Fanu) see INHERITANCE, The /
MYSTERIOUS UNCLE SILAS, The
UNCLE WAS A VAMPIRE (I) Embassy/Maxima-Cei Incom-Montflour
1959 Technicolor (TEMPI DURI PER I VAMPIRI. HARD TIMES
FOR VAMPIRES. HARD TIMES FOR DRACULA) D: Stefano
Steno. SP: Anton, Continenza, Verde. PH:Marco Scarpelli. Ref:
Orpheus 3:28. COF 4:38.11:20. Ital P. DDC II:354. Pic: COF
11:21. with Renato Rascel, Christopher Lee (vampire), Sylva
Koscina, Kai Fischer, Susanne Loret, Lia Zoppelli. Porter's

uncle turns out to be a vampire ("Dracula"). Sporadically amusing.

UNCONQUERED Para 1917 55m. Ref: MPN 15:3459. with Mabel
  Van Buren, Fannie Ward, Hobart Bosworth, Tully Marshall,
  Jane Wolfe. "Voodoo Queen" sends "Voodoo crazed" Negro after
  human sacrifice.

The UNDEAD AI/Balboa 1957 71m. D, P: Roger Corman. SP:
  Charles B. Griffith, Mark Hanna. PH: William Sickner. Mus:
  Ronald Stein. Ref: V 2/19/57. with Allison Hayes, Richard
  Garland, Richard Miller, Billy Barty, Mel Welles, Bruno ve
  Sota, Pamela Duncan, Val DuFour, Richard Devon. A hypnotist
  and his subject go back in time 1000 years to the time of her
  first incarnation. Odd, offbeat, slightly mixed-up, but fairly
  interesting Griffith-Corman.

UNDER THE FROZEN FALLS (B) G-B Instructional/Children's
  Entertainment Films 1948 44m. D: Darrell Catling. SP: J. H.
  Martin Cross. Adap: Mary C. Borer. Ref: MFB'48:48. with
  Harold Warrender, Ray Jackson, Tony Richardson. Cylinder in
  mine contains "invention more powerful than radium."

UNDER THE MOON OF MOROCCO (F) Vandal-Delac 1932 82m.
  (SOUS LA LUNE DU MAROC) D: Julien Duvivier. SP: Andre Reuze.
  From "Five Doomed Gentlemen" or "Les Cinq Gentlemen Maudits."
  Mus: Jacques Ibert. Ref: FDY. Photoplay'33. DDC I:190. II:66,
  233. III:69. with Harry Baur, Rene Lefebvre, Robert Le Vigan,
  Rosine Déréon. An Algerian beggar's "weird curse" proves fatal
  to three Europeans.

UNDER THE RED LIGHT Literatia 1914 28m. Ref: Bios 5/4/14.
  An inventor's "new curative element" restores his eyesight.

UNDER THE SEAS see 20,000 LEAGUES UNDER THE SEA (1907)

UNDERNEATH THE ARCHES (B) Twickenham 1937 72m. D: Redd
  Davis. Ref: MFB'37:56. with Bud Flanagan, Chesney Allen,
  Enid Stamp Taylor. "Peace gas" disrupts revolution.

UNDERSEA CITY see UNDERWATER CITY, The

The UNDERSEA KINGDOM Rep 1936 serial 12 episodes ('66 fea-
  ture-SHARAD OF ATLANTIS) D: B. Reeves Eason, Joseph Kane.
  SP: J. Rathmell, M. Geraghty, O. Drake, T. Knight. PH:W.
  Nobles, E. Lyons, Ref: Barbour. SF Film. Pic:SM 4:32. with
  Ray Corrigan (as Crash Corrigan), Lois Wilde, Monte Blue,
  William Farnum (Sharad), Lon Chaney, Jr., Boothe Howard,
  C. Montague Shaw, Lee Van Atta, Smiley Burnette, Lane Chandler, Jack Mulhall, Ralph Holmes, David Horsley, Raymond Hatton. Ray guns, death rays, "robotic Volkites," "rocket submarine," "reflectoplate televisors" and "rocket-powered Vol-
  planes" in Atlantis. "Nothing is safe with Crash Corrigan around!"

UNDERSEA MONSTER see VIKING WOMEN

The UNDERTAKER AND HIS PALS Howco/Eola 1967 color 60m. D, P:
  David C. Graham. SP: T. L. P. Swicegood. PH: A. Janczak. Art
  D: Mike McCloskey. Ref: V 10/18/67. with Robert Lowery, Ray
  Dennis, W. Ott, Rad Fulton. Similar in some ways to The LOVED
  ONE, more authentically crude, and with just as many laughs (i.e.,
  three or four). A man getting a screwdriver through the forehead is
  one of the laughs, which shows how far they had to go to get even that
  few. Technically very sloppy.

The UNDERWATER CITY Col/Neptune 1961 78m. (UNDERSEA CITY.

The AMPHIBIANS) D: Frank McDonald. SP: Owen Harris. East-
mancolor/Fantascope PH: Gordon Avil. Mus: Ronald Stein. Art
D: Don Ament. P: Alex Gordon. Ref: Clarens. FM 13:78.
Orpheus 3:27. PM. with William Lundigan, Julie Adams, Roy
Roberts, Carl Benton Reid, Chet Douglas, Kathie Browne. A
construction engineer is hired by the Halstead Institute of
Oceanography to construct an experimental underwater unit on the
ocean floor.

UNDINE   Than   1913   35m. Ref: SilentFF. Bios 2/13/13. Sea
nymphs avenge the death of one of their own.

UNDINE Bluebeard 1916 Ref: MPW 27:1196.

The UNDYING MONSTER Fox 1942 60m. (The HAMMOND
MYSTERY-Eng.) D: John Brahm. SP: Lillie Hayward, Michael
Jacoby, from the novel by Jessie Douglas Kerruish. PH: Lucien
Ballard. Mus: Emil Newman, David Raksin. Art D: Richard Day,
Lewis Creber. Ref: Clarens. MFB'46:97 FM 14:6. Pic: FanMo
3:25. with James Ellison, Heather Angel, John Howard, Bram-
well Fletcher, Heather Thatcher, Eily Malyon, Aubrey Mather,
Halliwell Hobbes, Alec Craig, Heather Wilde, Holmes Herbert,
Matthew Boulton. A small English village is terrorized by a
werewolf.

The UNEARTHLY Rep/AB-PT 1957 73m. D,P: Brooke L.
Peters. SP: Jane Mann, Geoffrey Dennis. PH: Merle Connell.
Mus sc: Henry Vars(e). Art D: Daniel Hall. Ref: FDY. with
John Carradine, Allison Hayes, Myron Healey, Roy Gordon,
Arthur Batanides, Tor Johnson. Mad scientist experimenting with
glands in search for secret of eternal life creates horde of
monsters. Pretty crummy.

The UNEARTHLY STRANGER (B) AI/Anglo Amalgamated/Independent
Artists 1963 D: John Krish. SP: Rex Carlton. PH: Reg Wyer. Mus:
Edward Williams. Ref: MFB. Pic: COF 5:52. with John Neville,
Gabriella Licudi, Philip Stone, Patrick Newell, Jean Marsh. A sci-
entist discovers that his wife is from another planet.

UNEASY FREEHOLD (book by D. Macardle) see UNINVITED, The

The UNEXPECTED GUEST UA 1947 59m. D: George Archainbaud.
SP: Ande Lamb. PH: Mack Stengler. Art D: Harvey T. Gillett.
Ref: HR 12/5/46. PM. Released 3/28/47. with William Boyd,
Andy Clyde, Una O'Connor, Ned Young, Robert H. Williams,
William Ruhl. Western: "Haunted" ranch, sliding panels, hidden
passageways, ghostly voices, "ghost messages."

The UNFAITHFUL WIFE Fox 1915 55m. D: J. Gordon Edwards.
SP: Mary Murillo. Ref: MPN 12/18/15. LC. with Robert B.
Mantell, Genevieve Hamper, Stuart Holmes, Warner Oland.
A nobleman entombed alive escapes.

UNFINISHED DESIRE (Korea) Dong Young Films/Hahn Kuk 1968
color/scope 100m. D: Yu Hyunmok. SP: Lee Sanghyun.
PH: Chang Sukjun. Ref: Korea Cinema'68. with Lee Soonjai,
Moon Hee, Yoon Ilbong, Chun Kaehyun, Kim Sukhoon, Cha
Youmi. Three tales. 1. Predestination: A man dies a strange
death after going against the will of his predestined wife.
2. Lamentation: A spirit of the sea is enchanted by a magic
flute. 3. Affection: non-fantasy.

UNGEHEUER VON LONDON CITY, Das see MONSTER OF LONDON

CITY, The
UNHEIMLICHE GESCHICHTEN   see HISTOIRES EXTRAORDINAIRES
   (1931)
UNHEIMLICHE MONCH, Der see SINISTER MONK, The
UNHEIMLICHEN HANDE DES DR. ORLAK, Die see HANDS OF
   ORLAC, The (1925)
UNHEIMLICHEN WUNSCHE, Der see SINISTER WISH, The
UNHOLY HOUR see WEREWOLF OF LONDON
UNHOLY LOVE see ALRAUNE (1928)
The UNHOLY NIGHT MGM 1929 95m. sound Ed: Grant Whytook.
   Titles: Joe Farnham. Art D: Cedric Gibbons. D: Lionel Barry-
   more. SP: Dorothy Farnum, Edwin Justus Mayer. From the
   story "The Green Ghost" by Ben Hecht. See also The GREEN
   GHOST. PH: Ira Morgan. Ref: AFI. Clarens. COF 3:30. FM 46:
   10. with Ernest Torrence, Dorothy Sebastian, Roland Young,
   Natalie Moorhead, Polly Moran, Sojin, George Cooper, John Mil-
   jan, Boris Karloff, John Loder, Lionel Belmore, John Roche,
   Richard Tucker, Richard Travers.   Legend of green ghost that
   holds that man died of disease which turned him green. Man mes-
   merized, then put into state of catalepsy. Seance that draws "dead"
   officers of regiment.
The UNHOLY THREE MGM 1925 80m. Ed: Daniel J. Gray. D, P:
   Tod Browning. SP: Waldemar Young, from the book "Tod Rob-
   bins" (?) by C. A. Robbins. Art D: Cedric Gibbons, Joseph
   Wright. PH: David Kesson. Ref: Clarens. with Lon Chaney,
   Mae Busch, Matt Moore, Victor McLaglen, Harry Earles, Mat-
   thew Betz, Percy Williams. Bizarre, well-acted story involving
   a ventriloquist, a midget, a strongman, and an ape.
The UNHOLY THREE MGM 1930 75m. Ed: Frank Sullivan. D: Jack
   Conway. SP: E. and J. C. Nugent. From the book "Tod Robbins"
   by C. A. Robbins.Art D: Cedric Gibbons. PH: Percy Hilburn.
   Ref: AFI. Clarens. FM 8:29. with Lon Chaney, Lila Lee, Elliott
   Nugent, Harry Earles, John Miljan, Ivan Linow, Crauford Kent.
   Pic: Pict Hist Talkies.   Remake of '25 film; Chaney's only all-
   talking picture. Sometimes quite clever and amusing, in small
   ways.
UNIDENTIFIED FLYING OBJECTS UA /Ivar 1956 Documentary
   (UFO) 92m. D: Winston Jones. SP: Frances Martin. PH: H. A.
   Anderson, C. Schaeffer, Ed Fitzgerald, B. Spielvogel. Mus:
   Ernest Gold. Narr: Tom Powers.
The UNINVITED Para 1944 98m. D: Lewis Allen. SP: Dodie Smith,
   from the novel "The Uninvited" or "Uneasy Freehold" by Dorothy
   Macardle. PH:Charles Lang. SP: also Frank Partos. Mus: Victor
   Young. Art D: Hans Dreier, Ernst Fegte. Process PH: Farciot
   Edouart. P: Charles Brackett. Ref: Academy. FM 10:28. 23:26.
   with Ray Milland, Ruth Hussey, Gail Russell, Cornelia Otis Skin-
   ner, Donald Crisp, Dorothy Stickney, Barbara Everest, Alan
   Napier, Ottola Nesmith, Ivan F. Simpson, Moyna Macgill, Queenie
   Leonard, Leyland Hodgson, Holmes Herbert, George Kirby,
   Elizabeth Russell, David Clyde.   A brother and sister buy a
   house overlooking the ocean and find out that it's haunted.
   Suspenseful, with the cheery scenes (though there are too many)
   well-alternated with the eerie ones, and the mystery skillfully

interwoven with the horror elements. The music is too insistent-
ly moody, and the humor is a little folksy at times, but it's a
smooth, highly professional production, and the material is good
enough to keep the smoothness from becoming dull.
The UNKNOWN MGM 1927 70m. D, P: Tod Browning. SP: Browning, Waldemar Young. Titles: Joe Farnham. Art D: Cedric Gib-
gons, Richard Day. PH: Merritt B. Gerstad. Ref: AFI. Clarens.
NYT 6/13/27. FD 6/26/27. MW 10:14. FM 8:29. PM: "Morbid."
Photoplay: "Macabre thrills." COF 15:22: Dyer. Pic: HM 4:2.
with Lon Chaney, Joan Crawford, Norman Kerry, Nick de Ruiz,
John George, Frank Lanning. For love of a woman a man has his
arms amputated.
The UNKNOWN Col 1946 70m. D: Henry Levin. SP: Julian Harmon,
Stuart Boylan, from the radio show "I Love a Mystery." PH:
Henry Freulich. Adap: Charles O'Neal, Dwight V. Babcock.
Mus D: Mischa Bakaleinikoff. Art D: George Brooks. Ref: FanMo
3:39: "Haunted Southern mansion, sinister grave robbers, secret
passages, and a prowling cloaked phantom of the night." with
Jeff Donnell, Jim Bannon, Karen Morley, Robert Wilcox, Barton
Yarborough, James Bell, Wilton Graff.
The UNKNOWN COUNTRY Lubin 1914 Ref: MPW 22:1114. Lee.
Spirits leave their bodies to possess other bodies.
UNKNOWN ISLAND Film Classics 1948 Cinecolor 76m. D: Jack
Bernhard. SP: Robert Shannon, Jack Harvey. PH: Fred Jack-
man, Jr. Mus: Ralph Stanley. Art D: Jerome Pycha, Jr. SpFX:
Howard A. Anderson, Ellis Burman. Makeup: Harry Ross. Ref:
FDY. FM 10:26. ModM 3:8. V 11/18/48. Pic: FM 66:23. with
Richard Denning, Barton MacLane, Virginia Grey, Dick Wessel,
Philip Reed. Prehistoric beasts and other monsters are dis-
covered on an island: giant sloth, tyrannosaurus, brontosaurus,
dimetrodon. Acceptable "B." Pleasant stereotypes--humans and
dinosaurs.
UNKNOWN LETTERS (by Stendhal) see CABINET OF DR.
CALIGARI, The
The UNKNOWN MAN OF SHANDIGOR (Swiss) Frajea 1967 90m.
(L'INCONNU DE SHANDIGOR) SP, D: Jean-Louis Roy. SP: also
Gabriel Arout. PH: Roger Bimpage. Mus: Alphonse Roy. Ref:
V 5/3/67. Positif 99:62. with Marie-France Boyer, Ben Car-
ruthers, Howard Vernon, Serge Gainsbourg. V: "Scientist who
has found a way to make atomic weapons unworkable is finally
devoured by some sort of sea monster he keeps in his pool."
UNKNOWN PEOPLE see SUPERMAN AND THE MOLE MEN
The UNKNOWN PURPLE Truart/West-Carlos 1923 90m. SP, D:
Roland West. SP: also Paul Schofield. From the play by West
and Carlyle Moore. Art D: Horace Jackson. PH: Oliver T.
Marsh. Ref: AFI. Wid's 8/25/23. NYT 9/16/18: Edward Van
Sloan in the stage play. with Stuart Holmes, Henry B. Walthall,
Alice Lake, Ethel Grey Terry, Brinsley Shaw, John Arthur,
Frankie Lee, Helen Ferguson, James Morrison. A ray of light
renders a man invisible.
The UNKNOWN TERROR Fox 1957 77m. D: Charles Marquis
Warren. SP: Kenneth Higgins. Mus sc & d: Raoul Kraushaar.
PH: Joseph Biroc. Art D: James W. Sullivan. Ref: FDY. with

John Howard, Mala Powers, Paul Richards, Sir Lancelot, May Wynn. A scientist conducting experiments in a cave creates a monster. Some movies just don't deserve their laughing-stock reputations. Others do. This does.

UNKNOWN TREASURES Sterling 1926 70m. D: Archie Mayo. SP: Charles A. Logue, from "The House Behind the Hedge" by Mary Spain Vigus. PH: Harry Davis. Ref: Movie Monsters. LC. FD 9/26/26. AFI. with Gladys Hulette, Robert Agnew, Jed Prouty, Gustav von Seyffertitz. Man trains ape to kill.

UNKNOWN WORLD Lippert 1951 73m. D, Ed: Terrell O. Morse. SP: Millard Kaufman. PH: Allen G. Siegler, Henry Freulich. Mus: Ernest Gold. Sets: Glenn Thompson. P: J. R. Rabin, I. A. Block. Mechanical FX: Willis Cook. SoundFX Ed: Marshall Pollock. Ref: V 10/23/51. Pic: SM 6:22. with Bruce Kellogg, Marilyn Nash, Jim Bannon, Victor Kilian, Otto Waldis, Dick Cogan. Six scientists drill to the center of the earth in a specially designed vehicle: Film is just one long bore.

UNMASKED Artclass 1929 sound 70m. D: Edgar Lewis. SP: Albert Cowles. Dial: Bert Ennis, Edward Clark. Based on the Craig Kennedy character created by Arthur B. Reeve. PH: T. Malloy, B. Harris, I. Browning. Ref: AFI. with Robert Warwick, Milton Krims, Sam Ash, Susan Conroy, Charles Slattery. Woman commits murder under East Indian mystic's hypnotic influence.

UNQUIET CORPSE, The (novel by W. Sloane) see WHEN THE DEVIL COMMANDS

The UNSEEN (F?) Eclair 1914 35m. Ref: Bios 4/30/14. "Scientist has the power of rendering himself invisible."

The UNSEEN Para 1945 80m. D: Lewis Allen. SP: Hagar Wilde, Raymond Chandler. Adap: Ken Englund, Wilde. From the book "Her Heart in Her Throat" by E. L. White. PH: John F. Seitz. Assoc P: John Houseman. Ref: Showmen's 2/24/45: "Eerie mystery...horror." Deserted house. MPH'45:2329: "Tangle of weird and terrifying circumstances." with Joel McCrea, Gail Russell, Herbert Marshall, Phyllis Brooks, Isobel Elsom, Mikhail Rasumny, Elisabeth Risdon, Victoria Horne, Norman Lloyd. Weak attempt by Allen to repeat the success of The UNINVITED.

UNSEEN, The (1961) see HOUSE OF MYSTERY

UNSEEN HANDS Associated Exhibitors 1924 70m. D: Jacques Jaccard. SP, P: W. C. Graves, Jr. Ref: AFI. with Wallace Beery, Joseph J. Dowling, Cleo Madison, Fontaine La Rue. Ghost scares man to death.

UNSICHTBAR GEHT DURCH DIE STADT, Ein see INVISIBLE MAN GOES THROUGH THE CITY, An

UNSICHTBARE, Der see INVISIBLE TERROR, The

UNSICHTBAREN KRALLENDES DES DR. MABUSE, Die see INVISIBLE DR. MABUSE, The

The UNTAMEABLE Univ 1923 55m. D: Herbert Blache. Continuity: Hugh Hoffman. PH: H. Oswald, Ben Kline. (The TWO SOULED WOMAN) From "The White Cat" by Gelette Burgess. Ref: AFI. with Gladys Walton, Malcolm McGregor, John Sainpolis, Etta Lee. Hypnotist gives woman split personality.

UNTAMED WOMEN UA/Jewell 1952 70m. D: W. Merle Connell. SP: George W. Sayre. PH: Glen Gano. Mus: Raoul Kraushaar.

SpFX,Art D: Paul Sprunck. Ref: FM 19:36. 27:14. FDY. with Doris
Merrick, Mikel Conrad, Morgan Jones, Autumn Rice. Four men
in a raft are washed ashore on an island of prehistoric monsters,
"Hairy Men," female descendants of the Druids, and flesh-eating
plants. The women all have goofy smiles, and the men all have
goofy lines ("Sure didn't have nothin' like this back on the farm"
"Not only your compass fell overboard, but your non compos
mentis as well"). Abysmal.
UOMO CHE RIDE, L' see MAN WHO LAUGHS, The (1965)
UOMO CHE VISSE DUE VOLTE, L' see SECRET OF DR.
CHALMERS, The
UOMO DI TOLEDO, L' see CAPTAIN FROM TOLEDO
UOMO IN NERO, L' see JUDEX (1963)
UP THE LADDER Univ-Jewel 1925 80m. D: Edward Sloman.
SP: Tom McNamara. Adap: Grant Carpenter. PH: Jackson Rose.
Ref: AFI. with Virginia Valli, Forrest Stanley, Margaret Living-
ston, Holmes Herbert, George Fawcett, Priscilla Moran. From
the play by Owen Davis. "Tele-vision-scope" invention.

VACATION IN RENO RKO 1946 60m. D, P: Leslie Goodwins.
SP: Charles E. Roberts, Arthur Ross. Story: Charles Kerr. PH:
George E. Diskant. Mus sc: Paul Sawtell. Art D: Albert
D'Agostino, Lucius O. Croxton. SpFX: Russell A. Cully. Ref:
TVK. V 10/10/46. with Jack Haley, Anne Jeffreys, Wally Brown,
Iris Adrian, Morgan Conway, Alan Carney, Matt McHugh, Myrna
Dell, Claire Carleton, Jason Robards, Matt Willis. An amateur
inventor's mine detector locates buried bank loot.
The VACUUM CLEANER (F) Pathe 1908 Ref: V&FI 8/1/08. Vacuum
cleaner draws people and animals into its spout.
The VACUUM TEST Imp (Univ) 1915 15m. D: Leon D. Kent. Ref:
MPW 26:2074. with J. Livingston, Constance Johnson. A man
almost dies in an inventor's "vacuum cabinet."
VAHA see BEYOND THE HORIZON
VALERIE AND THE WEEK OF WONDERS (Cz) c1969 color 85m.
(VALERIE A TYDEN DIVU. VALERIE AND HER WEEK OF
WANDERS) Czech State/Barrandov D: Jaromil Jires. Sp, Art D:
Ester Krumbachova, from a story by V. Nezval. PH: Jan Curik.
Mus: Lubos Fiser. Ref: V 8/19/70. MFB'71. with Jaroslava
Musil, Helena Anyzkova. A girl's grandmother becomes a vampire.
VALKOINEN PEURA see WHITE REINDEER, The
VALLE DE LOS HOMBRES DE PIEDRA, El see MEDUSA VS.
THE SON OF HERCULES
VALLE DELL'ECO TONANTE, La see HERCULES OF THE DESERT
The VALLEY OF BEAUTIFUL THINGS Victor 1917 SP: Fred Myton.
P: Lule Warrenton. Ref: MPW 31:904,1593. with Peggy Custer
(Sea Foam), Antrim Short (Prince Happy Day), Elsie Cort
(Zamba). Witch uses fairy child to lure and rob travellers,
casts spell over prince.
VALLEY OF EAGLES (B) Lippert/Independent Sovereign 1951 86m.
(The VALLEY OF THE EAGLES) SP,D: Terence Young. PH:

Harry Waxman. Art D: J. Elder Wills. Mus: Nino Rota. Ref:
MFB'51:345. with Jack Warner, Nadia Gray, Anthony Dawson,
John McCallum, Christopher Lee. A scientist discovers the
secret of extracting power from sound waves.
The VALLEY OF GWANGI WB-7A/Morningstar 1969 (1968)
  Technicolor 95m. (The LOST VALLEY. The VALLEY WHERE
  TIME STOOD STILL. GWANGI. GWONJEE. The VALLEY-TIME
  FORGOT) D: James O'Connolly. SP: William E. Bast. Add'l
  Material: Julian More. PH: Erwin Hillier. Mus sc & d: Jerome
  Moross. Art D: Gil Parrando. VisualFX: Ray Harryhausen. P:
  Charles H. Schneer. Ref: FM 22:31. 44:75. 50:5. withGustavo
  Rojo, James Franciscus, Gila Golan, Freda Jackson, Richard
  Carlson, Laurence Naismith. Valley of dinosaurs. Good use of
  sound effects to reinforce visual effects. Better-than-average
  animation epic thanks to several good touches.
The VALLEY OF LOST SOULS Independent 1923 60m. D: Caryl
  S. Fleming. SP: G. P. Proctor. Story: J. S. Drummond. PH:
  Frank Perugini. Ref: AFI. with Muriel Kingston, Victor Suther-
  land, Edward Roseman, Luis Alberni. A Mountie investigates a
  series of "ghost" killings.
VALLEY OF THE DRAGONS Col/ZRB 1962 79m. (PREHISTORIC
  VALLEY-Eng.) SP,D: Edward Bernds. From a story by Donald
  Zimbalist and "Hector Servadac" and "Off on a Comet" or "The
  Career of a Comet" by Jules Verne. PH: Brydon Baker. Mus:
  Ruby Raksin. Art D: Don Ament. SpFX: Dick Albain. Scenes
  from ONE MILLION B. C. Exec P: Al Zimbalist. Ref: FFacts.
  MFB'67:176. FM 13:64. 19:36. Mod M 3:73. SM 2:53. with
  Cesare Danova, Sean McClory, Joan Staley, Danielle De Metz,
  Gregg Martell, I. Stanford Jolley, Michael Lane. Comet, pre-
  historic fragment of earth, bearing mastodons, giant spider,
  Cave People, River People, etc.
VALLEY OF THE HEADLESS HORSEMAN see CURSE OF THE HEAD-
  LESS HORSEMAN
VALLEY OF THE MISTS see BEAST OF HOLLOW MOUNTAIN, The
VALLEY OF THE RESOUNDING ECHO, The see HERCULES OF
  THE DESERT
VALLEY OF THE STONE MEN, The see MEDUSA VS. THE SON
  OF HERCULES
VALLEY OF THE ZOMBIES Rep 1946 56m. D: Phil Ford. SP:
  Dorrell & Stuart McGowan. Story: Royal Cole, Sherman Lowe.
  PH: Reggie Lanning. Mus D: Richard Cherwin. Art D: Hilyard
  Brown. SpFX: Howard and Theodore Lydecker. Ref: FDY. Pic:
  STI 3:30. with Ian Keith, Robert Livingston, Adrian Booth, Wilton
  Graff, Charles Trowbridge, Thomas Jackson. A man thought
  dead returns as a zombie that needs blood transfusions to remain
  alive. Always cliched, sometimes cloddish dialogue ("Blood?
  That's a strange request"--"I'm a strange man, doctor"). No
  thrills. A few (intentional) laughs thanks to the mildly amusing
  leads.
VALLEY WHERE TIME STOOD STILL, The see VALLEY OF
  GWANGI, The
VAMPIRAS, Las see VAMPIRE GIRLS, The
The VAMPIRE (B) Searchlight 1913 Ref: Movie Monsters. Girl turns

into snake.
The VAMPIRE (F?) Eclair 1914 32m. Ref: Bios 3/26/14. A
psychologist bound by oath to a "mysterious order" must kill
his second wife with narcotics and a "huge vampire bat."
The VAMPIRE (Mex) AI-TV/Cinematografica, A.B.S.A. 1956
(El VAMPIRO) D: Fernando Méndez. SP: Ramón Obón, H.
Rodríguez. PH: Rosario Solano. Mus: Gustavo Carrión. Art D:
Günther Gerszo. Ref: Aventura. Clarens. MadM 4:32. Pic: FM-
A'69:20. with Abel Salazar, German Robles, Ariadna Welter,
José Luis Jiménez, Carmen Montejo. An important new film-
vampire ruling is made by The VAMPIRE A vampire must
"suck your blood twice" to turn you into a vampire. What you
might become if he sucked it a third time is too horrible to con-
template. Let alone the 127th time.
The VAMPIRE (Malayan) Keris Films 1957 110m. (PONTIANAK)
Sequel: REVENGE OF THE VAMPIRE. Ref: FEFN 8/9/57.
5/17/57. with Maria Menado (girl, mutate, vampire). Hunch-
backed-girl-transformed-by-magic-formula-into-beautiful-maiden
turns into a vampire when she tastes human blood. The village
doctor kills her by driving a nail through her head.
The VAMPIRE UA/Gramercy 1957 74m. (IT'S ALWAYS DARKEST
BEFORE THE DAWN. MARK OF THE VAMPIRE-TV) D: Paul
Landres. SP: Pat Fielder. PH: Jack M(a)cKenzie. Mus: Gerald
Fried. Makeup: Don Robertson. Ref: FDY. PM. FM 11:38. with
John Beal, Kenneth Tobey, Dabbs Greer, Arthur Gardner, Paul
Brinegar, Coleen Gray, Louise Lewis. Some pills turn a doctor
into a vampire. Run-of-the-mill.
VAMPIRE see LOVES OF CT. IORGA/VAMPYR
The VAMPIRE AND THE BALLERINA UA/CIF (I) 1960 (L'AMANTE
DEL VAMPIRO. The VAMPIRE'S LOVER. The DANCER AND
THE VAMPIRE) SP,D: Renato Polselli. SP: also Ernesto Gas-
taldi, Giuseppe Pellegrini. PH: Angelo Baistrocchi. Mus: Aldo
Piga. Art D: Amedeo Mellone. Ref: Bianco 8/60. Orpheus 3:29.
FM 10:10-11. PM. FFacts. Pic: FM 19:17. 46:64-69. with
Hélène Remy, Walter Brandi, Maria Luisa Rolando, Tina
Gloriani, I. Ravajoli, John Turner, Stefania Sabatini. Ballet-
school girls encounter vampires at a country home.
The VAMPIRE BAT Majestic 1933 67m. D: Frank Strayer. SP:
Edward T. Lowe. PH: Ira Morgan. Art D: Daniel Hall. Ed: Otis
Garrett. P: Phil Goldstone. Ref: MPH 1/28/33. MW 1:30. Pic:
FMO 6:8. with Lionel Atwill, Fay Wray, Melvyn Douglas, George
E. Stone, Maude Eburne, Dwight Frye, Robert Frazer, Lionel
Belmore, William V. Mong, Paul Weigel, Fern Emmett, Carl
Stockdale. Series of murders blamed on "vampire." Independent
cheapie doesn't have much to offer except opening shots of bats
just hanging around.
The VAMPIRE BEAST CRAVES BLOOD (B) Pacemaker/Tigon 1968
Eastmancolor 88m. (BLOOD BEAST FROM HELL. The BLOOD
BEAST TERROR. The DEATHSHEAD VAMPIRE) D: Vernon
Sewell. SP: Peter Bryan. PH: Stanley Long. SpFX: Roger Dicken.
Ref: MMF 18-19:14. FM 50:7. with Peter Cushing, Robert
Flemyng, Wanda Ventham, Vanessa Howard. Giant vampire moth.
VAMPIRE DES DR. DRACULA, Die see MARK OF THE WOLFMAN,
The

The VAMPIRE DOLL(J) Toho 1970 color/scope 71m. (CHI O SUU
NINGYO) D: Michio Yamamoto. SP: Ei Ogawa, Hiroshi Nagano.
PH: K. Hara. Mus: R. Manabe. Art D: Y. Honda. Ref: UFQ 50.
with Kayo Matsuo, Yukiko Kobayashi, Rin Nakao. "Ghostly events"
in a haunted house.
A VAMPIRE FOR TWO (Sp) Belmar 1965 scope 85m. (Un VAM-
PIRO PARA DOS) SP,D: Pedro Lazaga. SP: also J. M. Palacio(s).
PH: Eloy Mella. Mus: A. G. Abril. Art D: Martin Zerolo.
Ref: SpCinema'66. COF 10:49. with Gracita Morales, José L. L.
Vasquez, Fernando F. Gomez, Trini Alonso, Goyo Lebreros.
Newlyweds vs. vampires at the Baron of Rosenthal's ("The
Vampire of Dusseldorf" 's) home.
The VAMPIRE GIRLS (Mex) Col c1967 color (Las VAMPIRAS)
D: F. Curiel. Ref: D. Glut. Photon 21:29. FJA pic. with John
Carradine (vampire), Mil Mascaras, Pedro Armendariz, Martha
Romero, Maria Duval.
The VAMPIRE HAPPENING (G) Aquila (P.A.C.) 1971 color/scope
97m. (GEBISSEN WIRD NUR NACHTS--HAPPENING DER VAM-
PIRE. HAPPENING OF THE VAMPIRES) D: Freddie Francis.
SP: August Rieger, from an idea by K. H. Hummel. PH: Gerard
Vandenberg. Mus: Jerry Van Rooyen (or Rooyan). Ref:
V 8/4/71. 5/7/69:169. with Yvor Murillo, Ingrid Van Bergen,
Ferdy Mayne (Dracula).
The VAMPIRE LOVERS (B) AI/Hammer 1970 Technicolor 91m.
D: Roy Ward Baker. SP: Tudor Gates, from "Carmilla" by
Sheridan Le Fanu. Adap:Gates, Harry Fine, Michael Style. See
also LUST FOR A VAMPIRE. Scenes in The RETURN OF COUNT
YORGA. PH: Moray Grant. Mus: Harry Robinson. Ref: MFB.
with Ingrid Pitt, Pippa Steele, Peter Cushing, George Cole,
Kate O'Mara, Douglas Wilmer, Ferdy Mayne. Vampiress changes
names to cover her tracks as she goes from place to place.
After promising pre-credit sequence film becomes routine and
bad with annoying shock music, useless camera zooms, large
blocks of cliche dialogue, and uniformly bad performances.
VAMPIRE MAN (J) Shintoho 1959 scope 78m. (ONNA KYUKETSUKI.
MALE VAMPIRE) D: Nobuo Nakagawa. SP: Shin Nakazawa,
Katsuyoshi Nakatsu. PH: Yoshimi Hirano. Ref: UFQ 5. Pic:
FM 23:11. MMF 9:32a. with Shigeru Amachi, Yoko Mihara,
Keinosuke Wada, Junko Ikeuchi. A beautiful woman is kidnapped
by the blood-sucking Vampire (who "cannot stand moonlight") and
turned into a wax doll. Witch, "huge monster."
The VAMPIRE MOTH (J) Toho 1956 (KYUKETSU GA) 90m. Ref:
FEFN 4/13/56. FM 22:13. From a novel by Seishi Yokomizo.
withRyo Ikebe, Akio Kobori, Asami Kuji, Kinuko Ito. A detec-
tive solves a "series of murders the only clue to which are tooth
marks on the bodies of the victims and a bloodstained moth
which creeps on the corpse."
VAMPIRE NUE, La see NAKED VAMPIRE, The
The VAMPIRE OF CASTLE FRANKENSTEIN (Sp) Cinefilms 1970
color/scope 91m. (El VAMPIRO DE LA AUTOPISTA-Sp.
Der VAMPIR VON SchloB FRANKENSTEIN. The VAMPIRE OF
THE HIGHWAY) D: José Luis Madrid. PH: Francisco Madurga.
Mus: Angel Arteaga. Ref: SpCinema'71. Fernsehen 4/71. with

Valdemar Wohlfahrt, Patricia Loran, Luis Induni, Barta Barry,
Adela Tauler, Anastasio Campoy. Vampire, reincarnation of
famous baron, commits series of "strange crimes."
VAMPIRE OF NOTRE DAME, The see DEVIL'S COMMANDMENT,
The
The VAMPIRE OF THE CAVE (Malayan) Keris Films 1964 (The
VAMPIRE OF THE CIVET-CAT CAVE. PONTIANAK GUA MUSANG)
D: B. N. Rao.   Fifth in Keris' vampire series. Ref: M/TVM
9/64. with Suraya Haron.
The VAMPIRE OF THE DESERT 1913 26m. Ref: Bios 8/14/13.
Woman casts hypnotic spell.
VAMPIRE OF THE HIGHWAY, The see VAMPIRE OF CASTLE
FRANKENSTEIN, The
The VAMPIRE OF THE OPERA (I) 1961 (Il VAMPIRO DELL'OPERA.
MONSTER OF THE OPERA) D: Renato Polselli. Ref: Film 9/67.
FM 46:30-35. FanMo 6:31. with Vittoria Prada, Marc Maryn,
Giuseppe Addobati. Vampire haunts old, recently-reopened opera
house.
VAMPIRE PEOPLE see BLOOD DRINKERS, The
The VAMPIRE RETURNS (Malayan) Keris Films 1963 (PONTIANAK
KEMBALI) D: R. Estellia. Fourth in Keris' vampire series.
Ref: M/TVM 4/63. with Maria Menado, Malik Selamat.
VAMPIRE THRILLS (F) Les Films Modernes 1970 95m. (Le
FRISSON DES VAMPIRES) D: Jean Rollin. PH: Jean-Jacques
Renon. Ref: MMF 24:11. with Sandra Jullien, Michel Delahaye,
Jean-Marie Durand.
VAMPIRES, The see GOLIATH AND THE VAMPIRES
The VAMPIRE'S COFFIN (Mex) AI-TV/Salazar-Cinematografica,
A.B.S.A. 1957 (El ATAUD DEL VAMPIRO) D: Fernando Mendez.
SP: Ramón Obón. Story: R. Zenteno. PH: Rosalio Solano, Kurt
Dayton. Mus: Gustavo Carrión. Art D: Günther Gerszo, William
Hayden. P: Abel Salazar. Ref: Indice. SP: also Enrique
Rodriguez. with Salazar, Ariadna Welter, German Robles, An-
tonio Raxell, Yerye Beirute. A vampire is revived from the
dead. Robles is about as menacing a monster as The Giant Claw.
A good scene with shadows. The kind of movie in which an old
lady will, rather foolishly, step into an open iron maiden.
The VAMPIRE'S CURSE (Malayan) Keris Films 1958 CathayScope
(SUMPAH PONTIANAK) Ref: FEFN 11/29/57. 2/28/58. Vampire,
"Hantu Hutan" (Spectre of the Forest), "Hantu Galah" (Bamboo
Ghost), "Hantu Kelawar" (Bat Ghost).
A VAMPIRE'S DREAM (Braz) UCB/Sercine 1969 color 80m. (Um
SONHO DE VAMPIROS) SP, D: Ibere Cavalcanti. PH: Renato
Neumann. Art D: Maria Augusta. Ref: V 10/14/70. with Ankito,
Irma Alvarez (the vampire). Lampoon of vampire films.
The VAMPIRE'S GHOST Rep 1945 59m. D: Lesley Selander. SP:
John Butler, Leigh Brackett. PH: Robert Pittack, Ellis Thack-
eray. Mus D: Richard Cherwin. Art D: Russell Kimball. Ref:
FDY. MFB'46:155. Pic: WFC 3:48. with John Abbott (vampire),
Peggy Stewart, Grant Withers, Adele Mara, Emmett Vogan, Roy
Barcroft, Frank Jaquet. A vampire terrorizes an African trad-
ing village. Ineffective except for one unusual scene in which the
vampire shatters a mirror just by looking at it.

VAMPIRE'S LAST VICTIM, The see PLAYGIRLS AND THE VAM-
PIRE, The
VAMPIRE'S LOVER, The see VAMPIRE AND THE BALLERINA,
The
VAMPIRE'S NIECE, The see MALENKA
VAMPIRES OF PRAGUE see MARK OF THE VAMPIRE
VAMPIRES OVER LONDON see MY SON, THE VAMPIRE
VAMPIRES, THE ARCH CRIMINALS OF PARIS (F) Gaum 1916
serial (Les VAMPYRES) D: Louis Feuillade. Ref: FM 37:49.
COF 8:47.9:39. DDC II: 339. MPN 15:115, 3666, 3673, 4040. Pic:
DDC III:428. with Edmond Mathe. Ch. 3. The Ghost (Le Spectre).
Ch. 6. Satanas. "Electric gun," hypnotism; band of black-robed,
hooded super-criminals.
VAMPIRES VS. HERCULES, The see HERCULES IN THE HAUNTED
WORLD
VAMPIRI, I see DEVIL'S COMMANDMENT, The
VAMPIRO, El see VAMPIRE, The (Mex-1956)
VAMPIRO ACECHA, El see LURKING VAMPIRE, The
VAMPIRO DE LA AUTOPISTA, El see VAMPIRE OF CASTLE
FRANKENSTEIN, The
VAMPIRO DEL PIANETA ROSSO, Il see NOT OF THIS EARTH
VAMPIRO DELL'OPERA, Il see VAMPIRE OF THE OPERA, The
VAMPIRO PARA DOS, Un see VAMPIRE FOR TWO, A
VAMPIRO SANGRIENTO, El see BLOODY VAMPIRE, The
VAMPIRO Y EL SEXO, El see SANTO AND DRACULA'S
TREASURE
VAMPYR (F) 1932 ('34-U.S.) (VAMPIRE. The STRANGE ADVEN-
TURE OF DAVID GRAY. CASTLE OF DOOM) SP, D: Carl Drey-
er. SP: also Christian Jul. PH: Rudolph Maté. Mus: Wolfgang
Zeller. Art D: Hermann Warm. From "Carmilla" by Sheridan Le
Fanu. Sequence in DR. TERROR'S HOUSE OF HORRORS (1943).
P: Baron de Gunzburg. Ref: Clarens. Pic: COF 4:40. DDC II:
137. with Julian West (aka de Gunzburg), Sybille Schmitz, Henriette Gerard, Jan Hieronimko, Albert Bras, Maurice Schutz.
Dreams, shadows, phantoms, skeleton, vampire. There are at
least three (quite different) prints of VAMPYR circulating. One
(the CASTLE OF DOOM print) is atrociously dubbed. Another is
in German with subtitles in Lithuanian or something. Neither is
worth seeing. There is a third, properly-subtitled-in-English
print, which I have seen the last half of and which seems like it
might (unlike Dreyer's other, more-oppressively-arty films) be
worth seeing.
VAMPYR (Sp?) 1971 D: Pedro Portabella. Ref: VVoice 6/17/71.
with Christopher Lee. A semi-documentary study of the filming
of COUNT DRACULA, with homages to VAMPYR (Dreyer) and
NOSFERATU (Murnau).
VAMPYRES, Les see VAMPIRES, THE ARCH CRIMINALS OF
PARIS
VAMPYROS LESBOS - DIE ERBIN DES DRACULA see LESBIAN
VAMPIRES
VANISHING BODY, The see BLACK CAT, The (1934)
The VANISHING RIDERS Spectrum Pictures 1935 58m. D: Bob
Hill. SP: Oliver Drake. Ref: FD 7/2/35. MFB'41:155. with Bill

Cody, Bill Cody, Jr., Ethel Jackson, Donald Reed. Silver City, a supposedly haunted town; fake ghosts. Western.

The VANISHING SHADOW Univ 1934 serial 12 episodes D: Lew Landers (aka Louis Friedlander). SP: B. Dickey, G. Morgan, H. Manheim. Story: Ella O'Neill. Ref: Imagen. RVB. MW 10:21. Pic: FM 12:16,18.16:43.13:99. FanMo 5:37. Ch. 2. The Destroying Ray. "Belt of invisibility." with Onslow Stevens, Walter Miller, William Desmond, Monte Montague, William Steele, Tom London.

VANITY'S PRICE FBO/Gothic Pictures 1924 70m. D: Roy William Neill. Ass't. D: Josef von Sternberg. SP: Paul Bern. PH: Hal Mohr. Ref: AFI. Wid's 10/18/24. MPN 30:1525. V 10/15/24. with Anna Q. Nilsson, Stuart Holmes, Arthur Rankin. Viennese surgeon's treatment rejuvenates actress.

VARAN THE UNBELIEVABLE (J) Crown/Dallas/Toho 1958 ('62-U.S.) 70m. (BARAN. DAIKAIJU BARAN. The MONSTER BARAN) D: I. Honda SP: Shinichi Sekizawa. Idea: T. Kuronuma. Mus: Akira Ifukube. Art D: K. Shimizu. SpFX: Eiji Tsuburaya. Ref: Toho Films'59. FFacts. FEFN 7/4/58.10/17/58. COF 1:24. with Myron Healey, Kozo Nomura, A. Sonoda, K. Senda, Akihiko Hirata. A huge beast wipes out yet another tenth of Japan. The makers' idea of terror is stated by an extra who exclaims of Varan's approach: "There are thousands of people!" Imagine the horror if there were millions! Let alone 127.

VARGTIMMEN see HOUR OF THE WOLF

VASCO THE VAMPIRE Imp 1914 Ref: MPW 20:1012. "Vasco, the mysterious vampire," captures and hypnotizes a detective.

VEILED WOMAN, The see QUEEN OF BLOOD

VELDT, The (by R. Bradbury) see ILLUSTRATED MAN, The

The VELVET VAMPIRE New World 1971 Metrocolor 79m. (THROUGH THE LOOKING GLASS. The DEVIL IS A WOMAN) SP,D: Stephanie Rothman. SP: also Maurice Jules, Charles S. Swartz. PH: Daniel Lacambre. 2nd Ass't Cameraman: Les Otis. Mus: Clancy B. Grass, III, Roger Dollarhide. Art D: Teddi Petersen. Ref: V. Boxo. with Michael Blodgett, Celeste Yarnall (Diane Le Fanu), Sherry Miles, Jerry Daniels. Female vampire.

VENDETTA (F) Eclipse 1914 80m. D: Louis Mereanton. From the book by Marie Corelli. Ref: The Film Index. with Regina Badet. Man buried as dead regains consciousness.

VENDETTA Cosmopolitan/Famous Players 1922 D: Alan Crosland. SP: Frances Marion, from Marie Corelli's book. Ref: Lee. MPW 21:1064. MPN 26:3131. with Lionel Barrymore, Alma Rubens. Man "returns from the dead."

VENDETTA DI ERCOLE, La see GOLIATH AND THE DRAGON

VENDETTA DI LADY MORGAN, La see LADY MORGAN'S VENGEANCE

The VENETIAN AFFAIR MGM 1966 Metrocolor/scope 92m. D: Jerry Thorpe. SP: E. Jack Neuman, from a novel by Helen MacInnes. PH: Milton Krasner. Mus: Lalo Schifrin. Art D: George W. Davis, Leroy Coleman. SpVisFX: Carroll L. Sheppard. Ref: FFacts. MFB'67:14. with Robert Vaughn, Elke Sommer, Boris Karloff, Felicia Farr, Karl Boehm, Luciana Paluzzi, Joe De Santis, Wesley Lau, Roger C. Carmel, Edward Asner. Mind-controlling drug turns people into "robots." Vaughn acts like he actually

wanted to make something of this mess.
VENGANZA DEL AHORCADO, La see VENGEANCE OF THE
  HANGED, The
VENGANZA DEL RESUCITADO, La see VENGEANCE OF THE
  REVIVED CORPSE
VENGEANCE see BRAIN, The
VENGEANCE DU COLOSSE, La see VENUS AGAINST THE SON OF
  HERCULES
The VENGEANCE OF EDGAR POE (F) Lux 1912 30m. Ref: Bios
  1/2/13. Drug drives Poe insane.
VENGEANCE OF EGYPT (F) Gaum 1912 45m. Ref: MPW 14:251.
  Lee. "Blinking mummies," cursed ring.
VENGEANCE OF FU MANCHU (B) WB-7A/Babasdave 1967 color
  89m. D: Jeremy Summers. SP: Peter Welbeck. PH: John von
  Kotze. Mus sc & d: Malcolm Lockye(a)r. Art D: Scott Mac-
  Gregor, Peggy Gick. Ref: MFB '68:12. V 1/17/68. M/TVM
  12/67. with Christopher Lee, Douglas Wilmer, Tsai Chin, Horst
  Frank, Howard Marion Crawford, Maria Rohm, Noel Trevarthen,
  Wolfgang Kieling. Based on characters created by Sax Rohmer.
  Fu Manchu attempts to eliminate the police chiefs of the world.
VENGEANCE OF HERCULES see GOLIATH AND THE DRAGON
The VENGEANCE OF SHE (B) Fox/7A/Hammer 1967 DeLuxe color
  101m. (AYESHA, THE RETURN OF SHE. AYESHA, DAUGHTER
  OF SHE) D: Cliff Owen. SP: Peter O'Donnell. Based on the book
  "She" by H. Rider Haggard. PH: Wolfgang Suschitzky. Mus sc:
  Mario Nascimbene. Prod Des: Lionel Couch. Ref: MFB'68:80.
  COF 7:54.8:48. PM. with Olinka Berova, John Richardson,
  Edward Judd, Colin Blakely, Jill Melford, Noel Willman, Andre
  Morell. Girl lured to ancient city where pagan rituals are prac-
  ticed.
VENGEANCE OF THE DEAD (F) Pathe 1910 11m. Ref: Bios 10/13/10.
  Portrait of woman girl killed comes to life, points accusing finger,
  and steps out of the frame.
The VENGEANCE OF THE HANGED (Mex) Clasa 1958 (La VEN-
  GANZA DEL AHORCADO) Ref: FM 31:18. Witch conjures up
  creature.
The VENGEANCE OF THE REVIVED CORPSE (Mex) Clasa 1964
  (La VENGANZA DEL RESUCITADO) Ref: FDY'65. Lee.
VENTO DI MORTE see LAST MAN ON EARTH, The (1964)
The VENTURES OF MARGUERITE Kalem 1915 serial 16 episodes
  D: Hamilton Smith, J. E. Mackin, Robert Ellis. Ref: MPW'15:
  2239. CNW. with Marguerite Courtot, Richard Purdon. Electric
  torpedo deflector tested successfully.
VENUS AGAINST THE SON OF HERCULES (I) Embassy/Spa-Incei
  1962 color/Totalscope 92m. (MARTE, DIO DELLA GUERRA-I. La
  VENGEANCE DU COLOSSE-F. MARS, GOD OF WAR) SP,D:
  Marcello Baldi. SP: also Continenza. PH: Marcello Masciocchi.
  Mus: Gino Marinuzzi. Ref: Embassy catalogue. Index de la
  Cinématographie Française'65. Pic: MMF 9:80a. with Massimo
  Serato, Roger Browne, Jackie Lane, Linda Sini, Dante di Paolo.
  "Man-eating monster plants," spell.
VENUS IN FURS (I-G-B-U.S.) AI/Cineproduzioni-Terrafilmkunst-
  Commonwealth United 1969 Movielab/color/scope 86m.

513   Venusian

(PAROXISMUS-I. VENUS IN PELTZ-G.) D: Jess Franco (Hans
Billian?). SP: Franco, Marvin Wald, Leder, Fadda, Cuccia. PH:
Angelo Lotti. Mus: Manfred Mann, Mike Hugg. SpFX: Howard
A. Anderson. Ref: Ital P'69. V 5/6/70. with James Darren,
Barbara McNair, Maria Rohm, Klaus Kinski, Dennis Price,
Margaret Lee. A girl returns from the dead to kill her murder-
ers.
VENUSIAN, The see STRANGER FROM VENUS
VERGINE DI NORIMBERGA, La see HORROR CASTLE
VERLDENS UNDERGANG see END OF THE WORLD (1916)
VERLORENE ICH, Das see LOST SOUL, The
VERLORENE SCHATTEN, Der see LOST SHADOW, The
VERONIQUE'S LONG NIGHT (I) Mercurfin Italiana 1966 Eastman-
color (La LUNGA NOTTE DI VERONIQUE. BUT YOU WERE
DEAD) SP,D,PH: Gianni Vernuccio. SP: also Enzo Ferraris.
Mus sc & d: G. Gaslani. Ref: MFB'69:127. Ital P. with Alba
Rigazzi, Alex Morrison, Walter Pozzi (or Poggi). Female ghost
lures man to his death.
A VERY HONORABLE GUY F Nat 1934 62m. D: Lloyd Bacon. SP:
Earl Baldwin. From a story by Damon Runyan. PH: Ira Morgan.
Ref: Maltin. MPH 3/24/34. with Joe E. Brown, Alice White, Alan
Dinehart, Hobart Cavanaugh, Robert Barrat, Harold Huber,
Dubin & Warren, Robert Ellis, Dick Powell, Lee Shumway,
Clarence Muse, Wade Boteler, Paul Hurst. A mad doctor ex-
periments in rejuvenation.
VIAGGO AL CENTRO DELLA LUNA see TRIP TO THE CENTER
OF THE MOON
VIJ, The (by Gogol) see BLACK SUNDAY
The VIKING WOMEN AND THE SEA SERPENT AI/Malibu 1957
(VIKING WOMEN-Eng. The SAGA OF THE VIKING WOMEN AND
THEIR VOYAGE TO THE WATERS OF THE GREAT SEA SER-
PENT. UNDERSEA MONSTER) D,P: Roger Corman. SP: L.
Goldman. Story: Irving Block. PH: Monroe Askins. Mus: Albert
Glasser. Ref: MFB'58:146. with Abby Dalton, Susan Cabot, Brad
Jackson, June Kenn(e)y, Jonathan Haze, Richard Devon, Betsy
Jones-Morland. Gary Conway, Jay Sayer, Michael For(r)est. Not
recommended.
VILLA MILAGROSA (Fili) LVN D: Susana de Guzman. Ref: FEFN
2/14/58. 3/14/58. with Charito Solis (ghost), Nestor de Villa.
VILLAGE OF THE DAMNED (B) MGM 1960 Metroscope 78m. SP,
D: Wolf Rilla. SP: also Sterling Silliphant, George Barclay. From
the book "The Midwich Cuckoos" by John Wyndham. PH:
Geoffrey Faithfull. Mus: Ron Goodwin. Art D: Ivan King. SpFX:
Tom Howard. Ref: Clarens. PM. with George Sanders, Martin
Stephens, Barbara Shelley, Michael Gwynn, Laurence Naismith,
Jenny Laird, Rosamund Greenwood. A number of children pos-
sessing superhuman powers are born in the English village of
Midwich. VILLAGE has imaginative stretches and powerful bursts
of violence, but "human interest" angles in the plot and typical,
dull s-f-film dialogue weaken the film. (The weaknesses are
in the book too.)
VILLAGE OF THE GIANTS Emb 1965 color 82m. D,P: Bert I.
Gordon. SP: Alan Caillou, from H. G. Wells' novel "The Food

of the Gods. " PH: Paul C. Vogel. Mus: Jack Nitzsche. Ref:
FM 15:6. 41:66, MW 5:50. 8:55. with Tommy Kirk, Johnny Crawford, Beau Bridges, Ronny Howard, Joy Harmon, Tisha Sterling. Teenagers steal a concoction that turns them into giants.
The movie is in such execrable taste it's funny. There are
great and terrible moments like the sheriff's first look at the
giant teenagers ("Oh, for crying out loud, what's this?").
(Everyone reacts rather oddly to the giants.) Highly embarrassing at times.
The VILLAGE SCARE 1909 Ref: MPW'09:769. A "beast with the
form of a wolf" stalks through the streets of a hamlet. A learned
man says that the beast is a "prehistoric ornitholupus, an
animal half bird and half wolf. " It turns out to be a dog covered
with feathers.
The VILLAGE WITCH (F) Pathe 1906 Ref: SilentFF. V&FI 12/1/06.
"A witch curses a man who later saves her from some of the
village men. "-SF Film.
VIOL DU VAMPIRE, Le see QUEEN OF THE VAMPIRES, The
VIRGIN OF NUREMBERG, The (by F. Bogart) see HORROR CASTLE
VIRGINS FOR THE HANGMAN see BLOODY PIT OF HORROR
The VISION Educ 1926 22m. Technicolor From the painting "Speak,
Speak!" by John Millais. Ref: Nealon (The Film Index). with John
Roche. A beautiful woman haunts an ancient castle.
The VISION OF A CRIME Lubin 1907 Ref: MPW'07:90. A man
dreams of a "ghastly tragedy" In the morning he goes to the
site of the dream and discovers a corpse.
VISIT TO A SMALL PLANET Para 1960 85m. D: Norman
Taurog. SP: Edmund Beloin, Henry Garson, from Gore Vidal's
play. PH: Loyal Griggs. Mus: Leigh Harline. SpPhFX: John P.
Fulton. P: Hal Wallis. Ref: FFacts. with Jerry Lewis, Joan
Blackman, Earl Holliman, Fred Clark, Lee Patrick, Gale
Gordon, Jerome Cowan, John Williams, Barbara Lawson. An
alien on earth observes man's ways. Surprisingly consistent in
its level of humor, even if it is rather low.
VISITOR FROM VENUS see STRANGER FROM VENUS
VISITORS, The (book by N. Benchley) see SPIRIT IS WILLING, The
!VIVA LA AVENTURA! see HURRAH FOR ADVENTURE!
VOICE OF THE WHISTLER Col 1946 60m. SP, D: William Castle.
Story: Allan Rader. SP: also Wilfred H. Pettit. Based on the
radio program "The Whistler. " PH: George Meehan. Mus D:
Mischa Bakaleinikoff. Ref: FD 1/16/46. MPH 10/45: ad:
"Haunted lighthouse. " with Richard Dix, Lynn Merrick, Rhys
Williams, Tom Kennedy, Donald Woods, Egon Brecher, Gigi
Perreau (or Pirreau). "Psychological suggestion" to have man
murder.
The VOICE ON THE WIRE Univ 1917 serial 15 episodes D: Stuart
Paton.   Ref: MPN 15:3020. CNW. From a novel by Eustace Hale
Ball. with Ben Wilson, Neva Gerber, Francis McDonald, Joseph
W. Girard. Ch. 5. The Spectral Hand. 11. The Thought Ma-
chine. 15. The Living Death. Psychical research group called
"The Black Seven"; mummification; arm-grafting; projection
through space; disembodied hand.
VOLCANO MONSTER, The see GIGANTIS

VOODOO BLOOD BATH see I EAT YOUR SKIN
VOODOO BLOOD DEATH see CURSE OF THE VOODOO
VOODOO ISLAND UA/Bel Air/Oak 1957 76m. (L'ISOLA STREGATA
   DEGLI ZOMBIES-I. SILENT DEATH) D: Reginald LeBorg. SP:
   Richard Landau. Mus: Les Baxter. PH: William Margulies.
   SpFX: Jack Rabin, Louis DeWitt. Ref: Photon 21:12. PM. Pic:
   FM 60:55. with Boris Karloff, Murvyn Vye, Beverly Tyler,
   Elisha Cook, Jr., Rhodes Reason, Friedrich Ledebur. Expedi-
   tion runs up against black magic and man-eating plants on island.
   Dull horror movie; the end is too far from the beginning.
VOODOO MAN Mono 1944 62m. D: William Beaudine. SP: Robert
   Charles. PH: Marcel Le Picard. Mus: Edward Kay. Art D: Dave
   Milton. Ref: FDY. Pic: FanMo 3:61. COF 15:2. P: Sam Katzman,
   Jack Dietz. with Bela Lugosi, John Carradine, Wanda McKay,
   Henry Hall, Louise Currie, Michael Ames, Mary Currier, George
   Zucco. A mad doctor's wife becomes a zombie.
VOODOO WOMAN AI/Carmel 1957 77m. D: Edward L. Cahn. SP:
   V. I. Voss, Russ Bender. PH: Frederick E. West. Mus sc:
   Darrell Calker. Art D: Bart Carre. P: Alex Gordon. Ref: FDY.
   with Marla English, Tom Conway, Paul Blaisdell, Touch Connors,
   Lance Fuller, Paul Dubov, Martin Willis. Pic: FM 43:34. with
   the aid of a serum, a mad scientist attempts to create a zombie.
   One of AI's less memorable ones.
VOSTRO SUPER AGENTE, Il see FLIT
VOUS PIGEZ? see DIAMOND MACHINE, The
VOYAGE A LA PLANETE JUPITER see TRIP TO JUPITER, A
VOYAGE A TRAVERS L'IMPOSSIBLE see IMPOSSIBLE VOYAGE, The
VOYAGE AROUND A STAR see TRIP TO A STAR (F)
VOYAGE AU CENTRE DE LA TERRE see JOURNEY TO THE CENTER
   OF THE EARTH (1909)
VOYAGE AUTOMOBILE PARIS - MONTE CARLO EN DEUX HEURES,
   Le see AUTOMOBILE CHASE, The
VOYAGE AUTOUR D'UNE ETOILE see TRIP TO A STAR (F)
VOYAGE DANS LA LUNE, Un see TRIP TO THE MOON, A (1903)
VOYAGE DANS UNE ETOILE, Le see TRIP TO A STAR (F)
VOYAGE IMAGINAIRE, Le see IMAGINARY VOYAGE, The
VOYAGE OF THE "ARCTIC," or HOW CAPTAIN KETTLE DIS-
   COVERED THE NORTH POLE (B) Paul 1903 (The ADVEN-
   TUROUS VOYAGE OF THE ARCTIC) D: Walter R. Booth. Ref:
   Hist Brit Film. Brit Cinema. Similar to CONQUEST OF THE
   NORTH POLE.
VOYAGE TO A PREHISTORIC PLANET see STORM PLANET
VOYAGE TO A STAR see TRIP TO A STAR (I)
VOYAGE TO PREHISTORIC TIMES see JOURNEY TO THE BEGIN-
   NING OF TIME
VOYAGE TO THE BOTTOM OF THE SEA Fox 1961 color/scope
   105m. (JOURNEY TO THE BOTTOM OF THE SEA) SP,D,P:
   Irwin Allen. SP: also Charles Bennett. PH: Winton Hoch. Mus:
   Paul Sawtell, Bert Shefter. Underwater PH: John Lamb. Art D:
   Jack Martin Smith, Herman A. Blumenthal. Sets: Walter M.
   Scott, John Sturtevant. SpPhFX: L. B. Abbott. Ref: FFacts.
   Orpheus 3:29. PM. with Walter Pidgeon, Joan Fontaine, Peter
   Lorre, Robert Sterling, Barbara Eden, John Litel, Henry Daniell

(Dr. Zucco), Frankie Avalon, Michael Ansara, Regis Toomey, Howard McNear, Skip Ward. Meteor activity sets the Van Allen radiation belt afire. Fairly good special effects don't quite atone for a plot full of amazing coincidences, dull incidents, incredible theories, and ridiculous speeches.

VOYAGE TO THE END OF THE UNIVERSE (Cz) AI/Barrandov 1963 Agfacolor 81m. (IKARIE XB-1) SP, D: Jindrich Polak. SP: also Pavel Juracek. (IKARIE XB 1- ZA DVE STE LET KONGEM CERVNA) PH: Jan Kalis. Art D: Jan Zazvorka. Ref: Imagen. Clarens. PM. with Zdenek Stepanek, Radovan Lukavsky, Dana Medricka. A 25th-century spaceship is headed for the "green planet."

VOYAGE TO THE MOON (F?) Gaum 1906 D: Romeo Bosetti. Ref: Mitry II. SF Film.

VOYAGE TO THE MOON see TRIP TO THE MOON, A (1902)

VOYAGE TO THE PLANET OF PREHISTORIC WOMEN (U.S.-Russ) AI 1966 color (The GILL WOMAN. GILL-WOMEN OF VENUS) See also STORM PLANET. Narr: Peter Bogdanovich. D: Derek Thomas (aka Bogdanovich). The dumb dubbing and pointless narration make the movie satisfyingly terrible. ("I can't imagine anyone in their right minds would explore this planet" "Well, we're here and we're in our right minds.") A key work in Bogdanovich's career.

VUELVE EL DOCTOR SATAN see DR. SATAN AND BLACK MAGIC

VULCAN, SON OF JUPITER (I) Emb/Juno 1962 75m. (VULCANO FIGLIO DI GIOVE) D: Emmimo Salvi. SP: A. Molteni, G. Stafford. SpFX: R. Parapetti. with Gordon Mitchell, Bella Cortez, Furio Meniconi. Morlock-like monsters, lizard-man monsters, and nice music, unfortunately not for this picture. Lesser Salvi.

The VYNALEZ (U.S.-B-Canada) Para/Film Financial-Homeric-Iliad 1967 91m. (MANUTARA) SP, D, P: Lawrence Huntington. PH: Stephen Dade. Mus: Eric Spear. Art D: Duncan Sutherland. Ref: MFB'68:161. Boxo 2/6/67. COF 8:50. with Akim Tamiroff, Broderick Crawford, Robert Hutton, Diane Clare, Philip Friend, Patrick Holt. Schoolteacher sees huge bird with human head rise from open grave of Francis Real.

VYNALEZ ZKAKY   see FABULOUS WORLD OF JULES VERNE, The

WACHSFIGURENKABINETT   see WAXWORKS

The WACKY WORLD OF DR. MORGUS Sevin-Calongne 1962 Ref: New Orleans Times-Picayune 10/28/62. FJA. with Sid Noel, Thomas George, David Kleinberger, Jeanne Teslof, Dan Barton. Dr. Morgus invents an instant-people machine which turns people into sand and then returns them to normal. Bruno, ruler of Microvania, plans to smuggle 300 spies into the U.S. with the machine.

WAGES OF SIN (I) Vita 1908 16m. Ref: V&FI 9/12/08. Victim of cholera regains consciousness in the tomb.

The WAGES OF SIN Int'l 1916 (Beatrice Fairfax series #11) Ref: MPN 14:2869. with Grace Darling, Harry Fox, Betty Howe.

An invention, a "deadly infernal machine," kills a band of anarchists.

WAHA KE LOG (India) 1967 Songs: C. Ramachandra. Ref: Shankar's 4/2/67. with Tanuja. Chinese missiles over India thought to be spaceships. "Micro-transmitter."

WAILING ASTEROID, The (novel by M. Leinster) see TERROR-NAUTS, The

WAJAN, SON OF THE WITCH Mutual Motion Picture 1937 (U.S.-Balinese) 60m. D: Walter Spies. Story, P: Friedrich Dalsheim. P: also Victor Von Plessan. (BLACK MAGIC-Eng.) Ref: NYT 4/18/38. London Times: "The weird swaying of the trance-dancers and the visions of the priest have been brought out with great effect." An old witch is discovered to be the reincarnation of the Goddess of Death.

WAKING UP THE TOWN UA/Pickford 1925 70m. (END OF THE WORLD) D: James Cruze. PH: Arthur Edeson, Paul Perry. SP: James Cruze, Frank Condon. Ref: AFI. with C. McDowell, Alec B. Francis. FIR'60:506. Lee. with Jack Pickford, Norma Shearer, Herbert Pryor Dream: The destruction of the world.

The WALKING DEAD WB 1936 66m. D: Michael Curtiz. SP: Peter Milne, Lillie Hayward, Robert Adams, Ewart Adamson. PH: Hal Mohr. Reedited footage titled "Young Dr. Jekyll Meets Frankenstein" in ENSIGN PULVER. Ref: Clarens. FM 63:24. Pic: FM 56:11. with Boris Karloff, Marguerite Churchill, Ricardo Cortez, Barton MacLane, Warren Hull, Henry O'Neill, Ruth Robinson, Addison Richards, Eddie Acuff, Edmund Gwenn, Kenneth Harlan. A doctor brings an executed man back to life. Badly written, weakly directed.

WALKING NIGHTMARE, The see LIVING GHOST, The

WANGMAGWI see MONSTER WANGMAGWI

WANTED - A MUMMY (B) C&M 1910 9m. Ref: Bios 3/3/10. A man pretends to be a mummy.

WAR BETWEEN THE PLANETS see PLANET ON THE PROWL

The WAR GAME (B) BBC-TV/British Film Institute/Pathe Contemporary 1967 (1965) 50m. SP, D: Peter Watkins. PH: Peter Bartlett. Design: Tony Cornell, Anne Davey. Makeup: Lilias Munro. Nuclear warheads dropped on England. Confused and confusing. Switches tenses haphazardly. It's hard to tell whether some sequences are staged or spontaneous.

WAR-GODS OF THE DEEP (U.S.-B) AI 1965 color 85m. (WAR-LORDS OF THE DEEP. CITY UNDER THE SEA) D: Jacques Tourneur. SP: Charles Bennett, Louis Heyward. From Edgar Allan Poe's stories "City in the Sea" and "A Descent into the Maelstrom." PH: Stephen Dade. Mus: Stanley Black. SpFX: Frank George, Les Bowie. P: Daniel Haller. Ref: Bianco. MW 4:41. FanMo 4:15. Orpheus 3:29. COF 6:50. with Vincent Price, Tab Hunter, Susan Hart, David Tomlinson, John le Mesurier. Aquatic creature kidnaps girl, takes her to underwater city.

The WAR O'DREAMS Selig 1915 45m. D: E. A. Martin. Author: W. E. Wing. Ref: MPN 7/3/15. LC. SF Film. with Edwin Wallock, Lillian Hayward. Ether waves explode a bomb.

WAR OF INSECTS see GENOCIDE

WAR OF 1995, The see BEYOND THE TIME BARRIER

WAR OF THE COLOSSAL BEAST AI/Carmel 1958 68m. (The
   TERROR STRIKES-Eng. REVENGE OF THE COLOSSAL MAN)
   color scene D, P, SpFX: Bert I. Gordon. SP: George W. Yates.
   PH: Jack Marta. Mus: Albert Glasser. Ref: Imagen. FFacts.
   TVG. with Dean Parkin, Sally Fraser, Roger Pace, Russ Bender,
   Charles Stewart, George Becwar, Roy Gordon, June Jocelyn, Rico
   Alaniz. Authorities capture a deranged army officer who has
   grown to a height of 60 feet. Sequel to The AMAZING COLOSSAL
   MAN. Pretty dumb, but not as bad as some Gordons.
WAR OF THE GARGANTUAS (J) Maron/Benedict-Toho 1967 color/
   scope 88m. (FURANKENSHUTAIN NO KAIJU -SANDA TAI GAIRA
   or FURANKENSHUTAIN NO KAIJU - SANDA TAI GAILAH. DUEL
   OF THE GARGANTUAS. The FRANKENSTEIN BROTHERS:
   planned sequel. ADVENTURE OF GARGANTUAS. FRANKENSTEIN
   -ZWEIKAMPF DER GIGANTEN-G.) D: Inoshiro Honda. SP: Honda,
   K. Mabuchi. PH:Hajime Koizumi. SpFX: Eiji Tsuburaya. Ref:
   J Films'68. Pic: FM 46:2. with Kumi Mizuno, Kenji Sahara,
   Russ Tamblyn, Kipp Hamilton, Jun Tazaki.
WAR OF THE MONSTERS see GAMERA VS. BARUGON
WAR OF THE PLANETS see DEADLY DIAPHANOIDS, The /THIS
   ISLAND EARTH
WAR OF THE PRIMAL TRIBES see PRIMITIVE MAN, The
WAR OF THE SATELLITES AA 1958 66m. D, P: Roger Corman.
   SP: Lawrence Goldman. Story: Irving Block, Jack Rabin. PH:
   Floyd Crosby. Mus: Walter Greene. Art D: Daniel Haller. Ref:
   Clarens. SM 8:8. with Richard Miller, Susan Cabot, Richard
   Devon, Eric Sinclair, Robert Shayne, Jay Sayer, Mitzi McCall,
   Beech Dickerson. Aliens control a scientist's mind. One of Cor-
   man's worst.
WAR OF THE WORLDS Para 1953 Technicolor 85m. D: Byron
   Haskin. SP: Barre Lyndon. From the novel by H. G. Wells.
   PH: George Barnes. Mus: Leith Stevens. Art D: Hal Pereira,
   Albert Nozaki. SpFX: Gordon Jennings, Wallace Kelley, Paul
   Lerpae, Ivyl Burts, Jan Donela, Irmin Roberts. P: George
   Pal. Ref: FM 13:7.14:40. FDY. Pic: SM 2:23.4:28. with Gene
   Barry, Ann Robinson, Henry Brandon, Les Tremayne, Robert
   Cornthwaite, Jack Kruschen, William Phipps, Lewis Martin,
   Sandro Giglio. Martians invade earth. Good but repetitious special
   effects. The rest is pretty bad.
WAR OF THE ZOMBIES (I) AI/Galatea 1963 ('65-U.S.) Eastman-
   color/Totalscope 105m. (ROMA CONTRO ROMA. NIGHT STAR,
   GODDESS OF ELECTRA-TV) D, Ed: Giuseppe Vari. SP: Piero
   Pieretti, M. Sartarelli. PH: Gabor Pogany. Mus: Roberto
   Nicolosi. Art D: G. Giovannini. SpFX: Ugo Amadoro. Ref: MFB
   '65:94. Pic: FM 36:8. COF 7:53. with John Drew Barrymore,
   Susi Andersen, Ettore Manni, Philippe Hersent. An army of
   zombies threatens to overthrow ancient Rome. -TVG.
WARLORD OF CRETE, The see MINOTAUR, The (1960)
WARLORDS OF THE DEEP see WAR-GODS OF THE DEEP
The WARNING Triumph (Equitable) 1915 60m. D: Edmund Lawrence.
   Ref: Clarens. MPW 26:1847. MPN 12/11/15. with Henry Kolker,
   Lily Leslie, Christine Mayo. Several "allegorical scenes" show
   "the suffering of the damned."

WARNING FROM SPACE (J) Daiei 1956 90m. (UCHUJIN TOKYO NI
ARAWARU. The MYSTERIOUS SATELLITE. The COSMIC MAN
APPEARS IN TOKYO. SPACE MEN APPEAR IN TOKYO) D:
Koji Shima. SP: Hideo Oguni. From a novel by G. Nakajima.
PH: K. Watanabe. Ref: MFB'58:64. with Keizo Kawasaki, Toyomi
Karita, Shozo Nanbu. People of "Planet R" try to save world
from huge earthbound meteor. Very silly. Dubbed dialogue padded
by all sorts of "yes," "sorry," and "all right" s.
WARNING SHADOWS (G) Film Arts/Deutsche Film Union 1922
('28-U.S.) 70m. (SCHATTEN, EINE NACHTLICHE HALLUZINA-
TION. MONSTER OF THE SHADOWS) D: Arthur Robison. SP:
Rudolf Schneider. PH:Fritz Arno Wagner. Art D: Albin Gray. Ref:
SilentFF. Pic: Pict Hist Cinema. with Fritz Kortner, Fritz Rasp,
Ruth Weyher. People go through actions under shadow-theatre
manipulator's hypnotic spell.
The WARNING SIGNAL Ellbee 1926 60m. D: Charles Hunt. SP:
A. B. Barringer. PH: William Tuers. Ref: AFI. with Gladys
Hulette, Kent Mead, Joseph Girard, Clarence Burton. "Radio
device" invention.
WARWICK CASTLE (B) 1926 short (HAUNTED CASTLE series) D:
Fred Paul. Ref: Brit Cinema. V 2/24/26.
The WASP WOMAN Filmgroup 1959 (The BEE GIRL. INSECT
WOMAN) D, P: Roger Corman. SP: Leo Gordon. Mus: Fred
Katz. Art D: Daniel Haller. Ref: FFacts. with Susan Cabot, Fred
Eisley, Ray Gordon, Bruno ve Sota, Barboura Morris, Frank
Gerstle, Michael Mark, William Roerick. Ref: Orpheus 3:27, 36.
4:38. Woman's beauty treatments include use of serum of wasp
enzymes. Terrible. The attempts at suspense are pretty silly,
though a few scenes in a cosmetics firm have an air of credibility
about them, and Susan Cabot is good. One of Roger's worst.
WASTED LIVES Second Nat'l 1923 60m. D: Clarence Geldert.
Titles: William B. Laub. Ref: AFI. with Richard Wayne, Catherine
Murphy, Winter Hall, Lillian Leighton, Margaret Loomis.
"Vibrameter" invention saves woman's life.
The WATCHMAKER'S INVENTION (F) Gaum 1909 7m. Ref: Bios
10/28/09. Invention attached to people or objects makes them
perform eccentric movements.
WATER CYBORGS (J) Toei-Ram 1966 (KAITEI DAISENSO) D: Hajime
Sato. Ref: COF 9:45. Unij Bltn. with Shinichi Chiba, Franz
Gruber, Peggy Neal.
WATER OF LIFE, The (by the Bros. Grimm) see MAGIC FOUNTAIN,
The
WATER WITCH, The (by D. Duncan) see THING THAT COULDN'T
DIE, The
WAVE OF SPOOKS (F) Pathe 1908 Ref: F Index 11/21/08. "Infernal
regions," "Satanic Majesty," "spooks transformed into skeletons."
WAX MUSEUM see MYSTERY OF THE WAX MUSEUM
WAXWORKS (G) Neptun 1924 70m. (WACHSFIGURENKABINETT.
THREE WAX MEN) D: Paul Leni. SP: Henrik Galeen. PH:
Helmar Lerski. Art D: Leni, Ernst Stern, Alfred Jünge. Ref:
SilentFF. FM 23:25. Pic: Bianco 7-8/68:88g. with Emil Jannings,
Conrad Veidt, Werner Krauss, Wilhelm Dieterle, Olga von
Balieff, John Gottowt. Three stories: Springheeled Jack (aka Jack

the Ripper), Ivan the Terrible, Haroun al Raschid.
WAXWORKS see HOUSE OF WAX/HOUSE THAT DRIPPED BLOOD,
  The/MYSTERY OF THE WAX MUSEUM
WAY...WAY OUT Fox/Coldwater-Jerry Lewis 1966 color/scope
  101m. D: Gordon Douglas. SP: William Bowers, Laslo Vadnay.
  PH: William H. Clothier. Mus sc & d: Lalo Schifrin. Art D:
  Jack Martin Smith, Hilyard Brown. SpPhFX: L. B. Abbott,
  Emil Kosa, Jr. Narr: Col. John Powers. 2nd Unit D: Ray
  Kellogg. Scenes from FRANKENSTEIN (1931). Ref: FFacts.
  COF 12:7. PM. with Lewis, Connie Stevens, Robert Morley,
  Dick Shawn, Brian Keith, Anita Ekberg, Dennis Weaver, Alex
  d'Arcy, Linda Harrison, Howard Morris, Sig Ruman, James
  Brolin, Milton Frome. Man and wife team of astronauts sent
  to U.S. weather station on moon in 1994. Miserable. Lewis
  has one or two moments, but he can't seem to settle on a new
  character, though maybe it's a good thing since the ones he has
  dallied with lately have been pretty unpleasant and unfunny.
WEAK-KNEED FROM FEAR OF GHOST-CAT (J) Toei 1954
  (KAIBYO KOSHINUKE DAISODO) D: Torajiro Saito. Ref: Unij
  Bltn 31. with Achako Hanabishi, Michiko Hoshi. Ghost story.
WEAPONS OF DESTRUCTION see FABULOUS WORLD OF JULES
  VERNE, The
WEAPONS OF VENGEANCE (I-F) Cinecompar/CFdF 1963 Eastman-
  color/Euroscope 101m. (I DIAVOLI DI SPARTIVENTO-I. The
  FIGHTING LEGIONS-Eng. ARMS OF THE AVENGER. CURSE
  OF THE HAUNTED FOREST) D: Leopoldo Savono. PH: Pier
  Ludovico. Mus: F. De Masi. Ref: MFB'69:57. with John Barry-
  more, Jr., Giacomo Rossi Stuart, Scilla Gabel, Jany Clair,
  Michel Lemoine. "Haunted forest," "flying machine."
WEARY DEATH, The see DESTINY (1921)
WEDDED BENEATH THE WAVES (F) Gaum 1910 8m. Ref: Bios
  12/1/10. Giant fish swallows man and girl.
WEDDING FEAST AND GHOSTS (I) Cines c1908 7m. Ref:
  SilentFF. "Ghosts" chase newlyweds.
WEEKEND (F) Athos/Copernic/Ascot Cineraid 1967 Eastmancolor
  105m. (Le WEEKEND) SP, D: Jean-Luc Godard. PH: Raoul
  Coutard. Mus: Antoine Duhamel. Ed: Agnès Guillemot. with
  Mireille Darc, Jean Yanne, Jean-Pierre Kalfon, Valerie La-
  grange, Paul Gegauff, Jean Eustache, Jean-Pierre Leaud, Anne
  Wiazemsky. Hellish vision of materialistic society confronted by
  anarchy, cannibalism, revolution. Episodic, but some of the
  episodes are very powerful, and the film seems more like a
  film than, like other recent Godards, an experiment. Brief but
  ingenious homage ("Arizona Jules") to Renoir's great CRIME OF
  MR. LANGE and Truffaut's JULES AND JIM may be misplaced,
  but it doesn't go unappreciated.
WEEKEND AT THRACKLEY, A see HOT ICE
WEIRD DEATH TRAP AT UTSUNOMIYA (J) Shintoho 1956 (KAII
  UTSUNOMIYA TSURITENJO) D: Nobuo Nakagawa. Ref: Unij
  Bltn 31. with Ryuzaburo Ogasawara, Akemi Tsukushi. Ghost
  story.
WEIRD NEMESIS Victor 1915 30m. SP, D: Jacques Jaccard. Ref:
  MPW'15:554. MPN 7/24/15. with Alan Forrest. Hypnosis used

to frighten.

WEIRD TALES see KWAIDAN

WEIRD WOMAN Univ 1944 64m. (Inner Sanctum series) D:
Reginald LeBorg. Story,SP: Brenda Weisberg, Scott Darling.
From the novel "Conjure Wife" by Fritz Leiber, Jr. PH: Virgil
Miller. Mus: Paul Sawtell. Art D: John B. Goodman, Richard
Riedel. SpPH: John P. Fulton. Ref: Clarens. COF 2: 46. 7: 38.
ModM 1: 25. Pic: HM 5: 43. with Lon Chaney, Jr. , Anne Gwynne,
Evelyn Ankers, Elizabeth Russell, Ralph Morgan , Lois Collier,
Elisabeth Risdon, Kay Harding, Harry Hayden. Bride raised by
superstitious natives practices witchcraft to protect her professor
husband. Don't fall out of your chair when you hear stray bits
of snappy dialogue coming from an Inner Sanctum mystery. You'll
get your share of not-so-snappy lines too. (Coed's intellectual
crush on Prof. Chaney: "(sigh) He's so brilliant.") The horror is
actually fairly effective for a stretch in the middle, but everyone
is acting silly by the end, which should have come much sooner.

WELL, GRANDMA'S DEAD see OH, GRANDMOTHER'S DEAD!

WELT IST MEIN, Die! see INVISIBLE MAN GOES THROUGH THE
CITY, An

The WEREWOLF Bison 1913 Ref: Bios 3/26/14. White girl's
spirit, according to legend, lures hunters to destruction.

The WEREWOLF (F) 1923 (Le LOUP-GAROU) Ref: DDC II: 479.
FJA. with Jean Marau, Madeleine Guitty. A priest curses a
murderer, who becomes a werewolf.

The WEREWOLF (G) 1932 D: Friedrich Feher. Ref: The Film Index.
FIR'61: 392. From the novel "Der Schwarze Mann" by Alfred
Machard. with Magda Sonja, Vladimir Sokolov. "Werewolf."

The WEREWOLF Col/Clover 1956 83m. D: Fred F. Sears. SP:
Robert E. Kent, James B. Gordon. PH: Edwin Linden. Mus D:
Mischa Bakaleinikoff. Art D: Paul Palmentola. P: Sam Katzman.
Ref: FDY. TVG. with Steven Ritch, Joyce Holden, Don Megowan,
Eleanor Tanin, Kim Charney, Harry Lauter, George M. Lynn,
Don C. Harvey, Marjorie Stapp. Serum turns victim of auto acci-
dent into a werewolf. A must for Katzman-dud completists.

WEREWOLF IN A GIRLS' DORMITORY (I-Austrian) MGM/Royal
1961 82m. (LYCANTHROPUS-I. BEI VOLLMOND MORD-Aus.
Le MONSTRE AU FILLES or Le LYCANTHROPE-F. DEATH IN
THE FULL MOON. I MARRIED A WEREWOLF-Eng. MONSTER
AMONG THE GIRLS. The GHOUL IN SCHOOL. GHOUL IN A
GIRLS' DORMITORY) D: Paolo Huesch (aka Richard Benson).
SP: Ernesto Gastaldi (aka Julian Berry). PH: George Patrick.
Mus: F. Berman. Art D: Peter Travers. Ref: MFB'64: 107.
TVFFSB. S&S'68: 182. DDC III: 39,118. FM 37: 71. PM. with
Barbara Lass, Carl Schell, Maurice Marsac, Curt Lowens,
Maureen O'Connor, Alan Collins. Lycanthrope loose around girls'
corrective school. Mainly silly, with an acceptable shock sequence
or two.

WEREWOLF OF LONDON Univ 1935 75m. (UNHOLY HOUR-
Canada) D: Stuart Walker. SP: John Colton. Story: Robert Harris,
Harvey Gates. PH: Charles Stumar. Ref: Academy. V 5/15/35.
with Henry Hull, Warner Oland, Valerie Hobson, Spring Byington, Lester Matthews, Zeffie Tilbury, Ethel Griffies, J. M.

Kerrigan, Charlotte Granville, Lawrence Grant, Reginald Barlow, Clark Williams, Egon Brecher, Harry Stubbs, Tempe Piggott, David Thursby, Edwin Parker. A botanist travelling in Tibet encounters a werewolf. Some good scenes and some good uses of sound effects. Poor staging makes other scenes unintentionally funny.

WEREWOLF OF PARIS, The (novel by G. Endore) see CURSE OF THE WEREWOLF

WEREWOLF'S SHADOW (G-Sp) Atlas Int'l/Plata 1970 color/scope?/ Hi Fi (La NOCHE DE WALPURGIS) D: Leon Klimovski (or Klimowsky). Ref: M/TVM'71. V 5/12/71. with Gaby Fuchs, Paul Naschy, Barbara Capell, Patty Shepard, Yelena Samarina. Vampire.

WEREWOLVES ON WHEELS Fanfare 1971   85m. DeLuxecolor D: Michel Levesque. SP: David Kaufman, Levesque. PH: Isidore Mankofsky. Mus: Don Gere. Art D: Allen Jones. Ref: Boxo 10/4/71:10. V 10/13/71. with Stephen Oliver, Severn Darden, D. J. Anderson, Billy Gray, Barry McGuire. Werewolves, devil cult. Poor. Slow motion makes little ballets of the monsters' attacks, and if there's anything that isn't frightening, it's a dancing werewolf. The only thing that keeps the plot going is a queasy mystic who forebodes disaster every five minutes. Gray has a funny car-salesman shtick.

WEST OF ZANZIBAR MGM 1928 80m. silent and sound-effects prints. Ed: Harry Reynolds. D: Tod Browning. SP: Elliot Clawson, Waldemar Young. Titles: Joe Farnham. PH: Percy Hilburn. Art D: Cedric Gibbons. Remake: KONGO. Ref: AFI. FD 1/6/29. NYT 12/31/28. PM: "It will make you shudder." Pic: FM 8:28. with Lon Chaney ("White Voodoo"), Lionel Barrymore, Warner Baxter, Mary Nolan. From a play by K. Gordon and C. DeVonde. Skeleton in coffin turns into woman. Stage magician, superstitions. Chaney, terrific; gives life to plot.

WHAT! (I-F) Vox/Leone/Titanus/Francinor-PIP 1963 Technicolor D: Mario Bava (aka John M. Old). (La FRUSTA E IL CORPO-I. NIGHT IS THE PHANTOM-Eng. The WHIP AND THE BODY) SP: Ernesto Gastaldi (aka Julian Berry), R. Hugo, Martin Hardy. PH: Ubaldo Terzano. Art D: Ottavio Scotti. Ref: Clarens. Shriek 1:58. COF 12:30. with Daliah Lavi, Christopher Lee, Tony Kendall, Harriet White, Isli Oberon, Jacques Herlin. Castle seems to be haunted by ghost.

WHAT A CARVE UP! see NO PLACE LIKE HOMICIDE

WHAT A WHOPPER! (B) Viscount/Regal 1962 D: Gilbert Gunn. SP: Terry Nation. PH: Reg Wyer. Ref: British Films 1962. DDC II:480. III:223. with Carole Lesley, Adam Faith, Sidney James, Terence Longden, Marie France, Charles Hawtrey, Spike Milligan. Writer constructing his own "Loch Ness Monster" meets the real one.

WHAT AN EYE Univ 1924 22m. SP,D: Edward L. Luddy. Ref: MPN 30:2001. Lee. with Buddy Messinger. Creature with huge eye haunts neighborhood. Haunted house.

WHAT EVER HAPPENED TO AUNT ALICE Cinerama/Palomar 1969 Metrocolor 100m. D: Lee H. Katzin. SP: Theodore Apstein, from the novel "Forbidden Garden" by Ursula Curtiss. PH:

Joseph Biroc. Mus: Gerald Fried. Art D: William Glasgow. P:
Robert Aldrich. Ref: Film Bltn 7/7/69: ad: "Horror." LA
Times, FD: "Horror." HR 7/21/69. with Geraldine Page, Ruth
Gordon, Rosemary Forsyth, Robert Fuller, Mildred Dunnock,
Peter Bonerz, Claire Kelly. Widow hires women for companions,
"invests" their life savings for them, and kills them.
WHAT EVER HAPPENED TO BABY JANE? WB-7A 1962 132m.
   D,P: Robert Aldrich. SP: Lukas Heller, from the novel by
   Henry Farrell. Mus: Frank DeVol. Art D: William Glasgow.
   PH: Ernest Haller. Ref: Clarens. COF 3:4. PM. with
   Bette Davis, Joan Crawford, Victor Buono, Anna Lee, Dave
   Willock. Ex-child-star Baby Jane Hudson and her sister Blanche
   live in seclusion in an old mansion. Pretty good fun and Gothic
   games. "See if necessary"-Eric Rohmer.
WHAT EVER HAPPENED TO COUSIN CHARLOTTE? see HUSH,
   HUSH, SWEET CHARLOTTE
WHAT IT WILL BE (F) Lux 1910 6m. Ref: SilentFF. Doctor mixes
   liquids and powders to create a baby.
WHAT THE GODS DECREE (F) Eclair 1913 75m. Ref: MPW 18:
   924. with Charles Krauss, Josette Andriot. Hypnotism, statue
   of Kali that moves.
WHAT'S THE MATTER WITH HELEN? UA/Filmways-Raymax
   1971 DeLuxe color 101m. D: Curtis Harrington. SP: Henry Far-
   rell. PH: Lucien Ballard. Mus: David Raksin. Art D: Eugene
   Lourie. P: George Edwards. Ref: V 6/9/71. with Debbie
   Reynolds, Shelley Winters, Dennis Weaver, Agnes Moorehead,
   Logan Ramsey. "Shocker" à la Farrell's WHAT EVER HAP-
   PENED TO BABY JANE?
WHEEL OF FIRE see PYRO
WHEN DINOSAURS RULED THE EARTH (B) WB/Hammer 1970
   (1969) Technicolor 100m. SP,D: Val Guest. Screen treatment:
   J. B. Ballard. PH: Dick Bush. Mus: Mario Nascimbene. Art
   D: John Blezard. SpFX: Allan Bryce, Roger Dicken, Brian John-
   cock. Ref: MFB. with Victoria Vetri, Robin Hawdon, Magda
   Konopka. In prehistoric times the Rock tribe's ritual sacrifice
   to the sun is disrupted by cyclonic winds. Cute tricks with an
   animated baby dinosaur--a little too cute. But the main problem
   is too much cave men, too little dinosaurs. One dull chase goes
   on for almost a half hour.
WHEN JERRY COMES HOME (play by R. Brian) see ITCHING
   PALMS
WHEN QUACKEL DID HYDE Aywon 1920 From "The Strange
   Case of Dr. Jekyll and Mr. Hyde" by Robert Louis Stevenson.
   Ref: FM 34:55: comedy.
WHEN SOUL MEETS SOUL Ess 1912 15m. Ref: The Film Index.
   The mummy of an Egyptian princess is brought into the study of
   her reincarnated lover.
WHEN SOULS ARE TRIED Lubin 1915 15m. SP,D: Romaine
   Fielding. Ref: MPN 8/21/15. LC. with Fielding, Vinnie Burns,
   Jack Lawton. Inventor's "new oxygen helmet" saves man's life.
WHEN SPIRITS WALK Frontier 1914 17m. Ref: Bios 3/19/14.
   Haunted house, somnambulist cook.
WHEN THE DEVIL COMMANDS Col 1941 65m. (The DEVIL SAID

NO) D: Edward Dmytryk. SP: Robert D. Andrews, Milton Gunzburg, from the novel "The Edge of Running Water" or "The Unquiet Corpse" by William Sloane. PH: Allen G. Siegler. Ref: Clarens. FM 2:34. Pic: FM 46:54. with Boris Karloff, Amanda Duff, Anne Revere, Richard Fiske, Dorothy Adams, Walter Baldwin, Kenneth MacDonald. With a brain-wave machine Dr. Julian Blair tries to communicate with his dead wife. Mediocre at best.

WHEN THE MIND SLEEPS Kalem 1915 45m. Ref: Lee. MPW 24: 1786. with Myrtle Tannehill. Drug cures girl of mental illness.

WHEN THE MUMMY CRIED FOR HELP Nestor (Univ) 1915 Ref: MPN 1/16/15. with Lee Moran, Eddie Lyons. Man masquerades as mummy.

WHEN THE SPIRITS MOVED Nestor (Univ) 1915 15m. SP,D: Al Christie. Ref: LC. MPW 24:2159. MPN 7/3/15. with Lee Moran, Eddie Lyons, Victoria Forde. Man beset by "spirits."

WHEN WERE YOU BORN? WB 1938 65m. D: William McGann. SP: Anthony Coldeway. Story: Manley Hall. PH: L. W. O'Connell. Ref: Hollywood Spectator 6/25/38. with Margaret Lindsay, Anna May Wong, Lola Lane, Charles Wilson, James Stephenson, Jeffrey Lynn, Leonard Mudie, Frank Jaquet, Olin Howland, Maurice Cass. A man whose horoscope said he had only two days to live is murdered.

WHEN WOMEN HAD TAILS (I) Euro Int'l/Clesi 1970 color 110m. (QUANDO LE DONNE AVEVANO LA CODA) SP,D: Pasquale Festa Campanile. SP: also Lina Wertmuller, O. Jemma. M. Costa. PH: Franco Di Giacomo. Mus: Ennio Morricone. Art D: Enrico Yob. Ref: V 12/23/70. with Giuliano Gemma, Senta Berger, Frank Wolff, Francesco Mule. Prehistoric man's first encounter with prehistoric woman.

WHEN WORLDS COLLIDE Para 1951 Technicolor 81m. D: Rudolph Mate. SP: Sydney Boehm. From "When Worlds Collide" and "After Worlds Collide" by Edwin Balmer and Philip Wylie. PH: John F. Seitz. Mus: Leith Stevens. Art D: Hal Pereira, Albert Nozaki. Ref: Clarens. FM 13:7.14:40. P: George Pal. with Richard Derr, Barbara Rush, Peter Hanson, Judith Ames, John Hoyt, Mary Murphy, Laura Elliot(t), Frank Cady, Hayden Ro(a)rke. Planet on collision course with earth. Very juvenile s-f, but as such fairly efficient.

WHERE THE BULLETS FLY (B) Golden Era/Puck 1966 color 90m. D: John Gilling. SP: Michael Pittock. PH: David Holmes. Ref: MFB'66:188. with Tom Adams, Sidney James, Dawn Addams, Michael Ripper, Ronald Leigh-Hunt, Suzan Farmer, Garry Marsh, John Watson. "Spurium Apparatus" powers plane from nuclear unit. Sequel to The SECOND BEST SECRET AGENT IN THE WHOLE WIDE WORLD.

WHERE THE ELEPHANT STOOD see HAUNTED HOUSE (1957)

WHERE THE TRUTH LIES see WITCHCRAFT (1961)

WHIFFLE'S NIGHTMARE (F) CGPC/Pathe 1914 8m. Ref: MPW 14:696. "Haunted" house.

WHILE I LIVE (B) Dryhurst 1948 85m. (DREAM OF OLWEN) SP,D: John Harlow. From the play "This Game Garden" by Robert Bell. PH: F. A. Young. Ref: MFB'48:4. S&S'50:301. with Sonia Dresdel, Clifford Evans, Carol Raye, Patricia Burke,

Tom Walls. "Reincarnation": Servant insists girl's spirit is still present in house.
WHILE JOHN BOLT SLEPT   Edison 1914 Ref: The Film Index. Spirit wanders in "evil regions."
WHILE LONDON SLEEPS WB 1926 70m. D: H. P. Bretherton or Walter Morosco. SP: Morosco. PH: Frank Kesson. Ref: AFI. with Rin-Tin-Tin, Helene Costello, Walter Merrill, John Patrick, Carl Stockdale, De Witt Jennings, George Kotsonaros (The Monk), Otto Matieson. A criminal leader commands a murderous "man-beast monster."
WHILE PARIS SLEEPS Para/Hodkinson 1923 (1920) D: Maurice Tourneur. From "The Glory of Love" by "Pan" (aka Leslie Beresford). PH: René Guissart. Ref: Clarens. FM 8:25. with Lon Chaney, Mildred Manning, Jack Gilbert, J. Farrell Mac-Donald. Waxworks proprietor bent on revenging himself against young man by adding him to his exhibit.
WHIP AND THE BODY, The see WHAT!
The WHIRLING DISK Gold Seal (Univ) 1915 25m. SP: H. G. Stafford. Ref: MPW 4/17/15. MPN 4/24/15. Doctor employs disk to hypnotize girl into sensing his presence wherever she goes.
WHIRLING THE WORLDS see IMPOSSIBLE VOYAGE, The
WHISPERING DEAD BEAUTY (J) Daiei 1963 scope 83m. (SASA-YAKU SHIBIJIN) D: Sadao Murayama. SP: Kazuo Mejiro. PH: Nobuo Munekawa. Ref: UFQ. with Keizo Kawasaki, Masayo Banri, Yuko Hamada. Woman returns from the dead.
WHISPERING GHOSTS Fox 1942 57m. D: Alfred Werker. SP: Lou Breslow. Story: Philip MacDonald. PH: Lucien Ballard. Mus D: Emil Newman. Art D: Richard Day, Lewis Creber. Ref: FDY. Pic: ModM 1:30-1. MadM 9:16. with Milton Berle, Brenda Joyce, John Carradine, Arthur Hohl, Willie Best, Grady Sutton, Milton Parsons, Abner Biberman, Rene Riano, Charles Halton. Private eye in "haunted" house.
The WHISPERING SHADOW Mascot 1933 serial 12 episodes D: Colbert Clark, Albert Herman. SP: also G. Morgan, W. Gittens, H.Bimberg(?), B. Sarecky,N. S. Hall. PH: E. Miller, V. Scheurick. Ref: RVB. D. Glut. with Bela Lugosi, Henry B. Walthall, Karl Dane, Viva Tattersall, Robert Warwick, Roy D'Arcy, George Lewis, Lloyd Whitlock, Tom London, Lafe McKee, Jack Perrin. "Shadow" that projects image of himself, remote-control explosive, laboratory, wax museum. Lots of useless flashbacks, dumb lines ("That was a clever trick of yours"), and badly-staged fist fights. The hero has an appealing way of making a fool of himself.
WHISPERING SHADOWS Peacock-States Rights/Peerless 1922 72m. D: E. Chautard. Story: Walter Hackett. PH: Jacques Bizeul. Art D: Titles: William B. Loeb, Harry Chandlee. Ref: MPN '22:1767. with Lucy Cotton, Charles A. Stevenson, Robert Barrat, Mrs. Celestine Saunders (the medium), Philip Merivale. Girl warned by "unseen forces" at seance that someone is trying to harm her sweetheart.
The WHISPERING SKULL PRC 1944 52m. D: Elmer Clifton. SP: Harry Fraser. PH: Edward Kull. Mus: Lee Zahler. Ref: MFB '51:268. FDY. with Tex Ritter, Dave O'Brien, I. Stanford

Jolley, Guy Wilkerson, Henry Hall, Edward Cassidy. Masked rider tries to scare ranchers into selling land.

WHISPERING WIRES FOX 1926 75m. D: Albert Ray. SP: L. G. Rigby, from a play by Kate L. McLaurin and a story by Henry Leverage. Titles: William Conselman. PH: George Schneiderman. Ref: AFI. FIR'68:160. Photoplay 12/26: "You'll shiver and shake." with Anita Stewart, Edmund Burns, Mack Swain, Charles Sellon, Heinie Conklin, Maym(e) Kelso, Frank Campeau, Arthur Housman, Scott Welsh. Whispering voice on phone "foretells" two deaths. House with trap doors and secret passages.

WHISTLER, The see POWER OF THE WHISTLER/VOICE OF THE WHISTLER

WHISTLING IN DIXIE MGM 1942 73m. D: S. Sylvan Simon. SP: Nat Perrin. Follow-up to WHISTLING IN THE DARK; PH: Clyde De Vinna. Mus sc: Lennie Hayton. Art D: Cedric Gibbons. Add'l Dial: Wilkie Mahoney. Ref: V 10/28/42. NYT 12/31/42: Gloomy old Southern mansion. Showmen's 10/31/42: "Riot of ghosts and guffaws." with Red Skelton, Ann Rutherford, George Bancroft, Guy Kibbee, Diana Lewis, "Rags" Ragland, Lucien Littlefield, Pierre Watkin, Emmett Vogan, Peter Whitney, Hobart Cavanaugh.

WHISTLING IN THE DARK MGM 1941 77m. D: S. Sylvan Simon. SP: Robert MacGunigle, Harry Clork, Albert Mannheimer. From the play by E. C. Carpenter and Lawrence Gross. See also SCARED. Follow-up: WHISTLING IN DIXIE; WHISTLING IN BROOKLYN, straight mystery. PH: Sidney Wagner. Art D: Cedric Gibbons. Ref: V 7/29/41: Cult of "moon worshippers." Boxo 8/2/41: "Comedy and chills." with Red Skelton, Conrad Veidt, Ann Rutherford, Virginia Grey, "Rags" Ragland, Henry O'Neill, Eve Arden, Don Douglas, Don Costello, William Tannen, Reed Hadley, Lloyd Corrigan, George Carleton.

WHITE CARPET (by E. Wallace) see MAD EXECUTIONERS, The

WHITE CAT, The (by G. Burgess) see UNTAMEABLE, The

The WHITE FAN (J) Toei 1956 85m. (HAKUSEN-MIDARE KURO-KAMI Ref: FEFN 3/23/56. with C. Azuma, M. Bando, Y. Tashiro, Y. Hasegawa. "Ghost story": Warrior commits murder for love of court maid.

WHITE GHOST, The see GHOST OF THE WHITE LADY, The

The WHITE MOOR (Rumanian) Romfilm 1964 color 89m. SP,D: Ion Popescu Gopo. PH: Grigore Ionescu. Ref: V 7/21/65. with Florin Piersis, C. C. Codrescu. Witch turns into beautiful woman.

The WHITE PEARL Para/Famous Players 1915 Ref: NYT 10/11/15. with Marie Doro. Curse on pearl stolen from idol.

WHITE PONGO PRC 1945 74m. (CONGO PONGO. ADVENTURE UNLIMITED-Eng. La SFIDA DE KING KONG-I. BLOND GORIL-LA) D: Sam Newfield. SP: Raymond L. Shrock. PH: Jack Greenhalgh. Mus D: Leo Erdody. Art D: Edward C. Jewell. P: Sigmund Neufeld. Ref: MFB'48:93. FM 28:81. MPH. TVG. with Maris Wrixon, Richard Fraser, Lionel Royce, Al Eben, Gordon Richard, Milton Kibbee, Egon Brecher. White ape believed to be missing link kills man.

The WHITE REINDEER (Finnish) Seli Film 1952 75m. (VALKOINEN

PEURA) D, PH: Erik Blomberg. Mus: Eimar Englund. Ref:
V 5/13/53. DDC II: 311. with Mirjami Kuosmanen. Woman turns
into bewitched white reindeer of legend and attacks hunters. Okay
shock scenes highlight dull story.
WHITE SICKNESS (by K. Capek) see SKELETON ON HORSEBACK
The WHITE SPECTRE General 1914 40m. Ref: Bios 5/14/14.
"Spectre" part of scheme to upset operations of blackmailing
gang.
The WHITE WOLF Nestor (Univ) 1914 Ref: MPW 21:1818. Lee.
Wolf in trap turns into tribe's medicine man.
WHITE ZOMBIE UA/Amusement Securities Corp. 1932 73m. D:
Victor Halperin. SP: Garnett Weston. Inspired by the book
"The Magic Island" by William Seabrook. PH: Arthur Martinelli.
Mus: Abe Meyer. Ass't D: William Cody. Ed: Howard Mc-
Ler(n)on. Art & Technical credits: Ralph Berger, Jack Pierce.
P: Edward Halperin. Sequence in DR. TERROR'S HOUSE OF
HORRORS (1943). Ref: RVB. COF 8:22.15:24. FM 60:7. Pic:
FM 16:30.38:16. with Bela Lugosi, Madge Bellamy, John Har-
ron, Joseph Cawthorn, Robert Frazer, Clarence Muse, Brandon
Hurst, George Burr M(a)cAnnan, Claude Morgan, John Printz,
Annette Stone. A sugar mill on an island is run by zombies.
Lugosi has one of his finest scenes whittling away and chatting
casually with a paralyzed victim. An independently-made film,
this has a look very different from the studio-made horror movies
of the era, which is one reason it seems fresher today than most
of them. There are plenty of things (best not gone into) wrong
with the production too.
WHITHER MANKIND see THINGS TO COME
WHO GOES THERE? (story by J. W. Campbell, Jr.) see THING,
The
WHO IS GUILTY? (India-Hindi) Bimal Roy Productions 1958 136m.
(APRADHI KAUN?) D: Asit Sen. Ref: FEFN 2/21/58. with
Mala Sinha, Abhi Bhattacharjee, Jagirdar, Kammo. "Ghost com-
plicates" murder mystery.
WHO IS "NUMBER ONE"? Para 1917 serial 15 episodes D: Wil-
liam Bertram. Ref: MPN 16:3133. CNW. with Katherine Clif-
ford, Cullen Landis. Spell, ghostly phenomena, super-sub-
marine.
WHO KILLED AUNT MAGGIE? Rep 1940 70m. D: Arthur Lubin.
SP: Stuart Palmer. Add'l Dial: Hal Fimberg, Frank Gill, Jr.
From a novel by Medora Field. PH: Reggie Lanning. Mus D: Cy
Feuer. Art D: John Victor McKay. Ref: FD 11/1/40. V 10/25/40.
with John Hubbard, Wendy Barrie, Edgar Kennedy, Elizabeth Pat-
terson, Onslow Stevens, Walter Abel, Mona Barrie, Willie Best,
Milton Parsons, Tom Dugan, Joyce Compton. Old Southern man-
sion, disappearing body, tombstone salesman, "eerie" black cat,
secret room, and three murders.
WHO KILLED 'DOC' ROBBIN? UA-Hal Roach 1948 55m. (SINISTER
HOUSE-Eng.) D: Bernard Carr. SP: Dorothy Reid, Maurice
Geraghty. PH: John Boyle. Mus D: Heinz Roemheld. Art D:
Jerome Pycha, Jr. Sets: William Stevens. SpFX: Roy W. Seawright, Makeup: Burris Grimwood. Ref: MFB'51:378. HR. V.
with Virginia Grey, Don Castle, George Zucco, Whitford Kane,

Claire DuBrey, Grant Mitchell, Donald King. "Atomic firing
chamber," "haunted" house, sliding panels, gorilla, underground
tunnels, "ghosts."
WHO KILLED JESSIE? (Cz) Czech State Film 1965 80m. (KDO
CHCE ZABIT JESSII. WHO WANTS TO KILL JESSIE?) SP,D:
Milos Macourek, Vaclav Vorlicek. PH: Jan Nemecek. Mus:
S. Havelka. Ref: COF 10:50. F&F 11/66. V 8/3/66. M/TVM
6/66. with Jiri Sovak, Juraj Visny (superman), Dana Medricka.
A middleaged couple, both scientists, have discovered a method
of mind-reading via a drug and headphones that turn the dreams
or thoughts of the wearer into images on a telescreen.
WHO STOLE THE BODY (F) 1962 92m. (The BODY IS MISSING)
D: Jean Girault. Ref: Maltin. TVFFSB. with Francis Blanche,
Darry-Cowl, Elke Sommer, Clement Harari, Daniel Ceccaldi,
Mario David. Comedy-horror: House salesmen in old mansion
discover owner's body.
WHODUNIT? (India) 1964 (WOH KAUN THI?) Ref: Shankar's
2/16/64. with Sadhna. "Sadhna in several ghostly rebirths,"
"sinister houses, all sorts of odd noises and ghosts using
telephones."
WHOM THE GODS WISH TO DESTROY see SIEGFRIED (1967)
WHO'S GUILTY? Col 1945 serial 15 episodes (1946 79-minute
feature) D: Howard Bretherton, Wallace Grissell. SP: Ande
Lamb, George H. Plympton. PH: Ira H. Morgan. Mus: Lee
Zahler. P: Sam Katzman. Ref: MFB'46:155. Barbour. with
Robert Kent, Amelita Ward, Minerva Urecal, Tim Ryan, Jayne
Hazard, Belle Mitchell, Charles Middleton, Sam Flint, Jack
Ingram, Wheeler Oakman, Anthony Warde, Charles King. Eerie
old house, sliding panels, underground cellars, "spirit messages."
WIELKA, WIELKA I NAJWIEKSZA see BIG WORLD OF LITTLE
CHILDREN, The
WIETOTET MAN EINE DAME? see TARGET FOR KILLING
The WILD ASS'S SKIN (F) Pathe 1909 16m. From Balzac's "The
Wild Ass's Skin," "The Magic Skin," or "Le Peau de Chagrin."
Ref: Mitry II:124. with Paul Capellani?
WILD ASS'S SKIN, The (by Balzac) see DREAM CHEATER, The/
MAGIC SKIN, The/SINISTER WISH, The/SLAVE OF DESIRE
WILD BEAST OF CRETE, The see MINOTAUR, The (1960)
WILD IN THE STREETS AI 1968 Pathecolor 96m. D: Barry Shear.
SP: Robert Thom. From "The Day It All Happened, Baby" by
Thom. PH: Richard Moore. Mus sc: Les Baxter. Art D: Paul
Sylos. Ref: FFacts. V 5/8/68. FM 52:17. with Shelley Winters,
Christopher Jones, Diane Varsi, Ed Begley, Hal Holbrook,
Millie Perkins, Richard Pryor, Salli Sachse, Melvin Belli, Louis
Lomax, Dick Clark, Walter Winchell, Army Archerd, Bert
Freed, Kevin Coughlin, Michael Margotta, Paul Frees, Pamela
Mason. Teenagers capture political power in the United States.
Not too badly overrated. Fanciful, crude, and sometimes very
funny. The story goes haywire near the end when the mood be-
comes rather sour.
WILD JUNGLE CAPTIVE see JUNGLE CAPTIVE
WILD, WILD PLANET (I) MGM/Manley/Mercury/Southern Cross
1965 ('67-U.S.) color 93m. (I CRIMINALI DELLA GALASSIA.

CRIMINALS OF THE GALAXY) D,P: Antonio Margheriti (aka
Anthony Dawson). P: also Joseph Fryd. SP: Ivan Reiner, Moret-
ti. PH: Riccardo Pallottini. Ref: Ital P. PM. Pic: COF 12:48.
with Tony Russell, Lisa Gastoni, Carlo Giustini, Franco Nero,
Massimo Serato, Michel Lemoine, Moa Thai, Linda Sini.
Mysterious disappearances among the citizens of a city in the
future are linked with experiments in miniaturization.
The WILD WOMEN OF WONGO Tropical 1959 Pathecolor 72m.
D: James Wolcott. SP: Cedric Rutherford. PH: Harry Walsh.
Ref: FFacts. with Jean Hawkshaw Johnny Walsh, Ed Fury, Pat
Crowley. Ape-men vs. the natives of the island of Wongo.
The WILD WORLD OF BATWOMAN ADP 1966 SP,D,P: Jerry War-
ren. Ref: FJA poster. COF 10:49.11:49. with Katherine Victor,
George Andre, Steve Brodie, Lloyd Nelson, Richard Banks. Mad
doctor.
WILLARD Cinerama/BCO 1971 DeLuxe color 95m. D: Daniel
Mann. SP: Gilbert A. Ralston, from the book "Ratman's Note-
books" by Stephen Gilbert. Mus: Alex North. Art D: Howard
Hollander. PH: Robert B. Hauser. Ref: V 6/16/71. with Bruce
Davison, Ernest Borgnine, Elsa Lanchester, Sondra Locke,
Joan Shawlee, J. Pat O'Malley, Minta Durfee Arbuckle, Michael
Dante. Son of invalid mother trains rats to kill.
WILLIAM WILSON (by E. A. Poe) see STUDENT OF PRAGUE, The
(1913/1926/1935)/TALES OF MYSTERY AND IMAGINATION
WILLIE THE GHOST (F) Eclair 1911 7m. (WILLY FANTOME) Ref:
Bios 11/30/11. Mitry II:283. with Willy Saunders. "Ghost"
scares household.
WINDSOR CASTLE (B) 1926 short (HAUNTED CASTLES series)
D: Maurice Elvey. Ref: Brit Cinema. V 2/24/26.
WINGS OF DOOM see FLIGHT TO FAME
WINKLE'S GREAT DISCOVERY Cosmopolitan 1913 6m. Ref: Bios
5/22/13. Powder, when dusted on person, makes him violent
and quarrelsome.
WIRTSHAUS IM SPESSART, Das see COLD HEART, The (1923-
Wenter)
The WISHING MACHINE (Cz) Xerox Films/Ceskolovensky-Societe
Generale/Faroun Films/Bellucci/Gottwaldov 1968 (AUTOMAT
NA PRANI) SP,D: Josef Pinkava. Adap: Jiri Blazek. PH: J.
Kolin. Ref: Boxo 3/15/71. The Czechoslovak Film 1968. with
Milan Zeman. Machine nearly gets two kids to moon.
The WITCH (F) Melies/Star 1906 14m. (La FEE CARABOSSE, ou
LE POIGNARD FATAL) Ref: V&FI 12/22/06. FM 67:7. Witch
vows vengeance on troubadour. Phantoms emerge from grave-
yard tombs to frighten him. "Terrible monsters," gnomes.
The WITCH (F?) Le Lion 1909 10m. Ref: MPW'09:661. Bios
10/21/09. Witch transfers soul of girl to dummy. Imps,
phantoms, spell, hunchback.
The WITCH (Mex) Internacional Cinematografica 1954 (La BRUJA)
SP, D: Chano Urueta. Story: Alfredo Salazar. PH: Victor
Herrera. Mus: Raul Lavista. Ref: Indice. FM 2:14. Pic: FMO
1:33.5:37. FM-A'62:31. '69:22. with Lilia del Valle, Ramon Gay,
Julio Villarreal, Charles Rooner, Luis Aceves Castañeda.
The WITCH (Finnish) Sonney 1954 70m. D: Roland Hallstrom. SP:

Mika Waltari, from his play. PH: Esko Toyri. Art D: Lauri
Elo. Ref: FJA. Pic: FM 67:19. with Mirja Mane (the witch),
Toivo Makela, Hillevi Lagerstam, Aku Korhonen, Sakari Jurkka,
Helge Herala. An archaeologist and his wife find the remains
of a woman, buried 300 years, with a stake through her heart.
The stake is removed, and a live girl is later found in the same
spot.
WITCH, The see WITCH IN LOVE, The
WITCH AND WARLOCK see WITCHCRAFT (1964)
WITCH HAMMER see HAMMER FOR THE WITCHES
WITCH HOUSE see CRIMSON ALTAR, The
WITCH HOUSE, The see CURSE OF THE CRYING WOMAN, The
The WITCH IN LOVE (I) Arco/Interfilm 1966 103m. (La STREGA
IN AMORE. The WITCH. THE STRANGE OBSESSION-Eng.) SP,D:
Damiano Damiani. SP: also Liberatore. From the novel "Aura"
by Carlos Fuentes. PH: Leonida Barboni. Ref: Ital P. Boxo
8/4/69. F&F 12/68. with Richard Johnson, Rosanna Schiaffino,
Gian Maria Volonte, Sarah Ferrati. "Gothic gloom and horror";
old woman becomes young through witchcraft.
The WITCH-KILLER OF BLACKMOOR (Sp-G-I) Fénix/Terra/
Prodimex 1970 color/scope 96m. (El PROCESO DE LAS BRUJAS
or El JUEZ SANGRIENTO-Sp. Der HEXENTOTER VON BLACK-
MOOR-G. Il TRONO DI FUOCO-I. The THRONE OF FIRE. The
WITCHES' TRIAL. The BLOODY JUDGE) SP,D: Jesus Franco
(aka J. Frank Maura). SP: also E. Colombo, Anthony Scott
Veith. PH: Manuel Merino. Mus: Bruno Nicolai. Art D: G.
Sanabria. Ref: SpCinema '71. Fernsehen 7/70. Pic: COF 17:45.
with Christopher Lee, Maria Schell, Hans Haas, Maria Rohm,
Leo Genn, Margaret Lee, Milo Quesada, José María Prada,
Peter Martel, Diana Lorys. The Lord Chancellor under Jacob II
hunts down those accused of witchcraft.
The WITCH KISS (F) Pathe 1907 color 6m. Ref: V&FI 89:16. Lee.
The WITCH OF ABRUZZI Le Lion 1911 12m. Ref: Bios 8/31/11.
Girl falls under witch's spell.
The WITCH OF SEVILLE (I) Itala 1911 13m. (Il STREGA DE
SIVIGLIA) Ref: Bios 1/25/12. Wearer of witch's enchanted cap
possessed with "demoniac spirit."
WITCH OF THE DARK HOUSE Kalem 1916 (Episode 14 of The Girl
from 'Frisco series) Ref: MPN 14:3178. Old house, witch, trap
doors.
The WITCH OF THE GLEN (B) Warwick 1910 9m. Ref: Bios 1/6/10.
Witch's display of two "spirits" frightens men.
The WITCH OF THE MOUNTAINS Knickerbocker 1916 35m. Ref:
MPW 27:2066. with Marguerite Nichols, Gordon Sackville,
Richard Johnson. Spectre-like "witch" frightens men away from
cave.
The WITCH OF THE RUINS (F) Pathe 1910 Ref: MPW 6:751,834.
"Witch" strikes man unconscious with stick.
WITCH OF TIMBUKTU, The see DEVIL DOLL (1936)
WITCH WITHOUT A BROOM (U.S.-Sp) Producers Releasing Organi-
zation 1966 Movielab color/Cinemagic 86m. (Una BRUJA SIN
ESCOBA) D: José Elorietta (aka Joe Lacy). SP: Howard Berk.
PH: A. Nieva. Mus: J. G. Segurro. Art D: J. L. Bayonas.

Ref: SpCinema. P: Sid Pink. with Jeffrey Hunter, Maria
Perschy, Gustavo Rojo, Perla Cristal. Time travel to year
2100; "Outer Space maidens."
WITCHCRAFT (F) Para/SNEG-Marianne 1961 102m. Dyaliscope
(MALEFICES. BEWITCHED. WHERE THE TRUTH LIES) SP,D:
Henri Decoin. SP: also C. Accursi. Story: Boileau-Narcejac.
Dial: Albert Husson. PH: Marcel Grignon. Art D: P.-L.
Boutié. Ref: La Prod Cin Fr 1/62. MFB'69:105. DDC II:1.
V 4/11/62. with Juliette Gréco, Jean-Marc Bory, Robert
Dalban, Liselotte Pulver, Jacques Dacqmine. Man suspects
woman of using witchcraft to cause "accidents."
WITCHCRAFT (U.S.-B) Fox 1964 79m. (WITCH AND WARLOCK)
D: Don Sharp. SP: Harry Spalding. PH: Arthur Lavis. Mus:
Carlo Martelli. Art D: George Provis. P: Jack Parsons, Robert
Lippert. Ref: Orpheus 3:27. FFacts. with Lon Chaney, Jr.,
Jack Hedley, Viola Keats, Jill Dixon, David Weston, Yvette
Rees. Ref: Shriek 1:33. COF 6:56. PM. Bulldozers disrupt a
witch's grave. Film quickly becomes standard after an eerie
opening.
WITCHCRAFT (India) Madhu Pictures 1965 D: B. Vittalachari. Ref:
M/TVM 6/65. with Kanta Rao, Rajanala. "A look at Indian
sorcery."
WITCHCRAFT see DEVIL'S HAND, The (1962)/SORCERER, The
WITCHCRAFT '70 (I) AI/P.A.C.-Caravel 1969 95m. (75m.-U.S.)
(ANGELI BIANCHI...ANGELI NERI. The SATANISTS. MAGIC
REPORT) SP,D,ED: Luigi Scattini. PH: Claudio Racca (or Rocca).
Ref: M/TVM 4/69. MFB. Narr: Edmund Purdom. Documentary
on witchcraft: grave desecration, voodoo cults, etc.
WITCHCRAFT THROUGH THE AGES (Swedish) Svensk 1921 94m.
(HAXAN) SP,D: Ben Christensen. PH: Johan Ankarstjerne. Art
D: Holst-Jørgensen. Sets: Richard Louw. Ref: SilentFF. Pic:
DDC I:409. with Maren Pedersen, Astrid Holm, Elith Pio,
Oscar Stribolt, Christensen, Emmy Schøenfeld. Witches-as-cats,
witches-on-broomsticks, Black Masses, demons, love potions.
Very entertaining history/documentary, with a startling bit of
animation.
The WITCHES (I-F) De Laurentiis 1966 (Le STREGHE) "A Night
Like Any Other" episode: D: Vittorio De Sica. SP: Cesare
Zavattini, F. Carpi, E. Muzii. with Silvano Mangano, Clint
Eastwood, Armando Bottin (superman), Gianni Gori (Diabolik),
Paolo Gozlino (Mandrake), Angelo Santi (Flash Gordon), Piero
Torrisi (Batman). A husband competes with comic book charac-
ters for his wife's affections. Other Directors: Alberto Sordi,
Visconti, Bolognini, Rossi, Monicelli. PH: Giuseppe Rotunno.
also with Sordi, Annie Girardot, Veronique Vendell, Francisco
Rabal, Toto, Massimo Girotti. Ref: V 3/19/69. Ital P.
WITCHES, The see DEVIL'S OWN, The
The WITCHES' CAVERN Selig 1909 Ref: MPW. Wild Harry of the
woods thought to be witch's son; "half man and half monster."
The WITCHES' SPELL Urban 1910 Ref: Bios 6/30/10. A peasant
seized at a revel of witches and spirits is transformed into a
wild beast.
WITCHES' TRIAL, The see WITCH-KILLER OF BLACKMOOR, The

WITCHFINDER GENERAL (book by R. Bassett) see CONQUEROR
WORM, The
The WITCHING EYES Stern 1929 silent SP: Ernest Stern. Ref:
AFI. LC. "Curse," "witching hand," evil eye.
The WITCHING HOUR Frohman 1916 From the book "Caleb Powers."
Ref: MPN 14:3670. NYT 12/11/16. with C. Aubrey Smith,
Marie Shotwell. Man driven to kill owner of cat's eye pin.
Psychic power, telepathy.
The WITCHING HOUR Para 1921 80m. D: William D. Taylor.
PH: James Van Trees. SP: Julia Ivers. From the play by
Augustus Thomas. Ref: AFI. Exhibitors Herald. Lee. with
Elliott Dexter, Winter Hall, Edward Sutherland, Mary Alden,
Ruth Renick, Robert Cain. Hypnosis, telepathy.
The WITCHING HOUR Para 1934 69m. D: Henry Hathaway. SP:
Anthony Veiller, Salisbury Field. From the play by Augustus
Thomas. PH: Ben Reynolds. Ref: FD 4/9/34:13.4/28/34.
Photoplay 7/34. FM 24:64. with John Halliday, Sir Guy Standing,
William Frawley, John Larkin, Olive Tell, Richard Carle, Ralf
Harolde, Purnell Pratt, Selmer Jackson. Gambler unintentionally
hypnotizes his prospective son-in-law and causes him to commit
murder.
The WITCHMAKER Excelsior/Las Cruces-Arrow 1969 Technicolor/
scope 97m. SP,D,P: William O. Brown. PH: J. A. Morrill.
Mus sc: Jaime Mendoza-Nava. Exec P: L. Q. Jones. Ref:
V(d) 5/7/69. with Anthony Eisley, Thordis Brandt, Alvy Moore,
John Lodge, Diane Webber, Larry Vincent. A professor attempts
to communicate with the "forces of witchcraft" responsible for
eight murders.
The WITCH'S CAVE (F) Pathe 1906 6m. Ref: V&F Index 11/17/06.
Dream: Skeleton, appearing and disappearing figures.
The WITCH'S CURSE (I) Medallion/Palisade Int'l 1962 ('64-U.S.)
(MACISTE ALL'INFERNO) D: Riccardo Freda. Ref: Boxo 2/10/64.
TVG. Pic: FM 67:15. with Kirk Morris, Helen Chanel. Woman
condemned as witch casts spell on village. Fair backgrounds in
hell, but the dialogue in the foreground is distracting: "How is
it that a beautiful woman like you is down here?" "I've always
fought against evil, and I've always won."
The WITCH'S DONKEY (F) Pathe 1908 8m. Ref: MPW'09:29. Donkey
under witch's spell.
The WITCH'S MIRROR (Mex) AI-TV/Cinematografica, A. B. S. A.
1961 (El ESPEJO DE LA BRUJA) D: Chano Urueta. SP: Alfredo
Ruanova. PH: Jorge Stahl, Jr. Mus: G. C. Carrión. Art D:
Javier Torija. P: Abel Salazar. Ref: Indice. Aventura. TVG.
Pic: FM 23:13. with Rosita Arenas, Armando Calvo (or Antonio
Calve), Dina de Marco, Isabela Corona. With her magic powers,
a witch attempts to prevent a murder. The usual poor dubbing
and welter of cliches, but some fair shocks and picturesque
tricks make this one of the best of the myriad Mexican horror
movies of the '60's. That's not much, but it's something.
The WITCH'S SECRET (F) Pathe 1907 Ref: V&FI 1/11/08. Intruders into a witch's "mystic laboratory" are attacked by "white
capped figures" and ogres.
WITH HERCULES TO THE CENTER OF THE EARTH see

HERCULES IN THE HAUNTED WORLD
WITH THE MUMMIES' HELP Christie 1917 11m. Ref: MPN 15:
3625,3800. with Eddie Barry, Ethel Lynne, George French,
Margaret Gibson. A wife cures her husband of his craze for
collecting antiques by hiring two friends to pose as mummies.
They "come to life and scare the wits out of the faddist."
WITH THE SPIRITS HELP Nestor (Univ) 1916 Ref: MPN 14:2248.
with Lee Moran, Eddie Lyons, Priscilla Dean. Hypnotist in
house scared by noises.
WITHOUT A SOUL   see LOLA
WITHOUT WARNING   see STORY WITHOUT A NAME, The
The WIZARD Fox 1927 70m. D: Richard Rosson. Story,SP: Harry
O. Hoyt, Andrew Bennison. From "Balaoo" by Gaston Leroux.
PH: Frank B. Good. Ref: FDY. with Edmund Lowe, Leila
Hyams, Gustav von Seyffertitz, Barry Norton, George Kotsonaros,
Norman Trevor. A mad scientist grafts a face onto an ape.
WIZARD, The see MYSTERIOUS MAGICIAN, The
The WIZARD OF GORE Mayflower 1970 color 96m. D: Herschell
G. Lewis. SP: Allen Kahn. Ref: Boxo 12/7/70. with Ray
Sager, Judy Cler, Wayne Ratay. A magician literally saws a
woman in half. At the end the hero "becomes" the magician.
The WIZARD OF MARS American General 1964 color (JOURNEY
INTO THE UNKNOWN?) SP,D,P: David Hewitt.Technical Ad-
viser: Forrest J Ackerman. Ref: RVB. J. R. Duvoli. FM 11:
14.34:66.41:18. with John Carradine, Roger Gentry. Ancient
civilization discovered on Mars.
The WIZARD OF OZ Loew's Inc. 1939 Technicolor 101m.
D: Victor Fleming. SP: Noel Langley, Florence Ryerson, Edgar
Allan Woolf. From the story by L. Frank Baum. PH: Harold
Rosson. Mus: Harold Arlen. Lyrics: E. Y. Harburg. P: Mer-
vyn Leroy. Ref: FDY. Pic: TBG. with Judy Garland, Frank
Morgan, Ray Bolger, Bert Lahr, Jack Haley, Billie Burke,
Margaret Hamilton, Charley Grapewin. Witches, evil monkeys,
tin woodsman, lions, tigers, and bears. One of the best
musicals, this follows a good rule for musicals: Have music
most of the time. And it uses color just about as well as it has
ever been used.
WOH KAUN THI?   see WHODUNIT?
WOLF BLOOD Lee-Bradford 1925 70m. D: George Chesebro, George
Mitchell. SP: C. A. Hill. Ref: AFI. with Chesebro, Marguerite
Clayton, Ray Hanford, Roy Watson. A man fears he is becom-
ing "half beast" after receiving a transfusion of wolf's blood.
WOLF DOG Mascot 1933 serial D: Harry Fraser, Colbert Clark.
SP: Al Martin, Clark, W. Gittens. PH: H. Neumann, T.
Galligan. Ref: Imagen. with Rin-Tin-Tin, Jr., Frankie Darro,
George Lewis, Hale Hamilton, Stanley Blystone, Tom London,
Sara Paden, Lane Chandler, Dickie Moore, Henry B. Walthall.
Powerful ray.
The WOLF MAN Reliance 1915 Ref: MPW 9/18/15. "New glaze
for pottery"; "chemical solution which explodes, destroying the
laboratory."
The WOLF MAN Fox 1924 65m. Story: Reed Heustis. (The BEAST)
D: Edmund Mortimer. SP: Frederick and Fanny Hatton. PH:

Wolf   534

Don Short, Michael Farley. Ref: AFI, Photoplay 5/24. MPN
29:1210. with John Gilbert, Norma Shearer, Eugene Pallette,
Edgar Norton, Alma Francis. A man with a dual personality is
persuaded by his brother that he has murdered.
The WOLF MAN Univ 1941 71m. (DESTINY) D,P: George Waggner.
SP: Curt Siodmak. Mus: Charles Previn. PH: Joseph Valentine.
Art D: Jack Otterson. Makeup: Jack Pierce. Ref: Clarens. FM
11:20. 32:74. COF 6:17. with Claude Rains, Ralph Bellamy,
Evelyn Ankers, Lon Chaney, Jr., Warren William, Patric
Knowles, Bela Lugosi, Fay Helm, Maria Ouspenskaya, Le(y)land
Hodgson, Forrester Harvey, J. M. Kerrigan, Kurt Katch, Doris
Lloyd, Olaf Hytten, Harry Stubbs, Tom Stevenson, Eric Wilton,
Harry Cording, Ernie Stanton, Ottola Nesmith, Connie Leon, La
Riana, Caroline Cooke, Jessie Arnold, Margaret Fealy. A man
turns into a wolf whenever there's a full moon. The production
values don't come near balancing a lot of dull talk about good
and evil and minds and diseases, a contrived ending, and occa-
sional really bad lines ("There's something very tragic about that
man"). Pretty bad.
The WOLF OF THE MALVENEURS (F) 1943 85m. (Le LOUP DES
MALVENEUR) D: Guillaume Radot . PH: Pierre Montazel. Mus:
Thiriet. Ref: DDC III: 403. Rep Gen'47. with Madeleine Sologne,
Pierre Renoir, Gabrielle Dorziat. "Reginald de Malveneuer, the
last of his house, inhabits a sinister domain where strange bio-
logical experiences occur. He is haunted by the legend that says
that one of his ancestors, struck by the divine curse, was trans-
formed into a wolf."-Rep Gen.
WOLFE WIFE, The (play by A. Bertram) see ESTHER REDEEMED
WOLFMAN, The see CURSE OF THE WEREWOLF
WOLFMAN OF GALICIA, The see ANCINES WOODS, The
WOLF'S FOREST, The see ANCINES WOODS, The
WOLFSMENSCH, Der see MARK OF THE WOLFMAN, The
The WOMAN AND THE BEAST (Mex) Brooks & Enriquez 1958
(La MUJER Y LA BESTIA) D: Alfonso Corona Blake. SP,
Story: F. Galiana. Story: also Oscar Brooks. PH: Jack Draper.
Mus: Manuel Esperon. Ref: Indice. FJA still: horror. with
Ana Luisa Peluffo, Carlos Cores, Ruben Rojo, Fanny Schiller,
Andres Soler.
The WOMAN EATER (B) Col/Fortress 1957 ('59-U.S.) 70m. D:
Charles Saunders. SP: Brandon Fleming. PH: Ernest Palmer.
Mus: Edwin Astley. Makeup: Terry Terrington. Ref: MFB'58: 79.
FM-A'69:22: Exec P: Richard Gordon. with George Coulouris,
Vera Day, Joy Webster, Marpessa Dawn, Peter Wayn. A scientist
returns from the Amazon jungles with a tree that feeds on young
girls. Crummy.
WOMAN IN THE MOON see GIRL IN THE MOON
The WOMAN IN WHITE Gem (Univ) 1912 35m. Ref: Bios 1/23/13.
with Janet Salzburg. The impersonator of Lady Glyde dies and
is buried (as Lady Glyde). From the book by Wilkie Collins.
WOMAN IN WHITE, The (by W. Collins) see CRIMES AT THE
DARK HOUSE/TWIN PAWNS
The WOMAN OF EVERYONE (Braz) Servicine 1969 (A MULHER DE
TODES) SP, D: Rogerio Sganzerla. From a story by Egidio

Eccio. PH: Peter Overbeck. Mus: Ana Soralina. Ref: V 4/1/70.
with Helena Ines, Jo Soares. Woman with a "draculinian way of
making love," "vampirism."
WOMAN OF MYSTERY Blanche 1914 65m. SP,D: Alice Blanche.
Ref: MPW 20:362. Lee. with Vinnie Burns, Fraunie Fraunholz.
Dual personality, "spirit control."
WOMAN OF THE SNOW see KWAIDAN
The WOMAN WHO CAME BACK Rep 1945 68m. D: Walter Colmes.
SP: Les Willis, Dennis Cooper. Story: John Kafka. Idea: Philip
Yordan. PH: Henry Sharp. Mus sc: Edward Plumb. Art D:
Jacques Mapes. Ref: FDY. FM 67:14. with John Loder, Nancy
Kelly, Otto Kruger, Ruth Ford, Harry Tyler, J. Farrell Mac-
Donald, Emmett Vogan. A girl believes she has inherited the
curse of a witch ancestor.
The WOMAN WHO WOULDN'T DIE (B) WB 1965 84m. (CATACOMBS)
D: Gordon Hessler. SP: Daniel Mainwaring, from a book by Jay
Bennett. PH: Arthur Lavis. Mus: Carlo Martelli. Art D: George
Provis. P: Jack Parsons. Ref: PM. F&F 2/67. with Gary Mer-
rill, Jane Merrow, Neil McCallum, Georgina Cookson. Woman's
ghost seems to haunt cottage.
WOMAN WITH NO NAME, The see HER PANELED DOOR
WOMEN OF THE PREHISTORIC PLANET USA/Realart/Standard
Club 1966 DeLuxe color 87m. (PREHISTORIC PLANET WOMEN)
SP,D: Arthur C. Pierce. PH: Archie Dalzell. Art D: Paul
Sylos. P: Jack Broder, George Edwards. Ref: FFacts. Boxo
10/31/66. with Wendell Corey, Keith Larsen, Paul Gilbert, John
Agar, Merry Anders, Irene Tsu, Suzie Kaye. Commander of
spaceship returning to earth after 30-year journey finds himself in
"prehistoric climes."
WON THROUGH A MEDIUM Biog 1911 8m. Ref: Bios 12/28/11.
2/9/14. Nellie gets rid of suitor Clarence by frightening him
at seance.
The WONDERFUL CHAIR Brockliss 1910 7m. Ref: Bios 7/28/10.
Electrical apparatus holds burglar in chair.
The WONDERFUL CHARM (F) Melies 1908 Ref: F Index 11/7/08.
Wicked spirit tears arm and legs from man's body, returns
them in exchange for his soul
The WONDERFUL COAT (F) Lux 1909 5m. Ref: Bios 11/4/09.
Coat from tailor's shop makes man invulnerable.
The WONDERFUL ELECTRO-MAGNET Edison 1909 Ref: MPW'09:
807. Inventor's magnet "attracts" people.
A WONDERFUL FLUID (F) Pathe 1908 Ref: V&FI 8/8/08. Chemist's
fluid grows blossoms on bushes, hair on faces or heads.
WONDERFUL HAIR REMOVER (F) Gaum 1909 5m. Ref: Bios 1/13/10.
Quack sells hair remover which takes feathers off chickens, etc.
WONDERFUL MARRYING MIXTURE Walturdaw 1910 9m. Ref: Bios
8/25/10. "Causes dozens of weddings."
WONDERFUL PILLS (I) Cines 1909 Ref: Bios 3/31/10. Pills cure
laziness.
The WONDERFUL RAYS Savoia 1913 37m. Ref: Bios 7/17/13.
"Invention in electric vibrations" reenacts crime.
The WONDERFUL WORLD OF THE BROTHERS GRIMM MGM/
Cinerama 1962 Technicolor/Cinerama 135m. D,P: George Pal.

D: also Henry Levin. SP: Charles Beaumont, William Roberts,
David Harmon, from "The Brothers Grimm" or "Die Bruder
Grimm" by Hermann Gerstner. PH: Paul C. Vogel. Mus: Leigh
Harline. Art D: George W. Davis, Edward Carfagno. SpVisFX:
Gene Warren, Wah Chang, Tim Barr, Robert R. Hoag. Makeup:
William Tuttle. Ref: FFacts. COF 4:52. with Laurence Harvey,
Karl Boehm, Claire Bloom, Walter Slezak, Ian Wolfe, Otto
Kruger, Terry-Thomas, Buddy Hackett, Barbara Eden, Oscar
Homolka, Arnold Stang, Martita Hunt, Tammy Marihugh, Walter
Rilla, Yvette Mimieux, Russ Tamblyn, Jim Backus, Beulah
Bondi, Walter Brooke. The story of the Brothers Grimm, with
several of their stories enacted, including "The Singing Bone": A
servant slays a dragon. Enjoyable.
WONDERS OF THE UNIVERSE see OUR HEAVENLY BODIES
WOODCROFT CASTLE (B) 1926 short (HAUNTED CASTLES series)
D: Walter West. Ref: Brit Cinema. V 2/24/26.
WOODEN HEADED VETERAN (F) Pathe 8m. Ref: F Index 1/9/09.
1908 A veteran who lost his head in battle keeps a collection
of "headpieces" in a closet. "Grotesque looking one."
WOOED BY A WILDMAN Kalem 1915 color Ref: MPW'15:1258. MPN
3/13/15. Stone Age comedy.
WORK IS A FOUR LETTER WORD (B) Rank 1968 Technicolor 95m.
D: Peter Hall. SP: Jeremy Summers, based on Henry Livings'
play "Eh?" PH: Gil Taylor. Mus: Guy Woolfenden. Art D:
Philip Harrison. Ref: V(d) 6/12/68. with David Warner, Cilla
Black, Zia Mohyeddin, David Waller, Jan Holden, Elizabeth
Spriggs. "Monster machines" take on identity and will of their
own.
WORLD IS MINE, The! see INVISIBLE MAN GOES THROUGH THE
CITY, An
WORLD OF SPACE, The see BATTLE IN OUTER SPACE
The WORLD OF THE VAMPIRES (Mex) AI-TV/Cinematografica,
A.B.S.A. 1960 (El MUNDO DE LOS VAMPIROS) D: Alfonso
Corona Blake. SP: Ramón Obón. Story: Raul Zenteno. PH: Jack
Draper. Mus: G. C. Carrion. Art D: Javier Torija. P: Abel
Salazar. Ref: Indice. MadM 4:30. Pic: MW 6:45. FM 28:44.
with Mauricio Garces, Silvia Fournier, Erna Martha Bauman,
Jose Baviera. Dull vampire-menace and cheap camera tricks ex-
cept for a bat-with-a-woman's-head.
WORLD ON PARADE, The see TELEVISION SPY
The WORLD, THE FLESH AND THE DEVIL MGM 1959 95m. SP,D:
Ranald MacDougall. From the book "The Purple Cloud" by
Matthew P. Shiel. PH: Harold J. Mazorati. Mus: Miklos Rozsa.
Story: Ferdinand Reyher. Ref: FFacts. TVG. with Harry Bela-
fonte, Inger Stevens, Mel Ferrer. A nuclear holocaust leaves
three survivors. The awful and the striking are indiscriminately
mixed. Good one minute; bad the next. "Not worth bothering
about"-Claude Chabrol.
WORLD WAR III BREAKS OUT (J) Toei 1960 scope 77m. (DAI-
SANJI SEKAI TAISEN. YONJU-ICHI JIKAN NO KYOFU. 41 JIKAN
NO KYOFU) D: Shigeaki Hidaka. SP: Hisataka Kai. PH: Tadashi
Aramaki. Ref: UFQ 11. FEFN 1/61. J Films'62:91. TVG. with
Tatsuo Umemiya, Yayoi Furusato, Noribumi Fujishima, Yukiko

Nikaido, Michiko Hoshi. An American plane accidentally explodes
an atomic bomb over Korea.
The WORLD WILL SHAKE (F) CCEF 1941 110m. (Le MONDE
TREMBLERA. La REVOLTE DES VIVANTS. The DEATH PRE-
DICTOR) D: Richard Pottier. SP: Henri-Georges Clouzot, J.
Villard. Story: Charles Robert Dumas, R. F. Didelot. PH: R.
Lefevre. Art D: Perrier. Ref: Imagen. FJA. Rep Gen'47:
"Dr. Durand invents the "biometer" which measures the lifetime
of each individual. The consequences: universal disorder, assas-
sinations, suicides, economic disaster, etc." with Madeleine
Sologne, Armand Bernard, Erich von Stroheim, Claude Dauphin,
Roger Duchesne.
WORLD WITHOUT END AA 1956 Technicolor/scope 80m. SP,D:
Edward Bernds. PH: Ellsworth Fredricks. Mus sc & d: Leith
Stevens. Ass't D: Austen Jewell. Ref: FDY. SM 3:9. with
Hugh Marlowe, Nancy Gates, Rod Taylor, Lisa Montell, Nelson
Leigh, Shawn Smith, Paul Brinegar. Four scientists break through
the time barrier into the earth in the year 2508. The usual.
WORLD WITHOUT WOMEN see LAST WOMAN ON EARTH
The WORLD'S PROGRESS FROM STONE AGE TO AIRSHIPS (F)
Gaum 1909 Ref: Bios 3/10/10. Prehistoric man to present day.
WOT! NO GANGSTERS (B) Cine Film-Tex 1947 47m. D: E. W.
White. SP: C. H. Williamson. PH: Adolphe Burger, Oscar Burns.
Ref: MFB'47. with Mark Hambourg, Ronald Frankau, Claude
Dampier. Super-TV-set brings in events from the Balkans, etc.
WOULD YOU BELIEVE IT? (B) Nettlefold 1929 70m. silent D:
Walter Forde. SP: Forde, Harry Fowler Mear. PH: Geoffrey
Faithfull. Ref: SilentFF. with Forde, Arthur Stratton. "Wireless
control" tank demonstrated.
The WRAITH OF HADDON TOWERS Clipper 1915 45m. Ref: MPN
1/1/16. with Constance Crawley, Arthur Maude, Beatrice Van.
"Disembodied wraith" haunts locked room.
The WRESTLING WOMEN VS. THE AZTEC MUMMY (Mex) AI-TV/
Calderon 1964 (Las LUCHADORAS CONTRA LA MOMIA) D: Rene
Cardona. Story,SP: Alfredo Salazar. Story: also Guillermo
Calderon. PH: Ezequiel Carrasco. Mus: A. D. Conde. Ref:
Indice. with Lorena Velazquez, Armando Silvestre, Maria Eugenia
San Martin, Ramon Bugarini, Chucho Salinas. Wrestling women
Ruby and Loretta go after the Aztec mummy. "The Black Dragon"
sends two Oriental girls after them. The hero is worried: "I
don't see how Loretta's going to beat the Orientals--they're holy
terrors." Meanwhile, a bat turns into the mummy and then into
a spider. Unexpectedly, the mummy is effectively repellent, in
what must be its last stage of decay, and it has a fairly sicken-
ing groan.
The WRESTLING WOMEN VS. THE MURDERING ROBOT (Mex) 1969
color (Las LUCHADORAS CONTRA EL ROBOT ASESINO. El
ASESINO LOCO Y EL SEXO. The MAD MURDERER AND SEX.
SEX MONSTER) Ref: M/TVM 3/69. MMF 24. Cahiers #228.
with Joaquin Cordero, Regina Torne, Hector Lechuga, Carlos
Agosti, Pascual G. Pena.
WUNDER DER SCHOPFUNG see OUR HEAVENLY BODIES
WURDALAK, The (by A. Tolstoy) see BLACK SABBATH

WURGER VON SCHLOSS BLACKMOOR, Der see STRANGLER
OF BLACKMOOR CASTLE, The
WYLIE see EYE OF THE CAT
WYNALEZ ZKAZY see FABULOUS WORLD OF JULES VERNE, The

X   see X, THE MAN WITH X-RAY EYES
The X FROM OUTER SPACE (J) AI-TV/Shochiku 1967 color/scope
89m. (GILALA. UCHU DAIKAIJU GUIRARA) SP,D: Kazui Nihon-
matsu. SP: also Eibi Motomochi, M. Ishida. PH: S. Hirase.
Mus: Taku Izumi. Art D: S. Shigeta. SpFX: Hiroshi Ikeda.
Ref: UFQ 37. M/TVM 10/68. with Peggy Neal, Eiji Okada,
Shinichi Yanagisawa, Franz Gruber. A single cell from outer
space becomes a monster upon entering earth's atmosphere.
X + YY - FORMULA OF EVIL (G) Brünnstein-Film 1969 77m.
(NACKT SIND SEINE OPFER; X YY - FORMEL DES BOSEN)
D: Teja Piegeler, P. Jocic. Ref: Fernsehen 8/70: "Horror."
V 5/17/71:154: "Sexy-thriller." with Kai Fischer, Luba
Samardy.
The X-RAY FIEND (B) Smith 1897 Ref: SF Film. Professor's
machine shows skeletons of embracing lovers.
X, THE MAN WITH X-RAY EYES AI 1963 Pathecolor 80m. (The
MAN WITH X-RAY EYES. X) D,P: Roger Corman. SP: Robert
Dillon, Ray Russell. PH: Floyd Crosby. Mus: Les Baxter. Ref:
Clarens. with Ray Milland, Diana Van Der Vlis, Harold J. Stone,
John Hoyt, Don Rickles, John Dierkes. A doctor discovers a
serum that increases the power of sight. Grim, sometimes
imaginative, but ultimately ponderous s-f/fantasy.
X, THE UNKNOWN (B) WB/Hammer 1956 86m. D: Leslie Norman.
SP: Jimmy Sangster. PH: Gerald Gibbs. Mus sc: James Bernard.
Ref: FDY. Brit Cinema. with Dean Jagger, Edward Chapman, Leo
McKern, Michael Ripper, Anthony Newley, William Lucas, John
Harvey, Edward Judd. Dr. Royston discovers an invisible force
which lives on radioactivity. One of Hammer's lesser s-f/films.

YABU NO NAKA NO KURONEKO see BLACK CAT (1968)
YAMBAO see CRY OF THE BEWITCHED
YANGRILLA (India) Bhavnani 1938 (TIBBET-KA JADU) SP,D: M.
Bhavnani. Dial:Mohan. PH: D. K. Mistry. Mus: B. Prasad.
Ref: Moving Picture Monthly 7/38.10/38. with E. R. Rao,
Brown, Fatty Prasad. "Black magic": Lama's occult powers used
against scientist.
YE SHALL KNOW THEM (by Vercors) see SKULLDUGGERY
YEAR OF THE CANNIBALS (I) AI 1970 Ref: Film Bltn 6/71:27.
with Pierre Clementi, Britt Ekland. Futuristic version of
"Antigone."
YEAR 2889 AI-TV/Azalea 1968 color 80m. (2889. IN THE YEAR
2889) D,P: Larry Buchanan. SP: Harold Hoffman. PH: Robert

C. Jessup. Ref: M/TVM 10/68. TVG. RVB. with Paul Peterson, Charla Doarty, Quinn O'Hara, Bill Thurman. Survivors of a nuclear war are terrorized by a monster. Remake of DAY THE WORLD ENDED?

YEH RAAT PHIR NA AAYEGI (India) Darshan 1966 D: Brij. Ref: M/TVM 7/66. with S. Tagore, Mumtaz, Biswajeet. "Mystery girl who claims to be the soul of a dancer murdered 2,000 years ago mystifies archeologist and police."

The YELLOW FACE (B) Stoll 1921 20m. SP: William J. Elliott, from the story by Sir Arthur Conan Doyle. Ref: SilentFF. with Eille Norwood, Hubert Willis, Clifford Heatherley. (Adventures of Sherlock Holmes series) "Holmes solves the mystery of a cottage inhabited by a creature with a yellow face."

The YELLOW MENACE Serial Film Co. 1916 serial 16 episodes D: William Steiner. SP: Aubrey M. Kennedy. Ref: MPW 29: 1235.31:922. MPN 14:1577, 1891,3018. CNW. with Edwin Stevens, Florence Malone, J. A. Hall. Ch. 5. The Haunted House. 15. The Ray of Death. Hypnotism; tarantula attracted by odor to kill; blinding ray; new explosive, "quadrinolite"; "submarine air control device."

YELLOW PHANTOM see SHADOW OF CHINATOWN

The YELLOW TYPHOON F Nat 1920 70m. D: Edward Jose. SP: Monte Katterjohn. Story: Harold McGrath. Ref: MPW 44:1106. FIR'68:159. with Anita Stewart, Ward Crane, Donald MacDonald, George Fisher. Plans for invention to protect ships from submarine attacks delivered to the United States.

YEUX SANS VISAGE, Les   see HORROR CHAMBER OF DR. FAUSTUS, The

YO DORMI CON UN FANTASMA see I SLEPT WITH A GHOST

YOG - MONSTER FROM SPACE   see SPACE AMOEBA

YOKAI DAISENSO see SPOOK WARFARE

YOKAI HYAKU MONOGATARI see HUNDRED MONSTERS, The

YOKAI NO RANBU see EIGHT BRAVE BROTHERS

YOKU see HALF A LOAF

YONGARY - MONSTER FROM THE DEEP see MONSTER YONG-KARI

YONJU-ICHI JIKAN NO KYOFU see WORLD WAR III BREAKS OUT

YOSEI GORASU see GORATH

YOTSUYA GHOST STORY, The see ILLUSION OF BLOOD

YOTSUYA GHOST STORY NEW EDITION (J) 1928 (SHINPAN YOTSUYA KAIDAN) D: Daisuke Ito. Ref: Japan.

YOTSUYA KAIDAN see CURSE OF THE GHOST, The/GHOST OF YOTSUYA, The (1949/1956/1959)/ILLUSION OF BLOOD

YOTSUYA KAIDAN I & II see GHOST OF YOTSUYA, The (1949)

YOU ONLY LIVE TWICE (B) UA/Eon 1967 Technicolor/scope 116m. D: Lewis Gilbert. SP: Roald Dahl. From the novel by Ian Fleming. Add'l Material: Harold Jack Bloom. PH: Freddie Young. Mus sc & d: John Barry. Prod des: Ken Adam. Art D: Harry Pottle. SpFX: John Stears. 2nd Unit D: Peter Hunt. Ref: FFacts. PM. with Sean Connery, Donald Pleasence, Robert Hutton, Alexander Knox, Tsai Chin, Bernard Lee, Karin Dor, Mie Hama, Akiko Wakabayashi, Teru Shimada, Lois Maxwell, Charles Gray. Missile base in crater, spaceship that swallows rocket, collapsible autogyro. Better gimmicks and quips than usual for James Bond, though there aren't enough second-half highlights.

YOU SHALL KNOW THEM (by Vercors) see SKULLDUGGERY

YOU'LL FIND OUT RKO 1940 97m. (HERE COME THE BOOGIE MEN) D, P: David Butler. SP: James V. Kern. Story: Kern, Butler. PH: Frank Redmond. Mus: Roy Webb. Art D: Van Nest Polglase. SpFX: Vernon Walker. Ref: FD 11/14/40. COF 5:22. Pic: FanMo 3:60. with Boris Karloff, Peter Lorre, Kay Kyser, Bela Lugosi, Dennis O'Keefe, Helen Parrish, Ish Kabibble, Ginny Simms. Magic, mansion with secret passages, etc. Fair comedy-horror fun; at least it's fun to see Karloff, Lugosi, and Lorre together.

The YOUNG DIANA Cosmopolitan/Para 1922 85m. D: Albert Capellani, Robert Vignola. SP: Luther Reed, from a novel by Marie Corelli. PH: Harold Wenstrom. Art D: Joseph Urban. Ref: AFI. Clarens. MPW 57:530. Pic: FM 18:24-5. with Marion Davies, Pedro de Cordoba, Forrest Stanley, Gypsy O'Brien, Maclyn Arbuckle. A doctor discovers the elixir of eternal youth.

YOUNG DR. JEKYLL MEETS FRANKENSTEIN see WALKING DEAD The

YOUNG MAN, I THINK YOU'RE DYING see BEAST IN THE CELLAR, The

YOUNG MAN WITH THE CREAM TARTS (by R. L. Stevenson) see TROUBLE FOR TWO

The YOUNG, THE EVIL AND THE SAVAGE (I) AI/Super Int'l-B.G.A. 1968 Perfect Color/Cromoscope 82m. (NUDE...SI MUORE) D: Antonio Margheriti (aka Anthony Dawson). SP: Margheriti, Frank Bottar. Story: Simonelli. PH: F. Zucc(i)oli. Mus: Carlo Savina. Art D: Antonio Visone. Ref: MFB'71:145. V 8/68. with Michael Rennie, Mark Damon, Eleanor Brown, Sally Smith. Multiple-murder à la Hammer and the "AIP Poe shockers."

YOUR SINS COUNT (Polish) Iluzjon/Film Polski 1963 D: J. Zarzvcki. Ref: M/TVM 7/63: "Black-humor." with E. Krzyzewska. "Journalist invents a 'suicide club'."

YOUR SPECIAL AGENT FLIT see FLIT

YUKI-ONNA see KWAIDAN/SNOW GHOST

YUKON PATROL, The see KING OF THE ROYAL MOUNTED

YUMIHARI-ZUKI see CRESCENT MOON, The

YUREI HANJO-KI see MY FRIEND DEATH

YUREISEN, I & II see GHOST SHIP (1957)

YUSEI OJI see PRINCE OF SPACE, The

Z. 7 OPERATION REMBRANDT (Sp-G-I) Agata/Planet/CA. PI Film 1967 color/scope 98m. (Z. 7 OPERACION REMBRANDT) SP, D, Story: Giancarlo Romitelli. SP: also Ennio de Concini, R. Veller. PH: Guglielmo Mancori. Mus: Aldo Piga. Art D: Adolfo Cofiño. Ref: SpCinema'68. with Lang Jeffries, Laura Valenzuela,

Loredana Nusciak, Carlo Hinterman, Joaquín Hansen, Luis Peña, Mónica Randal. A famous German scientist is working on a machine capable of destroying great areas of land with bombardments of cosmic rays.
ZABIL JSEM EINSTEINA, PANOVE   see   I KILLED EINSTEIN, GENTLEMEN
ZAMBO THE APE MAN (India) Bhavnani 1937 157m. (SHER-E-JUNGLE) SP, D: M. Bhavnani. Sequel: SON OF ZAMBO. PH: R. M. Master. Ref: Filmindia 5/37/46. Dipali 9/10/37. Moving Picture Monthly 6/37:27: error: JUMBO. Pic: Filmindia 6/37:47. with S. B. Nayampally, Sarla. A scientist turns an "ape man monster" into a man.
ZANDORI'S SECRET (F) Warner's Features/Eclair 1914 Ref: Motography 1/9/15. 45m. with Renée Sylvaine. Serum cure for insanity.
ZAREX (Fili) LVN 1958 D: Richard Abelardo. Based on the comic strip appearing in Filipino Komiks. Ref: FEFN 4/18/58. Pic: FEFN 3/7/58. with Willie Sotelo, Jose Vergara, Carmencita Abad. "Science fiction thriller": vaporizers, etc.
ZBEHOVE A TULACI see DESERTERS AND THE NOMADS, The
A ZEPPELIN ATTACK ON NEW YORK Mutual 1917 11m. Ref: MPN 55:3474. "A flock of Zeppelins" bombs New York City.
ZERO IN THE UNIVERSE Film-Makers 1967 85m. D: George Moorse. SP: Moorse, Jock Livingston. Ref: FFacts. with Moorse, Livingston. Experimental: Two characters float through time as disembodied forces, one as a "space pioneer" at one point.
ZETA ONE (B) Tigon 1969 Eastmancolor 82m. D: Michael Cort. SP: Cort, Alastair McKenzie. Based on a story in "Zeta" magazine. PH: Jack Atchelor. Mus sc & d: Johnny Hawksworth. Art D: Martin Gascoigne. Ref: MFB'71:62. with Robin Hawdon, James Robertson Justice, Charles Hawtrey, Dawn Addams, Anna Gael. Extra-terrestrial race of super-women.
ZETTAI ZETSUMEI see KILLING BOTTLE, The
ZEX, THE ELECTRONIC FIEND see ELECTRONIC MONSTER, The
ZINDAGI AUR MAUT (India) Bundel Khand 1965 D: N. A. Ansari. Ref: M/TVM 7/65. Shankar's 5/16/65. "Horror": "Deserted houses, raucous orchestra." with Pradeep Kumar, Fariyal.
ZINGARO (India) Krishna Tone 1935 Ref: Dipali 7/12/35. with Gulab, Puspa, Johra. "Man made into a monster - Possessed the strength of 1001 men."
ZOMBIE, The see PLAGUE OF THE ZOMBIES
ZOMBIES see I EAT YOUR SKIN
ZOMBIES, The see PLAGUE OF THE ZOMBIES
ZOMBIES OF MORA TAU Col/Clover 1957 70m. (The DEAD THAT WALK-Eng.)D: Edward L. Cahn. SP: Raymond T. Marcus. Story: George Plympton. PH: Benjamin Kline. Mus D: Mischa Bakaleinikoff. Art D: Paul Palmentola. Ref: FM 2:16. PM. FDY. P: Sam Katzman. with Allison Hayes, Gregg Palmer, Autumn Russell, Ray Corrigan, Morris Ankrum, Gene Roth, Joel Ashley. A diving expedition travels to Africa to recover diamonds from a shipwreck guarded by zombies. Better-than-average Katzman dud--but still a dud.
ZOMBIES OF THE STRATOSPHERE Rep 1952 serial 12 episodes

(SATAN'S SATELLITES - '57 Feature) D: Fred C. Brannon. SP: Ronald Davidson. PH: John MacBurnie. SpFX: Howard and Theodore Lydecker. Ref: Barbour. TVG. Pic: ModM 2:62. SM 4:9. with Judd Holdren, Aline Towne, Wilson Wood, Lane Bradford, John Crawford, Leonard Nimoy (Narab), Tom Steele, Dale Van Sickel, Gayle Kellogg, Jack Shea. Zombies invade earth.

ZOMBIES ON BROADWAY RKO 1945 68m. (LOONIES ON BROADWAY-Eng.) D: Gordon Douglas. SP: Laurence Kimble, Robert Kent. From a story by Robert Faber and Charles Newman. PH: Jack Mackenzie. Mus sc: Roy Webb. Art D: Albert D'Agostino, Walter E. Keller. Ref: FDY. TVK. with Bela Lugosi (Prof. Renault), Wally Brown, Alan Carney, Sheldon Leonard, Ian Wolfe, Frank Jenks, Anne Jeffreys, Russell Hopton, Joseph Vitale, Louis Jean Heydt, Darby Jones. Two press agents travel to a West Indies isle to produce a zombie for a night club. A monkey has the funniest bit, imitating a zombie.

ZONTAR THE THING FROM VENUS AI-TV/Azalea 1966 color D, P: Larry Buchanan. SP:Buchanan, H. Taylor. Remake of IT CONQUERED THE WORLD. PH: Robert Alcott. Ref: TVG. L. Otis. with John Agar, Anthony Houston, Susan Bjurman, Patricia De Laney, Warren Hammack. A scientist is in league with a Venusian creature. Most of the cast are terrible, but Houston as the villain is incredible. Most of the lines are that way too: "Zontar's on his way, dear" "The world's been headed downhill for a long time" "Isn't it great having the only working tape deck in the world?" "You know, it's strange. Here we've worked hard all these years, and now it's ready to go. "

ZTRACENA TVAR see LOST FACE, The

ZUDORA Than 1914 serial 20 episodes (The TWENTY MILLION DOLLAR MYSTERY. ZUDORA IN THE TWENTY MILLION DOLLAR MYSTERY) D: Howell Hansell. (The DEMON SHADOW) Ref: MPN 1/16/15. Motography 12/26/14. 1/9/15. CNW. with James Cruze, Marguerite Snow, Harry Benham, Sidney Bracy. Ch. 5. The Secret of the Haunted Hills. 6. The Mystery of the Perpetual Glare. Powerful machine that absorbs and emits the sun's rays and destroys ships; fluid that photographs the countenance of anyone near it; Chinese hypnotist.

ZWERG NASE see DWARF NOSE

ZWOLFTE STUNDE, Die see TWELFTH HOUR, The

TITLES ANNOUNCED FOR RELEASE IN 1971-1972

The ALIEN Univ with D. Janssen
ALL-HALLOW'S EVE
AMERICAN ODYSSEY (U.S.-I) "s-f"
ANABELLE [sic] LEE General from Poe
APPOINTMENT WITH LUST Maron "horror"
ASYLUM

The BABY General "psychological-horror"
BARON BLOOD (The BLOOD BARON) with J. Cotton, E. Sommer
BARON MUNCHAUSEN (G)
BEN (Sequel to WILLARD)
BLACK CIRCLE (Dutch) Ref: V 5/12/71:182
BLACK MAGIC Clover "horror"
BLACK NOON CBS-TV
The BLESSING WAY WB witchcraft
BLOOD CROWD Chevron
BLOOD OF THE IRON MAIDEN H'w'd Star with Carradine, P.
    Duryea
BLOOD OF THE MAN DEVIL Medallion-TV
BLOOD WILL HAVE BLOOD werewolf
The BLOODY BENDERS MGM
BRAIN OF FRANKENSTEIN Kirt
BRAVE NEW WORLD
The BRIDE FROM HELL (HK) Ref: M/TVM'71.
BURKE AND HARE

CADAVER Harrington
CAGLIOSTRO (I-J)
CAPTAIN KRONUS - VAMPIRE HUNTER Hammer
CARNIVAL OF BLOOD (DEATH RIDES A CAROUSEL)
CASTLE OF GORE
CAT'S CRADLE
CHAMPIONS OF JUSTICE (Mex) with Blue Demon, "Medico Asesino."
A CLOCKWORK ORANGE
The CLONE
CONQUEST OF THE PLANET OF THE APES
COUNT EROTICA VAMPIRE
COVEN OF THE DAMNED Marlene
CRESCENDO WB "psychological horror"
CRUCIBLE OF HORROR (VELVET HOUSE) with M. Gough

The CULT   Maron "horror"
Le CULTE DU VAMPIRES   Rollin

DARK SIDE OF TOMORROW   Novik
The DAY THEY GAVE BABIES AWAY   TV-movie
De SADE AI   D: Franco
DEAD OF SUMMER   Plaza   futuristic
DEMON ANGELS   Fanfare   "horror"
DESTROY NORTHEAST   Kirt   s-f
DEVIL COMES FROM AKASAWA (G-Sp)   Franco
DEVIL'S CHOICE   General
DIABOLIC WEDDING   General   with M. O'Brien
The DINOSAUR GIRL   Hammer
The DISAPPEARANCE   Pal
DOC SAVAGE   series of films   Pal   with F. J Ackerman?
DR. JEKYLL AND MISS HYDE   EVI
DR. JEKYLL AND MR. HYDE   D: D. Curtis
DR. JEKYLL AND MRS. HYDE   Kirt
DR. JEKYLL AND SISTER HYDE
DR. PHIBES RISES AGAIN (sequel to The ABOMINABLE DR.
   PHIBES)
DOOMSDAY 2000 A.D.   (BARRACUDA 2000 A.D. /BLOOD SPORT)
DOOR INTO SUMMER   from Heinlein
DRACULA CHELSEA '72 (DRACULA '72)
DRACULA IN THE REALM OF TERROR   Marlene
DRACULA IN THE YEAR 2000   Marlene
DRACULA TODAY   Hammer
DRACULA VS. THE BEASTS OF ZARCON   Marlene with Carradine
DRACULA VS. THE TERROR OF ATLANTIS   Marlene
DRACULA'S CASTLE or WILL THE REAL COUNT DRACULA
   STAND UP?   Cardoza
The DUBIOUS DEATH (I)
DUNGEON OF THE DAMNED   Marlene

EARTH II   TV-movie
EARTHQUAKE 1980   Univ (EARTHQUAKE)
EASY VAMPIRE   Canyon
EDGE OF THE EARTH   Col-Krofft
EQUINOX (I) futuristic
The EROTIC LIFE OF SLEEPING BEAUTY (I)
The EXORCIST   Monash

The FACE EATERS   Marlene
The FAR BANKS   (F) Risi
The FEMALES (G)   Ref: V 6/30/71:36.
The FIRST OF JANUARY (The EDICT) with O. Reed, G. Chaplin
FLESH GORDON
FRANKENSTEIN   NBC-TV/Univ
FRANKENSTEIN: CURSE FROM THE GRAVE   Marlene
The FREEWALKERS   Panpiper

FRENZY Hitchcock
FROGS AI

G.O.O. AI Story: Matheson
GAMERA VS. LEOMAN
GARDEN OF THE MOON Manley (sfa GARDEN OF DR. KANA-
    SHIMA Manley/Toho "s-f" Ref: V 5/7/69?)
GAY VAMPIRES Fanfare
The GHOST'S REVENGE (HK)
GINGERBREAD HOUSE (Hansel and Gretel)
GODZILLA VS. THE SMOG MONSTER AI
GODZILLA'S REVENGE (TERROR OF GODZILLA) Maron
GOLDEN APPLES OF THE SUN
GOOD MORNING, BERENGER! Rembrandt (sfa WHO WANTS TO
    KILL JESSIE?)
GRAVESIDE STORY AI with Price

HEADLESS HUSBAND Kirt with B. Major
HELP, HELP, THE GLOBOLINKS
HERE COMES THE BLOB (SON OF BLOB. BEWARE OF THE
    BLOB. BEWARE! THE BLOB. sfa The BLOB?-V 9/29/71:24)
    D: L. Hagman.
HEXED (NIGHT OF THE WARLOCK) Cambist
HIGH PRIEST OF VAMPIRES Hammer
HORROR CREATURES OF THE PREHISTORIC WORLD
HOUSE OF EVIL AI
HOUSE OF THE SCREAMING TERROR Marlene
HOUSE OF THE SEVEN GABLES AI
HOW TO BECOME A VAMPIRE Benmar
A HOWLING IN THE WOODS CBS-TV

I CRAVE YOUR BLOOD Marlene
I, MONSTER (Jekyll and Hyde) Amicus
"IDAHO TRANSFER" P. Fonda
INFERNAL IDOL Cohen
IS THERE SEX AFTER DEATH?
ISLAND AT THE END OF THE WORLD BV "s-f"

JODIE Dundee devil

KING KONG - FRANKENSTEIN'S SON (J) Toho
The KOLCHAK TAPES ABC-TV with D. McGavin, C. Lynley.
    vampire

LADY FRANKENSTEIN (MADAME FRANKENSTEIN) New World (I)
    with J. Cotten
LAND OF 1000 MONSTERS Filmpeople

LEGACY OF BLOOD with Carradine, J. Morrow
LEGEND OF HORROR Ellman-General from Poe's "The Tell-Tale
  Heart."
LIVING DEAD (B) D: K. Sharp
LOGAN'S RUN Pal
LOVE BITE werewolf
LOVE - VAMPIRE STYLE (G) Ref: M/TVM 6/71. with E. Renzi,
  B. Skay, B. Valentin

MADMEN, MANIACS AND MONSTERS Ind-Int'l Ref: V 5/12/71:
  203: "Horror classics" with Karloff
The MAGICIAN Fox
The MAN WHO FELL TO EARTH Cannon
The MAN WITH THE TRANSPLANTED BRAIN Valcroze with
  J.-L. Trintignant
The MONK (G)
MOURIR A L'AUBE (F) Rollin vampires
MYSTERIOUS ISLAND (I) Rizzoli

NIGHT OF THE WITCH Cannon
NIGHTMARE BLOOD BATH with R. Carrol, S. Brady

El OMBRE OCULTO Ref: V 5/12/71:143.
The OMEGANS (U.S.-Fili) D: W. L. Wilder. SP: W. Wheeland.
  Ref: L. Otis
ONE FRIGHTFUL NIGHT Clover "horror"
The OTHER D: R. Mulligan

PENDRA - PRINCE OF DARKNESS Marlene
PHOBIA Spillane (Poe)
PIED PIPER OF HAMELIN Demy
PITCHFORK SP: J. E. McLarty
The PLANET VENUS (I) "political-fantasy"
POE Cannon
POSSESSION OF JOEL DELANEY
The POSSESSORS SP: Baxt
PROGENY OF THE ADDER AI
The PUPPET MASTERS

RED RIDING HOOD Omega
RETURN OF THE WITCHES (I)
The ROBOTS VS. THE BLOODY THING Marlene

SANTO EN LA VENGANZA DE LA MOMIA Ref: M/TVM 10/70
SARNAK - DEMON OF HELL Marlene
SCREAM OF TERROR (POINT OF TERROR) Crown "Mad rock
  star"
SCREAMING DEATH Marlene

SEA BEAST   United
The SECRET SEX LIFE OF DRACULA   Kirt
SHE WAS A HIPPIE VAMPIRE   ADP/Warren
SIEGFRIED IN THE COUNTRY OF THE KING OF DENMARK
   (sequel to The TERRIBLE QUICK SWORD OF SIEGFRIED)
SILENT RUNNING (RUNNING SILENT)   Univ
SINBAD IN INDIA (sequel to SEVENTH VOYAGE OF SINBAD)
   Harryhausen
The SIRENS OF TITAN   P. Williams
SLAUGHTERHOUSE-FIVE   Univ
SNOW WHITE AND THE SEVEN DWARFS   Omega
SOMETHING WICKED THIS WAY COMES   Peckinpah
The SPORE   United
STAR CHILD
STONE AGE WOMEN   Filmpeople
STOP! WB   "murder and mysticism"
STRANGER IN A STRANGE LAND
SUPER 3-D HORROR SHOW   Ind-Int'l
SWEETKILL

TALES FROM THE CRYPT   with R. Richardson
10,000 YEARS   AI   SP: C. Vaughn
TERROR BLOOD ORGY   Marlene
A THIRST FOR BLOOD   Clover   "horror"
TO LIVE AGAIN   Kirt
TONIGHT YOU SLEEP   Four Star
TOWER OF EVIL   Fanfare/R. Gordon
TOWER OF SIN   Maron   "Horror"
The TOY FACTORY (NECROMANCY/NECROMANCY - A LIFE FOR
   A LIFE)
12 plus 1 (I) Jekyll and Hyde sequence
TWINS OF EVIL   Gordon

VAMPIRE CIRCUS   Hammer
VAMPIRE LUST FOR BLOOD   Marlene
VAMPIRE PEOPLE   Hemisphere
VAMPIRE VIRGINS   Hammer
VAMPIRES (Russ)   D: G. Erschov, G. Kropachev. Ref: V 6/30/71:
   36.
VENOM
VIENNA STRANGLER
VILLAGE OF THE VAMPIRES   Hammer
VIRGIN WITCH(ES) (B)   Univista
VOODOO (I) D: Dellamano

The WEREWOLF MUST KILL!
WHEN THE EARTH CRACKED OPEN   Hammer
WHEN WOMEN LOST THEIR TALES   (sequel to WHEN WOMEN
   HAD TAILS)
WHO'S AFRAID OF THE BIG BAD WEREWOLF?

WITCH STORY Kirt
WORLD OF TWO MOONS Fox

ZORA "horrific" with Carradine

SHORTS (1930-1971), AND ANIMATED AND PUPPET FILMS

A HAUNTING WE WILL GO Univ 1939 cartoon 10m. Haunted
mill. Ref: FD 7/6/39.
The ABOMINABLE SNOWMAN Panda 1954 35m. Documentary
Ref: Lee.
ADVENTURES IN SPACE (G) 17m. "Space robot." Ref: Lee.
The ADVENTURES OF TOPO GIGIO (I) Cinecidi-Jolly 1961 Space-
ship. Ref: Imagen. Puppet.
The ADVENTURES OF ICHABOD AND MR. TOAD Disney 1950
animated
Narr: Basil Rathbone. From "The Legend of Sleepy Hollow"
and "The Wind in the Willows."
ADVENTURES OF LITTLE SAMURAI (J) Toei 1959 animated Witch,
sea monster, Ref: FEFN 11/59. UFQ 9.
ALAKAZAM (J) 1961 animated Monsters.
ALFALFA'S AUNT MGM 1939 11m. Ref: FD 1/24/39: "Spook
stuff."
ALICE'S SPOOKY ADVENTURE Disney 1924 cartoon "Spooks-
ville." Ref: SilentFF.
ANIMATED GENESIS 1949 cartoon Giant Spider. Ref: DDC II: 89.
ALL HALLOWE'EN (B) 1952 34m. Ghost. Ref: Lee. with
Diane Cilento.
AUTOMANIA 2000 cartoon Automation in the future.

BABES IN THE WOODS FBO 1925 cartoon 20m. Hansel and
Gretel. Ref: FD 9/20/25.
BAMBI MEETS GODZILLA short cartoon
BEAUTY AND THE BEAST animated 41m. "Monster." Ref:
TVFFSB.
BENNY'S BATHTUB (Danish) animated Ref: V 5/12/71:102.
Skeleton pirates.
BIRTH OF A ROBOT (B) 1934 animated puppet short Ref: Lee.
The BLACK CAT 1960 short cartoon Ref: FM 12:6.
BOBO THE HOBO AND HIS TRAVELING TROUPE IN THE LOST
SPACE SHIP 1953 15m. Ref: Imagen.
The BOLD DRAGON Dynamic 1954 15m. Ref: Lee. with Monty
Woolley.
The BOOGIE WOOGIE MEN Univ 1943 7m. animated "Ghost
convention." Ref: Showmen's 10/9/43.
BONZOLINO (B) Ward 1924 cartoon Bonzo as famous actor
Bon Chaney. Ref: SilentFF
BOTHERED BY A BEARD (B) Ref: MFB'46:1. 36m. Tod

Slaughter as Sweeney Todd.
The BRAIN INSPECTOR (F) Pathe 1910 Animation: Cohl. (Le
RETAPEUR DE CERVELLE. BRAINS REPAIRED) Ref: SilentFF.
Bios 2/16/11. Doctor's instrument allows him to examine pa-
tient's brain.
BRING 'EM BACK A LIE Univ 1935 20m. Ref: FM 10:19. with
Ben Turpin.
The BURNING OF A THOUSAND SUNS (F) Argos 1965 25m.
(La BRULERE DE MILLE SOLEILS) 30th century astronaut. Ref:
Imagen.

The CALICO DRAGON MGM 1935 8m. cartoon "Fearsome
dragon." Ref: FD 10/7/35.
The CASK OF AMONTILLADO Dynamic 1954 15m. with Monty
Woolley. Ref: Lee.
CERTAIN PROPHECIES (Hung) 1968 puppet short Aliens on
earth. Ref: S&S'68:184.
CHAMBER OF HORRORS 1916 (Mutt & Jeff series) cartoon Ref:
MPN 14:3331.
The CHEMIST Fox/Educ 1936 21m. Chemistry pupil's love potion;
formula for making animals grow. Ref: FD 10/21/36. with
Buster Keaton.
The CHILD AND THE BALL (Yugoslav) Zagreb 1960 cartoon short
(DECAK I LOPTA) City of the future. Ref: Imagen.
CHRISTOPHER'S INVISIBLE PLAYMATE 1955 short cartoon Ref:
DDC I:316.
CITIZEN IM 5 (Yugoslav) 1962 cartoon (GRADANIN IM 5) Robot.
Ref: Imagen.
The CLIFF MONSTER Golden Eagle 1962 "Monster." short Ref:
FanMo 3:32,62.HM 3:33: Paul Blaisdell.
COL. HEEZA LIAR AND THE GHOST Bray 1923 animated short
Ref: Lee.
COL. HEEZA LIAR , GHOST BREAKER Bray 1915 animated
Haunted house. Ref: MPN 2/13/15.
COL. HEEZA LIAR IN THE HAUNTED HOUSE Bray/Pathe 1915
animated Ref: MPN 3/6/15.
The COSMODROME OF 1999 (Cz) 1969 animated short Ref: M/TVM
4/70:23.
The CREATION OF THE WORLD (Cz) 1956 cartoon Devil. Ref:
DDC III:46.
CREEPS 1956 Knight's ghost, haunted castle. Ref: TVG. Movie
Comedy Teams. with The Three Stooges.
CUBBY'S STRATOSPHERE FLIGHT RKO 1934 animated Ref:
Imagen.
The CYBERNETIC GRANDMOTHER (Cz) Ref: DDC III:316. MMF
8:53. animated

DAVEY JONES' LOCKER AM&B 1903 puppet Skeleton. Ref:
Niver.
The DESERTED PLANET (Polish) 1962 (BEZLUDNA PLANETA)
cartoon Ref: Imagen.

DIRTY WORK MGM 1933 25m. Youth tonic. Ref: Lee. with
    Laurel and Hardy.
DR. HEIDEGGER'S EXPERIMENT(S) Dynamic 1954 Ref: Lee. with
    Monty Woolley. From the story by Hawthorne.
DR. JEKYLL AND MR. HYDE Pixilated Pix Ref: FM 11:39.
DR. JEKYLL AND MR. MOUSE MGM 1947 animated 8m. Ref:
    Lee.
DR. JEKYLL'S HIDE Univ 1932 short Ref: FM 34:55. MPH
    10/1/32.
DR. JERKYL'S HIDE WB 1955 7m. animated Ref: Lee.
DREAM WITHOUT AN END (Holland) 1964 short Comet approaching
    earth. Ref: Imagen.

The ENCHANTED SWORD Fox 1960 (sp) 74m. cartoon "Monsters."
    Ref: TVFFSB. COF 9:32.
EVOLUTION Ideal 1932 28m. Documentary. Prehistoric animals;
    footage from OUR HEAVENLY BODIES. Ref: FJA. MPH
    9/3/32.
EXPLORING EPHRAIM'S EXPLOIT 1915 cartoon New planet.
    Ref: MPW 9/25/15.
The EXTRAORDINARY ADVENTURES OF JULES VERNE (F) 1952
    short (Les AVENTURES EXTRAORDINAIRES DE JULES VERNE)
    Ref: DDC II:350.

FANTASIA RKO/Disney 1940 Bela Lugosi pantomimed "A Night on
    Bald Mountain" sequence. Ref: FM 12:6.40:29. COF 4:4. Pic:
    DDC II:81. "The Sorcerer's Apprentice," "The Rite of Spring."
FANTOCHE'S NIGHTMARE (F) animated (Le CAUCHEMAR DU
    FANTOCHE) D: Cohl. Ref: DDC I:444.
FELIX IN OUTER SPACE 1955 15m. cartoon Ref: Imagen.
FELIX SWITCHES WITCHES Educ 1927 10m. cartoon Witch's
    spell, "hobgoblins." Ref: FD 10/23/27.
FELIX THE CAT IN DRAGGIN' THE DRAGON 1928 10m. cartoon
    Ref: MPN 2/25/28.
The FIRST PAVILION (Polish) Film Polski 1964 short? Old man
    perfects system of shrinking people. Ref: M/TVM 8/64.
FLYING SAUCER DAFFY Col 1958 10m. Ref: Imagen. with the
    Three Stooges.
The FOX WITH NINE TAILS (J) Daiei 1968 cartoon Bewitched
    girl. Ref: MPH 12/18/68.
FRANKENSTEIN'S CAT Fox 1942 10m. cartoon Ref: Lee.
FRESH LOBSTER Man pursued by giant lobster: Dream. with
    Billy Bletcher.
The FRIEND (Polish) 1963 short (PRZYJACIEL) Robots, atomic war.
FRIENDLY SPIRITS Fox/Educ 1935 19m. "Haunted" house. Ref:
    FD 6/10/35.

A GAME (Bulgarian) animated 1970 Ref: M/TVM 8/70:21. "Evil
    magic bird."
GANDY GOOSE IN GHOST TOWN 1944 animated (The GHOST

TOWN) "Dracula." Ref: Photon 21:26.
GENTLEMAN JEKYLL AND DRIVER HYDE (Canadian) Int'l 1950
8m. Ref: MFB'50:145.
GERALD ON PLANET MOO 1955 cartoon short Ref: DDC I:316.
GERTIE THE DINOSAUR 1909 short animated/live action Sea
monster, pterodactyl, mammoth. with George McManus, Winsor
McKay (or McCay).
GERTIE THE DINOSAUR McKay imitation.
GET ALONG, LITTLE ZOMBIE Col 1946 20m. Ref: LC.
GHOST BUSTER Haunted house. with Gil Lamb.
The GHOST OF SACRAMENTO (Polish) 1962 cartoon (El FANTASMA
DE SACRAMENTO. DUCH ZAMZYSKA SACRAMENTO) Robot,
ghost. Ref: Imagen.
GHOST TALES RETOLD (B) 1938 series of shorts Ref: Brit
Cinema. D: W. A. Newman.
GHOSTS IS THE BUNK Para 1939 7m. Spooky hotel. Ref:
FD 7/14/39.
GIBUS THE MAGICIAN 6m. cartoon Live mummy. Ref: Belgian
Film Production:24.
GINGER NUTT'S FOREST DRAGON (B) 1950 Ref: MFB'50:94. 7m.
The GOLD GHOST Educ/Fox 1934 short Ref: FD 4/5/34. with
Buster Keaton.
GOLDEN SUPERMAN (Korea) 1968 animated 70m. "Sunlight
weapon," "evil Cooper Devil." Ref: Korea Cinema'68.
GOODNESS! A GHOST RKO 1940 16m. Ref: Lee. with Harry
Langdon.
GRAVE DIGGER'S AMBITIONS 1913 "shadow drama" Ref: Bios
5/18/13. Deal with the devil.
The GREEN PLANET (F) 1965 short Planet inhabited by semi-
humans. Ref: Imagen.
GULLIVER'S TRAVELS BEYOND THE MOON (J) 1965 Ref:
Imagen. PM.

HANSEL AND GRETEL RKO/Myerberg 1954 75m. puppet anima-
tion Ref: COF 10:41.
HAUNTED HOUSE Paul Terry 1925 Ref: LC.
HAUNTED HOUSE 1931 Mickey Mouse Ref: LC.
HAUNTED HOUSE 1939 12m. Vitaphone Ref: FD 6/28/39.
The HAUNTED MOUSE Looney Tune 1941 Ref: LC.
The HEADLESS HORSEMAN 1936 10m. cartoon Ref: FD 2/26/36.
HELP! (I) 1954 15m. From "William Wilson" by Poe. Ref: Lee.
FM 12:6.
HOST TO A GHOST RKO 1947 17m. Ref: Lee. with Edgar
Kennedy
HOUSE OF THE FUTURE cartoon Tex Avery Ref: DDC I:153.
The HOUSE OF TOMORROW MGM 1949 7m. Ref: Imagen.
HYPOTHESIS (Cz) 1963 short Possibilities of life on other planets.
Ref: Imagen.

ICARUS MON(T)GOLFIER WRIGHT 1963 18m. Ref: Imagen. MW
6:47. From Ray Bradbury's short story.

IN PARADISE (Polish) 1962 Ref: Imagen. Year 2000, astronaut,
    devil.
INSOMNIA (F) 1963 short Vampires. Ref: 70 Years. COF 8:47.
    Pierre Etaix.
INTERPLANETARY REVOLUTION (russ) 1924 animated Parody of
    AELITA. Ref: Lee.
The INVENTORS 1918 cartoon (Mutt & Jeff) "War invention."
    Ref: SilentFF.
The INVISIBLE MOUSE Disney Ref: Shriek 1:28.
The INVISIBLE MOUSE MGM 1947 Tom & Jerry Ref: Lee.

JASPER AND THE HAUNTED HOUSE Puppetoon Ref: HR 10/27/42.
JEEPERS CREEPERS Looney Tune 1939 7m. cartoon "Spook."
    Ref: FD 10/19/39.
La JETEE (F) Janus 1963 27m. Post-World War III. Ref: COF
    11:6.
JOHNNY THE GIANT KILLER Lippert 1953 70m. cartoon Giant,
    magic ray. Ref: COF 11:42.
JORINDE AND JORINGEL (G) 1920 cartoon Witch. Ref: SilentFF.
JULES VERNE (Bulgarian) c1960 D: Arcady. Short Ref: DDC
    I:108.
JUST SPOOKS Bray 1925 short cartoon Ref: LC.

The KID FROM MARS Para 1961 7m. cartoon Ref: Boxo 5/8/61.
KING KLUNK Univ 1933 cartoon 10m. Ref: MW 3:6. Imagen.
    MMF 6:62.
KITRO (J) Toei 44m. cartoon Boy turns people into monsters.
    Ref: UFQ 42.
KOKO IN 1999 1924 cartoon Year 1999. Ref: SilentFF.
KOKO'S HAUNTED HOUSE Para 1928 cartoon Ref: SilentFF.
KRAZY'S MAGIC Col 1938 7m. cartoon Old house, storm, mad
    magician. Ref: FD 5/25/38.
KRAZY'S RACE OF TIME Col 1937 7m. 1999 newsreel. Ref:
    FD 6/3/37.

The LAST MORNING OF EDGAR ALLAN POE (F) 1964 short
    Ref: Bulletin d'Information'68 (June-Aug.):111.
The LAUREL AND HARDY MURDER CASE Roach 1930 30m.
    British Film Institute Distribution Catalogue'62: "Old mansion,
    ghosts, murders."
LITTLE RED RIDING HOOD (B) Hepworth 1922 cartoon Ref:
    SilentFF.
LITTLE NORSE PRINCE VALIANT (J) Toei 1968 Villain has
    powers over wolves. Ref: UFQ 42.
LIVE GHOSTS MGM 1935 20m. "Haunted" ship. Ref: FD 1/15/35.
LONESOME GHOSTS RKO/Disney 1940 cartoon short Ref: Lee.
    Haunted house.
A LOST WORLD 1948 10m. From "The Lost World" by Doyle.
    Ref: Lee.

The MAD HOUSE Fox/Educ 1934 7m. cartoon Haunted house,
chemist's invisibility formula. Ref: FD 5/11/34.
MAD MONSTER PARTY Emb 1967 animated (Animagic) Franken-
stein's monster, Dracula, werewolf, The Creature, Dr. Jekyll
and Mr. Hyde, The Mummy, The Hunchback of Notre Dame, The
Invisible Man, robot. Boris Karloff.
The MAGIC BEAN Univ 1939 7m. Ref: FD 3/6/39. Jack and the
Beanstalk, giant cat.
MAGIC BOY (J) animated Ref: COF 10:46.
MAGIC VOYAGE OF SINBAD Ref: COF 10:46.
El MAGO DE LOS SUENOS (Sp) 1966 (The DREAM MAKER) Flying
saucer, Martian. animated? Ref: SpCinema'67.
MAGOO MEETS FRANKENSTEIN UPA 1959 6m. animated Ref:
MW 1:15.
MAN AND THE MOON BV 1955 animated and live action Ref:
Imagen. Lee. 60m. Outer space.
A MAN CALLED FLINTSTONE animated feature
MAN IN SPACE 35m. 1955 Disney Excerpts from GIRL IN THE
MOON cartoons showing future space flights; part of A TRIP
TO THE MOON (Melies).
MASQUE OF THE RED DEATH Zagreb From Poe's story. Ref:
B. Warren.
MEANWHILE, BACK ON EARTH 14m. Ref: SM 1:10. "Space
Age future."
MECHANICAL HANDY MAN Univ 1937 animated 7m. Robot. Ref:
Lee.
The MECHANICAL HORSE animated Ref: MPW 57:703.
The MECHANICAL MAN Univ 1932 10m. cartoon Ref: Lee.
MICKEY'S APE MAN RKO 1933 20m. Ref: LC.
MICKEY'S GALA PREMIERE Disney 1933 Frankenstein's
monster, Dracula. Ref: MW 1:18. DDC II:80.
MICKEY'S MECHANICAL MAN Disney 1933 10m. cartoon Ref: Lee.
MICROSPOOK Col 1949 16m. Gorilla, ghosts, old house. Ref:
Lee.
MIGHTY MOUSE series Fox Ref: Imagen. Photon 21:26. MIGHTY
MOUSE MEETS BAD BILL BUNION ("Dracula") ('45). MIGHTY
MOUSE MEETS JEKYLL AND HYDE CAT. A CAT'S TALE ('51).
A SOAPY OPERA ('52). A SWISS MISS ('51). ANTI-CATS ('50).
BEAUTY AND THE BEACH ('50). GOONS FROM THE MOON
('51). HANSEL AND GRETEL ('52). HAPPY HOLLAND ('52).
HERO FOR A DAY ('52). HOT RODS ('53). INJUN TROUBLE
('51). LAW AND ORDER ('50). MOTHER GOOSE'S BIRTHDAY
PARTY ('50). PREHISTORIC PERILS ('51). SPARE THE ROD
('53). STOP, LOOK AND LISTEN ('49). SUNNY ITALY ('50).
HELPLESS HIPPO ('53). MAGIC SLIPPER ('48). The RACKET
BUSTER ('48). The REFORMED WOLF ('54). WHEN MOUSE-
HOOD WAS IN FLOWER ('53).
MIRKO THE INVISIBLE (Bulgarian) 1961 puppet invisibility. Ref:
FEFN 2/61.
MR. MAGOO - MAN OF MYSTERY 1965 cartoon 96m. Ref: TVG.
Magoo as Dr. Frankenstein, Dr. Watson, Edmund Dantes, and
Dick Tracy. From the TV series.
MR. ROBIDA, TIME-EXPLORER (F) 1952 short Ref: DDC II:350.
Imagen.

MONIHARA (India) 1968 short "Ghost." Ref: Link 1/14/68.
MONSTER PRINCE (J) 1968 Ref: UFQ 41:38: "trick film." "Boy
    fights dinosaur."
The MOON (Russ) 1965 short Ref: COF 10:50. Soviet Film 9/65.
    Documentary.
MOONGLOW (Holland) cartoon Ref: DDC II:101: witch.
MOONSTRUCK (B) 1963 cartoon Ref: Imagen. Trip to moon in
    rocket.
MUMMY'S DUMMIES Col 1948 16m. Mummy. Ref: Lee. with
    The Three Stooges.
The MYSTERY OF PROFESSOR ZAZUL (Polish) 1962 short Ref:
    MMF 9. Robots.

NEW ADVENTURES OF THE SPACE EXPLORERS cartoon 102m.
    Ref: TVFFSB.
A NIGHT ON BALD MOUNTAIN (F) 1932 short Ref: DDC II:349:
    Monster.
NO. 00173 (Polish) 1966 Ref: M/TVM 9/67. short? "Robot world."

OBJECTIVE MOON (F?) 1962 cartoon Ref: TVFFSB. with Tin Tin.
OF STARS AND MEN Brandon 1963 feature-length cartoon Ref:
    Orpheus 4:38.
ONE LIVE GHOST 1936 21m. Ref: FD 11/3/36. Seance, "ghost."
The ORIGIN OF SCIENCE FICTION (I) 1963 short Ref: Imagen.
The ORPHAN BROTHER (J) Toei 1959 cartoon Ref: UFQ 9. Giant
    spider.
OUTER SPACE VISITOR Fox 1959 cartoon short Ref: Lee.

PALLE ALONE IN THE WORLD (Danish) Nordisk 1949 25m.
    Dream: Flight to moon in plane. Ref: MFB'50:192.
PANDA AND THE MAGIC SERPENT (J) 1961 Ref: TVG. Evil
    magician.
PARK OF GAMES (Sp) 1963 Ref: Imagen: vampirism?
PERCY, THE MECHANICAL MAN Bray 1916 animated Ref: Lee.
    Robot.
PETE'S HAUNTED HOUSE Bray 1926 cartoon short "Spooks and
    skeletons." Ref: MPW'26:427.
PIGS IS PIGS Vitaphone 1937 7m. cartoon Dream: ogre. Ref:
    FD 1/7/37.
PINOCCHIO Disney 1940 "Monstro" the Whale, "Pleasure Island"
    horror scenes.
PINOCCHIO IN OUTER SPACE Univ 1965 cartoon 71m. Ref:
    COF-A:6. PM. Monster crabs.
The PIT 1960-62 Abraham 30m. From Poe's "The Pit and the
    Pendulum." Ref: "The Horror Film."
The PIT AND THE PENDULUM (F) 1963 35m. From Poe's story.
    Ref: Avant-Scene du Cinema 11/66.
PLANET OF 3 ISLANDS (Polish) 1967 cartoon Robot. Ref: M/TVM
    2/68.

PLANET PEOPLE (Cz) 1964 "Strange planet. " Ref: M/TVM 8/64.
  short?
POPEYE MEETS SINBAD 1936 17m. Ref: FD 11/4/36.   The roc,
  dragon. cartoon.
POPEYE, THE ACE OF SPACE   Par   1953   cartoon short .
PORKY'S MOVIE MYSTERY   Vitaphone   1939   7m. cartoon Ref:
  FD 3/9/39. Mr. Motto vs. phantom, the Invisible Man, etc.
PREHISTORIC PORKY 1940   7m. cartoon Ref: Showmen's 11/2/40.
PRINCE BAJAJA (Cz) 1950 puppet animation   Monster. Good.
The PRINCESS WITH THE IRON FAN (Chinese) 1942 cartoon feature
  Ref: The XXth Century 1/42. Demon.
PRISONER OF THE BLUE PLANET (Cz) 1963 Ref: Imagen.
  Marionettes.
PROPS AND THE SPIRITS   Educ   1925   cartoon 10m.   Ref: FD 9/20/
  25. Medium brings spirits out of cabinet.
PUBLIC GHOST NO. 1   Roach   1935   Haunted House   Ref: Lee.
  with Charley Chase.
PUSS IN BOOTS   Principal   1936 6m.   "Monstrous ogre. " Ref:
  FD 3/12/36.

QUININE   1917   5m. cartoon Ref: MPN 15:3626. Dream à la Jack &
  the Beanstalk.

RED STAIN (Cz) 1963 14m. cartoon Ref: Lee. Robot.
RETURN TO GLENNASCAUL (Irish) 1951   23m. Ghost story. Ref:
  Lee. with Orson Welles.
The REVENGE OF THE GHOSTS (F) 1909 cartoon D: Cohl. Ref:
  DDC I: 444 .
The RISK (Polish) Semafor 1963 Ref: Imagen. Electronic brain.
ROBOT (Yugos) 1960 short marionettes   Robots.
The ROBOT 1932 cartoon Ref: Imagen. short.
ROBOT WRECKS   MGM   1941   Ref: SF Film.
ROCKET TO MARS   Para   1946   10m. Ref: Imagen.
ROUND TRIP TO MARS   Univ   1957   10m. cartoon Ref: Imagen
RUSSIAN ROCKET TO THE MOON (Russ) 1957 cartoon 2m. Ref:
  Lee.

SATAN'S WAITIN'   Hell, satan, etc. cartoon
The SAVAGE PLANET (F-Cz) 1969 cartoon feature Ref: V 5/7/69:
  109.
SCRAPPY'S GHOST STORY   1935   7m. cartoon Ref: FD 5/28/35.
  Ghosts: dream.
SCHTROUMPF A TOUT FAIRE (Belgian) 1966 cartoon Robot. Ref:
  Annuaire du Film Belge 66/67.
The SCREAM (I) 1965 13m. Emotion eliminated. Ref: Lee.
The SECRET OF MAGIC ISLAND (F) Emb 1958 ('65-U.S.) 66m.
  cartoon?   (The SECRET OF OUTER SPACE ISLAND. ONCE
  UPON A TIME) Ref: Lee.
SHEIKH CHILLI (India) 1938 short Ref: Dipali 1/21/38. Hindi ver-
  sion of Bengali short MAYA KAJAL. Messenger of Death.

SINBAD THE SAILOR (J) 1963 Ref: TVG. cartoon.
SIRENE (Belgian) cartoon Ref: Belgian Film Production: 86.
Prehistoric bird.
SIRENS (Belgian) cartoon 7m. Ref: Belgian Film Production: 100.
Sirens lure sailors.
The SKELETON DANCE Disney 1929 Ref: Pict Hist Cinema. cartoon short.
SKELETON FROLIC Col 1937 7m. cartoon Ref: FD 2/13/37.
Skeletons.
SKY HIGH WB 1931 10m. Ref: SF Film. LC. Futuristic plane.
SLEEPING BEAUTY Disney c1955 Ref: FM 12:6.
SLEEPING PRINCESS 1939 10m. cartoon Ref: Showmen's 12/2/39.
Witch's spell.
The SNAILS (F) (Les ESCARGOTS) Cartoon Giant snails. Ref:
COF 10:50.
The SNOW QUEEN Univ (russ) 1960 70m. cartoon.
SNOW WHITE & THE SEVEN DWARFS Disney 1937 Ref: FM 12:6.
The SORCERER'S APPRENTICE (F) 1935 10m. Ref: FD 4/16/35.
Phantoms.
The SPACE EXPLORERS cartoon 59m. Ref: TVFFSB.
SPACE SHIP SAPPY Col 1957 16m. Ref: Lee. Glut. with The
Three Stooges. Vampire-women.
The SPIRIT OF 1976 RKO 1935 20m. Ref: SF Film.
SPOOK SPORT 1940 (Canadian) Ref: DDC III:272.
SPOOKEASY Col 1930 10m. Ref: LC.
SPOOKS 1930 cartoon Ref: LC.
SPOOKS 1932 cartoon Ref: LC.
SPOOKS 1936 Ref: FD 6/10/36. 9m. Ghostly cabin.
SPOOKS with El Brendel(l), Tom Kennedy. "Haunted" warehouse.
SPOOKS Col 1952 20m. Ref: COF 5:51. Lee. 3-D with The
Three Stooges.
SPOOKY HOOKY MGM 1937 10m. Ref: FD 2/3/37. Spooky
schoolroom.
SPOOKY WOOKY Haunted country house. with Leon Errol.
The STARFISH (B) 1950 38m. Ref: MFB. Witch's curse.
A STONE AGE ADVENTURE Pathe 1915 cartoon 7m. Dionsaur
Ref: MPN 5/29/15.
A STONE AGE CARTOON Para 1940 cartoon 7m. Ref: Lee.
STONE AGE ROMEOS with The Three Stooges. Ref: TVG.
STRANGER THAN FICTION 1935 10m. Ref: FD 3/15/35. Haunted
church.
SUPER MOUSE series 1943 Ref: Lee. cartoon shorts.
SUPERMAN series 1941-43 cartoon shorts THE MUMMY
STRIKES. MECHANICAL MONSTERS ("giant flying robots").
Ref: Imagen. MW 10:23. FanMo 6:51.

The TELL-TALE HEART 1941 MGM 20m. Ref: FM 11:42.
From the story by Edgar Allan Poe. Fair.
The TELL-TALE HEART 1954 cartoon short Ref: DDC II:101.
Good. From Poe's story.
The TELL-TALE HEART 1966 short with Theodore Gottlieb. Ref:
FM 37:49.

10,000 YEARS B.C. 1917 puppet Ref: Lee.
A TERRIBLY STRANGE BED short
THAT OL'GHOST TRAIN Soundies 1942 10m. Ref: Lee.
THIRTY THOUSAND MILES UNDER THE SEA (J) Toei cartoon
1970 60m. Ref: UFQ 50. Robot-dragons.
THREE DIMENSIONAL MURDER Pete Smith Novelty Ref: FM 24:
67. Ed Payson as Frankenstein's monster.
THUNDERBIRDS ARE GO (B) puppet animation Ref: PM. V 7/24/68.
21st Century.
The TIN MAN MGM 1935 short Robot, "spooky house." Ref:
FD 3/23/35.
TO HEIR IS HUMAN with H. Langdon, Una Merkel. Old house,
"hauntings."
TORTICOLA VS. FRANKENSBERG (F) 1952 Ref: FM 28:20. Frank-
enstein-like monster.
TRANSYLVANIA 6-5000 Vampire. c1960 WB Ref: Photon 21:26.
A TRIP TO THE MOON Mo-Toy 1917 11m. puppet Ref: MPN 15:
3625.
A TRIP TO THE MOON 1934 11m. Ref: Imagen.
A TRIP TO THE MOON Lubin 1914 cartoon Ref: Bios 5/28/14.
A TRIP TO THE POLE (F) Pathe 1911 cartoon short Ref: SilentFF.
Subway to pole.
A TRIP THROUGH THE COSMOS (Polish) 1962 cartoon Ref: Imagen.
Earthman on another planet.
TUPAPAOO MGM 1938 11m. Ref: FD 6/27/38. South Seas is-
landers' "curse of the shooting star."
20,000 B.C. Terry Toons 1931 6m. Ref: Lee. cartoon.
TWIST AGAIN (Yugos) 1964 cartoon Ref: M/TVM 6/64. Stone Age.
The TWO-HEADED GIANT Fox 1939 7m. cartoon Ref: FD 8/15/39.
Jack the Giant Killer.

ULTRA 7 (J) Toei 1968 Ref: UFQ 42. 25m. Invasion from
space.
UP POPPED THE GHOST Para 1932 20m. Ref: LC.
UP TO MARS Para 1930 10m. cartoon Ref: Imagen.
UPSIDE DOWN PLANET (Cz) 1963 Ref: COF 6:30. short.

Le VAMPIRE (F) 1945 short D: Jean Painlevé. Documentary
Scenes from NOSFERATU. Ref: RVB. DDC II:347. Le Sur-
realisme au Cinema.
The VAMPIRE (Polish) 1968 Ref: S&S'68:184. Bianco 11/68.
M/TVM 8/69. 30m. Dance attended by "vampires."
VAMPIRES D'ALFAMA cartoon short Ref: MMF 13:67.
VAMPIRISME (F) 1967 Ref: MMF 18-19:9. with Alain Le Bris.
12m.
VENERA (Yugos) 1961 Ref: Imagen. marionettes Robot, rocket
to Venus.
VIP, MY SUPERMAN BROTHER (I) Ref: Ital P. 1966 cartoon.
VISITOR FROM SPACE (Yugos) cartoon Ref: F&F 10/66.
VOODOO FIRES Vitaphone 1939 Ref: FD 5/19/39. Voodooism
practiced on plantation.

VOODOO IN HARLEM Univ 1938 7m. Ref: FD 6/20/38. "Weird dances."

WALPURGIS NIGHT Kendall DeVally Operalogue
WE DO BELIEVE IN GHOSTS (B) 1946 36m. Ref: MFB'47:35. Real ghosts.
WE WANT OUR MUMMY Col 1938 Ref: Lee. with the Three Stooges. Mummy.
WHAT! NO MEN? WB 1935 short Ref: SF Film. Flight to Mars. with El Brendel.
WHEN MEN WERE MEN Pathe 1925 11m. cartoon Ref: FD 7/12/25. Dinosaurs.
WHITE SNAKE ENCHANTRESS (J) cartoon 1958 (HAKUJA-DEN) Ref: UFQ
WILLY McBEAN AND HIS MAGIC MACHINE (J) Magna 1965 94m. puppet Ref: COF 8:6. Time machine.
WOODPECKER FROM MARS Univ 1956 7m. cartoon Ref: Imagen.
The WORLD OF LITTLE IG (B) Halas & Batchelor 1963 8m. cartoon Life on an imaginary planet. Ref: TVG. Imagen.
The WORM TURNS UA 1937 10m. cartoon Chemist's formula gives animal great strength.

XANTIPA A SOKRATES (Cz) 1962 marionettes Ref: Imagen. 21st Century.

The YEAR 3003 (Yugos) Triglav Film 1962 marionettes Ref: Imagen. World of robots.
The YELLOW SUBMARINE 1968 cartoon feature Frankenstein's monster.

OUT LIST

Borderline Cases, Misleading Titles, Films with Slight
S-F/horror Elements, Further Research Necessary

[A "NO" indicates that the title has been considered for
the main sequence but discarded on the basis of research.]

[Title missing] (Fili) Ref: FEFN 1/24/58. 1958. Princess turns
into snake.

A-008, OPERATION EXTERMINATE (I) 1965 "Mysterious new in-
vention called Antiradar." Ref: Ital P. with I. Schoeller, A.
Lupo, J. Heston.
AADMI Ref: FEFN '58/'59. Deal with devil?
ABBYS OF PASSION (Mex) 1953 (WUTHERING HEIGHTS) D: Luis
Bunnel. Ref: FM 31:18.
ABSENT-MINDED MOTHER   Ref: Bios 5/4/14. Hair restorer?
Les ABYSSES (F) 1963 Ref: COF 6:52: "Socio-horror." COF 9:
39.
ACCIDENTS WILL HAPPEN   1903   Severed head. Ref: Niver.
The ACCURSED (B)   1957   with Christopher Lee.
The ACCURSED TOWER (F) 1900 Melies Ref: DDC III:350.
The ACCUSED (B)   1954   Old house. Ref: MFB'54:22.
ADALEN '31 Boys go to see "Frankenstein in London."
ADVENTURE(S) IN SPACE   Documentary s-f?   Ref: FIR'64:547.
ADVENTURES ON THE RYUKYUS (J) 1961 Invisible swordsmen.
Ref: FEFN 4/61.
AEROGRAD (Russ) 1935   NO--New Yorker 1/11/36. (FRONTIER.
AIR CITY)
AFRICA ADDIO 1967 Ref: Boxo: sadism.
AFTER THE FOG 1930   Ref: Photoplay: "Mary Philbin has another
role similar to her PHANTOM OF THE OPERA."
AFTERWARDS 1934 Clairvoyance. Ref: PM.
AGAIN THE WIZARD (G) 1965 Ref: FIR'67. 85.
L'AGE D'OR (Sp) 1930 Surrealistic.
AGENT END (Sp-I) Ref: SpCinema. "Rocket Airplane" in prepara-
tin.
AGENT 3S3, MASSACRE IN THE SUN (I-F-Sp) 1966 Deadly new
gas. Used? with G. Ardisson, F. Wolff, M. Lemoine. Ref:
Ital P.
AGENT 3S3, PASSPORT FOR HELL (I-F-Sp) 1965 Organization
called "The Black Scorpion." Ref: Ital P.
AGENT X-1-7, OPERATION "OCEAN" (I) 1965 "Electro-magnetic
cigarette-holder." Ref: Ital P.

AGENT Z55 (Sp) Ref: SpCinema'67. 1966. "Magnetophone."
The AIR HAWK 1925 MPN 30:2856. NO.
ALARM IN 5 BANKS (I) Ref: Annuario. New bank alarm.
The ALCHEMIST 1913 Ref: Bios 7/10/13. NO.
The ALCHEMIST AND THE DEMON (F) Melies 1906 (L'ALCHEM-
    ISTE PARAFARAGARAMUS ou LA CORNUE INFERNALE) Ref:
    Lee. Imp. (aka THE MYSTERIOUS RETORT?)
ALIAS BULLDOG DRUMMOND 1935 Ref: FD 9/10/35. "Hair
    raising...underground tunnels."
ALIAS JOHN PRESTON (B) 1955 with C. Lee. Ref: COF 6:4:
    Jekyll-Hyde personality?
The ALIBI (F) 1937 Ref: MFB'38:164: "Von Stroheim as the
    mysterious thought-reading Professor Winckler, the villain."
The ALIBI (B) 1941 Ref: MFB'42:57: "thought reader."
The ALIEN c1965 Ref: FM 32:20.33:50. Amateur s-f film shown
    on local TV.
The ALIENS' INVASION (B) 1905 Ref: DDC III:33.
ALL SOUL'S EVE 1921 Spirits. Ref: Lee.
ALONG THE MOONLIGHT TRAIL 1920 Ref: FM 63:28: footage
    from GHOST OF SLUMBER MOUNTAIN, The
The ALRAUNE 1913 Ref: Bios 7/31/13. NO.
AMADOR (Sp) 1965 Ref: MMF 13:47: Bluebeard.
An AMBASSADOR FROM THE DEAD 1915 Ref: Lee. NO.
An AMOROUS GHOST (Norwegian) 1947. Ref: DDC III:482.
The AMULET 1912 Ref: MPW 14:1340. Bios 3/20/13. NO.
ANGEL IN MY POCKET Ref: HR: "Haunted" graveyard. NO.
ANGEL OF DEATH Ref: Bios 10/30/13: allegory
ANGEL ON MY SHOULDER UA 1946 Devil
ANGEL ON THE AMAZON NO-V.
ANGELIC FRANKENSTEIN 1964 (POUR MESSIEURS SEULS) Ref:
    D. Glut. FM 63:24.
ANGKOR 1934 Ref: PM: "Silent weird jungle picture."
ANGRY GHOST (J) Ref: Japan.
AN(N)ABEL LEE 1921 Exhibitors Herald: Love story. NO.
The ANNIVERSARY Ref: PM. NO.
The ANNOUNCEMENT 1964 Ref: FM 29:8: "Melting man." N
ANONA'S BAPTISM 1913 Ref: Bios 5/15/13 Spirit.
ANOTHER THIN MAN 1939 Man "foresees" death. NO.
L'ANTIMIRACOLO (I) 1962 Ref: Ital P'63. Futuristic?
ANYONE CAN PLAY 1968 (LADIES AND LADIES) Ref: HR 9/18/68.
    Nightmare.
ANYTHING TO DECLARE (B) 1938 Ref: MFB'38:255. "Anti-gas
    formula."
ARABELLA AND THE WIZARD (F) 1913 Ref: Lee. Magic.
The ARGYLE CASE 1929 Ref: New Yorker 9/7/29: "sliding panels."
    NO.
AROUND THE WORLD IN 80 DAYS Ref: COF 6:31: Includes
    Melies' A TRIP TO THE MOON
The ARSENAL STADIUM MYSTERY Ref: Boy's Cinema 2/24/36?
    New poison.
AS IT WAS IN THE BEGINNING 1911 Ref: Lee. Magic, reincarna-
    tion.
The ASIAN SUN (G) 1921 Ref: SilentFF. Gold formula.

The ASTROLOGER'S DREAM (F?) 1905 Ref: SilentFF. S-f?
The ASSASSINATION BUREAU Zeppelin - minor element. Ref: V.
  HR.
El ASTRONAUTA (Sp) Ref: SpCinema'71. 1970. NO.
AT MIDNIGHT IN THE GRAVEYARD (Russ) 1910 Ref: RVB.
L'ATOMIQUE MONSIEUR PLACIDO (F) 1949 Ref: DDC II:430
ATTACK OF THE JUNGLE WOMAN 1959
AU DEVANT DES REVES (Russ) 1963 Ref: Musee du Cinema. S-f?
AUTOMATIC FALSE TEETH 1909 Ref: Bios 10/7/09. S-f?
The AUTOMATIC HOUSE 1915 Ref: MPN 2/13/15. MPW 24:466.
  NO.
The AUTOMATIC MONKEY Ref: F Index 5/1/09: ?
AUTOMATON OR ACROBAT? (F?) Pathe 1910 Ref: Bios 1/12/11: ?
AVENGING SHADOW 1928 Ref: Photoplay 6/28: NO.
AWFUL SCARE 1913 Ref: Bios 10/16/13: ?

BABY LOVE 1969 Ref: MFB'69:79: violence, sadism.
BACCHANALE 1970 Ref: V 7/1/70. "Spirit," "cloaked appari-
  tion."
BACK FROM THE DEAD 1912 (F) Ref: Bios 2/27/13: NO.
BACK FROM THE GRAVE 1914 Ref: Lee.
BAEFENGYI KUTT (Korea) 1956 Ref: FEFN 1/18/57. Spirit.
BAIT 1954 Ref: Halliwell. The devil.
The BANG SUN ENGINE 1915 Ref: MPN 11/27/15. Plans for
  engine.
BANDIT OF BAGDAD (India) c1931 Ref: Indian Cin.
BANISHED FROM PARADISE (UAR) 1964 Ref: V 7/14/65. Man
  rises from coffin.
The BAREFOOT EXECUTIVE Ape picks TV shows.
BARU, MAN OF THE JUNGLE (Mex) c1964 Fake apeman. Ref: Lee.
BARU'S SAVAGE WORLD (Mex) c1964 Ref: FanMo 4:15.
BATMAN DRACULA Warhol Ref: Film Comment 45:13.
BATTLE ON THE ROBOT CREATURES Florida-made?
BEACH HEAD Ref: RVB: British TV series episode (BRIDGEHEAD)
The BEAR AND THE GHOSTS (Cz) 1959 Ref: Modern Czechoslovak
  Film.
BEASTS OF MARSEILLES Ref: COF 7:8. MPH 7/25/59. War
  drama. Chamber of horrors?
BEAUTY AND THE BEAST 1903 Ref: Lee.
BEAUTY AND THE BEAST 1912 Non-fantasy. Ref: Lee.
BEAUTY AND THE BEAST (B) 1922 Ref: SilentFF. Non-fantasy.
The BEAUTY IN THE SEASHELL 1913 Ref: MPW 18:420. 4000-
  year-old woman.
BEAUTY OF THE DEVIL 1949 Comic version of "Faust."
BEBE AND HYPNOTISM (F) 1911 Ref: DDC II:338. D: Feuillade.
BED OF GRASS (Greek) 1957 Ref: Lee. "Witch."
BEDAZZLED 1967 Comic updating of "Faust" story.
The BEDFORD INCIDENT 1965 Ref: Halliwell. End-of-world
  implied.
BEDKNOBS AND BROOMSTICKS Ref: V 10/13/71: fantasy.
BEES IN PARADISE (B) 1944 Ref: Lee. Island run like bee hive.
BEES SAAL BAAD (India) Ref: Illustrated Weekly of India

7/5/64: "chiller."
BEFORE THE DELUGE (F) 1954 Ref: Menville. La Prod Cin Fr:
    NO.
BEFORE THE WHITE MAN CAME 1912 Spirit. Ref: FIR'66:221.
    Remake: HOPE LEGEND.
BEGINNING OF THE SERPENTINE (F) 1909 Ref: V&FI IV:4:8.
    Devil.
The BEGUILED   Ref: V 3/17/71: "Black comedy." MPH: "Hor-
    ror." NO. 1971
BEHIND THAT CURTAIN 1929 Ref: V 7/3/29: NO.
EBHIND THE MASK 1946 (The SHADOW BEHIND THE MASK. The
    SHADOW'S SHADOW) Ref: V. MPH. FanMo 6:47. NO.
BELL, BOOK AND CANDLE 1959 Love spell. NO. Ref: HR.
The BELLS 1913 Ref: SilentFF. NO.
BELOVED VAMPIRE 1917 Ref: RVB. "Vamp."
BELOW THE SEA 1933 (HELL'S CARGO) Ref: Photoplay 8/33: big
    octopus. V 6/6/33: NO. Harrison's 5/6/33: "Giant octopus."
BELSHAZZAR'S FEAST (F) 1905 Ref: SilentFF. Disembodied hand.
BESPOKE OVERCOAT (B) 1956.
BETTY BOOP'S PENTHOUSE Frankenstein monster?
BETWEEN EVENING AND MORNING (G) 1923 Ref: Deutsche. (Der
    SPUK EINER NACHT)
BETWEEN TWO WORLDS 1944 Ship of the dead.
BEWITCHED (Arg) 1941 (EMBRUJO)
The BEWITCHED OF THE WHITE MOUNTAINS (Arg) 1955 Ref:
    Cine Arg.
BEWITCHED PORTRAITS Ref: Bios 12/ı/10. 1910. NO.
BEWITCHED SPIRITS OF THE CASTLE OF WHITE WAX (J) Ref:
    Lee. (BYAKUROJO NO YOKI)
The BEWITCHER 1910 Ref: Bios 11/17/70. NO.
BEYOND 1921 Ref: Lee. Ghost.
BEYOND DEATH (F) 1922 Ref: DDC III:392.
BEYOND THE GRAVE (Hong Kong) 1955.
BEYOND THE GRAVE'S MYSTERIES 1913 Ref: Bios 10/9/13.
BEYOND THE RIVER (G) 1922 Spirit. Ref: SilentFF.
BEYOND TOMORROW 1940 Ref: V. TVG. Ghost has man returned
    to life. NO.
BHAKT PRAHLAD (India) 1934 Ref: Dipali 5/11/34:25: monster?
The BICYCLE AND THE WITCH (Danish) 1909 Ref: MPW'09:344:
    The WITCH AND THE CYCLE. NO.
BILLY VAN DEUSEN AND THE VAMPIRE 1916 Ref: MPN 13:875:
    vamp.
BIN BADAL BARSATT (India) 1963 Ref: M/TVM 9/63. Curse.
The BINNETTOSCOPE 1910 Ref: Bios 1/20/10: ?
BIRTH OF A RACE 1919 Ref: MPW 40:938: NO.
The BISHOP MURDER CASE Ref: AFI. hunchback.
The BIZARRE ONES Ref: Lee (Richardson): horror?
BLACK ANGELS Merrick Ref: COF 15:39.
The BLACK BOOK 1929 serial "Great hand"-The Serial.
BLACK BUTTERFLIES 1928 Ref: Lee: "great beyond."
BLACK CAT KILLINGS (J) 1958 Ref: FEFN 6/13/58: NO.
The BLACK COBRA (W.G.) 1963 Ref: FJA folder: "mysterious
    machine."

The BLACK EAGLE VS. THE MASKS OF DEATH (Mex) 1956 Ref: Indice.
BLACK FEAR 1916 Ref: MPN 1/1/16. Satan in vision.
BLACK GHOST 1932 (from the serial LAST FRONTIER) Ref: STI 1:20: Lon Chaney, Jr., as the hero, "Black Ghost."
BLACK GHOST (India) c1932 Ref: Indian Cin.
BLACK GOD AND WHITE DEVIL 1963 Ref:M/TVM 6/64. Cruel, fanatical sect.
BLACK MAGIC 1929 Ref: PM. Photoplay 10/29. V. ?
BLACK ORCHIDS 1916 Ref: MPN 15:116. MPW 31:98. Crystalgazer.
BLACK PANIC 1958 Wilder Ref: Orpheus 4:37. Made?
The BLACK PEARL 1929 Ref: V 3/20/29: NO.
The BLACK ROSE INN (J) 1968 (KUROBARANO YAKATA) Ref: M/TVM 11/68: "horror." shooting.
The BLACK VAMPIRE (Arg) 1953 (El VAMPIRO NEGRO)
BLACK WATERS 1929 Ref: PM. Photoplay 6/29. V. NO.
The BLACK WIDOW (G-Sp) 1963 Ref: German Pictures. SpCinema '65: NO.
BLACK WITCH (F) 1907 Ref: SilentFF: Magic.
The BLACKBIRD 1926 Ref: V 2/3/26. NO.
The BLISS OF MRS. BLOSSOM 1968 Dragon in daydream.
BLONDE VAMPIRE 1922 Ref: RVB. Vamp.
BLOOD LUST 1971 Karma Vampires?
BLOOD MANIA 1971 Ref: Boxo 2/8/71: "Horror." ?
BLOOD OF A POET (F) 1931 Ref: COF 5:40. NO.
The BLOOD OF PONTIANAK (Malayan) Shaw 1958 Ref: FEFN 11/22/57: announced for filming. Vampire.
BLOOD OF THE BEASTS (F) 1949 20m. Ref: COF 9:39: "horror."
BLOOD OF THE DOOMED
BLOOD OF THE WEREWOLF 1957 Ref: Lee. Alternate title?
BLOOD ON HIS SWORD (F) 1961 Ref: COF? "Witchcraft." NO.
BLOODLUST 1968 Ref: RVB. Vampires?
BLUE SKIES Billy DeWolfe imitates Frankenstein's monster.
BLUEBEARD (F) 1898 Ref: DDC II:383.III:503. Perrault.
BLUEBEARD (F) 1901 Ref: DDC II:383. Perrault. Melies
BLUEBEARD (F) 1907 Ref: Lee. SilentFF. c1910
BLUEBEARD 1909 Perrault. Ref: MPW 5:767: NO.
BLUEBEARD (F) 1936 short Ref: Lee. ?
BLUEBEARD (I) 1941 Ref: DDC I:265.
BLUEBEARD (F) 1951 Ref: DDC I:50.II:183.
BLUEBEARD (F) 1962 (LANDRU) NO.
BLUEBEARD'S TEN HONEYMOONS 1959 (B) Ref: PM: NO.
BOBBY TAKES UP SPIRITUALISM 1912 Ref: Bios 11/14/12: NO.
BOCCACCIO '70 (I) 1961 Giantess.
The BODY IS A SHELL 1956 Ref: FM 2:14. "Spiritualistic."
BONGO WOLF'S REVENGE 1970-71 with B. Wolf, J. Shapiro. No werewolf.
BOOM Reference to "vampire." Poet nicknamed the "angel of death."
BORDER PHANTOM 1937 Ref: FD 6/7/37: "Mystery atmosphere, deserted house."
BORDERLAND 1922 Ref: MPW 8/5/22. Spirit. NO.

BOSTON BLACKIE AND THE LAW 1946 Magician Ref: TVG. V. NO.
BOSTON BLACKIE'S RENDEZVOUS 1945(SURPRISE IN THE NIGHT) Ref: V 9/11/45: mad strangler.
The BOTTLE IMP (G) 1952 puppets Ref: Deutsche Filme 1952.
BOUT DE ZAN ET LE FANTOME (F) 1915 Ref: Mitry II:218.
The BOY AND THE DRAGON (Swedish) 1961 Ref: Lee.
The BOY AND THE PHYSIC (B) 1910 Ref: Bios 10/27/10: ?
The BOY AND THE PIRATES 1960 genie Ref: PM. D: B. I. Gordon. NO.
The BOY WITH GREEN HAIR 1948 fantasy
The BRAIN 1969 Ref: MFB: NO.
The BRAIN MACHINE (B) 1954 Ref: HR: NO.
The BRAIN STEALERS (Chinese) 1969 Ref: M/TVM 3/69:26.
BRAINS TRUST No. 3 (B) 1943 Ref: MFB'43:73. Questions on the Loch Ness Monster.
BREAKING THE SOUND BARRIER (B) Experimental plane. NO.
BREWSTER McCLOUD 1970 Flying apparatus.
BRENDA STARR, REPORTER 1945 serial Ch. 4. A Ghost Walks. 9. Dark Magic.
BRIDE OF THE SHADOWS (F) 1943 Ref: Fowler: NO.
The BRIDE WORE BLACK Ref: NYT: "horror." NO.
BRIGHT TOMORROW Ref: SM 1:16. S-f?
BRITISH INTELLIGENCE 1940 Ref: MPH: NO.
BROKEN SPELL 1910 Ref: Bios 6/23/10. NO.
BROOBA (J) 1956 Ape man? Ref: Lee.
BROTHER JOHN 1971 Man from another planet? Ref: HR 3/24/71: NO. V 3/24/71.
BULLDOG DRUMMOND IN AFRICA1938 Ref: FD 8/1/38. NYT 8/25/38: NO. England "supposedly" possesses radio-wave disintegrator.
The BULLY'S DOOM 1914 Ref: Bios 6/18/14. "Electric snuff."
The BURGOMEISTER (Australian) 1935 horror? Ref: Lee.
BURIED ALIVE 1940 D: V. Halperin. NO.
BURIED ALIVE (I) 1948 (La SEPOLTA VIVA) Ref: DDC I:270.
BURIED TREASURE 1921 Ref: NYT 2/14/21. Reincarnation.
The BURNING BRAZIER (F) 1923 Premonition. Fair.
BURY ME DEAD 1947 Ref: TVK. NO.
BUT DO NOT DELIVER US FROM EVIL 1970 Ref: V 5/26/71. "Black mass."
BYE, BYE BIRDIE Pills make turtle go fast.

The CABINET OF DR. LARIFARI (G) 1931 Ref: NYT. Musical-comedy.
The CABINET OF DR. SEGATO (G) 1924 Ref: Deutsche.
CABIRIA (I) 1913 Ref: NYT 6/2/14: Herculean giant.
CAESAR'S GHOST 1922 10m. Ref: Lee.
CAGLIOSTROS TOTENHAND (G) 1919 Ref: DDC III:170.
CALINO AMONG THE CANNIBALS 1909 Ref: Bios 1/13/10. Disembodied head dances.
The CALL OF THE DEMONS (Cz) 1968 Ref: The Czechoslovak Film '68: mystery. Sequel to MURDERER FROM BEYOND THE GRAVE.

CALL OF THE SAVAGE 1935 Ref: D. Glut. Cancer cure?
CAMP ON BLOOD ISLAND (B) 1958 NO.
CAN HEIRONYMOUS... Ref: Boxo 3/31/69. 1969 The devil,
    "Presence of death."
The CANDIDATE 1965 Ref: FM 63:24. Costume ball vampires,
    Frankenstein monster
CANDY 1968 "Outer space child"
CAPTAIN GHOST (I) 1954 (CAPITAN FANTASMA) Ref: DDC I:43.
CAPTAIN GRANT'S CHILDREN (F) 1901 Ref: DDC III:504.
CAPTAIN GRANT'S CHILDREN (Russ) 1938 Ref: FD 1/23/39. NO.
The CARELESS ANARCHIST 1915 Ref: MPW 9/18/15. "New ex-
    plosive."
CARMILLA (Swedish-J) 1968 Ref: M/TVM 1/69:42.
CAROUGE THE GHOUL (F) 1913 (or The AVENGER) Ref: Lee.
    Poisoner.
CARPET OF HORROR (W.G.I-Sp) 1962 Ref: FIR. TVK (Il TER-
    RORE DI NOTTE-I.)
CARRY ON SPYING (B) 1964 Ref: MFB'64:133. TVG. "Automation
    Plant."
CARTHAGE IN FLAMES (I) 1961 Monster? Ref: Lee. V. HR.
CASE OF THE BLACK PARROT 1941 Ref: MFB. Boxo 2/1/41. NO.
CASE OF THE BLACK CAT 1936 Ref: V. FD.
CASEY AND HIS NEIGHBOR'S GOAT 1903 Man returns to life.
CASEY'S FRIGHTFUL DREAM 1904 Ref: Niver. NO.
The CASTLE OF FEAR (F) 1912 Ref: DDC II:338. (Le CHATEAU
    DE LA PEUR)
CASTLE OF TERRORS (B) 1967 amateur Ref: FM 44:72. MW 3:
    37.4:25.
CASTLE OF THE LAST CHANCE (F) 1948 Ref: DDC III:311.
CASTLE OF THE SLOW DEATH (F) 1925 Ref: DDC II:127.
CASTLE OF THE TERRIFIED (Austrian) 1922 Ref: Osterr.
CASTLE VOGELOD (G) 1921 Ref: Clarens. Nightmare.
CASTLE VOGELOD (G) 1936 Ref: Lee.
CAT AND THE CANARY 1912 Ref: Lee: NO.
The CAT O'NINE TAILS Ref: MFB'71:120. Thriller.
The CAT THAT WAS CHANGED INTO A WOMAN 1913 Ref: Bios
    11/6/13. NO.
The CATACLYSM (Hung) 1934 Ref: SM 1:4: amateur space film.
CATHERINE (F) 1968 Ref: Fernsehen: "horror." M/TVM 2/69:
    adventure.
Il CAVALIERE INESISTENTE Ref: V 11/18/70. Invisible knight.
The CAVE DWELLERS Ref: MPW 22: NO.
CAVE GIRL F Nat 1921 Ref: Lee: NO.
CAVE MAN 1915 Ref: MPN 12/11/15. NO.
CAVE MAN 1926 Ref: Lee: NO. Photoplay 4/26.
CAVE MAN'S WOOING 1912 Ref: Bios 8/29/12: NO.
CENERI E VAMPRE (I) 1916 Ref: DDC II:302.
El CEREBRO INFERNAL (Mex) shooting Ref: M/TVM 2/67. D:
    C. Urueta. W/D. Reynoso.
CHARLIE CHAN AT THE RACE TRACK 1936 Ref: V 8/19/36:
    "Camera shoots strange dart."
CHARLIE CHAN IN CITY IN DARKNESS 1939 Ref: FD 12/20/39:
    NO.

CHARLIE CHAN IN HONOLULU 1938 with George Zucco. NO.
CHARLIE CHAN IN LONDON 1934 New airplane gadget tested Ref:
    MPH 9/22/34. ?
CHARLIE CHAN IN PANAMA 1940 with Lionel Atwill. NO.
CHARLIE CHAN ON BROADWAY 1937 Ref: COF 7:44. with Lon
    Chaney, Jr. ? NO.
Un CHIEN ANDALOU 1929 Surrealism Ref: COF 5:38.
CHINAMAN'S DREAM 1910 Ref: Bios 1/13/10. Monkey into imp.
The CHIPS ARE DOWN (F) 1947 ghost Ref: MFB'48:64. DDC II:316.
CHITTY, CHITTY, BANG BANG flying machine Ref: MFB'69:24:
    NO.
CHRISTA Ref: V 5/26/71. "Futuristic company."
CHRONICLE OF THE GRAY HOUSE (G) 1923 Ref: Clarens. Spirits.
CHRYSANTHEMUM AND THE DRAGON (J) Ref: J Films '68:60.
CIRCE (I) 1917 Ref: DDC III:148.
CIRCE THE ENCHANTRESS 1924 Ref: FD 9/14/24: NO.
CIRCUMSTANTIAL EVIDENCE 1935 Ref: FD 7/17/35. V 7/17/35.
    "Mysterious hand."
The CITY IN THE NAME OF GOD (J) Ref: V 10/29/69: fantasy.
    Ape goddess legend.
CIVILIZATION 1916 Ref: NYT 6/3/16. Vision of hell.
The CLAIRVOYANT (G) 1933 Ref: NYT 9/11/13. Mind-reading.
The CLAIRVOYANT SWINDLERS 1915 Ref: Motog 5/18/15: seance,
    secret passage.
The CLAYDON TREASURE MYSTERY (B) 1938 Ref: MFB 3/38.
    "General air of eerieness"
A CLEAR AND PRESENT DANGER s-f? TV movie?
CLEOPATRA'S DAUGHTER (I-F) 1960 Death-semblance serum. Ref:
    Ital P'60.
CLEOPATRE (F) Melies 1899 Ref: Movie Monsters. Mummy?
CLOWN AND POLICE (B) 1900 Ref: SilentFF. Dismembered bodies
    reassemble.
La CLOWNESSE FANTOME (F) 1902 Melies Ref: Mitry II.
COBRA GIRL (India) 1963 Ref: Shankar's 6/23/63: Jack the Giant
    Killer?
The COLLECTOR 1965 D: Wyler.
COLONEL MARCH INVESTIGATES (B) 1953 Ref: MFB. Conjuror.
    NO.
COMISSAR X: IN THE CLAWS OF THE GOLDEN DRAGON (Austrian)
    1966 Ref: Film Kunst 49:F4. "Perilous weapon."
The COMMITTE (B) 1968 Ref: MFB'68:177. Kafkaesque. Severed
    head.
COMPELLED TO BE A MAGICIAN (I) 1950 Ref: Ital P. Magician
    curses people.
CONFESSIONS OF AN OPIUM EATER 1963 Ref: PM. NO.
CONQUERING POWER 1921 Ref: Clarens. Ghoul visions.
CONQUEST OF MYCENE (I) 1963 Ref: TVK.
CONSCIENCE 1917 Ref: Lee. Lucifer.
A COOK IN TROUBLE (F) 1904 Ref: Niver. Devil.
Un COPLO DA RE (I) 1966 Ref: M/TVM 11/66. New radioactive
    substance. made? with Alan Steel, Pamela Tudor. D: Ray
    Morrison.
CORRIDOR OF MIRRORS (B) 1947 Ref: COF. NO.

The CORSICAN BROTHERS (B) 1898 Ref: 70 Years. Ghost.
The CORSICAN BROTHERS 1912 Ref: Bios 6/13/12. Spirit.
COSE DELL'ALTRO MONDO (I) 1939 Ref: DDC III:290.
COTTAGE TO LET (B) 1943 Ref: MPH 5/15/43. (BOMBSIGHT
  STOLEN)
The COUCH 1962 Ref: FFacts. NO.
COUNTRY WITHOUT STARS (F) 1946 Ref: Fowler. S&S'46:51:
  fantasy. NO.
A COUP OF 1000 MILLIARDS (I) Ref: Ital P'66: "nuclear engine of
  ship. "
The COWARDLY WAY 1915 Ref: MPN 11/20/15. Spirit. NO.
The CRAVING Ref: MPW 19:448. New explosive.
CRAZY PARADISE (Danish) 1965 Ref: COF 9:6. Chicken eggs im-
  part sexual potency.
The CREATURE FROM TAGANARA Ref: COF 10:50. alternate
  title?
CREATURES OF THE RED PLANET 1968 AI-TV Ref: TVFFSB 90m.
  "S-f. "with John Carradine. Mad scientist.   aka WIZARD OF
  MARS? HORROR OF THE BLOOD MONSTERS?
CRIME EXPERT (B) 1940 Ref: TVK: "Eerie thriller. "
CRIME RING 1938 Ref: MFB'38:220: "Rather macabre, light humor
  is supplied by one crook's fear of ghosts. " ?: FD 7/27/38.
  Boxo 7/2/38. MPH 7/30/28. Showmen's 7/2/38. NYT 7/22/38.
  V. HR. (The FORTUNEERS. CHEATING THE STARS)
The CRIMINAL LIFE OF ARCHIBALDO DE LA CRUZ (Mex) 1955
  Ref: FM 31:18. MFB'60:164 (El ENSAYO DE UN CRIMEN) "Death-
  dealing" music box.
The CRIMSON FLASH 1927 serial Ch. 2. The Ghost Takes a Hand.
  Ref: LC.
CROSSROADS (J) 1928 Ref: Richie: "The cat turns into a great and
  mythic beast"
The CROUCHING BEAST 1936 Ref: NYT. Spy. NO.
The CRUCIBLE (F) 1958 "witchcraft" NO.
CRY OF THE VAMPIRE (I?) 1962 Ref: Photon 21:27. made? (L'UR-
  LO DEL VAMPIRO)
The CRYSTAL GAZER Ref: MPN 16:1151. Hypnotism. NO.
CUATRO PASOS EN LA LUNA (Arg?) Ref: Heraldo'69:487. "The
  race for the conquest of the universe"?
CUL-DE-SAC "black comedy"
CUPID'S STOLEN ARROWS (F) 1912 Ref: Lee. Evil spirit steals
  cupid's arrows.
The CURSE Domino 1913 Ref: MPW 18:1476. "witchcraft" NO.
The CURSE Powers 1913 Ref: Bios 9/4/13: NO.
The CURSE SCAGL 1913 Ref: Bios'13:909: NO.
The CURSE OF IKU 1918 Ref: MPW 35:1865: NO.
CURSE OF THE DEVIL DOCTOR Ref: FM 42:59: TV?
CURSE OF THE HEADLESS DEMON Ref: FM 50:9 (PLAGUE OF THE
  UNDEAD. MENACE OF THE UNDEAD. MARK OF DRACULA)
  with Chaney, Jr., Carradine, Lieber, Jr.
CURSE OF THE HIDDEN VAULT (W.G.) 1964 Ref: FIR.
CURSE OF THE YELLOW SNAKE (W.G.) 1963. NO.
CURSE OF THE WITCH (Austrian) 1920 Ref: Osterr. (Der FLUCH
  DER HEXE)

The CURSE OF VERERBUNG (G) 1934 Ref: DDC I:49. (DER FLUCH
DER VERERBUNG)
The CURSED CAGE 1909 Ref: MPW'09:737. Witch's vision. NO.
The CURSED JEWEL (Braz) 1920 Ref: DDC I:268. (Le BIJOU
MAUDIT)

DADDY'S GONE A-HUNTING Ref: MFB'69:214: melodrama.
The DAGGER DEVIL (India) Ref: Moving Picture Monthly 3/34:
"thriller."
DAKKI THE VAMPIRE (J) Ref: Cinema Yearbook of Japan'36/'37.
DAKU MANSOOR (India) Ref: Dipali 5/31/35: spirit.
DAMN YANKEES 1958 deal with devil (WHAT LOLA WANTS).
DAN GREEGAN'S GHOST 1913 Ref: Lee. NO.
The DANCE AT ALECK FONTAINE'S Ref: MPN 3/6/15. "Ghost"
scares man.
The DANCER OF PARIS 1926 Ref: Photoplay 5/26. FM 37:31. NO.
The DANGER (Polish) 1964 Ref: Lee:s-f?
DANGER TOMORROW (B) 1961 Murder, visions.
DANGEROUS GAME 1941 Insane asylum. Ref: TVK.
DANGEROUS INTRUDER 1945 Ref: TVG. V. HR. Maniac. NO.
DANGEROUS WATERS 1919 Ref: Exhibitors Herald. Dream of
death.
DANGEROUSLY YOURS 1933 Ref: NYT. Harrisons. Seance, jewel
thieves. NO.
DANGERS OF THE CANADIAN MOUNTED 1948 serial Liquid
diamonds.
DANSE MACABRE (Hung) 1958 Ref: DDC III:55.
DANSE VAMPIRESQUE (Danish) 1912 Ref: DDC.
DANTE'S INFERNO 1910 Ref: FM 67:11.
DANTE'S INFERNO 1911 Ref: FM 67:11.
DARE DEVILS IN DANGER 1916 Ref: MPN 14:792: plans for "self-
aiming gun."
DAREDEVIL IN THE CASTLE (J) 1961 Ref: J Films. "Occult pow-
ers."
DARK STREETS OF CAIRO 1940 (STREETS OF CAIRO) Ref: FD.
V. PM. NO.
DARNA AT ANG BABAING TUOD (Fili) Ref: M/TVM 6/65.
DARNA AT ANG PLANETMAN Ref: FJA.
DARWIN WAS RIGHT 1924 Ref: FD 10/26/24: fake elixir.
DAUGHTER OF DARKNESS (B) 1948 Ref: British Film Annual'49:
NO.
The DAUGHTER OF PONTIANAK Ref: FEFN 11/22/57: announced
for filming.
DAUGHTER OF THE JUNGLE1949 Ref: MPH 3/19/49: NO. PM.
Voodoo.
DAWN EXPRESS 1942 Ref: TVG: secret formula.
DAY OF WRATH (Danish?) "Witch." NO.
DAYBREAK (B) 1947 Ref: MFB'48:72. NO.
DAYS OF THRILLS AND LAUGHTER 1961 Scenes from The MAN
FROM BEYOND.
The DEAD ALIVE (B) 1913 Ref: MPW 16:363: NO. Bios 8/14/13.
DEAD RINGER Ref: COF 5:4. (WHO IS BURIED IN MY GRAVE-

India) NO.
DEADWOOD DICK 1940 serial Ch. 2. Who is the Skull?
DEAL WITH THE DEVIL (Cz) 1967 Ref: Czechoslavak Film 1968.
  Comedy. Fantasy.
DEAR OLD GIRL Ref: MPN 1/16/15: spirit. NO.
DEATH BY HANGING (J) Ref: MFB'71:76: murder victim "becomes
  visible."
DEATH IN THE AIR Ref: FD 2/15/37. Masked madman machine-
  guns planes.
DEATH IS A WOMAN Ref: F&F 6/67:26.
The DEATH KISS 1933 with Bela Lugosi, David Manners, Edward
  Van Sloan. Ref: NYT. Clarens. Harrison's 2/4/33. FM 27:22.
  MPH 12/24/32: NO. Photoplay 1/33. COF 8:22. Mystery.
  "Atmosphere."
DEATH OCCURRED LAST NIGHT Ref: MFB'71:122. Bizarre.
DEATH OF TARZAN (Cz) 1962 Ref: FFacts: man raised as ape.
  Fair. (DEATH OF THE APE-MAN)
DECISION AGAINST TIME (B) 1957 Ref: TVG. "New rocket-pro-
  pelled transport plane."
The DEFORMED (HK) Ref: FEFN 2/61: "Beauty and the beast."
DEMON AND THE DOCTOR Hemisphere Ref: V 4/29/70:176.
DEMON OF BLOOD Ref: V 4/29/70:196.
DEMON OF THE HIMALAYAS (F) 1934 Ref: DDC III:52.
DEMONIACAL DARLING (G) 1950 Ref: DDC III:35.
DEMONS AND MAN D: Oswald. Ref: FIR'58:445.
DEN OF SPIRITS (F) 1901 Melies Ref: DDC III:350.
DENS OF EVIL Horror-comedy?
DENSHICHI, THE SLEUTH Ref: FEFN 6/1/56: "female fox"-
  killer?
DERBY-KA-SHIKAR (India) Ref: Dipali 11/29/35: monster-hand?
The DERVISH'S DANCE Ref: MPW'07:393: man cursed to dance.
The DESERT GHOST Ref: MPN 15:2521 1917 NO.
The DESERT HAWK Col 1944 serial crystal ball NO.
DESERT HELL Ref: HR 6/10/58. "Phantom" killers. NO.
DESTINY 1944 Ref: FD. MPH: fantasy touches. Originally part of
  FLESH AND FANTASY?
The DEVIL 1908 Ref: Niver: devil.
DEVIL AND THE MAN FROM SMALAND Ref: Sweden I.
DEVIL BEAR 1929 horror? Ref: S&S'58/9.
The DEVIL CHECKS UP (B) 1941 Ref: Boxo: NO.
The DEVIL FROM MUEHLENBURG (E.G.) Ref: Thought 11/7/59:
  "Good spirits."
DEVIL GODDESS 1955 Ref: COF-A:38. FD 9/2/55. NO.
The DEVIL IN LOVE (I) 1966 Ref: Ital P: NO.
The DEVIL IN THE STUDIO (B) 1901 Ref: Brit Cinema.
DEVIL IN VELVET Ref: Boxo 4/7/69. Trial of Marquis De Sade.
DEVIL MONSTER 1937 (The SEA FIEND) Ref: MFB 1/38: NO.
  "Giant devil fish."
The DEVIL TO PAY 1920 Ref: Exhibitors Herald. Man revived after
  hanging.
The DEVIL WITH HITLER Ref: FM 67:11: devil. V. HR, NO.
The DEVIL-WOMAN (Austrian) 1915 Ref: Osterr: "Fantastic story
  of Hell."

DEVILS (Cz) Ref: V 9/17/69: devils.
The DEVILS (B) 1971 Ref: V 7/14/71.
The DEVIL'S BONDWOMAN 1916 Ref: MPN 14:3330: visions of hell.
The DEVIL'S BOARD (F) Melies 1904 (La PLANCHE DU DIABLE)
The DEVIL'S ENVOYS (F) 1942 Agents of devil. Ref: FM 67:11.
The DEVIL'S EYE (Swedish) 1960 Satan, Don Juan.
The DEVIL'S HAND (F) 1922 (La MAIN DU DIABLE) Ref: DDC II:
   279.
DEVIL'S HAUNT GATE (Russ) Ref: Soviet Cinema:319.
DEVIL'S ISLAND 1939 Karloff. Drama.
The DEVIL'S LONGEST NIGHT (Belg)1971 Ref: V 10/6/71: horror?
The DEVIL'S PASSION (Polish) 1928 Ref: FD 5/27/28: NO.
   Hypnotism.
The DEVOTED APE Ref: Bios 12/15/10: tears bars apart.
DEVOTION Ref: Halliwell. Dreams of Death.
El DIABLO COJUELO Ref: SpCinema'71. Devil.
The DIABOLICAL LODGER (F) 1909 Ref: DDC III:353.
DIABOLICAL MAGIC (F) Melies 1898 Ref: Mitry II.
DIABOLICAL VENGEANCE (F) 1918 Ref: DDC III:258.
La DIABOLIKA LADY (I) RTB Int'l Ref: M/TVM 3/66. with
   C. Lee, B. Steele. "Terror." Not made?
DIABOLO NIGHTMARE (B) 1907 Ref: Brit Cinema.
Der DIAMANT DES TODES (Austrian) 1919 Ref: Osterr.
The DIAMOND MASTER 1914 Eclair Ref: SF Film. ?
DICK BARTON, DETECTIVE (B) 1948 Ref: COF-A:39. NO.
DINOSAUR Shaw Ref: FEFN 12/23/55:8.
The DINOSAURS Ref: FM 63:28. Documentary.
The DIVER'S REMORSE Ref: MPW'09:545: apparition.
DIYOSA (Fili) Ref: FEFN 4/26/57: evil sorceress.
DR. COOK'S GARDEN 1971 ABC-TV Ref: TVG: suspense drama.
DR. DOLITTLE 1967 Ref: PM: Great Pink Sea Snail.
DR. JACK 1923 Ref: MPN 1/6/23: doctor impersonates lunatic.
   NO. Wid's.
DR. JEKYLL 1917 Ref: Film 9/67. Made?
DR. JEKYLL (I) 1964 (1951?) D: Guardamagna (Scoffi?). Ref: FM
   34:55. Movie Monsters. Made?
DR. JEKYLL AND MADAM HYDE 1917 Ref: Film 9/67. ?
DR. JEKYLL AND MR. HYDE ABC-TV 1968 Ref: TVG. with Jack
   Palance. TV drama shown as movie in some areas.
DR. KILLEM'S DOPE Ref: Motog 12/26/14: soothes patient.
DR. MABUSE (F) 1953 (Le DOCTEUR MABUSE) Ref: DDC II:317.
   with C. Farell. ?
DR. PHANTOM, THE SCIENTIFIC SLEUTH1902 Ref: G. Dorst.
DOCTOR POLLY Ref: Bios 6/4/14: ghost?
DR. SYN (B) 1937 Ref: FD 10/21/37: non-horror version of NIGHT
   CREATURES.
DOCTOR X (Fili) c1940 Ref: Motion Pictures in the Philippines.
A DOG IN ORBIT (Sp) 1967 Ref: SpCinema'67: NO.
DOLLAR DOWN 1925 Ref: AFI: invention.
La DOLOROSA 1934 Ref: V 7/28/71: sf?
DON JUAN 1908 Ref: MPW'08:497: ghost scene.
DON JUAN TENORIO (Spanish-language) Ref: NYT 12/28/37:
   "Spooky scenes."

DON'T TAKE IT TO HEART (B) 1944 Ref: MFB'44:127: Ghost. NO.
DOOR-TO-DOOR MANIAC c1965
Der DOPPELGANGER (G) 1934 Ref: FIR'67:77.
DORIKTHE DONGALU Ref: M/TVM 12/64: s-f. shooting.
DOROTHY AND THE SCARECROW Ref: Bios 6/9/10: NO.
DOUBLE CROSS (India) 1938 Ref: Filmindia 1/39. Artificial-
    diamond formula.
The DOUBLE TERROR (F) 1920 (La DOUBLE EPOUVANTE) Ref:
    DDC III:197.
DOUBLING WITH DANGER Ref: V 9/29/26: "war machine" papers.
DRACULA (Russ) Ref: FM 23:43: film or play?
DRACULA MEETS THE OUTER SPACE CHICKS 1968 Ref: RVB. ?
DRAGON SKY (F) 1964 Ref: Boxo 9/28/64: spirits.
The DRAGONS OF VILLARS (F) 1903 Ref: FIR'64:142.
DRAGONWYCK 1946 Ref: Maltin: "chiller." FD 2/28/46: NO.
The DREAM (Yugos) Ref: V: "dead men coming back to life."
DREAM OF A RAREBIT FIEND 1906 Ref: SilentFF: nightmare.
DREAM OF THE STARS Ref: SM 2:31.3:22. ?
DREAM STREET 1921 Hell visions, dragon.
The DREAM WOMAN Ref: Bios 6/18/14: from Wilkie Collins. ??
DREAMS OF DEATH (G) 1950 Ref: S&S'51:40: Gothic fantasy.
DRUMS OF THE CONGO Ref: NYT. Meteorite metal necessary for
    war instruments.
A DUAL PERSONALITY Ref: Bios 5/23/12. NO.
The DUALITY OF MAN 1910 Wrench Ref: Movie Monsters: split per-
    sonality?
DUE MARINES E UN GENERALE Ref: Annuario. (I) New weapon.
DUGO NG VAMPIRA Ref: M/TVM 8/69:35.
The DUKE'S GOOD JOKE (F) Melies Sorcerer.
DUNGEON MASTER 1968 Ref: RVB: vampire?

EARTH LIGHT (F) 1969 Ref: V 4/29/70:73: sf. V 4/1/70: NO.
EARTHBOUND 1920 Ref: Exhibitors Herald. Ghost. NO.
EARTHBOUND 1940 Ghost. NO.
ECCE HOMO (I) c1970 Gaburro End-of-the-world drama?
ECCO Ref: COF-A:6: "Paris' famed Grand Guignol horror theater,
    a Black Mass."
ECOLOGY OF A CRIME (I) Ref: V 10/6/71: sf?
EDEN AND AFTER Ref: COF 16:15: fantasy. Death.
EDGAR ALLAN POE 1909 Ref: FM 11:40. SilentFF. "Raven." NO.
EIGHTY STEPS TO JONAH Ref: Film Bltn 10/27/69: horror.
Die ELF TEUFEL (G) 1927 Ref: DDC II:401.
The ELECTRIC ALARM Ref: MPN 5/29/15:sf?
ELECTRIC BATTERY MACHINE Ref: Bios 1/12/11. Man "shocks"
    others with machine.
ELMO, THE MIGHTY 1919 serial Ref: CNW: Friendly "Phantom
    Menace of Mad Mountain."
The EMBODIED THOUGHT 1916 Ref: MPN 13:869. MPW 27:654.
    Phantasm. NO.
The EMPEROR JONES 1933 Ref: NYT. Photoplay 12/33. Voodoo
    drums.
ENCHANTED BOOTS Ref: MPW'08:328. Devil.

END OF AGENT W4C (Cz) Ref: Thought 4/20/68. Military plans
  for Venus?
END OF THE WORLD Ref: Bios 6/2/10: NO.
END OF THE WORLD 1913 NO
END OF THE WORLD 1924
END OF THE WORLD (I) 1964 Ref: Ital P: ?
Les ENFANTS TERRIBLES (F) 1950 Ref: COF 5:40: "eerie,
  macabre"
EQUINOZIO Ref: M/TVM #6, 1971: "apparitions"
ERCOLE CONTRO MOLOCH (HERCULES AGAINST MOLOCH.
  HERCULES ATTACKS-Eng.) (I-F) 1962 Ref: Ital P'63: "Monster"
  Moloch, king's son. MFB'65:91. sfa CONQUEST OF MYCENE?
  with G. Scott, A. Dominici, A. Panaro, R. Neri.
The EROTIC CIRCUS Ref: RVB: sadism.
ESCAPE IN THE FOG 1945 Prophetic dream.
The ETERNAL MASK (G-Swiss) 1936 Ref: FM 23:24. NYT: dream
  phantoms.
The ETERNAL SIN 1917 Ref: MPN 15:2036: curse.
An EVENING WITH THE ROYAL BALLET 1966 Ref: Boxo 12/20/65:
  sequence from "Sleeping Beauty."
EVERYTHING'S DUCKY 1961 Ref: FFacts. V 11/18/61: two men on
  satellite: minor element.
The EVIL EYE Ref: Bios 1/22/14: NO.
The EVIL EYE 1916 Ref: FIR'65:568. NO.
The EVIL EYE 1920 serial Ref: MPW'20:143: House where the
  "evil eye" causes those who defy him to "drink of the waters of
  blindness. "
The EVIL EYE (I) 1964 Ref: F&F 9/65: eerie house, stormy night.
  D: Bava. Poor.
EVOLUTION OF MAN 1921 Ref: MPW index: aka JACK THE MAN-
  APE.
EVOLUTION OF MAN 1925
EXPERIMENT IN NIGHTMARE Ref: COF 17:24: 5-minute plug for
  The NIGHT WALKER
The EXPERIMENTS OF YALON (G) 1966 Ref: FM 39:52. 80:44:
  amateur.
EXPLOSION OF A MOTOR CAR (B) 1900 Ref: SilentFF: fantasy.
The EXTERMINATING ANGEL (Mex) 1962 "See if necessary"-Eric
  Rohmer. People trapped in house. Good.
The EXTERMINATORS 1966 Ref: MFB'66:108: "weird" landscape
EXTINCT MONSTERS? Ref: NYT? 1922?
EXTRACONJUGALE (I?) Ref: V 2/24/65: "The Shower": "twist at
  finale" sf? Movies Int'l #5: futuristic?
The EXTRAORDINARY SEAMAN Ref: V 1/22/69: ghost.
EYE OF EVIL 1967 Ref: ad: second feature for SHE FREAK in
  Sacramento
EYE OF THE ALIEN (Uruguay) Ref: COF 10:48
EYES OF MYSTERY 1918 D: Tod Browning Ref: FM 22:41. MPW
  35:867: sliding panels, secret stairway, portrait with peepholes.
  NO.
The EYES THAT KILL (F) 1912 (Les YEUX QUI MEURENT) Ref:
  DDC II:338. Feuillade.

The FACE OF DEATH (Mex) c1965 Ref: Lee: ?
The FACE OF MEDUSA (Greek) Ref: V 7/12/67:NO.
FACES IN THE DARK (B) 1961 Ref: Speed: thriller.
The FAIRY FOX AND GHOST Ref: B. Warren.
FAIRY, GHOST AND VIXEN (HK-Chinese) Ref: M/TVM 7/65.
FAITH, HOPE AND WITCHCRAFT (Danish) 1960 Ref: V 7/27/60:
   NO.
The FALL OF THE HOUSE OF USHER 1942 D: C. Harrington,
   amateur.
FALL OF THE HOUSE OF USHER 1955 Ref: FIR'61:568. experi-
   mental?
The FALSE MAGISTRATE (F) 1914 (FANTOMAS V) Ref: DDC II:
   339.
FAME AND THE DEVIL (F?) 1950 Ref: HR 5/2/52: NO. devil.
FANTASMA 1914 Ref: LC.
FANTASMAGORIE (F) c1963 Ref: COF 9:39. MMF 7:65c. with
   E. Scob. Vampire. short?
FANTASMAGORICAL ILLUSIONS (F) 1898 Ref: SilentFF. Conjuror
   splits boy in two with axe.
FANTASMAS EN LA CASA (Sp) 1958 Ref: Spanish Annual'63:345.
The FANTASTIC GOBLIN PUSSYCAT Ref: M/TVM 4/70:45.
The FANTASTIC NIGHT (F) 1942 Ref: Lee. Fantasy.
FANTASY 1927 Ref: LC. Based on "Old Applejoy's Ghost."
FANTOMAS (F) 1913 Ref: MPW 17:470. DDC II:339.
FANTOMAS (F) 1930 Ref: DDC III:60. V 3/20/34: "shrieks"
FANTOMAS (F) 1947 Ref: DDC III:315.
FANTOMAS CONTRE FANTOMAS (F) 1914 Ref: DDC II:339.
FANTOMAS CONTRE FANTOMAS (F) 1947 Ref: DDC II:201.
Le FANTOME DU CAVEAU (Danish) 1910 Ref: Mitry V:144.
FASTER, PUSSYCAT, KILL KILL Ref: Boxo'66: sadism.
The FATAL FORTUNE 1919 serial Ref: CNW: Villain, the "Face-
   less Terror."
The FATAL WARNING 1929 serial Ref: CNW. with Karloff. Ch. 7.
   The House of Horror.
FAUST (F) 1922 D, SP: Gerard Bourgeois. Ref: Mitry II.
FAUST (I) c1963 Ref: COF 12:30. FM 26:13. COF 6:11. (KATAR-
   SIS) Not finished.
FAUST AND MARGUERITE (F) Ref: Bios 6/30/10: NO.
FAUST FAMILY OF ACROBATS 1901
Le FAUX VALDEMAR (Danish) 1914 Ref: DDC I:67.
The FEAR CHAMBER Ref: FM 54:6. with Karloff. Completed?
The FEATHERED SERPENT 1948 Ref: COF 9:33: flying serpent.
   MPH 2/12/49: NO.
FEATHERTOP 1916 Ref: MPN 13:2551: NO.
FEET OF CLAY 1924 Ref: Wid's 9/27/24: Dead attempt to return
   to life.
The FEMALE OF THE SPECIES (VIOLA) Ref: Spectre 17:7: horror.
   SP: Richard Davis.
FENCE OF TERROR Ref: SpCinema'69: "apparition"?
The FERRET 1915 Ref: Lee: split personality.
FIDDLERS THREE (B) 1944 Ref: COF 9:33. People struck by
   lightning transported in time.
The FIEND THAT WALKED THE WEST Ref: FFacts: sadism. Fan

Mo 4:63: advertised as horror
FIEND WITH THE ELECTRONIC BRAIN AI-TV 1968 Ref: TVFFSB.
 with Carradine. (sfa ASTRO-ZOMBIES?)
15-MINUTE NAP Ref: Bios 12/1/10. Umbrella carries man into
 air.
50,000 B.C. Ref: V 4/29/70:196.
FIGHT THAT GHOST   Toddy 1952 Ref: FDY.
FIGHTING SEA MONSTERS 1943 Ref: CB.
FIGURES IN A LANDSCAPE Ref: MFB'71: "nightmare world of
 pursuit."
A FINAL RECKONING 1929 serial Ref: CNW. Ch. 11. The Living
 Dead.
FIRE WOMAN (Korea) 1970 Ref: V 10/6/71: horror?
FIRST MAN TO THE MOON 1920 Ref: LC.
FISH AND THE FISHERS Ref: Bios 10/21/09: "monstrous fish."
FIVE BEAUTIFUL WITCHES Ref: B. Warren.
FIVE BLOODY GRAVES Ref: Boxo 4/5/71: Voice of Death.
 Western.
FIVE MILLION B.C. Ref: COF 7:52. not made.
5000 FINGERS OF DR. T 1953 hypnotism.
FIVE WEEKS IN A BALLOON 1962
FLAMING BARRIERS 1924 Ref: AFI: invention.
The FLASHLIGHT Ref: MPN 15:3314. camera invention.
The FLAT (B) 1921 Ref: SilentFF.
FLESH AND BLOOD 1922 Ref: Lee: Chaney as mad killer.
FLIGHT OF THE LOST BALLOON 1960 Ref: SF Film. V 11/1/61
 (CLEOPATRA & THE CYCLOPS)
The FLOATING DEATH Ref: MPN 6/26/15: spirits.
FLOWER THIEF Ref: Boxo 4/11/63: "giant"?
FLOWERY PHANTASM Ref: XXth Century 6/43: NO.
The FLYING DUTCHMAN (E.G.) 1965 Ref: M/TVM 7/6. Lee:
 "ship of the dead."
The FLYING SAUCER (J) Shintoho 195- Ref: Lee. alternate title?
FLYING SAUCERS (G) 1954 (FLIEGEN DE UNTERTASSEN) Ref:
 FJA folder. amateur?
FOG 1934 Ref: Photoplay: clairvoyant, strangler V 1/9/34: NO.
The FOOL Ref: MPN 13:3935: invention 1916
A FOOL AND DEATH (Austrian) 1920 Ref: Osterr. "Reawakening
 from death"?
FOOTSTEPS IN THE FOG 1955 Ref: COF 5:46.9:36. suspense. NO.
FOOTSTEPS IN THE NIGHT (B) 1933 Ref: FD 5/10/33: plans for
 device; castle.
FORBIDDEN ADVENTURE 1934 (INYAH, THE JUNGLE GODDESS)
The FORBIDDEN ROOM 1919 with Chaney
FORBIDDEN VENUS (I) 1964 Ref: Ital P: "the skeletons strip...
 Grand Guignol"
The FORERUNNERS (Russ) 1962 Ref: Imagen: cosmonaut training?
The FOREST VAMPIRES 1914 Ref: MPW 20:868: robber band. NO.
The FORGER (B) 1929 Ref: FIR'67:76.
The FORGER OF LONDON (Il CASTELLO DELL'ORRORE-I.)
 (W.G.) 1961 Ref: FIR'67:80.
FORTRESS OF THE DEAD 1965
48 HOURS TO LIVE (B-SWEDISH) 1959 Ref: COF 9:36. MPH

10/8/60: NO. robot?
The FOSTER BROTHER Ref: MPN 2/6/15: cancer cure secret.
The FOURPOSTER ghosts
FRANK N. STEIN 1952 Ref: RVB. short?
FRANKENSTEIN CHERIE 1967 Ref: FM 63:24.
FRANKENSTEIN MEETS THE HELL'S ANGELS 1971?
FRANKENSTEIN'S EXPERIMENT Ref: MW 4:25. amateur
FRANKENSTEIN'S TRESTLE 1902 Ref: FM 24:3: NO.
The FREEZING MIXTURE Ref: Bios 11/3/10: ?
The FRIGHTENING (F) 1910 (L'EPOUVANTE) Ref: DDC II:234.
The FROG (B) 1931
The FROG (B) 1937
FROM MORN TILL MIDNIGHT (G) 1922 Ref: Fantastique: NO.
The FUGITIVE 1940 Ref: FM 12:13.

The GABLES MYSTERY Ref: MFB'38: V 4/3/32. NO.
The GALLERY OF MONSTERS (F) 1924 Ref: DDC III:34, 312, 409,
    422.
La GARDE FANTOME (F) 1904 Velle Ref: Mitry II.
The GARDEN OF SHADOWS 1916 Ref: MPN 14:458: child's spirit.
GARDIENS DE PHARE (F) 1929 Ref: 70 Years: "Grand Guignol."
GASLIGHT (B) 1941 Ref: NYT 11/11/52. suspense
GASLIGHT 1944 Ref: COF 16:25. suspense with a few horror
    touches.
GASLIGHT FOLLIES 1958 with Chaney.
A GATHERING OF EAGLES sf?
GAULOISES BLEUES Ref: Boxo 6/16/69: "Death"?
GDZIE JESTES LUIZO? (Polish) 1964 Ref: Imagen. saucer?
GEMINI-12/CAPE CANAVERAL Ref: FJA sf?
GENII OF FIRE(F) Melies 1908
GENOSSE MUNCHAUSEN Ref: Imagen. Rocket to Venus falls on
    English isle
GENTLEMEN WITHOUT UMBRELLAS (Rumania) Ref: M/TVM 1/70:
    chemical invention
GERGASI (Malayan) Ref: FEFN 10/10/58: "legendary giant"?
GERM IN THE KISS Ref: MPW 19:594. 1914 ?
GET ON WITH IT Ref: Boxo 6/24/63: Message beamed from
    satellite
GHALTA PUTLA (India) 1935 Ref: Moving Picture 7/35:2: "Frank-
    enstein touch"
A GHASTLY TALE c1938 Ref: FD 6/28/39: "psychological murder
    theme."
The GHOST (B) 1898 Ref: DDC II:448.
The GHOST (F) Pathe Ref: Bios 9/8/10: NO.
The GHOST (Mex) 1961 (El FANTASMA) Ref: Lee. with Chaney, Jr.
The GHOST AND DONA JUANITA (Sp) 1944 Ref: DDC II:234.
GHOST APPEARS IN VALLEY (J) Ref: FEFN 11/61: ?
GHOST BARON (Swedish) 1927 Ref: DDC: I:240.
    GHOST CITY 1922 Ref: FDY 2/26/22.
The GHOST CITY 1923 serial Ref: LC.
GHOST CITY 1932 Ref: V 3/22/32: NO.
The GHOST COMES HOME 1940   NO.

GHOST FOR SALE (Swedish) 1939 Ref: DDC. (SPOKE TILL SALU)
The GHOST GIRLS Univ. 1919 Ref: MPW 34:464: NO. (GHOST GIRL)
GHOST IN A CAB (J) Ref: FEFN 6/22/56: NO.
The GHOST KING (I) 1914 Ref: DDC II:302.
GHOST LOVE (HK) Ref: FEFN 7/27/56: ?
GHOST MORNING Ref: LATimes 3/70
The GHOST OF ALGIERS (F) Melies 1906 Ref: DDC III:352.
GHOST OF CROSSBONE CANYON Ref: MFB'52:178.
The GHOST OF ELISHA DOOM (Yugos) Ref: FanMo 6:41. ModM 3:8.
The GHOST OF GRANLEIGH 1913 Ref: Bios 11/13/13: ghost.
The GHOST OF HIDDEN VALLEY Ref: HR 4/25/47: NO.
The GHOST OF IOWA Ref: M/TVM 4/70:44. (J)
GHOST OF MONK'S ISLAND (B) 1966 Ref:MFB'68:9: NO.
The GHOST OF SAMARA (UAR) 1959 Ref: Sadoul:283.
GHOST OF SELF Ref: Bios 3/19/14: NO.
GHOST OF THE INDIAN OCEAN 1923 Ref: Deutsche.
GHOST OF THE JUNGLE Ref: MPW 28:2293: spirit.
GHOST OF THE OVEN 1910 Ref: MPW 7:1007: NO.
GHOST OF THE OVEN (Malayan) Ref: FEFN 7/26/57: announced
    "horror"
GHOST OF THE VAULT Ref: Bios 2/16/11: NO.
GHOST PARADE 1931 short
The GHOST PATROL 1923 Ref: MPN 27:472: NO.
GHOST REPORTER (Swedish) 1941 Ref: DDC II:228.
GHOST RIDER 1935 Ref: TVFFSB.
GHOST RIDER 1943 Ref: V. HR: NO.
GHOST SHIP 1943 Lewton Ref: V 12/7/43:NO.
The GHOST THAT WALKS ALONE 1944 Ref: HR. V. NO.
GHOST TRAIN 1903 Ref: Niver: NO.
GHOST TRAIN (J) Ref: Japan.
GHOST VALLEY RAIDERS 1940
GHOST WAGON 1916 fantasy
GHOSTS (B) 1912 Ref: Lee: Ibsen.
GHOSTS 1915 Ref: Lee: Ibsen.
GHOSTS (G) 1939 Ref: Lee: Ibsen.
The GHOSTS (Polish) 1960 Ref: DDC I:417.
GIANT OF EVIL ISLAND (I) 1964 Ref: TVK: NO.
The GIANT DEVIL (F) Melies 1901 Ref: DDC III:350.
GIANT OF MARATHON Ref: PM: NO.
The GIANT'S THREE GOLDEN HARES Ref: TVG.
Il GIOCO DELLA TORRE (I) D.C. Ref: M/TVM 7/65: "Terror tale
    set in ancient castle." with G. Medici, Rita Klein. D: Angelo
    Dorigo. made?
GIRL AND THE CORPSE (I) 1919 Ref: DDC II:430.
The GIRL AND THE DINOSAUR O'Brien Ref: Lee.
GIRL OF THE BERSAGLIERE (I) 1966 Ref: Ital P. Spirit
GIRL OF THE CURSED WOOD 1937 (La FILLE DU BOIS MAUDIT)
GIRL ON A CHAIN GANG Ref: COF 9:43: asdism.
GLASS BOTTOM BOAT Ref: COF 10:47: robot cleaner.
The GLASS CAGE Ref: COF 7:46. 1962
The GLASS CEILING (Sp) 1970 Ref: V 5/12/71: GASLIGHT-type.
A GLASS OF GOAT'S MILK (B) 1909 Ref: SilentFF. Milk turns
    man into goat.

The GLASS TOWER 1957 Ref: COF 10:38: The COLLECTOR-type.
The GLITTERING CURSE (Austrian) 1921 Ref: Osterr: Diamond
    brings disaster?
GLOVES (B) c1914 Ref: SilentFF: gloves make objects vanish.
The GO-BETWEEN "curse," witchcraft.
GOD, MAN AND THE DEVIL   1950 Ref: Lee.
GOLD SPIDER Ref: Bios 11/18/09: "Gold-coining spider."
GOLDEN BOY SUBDUES MONSTERS (Mandarin) Ref: B. Warren.
The GOLDEN HAIR (India) Ref: The Lighthouse 2/19/38: undersea
    kingdom.
The GOLDEN KEY (Cz) 1922 Ref: EncicDS III:364: Karel Capek
    story.
GOLDEN PEACOCK CASTLE (J) Ref: UFQ 14. 1961 wizard.
The GOLDEN WEB 1926 Ref: MPW 82:113: eccentric inventor. with
    Karloff.
GOLDSTEIN 1964 Ref: Consumer Bulletin.
GOLIATH AND THE BARBARIANS
GOLPE DE MIL MILLONES Ref: SpCinema'67: ray gun?
GOOD NEIGHBOR SAM 1964 Ref: FM 63:24: Frankenstein monster
    on billboard.
GOOD SOLDIER SCHWEIK 1926 seance brings ghosts.
GOODBYE GEMINI Ref: Film Bltn 10/5/70: horror.
The GOPHER Ref: MPN 8/21/15: "scientific device," underground
    house
GORDON OF GHOST CITY serial
La GORGONA (I) 1914 Ref: DDC III:112.
The GORILLA (B) 1914 Ref: RVB.
GORILLA MAN 1942 NO
GOVERNMENT AGENTS VS. PHANTOM LEGION 1951 serial Ref:
    D. Glut: NO.
GOVERNOR'S GHOST Ref: MPW 19:1076: NO.
GOTO, ISLAND OF LOVE Ref: MFB'69:257: totalitarian island.
GRAN GOLPE DENIZA Ref: SpCinema'69: radar system.
GRAND GUIGNOL Ref: COF 7:50.
The GRASSHOPPER "Japanese" s-f movie on TV.
The GRAY GHOST 1917 serial Ch. 6. The House of Mystery.
The GRAY WOLF'S GHOST 1919 NO.
GREAT BLOW TO HER MAJESTY'S SERVICE (Sp-I) Ref: SpCinema:
    radar.
The GREAT CHASE 1961 Ref: COF 10:39: clips from silent
    PERILS OF PAULINE
The GREAT GABBO 1929 Ref: COF-A:44. NYT: NO.
The GREAT IMPERSONATION 1921 Ref: MPN 24:1917: insanity.
    NO.
The GREAT IMPERSONATION 1942 Ref: V: NO.
The GREAT MELIES (F) 1951 D: Franju. (GEORGES MELIES)
    30m. Includes A TRIP TO THE MOON.
The GREAT UNKNOWN (G) 1927 Ref: Deutsche. From "The
    Sinister Man."
The GREATEST QUESTION 1919 Ref: NYorker 2/13/71: ghost.
The GREATEST TRUTH (G) 1922 reincarnation Ref: MPW 57:450.
The GRINNING SKULL 1916 Ref: MPW 27:1498: NO.
GRISSLY'S MILLIONS 1945 Ref: V. HR. MFB'45:48. NO.

GROTESQUES (F) 1908 Ref: Lee: puppets in grotesque costumes
GROTTO OF TORTURE Ref: Lee. 1912.
GUEST IN THE HOUSE 1944 Ref: COF 10:40.
GUGUSSE ET BELZEBUTH (F) 1901 Melies Ref: Mitry II.
GULLIVERS REISEN (Austrian) 1924 Ref: Osterr.
GULLIVER'S VOYAGE TO LILLIPUT AND THE LAND OF THE
    GIANTS(F) 1902 Melies
GYPSY GIRL Ref: ModM 3:5: "cemetery sequences."
GYPSY's REVENGE Ref: MPW'08:82. Apparition.

Un HACHA PARA LA LUNA DE MIEL Ref: SpCinema'71: ax
    murderer
HAMLET or KHUN KA KHUN (India) c1932 Ref: Indian Cin.: 171.
The HAND (B) 1961 Ref: COF 10:40. NO.
HAND OF HORROR 1914 Ref: Lee. NO.
The HAND OF VENGEANCE 1918 serial Ch. 4. The Grey Lady.
    5. The League of Silence. 6. The Mysterious Manor.
HANDS UP 1918 serial Ref: CNW: NO.
The HANGED MAN 1964 Ref: COF 10:40: superstitions.
The HANGMAN AND THE WITCH Ref: TVFFSB. "witch"
HANSEL AND GRETEL 1919 NO.
HANSEL AND GRETEL 1951 16mm. 59m. Ref: LC.
HANTU PENANGGAL (Malayan) Ref: FEFN 7/26/57: announced.
    Flying head lives on the blood of women.
HAPPY LAND 1943 ghost
The HATE OF THE SORCERER (F) 1913 Ref: DDC I:287.
The HAUNTED (HK-Chinese) Ref: M/TVM 1/67.
HAUNTED BACHELOR 1912 Ref: Lee.
HAUNTED BARN (Australian) 1931
HAUNTED BRIDE Ref: Bios 2/12/14: NO.
HAUNTED BY HAWKEYE Ref: Bios 5/15/13: ?
HAUNTED BY THE COPS (F) 1909 Ref: Lee: NO.
HUUNTED CASTLE (G) c1962 Ref: FM 17:6.
HAUNTED ENGLAND (B) 1961 Ref: Sarris.
The HAUNTED HAT 1909 Ref: Niver: NO.
HAUNTED HONEYMOON (B) 1940 Ref: NYT 10/31/40: NO.
HAUNTED LOUNGE Ref: F Index 1/9/09: NO.
HAUNTED RANGE Ref: Bios 6/13/12: NO.
HAUNTED ROCKER 1912 Ref: SilentFF: NO.
HAUNTED SHIP 1927 Ref: Lee: NO.
The HAUNTED TOMB Gorgon 1964 Ref: MadM 9:9. Werewolf.
    amateur?
HAUNTED VALLEY 1923 serial Ref: Lee.
HAUNTED WELL Ref: Bios 9/15/10: NO.
HAUNTING EYE Ref: Motography 4/10/15: ?
HAUNTING FEAR 1915 Ref: Lee: NO.
Der HAUPT DER MEDUSA (Austrian) 1919 Ref: Osterr.
HAVAI KHATOLA (India) Ref: Filmindia 11/46: "Magic picture with
    chills."
HAVING A WILD WEEKEND (B) 1965 Ref: F&F 8/65: Frankenstein
    monster disguise
HAWK OF THE WILDERNESS 1938 serial Ref: COF 16:52: dinosaurs.

580 Out Lists

D. Glut: NO.
HE DID NOT DIE   Ref: Bios 4/28/10: NO.
HE LIVED TO KILL Ref: Screen World'57. with Lugosi
HEAD Ref: V 11/6/68. Lugosi (and Karloff?) clip
HEAVEN CAN WAIT 1943 devil
HEAVENS ABOVE (B) Rocket ride
HELICOPTER SPIES Ref: SF Film: "Thermal Prism."
HELL AND HIGH WATER Ref: HR 2/2/54: atomic explosion.
The HELL DIGGERS 1921 Ref: FIR'66:229: invention.
The HELLFIRE CLUB (B) cult Ref: Boxo 10/21/63: NO.
HELLO, MARS 1922 Ref: Lee.
The HELLSTROM CHRONICLE scenes from THEM! borderline-sf
HERCULES & THE PRINCESS OF TROY (I) 1966 Ref: FM 38:66. TV-
    show or -movie?
HERCULES & THE TYRANTS OF BABYLON (I) 1964 Ref: Ital P:
    sorceress.
HERITAGE OF BEAUCITRON Ref: COF 6:31: "fantasy"
HEROES OF THE WILD 1927 serial Ch. 7. The Clutching Hand.
Der HERR DES MONDES Ref: Osterr: "Utopisches." 1922
Der HERR VOM ANDERN STERN (G) 1948 Ref: Deutsche Filme
    1952.
HIAWATHA Ref: Bios 7/21/10: NO.
HIAWATHA Ref: Movie Monsters: werewolf? 1913 MPW 15:980: NO.
HIDDEN DANGERS 1920 serial Ch.1. The Evil Spell.
HIDDEN ENEMY steel formula
HIDDEN POWER Ref: Boy's Cinema 2/24/60: new explosive
The HIDDEN ROOM (B) Ref: COF.
HIGH SEASON FOR SPIES Ref: TVG. Metal Alloy.
HIGH WIND IN JAMAICA Ref: COF 10:42: horror.
HIGHFLYTE'S AEROPLANE (F) 1910 Ref: SilentFF. Fantasy
The HILLS OF DONGEAL (B) 1947 Ref: COF 10:42: eerie. MFB'47:
    127: NO.
The HINDOO'S CURSE 1912 Ref: SilentFF: NO.
HIS GREAT UNCLE'S SPIRIT Ref: MPW 11:804. 1912 NO.
HIS GUIDING SPIRIT 1913 Ref: MPW 19:450: NO.
HIS LAST 12 HOURS (I) Ref: V 11/18/53: dead man returns to life.
    NO.
HIS PHANTOM SWEETHEART 1915 Ref: FIR'68:157: dream. NO.
HIS PREHISTORIC BLUNDER Ref: MPW 57:454. 1922 ?
The HOBGOBLIN (G) 1924 Ref: Deutsche. From Cazote?
HOLD ON! Ref: COF 10:6. FFacts. NO.
HOLD THAT HYPNOTIST 1957 (OUT OF THIS WORLD) hypnotism
A HOLE IN THE WALL (F) 1930 Ref: DDC III:356.
HOLIDAY IN THE CARRIBBEAN (Sp) Ref: SpCinema'59. voodoo
    ceremony
HOLLYWOOD BLUE KING KONG excerpts
The HONEYMOON MACHINE Ref: Boxo 7/17/61: used to beat
    roulette wheel
HONEYMOON OF HORROR 1964 Ref: TVFFSB: horror. with R.
    Parsons. MMF 18-19:104.
The HON. MR. JAP VAN WINKLE 1919 Ref: SilentFF: fantasy.
The HOODED TERROR (B) 1938 Ref: MFB'38: NO.
A HOPI LEGEND 1913 Ref: FIR'66:223. Spirits. Remake of

BEFORE THE WHITE MAN CAME
HORRIBLE MIDNIGHT (J) 1958 Ref: J Films'60:94.
HORRIBLE NIGHT (G) 1921 (GRAUSIGE NACHTE) Ref: DDC III:257.
HORROR (Hung) 1965 Ref: ModM 3:5. COF 10:48. Film 11/68.
  short?
HORROR OF MARS Ref: Miami Herald 4/5/68.
HOT MONEY 1936 gas substitute
HOT SPRING GHOST (J) Ref: FJA.
The HOUR of 13
HOUSE GOBLIN (Swedish) c1946 Ref: Lee.
HOUSE OF FEAR 1915 Ref: MPW 26:1845. NO. MPN 12/1/15: death
  symbol
HOUSE OF A 1000 CANDLES Ref: FD 4/3/36: spy. NO.
HOUSE OF A 1000 TREMBLES Ref: LC. 1922
HOUSE OF DANGER 1934 Ref: Film World'51/2: mystery.
HOUSE OF EVIL with Karloff completed?
The HOUSE OF FEAR (F) 1927 Ref: DDC III:141.
HOUSE OF GHOSTS (UAR) 1951 Ref: Sadoul.
HOUSE OF MENACE 1935 Ref: MPH 12/7/35: NO. (KIND LADY)
HOUSE OF MYSTERY Ref: MPW'13:843. Trap doors. NO.
The HOUSE OF MYSTERY (F) 1922 Ref: DDC II:234.
The HOUSE OF MYSTERY (F) 1934 Ref: Rep Gen'47: NO.
HOUSE OF TERROR 1908 Ref: Lee: NO.
HOUSE OF THE DEAD (G) Ref: Orpheus 2:19.
HOUSE OF THE SPANIARD (B) 1936 Ref: TVFFSB: "mysterious
  mansion"
HOW TO FRAME A FIGG computer
HOW TO STOP A MOTOR CAR (B) 1902 Ref: SilentFF: sadism
HOW TO STUFF A WILD BIKINI 1965 Ref: COF 8:6: fantasy
  touches.
The HUMAN CLOCK Ref: MPW'07:220: fantasy.
HUMAN SACRIFICE Ref: MPW 10:109: NO.
HUMAN SOUL 1914 Ref: Lee: spirit. NO.
HUMAN TORPEDOES (J) Ref: UFQ 40: sf?
The HUNCHBACK FIDDLER Ref: Bios 12/23/09: sea spirits.
The HUNGRY MOTOR-CAR Ref: Bios 1/27/10: fantasy.
The HUNCHBACK OF SOHO (G) 1966 Ref: FIR'67:183. B. Warren:
  NO.
The HUNTED SAMURAI (J) 1970 Ref: LATimes 7/10/71: magician.
  V 7/21/71. (The HAUNTED SAMURAI)
The HUNTER'S DREAM 1911 Ref: MPW 8:718: nightmare.
HUNTINGTOWER (B) 1928 Ref: V 3/21/28: NO. Ghost?
The HURRICANE AT PILGRIM HILL 1953 Ref: Lee. Hurricane
  "conjured up. "
The HUSBAND OF PONTIANAK (Malayan) Ref: FEFN 11/22/57:
  announced. Vampire.
HYPNOSE (Austrian) 1919 Ref: Osterr.
HYPNOTISING THE HYPNOTIST Ref: Bios 3/7/12: NO.
The HYPNOTIST 1911 Ref: MPW 10:830: "Swengually, " NO.
The HYPNOTIST Ref: Bios 9/5/12: NO. Lubin.
The HYPNOTIST Ref: Bios 7/24/13: NO. Nordisk.
The HYPNOTIC MIRROR Ref: Bios 10/14/09: NO.

I, MARQUIS DE SADE Ref: LATimes 8/6/71.
I DISCOVERED HEAVEN (India) Ref: FEFN 9/60: kingdom of death.
I KILLED RASPUTIN Ref: MFB'69:33: NO.
I WAKE UP SCREAMING 1942 Ref: RVB: NO.
ICE STATION ZEBRA 1968 New photographic emulsion.
ICT WOLLT' ICH WARE FRANKENSTEIN (U.S.-I) 1970? Ref:
    Fernsehen 5/71: D: Dan Ash. with Dustin Hoffman, Elsa
    Martinelli. (aka MADIGAN'S MILLIONS?)
IF A GHOST DIES (J) Ref: Cinema Ybk. of Japan'36/7.
I'LL NEVER FORGET YOU 1951 Ref: FM 7:42. NO.
ILLUSION 1927 Ref: NYTimes: illusionist. NO.
L'ILLUSIONNISTE DOUBLE ET LA TETE VIVANTE (F) 1900 Melies
    Ref: Mitry II.
IM BANNE DES UNHEIMLICHEN (G) Ref: Film 7/68.
I'M FROM THE CITY 1938 Ref: FD 6/28/38: hypnotism.
The IMAGE MAKER 1916 Ref: MPW 31:541. Reincarnation. NO.
IMAGE OF LOVE c1964 Ref: Ref: COF 7:49: ONE MILLION B.C.
    sequence, stills of Karloff, Lorre.
IMPASSIVE FOOTMAN (B) 1932 Ref: MFB'48:171: man scared to
    death.
IN SEARCH OF THE CASTAWAYS (F) 1914 Ref: LC.
IN SEARCH OF THE CASTAWAYS 1962 Ref: COF 11:36.
IN THE CLUTCHES OF THE HINDU 1920 serial Ref: MPN 22:4015.
    Ch. 1. Under Hypnotic Power. ?
IN THE DAYS OF WITCHCRAFT 1909 NO.
IN THE DAYS OF WITCHCRAFT 1913 Ref: MPW 16:505: NO.
IN THE DEAD OF NIGHT 1916 Ref: LC.
Les INCONNUS DE LA MAISON (F) 1944: Ref: Lee. ?
The INCREDIBLE CREEPING MONSTERS ?
The INCREDIBLE INVASION with Karloff. Completed?
The INCREDIBLE MR. LIMPET 1964 Ref: COF 5:45.
The INDIAN TOMB (F) 1937 Ref: DDC III:337. Lee: NO.
INFERNO (Austrian) 1920 Ref: Osterr: satan.
INNER SANCTUM 1948 clairvoyant.
AN INNOCENT VAMPIRE Ref: MPN 13:3271. 1916
An INNOCENT WITCH (J) 1966 Ref: UFQ. Medium, witch.
The INN WHERE NO MAN RESTS (F) Melies Ref: Niver: fantasy.
The INSANE DEMONS OF TOPANGA CANYON c1964 Ref: MadM
    9:41. ?
The INSECT PLAY (B) 1960 BBC-TV 91m.
INTERNATIONAL CRIME 1938 Ref: MFB '38:159: eerie atmosphere.
INTRIGUES OF LOS ANGELES (I) 1964 Ref: ITal P: sf?
The INVASION OF THE PREHISTORIC BEASTS Ref: FM 42:59.
INVASIONE (I) 1964 Ref: Imagen: futuristic?
The INVISIBLE Ref: Bios 8/8/12: invisibility powder.
INVISIBLE BLACK HANDS (J) Ref: UFQ 8: NO.
INVISIBLE CYCLIST Ref: Bios 8/1/12: NO.
INVISIBLE DEATH (F) 1917 Ref: DDC I:316.
INVISIBLE ENEMY Ref: MFB'38:201: "eerie." HR. V: NO.
The INVISIBLE GOLDEN MAN Ref: M/TVM 3/68:29.
INVISIBLE HAND Ref: Bios 4/9/14: mysterious figure.
INVISIBLE HAND 1919 serial Ref: FIR'67:339.
INVISIBLE MAGIC SWORD (J) Ref: Cinema Ybk. of Japan '36/7.

The INVISIBLE MENACE 1937 NO.
INVISIBLE MR. UNMEI (J) Ref: MFB'52: NO.
The INVISIBLE WOMAN (F) 1932 Ref: Rep Gen'47: NO.
INVISIBLE WRESTLER 1911 Ref: MPW'11:648: invisibility through
    magic.
Les INVISIBLES (F) 1906 Ref: DDC II:383. Mitry II. D: Gaston
    Velle.
INVITATION TO LUST 1968 Ref: J. R. Duvoli: drug induces pas-
    sion.
INVITATION TO THE ENCHANTED TOWN (J) 1961 Ref: UFQ 12:
    wizards, supernatural.
IRON FAN AND MAGIC SWORD Ref: LATimes 7/28/71.
ISABELL, A DREAM (I) 1958 Ref: FM 54:8. 63:24. 80:26. Dracula,
    Frankenstein monster, mummy. ?
ISLAND OF DOOMED MEN 1940 Ref: TVK: sadism. NO. with P.
    Lorre.
ISLAND OF HORRORS (J) 1970 Ref: UFQ 51: torture.
ISLAND OF LOST MEN 1939 Remake of WHITE WOMAN.
ISLAND OF LOVE Ref: Boxo '63: horror-film producer.
ISLE OF THE DEAD (F) 1924 Ref: DDC II:127.
ISMAIL YASSINE AS TARZAN (UAR) 1958
ISMAIL YASSINE AT THE WAXWORKS (UAR) 1957
ISSUMBOSHI (J) c1955 Ref: Lee: horror? dwarf?
IT HAPPENED TOMORROW 1944 Supernatural.
IT'S A WONDERFUL LIFE 1946 fantasy "A masterpiece"--William
    S. Pechter. One of the greatest American films.
IT'S CALLED ROBERT (Russ) 1968 Ref: RVB. V 7/10/68.

JADU-I-KISMET (India) Ref: Filmindia 4/44: "Chills and magic."
JAMAICA INN 1939 Ref: PM: "horror."
JAMAICA RUN 1953 Ref: COF 11:40: voodoo overtones.
JAMES TONT: OPERATION GOLDSINGER (W.G.) 1966 Ref: TVG:
    criminal Goldsinger.
JANE EYRE (I) 1910 Ref: Bios 6/23/10.
JANE EYRE 1914 Ref: Bios 5/7/14. MPW 19:810: "Spooky situations."
JANE EYRE 1915 Ref: MPN 7/31/15.
JANE EYRE 1921 Ref: LC. FDY.
JANE EYRE 1934 Ref: Photoplay'34.
JANE EYRE 1944 Ref: FD 2/3/44.
JANE EYRE 1957 Ref: COF 11:42.
JANE EYRE 1971 Ref: MFB'71:75. TVG.
JANWAR (India) Ref: Shankar's 4/18/65: "cavemen"?
JASSY (B) 1947 Ref: HR 2/5/48: girl with psychic powers.
JEDDA THE UNCIVILIZED "Almost mystic" chanting of natives
    drives warrior insane: pressbook.
JENNIFER 1953 suspense
JERRY LAND, SPY-HUNTER (I-G-Sp) 1966 Ref: Ital P: "Formula
    for ionum engines."
JIGGS AND MAGGIE OUT WEST 1950 Ref: TVG: ghost town.
JOAN OF THE ANGELS? (Polish)1960 Based on the same historical
    incident as The DEVILS.
JOHNNY ALLEGRO Ref: Dimmitt. Loosely based on Richard

Connell's "The Most Dangerous Game." RVB: NO.
The JOHNSTOWN MONSTER (B) CFF Ref: M/TVM.
The JONAH MAN, or THE TRAVELLER BEWITCHED (B) 1904 Ref:
   SilentFF. NO.
JONES' PATENT MOTOR (B) 1906 Ref: SF Film.
JORINDE AND JORINGEL (G) 1922 Ref: Lee.
JOSEPH, APE WITH THE HUMAN BRAIN Ref: Bios 5/7/14: NO:
   "Animal study."
JOSEPH KILIAN (Cz) 1964 Ref: COF 6:56: political-fantasy.
The JOURNEY TO COSMATOM Ref: Children's Features:138:
   flight to moon "via imagination"
JOURNEY TO THE MOON (UAR) 1958 Ref: Sadoul.
JOURNEY TO THE STARS 1963 Ref: SM 8:7. Documentary.
JOY OF TORTURE (J) Ref: M/TVM 4/69:26: tortures.
JULIA AND THE COELECANTH (Sp) 1961 Ref: SpCinema'62:
   prehistoric fish.
JULIE 1956 Ref: COF 11:42: macabre ending.
JUNGLE BOOK 1942 Ref: FM 12:6: White cobra a monster.
JUNGLE DRUMS OF AFRICA 1953 serial Ch. 4. Voodoo Vengeance.
JUNGLE GIRL 1941 serial Ch. 1. Death By Voodoo.
JUNGLE HELL 1956 Ref: L. Richardson: sf.
JUNGLE PRINCESS 1936 Ref: Lee: giant ape.
JUNGLE TREASURE (B) 1951 Ref: COF 11:43: ghost.
JUNIOR G-MEN serial Ref: Showmen's 8/3/40: explosive formula.
JUPITER (F) 1971 Ref: MMF 24. V 5/12/71:74.
JUST LIKE A WOMAN (B) 1967 Ref: F&F 5/67: horror scene.
JUVE VS. FANTOMAS (F) 1913 Part II: The Haunted Villa: sup-
   posedly haunted room. Fair.
JUWELEN (Austrian) 1930 Ref: Osterr. From E. T.A. Hoffmann.

KAPAL KUNDALA (India) Ref: The Indian Film: horror? Filmindia:
   NO.
KAYE (F-Yug) Ref: Boxo 4/7/69: "strange murders."
KEEP'EM FLYING Ref: COF 5:46: scary sequence.
KEEP SMILING 1925 Ref: AFI: invention.
KILL OR BE KILLED Ref: Halliwell: similar to "The Most
   Dangerous Game."
KILLING THE DEVIL (Cz) Ref: V 10/14/70: devil.
KING OF ATLANTIS Ref: FanMo 6:41. O. Welles.
The KING OF DENMARK (Name of the Game episode) Ref: TVG:
   "Eerie mystery."
KING OF THE CIRCUS 1920 serial Ref: LC: CH. 10. The Mystic's
   Power.
KING OF THE JUNGLE 1927 Ref: LC. Ch. 8. The Giant Ape Strikes.
The KINGDOM OF NOSEY LAND Ref: MPN 11/27/15: witch.
The KISS DOCTOR Ref: MPN 3/17/28: caveman bit.
KISS, KISS, KILL KILL (W.G.) 1966 Ref: TVG: sf.
KISS ME DEADLY 1955 Ref: V 4/20/55: "some kind of fissionable
   material."
KISS OF THE DEAD (I) 1948 Ref: DDC I:270.
KISS OF THE VAMPIRE 1915 Ref: RVB.
KNIGHT OF THE BLACK ART (F) Melies Magician.

KNIVES OF THE AVENGER (I) Ref: Ital P: prophecy. 1965 D: Bava.
KRIMINAL (I?) 1967 Ref: Ital P'66: NO. Skeleton-mask.
KURFURSTENDAMM (G) 1919 Ref: Lee. Satan.

Le LABORATOIRE DE MEPHISTO (F) Melies 1896 Ref: F&F 11/68.
   SF Film.
LABYRINTH (G) 1960 Ref: DDC II:314: fantasy.
LADY IN DEATH HOUSE 1944 Ref: V. HR. NO.
LADY OF THE NIGHT 1925 Ref: AFI: invention.
LADY MACBETH (I) 1917 Ref: Mitry V:11.
LAND OF THE MIST (B) 1935 Ref: FJA. Made?
LANDRU (Austrian) 1923 Ref: Osterr.
LARSAN'S LAST INCARNATION 1914 From Leroux.
The LAST DAYS OF POMPEII Ref: V 10/3/13: Potion makes man
   go mad.
The LAST MAN Ref: SilentFF. 1924. "Crazed scientist."
The LAST NIGHT (Russ) 1937 Ref: Menville: sf? Lee: NO.
LAST YEAR AT MARIENBAD From sf novel "The Morals Invention."
The LATEST IN VAMPIRES 1916 Ref: MPN. vamp
The LAUGHING WOMAN Ref: Boxo 6/29/70: torture.
LEAGUE OF THE PHANTOMS (I) 1914 Ref: Lee.
LEGACY OF HORROR (G) 1964 Ref: FIR'67:84.
LEGEND OF BLOOD MOUNTAIN Ref: Miami Herald 4/5/68.
LEGEND OF HORROR Ref: COF 8:48.
LEGEND OF ORPHEUS (F) 1909 Ref: Lee.
LEGEND OF THE EVERGLADE Ref: Bios 6/19/13: spirit.
LEGEND OF THE ICY HEART (Russ) Ref: Orient. Spell.
LEMMY FOR THE WOMEN (F) 1962 Ref: FIR'68: secret laboratory.
LEOPARD MEN OF AFRICA 1940.
LIFE AFTER DEATH (India) c1932 Ref: Indian Cin.:157.
LIFE RETURNS 1935 Ref: FD 1/2/35: sf-documentary?
The LIGHTNING RAIDER serial Ref: LC. 1919.
LIGHTS OUT 1923 Ref: V 10/25/23: NO.
LILITH AND LY (Austrian) 1919 Ref: Osterr: "Vampirismus." ?
   SP: Fritz Lang.
LIO EN EL LABORATORIO Ref: SpCinema'68.
LIQUEFACTION DES CORPS DURS (F) 1909 Ref: DDC I:404. de
   Chomon.
The LITTLE SINGING TREE (G) 1965 short? Giant fish, evil dwarf
   Ref: Positif 70:41 color (Le PETIT ARBRE CHANTE)
The LIVER EATERS. Florida
The LIVING MUMMY (Swedish) 1918 Ref: Sweden I.
The LITTLE MAPIRE   (G) 1968 Ref: Germany. (Der KLEINE
   VAMPIRE. LITTLE BOY)
The LIVING DEAD MAN (F) 1912 Ref: DDC II:338. D: Feuillade.
The LIVING GHOST (J) 1928 Ref: DDC III:130.
LIZARD IN A WOMAN'S SKIN suspense
LO QUE DE AYER A HOY (Mex) Aventura: sf?
LOCK UP YOUR DAUGHTERS 1958 Ref: MFB 5/59: Clips from six
   of Lugosi's Monograms. 50m.
The LODGER (Polish) 1967 Ref: Film Polski: seances.
LOHENGRIN (G) 1916 Ref: DDC III:427.
LOHENGRIN (I) 1936 Ref: DDC II:73.

LOLITA Ref: FM 63:24: CURSE OF FRANKENSTEIN excerpt.
LONDON BY NIGHT 1937 Ref: Motion Picture Reviews: "macabre
  mystery"
LORD ARTHUR SAVILE'S CRIME (Hung) 1919 Ref: DDC?
LORD OF THE FLIES (B) 1963 Ref: COF 4:5.
LOST HORIZON 1937
The LOST PLANET (G) 1968 Ref: RVB: from TV series.
The LOST SECRET 1915 Ref: MPW 9/25/15: new explosive.
LOST VOLCANO 1950 Ref: COF 14:49. HR 6/23/50: footage from
  ONE MILLION B.C.
LOVE AFTER DEATH (Mex) Ref: Photon 21:29 (De VANPIER VAN
  NEW YORK) Premature burial.
LOVE HATE LOVE 1971 ABC-TV suspense
The LOVES OF EDGAR ALLAN POE 1942.
LUCIFER (Austrian) 1921 Ref: Osterr.
The LUCKY GHOST 1941 Ref: The Negro in Film.
The LUNATICS (F) 1914 Ref: The Film Index: NO.
LUNATICS IN POWER 1909 Ref: F Index 5/15/09: NO.
LURED 1947 NO.

M (G) 1931 Ref: Photoplay 6/33: horror. (The VAMPIRE OF DUS-
  SELDORF)
M 1950 Remake of '31 M.
MAANGALYA Ref: FEFN '58/'59: supernatural
The MACABRE TRACK (Mex)   LATimes 1/23/69.
MACABRO (U.S.-I) c1966
MACISTE CONTRE LA MORT (I) 1916/1920 Ref: DDC II:234.
MACISTE, GLADIATOR OF SPARTA (I-F) 1964 Ref: Ital P: "Giant
  gorilla."
MADAM SATAN Ref: V 10/6/30. NYT 10/6/30. FD 10/5/30. B.
  Warren: mechanically-choreographed dance. A la METROPOLIS.
The MAD MINSTREL Ref: HM 7:43: c1963. Titan
The MAD ROOM Ref: FFacts: NO.
MAD VAMPIRE   Florida
The MADMAN (Canadian) 1962 From "The Horla." Ref: Lee.
MADONNA OF THE SEVEN MOONS Ref: Maltin: "strange gypsy
  curse"
The MAGGOT CREATURES   Florida
MAGIC FLUTE Ref: Bios 9/22/10. (F) Flute makes dead man rise.
MAGIC HANDKERCHIEF (F) 1908 Ref: Lee: invisibility.
MAGIC THROUGH THE AGES (F) Melies Ref: DDC III:352.
The MAGICIAN (F) 1932 Ref: DDC II:428.
MAGNETIC FLUID Ref: Bios 2/15/12. (F)
MAHASATI SAVITRI (India) Ref: FEFN 8/31/56: man returns from
  dead
MAID OF SALEM 1937 "witch" NO.
MALAMONDO (I) 1964 Ref: Ital P.
Le MALEFICE (F) 1912 Ref: DDC II:338. Feuillade.
Il MALEFICO ANELLO (I) 1916 Ref: DDC II:302.
MALOMBRA (I) 1916
MALOMBRA (I) 1942 Ref: Le Surrealisme au Cinema: ghosts.
MAMMOTH INSECTS Ref: FM 42:59.

MAMMY'S GHOST Ref: Bios 6/8/11: NO.
MAMMY'S ROSE Ref: MPN 13:726: "land of spirits"
The MAN IN THE MIRROR (B) 1936 Ref: FM 10:26. Fantasy.
The MAN-MIRROR (G) 1923 Ref: DDC I:300.
MAN-MONKEY (F) 1907 Ref: Lee.
The MAN WHO DISAPPEARED 1914 serial Ref: LC. Ch. 9. The
   Living Dead.
The MAN WHO STOLE THE MOON Ref: SF in the Cinema:70.
   Futuristic plane?
The MAN WHO RETURNED TO LIFE 1942 Ref: V 2/19/42: NO.
MAN WITH A CLOAK 1951 Edgar Allan Poe.
The MAN WITH A THOUSAND INVENTIONS (F) Melies Ref: DDC
   III:353.
The MAN WITH THE IRON HEART Ref: MPN 9/4/15: Death per-
   sonified.
MAN WITH THE GOLDEN FIST Ref: Ital P'67: radioactive dust?
MAN WITHOUT A CONSCIENCE Ref: MFB'43:54. Deranged gangster,
   "The Ghost."
The MANIAC (B) 1963 Ref: FFacts: NO.
The MANIAC BARBER 1902 Ref: Niver: severed head.
Der MANN AUF DEM KOMETEN (G) 1924 Ref: Deutsche.
The MANNIKIN (Swedish) 1962 Ref: COF 5:4: macabre.
The MANSION OF MYSTERY 1927 serial Ref: CNW.
MARAT/SADE Ref: PM. NO.
MARGUERITE AND FAUST (G-Aust) D: Richard Oswald?
MARIA MARTEN (B) 1899 Ref: Hist Brit Film.
MARIA MARTEN (B) 1904 Ref: DDC II:449.
MARIA MARTEN (B) 1914 Ref: Lee. DDC II:189.
MARIA MARTEN (B) 1928 Ref: Brit Cinema.
MARIE CHANTAL VS. DR. KHA 1965 Ref: V 10/6/65. La Prod
   Cin Fr: virus?
The MARK OF THE PHANTOM (Hung) 1920 Ref: DDC II:324.
The MARKET OF SOULS 1919 Ref: MPN 20:2467: ghost bit.
MARKETA LAZAROVA (Cz) 1968 Ref: S&S'68:185: "horror build-up"
MARS(F) 1908 Ref: DDC I:404. De Chomon.
MARY JANE'S MISHAP (B) 1902 Ref: 70 Years. Ghost.
The MASKED MENACE 1927 Ref: LC.
The MASK OF DEATH (Mex) Ref: FEFN 6/61: NO.
MASK OF HORROR (F) 1912 Ref: DDC II:416.
MASK OF THE RED DEATH (I) 1911 Ref: The Film Index: NO.
MASTER MAN (India) Ref: The Lighthouse 5/21/38. Jekyll & Hyde?
   Doubt.
MATA SHAITAN (Malayan) Ref: M/TVM 5/62: "horror." shooting.
MAYA KAJAL (India) Ref: Dipali 2/19/37: spirit.
MATCHLESS 1967 Ref: PM. Ring of invisibility.
Les MAUDITS SAUVAGES (Canadian) Ref: V 6/9/71.
MEDIUM SPIRITS Ref: LC. 1921.
MEET MR. LUCIFER (B) 1954 Ref: MFB: NO.
MELCHIOR, DAS MEDIUM (Austrian) 1919 Ref: Osterr.
The MELOMANIAC (F) 1903 Ref: Niver. Severed head.
MEMENTO Ref: FM 63:24. RVG. (F) 1968. Frankenstein monster
   model kit.
MEMORIAS DE UNA VAMPIRESA (Mex) 1945 Ref: Indice.

MENACE 1934 Ref: Photoplay. TVK. Thriller.
MEPHISTO'S AFFINITY Ref: MPW'08:547. Devil.
MEPHISTOS CARNIVAL (Austrian) 1919 Ref: Osterr.
MEPHISTO'S PLIGHT (B) Ref: Bios 4/27/11.
MERCY ISLAND Ref: PM: "horror film." FD 10/9/41: NO.
The MESMERIST (B) 1898 Ref: DDC II:448.
MESSIAH Ref: V 7/28/71. sf?
MESSAGE FROM THE MOON Ref: Bios 6/18/14: NO.
MESSENGER FROM THE MOON (J) Ref: FEFN 6/22/56.
METEORANGO KID, INTERGALACTIC HERO (Braz) 1969 Ref:
    V 4/29/70:167.
MGM'S BIG PARADE OF COMEDY Ref: COF 6:50: "horror films...
    Tod Browning at work on his set."
The MIBSTER AND THE MONSTER Milligan Ref: V.
MIDGET AND GIANT (F) Melies 1901 Ref: DDC III:350.
MIDNIGHT COWBOY sf-film on theatre screen.
The MIDNIGHT GHOST (UAR) 1946 Ref: Sadoul.
MIDNIGHT IN BOMBAY Ref: Filmindia 3/48: pendulum torture.
MIDNIGHT LACE Ref: FM 26:9. suspense.
MIDNIGHT MYSTERY 1930 Ref: NYT. V 6/4/30. NO.
MIDNIGHT PHANTOM 1935 Ref: FD 11/21/35: NO.
MIDWINTER SACRIFICE (Swedish) 1946 short "eerie."
A MILLION DOLLARS FOR SEVEN ASSASSINS (I) Ref: Ital P:
    "New form of propulsion."
The MIRROR OF CAGLIOSTRO (F) 1899 Ref: DDC III:350.
The MISCHIEVOUS ELF Ref: Bios 2/10/10. Elf, witch.
MISFORTUNES OF AN AERONAUT (F) 1900 Ref: Imagen.
MISION SPECIAL EN CARACAS Ref: SpCinema'67: new type bomb.
The MISSING LADY 1946 NO.
The MISSING LINK (B) 1917.
The MISSING LINK (UAR) 1949.
MISSION INTERPLAN (W.G.) 1962 Ref: SM 5:8. FJA. amateur.
MR. JARR'S MAGNETIC FRIEND Ref: MPW 4/17/15.
MR. MOTO TAKES A VACATION 1939 Ref: Hollywood Spectator:
    atmospheric.
MR. VAMPIRE 1916 Ref: DDC II:371.
MR. WU 1927 Ref: FD 5/22/27: severed head. NO. FM 24:8.
MR. WU (Spanish version of above)
MR. X Ref: Moving Picture Monthly 12/38: man revived from dead.
MODERN LOVE POTION (B) Ref: Bios 9/15/10: ?
MODERN JEKYLL AND HYDE 1914 Ref: Bios 3/12/14: NO.
The MODERN ROCAMBOLE (I) 1918 Ref: DDC III:285.
MODERN TIMES 1936 Ref: FD 2/7/36: NO. Satire on automation.
MONDO BALORDO Narr: Karloff. Ref: FFacts: NO.
MONDO BIZARRO   "Voodoo ritual"
MONDO CANE (I)
MONDO FREUDO "Black mass"
MONDO PAZZO
MONICA STOP (Sp) Ref: SpCinema: sf?
MONJA, CASADA, VIRGEN Y MARTIR (Mex) 1935 Ref: Aventura:
    horror?
MONKEY INTO MAN (B) Ref: V 4/17/40: "Animal life from Stone
    Age to present."

The MONSTER (Chinese) 1927 Ref: DDC I:402.
The MONSTER (Egyptian) 1953 Ref: Index des Films Egyptiens '53-
    '55: NO.
The MONSTER AND THE GIRL Ref: MPW 19:1694: NO.
MONSTER BEAST Ref: Miami Herald 5/11/68.
The MONSTER FROM 1000 A.D. Ref: FM 42:59.
MONSTER OF THE ISLAND (I) 1953 Ref: COF 9:16. Drama with
    Karloff.
MONSTERS OF THE DEEP 1931 Ref: PM. Photoplay: "giant devil-
    fish."
MOON MAN (B) 1905 Ref: SilentFF: fantasy.
MOON-ROBBERS (Polish) 1962 Ref: MMF 9:24: fantasy.
MOON WOLF 1964 Ref: FFacts: "launch project."
MOONLIGHT MURDER 1936 swami
The MOONSTONE OF FEZ Ref: MPW 21:104: NO: mystery.
MORE THAN A MIRACLE 1967 Ref: MFB'69:193: witches' spell of
    paralysis.
MORGAN (B) clips from KING KONG.
Il MOSCHETTIERE FANTASMA (I) 1952 Ref: DDC III:215.
MOUNTAIN OF FEAR (Yug) 1964 Ref: MFB: witch.
MOUNTAIN WITCH 1913 Ref: Bios 4/24/13: NO.
The MUD CURE Ref: MPN 14:1895. 1916 sf?
LA MUERTA ESPERA EN ATENAS Ref: SpCinema'67: "new nuclear
    superbomb."
Las MUJERES MANDAN (Mex) Ref: Aventura. 1936 ?
The MUMMY (F) 1909 Ref: DDC II:461.
The MUMMY (F) 1913 Ref: DDC II:339. Feuillade.
The MUMMY 1923 short Ref: LC.
The MUMMY (Egyptian) Ref: V 7/28/71.
The MUMMY AND THE HUMMINGBIRD Ref: MPN 11/27/15: NO.
The MUMMY INTERFERES (Hung) Ref: M/TVM 5/67.1/68:
    "Satire on crime drama."
MURDER A LA MOD Ref: V 4/26/68: "horror."
MURDER AT THE BASKERVILLES (B) 1938 Ref: FD 6/18/41:
    mystery.
MURDER IN THE MUSEUM 1934 Ref: FD 6/27/34: "freak museum."
The MURDER OF MR. DEVIL (Cz) Ref: COF 16:15.
MURDERER FROM BEYOND THE GRAVE (Cz) Ref: Czechoslovak
    Film 3: mystery.
MUSIC ON MARS (Cz) 1954 Ref: DDC III:147.
MUTANO THE HORRIBLE (W.G.) 1961 Ref: FM 17:28.19:12. FJA.
    amateur sequel: EXPERIMENTS OF YALON.
MY BRIDE IS A GHOST (Arg) 1944 Ref: DDC III:77.
MY MOTHER-IN-LAW IS AN ATOMIC BOMB (UAR) 1952 Ref: Cinema
    Arab Countries.
The MYSTERIES OF PARIS 1913,1922,1935,1943,1962 versions:
    borderline horror.
The MYSTERIOUS ARMOR (F) 1907 Ref: MPW'07:583: magic.
The MYSTERIOUS CREATURE (Danish) 1914 Ref: DDC I:67.
A MYSTERIOUS DISLOCATION(F) 1901 Ref: SilentFF: severed limbs.
MYSTERIOUS FLAMES Ref: MPW'08:547: devil. (F)
The MYSTERIOUS ISLAND (India) Ref: FEFN 7/27/56.
The MYSTERIOUS PILOT 1937 serial Ref: Barbour. Ch. 11. The

Haunted Mill.
The MYSTERIOUS PEARL 1921 serial Ch. 2. The Brass Spectre.
The MYSTERIOUS VILLA (G) 1913 Ref: DDC III:337.
The MYSTERIOUS X (Danish) 1913 Ref: DDC II:8.
MYSTERY HOUSE 1938 Ref: FD 6/1/38: NO.
MYSTERY MANSION 1928 short Ref: LC.
MYSTERY OF CORBY CASTLE (G) 1914.
The MYSTERY OF EDWIN DROOS 1914 (B) Ref: MPW 22:501,410.
The MYSTERY OF MR. X 1934 Ref: TVG. TVK. Mystery.
The MYSTERY OF THE COBRA (Mex) Ref: FJA: ape-man?
MYSTERY OF THE DOUBLE CROSS 1917 serial Ch. 6. The Dead
   Come Back.
MYSTERY OF THE HOODED HORSEMAN 1937 Ref: FD 7/30/37:
   NO.
The MYSTERY OF THE TAPESTRY ROOM Ref: MPN 8/28/15:
   killer in black, panels
MYSTERY OF THE YELLOW ROOM (F) 1913 Ref: Bios 4/10/13: NO.
The MYSTIC RING (B) 1912 Ref: SilentFF. Dream: devil, ring of
   invisibility.

NABONGA 1944 (NABONGA, FILS DE KING KONG-Belgium) Ref:
   MPH'44:1783: NO. Girl brought up by gorilla. (JUNGLE WITCH.
   NABOB. GIRL AND THE GORILLA) Ref: HR 11/16/45. FM 66:23.
   28:81. 33:14.
NACHT DER GRAUENS (G) 1912 Ref: Germany.
Die NACHT DES SCHRECKENS (G) Ref: Deutsche.
NAGASALITANG (Fili) Ref: FEFN 6/61: "horror." announced. D:
   Pablo Santiago.
NAGIN (India) Ref: Thought 1/15/55: "Dantesque hell."
NAKED EDGE Ref: Boxo 6/26/61: ad: compared to PSYCHO.
NAKED JUNGLE 1954.
NAKED TERROR 1961 Ref: C. Bulletin: Documentary. Witchcraft.
The NAKED WITCH Ref: Boxo 3/6/67. D: Andy Milligan.
NAMAHAGE, THE DEMONS Ref: FEFN 2/61:57: NO. Orpheus
   4:38.
NANCY DREW AND THE HIDDEN STAIRCASE Ref: FD 11/2/39.
   V. ?
The NANNY (B) Ref: Boxo 10/25/65: NO.
The NARCOTIC SPECTRE Ref: Bios 4/23/14:?
NARROW ESCAPE Ref: Bios 4/30/14: "fearsome Macbethian
   crone."
NECKLACE OF THE DEAD (G?) 1919 Ref: FM 34:45. FMO 2:9:
   horror. with Lugosi.
NECROPHAGUS (Sp) Ref: V 10/6/71: horror?
NEUTRON CONTRA EL CREMINAL SADICO (Mex) Ref: LATimes.
NEW ABSURD WRESTLING MATCHES (F) 1900 woman dismembered.
The NEW ROCAMBOLE (F) 1913 Ref: DDC II:64.
NEXT! (I-Sp) Ref: V 8/11/71: "shock-pic." Boxo 8/9/71:
   "horror."?
NICK CARTER E IL TRIFOGLIO ROSSO (I) 1966 Ref: Annuario.
   New weapons.
NICK CARTER, MASTER DETECTIVE Ref: NYT 12/14/39: plans

for rocket plane.
A NIGHT IN TRANSYLVANIA (Hung) 1941 Ref: EncicDS IX:1247.
NIGHT OF THE BEAST Taurus 1966 Ref: MMF 13:60. FM 37:49.
    (The WIDDERBURN HORROR) with Carradine, Chaney, J. Thor,
    M. Shinn. D: H. Daniels. made?
NIGHT OF THE DAMNED (I) Ref: M/TVM'71: "terror."
NIGHTMARE (Swedish) 1965 Ref: MFB'69:148: suspense.
NINE DAYS IN ONE YEAR (Russ) Ref: SF in the Cinema.
NINE LIVES OF A CAT Ref: MPW'07:362: cat put through sausage
    machine.
NINE SUPERMEN (Fili?) Ref: LATimes 5/25/71.
NO MORE SPOOKS (Cz) 1953 Ref: Modern Cz. Film.
NOCTURNAL HORROR (Cz) 1915 Ref: EncicDS III:364.
NOVEL NAVIGATION (F) Ref: Bios 2/3/10: cab plus sail flies
    into air.

O.K. NERO (I) Ref: Ital P'51: dream: sorcerer's hate potion.
OSS 117--MISSION FOR A KILLER (F) 1965 Ref: FFacts'66:
    hypnotic trance.
OCTAVIUS Ref: Bios 6/12/13: ghost?
The OGRE AND THE GIRL Ref: Lee: NO. 1915.
The OGRE OF ATHENS (Greek) 1955 Ref: DDC II:458.
The OGRE'S KITCHEN (F) 1908 Ref: DDC III:352.
OH, MR. PORTER (B) 1938 Ref: Halliwell: gun-runners pose as
    ghosts.
OH, MUMMY 1927 Ref: Lee. short.
OHYAKU THE FEMALE DEMON (J) Ref: COF 15:16. D: Ishikawa, Y.
OLD MOTHER RILEY'S GHOSTS (B) Ref: TVFFSB. 1941.
The OLD WOODMAN Ref: Bios 10/21/09: "image of Death."
The OLD WOODMAN Ref: Bios 1/13/10: devil.
OLGA'S GIRLS 1964 Ref: COF 8:6: torture.
ON SUCH A NIGHT Ref: NYT. FD 8/16/37. Old mansion. NO
ON THE STORMY HILL (Korea) Ref: FEFN 11/60: from "Wuthering
    Heights."
ON THE STROKE OF 12 Ref: Motog 3/6/15: invention.
ON THE THRESHHOLD OF SPACE 1956.
The ONE-EYED SOLDIERS (Yug-U.S.-B) Ref: MFB'69. 1966.
ONE IN A MILLION 1937 Ref: Movie Comedy Teams: impression
    of the Monster.
ONE MILLION AC/DC Ref: L. Richardson: horror.
OPERATION ABDUCTION (F) 1961 Ref: TVG: new rocket fuel.
OPERATION DIPLOMATIC PASSPORT Ref: TVFFSB: synthetic
    petroleum.
OPERATION DOUBLE CROSS 1965 Ref: TVFFSB: "atomic cannon"
    with M. Mell, Vernon.
OPERATION GOLDSEVEN (I-Sp) 1966 Ref: Ital P. serum.
OPERATION TOP SECRET Ref:TVFFSB:"project that will return
    rockets to earth."
OPERATION TURNTABLE (W.G.) 1966 Ref: TVG. Arch-criminal
    Goldsinger.
OPERATION WARHEAD Ref: TVFFSB: transistorized bomb.
ORAMUNDE Ref: FanMo 5:40: "silent horror film."

ORPHEUS IN THE UNDERWORLD Ref: Sweden I: 1909.
The OTHER BOARDING SCHOOL (Sp) 1970 Ref: SpCinema'71: NO.
V 5/12/71: spoof of The BOARDING SCHOOL.
OUR MOTHER'S HOUSE 1967 seance. Ref: PM.
OUT OF THE MIST (G) c1927 Ref: Lee: curse? Orpheus 2:20.
The OUTSIDE WOMAN Ref: MPW 49:108: grotesque statue.
OUTWARD BOUND 1930 Ref: Photoplay 11/30.
The OVERCOAT (Russ) Ref: EncicDS IX:1346. 1926 From Gogol.
The OWL WITCH 1927 short Ref: The Film Spectator 2/19/27:
legend.

PADMINI (India) 1948 Ref: Filmindia 9/48: fake ghost.
PALKI (India) Ref: Shankar's 5/21/67: people return from the
dead?
PALMY DAYS seance Ref: Halliwell.
PANCHA DELIMA (Singapore) Ref: FEFN 7/5/57: "curse"
PANDEMONIUM Ref: NYorker 5/1/71:33: devil cult. with Candy
Darling.
PANIC IN THE CITY Ref: MFB'69:148:nuclear bomb.
PANFOCUS Ref:M/TVM 10/70: reincarnation.
PANOPTICUM (Austrian) 1959 Ref: FEFN 9/59: Girl under charla-
tan's "evil influence." experimental.
The PANTHER'S CLAW Ref: Boxo 4/4/42:NO.
PARACELSUS (G) 1943 Ref: Deutscher: NO.
PARIS DOES NOT EXIST Opera/Lycanthrope Ref: M/TVM 4/69:
clairvoyant.
PARIS NOUS APPARTIENT Ref: S&S'68:212: sf?
PARISIENNE AND THE PRUDES Ref: MMF 13:44: futuristic?
PARTNER Ref: V 9/18/68.
PATENT 95-75 (F) Ref: Rep Gen'47: new-type plane?
The PATH THAT LEADS TO HEAVEN (Swedish) 1942 Ref: S&S
'46:30: demons?
PAUL SLEUTH AND THE MYSTIC 7 Ref: Bios 6/4/14: NO.
PAYING THE PRICE Ref: MPN 14:626. 1916.. New explosive.
PEANUTS AND POWDER Ref: Pictures and the Picturegoer
8/12/16: explosive.
PEER GYNT Ref: FM 35:20. 85m. Goblins, trolls.
PFUT THE LITTLE GHOST (Braz) 1967 Ref: La Saison Cin. '68.
The PHANTOM (I) 1909 Ref: Lee.
The PHANTOM (G) Murnau Ref: S&S Index: NO. COF 16:31.
PHANTOM BUSTER 1927 Ref: FD 8/21/27: NO.
The PHANTOM CARAVAN 1954 Ref: L. Otis. Film Review 55/56:
horde of murderers.
PHANTOM COWBOY Ref: V 4/2/41: NO.
PHANTOM EXPRESS Ref: Photoplay 11/32. MFB'39:48: "ghost
train."
The PHANTOM GONDOLA (F) 1936 Ref: London Times 6/22/36:
"macabre."
The PHANTOM KNIGHT Ref: Bios 7/27/11.
The PHANTOM LADY (F) Melies 1904 Ref: DDC III:352.
The PHANTOM LADY (Arg) 1945 Ref: DDC I:113.
PHANTOM LIGHT (B) 1935 Ref: London Times 7/8/35: NO.

PHANTOM OF CHINATOWN Ref: V 1/1/41: NO.
PHANTOM OF 42ND STREET 1945. NO.
PHANTOM OF MORRISVILLE Ref:M/TVM 8/66: "Spoof of oldtime hair-raising thriller."
PHANTOM OF PARIS 1931 NO.
PHANTOM PATROL Ref: V 7/28/37: NO.
PHANTOM SHIP Ref: Lee: telepathy. Bios 5/8/13: NO.
The PHANTOM SHIP (B) 1936 Ref: Lee. FM 20:25. NO.
The PHANTOM STRIKES (B) 1938 Ref: FD 11/17/39. FIR'67:78. MFB'39:1:"Conveys horror." From "The Ringer" by E. Wallace.
PHANTOM'S HOTEL (F) 1932 Ref: DDC III:477.
The PHANTOMS HURRY (Rumania) Ref: M/TVM 6/67. V 5/8/68: Russian? mystery.
A PIECE OF CAKE Ref: MFB'48:155: devil?
PIERROT ET LE FANTOME (F) 1898 Ref: DDC II:383.
PINOCCHIO (I) Ref: Mitry V: 1909. Bios 11/23/11: puppet?
PLUNDER 1922 serial Ref: Lee: gorilla.
POISON BELT 1935 (B) Ref: FJA.
POLIDOR AS A GIANT Ref: Bios 3/19/14: ?
PONTIANAK (Mandarin) Ref: FEFN 8/1/58.
PONTIANAK MEETS THE OILY MAN (Malaya) Ref: FEFN 11/22/57: announced. Shaw.
PONTIANAK STRIKES AGAIN (Malaya) Shaw Ref: FEFN 11/22/57: announced.
A POOR KNIGHT AND THE DUKE'S DAUGHTER (F) Ref: MPW'08: 548: witch.
POOR LITTLE RICH GIRL silent Ref: Lee: "two-faced thing" in dream.
PORT OF GHOSTS (I) 1912 Ref: DDC III:112.
PORTRAIT OF HELL (U) Ref: Hollywood Citizen-News: 11/26/69: ghost.
PORTRAIT-ROBOT (F) 1962 Ref: V 11/21/62: NO.
POSITION WANTED (I) Ref: Ital P'51: spirit, medium.
POWER OF EVIL (Armenian) 1929 Ref: NYT. "witch" NO.
PREHISTORIC ANIMALS Ref: NYT? 1922?
A PREHISTORIC LOVE STORY (B) 1915 Ref: Brit Cinema.
PREHISTORIC MAN Ref: Bios 1/12/11: NO.
PREHISTORIC MAN 1924 Ref: LC.
The PREVIEW MURDER MYSTERY Ref: Motion Picture Reviews: "eerie atmosphere" MPH 2/15/36: NO.
The PRIMEVAL TEST 1914 Ref: Lee. ?
PRIMITIVE LOVE (I) 1965 Ref: La Saison Cin'67. ?
PRINCE OF DARKNESS Ref: M/TVM 9/67. "The Man from U.N.C.L.E." TV show released theatrically overseas.
The PRINCESS YANG (J) 1955 Ref: Japanese Movies: spirit.
The PRISONER 1923 From "Castle Craneycrow" by G. B. McCutcheon. Ref: AFI: NO.
The PRIVATE LIFE OF SHERLOCK HOLMES (B) 1970 Ref: MFB '71:11. Fake Loch Ness monster.
The PRIVATE LIVES OF ADAM AND EVE 1960 Ref: FFacts. Dream: devil.
PROFESSOR, BEWARE 1938 Ref: Hollywood Spectator.
PROF. VAMAN (India) Ref: Dipali 8/18/39: science-mystery.

Il PROGRESSO DELLA VAMPIRO (I) Ref: COF 16:41.
PSYCHO A GO GO Ref: COF 10:48. Boxo 9/20/66: NO.
PSYCHO-CIRCUS (B) 1967 Grotesque masks. NO.
PSYCHOMANIA 1964 Ref: TVG: demented killer.
PULGARCITO Ref: Grafica 7/8/62:36: giant?
PURSUIT OF PHANTOM Ref: MPW 10/10/14: NO.
PUSS IN BOOTS Ref: F Index 11/21/08: Cat transforms into man-
  size cat-being.

QUEEN ELIZABETH 1912 Prediction of death.
QUEEN OF SPADES (I) Ref: Bios 2/20/13: NO.
QUEEN OF SPADES (Greek) Ref: M/TVM 10/66: NO.
QUEEN OF THE JUNGLE Ref: Lee: radio beam in idol eye. 1935.

R. U. R. (I) 1958 Ref: Orpheus 3:35: not made.
Die RACHE DER PHARAONEN (Austrian) 1925 Ref: Osterr.
Die RACHE DES FAKIRS (Aus) 1918 Ref: Osterr.
RAMBHAKTA HANUMAN (India) Ref: Filmindia 12/48: monkey-king.
RAMIR (Fili) Ref: FEFN 6/6/58: prediction of death.
RASHOMON (J) 1951 Ghost, medium.
RASPUTIN (Austrian) 1925 Ref: Osterr.
RAT PFINK AND BOO BOO Ref: Boxo 11/7/66. COF 10:29.
REACH FOR THE PLANETS dionsaurs Ref: FJA folder. Amateur?
The RED CIRCLE 1915 serila Ref: CNW: curse.
RED HELL AND TWO BELOW ZERO 1962 Ref: Take One II:6:11.
  Boxo. Sf? (RED HELL AND TWO BEFORE ZERO)
The RED INN (F) 1928 Ref: MMF 9:18: "Film de terreur."
The RED INN (F) 1951 Ref: TVK.
The RED SIGNAL 1948 "Grand guignol" Ref: DDC III:209.
The RED SKELETON (Chinese) 1921 Ref: DDC I:401.
REGGAE (B) Ref: MFB'71:82. clips from KING KONG.
The RELUCTANT ASTRONAUT Ref: V 1/18/67. PM. NO.
The RELUCTANT SADIST
REPORTED MISSING Ref: V 9/1/37: NO.
RESCUED c1965 Ref: FM 32:10: amateur.
RETANDO LA MUERTE Ref: LATimes.
The RETURN OF PETER GRIMM 1926
The RETURN OF PETER GRIMM 1935
RETURN OF THE FROG (B) 1939 Ref: FD 10/11/39. Advertised as
  horror.
The REVENANT (F) 1913 Ref: DDC II:339. Feuillade
The REVENANT (F) 1918 Ref: DDC I:180.
A REVENANT (F) 1946 Ref: MFB'48:132: NO.
The REVENGE OF DR. KUNG (G-Sp?) Ref: Film 4/68.
REVENGE OF THE DEAD (Austrian) 1916 Ref: DDC.
RIDERS OF THE WHISTLING SKULL Ref: FD 6/3/37: NO.
RIDERS OF THE WITCH (Mex)c1968 Ref: LATimes 5/4/68.
RIGHT TO THE HEART (Canadian) Ref: V 6/4/69: NO.
The RINGER (B) 1929 Ref: FIR'67:76.
The RINGER (B) 1932 Ref: FIR'67:76.
The RINGER (B) 1951 Ref: FIR'67:79. MFB: NO.

RIO 70 Ref: SpCinema'71. Non-sf sequel to The MILLION EYES OF
SUMURU.
Il RISVEGLIO DI DRACULA (I) c1964 aka HOUSE OF DRACULA?-
D. Glut.
The RITE (SWEDISH) Ref: MFB'71:124: "sinister masks."
The ROAD TO MANDALAY 1926 Ref: V 6/30/26: "Grand Guignol
... morbid"
The ROAD TO RUIN Ref: Bios 6/19/13: "woman vampire... ghostly
residents."
The ROAD TO YESTERDAY 1925 Ref: FJA: caveman flashback bit.
ROBERT HYDE'S DOUBLE LIFE Ref: Bios 7/10/10: NO.
ROBERT THE DEVIL Ref: Bios 8/4/10: NO. Enchanted plant.
ROBOT-AGENT X-2 (J) Ref: M/TVM 4/70:38.
ROBOTS (F) 1932 Ref: DDC II:74. experimental?
ROBOTS FROM MARS Florida.
ROCAMBOLE (F) 1913,1924,1933,1946, & 1962 versions.
A ROCKET FROM CALABUCH (Sp-I) Ref: MFB'58:55: NO.
ROCKETFLIGHT TO THE MOON (Bavarian) 1941 (SPACESHIP #1
STARTS) Ref: FJA: probably not finished. SM 1:54. 2:32.
The ROMANCE OF THE MUMMY (I) 1915 Ref: DDC III:112.
ROMANCE ROAD 1925 Ref: AFI: invention.
ROSE O' SALEM TOWN 1910 Ref: "witchcraft"
ROSE OF THE WORLD 1918 Ref: FIR'64:562.
ROSEANNA (Swedish) 1967 Ref: MFB'69:28: nocturnal killer.
ROULETABILLE CONTRE LA DAME DE PIQUE (F) 1946 Ref:
DDC III:353.
RUMPELSTILZCHEN (Austrian) 1923 Ref: Osterr.
RUN FOR THE HILLS 1953 Ref: V 6/25/53: NO.
RUN FOR THE SUN 1956 Ref: RVB: NO. Similar to "The Most
Dangerous Game."
RUNAWAY JANE 1915 serial Ch. 12. The Spirit of the Marsh. Ref:
Motog 4/10/15: NO.
The RUNT 1915 Ref: MPW 9/25/15: spirit.
The RUNWAY (F) c1964 Ref: SM 8:7: time travel. made?

SABAASH MEENA (India) Ref: FEFN 10/25/57: demon possession.
shooting.
SABOTAGE (B) 1936? Ref: SF Film: ray?
SACRILEGE Ref: LATimes. The devil?
SADISMO Ref: V: NO.
The SADIST 1963 Ref: COF 5:5.
The SAINT'S DOUBLE TROUBLE 1940 with Lugosi. NO.
SALLY'S HOUNDS Ref: Boxo 4/7/69: spell?
SALOME'73 (I) 1964 Ref: Ital P: youth potion.
SAM, THE FRIENDLY VAMPIRE Florida.
SAMSON AND THE SEA BEASTS (I) 1962 Ref: TVK: NO.
SAN DIEGO, I LOVE YOU Ref: MPH 9/9/44: new explosive.
SANDOKAN THE GREAT (I-F-Sp) 1964 Ref: Ital P. Death-semblance
serum.
SANTA CLAUS' BUSY DAY 1906 Ref: SF Film: "Man in the Moon."
SANTO CONTRA LOS ASESINOS DE LA MAFIA (Mex-Sp) Ref:
SpCinema'71: NO.

El SANTO CONTRA LOS CAZADORES DE CABEZAS (Mex) Ref:
   M/TVM 12/69.
El SANTO CONTRA LOS JINETES DEL TERROR Ref: M/TVM
   5/70: shooting.
SANTO CONTRA LOS VILLANOS DEL RING (Mex) Ref: M/TVM
   3/66: shooting.
SANTO EN EL MUNDO DE LOS MUERTOS (Mex) Ref: M/TVM
   3/69: shooting.
SANTO IN THE HOTEL OF THE DEAD (Mex) Ref: FDY'64: Lee.
SATAN FINDS MISCHIEF (F) c1908 Ref: SilentFF: Satan.
SATAN IN SOFIA (Bulg) 1921 Ref: Lee. From the German film
   KURFURSTENDAMM.
SATAN ON A RAMPAGE Ref: MPW'11:391: Satan.
SATAN ON MISCHIEF BENT Ref: Bios 6/29/11.
SATAN TRIUMPHS (Russ) silent Ref: EncicDS IX:1342: from
   Tolstoy. Mystical.
El SATANICO (Mex) 1967 Ref: LATimes 2/26/68. FJA: midget
   master criminal.
SATANIS, THE DEVIL'S MASS Ref: V 3/11/70. Documentary on A.
   LaVey.
The SATANIST Ref: LATimes.
SATAN'S RIVAL Ref: MPW'11:391: Satan.
El SATELITE CHIFLADO (Arg) 1956 Ref: Hist del Cine Arg.
SATI SAVITRI (India) 1948 Ref: Lee. Tortures of hell.
SAVED FROM THE VAMPIRE 1914 Ref: RVB.
The SCANDALOUS ADVENTURES OF BURAIKAN (J) Ref: World
   Cinema 12/4/70: "He is rocketed to the moon...on..fireworks."
   J.C. Mahoney.
SCARABUS (Belg) Ref: V 7/28/71: sf?
SCARE THEIR PANTS OFF 1968 Ref: L. Richardson: horror.
SCARED STIFF 1945 Ref: V. HR. NO.
The SCARLET GHOST serial Ref: FM 41:63: The MAN WITH THE
   DEATHMASK-Germany.
SCIENTIST'S NIGHTMARE (F) Ref: Bios 3/10/10: ?
SCRATCH HARRY Ref: Boxo 8/4/69: devil (The EROTIC THREE)
SCREAM IN THE NIGHT 1936 Ref: MPH 12/28/35:101: ? MFB 12/
   50.
The SCREEN OF CAGLIOSTRO (Sp) 1910 Ref: DDC I: 404.
SE DA COMER E EL HOTEL ELECTRICO (Sp) 1905 Ref: DDC
   I:403. Sfa The ELECTRIC HOTEL?
The SEA DEVIL Ref: FD 4/2/36: "sea monster."
The SEA GHOST Ref: MPN 7/3/15: ghost scene.
The SEALED ROOM c1905 Ref: FM 36:53: "sinister."
SEANCE ON A WET AFTERNOON (B) 1965 Ref: PM: medium.
SEBASTIAN 1968 Ref: J. R. Duvoli: "Mysterious satellite."
SECRET AGENT SUPERDRAGON (I) 1966 Ref: Ital P. "Powerful
   drug."
The SECRET FORMULA (F) 1913 Ref: MPW 17:232: cement
   formula.
The SECRET FORMULA Ref: MPW '15:1358: explosive
The SECRET KINGDOM 1916 serial Ref: MPN 14:3864. Ch. 7. The
   Ghost Ship. 11. The White Witch.
The SECRET MAN Ref: MFB'59: new missile.

Secret   597

The SECRET OF CASTLE MONROE (I) 1914 Ref: DDC III:354.
The SECRET OF DEATH VALLEY Ref: V&FI 9/15/06: visions of
   dead friend.
SECRET OF THE BLACK TRUNK (W.G.) 1962 Laboratory, under-
   ground passages. (Das SCHLOSS DES SCHRECKENS)
SECRET OF THE LOCH (B) 1957? Ref: COF 3:36. RVB. made?
The SECRET OF TWO OCEANS (Russ) 1957 Ref: MFB'58:24: ?
   super-sub?
The SECRET ROOM Ref: Bios 9/15/10:?
The SECRET SEVEN Ref: MPH 8/17/40: NO.
SECRET VENTURE (B) 1955 Ref: TVK: "new jet fuel." D: R. G.
   Springsteen.
SECRETS OF CHINATOWN 1935 Ref: FD 2/20/35: secret Oriental
   society.
La SENAL DEL VAMPIRO (Arg) Ref: Imparcial Film 12/10/42:
   announced for '43.
SERPENT WOMAN Ref: Bios 11/27/13: NO.
Le SEUIL DU VIDE (F) 1971 Ref: V 10/6/71: horror?
SEVEN DAYS TO NOON (B) 1950 Ref: TVG: "super-bomb."
SEVEN DOORS TO DEATH 1944 mystery.
7 SURPRISES Ref: TVG: ad: "horror."
7 WONDERS OF HONJO (J) Ref: Lee: ghost film?
The SEVENTH CONTINENT (Yus-G) 1967 Ref: PM: Children dis-
   cover new island.
SEX AND ASTROLOGY New World "the occult."
The SEX MACHINE mechanical man?
SEXY MAGICO c1966
The SHADOW LAUGHS 1933 Ref: PM: mystery. FD 3/27/33.
   TVFFSB.
The SHADOW RETURNS 1946 Ref: FanMo 6:47.
The SHADOW STRIKES 1937 Ref: FD 7/9/37. MPH. V. NYT 9/13/37.
   Boxo 6/26/37: "chilliest." From "The Ghost of the Manor." MFB
   '37.
The SHADOW WITHIN (J) 1970 Ref: UFQ 50: "Psychological thriller."
The SHADOWGRAPH MACHINE Ref: MPN 6/26/15: miniature pro-
   jector.
SHADOWS (F) Ref: V 7/28/71: sf?
SHADOWS OF OUR FORGOTTEN ANCESTORS (Russ) 1965 Ref:
   MFB'68:174. COF 10:6.
The SHAGGY DOG 1959 fantasy.
SHAKUNTALA Ref: Indian Films'61:12. curse.
The SHANGHAI CHEST 1948 Eerie graveyard scene.
SHE FOUND THE SUPERNATURAL Ref: LATimes 8/15/69.
SHE-GODS OF SHARK REEF 1958 Ref: FFacts.
SHE WAS SOME VAMPIRE Ref: Motography 7/22/16: vamp.
SHERLOCK HOLMES' FATAL HOUR 1931 Ref: MPH 7/18/31: NO.
SHINBONE ALLEY Ref: Photon 21:43: vampire moths.
SHOCK CORRIDOR Ref: FD 7/3/63: NO.
The SHOES OF THE FISHERMAN Ref: LATimes: "near future."
SHORTY LAYS A JUNGLE GHOST Ref: MPN 15:2864:? 1917.
A SHRIEK IN THE NIGHT 1915 Ref: MPW 9/18/15: NO.
The SIBERIAN LADY MACBETH (Yug) Ref: FEFN 8/62. From
   Shakespeare.

The SIGN OF FOUR 1932 Ref: NYT: NO.
SIGN OF THE ZOMBIES c1940 made? serial.
The SILENT ACCUSER 1924 Ref: Wid's 11/22/24: man haunted by
  dog's "ghost."
SILENT NIGHT, LONELY NIGHT Ref: FM 63:24. footage from
  "Frankenstein" film
SILENT PLANET Florida?
SIMON OF THE DESERT (Mex) Ref: MFB'69:96. 1965 The devil as
  temptress. A great comedy. Incredibly funny.
SIMPLY TERRIFIC (B) Ref: MFB'38: hangover cure.
The SIN OF NORA MORAN 1933 Ref: Harrison's 12/23/33: spirit.
SING AS WE GO 1934 Ref: London Times 9/17/34: side-shows.
  MMF.
SING, BABY, SING Ref: FIR: Jekyll and Hyde parody sequence.
SINGAPUR Ref: SpCinema'67: super-bomb formula.
The SINISTER GUEST (G) 1922 Ref: DDC II:161.
The SINISTER MAN (B) Ref: MFB'62:26: NO.
The SINNER AND THE WITCH (Sp) Ref: SpCinema'65: NO.
SIR, YOU ARE A WIDOWER (Cz) Ref: V 7/28/71: sf?
The SIREN'S NECKLACE Ref: Bios 11/18/09: siren, Neptune.
The SIREN'S SONG Ref: FIR'68:286. curse.
A SISTER TO SALOME 1920 Ref: MPN 22:1005: "dream: ancient
  Roman" reincarnated.
SIVA THE INVISIBLE (F) 1904 Ref: Imagen: invisibility.
The SIX MOTHERS-IN-LAW OF BLUEBEARD (Arg) 1945.
The SIX WIVES OF BLUEBEARD (I) 1950 Ref: DDC III:245.
The SKELETON Ref: Bios 4/3/13: ? 1912 Powers.
The SKELETON Ref: FIR'66:224: NO. Univ.
The SKULL OF THE PHAROAH'S DAUGHTER (G) 1921 Ref: DDC
  III:124.
SKY ALTITUDE 1936 serial Ref: FanMo 2:64. FIR'63:126. Hoax.
SKY ALTITUDE MEETS ZOLTAR 1938 serial Ref: FanMo 2:64.
  ModM. 3:23. Hoax.
SKY ALTITUDE VS. MANIAC MASTER 1940 serial Ref: FanMo
  2:64. Hoax.
SKY RAIDERS serial 1941 Ref: Showmen's: "new pursuit plane."
SKYPORT (Canadian) 1966? Ref: Lee: sf?
SLEEP MY LOVE 1948 Ref: TVG.
The SLEEPING BEAUTY (I) 1941 Ref: DDC III:460.
SLEEPING BEAUTY 1959 BV Unreleased live-action version of
  the Disney cartoon with Ed Kemmer.
SMALL TOWN STUFF Ref: MPN 14:2868: fake ghost.
The SMALL WITCH (UAR) 1963.
A SMART CAPTURE Ref: MPW'07:124: fantasy.
SMITH VISITS THE MOON Ref: Bios 1/22/14: NO.
SMUGGLERS IN THE GHOST LAND (J) 1961 Ref: J Films'62: ?
SNAKE GIRL MORTALIZED (HK) Ref: FEFN 5/10/57: shooting.
The SNAKE PRINCESS (J) 1938 Ref: DDC III:130,167.
SNAKE QUEEN AND SHAKE IN THE TEMPLE (Mandarin) Ref:
  FEFN 4/13/56: ?
SNAKY WOMAN (Mandarin) Ref: Singapore Straits-Times 10/16/70.
The SNOB'S ENCHANTED UMBRELLA Ref: Bios 5/28/14:
  "Veritable Frankenstein" of an umbrella.

The SNOW MAIDEN (Russ) Ref: M/TVM 6/69: fairy tale.
SNUFFY SMITH, YARDBIRD 1941 Ref: Lee: "spirit liquid."
SOCIETY WITCH Ref: Bios 1/2/13: NO.
SODUM UND GOMORRAH (Austrian) 1921 Ref: Osterr:"Monster-
    film."
A SOLITARY CHILD (B) 1962 (1957?) Ref: Speed: GASLIGHT-type.
SOLUNA (Arg) Ref: V 10/16/68: primitive sorcery.
SON OF HERCULES AND FIVE GIANTS Ref: TVFFSB.
SON OF HERCULES IN THE LAND OF DARKNESS Ref: TVK: sub-
    terranean city.
SON OF SKY ALTITUDE Ref: FanMo 2:64. Hoax-D. Glut.
SON OF THE EXECUTIONER Ref: MPW 8:547. 1911 Witch, magic
    sword.
SON OF THE GUARDSMEN Ref: The Serial: pendulum torture.
SONATAS Ref: MMF 9:18: demon possession. short?
SONNY'S FLIGHT TO THE MOON Ref: Sm 8:6. amateur?
The SORCERER OF ATHENS (Greek) 1931 Ref: DDC II:458.
The SORCERER OF THE SKY (F) 1948 Ref: DDC III:119.
SORCERER'S APPRENTICE (F) 1933 Ref: DDC II:482. short?
The SORCERER'S VILLAGE Ref: PM. Semi-documentary.
The SORCERESS (BLONDE WITCH) Ref: MFB'58:158: "witch"?
SORCERY (G) 1954 Ref: DDC III:240.
SO'S YOUR OLD MAN 1926 Ref: AFI: unbreakable glass.
SOUL OF THE BEAST 1923 Ref: V 5/24/23: fake ape-woman.
SOWBHAGYAVATHI (India) Ref: FEFN 11/15/57: the underworld.
SPACE AGE BEAVER Ref: LATimes 2/8/68.
SPACE MISSION: ZERO HOUR (I) Ref: M/TVM 9/69.
SPACE PROBE TAURUS Ref: M/TVM 3/68:29: documentary.
SPACE STATION K-9 (Russ) 1961 Ref: Imagen. short?
SPACE WOMEN c1961 Ref: SM 2:11. released?
The SPANISH CAPE MYSTERY 1935 Ref: V. FD 10/9/35. PM. NO.
SPECIAL CIPHER (Sp-I) Ref: SpCinema'68: anti-gravity formula.
SPECTER OF THE ROSE 1946 Ref: Lee: dual personality.
The SPECTRE (F) 1899 Melies Ref: DDC III:350.
The SPECTRE BRIDEGROOM 1913 Ref: Bios 5/8/13: NO.
SPEED 1936 Ref: STI 8: futuristic cars.
SPEED QUEEN Ref: Filmindia 3/47:58: "Atomic speed thrills."
SPEED SPOOK 1924 Ref: Photoplay 5/25: NO.
SPELL OF THE CIRCUS 1930 serial CH. 1. A Menacing Monster.
    2. The Phantom Shadow.
SPELLBOUND BY THE WEIRD ONE Ref: V 5/8/68. (W.G.)
SPIES KILL SILENTLY (Sp-I) 1967 Ref: SpCinema'67: cancer cure
    sought.
The SPIRIT HAND 1911 Ref: MPW 8:546: NO.
SPIRITISME ABRACADABRANT (F) 1900 Melies.
SPIRITISME FIN DE SIECLE (F) 1900 Melies Ref: Mitry II.
SPIRITS HAVE ORDAINED (F) Ref: Bios 7/20/11: seance. NO.
SPIRITS IN THE KITCHEN 1902 Ref: Niver: NO.
The SPIRITUALIST PHOTOGRAPHER (F) Melies 1903 (sfa Le
    PORTRAIT SPIRITE) 1903?-Mitry II)
SPIRITUALISTIC MEETING (F) Melies 1905.
The SPOOK COTTAGE (J) Ref: Toho Films '61: NO.
SPOOK TOWN 1944 Ref: MPH'44:1890: NO.

SPORTING YOUTH 1930 serial Ref:LC. Ch. 5. Live Ghost.
  11. Halloween.
SPRING (Russ) 1927 Ref: FJA: liquid nuclear energy?
SPY IN THE SKY 1958 Ref: FFacts. Ad: "The enemy that watches
  behind the veil of space." PM.
The SPY WHO CAME FROM THE SEA Ref: Ital P'66:missile
The STALKING MOON 1968 Ref: Life. PM. NO.
STANLEY AMONG THE VOODOO WORSHIPPERS Ref: MPN
  12/11/15: NO.
The STAR GLOBETROTTER (B) 1908 Ref: Brit Cinema. Booth.
STAR OF ASIA (India) Ref: Moving Picture Monthly 8/37: crown of
  invisibility.
STARK FEAR Ref: Boxo 10/7/63: NO.
STAY TUNED FOR TERROR (U.S.-Arg) Ref:Heraldo'68:608 D: E.
  Vieyra.
The STONE AGE Ref: LC. 1922.
The STONE KINGDOM (Fili) Ref: FEFN 3/29/57: cave men?
The STONE RIDER (G) 1923 Ref: SilentFF: couple turned to stone.
STORIES FROM BEHIND LOCKED DOORS Ref: Film User 10/68:58:
  "horror." with M. Dunnock, M. Hamilton.
STORIES OF CAPEK (Cz) 1947 Ref: EncicDS IX:61.
STORY OF THE GOBLIN CAT (J) Ref: FM 25:10: aka?
The STORY OF VERNON AND IRENE CASTLE ghost bit Ref: J.
  Shapiro.
STOUT AND THYNNE, SPIRITUALISTS Ref: Bios 12/12/12: NO.
STOUT'S BAD QUARTER OF AN HOUR Ref: Bios 11/13/13: ghost?
The STRANGE COUNTESS (G) 1961 Ref: FM 28:3: horror?
The STRANGE GIRL (G) 1913 Ref: Orpheus 2:31: fantasy.
STRANGE ILLUSION 1945 Ref: PM. TVG. Premonitions.
The STRANGLER Ref: HR 2/9/43 (B) NO.
The STRANGLER 1964 Ref: MadM 8:3. COF 9:30. NO.
STRANGLER OF THE TOWER (G) Ref: FDY'66. TVG. cult.
STREET OF SHADOWS Ref: FJA poster (Der VAMPYR VON SOHO-
  G.)
STUDIUM (Hung) Ref: V 7/28/71: sf?
Los SUBDESARROLLADOS Ref: SpCinema'69: "robot drawings."
The SUBURBAN-BUNKUM-MICROBE-GUYOSCOPE (B) 1903 Ref:
  DDC III:33.
SUDDEN TERROR Ref: Film Bltn 2/8/71: shock-suspense. NO.
SUFFERING IN CRIME Ref: SpCinema'68: mad boy amputates vic-
  tim's hands.
The SUICIDE CLUB 1909 Ref: DDC II:464. Niver: NO.
The SUICIDE CLUB (B) 1932 Ref: DDC II:189: ?
The SUICIDE CLUB (Mex) c1970 Ref: LATimes 6/14/71. Suicide
  motorcycle club.
SUN AND SHADOW (Bulgarian) 1961 Ref: Films on 8&16. Dream:
  atomic-destruction sequence.
SUPERSEVEN CALLING CAIRO (I-F) 1965 Ref: Ital P: "Newly
  discovered radioactive substance."
SUPREME POWER Ref: Bios 1/16/13: angel of death.
The SUPREME TEMPTATION Ref: MPN 13:1920: catalepsy.
SWAMP CREATURE Florida.
SWEDISH PORTRAITS Ref: Film in Sweden 1/65: monster?

SWEET CHARITY Ref: FM 63:24: footage from "Frankenstein" film.
SWEET HUNTERS 1969 Ref: Photon 21:29: vampirism?
SWEET VENGEANCE Ref: S Union: "spine-tingling."
SWORD OF DOOM (J) Ref: PM: psychopathic samurai killer.
The SYSTEM OF DR. SOUFLAMORT (F) Ref: DDC III:352. Melies.

TABOOS OF THE WORLD (I) Ref: FM 43:69.
TALE OF TORTURE Ref: FDY: (I) Int'l Ent. Corp.
TALES OF BLOOD AND HORROR Ref: FJA. D, P: Maurice Dawson. Narr: Peter Cushing. (I) Titan Ref: Photon 21:29. Vampire. made?
TALKATIVE LADY Ref: Bios 12/30/09: Doctor makes dumb wife talk--constantly.
The TAME CAT Ref: AFI: magic. 1921.
TANNHAUSER Ref: MPW 17:358: spell.
TANKS (B) 1916 Ref: SF Film.
TAROT Ref: TVG: "occult practitioners." "Name of the Game" episode.
TARZAN AND THE GOLDEN LION 1927 Ref: FM 2:31. Lee: secret city. with Karloff.
TARZAN ESCAPES Ref: FM 13:58: vampire bats. Originally to feature dinosaurs.
TASKS OF HERCULES Ref: Bios 5/26/10: ?
TAUR THE MIGHTY (I) 1962 Ref: TVG.
The TEAR THAT BECAME A PEARL Ref: Thought 2/10/68: ghost, "space capsule dance number."
TECHNIQUE OF A SPY (Sp) Ref: SpCinema'68: ray?
TEENAGE STRANGLER Ref: RVB: NO. 1964
TEESRI MANZIL (India) Ref: Shankar's 11/20/66: "Frightening scenes... sudden screams, creaking doors."
The TEMPTATION OF BARBIZON Ref: S&S'46:51: devil, angel. Rep Gen'47:518.
TEN BROTHERS CONQUERING A DEMON (Chinese) Ref: FJA pamphlet: announced. Giant fish.
TENDER ENEMY Ref: FD 4/9/38: "trio of ghosts."
The TERRIBLE TURKISH EXECUTIONER (F) 1904 Ref: Nivers: severed head.
The TERROR FROM THE TOMB Ref: FM 7:12. amateur?
TERROR IN THE JUNGLE Ref: V 11/20/68: toy tiger turns into a real one.
TERROR MOUNTAIN 1928.
TERROR OF PONTIANAK (Malayan) Shaw Ref: FEFN 11/22/57: announced.
TERROR OF ROME AGAINST THE SON OF HERCULES (I) 1963 Ref: TVG: "giant gorilla."
TERROR OF THE BLOODHUNTERS 1963 NO.
TERROR SHIP (B) 1954 new atomic substance.
TERROR STRIKES ROME (I) Ref: TVFFSB: man injected with plague.
TERRY AND THE PIRATES 1940 serial Ref: Showmen's 4/20/40. trained gorilla.

The TESTAMENT OF FRANKENSTEIN Ref: Movie Monsters: 1964.
  Ref: FM 63:24. with G. Landry, G. Vallis. D: J. L. Madrid.
TEX GRANGER 1948 serial Ch. 8. Mystery of the Silver Ghost.
THAT COLD DAY IN THE PARK Ref: Film Bltn 6/69: horror.
THAT GHOST OF MY HUSBAND (I) 1950 Ref: DDC I:338.
THERE DWELT ON EARTH AN ALIEN Florida.
The THERMO-NUCLEAR MAN Ref: MMF 13:44: experimental.
THEY CAME TO A CITY (B) Ref: NYorker 2/24/45.
THEY DRIVE BY NIGHT (B) 1939 Ref: MFB'39: "eerie...creepy."
THEY NEVER DIE (G) Ref: FM 26:10: shooting.
THIEF OF BAGDAD (India) Ref: FEFN 10/25/57: shooting.
THIEF ON THE LOOSE (J) 1970 animated "ghost" bit.
The THIRD EYE 1920 serial Ch. 10. The House of Terrors.
The THIRD PART OF THE NIGHT Ref: V 9/22/71: apparitions. NO.
The THIRD VOICE horror? NO. 1960.
13 FRIGHTENED GIRLS 1963 NO.
36 KILLERS (HK) Ref: V 10/6/71: horror?
THOMAS AND THE BEWITCHED (I) Ref: V 10/14/70: seance.
THOMAS, THE RESTLESS ONE (F-Belg) Ref: V 10/16/68: "strange
  beings."
THOSE MAGNIFICENT MEN IN THEIR FLYING MACHINES caveman
  bit.
A THOUSAND AND ONE WOMEN (I) Ref: Ital P:"the death strip-
  tease, ghosts."
THREE (Yug) Ref: M/TVM 7/66: "encounter with death."
THREE-EYES MONSTER (J) Ref: FM 28:11. aka?
THREE FANTASTIC STORIES (Arg) 1963 Ref: Tempo de Cine 18-
  19/'61. "parapsychological phenomena."
THREE FORTUNATE UNFORTUNATES (Mex?) Ref: FJA pressbook:
  ghosts?
The THREE MAGICIANS (J) Ref: MMF 9:32.
The THREE PASSIONS Ref: FM-A'62:77.
THREE STEPS IN THE DARK (B) Ref: MFB'53:136. horror?
The THREE STOOGES GO AROUND THE WORLD IN A DAZE
  Ref: Imagen. V: NO: "sumo giant."
The THREE WISE MEN Ref: MPN 13:2722: dream: devil.
The THREE WORLD OF GULLIVER (B-Sp-U.S.) Ref: PM. giants.
The THRILL KILLERS Ref: COF 6:59.8:6: "gruesome."
THRONE OF BLOOD (J) 1957 from "Macbeth." (CASTLE OF THE
  SPIDER'S WEB)
THROUGH FIRE AND WATER (Russ) Ref: Soviet Film 7/68: witches.
THUNDERBALL hydrofoil/jet pack.
THURSDAY'S CHILD (B) Frankenstein-monster bit? Ref: D. Glut:
  NO.
TICKET OF LEAVE MAN (B) Ref: MFB 11/30/37: bizarre ending.
TICKLISH TIMOTHY Ref: Bios 9/9/09: tickling brings man back to
  life.
TIDES OF RETRIBUTION Ref: MPN 12/25/15: invention.
The TIGER BAND 1920 serial Ref: CNW. Ch. 15. The Masked Man's
  Claws.
TIKI TIKI Ref: V 10/6/71: animated & live King Kong?
TIM TYLER'S LUCK 1937 Ref: D. Glut: new-type tank?
The TIN GHOST 1926 Ref: LC.

TIRA A SEGNO PER UCCIDERE (I-Austrian) Ref: M/TVM 10/66: "sf" with S. Granger, S. Gabel.
TO OBLIGE A VAMPIRE 1917 Ref: MPN 15:3165: vamp.
TO TRAP A SPY Ref: Boxo 2/21/66: NO.
TOM THUMB IN LOVE Ref: Bios 9/15/10: giantess.
TONIGHT'S THE NIGHT (B) 1955 Ref: J. Shapiro: ghost bit.
TONS OF MONEY (B) 1924 Ref: SilentFF: new explosive.
TONTOLINI AND THE DONKEY (I) Ref: Bios 11/9/11: balloons carry man into air.
TOO MUCH MOTHER-IN-LAW Ref: MPW'07:238: devil, spirits, Hades.
TOP SECRET (B) Ref: HR 2/22/51: formula.
TOP SECRET (B) 1953 sf? Ref: Film Review: NO.
TOPO GIGIO AND THE MISSILE WAR Ref: V 8/16/68.
TOPPER 1937 Ref: FD 7/12/37: NO.
TOPPER TAKES A TRIP Ref: FD 1/5/39: NO.
TORCH RIDERS Ref: SpCinema'67: "monkey which they call Kink-Kong."
La TORRE DE LOS SUPLICIOS (Mex) Ref: Aventura: ?
Le TOUT PETIT FAUST (F) 1910 Ref: DDC I:444.
TOWER OF LONDON (F) Melies 1905.
TOWER OF NESLE (F) Ref: MPW'09:416.
TRACKED BY A VAMPIRE 1914 Ref: MPW 20:1320: vamp.
The TRADE OF THE VAMPIRE (F) 1950 Ref: Film 9/67. Movie Monsters.
Un TRAIN DANS LA NUIT (F) 1934 Ref: Rep Gen'47:530: "ghost train " endowed with "mise en scene hallucinante."
TRAIN DES SUICIDES (F) Ref: Le Surrealisme: "terreur."
The TRAIN OF SPECTRES (I) 1913 Ref: DDC III:112. (GHOST TRAIN)
The TRAMP Ref: COF 9:46: horror?
The TRANSPLANT (I-Sp) 1969 Ref: Heraldo'70:709. SpCinema'71.
The TRAP 1946 Ref: MFB'47: "ghostly happenings in isolated house." V. HR: NO.
TRAP FOR SEVEN SPIES (Sp-I) Ref: SpCinema'68: "Most Dang. Game" bit.
TRAPPED BY THE CAMERA 1914 Ref: MPW 22:644: gadgets. NO.
The TRAVELING EXECUTIONER Ref: Motion Picture Exhibitor 12/9/70: plan to revive dead.
The TRIAL (F-G-I) Ref: V: NO. COF 4:5. 1963.
TRILOGY Ref: V. HR: NO: nanny beset by imaginary child.
The TRIP 1967 horror bits.
A TRIP TO THE MOON (Mex) 1957 Ref: Indice.
A TRIP WITH DRACULA Ref: Photon 21:30: underground film.
TROIKA Ref: V 12/10/69: bug-like creature.
The TSAR'S BRIDE Ref: MFB'69:220: potion. NO.
TU IMAGINES ROBINSON Ref: M/TVM 4/69: sf?
TUMBLEDOWN RANCH IN ARIZONA Ref: Boxo 5/8/43? Dream.
The TUNNEL UNDER THE WORLD Ref: M/TVM 8/69.
12 PAST 12 (G) 1964 Ref: FIR'67:84: "A weird, sadistic film."
26TH VOYAGE TO MARS (W.G.) Ref: FJA folder. amateur?
TWILIGHT OF TERROR (F) 1922 Ref: DDC II:389.
TWO GIRLS FROM THE RED STAR (Aust-G-F) Ref: Film Kunst

49:F2: "miracle weapon."
TWO LITTLE URCHINS (F) 1921 Ref: DDC. 4. Back from the
    grave.
The TWO ROADS 1916 Ref: MPN 14:3866: alloy like gold.

ULTUS AND THE SECRET OF THE NIGHT (B) 1917 Ref: Hist Brit
    Film: "mystery house."
ULTUS: THE MAN FROM THE DEAD (B) Ref: Hist. Brit Film.
UNA SULL'ALTRA Ref: MFB'71:69: compared to DIABOLIQUE.
The UNATTAINABLE Ref: MPN 14:1397. 1916 Plague cure for
    sheep: minor element.
UNCLE ABDU'S GHOST (UAR) 1952 Ref: Sadoul.
UNDERGROUND (B) 1928 Ref: V 2/27/29. SilentFF: NO.
UNDRESSING EXTRAORDINARY Ref: Hist Brit Film: skeleton.
The UNDYING FLAME 1917 Ref: MPN 15:3619: NO. Movie Monsters:
    mummy.
Der UNHEIMLICHE (G) 1968 Ref: Film 4/68.
UNIVERSAL IKE, JR;, AND THE VAMPIRE Ref: MPW 20:viii. 1914.
UNKNOWN DANGERS 1926 Ref: AFI: Gang's headquarters in Ghost
    House.
The UNKNOWN MONSTER 1914 Ref: MPW 19:1070: NO.
UNMAN, WITTERING AND ZIGO Ref: Film Bltn 6/71: "psychological
    horror."
UP IN SMOKE 1957 Ref: FDY. Comedy: deal with devil.
UPPER-SEVEN, THE DEVIL'S AGENT (I) 1965 Ref: Ital P: missile
    base?
URGE TO KILL (B) 1964 Ref: FIR'67:83: "Almost a re-working of
    "The Lodger"."
URSUS IN THE LAND OF FIRE Ref: MFB'64:109: "invention."

VALI Ref: MFB'71:126: sorceress.
The VALLEY OF FEAR (G-F-I) 1962 Ref: Bianco 6/63. FM 27:11.
    NO.
The VALLEY OF GHOSTS (B) 1929 Ref: Brit Cinema. FIR'67:76.
VALLEY OF MYSTERY 1967 Ref: PM: witchcraft overtones.
VAMPIRA (Fili) Ref: FEFN 2/61: announced.
La VAMPIRA INDIANA (I) 1913 Ref: Mitry V:107.
The VAMPIRE Messter Ref: Bios 8/3/11: vamp.
The VAMPIRE Selig Ref: Bios 1/5/11: vamp.
The VAMPIRE Kalem 1913 "Vampire" disguised as wood nymph.
VAMPIRE 1920 vamp?
Le VAMPIRE (F) 1925? Ref: RVB: clips from NOSFERATU?
The VAMPIRE 1928 ? Ref: RVB.
The VAMPIRE (F) 1951 Ref: Lee: jets.
VAMPIRE A LA MODE 1928.
VAMPIRE BAT AND ARMADILLO Ref: Bios: documentary. 1914.
VAMPIRE DANCE (Danish) 1912 Ref: DDC II:8.
VAMPIRE DANCER 1912 vamp?
VAMPIRE LOVE (HK-Thai) Ref: FEFN 3/22/57: shooting.
The VAMPIRE OF DUSSELDORF (F-Sp-I) 1964 Ref: SpCinema '66:
    night murderer. Heraldo 9/1/65: M remake.

VAMPIRE OUT OF WORK 1916 vamp?
The VAMPIRE WITCH (G) c1963 Ref: MMF 9:18: "un curieux film."
The VAMPIRE'S CLUTCH 1914 vamp?
VAMPIRES LOVE 1969 Ref: RVB.
A VAMPIRE'S NOSTALGIA (Yug) 1968 Ref: Eastern Europe.
VAMPIRES OF THE COAST Ref: F Index 1/30/09: outlaws.
VAMPIRES OF THE NIGHT Ref: Bios 9/25/13: criminals.
The VAMPIRES OF WARSAW (Polish) 1925 Ref: DDC I:234.
VAMPIRE'S TOMB Ref: FM 23:43. WFC 3:53: Lugosi died before
    making.
The VAMPIRE'S TOWER Ref: Bios 2/15/14: NO.
The VAMPIRE'S TRAIL Kalem 1914.
VAMPIRESAS (Sp) 1962 Ref: Annuario Español: NO.
VAMPYR(E)N (Swedish) 1912 Ref: DDC III:123, 481. Lee.
The VANISHING AMERICAN cave man bit.
The VANISHING DAGGER 1920 serial Ch. 15. The Great Pendulum.
    Ref: LC.
VANISHING TRAILS 1920 serial Ref: CNW: "eerie." Ch. 10. The
    Mansion of Mystery.
The VANISHING WOMEN (F) 1959 Ref: Bianco. (I VAMPIRI DEL
    SESSO-I) MFB: NO.
The VEIL (Pakistani) Ref: Lee: fake ghost.
The VEILED MYSTERY Ref: FIR'67:339. 1920 serial Ch. 10. A
    Demon's Device.
VELVET FINGERS 1920 serial Ref: CNW. Ch. 13. The Hidden Room.
The VENGEANCE OF CRIMILDA Ref: V 10/6/71: horror?
VENGEANCE OF FU MANCHU (Fili?) 1967 Ref: M/TVM 9/67.
VENGEANCE OF MAGNUS VANN (B) c1942 with T. Slaughter. aka?
VERA, THE MEDIUM Ref: MPW 29:2075: NO.
The VESTRIS Ref: FM 50:60. with Karloff?
The VILLAGE CUT-UP Ref: V&FI 7/7/06: fake ghost.
The VILLAGE VAMPIRE 1916 Ref: MPN: "vampire" heads gang of
    crooks.
VIRGIN VAMPIRE (W.G.) Roxy 1970 Ref: Photon 21:31.
The VISCOUNT (F-SP-I) Ref: FFacts: NO. "matter destroyer"?
VISIT TO A NEW PLANET Ref: LATimes 6/6/69.
The VISITOR Florida sf?
La VITA DI UNA RATA MORTA (Cz) c1907 Ref: EncicDS III:364: sf?
VOICE FROM THE BEYOND (Polish) Ref: S&S'63.
VOODOO 1933 Ref: NYTimes: "witchcraft."
VOODOO DOCTOR c1954 Ref: WFC 3:53. with Lugosi. made?
VOODOO TIGER 1952. Ref: MFB'53. V. HR. NO.
VOODOO VENGEANCE 1913 Ref: MPW 16:1237: NO.
VOODOO VILLAGE 1963 documentary.
Le VOYAGE DU FILS DE DIABLE A PARIS (F) 1907 Ref: Mitry II.
VOYAGE INTO SPACE AI-TV Ref: Photon 21:5.
VULTURES ARE MOURNING (Mex) Ref: ModM 3:5: macabre.

WR, MISTERISTE ORGANIZMA (Yus) Ref: V 6/9/71: severed head
    speaks.
WAIT UNTIL DARK 1967 shock-suspense.
WAKE UP! OR A DREAM OF TOMORROW 1914 Ref: ?

The WALKING CORPSE (HK-Mandarin) Ref: FEFN 3/22/57: ?
WALPURGISNACHT (G) 1926 Ref: Deutsche.
WALPURGISZAUBER (Aus) 1923 Ref: Osterr.
WANTED FOR MURDER (B) 1945 Ref: PM: "demented strangler."
WAR (Yug) 1960 Ref: Jadran Film: sf?
The WAR EAGLE c1939 Ref: ModM 4:56: unfinished.
WAR WITH THE NEWTS (Cz-I) 1958 Ref: Orpheus 3:35: not made.
WARFARE OF THE FLESH 1917 Ref: MPN 15:2858: Dream: cave
    man bit.
WAS SHE A VAMPIRE? Univ 1915 Ref: RVB.
The WAY TO PARADISE Ref: V 8/18/71: man haunted by visions.
WE MARTIANS (Russ) Ref: M/TVM 2/67.
The WEIRD TRANSFORMATION OF ALEX ROSCHER (G) 1945
    Ref: DDC.
WEIRD, WICKED WORLD ABC 1966.
WHAT'S SO BAD ABOUT FEELING GOOD? 1968 Ref: PM: toucan
    with rare virus.
WHEN DUMBLEIGH SAW THE JOKE Ref: Motog 4/10/15: man
    returns to life.
WHEN GHOST MEETS GHOST Ref: Bios 6/19/13: two ghosts.
WHEN LILIAN WAS LITTLE RED RIDING HOOD Ref: Bios 8/28/13:
    NO.
WHEN THE DEAD RETURN Ref: Bios'11: NO.
WHEN THE DEVIL DRIVES (B) 1907 Ref: SilentFF. devil.
WHEN THE MAN IN THE MOON SEEKS A WIFE(B) 1908 Ref: SF
    Film: fantasy.
WHERE EAST IS EAST Ref: Photoplay 6/29: "A touch of Kipling and
    Poe."
WHERE IS LOUISA (Polish) 1968 sf?
WHERE THE DEVIL CANNOT GET (Cz) 1959 Ref: Modern Cz. Film:
    Comedy. Witch.
WHIRLPOOL 1949 Ref: FD 11/28/49: woman in power of hypnotist.
WHIRLPOOL (Danish) Ref: Boxo 9/14/70. V 9/1/70: necrophilia.
    Film Bltn 9/7/70.
WHIRLWIND (J) 1964 Ref: UFQ: sorceress, wizard.
The WHITE COCKATOO Ref: V 1/15/35: NO. FD 1/12/35: "eerie
    French hotel."
The WHITE FLOWER 1923 Ref: AFI: curse.
The WHITE GORILLA Ref: V 12/3/47(45?): NO.
The WHITE HORSEMAN 1921 serial Ref: LC. Ch. 3. The Mummy
    Man.
WHITE PANTS WILLIE Ref: Photoplay 10/27: "magnetic bumper."
WHITE SMOKE Ref: Bios 6/25/14: "powerful chemical."
The WHITE WITCH (B) 1913 Ref: RVB.
WHITE WOMAN 1933 Ref: Photoplay: "horror...blood-curdling."
    V 11/21/33:?
WHY RUSSIANS ARE REVOLTING Ref: Boxo 6/22/70: clips from
    the Barrymore DR. JEKYLL AND MR. HYDE.
WIDECOMBE FAIR (B) 1928 Ref: SilentFF: fake ghost.
The WIFE AND THE VAMPIRE (India) c1931 Ref: Indian Cin:145.
    Vamp?
WILBUR AND THE BABY FACTORY sf?
The WILD OLIVE Ref: MPN 6/26/15: hallucination.

WILD ORANGES Ref: V 3/5/24: NO. Giant halfwit. Melodrama.

WILD, WILD WORLD 1966 Sokoler.

WILL OF THE WISP(J) Ref: FEFN 7/27/56: "unearthly light around bodies."

WILLIE AND THE WILD MAN Ref: Bios 10/23/13: ?

WILLY ROI DES SORCIERS Ref: Mitry II:283. 1912.

WINK OF AN EYE 1958 Ref: Lee: horror? FD. V 6/11/58: NO.

The WINKING IDOL 1926 serial Ch. 1. The Eye of Evil. Ref: LC.

The WISHING CHARM Ref: MPW'09:357. Satan.

The WITCH (I) 1907 Ref: V&FI 131:10.

The WITCH (F) 1908 Ref: Lee: NO.

The WITCH Vita 1908 Ref: F Index 10/24/08: NO.

The WITCH Ref: MPW 18:424: NO. 1913.

The WITCH 1913 Ref: MPW 17:354: NO.

The WITCH 1914 Ref: LC.

The WITCH Ref: Bios 3/19/14. American Standard NO.

The WITCH 1916 Ref: MPN 13:1472: witch makes man fall in love with her.

WITCH (F-Swedish) 1957 Ref: Sweden I.

WITCH FROM BENEATH THE SEA Ref: TVFFSB. Miami Herald 1/13/68 (MARIZANIA)

WITCH GIRL Ref: MPW 22:643: NO. 1914.

WITCH OF LANADOR Florida.

WITCH OF SALEM TOWN 1915 Ref: Lee: NO.

WITCH OF THE AIRPORT (J) Ref: FEFN 12/59: NO.

WITCH OF THE EVERGLADES Ref: Bios 6/29/11: NO.

The WITCH OF THE RANGE Ref: Bios 7/27/11: NO.

The WITCH OF THE WELSH MOUNTAINS (B) Ref: RVB. 1915.

WITCH WOMAN 1917 Ref: LC.

WITCH WOMAN (Danish) 1920 Ref: SilentFF: NO. (The WITCH) Dreyer.

WITCHCRAFT (I) Ref: Bios 10/24/12.

WITCHCRAFT 1916 Ref: MPN 14:2710: NO.

WITCHCRAFT (I) 1952 Scalera Ref: FDY?

WITCHCRAFT (Arg-Sp-Mex) c1955 (MALEFICES)

WITCHES' NIGHT (Swedish) Ref: Sweden I.

The WITCH'S FIDDLE (B) 1924 Ref: SilentFF: bewitched fiddle.

The WITCH'S LOVE Ref: SpCinema'68: supposed phantom haunts girl: minor element.

The WITCH'S REVENGE (F) Melies 1903 Ref: FM 67:7.

The WITCH'S SPECTACLES Ref: Bios 2/26/14 & 8/5/09: NO.

The WIZARD (G) 1932 Ref: FIR'67:76.

The WIZARD OF OZ 1908 Ref: Lee.

The WIZARD OF OZ Ref: Bios 5/26/10:?

The WIZARD OF OZ 1915 series.

The WIZARD OF OZ Ref: NYTimes 4/14/25: no witch? SilentFF.

The WOLF-MAN 1918 Polifilms.

WOLF MAN Sunset 1924 Ref: AFI.

WOLF WOMAN c1962 Ref: FanMo 4:15. made? with L. LaPlanche.

A WOMAN IN GREY 1920 serial Ref: CNW: Ch. 1. The House of Mystery.

The WOMAN IN WHITE Ref: Bios 1/16/13: NO.

The WOMAN IN WHITE 1917 Ref: MPN 16:115: NO.

The WOMAN IN WHITE 1929 Ref: MPN 41: "mystery." NO.
The WOMAN IN WHITE 1948 Ref: TVG.
WOMAN IN WHITE 1949 Ref: Sweden I.
The WOMAN OF MYSTERY Ref: MPN 1/1/16: explosive. ?
WOMAN WITHOUT A HEAD (Mex) 1944 Ref: Aventura: detective Fu-
    Man-Chu. Others in series: El MUSEO DEL CRIMEN (1944);
    El ESPECTRO DE LA NOVIA, El AS NEGRO. Indice: La CASA
    EMBRUJADA (1944).
WOMEN...OH, WOMEN! (J) 1963 Ref: UFQ: devil-mask.
The WORLD OF ABBOTT AND COSTELLO 1965 Ref: COF 7:46:
    includes horror scenes.
The WORLD OF APU Characters watch Indian "demon" film.
The WORLD OF DRUGS (Mex) Ref: FM 33:10: weird scenes.
The WRECKING CREW Ref: MFB'69:63. F&F 4/69: helicopter with
    automatic control?

X-RAY GLASSES Ref: MPW'09:809: "magic spectacles."

The YELLOW CLAW (B) 1921 Ref: SilentFF. From Sax Rohmer
    story.
YOGI (G) 1916 Ref: Orpheus 3:47. EncicDS IX:1881: invisibility.
The YOGI Ref: MPW: fake medium. 1917?
YOU SAID A MOUTHFUL Ref: MPH 11/19/32. TVK: "nonsinkable
    bathing suit." NO.
YOU'LL NEVER SEE ME AGAIN (B) 1959 Ref: TVG: "horrifying
    dreams."
YOU'RE TELLING ME 1934 puncture-proof tire.
YPOTRON (Sp-I) Ref: SpCinema'68: invention. MFB'68:153.

ZAMBA 1949 Ref: V. HR: NO.
ZIMBO (India) Ref: FEFN 9/5/58: "Tarzan"-type.
ZIMBO COMES TO TOWN (India) Ref: FEFN 9/60: wild ape
    trained.
ZOTZ! (U.S.-B) 1962 Ref: PM: mystical power.
ZVENIGORA (Russ) 1927 fantasy scene?

REFERENCES

Books

The American Film Institute Catalog of Motion Pictures Produced in
   the United States: Feature Films 1921-1930. New York: R.R.
   Bowker Company, 1971.
Annuario del Cinema Italiano 1966-1967. Rome: Centro Studi di Cul-
   tura, Economia e Divulgazione del Cinema, 1967.
Ayala Blanco, Jorge. Aventura del Cine Mexicano. Mexico: Ediciones
   Era, 1968.
Barbour, Alan G. The Serials of Columbia. Kew Gardens, N.Y.:
   Screen Facts Press, 1967:
   _____. The Serials of Republic. Kew Gardens, N.Y. Screen Facts
   Press, 1965.
Baxter, John. Science Fiction in the Cinema. New York: A.S. Barnes;
   London: A. Zwemmer, 1970.
Bessy, Maurice and Chardans, Jean-Louis. Dictionnaire du Cinéma
   et de la Télévision. Paris: Jean-Jacques Pauvert, 1965-1967.
   Three volumes.
Blum, Daniel. Screen World. New York: Crown Publishers, 1952-1965.
British Film Institute (Distribution) Catalogue. London: 1962.
Bucher, Felix. Germany. London: A. Zwemmer, 1970.
Clarens, Carlos. An Illustrated History of the Horror Film. New
   York: Putnam, 1967.
Cowie, Peter. 70 Years of Cinema. South Brunswick, N.J.: A.S.
   Barnes, 1969.
Dimmitt, Richard Bertrand. A Title Guide to the Talkies. New York:
   Scarecrow Press, 1965. Two volumes.
Eisner, Lotte H. The Haunted Screen. Berkeley: University of
   California Press, 1969.
Enciclopedia dello Spettacolo. Rome: Unione Editoriale, 1958.
Everson, William K. The Bad Guys. New York: Citadel Press, 1964.
Fantastique et Réalisme dans le Cinéma Allemand 1912-1933. Brus-
   sels: Musée du Cinéma, 1969.
Fernett, Gene. Next Time Drive Off the Cliff! Cocoa, Fla.:
   Cinememories Pub. Co., 1968.
Film Daily Yearbook of Motion Pictures. New York: John W. Alicoate,
   1930-1969.
The Film Index: V.I.: The Film as Art. New York: Museum of Modern
   Art Film Library and H.W. Wilson Company, 1941.
Fowler, Roy. The Film in France. London: Pendulum Publications,
   1946.
Fritz, Walter. Die Osterreichischen Spielfilme der Stummfilmzeit
   1907-1930. Vienna: Osterreichischen Gesellschaft für Filmwissen-

schaft, 1967.
_____. Die Osterreichischen Spielfilme der Tonfilmzeit 1929-1938.
Vienna: Osterreichischen Gesellschaft für Filmwissenschaft, 1968.
Fuente, Maria Isabel de la. Indice Bibliografico del Cine Mexicano,
Vol. I (1930-1965). Mexico City: Talleves de Editorial America,
1967.
Gasca, Luis. Imagen y Ciencia Ficción. San Sebastian: XIV
Festival Internacional del Cine, 1966.
German Pictures 1963/64. Wiesbaden: Spitzenorganisation der
Filmwirtschaft, 1964.
Gifford, Denis. British Cinema. London: A. Zwemmer; New York:
A. S. Barnes, 1968.
_____. Movie Monsters. London: Studio Vista; New York: Dutton,
1969.
_____. Science Fiction Film. Studio Vista; New York: Dutton,
1971.
Halliwell, Leslie. The Filmgoer's Companion. New York: Hill &
Wang, 1967.
Holmes, Winifred. Orient: A Survey of Films. London: British
Film Institute, 1959.
Index de la Cinématographie Française. Paris: Cinématographie
Française, 1951-1966.
The Indian Cinematograph Year Book of 1938. Bombay: Motion
Picture Society of India, 1938.
Italian Production. Rome: Unitalia, 1950-51, 1959-1969.
Japanese Films. Tokyo: Unijapan Film, 1962-.
Jones, Jack R. Fantasy Films and Their Fiends. Oklahoma City,
Okla.: 1964.
Korea Cinema. Seoul: Motion Picture Producers Association, 1967.
Kraatz, Karl L. Deutscher Filmkatalog 1930-1945. Frankfurt-am-
Main: Transit-Film Gesellschaft [1969?]
Kyrou, Adonis. Le Surréalisme au cinéma. [Paris?] Le Terrain
Vague, 1963.
Lamprecht, Gerhard. Deutsche Stummfilme 1923-1926, 1927-1931.
Berlin: Deutsche Kinemathek, 1967. Two volumes.
Low, Rachel. The History of the British Film 1896-1906, 1914-1918.
London: Allen and Unwin, 1950.
Maltin, Leonard. TV Movies. New York: New American Library,
1969.
Menville, Douglas. The Science-Fiction Film. (Master's thesis).
University of Southern California, Los Angeles, 1959.
Mitry, Jean. Filmographie Universelle, Vol. II, part I; Vol. V.
Paris: Institut des Hautes Etudes Cinématographiques, 1964.
Motion Pictures: 1894-1912, 1912-1939, 1940-1949, 1950-1959.
Washington, D.C.: Library of Congress Register of Copyrights,
1953, 1951, 1953, 1960.
Nealon, Jack. The American Horror Film since 1930. (Master's
thesis.) University of Southern California, Los Angeles, 1953.
Niver, Kemp. Motion Pictures From the Library of Congress Paper
Print Collection, 1894-1912. Berkeley: University of California
Press, 1967.
Noble, Peter, ed. British Film Yearbook 1947-48, 1949-50. London:
British Yearbooks, 1949, 1950.

Picture History of the Cinema. New York: Macmillan, 1960.
Répertoire Général des Films. [Analyse Général des Films]. Paris: Centrale Catholique du Cinéma et de la Radio, 1944-.
Sadoul, Georges. Cinema in the Arab Countries. Bierut: Inter-Arab Centre of Cinema & Television, 1966.
Scheuer, Steven H. TV Key Movie Guide. New York: Bantam Books, 1958, 1968.
The Spanish Cinema. Madrid: Uniespaña, 1959-.
Television Feature Film Source Book. New York: Broadcast Information Bureau, winter/spring 1971.

Periodicals

Bianco e Nero. Rome: Centro Sperimentale di Cinematografia, 1960-1968.
The Bioscope. London: 1909-1914.
Bizarre: Cinéma Fantastique. #24-25. Paris: Libraire du Palimugre, 1962.
Boxoffice. New York: Associated Publications, 1934-.
Boy's Cinema. London: 1932-1935.
Cahiers du Cinéma. Paris: Editions de l'Etoile, 1956-.
Castle of Frankenstein. New York: Gothic Castle Pub. Co., 1962-.
Cine Argentino 1968. Buenos Aires: Instituto Nacional de Cinematografia, 1968.
El Cine Grafico. Mexico City: Antonio J. Olea, 1941.
Ciné Nouvelles. Cairo, 1953.
Dipali. Calcutta: 1934-1941.
The Edison Kinetogram. Orange, N.J.: Thomas A. Edison, Inc., 1912-1913.
Famous Monsters. New York: Warren Pub. Co., 1958-.
Fantastic Monsters. Topanga, Cal. Black Shield Publications, 1962-1964.
Far East Film News [Movie/TV Marketing]. Tokyo: Rengo Film News, 1955-.
Fernsehen und Film [Film]. Hanover: Friedrich Verlag, 1967-.
Film Bulletin. Philadelphia: Wax Publications, 1969-.
Film Daily. New York: Charles A. Alicoate, 1925-1968.
Film Facts. New York: American Film Institute, Ernest Parmentier, 1958-.
The Film Index [Views and Film Index]. New York: Films Pub. Co., 1906-1908.
Filmcritic. Bombay: R.R. Rishi, 1951.
Filmfare. The Times of India, 1953.
Filmindia. Bombay: Filmindia Publications, 1934-.
Films and Filming. London: Hansom Books, 1954-.
Films in Review. New York: Henry Hart, 1954-.
For Monsters Only. Valley Stream, N.Y.: Major Magazines, 1965-67.
Harrison's Reports. New York: P.S. Harrison, 1932-35.
Heraldo del Cine. Buenos Aires, 1940-.
The Hollywood Reporter. Hollywood, Cal.: Hollywood Reporter Corp., 1933-.

Horror Monsters. Derby, Conn.: Charlton Publications, 1961-66.
Imparcial Film. Buenos Aires.
Jadran Film. Zagreb, Yugoslavia.
The Lighthouse. Bombay: 1936-38.
Mad Monsters. Derby, Conn.: Charlton Publications, 1961-66.
Midi-Minuit Fantastique. Paris: Le Terrain Vague, 1962-.
Modern Czechoslovak Film. Prague: Artia, in cooperation with the Czechoslovak Film Institute, 1963-.
Modern Monsters. Los Angeles: Prestige Publications, [1963?-1967?]
The Modesto Bee. Modesto, Cal.: McClatchy Newspapers, 1965-.
Monster Mania. New York: Renaissance Productions, 1966-67.
Monster World. New York: Warren Pub. Co., [1964?-1966?]
Monsters and Heroes. M&H Publications, 1967-.
The Monthly Film Bulletin. London: British Film Institute, 1937-.
Motion Picture Herald [Exhibitors Herald]. New York: Quigley Pub. Co., 1919-68.
Motion Picture News. New York: Motion Picture News, 1914-30.
Motography. Chicago: 1911-15.
The Moving Picture Monthly. Bombay: D. Dwivedi, 1934-38.
Moving Picture World. New York: Chalmers Pub.Co., 1907-26.
The New York Times. New York: The New York Times Co., 1913-.
Parents' Magazine. New York: The Parents' Institute, 1930-.
Photoplay. Chicago: Photoplay Pub. Co., 1924-35.
Positif. Paris. Editions Le Terrain Vague, 1965-66.
The Sacramento Bee. Sacramento, Cal.: McClatchy Newspapers, 1960-.
Showmen's Trade Review. Philadelphia: Showmen's Trade Reviews, 1938-57.
Shriek. London: House of Horror, [1963?]-1966.
Sight and Sound. London: British Film Institute, 1932-.
Sound and Shadow. Madras, India: 1932-36.
Spaceman. Philadelphia: Warren Pub. Co., [1963?-1965?]
Thought. New Delhi: Siddhartha Publications, 1954-56.
Toho Films. Tokyo: Toho Co., 1958-.
TV Guide. Radnor, Pa.: Triangle Publications, 1960-.
Unijapan Bulletin. Tokyo: Unijapan Films, 1965-.
Unijapan Film Quarterly. Tokyo: Unijapan Film., 1958-.
Variety. New York: Variety, Inc., 1920-.
The Village Voice. New York: Village Voice, Inc., 1970-.
Wid's Weekly. Hollywood, Cal.: 1923-.